For Reference

Not to be taken from this room

The Who, What, *and* Where *of* America

Understanding the American Community Survey

Tenth Edition
2023

Edited by
Shana Hertz Hattis

 **Bernan** Press

Lanham • Boulder • New York • London

Published by Bernan Press
An imprint of The Rowman & Littlefield Publishing Group, Inc.
4501 Forbes Boulevard, Suite 200, Lanham, Maryland 20706
www.rowman.com

86-90 Paul Street, London EC2A 4NE

ISBN 9781636710785 (cloth) | ISBN 9781636710792 (ebook)

Contents

Page

Preface

The 2010 census was different from any census in recent memory. All American households answered a simple questionnaire with ten questions. No longer did some people get the "long form," which included dozens of detailed questions about employment, education, income, previous residence, housing characteristics, and more. The data gleaned from these important questions have long been used by federal, state, and local governments to evaluate their populations and program needs; by large and small businesses and nonprofit organizations for a variety of planning and location purposes; and by academic researchers to study trends in social and economic conditions. However, the cost, timeliness, and quality of the traditional long form data made it necessary to develop a new data collection strategy for gathering economic and demographic characteristics of the nation.

The "long form" has been replaced by the American Community Survey (ACS). Under development for more than a decade, the ACS is an ongoing survey of the American people that ushered in a new era in social and economic data analysis. The census "long form" provided detailed estimates of social and economic characteristics every ten years. The ACS collects this same information on a rolling basis. It takes five years of ACS responses to accumulate a sample almost as large as the census "long form" collected at a single point in time. But data users now have the ability to study these characteristics and trends throughout the decade—annually for some areas.

Because the ACS is a sample survey, large numbers of sample cases are needed before reliable estimates can be made for small populations. Each year's sample is large enough to produce estimates for the nation, all the states, most metropolitan areas, and many counties and cities. The tables in this volume include single-year estimates for 2021 (the most current year available) for the United States, all states, all metropolitan areas, as well as counties and cities with populations of 65,000 or more.

The richness of the ACS data can be accessed in varying degrees. Much more subject matter detail is available for large geographic areas, partly because reliable estimates for large areas can be produced with smaller samples and partly because more data must be suppressed for the smaller areas to protect the confidentiality of the respondents. Although the county and city data in this book have traditionally been derived from a special ACS 1-year supplemental file that is less detailed than the standard 1-year file for areas with populations of 65,000 or more, these data were not available for 2021 at the time of publication. Data thus are for communities with populations of 65,000 or more.

This book is designed to include a sampling of key information but also to guide users through the process of using the Census Bureau's website to expand on the information included here. The state tables in this book include more than three hundred data items. The metropolitan area, county, and city tables include forty-eight data items. The data in the tables are a small selection that show what is available for the geographic areas in the book. Every column includes an ACS Table Number that enables users to find the original data on the Census Bureau's website. The selection in this book is limited because the county and city data are from the less detailed supplemental file. Much more information is available in the standard 1-year file for analysis of larger cities and counties or for analysis of specific racial or ethnic groups if those groups have large populations in a particular city or county. Furthermore, as the 5-year data are also available, additional information can be found for the cities and counties in this book, and for all cities and counties in the nation, no matter how small.

One of the most notable differences between the census "long form" and the ACS is the time frame of the estimates. We are accustomed to the census data that give us specific information every ten years, a snapshot of the country on April 1. The ACS multiyear estimates are different as the Census Bureau surveys nearly 300,000 households every month. The data in this book are from the ACS 1-year 2021 estimates, which are produced from the twelve calendar months of survey data collection. The estimates reported here represent an "average" population profile over the twelve months of 2021. The sample cases are spread evenly throughout the year rather than the "point in time" decennial census estimates reported as of April 1.

To help in the understanding of these estimates, we have included a measure of population change for each geographic area. These are from the 2010 census and the 2019 estimates, showing the actual population growth or decline in each geographic area. Each table shows population characteristics as estimated for 2019. It should be remembered that the decennial census and the Census Bureau's Population Estimates Program provide the official population counts that underlie the ACS sample. If an area experienced unusually large population growth or decline, we should understand that these short-term population impacts may not be reflected in the ACS period estimates. Changes due to a city annexing a large tract of land, many people moving into a new development, or many people leaving the area because of a plant closing may be hidden in the short-term.

With the ACS, there is always a trade-off between data currency and data reliability. More current 1-year estimates come from smaller samples and therefore have larger margins of error. Estimates from the 5-year data are based on five times the sample size and have smaller margins of error but, of course, they do not represent as current a period. Earlier editions of *The Who, What, and Where of America* relied on the Census Bureau's 3-year (2010–2012) estimates because of the larger sample size and smaller margins of error inherent in the longer period estimates. Due to the elimination of the 3-year data series, the current volume reports the results of the 1-year 2019 data. Users may want to compare data among the editions but should use caution as there will be more sample variability in the 2019 data and small differences may not be meaningful. Users will also notice that there are a number of geographic areas where the estimates are not available due to the Census Bureau's data disclosure rules.

Finally, it is always critical to remember that all estimates are subject to sampling error. On the Census Bureau's website, every ACS number is accompanied by its margin of error. In the interests of space and simplicity, this book does not include the margins of error, but all users are encouraged to consult the Census Bureau's website and to understand some basics: small differences are very likely to represent no difference at all, do not draw conclusions from small numbers, use these numbers as a starting point to explore the wealth of information from the ACS.

Introduction

The American Community Survey (ACS) has ushered in the most substantial change in the decennial census in more than sixty years. It replaced the decennial census "long form" in 2010, providing more current data throughout the decade by collecting long-form-type information annually rather than only once every ten years. The ACS provides annual data for states, metropolitan areas, and large cities and counties and combines multiple years of survey responses to produce data for midsize communities. Very small communities (under 20,000 population) and statistical areas like census tracts and ZIP code tabulation areas require five years of survey responses to yield characteristic estimates.

The ACS gathers demographic, social, economic, housing and financial information about the nation's people and communities on a continuous basis. The ACS is an ongoing survey conducted by the U.S. Census Bureau in every county, American Indian and Alaska Native Area, and Hawaiian Home Land in the United States. The ACS is also conducted as the Puerto Rico Community Survey in every municipality in Puerto Rico. As the largest survey in the United States, it is the only source of small-area data on a wide range of important social and economic characteristics for all communities in the country. After years of planning, development, and a demonstration period, the ACS began nationwide full implementation in 2005.

Information about the ACS is available on the Census Bureau's website. The ACS main page is https://www.census.gov/programs-surveys/acs. Data from the ACS is available at https://data.census.gov.

A vast amount of information is collected in the ACS. In this publication, selections of these data have been assembled in various tables by subject and geographic type.

Volume Organization

The data tables in this book contain a representative selection of information from the ACS.

Part A: Who contains the following subjects: age, race/ethnicity, and household structure, among others.

Part B: What contains the following subject areas: education, employment, and income.

Part C: Where comprises data on: migration, housing, and transportation.

Within each part are four tables: Table 1 has data for the 50 states and the District of Columbia, Table 2 has data for all counties with populations of 65,000 or more, Table 3 has data for all the nation's metropolitan statistical areas, and Table 4 has data for all cities with populations of 65,000 or more. Counties and cities are listed alphabetically by state. Metropolitan areas are listed alphabetically, and metropolitan divisions are listed alphabetically within the metropolitan statistical area of which they are components.

In addition, each part is preceded by highlights and ranking tables that show how areas diverge from the national norm as well as the differences among small areas. These research aids are invaluable for helping people understand what the census data tell us about who we are, what we do, and where we live.

In the following sections, information about the ACS and how to use the data is included, much of it excerpted from the wealth of information available on the Census Bureau's website. Especially helpful are the instructions, definitions, and guidelines on using the data in the section on "Guidance for Data Users."

Readers are encouraged to explore the Census Bureau's website to expand on the information contained here and to keep up to date with this constantly changing dataset.

Shana Hertz Hattis is an editor with over a decade of experience in statistical and government research publications. Past titles include *State Profiles: The Population and Economy of Each U.S. State*, *Housing Statistics of the United States*, and *Justice Statistics: An Extended Look at Crime in the United States*. She earned her bachelor of science in journalism and master of science in education degrees from Northwestern University.

Understanding the American Community Survey

Every ten years since 1790, as required by the U.S. Constitution, Congress has authorized funds to conduct a national census of the U.S. population. From 1960 through 2000, censuses have consisted of:

- a "short form," which included basic questions about age, sex, race, Hispanic origin (since 1980), household relationship, and owner/renter status, and

- a "long form" used for a sample of approximately one of every six households that included not only the basic short-form questions but also detailed questions about socioeconomic and housing characteristics.

Beginning with the 2010 census, the American Community Survey (ACS) replaced the decennial census "long form" by collecting long-form-type information annually rather than only once every ten years, providing more current data throughout the decade. The 2010 Census counted the population to support the constitutional mandate—to provide population counts needed to apportion the seats in the U.S. House of Representatives. The ACS data now provide, for the first time, a regular stream of updated information for states and local areas, revolutionizing the way we use data to understand our communities. It produces social, housing, and economic characteristics for demographic groups, even for geographic areas as small as census tracts and block groups.

Some Key Facts about the ACS

- The ACS annually provides the same kind of detailed information previously available only every ten years from the census. The ACS is conducted under the authority of Title 13, United States Code, Sections 141 and 193.

- All answers are confidential. Any Census Bureau employee who violates that confidentiality is subject to a jail term, a fine, or both.

- The Census Bureau may use the information it collects only for statistical purposes.

- Addresses are selected at random from the Master Address File to represent similar households in the area. Nearly 300,000 addresses are selected each month and the survey is conducted by mail, telephone, and personal visit. Response to this survey is required by federal statute Section 221 of Title 13.

- Approximately 3.0 percent of U.S. households are surveyed each year. A sample of group quarters (nursing homes, college dormitories, etc.) is included in the ACS as well.

- While the ACS sample size approximates the traditional long-form census sample, it is a smaller sample resulting in somewhat larger margins of error.

The traditional long-form census taken once a decade provided the socioeconomic portrait of the nation and communities but that portrait was fixed in time for ten years. Data from the ACS provides a regular update to that portrait that is used for a variety of purposes including monitoring the well-being of America's older population, children and families, tracking trends in disability, analyzing the growth in the number of grandparents responsible for their grandchildren, determining the economic well-being of the elderly and working-poor families, and tracking social, economic, and demographic changes in the general U.S. population.

The ACS provides critical information for communities on a current basis when they need it most. But the ACS is still a relatively new data collection instrument and a different measure of the characteristics of the population and households. Researchers are still working to understand the differences from the traditional census data, so it is good to be cautious in the interpretation of differences between areas and across time. Small differences may not be meaningful. On the other hand, the ACS provides annual estimates and the frequency of updates and currency of the data far outweigh waiting ten years for new results.

New Opportunities

The main benefits of the ACS are timeliness and access to annual data for states, local areas, and small population subgroups. The ACS delivers useful, relevant data, similar to data from previous census long forms, but updated every year rather than every ten years. The ACS provides comparable information across and within states for program evaluation and use in funding formulas.

- ACS information is often used to determine the placement of new schools, senior residential services, hospitals, and highways.

- ACS provides information for tracking the well-being of children, families, and the elderly allowing service providers to better target populations in need.

- The data will improve the distribution of aid through federal, state, and local governments. More than $400 billion in federal program funds are distributed each year based, in whole or in part, on census and ACS data.

- The data are used by community programs, such as those for the elderly, libraries, hospitals, banks, and other organizations.

- The data are used by transportation planners to evaluate peak volumes of traffic in order to reduce congestion, plan for parking, and develop plans for carpooling and flexible work schedules.

- Corporations, small businesses, and individuals use these data to develop business plans, to set strategies for expansion or starting a business, and to determine trends in their service areas to meet current and future needs.

- Small towns and rural communities have much to gain from the ACS. Lacking the staff and resources to conduct their own research, many local communities have relied on decennial census information that became increasingly outdated throughout the decade, or used local administrative records that are not comparable with information collected in neighboring areas.

- The ACS also provides tools for those who want to conduct their own research. The ACS includes a Public Use Microdata Sample (PUMS) file each year that enables researchers to create custom universes and tabulations from individual ACS records that have been stripped of personally identifiable information.

- Because the ACS data collection occurs every month, the Census Bureau uses professional, highly trained, permanent interviewers who have improved the accuracy of ACS data compared with those from the decennial census long-form sample. This strategy has effectively reduced the number of refusals to complete the ACS questionnaire and allows interviewers to obtain more complete information than decennial census interviewers.

New Challenges

The main challenges for ACS data users are understanding and using multiyear estimates and the relatively large margins of error associated with ACS data for smaller geographic areas and subgroups of the population.

- ACS data are produced every year, but the sample size of the ACS is smaller than that of the Census 2000 long form sample. Data users need to pay more attention to the margin of error.

- Data users have access to 5-year estimates of ACS data. The sample size based on 5-year period estimates of ACS data is still smaller than the long-form sample in the decennial census, resulting in larger margins of error in the ACS 5-year estimates.

- Prior to the 2014 data release, the ACS produced 1-year, 3-year, and 5-year estimates so areas of 65,000 population or more received three separate estimates of the same characteristic every year. For example, a large city would receive 1-year, 3-year and 5-year estimates of the number of persons 65 and over in poverty. Data users had to decide which datasets were appropriate for their needs.

- As of 2014, the Census Bureau eliminated all 3-year estimates products as a cost saving measure. In 2017, a 1-year Supplemental file was released for areas with populations of 20,000 or more. The supplemental file contains less detail then the standard 1-year file but provides 1-year data for many additional cities and counties. Areas below 20,000 will continue to only receive estimates based on five years of data collection. Large areas of 65,000 or more will now only have two separate estimates rather than three. The historical 3-year data are still available.

- Data users will need to be aware of the implications of multiyear estimates, particularly in analyzing employment and income data that will span a full year or even a 5-year period.

- The 5-year estimates will not reflect short-term changes in the population or economy of an area. A recession is a good example because the 5-year ACS estimates might span both the fall into recession and the resulting growth coming out.

The ACS includes several questions that are very similar to those collected in other federal surveys—especially the Current Population Survey (CPS), the American Housing Survey, and the Survey of Income and Program Participation. In some cases, there are clear guidelines about which data to use. For example, the CPS is the official source of income and poverty data. It includes detailed questions on these topics and should be used in reporting national trends in these subject areas. The Census Bureau recommends that ACS information on income and poverty be used to supplement CPS data for areas below the state level and for population subgroups (such as age, sex, race, Hispanic origin, type of household) at the state level. More information on income and poverty can be found on the Census website at https://www.census.gov/topics/income-poverty.html. For states, generally the Census Bureau recommends using the ACS, though the CPS is still valuable as a source for examining historical state income and poverty trends.

Data Collection versus Data Reporting

Results from the ACS are reported each year which is a major advantage over the traditional long-form data from the decennial census. But unlike the release of data only once every ten years in the decennial census, the annual release of data from the ACS can be quite confusing. The ACS sample size is such that the reliability of the data is greatly affected by the length of the data collection period and the size of geographic reporting areas. In survey sampling, it is well understood that larger samples yield more reliable estimates with smaller margins of error. In order to produce reliable estimates from the ACS, it is necessary to collect the data over differing periods of time in order to provide estimates for all areas, including small areas like census tracts.

Each set of period estimates is released each year, generally between September and December, and reflect data collection ending in the previous calendar year. Thus, the collection year 2017 1-year estimates were released in September of 2018, the 1-year Supplemental estimates followed in October, and the 2013–2017 5-year estimates were released in December 2018.

The ACS Sample

The ACS is sent each month to a sample of over 290,000 addresses in the United States and Puerto Rico, or about 3.5 million a year, resulting in more than 2.2 million final interviews. The sample represents all housing units and group quarters in the United States and Puerto Rico. (Group quarters include places such as college dormitories, prisons, military barracks, and nursing homes.) The addresses are selected from the Census Bureau's Master Address File (MAF), which is also the basis for the decennial census.

The annual ACS sample is smaller than that of the Census 2000 long-form sample, which included about 18 million housing units. As a result, the ACS needs to combine population or housing data from multiple years to produce reliable numbers for small counties, neighborhoods, and other local areas. To provide information for communities each year, the ACS provides 1- and 5-year estimates.

The ACS sample is not spread evenly across all areas but includes a larger proportion of addresses in sparsely populated rural communities and American Indian reservations and a lower proportion in densely populated areas. Over a 5-year period, the ACS will sample more than 15 million addresses and complete interviews for about 11 million. This sample is sufficient to produce estimates

for small geographic areas, such as neighborhoods and sparsely populated rural counties though the estimates will have larger margins of error than the census long-form data. In a 5-year period no address will be selected for the ACS more than once, and many addresses will never be selected for the survey. It's important to remember that the sample is address-based so while a given address will not be in sample again for at least five years, it is possible that individuals who move or have a second home could be surveyed more than once.

Geography

The ACS data are tabulated for a variety of geographic areas ranging in size from broad geographic regions (Northeast, Midwest, South, and West) to cities, towns, neighborhoods, and census block groups. Before December 2008, the ACS data were only available for geographic areas with at least 65,000 people, including regions, divisions, states, the District of Columbia, Puerto Rico, congressional districts, Public Use Microdata Areas (PUMAs)—census-constructed geographic areas, each with approximately a population of 100,000—and many large counties, metropolitan areas, cities, school districts, and American Indian areas. Starting in December 2008, 3-year estimates became available for all areas with at least 20,000 residents, and in 2010, 5-year estimates for geographic areas down to the block group level became available. One-, three-, and five-year estimates—three sets of numbers—were available and were refreshed every year up until the 2014 data release. Less populous areas—those under 20,000—receive only 5-year estimates. Areas of 20,000 or more receive 1-year estimates, but areas between 20,000 and 65,000 receive less detailed information in the supplemental estimates while those with populations of 65,000 or more continue to receive the very detailed 1-year estimates.

The data tables in this book contain data from the 1-year 2017 estimates. These tables are based on the 2010 tabulation geography for political and statistical areas, the same definitions as the 2010 Census. Changes in area boundaries can occur as a result of annexation, new incorporation or disincorporation of cities, towns, and places. For multiyear estimates, the Census Bureau reports the data based on the most current geographic boundaries incorporating any changes occurring in the multiyear period.

Data Comparability

Since the ACS data are collected continuously, they are not always comparable with long-form data that was collected from the decennial census. For example, both surveys asked about employment status during the week prior to the survey. However, data from the decennial census were typically collected between March and July with a reference date of April 1, whereas data from the

ACS are collected nearly every day and reflect employment throughout the year. Other factors that may also have an impact on the data include seasonal variation in population and minor differences in question wording and question order.

While the categories of income by source are comparable with the decennial long-form data, the monthly collection of ACS data results in a significant difference in concept. In the decennial census, income referred to the previous calendar year whereas in the ACS it refers to the previous 12-month period. Most people have a better understanding of what their calendar year income is, especially since the census is taken around tax time. With the ACS, individuals have to report income for a different period each month. A response to the survey in October of the year will report income from October of the previous year through September of the current year. This may require respondents to actually compute their 12-month income.

In 2006, the ACS began including samples of the population living in group quarters (e.g., jails, college dormitories, and nursing homes) for the first time. As a result, the ACS data from 2008 through 2017 may not be comparable with data from earlier ACS surveys. This is especially true for estimates of young adults and the elderly, who are more likely than other groups to be living in group quarters facilities.

One of the most important uses of the ACS estimates is to make comparisons between estimates—over time or across areas. Several key types of comparisons are of general interest to users:

- Comparisons of estimates from different geographic areas within the same time period (e.g., comparing the proportion of seniors below the poverty level in two counties).

- Comparisons of estimates for the same geographic area across time periods (e.g., comparing the proportion of people below the poverty level in a metropolitan area for 2015 and 2017).

- Comparisons of ACS estimates with the corresponding estimates from past decennial census samples (e.g., comparing the proportion of people below the poverty level in a county in 2017 compared with 2010 and 2000).

A number of conditions must be met when comparing survey estimates:

- When comparing data for different geographic areas, always use the same period estimates. When comparing data for an area which only have 5-year estimates to an area with 1- and 5-year estimates, it is important to compare only the 5-year estimates.

- When comparing over time for the same geographic area, again, only compare like-year period estimates. For example, it is not appropriate to compare a 1-year estimate for 2017 to a 5-year estimate for 2013–2017.

- Of primary importance is that the comparison takes into account the sampling error associated with each estimate, thus determining whether the observed differences between estimates are statistically significant. Statistical significance means that there is statistical evidence that a true difference exists within the full population, and that the observed difference is unlikely to have occurred by chance due to sampling. A method for determining statistical significance when making comparisons, as well as considerations associated with the various types of comparisons, can be found in Sections 4 and 7 of the *ACS General Handbook*: https://www.census.gov/programs-surveys/acs/guidance/handbooks/general.html.

- The statistical properties of survey samples like the ACS are dependent upon independence of samples. In the ACS multiyear period estimates, the estimates are based on the sampled households for each year. That means that when comparing estimates for the period 2009–2011 to 2010–2012, two thirds of the sample cases are the same households—those surveyed in 2010 and 2011. The only different (independent) households are those taken in 2009 and 2012. When comparisons over time are made, it is best to compare non-overlapping samples. That is, compare estimates for 2007–2009 to the period 2010–1012 because both periods contain independent household samples. To meet this criterion for the use of the most recent 5-year estimates (2013–2017), data users should use the 2008–2012 data to make time series comparisons.

Finally, the decennial census and the ACS have different residency rules. In the decennial census, population is tabulated by their "usual place of residence" typically where they spend six months or more of the year. This is subject to some seasonal variation due to persons with dual residences. In the ACS, there is a 2-month residency rule. That is, if the respondent has been in the sampled housing unit for two months or expects to be resident there for two months they are captured in the survey. This can have an impact on communities with highly seasonal populations and college communities.

Subjects Covered

The topics covered by the ACS focus on demographic, social, economic, and housing characteristics. These topics are virtually the same as those covered by the 2000 census long-form sample data.

Demographic Characteristics

Age, Sex, Hispanic Origin, Race, and Relationship to Householder (e.g., spouse)

Social Characteristics

Marital Status and Marital History, Fertility, Grandparents as Caregivers, Ancestry, Place of Birth, Citizenship and Year of Entry, Language Spoken at Home, Educational Attainment and School Enrollment, Residence One Year Ago, Veteran Status, Period of Military Service, VA Service-Connected Disability Rating, and Disability

Economic Characteristics

Income, Food Stamps Benefit, Labor Force Status, Industry, Occupation, Class of Worker, Place of Work and Journey to Work, Work Status Last Year, Vehicles Available, and Health Insurance Coverage

Housing Characteristics

Year Structure Built, Units in Structure, Year Moved Into Unit, Rooms, Bedrooms, Kitchen Facilities, Plumbing Facilities, House Heating Fuel, Telephone Service Available, and Farm Residence

Financial Characteristics

Tenure (Owner/Renter), Housing Value, Rent, and Selected Monthly Owner Costs

Availability of ACS Estimates

The ACS began in 1996 and has expanded each subsequent year. From 2000 through 2004, the sample included between 740,000 and 900,000 addresses annually. In 2005, the ACS shifted from a demonstration program to the full sample size and design. It became the largest household survey in the United States, with an annual sample size of about three million addresses. Beginning with 2005, the ACS single-year estimates are available for geographic areas with a population of 65,000 or more. Less detailed single-year supplemental estimates were first released in 2014 for areas of 20,000 or more and are expected to continue. Three-year period estimates for areas of 20,000 or more were first released for the 2005–2007 time period and there are annual 3-year estimates through the 2011–2013 period. 5-year estimates for all areas were first released

in 2010 and are available for every subsequent year with 2017 being the most current as of this writing. The ACS will continue to accumulate samples over 5-year intervals to produce estimates for smaller geographic areas, including census tracts and block groups.

Annually, the ACS produces updated, single-year estimates of demographic, housing, social, and economic characteristics for all states, as well as for larger counties, cities, metropolitan and urban areas, and congressional districts. Geographic areas must have a minimum population of 65,000 to qualify for detailed estimates based on a single year's sample, and a minimum population of 20,000 to qualify for supplemental estimates. Every state, metropolitan area, and congressional district meets the 65,000 threshold and therefore new single year estimates are released each year for these areas. Some school districts, townships, and American Indian and Alaska Native areas also meet this population threshold.

For areas with populations of at least 20,000, the Census Bureau produces 1-year supplemental estimates, and until 2013 produced estimates using data collected over a 3 year period. The 3-year estimates are available through the 2011–2013 collection period (released in 2014). However, the Census Bureau is no longer producing the 3-year data products. For rural areas and city neighborhoods (including census tracts and block groups) with fewer than 20,000 people, the Census Bureau produces estimates using data collected over a 5-year period and updates these multi-year estimates every year. ACS data are released annually, about nine months after the end of each calendar year of data collection.

For most geographic areas—including three-quarters of all counties, most school districts, and most cities, towns, and American Indian reservations—the only detailed estimates are the 5-year estimates because of their population size. Because some federal grant programs allocate funds directly to these areas, Congress can use the 5-year estimates to evaluate needs at the relevant geographic level, compare characteristics between areas within and among states, and analyze how various formulas distribute funds. The vast majority of areas will receive only 5-year detailed estimates. In partnership with the states, the Census Bureau created *Public Use Microdata Areas (PUMAs)*, which are special, non-overlapping areas within a state, each with a population of about 100,000. These areas will have annual 1-year estimates.

Definitions of these geographic areas are at https://www. census.gov/programs-surveys/acs/geography-acs/concepts-definitions.html.

Using the ACS

Differences between the ACS and the Decennial Census

While the main function of the decennial census is to provide *counts* of people for the purpose of congressional apportionment and legislative redistricting, the primary purpose of the ACS is to measure the changing social and economic *characteristics* of the U.S. population. As a result, the ACS does not provide official counts of the population though users of the data will report the estimate results as though they were counts. In non-decennial census years, the Census Bureau's Population Estimates Program continues to be the official source for annual population totals, by age, race, Hispanic origin, and sex. The ACS sample estimates are controlled to match the decennial census and the Census Bureau's annual population estimates by selected age, sex, race, and Hispanic origin categories. For more information about population estimates, visit the Census Bureau's website at https://www.census.gov/programs-surveys/popest.html.

There are many similarities between the methods used in the traditional decennial census sample and the ACS but there are also a number of differences in collection method and concepts. Response to both the ACS and decennial census is required by law, a factor that helps improve overall response. Both the ACS and the decennial census sample data are based on information from a sample of the population. The data from the Census 2000 sample of about one-sixth of the population were collected using a "long-form" questionnaire, whose content was the model for the ACS. The sample for the ACS is somewhat smaller, approximately 1 in 7 households, resulting in larger margins of error.

While some differences exist in the specific Census 2000 long-form question wording and that of the ACS, most questions are identical or nearly identical. Differences in the design and implementation of the two surveys are noted below with references provided to a series of evaluation studies that assess the degree to which these differences are likely to impact the estimates. The ACS produces period estimates (covering one or five years of data collection) so these estimates do not measure characteristics for the same time frame as the decennial census estimates, which are interpreted to be a snapshot as of April 1 of the census year.

Some data items were collected by both the ACS and the Census 2000 long form with slightly different definitions or reference periods that could affect the comparability of the estimates for these items. One example is annual costs for a mobile home. Census 2000 included installment loan costs in the total annual costs but the ACS does not. In this example, the ACS could be expected to yield smaller estimates than Census 2000.

While some differences were a part of the census and survey design objectives, other differences observed between ACS and census results were not by design, but due to nonsampling error—differences related to how well the surveys were conducted. The ACS and the census experience different levels and types of coverage error, different levels and treatment of housing unit and questionnaire item nonresponse, and different instances of measurement and processing error. Both Census 2000 and the ACS had similarly high levels of survey coverage and low levels of unit nonresponse. Higher levels of unit nonresponse were found in the nonresponse follow-up stage of Census 2000 while lower levels of item nonresponse were found in the ACS due to a permanent staff of trained interviewers.

Census Bureau analysts have compared sample estimates from Census 2000 with 1-year ACS estimates based on data collected in 2000 and 3-year ACS estimates based on data collected in 1999–2001 in selected counties. In general, ACS estimates were found to be quite similar to those produced from decennial census data.

Detailed information about the ACS methodology can be found at https://www.census.gov/programs-surveys/acs/methodology.html.

Residence Rules

The fundamentally different purposes of the ACS and the census, and their timing, led to important differences in the choice of data collection methods. For example, the residence rules for a census or survey determine the sample unit's occupancy status and household membership at the time of collection. Defining the rules in a dissimilar way can affect those two very important estimates. The 2010 census residence rules, which determined where people should be counted, were based on the principle of "usual residence" on April 1, 2010, in keeping with the focus of the census on the requirements of congressional apportionment and state redistricting. To accomplish this, the decennial census attempts to restrict and determine a principal place of residence on one specific date for everyone enumerated. The ACS residence rules are based on a "current residence" concept since data are collected continuously throughout the entire year with responses provided relative to the continuously changing survey interview dates. Under this concept, anyone who is living or staying at an address for two months or more is considered a resident of that address. This method is consistent with the goal of the ACS to produce estimates that reflect annual averages of the characteristics of all areas.

Residence rules determine which individuals are considered to be residents of a particular housing unit or group quarters. While many people have definite ties to a single housing unit or group quarters, some people may stay in different places for significant periods of time over the course of the year. The differences in the ACS and census data, as a consequence of the different residence rules, are most likely minimal for most areas and most characteristics. However, for certain segments of the population the usual and current residence concepts could result in different residence decisions. The older population is one of those segments as many retired and active seniors maintain dual residences. Appreciable differences may occur in areas where large proportions of the total population spend several months of the year in what would not be considered their residence under decennial census rules. In particular, data for areas that include large beach, lake, or mountain vacation areas may differ appreciably between the census and the ACS if populations live there for more than two months. In addition, in the decennial census college students are to be counted at the location of the college rather than their parent's home. However, during summer months, college students can meet the two-month residency rule for the ACS and be counted along with their parents rather than at the college.

For the past several censuses, decennial census residence rules were designed to produce an accurate count of the population as of Census Day, April 1, while the ACS residence rules were designed to collect representative information to produce annual average estimates of the characteristics of all types of areas. The residence rules governing the census enumerations of people in group quarters depend on the type of group quarter and, where permitted, whether people claim a "usual residence" elsewhere. The ACS applies a straight de facto residence rule to every type of group quarter. Everyone living or staying in a group quarter on the day it is visited by an ACS interviewer is eligible to be sampled and interviewed for the survey.

Reference Periods

Estimates produced by the ACS are not measuring exactly what decennial samples have been measuring. The ACS yearly samples, spread over twelve months, collect information that is anchored to the day on which the sampled unit was interviewed, whether it is the day that a mail questionnaire is completed or the day that an interview is conducted by telephone or personal visit. Individual questions with time references such as "last week" or "the last 12 months" all begin the reference period as of this interview date. Even the information on types and amounts of income refers to the twelve months prior to the day the question is answered. ACS interviews are conducted just about every day of the year, and all of the estimates that the survey releases are considered to be averages for a specific time period. The 1-year estimates reflect the full calendar year; 5-year estimates reflect the full 60-month period.

Most decennial census sample estimates are anchored in this same way to the reference date of April 1. The most obvious difference between the ACS and the census is the overall time frame in which they are conducted. The census enumeration time period is less than half the time period used to collect data for each single-year ACS estimate. But a more important difference is that the distribution of census enumeration dates are highly clustered in March and April (when most census mail returns were received) with additional, smaller clusters seen in May and June (when nonresponse follow-up activities took place).

This means that the data from the decennial census, intended to reflect the characteristics of the population and housing on April 1, tend to describe the characteristics in the March through June time period (with an over-representation of March/April). The ACS data describe the characteristics nearly every day over the full calendar year. For employment and income estimates, the decennial census referred to the prior calendar year for all respondents, while the ACS asks about the twelve months preceding the interview.

Individual tables can be compared with the table comparison tool or you can download the entire comparison table.

Some specific differences in reference periods between the ACS and the decennial census are described below. Users should consider the potential impact these different reference periods could have on distributions when comparing ACS estimates with Census 2000. As we get further and further away from use of the 2000 data and compare current ACS data to prior years' ACS data, these differences have become less important.

- **Income Data**: To estimate annual income, the Census 2000 long-form sample used the calendar year prior to Census Day as the reference period, and the ACS uses the twelve months prior to the interview date as the reference period. Thus, while Census 2000 collected income information for calendar year 1999, the ACS collects income information for the twelve months preceding the interview date. The responses are a mixture of twelve reference periods ranging from, in the case of the 2016 ACS single-year estimates, the full calendar year 2015 through November 2016. The ACS income responses for each of these reference periods are individually inflation-adjusted to represent dollar values for the ACS collection year. Further inflation adjustments are made to the 3- and 5-year estimates to reflect dollar values of the final year of the estimate. It's important to note that the rotating reference period for income can result in misreporting. The calendar year reference period of the decennial census coincides with an individual's annual salary and is also collected around tax time. Respondents will have a good idea of what their annual salary is. In the ACS, the respondent has to calculate their income for the previous twelve months, a figure which can vary considerably throughout the year.

- **School Enrollment**: The school enrollment question on the ACS asks if a person had "at any time in the last 3 months attended a school or college." A consistent 3-month reference period is used for all interviews. In contrast, Census 2000 asked if a person had "at any time since February 1 attended a school or college." Since Census 2000 data were collected from mid-March to late-August, the reference period could have been as short as about six weeks or as long as seven months.

- **Utility Costs**: The reference periods for two utility cost questions—gas and electricity—differ between Census 2000 and the ACS. The census asked for annual costs, while the ACS asks for the utility costs in the previous month.

Period Estimates

The ACS produces period estimates of socioeconomic and housing characteristics. It is designed to provide estimates that describe the average characteristics of an area over a specific time period. In the case of ACS single-year estimates, the period is the calendar year (e.g., the 2017 ACS covers January through December 2017). In the case of ACS five-year estimates, the period is January 2013 through December 2017). The ACS five-year estimates are similar in many ways to the ACS single-year estimates, but they encompass a longer time period.

The differences in time periods between single-year and multiyear ACS estimates affect decisions about which set of estimates should be used for a particular analysis. While one may think of these estimates as representing average

characteristics over a single calendar year or multiple calendar years, it must be remembered that the 1-year estimates are not calculated as an average of twelve monthly values and the five-year estimates are not calculated as the average of 60 monthly values, nor are the five-year estimates calculated as the average of five single-year estimates. Rather, the ACS collects survey information continuously nearly every day of the year and then aggregates the results over a specific time period—one year or five years. The data collection is spread evenly across the entire period represented so as not to over-represent any particular month or year within the period.

Because ACS estimates provide information about the characteristics of the population and housing for areas over an entire time frame, ACS single-year and multiyear estimates contrast with "point-in-time" estimates, such as those from the decennial census long-form samples or monthly employment estimates from the Current Population Survey (CPS), which are designed to measure characteristics as of a certain date or narrow time period. For example, Census 2000 was designed to measure the characteristics of the population and housing in the United States based upon data collected around April 1, 2000, and thus its data reflect a narrower time frame than ACS data. The monthly CPS collects data for an even narrower time frame, the week containing the 12th of each month.

Most areas have consistent population characteristics throughout the calendar year, and their period estimates may not look much different from estimates that would be obtained from a "point-in-time" survey design. However, some areas may experience changes in the estimated characteristics of the population, depending on when in the calendar year the measurement occurred. For these areas, the ACS period estimates (even for a single-year) may noticeably differ from "point-in-time" estimates. The impact will be more noticeable in smaller areas where changes such as a factory closing can have a large impact on population characteristics, in areas with seasonal population shifts, and in areas with a large natural event such as Hurricane Katrina's impact on the New Orleans area.

This logic can be extended to better interpret five-year estimates where the periods involved are much longer. If, over the full period of time there have been major or consistent changes in certain population or housing characteristics for an area, a period estimate for that area could differ markedly from estimates based on a "point-in-time" survey. The tables in this book were prepared from the 1-year 2017 survey results. Some areas will have experienced a more rapid recovery from the recession while others still continue to struggle and haven't returned to previous levels of growth. Strong growth between the 2000 and 2010 censuses may be replaced by a slowdown in the most recent years

Single-year estimates provide more current information about areas that have changing population and/or housing characteristics because they are based on the most current data—survey responses from the past calendar year. In contrast, multiyear estimates provide less current information because they are based on both survey responses from the previous year and responses that are up to five years old. As noted earlier, for many areas with minimal change taking place, using the "less current" sample used to produce the multiyear estimates may not have a substantial influence on the estimates. However, in areas experiencing major changes over a given time period, the multiyear estimates may be quite different from the single-year estimates for any of the individual years. Single-year and multiyear estimates are not expected to be the same because they are based on data from two different time periods. This will be true even if the ACS single year is the midyear of the ACS multiyear period (e.g., 2015 single year, 2013–2017 multiyear).

Multiyear estimates are based on larger sample sizes and are therefore more reliable

The five-year estimates are based on five times as many sample cases as the one-year estimates. For some characteristics this increased sample is needed for the estimates to be reliable enough for use in certain applications. For other characteristics the increased sample may not be necessary.

Multiyear estimates are the only type of detailed estimates available for geographic areas with populations of less than 20,000. Users may think that they only need to use multiyear estimates when they are working with small areas, but this isn't the case. Estimates for large geographic areas benefit from the increased sample, resulting in more precise estimates of population and housing characteristics, especially for subpopulations within those areas. In addition, users may determine that they want to use single-year estimates, despite their reduced reliability, as building blocks to produce estimates for meaningful higher levels of geography. These aggregations will similarly benefit from the increased sample sizes and gain reliability.

The important thing to keep in mind is that ACS single-year estimates describe the population and characteristics of an area for the full year, not for any specific day or period within the year. The ACS multiyear estimates describe the population and characteristics of an area for the full five-year period, not for any specific day, period, or year within the multiyear time period.

Deciding Which ACS Estimate to Use

Three primary uses of ACS estimates are:

- to understand the characteristics of the population of an area for local planning needs,

- to make comparisons across areas, and

- to assess change over time in an area.

Local planning could include making local decisions such as where to place schools or hospitals, determining the need for senior services or transportation, and carrying out other infrastructure analysis. In the past, decennial census sample data provided the most comprehensive information. However, the currency of those data suffered through the intercensal period, and the ability to assess change over time was limited. ACS estimates greatly improve the currency of data for understanding the characteristics of housing and population and enhance the ability to assess change over time. At the same time, small differences between ACS estimates can lead to misinterpretation due to larger margins of error.

Several key factors can help users decide whether to use single-year or multiyear ACS estimates for areas where both are available:

- intended use of the estimates

- required precision, or reliability, of the estimates

- currency of the estimates

All of these factors, along with an understanding of the differences between single-year and multiyear ACS estimates, should be taken into consideration when deciding which set of estimates to use.

For users analyzing estimates for areas of different size and for different time periods, it is important to recognize that three-year estimates for areas of any size were eliminated in the 2014 ACS product release. Three year estimates had been available for areas of 20,000 or more so it is still possible to analyze the 3-year data for time periods prior to 2014. For the smallest of geographic areas (under 20,000 population), the only option is to use the 5-year ACS estimates. When comparing areas of different size, it is critical that users only make comparisons between similar period estimates. Even if the study area has one-year estimates, it is not appropriate to compare the one-year estimate to a five-year estimate from a different area.

The release of one-year supplemental estimates has greatly improved the availability of ACS data for many geographic areas. The supplemental estimates consist of 58 detailed tables tabulated on the one-year microdata for geographies with populations of 20,000 or more. These supplemental estimates are available for the same geographic summary levels as those in the ACS 1-year dataset.

The key trade-off to be made in deciding whether to use single-year or multiyear estimates is between currency and precision. In general, the single-year estimates are preferred, as they will be more relevant to the current conditions. However, the user must take into account the level of uncertainty present in the single-year estimates, which may be large for small subpopulation groups and rare characteristics. While single-year estimates offer more current estimates, they also have higher sampling variability. One measure, the coefficient of variation (CV) can help you determine the fitness for use of a single-year estimate in order to assess if you should opt instead to use the multiyear estimate. The CV is calculated as the ratio of the standard error of the estimate to the estimate, times 100. A single-year estimate with a small CV is usually preferable to a multiyear estimate as it is more up to date. However, multiyear estimates are an alternative option when a single-year estimate has an unacceptably high CV. Single-year estimates for small subpopulations (e.g., grandparents 65 and over who are responsible for grandchildren) will typically have larger CVs. In general, multiyear estimates are preferable to single-year estimates when looking at estimates for small subpopulations.

For the complete discussion on deciding which estimates to use and on calculating the CV, see Section 7 of the *ACS General Handbook*: https://www.census.gov/programs-surveys/acs/guidance/handbooks/general.html.

Users are encouraged to make comparisons between sequential single-year estimates. Comparison profiles are available beginning with the 2007 single-year data. These profiles identify statistically significant differences between each year from 2007 through the most recently released year.

Caution is needed when using multiyear estimates for estimating year-to-year change in a particular characteristic. This is because roughly four-fifths of the respondents in a

5-year estimate overlap with the respondents in the next year's 5-year estimate period. When comparing 5-year estimates from 2011–2015 with those from 2012–2016, the differences in overlapping multiyear estimates are driven by differences in the non-overlapping years (i.e., 2011 and 2016). A more appropriate comparison of change over time would be comparing the 2008–2012 5-year estimate to the 2013–2017 5-year estimate because they include responses from totally independent samples. Comparison of overlapping periods should be made with caution.

Users who are interested in comparing overlapping multiyear period estimates should refer to Section 4 of the *ACS General Handbook* for more information: https://www.census.gov/programs-surveys/acs/guidance/handbooks/general.html.

Multiyear estimates are likely to confuse some data users, in part because of their statistical properties, and in part because this is a new product from the Census Bureau. The ACS will provide all states and communities that have at least 65,000 residents with single-year estimates of demographic, housing, social, and economic characteristics—a boon to government agencies that need to budget and plan for public services like transportation, medical care, and schools. For geographic areas with smaller populations, the one-year supplemental estimates will provide even greater opportunities. For very small communities, several years of data will be pooled together to create reliable five-year estimates.

Multiyear estimates should, in general, be used when single-year estimates have large CVs or when the precision of the estimates is more important than the currency of the data. Multiyear estimates should also be used when analyzing data for smaller geographies and smaller population subgroups in larger geographies. Multiyear estimates are also of value when examining change over non-overlapping time periods and for smoothing data trends over time.

Single-year estimates should, in general, be used for larger geographies and populations when currency is more important than the precision of the estimates. Single-year estimates should be used to examine year-to-year change for estimates with small CVs. Given the availability of a single-year estimate, calculating the CV provides useful information to determine if the single-year estimate should be used. For areas believed to be experiencing rapid changes in a characteristic, single-year estimates should generally be used rather than multiyear estimates as long as the CV for the single-year estimate is reasonable for the specific usage.

Local area variations may occur due to rapidly occurring changes. Multiyear estimates will tend to be insensitive to such changes when they first occur. Single-year estimates, if associated with sufficiently small CVs, can be very valuable in identifying and studying such phenomena.

Data users also need to use caution in looking at trends involving income or other measures that are adjusted for inflation, such as rental costs, home values, and energy costs. Note that inflation adjustment is based on a national-level consumer price index: it does not adjust for differences in costs of living across different geographic areas.

Section 10 of the *ACS General Handbook* provides information on the adjustment of single-year and multiyear ACS estimates for inflation: https://www.census.gov/programs-surveys/acs/guidance/handbooks/general.html.

Margin of Error

All data that are based on samples, such as the ACS and the census long-form samples, include a range of uncertainty. Two broad types of error can occur: sampling error and nonsampling error. Nonsampling errors can result from mistakes in how the data are reported or coded, problems in the sampling frame or survey questionnaires, or problems related to nonresponse or interviewer bias. The Census Bureau tries to minimize nonsampling errors by using trained interviewers and by carefully reviewing the survey's sampling methods, data processing techniques, and questionnaire design.

Section 7 of the *ACS General Handbook* includes a more detailed description of different types of errors in the ACS and other measures of ACS quality: https://www.census.gov/programs-surveys/acs/guidance/handbooks/general.html.

Sampling error occurs when data are based on a sample of a population rather than the full population. Sampling error is easier to measure than nonsampling error and can be used to assess the statistical reliability of survey data. For any given area, the larger the sample and the more months included in the data, the greater the confidence in the estimate. The Census Bureau reports the 90-percent confidence interval on all ACS estimates produced since 2005. Beginning with the release of the 2006 ACS data, *margins of error (MOE)* are now provided for every ACS estimate. Ninety percent confidence intervals define a range expected to contain the *true* value of an estimate with a level of confidence of 90 percent. Margins of error are easily converted into these confidence ranges. By adding and subtracting the margin of error from the point estimate, we can calculate the 90-percent confidence interval for an estimate. Therefore, we can be 90 percent confident that the true number falls between the lower-bound interval and the upper-bound interval.

Detailed information about sampling error and instructions for calculating confidence intervals and margins of error are included in Section 7 of the *ACS General Handbook*. The margin of error around an estimate is important because it helps one draw conclusions about the data. Small differences between two estimates may not be statistically significant if the confidence intervals of those estimates overlap. However, the Census Bureau cautions data users not to rely on overlapping confidence intervals as a test for statistical significance, because this method will not always produce accurate results. Instead, the Census Bureau recommends following the detailed instructions for conducting statistical significance tests in Section 7 of the *ACS General Handbook*.

In some cases, data users will need to construct custom ACS estimates by combining data across multiple geographic areas or population subgroups or it may be necessary to derive a new percentage, proportion, or ratio from published ACS data. In such cases, additional calculations are needed to produce confidence intervals and margins of error for the derived estimates. Section 8 of the *ACS General Handbook* provides detailed instructions on how to make these calculations. Note that these error measures do not tell us about the magnitude of nonsampling errors.

Accessing ACS Data Online

All ACS data are available through the Census Bureau's Data Explorer website at https://data.census.gov/cedsci. From the home page, there is a search box that leads to both general and advanced searches, as well as links to lists of tables and maps that can be modified to user preference.

Basic information on using the functions and features of Census Explorer can be found at https://www.census.gov/data/what-is-data-census-gov.html.

The various ACS data products are described below.

- **Geographic comparison tables.** Those interested in geographic comparisons for areas other than states may be interested in the *geographic comparison tables*, which allow comparison of ACS data across a variety of geographic areas, including metropolitan areas, cities, counties, and congressional districts.

- **Subject tables.** These are similar to *data profiles* but are specific to a more detailed characteristic or topic (e.g., employment, education, and income). *Subject tables* provide pre-tabulated numbers and percentages for a wide variety of topics, often available separately by age (60 and over and 65 and over), gender, or race/ethnicity.

- **Selected population profiles.** The most detailed race/ethnic data are available through the *selected population profiles*, which provide summary tables separately for more than 400 detailed race, ethnic, tribal, ancestry, and country of birth groups.

- **Comparison profiles.** The *comparison profiles* show data side-by-side from multiple years, indicating where there is a statistically significant difference between the two sets of estimates. Comparison profiles are only available for 1-year estimates.

- **Thematic maps.** The *thematic maps* provide graphic displays of the data available through the various tables. Different shades of color are used to display variations in the data across geographic areas. Data users can also highlight areas with statistically different values from a selected state, county, or metropolitan area of interest. If a mapping option is available, it will display as an option when you view a table.

The ACS data are complex and cover a broad range of topics and geographic areas. Because this is a relatively new survey, many people do not fully understand how to interpret and use the ACS data. The key points are summarized below.

- Use caution in comparing ACS data with data from the decennial census or other sources. Every survey uses different methods, which could affect the comparability of the numbers. Some characteristics in the ACS, such as income, reflect a different reference period from the traditional long-form census.

- The ACS was designed to provide estimates of the characteristics of the population, not to provide counts of the population in different geographic areas or population subgroups. However, counts of the population are often what is required by grant applications and researchers and is primarily what is provided in this publication.

- Be careful in drawing conclusions about small differences between two estimates because they may not be statistically different. Statistical testing should always be considered based on the sensitivity of conclusions to differences in the data results. Users can check the table on Census Explorer to review the margin of error.

- Data users need to be careful not to interpret annual fluctuations in the data as long-term trends. Again, statistical testing is necessary to determine if annual fluctuations are real or merely a result of the sample.

- Use caution in comparing data from 2006 and later surveys with data from the 2000–2005 surveys. Unlike earlier surveys, the 2006 and later ACS surveys include samples of the population living in group quarters (e.g., college dorms and nursing homes), so the data may not be comparable, especially for young adults and the elderly, who are more likely than other age groups to be living in group quarters facilities.

- The questionnaire series to define disability changed in 2008 making it impossible to compare disability status for periods before that date.

- Data users should not interpret or refer to multi-year period estimates as estimates of the middle year or last year in the series. For example, a 2013–2017 estimate is not a "2015 average."

- Data users should always be consistent in comparing similar period estimates over time or between geographic areas. Compare 1-year to 1-year, 3-year to 3-year and 5-year to 5-year estimates. Since geographic areas of different population size have different period estimates available, always make comparisons using the same period estimate. Do not compare a 1-year estimate for a large population size area to a 5-year estimate for a small area or census tract.

- Due to reductions in funding authorization for data products, the Census Bureau has eliminated the 3-year ACS estimates. The last set of 3-year estimates covered the period 2011–2013.

- Data users should *not* rely on overlapping confidence intervals as a test for statistical significance because this method will not always provide an accurate result.

Who
Age, Race/Ethnicity, and Household Structure

Who: Age, Race/Ethnicity, and Household Structure

Every ten years, the census measures changes in the American population: shifts in race and ethnic groups, changing age patterns, migration among cities and regions, and changes in the predominant household structures. In the years between censuses, the American Community Survey is used to discover the details of these changes and the changes that are occurring in the new decade. In earlier decades, these detailed characteristics could not be updated until the next decennial census. The ACS provides annual detailed information about states, metropolitan areas, and other geographic entities with populations of 65,000 or more. In addition, a supplemental one-year data file is released annually (with the exception of 2020 due to the COVID-19 pandemic) for geographic areas with populations of 20,000 or more. These supplemental tables are less detailed than the standard one-year data so that smaller geographic areas can be tallied without compromising the confidentiality of the data. For smaller areas with fewer than 20,000 residents, five-year estimates are available, providing a regular stream of detailed social, housing, and economic characteristics for demographic groups. All tables in this book use 2021 one-year data from the 1-year ACS tables, with the exception of the population change estimates, which use 2019 and 2010 data. The number of counties and cities included in this publication is limited, as the supplemental tables were not available at the time this edition went to press.

One of the American Community Survey's most valuable aspects is that it allows users to compare their city or town against other local areas or against the United States. It highlights the differences among small areas within the United States. National trends are not mirrored in every community. Some places are changing even faster than the national picture; others are lagging or even going in a different direction. It is important for people to know how their locality fits into the national picture. These tables offer Americans information needed to compare various areas to see how they differ and how they are similar.

Population

Although the ACS has replaced the census long form as the key source of detailed social and economic characteristics, the official population estimates are still developed through the Census Bureau's Population Estimates Program. After the 2010 census, all ACS estimates were adjusted to reflect the new population count. The ACS single-year estimates are based on the official total population estimates from the Population Estimates Program. For states, metropolitan areas, and counties, the ACS total population is usually the same as the official population estimate, but the city populations often differ because of weighting and adjustments, and there are some cities (as well as counties) in this book with ACS populations below 20,000. The ACS includes census designated places (CDPs)—and we include them in this book—but they are not included in the Population Estimates Program.

Ten states had populations of 10 million or more in 2021, led by California with nearly 40 million and Texas with nearly 30 million. More than half of the nation's population lived in these ten states. Another five states and the District of Columbia had populations of less than 1 million, representing 1.3 percent of the nation's population. Between 2010 and 2019, the United States' population increased 6.3 percent. The District of Columbia grew by 17.3 percent in those 9 years, more than any of the states, while Texas added 15.3 percent to its already large population. Due to a boom in oil extraction, North Dakota's population grew by 13.3 percent. The populations of Arizona, Utah, Florida, Colorado, Idaho, North Carolina, Nevada, Oregon, South Carolina, and Washington also increased by more than 10 percent. Overall, 20 states and the District of Columbia had population growth above the national average. Four states had population growth of less than one percent, and four states lost population. West Virginia had the largest decrease at 3.3 percent, a loss of nearly 60,000 people.

About 37 percent of the U.S. population resided in the 75 most populous counties in 2021. Forty-seven of these counties had populations exceeding 1 million. These 45 large counties were home to 29 percent of Americans. Los Angeles County was, by far, the most populous county in the nation, with nearly 10 million residents. New York City consists of five counties which together total nearly 8.5 million people. Four of these counties are in the top 30.

Almost 290 million people, or about 88 percent of the population, lived in the nation's 390 metropolitan statistical areas (including those in Puerto Rico). Nearly one-third of the U.S. population resided in the 15 most populous metropolitan areas, those with about 4 million people or more. Fifty-three metropolitan areas had populations of 1 million or more. Seventeen metropolitan areas had growth rates of 20 percent or more between 2010 and 2019 (the most recent year for which data are available). The highest growth rate was 41.7 percent in The Villages, Florida. Among metropolitan areas of more than 1 million people, the largest growth was 29.8 percent in Austin-Round Rock-Georgetown, Texas, followed by Raleigh, North Carolina, at 23.0 percent, and Orlando, Florida, at 22.2 percent. With just over 7 million people, the Houston-The Woodlands-Sugar Land, Texas, metropolitan area is the fifth largest in the nation, and it increased by 19.4 percent between 2010 and 2019. About 40 percent of the metropolitan areas had growth rates exceeding the national rate of 6.3 percent, while 86 areas lost population, with Pine Bluff, Arkansas losing 12.4 percent of its population. Seven metropolitan areas with over a million residents experienced population losses—Birmingham-Hoover, Alabama (5.2 percent); Detroit-Dearborn-Livonia, Michigan (3.7 percent); Pittsburgh, Pennsylvania (1.6 percent); Cleveland-Elyria, Ohio

(1.4 percent); Rochester, New York (0.9 percent); Buffalo-Cheektowaga, New York (0.7 percent); and Hartford-East Hartford-Middletown, Connecticut (0.6 percent).

Thirty-seven cities had populations of 500,000 or more in 2021, including 9 with populations of 1 million or more. With more than 8 million people, New York is, by far, the largest city. Los Angeles is second, with nearly 4 million people, and Chicago's 2.7 million people still outnumber the fast-growing Houston's 2.3 million.

Age

In 2021, the United States' median age was 38.8 years, with half of the people older and half the people younger. Sixteen states had median ages of 40 or higher, topped by Maine, at 44.7 years. Utah had the lowest median age, at

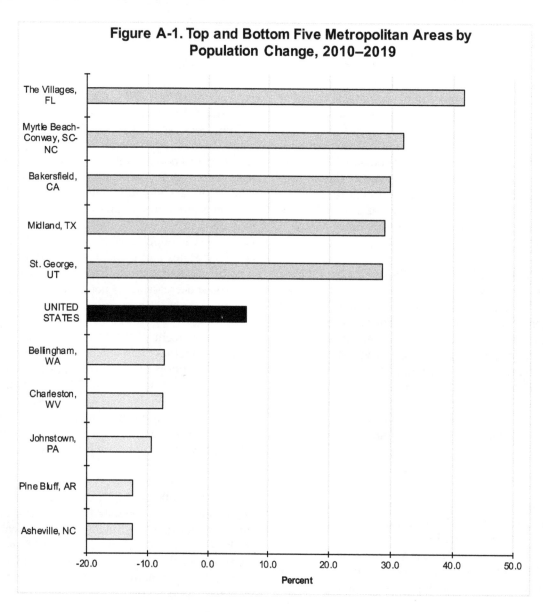

Figure A-1. Top and Bottom Five Metropolitan Areas by Population Change, 2010–2019

31.8 years. Only Utah and the District of Columbia had median ages lower than 35 years. Nearly 30 percent of Utah's population was under age 18, compared with 22.1 percent for the nation as a whole. At the other extreme, only about 19 percent of the District of Columbia's population was under 18 years, despite its relatively low median age of 34.8. Over 41 percent of the District of Columbia's population was in the 25- to 44-year old age group, well above the national level of 35.9 percent. In the District of Columbia, Vermont, Maine, New Hampshire, Rhode Island, Massachusetts, and Florida, children under 18 years old accounted for less than 20 percent of their populations. In Delaware, Florida, West Virginia, Vermont, and Maine, over 20 percent of residents were 65 years or older, and 25 other states had levels above the national proportion of 16.8 percent. In two states and Puerto Rico, 2.4 percent or more of the population was 85 years old and over, while only Alaska had less than 1 percent in that age group.

Three metropolitan areas had more than 32 percent residents under the age of 18. Two were located in Texas, and one was located in Utah. Five metropolitan areas had at least one in three residents who were over age 65, all of them in Florida. By far, the highest proportion was in The Villages, where 59.5 percent of residents were age 65 or older.

Eighteen of the selected counties for which 2021 data were available had median ages of 50 or older. The most populous was Sarasota County, Florida, with more than 445,000 residents; Collier County, Florida; Yavapai County, Arizona; Sussex County, Delaware; Barnstable County, Massachusetts; and Mohave County, Arizona, all had more than 200,000 residents. Two counties, both in Utah, had median ages under 26. In 11 counties, at least 30 percent of the population was under age 18; four of these counties were in Texas, three were in Utah, and one each in Washington, Idaho, California, and New Mexico.

The median age in five of the 640 cities surveyed was 60 years or more. All of these cities were located in Florida. In 2021, of the nearly 640 cities surveyed, 13 had 25 percent or more of their populations consisting of people 65 years and older. Nationally, this age group accounted for 16.5 percent of the population. In one city surveyed, more than half of the residents were under 18 years old: Lakewood, New Jersey, which has large Orthodox Jewish communities. Twenty-two cities had between 30 and 41 percent of their populations under 18, with the majority in Utah, California, and Texas. Seven of the surveyed cities, many of them college towns, had median ages of 25 years or less.

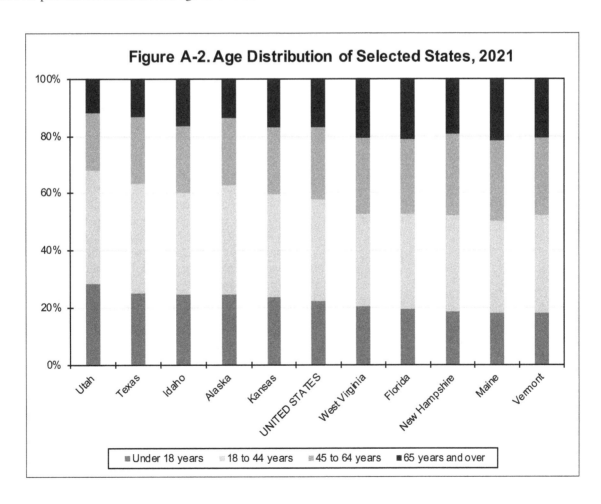

Figure A-2. Age Distribution of Selected States, 2021

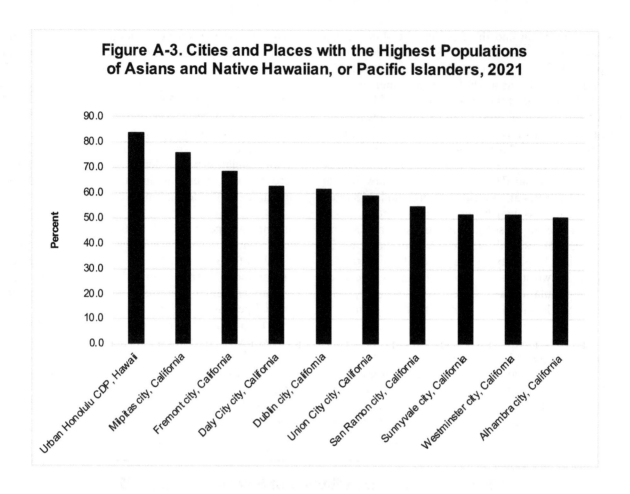

Figure A-3. Cities and Places with the Highest Populations
of Asians and Native Hawaiian, or Pacific Islanders, 2021

The working-age population is generally considered to include people between the ages of 16 and 64, but another definition includes only ages 25 to 64 to exclude the many 18- to 24-year-olds who are in school or training situations. Nationally, 52.1 percent of the population was in this latter category. Thirty-nine surveyed cities had proportions of working-age population that exceeded 50 percent. In 20 cities, fewer than 30 percent of residents were between the ages of 25 and 64. These were mostly retirement communities and college towns.

Race/Ethnicity

Probably the most visible place-based demographic difference is in racial and ethnic composition. Seen from afar, the U.S. population may be a melting pot, but at close range it varies widely. For example, more than 90 percent of the population of Maine, Vermont, and West Virginia was non-Hispanic White. In contrast, Hawaii, the District of Columbia, California, Maryland, New Mexico, Texas, and Nevada are all "majority minority" states, with non-Hispanic Whites making up less than 50 percent of their populations. Almost half of the District of Columbia's residents were Black. Nearly 21 percent of Alaskan residents

were American Indian or Alaska Native alone or in combination. More than four in five Hawaiian residents were Asian, Native Hawaiian, or other Pacific Islander. In New Mexico, just over half of the population was Hispanic or Latino.

Nineteen metropolitan areas—all relatively small—had populations consisting of 95 percent or more of White alone or in combination (including both Hispanic and non-Hispanic.) In the Honolulu metropolitan area, about 86 percent of the population identified as Asian, Native Hawaiian, or Pacific Islander.[1] Albany, Georgia, was a majority Black metropolitan areas, with more than half of their populations identifying as Black alone or in combination. In another 11 metropolitan areas—all in the South—more than 40 percent of the residents were Black. The Memphis TN-MS-AR metropolitan area was the only one with more than 1 million residents. Hispanic or Latino residents make up a majority in 21 metropolitan areas, the largest of which are Riverside-San Bernardino-Ontario, California, with 4.65 million residents, and San

---

[1] There is some double counting of persons who identified with both groups ("Asian alone or in combination" and "Native Hawaiian or Pacific Islander alone or in combination").

Figure A-4. Foreign-Born U.S. Residents, by County, 2021

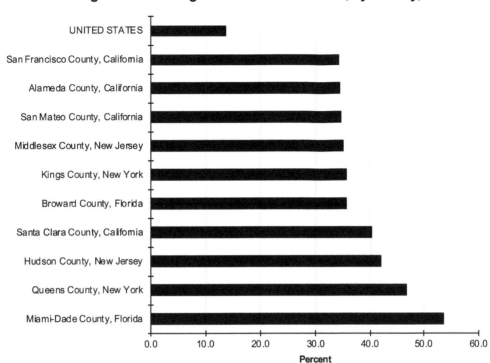

Antonio-New Braunfels, Texas, with nearly 2.6 million residents. [2] In another 10 metropolitan areas, the proportion of Hispanic or Latino residents is between 40 and 50 percent. These include Los Angeles-Long Beach-Anaheim, with 13.2 million residents and Miami-Fort Lauderdale-Pompano Beach, with nearly 6.2 million.

Thirty-five of the limited number of cities surveyed for 2021 had White populations of 90 percent or higher. There were 12 cities where more than 90 percent of the residents identified as Hispanic or Latino; these were in Puerto Rico, California, Texas, and Florida. In four cities, more than 80 percent of residents were Black or African American alone. Detroit's population was 79.7 percent Black or African American, the highest level among the largest cities. In five cities—one in Hawaii and four in California—more than 60 percent of residents were Asian, Hawaiian or Pacific Islander.

Foreign-Born Populations and Foreign Languages

Nationally, 13.6 percent of the population was foreign born. Nearly 27 percent of California's population was foreign born, and New York, New Jersey, and Florida, had

___
[2] Hispanic or Latino persons may be of any race. Most self-identify as "White" or "some other race."

levels at 20 percent or more. West Virginia had the lowest proportion of foreign-born residents at 1.6 percent, while Mississippi and Montana both had levels below three percent.

In 12 counties, one-third or more of the residents were foreign born. Eight of these counties had more than a million residents; the percentage of foreign-born residents were led by Miami-Dade County, Florida with 53.6 percent, and Queens County, New York, with 46.8 percent. Thirty-two metropolitan areas had foreign-born populations of 20 percent or more. The Miami and San Jose metropolitan areas had the highest proportions, both at more than 39 percent, and just under one-third of residents in Los Angeles and San Francisco were foreign born.

Of the 640 cities for which 2021 data were available, 352 had foreign-born proportions that exceeded the U.S. average. Eight cities had majority foreign-born residents. More than 60 percent of the residents of Hialeah and Doral, Florida, were foreign born. Three cities of more than 100,000 had majority foreign-born populations: Hialeah and Miami, Florida, and Glendale, California.

Nearly one in five American households spoke a language other than English at home (in addition to or instead of English). California had the highest proportion—almost

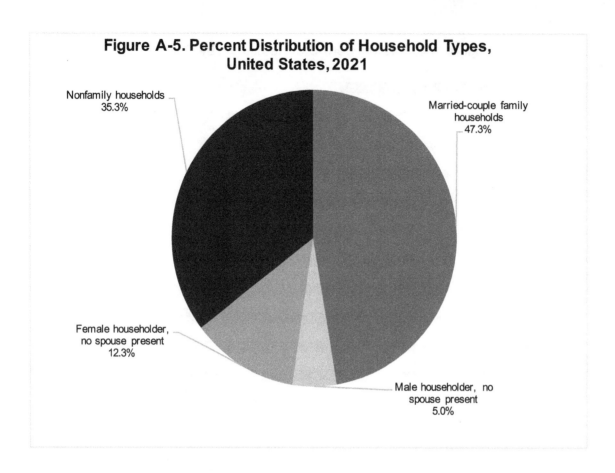

Figure A-5. Percent Distribution of Household Types, United States, 2021

Nonfamily households
35.3%

Married-couple family households
47.3%

Female householder, no spouse present
12.3%

Male householder, no spouse present
5.0%

46 percent of households—while between 35 and 40 percent of households in New Mexico and Texas spoke another language at home. Spanish-speaking households were most prevalent in New Mexico (29.4 percent), Texas (29.3 percent), California (26.6 percent), and Florida (22.2 percent). In Hawaii, 28.9 percent of households spoke languages other than English and Spanish, and 19.0 percent of California households were in this group. More than 30 percent of households in New York and New Jersey spoke languages other than English, with roughly half of them speaking Spanish and half speaking other languages at home. In just over 8 percent of California households and over 6 percent of New York, Texas, Massachusetts, and Florida households, no adult spoke English well. West Virginia and Mississippi had the lowest proportions of households speaking a language other than English, both under 5 percent.

Household Structure

Places that differ from the national age portrait also differ from the nation's household portrait. Almost two-thirds of the nation's households were family households (people related by birth, marriage, or adoption), and 47.3 percent of all households were married-couple family households. Nonfamily households included people living alone or with

unrelated people. In some areas, people lived predominantly in married-couple households, while others were dominated by male- and female-headed family households (no spouse present) or by nonfamily households.

Nearly 36 percent of the nation's households are made up of nonfamily households—people living alone, or with other, unrelated adults. Thirty-four states, Puerto Rico, and the District of Columbia had proportions of nonfamily households that exceeded this national level. Nearly 60 percent of the District of Columbia's households were nonfamily households, many of them one-person households. Nationally, 28.3 percent of households consisted of a person living alone.

Although there were large numbers of single-person households in every age group, Vermont, Maine, West Virginia, Pennsylvania, and Rhode Island had the highest proportions of persons over 65 years old living alone (all at or above 13.0 percent) while Florida, Montana, Connecticut, Ohio, Delaware, New Mexico, and New York all had levels above 12.5 percent.

About 7.2 percent of householders were unmarried partner couples, ranging from 4.7 percent in Mississippi to 10.7 percent in Vermont. Same-sex unmarried couples comprised 0.4 percent of all households, while married same-sex couples were estimated to be about 0.6 percent of all households in 2021.

In the United States, just over 34 percent of adults had never married by 2021. The District of Columbia had the highest proportion of never married residents at 55.3 percent, and 14 states had rates above the national level, led by New York, California, Massachusetts, and Rhode Island, all above 37 percent. Puerto Rico had a rate of 43.2 percent. Utah and Idaho had the highest percentages of currently married residents, at 56.4 and 55.9 percent, respectively. Nationally, just under half of all persons are currently married, but 17 states, Puerto Rico, and the District of Columbia have lower proportions. West Virginia and Arkansas had the highest proportions of divorced residents among states, at 13.3 percent each, while more than 12.5 percent were divorced in six more states. New Jersey, California, and Utah had the lowest proportions of divorced individuals, all under 9 percent.

In seven metropolitan areas in the area excluding Puerto Rico, 20 percent or more of households were female-headed families, compared with 12.3 percent for the nation as a whole. Nationally, 47.5 percent of households were married-couple families. In four metropolitan areas, most in Utah and Idaho, married-couple families equaled or exceeded 60 percent of households. The proportion was less than 40 percent in 13 metropolitan areas, some with large student populations.

Among the states, Utah had the highest average household size—2.99 persons per household, followed by Hawaii and California with 2.86 persons per household each. The District of Columbia (1.98 persons per household), Maine (2.25 persons per household), and Vermont (2.29 persons per household) had the lowest average household sizes. The national average was 2.54 persons per household.

Just over 65 percent of households with children were married-couple family households. Utah had the highest proportion—78.9 percent—and the District of Columbia had the lowest proportion, 52.6 percent. Just over 30 percent of American households included children under 18 years old in 2021, with proportions ranging from 38.3 percent in Utah to 18.8 percent in the District of Columbia, 23.6 percent in Puerto Rico, and 24.1 percent in Maine.

Nationally, 41.5 percent of households included someone 60 years old or older in 2021. Just under half of the states (plus Puerto Rico at 53.2 percent) had higher proportions, led by Hawaii, Florida, Delaware, Maine, West Virginia, and New Hampshire, all with more than 45 percent. In the District of Columbia and Utah, less than one-third of households include someone over 60 years of age. In 82 of the selected counties for which 2021 data were available, more than half of the households included someone age 60 years or over, led by Sumter County, Florida where 81.4 percent of the households included this age group. Arlington County, Virginia; Travis County, Texas; Utah County, Utah; Midland County, Texas; and Onslow County, North Carolina, count fewer than 25 percent of their households with people 60 years old or older. These counties generally have large student and military populations. Among the 75 largest cities, only 6 exceed the national level of 41.5 percent of households with persons age 60 or over: San Juan zona urbana, Puerto Rico, with 50.7 percent; Urban Honolulu CDP, Hawaii, with 49.4 percent of households; Scottsdale, Arizona, with 47.3 percent; Henderson, Nevada, with 44.4 percent of households; St. Petersburg, Florida, with 43.3 percent; and New York, New York, with 41.7 percent of households. In Austin, Texas, only 22.7 percent of households include this older age group, while Seattle, Washington; Minneapolis, Minnesota; Denver, Colorado; Irvine, California; and Charlotte, North Carolina, all have levels below 28 percent.

State Rankings, 2021

Selected Rankings

Population rank	State	Total population [A-1, col 1]	Percent change rank	State	Percent change, 2010 to 2019 [A-1, col 2]	Percent White alone, not Hispanic or Latino Rank	State	Percent White alone, not Hispanic or Latino [A-1, col 11]
	UNITED STATES........................	331,893,745		UNITED STATES........................	6.3		UNITED STATES.........	58.1
1	California..............................	39,237,836	1	District of Columbia.................	15.3	1	Vermont....................	90.6
2	Texas	29,527,941	2	Texas	12.6	2	West Virginia.............	90.4
3	Florida.................................	21,781,128	3	North Dakota	12.3	3	Maine.......................	90.0
4	New York..............................	19,835,913	4	Utah	12.2	4	New Hampshire..........	87.3
5	Pennsylvania	12,964,056	5	Florida	11.6	5	Montana....................	83.8
6	Illinois	12,671,469	6	Colorado	11.5	6	Iowa........................	83.0
7	Ohio	11,780,017	7	Nevada	11.0	7	Kentucky..................	82.7
8	Georgia	10,799,566	8	Washington	10.1	8	North Dakota............	82.3
9	North Carolina	10,551,162	9	Arizona	9.8	9	Wyoming...................	81.5
10	Michigan	10,050,811	10	Idaho	9.5	10	South Dakota	80.0
11	New Jersey	9,267,130	11	South Carolina....................	8.6	11	Wisconsin..................	79.0
12	Virginia	8,642,274	12	Oregon	8.1	12	Idaho.......................	78.7
13	Washington	7,738,692	13	North Carolina	7.7	13	Minnesota.................	76.9
14	Arizona	7,276,316	14	Georgia	7.6	14	Indiana.....................	76.6
15	Massachusetts	6,984,723	15	Delaware	7.1	14	Missouri....................	76.6
16	Tennessee............................	6,975,218	16	South Dakota	6.8	14	Ohio........................	76.6
17	Indiana	6,805,985	17	Montana	6.2	17	Nebraska..................	76.4
18	Missouri...............................	6,168,187	18	California	6.1	18	Utah........................	76.0
19	Maryland	6,165,129	19	Virginia	5.9	19	Pennsylvania.............	73.6
20	Wisconsin.............................	5,895,908	20	Tennessee	5.8	20	Kansas.....................	73.4
21	Colorado	5,812,069	21	Minnesota	5.1	21	Michigan...................	72.9
22	Minnesota	5,707,390	21	Nebraska	5.1	22	Tennessee.................	72.1
23	South Carolina	5,190,705	23	Hawaii	4.9	23	Oregon.....................	72.0
24	Alabama...............................	5,039,877	24	Maryland	4.8	24	Rhode Island..............	68.9
25	Louisiana	4,624,047	24	Massachusetts	4.8	25	Arkansas..................	68.2
26	Kentucky	4,509,394	24	Oklahoma	4.8	26	Massachusetts	67.5
27	Oregon	4,246,155	27	Alaska	4.2	27	Colorado...................	65.2
28	Oklahoma	3,986,639	28	Louisiana	3.3	28	Washington	64.3
29	Connecticut..........................	3,605,597	29	Iowa	3.2	29	Alabama....................	64.2
30	Utah....................................	3,337,975	30	Arkansas	3.0	30	Oklahoma..................	62.8
31	Iowa....................................	3,193,079	31	Indiana	2.8	31	Connecticut...............	62.7
32	Nevada	3,143,991	31	Wyoming	2.8	32	South Carolina...........	62.6
33	Arkansas..............................	3,025,891	33	Kentucky	2.6	33	North Carolina...........	60.9
34	Mississippi	2,949,965	34	New Jersey	2.4	34	Delaware..................	59.3
35	Kansas.................................	2,934,582	34	New York	2.4	35	Virginia....................	59.2
36	New Mexico	2,115,877	36	Kansas	2.1	36	Illinois.....................	58.9
37	Nebraska	1,963,692	36	Missouri	2.1	37	Alaska	57.9
38	Idaho	1,900,923	38	Alabama	2.0	38	Louisiana..................	56.9
39	West Virginia	1,782,959	38	New Hampshire	2.0	39	Mississippi	55.4
40	Hawaii.................................	1,441,553	40	Wisconsin	1.9	40	New York..................	53.5
41	New Hampshire......................	1,388,992	41	New Mexico	1.4	41	New Jersey................	52.1
42	Maine..................................	1,372,247	42	Ohio	1.1	42	Arizona....................	52.0
43	Montana...............................	1,104,271	43	Michigan	0.8	43	Florida.....................	51.1
44	Rhode Island.........................	1,095,610	43	Pennsylvania	0.8	44	Georgia....................	50.2
45	Delaware..............................	1,003,384	45	Maine	0.6	45	Maryland..................	47.8
46	South Dakota	895,376	45	Rhode Island	0.6	46	Nevada....................	45.2
47	North Dakota.........................	774,948	47	Mississippi	0.5	47	Texas	39.4
48	Alaska..................................	732,673	48	Connecticut	0.4	48	District of Columbia....	36.4
49	District of Columbia.................	670,050	49	Illinois	-0.2	49	New Mexico	34.9
50	Vermont...............................	645,570	50	Vermont	-0.3	50	California..................	34.3
51	Wyoming..............................	578,803	51	West Virginia	-2.0	51	Hawaii.....................	20.8

State Rankings, 2021

Selected Rankings

Percent Black or African American rank	State	Percent Black or African American alone or in combination [A-1, col 4]	Percent American Indian/ Alaska Native rank	State	Percent American Indian/ Alaska Native alone or in combination [A-1, col 5]	Percent Asian rank	State	Percent Asian alone or in combination [A-1, col 6]
	UNITED STATES.........................	14.2		UNITED STATES.......................	2.6		UNITED STATES.........	7.1
1	District of Columbia....................	47.1	1	Alaska	20.7	1	Hawaii	56.5
2	Mississippi	37.7	2	Oklahoma...............................	14.6	2	California...................	17.8
3	Georgia	33.4	3	New Mexico	12.8	3	Washington	12.3
4	Louisiana	33.2	4	South Dakota	10.5	4	Nevada	11.3
5	Maryland	32.3	5	Montana	8.3	5	New Jersey	11.1
6	Alabama	27.3	6	North Dakota	7.1	6	New York...................	9.9
7	South Carolina..........................	26.9	7	Arizona..................................	6.0	7	Alaska	9.0
8	Delaware	24.3	8	Wyoming................................	4.2	8	Virginia	8.5
9	North Carolina..........................	22.6	8	Oregon..................................	4.2	9	Massachusetts	8.3
10	Virginia	21.2	10	Washington	3.5	10	Maryland	8.0
11	Florida	17.7	11	Colorado	3.3	11	Illinois	6.8
12	New York..................................	17.6	11	California...............................	3.3	12	Oregon......................	6.6
13	Tennessee	17.4	13	Idaho....................................	3.2	13	Texas	6.3
14	Arkansas	16.2	13	Nevada	3.2	14	Minnesota	6.2
15	New Jersey	15.5	15	Kansas	3.1	15	Connecticut................	5.8
16	Michigan	15.4	16	North Carolina	3.0	15	District of Columbia....	5.8
17	Illinois	15.2	17	Hawaii	2.8	17	Georgia	5.3
18	Ohio	14.3	17	Arkansas	2.8	18	Delaware	5.1
19	Connecticut..............................	13.8	19	Utah	2.5	19	Arizona......................	4.8
20	Texas	13.7	20	Nebraska	2.4	19	Colorado	4.8
21	Pennsylvania	12.8	20	Georgia	2.4	21	Pennsylvania	4.4
22	Missouri...................................	12.4	20	Texas	2.4	22	Michigan	4.1
23	Nevada	11.9	20	Delaware	2.4	22	Rhode Island..............	4.1
24	Indiana	10.8	24	Mississippi	2.3	24	Utah	4.0
25	Massachusetts	10.1	24	Minnesota	2.3	25	North Carolina	3.9
26	Oklahoma.................................	9.6	24	Kentucky	2.3	26	Florida	3.8
27	Kentucky	9.0	27	Missouri................................	2.2	26	Kansas	3.8
28	Rhode Island.............................	8.8	27	Louisiana	2.2	28	Wisconsin..................	3.7
29	Minnesota	8.5	29	Alabama	2.1	29	New Hampshire	3.5
30	Wisconsin	7.6	29	Illinois	2.1	30	Nebraska	3.4
31	Kansas	7.5	31	Virginia	2.0	31	Oklahoma..................	3.2
32	California..................................	7.3	31	Tennessee	2.0	32	Ohio	3.1
33	Arizona.....................................	6.3	31	Wisconsin	2.0	32	Iowa	3.1
33	Nebraska	6.3	31	Indiana	2.0	34	Indiana	3.0
35	Washington	5.9	35	South Carolina........................	1.9	35	Missouri....................	2.8
36	Colorado	5.7	35	Vermont	1.9	36	New Mexico	2.7
37	Alaska	5.3	37	West Virginia	1.8	37	Idaho........................	2.5
38	Iowa	5.1	37	New York...............................	1.8	37	Vermont	2.5
39	West Virginia	4.3	37	Michigan	1.8	39	Tennessee	2.4
40	North Dakota............................	4.1	37	Iowa	1.8	40	South Carolina...........	2.3
41	Hawaii	3.7	41	Maryland...............................	1.7	41	South Dakota	2.3
42	New Mexico	3.5	41	Maine....................................	1.7	41	Louisiana	2.3
43	Oregon.....................................	3.2	43	Ohio	1.6	43	Arkansas	2.2
43	South Dakota	2.9	44	District of Columbia.................	1.5	44	North Dakota.............	2.1
45	New Hampshire	2.7	44	Connecticut............................	1.5	44	Kentucky	2.1
46	Maine.......................................	2.2	44	Rhode Island...........................	1.5	46	Maine........................	1.9
47	Utah	2.1	47	Florida	1.4	46	Alabama	1.9
47	Vermont	2.0	48	New Jersey	1.3	48	Wyoming...................	1.6
49	Wyoming..................................	1.6	49	New Hampshire	1.2	48	Mississippi	1.6
50	Idaho.......................................	1.3	49	Pennsylvania	1.2	50	Montana	1.5
51	Montana	1.0	51	Massachusetts	1.1	51	West Virginia	1.2

State Rankings, 2021

Selected Rankings

Percent Hispanic or Latino rank	State	Percent Hispanic or Latino rank [A-1, col 9]	Median age rank	State	Median age, years [A-1, col 23]	Average household size rank	State	Average household size [A-1, col 43]
	UNITED STATES......	18.8		UNITED STATES......	38.8		UNITED STATES......	2.54
1	New Mexico	50.1	1	Maine	44.7	1	Utah	2.99
2	California	40.2	2	New Hampshire	43.1	2	California	2.86
2	Texas	40.2	3	Vermont	42.9	2	Hawaii	2.86
4	Arizona	32.3	4	Florida	42.8	4	Idaho	2.70
5	Nevada	29.9	4	West Virginia	42.8	5	Texas	2.68
6	Florida	26.8	6	Delaware	41.6	6	Georgia	2.64
7	Colorado	22.3	7	Connecticut	41.1	7	Alaska	2.61
8	New Jersey	21.5	8	Pennsylvania	40.9	7	Nevada	2.61
9	New York	19.5	9	Rhode Island	40.6	9	New Jersey	2.60
10	Illinois	18.0	10	New Jersey	40.3	10	Maryland	2.56
11	Connecticut	17.7	11	Hawaii	40.2	11	Mississippi	2.54
12	Rhode Island	17.1	11	Michigan	40.2	12	Arizona	2.53
13	Utah	14.8	11	South Carolina	40.2	13	Louisiana	2.52
14	Oregon	14.0	14	Montana	40.1	13	New York	2.52
15	Washington	13.7	14	Oregon	40.1	13	Virginia	2.52
16	Idaho	13.3	14	Wisconsin	40.1	16	Oklahoma	2.51
17	Massachusetts	12.8	17	Massachusetts	39.9	16	Washington	2.51
18	Kansas	12.7	18	Alabama	39.8	18	Alabama	2.50
19	Nebraska	11.9	18	New York	39.8	19	Arkansas	2.49
20	Oklahoma	11.7	20	Ohio	39.6	19	Florida	2.49
21	District of Columbia	11.5	21	North Carolina	39.4	19	New Mexico	2.49
22	Hawaii	11.1	22	Maryland	39.3	22	Illinois	2.48
22	Maryland	11.1	23	Missouri	39.2	23	Delaware	2.47
24	Wyoming	10.6	23	Tennessee	39.2	23	Indiana	2.47
25	Virginia	10.2	25	Kentucky	39.1	23	Kansas	2.47
26	North Carolina	10.1	25	New Mexico	39.1	23	South Carolina	2.47
26	Delaware	10.1	27	Illinois	39.0	27	Colorado	2.46
28	Georgia	10.0	27	Wyoming	39.0	27	Kentucky	2.46
29	Pennsylvania	8.4	29	Minnesota	38.8	27	New Hampshire	2.46
30	Arkansas	8.2	29	Virginia	38.8	27	North Carolina	2.46
31	Indiana	7.6	31	Nevada	38.7	27	Tennessee	2.46
32	Wisconsin	7.5	32	Arizona	38.6	32	Connecticut	2.45
33	Alaska	7.1	32	Mississippi	38.6	32	Minnesota	2.45
34	Iowa	6.6	34	Arkansas	38.5	34	Massachusetts	2.44
35	South Carolina	6.3	34	Iowa	38.5	34	Nebraska	2.44
36	Tennessee	6.0	36	Indiana	38.2	34	Oregon	2.44
37	Minnesota	5.8	36	Washington	38.2	37	Michigan	2.43
38	Michigan	5.6	38	Louisiana	38.0	37	Missouri	2.43
39	Louisiana	5.5	39	California	37.6	39	South Dakota	2.42
40	Alabama	4.7	39	Colorado	37.6	40	West Virginia	2.41
41	Missouri	4.6	39	South Dakota	37.6	41	Montana	2.40
42	New Hampshire	4.3	42	Georgia	37.5	41	Pennsylvania	2.40
42	Montana	4.3	43	Idaho	37.3	43	Rhode Island	2.39
42	Ohio	4.3	43	Kansas	37.3	44	Iowa	2.38
45	South Dakota	4.2	45	Nebraska	37.2	44	Ohio	2.38
45	North Dakota	4.1	45	Oklahoma	37.2	46	Wisconsin	2.35
47	Kentucky	3.9	47	North Dakota	35.8	47	North Dakota	2.33
48	Mississippi	3.2	48	Alaska	35.6	47	Wyoming	2.33
49	Vermont	2.0	49	Texas	35.5	49	Vermont	2.29
50	Maine	1.9	50	District of Columbia	34.8	50	Maine	2.25
51	West Virginia	1.7	51	Utah	31.8	51	District of Columbia	1.98

State Rankings, 2021

Selected Rankings

Never married rank	State	Percent never married [A-1, col 33]	Now married (includes separated) rank	State	Percent now married (includes separated) [A-1, col 34]	Divorced rank	State	Percent divorced [A-1, col 36]
	UNITED STATES......................	34.2		UNITED STATES......................	49.7		UNITED STATES......................	10.6
1	District of Columbia................	55.3	1	Utah..............................	56.4	1	West Virginia.........................	13.3
2	New York.............................	38.7	2	Idaho..............................	55.9	1	Arkansas...........................	13.3
3	California.............................	38.2	3	Wyoming........................	55.2	3	Maine..............................	13.2
4	Massachusetts.....................	37.5	4	Nebraska.........................	53.2	4	New Mexico	12.8
5	Rhode Island.......................	37.4	5	Kansas............................	52.6	4	Nevada.............................	12.8
5	Louisiana	36.4	5	South Dakota	52.6	6	Oregon.............................	12.7
7	Illinois................................	36.1	7	New Hampshire	52.5	7	Oklahoma..........................	12.6
8	Connecticut.........................	35.9	8	Maine..............................	52.4	7	Kentucky...........................	12.6
9	Maryland............................	35.6	9	Iowa...............................	52.3	9	Florida	12.5
10	Georgia	35.2	10	Montana	52.1	9	Indiana.............................	12.5
11	New Mexico	35.1	11	Washington.......................	52.1	11	Wyoming...........................	12.3
12	Nevada...............................	35.0	12	Texas	51.8	12	Alabama............................	12.2
13	Mississippi	34.6	13	Minnesota	51.7	13	Idaho...............................	11.9
14	New Jersey	34.4	14	New Jersey	51.5	13	Montana	11.9
14	Pennsylvania........................	34.4	14	Colorado	51.5	13	Ohio................................	11.9
16	Delaware	34.1	16	Virginia............................	51.4	13	Tennessee..........................	11.9
17	Hawaii................................	34.0	17	North Dakota.....................	51.2	17	Missouri............................	11.8
18	Michigan.............................	33.9	18	Missouri...........................	51.1	18	Louisiana...........................	11.7
19	North Dakota........................	33.8	19	Arkansas...........................	50.9	18	New Hampshire	11.7
20	Alaska................................	33.6	19	Hawaii.............................	50.9	20	Arizona.............................	11.6
21	Texas	33.4	21	Kentucky	50.9	21	Mississippi	11.5
21	Ohio..................................	33.4	22	Alaska.............................	50.8	21	Michigan...........................	11.5
23	Virginia...............................	33.3	22	Wisconsin.........................	50.8	23	Vermont............................	11.4
23	Minnesota	33.3	24	Oklahoma.........................	50.7	23	Washington	11.4
23	Colorado	33.3	24	Tennessee.........................	50.7	25	Alaska..............................	11.3
26	Wisconsin............................	33.2	24	North Carolina	50.7	25	Georgia	11.3
27	Arizona...............................	33.1	24	West Virginia......................	50.7	27	Colorado	11.1
28	Vermont..............................	32.9	28	Indiana............................	50.4	28	Kansas..............................	11.0
28	North Carolina......................	32.9	28	Vermont...........................	50.4	29	Wisconsin	10.8
30	South Carolina......................	32.8	30	Arizona............................	50.2	29	Rhode Island.......................	10.8
31	Oregon...............................	32.5	31	South Carolina	50.1	31	North Carolina	10.7
32	Washington..........................	32.2	32	Oregon............................	50.0	32	Iowa................................	10.5
33	South Dakota	32.0	33	Pennsylvania......................	49.8	32	South Carolina	10.5
34	Alabama..............................	31.7	34	Delaware	49.7	34	Nebraska	10.4
34	Iowa..................................	31.7	35	Florida	49.3	34	Connecticut........................	10.4
34	Florida	31.7	35	Maryland..........................	49.3	36	Minnesota	10.1
37	Utah..................................	31.5	37	Alabama...........................	49.0	37	Virginia.............................	10.0
38	Indiana...............................	31.4	38	Michigan	48.9	38	Texas	9.9
39	Nebraska	31.2	39	Illinois.............................	48.8	38	South Dakota	9.9
40	Tennessee............................	31.1	40	Ohio...............................	48.7	38	Delaware	9.9
40	Missouri..............................	31.1	41	Connecticut.......................	48.4	41	Maryland...........................	9.8
42	Kansas................................	30.7	42	Georgia	48.3	41	North Dakota......................	9.8
43	New Hampshire	30.6	42	California..........................	48.3	43	Pennsylvania.......................	9.7
43	Montana	30.6	44	Massachusetts	48.1	44	Illinois..............................	9.6
45	Oklahoma............................	30.4	45	Mississippi	47.0	45	Hawaii..............................	9.4
46	Kentucky.............................	29.9	46	Nevada............................	46.8	46	District of Columbia...............	9.3
47	Arkansas.............................	29.2	47	New York..........................	46.5	47	Massachusetts	9.2
48	West Virginia........................	28.7	48	New Mexico	46.3	48	New York	9.1
49	Maine.................................	28.6	28	Rhode Island......................	46.3	49	California...........................	8.9
50	Wyoming.............................	27.5	50	Louisiana	45.7	50	Utah................................	8.6
51	Idaho.................................	27.4	51	District of Columbia..............	31.5	51	New Jersey	8.5

State Rankings, 2021

Selected Rankings

Foreign born rank	State	Percent foreign born [A-1, col. 37]	Spanish-speaking households rank	State	Percent Spanish-speaking households [A-1, col. 39]	Households where no adult speaks English well rank	State	Percent households where no adult speaks English well [A-1, col. 41]
	UNITED STATES..................	13.6		UNITED STATES..................	12.8		UNITED STATES..................	4.2
1	California..................	26.6	1	New Mexico..................	29.4	1	California..................	8.3
2	New Jersey..................	23.0	2	Texas..................	29.3	2	New York..................	7.4
3	New York..................	22.3	3	California..................	26.6	3	New Jersey..................	6.9
4	Florida..................	21.2	4	Florida..................	22.2	4	Texas..................	6.8
5	Hawaii..................	18.8	5	Arizona..................	20.4	5	Florida..................	6.7
6	Nevada..................	18.4	6	Nevada..................	18.9	6	Massachusetts..................	6.1
7	Massachusetts..................	17.6	7	New Jersey..................	16.8	7	Rhode Island..................	5.7
8	Texas..................	17.2	8	New York..................	14.7	8	Hawaii..................	5.5
9	Maryland..................	15.9	9	Connecticut..................	13.3	9	New Mexico..................	5.3
10	Connecticut..................	15.2	10	Rhode Island..................	12.8	9	Connecticut..................	5.3
11	Washington..................	14.8	11	Illinois..................	12.3	11	Nevada..................	5.0
12	Rhode Island..................	14.5	12	Utah..................	11.9	12	Illinois..................	4.3
13	Illinois..................	14.2	13	Colorado..................	11.2	13	Arizona..................	3.8
14	District of Columbia..................	13.3	14	Massachusetts..................	9.9	13	Washington..................	3.8
15	Arizona..................	12.6	15	Idaho..................	9.5	15	District of Columbia..................	3.4
16	Virginia..................	12.4	16	District of Columbia..................	8.6	16	Maryland..................	3.3
17	Delaware..................	10.1	17	Oregon..................	8.4	17	Nebraska..................	2.8
18	Georgia..................	10.0	18	Washington..................	8.3	18	Pennsylvania..................	2.6
19	Colorado..................	9.8	19	Maryland..................	8.1	18	Virginia..................	2.6
20	Oregon..................	9.7	20	Kansas..................	7.6	18	Georgia..................	2.6
21	New Mexico..................	9.1	20	Georgia..................	7.6	21	Colorado..................	2.5
22	Minnesota..................	8.5	22	Nebraska..................	7.4	22	Kansas..................	2.4
23	Utah..................	8.3	23	Oklahoma..................	7.3	23	Oregon..................	2.3
24	North Carolina..................	8.2	23	Delaware..................	7.3	24	Delaware..................	2.2
25	Alaska..................	8.1	23	Virginia..................	7.3	24	Utah..................	2.2
26	Nebraska..................	7.4	26	North Carolina..................	7.0	24	North Carolina..................	2.2
27	Pennsylvania..................	7.2	27	Pennsylvania..................	5.6	24	Alaska..................	2.2
28	Kansas..................	6.9	28	Wyoming..................	5.5	24	Minnesota..................	2.2
28	Michigan..................	6.8	29	Arkansas..................	5.1	29	Idaho..................	2.0
30	Idaho..................	6.1	30	Indiana..................	4.9	30	Oklahoma..................	1.9
31	New Hampshire..................	5.9	31	Alaska..................	4.8	31	Michigan..................	1.6
32	Oklahoma..................	5.8	32	Wisconsin..................	4.7	31	Tennessee..................	1.6
33	Indiana..................	5.6	33	South Carolina..................	4.4	33	Indiana..................	1.5
34	Iowa..................	5.4	34	Tennessee..................	4.2	33	Louisiana..................	1.5
35	Tennessee..................	5.3	35	Iowa..................	4.1	33	Iowa..................	1.5
36	South Carolina..................	5.2	36	Louisiana..................	3.9	33	Ohio..................	1.5
37	Wisconsin..................	5.1	37	Minnesota..................	3.8	37	Arkansas..................	1.4
38	Ohio..................	5.0	38	Hawaii..................	3.6	37	Kentucky..................	1.4
39	Arkansas..................	4.7	39	Michigan..................	3.2	39	Wisconsin..................	1.3
40	North Dakota..................	4.4	39	Alabama..................	3.2	40	South Carolina..................	1.2
41	Louisiana..................	4.3	41	North Dakota..................	2.9	41	Alabama..................	1.1
42	Vermont..................	4.2	41	Ohio..................	2.9	42	North Dakota..................	1.0
43	Maine..................	4.1	41	Missouri..................	2.9	42	Missouri..................	1.0
43	Missouri..................	4.1	44	South Dakota..................	2.8	42	New Hampshire..................	1.0
45	Kentucky..................	4.0	44	Kentucky..................	2.8	42	Maine..................	1.0
46	Alabama..................	3.5	46	New Hampshire..................	2.7	46	Mississippi..................	0.8
46	South Dakota..................	3.5	47	Mississippi..................	2.4	46	Wyoming..................	0.8
48	Wyoming..................	3.4	48	Montana..................	1.9	46	South Dakota..................	0.8
49	Montana..................	2.2	49	Vermont..................	1.4	49	Vermont..................	0.6
50	Mississippi..................	2.1	50	West Virginia..................	1.2	50	Montana..................	0.4
51	West Virginia..................	1.6	50	Maine..................	1.2	51	West Virginia..................	0.3

State Rankings, 2021

Selected Rankings

Married-couple families rank	State	Percent married-couple families [A-1, col. 45]	Female householders rank	State	Percent female householders [A-1, col. 47]	One-person households rank	State	Percent one-person households [A-1, col. 49]
	UNITED STATES.....................	47.3		UNITED STATES.....................	12.3		UNITED STATES.....................	28.3
1	Utah............................	59.3	1	Mississippi.............	16.9	1	District of Columbia................	48.2
2	Idaho..........................	55.6	2	Louisiana..............	16.0	2	North Dakota................	33.2
3	New Hampshire.................	52.3	3	Georgia...............	15.0	3	Ohio.....................	31.1
4	Hawaii........................	50.6	3	Alabama...............	14.1	4	Wyoming..............	30.9
5	New Jersey....................	50.4	5	Maryland..............	13.8	4	New Mexico............	30.9
6	Wyoming.......................	49.8	6	New York...............	13.7	4	New York..............	30.9
6	Nebraska......................	49.8	6	South Carolina..........	13.7	4	Alabama..............	30.9
6	Washington....................	49.8	8	New Mexico............	13.6	8	Louisiana..............	30.7
9	Kansas........................	49.5	9	Texas.................	13.5	9	Illinois................	30.6
9	Texas.........................	49.5	10	California.............	13.1	10	Nebraska..............	30.4
11	Minnesota.....................	49.2	10	Connecticut............	13.1	10	Rhode Island...........	30.4
12	Iowa..........................	49.1	11	District of Columbia.....	13.0	12	Wisconsin.............	30.3
13	South Dakota..................	49.0	13	Florida................	12.9	13	South Dakota...........	30.2
14	Virginia......................	48.9	13	Delaware..............	12.9	13	Pennsylvania...........	30.2
15	Montana.......................	48.8	15	Arkansas.............	12.8	13	Iowa..................	30.2
16	Colorado......................	48.6	16	Nevada...............	12.7	13	Michigan..............	30.2
17	Maine.........................	48.5	16	New Jersey............	12.7	17	Missouri..............	30.1
17	California....................	48.5	18	North Carolina.........	12.6	18	Kansas...............	30.0
19	Vermont.......................	48.4	19	Tennessee.............	12.5	19	Maine................	29.9
20	Indiana.......................	48.0	20	Ohio.................	12.3	19	West Virginia..........	29.9
21	Alaska........................	47.9	20	Hawaii................	12.3	21	Mississippi............	29.7
22	West Virginia.................	47.8	22	Kentucky..............	12.2	22	North Carolina.........	29.4
22	Arkansas......................	47.8	23	Oklahoma..............	12.1	23	Oklahoma..............	29.3
24	Arizona.......................	47.7	24	Rhode Island...........	12.0	24	Montana..............	29.2
24	Missouri......................	47.7	24	Arizona...............	12.0	24	Tennessee.............	29.2
26	Kentucky......................	47.6	26	Illinois...............	11.9	26	Minnesota.............	29.1
27	Wisconsin.....................	47.5	26	Massachusetts..........	11.9	26	Indiana...............	29.1
28	Oregon........................	47.4	28	Michigan..............	11.6	26	South Carolina.........	29.1
29	North Carolina................	47.3	28	Pennsylvania...........	11.6	29	Delaware..............	29.0
29	Oklahoma......................	47.3	30	Virginia...............	11.5	30	Connecticut...........	28.8
31	Delaware......................	47.1	31	Indiana...............	11.2	31	Arkansas..............	28.7
31	Maryland......................	47.1	31	West Virginia..........	11.2	32	Alaska...............	28.6
31	Tennessee.....................	47.1	33	Missouri..............	11.0	33	Kentucky..............	28.5
34	South Carolina................	47.0	34	Alaska................	10.1	33	Massachusetts.........	28.5
34	Georgia.......................	47.0	35	Kansas................	9.7	35	Florida...............	28.4
36	Pennsylvania..................	46.9	35	Oregon...............	9.7	36	Virginia..............	28.3
37	Connecticut...................	46.5	35	Washington............	9.7	37	Oregon...............	28.1
38	Florida.......................	46.4	35	Wisconsin.............	9.7	38	Nevada...............	28.0
39	Michigan......................	46.3	39	Colorado..............	9.4	39	Maryland..............	27.9
40	Illinois......................	46.1	40	Maine.................	9.1	39	Colorado..............	27.9
40	North Dakota..................	46.1	41	Minnesota.............	8.9	41	Vermont..............	27.9
42	Massachusetts.................	46.0	41	Nebraska..............	8.9	42	Washington............	27.1
42	Alabama.......................	46.0	41	New Hampshire.........	8.9	43	Georgia...............	26.8
44	Ohio..........................	44.7	44	Iowa.................	8.8	44	Arizona...............	26.3
45	Rhode Island..................	44.2	45	Vermont...............	8.7	45	New Jersey............	26.2
45	Mississippi...................	44.2	46	Idaho.................	8.6	46	New Hampshire.........	25.9
47	Nevada........................	43.8	46	Utah.................	8.6	47	Texas................	25.6
48	New Mexico....................	42.9	48	South Dakota..........	8.3	48	Hawaii...............	24.6
49	New York......................	42.7	49	Montana...............	8.1	49	Idaho................	24.2
50	Louisiana.....................	42.4	50	Wyoming..............	7.7	50	California............	24.0
51	District of Columbia..........	24.2	51	North Dakota..........	7.6	51	Utah.................	20.6

County Rankings, 2021

Selected Rankings

Population rank	County	Total population [A-2, col 1]	Median age rank	County	Median age [A-2, col 8]
	UNITED STATES...	331,893,745		UNITED STATES...	38.8
1	Los Angeles County, California	9,829,544	1	Sumter County, Florida	68.4
2	Cook County, Illinois	5,173,146	2	Charlotte County, Florida	60.4
3	Harris County, Texas..	4,728,030	3	Citrus County, Florida.......................................	57.8
4	Maricopa County, Arizona	4,496,588	4	Sarasota County, Florida	57.0
5	San Diego County, California	3,286,069	5	Brunswick County, North Carolina	56.1
6	Orange County, California	3,167,809	6	Yavapai County, Arizona	55.3
7	Miami-Dade County, Florida...............................	2,662,777	7	Indian River County, Florida.............................	55.1
8	Kings County, New York	26,41,052	8	Barnstable County, Massachusetts	54.6
9	Dallas County, Texas	2,586,050	9	Highlands County, Florida	54.4
10	Riverside County, California	2,458,395	10	Mohave County, Arizona	53.4
11	Queens County, New York	2,331,143	10	Flagler County, Florida......................................	53.4
12	Clark County, Nevada	2,292,476	12	Martin County, Florida.....................................	53.3
13	King County, Washington	2,252,305	13	Collier County, Florida......................................	52.7
14	San Bernardino County, California	2,194,710	14	Sussex County, Delaware	51.8
15	Tarrant County, Texas	2,126,477	15	Cape May County, New Jersey	51.6
16	Bexar County, Texas	2,028,236	16	Clallam County, Washington.............................	51.5
17	Broward County, Florida	1,930,983	17	Carteret County, North Carolina	50.3
18	Santa Clara County, California	1,885,508	18	Nevada County, California	50.2
19	Wayne County, Michigan	1,774,816	19	Manatee County, Florida..................................	49.9
20	Alameda County, California	1,648,556	20	Lee County, Florida	49.5
21	Middlesex County, Massachusetts......................	1,614,742	21	Pinellas County, Florida	49.1
22	Sacramento County, California	1,588,921	21	Horry County, South Carolina	49.1
23	New York County, New York.............................	1,576,876	23	Marion County, Florida.....................................	48.5
24	Philadelphia County, Pennsylvania.....................	1,576,251	23	Josephine County, Oregon	48.5
25	Suffolk County, New York	1,526,344	25	Monroe County, Florida....................................	48.2
26	Palm Beach County, Florida	1,497,987	25	Aroostook County, Maine	48.2
27	Hillsborough County, Florida.............................	1,478,194	27	Santa Fe County, New Mexico...........................	47.9
28	Bronx County, New York	1,424,948	28	Hernando County, Florida.................................	47.8
29	Orange County, Florida	1,422,746	28	Berkshire County, Massachusetts	47.8
30	Nassau County, New York	1,390,907	30	Chatham County, North Carolina.......................	47.7
31	Franklin County, Ohio.......................................	1,321,414	31	Litchfield County, Connecticut	47.6
32	Travis County, Texas	1,305,154	31	Beaufort County, South Carolina	47.6
33	Oakland County, Michigan................................	1,270,017	33	Henderson County, North Carolina	47.4
34	Hennepin County, Minnesota............................	1,267,416	34	Armstrong County, Pennsylvania.......................	47.3
35	Cuyahoga County, Ohio....................................	1,249,387	34	Westmoreland County, Pennsylvania	47.3
36	Allegheny County, Pennsylvania........................	1,238,090	36	Warren County, New York	47.2
37	Salt Lake County, Utah.....................................	1,186,421	36	Oconee County, South Carolina	47.2
38	Contra Costa County, California	1,161,413	38	Franklin County, Massachusetts	47.1
39	Wake County, North Carolina	1,150,204	38	Bedford County, Virginia	47.1
40	Fairfax County, Virginia....................................	1,139,720	38	James City County, Virginia	47.1
41	Mecklenburg County, North Carolina..................	1,122,276	41	Brevard County, Florida....................................	47.0
42	Collin County, Texas..	1,109,462	41	Guaynabo Municipio, Puerto Rico	47.0
43	Fulton County, Georgia	1,065,334	43	Marin County, California...................................	46.9
44	Montgomery County, Maryland	1,054,827	43	Nassau County, Florida....................................	46.9
45	Pima County, Arizona	1,052,030	45	Somerset County, Pennsylvania.........................	46.8
46	Fresno County, California	1,013,581	46	Middlesex County, Connecticut.........................	46.7
47	Honolulu County, Hawaii	1,000,890	46	Lake County, Florida..	46.7
48	Duval County, Florida.......................................	999,935	46	Volusia County, Florida....................................	46.7
49	Westchester County, New York	997,895	46	Douglas County, Oregon...................................	46.7
50	St. Louis County, Missouri	997,187	46	Newport County, Rhode Island..........................	46.7
51	Marion County, Indiana	971,102	51	Hunterdon County, New Jersey	46.4
52	Gwinnett County, Georgia	964,546	52	Washington County, Rhode Island	46.2
53	Fairfield County, Connecticut	959,768	53	Cambria County, Pennsylvania	46.0
54	Pinellas County, Florida	956,615	54	Putnam County, Florida....................................	45.9
55	Prince George's County, Maryland	955,306	55	Greene County, Tennessee	45.8
56	Bergen County, New Jersey	953,819	56	El Dorado County, California	45.7
57	Erie County, New York.....................................	950,683	57	Fayette County, Pennsylvania	45.6
58	Denton County, Texas......................................	941,647	58	Garland County, Arkansas................................	45.5
59	Milwaukee County, Wisconsin	928,059	58	Clearfield County, Pennsylvania	45.5
60	Pierce County, Washington	925,708	60	Palm Beach County, Florida..............................	45.4
61	DuPage County, Illinois....................................	924,885	60	St. Lucie County, Florida..................................	45.4
62	Shelby County, Tennessee	924,454	60	Geauga County, Ohio.......................................	45.4
63	Kern County, California	917,673	63	York County, Maine	45.3
64	Hartford County, Connecticut............................	896,854	63	Burke County, North Carolina	45.3
65	Hidalgo County, Texas......................................	880,356	63	Wilkes County, North Carolina	45.3
66	Macomb County, Michigan................................	876,792	63	San Juan Municipio, Puerto Rico	45.3
67	El Paso County, Texas......................................	867,947	67	Lincoln County, North Carolina	45.2
68	New Haven County, Connecticut	863,700	67	Carbon County, Pennsylvania	45.2
69	Worcester County, Massachusetts.....................	862,029	67	Sullivan County, Tennessee..............................	45.2
70	Middlesex County, New Jersey	860,807	70	Lapeer County, Michigan	45.1
71	Montgomery County, Pennsylvania	860,578	71	Rockingham County, North Carolina	45.1
72	Fort Bend County, Texas..................................	858,527	71	Roanoke County, Virginia	45.1
73	Essex County, New Jersey................................	854,917	71	Arecibo Municipio, Puerto Rico	45.1
74	Baltimore County, Maryland..............................	849,316	74	Walton County, Florida	45.0
75	Ventura County, California................................	839,784	74	Crow Wing County, Minnesota..........................	45.0

County Rankings, 2021

Selected Rankings

Foreign born rank	County	Percent foreign born [A-2, col. 18]	Married-couple families rank	County	Percent married-couple families [A-2, col. 22]
	UNITED STATES...............................	13.6		UNITED STATES...............................	47.3
1	Miami-Dade County, Florida..........................	53.6	1	Oldham County, Kentucky	71.6
2	Queens County, New York	46.8	2	Forsyth County, Georgia	71.0
3	Hudson County, New Jersey.........................	42.0	3	Utah County, Utah	70.2
4	Santa Clara County, California	40.3	4	Rockwall County, Texas.............................	69.9
5	Broward County, Florida	35.6	5	Williamson County, Tennessee	69.2
5	Kings County, New York	35.6	6	Tooele County, Utah	68.6
7	Middlesex County, New Jersey	34.9	7	Union County, North Carolina......................	67.9
8	San Mateo County, California	34.6	8	Washington County, Utah...........................	67.3
9	Alameda County, California	34.3	9	Loudoun County, Virginia...........................	66.4
9	San Francisco County, California	34.3	10	Delaware County, Ohio..............................	66.1
11	Bronx County, New York	33.7	11	Hunterdon County, New Jersey	66.0
12	Los Angeles County, California	33.3	12	Fort Bend County, Texas............................	65.8
13	Montgomery County, Maryland	32.9	13	Fayette County, Georgia	65.4
14	Union County, New Jersey...........................	32.8	14	York County, Virginia................................	65.3
15	Fort Bend County, Texas.............................	32.1	15	Parker County, Texas................................	65.0
16	Passaic County, New Jersey.........................	30.8	16	Paulding County, Georgia	64.8
17	Bergen County, New Jersey	30.5	17	Cache County, Utah..................................	64.5
18	Orange County, California	30.4	18	Douglas County, Colorado	64.2
19	Fairfax County, Virginia	29.9	19	Carroll County, Maryland	63.8
20	Suffolk County, Massachusetts.....................	29.7	19	Scott County, Minnesota............................	63.8
21	Essex County, New Jersey............................	29.5	21	Jackson County, Georgia............................	63.5
22	Imperial County, California	29.2	22	Hamilton County, Indiana..........................	63.3
23	Starr County, Texas	29.0	22	Johnson County, Texas..............................	63.3
23	Monterey County, California	29.0	24	St. Johns County, Florida............................	63.2
25	New York County, New York........................	28.1	25	Stafford County, Virginia............................	62.7
26	Somerset County, New Jersey	27.8	25	Davis County, Utah	62.7
27	Palm Beach County, Florida.........................	27.3	27	Livingston County, Michigan	62.4
27	Gwinnett County, Georgia	27.3	28	Ellis County, Texas	62.2
29	Osceola County, Florida..............................	26.9	29	Comal County, Texas................................	62.1
30	Harris County, Texas	26.3	30	Saline County, Arkansas............................	61.9
31	Prince William County, Virginia	26.2	30	Medina County, Ohio................................	61.9
32	Webb County, Texas..................................	25.8	30	Cherokee County, Georgia	61.9
33	Hidalgo County, Texas................................	25.6	33	Boone County, Indiana..............................	61.8
33	Loudoun County, Virginia............................	25.6	33	Collin County, Texas.................................	61.8
33	Richmond County, New York	25.6	35	Geauga County, Ohio................................	61.3
36	Merced County, California...........................	25.5	36	James City County, Virginia.........................	61.1
37	Contra Costa County, California	25.2	37	Warren County, Ohio................................	61.0
38	Dallas County, Texas	25.1	38	Nassau County, New York	60.9
39	King County, Washington	25.0	39	Cabarrus County, North Carolina	60.7
39	Collier County, Florida................................	25.0	39	Chatham County, North Carolina.................	60.7
41	Westchester County, New York	24.6	41	Ozaukee County, Wisconsin	60.6
42	Howard County, Maryland	24.2	41	Somerset County, New Jersey	60.6
43	Prince George's County, Maryland	24.0	41	Rockland County, New York	60.6
44	San Joaquin County, California	23.8	44	Calvert County, Maryland	60.5
45	Alexandria city, Virginia..............................	23.7	44	Coweta County, Georgia	60.5
46	Tulare County, California.............................	23.4	44	Allegan County, Michigan..........................	60.5
47	Orange County, Florida	23.0	44	Montgomery County, Texas........................	60.5
47	Yuma County, Arizona................................	23.0	48	Howard County, Maryland	60.3
47	Napa County, California..............................	23.0	49	Wright County, Minnesota	60.2
50	El Paso County, Texas................................	22.9	50	Fauquier County, Virginia...........................	60.1
51	Cameron County, Texas	22.9	51	Hancock County, Indiana	59.9
52	Sutter County, California	22.6	51	Hendricks County, Indiana	59.9
52	Fairfield County, Connecticut.......................	22.6	51	Carver County, Minnesota	59.9
54	Mercer County, New Jersey.........................	22.5	54	Benton County, Arkansas...........................	59.7
54	Middlesex County, Massachusetts.................	22.5	54	Kaufman County, Texas.............................	59.7
56	San Diego County, California	22.4	56	Columbia County, Georgia.........................	59.5
57	Nassau County, New York...........................	22.3	56	Christian County, Missouri	59.5
58	Santa Barbara County, California	22.1	58	Hanover County, Virginia...........................	59.4
58	Arlington County, Virginia...........................	22.1	58	Rockingham County, Virginia......................	59.4
60	Riverside County, California	22.0	60	San Benito County, California......................	59.3
60	Collin County, Texas..................................	22.0	61	Waukesha County, Wisconsin	59.2
62	Stanislaus County, California........................	21.8	61	Spotsylvania County, Virginia	59.2
62	Ventura County, California	21.8	61	Washington County, Minnesota	59.2
64	Yolo County, California...............................	21.6	61	Morris County, New Jersey.........................	59.2
65	Sacramento County, California	21.4	65	Bedford County, Virginia............................	59.1
66	Clark County, Nevada................................	21.3	66	Chester County, Pennsylvania	59.0
66	Ector County, Texas...................................	21.3	66	Ottawa County, Michigan	59.0
66	San Bernardino County, California	21.3	68	Denton County, Texas...............................	58.9
69	San Benito County, California	21.2	69	Placer County, California............................	58.8
69	Cook County, Illinois	21.2	70	Shelby County, Alabama	58.7
71	Rockland County, New York........................	20.5	71	Livingston Parish, Louisiana........................	58.5
72	Honolulu County, Hawaii	20.4	72	Flagler County, Florida...............................	58.4
73	Solano County, California............................	20.3	72	Rogers County, Oklahoma	58.4
73	Forsyth County, Georgia	20.3	74	McHenry County, Illinois............................	58.3
75	Franklin County, Washington.......................	20.2	74	Maury County, Tennessee	58.3

County Rankings, 2021

Selected Rankings

Female householder rank	County	Percent female householders [A-1, col. 21]	One-person households rank	County	Percent one-person households [A-2, col. 26]
	UNITED STATES............................	12.3		**UNITED STATES**............................	28.3
1	Clayton County, Georgia........................	29.4	1	District of Columbia, District of Columbia	48.2
2	Bronx County, New York	28.5	1	New York County, New York.......................	48.2
3	Starr County, Texas	26.9	3	St. Louis city, Missouri	47.5
4	Spalding County, Georgia........................	24.7	3	Alexandria city, Virginia	46.5
5	McKinley County, New Mexico..................	24.5	5	Richmond city, Virginia	46.2
5	Portsmouth city, Virginia	24.5	6	Orleans Parish, Louisiana........................	45.1
7	Hinds County, Mississippi	23.8	7	Baltimore city, Maryland........................	42.4
7	Dougherty County, Georgia	23.8	8	Douglas County, Kansas	41.9
9	Webb County, Texas	23.7	9	Arlington County, Virginia	41.7
10	Kings County, California	22.9	10	Dougherty County, Georgia	41.0
11	St. Landry Parish, Louisiana..................	22.9	11	Roanoke city, Virginia	39.8
12	Montgomery County, Alabama................	22.8	12	Allegany County, Maryland	39.2
12	Richmond County, Georgia.....................	22.8	12	Cuyahoga County, Ohio..........................	39.2
14	Hidalgo County, Texas	22.2	14	Denver County, Colorado.	38.9
15	Robeson County, North Carolina..............	22.0	15	Natrona County, Wyoming	38.6
15	Harrison County, Texas	22.0	16	Pitt County, North Carolina	38.4
15	Douglas County, Georgia	22.0	17	Orangeburg County, South Carolina	37.7
18	Orangeburg County, South Carolina	21.6	18	Cass County, North Dakota	37.3
19	Apache County, Arizona	21.5	18	Monroe County, Indiana	37.3
20	Muscogee County, Georgia.....................	21.3	20	Suffolk County, Massachusetts	37.2
21	Bibb County, Georgia...........................	21.3	21	Philadelphia County, Pennsylvania.........	37.1
22	Ouachita Parish, Louisiana	21.0	22	San Francisco County, California............	37.0
23	Imperial County, California	20.7	23	Newport News city, Virginia	36.9
24	Merced County, California	20.6	23	Sangamon County, Illinois...................	36.9
25	Philadelphia County, Pennsylvania	20.0	23	Burleigh County, North Dakota..............	36.9
26	Henry County, Georgia	19.9	26	Belmont County, Ohio.........................	36.8
26	Baltimore city, Maryland......................	19.9	26	Chautauqua County, New York..............	36.8
26	Umatilla County, Oregon......................	19.9	28	Pinellas County, Florida	36.5
29	Franklin County, Washington	19.8	29	Macon County, Illinois........................	36.4
30	Shelby County, Tennessee.....................	19.7	30	Tompkins County, New York..................	36.3
30	Elmore County, Alabama	19.7	31	Lucas County, Ohio.............................	36.3
32	Rockdale County, Georgia.....................	19.6	32	Hamilton County, Ohio........................	36.0
33	El Paso County, Texas	19.5	32	Norfolk city, Virginia	36.0
34	Caddo Parish, Louisiana	19.3	34	Fulton County, Georgia........................	35.9
35	Tulare County, California	19.2	35	Cochise County, Arizona	35.7
35	Cameron County, Texas........................	19.2	36	Cattaraugus County, New York	35.6
37	Passaic County, New Jersey...................	19.1	36	Oneida County, New York.....................	35.6
37	Valencia County, New Mexico	19.1	38	Allegheny County, Pennsylvania............	35.5
39	San Juan County, New Mexico	19.0	39	Milwaukee County, Wisconsin	35.4
39	Bulloch County, Georgia.......................	19.0	40	Mahoning County, Ohio.......................	35.3
41	Liberty County, Georgia	18.9	40	Vermilion County, Illinois.....................	35.3
41	Madison County, Tennessee...................	18.8	40	Sullivan County, New York....................	35.3
43	Lauderdale County, Mississippi..............	18.6	43	Ingham County, Michigan.....................	35.2
43	Troup County, Georgia	18.6	43	Bay County, Michigan	35.2
43	San Patricio County, Texas....................	18.6	45	Shawnee County, Kansas......................	35.1
46	Essex County, New Jersey.	18.5	46	Champaign County, Illinois...................	35.0
47	Hampton city, Virginia	18.4	47	Albany County, New York.....................	34.9
48	Prince George's County, Maryland	18.2	47	Erie County, New York.........................	34.9
49	Madera County, California	17.9	47	Putnam County, Florida........................	34.9
49	Jefferson County, Texas	17.9	47	Durham County, North Carolina.............	34.9
49	Houston County, Alabama.....................	17.9	47	Fayette County, Kentucky	34.9
52	Wayne County, Michigan......................	17.8	47	Jefferson County, Alabama	34.9
52	Lowndes County, Georgia.....................	17.8	47	Vigo County, Indiana	34.9
52	Lake County, Indiana..........................	17.8	47	Vanderburgh County, Indiana	34.9
55	East Baton Rouge Parish, Louisiana.........	17.7	55	Richmond County, Georgia....................	34.8
56	Miami-Dade County, Florida..................	17.6	55	Bibb County, Georgia..........................	34.8
56	Kings County, New York	17.6	55	Lowndes County, Georgia.....................	34.8
58	Putnam County, Florida........................	17.4	55	Hinds County, Mississippi	34.8
58	Mobile County, Alabama......................	17.4	55	Caldwell County, North Carolina............	34.8
60	Hampden County, Massachusetts	17.3	60	Davidson County, Tennessee	34.7
61	Glynn County, Georgia	17.2	60	Harrison County, West Virginia	34.7
62	Madison County, Mississippi	17.1	60	Androscoggin County, Maine.................	34.7
62	Osceola County, Florida	17.1	63	Broome County, New York....................	34.6
64	Cumberland County, New Jersey.............	17.0	64	Multnomah County, Oregon..................	34.5
64	Bowie County, Texas...........................	17.0	64	Walker County, Texas..........................	34.5
64	Newton County, Georgia......................	17.0	66	Sullivan County, Tennessee..................	34.4
64	Yuba County, California	17.0	67	Indian River County, Florida.	34.3
68	Yuma County, Arizona.........................	16.9	67	Ramsey County, Minnesota	34.3
68	Wilson County, North Carolina	16.9	67	Marion County, Indiana.......................	34.3
68	Coryell County, Texas..........................	16.9	67	Laramie County, Wyoming	34.3
68	Cumberland County, North Carolina	16.8	67	Montgomery County, Ohio....................	34.3
72	Chatham County, Georgia.....................	16.7	72	Erie County, Pennsylvania....................	34.2
72	Harrison County, Mississippi	16.7	72	Cook County, Illinois	34.2
72	Fresno County, California	16.7	72	Sheboygan County, Wisconsin	34.2
72	Talladega County, Alabama...................	16.7	72	Sumter County, South Carolina..............	34.2

Metropolitan Area Rankings, 2021

Selected Rankings

Population rank	Area name	Total population [A-3, col 1]	Median age rank	Area name	Median age [A-3, col 8]
	UNITED STATES............	331,893,745		UNITED STATES............	38.8
1	New York-Newark-Jersey City, NY-NJ-PA	19,216,182	1	The Villages, FL	68.4
2	Los Angeles-Long Beach-Anaheim, CA	13,214,799	2	Punta Gorda, FL	60.4
3	Chicago-Naperville-Elgin, IL-IN-WI	9,457,867	3	Homosassa Springs, FL	57.8
4	Dallas-Fort Worth-Arlington, TX	7,573,136	4	Prescott Valley-Prescott, AZ	55.3
5	Houston-The Woodlands-Sugar Land, TX	7,066,140	5	Sebastian-Vero Beach, FL	55.1
6	Washington-Arlington-Alexandria, DC-VA-MD-WV	6,280,697	6	Barnstable Town, MA	54.6
7	Miami-Fort Lauderdale-Pompano Beach, FL	6,166,488	7	Sebring-Avon Park, FL	54.4
8	Philadelphia-Camden-Wilmington, PA-NJ-DE-MD	6,102,434	8	North Port-Sarasota-Bradenton, FL	53.9
9	Atlanta-Sandy Springs-Alpharetta, GA	6,018,744	9	Lake Havasu City-Kingman, AZ	53.4
10	Phoenix-Mesa-Chandler, AZ	4,948,203	10	Naples-Marco Island, FL	52.7
11	Boston-Cambridge-Newton, MA-NH	4,873,019	11	Ocean City, NJ	51.6
12	San Francisco-Oakland-Berkeley, CA	4,731,803	12	Myrtle Beach-Conway-North Myrtle Beach, SC-NC	50.7
13	Riverside-San Bernardino-Ontario, CA	4,650,631	13	Cape Coral-Fort Myers, FL	49.5
14	Detroit-Warren-Dearborn, MI	4,319,629	14	Grants Pass, OR	48.5
15	Seattle-Tacoma-Bellevue, WA	3,979,845	14	Ocala, FL	48.5
16	Minneapolis-St. Paul-Bloomington, MN-WI	3,640,043	16	Deltona-Daytona Beach-Ormond Beach, FL	48.3
17	San Diego-Chula Vista-Carlsbad, CA	3,338,330	16	Port St. Lucie, FL	48.3
18	Tampa-St. Petersburg-Clearwater, FL	3,194,831	18	Santa Fe, NM	47.9
19	Denver-Aurora-Lakewood, CO	2,967,239	19	Pittsfield, MA	47.8
20	St. Louis, MO-IL	2,801,423	20	Hilton Head Island-Bluffton, SC	47.2
21	Baltimore-Columbia-Towson, MD	2,800,053	21	Palm Bay-Melbourne-Titusville, FL	47.0
22	Charlotte-Concord-Gastonia, NC-SC	2,636,883	21	San Germán, PR	47.0
23	Orlando-Kissimmee-Sanford, FL	2,608,147	23	Salisbury, MD-DE	46.7
24	San Antonio-New Braunfels, TX	2,550,960	24	Glens Falls, NY	46.2
25	Portland-Vancouver-Hillsboro, OR-WA	2,493,221	25	Guayama, PR	46.0
26	Sacramento-Roseville-Folsom, CA	2,363,730	25	Johnstown, PA	46.0
27	Pittsburgh, PA	2,317,600	27	Kingsport-Bristol, TN-VA	45.7
28	Las Vegas-Henderson-Paradise, NV	2,266,715	28	Hot Springs, AR	45.5
29	Austin-Round Rock-Georgetown, TX	2,227,083	29	Aguadilla-Isabela, PR	45.3
30	Cincinnati, OH-KY-IN	2,219,750	30	Arecibo, PR	44.8
31	Kansas City, MO-KS	2,155,068	31	Asheville, NC	44.8
32	Columbus, OH	2,122,271	31	Weirton-Steubenville, WV-OH	44.8
33	Indianapolis-Carmel-Anderson, IN	2,076,531	33	Yauco, PR	44.7
34	Cleveland-Elyria, OH	2,048,449	34	Kingston, NY	44.5
35	San Jose-Sunnyvale-Santa Clara, CA	1,990,660	35	Mayagüez, PR	44.4
36	Nashville-Davidson--Murfreesboro--Franklin, TN	1,933,860	36	Beckley, WV	44.2
37	Virginia Beach-Norfolk-Newport News, VA-NC	1,765,031	37	Youngstown-Warren-Boardman, OH-PA	44.0
38	Providence-Warwick, RI-MA	1,624,578	38	Bay City, MI	43.9
39	Milwaukee-Waukesha, WI	1,575,179	38	Daphne-Fairhope-Foley, AL	43.9
40	Jacksonville, FL	1,559,514	38	Gettysburg, PA	43.9
41	Oklahoma City, OK	1,408,950	38	Wheeling, WV-OH	43.9
42	Raleigh-Cary, NC	1,390,785	42	San Juan-Bayamón-Caguas, PR	43.8
43	Memphis, TN-MS-AR	1,344,910	43	East Stroudsburg, PA	43.7
44	Richmond, VA	1,290,866	43	Parkersburg-Vienna, WV	43.7
45	New Orleans-Metairie, LA	1,270,530	45	Altoona, PA	43.6
46	Louisville/Jefferson County, KY-IN	1,266,389	46	Roanoke, VA	43.6
47	Salt Lake City, UT	1,232,696	46	Portland-South Portland, ME	43.5
48	Hartford-East Hartford-Middletown, CT	1,204,877	48	Charleston, WV	43.4
49	Buffalo-Cheektowaga, NY	1,127,983	49	Carson City, NV	43.3
50	Birmingham-Hoover, AL	1,090,435	50	Hickory-Lenoir-Morganton, NC	43.2
51	Grand Rapids-Kentwood, MI	1,077,370	51	Sierra Vista-Douglas, AZ	43.2
52	Rochester, NY	1,069,644	52	Bloomsburg-Berwick, PA	43.1
53	Tucson, AZ	1,047,279	53	Ponce, PR	43.0
54	Fresno, CA	999,101	54	Kahului-Wailuku-Lahaina, HI	42.9
55	Tulsa, OK	998,655	54	Niles, MI	42.9
56	Urban Honolulu, HI	974,563	54	Staunton, VA	42.9
57	Omaha-Council Bluffs, NE-IA	949,726	57	Monroe, MI	42.8
58	Worcester, MA-CT	947,404	57	Pittsburgh, PA	42.8
59	Bridgeport-Stamford-Norwalk, CT	943,332	59	Johnson City, TN	42.7
60	Greenville-Anderson, SC	920,477	59	Napa, CA	42.7
61	Albuquerque, NM	914,480	59	Santa Rosa-Petaluma, CA	42.7
62	Bakersfield, CA	900,202	62	Bend, OR	42.6
63	Albany-Schenectady-Troy, NY	880,381	63	Lewiston, ID-WA	42.5
64	Knoxville, TN	869,525	64	Cumberland, MD-WV	42.4
65	McAllen-Edinburg-Mission, TX	868,707	64	Huntington-Ashland, WV-KY-OH	42.4
66	Baton Rouge, LA	854,884	66	Tampa-St. Petersburg-Clearwater, FL	42.3
67	New Haven-Milford, CT	854,757	66	Wausau-Weston, WI	42.3
68	Oxnard-Thousand Oaks-Ventura, CA	846,006	68	Atlantic City-Hammonton, NJ	42.2
69	Allentown-Bethlehem-Easton, PA-NJ	844,052	68	Bangor, ME	42.2
70	El Paso, TX	843,725	70	Chambersburg-Waynesboro, PA	42.1
71	Columbia, SC	839,039	70	Elmira, NY	42.1
72	North Port-Sarasota-Bradenton, FL	836,995	70	Medford, OR	42.1
73	Dayton-Kettering, OH	807,611	70	Rocky Mount, NC	42.1
74	Charleston-North Charleston, SC	802,122	70	Scranton--Wilkes-Barre, PA	42.1
75	Greensboro-High Point, NC	771,851	75	Miami-Fort Lauderdale-Pompano Beach, FL	42.0

Metropolitan Area Rankings, 2021

Selected Rankings

Foreign born rank	Area name	Percent foreign born [A-3, col. 15]	One-person households rank	Area name	Percent one-person households [A-3, col. 22]
	UNITED STATES............................	13.6		UNITED STATES............................	28.3
1	Miami-Fort Lauderdale-Pompano Beach, FL	41.5	1	Lawrence, KS	41.9
2	San Jose-Sunnyvale-Santa Clara, CA	39.6	2	Casper, WY	38.6
3	Los Angeles-Long Beach-Anaheim, CA	32.6	3	Greenville, NC	38.4
4	San Francisco-Oakland-Berkeley, CA	31.2	4	Cumberland, MD-WV	36.8
5	New York-Newark-Jersey City, NY-NJ-PA	29.4	5	Decatur, IL	36.4
6	El Centro, CA	29.2	6	Ithaca, NY	36.3
7	Salinas, CA	29.0	6	Fargo, ND-MN	36.3
8	Laredo, TX	25.8	8	Springfield, IL	36.0
9	McAllen-Edinburg-Mission, TX	25.6	9	Sierra Vista-Douglas, AZ	35.7
10	Merced, CA	25.5	10	Bloomington, IN	35.6
11	Naples-Marco Island, FL	25.0	11	Carbondale-Marion, IL	35.4
12	Houston-The Woodlands-Sugar Land, TX	24.1	12	Danville, IL	35.3
13	Stockton, CA	23.8	13	Carson City, NV	35.2
14	Visalia, CA	23.4	13	Bay City, MI	35.2
15	El Paso, TX	23.0	13	Cleveland-Elyria, OH	35.2
15	Yuma, AZ	23.0	16	Lewiston, ID-WA	34.8
15	Napa, CA	23.0	17	Lewiston-Auburn, ME	34.7
15	Washington-Arlington-Alexandria, DC-VA-MD-WV	23.0	18	Albany, GA	34.6
19	Brownsville-Harlingen, TX	22.9	18	Wheeling, WV-OH	34.6
20	Bridgeport-Stamford-Norwalk, CT	22.6	20	Champaign-Urbana, IL	34.5
21	Trenton-Princeton, NJ	22.5	21	Topeka, KS	34.4
22	San Diego-Chula Vista-Carlsbad, CA	22.4	21	Toledo, OH	34.4
23	Santa Maria-Santa Barbara, CA	22.1	23	Sebastian-Vero Beach, FL	34.3
24	Modesto, CA	21.8	23	Utica-Rome, NY	34.3
24	Oxnard-Thousand Oaks-Ventura, CA	21.8	23	Cheyenne, WY	34.3
26	Riverside-San Bernardino-Ontario, CA	21.7	23	Buffalo-Cheektowaga, NY	34.3
27	Las Vegas-Henderson-Paradise, NV	21.3	27	Erie, PA	34.2
27	Odessa, TX	21.3	27	Sheboygan, WI	34.2
29	Urban Honolulu, HI	20.4	29	State College, PA	34.1
30	Vallejo, CA	20.3	30	Sumter, SC	33.9
31	Orlando-Kissimmee-Sanford, FL	20.1	31	Valdosta, GA	33.8
32	Seattle-Tacoma-Bellevue, WA	20.0	31	Bismarck, ND	33.8
33	Fresno, CA	19.7	31	Homosassa Springs, FL	33.8
33	Bakersfield, CA	19.7	31	Weirton-Steubenville, WV-OH	33.8
35	Boston-Cambridge-Newton, MA-NH	19.5	35	Binghamton, NY	33.7
36	Kahului-Wailuku-Lahaina, HI	19.2	35	New Orleans-Metairie, LA	33.7
37	Dallas-Fort Worth-Arlington, TX	19.1	35	Charlottesville, VA	33.7
38	Yuba City, CA	19.0	38	Pittsburgh, PA	33.5
39	Sacramento-Roseville-Folsom, CA	18.8	38	Santa Fe, NM	33.5
40	Santa Cruz-Watsonville, CA	18.2	38	La Crosse-Onalaska, WI-MN	33.5
41	Hanford-Corcoran, CA	18.1	41	Ames, IA	33.4
42	Cape Coral-Fort Myers, FL	18.0	42	Anniston-Oxford, AL	33.3
43	Chicago-Naperville-Elgin, IL-IN-WI	17.8	42	Great Falls, MT	33.3
43	Madera, CA	17.8	44	Johnstown, PA	33.3
45	Yakima, WA	17.5	45	Mansfield, OH	33.2
46	Santa Rosa-Petaluma, CA	17.1	45	Monroe, LA	33.2
47	Gainesville, GA	16.2	45	Bloomington, IL	33.2
48	Port St. Lucie, FL	16.0	48	Pittsfield, MA	33.1
48	Atlantic City-Hammonton, NJ	16.0	49	Youngstown-Warren-Boardman, OH-PA	33.0
50	Austin-Round Rock-Georgetown, TX	15.7	49	Florence, SC	33.0
51	Las Cruces, NM	15.0	51	Hammond, LA	32.9
52	Tampa-St. Petersburg-Clearwater, FL	14.8	51	Duluth, MN-WI	32.9
52	New Haven-Milford, CT	14.8	51	Terre Haute, IN	32.9
54	Kennewick-Richland, WA	14.5	54	Evansville, IN-KY	32.8
55	Dalton, GA	14.4	55	Jackson, MI	32.7
56	Providence-Warwick, RI-MA	14.2	55	Columbia, MO	32.7
56	Grand Island, NE	14.2	57	Flint, MI	32.6
58	Atlanta-Sandy Springs-Alpharetta, GA	13.8	57	Wilmington, NC	32.6
59	Carson City, NV	13.7	57	Kalamazoo-Portage, MI	32.6
60	Midland, TX	13.6	60	Madison, WI	32.5

Metropolitan Area Rankings, 2021—*Continued*

Selected Rankings

Foreign born rank	Area name	Percent foreign born [A-3, col. 15]	One-person households rank	Area name	Percent one-person households [A-3, col. 22]
61	Phoenix-Mesa-Chandler, AZ	13.4	60	Johnson City, TN	32.5
61	Hartford-East Hartford-Middletown, CT	13.4	60	Lafayette-West Lafayette, IN	32.5
63	Reno, NV	13.3	60	Macon-Bibb County, GA	32.5
64	Sioux City, IA-NE-SD	12.9	64	Waterloo-Cedar Falls, IA	32.4
65	Sebring-Avon Park, FL	12.8	64	Brunswick, GA	32.4
66	Sierra Vista-Douglas, AZ	12.6	64	Shreveport-Bossier City, LA	32.4
66	Raleigh-Cary, NC	12.6	67	Asheville, NC	32.3
66	Wenatchee, WA	12.6	67	Walla Walla, WA	32.3
69	Portland-Vancouver-Hillsboro, OR-WA	12.5	67	Dayton-Kettering, OH	32.3
70	Worcester, MA-CT	12.4	67	Kingsport-Bristol, TN-VA	32.3
71	Denver-Aurora-Lakewood, CO	12.3	71	Akron, OH	32.2
71	North Port-Sarasota-Bradenton, FL	12.3	71	Roanoke, VA	32.2
73	Ann Arbor, MI	12.2	71	Muncie, IN	32.2
73	Salt Lake City, UT	12.2	71	Pine Bluff, AR	32.2
75	San Antonio-New Braunfels, TX	12.1	75	Rocky Mount, NC	32.1
			75	Saginaw, MI	32.1
			75	Niles, MI	32.1

City Rankings, 2021

Selected Rankings

Population rank	City	Total population, [A-4, col 1]	Median age rank	City	Median age [A-4, col 8]
	UNITED STATES..	331,893,745		UNITED STATES..	38.8
1	New York city, New York...........................	8,467,513	1	The Villages CDP, Florida.........................	74.1
2	Los Angeles city, California......................	3,849,306	2	Port Charlotte CDP, Florida......................	56.3
3	Chicago city, Illinois................................	2,696,561	3	Delray Beach city, Florida........................	51.0
4	Houston city, Texas.................................	2,287,047	4	Palm Coast city, Florida...........................	50.8
5	Phoenix city, Arizona...............................	1,624,539	5	North Port city, Florida............................	50.6
6	Philadelphia city, Pennsylvania................	1,576,251	6	Cape Coral city, Florida...........................	49.7
7	San Antonio city, Texas...........................	1,451,863	7	Scottsdale city, Arizona...........................	49.5
8	San Diego city, California.........................	1,381,600	8	Clearwater city, Florida...........................	49.0
9	Dallas city, Texas....................................	1,288,441	9	Newport Beach city, California..................	48.4
10	San Jose city, California...........................	983,530	10	Boca Raton city, Florida...........................	48.0
11	Austin city, Texas....................................	964,000	11	Livonia city, Michigan..............................	47.3
12	Jacksonville city, Florida..........................	954,624	12	Mission Viejo city, California....................	46.9
13	Fort Worth city, Texas.............................	940,437	12	Guaynabo zona urbana, Puerto Rico..........	46.9
14	Columbus city, Ohio................................	907,310	14	Carlsbad city, California...........................	46.3
15	Indianapolis city (balance), Indiana...........	882,327	14	Largo city, Florida...................................	46.3
16	Charlotte city, North Carolina...................	879,697	16	Hialeah city, Florida................................	46.1
17	San Francisco city, California....................	815,201	17	Deerfield Beach city, Florida.....................	46.0
18	Seattle city, Washington..........................	733,904	18	Yorba Linda city, California.......................	45.4
19	Denver city, Colorado..............................	711,463	18	San Juan zona urbana, Puerto Rico............	45.4
20	Oklahoma City city, Oklahoma..................	687,691	20	Fort Lauderdale city, Florida.....................	45.1
21	Nashville-Davidson metropolitan government (balance), Tennessee	678,845	21	Walnut Creek city, California.....................	44.9
22	El Paso city, Texas...................................	678,422	22	Pembroke Pines city, Florida.....................	44.8
23	Washington city, District of Columbia	670,050	23	Southfield city, Michigan..........................	44.7
24	Boston city, Massachusetts......................	654,281	24	Spring Hill CDP, Florida............................	44.5
25	Las Vegas city, Nevada............................	646,776	25	Daly City city, California...........................	44.4
26	Portland city, Oregon..............................	642,218	25	Boynton Beach city, Florida......................	44.4
27	Detroit city, Michigan..............................	632,589	27	Hemet city, California..............................	44.3
28	Louisville/Jefferson County metro government (balance), Kentucky........	628,577	28	Pleasanton city, California........................	44.2
29	Memphis city, Tennessee.........................	628,118	28	Caguas zona urbana, Puerto Rico..............	44.2
30	Baltimore city, Maryland..........................	576,498	30	Torrance city, California...........................	44.1
31	Milwaukee city, Wisconsin........................	569,326	31	Huntington Beach city, California...............	44.0
32	Albuquerque city, New Mexico..................	562,591	31	Redondo Beach city, California..................	44.0
33	Fresno city, California..............................	544,500	31	New Rochelle city, New York......................	44.0
34	Tucson city, Arizona................................	543,215	34	Bethesda CDP, Maryland..........................	43.9
35	Sacramento city, California......................	525,028	34	Troy city, Michigan..................................	43.9
36	Mesa city, Arizona...................................	509,492	36	Loveland city, Colorado...........................	43.8
37	Kansas City city, Missouri.........................	508,415	36	Ponce zona urbana, Puerto Rico................	43.8
38	Atlanta city, Georgia...............................	496,480	38	Tamarac city, Florida...............................	43.7
39	Omaha city, Nebraska..............................	487,299	38	Urban Honolulu CDP, Hawaii.....................	43.7
40	Colorado Springs city, Colorado................	483,969	38	Skokie village, Illinois..............................	43.7
41	Raleigh city, North Carolina......................	469,502	38	Independence city, Missouri......................	43.7
42	Virginia Beach city, Virginia......................	457,672	42	Thousand Oaks city, California..................	43.5
43	Long Beach city, California.......................	456,063	42	Union City city, California.........................	43.5
44	Miami city, Florida..................................	439,906	42	Arlington Heights village, Illinois...............	43.5
45	Oakland city, California............................	433,797	45	Kendall CDP, Florida................................	43.4
46	Minneapolis city, Minnesota.....................	425,338	45	Bayamón zona urbana, Puerto Rico...........	43.4
47	Tulsa city, Oklahoma...............................	411,905	45	Carolina zona urbana, Puerto Rico.............	43.4
48	Bakersfield city, California........................	407,581	48	San Leandro city, California......................	43.3
49	Wichita city, Kansas................................	395,707	49	Camarillo city, California..........................	43.1
50	Arlington city, Texas................................	392,802	49	Highlands Ranch CDP, Colorado................	43.1
51	Aurora city, Colorado..............................	389,675	49	Port St. Lucie city, Florida	43.1
52	Tampa city, Florida..................................	387,037	52	Simi Valley city, California........................	43.0
53	New Orleans city, Louisiana......................	376,971	52	Mount Pleasant town, South Carolina........	43.0
54	Cleveland city, Ohio................................	368,006	54	Indio city, California................................	42.9
55	Anaheim city, California...........................	345,935	55	Castro Valley CDP, California....................	42.8
56	Urban Honolulu CDP, Hawaii.....................	345,532	56	Peoria city, Arizona.................................	42.7
57	Henderson city, Nevada...........................	322,202	56	Melbourne city, Florida............................	42.7
58	Stockton city, California...........................	322,107	56	Miami Beach city, Florida.........................	42.7
59	Lexington-Fayette urban county, Kentucky.......	321,793	59	Novi city, Michigan..................................	42.6
60	San Juan zona urbana, Puerto Rico............	320,456	59	Flower Mound town, Texas.......................	42.6
61	Corpus Christi city, Texas.........................	317,768	61	Santa Fe city, New Mexico.......................	42.5
62	Riverside city, California...........................	317,257	61	Lorain city, Ohio.....................................	42.5
63	Santa Ana city, California.........................	309,468	61	The Woodlands CDP, Texas......................	42.5
64	Orlando city, Florida................................	309,193	64	Burbank city, California............................	42.4
65	Irvine city, California...............................	309,014	54	Ellicott City CDP, Maryland......................	42.4
66	Cincinnati city, Ohio................................	308,913	66	Decatur city, Illinois................................	42.3
67	Newark city, New Jersey..........................	307,216	66	Bloomington city, Minnesota....................	42.3
68	St. Paul city, Minnesota...........................	307,176	66	Clifton city, New Jersey...........................	42.3
69	Pittsburgh city, Pennsylvania....................	300,454	69	West Palm Beach city, Florida...................	42.2
70	Greensboro city, North Carolina................	298,250	70	Lake Forest city, California.......................	42.1
71	St. Louis city, Missouri.............................	293,310	70	Daytona Beach city, Florida......................	42.1
72	Lincoln city, Nebraska..............................	292,648	72	Wilmington city, North Carolina.................	42.0
73	Anchorage municipality, Alaska.................	288,121	72	Warwick city, Rhode Island.......................	42.0
74	Plano city, Texas.....................................	287,037	72	Missouri City city, Texas...........................	42.0
75	Durham city, North Carolina.....................	285,439	75	Westminster city, California......................	41.9
			75	St. Petersburg city, Florida.......................	41.9
			75	Westland city, Michigan...........................	41.9

City Rankings, 2021

Selected Rankings

Foreign born rank	City	Percent foreign born [A-4, col. 18]	One-person households rank	City	Percent one-person households [A-4, col. 26]
	UNITED STATES..	13.6		UNITED STATES..	28.3
1	Hialeah city, Florida.............................	71.7	1	Miami Beach city, Florida.........................	48.7
2	Doral city, Florida...............................	65.6	2	Washington city, District of Columbia	48.2
3	Union City city, New Jersey	57.9	3	St. Louis city, Missouri...........................	47.5
4	Miami city, Florida..............................	57.5	4	Albany city, New York.............................	47.2
5	Miami Beach city, Florida........................	52.9	5	Bloomington city, Indiana........................	46.7
6	Milpitas city, California.........................	51.9	6	Alexandria city, Virginia........................	46.5
7	Weston city, Florida.............................	51.7	7	Greenville city, North Carolina	46.4
8	Glendale city, California.........................	50.7	8	Richmond city, Virginia..........................	46.2
9	Union City city, California	50.0	8	Cincinnati city, Ohio............................	46.2
10	Sunnyvale city, California........................	49.9	8	Cleveland city, Ohio.............................	46.2
11	Daly City city, California.........................	49.8	11	Wilmington city, Delaware	46.0
12	Fremont city, California..........................	49.1	12	Lawrence city, Kansas...........................	45.8
13	Elizabeth city, New Jersey	48.3	13	Santa Monica city, California.....................	45.3
14	Redmond city, Washington.......................	48.2	14	West Des Moines city, Iowa.......................	45.1
15	Garden Grove city, California.....................	47.7	14	New Orleans city, Louisiana......................	45.1
16	El Monte city, California.........................	46.8	16	Kalamazoo city, Michigan........................	45.0
17	Baldwin Park city, California.....................	45.3	17	Birmingham city, Alabama.......................	44.6
18	Lawrence city, Massachusetts....................	44.7	18	Atlanta city, Georgia............................	44.5
19	Westminster city, California......................	44.3	19	Southfield city, Michigan........................	44.3
20	Santa Clara city, California	43.2	19	Syracuse city, New York..........................	43.3
21	Paterson city, New Jersey	43.0	21	Albany city, Georgia............................	43.2
22	Tamarac city, Florida............................	42.9	22	Springfield city, Illinois..........................	42.8
23	Cicero town, Illinois.............................	42.8	23	Baltimore city, Maryland.........................	42.4
24	South Gate city, California.......................	42.7	24	Pittsburgh city, Pennsylvania....................	42.2
25	Irving city, Texas................................	42.3	25	Decatur city, Illinois............................	42.0
26	Mountain View city, California	42.2	26	Westland city, Michigan.........................	41.9
26	Dublin city, California...........................	42.2	27	Arlington CDP, Virginia..........................	41.7
28	Alhambra city, California........................	42.1	27	Fargo city, North Dakota.........................	41.7
29	Bellevue city, Washington........................	42.0	27	Largo city, Florida..............................	41.7
30	Malden city, Massachusetts......................	41.9	30	Rochester city, New York.........................	41.5
31	Santa Ana city, California	41.5	30	Greenville city, South Carolina...................	41.5
32	Hayward city, California..........................	41.4	32	Bismarck city, North Dakota......................	41.4
33	Passaic city, New Jersey	41.3	33	Madison city, Wisconsin.........................	41.3
34	San Jose city, California..........................	40.8	34	Evansville city, Indiana..........................	41.2
35	East Los Angeles CDP, California	40.6	34	Detroit city, Michigan...........................	41.2
36	Irvine city, California............................	40.4	34	Toledo city, Ohio...............................	41.2
37	Jersey City city, New Jersey......................	40.2	34	Minneapolis city, Minnesota.....................	41.2
38	Germantown CDP, Maryland......................	39.9	38	Gainesville city, Florida.........................	41.1
39	Salinas city, California...........................	39.4	39	Asheville city, North Carolina....................	41.0
40	Town 'n' Country CDP, Florida....................	39.3	39	Topeka city, Kansas.............................	41.0
40	Sunrise city, Florida.............................	39.3	39	Deerfield Beach city, Florida	41.0
42	Miami Gardens city, Florida......................	39.1	42	Wilmington city, North Carolina..................	40.9
42	Lauderhill city, Florida...........................	39.0	43	Fort Lauderdale city, Florida.....................	40.8
43	Hollywood city, Florida..........................	39.0	44	Akron city, Ohio	40.5
43	Gaithersburg city, Maryland.....................	38.9	44	Cambridge city, Massachusetts	40.5
45	Miramar city, Florida............................	38.6	46	Knoxville city, Tennessee........................	40.3
47	San Leandro city, California......................	38.3	47	Portland city, Maine............................	40.1
47	Kendall CDP, Florida.............................	38.3	47	Delray Beach city, Florida........................	40.1
49	Mount Vernon city, New York	37.9	47	Buffalo city, New York...........................	40.1
49	West Covina city, California......................	37.9	47	Salt Lake City city, Utah..........................	40.1
51	Clifton city, New Jersey	37.3	51	Seattle city, Washington.........................	40.0
52	Lynwood city, California..........................	37.1	52	Roanoke city, Virginia	39.8
53	Anaheim city, California..........................	36.8	53	Springfield city, Missouri........................	39.5
54	Centreville CDP, Virginia.........................	36.7	53	Dayton city, Ohio...............................	39.5
55	Pembroke Pines city, Florida.....................	36.6	55	Flint city, Michigan.............................	39.4
56	New York city, New York.........................	36.4	56	Lansing city, Michigan...........................	39.3
57	Sammamish city, Washington	36.3	57	San Juan zona urbana, Puerto Rico	39.2
58	Rockville city, Maryland..........................	36.2	57	Chicago city, Illinois............................	39.2
58	San Ramon city, California	36.0	59	Austin city, Texas...............................	39.1
60	Los Angeles city, California	35.9	59	Columbia city, South Carolina....................	39.1
61	Sugar Land city, Texas...........................	35.9	59	East Orange city, New Jersey	39.1
61	Homestead city, Florida..........................	35.9	62	Green Bay city, Wisconsin........................	38.9
61	Palo Alto city, California.........................	35.9	62	Mobile city, Alabama	38.9
64	Hawthorne city, California........................	35.8	62	Daytona Beach city, Florida......................	38.9
64	Deerfield Beach city, Florida	35.8	62	Denver city, Colorado...........................	38.9
66	Norwalk city, California..........................	35.7	66	New Haven city, Connecticut.....................	38.8
66	Dale City CDP, Virginia...........................	35.7	66	Lafayette city, Indiana..........................	38.8
68	Newark city, New Jersey.........................	35.4	68	Dallas city, Texas...............................	38.7
69	Carson city, California...........................	35.3	68	St. Petersburg city, Florida.......................	38.7
70	Silver Spring CDP, Maryland......................	34.8	68	Peoria city, Illinois..............................	38.7
70	Chino Hills city, California	34.8	68	West Palm Beach city, Florida....................	38.7
72	Tustin city, California............................	34.6	72	Lorain city, Ohio...............................	38.5
73	Kissimmee city, Florida..........................	34.5	73	Boston city, Massachusetts.......................	38.3
73	Oxnard city, California...........................	34.5	73	Waterloo city, Iowa.............................	38.3
75	Waukegan city, Illinois...........................	34.3	75	Ames city, Iowa................................	38.2
75	San Francisco city, California.....................	34.3	75	Erie city, Pennsylvania..........................	38.2
			75	Miami city, Florida..............................	38.2
			75	Santa Fe city, New Mexico........................	38.2

Table A-1. States — Who: Age, Race/Ethnicity, and Household Structure, 2021

	STATE	Total population	Percent change, 2010–2019	Race alone or in combination (percent)						Percent Hispanic or Latino	Percent two or more races	Percent White alone, not Hispanic or Latino
				White	Black or African American	American Indian or Alaska Native	Asian	Native Hawaiian or Pacific Islander	Some other race			
State code	ACS table number:	B01003	Census PEP	B02008	B02009	B02010	B02011	B02012	B02013	B03003	B02001	B01001H
	Column number:	1	2	3	4	5	6	7	8	9	10	11

Table A-1. States — Who: Age, Race/Ethnicity, and Household Structure, 2021—*Continued*

	STATE	Total population	Population by age (percent)								+/- U.S. percent under 18 years	+/- U.S. percent 65 years and over	Percent female
			Under 5 years	5 to 17 years	18 to 24 years	25 to 44 years	45 to 64 years	65 to 84 years	85 years and over			
State code	ACS table number:	B01001	B01001	B01001	B01001	B01001	B01001	B01001	B01001	B01001	B01001	B01001
	Column number:	12	13	14	15	16	17	18	19	20	21	22

Table A-1. States — Who: Age, Race/Ethnicity, and Household Structure, 2021—*Continued*

	STATE	Median age								
		Total population	White alone, not Hispanic or Latino	Black alone	American Indian or Alaska Native alone	Asian alone	Native Hawaiian or Pacific Islander alone	Some other race alone	Two or more races	Hispanic or Latino
State code	ACS table number:	B01002	B01002H	B01002B	B01002C	B01002D	B01002E	B01002F	B01002G	B01002I
	Column number:	23	24	25	26	27	28	29	30	31

Table A-1. States — Who: Age, Race/Ethnicity, and Household Structure, 2021—*Continued*

	STATE	Total population, 15 years and over	Marital status of population 15 years and over (percent)				Foreign born (percent of total population)	Languages spoken (percent of households)			
			Never married	Now married (includes separated)	Widowed	Divorced		English only	Spanish, with or without English	Other languages, with or without English	Limited English-speaking household
State code	ACS table number:	B12001	B12001	B12001	B12001	B12001	C05002	C16002	C16002	C16002	C16002
	Column number:	32	33	34	35	36	37	38	39	40	41

Table A-1. States — Who: Age, Race/Ethnicity, and Household Structure, 2021—*Continued*

					Household type (percent of all households)								
					Family households				Nonfamily households			Unmarried partner households		
	STATE	Total households	Average household size	Total family households	Married-couple families	Male householder families (no spouse)	Female householder families (no spouse)	Total nonfamily households	Total one-person households	One person households age 65 or over	Total unmarried cohabiting partner households	Same-sex cohabiting partner households	Same-sex married partner households
State code	ACS table number:	B11001	B25010	B11001	B11001	B11001	B11001	B11001	B11001	B11010 / B11001	B11009	B11009	B11009
	Column number:	42	43	44	45	46	47	48	49	50	51	52	53

Table A-1. States — Who: Age, Race/Ethnicity, and Household Structure, 2021—*Continued*

		Households with people under 18 years old				Households with people 60 years and over				
			Household type (percent)				Household type (percent)			
	STATE	Total households with children	Married-couple families	Male householder families (no spouse)	Female householder families (no spouse)	Total households with people 60 years and over	Married-couple families	Male householder families (no spouse)	Female householder families (no spouse)	Nonfamily households
State code	ACS table number:	C11005	C11005	C11005	C11005	B11006	B11006	B11006	B11006	B11006
	Column number:	54	55	56	57	58	59	60	61	62

Table A-2. Counties — Who: Age, Race/Ethnicity, and Household Structure, 2021

				Population by age (percent)						Race alone or in combination (percent)					
	STATE County	Total population	Percent change, 2010–2019	Under 18 years	18 to 24 years	25 to 44 years	45 to 64 years	65 years and over	Median age	White	Black or African American	American Indian and Alaska Native	Asian	Native Hawaiian or Other Pacific Islander	Some other race
STATE County code	ACS table number:	B01003	Population Estimates	B01001	B01001	B01001	B01001	B01001	B01002	B02008	B02009	B02010	B02011	B02012	B02013
	Column number:	1	2	3	4	5	6	7	8	9	10	11	12	13	14

Table A-2. Counties — Who: Age, Race/Ethnicity, and Household Structure, 2021—*Continued*

								Household type (percent of all households)						Percent of households with people age 60 years and over
								Family households				Nonfamily households		
	STATE County	Two or more races (percent)	Hispanic or Latino (percent)	Native, born in state of residence (percent)	Foreign born (percent)	Non-citizens (percent)	Total house-holds	Total	Married couple	Male house-holder	Female house-holder	Total	One-person house-holds	
STATE County code	ACS table number:	B02001	B03003	B05002	B05002	B05002	B11001	B11001	B11001	B11001	B11001	B11001	B11001	B11006
	Column number:	15	16	17	18	19	20	21	22	23	24	25	26	27

Table A-3. Metropolitan Areas — Who: Age, Race/Ethnicity, and Household Structure, 2021

Metropolitan area / division code	Metropolitan area / division	Total population	Percent change, 2010–2019	Population by age (percent)					Median age	Race alone or in combination (percent)				Hispanic or Latino (percent)
				Under 18 years	18 to 24 years	25 to 44 years	45 to 64 years	65 years and over		White	Black or African American	Asian + Native Hawaiian or Other Pacific Islander	American Indian and Alaska Native + Some other race	
	ACS table number:	B01003	Population Estimates	B01001	B01001	B01001	B01001	B01001	B01002	B02008	B02009	B02011 + B02012	B02010 + B02013	B03003
	column number:	1	2	3	4	5	6	7	8	9	10	11	12	13

Table A-3. Metropolitan Areas — Who: Age, Race/Ethnicity, and Household Structure, 2021—*Continued*

Metropolitan area / division code	Metropolitan area / division	Born in state of residence (percent)	Foreign born (percent)	Total households	Household type (percent of all households)							Percent of households with people age 60 years and over
					Family households				Nonfamily households			
					Total	Married-couple	Male householder	Female householder	Total	One-person households		
	ACS table number:	B05002	B05002	B11001	B11001	B11001	B11001	B11001	B11001	B11001		B11006
	column number:	14	15	16	17	18	19	20	21	22		23

Table A-4. Cities — Who: Age, Race/Ethnicity, and Household Structure, 2021

STATE and place code	STATE Place	Total population	Percent change, 2014–2019	Population by age (percent)					Median age	Race alone or in combination (percent)					
				Under 18 years	18 to 24 years	25 to 44 years	45 to 64 years	65 years and over		White	Black	American Indian and Alaska Native	Asian	Native Hawaiian or Other Pacific Islander	Some other race
	ACS table number:	B01003	Population Estimates	B01001	B01001	B01001	B01001	B01001	B01002	B02008	B02009	B02010	B02011	B02012	B02013
FIPS	column number:	1	2	3	4	5	6	7	8	9	10	11	12	13	14

Table A-4. Cities — Who: Age, Race/Ethnicity, and Household Structure, 2021—*Continued*

STATE and place code	STATE Place	Two or more races (percent)	Hispanic or Latino (percent)	Native, born in state of residence (percent)	Foreign born (percent)	Non-citizens (percent)	Total households	Household type (percent of all households)						Percent of households with people age 60 years and over
								Family households				Nonfamily households		
								Total	Married-couple	Male householder	Female householder	Total	One-person households	
	ACS table number:	B02001	B03003	B05002	B05002	B05002	B11001	B11001	B11001	B11001	B11001	B11001	B11001	B11006
FIPS	column number:	15	16	17	18	19	20	21	22	23	24	25	26	27

Table A-1. States — Who: Age, Race/Ethnicity, and Household Structure, 2021

State code	STATE	Total population	Percent change, 2010–2019	White	Black or African American	American Indian or Alaska Native	Asian	Native Hawaiian or Pacific Islander	Some other race	Percent Hispanic or Latino	Percent two or more races	Percent White alone, not Hispanic or Latino
	ACS table number:	B01003	Census PEP	B02008	B02009	B02010	B02011	B02012	B02013	B03003	B02001	B01001H
	Column number:	1	2	3	4	5	6	7	8	9	10	11
0	UNITED STATES.............	331,893,745	6.3	72.9	14.2	2.6	7.1	0.5	16.2	18.8	12.6	58.1
1	Alabama......................	5,039,877	2.0	69.6	27.3	2.1	1.9	0.2	4.3	4.7	5.0	64.2
2	Alaska	732,673	4.2	71.3	5.3	20.7	9.0	2.5	6.0	7.1	13.3	57.9
4	Arizona........................	7,276,316	9.8	77.6	6.3	6.0	4.8	0.4	25.9	32.3	20.1	52.0
5	Arkansas......................	3,025,891	3.0	79.5	16.2	2.8	2.2	0.5	9.2	8.2	9.9	68.2
6	California.....................	39,237,836	6.1	57.1	7.3	3.3	17.8	0.8	34.2	40.2	19.0	34.3
8	Colorado......................	5,812,069	11.5	84.8	5.7	3.3	4.8	0.4	17.1	22.3	14.9	65.2
9	Connecticut.................	3,605,597	0.4	75.7	13.8	1.5	5.8	0.2	15.6	17.7	11.6	62.7
10	Delaware	1,003,384	7.1	68.9	24.3	2.4	5.1	0.3	9.5	10.1	9.4	59.3
11	District of Columbia........	670,050	15.3	45.8	47.1	1.5	5.8	0.1	10.3	11.5	9.6	36.4
12	Florida........................	21,781,128	11.6	74.1	17.7	1.4	3.8	0.2	22.9	26.8	19.1	51.1
13	Georgia.......................	10,799,566	7.6	59.5	33.4	2.4	5.3	0.2	8.7	10.0	8.8	50.2
15	Hawaii.........................	1,441,553	4.9	42.9	3.7	2.8	56.5	26.4	6.0	11.1	26.3	20.8
16	Idaho..........................	1,900,923	9.5	90.5	1.3	3.2	2.5	0.4	12.0	13.3	9.4	78.7
17	Illinois........................	12,671,469	-0.2	71.8	15.2	2.1	6.8	0.1	15.8	18.0	11.1	58.9
18	Indiana.......................	6,805,985	2.8	85.0	10.8	2.0	3.0	0.1	6.9	7.6	7.4	76.6
19	Iowa...........................	3,193,079	3.2	90.9	5.1	1.8	3.1	0.3	6.0	6.6	6.8	83.0
20	Kansas........................	2,934,582	2.1	86.1	7.5	3.1	3.8	0.2	10.5	12.7	10.6	73.4
21	Kentucky	4,509,394	2.6	89.3	9.0	2.3	2.1	0.2	3.9	3.9	6.3	82.7
22	Louisiana	4,624,047	3.3	63.9	33.2	2.2	2.3	0.1	5.6	5.5	6.7	56.9
23	Maine.........................	1,372,247	0.6	95.9	2.2	1.7	1.9	0.1	3.9	1.9	5.5	90.0
24	Maryland	6,165,129	4.8	55.8	32.3	1.7	8.0	0.2	10.8	11.1	8.0	47.8
25	Massachusetts	6,984,723	4.8	78.7	10.1	1.1	8.3	0.1	14.2	12.8	11.2	67.5
26	Michigan	10,050,811	0.8	80.6	15.4	1.8	4.1	0.1	5.5	5.6	7.0	72.9
27	Minnesota	5,707,390	5.1	84.3	8.5	2.3	6.2	0.1	5.9	5.8	6.9	76.9
28	Mississippi	2,949,965	0.5	60.8	37.7	2.3	1.6	0.2	3.1	3.2	5.1	55.4
29	Missouri	6,168,187	2.1	84.7	12.4	2.2	2.8	0.3	5.6	4.6	7.6	76.6
30	Montana	1,104,271	6.2	91.3	1.0	8.3	1.5	0.2	4.3	4.3	6.3	83.8
31	Nebraska	1,963,692	5.1	86.8	6.3	2.4	3.4	0.2	10.1	11.9	8.7	76.4
32	Nevada	3,143,991	11.0	65.7	11.9	3.2	11.3	1.5	25.2	29.9	17.5	45.2
33	New Hampshire..............	1,388,992	2.0	94.1	2.7	1.2	3.5	0.1	5.2	4.3	6.4	87.3
34	New Jersey	9,267,130	2.4	65.2	15.5	1.3	11.1	0.2	19.7	21.5	12.1	52.1
35	New Mexico	2,115,877	1.4	71.4	3.5	12.8	2.7	0.3	38.5	50.1	27.5	34.9
36	New York......................	19,835,913	2.4	64.0	17.6	1.8	9.9	0.2	18.2	19.5	10.7	53.5
37	North Carolina...............	10,551,162	7.7	70.1	22.6	3.0	3.9	0.2	9.2	10.1	8.4	60.9
38	North Dakota.................	774,948	12.3	89.0	4.1	7.1	2.1	0.5	3.9	4.1	6.1	82.3
39	Ohio...........................	11,780,017	1.1	83.4	14.3	1.6	3.1	0.2	4.4	4.3	6.4	76.6
40	Oklahoma.....................	3,986,639	4.8	78.8	9.6	14.6	3.2	0.3	8.7	11.7	14.0	62.8
41	Oregon........................	4,246,155	8.1	85.9	3.2	4.2	6.6	0.8	12.4	14.0	11.8	72.0
42	Pennsylvania.................	12,964,056	0.8	81.1	12.8	1.2	4.4	0.1	7.9	8.4	7.0	73.6
72	Puerto Rico...................	3,263,584	-14.3	60.3	13.4	2.2	0.3	0.0	64.3	99.2	35.8	0.5
44	Rhode Island.................	1,095,610	0.6	80.6	8.8	1.5	4.1	0.3	17.7	17.1	11.9	68.9
45	South Carolina...............	5,190,705	8.6	69.7	26.9	1.9	2.3	0.2	5.9	6.3	6.6	62.6
46	South Dakota	895,376	6.8	86.6	2.9	10.5	2.3	0.2	3.9	4.2	6.0	80.0
47	Tennessee	6,975,218	5.8	79.4	17.4	2.0	2.4	0.2	5.8	6.0	6.8	72.1
48	Texas..........................	29,527,941	12.6	70.9	13.7	2.4	6.3	0.2	31.4	40.2	23.9	39.4
49	Utah...........................	3,337,975	12.2	88.4	2.1	2.5	4.0	1.6	11.8	14.8	9.5	76.0
50	Vermont	645,570	-0.3	95.9	2.0	1.9	2.5	0.1	3.1	2.0	5.1	90.6
51	Virginia.......................	8,642,274	5.9	69.4	21.2	2.0	8.5	0.3	9.1	10.2	9.5	59.2
53	Washington	7,738,692	10.1	78.1	5.9	3.5	12.3	1.4	12.3	13.7	12.4	64.3
54	West Virginia	1,782,959	-2.0	95.6	4.3	1.8	1.2	0.1	2.4	1.7	5.0	90.4
55	Wisconsin.....................	5,895,908	1.9	87.4	7.6	2.0	3.7	0.1	7.0	7.5	7.4	79.0
56	Wyoming......................	578,803	2.8	92.6	1.6	4.2	1.6	0.1	8.5	10.6	8.1	81.5

'^ = Either no sample observations or too few sample observations were available to compute an estimate, or a ratio of medians cannot be calculated because one or both of the median estimates falls in the lowest interval or upper interval of an open-ended distribution.
NA = Not available.

Table A-1. States — Who: Age, Race/Ethnicity, and Household Structure, 2021—*Continued*

State code	STATE	Total population	Population by age (percent)							+/- U.S. percent under 18 years	+/- U.S. percent 65 years and over	Percent female
			Under 5 years	5 to 17 years	18 to 24 years	25 to 44 years	45 to 64 years	65 to 84 years	85 years and over			
	ACS table number:	B01001	B01001	B01001	B01001	B01001	B01001	B01001	B01001	B01001	B01001	B01001
	Column number:	12	13	14	15	16	17	18	19	20	21	22
0	**UNITED STATES**.............	331,893,745	5.6	16.5	9.1	26.8	25.2	15.0	1.8	0.0	0.0	50.5
1	Alabama.....................	5,039,877	5.8	16.5	9.3	25.2	25.7	16.0	1.6	0.1	0.8	51.5
2	Alaska	732,673	6.3	18.2	9.2	29.4	23.5	12.5	0.9	2.4	-3.4	47.7
4	Arizona.....................	7,276,316	5.5	16.7	9.4	26.3	23.8	16.6	1.8	0.1	1.5	50.1
5	Arkansas....................	3,025,891	5.9	17.3	9.4	25.4	24.6	15.6	1.7	1.2	0.6	50.6
6	California...................	39,237,836	5.6	16.7	9.1	28.7	24.7	13.5	1.7	0.3	-1.6	50.0
8	Colorado....................	5,812,069	5.3	16.1	9.0	30.1	24.3	13.7	1.4	-0.7	-1.7	49.4
9	Connecticut.................	3,605,597	4.9	15.2	9.5	25.0	27.3	15.7	2.3	-1.9	1.2	51.0
10	Delaware	1,003,384	5.3	15.5	8.3	25.0	25.8	18.2	1.9	-1.3	3.3	51.6
11	District of Columbia........	670,050	6.1	12.7	9.8	38.3	20.4	11.2	1.5	-3.3	-4.0	52.4
12	Florida......................	21,781,128	5.0	14.7	7.9	25.1	26.1	18.7	2.4	-2.4	4.3	50.8
13	Georgia.....................	10,799,566	5.8	17.6	9.7	27.0	25.3	13.4	1.3	1.3	-2.1	51.2
15	Hawaii......................	1,441,553	5.6	15.5	8.0	27.0	24.3	17.1	2.5	-1.0	2.8	49.7
16	Idaho.......................	1,900,923	5.9	18.8	9.1	26.3	23.3	14.9	1.6	2.6	-0.3	49.8
17	Illinois.....................	12,671,469	5.6	16.5	9.0	26.8	25.5	14.8	1.8	0.0	-0.2	50.6
18	Indiana	6,805,985	6.0	17.3	9.7	25.8	24.8	14.7	1.7	1.2	-0.4	50.4
19	Iowa........................	3,193,079	5.9	17.2	10.0	25.0	24.1	15.6	2.2	1.0	1.0	49.8
20	Kansas......................	2,934,582	6.1	17.9	9.9	25.7	23.7	14.8	1.9	1.8	-0.1	49.8
21	Kentucky....................	4,509,394	5.7	16.8	9.2	25.6	25.6	15.4	1.7	0.4	0.2	50.6
22	Louisiana...................	4,624,047	6.1	17.3	9.2	26.7	24.2	15.0	1.6	1.3	-0.2	51.1
23	Maine.......................	1,372,247	4.4	13.7	7.8	24.3	28.0	19.5	2.1	-3.9	4.9	50.9
24	Maryland....................	6,165,129	5.7	16.4	8.6	26.7	26.3	14.5	1.8	0.0	-0.5	51.3
25	Massachusetts...............	6,984,723	5.0	14.5	9.9	26.9	26.3	15.3	2.1	-2.6	0.6	51.2
26	Michigan	10,050,811	5.4	16.0	9.2	25.2	26.1	16.2	1.9	-0.7	1.3	50.5
27	Minnesota	5,707,390	5.8	17.1	8.8	26.5	25.0	14.9	1.9	0.8	0.0	49.9
28	Mississippi	2,949,965	5.9	17.6	9.8	25.1	24.8	15.3	1.5	1.4	0.0	51.3
29	Missouri....................	6,168,187	5.7	16.7	9.0	25.9	25.0	15.7	1.9	0.3	0.8	50.6
30	Montana	1,104,271	5.1	16.2	9.3	25.4	24.4	17.8	1.8	-0.8	2.9	49.2
31	Nebraska	1,963,692	6.3	18.2	9.6	26.0	23.4	14.5	2.0	2.5	-0.4	49.8
32	Nevada	3,143,991	5.6	16.6	8.1	28.2	25.1	15.1	1.4	0.1	-0.3	49.6
33	New Hampshire..............	1,388,992	4.5	14.0	9.0	24.8	28.5	17.4	1.8	-3.7	2.5	50.1
34	New Jersey	9,267,130	5.6	16.2	8.3	26.0	27.0	14.9	2.0	-0.3	0.1	50.8
35	New Mexico	2,115,877	5.4	16.9	9.1	26.2	23.9	16.6	1.9	0.2	1.7	50.3
36	New York	19,835,913	5.5	15.2	8.8	27.0	26.0	15.4	2.1	-1.4	0.7	51.1
37	North Carolina..............	10,551,162	5.5	16.3	9.5	25.9	25.8	15.4	1.6	-0.3	0.2	51.2
38	North Dakota...............	774,948	6.6	17.0	11.0	27.2	22.2	13.9	2.1	1.5	-0.8	48.4
39	Ohio........................	11,780,017	5.7	16.4	9.0	25.5	25.6	15.9	1.9	0.0	1.0	50.7
40	Oklahoma...................	3,986,639	6.1	18.0	9.8	26.5	23.5	14.6	1.6	1.9	-0.6	50.2
41	Oregon......................	4,246,155	5.0	15.3	8.4	28.0	24.7	16.8	1.8	-1.9	1.8	50.0
42	Pennsylvania................	12,964,056	5.2	15.4	8.7	25.5	26.1	16.8	2.3	-1.5	2.2	50.6
72	Puerto Rico	3,263,584	3.2	13.5	9.7	24.6	26.3	19.7	3.0	-5.4	5.9	52.7
44	Rhode Island...............	1,095,610	4.8	14.2	10.4	26.0	26.4	16.0	2.3	-3.1	1.5	51.0
45	South Carolina..............	5,190,705	5.3	16.2	9.2	25.3	25.4	17.0	1.6	-0.6	1.8	51.4
46	South Dakota	895,376	6.5	18.2	9.4	24.9	23.4	15.6	2.0	2.5	0.8	49.5
47	Tennessee...................	6,975,218	5.7	16.3	8.9	26.4	25.6	15.4	1.6	-0.1	0.2	51.1
48	Texas.......................	29,527,941	6.4	18.8	9.6	28.4	23.5	11.9	1.2	3.2	-3.6	50.1
49	Utah........................	3,337,975	7.0	21.3	11.4	28.5	20.1	10.5	1.1	6.2	-5.2	49.2
50	Vermont	645,570	4.2	13.9	10.2	24.0	27.1	18.5	2.1	-4.0	3.8	50.4
51	Virginia	8,642,274	5.6	16.2	9.5	27.0	25.5	14.6	1.7	-0.3	-0.5	50.5
53	Washington.................	7,738,692	5.6	16.1	8.6	29.3	24.3	14.6	1.6	-0.4	-0.6	49.6
54	West Virginia...............	1,782,959	5.0	15.3	8.8	23.8	26.5	18.7	2.0	-1.8	3.9	50.2
55	Wisconsin...................	5,895,908	5.3	16.3	9.2	25.2	26.1	15.9	2.0	-0.5	1.1	49.9
56	Wyoming....................	578,803	5.2	17.5	9.0	26.0	24.3	16.0	1.9	0.6	1.1	48.9

'^ = Either no sample observations or too few sample observations were available to compute an estimate, or a ratio of medians cannot be calculated because one or both of the median estimates falls in the lowest interval or upper interval of an open-ended distribution.
NA = Not available.

Table A-1. States — Who: Age, Race/Ethnicity, and Household Structure, 2021—*Continued*

	STATE	Total population	White alone, not Hispanic or Latino	Black alone	American Indian or Alaska Native alone	Asian alone	Native Hawaiian or Pacific Islander alone	Some other race alone	Two or more races	Hispanic or Latino
State code	ACS table number:	B01002	B01002H	B01002B	B01002C	B01002D	B01002E	B01002F	B01002G	B01002I
	Column number:	23	24	25	26	27	28	29	30	31
0	**UNITED STATES**.............	38.8	43.9	35.3	33.1	38.4	33.7	31.7	29.5	30.5
1	Alabama........................	39.8	43.3	35.9	34.7	37.6	41.6	24.4	27.5	23.5
2	Alaska..........................	35.6	40.1	30.7	30.1	36.7	24.9	30.8	24.2	27.5
4	Arizona........................	38.6	48.9	32.9	31.7	38.7	34.1	31.0	28.6	29.0
5	Arkansas.......................	38.5	42.7	33.4	33.7	34.1	26.4	27.4	28.1	24.8
6	California......................	37.6	46.6	37.2	34.2	40.5	36.9	31.8	30.1	30.9
8	Colorado	37.6	41.5	33.3	36.4	37.3	30.5	33.0	28.8	29.5
9	Connecticut...................	41.1	48.2	35.7	36.6	35.9	NA	33.3	28.6	30.5
10	Delaware	41.6	49.2	38.4	34.7	37.4	35.1	33.8	25.0	26.8
11	District of Columbia........	34.8	34.8	37.4	42.5	35.1	^	30.5	31.5	32.0
12	Florida	42.8	51.3	34.8	38.5	41.1	38.3	35.2	37.6	37.3
13	Georgia	37.5	42.6	35.0	30.2	37.2	33.9	28.4	27.0	27.2
15	Hawaii..........................	40.2	45.9	30.9	32.8	50.2	34.3	34.3	29.2	26.2
16	Idaho...........................	37.3	40.3	24.7	30.3	37.0	35.0	30.6	29.8	26.5
17	Illinois.........................	39.0	43.7	35.6	34.6	37.8	39.1	32.0	28.3	30.0
18	Indiana.........................	38.2	41.2	33.0	37.7	31.1	26.9	28.4	24.8	25.8
19	Iowa............................	38.5	41.5	28.9	28.5	32.1	23.5	29.5	22.6	23.7
20	Kansas..........................	37.3	40.9	34.4	31.7	34.4	27.6	28.5	23.5	25.4
21	Kentucky	39.1	41.2	33.7	35.1	33.6	24.5	28.3	27.1	25.1
22	Louisiana	38.0	42.0	34.4	35.4	35.7	34.8	29.9	27.7	29.9
23	Maine...........................	44.7	46.5	23.1	41.9	37.7	NA	34.8	33.0	30.5
24	Maryland	39.3	44.5	38.1	33.5	39.8	39.6	29.9	27.8	29.5
25	Massachusetts	39.9	45.3	34.7	37.3	35.7	NA	32.5	28.3	29.7
26	Michigan.......................	40.2	43.7	34.6	35.5	35.8	39.0	31.7	24.9	27.0
27	Minnesota	38.8	42.6	28.7	30.8	31.9	39.3	30.0	23.1	26.2
28	Mississippi	38.6	42.2	35.1	29.0	39.7	19.7	23.1	27.7	26.7
29	Missouri........................	39.2	41.8	34.2	31.4	35.4	34.3	29.1	26.4	26.2
30	Montana	40.1	42.4	28.3	28.2	26.9	67.5	33.8	30.2	25.7
31	Nebraska	37.2	40.9	30.7	27.0	32.6	29.1	27.7	23.2	24.7
32	Nevada.........................	38.7	47.8	33.6	35.1	43.7	33.5	30.7	29.1	29.9
33	New Hampshire	43.1	45.5	31.4	NA	34.9	^	35.9	27.9	29.2
34	New Jersey	40.3	46.5	36.8	36.0	39.0	47.5	34.0	32.2	33.3
35	New Mexico	39.1	51.4	33.6	33.7	36.1	51.4	37.8	32.1	33.2
36	New York.......................	39.8	44.3	37.5	33.7	38.8	34.0	34.4	32.7	33.9
37	North Carolina................	39.4	44.2	37.3	35.8	35.6	32.0	26.7	25.0	25.3
38	North Dakota.................	35.8	38.5	25.7	27.7	33.9	27.7	31.4	21.4	26.0
39	Ohio............................	39.6	42.6	33.7	39.6	35.3	30.5	30.9	24.0	26.5
40	Oklahoma......................	37.2	42.4	34.0	30.9	34.1	23.4	28.4	25.0	24.5
41	Oregon.........................	40.1	44.2	32.2	33.4	38.3	30.6	30.2	29.0	27.6
42	Pennsylvania..................	40.9	45.2	35.0	32.4	36.5	40.2	30.5	25.1	28.0
72	Puerto Rico....................	44.1	54.3	46.5	41.0	49.4	^	41.8	45.4	44.1
44	Rhode Island..................	40.6	47.0	35.1	32.1	34.7	34.3	31.4	28.3	29.2
45	South Carolina................	40.2	44.6	36.3	32.0	37.8	46.9	28.8	25.6	26.7
46	South Dakota	37.6	41.2	29.0	25.1	31.6	39.8	27.0	22.5	23.7
47	Tennessee.....................	39.2	42.3	35.3	34.0	36.0	NA	25.8	25.4	25.2
48	Texas	35.5	42.4	34.0	33.7	36.9	35.5	31.3	30.2	29.9
49	Utah............................	31.8	33.9	25.8	32.5	33.7	29.7	28.6	23.8	26.2
50	Vermont	42.9	44.3	25.7	32.6	33.5	^	40.6	29.6	36.0
51	Virginia........................	38.8	42.7	37.4	31.6	38.6	30.1	30.1	26.5	29.3
53	Washington...................	38.2	43.2	33.2	30.7	36.8	31.3	28.1	26.1	26.1
54	West Virginia.................	42.8	44.0	42.3	38.0	37.3	45.4	29.8	24.8	23.6
55	Wisconsin......................	40.1	44.0	30.4	35.4	30.6	26.5	28.7	24.6	25.7
56	Wyoming.......................	39.0	41.1	29.2	31.1	33.0	^	33.7	34.7	28.9

^ = Either no sample observations or too few sample observations were available to compute an estimate, or a ratio of medians cannot be calculated because one or both of the median estimates falls in the lowest interval or upper interval of an open-ended distribution.
NA = Not available.

State code	STATE	Total population, 15 years and over	Marital status of population 15 years and over (percent)				Foreign born (percent of total population)	Languages spoken (percent of households)			
			Never married	Now married (includes separated)	Widowed	Divorced		English only	Spanish, with or without English	Other languages, with or without English	Limited English-speaking household
	ACS table number:	B12001	B12001	B12001	B12001	B12001	C05002	C16002	C16002	C16002	C16002
	Column number:	32	33	34	35	36	37	38	39	40	41
0	UNITED STATES..............	271,400,195	34.2	49.7	5.5	10.6	13.6	77.5	12.8	9.7	4.2
1	Alabama.........................	4,113,516	31.7	49.0	7.1	12.2	3.5	94.4	3.2	2.5	1.1
2	Alaska	581,897	33.6	50.8	4.2	11.3	8.1	82.0	4.8	13.2	2.2
4	Arizona.........................	5,951,507	33.1	50.2	5.1	11.6	12.6	71.5	20.4	8.1	3.8
5	Arkansas........................	2,445,206	29.2	50.9	6.6	13.3	4.7	92.3	5.1	2.6	1.4
6	California.......................	32,021,241	38.2	48.3	4.6	8.9	26.6	54.5	26.6	19.0	8.3
8	Colorado	4,793,694	33.3	51.5	4.1	11.1	9.8	82.3	11.2	6.4	2.5
9	Connecticut....................	3,018,535	35.9	48.4	5.4	10.4	15.2	74.5	13.3	12.3	5.3
10	Delaware.......................	832,027	34.1	49.7	6.3	9.9	10.1	84.4	7.3	8.3	2.2
11	District of Columbia........	559,673	55.3	31.5	3.8	9.3	13.3	80.2	8.6	11.2	3.4
12	Florida	18,251,571	31.7	49.3	6.4	12.5	21.2	68.8	22.2	9.0	6.7
13	Georgia	8,731,410	35.2	48.3	5.2	11.3	10.0	84.8	7.6	7.6	2.6
15	Hawaii..........................	1,184,801	34.0	50.9	5.7	9.4	18.8	67.5	3.6	28.9	5.5
16	Idaho...........................	1,515,845	27.4	55.9	4.8	11.9	6.1	86.6	9.5	3.9	2.0
17	Illinois..........................	10,376,721	36.1	48.8	5.5	9.6	14.2	76.5	12.3	11.2	4.3
18	Indiana.........................	5,500,676	31.4	50.4	5.7	12.5	5.6	90.1	4.9	5.0	1.5
19	Iowa............................	2,588,040	31.7	52.3	5.5	10.5	5.4	91.3	4.1	4.6	1.5
20	Kansas..........................	2,354,938	30.7	52.6	5.7	11.0	6.9	87.8	7.6	4.6	2.4
21	Kentucky	3,672,905	29.9	50.9	6.6	12.6	4.0	93.9	2.8	3.3	1.4
22	Louisiana.......................	3,725,807	36.4	45.7	6.3	11.7	4.3	90.6	3.9	5.4	1.5
23	Maine...........................	1,168,883	28.6	52.4	5.8	13.2	4.1	92.1	1.2	6.7	1.0
24	Maryland	5,042,297	35.6	49.3	5.4	9.8	15.9	78.7	8.1	13.3	3.3
25	Massachusetts	5,871,307	37.5	48.1	5.1	9.2	17.6	73.0	9.9	17.2	6.1
26	Michigan	8,287,187	33.9	48.9	5.7	11.5	6.8	89.3	3.2	7.5	1.6
27	Minnesota	4,628,858	33.3	51.7	4.8	10.1	8.5	87.5	3.8	8.7	2.2
28	Mississippi	2,382,518	34.6	47.0	6.9	11.5	2.1	95.7	2.4	2.0	0.8
29	Missouri........................	5,026,699	31.1	51.1	6.0	11.8	4.1	92.8	2.9	4.4	1.0
30	Montana	910,599	30.6	52.1	5.4	11.9	2.2	94.3	1.9	3.8	0.4
31	Nebraska	1,563,814	31.2	53.2	5.2	10.4	7.4	88.2	7.4	4.4	2.8
32	Nevada	2,567,541	35.0	46.8	5.4	12.8	18.4	69.0	18.9	12.1	5.0
33	New Hampshire	1,180,473	30.6	52.5	5.2	11.7	5.9	90.0	2.7	7.3	1.0
34	New Jersey	7,606,368	34.4	51.5	5.5	8.5	23.0	65.5	16.8	17.7	6.9
35	New Mexico	1,728,213	35.1	46.3	5.7	12.8	9.1	62.8	29.4	7.8	5.3
36	New York.......................	16,443,249	38.7	46.5	5.6	9.1	22.3	68.5	14.7	16.8	7.4
37	North Carolina...............	8,660,874	32.9	50.7	5.7	10.7	8.2	87.8	7.0	5.2	2.2
38	North Dakota.................	620,127	33.8	51.2	5.2	9.8	4.4	90.7	2.9	6.4	1.0
39	Ohio............................	9,636,748	33.4	48.7	6.0	11.9	5.0	91.2	2.9	5.9	1.5
40	Oklahoma......................	3,195,710	30.4	50.7	6.3	12.6	5.8	88.5	7.3	4.1	1.9
41	Oregon.........................	3,540,546	32.5	50.0	4.9	12.7	9.7	83.7	8.4	7.8	2.3
42	Pennsylvania..................	10,766,654	34.4	49.8	6.1	9.7	7.2	87.0	5.6	7.4	2.6
72	Puerto Rico....................	2,833,104	43.2	34.0	8.1	14.7	2.7	3.7	96.2	0.2	68.5
44	Rhode Island..................	925,558	37.4	46.3	5.5	10.8	14.5	75.9	12.8	11.3	5.7
45	South Carolina...............	4,276,713	32.8	50.1	6.6	10.5	5.2	92.0	4.4	3.5	1.2
46	South Dakota	711,925	32.0	52.6	5.5	9.9	3.5	92.2	2.8	4.9	0.8
47	Tennessee	5,707,432	31.1	50.7	6.3	11.9	5.3	92.1	4.2	3.7	1.6
48	Texas	23,373,981	33.4	51.8	4.8	9.9	17.2	62.9	29.3	7.8	6.8
49	Utah	2,561,556	31.5	56.4	3.5	8.6	8.3	80.5	11.9	7.6	2.2
50	Vermont........................	550,276	32.9	50.4	5.3	11.4	4.2	92.3	1.4	6.3	0.6
51	Virginia.........................	7,088,043	33.3	51.4	5.3	10.0	12.4	82.3	7.3	10.4	2.6
53	Washington....................	6,346,203	32.2	52.1	4.4	11.4	14.8	77.9	8.3	13.8	3.8
54	West Virginia	1,486,191	28.7	50.7	7.3	13.3	1.6	96.6	1.2	2.2	0.3
55	Wisconsin......................	4,852,416	33.2	50.8	5.2	10.8	5.1	90.6	4.7	4.7	1.3
56	Wyoming.......................	471,226	27.5	55.2	5.0	12.3	3.4	91.2	5.5	3.3	0.8

'^ = Either no sample observations or too few sample observations were available to compute an estimate, or a ratio of medians cannot be calculated because one or both of the median estimates falls in the lowest interval or upper interval of an open-ended distribution.
NA = Not available.

Table A-1. States — Who: Age, Race/Ethnicity, and Household Structure, 2021—*Continued*

				Household type (percent of all households)									
				Family households				Nonfamily households			Unmarried partner households		
	STATE	Total households	Average household size	Total family households	Married-couple families	Male householder families (no spouse)	Female householder families (no spouse)	Total nonfamily households	Total one-person households	One person households age 65 or over	Total unmarried cohabiting partner households	Same-sex cohabiting partner households	Same-sex married partner households
	ACS table number:	B11001	B25010	B11001	B11001	B11001	B11001	B11001	B11001	B11010/ B11001	B11009	B11009	B11009
State code	Column number:	42	43	44	45	46	47	48	49	50	51	52	53
0	UNITED STATES.............	127,544,730	2.54	64.7	47.3	5.0	12.3	35.3	28.3	11.3	7.2	0.4	0.6
1	Alabama.....................	1,967,559	2.50	64.6	46.0	4.6	14.1	35.4	30.9	12.4	4.8	0.3	0.3
2	Alaska	271,311	2.61	63.5	47.9	5.5	10.1	36.5	28.6	8.7	8.5	0.2	0.4
4	Arizona......................	2,817,723	2.53	65.5	47.7	5.8	12.0	34.5	26.3	11.1	8.6	0.5	0.7
5	Arkansas....................	1,183,675	2.49	65.7	47.8	5.1	12.8	34.3	28.7	11.9	6.2	0.3	0.3
6	California...................	13,429,063	2.86	68.1	48.5	6.4	13.1	31.9	24.0	9.5	7.9	0.5	0.8
8	Colorado....................	2,313,042	2.46	62.6	48.6	4.6	9.4	37.4	27.9	9.6	7.6	0.5	0.6
9	Connecticut................	1,428,313	2.45	64.2	46.5	4.5	13.1	35.8	28.8	12.7	7.3	0.5	0.7
10	Delaware....................	395,656	2.47	64.8	47.1	4.8	12.9	35.2	29.0	12.6	6.4	0.3	1.0
11	District of Columbia........	319,565	1.98	40.3	24.2	3.1	13.0	59.7	48.2	11.7	7.8	1.1	1.5
12	Florida......................	8,565,329	2.49	64.3	46.4	5.0	12.9	35.7	28.4	12.8	7.5	0.5	0.7
13	Georgia	4,001,109	2.64	66.9	47.0	4.8	15.0	33.1	26.8	9.7	6.1	0.5	0.5
15	Hawaii	490,080	2.86	68.3	50.6	5.4	12.3	31.7	24.6	11.0	7.7	0.7	0.7
16	Idaho........................	693,882	2.70	68.7	55.6	4.5	8.6	31.3	24.2	11.0	6.5	0.2	0.3
17	Illinois......................	4,991,641	2.48	62.8	46.1	4.8	11.9	37.2	30.6	12.0	6.9	0.4	0.5
18	Indiana......................	2,680,694	2.47	64.1	48.0	4.9	11.2	35.9	29.1	11.1	7.7	0.4	0.5
19	Iowa.........................	1,300,467	2.38	62.1	49.1	4.2	8.8	37.9	30.2	12.2	7.6	0.2	0.3
20	Kansas.......................	1,159,026	2.47	63.9	49.5	4.7	9.7	36.1	30.0	12.0	6.3	0.3	0.2
21	Kentucky....................	1,785,682	2.46	64.9	47.6	5.1	12.2	35.1	28.5	11.5	7.1	0.4	0.4
22	Louisiana	1,783,924	2.52	63.8	42.4	5.4	16.0	36.2	30.7	12.0	6.7	0.3	0.4
23	Maine........................	593,626	2.25	61.5	48.5	3.9	9.1	38.5	29.9	13.4	9.2	0.5	0.6
24	Maryland....................	2,355,652	2.56	65.8	47.1	4.9	13.8	34.2	27.9	10.9	6.2	0.3	0.6
25	Massachusetts...............	2,759,018	2.44	62.3	46.0	4.5	11.9	37.7	28.5	11.9	7.7	0.4	0.8
26	Michigan	4,051,798	2.43	62.9	46.3	5.0	11.6	37.1	30.2	12.4	7.4	0.3	0.4
27	Minnesota...................	2,281,033	2.45	62.6	49.2	4.5	8.9	37.4	29.1	11.6	8.5	0.4	0.5
28	Mississippi..................	1,129,611	2.54	65.8	44.2	4.7	16.9	34.2	29.7	12.1	4.7	0.2	0.3
29	Missouri.....................	2,468,726	2.43	63.0	47.7	4.4	11.0	37.0	30.1	11.9	7.0	0.4	0.4
30	Montana.....................	448,949	2.40	61.4	48.8	4.5	8.1	38.6	29.2	12.8	8.3	0.3	0.2
31	Nebraska	785,982	2.44	63.0	49.8	4.3	8.9	37.0	30.4	12.0	6.5	0.3	0.4
32	Nevada	1,191,380	2.61	63.3	43.8	6.7	12.7	36.7	28.0	10.7	9.1	0.4	0.7
33	New Hampshire.............	548,026	2.46	65.9	52.3	4.7	8.9	34.1	25.9	11.7	8.9	0.3	0.6
34	New Jersey..................	3,497,945	2.60	68.0	50.4	4.9	12.7	32.0	26.2	11.5	6.8	0.2	0.6
35	New Mexico	834,007	2.49	62.7	42.9	6.1	13.6	37.3	30.9	12.6	8.3	0.5	0.6
36	New York....................	7,652,666	2.52	61.6	42.7	5.2	13.7	38.4	30.9	12.6	7.4	0.5	0.7
37	North Carolina..............	4,179,632	2.46	64.3	47.3	4.3	12.6	35.7	29.4	11.1	6.4	0.4	0.4
38	North Dakota...............	322,511	2.33	59.1	46.1	5.4	7.6	40.9	33.2	11.2	7.3	0.1	0.3
39	Ohio.........................	4,832,922	2.38	61.8	44.7	4.8	12.3	38.2	31.1	12.7	7.8	0.4	0.4
40	Oklahoma...................	1,547,967	2.51	64.6	47.3	5.2	12.1	35.4	29.3	11.6	6.6	0.4	0.4
41	Oregon......................	1,702,599	2.44	61.9	47.4	4.8	9.7	38.1	28.1	11.8	9.0	0.5	0.7
42	Pennsylvania................	5,228,956	2.40	63.1	46.9	4.6	11.6	36.9	30.2	13.1	7.5	0.4	0.4
72	Puerto Rico	1,165,982	2.77	63.4	34.5	6.6	22.3	36.6	31.3	16.3	10.9	0.3	0.2
44	Rhode Island................	440,170	2.39	61.0	44.2	4.8	12.0	39.0	30.4	13.0	8.5	0.4	0.7
45	South Carolina..............	2,049,972	2.47	65.2	47.0	4.5	13.7	34.8	29.1	11.8	5.8	0.3	0.4
46	South Dakota	356,887	2.42	62.0	49.0	4.6	8.3	38.0	30.2	12.3	7.5	0.1	0.3
47	Tennessee...................	2,770,395	2.46	64.4	47.1	4.8	12.5	35.6	29.2	11.5	6.6	0.3	0.4
48	Texas........................	10,796,247	2.68	68.3	49.5	5.3	13.5	31.7	25.6	8.5	6.3	0.4	0.6
49	Utah.........................	1,101,499	2.99	72.5	59.3	4.6	8.6	27.5	20.6	7.1	5.2	0.3	0.6
50	Vermont	270,163	2.29	61.1	48.4	4.0	8.7	38.9	27.9	12.9	10.7	0.3	0.7
51	Virginia......................	3,331,461	2.52	65.0	48.9	4.6	11.5	35.0	28.3	10.9	6.2	0.3	0.5
53	Washington.................	3,022,255	2.51	64.1	49.8	4.6	9.7	35.9	27.1	10.1	8.6	0.4	0.7
54	West Virginia................	722,201	2.41	64.0	47.8	5.0	11.2	36.0	29.9	13.3	6.4	0.3	0.3
55	Wisconsin....................	2,449,970	2.35	61.8	47.5	4.7	9.7	38.2	30.3	12.0	8.2	0.3	0.4
56	Wyoming....................	242,763	2.33	62.1	49.8	4.6	7.7	37.9	30.9	11.1	6.8	0.5	0.4

'^ = Either no sample observations or too few sample observations were available to compute an estimate, or a ratio of medians cannot be calculated because one or both of the median estimates falls in the lowest interval or upper interval of an open-ended distribution.
NA = Not available.

		Households with people under 18 years old				Households with people 60 years and over				
			Household type (percent)				Household type (percent)			
State code	STATE	Total households with children	Married-couple families	Male householder families (no spouse)	Female householder families (no spouse)	Total households with people 60 years and over	Married-couple families	Male householder families (no spouse)	Female householder families (no spouse)	Nonfamily households
	ACS table number:	C11005	C11005	C11005	C11005	B11006	B11006	B11006	B11006	B11006
	Column number:	54	55	56	57	58	59	60	61	62
0	UNITED STATES............	37,661,807	65.1	9.1	25.0	52,911,453	48.0	4.0	9.5	38.4
1	Alabama........................	566,528	61.3	8.5	29.7	838,409	45.8	3.8	10.5	39.8
2	Alaska..........................	86,062	67.0	9.3	22.3	98,385	47.8	5.1	7.2	39.9
4	Arizona.........................	828,188	62.9	11.2	24.8	1,216,988	50.5	3.8	8.8	36.9
5	Arkansas.......................	370,809	62.0	9.4	27.4	488,704	47.0	3.8	9.1	40.0
6	California......................	4,376,572	66.6	10.0	22.6	5,559,932	48.8	6.0	12.0	33.3
8	Colorado	655,933	70.4	8.7	20.0	847,023	50.1	4.0	7.6	38.4
9	Connecticut...................	405,492	64.7	8.3	26.4	630,003	46.4	3.8	9.8	40.1
10	Delaware.......................	105,186	62.4	9.2	28.2	187,818	49.2	3.8	8.6	38.5
11	District of Columbia........	60,217	52.6	5.6	40.5	96,415	22.3	3.7	17.2	56.8
12	Florida..........................	2,225,531	61.3	9.5	28.2	4,092,053	48.4	3.9	9.4	38.4
13	Georgia........................	1,273,334	61.7	8.1	29.5	1,529,712	48.7	3.9	11.4	35.9
15	Hawaii..........................	149,570	69.4	8.8	21.2	245,832	49.1	5.4	13.3	32.2
16	Idaho...........................	227,024	72.4	9.6	17.0	285,824	54.7	2.2	5.8	37.3
17	Illinois..........................	1,443,661	65.7	8.9	24.5	2,019,613	46.3	3.8	9.3	40.7
18	Indiana	797,631	65.2	9.2	24.2	1,071,094	47.9	3.3	8.4	40.5
19	Iowa............................	372,532	68.4	9.4	21.2	533,060	50.9	2.1	5.0	42.0
20	Kansas..........................	351,413	68.0	9.2	21.8	460,277	50.2	2.7	6.1	41.0
21	Kentucky.......................	535,332	63.3	9.6	25.9	737,180	46.9	4.3	9.7	39.0
22	Louisiana......................	538,166	55.4	10.1	34.0	739,655	43.5	4.3	11.9	40.3
23	Maine...........................	142,937	66.9	9.1	22.5	278,519	49.0	2.6	5.6	42.7
24	Maryland.......................	719,289	64.7	8.3	25.9	977,605	47.4	4.2	10.9	37.5
25	Massachusetts................	772,250	66.8	7.8	24.6	1,170,977	46.9	3.9	9.1	40.1
26	Michigan	1,104,257	63.7	9.8	25.4	1,740,164	47.3	3.5	8.5	40.6
27	Minnesota	655,004	69.9	9.3	19.8	906,671	50.5	2.6	5.8	41.1
28	Mississippi....................	342,962	56.7	7.7	34.9	486,767	43.5	3.7	12.5	40.3
29	Missouri........................	696,884	65.2	8.8	24.8	1,025,641	48.5	3.4	7.2	40.9
30	Montana	112,481	68.3	10.4	19.8	199,042	50.9	3.0	6.3	39.7
31	Nebraska.......................	232,841	69.4	9.1	20.4	303,718	50.5	2.5	5.3	41.7
32	Nevada.........................	352,763	60.7	12.2	26.0	492,238	45.0	5.7	9.5	39.8
33	New Hampshire..............	145,490	70.2	9.1	19.5	250,774	53.3	4.0	5.6	37.1
34	New Jersey	1,092,567	70.4	7.5	21.5	1,517,330	48.5	4.1	10.5	37.0
35	New Mexico...................	240,483	56.1	12.5	30.9	369,586	45.2	4.6	9.1	41.0
36	New York.......................	2,065,681	63.7	8.8	26.7	3,387,943	43.1	4.8	11.8	40.3
37	North Carolina................	1,194,312	63.5	8.0	27.5	1,696,083	48.7	3.2	9.4	38.6
38	North Dakota..................	85,239	68.2	11.0	19.6	115,722	49.7	2.7	4.2	43.4
39	Ohio.............................	1,352,498	61.5	9.7	27.9	2,021,585	45.4	3.5	8.2	42.9
40	Oklahoma......................	478,816	63.3	9.9	25.8	616,267	47.1	3.8	8.7	40.4
41	Oregon.........................	462,220	67.4	10.4	21.3	712,851	48.9	3.2	7.3	40.6
42	Pennsylvania..................	1,404,977	64.7	9.2	25.3	2,322,451	47.3	3.5	8.5	40.6
72	Puerto Rico....................	275,243	38.6	13.9	47.3	620,085	37.2	4.8	16.2	41.8
44	Rhode Island..................	113,777	64.1	7.0	27.7	195,071	45.8	4.4	7.8	42.0
45	South Carolina...............	579,540	60.5	8.1	30.7	891,527	48.5	3.3	9.8	38.4
46	South Dakota	103,442	67.6	9.6	20.9	146,806	51.6	3.0	4.0	41.5
47	Tennessee.....................	794,247	63.3	8.5	27.2	1,137,557	47.8	3.6	9.5	39.1
48	Texas	3,756,798	66.5	8.2	24.7	3,828,316	50.4	4.4	11.2	34.0
49	Utah.............................	421,678	78.9	6.4	14.1	361,811	57.5	3.9	7.8	30.8
50	Vermont........................	66,142	67.0	9.6	22.8	121,172	50.3	2.1	5.9	41.7
51	Virginia.........................	1,003,448	68.0	8.2	23.0	1,345,452	49.5	3.8	9.1	37.6
53	Washington....................	877,863	69.7	9.2	20.3	1,179,715	51.1	3.5	7.6	37.8
54	West Virginia	188,074	63.0	9.8	26.5	335,452	48.9	4.2	8.1	38.8
55	Wisconsin......................	663,169	64.7	10.6	23.8	1,001,472	49.6	2.8	5.7	41.9
56	Wyoming.......................	70,497	69.9	10.0	19.2	97,191	52.4	3.5	4.2	39.8

'^ = Either no sample observations or too few sample observations were available to compute an estimate, or a ratio of medians cannot be calculated because one or both of the median estimates falls in the lowest interval or upper interval of an open-ended distribution.
NA = Not available.

This page is intentionally left blank

Table A-2. Counties — Who: Age, Race/Ethnicity, and Household Structure, 2021

				Population by age (percent)						Race alone or in combination (percent)					
STATE County code	STATE County	Total population	Percent change, 2010–2019	Under 18 years	18 to 24 years	25 to 44 years	45 to 64 years	65 years and over	Median age	White	Black or African American	American Indian and Alaska Native	Asian	Native Hawaiian or Other Pacific Islander	Some other race
	ACS table number:	B01003	Population Estimates	B01001	B01001	B01001	B01001	B01001	B01002	B02008	B02009	B02010	B02011	B02012	B02013
	Column number:	1	2	3	4	5	6	7	8	9	10	11	12	13	14
00000	**UNITED STATES**	331,893,745	6.3	22.1	9.1	26.8	25.2	16.8	38.8	72.9	14.2	2.6	7.1	0.5	16.2
01000	**ALABAMA**	5,039,877	2.0	22.2	9.3	25.2	25.7	17.6	39.8	69.6	27.3	2.1	1.9	0.2	4.3
01003	Baldwin County, Alabama	239,294	22.5	21.2	6.6	23.4	27.5	21.4	43.9	87.6	9.7	1.6	1.5	-	4.7
01015	Calhoun County, Alabama	115,972	-4.2	21.6	10.4	24.3	25.4	18.2	40.2	75.4	20.3	3.9	1.7		4.4
01043	Cullman County, Alabama	89,496	4.2	22.0	8.3	24.3	26.5	18.9	40.5	94.4	1.7	1.4	0.8	-	4.7
01049	DeKalb County, Alabama	71,813	0.6	24.4	7.6	22.9	27.6	17.4	40.2	87.2	2.0	5.5	-		10.6
01051	Elmore County, Alabama	89,304	2.4	22.2	7.8	26.5	26.7	16.7	40.0	77.7	23.4	1.1	-		1.7
01055	Etowah County, Alabama	103,162	-2.1	21.6	8.6	23.8	26.9	19.1	41.5	81.6	17.2	1.7	1.0	-	4.5
01069	Houston County, Alabama	107,458	4.3	22.8	7.7	25.4	25.6	18.5	40.5	69.6	29.2	1.5	1.7	-	3.5
01073	Jefferson County, Alabama	667,820	0.0	22.9	8.7	27.2	24.6	16.6	38.3	52.0	44.2	1.1	2.2	0.2	4.2
01077	Lauderdale County, Alabama	94,043	0.0	20.1	10.9	23.1	25.6	20.3	40.0	90.3	8.0	3.7	1.1	-	3.1
01081	Lee County, Alabama	177,218	17.3	21.0	16.6	26.5	22.9	12.9	33.3	72.4	23.8	1.4	4.8	-	3.5
01083	Limestone County, Alabama	107,517	19.5	22.0	7.7	27.8	26.7	15.8	40.8	85.1	11.4	5.3	2.3	1.4	5.0
01089	Madison County, Alabama	395,211	11.4	21.7	9.1	26.9	26.7	15.6	39.6	71.5	26.1	2.9	3.7	0.3	4.5
01095	Marshall County, Alabama	98,228	4.0	25.6	8.4	24.2	24.9	17.0	37.8	87.8	3.6	3.6	0.9	-	10.1
01097	Mobile County, Alabama	413,073	0.1	23.4	8.8	26.0	24.8	17.0	38.8	59.1	37.5	1.6	2.5	-	3.1
01101	Montgomery County, Alabama	227,434	-1.3	23.8	9.4	27.1	23.7	16.0	37.2	34.9	61.0	0.8	3.7	-	3.3
01103	Morgan County, Alabama	123,668	0.2	23.1	7.6	24.9	26.0	18.4	40.8	80.2	14.5	3.3	-	-	9.2
01115	St. Clair County, Alabama	92,748	7.1	22.3	7.4	25.4	26.9	18.0	41.3	83.1	12.2	3.9	3.0		5.1
01117	Shelby County, Alabama	226,902	11.6	22.8	8.3	25.6	26.9	16.4	40.6	NA	NA	NA	NA	NA	NA
01121	Talladega County, Alabama	81,524	-2.8	20.7	8.2	25.1	27.1	18.8	42.9	66.9	32.4	3.4	0.6	-	2.6
01125	Tuscaloosa County, Alabama	227,007	7.6	21.1	15.6	26.6	22.5	14.3	34.4	64.9	33.4	0.8	2.2	-	3.7
02000	**ALASKA**	732,673	4.2	24.5	9.2	29.4	23.5	13.4	35.6	71.3	5.3	20.7	9.0	2.5	6.0
02020	Anchorage Municipality, Alaska	288,121	-1.3	23.9	9.5	31.2	22.7	12.7	35.2	70.2	8.3	13.5	13.3	4.4	6.8
02090	Fairbanks North Star Borough, Alaska	95,593	-0.8	23.5	12.3	30.4	21.2	12.6	32.0	82.5	7.0	12.1	6.3	0.8	7.5
02170	Matanuska-Susitna Borough, Alaska	110,686	21.7	26.2	7.6	28.4	24.5	13.2	36.9	87.3	2.4	12.0	3.5	1.4	5.8
04000	**ARIZONA**	7,276,316	9.8	22.2	9.4	26.3	23.8	18.3	38.6	77.6	6.3	6.0	4.8	0.4	25.9
04001	Apache County, Arizona	65,623	0.5	26.6	8.7	24.1	23.7	16.9	35.9	22.6	2.7	72.6	-		5.4
04003	Cochise County, Arizona	126,050	-4.1	21.2	8.1	23.2	23.8	23.8	43.2	85.7	6.0	3.5	4.0	-	26.7
04005	Coconino County, Arizona	145,052	6.7	20.0	19.7	24.6	21.6	14.0	33.0	62.7	2.2	28.6	2.9	0.4	12.8
04013	Maricopa County, Arizona	4,496,588	17.5	23.0	9.2	27.9	24.1	15.8	37.3	77.5	7.4	3.6	5.9	0.5	26.2
04015	Mohave County, Arizona	217,692	6.0	16.4	5.6	18.6	28.0	31.3	53.4	90.0	2.1	4.0	2.1	0.4	13.1
04017	Navajo County, Arizona	108,147	3.2	25.6	7.5	23.1	23.6	20.2	38.4	53.5	2.4	45.3	0.6	-	8.1
04019	Pima County, Arizona	1,052,030	6.8	20.3	11.4	24.9	22.7	20.7	39.1	77.6	5.7	5.5	4.5	0.3	28.6
04021	Pinal County, Arizona	449,557	23.2	22.2	7.7	26.4	22.8	21.0	39.8	78.9	7.3	7.3	2.4	0.6	20.9
04025	Yavapai County, Arizona	242,253	11.4	15.6	6.2	18.0	26.4	33.8	55.3	91.9	1.5	2.9	2.2	0.3	14.4
04027	Yuma County, Arizona	206,990	9.2	25.1	10.2	25.4	19.9	19.4	35.4	79.4	3.2	3.0	1.9	0.3	59.4
05000	**ARKANSAS**	3,025,891	3.0	23.3	9.4	25.4	24.6	17.4	38.5	79.5	16.2	2.8	2.2	0.5	9.2
05007	Benton County, Arkansas	293,692	26.1	25.6	8.4	29.3	23.2	13.5	35.8	87.9	2.9	3.4	5.7	1.0	27.4
05031	Craighead County, Arkansas	112,218	14.4	25.2	10.5	29.3	21.2	13.8	33.6	78.7	17.2	2.9	1.9	-	6.2
05045	Faulkner County, Arkansas	125,106	11.3	22.5	15.2	26.8	22.4	13.0	33.3	84.7	13.5	1.6	1.9	-	4.0
05051	Garland County, Arkansas	100,330	3.5	19.8	6.9	22.6	26.7	24.0	45.5	90.2	9.8	2.3	1.1	-	2.4
05069	Jefferson County, Arkansas	65,861	-13.7	21.9	9.3	25.8	24.5	18.5	39.3	42.5	56.9	0.8	-	-	3.3
05085	Lonoke County, Arkansas	74,722	7.2	25.0	7.8	28.1	24.8	14.3	36.8	91.8	7.2	2.2	1.5	-	3.3
05119	Pulaski County, Arkansas	397,821	2.4	23.3	8.4	27.5	24.5	16.4	37.7	56.2	39.3	1.2	2.8	-	6.1
05125	Saline County, Arkansas	125,233	14.3	22.9	8.0	26.2	24.7	18.2	40.6	87.8	10.0	1.2	1.8	-	3.7
05131	Sebastian County, Arkansas	128,400	-11.6	23.4	10.3	24.7	25.8	15.8	37.4	77.7	8.4	4.4	6.3	-	12.8
05143	Washington County, Arkansas	250,057	17.8	23.9	14.1	28.2	21.4	12.5	32.8	86.7	4.9	3.8	3.9	3.2	21.4
05145	White County, Arkansas	77,207	2.2	23.1	11.4	24.5	24.8	16.2	38.0	95.0	4.0	3.9	1.4	-	6.1
06000	**CALIFORNIA**	39,237,836	6.1	22.4	9.1	28.7	24.7	15.2	37.6	57.1	7.3	3.3	17.8	0.8	34.2
06001	Alameda County, California	1,648,556	10.7	20.1	7.8	31.6	25.6	14.9	38.8	40.8	11.9	2.2	36.6	1.5	19.8
06007	Butte County, California	208,309	-0.4	20.4	14.2	25.0	22.0	18.4	36.8	85.3	3.3	5.0	6.9	0.5	13.9
06013	Contra Costa County, California	1,161,413	10.0	22.2	7.9	26.4	26.9	16.7	40.4	56.2	11.0	3.3	22.2	1.1	22.8
06017	El Dorado County, California	193,221	6.5	19.7	6.8	22.7	28.3	22.5	45.7	87.8	1.6	3.2	8.2	0.7	11.9
06019	Fresno County, California	1,013,581	7.4	28.2	9.6	28.4	21.3	12.6	33.1	60.5	6.3	3.2	12.5	0.4	46.9
06023	Humboldt County, California	136,310	0.7	19.0	12.0	25.5	24.0	19.5	39.9	84.4	3.2	9.1	5.2	0.7	13.2

STATE County code	STATE County	Two or more races (percent)	Hispanic or Latino (percent)	Native, born in state of residence (percent)	Foreign born (percent)	Non-citizens (percent)	Total house-holds	Family households Total	Married couple	Male house-holder	Female house-holder	Nonfamily households Total	One-person house-holds	Percent of households with people age 60 years and over
	ACS table number:	B02001	B03003	B05002	B05002	B05002	B11001	B11001	B11001	B11001	B11001	B11001	B11001	B11006
	Column number:	15	16	17	18	19	20	21	22	23	24	25	26	27
00000	**UNITED STATES**.....................	12.6	18.8	58.0	13.6	6.6	127,544,730	64.7	47.3	5.0	12.3	35.3	28.3	41.5
01000	**ALABAMA**	5.0	4.7	69.2	3.5	2.0	1,967,559	64.6	46.0	4.6	14.1	35.4	30.9	42.6
01003	Baldwin County, Alabama..........	5.0	4.8	54.3	3.3	1.7	94,105	65.6	53.8	4.3	7.6	34.4	30.2	48.6
01015	Calhoun County, Alabama.........	5.5	4.2	68.3	2.9	1.9	44,631	62.5	41.9	4.9	15.7	37.5	33.3	43.0
01043	Cullman County, Alabama	3.2	4.7	75.1	1.9	1.3	35,131	71.9	56.8	5.0	10.1	28.1	23.7	40.7
01049	DeKalb County, Alabama............	5.4	15.8	71.2	7.9	7.0	24,979	67.7	52.9	4.3	10.6	32.3	29.4	47.5
01051	Elmore County, Alabama	4.0	3.1	73.5	1.9	1.5	32,108	69.2	44.1	5.4	19.7	30.8	27.6	40.6
01055	Etowah County, Alabama............	5.4	4.6	77.9	1.6	1.2	38,006	64.2	44.6	5.5	14.1	35.8	31.2	47.2
01069	Houston County, Alabama	4.9	3.6	63.3	1.8	0.9	44,058	65.9	43.1	5.0	17.9	34.1	29.4	43.9
01073	Jefferson County, Alabama	3.7	4.3	75.4	3.6	2.0	270,147	59.7	38.7	4.5	16.5	40.3	34.9	40.1
01077	Lauderdale County, Alabama	6.2	3.1	72.7	2.1	1.5	38,250	66.8	49.3	5.8	11.7	33.2	28.3	44.9
01081	Lee County, Alabama.................	4.9	3.9	49.0	6.3	3.5	67,358	63.9	48.1	5.7	10.1	36.1	27.5	32.3
01083	Limestone County, Alabama	9.6	6.5	64.0	5.0	1.9	40,685	68.0	54.5	4.1	9.3	32.0	27.9	42.5
01089	Madison County, Alabama..........	7.9	5.5	51.8	5.4	2.4	164,493	65.5	49.4	4.4	11.7	34.5	29.0	37.5
01095	Marshall County, Alabama..........	5.9	15.6	68.1	7.2	5.8	36,003	68.6	49.2	6.0	13.5	31.4	26.7	41.8
01097	Mobile County, Alabama............	3.5	3.1	73.9	3.4	1.7	162,963	63.3	41.6	4.4	17.4	36.7	32.3	40.7
01101	Montgomery County, Alabama...	3.6	3.9	70.8	5.6	3.9	92,407	61.7	34.3	4.6	22.8	38.3	33.3	37.3
01103	Morgan County, Alabama...........	7.1	9.0	68.6	4.5	3.9	47,558	65.4	50.7	4.0	10.6	34.6	31.4	45.2
01115	St. Clair County, Alabama...........	NA	NA	77.2	0.8	0.1	33,093	68.2	51.9	3.9	12.4	31.8	28.0	42.5
01117	Shelby County, Alabama.............	7.0	6.0	63.7	4.7	2.5	86,970	72.3	58.7	4.6	9.1	27.7	23.4	38.9
01121	Talladega County, Alabama.........	5.6	2.6	80.5	1.3	0.9	33,775	63.9	42.1	5.0	16.7	36.1	32.3	46.8
01125	Tuscaloosa County, Alabama.......	4.7	4.2	72.2	3.6	2.4	86,694	65.0	46.6	4.0	14.4	35.0	29.1	37.5
02000	**ALASKA**	13.3	7.1	42.9	8.1	2.9	271,311	63.5	47.9	5.5	10.1	36.5	28.6	36.3
02020	Anchorage Municipality, Alaska ..	14.9	9.7	39.5	11.0	3.8	109,584	62.6	46.1	5.7	10.8	37.4	30.1	33.1
02090	Fairbanks North Star Borough, Alaska	15.3	8.4	34.8	6.7	2.5	36,426	61.9	51.7	2.2	8.1	38.1	30.4	28.8
02170	Matanuska-Susitna Borough, Alaska	11.5	5.6	42.5	3.5	1.1	40,997	71.6	55.2	7.0	9.4	28.4	21.1	35.8
04000	**ARIZONA**	20.1	32.3	39.9	12.6	7.4	2,817,723	65.5	47.7	5.8	12.0	34.5	26.3	43.2
04001	Apache County, Arizona	4.5	7.1	70.2	2.7	1.7	19,875	67.1	41.4	4.3	21.5	32.9	29.1	51.2
04003	Cochise County, Arizona............	24.6	35.9	37.0	12.6	5.8	49,952	59.7	46.0	4.2	9.4	40.3	35.7	52.5
04005	Coconino County, Arizona	8.9	14.9	56.1	5.0	3.0	55,145	60.1	45.0	3.9	11.2	39.9	24.5	37.9
04013	Maricopa County, Arizona	20.2	32.0	38.7	13.9	7.4	1,708,034	65.8	48.0	5.9	11.9	34.2	25.6	38.9
04015	Mohave County, Arizona	10.6	17.7	17.2	7.9	2.7	102,398	64.0	47.0	4.6	12.4	36.0	29.2	61.1
04017	Navajo County, Arizona	9.4	12.1	68.2	2.5	1.1	40,087	71.2	47.2	9.3	14.7	28.8	25.7	51.9
04019	Pima County, Arizona	20.7	38.5	43.3	11.4	4.8	433,148	61.8	44.0	5.9	11.9	38.2	29.7	45.1
04021	Pinal County, Arizona.................	16.8	31.4	40.2	9.1	4.8	155,161	73.3	53.7	6.6	13.0	26.7	21.0	49.9
04025	Yavapai County, Arizona	12.4	15.3	30.5	7.8	4.0	112,075	62.8	50.3	4.9	7.6	37.2	29.3	61.6
04027	Yuma County, Arizona	46.4	65.5	39.3	23.0	12.1	74,981	74.7	52.6	5.1	16.9	25.3	19.2	45.3
05000	**ARKANSAS**	9.9	8.2	60.5	4.7	3.2	1,183,675	65.7	47.8	5.1	12.8	34.3	28.7	41.3
05007	Benton County, Arkansas............	27.6	17.6	42.1	11.1	7.7	106,553	75.5	59.7	4.9	10.9	24.5	20.2	32.5
05031	Craighead County, Arkansas.......	6.2	5.5	70.3	1.8	1.3	42,186	67.3	47.8	5.7	13.8	32.7	27.8	33.5
05045	Faulkner County, Arkansas..........	5.5	4.5	71.6	3.1	1.4	48,497	64.5	50.0	4.5	10.0	35.5	25.9	29.7
05051	Garland County, Arkansas..........	6.1	6.4	54.0	2.6	1.4	42,077	62.5	43.3	7.9	11.3	37.5	31.1	50.4
05069	Jefferson County, Arkansas	4.8	2.5	77.1	2.8	2.0	24,319	62.2	40.3	6.4	15.5	37.8	33.9	49.0
05085	Lonoke County, Arkansas............	6.0	5.0	67.0	2.9	1.8	27,880	73.1	55.1	6.8	11.3	26.9	21.9	37.6
05119	Pulaski County, Arkansas	5.2	6.5	67.8	5.0	3.0	172,100	61.9	41.7	3.8	16.4	38.1	31.2	37.9
05125	Saline County, Arkansas..............	4.3	5.7	64.2	2.1	0.7	49,768	73.4	61.9	4.4	7.0	26.6	23.6	39.2
05131	Sebastian County, Arkansas	8.8	15.4	54.4	8.9	3.3	51,472	64.1	45.7	5.5	13.0	35.9	27.2	40.9
05143	Washington County, Arkansas	22.8	17.5	51.2	10.8	7.8	94,220	62.8	45.7	5.9	11.2	37.2	28.2	32.1
05145	White County, Arkansas..............	10.2	4.8	65.3	1.9	1.4	29,359	67.4	54.1	2.3	11.0	32.6	24.7	41.1
06000	**CALIFORNIA**	19.0	40.2	56.1	26.6	12.4	13,429,063	68.1	48.5	6.4	13.1	31.9	24.0	41.4
06001	Alameda County, California	11.6	22.4	48.4	34.3	15.3	589,180	65.1	49.2	4.9	11.1	34.9	25.9	39.1
06007	Butte County, California	13.8	18.4	74.0	8.2	3.8	81,353	60.2	41.2	6.6	12.5	39.8	26.8	40.7
06013	Contra Costa County, California .	15.0	26.8	56.2	25.2	10.6	411,560	72.5	55.0	4.9	12.6	27.5	21.3	44.0
06017	El Dorado County, California.......	11.7	13.8	66.1	9.6	2.8	74,909	69.9	55.5	4.1	10.3	30.1	23.9	50.2
06019	Fresno County, California............	28.4	54.7	69.9	19.7	10.1	322,646	71.7	46.4	8.6	16.7	28.3	22.5	38.0
06023	Humboldt County, California	14.8	12.9	69.6	6.5	3.1	55,184	52.0	38.3	4.8	9.0	48.0	34.0	41.0

Table A-2. Counties — Who: Age, Race/Ethnicity, and Household Structure, 2021—*Continued*

				Population by age (percent)						Race alone or in combination (percent)					
	STATE County	Total population	Percent change, 2010– 2019	Under 18 years	18 to 24 years	25 to 44 years	45 to 64 years	65 years and over	Median age	White	Black or African American	American Indian and Alaska Native	Asian	Native Hawaiian or Other Pacific Islander	Some other race
STATE County code	ACS table number:	B01003	Population Estimates	B01001	B01001	B01001	B01001	B01001	B01002	B02008	B02009	B02010	B02011	B02012	B02013
	Column number:	1	2	3	4	5	6	7	8	9	10	11	12	13	14
	CALIFORNIA—Cont.														
06025	Imperial County, California	179,851	3.8	28.3	9.8	27.3	20.9	13.6	32.8	42.8	5.8	3.2	2.1	-	76.1
06029	Kern County, California	917,673	7.2	28.7	10.0	28.6	21.3	11.4	32.5	69.9	6.7	3.2	6.3	0.4	40.2
06031	Kings County, California	153,443	-0.0	27.0	10.2	32.2	19.9	10.7	32.2	59.3	8.3	2.9	5.4	0.7	48.2
06033	Lake County, California..............	68,766	-0.4	20.4	7.9	23.3	24.2	24.2	43.9	82.2	3.3	5.0	2.2	1.8	19.7
06037	Los Angeles County, California ...	9,829,544	2.2	21.1	8.9	29.9	25.5	14.6	37.8	48.4	9.3	3.5	17.0	0.6	42.9
06039	Madera County, California.........	159,410	4.3	27.6	9.3	26.2	22.0	14.9	35.1	58.9	4.0	4.1	3.5	0.6	52.5
06041	Marin County, California.............	260,206	2.5	19.2	6.7	21.0	29.4	23.7	46.9	80.3	4.1	1.3	9.0	0.6	16.5
06045	Mendocino County, California......	91,305	-1.2	21.1	7.0	24.4	23.8	23.8	42.4	78.9	1.7	7.8	2.9	1.0	23.9
06047	Merced County, California	286,461	8.6	29.1	11.2	27.4	20.6	11.7	31.8	41.9	4.6	3.2	8.5	0.4	55.3
06053	Monterey County, California......	437,325	4.6	25.9	9.7	27.3	22.7	14.5	35.4	45.2	3.4	2.3	8.0	1.0	55.5
06055	Napa County, California.............	136,207	0.9	19.7	8.7	24.9	26.4	20.4	42.7	72.7	3.2	3.6	10.7	0.5	27.6
06057	Nevada County, California..........	103,487	1.0	16.9	5.4	21.4	28.4	27.9	50.2	93.4	0.7	2.9	4.8	-	10.1
06059	Orange County, California...........	3,167,809	5.5	21.4	8.7	27.4	26.7	15.7	39.2	58.4	2.8	2.2	25.1	0.7	28.2
06061	Placer County, California............	412,300	14.3	22.1	7.2	24.4	26.2	20.1	42.3	83.2	3.2	2.2	12.1	1.3	13.6
06065	Riverside County, California	2,458,395	12.8	24.6	9.4	27.3	23.8	14.9	36.6	55.6	8.4	3.3	8.7	0.8	45.6
06067	Sacramento County, California ...	1,588,921	9.4	23.3	8.2	29.6	24.2	14.7	37.2	57.0	13.0	3.9	20.8	1.8	19.8
06069	San Benito County, California	66,677	13.6	26.0	8.2	28.3	24.3	13.2	35.4	73.5	0.0	4.1	7.0	2.5	54.5
06071	San Bernardino County, California.................	2,194,710	7.1	26.0	9.8	28.8	23.2	12.1	34.3	52.2	10.1	3.7	9.9	0.8	45.5
06073	San Diego County, California......	3,286,069	7.9	21.3	9.8	30.2	23.9	14.9	36.9	68.6	6.7	2.9	15.2	0.9	28.8
06075	San Francisco County, California .	815,201	9.5	14.0	6.5	36.4	25.6	17.5	40.4	49.9	6.7	1.7	39.8	0.9	14.2
06077	San Joaquin County, California ...	789,410	11.2	26.7	9.4	27.7	23.0	13.2	35.0	52.3	9.2	7.5	21.1	1.5	37.3
06079	San Luis Obispo County, California.................	283,159	5.0	17.5	14.8	23.2	22.9	21.5	40.2	87.5	2.9	2.2	6.0	0.5	20.0
06081	San Mateo County, California	737,888	6.7	19.9	7.0	28.9	26.8	17.5	40.8	51.4	3.6	2.5	35.1	1.9	20.5
06083	Santa Barbara County, California	446,475	5.3	22.1	15.0	25.0	21.8	16.0	34.6	72.7	2.9	3.4	7.6	0.5	39.8
06085	Santa Clara County, California ...	1,885,508	8.2	21.2	8.2	30.3	25.8	14.5	38.2	45.5	3.5	2.2	42.7	0.8	22.3
06087	Santa Cruz County, California	267,792	4.1	18.6	14.4	23.9	24.7	18.3	39.0	73.4	2.1	4.0	7.2	0.1	30.2
06089	Shasta County, California...........	182,139	1.6	21.8	7.6	24.5	25.2	21.0	41.8	90.1	2.6	5.1	5.0	0.6	10.5
06095	Solano County, California	451,716	8.3	21.9	8.3	27.8	25.0	16.9	38.9	52.6	17.3	2.8	20.0	2.2	23.5
06097	Sonoma County, California	485,887	2.2	19.1	7.9	25.7	26.2	21.1	42.1	76.6	2.8	4.5	7.0	1.0	23.5
06099	Stanislaus County, California......	552,999	7.0	26.9	9.2	27.5	22.7	13.5	34.7	69.3	4.4	3.9	7.6	1.2	43.6
06101	Sutter County, California	99,063	2.4	24.8	8.8	26.6	23.7	16.1	36.8	59.9	4.0	5.2	18.7	1.4	30.5
06103	Tehama County, California..........	65,498	2.6	24.8	8.2	21.6	24.3	21.1	40.7	87.6	1.5	5.5	2.2	-	21.0
06107	Tulare County, California............	477,054	5.4	30.2	10.2	27.1	20.9	11.7	31.7	65.3	2.5	4.4	4.6	0.3	53.1
06111	Ventura County, California..........	839,784	2.8	22.2	8.8	26.2	26.1	16.7	39.0	76.7	3.1	4.4	9.6	0.6	32.0
06113	Yolo County, California	216,986	9.8	20.4	19.8	25.5	21.0	13.3	32.7	67.6	4.9	3.2	18.3	0.6	25.7
06115	Yuba County, California..............	83,421	9.0	27.5	9.4	28.7	21.2	13.3	34.1	69.6	6.2	6.3	10.4	1.5	27.3
08000	**COLORADO**	5,812,069	11.5	21.4	9.0	30.1	24.3	15.1	37.6	84.8	5.7	3.3	4.8	0.4	17.1
08001	Adams County, Colorado..........	522,140	17.2	25.3	9.0	31.5	23.2	11.0	34.8	75.5	4.9	4.8	5.4	0.3	31.3
08005	Arapahoe County, Colorado	654,900	14.8	22.8	8.0	30.5	24.6	14.0	37.2	73.8	13.7	2.6	8.0	0.5	17.3
08013	Boulder County, Colorado...........	329,543	10.7	18.1	14.1	26.8	25.1	15.9	38.2	91.5	2.0	1.5	6.5	0.5	12.4
08014	Broomfield County, Colorado......	75,325	26.1	21.0	8.0	29.9	26.0	15.0	38.9	86.2	2.3	1.9	8.1	-	11.6
08031	Denver County, Colorado...........	711,463	21.2	18.6	8.1	40.0	21.1	12.1	35.1	75.8	11.1	3.2	5.4	0.3	23.3
08035	Douglas County, Colorado	368,990	23.0	24.0	7.7	27.0	28.2	13.2	39.3	89.4	2.6	1.9	7.4	0.2	9.2
08041	El Paso County, Colorado..........	737,867	15.8	23.4	10.6	29.8	22.8	13.5	34.9	85.0	9.0	3.7	5.3	1.1	13.4
08059	Jefferson County, Colorado.........	579,581	9.0	18.9	7.3	30.3	26.1	17.4	40.2	91.2	2.2	2.9	4.2	0.2	12.7
08069	Larimer County, Colorado..........	362,533	19.1	18.7	13.8	28.0	22.7	16.8	36.4	92.7	2.6	3.0	3.1	0.3	9.9
08077	Mesa County, Colorado.............	157,335	5.1	20.9	9.0	25.3	24.1	20.6	41.1	95.4	1.5	3.4	1.7	-	12.6
08101	Pueblo County, Colorado...........	169,622	5.9	22.1	8.7	25.4	24.5	19.2	40.0	88.9	2.8	5.4	1.8	-	19.6
08123	Weld County, Colorado	340,036	28.3	25.7	9.1	29.5	23.1	12.5	35.2	85.8	2.7	4.0	2.8	0.3	20.5
09000	**CONNECTICUT**	3,605,597	0.4	20.2	9.5	25.0	27.3	18.0	41.1	75.7	13.8	1.5	5.8	0.2	15.6
09001	Fairfield County, Connecticut....	959,768	2.9	21.9	9.0	24.5	28.1	16.5	41.2	71.2	14.2	1.3	6.8	0.2	20.5
09003	Hartford County, Connecticut....	896,854	-0.3	20.8	8.8	26.4	26.3	17.7	40.0	70.9	18.3	1.2	7.1	0.1	14.9
09005	Litchfield County, Connecticut....	185,000	-5.1	17.6	6.9	22.8	30.0	22.7	47.6	93.6	3.2	1.1	2.7	-	8.1
09007	Middlesex County, Connecticut...	164,759	-2.0	16.6	8.8	22.8	30.1	21.8	46.7	90.1	7.0	1.6	4.0	-	8.3
09009	New Haven County, Connecticut	863,700	-0.9	19.9	9.6	25.8	26.5	18.1	40.5	72.0	16.5	1.2	5.2	0.3	17.4

								Household type (percent of all households)						
								Family households				Nonfamily households		Percent of households with people age 60 years and over
STATE County code	STATE County	Two or more races (percent)	Hispanic or Latino (percent)	Native, born in state of residence (percent)	Foreign born (percent)	Non-citizens (percent)	Total households	Total	Married couple	Male householder	Female householder	Total	One-person households	
	ACS table number:	B02001	B03003	B05002	B05002	B05002	B11001	B11001	B11001	B11001	B11001	B11001	B11001	B11006
	Column number:	15	16	17	18	19	20	21	22	23	24	25	26	27
	CALIFORNIA—Cont.													
06025	Imperial County, California	27.1	85.8	62.4	29.2	14.5	47,849	77.0	48.5	7.9	20.7	23.0	20.2	47.5
06029	Kern County, California	25.4	56.1	68.5	19.7	11.2	282,963	73.3	48.7	8.0	16.5	26.7	21.5	37.7
06031	Kings County, California	23.7	56.6	65.6	18.1	12.2	43,143	80.0	50.5	6.6	22.9	20.0	15.3	34.7
06033	Lake County, California	13.1	23.9	64.6	11.8	5.6	27,472	64.1	44.6	6.2	13.2	35.9	29.9	53.5
06037	Los Angeles County, California	20.2	49.1	52.5	33.3	14.9	3,375,587	65.7	43.4	7.5	14.8	34.3	25.9	40.4
06039	Madera County, California	22.9	60.2	69.5	17.8	10.4	44,048	74.7	48.1	8.7	17.9	25.3	19.8	48.5
06041	Marin County, California	11.3	16.8	50.0	19.5	9.8	103,378	61.8	49.4	4.1	8.4	38.2	29.7	52.0
06045	Mendocino County, California	15.2	27.2	65.8	11.8	7.0	34,273	59.0	38.0	7.9	13.1	41.0	33.7	54.9
06047	Merced County, California	12.9	62.5	66.4	25.5	15.4	84,967	75.8	47.7	7.5	20.6	24.2	19.7	37.6
06053	Monterey County, California	14.5	60.4	55.2	29.0	21.3	133,224	71.9	49.7	7.4	14.8	28.1	20.9	43.8
06055	Napa County, California	17.1	35.6	57.1	23.0	10.0	49,979	67.9	52.3	7.3	8.3	32.1	24.9	47.6
06057	Nevada County, California	10.8	10.1	65.7	5.7	2.1	42,679	60.6	51.3	2.3	7.0	39.4	27.7	58.2
06059	Orange County, California	16.4	34.1	52.8	30.4	12.8	1,077,193	70.8	53.5	5.6	11.7	29.2	21.4	42.4
06061	Placer County, California	13.6	15.2	65.7	11.8	4.6	155,945	71.6	58.8	4.3	8.5	28.4	22.6	45.5
06065	Riverside County, California	20.8	51.6	61.9	22.0	9.8	765,673	75.0	54.1	6.6	14.3	25.0	19.6	44.4
06067	Sacramento County, California	14.5	24.4	61.8	21.4	7.9	571,949	65.0	46.2	6.4	12.4	35.0	25.9	39.8
06069	San Benito County, California	38.8	62.0	68.3	21.2	11.7	20,307	76.9	59.3	7.5	10.0	23.1	18.8	41.5
06071	San Bernardino County, California	20.7	55.8	65.7	21.3	10.0	675,929	75.5	50.5	8.5	16.5	24.5	18.6	39.1
06073	San Diego County, California	21.8	34.8	51.3	22.4	9.1	1,162,896	65.6	48.8	5.3	11.5	34.4	24.9	39.0
06075	San Francisco County, California	11.7	15.7	41.6	34.3	13.4	350,796	48.5	37.4	3.3	7.9	51.5	37.0	36.4
06077	San Joaquin County, California	22.7	43.0	64.7	23.8	10.6	241,760	75.2	51.4	9.0	14.8	24.8	19.9	41.2
06079	San Luis Obispo County, California	17.8	23.8	67.2	9.9	5.4	107,571	63.9	50.1	5.2	8.6	36.1	26.2	50.4
06081	San Mateo County, California	13.4	24.0	49.7	34.6	14.2	264,135	68.6	54.1	5.0	9.5	31.4	24.6	42.5
06083	Santa Barbara County, California	26.3	47.2	57.7	22.1	13.1	150,550	64.9	46.6	6.3	12.1	35.1	24.2	43.5
06085	Santa Clara County, California	15.8	25.0	45.5	40.3	18.6	650,593	70.2	54.3	5.4	10.6	29.8	22.0	37.8
06087	Santa Cruz County, California	16.2	34.4	61.2	18.2	10.7	97,353	64.9	49.8	4.7	10.4	35.1	23.9	48.9
06089	Shasta County, California	12.4	11.4	72.3	4.3	1.7	71,506	60.2	43.3	4.8	12.1	39.8	27.7	47.6
06095	Solano County, California	16.0	28.6	57.7	20.3	8.6	157,617	69.7	49.1	6.9	13.7	30.3	24.1	45.7
06097	Sonoma County, California	13.9	28.3	63.5	17.1	8.7	190,586	64.2	49.7	4.9	9.6	35.8	26.2	48.1
06099	Stanislaus County, California	28.6	49.5	67.7	21.8	11.6	174,209	75.3	51.2	8.3	15.8	24.7	19.7	38.6
06101	Sutter County, California	18.8	32.9	60.6	22.6	11.5	33,655	71.8	48.3	8.8	14.7	28.2	22.4	47.8
06103	Tehama County, California	18.0	27.3	76.3	6.9	3.7	23,950	66.4	45.4	6.0	15.0	33.6	26.2	52.6
06107	Tulare County, California	28.8	66.7	67.8	23.4	14.7	143,541	78.4	49.9	9.3	19.2	21.6	16.6	37.1
06111	Ventura County, California	25.1	44.1	60.1	21.8	10.2	279,168	70.7	53.6	5.3	11.7	29.3	22.4	47.6
06113	Yolo County, California	18.4	32.6	60.4	21.6	10.4	76,844	61.3	44.9	5.0	11.4	38.7	22.2	34.7
06115	Yuba County, California	20.0	30.5	67.8	14.6	5.6	27,942	75.5	47.0	11.6	17.0	24.5	19.5	42.6
08000	**COLORADO**	14.9	22.3	42.2	9.8	4.8	2,313,042	62.6	48.6	4.6	9.4	37.4	27.9	36.6
08001	Adams County, Colorado	20.8	41.8	51.5	16.0	10.4	183,023	69.7	50.0	6.8	12.9	30.3	22.5	32.7
08005	Arapahoe County, Colorado	14.7	20.6	39.7	15.8	7.8	250,041	62.8	46.6	4.9	11.2	37.2	28.9	35.9
08013	Boulder County, Colorado	13.5	14.1	33.3	10.2	5.0	135,607	56.2	44.5	4.9	6.8	43.8	29.8	36.5
08014	Broomfield County, Colorado	9.7	13.5	38.6	9.9	4.4	30,161	65.6	50.7	4.1	10.9	34.4	25.4	36.8
08031	Denver County, Colorado	17.7	29.0	38.4	14.2	7.7	326,634	46.8	33.8	3.5	9.5	53.2	38.9	27.0
08035	Douglas County, Colorado	9.4	9.7	37.4	8.6	3.4	136,238	75.6	64.2	4.6	6.9	24.4	18.8	34.9
08041	El Paso County, Colorado	15.2	18.4	30.7	7.0	2.5	282,904	67.7	52.0	5.4	10.3	32.3	23.5	34.3
08059	Jefferson County, Colorado	12.5	15.9	45.2	6.5	2.4	239,823	62.9	50.8	4.1	7.9	37.1	27.5	39.9
08069	Larimer County, Colorado	10.3	12.4	38.1	6.0	2.4	152,123	59.3	49.9	2.4	7.1	40.7	26.3	36.6
08077	Mesa County, Colorado	13.4	15.3	52.0	3.3	2.0	63,796	64.3	48.4	5.2	10.8	35.7	29.5	47.1
08101	Pueblo County, Colorado	18.0	43.7	61.3	4.2	2.2	69,078	62.8	43.1	6.3	13.4	37.2	31.6	45.2
08123	Weld County, Colorado	14.9	30.6	49.9	8.9	5.1	119,502	72.8	58.0	5.1	9.7	27.2	20.0	34.8
09000	**CONNECTICUT**	11.6	17.7	53.8	15.2	6.8	1,428,313	64.2	46.5	4.5	13.1	35.8	28.8	44.1
09001	Fairfield County, Connecticut	13.0	21.3	42.2	22.6	10.5	357,271	67.2	51.2	3.6	12.4	32.8	26.6	43.8
09003	Hartford County, Connecticut	11.8	19.4	55.8	15.0	6.1	360,140	63.2	44.0	4.7	14.5	36.8	30.1	43.0
09005	Litchfield County, Connecticut	7.8	8.1	64.0	8.5	4.1	77,106	67.5	52.7	4.8	10.0	32.5	26.8	53.2
09007	Middlesex County, Connecticut	9.1	7.1	62.1	9.8	3.2	69,789	61.2	51.0	2.8	7.5	38.8	30.8	46.6
09009	New Haven County, Connecticut	11.9	20.2	58.5	14.8	6.6	349,089	62.4	42.2	5.4	14.8	37.6	30.5	43.7

Table A-2. Counties — Who: Age, Race/Ethnicity, and Household Structure, 2021—*Continued*

STATE County	Total population	Percent change, 2010–2019	Population by age (percent) Under 18 years	18 to 24 years	25 to 44 years	45 to 64 years	65 years and over	Median age	Race alone or in combination (percent) White	Black or African American	American Indian and Alaska Native	Asian	Native Hawaiian or Other Pacific Islander	Some other race
ACS table number:	B01003	Population Estimates	B01001	B01001	B01001	B01001	B01001	B01002	B02008	B02009	B02010	B02011	B02012	B02013
Column number:	1	2	3	4	5	6	7	8	9	10	11	12	13	14
CONNECTICUT—Cont.														
New London County, Connecticut	268,805	-3.2	19.1	9.8	24.9	26.9	19.2	41.6	84.2	9.9	3.4	5.3	0.2	10.6
Tolland County, Connecticut	150,293	-1.3	16.2	20.3	20.5	25.8	17.2	37.9	87.6	5.0	1.5	6.0	0.8	7.4
Windham County, Connecticut	116,418	-1.4	19.3	9.8	25.2	28.1	17.6	40.8	93.5	3.1	3.5	1.9	-	12.5
DELAWARE	1,003,384	7.1	20.8	8.3	25.0	25.8	20.1	41.6	68.9	24.3	2.4	5.1	0.3	9.5
Kent County, Delaware	184,149	11.4	23.0	9.6	25.7	23.9	17.8	38.8	66.0	30.9	2.1	3.3	-	7.4
New Castle County, Delaware	571,708	3.8	21.3	9.0	27.2	25.9	16.6	39.1	63.9	27.0	3.0	7.1	-	10.2
Sussex County, Delaware	247,527	18.8	18.0	5.9	19.3	26.8	29.8	51.8	82.4	12.9	1.1	1.6	0.5	9.5
DISTRICT OF COLUMBIA	670,050	15.3	18.8	9.8	38.3	20.4	12.8	34.8	45.8	47.1	1.5	5.8	0.1	10.3
District of Columbia	670,050	15.3	18.8	9.8	38.3	20.4	12.8	34.8	45.8	47.1	1.5	5.8	0.1	10.3
FLORIDA	21,781,128	11.6	19.7	7.9	25.1	26.1	21.1	42.8	74.1	17.7	1.4	3.8	0.2	22.9
Alachua County, Florida	279,238	8.8	18.2	20.0	26.3	20.5	15.0	32.8	71.0	21.4	1.1	7.5	0.3	9.6
Bay County, Florida	179,168	3.5	20.7	7.0	26.2	28.2	17.9	41.1	84.2	12.2	2.3	3.6	0.5	5.7
Brevard County, Florida	616,628	10.8	18.2	6.8	22.8	28.0	24.2	47.0	82.3	12.4	1.1	3.9	0.4	10.8
Broward County, Florida	1,930,983	11.7	21.0	7.5	26.6	27.5	17.5	41.3	60.6	32.0	1.4	4.7	0.2	25.5
Charlotte County, Florida	194,843	18.1	11.9	4.9	15.5	27.1	40.7	60.4	89.9	6.6	0.8	1.8	-	7.3
Citrus County, Florida	158,083	6.0	14.5	5.0	17.8	26.0	36.7	57.8	93.9	3.6	2.3	2.2	-	4.5
Clay County, Florida	222,361	14.9	23.0	8.4	24.2	27.3	17.1	40.9	81.1	11.7	3.7	4.3	0.2	12.0
Collier County, Florida	385,980	19.7	16.5	6.3	19.0	25.2	33.0	52.7	84.3	7.7	1.3	2.0	0.4	25.9
Columbia County, Florida	70,385	6.2	21.6	9.1	25.3	25.3	18.7	39.8	80.6	14.2	7.1	0.9	0.5	8.6
Duval County, Florida	999,935	10.8	22.6	8.5	29.5	24.5	14.9	36.8	61.0	31.8	1.6	6.3	0.2	10.5
Escambia County, Florida	322,390	7.0	21.1	11.0	26.0	24.3	17.6	38.5	72.8	24.8	2.5	4.8	0.4	5.5
Flagler County, Florida	120,932	20.3	16.5	6.1	17.4	28.8	31.1	53.4	83.2	11.3	0.8	3.3	-	10.1
Hernando County, Florida	200,638	12.2	18.6	6.1	22.5	26.1	26.8	47.8	85.5	7.4	1.2	2.0	-	16.3
Highlands County, Florida	103,296	7.5	16.6	5.6	17.9	23.7	36.1	54.4	80.6	12.4	3.1	1.8	-	15.1
Hillsborough County, Florida	1,478,194	19.7	22.0	8.6	29.1	25.3	14.8	37.9	69.3	19.4	1.4	5.6	0.2	25.2
Indian River County, Florida	163,662	15.9	15.4	6.8	16.8	26.5	34.5	55.1	84.7	10.2	1.3	2.0	-	13.0
Lake County, Florida	395,804	23.6	19.4	6.6	22.2	25.4	26.5	46.7	84.0	12.8	1.2	2.8	-	16.1
Lee County, Florida	787,976	24.5	17.3	6.8	21.2	25.7	29.0	49.5	85.3	9.6	1.2	2.3	0.3	20.1
Leon County, Florida	292,817	6.6	18.8	20.9	25.2	20.5	14.6	32.0	63.7	32.7	1.7	4.6	0.2	6.6
Manatee County, Florida	412,703	24.9	17.6	6.5	20.7	26.9	28.2	49.9	82.9	10.1	1.4	2.8	-	14.9
Marion County, Florida	385,915	10.3	18.6	6.5	20.9	25.4	28.7	48.5	82.6	14.8	1.9	2.8	-	11.9
Martin County, Florida	159,942	10.0	16.5	6.6	17.8	27.4	31.7	53.3	89.6	6.2	1.0	2.2	-	13.7
Miami-Dade County, Florida	2,662,777	8.8	20.2	8.1	27.2	27.7	16.9	40.9	73.1	17.4	0.8	2.1	0.1	57.2
Monroe County, Florida	82,170	1.6	15.1	6.0	24.2	31.5	23.2	48.2	87.0	9.2	1.0	2.6	-	19.6
Nassau County, Florida	94,189	20.9	19.1	7.2	22.5	26.7	24.5	46.9	91.7	5.7	1.2	2.5	-	5.3
Okaloosa County, Florida	213,255	16.5	22.4	8.8	28.1	24.4	16.3	37.6	82.3	11.9	2.4	5.7	1.0	10.0
Orange County, Florida	1,422,746	21.6	21.6	9.9	30.9	24.8	12.8	36.6	63.6	23.4	1.7	6.7	0.3	29.3
Osceola County, Florida	403,282	39.8	24.2	9.2	29.0	24.2	13.5	36.7	54.0	14.9	1.2	3.6	-	49.2
Palm Beach County, Florida	1,497,987	13.4	19.0	7.2	23.4	25.9	24.5	45.4	69.6	20.7	1.2	3.6	0.1	22.3
Pasco County, Florida	584,067	19.2	20.4	7.0	24.0	26.5	22.1	43.8	84.2	8.5	1.6	4.1	0.2	14.5
Pinellas County, Florida	956,615	6.4	15.7	6.3	23.5	28.7	25.8	49.1	83.3	11.8	1.1	4.4	0.2	9.3
Polk County, Florida	753,520	20.4	22.1	8.3	25.9	23.9	19.8	39.9	66.6	17.2	1.4	2.3	0.1	25.2
Putnam County, Florida	74,167	0.2	21.3	6.5	20.7	27.7	23.8	45.9	82.4	17.7	1.2	1.0	-	11.3
St. Johns County, Florida	292,466	39.3	21.8	7.0	22.3	28.4	20.6	44.4	90.0	6.0	0.7	4.5	-	7.7
St. Lucie County, Florida	343,579	18.2	19.7	7.1	22.8	25.8	24.5	45.4	71.6	23.2	1.3	2.4	-	14.9
Santa Rosa County, Florida	193,998	21.8	21.9	7.1	27.0	27.6	16.4	40.8	89.5	7.4	2.3	3.7	0.7	6.4
Sarasota County, Florida	447,057	14.3	14.0	5.6	17.4	25.9	37.1	57.0	91.4	5.1	0.7	2.5	0.2	10.4
Seminole County, Florida	470,093	11.6	20.8	7.9	28.6	26.3	16.4	39.8	75.3	14.7	1.5	6.1	0.3	20.3
Sumter County, Florida	135,638	41.7	7.0	2.4	11.9	20.4	58.3	68.4	90.4	5.8	2.3	1.5	-	5.9
Volusia County, Florida	564,412	11.9	17.6	8.1	22.3	27.0	25.1	46.7	77.4	12.5	1.1	2.4	0.0	14.2
Walton County, Florida	80,069	34.6	20.5	4.8	24.6	30.1	20.0	45.0	91.8	5.4	2.0	1.9	-	6.3
GEORGIA	10,799,566	7.6	23.4	9.7	27.0	25.3	14.7	37.5	59.5	33.4	2.4	5.3	0.2	8.7
Barrow County, Georgia	86,658	20.0	25.4	8.2	27.5	25.9	13.0	36.9	75.1	15.0	2.9	4.5	-	10.1
Bartow County, Georgia	110,843	7.6	23.2	8.6	26.8	27.0	14.4	39.7	84.3	13.2	1.9	1.8	-	6.4
Bibb County, Georgia	156,762	-1.5	24.2	10.7	25.8	23.3	16.0	35.7	39.3	57.2	0.8	2.6	-	3.8

							Household type (percent of all households)						Percent of households with people age 60 years and over
							Family households				Nonfamily households		
STATE County code	STATE County	Two or more races (percent)	Hispanic or Latino (percent)	Native, born in state of residence (percent)	Foreign born (percent)	Non-citizens (percent)	Total house-holds	Total	Married couple	Male house-holder	Female house-holder	Total	One-person house-holds	
	ACS table number:	B02001	B03003	B05002	B05002	B05002	B11001	B11001	B11001	B11001	B11001	B11001	B11001	B11006
	Column number:	15	16	17	18	19	20	21	22	23	24	25	26	27
	CONNECTICUT—Cont.													
09011	New London County, Connecticut	11.4	12.0	53.5	7.8	2.6	110,950	63.0	45.2	5.4	12.4	37.0	30.0	43.3
09013	Tolland County, Connecticut	7.4	6.6	58.0	7.8	3.5	58,244	62.2	50.1	2.6	9.5	37.8	24.5	42.7
09015	Windham County, Connecticut	12.4	12.7	52.3	4.6	2.9	45,724	65.5	45.2	6.0	14.4	34.5	26.1	43.5
10000	**DELAWARE**	9.4	10.1	44.0	10.1	5.1	395,656	64.8	47.1	4.8	12.9	35.2	29.0	47.5
10001	Kent County, Delaware	9.6	7.8	48.8	7.5	2.6	70,167	67.3	50.7	3.2	13.4	32.7	26.7	45.6
10003	New Castle County, Delaware	10.0	11.0	43.8	12.0	5.5	220,758	61.9	43.4	4.9	13.6	38.1	31.4	42.1
10005	Sussex County, Delaware	7.9	9.6	35.5	7.7	3.4	104,731	69.3	52.7	5.5	11.0	30.7	25.4	60.0
11000	**DISTRICT OF COLUMBIA**	9.6	11.5	37.2	13.3	6.2	319,565	40.3	24.2	3.1	13.0	59.7	48.2	30.2
11001	District of Columbia	9.6	11.5	37.2	13.3	6.2	319,565	40.3	24.2	3.1	13.0	59.7	48.2	30.2
12000	**FLORIDA**	19.1	26.8	35.8	21.2	9.0	8,565,329	64.3	46.4	5.0	12.9	35.7	28.4	47.8
12001	Alachua County, Florida	9.9	11.0	52.3	10.4	4.6	108,189	52.8	39.0	4.1	9.7	47.2	34.0	37.7
12005	Bay County, Florida	8.0	7.4	40.6	8.9	4.5	79,532	66.2	47.4	5.7	13.1	33.8	24.5	41.5
12009	Brevard County, Florida	10.2	11.6	31.8	9.7	3.3	254,314	63.2	47.6	4.6	11.0	36.8	30.8	51.6
12011	Broward County, Florida	22.6	32.0	36.0	35.6	13.3	747,715	63.2	42.9	5.8	14.5	36.8	29.0	43.6
12015	Charlotte County, Florida	6.5	8.2	19.3	9.9	4.3	88,988	65.9	54.6	4.3	7.0	34.1	27.3	69.7
12017	Citrus County, Florida	5.8	6.7	32.2	4.4	0.7	68,269	60.4	47.2	4.2	8.9	39.6	33.8	69.7
12019	Clay County, Florida	12.4	11.1	45.5	6.1	1.9	80,459	73.0	54.6	3.9	14.5	27.0	20.2	44.6
12021	Collier County, Florida	20.6	29.0	21.9	25.0	11.5	163,943	68.2	55.5	3.9	8.8	31.8	26.2	60.4
12023	Columbia County, Florida	11.4	6.9	60.2	4.3	2.3	27,545	66.5	49.1	4.7	12.8	33.5	25.3	45.6
12031	Duval County, Florida	10.4	11.3	46.8	12.0	4.9	406,301	60.3	40.1	4.8	15.3	39.7	31.5	37.0
12033	Escambia County, Florida	9.7	6.4	46.4	5.2	2.5	126,980	62.8	42.0	6.2	14.6	37.2	30.2	42.9
12035	Flagler County, Florida	8.6	11.4	27.9	11.4	3.3	48,187	72.9	58.4	4.5	10.0	27.1	20.9	63.8
12053	Hernando County, Florida	11.9	16.2	32.2	7.2	2.2	81,497	68.8	49.6	5.8	13.4	31.2	23.1	57.9
12055	Highlands County, Florida	12.6	22.1	36.8	12.8	6.7	46,166	66.1	50.6	3.9	11.6	33.9	28.9	62.2
12057	Hillsborough County, Florida	19.7	30.3	38.8	19.2	8.6	578,259	62.6	44.3	5.3	13.0	37.4	29.6	36.5
12061	Indian River County, Florida	10.9	13.3	33.7	8.1	2.7	69,974	61.6	46.8	3.9	10.8	38.4	34.3	63.7
12069	Lake County, Florida	16.5	17.9	35.0	8.5	2.5	156,435	66.1	51.5	3.7	11.0	33.9	29.0	55.7
12071	Lee County, Florida	17.9	23.8	26.7	18.0	7.1	320,466	65.5	52.3	3.9	9.3	34.5	28.3	56.6
12073	Leon County, Florida	8.7	7.0	59.5	7.4	2.7	121,423	52.6	35.0	5.2	12.5	47.4	31.2	34.3
12081	Manatee County, Florida	11.8	17.1	31.4	13.3	5.5	163,520	63.8	51.4	2.9	9.5	36.2	29.6	58.7
12083	Marion County, Florida	12.2	15.5	39.4	9.5	3.3	157,348	67.2	48.7	5.5	13.0	32.8	27.8	57.4
12085	Martin County, Florida	12.2	14.6	30.1	9.7	4.9	69,719	61.9	48.4	3.6	9.9	38.1	32.0	61.9
12086	Miami-Dade County, Florida	49.9	69.1	32.8	53.6	20.1	963,477	67.7	42.9	7.1	17.6	32.3	25.8	43.8
12087	Monroe County, Florida	18.7	25.7	33.0	19.0	6.9	36,078	58.2	44.6	5.8	7.8	41.8	29.9	48.3
12089	Nassau County, Florida	7.3	5.2	45.9	4.4	0.8	40,276	71.5	57.0	5.2	9.3	28.5	23.2	51.4
12091	Okaloosa County, Florida	11.1	10.2	30.5	7.8	3.8	84,497	66.8	51.7	3.6	11.5	33.2	28.1	41.5
12095	Orange County, Florida	23.7	33.1	34.8	23.0	11.4	512,496	67.0	45.6	5.8	15.7	33.0	24.0	34.4
12097	Osceola County, Florida	21.8	56.3	26.3	26.9	14.3	133,330	75.9	54.2	4.6	17.1	24.1	19.8	38.4
12099	Palm Beach County, Florida	16.9	23.9	30.1	27.3	11.0	595,447	62.5	45.5	5.2	11.9	37.5	30.5	52.5
12101	Pasco County, Florida	12.0	18.1	36.1	11.5	4.6	230,060	63.4	48.5	4.0	10.9	36.6	30.3	49.6
12103	Pinellas County, Florida	9.7	10.6	33.1	11.8	3.5	419,798	55.0	41.6	3.7	9.7	45.0	36.5	52.6
12105	Polk County, Florida	12.2	27.4	44.0	10.4	5.6	276,469	67.7	47.7	5.2	14.9	32.3	24.5	47.2
12107	Putnam County, Florida	12.6	10.7	61.7	4.5	3.2	29,765	58.9	33.2	8.2	17.4	41.1	34.9	57.5
12109	St. Johns County, Florida	8.9	8.3	32.1	8.6	3.2	109,147	74.7	63.2	3.3	8.1	25.3	20.0	46.0
12111	St. Lucie County, Florida	12.4	21.1	34.0	19.0	5.8	131,235	66.8	48.7	5.9	12.3	33.2	27.8	56.2
12113	Santa Rosa County, Florida	8.9	6.4	36.0	5.4	1.2	71,722	73.4	57.2	4.5	11.7	26.6	22.9	44.0
12115	Sarasota County, Florida	9.8	10.1	23.6	11.3	3.1	204,018	60.2	50.5	2.7	7.0	39.8	31.8	65.0
12117	Seminole County, Florida	16.9	23.3	37.3	15.0	5.4	188,239	67.1	48.1	4.7	14.3	32.9	24.9	39.4
12119	Sumter County, Florida	5.8	6.2	20.8	5.3	1.5	68,792	61.7	57.2	0.7	3.8	38.3	31.6	81.4
12127	Volusia County, Florida	7.1	16.1	34.4	8.3	3.5	243,344	60.8	44.0	5.3	11.6	39.2	30.8	54.1
12131	Walton County, Florida	7.0	6.8	30.2	5.9	0.8	33,941	65.6	57.4	2.0	6.3	34.4	28.3	49.1
13000	**GEORGIA**	8.8	10.0	54.4	10.0	5.5	4,001,109	66.9	47.0	4.8	15.0	33.1	26.8	38.2
13013	Barrow County, Georgia	7.7	14.1	56.0	9.0	5.0	30,194	75.1	52.2	7.1	15.8	24.9	21.0	34.4
13015	Bartow County, Georgia	7.5	9.8	64.5	5.0	3.7	38,903	72.0	57.9	4.2	9.9	28.0	22.8	40.6
13021	Bibb County, Georgia	3.6	3.9	75.1	2.8	1.3	57,677	59.1	33.7	4.1	21.3	40.9	34.8	41.1

Table A-2. Counties — Who: Age, Race/Ethnicity, and Household Structure, 2021—*Continued*

STATE County code	STATE County	Total population	Percent change, 2010–2019	Population by age (percent)					Median age	Race alone or in combination (percent)					
				Under 18 years	18 to 24 years	25 to 44 years	45 to 64 years	65 years and over		White	Black or African American	American Indian and Alaska Native	Asian	Native Hawaiian or Other Pacific Islander	Some other race
STATE County code	ACS table number:	B01003	Population Estimates	B01001	B01001	B01001	B01001	B01001	B01002	B02008	B02009	B02010	B02011	B02012	B02013
	Column number:	1	2	3	4	5	6	7	8	9	10	11	12	13	14
	GEORGIA—Cont.														
13031	Bulloch County, Georgia	82,442	13.4	18.5	26.6	22.5	20.6	11.9	28.6	69.0	29.5	3.0	2.2	-	4.7
13045	Carroll County, Georgia	121,968	8.6	23.7	11.6	27.0	23.7	13.9	34.6	76.4	17.6	3.9	1.1	-	8.9
13047	Catoosa County, Georgia	68,397	5.7	22.9	7.0	25.4	26.2	18.5	40.1	95.3	2.4	2.1	1.8	-	5.1
13051	Chatham County, Georgia	296,329	9.2	20.6	10.9	29.0	22.8	16.8	36.9	54.6	42.9	1.2	3.8	-	6.3
13057	Cherokee County, Georgia.........	274,615	20.7	23.1	8.8	24.7	27.9	15.5	40.8	86.0	7.6	4.1	3.4	0.6	8.8
13059	Clarke County, Georgia..............	128,711	10.0	16.5	26.3	27.4	17.9	11.9	29.3	64.7	26.7	3.0	4.6	-	10.5
13063	Clayton County, Georgia............	297,100	12.7	27.2	9.6	29.1	24.0	10.2	33.7	16.7	73.6	2.4	6.0	-	10.9
13067	Cobb County, Georgia	766,802	10.5	22.7	8.9	28.8	26.3	13.3	37.7	59.6	29.0	2.9	6.6	0.2	13.5
13073	Columbia County, Georgia.........	159,639	26.3	25.2	9.8	25.0	25.3	14.7	37.6	73.0	19.5	1.7	5.7	-	9.1
13077	Coweta County, Georgia	149,956	16.6	23.3	7.7	26.0	28.5	14.5	38.9	80.6	17.4	3.1	2.8	-	6.1
13089	DeKalb County, Georgia	757,718	9.7	22.6	8.3	30.9	24.7	13.6	36.6	36.0	55.3	2.8	7.7	0.3	8.1
13095	Dougherty County, Georgia	84,844	-7.0	23.5	12.0	24.7	22.9	16.9	37.4	26.9	71.8	1.4	1.3	-	2.9
13097	Douglas County, Georgia...........	145,814	10.5	25.1	9.6	26.2	26.8	12.3	37.3	43.1	53.9	1.1	2.1	-	6.9
13103	Effingham County, Georgia.........	66,741	23.1	25.9	7.5	27.5	27.6	11.5	36.3	81.0	17.1	0.7	2.5	-	5.4
13113	Fayette County, Georgia	120,574	7.4	22.7	9.5	20.3	28.5	18.9	42.5	67.9	27.7	1.3	7.7	-	6.5
13115	Floyd County, Georgia	98,771	2.3	22.6	11.3	23.9	25.5	16.7	38.5	79.1	14.9	4.2	1.8	-	11.0
13117	Forsyth County, Georgia	260,206	39.2	26.2	7.8	25.4	28.2	12.3	39.4	75.1	6.0	2.8	18.3	0.5	8.7
13121	Fulton County, Georgia..............	1,065,334	15.6	21.0	10.0	31.5	25.1	12.4	36.0	46.9	44.3	2.1	8.8	0.1	6.4
13127	Glynn County, Georgia	84,739	7.1	21.1	8.2	23.8	24.6	22.3	40.9	69.8	25.0	1.7	2.0	-	8.0
13135	Gwinnett County, Georgia..........	964,546	16.3	26.3	9.2	27.1	26.4	11.0	36.0	46.6	31.8	1.9	14.2	0.2	19.5
13139	Hall County, Georgia.................	207,369	13.8	24.3	9.0	25.1	26.1	15.4	38.2	83.4	8.9	1.8	2.6	0.2	24.8
13151	Henry County, Georgia	245,235	15.0	25.1	9.1	26.4	27.0	12.4	37.0	43.2	53.4	3.3	4.3	-	6.3
13153	Houston County, Georgia...........	166,829	12.8	25.3	9.0	28.5	24.2	13.0	36.9	59.6	35.4	2.0	5.2	-	3.9
13157	Jackson County, Georgia............	80,286	20.7	25.4	8.5	25.6	26.2	14.3	38.6	86.4	8.9	0.6	2.9	-	8.3
13179	Liberty County, Georgia	65,711	-3.2	28.5	15.2	29.7	16.2	10.5	27.9	50.2	48.7	1.3	3.5	-	9.6
13185	Lowndes County, Georgia..........	119,276	7.5	24.6	16.3	26.8	19.3	13.0	31.1	58.3	39.1	1.3	3.2	-	4.4
13215	Muscogee County, Georgia.........	205,617	3.1	24.8	9.6	29.2	22.2	14.1	34.7	45.0	49.9	1.5	3.7	0.7	7.8
13217	Newton County, Georgia	115,355	11.8	25.5	8.8	26.2	26.2	13.2	37.4	50.2	53.6	2.5	1.7	-	5.0
13223	Paulding County, Georgia	173,780	18.5	25.6	8.4	28.3	25.6	12.1	36.8	74.1	25.2	1.4	2.4	-	6.4
13245	Richmond County, Georgia.........	205,673	1.0	22.8	11.0	28.4	22.7	15.0	35.3	40.1	60.2	1.5	3.1	-	4.9
13247	Rockdale County, Georgia..........	94,082	6.7	24.0	8.3	23.7	28.6	15.3	38.8	33.2	61.2	3.0	2.3	-	7.8
13255	Spalding County, Georgia	67,909	4.1	23.4	7.7	25.1	24.8	19.0	39.0	62.3	37.9	-	-	-	4.4
13285	Troup County, Georgia...............	69,720	4.3	23.1	5.6	31.8	23.0	16.5	38.5	60.2	37.4	1.4	2.6	-	3.9
13295	Walker County, Georgia	68,510	1.5	21.4	7.0	25.4	26.3	19.9	41.9	NA	NA	NA	NA	NA	NA
13297	Walton County, Georgia.............	99,853	12.9	24.0	9.2	23.6	25.8	17.4	39.2	77.9	18.4	4.1	2.0	1.8	5.3
13313	Whitfield County, Georgia	102,848	2.0	25.1	10.0	26.4	23.8	14.7	36.1	81.2	4.5	3.2	1.8	-	18.9
15000	**HAWAII**	1,441,553	4.9	21.1	8.0	27.0	24.3	19.6	40.2	42.9	3.7	2.8	56.5	26.4	6.0
15001	Hawaii County, Hawaii...............	202,906	8.9	21.1	6.2	24.2	25.6	22.9	44.0	54.6	3.1	3.6	44.2	33.9	7.8
15003	Honolulu County, Hawaii	1,000,890	2.2	21.0	8.8	27.8	23.7	18.8	39.0	38.3	4.3	2.7	60.8	24.8	5.6
15007	Kauai County, Hawaii.................	73,454	7.8	21.6	6.8	26.5	23.6	21.3	40.6	55.0	0.7	3.6	53.6	31.0	4.2
15009	Maui County, Hawaii	164,268	8.1	21.5	6.0	25.7	26.9	19.8	42.9	50.6	1.8	2.6	46.6	25.1	7.0
16000	**IDAHO**	1,900,923	9.5	24.7	9.1	26.3	23.3	16.5	37.3	90.5	1.3	3.2	2.5	0.4	12.0
16001	Ada County, Idaho....................	511,931	22.7	22.6	8.2	28.8	24.8	15.5	38.2	90.9	2.1	2.4	4.5	0.3	8.4
16005	Bannock County, Idaho..............	88,263	6.0	25.3	11.0	27.1	21.8	14.8	35.0	91.6	1.4	5.1	2.4	-	5.9
16019	Bonneville County, Idaho	127,930	14.2	30.0	8.0	27.4	21.3	13.4	33.7	91.7	1.5	1.3	1.8	-	11.4
16027	Canyon County, Idaho	243,115	21.7	27.1	9.1	27.3	22.1	14.5	34.6	84.4	1.3	2.9	2.0	1.0	22.6
16055	Kootenai County, Idaho	179,789	19.6	22.7	7.6	25.2	24.9	19.5	40.5	96.1	0.8	3.5	1.9	0.3	6.0
16083	Twin Falls County, Idaho	92,243	12.5	27.1	9.4	26.1	21.0	16.5	35.9	89.2	0.7	3.7	3.2	-	17.3
17000	**ILLINOIS**	12,671,469	-0.2	22.1	9.0	26.8	25.5	16.6	39.0	71.8	15.2	2.1	6.8	0.1	15.8
17019	Champaign County, Illinois	205,943	4.3	19.1	22.8	25.0	19.8	13.4	31.0	73.5	15.7	1.9	11.8	-	6.4
17031	Cook County, Illinois..................	5,173,146	-0.9	21.5	8.5	29.7	24.7	15.6	37.8	55.7	24.2	2.0	8.9	0.1	22.9
17037	DeKalb County, Illinois	100,414	-0.3	21.6	15.5	27.4	22.1	13.4	32.9	84.7	7.8	4.2	3.7	-	9.6
17043	DuPage County, Illinois	924,885	0.7	22.4	8.3	25.9	26.7	16.8	40.0	76.0	6.0	1.2	14.2	0.1	13.3
17089	Kane County, Illinois	515,588	3.3	24.4	9.0	25.1	26.6	14.8	39.0	75.9	6.1	2.9	5.2	0.2	30.1
17091	Kankakee County, Illinois	106,601	-3.2	22.4	11.0	23.7	24.6	18.4	39.3	81.4	16.0	1.5	2.1	-	6.1
17093	Kendall County, Illinois	134,867	12.4	27.6	9.8	25.4	26.5	10.7	35.9	86.0	7.3	2.9	4.7	-	19.4
17097	Lake County, Illinois	711,239	-1.0	23.5	10.1	24.1	27.0	15.4	38.8	75.4	8.5	2.7	9.5	0.1	19.5

STATE County code	STATE County	Two or more races (percent)	Hispanic or Latino (percent)	Native, born in state of residence (percent)	Foreign born (percent)	Non-citizens (percent)	Total house-holds	Family households Total	Married couple	Male house-holder	Female house-holder	Nonfamily households Total	One-person house-holds	Percent of households with people age 60 years and over
	ACS table number:	B02001	B03003	B05002	B05002	B05002	B11001	B11001	B11001	B11001	B11001	B11001	B11001	B11006
	Column number:	15	16	17	18	19	20	21	22	23	24	25	26	27
	GEORGIA—Cont.													
13031	Bulloch County, Georgia	7.2	4.5	64.8	2.7	1.5	29,318	55.8	34.1	2.7	19.0	44.2	26.1	31.4
13045	Carroll County, Georgia	7.9	7.5	69.6	5.1	3.0	43,859	71.0	48.0	7.8	15.3	29.0	24.6	37.0
13047	Catoosa County, Georgia	6.9	3.6	32.0	3.0	0.7	26,864	73.7	55.0	4.5	14.1	26.3	19.0	43.0
13051	Chatham County, Georgia	8.5	6.8	53.5	6.7	3.2	121,028	63.6	42.4	4.4	16.7	36.4	27.0	39.7
13057	Cherokee County, Georgia	9.0	11.3	47.2	9.6	5.5	100,023	74.9	61.9	4.0	9.0	25.1	19.4	40.5
13059	Clarke County, Georgia	9.3	11.2	53.6	9.7	5.3	55,332	46.7	34.1	3.9	8.8	53.3	32.4	29.2
13063	Clayton County, Georgia	9.1	13.5	49.2	11.9	6.0	106,249	69.7	35.1	5.2	29.4	30.3	25.4	31.7
13067	Cobb County, Georgia	11.1	13.7	41.2	14.5	7.8	292,841	65.9	49.4	5.0	11.5	34.1	26.2	34.5
13073	Columbia County, Georgia	8.2	7.6	47.4	6.8	2.9	51,178	75.3	59.5	5.4	10.4	24.7	22.5	39.9
13077	Coweta County, Georgia	9.8	7.7	52.5	5.0	2.1	55,729	76.8	60.5	3.2	13.0	23.2	19.6	40.3
13089	DeKalb County, Georgia	9.1	8.6	45.2	15.3	7.1	273,981	57.2	37.2	4.8	15.1	42.8	34.0	35.6
13095	Dougherty County, Georgia	4.2	3.2	78.0	1.5	0.7	34,835	55.1	26.5	4.8	23.8	44.9	41.0	43.1
13097	Douglas County, Georgia	7.0	11.1	48.4	8.1	2.7	51,441	73.4	47.7	3.7	22.0	26.6	23.4	32.4
13103	Effingham County, Georgia	6.6	5.9	57.2	1.9	0.7	23,373	73.8	57.8	5.0	11.0	26.2	22.6	36.6
13113	Fayette County, Georgia	8.8	7.9	39.6	11.7	5.3	43,689	81.8	65.4	3.9	12.5	18.2	16.3	46.7
13115	Floyd County, Georgia	10.5	12.1	75.2	5.4	3.3	35,417	68.2	47.9	4.7	15.7	31.8	25.7	41.9
13117	Forsyth County, Georgia	10.0	9.8	39.3	20.3	10.8	86,475	83.9	71.0	5.1	7.8	16.1	13.0	31.3
13121	Fulton County, Georgia	8.0	7.3	41.7	13.0	6.7	467,735	52.7	36.5	3.3	12.8	47.3	35.9	30.1
13127	Glynn County, Georgia	7.8	6.9	56.0	6.8	4.3	34,137	63.0	41.8	4.1	17.2	37.0	31.6	50.8
13135	Gwinnett County, Georgia	13.3	22.2	38.1	27.3	12.6	323,014	75.1	56.2	5.4	13.6	24.9	20.3	34.1
13139	Hall County, Georgia	21.3	29.5	53.0	16.2	10.4	72,454	69.9	52.7	5.1	12.1	30.1	24.1	41.4
13151	Henry County, Georgia	9.3	7.9	55.3	7.0	1.0	84,978	72.2	46.2	6.0	19.9	27.8	23.7	34.8
13153	Houston County, Georgia	5.8	6.9	55.1	6.8	4.1	60,815	71.5	47.3	9.1	15.1	28.5	25.7	34.2
13157	Jackson County, Georgia	7.1	9.6	61.5	5.0	2.0	25,272	80.8	63.5	4.1	13.2	19.2	15.3	42.5
13179	Liberty County, Georgia	13.5	12.6	37.3	6.5	3.4	23,883	72.3	47.2	6.2	18.9	27.7	23.1	28.5
13185	Lowndes County, Georgia	6.3	6.3	57.2	3.3	1.3	45,139	58.5	37.7	3.0	17.8	41.5	34.8	32.6
13215	Muscogee County, Georgia	7.9	8.2	56.1	4.8	2.2	82,663	62.5	35.0	6.2	21.3	37.5	32.6	35.0
13217	Newton County, Georgia	9.1	1.6	62.9	3.8	0.7	41,515	78.3	55.0	6.3	17.0	21.7	17.7	40.1
13223	Paulding County, Georgia	8.9	8.0	51.6	5.8	2.6	58,025	82.6	64.8	4.7	13.0	17.4	14.6	34.3
13245	Richmond County, Georgia	8.3	5.3	61.4	3.2	0.8	74,476	58.4	31.9	3.7	22.8	41.6	34.8	41.8
13247	Rockdale County, Georgia	6.9	10.7	52.7	11.0	3.9	33,141	69.7	46.2	4.0	19.6	30.3	24.4	44.3
13255	Spalding County, Georgia	5.7	5.5	70.2	3.5	1.5	25,696	74.1	44.6	4.9	24.7	25.9	22.3	48.8
13285	Troup County, Georgia	4.7	4.0	67.4	5.5	4.1	26,768	67.7	46.4	2.7	18.6	32.3	26.8	36.2
13295	Walker County, Georgia	NA	NA	39.7	0.2	0.0	26,315	66.2	50.5	2.9	12.8	33.8	29.1	44.9
13297	Walton County, Georgia	8.1	5.8	62.4	3.9	1.1	35,628	77.1	55.8	6.4	14.9	22.9	18.0	44.9
13313	Whitfield County, Georgia	9.3	37.3	59.4	18.7	11.4	35,746	74.2	54.4	8.1	11.8	25.8	23.1	40.1
15000	**HAWAII**	26.3	11.1	52.3	18.8	7.9	490,080	68.3	50.6	5.4	12.3	31.7	24.6	50.2
15001	Hawaii County, Hawaii	31.0	13.8	53.5	11.6	5.9	72,194	68.1	49.0	6.2	12.9	31.9	25.5	55.4
15003	Honolulu County, Hawaii	25.3	10.4	51.5	20.4	7.3	338,093	68.7	51.7	4.9	12.0	31.3	24.4	47.8
15007	Kauai County, Hawaii	30.6	11.8	56.3	15.1	6.0	23,464	69.7	46.0	8.5	15.3	30.3	20.9	57.2
15009	Maui County, Hawaii	24.8	12.1	48.7	19.2	8.6	56,319	66.0	48.1	6.2	11.7	34.0	26.5	54.7
16000	**IDAHO**	9.4	13.3	46.1	6.1	3.3	693,882	68.7	55.6	4.5	8.6	31.3	24.2	41.2
16001	Ada County, Idaho	7.7	9.1	38.8	6.6	3.5	196,255	66.8	54.7	3.8	8.2	33.2	23.5	36.9
16005	Bannock County, Idaho	6.7	9.6	59.5	3.3	1.7	33,557	64.6	47.8	4.6	12.2	35.4	29.0	39.6
16019	Bonneville County, Idaho	7.8	14.0	54.6	3.3	1.7	42,905	67.2	55.3	4.0	8.0	32.8	28.0	36.5
16027	Canyon County, Idaho	14.0	25.7	46.7	10.2	4.9	82,667	74.4	57.6	5.9	10.8	25.6	18.3	36.5
16055	Kootenai County, Idaho	8.1	5.4	29.3	2.1	0.6	67,771	68.5	57.2	3.5	7.8	31.5	23.6	45.9
16083	Twin Falls County, Idaho	12.5	17.8	51.0	8.7	4.0	34,311	66.3	52.8	4.9	8.6	33.7	29.8	41.2
17000	**ILLINOIS**	11.1	18.0	67.4	14.2	6.4	4,991,641	62.8	46.1	4.8	11.9	37.2	30.6	40.5
17019	Champaign County, Illinois	9.2	6.6	67.6	11.8	8.3	84,248	52.5	38.3	3.0	11.2	47.5	35.0	31.5
17031	Cook County, Illinois	13.2	26.0	61.2	21.2	9.8	2,072,143	58.3	40.1	4.8	13.4	41.7	34.2	38.6
17037	DeKalb County, Illinois	9.4	12.6	77.6	7.1	3.9	38,916	65.6	46.4	4.0	15.2	34.4	23.8	34.6
17043	DuPage County, Illinois	10.4	15.0	63.3	19.8	7.9	350,639	69.7	56.1	4.1	9.5	30.3	25.1	41.1
17089	Kane County, Illinois	19.7	32.7	64.8	16.9	8.9	183,427	72.6	56.2	6.2	10.1	27.4	21.9	40.2
17091	Kankakee County, Illinois	6.4	11.6	81.8	4.0	1.8	41,020	64.5	45.8	5.2	13.5	35.5	26.5	43.5
17093	Kendall County, Illinois	20.2	21.7	76.9	10.6	6.4	44,208	77.7	54.9	10.8	12.0	22.3	12.0	33.0
17097	Lake County, Illinois	14.8	23.1	58.9	19.0	9.4	254,744	71.9	57.0	4.3	10.6	28.1	23.2	40.4

Table A-2. Counties — Who: Age, Race/Ethnicity, and Household Structure, 2021—*Continued*

STATE County	Total population	Percent change, 2010–2019	Population by age (percent)						Race alone or in combination (percent)					
			Under 18 years	18 to 24 years	25 to 44 years	45 to 64 years	65 years and over	Median age	White	Black or African American	American Indian and Alaska Native	Asian	Native Hawaiian or Other Pacific Islander	Some other race
ACS table number:	B01003	Population Estimates	B01001	B01001	B01001	B01001	B01001	B01002	B02008	B02009	B02010	B02011	B02012	B02013
STATE County code — Column number:	1	2	3	4	5	6	7	8	9	10	11	12	13	14
ILLINOIS—Cont.														
17099 LaSalle County, Illinois	108,965	-4.6	20.8	7.9	24.8	26.6	19.9	41.8	93.6	2.2	2.0	1.4	-	8.9
17111 McHenry County, Illinois	311,122	-5.9	22.8	8.1	24.7	28.8	15.7	40.6	92.5	2.5	1.3	4.3	-	12.0
17113 McLean County, Illinois	170,889	-2.3	21.2	17.7	24.8	21.8	14.5	33.9	85.2	9.3	1.3	5.7	-	4.3
17115 Macon County, Illinois	102,432	-5.7	22.2	8.7	23.4	25.0	20.6	41.5	81.8	18.3	3.5	1.5	-	2.5
17119 Madison County, Illinois	264,490	-0.3	21.7	8.4	25.2	26.5	18.2	40.5	90.7	9.0	2.6	1.5	0.2	3.5
17143 Peoria County, Illinois	179,432	3.9	23.9	8.9	25.5	23.9	17.8	38.6	77.5	19.8	3.0	5.1	-	5.2
17161 Rock Island County, Illinois	142,909	-3.8	22.4	9.0	23.7	24.4	20.5	41.1	80.8	11.4	3.3	3.2	-	10.8
17163 St. Clair County, Illinois	254,796	-3.8	23.4	7.7	25.9	26.1	17.0	40.1	69.1	30.1	4.7	2.5	-	4.3
17167 Sangamon County, Illinois	194,734	-1.4	22.1	7.7	25.0	26.4	18.8	40.8	84.8	13.9	2.0	2.8	-	2.6
17179 Tazewell County, Illinois	130,413	-2.7	22.5	7.1	25.2	25.9	19.3	41.7	97.0	1.8	1.2	1.4	-	2.7
17183 Vermilion County, Illinois	73,095	-7.2	23.4	6.7	24.3	25.7	19.9	41.0	83.5	15.6	0.6	1.2	-	4.7
17197 Will County, Illinois	697,252	1.9	24.0	9.1	25.5	27.4	14.0	39.0	73.0	13.4	1.6	7.3	0.1	16.3
17199 Williamson County, Illinois	66,879	0.4	20.9	7.2	26.5	25.9	19.4	41.7	94.0	3.9	2.9	1.8	-	2.9
17201 Winnebago County, Illinois	283,119	-4.3	23.5	8.2	24.6	25.4	18.4	39.3	77.5	16.5	1.8	3.6	-	12.5
18000 **INDIANA**	6,805,985	2.8	23.3	9.7	25.8	24.8	16.4	38.2	85.0	10.8	2.0	3.0	0.1	6.9
18003 Allen County, Indiana	388,608	6.7	25.5	9.0	27.0	23.5	15.1	36.2	81.2	12.3	2.7	5.6	0.1	7.9
18005 Bartholomew County, Indiana	82,475	9.1	24.2	7.2	28.1	24.3	16.3	37.0	85.7	3.2	1.3	8.4	-	6.4
18011 Boone County, Indiana	73,052	19.8	25.4	6.9	26.5	27.1	14.2	39.2	92.6	3.2	1.6	3.3		3.9
18019 Clark County, Indiana	122,738	7.3	22.2	7.4	27.8	25.6	17.0	39.1	88.2	10.5	1.9	1.7	-	4.9
18035 Delaware County, Indiana	111,871	-3.0	18.3	20.4	21.2	22.8	17.2	35.2	93.1	6.8	3.1	2.0	-	2.1
18039 Elkhart County, Indiana	206,921	4.4	27.3	9.1	24.8	23.3	15.5	36.0	84.5	7.3	1.1	1.7	-	15.3
18043 Floyd County, Indiana	80,454	5.3	22.2	7.9	26.7	26.8	16.4	39.5	92.6	6.8	0.9	1.7	-	4.2
18053 Grant County, Indiana	66,263	-6.1	21.2	12.0	22.8	24.2	19.7	40.5	93.2	5.5	4.8	-	-	3.8
18057 Hamilton County, Indiana	356,650	23.1	25.8	7.8	27.1	26.0	13.4	37.5	87.7	5.6	1.5	7.2	-	5.0
18059 Hancock County, Indiana	81,789	11.7	23.5	6.8	26.3	26.3	17.1	40.3	96.2	5.0	0.7	1.5	-	3.4
18063 Hendricks County, Indiana	179,355	17.1	24.4	8.3	26.9	26.1	14.4	38.9	85.0	9.0	2.6	3.6	-	4.3
18067 Howard County, Indiana	83,687	-0.3	21.9	8.3	24.0	26.4	19.4	41.5	90.6	7.7	4.7	2.1	-	3.9
18081 Johnson County, Indiana	164,298	13.3	24.5	8.2	28.0	24.3	15.1	38.5	91.0	4.2	0.5	5.6	-	2.8
18085 Kosciusko County, Indiana	80,106	2.7	23.7	8.8	25.3	24.4	17.7	38.5	94.4	1.7	0.7	1.9	-	8.1
18089 Lake County, Indiana	498,558	-2.1	23.3	8.5	25.2	25.6	17.3	39.6	66.6	23.8	2.8	2.0	0.1	18.2
18091 LaPorte County, Indiana	112,390	-1.4	21.5	8.2	25.6	26.3	18.4	40.7	86.5	12.1	3.0	1.0	-	7.2
18095 Madison County, Indiana	130,782	-1.6	21.3	8.1	25.9	26.3	18.5	41.2	91.3	7.3	4.0	1.0	-	3.2
18097 Marion County, Indiana	971,102	6.8	24.7	9.3	30.0	22.9	13.1	34.5	61.9	30.9	1.5	4.9	0.2	9.9
18105 Monroe County, Indiana	139,875	7.6	15.6	26.7	24.6	19.2	13.9	30.2	89.5	5.0	2.7	6.7	-	2.8
18109 Morgan County, Indiana	72,206	2.3	22.3	7.3	23.1	29.5	17.8	42.4	98.3	0.4	1.5	1.0	0.4	2.9
18127 Porter County, Indiana	174,243	3.7	21.3	8.6	26.3	25.9	17.8	40.9	92.0	5.3	0.9	2.0	-	7.7
18141 St. Joseph County, Indiana	272,212	-1.3	23.4	11.2	25.3	23.5	16.6	37.6	81.9	16.0	1.4	3.3	0.2	8.7
18157 Tippecanoe County, Indiana	187,076	13.3	20.3	23.5	25.3	18.8	12.1	28.9	83.5	7.2	2.1	8.1	-	8.2
18163 Vanderburgh County, Indiana	179,987	1.0	21.6	10.1	26.5	24.2	17.6	38.4	87.7	10.7	2.7	1.9	0.3	3.5
18167 Vigo County, Indiana	105,994	-0.8	20.1	15.3	24.7	23.4	16.5	36.5	89.2	9.0	0.8	2.6	-	3.7
18177 Wayne County, Indiana	66,456	-4.4	22.4	10.1	22.0	26.6	18.9	41.7	93.4	5.6	3.2	1.3	-	3.7
19000 **IOWA**	3,193,079	3.2	23.1	10.0	25.0	24.1	17.8	38.5	90.9	5.1	1.8	3.1	0.3	6.0
19013 Black Hawk County, Iowa	130,368	0.1	22.0	14.3	25.0	24.1	17.6	36.1	84.7	11.5	2.5	3.6	-	4.9
19049 Dallas County, Iowa	103,796	41.3	26.8	7.3	31.6	22.2	12.1	35.6	90.6	3.9	1.4	5.0	-	8.4
19061 Dubuque County, Iowa	98,718	3.9	22.7	9.9	24.1	24.5	18.9	39.4	94.4	4.6	0.6	1.9	0.7	2.4
19103 Johnson County, Iowa	154,748	15.5	19.7	20.3	28.1	19.0	13.0	30.9	84.2	9.4	2.5	7.4	-	5.8
19113 Linn County, Iowa	228,939	7.3	22.8	9.5	26.0	25.0	16.7	39.0	89.0	9.0	1.0	3.2	-	4.0
19153 Polk County, Iowa	496,844	13.8	24.5	8.8	29.5	23.5	13.7	36.3	83.8	9.3	0.9	6.0	0.1	7.4
19155 Pottawattamie County, Iowa	93,304	0.1	22.3	9.7	24.3	25.1	18.7	40.4	95.2	3.4	1.4	0.9	-	7.5
19163 Scott County, Iowa	174,170	4.7	23.5	8.4	25.8	25.3	16.9	39.1	89.2	9.1	2.4	3.7	-	6.2
19169 Story County, Iowa	99,472	8.5	16.4	31.0	21.6	17.8	13.3	26.6	90.6	3.6	2.4	7.1	-	3.8
19193 Woodbury County, Iowa	105,607	0.9	26.2	9.9	25.2	23.8	14.9	36.8	86.6	7.6	3.5	3.5	-	16.3
20000 **KANSAS**	2,934,582	2.1	23.9	9.9	25.7	23.7	16.7	37.3	86.1	7.5	3.1	3.8	0.2	10.5
20015 Butler County, Kansas	67,889	1.6	24.8	8.9	25.2	24.8	16.4	37.8	94.3	3.1	2.1	2.0	0.5	5.6
20045 Douglas County, Kansas	119,363	10.3	17.5	21.3	27.9	19.5	13.7	32.3	89.1	6.4	4.1	5.9	-	5.2
20091 Johnson County, Kansas	613,219	10.7	23.7	7.9	27.9	25.0	15.5	38.4	86.8	6.4	1.2	6.3	0.3	8.1

							Household type (percent of all households)						
							Family households				Nonfamily households		Percent of households with people age 60 years and over
STATE County	Two or more races (percent)	Hispanic or Latino (percent)	Native, born in state of residence (percent)	Foreign born (percent)	Non-citizens (percent)	Total house-holds	Total	Married couple	Male house-holder	Female house-holder	Total	One-person house-holds	
STATE County code	ACS table number:	B02001	B03003	B05002	B05002	B05002	B11001	B11001	B11001	B11001	B11001	B11001	B11001	B11006
	Column number:	15	16	17	18	19	20	21	22	23	24	25	26	27
	ILLINOIS—Cont.													
17099	LaSalle County, Illinois................	8.0	10.6	84.8	3.1	1.6	44,972	61.1	45.9	3.7	11.6	38.9	33.9	45.8
17111	McHenry County, Illinois	12.1	14.7	72.6	9.2	3.7	116,768	72.7	58.3	5.3	9.0	27.3	23.3	43.0
17113	McLean County, Illinois..............	5.6	5.4	73.3	7.6	4.5	69,263	55.7	44.7	1.7	9.2	44.3	33.2	33.2
17115	Macon County, Illinois................	7.3	2.6	80.1	2.4	1.6	43,914	58.1	42.7	3.5	12.0	41.9	36.4	46.4
17119	Madison County, Illinois.............	6.9	3.7	67.8	1.8	0.6	109,818	61.9	45.2	5.8	10.9	38.1	32.1	42.7
17143	Peoria County, Illinois................	9.3	5.4	73.0	8.8	5.6	79,307	59.9	42.3	4.5	13.0	40.1	33.7	37.6
17161	Rock Island County, Illinois........	9.5	13.7	65.6	9.4	4.4	60,187	59.7	42.6	4.3	12.8	40.3	33.4	45.1
17163	St. Clair County, Illinois	9.1	4.6	55.1	3.2	1.4	98,926	65.7	47.2	4.1	14.4	34.3	30.3	42.1
17167	Sangamon County, Illinois...........	5.9	2.6	81.3	3.4	1.7	84,414	57.1	40.5	4.0	12.6	42.9	36.9	42.2
17179	Tazewell County, Illinois	4.3	2.6	85.2	1.3	0.3	55,208	63.9	49.7	4.5	9.6	36.1	31.5	41.8
17183	Vermilion County, Illinois............	5.4	5.6	83.1	3.0	0.5	29,007	57.6	41.0	4.3	12.4	42.4	35.3	45.6
17197	Will County, Illinois	10.5	18.9	72.9	12.5	5.2	242,530	73.7	57.1	5.6	11.1	26.3	21.6	37.9
17199	Williamson County, Illinois	5.4	2.9	79.8	2.5	1.6	27,361	62.0	46.3	3.2	12.5	38.0	32.1	43.8
17201	Winnebago County, Illinois	11.5	14.4	69.7	8.3	3.6	115,282	63.6	43.3	6.0	14.3	36.4	29.9	43.2
18000	**INDIANA**	7.4	7.6	67.7	5.6	3.1	2,680,694	64.1	48.0	4.9	11.2	35.9	29.1	40.0
18003	Allen County, Indiana.................	9.6	8.1	65.4	7.8	4.0	154,866	63.1	46.7	4.7	11.7	36.9	29.4	37.2
18005	Bartholomew County, Indiana.....	4.6	8.0	69.7	10.2	7.7	32,518	67.5	53.8	3.8	10.0	32.5	25.9	36.9
18011	Boone County, Indiana...............	4.9	3.6	73.7	3.0	1.5	28,048	72.9	61.8	3.4	7.7	27.1	19.0	39.7
18019	Clark County, Indiana	6.4	6.0	50.9	3.7	2.4	50,153	62.9	44.4	6.7	11.7	37.1	31.0	37.8
18035	Delaware County, Indiana...........	6.7	2.8	76.6	1.3	0.7	45,977	59.0	42.3	5.2	11.4	41.0	32.2	39.0
18039	Elkhart County, Indiana..............	9.9	17.6	67.5	8.7	4.3	69,015	72.5	54.9	5.4	12.2	27.5	24.1	40.9
18043	Floyd County, Indiana................	6.4	3.9	49.7	3.1	2.2	30,846	64.3	50.8	4.0	9.5	35.7	30.3	39.3
18053	Grant County, Indiana................	8.1	4.9	75.4	2.9	1.9	26,342	65.3	45.9	7.0	12.4	34.7	28.1	43.3
18057	Hamilton County, Indiana	6.8	4.6	57.7	9.3	4.8	132,255	73.4	63.3	4.1	6.1	26.6	22.8	33.2
18059	Hancock County, Indiana	6.1	3.1	70.3	1.4	0.4	32,661	73.6	59.9	6.2	7.6	26.4	21.4	42.6
18063	Hendricks County, Indiana	4.8	4.7	62.5	6.2	1.9	65,751	73.9	59.9	5.6	8.4	26.1	20.5	36.5
18067	Howard County, Indiana	8.5	3.9	75.0	2.9	1.1	36,530	68.6	47.2	9.0	12.4	31.4	25.7	40.5
18081	Johnson County, Indiana............	4.2	4.0	70.3	5.7	2.3	62,116	70.7	56.7	5.7	8.2	29.3	24.2	36.0
18085	Kosciusko County, Indiana	6.7	8.6	71.9	4.3	2.2	31,523	70.9	57.1	4.3	9.6	29.1	23.2	42.7
18089	Lake County, Indiana	12.7	20.4	55.0	7.1	2.9	192,256	67.0	42.9	6.3	17.8	33.0	27.9	44.2
18091	LaPorte County, Indiana	9.2	7.3	73.2	2.2	0.9	43,445	64.9	45.4	5.0	14.5	35.1	28.0	47.0
18095	Madison County, Indiana............	6.6	4.8	75.2	1.7	0.7	53,910	62.8	44.7	5.4	12.7	37.2	29.6	45.2
18097	Marion County, Indiana	8.8	11.3	65.9	10.8	7.6	394,717	56.4	37.3	3.9	15.2	43.6	34.3	34.4
18105	Monroe County, Indiana	6.3	3.8	58.6	7.2	4.9	56,714	48.2	36.2	3.2	8.8	51.8	37.3	32.4
18109	Morgan County, Indiana	4.2	1.9	81.2	1.0	0.6	26,821	71.8	53.6	5.5	12.8	28.2	20.5	46.1
18127	Porter County, Indiana	7.7	11.0	63.2	3.9	1.6	68,266	68.7	53.7	4.5	10.4	31.3	25.3	41.2
18141	St. Joseph County, Indiana	10.7	9.8	62.9	6.2	3.1	107,076	61.4	44.9	4.6	11.9	38.6	32.1	41.1
18157	Tippecanoe County, Indiana........	8.5	9.2	58.7	9.7	6.4	73,525	51.7	39.8	3.6	8.4	48.3	33.6	29.1
18163	Vanderburgh County, Indiana	6.5	3.1	71.3	2.7	1.5	79,215	58.1	39.8	5.3	13.1	41.9	34.9	40.4
18167	Vigo County, Indiana	4.9	3.0	72.6	2.7	1.2	42,140	55.1	38.0	4.5	12.6	44.9	34.9	41.1
18177	Wayne County, Indiana...............	6.4	3.4	73.6	3.0	2.7	26,452	62.0	43.0	3.8	15.1	38.0	34.0	43.8
19000	**IOWA**	6.8	6.6	69.7	5.4	3.0	1,300,467	62.1	49.1	4.2	8.8	37.9	30.2	41.0
19013	Black Hawk County, Iowa	5.8	4.9	73.9	6.5	2.7	53,951	56.1	44.2	3.8	8.2	43.9	33.9	38.8
19049	Dallas County, Iowa	8.8	6.5	68.5	8.8	3.0	41,681	60.2	49.0	3.5	7.7	39.8	31.8	29.0
19061	Dubuque County, Iowa	4.7	2.9	76.8	2.7	1.8	40,482	64.8	52.7	4.2	7.9	35.2	27.5	40.6
19103	Johnson County, Iowa................	8.4	6.0	60.0	8.7	4.5	61,301	53.7	45.6	1.7	6.5	46.3	29.9	31.0
19113	Linn County, Iowa.....................	6.2	3.7	74.6	5.3	2.6	94,884	62.4	47.3	4.7	10.4	37.6	30.6	39.6
19153	Polk County, Iowa.....................	7.1	9.1	66.3	9.8	5.0	203,390	61.7	47.0	4.6	10.1	38.3	29.8	35.2
19155	Pottawattamie County, Iowa.......	8.7	8.7	54.2	4.4	2.6	37,930	61.9	47.0	4.3	10.6	38.1	32.2	43.2
19163	Scott County, Iowa	10.2	7.4	57.7	3.8	1.4	72,128	60.9	45.8	4.7	10.4	39.1	30.9	38.5
19169	Story County, Iowa	7.2	4.0	63.4	6.4	4.0	38,868	48.1	40.7	1.1	6.3	51.9	33.4	31.8
19193	Woodbury County, Iowa.............	17.4	18.6	63.0	12.0	6.0	41,327	67.5	48.2	6.8	12.5	32.5	24.9	38.6
20000	**KANSAS**	10.6	12.7	59.2	6.9	4.2	1,159,026	63.9	49.5	4.7	9.7	36.1	30.0	39.7
20015	Butler County, Kansas................	7.1	5.5	68.5	2.6	1.2	24,545	69.6	54.9	3.7	11.0	30.4	25.9	41.0
20045	Douglas County, Kansas.............	10.3	6.7	52.5	5.5	3.6	49,759	49.7	37.6	3.2	8.8	50.3	41.9	30.3
20091	Johnson County, Kansas	8.6	8.2	42.4	8.7	3.8	245,646	67.4	56.8	3.8	6.8	32.6	25.3	35.1

Table A-2. Counties — Who: Age, Race/Ethnicity, and Household Structure, 2021—*Continued*

			Population by age (percent)						Race alone or in combination (percent)					
STATE County	Total population	Percent change, 2010–2019	Under 18 years	18 to 24 years	25 to 44 years	45 to 64 years	65 years and over	Median age	White	Black or African American	American Indian and Alaska Native	Asian	Native Hawaiian or Other Pacific Islander	Some other race
ACS table number:	B01003	Population Estimates	B01001	B01001	B01001	B01001	B01001	B01002	B02008	B02009	B02010	B02011	B02012	B02013
Column number:	1	2	3	4	5	6	7	8	9	10	11	12	13	14
KANSAS—Cont.														
20103 Leavenworth County, Kansas......	82,184	7.3	23.7	8.3	26.9	25.3	15.8	37.5	89.0	11.1	4.6	2.4	-	7.8
20161 Riley County, Kansas..................	72,208	4.4	16.5	29.6	27.2	16.1	10.6	26.3	86.3	7.9	2.9	5.6	-	5.5
20173 Sedgwick County, Kansas	523,828	3.5	25.2	9.2	26.9	23.2	15.5	35.9	80.6	11.0	3.5	5.4	0.2	13.1
20177 Shawnee County, Kansas............	178,264	-0.6	23.3	8.1	25.6	23.7	19.4	38.4	84.6	11.2	2.8	2.4	-	9.7
20209 Wyandotte County, Kansas........	167,046	5.0	27.6	9.1	27.3	22.9	13.1	34.7	57.7	23.5	3.2	5.8	-	25.7
21000 **KENTUCKY**	4,509,394	2.6	22.5	9.2	25.6	25.6	17.0	39.1	89.3	9.0	2.3	2.1	0.2	3.9
21015 Boone County, Kentucky.............	137,412	12.4	25.7	7.6	27.0	25.8	13.9	37.9	91.4	2.6	3.3	3.2	-	6.0
21029 Bullitt County, Kentucky.............	82,918	9.9	21.2	7.6	25.9	28.6	16.7	41.5	NA	NA	NA	NA	NA	NA
21037 Campbell County, Kentucky........	93,050	3.6	20.5	9.2	28.1	25.4	16.8	38.5	95.6	3.0	1.7	1.6	-	3.3
21047 Christian County, Kentucky........	72,357	-4.7	27.4	15.8	27.9	16.4	12.5	28.7	72.0	24.0	2.4	1.0	-	5.3
21059 Daviess County, Kentucky..........	103,063	5.0	24.0	8.4	25.0	24.8	17.8	39.3	92.2	4.9	2.4	2.3	-	3.8
21067 Fayette County, Kentucky..........	321,793	9.2	20.7	14.0	28.0	22.9	14.3	35.3	79.0	15.1	3.1	5.2	-	7.2
21093 Hardin County, Kentucky...........	111,607	5.1	24.7	8.6	26.8	24.6	15.3	37.8	84.3	14.5	2.3	4.0	-	4.4
21111 Jefferson County, Kentucky........	777,874	3.5	22.0	8.5	27.6	24.9	17.0	38.5	74.5	23.6	2.9	4.2	0.1	6.1
21117 Kenton County, Kentucky...........	169,495	4.6	23.4	7.5	28.9	25.1	15.1	38.2	92.5	4.8	2.4	1.9	-	4.2
21145 McCracken County, Kentucky.....	67,454	12.1	22.2	7.7	23.9	25.4	20.8	42.7	87.2	12.6	1.4	1.2	-	3.0
21151 Madison County, Kentucky........	94,666	-1.1	20.9	17.4	24.5	23.2	14.0	33.9	93.4	5.5	1.0	1.6	-	3.8
21185 Oldham County, Kentucky..........	68,685	10.7	24.4	8.4	25.4	27.7	14.1	40.7	93.1	5.1	1.3	2.2	-	4.7
21199 Pulaski County, Kentucky...........	65,423	3.0	22.2	7.1	24.4	26.9	19.4	40.9	NA	NA	NA	NA	NA	NA
21227 Warren County, Kentucky..........	137,212	16.8	23.2	16.1	25.7	22.1	12.9	32.4	83.2	9.7	2.2	5.7	-	4.3
22000 **LOUISIANA**	4,624,047	3.3	23.4	9.2	26.7	24.2	16.6	38.0	63.9	33.2	2.2	2.3	0.1	5.6
22005 Ascension Parish, Louisiana........	128,369	18.1	26.5	7.6	29.3	23.3	13.4	35.8	69.9	24.9	0.8	1.8	-	6.6
22015 Bossier Parish, Louisiana.............	129,144	8.6	24.8	9.1	28.7	22.6	14.9	36.0	72.3	26.0	1.0	2.6	-	5.8
22017 Caddo Parish, Louisiana.............	233,092	-5.8	23.4	8.3	25.5	24.2	18.6	40.4	47.7	50.9	1.2	1.7	0.2	2.6
22019 Calcasieu Parish, Louisiana........	205,282	5.5	24.7	8.5	26.7	24.4	15.8	37.5	72.2	26.0	1.0	1.7	-	5.3
22033 East Baton Rouge Parish, Louisiana	453,301	-0.0	22.7	13.3	26.8	21.8	15.4	34.7	47.1	48.0	1.0	3.9	-	5.0
22045 Iberia Parish, Louisiana................	68,975	-4.7	25.9	8.5	23.8	25.3	16.6	38.7	65.2	33.2	1.6	2.9	-	5.0
22051 Jefferson Parish, Louisiana	433,688	-0.0	22.2	7.3	26.5	25.5	18.4	40.2	62.4	28.5	2.4	5.0	-	14.4
22055 Lafayette Parish, Louisiana.........	244,205	10.3	23.7	9.4	29.2	23.3	14.3	36.3	70.0	28.2	0.8	2.7	-	5.8
22057 Lafourche Parish, Louisiana........	97,504	1.3	23.0	8.5	25.5	25.1	17.9	39.6	81.5	15.5	5.1	1.3	-	3.1
22063 Livingston Parish, Louisiana........	145,830	10.0	25.5	8.8	27.6	24.5	13.5	36.5	92.7	6.8	4.3	-	-	7.5
22071 Orleans Parish, Louisiana.............	376,971	13.5	19.8	8.2	30.9	24.5	16.6	38.3	37.1	59.6	1.7	3.6	0.1	5.3
22073 Ouachita Parish, Louisiana.........	158,768	-0.3	24.4	10.0	25.7	24.0	15.8	36.8	60.6	37.1	2.2	1.3	-	2.5
22079 Rapides Parish, Louisiana...........	128,654	-1.5	24.6	8.4	25.3	25.0	16.7	38.8	64.5	32.8	1.8	1.7	-	4.2
22097 St. Landry Parish, Louisiana........	82,071	-1.5	26.6	8.7	26.3	21.4	17.0	37.9	59.4	38.2	4.6	-	-	3.8
22103 St. Tammany Parish, Louisiana.....	269,388	11.4	23.7	7.4	25.0	25.9	18.0	40.6	83.7	13.7	2.2	2.1	-	7.2
22105 Tangipahoa Parish, Louisiana.......	135,217	11.3	24.6	11.6	25.8	21.9	16.1	35.6	67.7	31.0	0.8	1.6	-	4.2
22109 Terrebonne Parish, Louisiana.......	108,708	-1.3	24.9	7.7	26.2	25.4	15.7	37.7	72.7	20.8	9.2	2.3	-	4.2
23000 **MAINE**	1,372,247	0.6	18.2	7.8	24.3	28.0	21.7	44.7	95.9	2.2	1.7	1.9	0.1	3.9
23001 Androscoggin County, Maine......	111,034	0.5	21.0	8.8	24.9	26.8	18.5	40.8	94.1	4.8	2.5	1.7	-	3.6
23003 Aroostook County, Maine..........	66,859	-6.7	18.3	7.3	20.6	29.0	24.9	48.2	97.0	1.7	2.7	0.8	-	1.8
23005 Cumberland County, Maine........	305,231	4.7	18.1	8.2	27.2	26.9	19.5	41.8	93.3	4.0	0.9	3.3	-	5.4
23011 Kennebec County, Maine...........	124,486	0.1	18.4	8.8	24.2	28.0	20.6	44.1	96.8	1.3	1.5	1.5	-	3.2
23019 Penobscot County, Maine	152,765	-1.2	17.8	10.6	24.5	27.8	19.4	42.2	96.0	1.7	2.2	1.6	-	3.6
23031 York County, Maine..................	214,591	5.3	18.1	7.1	24.6	28.7	21.6	45.3	96.1	1.7	1.5	1.9	-	6.1
24000 **MARYLAND**	6,165,129	4.8	22.1	8.6	26.7	26.3	16.3	39.3	55.8	32.3	1.7	8.0	0.2	10.8
24001 Allegany County, Maryland........	67,729	-6.2	16.5	13.2	24.9	25.1	20.4	41.3	88.8	10.1	0.6	1.4	-	1.8
24003 Anne Arundel County, Maryland.	590,336	7.7	22.3	8.4	28.0	25.9	15.5	38.4	71.9	20.5	1.9	5.7	0.2	8.2
24005 Baltimore County, Maryland........	849,316	2.8	21.8	8.7	25.9	25.6	17.9	39.9	59.9	32.6	1.5	7.3	0.3	5.9
24009 Calvert County, Maryland	93,928	4.3	23.1	7.9	23.9	28.1	17.0	40.5	84.2	15.5	1.6	3.2	-	6.6
24013 Carroll County, Maryland	173,873	0.8	21.9	8.2	24.0	28.4	17.5	41.3	92.4	5.2	0.9	3.0	-	3.5
24015 Cecil County, Maryland..............	103,905	1.7	22.0	7.8	24.8	28.7	16.7	41.3	88.3	9.3	1.1	2.0	-	5.7
24017 Charles County, Maryland..........	168,698	11.4	23.5	8.6	26.2	28.8	12.9	39.0	42.1	54.9	2.7	5.5	0.3	5.1
24021 Frederick County, Maryland	279,835	11.2	23.3	8.1	26.7	27.0	15.0	38.8	81.8	11.0	2.2	7.2	0.7	10.3
24025 Harford County, Maryland	262,977	4.3	22.3	8.1	25.5	27.2	16.9	39.6	80.3	16.8	2.0	4.7	0.5	4.9
24027 Howard County, Maryland..........	334,529	13.4	24.1	7.9	26.4	26.9	14.7	39.9	54.5	22.5	0.9	21.7	-	7.6

Table A-2. Counties — Who: Age, Race/Ethnicity, and Household Structure, 2021—*Continued*

STATE County code	STATE County	Two or more races (percent)	Hispanic or Latino (percent)	Native, born in state of residence (percent)	Foreign born (percent)	Non-citizens (percent)	Total households	Family households Total	Married couple	Male householder	Female householder	Nonfamily households Total	One-person households	Percent of households with people age 60 years and over
ACS table number:		B02001	B03003	B05002	B05002	B05002	B11001	B11001	B11001	B11001	B11001	B11001	B11001	B11006
Column number:		15	16	17	18	19	20	21	22	23	24	25	26	27
	KANSAS—Cont.													
20103	Leavenworth County, Kansas	11.7	7.7	49.8	2.9	1.8	29,963	70.0	57.3	4.9	7.7	30.0	22.6	38.5
20161	Riley County, Kansas	8.5	8.7	48.2	7.4	4.8	27,866	54.2	48.7	0.3	5.2	45.8	31.4	27.4
20173	Sedgwick County, Kansas	12.8	15.7	63.7	7.8	4.1	203,656	64.3	46.1	6.1	12.1	35.7	30.5	38.4
20177	Shawnee County, Kansas	10.2	13.4	69.9	4.3	2.8	74,908	58.7	43.2	4.8	10.7	41.3	35.1	43.9
20209	Wyandotte County, Kansas	15.4	30.8	52.6	16.8	11.3	62,538	64.5	41.6	6.6	16.2	35.5	28.6	37.0
21000	**KENTUCKY**	6.3	3.9	68.3	4.0	2.5	1,785,682	64.9	47.6	5.1	12.2	35.1	28.5	41.3
21015	Boone County, Kentucky.............	6.6	4.7	49.6	5.9	3.2	50,728	69.2	53.8	4.9	10.5	30.8	24.4	35.9
21029	Bullitt County, Kentucky.............	NA	NA	83.5	1.6	1.1	30,979	70.8	54.5	4.8	11.4	29.2	23.8	42.5
21037	Campbell County, Kentucky........	5.0	2.4	59.2	2.2	1.3	39,048	61.5	46.5	4.2	10.8	38.5	30.0	39.7
21047	Christian County, Kentucky........	5.9	8.5	50.8	2.6	0.9	25,317	64.1	44.2	4.7	15.2	35.9	29.6	33.9
21059	Daviess County, Kentucky	5.7	3.5	73.2	3.8	2.6	41,246	64.5	45.6	5.1	13.8	35.5	29.6	42.1
21067	Fayette County, Kentucky	9.3	7.5	57.9	9.8	6.2	139,303	53.8	38.6	4.3	10.9	46.2	34.9	33.5
21093	Hardin County, Kentucky...........	7.7	6.1	56.2	3.8	1.7	42,714	64.1	45.6	4.9	13.5	35.9	29.7	38.2
21111	Jefferson County, Kentucky........	10.2	6.6	65.1	9.3	5.4	331,104	59.7	41.0	5.1	13.6	40.3	32.6	39.3
21117	Kenton County, Kentucky	6.0	3.7	58.3	3.0	1.5	68,073	63.5	46.6	6.2	10.7	36.5	28.9	37.3
21145	McCracken County, Kentucky.....	5.4	2.9	60.5	2.4	0.7	25,531	66.4	53.2	1.6	11.6	33.6	26.9	49.3
21151	Madison County, Kentucky.........	5.1	2.8	69.2	2.9	1.3	36,052	65.5	49.6	2.3	13.6	34.5	27.0	34.9
21185	Oldham County, Kentucky	6.4	4.1	55.5	5.4	1.5	22,895	79.3	71.6	2.1	5.6	20.7	16.5	34.5
21199	Pulaski County, Kentucky	NA	NA	NA	NA	NA	25,509	64.9	45.9	3.3	15.6	35.1	31.2	47.5
21227	Warren County, Kentucky	5.6	5.7	60.2	8.5	5.2	53,093	65.0	44.9	6.9	13.3	35.0	29.0	32.9
22000	**LOUISIANA**	6.7	5.5	77.6	4.3	2.5	1,783,924	63.8	42.4	5.4	16.0	36.2	30.7	41.5
22005	Ascension Parish, Louisiana........	3.9	6.4	83.4	4.6	2.9	48,129	73.6	53.1	6.1	14.4	26.4	22.6	35.3
22015	Bossier Parish, Louisiana.............	7.7	7.0	60.3	3.7	2.2	49,418	64.2	45.2	6.1	12.9	35.8	30.7	39.4
22017	Caddo Parish, Louisiana.............	4.1	3.1	78.7	1.4	0.8	96,369	61.7	35.3	7.1	19.3	38.3	34.1	42.1
22019	Calcasieu Parish, Louisiana.........	5.9	4.2	80.4	4.2	3.3	71,511	68.5	50.4	4.0	14.2	31.5	26.5	43.3
22033	East Baton Rouge Parish, Louisiana	4.9	4.6	78.1	6.1	3.6	175,731	59.7	37.6	4.5	17.7	40.3	32.1	37.5
22045	Iberia Parish, Louisiana................	7.2	4.4	86.3	3.0	1.6	25,440	66.3	45.6	8.1	12.6	33.7	27.8	46.6
22051	Jefferson Parish, Louisiana	11.8	15.3	70.1	13.6	7.7	179,775	62.4	40.3	5.8	16.3	37.6	32.5	44.1
22055	Lafayette Parish, Louisiana	6.8	4.7	81.4	4.5	3.3	97,877	63.0	44.9	3.8	14.3	37.0	31.1	33.8
22057	Lafourche Parish, Louisiana	6.5	4.6	90.4	2.2	0.9	38,111	64.9	47.5	4.2	13.1	35.1	30.8	43.8
22063	Livingston Parish, Louisiana........	11.3	4.7	75.2	3.4	2.9	51,960	78.0	58.5	6.1	13.4	22.0	18.1	38.6
22071	Orleans Parish, Louisiana.............	6.3	5.7	68.9	5.7	2.8	158,827	46.8	27.3	3.8	15.8	53.2	45.1	39.4
22073	Ouachita Parish, Louisiana	3.7	2.4	79.7	1.8	0.9	61,594	63.7	37.3	5.4	21.0	36.3	31.4	39.7
22079	Rapides Parish, Louisiana	4.9	3.6	80.6	3.2	1.7	48,405	65.9	44.0	5.3	16.6	34.1	29.0	43.4
22097	St. Landry Parish, Louisiana........	7.3	2.6	88.2	3.1	1.8	32,213	65.9	35.3	7.6	22.9	34.1	28.2	45.8
22103	St. Tammany Parish, Louisiana.....	9.1	6.2	72.8	4.5	2.5	103,543	71.8	55.5	5.2	11.0	28.2	24.6	44.4
22105	Tangipahoa Parish, Louisiana.......	5.1	4.7	80.5	0.8	0.4	49,915	61.3	39.6	5.6	16.1	38.7	32.9	38.9
22109	Terrebonne Parish, Louisiana	9.1	5.5	85.4	2.4	1.4	43,996	69.7	48.5	6.8	14.4	30.3	24.9	40.0
23000	**MAINE**	5.5	1.9	61.6	4.1	1.6	593,626	61.5	48.5	3.9	9.1	38.5	29.9	46.9
23001	Androscoggin County, Maine......	6.4	2.1	71.3	4.2	2.3	46,323	59.0	47.4	3.1	8.5	41.0	34.7	43.0
23003	Aroostook County, Maine	4.0	1.6	73.7	4.9	2.2	30,220	64.7	48.6	5.5	10.6	35.3	27.6	50.0
23005	Cumberland County, Maine........	6.7	2.3	52.3	6.6	3.1	129,977	58.6	48.4	2.9	7.2	41.4	31.4	43.2
23011	Kennebec County, Maine............	4.3	1.9	69.1	2.6	1.0	53,803	63.9	47.2	5.2	11.4	36.1	29.2	44.9
23019	Penobscot County, Maine	5.1	1.7	67.3	3.6	1.5	65,441	59.4	47.1	2.9	9.3	40.6	30.7	41.3
23031	York County, Maine	6.7	2.0	48.3	3.7	1.3	90,907	64.7	49.6	5.5	9.6	35.3	27.9	47.7
24000	**MARYLAND**	8.0	11.1	47.4	15.9	7.4	2,355,652	65.8	47.1	4.9	13.8	34.2	27.9	41.5
24001	Allegany County, Maryland........	2.7	2.1	70.7	2.6	1.5	28,535	53.6	38.4	4.5	10.7	46.4	39.2	40.9
24003	Anne Arundel County, Maryland.	7.7	9.0	51.1	9.6	4.3	225,064	69.9	54.6	4.8	10.4	30.1	23.9	39.5
24005	Baltimore County, Maryland.......	6.6	6.2	64.3	12.1	4.4	332,529	64.2	44.5	4.7	15.0	35.8	29.4	44.4
24009	Calvert County, Maryland	11.1	4.8	50.0	3.0	0.9	33,994	77.1	60.5	6.8	9.7	22.9	19.6	42.7
24013	Carroll County, Maryland	5.0	4.3	64.9	4.8	1.9	64,161	76.6	63.8	4.4	8.4	23.4	20.3	43.8
24015	Cecil County, Maryland..............	6.5	4.9	47.0	4.1	2.2	41,000	66.6	48.8	8.1	9.7	33.4	26.3	43.3
24017	Charles County, Maryland..........	9.1	7.0	39.9	8.7	3.2	59,481	73.0	52.6	5.3	15.1	27.0	23.5	37.7
24021	Frederick County, Maryland	12.4	11.3	50.1	11.5	4.4	103,685	71.0	55.5	5.3	10.2	29.0	22.7	39.9
24025	Harford County, Maryland..........	7.0	5.1	65.9	6.0	2.1	101,196	71.7	57.2	3.9	10.6	28.3	22.1	41.2
24027	Howard County, Maryland	7.0	7.6	39.7	24.2	7.9	120,546	76.7	60.3	4.4	12.0	23.3	18.2	38.0

Table A-2. Counties — Who: Age, Race/Ethnicity, and Household Structure, 2021—*Continued*

STATE County	Total population	Percent change, 2010–2019	Population by age (percent)					Median age	Race alone or in combination (percent)					
			Under 18 years	18 to 24 years	25 to 44 years	45 to 64 years	65 years and over		White	Black or African American	American Indian and Alaska Native	Asian	Native Hawaiian or Other Pacific Islander	Some other race
ACS table number:	B01003	Population Estimates	B01001	B01001	B01001	B01001	B01001	B01002	B02008	B02009	B02010	B02011	B02012	B02013
Column number:	1	2	3	4	5	6	7	8	9	10	11	12	13	14
MARYLAND—Cont.														
24031 Montgomery County, Maryland..	1,054,827	8.1	22.9	7.7	26.1	26.8	16.6	40.0	51.4	21.2	1.4	17.8	0.2	19.6
24033 Prince George's County, Maryland	955,306	5.3	22.1	9.2	27.6	26.6	14.5	38.4	17.7	63.9	1.8	5.2	0.1	19.8
24037 St. Mary's County, Maryland	114,468	7.9	23.8	8.9	27.1	26.5	13.8	37.2	81.1	16.5	1.6	4.1	-	7.6
24043 Washington County, Maryland....	154,937	2.5	21.6	8.1	26.2	26.2	17.9	40.7	84.8	14.3	2.7	2.6	-	5.4
24045 Wicomico County, Maryland	103,980	4.9	22.3	15.2	22.2	24.4	16.0	35.9	68.5	26.8	3.2	3.7	-	6.8
24510 Baltimore city, Maryland	576,498	-4.4	20.3	9.3	32.1	23.5	14.8	36.1	32.3	63.2	1.8	3.5	0.2	5.8
25000 **MASSACHUSETTS**	6,984,723	4.8	19.5	9.9	26.9	26.3	17.4	39.9	78.7	10.1	1.1	8.3	0.1	14.2
25001 Barnstable County, Massachusetts	232,411	-1.3	14.5	6.2	18.7	28.4	32.3	54.6	90.8	4.3	1.3	2.2	-	8.4
25003 Berkshire County, Massachusetts	128,657	-4.8	16.2	9.1	21.6	28.6	24.6	47.8	94.1	5.1	0.8	2.3	-	5.0
25005 Bristol County, Massachusetts	580,164	3.1	20.5	8.7	25.7	27.5	17.5	41.3	85.2	8.1	1.2	3.2	-	13.5
25009 Essex County, Massachusetts	807,074	6.2	20.9	8.9	25.3	27.1	17.9	40.9	79.2	6.7	1.2	4.4	0.1	21.5
25011 Franklin County, Massachusetts	71,015	-1.7	16.7	7.3	23.6	28.2	24.2	47.1	94.3	2.6	1.3	2.5	-	5.3
25013 Hampden County, Massachusetts	462,718	0.6	21.2	9.9	25.6	25.7	17.6	39.9	80.2	12.5	1.5	3.4	-	22.6
25015 Hampshire County, Massachusetts	161,572	1.7	14.2	24.2	20.3	22.4	18.8	36.4	89.2	4.7	1.0	6.2	0.2	6.7
25017 Middlesex County, Massachusetts	1,614,742	7.2	19.6	9.6	28.9	26.0	15.9	38.9	76.8	6.9	0.8	15.1	0.1	10.9
25021 Norfolk County, Massachusetts	724,505	5.4	20.6	8.7	26.2	27.1	17.4	40.6	77.3	9.2	0.7	13.7	0.1	7.1
25023 Plymouth County, Massachusetts	533,003	5.3	20.8	8.3	23.3	28.6	19.0	42.7	83.0	12.4	0.7	2.3	0.1	11.1
25025 Suffolk County, Massachusetts....	771,245	11.3	16.3	13.7	35.6	21.5	12.9	33.8	60.0	26.8	1.8	10.3	0.1	24.4
25027 Worcester County, Massachusetts	862,029	4.0	20.7	9.3	25.8	27.7	16.5	40.0	82.9	7.7	1.0	5.9	0.2	13.6
26000 **MICHIGAN**	10,050,811	0.8	21.4	9.2	25.2	26.1	18.1	40.2	80.6	15.4	1.8	4.1	0.1	5.5
26005 Allegan County, Michigan	120,950	6.0	23.7	7.4	24.3	27.1	17.6	40.1	95.0	2.4	1.5	1.3	-	7.2
26017 Bay County, Michigan	102,985	-4.3	19.0	8.2	23.7	27.3	21.7	43.9	96.6	4.2	2.1	1.1	-	4.6
26021 Berrien County, Michigan	153,101	-2.2	21.6	8.1	23.0	26.4	20.9	42.9	80.2	15.8	1.4	2.7	-	6.6
26025 Calhoun County, Michigan	133,819	-1.5	22.7	9.1	24.1	26.0	18.2	40.3	85.0	12.6	2.8	3.3	-	5.8
26037 Clinton County, Michigan	79,426	5.6	21.5	8.3	24.7	27.2	18.3	41.5	95.4	2.8	2.0	2.2	0.2	3.5
26045 Eaton County, Michigan	108,944	2.3	20.5	8.0	25.8	25.6	20.1	40.9	89.7	8.4	1.3	2.9	0.4	5.6
26049 Genesee County, Michigan	404,208	-4.7	22.3	8.2	24.6	26.6	18.3	40.3	77.7	22.1	1.5	1.5	-	2.7
26055 Grand Traverse County, Michigan	95,860	7.0	19.9	7.1	24.8	26.9	21.3	43.4	96.9	1.4	2.1	1.2	-	2.0
26065 Ingham County, Michigan	284,034	4.1	19.7	18.3	26.8	20.7	14.5	33.8	79.3	15.2	2.2	7.7	0.3	7.2
26067 Ionia County, Michigan	67,197	1.2	23.3	8.1	27.0	26.0	15.5	39.7	94.8	5.6	1.8	-	-	3.5
26075 Jackson County, Michigan	160,050	-1.1	21.4	7.6	25.9	26.6	18.5	40.9	90.1	10.4	1.2	1.3	-	4.9
26077 Kalamazoo County, Michigan	261,108	5.9	21.5	15.6	25.3	22.1	15.6	34.7	83.2	13.9	1.7	3.3	0.4	5.3
26081 Kent County, Michigan	658,046	9.0	23.7	9.2	29.1	23.6	14.5	36.0	82.3	12.5	1.2	4.3	0.1	10.5
26087 Lapeer County, Michigan	88,513	-0.8	20.0	7.9	22.1	30.6	19.5	45.1	96.5	1.7	2.0	1.0	-	3.9
26091 Lenawee County, Michigan	98,956	-1.4	20.8	8.7	23.9	26.7	19.9	42.0	93.9	4.1	1.5	0.9	0.3	8.0
26093 Livingston County, Michigan	195,014	6.1	20.8	7.5	23.1	29.7	18.9	43.6	97.9	1.0	1.2	1.5	-	3.0
26099 Macomb County, Michigan	876,792	3.9	20.8	7.8	25.9	27.6	17.9	41.2	80.8	14.6	1.2	5.7	0.1	3.6
26103 Marquette County, Michigan	66,103	-0.6	17.3	14.9	23.8	23.7	20.3	39.5	95.7	2.6	3.2	1.3	-	2.7
26111 Midland County, Michigan	83,457	-0.6	20.9	8.2	25.4	26.0	19.5	41.1	94.0	2.0	1.0	2.8	-	5.5
26115 Monroe County, Michigan	155,274	-1.0	21.1	8.1	23.2	27.9	19.8	42.8	96.3	3.7	1.2	1.0	-	4.9
26117 Montcalm County, Michigan	67,220	0.9	21.9	8.1	24.4	27.4	18.2	41.1	95.1	3.7	0.9	0.2	-	4.4
26121 Muskegon County, Michigan	176,511	0.8	22.8	8.5	25.3	24.9	18.5	39.8	83.6	15.7	2.0	1.0	0.1	6.1
26125 Oakland County, Michigan	1,270,017	4.6	20.4	7.9	26.2	27.6	17.8	41.6	76.8	14.9	1.2	9.3	0.2	5.8
26139 Ottawa County, Michigan	299,157	10.6	23.5	13.1	24.6	23.0	15.7	36.2	91.2	2.7	1.3	3.4	0.4	8.4
26145 Saginaw County, Michigan	189,591	-4.8	21.6	9.3	23.8	25.5	19.7	40.9	75.6	21.1	1.5	1.6	-	7.2
26147 St. Clair County, Michigan	160,053	-2.4	20.5	7.3	22.7	29.9	19.7	44.6	95.7	3.8	1.2	1.2	-	2.9
26155 Shiawassee County, Michigan	67,877	-3.6	21.0	7.8	23.6	28.2	19.4	43.3	97.3	1.5	1.6	0.7	-	2.1
26159 Van Buren County, Michigan	75,658	-0.8	23.1	7.4	22.6	28.2	18.7	40.9	90.7	4.8	3.2	1.3	-	11.7
26161 Washtenaw County, Michigan	369,390	6.6	18.4	17.8	26.0	22.7	15.0	34.8	77.6	13.9	1.5	10.6	0.2	4.9
26163 Wayne County, Michigan	1,774,816	-3.9	23.7	8.3	26.4	25.4	16.2	37.9	55.7	39.6	1.5	4.4	0.1	6.1
27000 **MINNESOTA**	5,707,390	5.1	22.9	8.8	26.5	25.0	16.8	38.8	84.3	8.5	2.3	6.2	0.1	5.9
27003 Anoka County, Minnesota	367,018	7.9	23.8	7.7	26.7	26.8	15.1	38.8	82.3	10.3	1.8	6.9	0.1	5.4
27013 Blue Earth County, Minnesota	69,280	5.7	19.5	21.1	24.8	19.4	15.2	31.8	91.9	4.5	2.2	3.1	-	4.1
27019 Carver County, Minnesota	108,626	15.4	25.7	9.1	25.0	26.9	13.3	38.6	92.9	3.2	1.1	4.4	-	5.0

Table A-2. Counties — Who: Age, Race/Ethnicity, and Household Structure, 2021—*Continued*

		Two or more races (percent)	Hispanic or Latino (percent)	Native, born in state of residence (percent)	Foreign born (percent)	Non-citizens (percent)	Total house-holds	Household type (percent of all households)						Percent of households with people age 60 years and over
								Family households				Nonfamily households		
								Total	Married couple	Male house-holder	Female house-holder	Total	One-person house-holds	
STATE County code	STATE County	ACS table number: B02001	B03003	B05002	B05002	B05002	B11001	B11001	B11001	B11001	B11001	B11001	B11001	B11006
	Column number:	15	16	17	18	19	20	21	22	23	24	25	26	27
	MARYLAND—Cont.													
24031	Montgomery County, Maryland ..	10.6	20.1	25.9	32.9	14.1	388,396	68.9	53.4	4.4	11.2	31.1	25.7	42.3
24033	Prince George's County, Maryland	7.5	20.4	26.2	24.0	13.3	346,127	63.5	38.7	6.6	18.2	36.5	29.9	40.7
24037	St. Mary's County, Maryland	10.1	5.7	45.2	5.6	2.2	42,078	69.3	54.7	3.8	10.8	30.7	24.4	36.6
24043	Washington County, Maryland....	8.8	6.5	63.5	5.5	2.5	60,215	63.6	44.9	5.7	12.9	36.4	29.2	44.6
24045	Wicomico County, Maryland.......	8.8	5.8	63.8	10.0	5.2	40,577	63.0	43.2	3.6	16.2	37.0	28.4	42.1
24510	Baltimore city, Maryland..............	6.2	6.0	65.8	8.0	3.8	254,370	48.2	23.9	4.4	19.9	51.8	42.4	36.8
25000	**MASSACHUSETTS**	11.2	12.8	59.4	17.6	7.8	2,759,018	62.3	46.0	4.5	11.9	37.7	28.5	42.4
25001	Barnstable County, Massachusetts	6.6	3.6	58.3	10.2	5.1	104,733	63.7	48.7	3.4	11.6	36.3	30.0	62.8
25003	Berkshire County, Massachusetts	7.2	5.5	62.5	5.9	2.0	57,765	58.9	45.7	4.7	8.5	41.1	33.1	51.7
25005	Bristol County, Massachusetts.....	9.6	9.3	64.8	13.6	5.4	233,531	64.6	44.5	5.3	14.8	35.4	28.4	42.8
25009	Essex County, Massachusetts	12.2	23.3	62.4	18.6	8.6	309,972	66.4	46.9	5.4	14.1	33.6	27.1	44.7
25011	Franklin County, Massachusetts ..	5.6	4.7	69.0	4.8	2.3	30,374	60.8	43.2	6.3	11.3	39.2	32.6	52.6
25013	Hampden County, Massachusetts	17.8	27.3	63.2	9.7	3.6	184,544	61.8	38.9	5.6	17.3	38.2	29.7	43.5
25015	Hampshire County, Massachusetts	7.5	6.4	61.0	8.3	3.4	60,870	58.3	46.3	3.5	8.5	41.7	29.5	46.5
25017	Middlesex County, Massachusetts	9.6	8.6	52.6	22.5	10.8	632,831	62.6	50.0	3.6	9.0	37.4	27.0	39.1
25021	Norfolk County, Massachusetts ...	7.6	5.5	59.9	19.0	7.8	280,067	64.9	51.6	4.2	9.1	35.1	26.6	42.7
25023	Plymouth County, Massachusetts	8.9	4.5	74.5	10.3	3.4	202,084	69.3	52.3	4.7	12.4	30.7	24.2	47.9
25025	Suffolk County, Massachusetts....	19.2	23.8	42.5	29.7	14.9	315,257	46.6	29.2	4.1	13.3	53.4	37.2	32.6
25027	Worcester County, Massachusetts	10.6	12.8	65.4	13.4	6.1	333,435	66.0	48.7	4.9	12.4	34.0	26.5	41.4
26000	**MICHIGAN**	7.0	5.6	76.2	6.8	3.2	4,051,798	62.9	46.3	5.0	11.6	37.1	30.2	42.9
26005	Allegan County, Michigan..........	7.2	7.9	80.9	2.9	1.6	44,479	74.9	60.5	4.9	9.4	25.1	20.1	43.3
26017	Bay County, Michigan................	7.7	5.8	88.8	1.3	0.1	45,487	57.0	44.1	4.4	8.5	43.0	35.2	47.4
26021	Berrien County, Michigan...........	6.4	6.1	58.4	5.3	2.6	65,764	61.6	45.9	4.3	11.4	38.4	32.1	48.4
26025	Calhoun County, Michigan	9.4	5.8	78.1	3.6	1.8	53,482	64.3	45.6	7.5	11.2	35.7	30.6	43.0
26037	Clinton County, Michigan	5.4	4.9	84.6	2.3	1.1	30,952	69.0	57.6	4.5	6.9	31.0	22.9	40.4
26045	Eaton County, Michigan..............	8.1	5.9	81.2	5.5	1.9	45,137	62.5	47.6	4.6	10.2	37.5	30.5	44.9
26049	Genesee County, Michigan	5.1	3.9	83.1	3.0	1.1	167,895	60.7	41.6	4.2	14.9	39.3	32.6	44.1
26055	Grand Traverse County, Michigan	3.7	3.2	74.9	2.1	0.5	40,083	63.7	49.7	4.6	9.3	36.3	28.2	45.0
26065	Ingham County, Michigan...........	10.6	8.2	73.3	8.8	4.1	115,752	52.6	37.1	4.3	11.2	47.4	35.2	34.0
26067	Ionia County, Michigan...............	6.0	5.2	89.2	1.5	0.3	23,531	65.9	48.7	7.6	9.5	34.1	27.1	39.9
26075	Jackson County, Michigan...........	7.4	3.9	84.3	1.3	0.7	61,937	62.3	44.9	6.5	10.9	37.7	32.7	45.1
26077	Kalamazoo County, Michigan	7.2	5.6	75.9	5.0	2.0	105,642	56.4	42.1	4.4	9.9	43.6	32.6	36.7
26081	Kent County, Michigan	10.2	11.3	74.3	8.6	4.6	253,092	65.2	49.8	4.8	10.6	34.8	26.9	35.6
26087	Lapeer County, Michigan	4.9	5.1	85.6	2.4	1.3	34,447	70.8	57.4	4.3	9.0	29.2	25.4	47.5
26091	Lenawee County, Michigan.........	8.2	8.6	74.5	3.1	1.1	38,963	65.3	50.3	4.0	11.0	34.7	29.6	44.7
26093	Livingston County, Michigan.......	4.4	2.8	81.4	2.6	0.9	75,370	73.4	62.4	3.2	7.8	26.6	21.1	44.7
26099	Macomb County, Michigan.........	5.6	2.9	77.8	11.3	3.1	358,011	64.1	46.2	5.7	12.3	35.9	29.6	43.5
26103	Marquette County, Michigan	5.2	1.7	78.2	2.1	0.8	27,290	57.8	46.3	5.2	6.4	42.2	32.5	44.3
26111	Midland County, Michigan..........	5.4	3.3	78.7	3.7	1.4	35,453	64.8	50.3	3.5	11.1	35.2	29.7	42.3
26115	Monroe County, Michigan	6.8	4.0	62.0	2.1	0.8	61,574	65.2	50.8	5.8	8.7	34.8	29.2	47.0
26117	Montcalm County, Michigan........	4.1	3.9	87.8	1.8	1.2	23,745	70.1	52.3	5.1	12.7	29.9	24.2	45.3
26121	Muskegon County, Michigan	8.4	6.2	85.7	1.4	0.5	67,707	67.4	47.1	5.8	14.4	32.6	25.5	44.5
26125	Oakland County, Michigan..........	7.6	4.7	70.7	12.2	5.5	530,383	63.6	49.3	4.3	10.0	36.4	30.0	40.9
26139	Ottawa County, Michigan..........	7.2	10.4	79.4	5.2	2.2	110,045	70.4	59.0	3.8	7.7	29.6	21.9	38.2
26145	Saginaw County, Michigan	7.0	9.2	84.8	2.1	1.1	80,146	60.2	41.3	3.5	15.4	39.8	32.1	44.6
26147	St. Clair County, Michigan	4.6	3.7	86.5	2.0	0.9	66,324	67.8	48.9	6.8	12.1	32.2	25.7	44.3
26155	Shiawassee County, Michigan	3.1	3.0	86.9	1.2	0.6	28,226	64.1	47.0	8.2	8.8	35.9	30.2	44.6
26159	Van Buren County, Michigan.......	11.2	12.3	71.3	5.3	4.0	28,457	69.3	53.4	5.1	10.9	30.7	24.5	48.4
26161	Washtenaw County, Michigan	8.0	5.2	60.6	12.2	6.5	149,133	57.0	44.3	3.3	9.4	43.0	29.7	36.1
26163	Wayne County, Michigan............	7.0	6.5	75.9	9.6	3.6	695,038	60.5	36.4	6.2	17.8	39.5	33.8	42.0
27000	**MINNESOTA**	6.9	5.8	67.7	8.5	3.7	2,281,033	62.6	49.2	4.5	8.9	37.4	29.1	39.7
27003	Anoka County, Minnesota	6.0	5.3	70.3	9.8	3.7	135,265	69.2	55.5	4.1	9.6	30.8	24.3	40.3
27013	Blue Earth County, Minnesota.....	5.9	4.3	77.5	5.6	2.1	27,604	57.2	45.3	4.8	7.1	42.8	25.2	32.8
27019	Carver County, Minnesota	6.2	4.5	68.0	4.7	1.8	40,141	73.8	59.9	4.3	9.6	26.2	19.2	35.1

Table A-2. Counties — Who: Age, Race/Ethnicity, and Household Structure, 2021—*Continued*

	STATE County	Total population	Percent change, 2010–2019	Population by age (percent)					Median age	Race alone or in combination (percent)					
				Under 18 years	18 to 24 years	25 to 44 years	45 to 64 years	65 years and over		White	Black or African American	American Indian and Alaska Native	Asian	Native Hawaiian or Other Pacific Islander	Some other race
STATE County code	ACS table number:	B01003	Population Estimates	B01001	B01001	B01001	B01001	B01001	B01002	B02008	B02009	B02010	B02011	B02012	B02013
	Column number:	1	2	3	4	5	6	7	8	9	10	11	12	13	14
	MINNESOTA—Cont.														
27027	Clay County, Minnesota............	65,574	8.9	24.8	12.7	26.7	21.7	14.1	35.0	92.2	4.2	4.4	2.3	-	3.4
27035	Crow Wing County, Minnesota...	67,270	4.1	21.1	6.6	22.3	26.6	23.4	45.0	97.9	1.6	1.3	1.0	-	2.9
27037	Dakota County, Minnesota	442,038	7.6	24.2	7.6	27.0	26.0	15.3	38.5	82.9	9.9	1.4	6.5	0.1	7.8
27053	Hennepin County, Minnesota.....	1,267,416	9.8	21.8	8.3	30.7	24.2	15.1	37.4	75.4	15.8	2.1	8.7	0.1	7.2
27109	Olmsted County, Minnesota.......	163,436	9.7	24.4	8.9	27.3	23.8	15.7	37.5	83.9	8.7	0.9	7.2	-	5.2
27123	Ramsey County, Minnesota........	543,257	8.2	23.3	9.4	29.6	22.5	15.3	35.8	67.6	15.3	1.9	16.6	0.2	7.6
27131	Rice County, Minnesota	67,262	4.4	21.4	14.1	23.7	24.5	16.2	38.9	87.7	6.5	3.6	1.9		7.9
27137	St. Louis County, Minnesota.......	199,182	-0.6	18.9	12.8	22.9	24.9	20.6	41.3	94.6	2.5	3.6	1.7	-	2.6
27139	Scott County, Minnesota............	153,268	14.7	26.1	8.0	27.3	26.9	11.7	37.4	83.1	7.2	1.5	7.8	-	6.2
27141	Sherburne County, Minnesota	99,074	9.9	25.7	7.9	27.2	26.8	12.4	38.6	94.6	2.1	3.8	2.2	-	5.4
27145	Stearns County, Minnesota........	158,947	6.9	23.5	15.0	23.3	22.7	15.4	34.2	86.8	10.2	0.8	2.9	-	3.7
27163	Washington County, Minnesota..	272,256	10.2	24.2	7.8	24.9	27.1	15.9	40.0	84.8	6.8	1.2	8.3	0.1	4.9
27171	Wright County, Minnesota..........	144,845	11.0	27.1	7.2	25.8	26.3	13.7	38.6	95.8	3.7	0.8	2.2		4.1
28000	**MISSISSIPPI**	2,949,965	0.5	23.5	9.8	25.1	24.8	16.8	38.6	60.8	37.7	2.3	1.6	0.2	3.1
28033	DeSoto County, Mississippi	188,633	14.7	25.1	8.7	27.4	25.1	13.8	37.5	63.9	33.2	0.6	2.2	-	5.7
28035	Forrest County, Mississippi	77,875	-0.0	22.9	17.7	22.5	22.9	13.9	33.0	64.6	35.6	2.7	1.6	-	3.1
28047	Harrison County, Mississippi.......	209,396	11.2	23.7	9.0	26.2	24.8	16.3	37.5	72.6	24.9	4.6	4.8	0.7	5.1
28049	Hinds County, Mississippi............	222,679	-5.5	23.7	10.4	26.4	23.8	15.7	36.7	25.6	74.0	1.4	0.8	-	1.2
28059	Jackson County, Mississippi........	143,987	2.8	23.0	7.1	26.1	27.5	16.4	39.9	74.9	19.9	4.0	2.9	-	5.7
28067	Jones County, Mississippi	66,744	0.5	23.8	10.6	22.6	25.0	17.9	40.2	69.5	28.6	-	-	-	4.3
28073	Lamar County, Mississippi	65,353	13.8	24.7	8.1	28.1	25.3	13.9	37.0	75.5	24.5	1.3	4.1	-	1.8
28075	Lauderdale County, Mississippi....	72,088	-7.6	23.4	7.7	25.7	25.1	18.1	40.4	54.8	45.2	1.6	1.3	-	3.1
28081	Lee County, Mississippi	82,883	3.0	25.3	7.8	26.8	24.7	15.4	37.9	66.8	32.3	0.4	0.6	-	3.3
28089	Madison County, Mississippi	109,813	11.6	23.5	9.1	26.9	26.4	14.2	39.6	60.3	37.2	1.2	3.0	-	3.2
28121	Rankin County, Mississippi	158,096	9.6	22.7	8.0	27.9	24.8	16.6	39.1	75.3	21.8	2.2	1.6	-	2.8
29000	**MISSOURI**	6,168,187	2.1	22.4	9.0	25.9	25.0	17.6	39.2	84.7	12.4	2.2	2.8	0.3	5.6
29019	Boone County, Missouri..............	185,840	11.0	20.6	17.8	27.4	20.9	13.3	32.6	84.0	12.2	1.2	6.0	-	2.8
29021	Buchanan County, Missouri.........	83,853	-2.1	22.5	9.1	26.8	24.8	16.8	38.5	88.4	8.0	2.4	2.4	-	6.1
29031	Cape Girardeau County, Missouri	82,113	4.2	21.4	13.6	25.1	22.6	17.2	36.7	91.7	6.3	4.9	2.3	-	3.4
29037	Cass County, Missouri................	109,638	6.3	24.0	7.6	24.6	26.0	17.8	39.8	92.6	5.9	1.3	1.3	1.3	6.2
29043	Christian County, Missouri..........	91,499	14.4	24.9	7.5	25.8	26.4	16.4	40.2	97.1	2.3	1.3	1.2	1.1	2.8
29047	Clay County, Missouri................	255,518	12.6	23.8	7.6	29.0	24.9	14.8	37.5	86.4	9.8	1.8	3.2	-	6.8
29051	Cole County, Missouri................	77,205	1.0	22.2	8.5	27.2	24.5	17.6	39.4	86.3	11.5	3.4	2.0	-	3.7
29071	Franklin County, Missouri...........	105,231	2.4	22.6	7.3	23.7	27.7	18.7	42.5	97.8	1.7	0.9	1.5	-	7.7
29077	Greene County, Missouri............	300,865	6.5	20.8	13.3	26.1	22.9	17.0	36.5	94.0	2.7	4.0	2.7	-	4.0
29095	Jackson County, Missouri	716,862	4.3	23.3	8.2	28.6	24.1	15.8	37.0	70.2	25.0	2.1	2.8	0.6	8.7
29097	Jasper County, Missouri	123,155	3.3	24.7	9.3	26.7	23.3	16.0	37.0	92.4	2.8	3.7	2.0	1.3	7.7
29099	Jefferson County, Missouri	227,771	2.9	22.8	7.3	26.1	27.6	16.2	40.4	97.0	2.1	1.0	1.3	-	10.4
29165	Platte County, Missouri	108,569	16.9	23.4	7.9	27.5	25.8	15.5	38.8	87.5	9.7	2.2	3.7	-	6.5
29183	St. Charles County, Missouri.......	409,981	11.5	22.8	8.2	26.6	26.2	16.3	39.7	92.1	4.7	2.6	3.6	0.2	4.7
29187	St. Francois County, Missouri	67,541	2.8	21.2	7.3	27.4	26.7	17.4	41.0	96.5	3.1	2.5	2.0	-	1.5
29189	St. Louis County, Missouri	997,187	-0.5	22.1	8.2	25.4	25.4	18.8	40.3	69.3	26.2	0.9	5.7	0.1	6.3
29510	St. Louis city, Missouri...............	293,310	-5.9	18.4	8.5	34.4	23.7	15.0	36.8	50.7	45.4	1.2	4.2	-	4.7
30000	**MONTANA**	1,104,271	6.2	21.3	9.3	25.4	24.4	19.7	40.1	91.3	1.0	8.3	1.5	0.2	4.3
30013	Cascade County, Montana..........	84,511	0.0	22.7	8.5	26.0	23.6	19.3	38.6	90.5	2.9	6.7	1.9	-	6.6
30029	Flathead County, Montana..........	108,454	14.2	21.7	6.3	25.2	26.0	20.8	43.0	98.0	0.4	4.0	0.8	-	5.2
30031	Gallatin County, Montana..........	122,713	27.8	19.2	15.7	30.7	20.9	13.4	34.2	94.8	0.7	2.2	2.7	-	5.6
30049	Lewis and Clark County, Montana	72,223	9.5	20.6	8.1	25.6	25.9	19.8	40.6	96.8	0.8	4.2	1.1	-	2.9
30063	Missoula County, Montana	119,533	9.4	18.4	12.7	30.1	22.2	16.6	37.4	93.2	1.0	4.2	2.9	-	3.6
30111	Yellowstone County, Montana	167,146	9.0	23.4	7.7	26.8	24.3	17.8	38.0	92.0	1.3	6.2	1.6	0.2	5.1
31000	**NEBRASKA**	1,963,692	5.1	24.6	9.6	26.0	23.4	16.4	37.2	86.8	6.3	2.4	3.4	0.2	10.1
31055	Douglas County, Nebraska.........	585,008	10.5	25.3	9.1	28.9	23.0	13.7	35.5	79.0	12.9	2.1	5.2	0.2	11.6
31109	Lancaster County, Nebraska.......	324,514	11.8	22.5	15.1	26.2	21.6	14.7	34.2	88.7	5.9	2.0	5.6	-	6.3
31153	Sarpy County, Nebraska.............	193,418	17.9	26.8	8.1	29.3	23.4	12.4	36.1	87.7	5.8	1.7	4.2	0.2	8.8

							Household type (percent of all households)							
							Family households					Nonfamily households		Percent of households with people age 60 years and over
STATE County	Two or more races (percent)	Hispanic or Latino (percent)	Native, born in state of residence (percent)	Foreign born (percent)	Non-citizens (percent)	Total households	Total	Married couple	Male householder	Female householder	Total	One-person households	
ACS table number:	B02001	B03003	B05002	B05002	B05002	B11001	B11001	B11001	B11001	B11001	B11001	B11001	B11006
STATE County code / Column number:	15	16	17	18	19	20	21	22	23	24	25	26	27
MINNESOTA—Cont.													
27027 Clay County, Minnesota..............	6.8	5.0	45.0	4.2	2.8	26,236	59.5	47.6	4.5	7.3	40.5	33.2	34.1
27035 Crow Wing County, Minnesota...	4.4	1.7	76.1	1.5	0.6	27,753	67.3	54.6	5.6	7.1	32.7	26.3	49.4
27037 Dakota County, Minnesota.........	7.8	7.8	64.2	10.0	3.4	170,696	67.7	53.8	5.1	8.9	32.3	25.1	39.1
27053 Hennepin County, Minnesota......	8.5	7.1	56.7	13.8	6.1	532,149	54.9	42.5	4.3	8.2	45.1	33.5	35.6
27109 Olmsted County, Minnesota........	5.6	5.5	60.3	10.3	3.6	65,122	63.1	52.0	3.2	7.8	36.9	29.0	35.1
27123 Ramsey County, Minnesota........	8.2	7.7	59.8	15.7	5.3	218,817	56.4	40.3	4.1	11.9	43.6	34.3	37.8
27131 Rice County, Minnesota	7.3	9.0	69.4	7.9	5.7	23,779	68.3	50.6	5.3	12.5	31.7	25.6	41.3
27137 St. Louis County, Minnesota........	5.0	1.9	76.8	2.1	1.1	85,576	56.1	42.5	4.5	9.2	43.9	32.8	43.2
27139 Scott County, Minnesota.............	5.5	5.8	69.9	10.8	4.3	55,327	77.5	63.8	5.0	8.8	22.5	17.4	33.0
27141 Sherburne County, Minnesota	8.2	3.1	81.8	2.8	1.0	34,738	71.6	57.3	4.3	10.0	28.4	22.0	35.9
27145 Stearns County, Minnesota	4.5	3.9	77.6	7.3	4.2	62,168	62.2	48.5	5.0	8.7	37.8	27.7	36.1
27163 Washington County, Minnesota..	5.8	4.8	67.4	9.0	2.9	102,421	73.3	59.2	4.2	9.9	26.7	20.8	39.4
27171 Wright County, Minnesota..........	6.6	3.4	80.0	1.8	0.8	52,260	71.9	60.2	3.2	8.4	28.1	20.3	34.3
28000 **MISSISSIPPI**	5.1	3.2	71.5	2.1	1.2	1,129,611	65.8	44.2	4.7	16.9	34.2	29.7	43.1
28033 DeSoto County, Mississippi	5.5	5.3	36.1	3.9	1.8	68,966	69.8	52.7	5.1	12.0	30.2	26.4	38.2
28035 Forrest County, Mississippi	7.9	3.3	73.2	2.9	2.4	30,600	60.5	38.0	6.3	16.2	39.5	31.7	34.5
28047 Harrison County, Mississippi........	10.8	5.7	54.2	4.2	1.6	81,224	66.9	45.3	4.9	16.7	33.1	28.9	43.5
28049 Hinds County, Mississippi..........	2.4	1.6	79.5	2.0	1.4	91,067	60.5	31.5	5.3	23.8	39.5	34.8	38.8
28059 Jackson County, Mississippi.........	6.6	7.2	58.7	3.4	1.7	56,984	66.9	47.0	5.0	14.9	33.1	27.0	39.5
28067 Jones County, Mississippi	5.3	4.8	79.1	3.8	2.9	23,506	64.6	44.0	4.3	16.3	35.4	30.0	50.4
28073 Lamar County, Mississippi	6.6	1.2	68.2	1.8	0.8	25,688	75.4	58.1	4.2	13.0	24.6	20.2	33.4
28075 Lauderdale County, Mississippi....	5.8	2.4	77.1	1.5	0.3	28,212	64.8	43.1	3.1	18.6	35.2	32.2	46.1
28081 Lee County, Mississippi	3.4	3.2	76.9	1.5	0.3	32,722	73.0	54.8	5.1	13.1	27.0	24.1	44.0
28089 Madison County, Mississippi	4.7	3.2	74.2	4.9	2.8	42,558	73.9	50.0	6.8	17.1	26.1	20.1	36.1
28121 Rankin County, Mississippi	3.8	2.7	74.8	1.8	0.9	59,894	70.6	56.1	2.9	11.6	29.4	23.9	41.4
29000 **MISSOURI**	7.6	4.6	65.9	4.1	2.1	2,468,726	63.0	47.7	4.4	11.0	37.0	30.1	41.5
29019 Boone County, Missouri.............	5.9	3.7	60.1	6.3	3.0	75,036	55.0	43.7	2.6	8.8	45.0	32.9	32.6
29021 Buchanan County, Missouri.........	6.7	7.1	70.3	3.7	2.4	33,334	55.8	39.8	3.9	12.1	44.2	33.9	39.3
29031 Cape Girardeau County, Missouri	7.7	2.6	71.4	2.1	1.3	32,800	61.6	46.3	6.1	9.2	38.4	30.3	42.5
29037 Cass County, Missouri..................	8.2	5.0	61.9	1.5	0.5	42,361	70.6	54.5	5.3	10.8	29.4	25.9	41.9
29043 Christian County, Missouri...........	5.9	3.5	60.1	1.7	0.8	34,116	70.8	59.5	5.3	6.1	29.2	23.2	41.5
29047 Clay County, Missouri...................	7.5	7.5	59.9	5.9	2.1	100,737	67.1	52.3	3.8	11.0	32.9	27.0	35.3
29051 Cole County, Missouri..................	6.5	3.2	77.3	1.8	0.2	29,522	62.0	47.1	2.3	12.6	38.0	32.8	43.6
29071 Franklin County, Missouri............	9.7	2.0	77.4	1.1	0.5	41,301	67.3	54.2	4.8	8.2	32.7	25.7	47.4
29077 Greene County, Missouri.............	7.3	4.2	60.0	3.7	2.0	130,986	57.9	44.3	2.7	10.9	42.1	31.7	35.7
29095 Jackson County, Missouri............	8.8	9.7	59.2	5.7	3.6	302,965	58.4	40.8	3.9	13.8	41.6	32.6	37.6
29097 Jasper County, Missouri	9.0	8.8	60.4	4.4	2.5	47,864	66.0	48.1	4.3	13.6	34.0	24.8	41.2
29099 Jefferson County, Missouri	11.5	2.3	80.3	1.9	0.6	88,806	70.7	53.7	6.4	10.6	29.3	22.9	40.1
29165 Platte County, Missouri	9.3	6.8	47.7	7.3	2.4	43,201	69.4	56.2	3.9	9.3	30.6	25.6	37.8
29183 St. Charles County, Missouri	7.7	3.6	68.4	4.5	1.8	157,907	71.2	58.2	4.9	8.1	28.8	22.5	39.7
29187 St. Francois County, Missouri	5.6	0.7	80.5	1.7	0.5	25,030	63.1	45.1	7.3	10.7	36.9	33.0	42.5
29189 St. Louis County, Missouri	8.1	3.1	67.8	7.2	3.1	412,833	62.1	45.4	4.2	12.4	37.9	32.0	43.1
29510 St. Louis city, Missouri................	5.8	4.4	67.7	6.2	2.8	139,736	42.2	22.6	4.4	15.2	57.8	47.5	34.0
30000 **MONTANA**	6.3	4.3	53.4	2.2	1.0	448,949	61.4	48.8	4.5	8.1	38.6	29.2	44.3
30013 Cascade County, Montana..........	8.4	5.2	55.7	1.7	0.6	34,303	61.2	51.7	3.3	6.2	38.8	33.3	43.3
30029 Flathead County, Montana..........	8.1	3.4	44.6	2.7	1.2	42,900	67.0	55.1	3.7	8.2	33.0	23.8	46.9
30031 Gallatin County, Montana..........	5.8	4.5	39.1	4.5	2.3	48,796	54.4	48.3	1.9	4.3	45.6	24.4	30.3
30049 Lewis and Clark County, Montana	5.6	3.8	55.3	1.2	0.5	31,208	61.5	44.6	7.4	9.5	38.5	32.1	44.5
30063 Missoula County, Montana	4.9	3.8	45.2	2.9	1.2	51,957	56.5	42.2	4.4	9.9	43.5	28.8	37.5
30111 Yellowstone County, Montana	6.2	6.3	58.7	2.1	1.4	69,001	64.4	48.7	7.1	8.6	35.6	27.1	41.2
31000 **NEBRASKA**	8.7	11.9	64.7	7.4	4.3	785,982	63.0	49.8	4.3	8.9	37.0	30.4	38.6
31055 Douglas County, Nebraska.........	10.4	13.5	60.0	9.7	5.7	236,106	60.2	44.8	4.5	11.0	39.8	32.6	33.7
31109 Lancaster County, Nebraska........	8.2	7.8	65.6	7.5	4.2	131,417	58.4	46.1	3.7	8.7	41.6	32.3	34.0
31153 Sarpy County, Nebraska..............	8.0	11.0	55.7	6.0	2.6	72,428	70.7	56.5	4.6	9.5	29.3	23.2	33.1

Table A-2. Counties — Who: Age, Race/Ethnicity, and Household Structure, 2021—*Continued*

				Population by age (percent)						Race alone or in combination (percent)					
	STATE County	Total population	Percent change, 2010–2019	Under 18 years	18 to 24 years	25 to 44 years	45 to 64 years	65 years and over	Median age	White	Black or African American	American Indian and Alaska Native	Asian	Native Hawaiian or Other Pacific Islander	Some other race
STATE County code	ACS table number:	B01003	Population Estimates	B01001	B01001	B01001	B01001	B01001	B01002	B02008	B02009	B02010	B02011	B02012	B02013
	Column number:	1	2	3	4	5	6	7	8	9	10	11	12	13	14
32000	**NEVADA**	3,143,991	11.0	22.2	8.1	28.2	25.1	16.5	38.7	65.7	11.9	3.2	11.3	1.5	25.2
32003	Clark County, Nevada	2,292,476	16.2	22.7	8.1	28.8	25.0	15.4	38.1	60.3	15.2	2.7	13.4	1.8	26.6
32031	Washoe County, Nevada	493,392	11.9	21.2	8.6	28.2	24.8	17.2	38.8	76.1	3.6	3.2	7.8	1.1	23.6
33000	**NEW HAMPSHIRE**	1,388,992	2.0	18.4	9.0	24.8	28.5	19.3	43.1	94.1	2.7	1.2	3.5	0.1	5.2
33005	Cheshire County, New Hampshire	77,329	-1.3	17.9	11.0	23.2	26.9	21.0	42.8	97.6	2.1	1.3	2.0	-	2.4
33009	Grafton County, New Hampshire	92,201	0.9	16.0	13.1	22.3	26.5	22.1	43.0	93.2	1.8	1.1	4.7		3.3
33011	Hillsborough County, New Hampshire	424,079	4.1	19.9	8.4	26.9	27.9	16.9	41.0	90.1	4.6	1.0	5.4	0.2	8.2
33013	Merrimack County, New Hampshire	155,238	3.4	18.4	8.8	25.7	27.9	19.1	42.9	95.9	2.5	1.2	3.0	-	3.3
33015	Rockingham County, New Hampshire	316,947	4.9	18.8	7.3	24.3	30.4	19.1	44.5	95.3	1.5	0.7	2.9		5.5
33017	Strafford County, New Hampshire	132,416	6.1	17.2	15.7	25.3	25.8	16.0	37.7	95.5	2.1	3.2	2.5	-	4.9
34000	**NEW JERSEY**	9,267,130	2.4	21.8	8.3	26.0	27.0	16.9	40.3	65.2	15.5	1.3	11.1	0.2	19.7
34001	Atlantic County, New Jersey	274,966	-4.0	20.9	8.7	23.7	27.5	19.2	42.2	67.1	17.1	1.8	9.2	-	17.8
34003	Bergen County, New Jersey	953,819	3.0	21.0	8.0	24.9	28.3	17.8	42.2	67.7	8.2	1.3	18.2	0.1	18.9
34005	Burlington County, New Jersey	464,269	-0.8	20.6	8.1	25.6	28.1	17.7	41.8	72.4	19.9	1.4	7.1	0.1	8.7
34007	Camden County, New Jersey	523,771	-1.4	22.7	8.0	27.2	25.9	16.2	38.6	61.4	21.9	1.4	7.4	0.2	16.9
34009	Cape May County, New Jersey	95,661	-5.4	16.9	5.7	20.8	29.0	27.6	51.6	90.9	6.1	1.0	1.4	-	7.4
34011	Cumberland County, New Jersey	153,627	-4.7	24.2	8.2	26.7	25.0	15.9	37.7	66.3	23.6	2.4	2.0	-	28.6
34013	Essex County, New Jersey	854,917	1.9	23.7	8.5	27.6	26.1	14.2	38.1	37.7	40.9	1.2	7.1	0.1	25.3
34015	Gloucester County, New Jersey	304,477	1.2	21.5	8.8	25.5	27.6	16.7	41.0	81.6	12.4	0.6	4.1	0.2	7.2
34017	Hudson County, New Jersey	702,463	6.0	20.3	7.2	36.9	23.0	12.6	36.1	53.5	15.8	1.8	17.5	-	37.9
34019	Hunterdon County, New Jersey	129,924	-3.1	18.4	7.8	22.4	31.7	19.7	46.4	89.3	3.9	1.2	4.8	-	8.0
34021	Mercer County, New Jersey	385,898	0.3	21.2	11.1	25.1	26.7	16.0	39.8	58.8	22.1	1.0	14.0	0.1	15.0
34023	Middlesex County, New Jersey	860,807	1.9	21.6	9.1	26.9	26.6	15.9	39.5	50.2	12.5	1.9	26.1	0.3	19.8
34025	Monmouth County, New Jersey	645,354	-1.8	20.8	8.4	22.6	29.6	18.7	43.7	82.9	7.8	1.0	6.5	-	11.0
34027	Morris County, New Jersey	510,981	-0.1	20.6	8.3	24.3	29.1	17.8	42.7	78.7	4.5	0.5	12.2	-	14.6
34029	Ocean County, New Jersey	648,998	5.3	24.7	7.4	21.4	24.2	22.3	41.5	90.8	4.6	0.9	2.6	0.3	8.2
34031	Passaic County, New Jersey	518,117	0.1	23.7	9.4	26.1	25.5	15.3	38.0	62.6	12.7	1.5	6.6	0.3	40.1
34033	Salem County, New Jersey	65,046	-5.6	21.8	8.1	22.8	28.1	19.2	43.0	78.4	16.9	0.5	1.6	1.3	8.8
34035	Somerset County, New Jersey	345,647	1.7	21.3	8.1	24.3	29.6	16.6	42.2	61.3	11.5	1.4	21.3	0.2	14.3
34037	Sussex County, New Jersey	145,543	-5.9	19.3	7.6	23.6	30.8	18.7	44.3	92.5	3.4	1.7	2.2	-	10.7
34039	Union County, New Jersey	572,114	3.7	23.4	8.2	26.4	27.0	14.9	39.2	52.1	23.0	1.2	6.2	0.2	31.9
34041	Warren County, New Jersey	110,731	-3.2	19.2	7.9	23.1	31.1	18.7	44.8	87.3	6.9	0.6	3.7	-	10.7
35000	**NEW MEXICO**	2,115,877	1.4	22.3	9.1	26.2	23.9	18.5	39.1	71.4	3.5	12.8	2.7	0.3	38.5
35001	Bernalillo County, New Mexico	674,393	2.5	20.9	9.0	28.2	24.5	17.4	39.3	76.1	4.7	8.7	4.8	0.5	37.5
35013	Doña Ana County, New Mexico	221,508	4.3	23.5	13.8	25.4	20.9	16.3	34.6	64.0	2.8	3.5	1.6	-	56.7
35025	Lea County, New Mexico	73,004	9.8	30.3	8.5	31.9	18.0	11.3	32.2	81.1	4.6	2.5	0.6	-	55.8
35031	McKinley County, New Mexico	71,780	-0.2	27.2	8.9	28.1	23.3	12.5	33.4	13.9	1.4	84.0	1.3	-	12.1
35035	Otero County, New Mexico	68,537	5.8	22.5	10.3	27.2	22.2	17.8	37.0	78.3	5.1	8.2	3.6		34.9
35043	Sandoval County, New Mexico	151,369	11.5	22.1	7.5	26.0	25.1	19.3	40.3	73.5	4.4	17.0	3.3	0.4	29.9
35045	San Juan County, New Mexico	120,993	-4.7	25.4	9.0	25.3	24.2	16.1	36.9	44.6	0.9	42.6	0.9	-	18.4
35049	Santa Fe County, New Mexico	155,201	4.3	16.8	7.0	23.2	26.3	26.7	47.9	77.3	1.6	5.5	2.3	-	41.4
35061	Valencia County, New Mexico	77,190	0.2	22.6	8.4	27.5	22.5	19.0	38.9	80.8	1.6	12.5	1.6	-	49.8
36000	**NEW YORK**	19,835,913	2.4	20.7	8.8	27.0	26.0	17.5	39.8	64.0	17.6	1.8	9.9	0.2	18.2
36001	Albany County, New York	313,743	0.4	18.1	13.7	26.3	24.0	17.8	38.6	76.9	14.7	1.1	8.3	0.4	6.4
36005	Bronx County, New York	1,424,948	2.4	24.5	9.4	28.1	24.0	14.0	35.6	22.3	39.8	4.0	4.9	0.3	48.6
36007	Broome County, New York	197,240	-5.0	19.3	13.3	22.5	25.1	19.8	40.3	87.3	8.7	0.9	5.4	-	4.0
36009	Cattaraugus County, New York	76,426	-5.2	21.4	9.5	21.5	27.1	20.5	42.1	94.3	2.7	4.8	0.4	-	4.0
36011	Cayuga County, New York	75,880	-4.3	18.8	7.2	25.1	28.3	20.6	44.2	92.4	4.9	1.9	1.1	-	5.3
36013	Chautauqua County, New York	126,807	-5.9	20.1	8.6	23.1	27.4	20.8	43.2	92.6	5.2	2.1	0.9	-	6.6
36015	Chemung County, New York	83,045	-6.0	20.5	7.4	25.6	27.1	19.4	42.1	90.8	8.7	0.8	2.1	-	3.8
36019	Clinton County, New York	79,596	-2.0	18.1	12.3	25.3	26.3	18.0	40.6	93.5	4.6	1.7	1.1	-	3.3
36027	Dutchess County, New York	297,112	-1.1	18.4	10.4	24.2	28.4	18.6	42.6	80.2	12.7	1.9	4.6	0.2	12.5
36029	Erie County, New York	950,683	-0.0	20.2	8.9	26.3	25.9	18.8	40.3	79.9	14.6	1.2	4.9	0.1	5.8

STATE County							Household type (percent of all households)						Percent of households with people age 60 years and over
							Family households				Nonfamily households		
	Two or more races (percent)	Hispanic or Latino (percent)	Native, born in state of residence (percent)	Foreign born (percent)	Non-citizens (percent)	Total house-holds	Total	Married couple	Male house-holder	Female house-holder	Total	One-person house-holds	
ACS table number:	B02001	B03003	B05002	B05002	B05002	B11001	B11001	B11001	B11001	B11001	B11001	B11001	B11006
Column number:	15	16	17	18	19	20	21	22	23	24	25	26	27
NEVADA	17.5	29.9	27.2	18.4	9.8	1,191,380	63.3	43.8	6.7	12.7	36.7	28.0	41.3
32003 Clark County, Nevada	18.5	32.3	25.0	21.3	9.7	854,289	63.4	42.6	6.8	14.0	36.6	28.2	39.8
32031 Washoe County, Nevada	14.5	25.9	34.5	13.4	6.8	198,018	60.4	43.7	6.6	10.1	39.6	27.9	41.0
NEW HAMPSHIRE	6.4	4.3	40.6	5.9	2.7	548,026	65.9	52.3	4.7	8.9	34.1	25.9	45.8
33005 Cheshire County, New Hampshire	4.7	2.3	42.0	2.5	0.8	28,266	60.4	49.1	2.2	9.2	39.6	30.9	52.3
33009 Grafton County, New Hampshire	4.1	2.7	41.1	5.8	2.8	35,199	60.3	46.7	4.0	9.6	39.7	31.3	49.8
33011 Hillsborough County, New Hampshire	9.0	7.9	40.4	9.8	3.8	167,899	66.0	51.6	5.4	8.9	34.0	25.1	41.7
33013 Merrimack County, New Hampshire	5.3	2.5	55.3	3.6	1.7	58,733	67.1	50.1	6.8	10.2	32.9	25.0	46.4
33015 Rockingham County, New Hampshire	5.8	3.6	31.3	5.2	1.8	127,882	69.7	56.5	3.6	9.6	30.3	23.2	46.1
33017 Strafford County, New Hampshire	8.1	3.0	43.5	3.8	1.6	52,067	65.0	52.7	5.9	6.5	35.0	24.3	39.1
NEW JERSEY	12.1	21.5	51.5	23.0	9.7	3,497,945	68.0	50.4	4.9	12.7	32.0	26.2	43.4
34001 Atlantic County, New Jersey	12.0	19.9	56.7	16.0	6.8	112,299	62.9	42.3	6.6	14.0	37.1	30.2	50.2
34003 Bergen County, New Jersey	13.1	22.0	42.2	30.5	10.4	352,030	71.6	55.9	4.1	11.6	28.4	24.1	46.0
34005 Burlington County, New Jersey	8.7	9.2	54.1	9.8	3.4	175,859	68.4	52.3	4.7	11.5	31.6	25.8	44.5
34007 Camden County, New Jersey	8.4	18.5	53.0	11.6	5.6	201,158	65.0	44.9	5.7	14.4	35.0	27.3	41.5
34009 Cape May County, New Jersey	6.4	8.4	48.6	5.0	1.5	48,860	65.4	53.0	4.5	7.9	34.6	29.4	51.7
34011 Cumberland County, New Jersey	22.0	33.0	68.2	10.9	7.2	53,883	67.2	42.9	7.2	17.0	32.8	24.6	42.5
34013 Essex County, New Jersey	11.4	24.3	47.1	29.5	13.6	322,453	64.7	40.0	6.2	18.5	35.3	30.5	38.0
34015 Gloucester County, New Jersey	5.5	7.4	58.1	6.1	1.8	112,502	72.5	54.5	5.5	12.5	27.5	21.4	44.1
34017 Hudson County, New Jersey	25.0	42.5	35.8	42.0	20.1	292,000	58.3	39.0	5.4	13.8	41.7	31.3	31.3
34019 Hunterdon County, New Jersey	7.2	7.8	60.5	10.7	3.6	51,292	76.9	66.0	4.3	6.6	23.1	20.3	47.5
34021 Mercer County, New Jersey	10.3	19.4	51.1	22.5	10.4	143,970	64.5	48.6	3.4	12.5	35.5	29.9	43.5
34023 Middlesex County, New Jersey	10.3	22.7	43.3	34.9	15.7	307,831	71.9	55.4	5.2	11.3	28.1	22.4	41.6
34025 Monmouth County, New Jersey	8.7	11.4	57.8	12.9	4.3	250,738	68.8	54.7	4.0	10.1	31.2	26.7	46.9
34027 Morris County, New Jersey	10.2	14.3	56.9	19.1	7.7	192,847	70.8	59.2	3.8	7.9	29.2	23.3	44.6
34029 Ocean County, New Jersey	7.0	9.8	67.8	8.2	3.3	240,736	67.1	52.9	4.6	9.6	32.9	27.8	53.4
34031 Passaic County, New Jersey	22.4	43.7	51.1	30.8	13.8	177,063	71.8	46.9	5.8	19.1	28.2	23.5	43.8
34033 Salem County, New Jersey	7.4	10.5	61.5	3.5	1.3	24,973	61.6	44.3	4.2	13.2	38.4	31.3	47.6
34035 Somerset County, New Jersey	9.0	15.8	49.9	27.8	10.6	130,939	72.2	60.6	2.9	8.7	27.8	22.4	43.1
34037 Sussex County, New Jersey	9.7	10.5	68.8	8.6	2.6	58,767	71.8	57.6	5.3	8.9	28.2	21.7	47.1
34039 Union County, New Jersey	14.0	33.6	47.8	32.8	15.4	201,392	70.7	49.4	5.5	15.7	29.3	24.8	41.5
34041 Warren County, New Jersey	8.7	11.4	64.4	11.0	4.1	46,353	66.7	51.7	4.9	10.1	33.3	27.5	45.7
NEW MEXICO	27.5	50.1	53.8	9.1	5.1	834,007	62.7	42.9	6.1	13.6	37.3	30.9	44.3
35001 Bernalillo County, New Mexico	30.3	50.9	52.5	9.8	4.7	285,185	59.2	40.0	5.2	13.9	40.8	33.8	40.3
35013 Doña Ana County, New Mexico	28.3	69.3	46.2	15.0	7.4	85,021	63.7	42.3	8.0	13.5	36.3	29.7	39.8
35025 Lea County, New Mexico	44.1	62.4	44.7	20.1	17.7	24,390	70.4	52.6	2.5	15.3	29.6	22.8	35.4
35031 McKinley County, New Mexico	9.9	14.6	79.1	2.4	1.8	20,949	66.9	28.7	13.7	24.5	33.1	26.6	44.1
35035 Otero County, New Mexico	28.3	39.7	40.7	9.9	4.8	24,034	69.2	49.4	5.8	14.0	30.8	25.3	41.9
35043 Sandoval County, New Mexico	26.0	41.2	52.8	4.5	1.8	56,655	73.3	56.3	5.5	11.5	26.7	21.5	44.9
35045 San Juan County, New Mexico	7.1	21.8	63.7	3.8	2.4	40,844	68.5	40.4	9.1	19.0	31.5	25.7	46.4
35049 Santa Fe County, New Mexico	26.5	50.5	47.6	9.8	4.6	70,152	58.8	43.2	4.4	11.2	41.2	33.5	52.2
35061 Valencia County, New Mexico	41.4	61.8	63.3	8.3	5.2	28,875	65.3	36.4	9.8	19.1	34.7	30.5	51.6
NEW YORK	10.7	19.5	63.1	22.3	9.1	7,652,666	61.6	42.7	5.2	13.7	38.4	30.9	44.3
36001 Albany County, New York	7.0	6.6	71.6	10.2	4.4	132,171	54.6	40.5	2.9	11.2	45.4	34.9	41.1
36005 Bronx County, New York	16.8	56.4	53.4	33.7	15.4	533,004	64.0	26.6	8.9	28.5	36.0	31.6	41.7
36007 Broome County, New York	5.9	4.8	73.4	7.0	2.9	84,452	55.8	40.5	5.2	10.1	44.2	34.6	44.9
36009 Cattaraugus County, New York	6.2	2.4	83.3	1.1	0.3	32,562	59.0	41.9	6.7	10.4	41.0	35.6	49.5
36011 Cayuga County, New York	5.6	3.3	85.6	2.6	1.0	32,392	63.1	43.0	7.7	12.5	36.9	28.8	48.5
36013 Chautauqua County, New York	6.1	8.1	74.9	2.3	0.9	53,309	56.2	39.8	5.2	11.2	43.8	36.8	47.6
36015 Chemung County, New York	6.1	3.6	76.6	3.1	1.4	35,407	59.2	45.2	3.6	10.4	40.8	32.0	45.4
36019 Clinton County, New York	4.2	3.0	77.8	3.2	1.8	33,860	63.4	47.8	7.3	8.4	36.6	28.6	41.2
36027 Dutchess County, New York	10.8	13.8	70.7	10.0	4.1	118,175	63.1	49.0	4.1	10.0	36.9	29.6	46.9
36029 Erie County, New York	6.0	6.0	80.5	7.1	2.5	412,870	57.4	39.7	4.8	12.9	42.6	34.9	43.3

Table A-2. Counties — Who: Age, Race/Ethnicity, and Household Structure, 2021—*Continued*

STATE County	Total population	Percent change, 2010–2019	Population by age (percent)					Median age	Race alone or in combination (percent)					
			Under 18 years	18 to 24 years	25 to 44 years	45 to 64 years	65 years and over		White	Black or African American	American Indian and Alaska Native	Asian	Native Hawaiian or Other Pacific Islander	Some other race
ACS table number:	B01003	Population Estimates	B01001	B01001	B01001	B01001	B01001	B01002	B02008	B02009	B02010	B02011	B02012	B02013
STATE County code / Column number:	1	2	3	4	5	6	7	8	9	10	11	12	13	14
NEW YORK—Cont.														
36045 Jefferson County, New York	116,295	-5.5	23.5	11.3	29.1	21.7	14.5	34.7	88.7	8.2	1.2	3.4	0.6	6.9
36047 Kings County, New York	2,641,052	2.2	22.7	7.5	31.6	23.0	15.1	36.3	44.4	33.0	1.9	13.8	0.2	18.7
36053 Madison County, New York	67,658	-3.4	19.0	12.8	21.2	27.3	19.7	42.1	95.6	1.4	2.2	1.4	-	4.3
36055 Monroe County, New York	755,160	-0.3	20.5	9.6	26.2	25.4	18.3	39.4	77.3	17.1	1.2	4.6	-	8.0
36059 Nassau County, New York	1,390,907	1.3	21.5	8.3	24.1	27.7	18.4	41.8	66.9	13.3	0.9	12.7	0.1	16.6
36061 New York County, New York	1,576,876	2.7	14.7	8.4	34.5	24.1	18.3	39.3	57.2	17.9	1.5	13.7	0.2	23.5
36063 Niagara County, New York	211,653	-3.3	19.9	8.0	23.9	27.5	20.6	43.1	90.0	9.5	2.3	1.8	-	2.6
36065 Oneida County, New York	230,274	-2.6	21.3	9.1	24.1	26.0	19.4	41.0	89.2	6.7	2.8	4.7	-	6.9
36067 Onondaga County, New York	473,236	-1.4	21.1	10.1	25.1	25.6	18.0	39.4	82.3	13.9	1.7	4.7	0.1	6.0
36069 Ontario County, New York	112,508	1.7	19.4	8.6	22.6	27.4	22.0	44.3	94.0	4.7	0.9	2.1	-	4.9
36071 Orange County, New York	404,525	3.3	25.7	10.1	24.3	25.5	14.4	37.1	71.7	15.2	2.5	4.1	0.1	18.3
36075 Oswego County, New York	117,387	-4.1	20.4	11.3	22.9	28.2	17.3	41.3	96.4	1.8	1.0	1.2	0.2	4.8
36079 Putnam County, New York	97,936	-1.4	19.2	7.5	24.8	29.4	19.1	44.0	81.7	5.3	2.1	2.7	-	18.1
36081 Queens County, New York	2,331,143	1.0	19.9	7.2	28.6	26.9	17.3	40.4	36.8	19.8	1.8	27.5	0.4	28.3
36083 Rensselaer County, New York	160,232	-0.4	19.2	9.5	26.7	26.5	18.0	40.0	86.2	9.5	0.8	3.7	-	6.8
36085 Richmond County, New York	493,494	1.6	21.7	8.2	25.9	27.3	17.0	40.9	70.9	11.9	1.2	13.0	-	15.6
36087 Rockland County, New York	339,227	4.5	29.2	9.1	23.0	23.0	15.6	35.2	73.3	14.5	1.2	7.0	-	15.8
36089 St. Lawrence County, New York	108,051	4.7	20.0	13.2	22.4	26.2	18.2	39.1	95.0	3.2	1.1	1.6	-	3.0
36091 Saratoga County, New York	237,359	0.4	19.3	7.7	25.1	28.7	19.3	43.5	95.1	2.5	2.0	2.5	0.1	4.4
36093 Schenectady County, New York	158,089	-5.3	21.6	8.9	25.7	26.3	17.5	40.4	79.0	14.1	2.5	6.8	0.3	9.7
36101 Steuben County, New York	92,948	-3.6	21.5	7.2	23.4	27.6	20.3	43.3	96.7	2.8	1.1	2.3	-	2.1
36103 Suffolk County, New York	1,526,344	-1.1	20.7	8.7	24.1	28.8	17.6	43.2	79.0	9.2	1.4	5.1	0.1	17.9
36105 Sullivan County, New York	79,806	-2.7	20.6	8.9	22.4	29.8	18.3	43.2	82.2	9.2	4.9	2.4	-	13.6
36109 Tompkins County, New York	105,162	0.6	12.0	31.2	20.1	21.4	15.3	31.4	81.0	5.9	1.1	11.6	-	5.5
36111 Ulster County, New York	182,951	-2.7	17.2	8.0	25.3	28.9	20.7	44.5	87.2	8.4	1.6	2.9	0.2	14.5
36113 Warren County, New York	65,618	-2.7	18.0	6.2	23.4	28.4	24.1	47.2	96.6	2.2	0.6	1.3	-	3.9
36117 Wayne County, New York	90,923	-4.1	20.9	7.1	22.8	28.8	20.3	43.8	93.6	3.5	1.5	1.1	-	6.9
36119 Westchester County, New York	997,895	1.9	21.4	8.6	24.5	27.7	17.8	41.6	64.7	17.3	1.6	7.3	0.1	24.2
37000 **NORTH CAROLINA**	10,551,162	7.7	21.8	9.5	25.9	25.8	17.0	39.4	70.1	22.6	3.0	3.9	0.2	9.2
37001 Alamance County, North Carolina	173,877	12.2	22.2	11.3	23.1	26.5	16.9	39.6	71.0	21.8	2.5	3.0	-	11.9
37019 Brunswick County, North Carolina	144,215	32.9	13.9	6.0	17.6	28.5	33.9	56.1	87.7	10.5	1.7	1.0	-	5.2
37021 Buncombe County, North Carolina	271,534	9.6	17.9	7.9	26.5	26.4	21.4	42.9	92.8	7.1	1.4	1.9	0.2	7.5
37023 Burke County, North Carolina	87,611	-0.5	18.0	8.6	23.0	28.7	21.7	45.3	86.9	6.5	2.4	4.1	-	5.9
37025 Cabarrus County, North Carolina	231,278	21.6	25.3	9.1	25.1	26.8	13.8	37.4	70.9	23.0	1.2	6.2	-	9.6
37027 Caldwell County, North Carolina	80,463	-1.0	20.1	8.4	22.4	28.4	20.7	43.8	91.7	6.0	0.9	1.6	-	6.5
37031 Carteret County, North Carolina	68,541	4.5	16.6	6.7	20.8	29.4	26.5	50.3	91.7	3.4	4.8	1.7	0.5	4.5
37035 Catawba County, North Carolina	161,723	3.4	21.8	8.3	23.6	27.6	18.7	41.4	84.1	8.7	3.0	5.7	-	9.7
37037 Chatham County, North Carolina	77,889	17.3	19.5	7.5	20.6	27.3	25.1	47.7	80.9	12.2	1.0	3.3	-	12.5
37045 Cleveland County, North Carolina	100,359	-0.1	22.2	8.8	23.2	27.2	18.6	40.9	79.6	20.1	3.0	1.3	-	5.8
37049 Craven County, North Carolina	100,674	-1.3	21.5	11.9	24.4	22.1	20.1	37.4	74.1	22.2	1.0	3.8	-	4.1
37051 Cumberland County, North Carolina	335,508	5.0	25.1	12.6	29.4	20.2	12.7	31.8	51.5	41.4	3.7	4.0	0.7	10.9
37057 Davidson County, North Carolina	170,637	2.9	21.8	7.3	22.7	29.4	18.8	43.4	87.6	11.2	1.3	2.0	-	6.2
37063 Durham County, North Carolina	326,126	20.1	19.9	10.1	32.2	23.4	14.4	36.3	51.8	36.6	1.8	6.6	0.1	13.3
37067 Forsyth County, North Carolina	385,523	9.0	22.7	9.8	25.3	25.6	16.6	38.6	64.1	28.6	2.4	3.0	0.1	11.9
37069 Franklin County, North Carolina	71,703	15.0	21.9	8.6	24.3	28.3	17.0	40.8	66.7	25.9	1.7	1.1	-	9.4
37071 Gaston County, North Carolina	230,856	8.9	22.5	7.9	25.9	27.4	16.3	40.4	77.7	19.9	1.5	2.3	0.1	7.1
37081 Guilford County, North Carolina	542,410	10.0	22.2	10.8	25.9	25.2	15.9	37.9	54.5	37.8	1.8	6.3	-	8.1
37085 Harnett County, North Carolina	135,966	18.6	25.5	8.5	29.5	23.1	13.5	35.5	71.0	23.1	3.9	2.0	1.4	8.4
37089 Henderson County, North Carolina	116,829	10.0	18.7	5.8	22.6	26.9	26.0	47.4	91.0	5.1	1.0	1.9	-	9.1
37097 Iredell County, North Carolina	191,968	14.0	22.5	7.7	25.0	28.5	16.3	40.7	83.4	11.2	3.7	3.3	-	9.2
37101 Johnston County, North Carolina	226,504	24.0	25.3	7.9	27.4	25.6	13.8	37.9	72.9	18.1	2.2	1.7	-	12.5
37109 Lincoln County, North Carolina	89,670	10.0	20.7	7.0	22.2	30.4	19.7	45.2	93.1	3.7	4.2	1.1	-	7.0

Table A-2. Counties — Who: Age, Race/Ethnicity, and Household Structure, 2021—*Continued*

STATE County	Two or more races (percent)	Hispanic or Latino (percent)	Native, born in state of residence (percent)	Foreign born (percent)	Non-citizens (percent)	Total house-holds	Family households				Nonfamily households		Percent of households with people age 60 years and over
							Total	Married couple	Male house-holder	Female house-holder	Total	One-person house-holds	
ACS table number:	B02001	B03003	B05002	B05002	B05002	B11001	B11001	B11001	B11001	B11001	B11001	B11001	B11006
STATE County code Column number:	15	16	17	18	19	20	21	22	23	24	25	26	27
NEW YORK—Cont.													
36045 Jefferson County, New York........	7.9	7.7	66.1	4.4	1.1	48,628	63.8	49.6	4.9	9.3	36.2	27.4	34.4
36047 Kings County, New York	11.1	18.8	48.5	35.6	13.3	1,001,868	59.7	37.1	5.0	17.6	40.3	30.0	39.5
36053 Madison County, New York	5.0	2.5	82.9	2.5	1.2	25,294	63.6	51.4	3.6	8.6	36.4	29.5	48.1
36055 Monroe County, New York..........	7.7	9.6	73.6	8.5	3.2	318,883	58.3	40.7	4.7	12.9	41.7	33.1	41.8
36059 Nassau County, New York...........	9.9	17.6	70.9	22.3	6.4	459,452	76.1	60.9	4.1	11.0	23.9	20.0	51.5
36061 New York County, New York.......	13.0	26.4	44.0	28.1	12.5	737,575	40.7	26.0	3.5	11.2	59.3	48.2	38.0
36063 Niagara County, New York	5.8	3.7	84.2	3.0	1.0	90,975	62.6	43.4	5.3	14.0	37.4	31.3	44.9
36065 Oneida County, New York...........	10.1	6.6	79.6	7.7	3.3	93,373	57.4	40.4	5.4	11.6	42.6	35.6	45.8
36067 Onondaga County, New York	8.1	5.5	75.7	7.3	3.0	198,132	58.4	40.5	5.0	12.8	41.6	33.5	43.2
36069 Ontario County, New York	6.4	5.2	78.2	4.0	1.4	47,607	62.9	47.7	4.7	10.5	37.1	27.4	48.2
36071 Orange County, New York	10.6	22.6	69.6	11.7	3.9	137,561	71.7	57.0	5.1	9.7	28.3	23.6	41.9
36075 Oswego County, New York	5.3	2.9	84.2	2.4	1.0	46,924	65.3	47.9	7.6	9.8	34.7	26.5	41.9
36079 Putnam County, New York	7.2	17.7	71.2	14.3	4.8	35,166	74.1	58.1	5.8	10.2	25.9	21.4	50.9
36081 Queens County, New York	13.5	28.1	45.3	46.8	19.3	820,686	64.9	42.9	6.4	15.6	35.1	28.2	46.5
36083 Rensselaer County, New York......	6.9	5.4	78.0	5.9	2.3	66,431	60.5	43.7	4.9	11.8	39.5	31.1	42.0
36085 Richmond County, New York	12.0	18.7	68.0	25.6	8.1	170,762	70.5	50.4	5.5	14.6	29.5	24.9	48.1
36087 Rockland County, New York	9.9	18.8	65.4	20.5	7.7	102,609	75.5	60.6	4.6	10.4	24.5	21.8	46.9
36089 St. Lawrence County, New York ..	3.7	2.4	81.3	3.2	1.4	42,298	61.9	47.5	3.5	10.9	38.1	30.7	44.7
36091 Saratoga County, New York	6.3	3.5	75.5	5.0	1.4	100,226	63.9	49.8	4.5	9.6	36.1	27.7	43.1
36093 Schenectady County, New York ..	11.5	7.8	73.6	10.2	3.6	66,910	58.0	42.5	4.7	10.9	42.0	31.7	44.2
36101 Steuben County, New York........	4.3	1.8	81.8	2.2	1.0	39,500	60.6	47.6	3.4	9.6	39.4	32.3	45.0
36103 Suffolk County, New York	11.9	20.7	75.0	16.5	7.1	511,951	71.8	55.5	5.4	11.0	28.2	22.7	50.7
36105 Sullivan County, New York	11.9	17.4	67.3	12.9	6.1	32,529	56.3	43.7	2.3	10.3	43.7	35.3	44.9
36109 Tompkins County, New York	4.7	5.5	54.7	11.2	6.8	44,469	48.4	36.9	3.4	8.1	51.6	36.3	34.8
36111 Ulster County, New York.............	13.4	11.1	73.3	7.2	2.1	75,053	60.1	44.5	4.7	10.8	39.9	30.4	49.4
36113 Warren County, New York	4.5	2.9	77.1	3.8	1.2	29,729	61.6	47.4	4.6	9.6	38.4	30.0	46.3
36117 Wayne County, New York	6.1	4.8	84.6	3.1	1.1	38,634	65.3	51.3	4.8	9.2	34.7	24.9	46.4
36119 Westchester County, New York...	13.9	25.9	58.8	24.6	9.6	371,736	68.4	52.0	4.5	11.9	31.6	27.5	46.4
37000 **NORTH CAROLINA**	8.4	10.1	56.0	8.2	4.9	4,179,632	64.3	47.3	4.3	12.6	35.7	29.4	40.6
37001 Alamance County, North Carolina..................................	9.3	13.7	64.8	8.4	4.7	69,343	65.1	46.6	4.4	14.1	34.9	30.7	41.0
37019 Brunswick County, North Carolina..................................	5.7	5.1	41.9	3.8	1.5	65,337	68.3	55.2	5.2	7.9	31.7	25.8	63.9
37021 Buncombe County, North Carolina..................................	10.7	7.2	47.9	5.4	2.8	97,345	59.1	45.6	3.3	10.2	40.9	33.1	46.7
37023 Burke County, North Carolina	5.8	6.9	67.8	4.5	2.3	35,709	69.8	50.3	6.5	13.0	30.2	25.4	51.1
37025 Cabarrus County, North Carolina	10.6	11.7	50.1	9.7	6.0	73,486	75.4	60.7	3.6	11.1	24.6	22.0	37.2
37027 Caldwell County, North Carolina.	6.5	6.5	76.1	2.7	1.5	32,600	61.8	43.5	4.2	14.1	38.2	34.8	47.0
37031 Carteret County, North Carolina .	5.9	4.7	54.0	3.8	1.6	30,589	71.0	55.7	5.3	10.0	29.0	25.0	55.1
37035 Catawba County, North Carolina	10.8	10.5	63.1	6.3	3.9	64,302	66.2	49.7	4.4	12.1	33.8	26.9	45.5
37037 Chatham County, North Carolina	9.2	12.2	47.4	9.8	7.3	31,474	71.8	60.7	3.0	8.1	28.2	24.5	55.1
37045 Cleveland County, North Carolina	9.1	4.4	73.5	2.1	1.1	40,296	66.7	46.9	6.5	13.3	33.3	27.5	43.7
37049 Craven County, North Carolina ...	5.0	8.0	51.4	2.8	1.4	42,139	63.4	46.1	5.0	12.3	36.6	30.8	46.5
37051 Cumberland County, North Carolina..................................	11.1	12.7	42.7	6.8	3.0	129,898	62.3	41.5	4.0	16.8	37.7	32.9	33.0
37057 Davidson County, North Carolina	8.0	8.0	66.9	5.5	2.9	66,245	69.3	52.5	4.7	12.1	30.7	25.5	44.4
37063 Durham County, North Carolina..	9.6	13.8	45.5	14.8	8.6	138,497	55.7	39.2	4.2	12.2	44.3	34.9	32.8
37067 Forsyth County, North Carolina ...	9.1	13.9	56.1	8.9	5.4	155,985	61.0	43.3	4.3	13.4	39.0	33.2	40.5
37069 Franklin County, North Carolina..	4.9	9.6	59.5	4.4	3.6	26,689	70.9	53.6	1.9	15.4	29.1	21.7	42.8
37071 Gaston County, North Carolina...	7.9	8.3	64.3	5.1	2.8	93,913	63.4	44.2	5.2	14.0	36.6	28.8	40.7
37081 Guilford County, North Carolina .	7.5	8.9	55.8	10.5	5.0	212,574	62.4	43.1	3.5	15.8	37.6	30.6	39.9
37085 Harnett County, North Carolina..	9.1	14.0	54.0	5.7	3.2	49,555	70.6	52.8	5.3	12.4	29.4	23.9	34.3
37089 Henderson County, North Carolina..................................	8.1	10.8	43.8	6.5	3.4	50,136	64.2	50.7	2.6	10.9	35.8	31.4	50.8
37097 Iredell County, North Carolina.....	10.2	8.5	49.5	6.7	3.4	73,434	67.6	52.7	5.3	9.6	32.4	27.9	41.5
37101 Johnston County, North Carolina	7.3	14.9	57.1	6.7	4.8	82,113	71.9	53.0	7.1	11.7	28.1	23.1	36.7
37109 Lincoln County, North Carolina ...	8.7	7.7	56.1	5.4	2.4	36,361	75.3	57.8	4.5	13.0	24.7	19.8	48.5

Part A — Who 53

Table A-2. Counties — Who: Age, Race/Ethnicity, and Household Structure, 2021—*Continued*

STATE County code	STATE County	Total population	Percent change, 2010–2019	Population by age (percent)					Median age	Race alone or in combination (percent)					
				Under 18 years	18 to 24 years	25 to 44 years	45 to 64 years	65 years and over		White	Black or African American	American Indian and Alaska Native	Asian	Native Hawaiian or Other Pacific Islander	Some other race
	ACS table number:	B01003	Population Estimates	B01001	B01001	B01001	B01001	B01001	B01002	B02008	B02009	B02010	B02011	B02012	B02013
	Column number:	1	2	3	4	5	6	7	8	9	10	11	12	13	14
	NORTH CAROLINA—Cont.														
37119	Mecklenburg County, North Carolina	1,122,276	20.7	22.8	8.9	31.8	24.5	11.9	35.7	54.0	33.6	1.4	7.2	0.2	13.4
37125	Moore County, North Carolina	102,763	14.3	21.4	6.5	22.8	24.9	24.3	44.0	83.6	12.8	1.7	2.2	-	7.9
37127	Nash County, North Carolina	95,176	-1.6	21.9	9.0	22.8	27.2	19.1	41.5	50.7	42.4	1.3	1.3	-	7.7
37129	New Hanover County, North Carolina	229,018	15.7	17.8	11.7	26.2	25.5	18.8	40.5	85.5	11.4	4.4	2.4	-	5.8
37133	Onslow County, North Carolina	206,160	11.3	24.3	21.9	27.7	16.6	9.6	27.3	80.0	16.7	4.9	3.9	1.1	8.4
37135	Orange County, North Carolina	148,884	11.0	18.7	18.2	22.5	24.8	15.8	37.4	77.1	12.7	2.1	9.0	0.5	8.9
37147	Pitt County, North Carolina	172,169	7.5	20.9	18.1	25.7	21.0	14.3	33.0	57.0	37.3	0.9	2.6	-	6.4
37151	Randolph County, North Carolina	145,172	1.4	22.7	8.2	23.4	28.0	17.8	41.6	87.6	5.6	3.7	1.9	-	11.4
37155	Robeson County, North Carolina	116,328	-2.6	25.0	10.4	23.7	25.0	15.9	36.9	26.8	24.3	43.3	1.0	-	9.0
37157	Rockingham County, North Carolina	91,266	-2.8	20.2	5.7	23.9	29.2	21.0	45.1	80.6	17.0	4.0	-	-	6.9
37159	Rowan County, North Carolina	148,150	2.6	21.9	8.8	24.0	27.6	17.8	41.2	82.0	14.9	4.1	1.3	-	8.8
37171	Surry County, North Carolina	71,152	-2.6	21.2	6.7	22.3	29.0	20.9	44.8	92.2	3.3	1.8	-	-	8.5
37179	Union County, North Carolina	243,648	19.2	25.9	9.4	23.3	28.0	13.3	39.2	77.9	13.4	2.4	4.7	-	10.3
37183	Wake County, North Carolina	1,150,204	23.4	23.2	9.0	29.5	25.8	12.5	37.4	67.3	21.6	1.5	9.2	0.1	10.2
37191	Wayne County, North Carolina	116,835	0.4	23.9	9.4	26.0	23.8	16.9	38.1	61.3	30.9	3.4	2.5	0.5	13.4
37193	Wilkes County, North Carolina	65,806	-1.3	20.0	7.1	22.3	28.0	22.5	45.3	94.1	3.1	3.5	-	-	7.9
37195	Wilson County, North Carolina	78,369	0.7	23.0	7.3	25.9	24.9	19.0	41.3	51.1	40.3	1.1	1.4	-	11.2
38000	**NORTH DAKOTA**	774,948	12.3	23.6	11.0	27.2	22.2	16.0	35.8	89.0	4.1	7.1	2.1	0.5	3.9
38015	Burleigh County, North Dakota	98,933	17.6	22.8	8.8	27.2	24.2	16.9	38.5	91.4	3.0	4.6	1.9	-	3.5
38017	Cass County, North Dakota	186,562	21.5	22.7	13.6	30.2	20.7	12.8	33.6	88.2	7.4	3.1	3.5	-	2.9
38035	Grand Forks County, North Dakota	72,705	3.9	21.7	19.4	26.9	18.9	13.2	31.0	89.8	5.4	5.4	3.6	1.2	3.3
38101	Ward County, North Dakota	69,071	9.7	23.6	14.0	30.2	19.1	13.1	32.3	90.2	6.7	4.8	2.7	-	6.8
39000	**OHIO**	11,780,017	1.1	22.1	9.0	25.5	25.6	17.8	39.6	83.4	14.3	1.6	3.1	0.2	4.4
39003	Allen County, Ohio	101,670	-3.7	23.0	10.1	24.1	24.0	18.8	39.9	85.6	13.3	3.7	1.2	-	3.3
39007	Ashtabula County, Ohio	97,337	-4.2	21.9	7.4	23.5	26.8	20.3	42.8	93.9	5.4	0.9	0.7	-	5.9
39013	Belmont County, Ohio	65,849	-4.8	19.2	6.9	24.6	27.7	21.6	44.3	95.1	5.5	0.6	-	-	1.8
39017	Butler County, Ohio	390,234	4.1	23.4	12.6	23.9	24.7	15.4	37.3	85.4	9.5	2.2	4.8	-	5.7
39023	Clark County, Ohio	135,633	-3.1	22.5	8.6	23.3	25.9	19.7	41.1	90.1	11.2	1.7	1.1	-	3.4
39025	Clermont County, Ohio	209,642	4.6	22.4	8.3	25.2	26.6	17.5	40.3	96.1	2.7	0.7	1.9	-	2.7
39029	Columbiana County, Ohio	101,310	-5.5	20.4	7.5	22.5	28.2	21.4	44.6	97.2	2.4	2.9	0.4	-	1.9
39035	Cuyahoga County, Ohio	1,249,387	-3.5	20.6	8.4	26.5	25.5	19.0	40.2	64.1	31.9	1.2	4.1	0.3	6.3
39041	Delaware County, Ohio	220,740	20.1	25.3	7.9	25.3	26.7	14.8	39.6	87.2	5.3	0.8	9.2	-	3.4
39043	Erie County, Ohio	74,852	-3.6	20.1	6.9	23.1	25.9	23.9	44.9	87.6	11.4	0.9	1.0	-	8.6
39045	Fairfield County, Ohio	161,064	7.8	24.0	8.1	25.6	26.6	15.7	38.9	89.1	8.8	3.3	2.9	-	3.4
39049	Franklin County, Ohio	1,321,414	13.2	23.3	9.6	31.7	22.7	12.7	34.7	67.7	26.5	1.4	7.0	0.3	6.5
39055	Geauga County, Ohio	95,565	0.3	22.5	7.8	19.5	28.8	21.5	45.4	98.0	1.3	1.3	0.5	-	4.8
39057	Greene County, Ohio	168,412	4.6	20.7	11.3	25.1	24.5	18.4	38.8	87.9	9.1	1.3	4.1	-	4.2
39061	Hamilton County, Ohio	826,139	1.9	23.0	9.2	27.7	24.0	16.0	36.9	69.8	28.1	1.2	3.5	0.2	3.7
39063	Hancock County, Ohio	74,656	1.3	21.5	8.6	26.0	25.2	18.6	39.9	93.0	2.4	1.1	2.6	-	5.8
39085	Lake County, Ohio	232,023	0.0	19.5	7.7	23.9	27.9	21.1	44.2	92.3	6.7	1.1	2.1	-	4.8
39089	Licking County, Ohio	180,401	6.2	22.8	9.7	23.8	26.4	17.2	39.7	91.8	6.0	1.2	3.7	-	2.2
39093	Lorain County, Ohio	315,595	2.8	21.8	8.3	23.5	27.2	19.2	41.9	87.4	10.1	1.7	1.9	-	10.2
39095	Lucas County, Ohio	429,191	-3.0	23.1	8.5	26.1	25.2	17.1	38.5	77.3	20.7	3.2	2.3	0.4	5.6
39099	Mahoning County, Ohio	226,762	-4.2	20.2	8.3	23.6	26.2	21.8	42.9	81.8	17.7	1.1	1.2	-	6.3
39101	Marion County, Ohio	65,291	-2.1	21.3	7.4	25.2	26.9	19.2	41.0	93.5	6.6	3.0	0.8	-	3.0
39103	Medina County, Ohio	183,092	4.3	21.6	7.7	23.4	28.2	19.0	42.8	96.5	2.3	0.6	1.8	-	3.3
39109	Miami County, Ohio	109,264	4.4	23.2	6.9	24.1	26.1	19.7	41.8	94.2	4.4	0.7	2.1	-	3.0
39113	Montgomery County, Ohio	535,840	-0.6	22.1	9.3	25.7	24.5	18.4	39.0	75.3	23.3	1.0	3.4	0.4	3.6
39119	Muskingum County, Ohio	86,408	0.2	22.3	9.3	24.2	26.3	17.8	40.2	96.4	6.9	1.0	-	-	1.4
39133	Portage County, Ohio	162,382	0.6	18.5	15.2	22.2	26.1	18.0	40.1	93.2	5.4	2.2	2.6	-	3.3
39139	Richland County, Ohio	125,195	-2.7	21.9	8.2	24.6	25.3	20.1	40.7	90.4	9.2	3.6	1.3	-	3.2
39141	Ross County, Ohio	76,891	-1.8	21.1	7.5	26.1	27.7	17.6	41.6	95.1	5.8	3.1	-	-	1.7
39145	Scioto County, Ohio	73,346	-5.3	21.9	8.7	24.8	25.7	18.8	39.7	97.6	3.8	1.5	0.7	-	1.8

Table A-2. Counties — Who: Age, Race/Ethnicity, and Household Structure, 2021—*Continued*

							Household type (percent of all households)						Percent of households with people age 60 years and over
							Family households				Nonfamily households		
STATE County	Two or more races (percent)	Hispanic or Latino (percent)	Native, born in state of residence (percent)	Foreign born (percent)	Non-citizens (percent)	Total house-holds	Total	Married couple	Male house-holder	Female house-holder	Total	One-person house-holds	
STATE County code	ACS table number: B02001	B03003	B05002	B05002	B05002	B11001	B11001	B11001	B11001	B11001	B11001	B11001	B11006
	Column number: 15	16	17	18	19	20	21	22	23	24	25	26	27
	NORTH CAROLINA—Cont.												
37119	Mecklenburg County, North Carolina..............	9.1	14.1	40.0	16.0	9.5	458,344	58.5	41.0	4.3	13.2	41.5	33.4	29.0
37125	Moore County, North Carolina....	7.8	7.4	48.9	4.7	2.0	43,554	65.3	50.3	5.2	9.8	34.7	30.9	49.7
37127	Nash County, North Carolina......	3.5	7.8	71.6	4.3	3.1	38,029	62.7	45.2	2.2	15.3	37.3	33.0	46.3
37129	New Hanover County, North Carolina..............	8.4	6.2	47.2	4.6	2.4	103,762	54.8	45.7	3.1	6.0	45.2	33.8	38.1
37133	Onslow County, North Carolina ..	13.3	13.4	34.3	4.7	1.7	73,121	70.6	55.4	3.2	12.0	29.4	25.6	26.6
37135	Orange County, North Carolina...	9.8	8.8	43.8	11.8	5.7	56,263	59.0	49.1	2.3	7.6	41.0	30.3	39.2
37147	Pitt County, North Carolina.........	4.0	6.9	66.9	4.7	3.0	75,578	50.4	30.2	6.0	14.2	49.6	38.4	33.0
37151	Randolph County, North Carolina	10.5	12.7	66.1	5.9	4.5	55,948	67.9	51.5	4.9	11.5	32.1	28.5	45.0
37155	Robeson County, North Carolina.	4.3	9.3	82.1	4.7	3.6	43,529	65.5	36.8	6.6	22.0	34.5	30.1	41.5
37157	Rockingham County, North Carolina..............	9.8	6.6	72.6	3.2	2.3	38,481	63.5	44.7	5.2	13.6	36.5	33.0	48.3
37159	Rowan County, North Carolina ...	10.3	10.1	61.7	5.7	3.5	57,024	67.7	49.1	4.5	14.1	32.3	25.3	44.4
37171	Surry County, North Carolina	7.2	11.8	69.3	5.9	4.7	30,317	72.4	54.7	5.5	12.2	27.6	23.9	46.5
37179	Union County, North Carolina.....	8.1	12.0	44.9	10.8	5.6	83,407	82.4	67.9	4.2	10.2	17.6	14.6	38.0
37183	Wake County, North Carolina	9.0	10.5	42.4	14.3	7.5	439,911	66.2	52.2	3.5	10.5	33.8	25.9	31.8
37191	Wayne County, North Carolina....	11.5	13.3	61.2	8.0	6.0	46,932	65.5	42.3	7.3	15.9	34.5	28.3	42.0
37193	Wilkes County, North Carolina	8.4	7.1	80.1	3.3	2.5	26,770	68.4	50.5	6.0	11.9	31.6	26.9	46.6
37195	Wilson County, North Carolina ...	5.0	11.4	68.4	7.0	4.8	32,868	63.5	40.5	6.1	16.9	36.5	32.2	42.7
38000	**NORTH DAKOTA**	6.1	4.1	61.8	4.4	2.6	322,511	59.1	46.1	5.4	7.6	40.9	33.2	35.9
38015	Burleigh County, North Dakota ...	4.9	2.9	72.0	2.5	1.1	39,295	56.9	45.2	5.3	6.4	43.1	36.9	40.0
38017	Cass County, North Dakota.........	4.9	3.1	55.0	7.8	4.3	83,761	55.0	39.7	5.1	10.2	45.0	37.3	29.1
38035	Grand Forks County, North Dakota	6.3	4.9	54.7	6.0	3.8	31,152	50.7	37.7	3.1	9.8	49.3	31.9	27.6
38101	Ward County, North Dakota........	9.8	7.0	54.6	3.3	1.6	28,795	58.9	45.5	6.8	6.6	41.1	28.6	29.1
39000	**OHIO**	6.4	4.3	74.7	5.0	2.3	4,832,922	61.8	44.7	4.8	12.3	38.2	31.1	41.8
39003	Allen County, Ohio	6.8	3.7	81.6	2.5	0.9	41,021	62.7	45.1	5.1	12.4	37.3	30.1	43.7
39007	Ashtabula County, Ohio.............	6.9	4.8	80.4	2.2	1.4	39,915	62.4	42.5	7.3	12.6	37.6	29.9	48.6
39013	Belmont County, Ohio	3.8	1.4	51.6	0.8	0.2	26,949	58.2	41.6	4.9	11.8	41.8	36.8	47.7
39017	Butler County, Ohio	7.9	5.4	69.7	7.0	4.0	146,057	64.6	48.3	5.1	11.2	35.4	27.7	40.6
39023	Clark County, Ohio	6.8	3.8	79.9	2.1	1.1	57,013	62.3	42.2	7.3	12.8	37.7	31.4	45.4
39025	Clermont County, Ohio..............	3.9	2.2	72.1	2.7	1.2	84,219	65.4	49.4	5.4	10.6	34.6	26.5	44.9
39029	Columbiana County, Ohio..........	5.2	0.6	78.0	0.9	0.5	41,047	63.1	44.2	6.8	12.1	36.9	31.1	46.2
39035	Cuyahoga County, Ohio.............	7.2	6.6	73.4	7.3	2.9	557,572	53.7	34.8	4.3	14.6	46.3	39.2	43.4
39041	Delaware County, Ohio..............	5.7	3.0	68.7	8.4	3.5	80,640	76.9	66.1	3.4	7.4	23.1	19.0	34.6
39043	Erie County, Ohio.....................	9.5	4.8	79.5	2.2	1.1	32,926	63.1	45.0	4.1	14.0	36.9	32.5	50.4
39045	Fairfield County, Ohio	7.0	2.6	78.4	4.4	2.2	59,818	72.3	55.4	4.4	12.5	27.7	22.8	39.3
39049	Franklin County, Ohio................	8.2	6.2	64.8	12.7	6.2	549,475	58.5	39.0	5.1	14.4	41.5	31.2	32.2
39055	Geauga County, Ohio	5.9	1.8	79.0	2.7	0.6	35,431	73.9	61.3	6.0	6.6	26.1	22.1	49.9
39057	Greene County, Ohio	6.4	3.2	62.1	5.5	1.8	67,822	64.3	51.7	5.1	7.5	35.7	27.4	41.1
39061	Hamilton County, Ohio	6.0	3.9	71.8	5.8	3.2	353,674	55.2	38.3	3.5	13.4	44.8	36.0	36.4
39063	Hancock County, Ohio	4.9	6.2	75.0	3.7	1.0	31,951	65.2	50.0	5.4	9.8	34.8	25.9	41.2
39085	Lake County, Ohio.....................	6.2	5.0	79.6	5.7	2.0	99,990	62.7	49.2	2.9	10.7	37.3	29.8	48.4
39089	Licking County, Ohio..................	4.6	2.3	75.8	3.6	1.2	67,761	70.5	53.3	4.8	12.3	29.5	22.3	43.0
39093	Lorain County, Ohio....................	10.9	10.8	77.6	2.4	1.0	124,879	62.4	45.6	4.8	12.0	37.6	31.9	44.4
39095	Lucas County, Ohio....................	8.9	7.8	75.6	4.5	1.6	184,315	56.2	37.6	4.7	14.0	43.8	36.3	40.3
39099	Mahoning County, Ohio	7.2	7.0	79.1	2.0	0.9	98,924	59.0	39.5	5.4	14.1	41.0	35.3	46.9
39101	Marion County, Ohio	6.2	3.1	82.2	1.2	0.4	24,692	63.5	44.9	6.1	12.4	36.5	28.5	45.5
39103	Medina County, Ohio.................	4.5	2.6	78.4	3.6	1.1	72,233	72.7	61.9	4.0	6.8	27.3	23.3	44.2
39109	Miami County, Ohio...................	4.4	2.0	79.2	4.0	1.6	43,896	66.0	54.6	4.4	6.9	34.0	29.6	45.4
39113	Montgomery County, Ohio	6.2	3.6	70.3	5.0	2.3	226,787	58.0	39.2	4.5	14.2	42.0	34.3	42.3
39119	Muskingum County, Ohio..........	5.5	1.3	87.6	0.2	0.1	33,876	61.0	40.9	7.4	12.7	39.0	32.9	45.0
39133	Portage County, Ohio	6.1	2.2	79.8	2.7	1.0	63,096	62.4	45.1	6.3	11.0	37.6	30.4	45.7
39139	Richland County, Ohio	7.3	2.2	80.6	1.9	0.3	49,536	61.9	48.7	3.2	10.0	38.1	33.2	46.6
39141	Ross County, Ohio	6.1	1.2	85.3	0.5	0.3	30,550	66.1	47.7	4.3	14.1	33.9	28.3	41.1
39145	Scioto County, Ohio...................	5.2	1.6	84.3	0.6	0.3	27,496	65.6	44.6	5.2	15.8	34.4	29.5	46.8

Table A-2. Counties — Who: Age, Race/Ethnicity, and Household Structure, 2021—*Continued*

STATE County	Total population	Percent change, 2010–2019	Population by age (percent)					Median age	Race alone or in combination (percent)					
			Under 18 years	18 to 24 years	25 to 44 years	45 to 64 years	65 years and over		White	Black or African American	American Indian and Alaska Native	Asian	Native Hawaiian or Other Pacific Islander	Some other race
ACS table number:	B01003	Population Estimates	B01001	B01001	B01001	B01001	B01001	B01002	B02008	B02009	B02010	B02011	B02012	B02013
Column number:	1	2	3	4	5	6	7	8	9	10	11	12	13	14

STATE County code

	OHIO—Cont.														
39151	Stark County, Ohio	373,834	-1.3	21.5	8.4	23.8	26.1	20.2	41.5	91.6	10.2	1.5	1.5	0.1	2.8
39153	Summit County, Ohio	537,633	-0.1	20.8	8.1	25.7	26.5	18.9	41.4	81.7	15.4	2.9	4.9	0.1	3.7
39155	Trumbull County, Ohio	201,335	-5.9	20.5	8.2	22.0	27.3	22.1	44.6	91.0	10.5	1.0	0.9	-	3.1
39157	Tuscarawas County, Ohio	92,500	-0.6	22.8	7.7	24.0	25.7	19.9	40.9	98.5	1.7	0.6	0.5	-	3.4
39165	Warren County, Ohio	246,553	10.3	23.9	7.8	25.7	27.4	15.2	39.3	88.1	4.6	1.9	6.7	0.1	3.7
39169	Wayne County, Ohio	116,710	1.0	23.7	10.5	22.6	24.6	18.6	39.9	96.4	1.8	1.0	1.3	-	2.3
39173	Wood County, Ohio	132,472	4.2	20.3	16.5	23.6	23.6	16.0	36.0	93.3	3.3	1.8	2.5	0.2	6.0
40000	**OKLAHOMA**	3,986,639	4.8	24.0	9.8	26.5	23.5	16.2	37.2	78.8	9.6	14.6	3.2	0.3	8.7
40017	Canadian County, Oklahoma	161,737	28.4	25.8	8.6	29.9	21.6	14.1	35.7	85.1	5.0	7.7	4.0	0.3	9.1
40027	Cleveland County, Oklahoma......	297,597	11.0	20.9	13.9	28.3	22.4	14.4	35.7	83.0	7.9	9.7	6.3	0.2	7.5
40031	Comanche County, Oklahoma......	122,063	-2.7	24.2	12.4	29.5	20.4	13.5	33.0	70.6	19.5	11.7	4.6	0.8	9.8
40037	Creek County, Oklahoma............	72,029	2.2	23.3	7.9	24.5	26.1	18.3	40.5	84.4	3.6	17.0	1.1	-	4.6
40101	Muskogee County, Oklahoma	66,146	-4.2	24.5	9.1	26.3	23.0	17.1	37.6	65.7	12.9	27.4	1.2	-	6.0
40109	Oklahoma County, Oklahoma......	798,575	11.0	25.3	9.2	28.4	22.7	14.3	35.4	72.2	18.2	8.2	4.6	0.3	11.7
40119	Payne County, Oklahoma............	81,989	5.7	18.9	25.3	24.2	18.1	13.4	28.6	85.3	5.3	10.7	5.1		3.4
40125	Pottawatomie County, Oklahoma	73,019	4.5	23.1	10.1	25.1	24.8	16.8	38.4	82.2	4.7	19.0	1.5	-	4.8
40131	Rogers County, Oklahoma	96,695	6.4	23.2	8.0	25.8	25.9	17.1	39.5	82.5	1.7	21.2	2.1	-	5.5
40143	Tulsa County, Oklahoma	672,858	8.0	25.1	8.8	27.7	23.3	15.1	36.2	75.7	12.6	12.1	4.5	0.3	11.6
40145	Wagoner County, Oklahoma.......	84,050	11.2	23.7	8.5	25.8	25.3	16.7	39.0	82.6	5.3	17.5	2.3	-	9.5
41000	**OREGON**	4,246,155	8.1	20.2	8.4	28.0	24.7	18.6	40.1	85.9	3.2	4.2	6.6	0.8	12.4
41003	Benton County, Oregon..............	96,017	8.7	15.7	22.8	23.5	20.2	17.9	33.5	88.2	2.1	2.3	9.5	0.6	6.9
41005	Clackamas County, Oregon.........	422,537	11.2	21.2	7.0	26.2	26.5	19.1	41.9	88.9	2.2	2.6	7.1	0.5	10.8
41017	Deschutes County, Oregon	204,801	25.3	19.3	6.1	27.7	26.2	20.7	42.6	93.7	1.1	2.6	2.7	0.4	7.0
41019	Douglas County, Oregon	111,978	3.1	19.4	5.8	22.9	25.7	26.3	46.7	94.6	0.8	4.9	2.7	0.2	8.7
41029	Jackson County, Oregon	223,734	8.7	20.5	7.2	25.3	24.1	22.9	42.1	91.0	1.7	3.7	3.0	0.1	13.5
41033	Josephine County, Oregon	88,346	5.8	18.9	5.8	22.2	26.0	27.1	48.5	96.7	0.0	5.5	1.8	-	7.4
41035	Klamath County, Oregon	70,164	2.8	22.0	7.8	24.0	24.9	21.4	40.9	89.5	0.0	10.0	0.9	-	8.5
41039	Lane County, Oregon..................	383,189	8.6	17.9	11.6	26.3	23.7	20.5	40.5	91.9	2.5	4.0	4.9	0.6	7.8
41043	Linn County, Oregon...................	129,839	11.2	22.4	8.2	24.9	25.3	19.2	40.3	93.1	1.5	4.2	2.3	-	8.9
41047	Marion County, Oregon..............	347,119	10.3	24.0	9.1	27.3	23.3	16.4	37.1	81.3	2.3	6.6	3.8	1.7	25.0
41051	Multnomah County, Oregon	803,377	10.5	18.0	7.8	35.3	24.7	14.3	38.4	80.3	7.8	3.5	10.5	1.3	10.3
41053	Polk County, Oregon..................	89,164	14.2	22.2	11.9	25.0	22.2	18.7	37.4	86.8	1.3	4.5	4.3	0.4	12.0
41059	Umatilla County, Oregon	79,988	2.7	24.8	8.8	27.3	22.2	17.0	37.4	81.6	1.4	5.7	2.0	0.3	20.2
41067	Washington County, Oregon.......	600,811	13.6	21.9	8.1	30.9	24.8	14.3	38.1	75.3	4.0	3.3	14.5	1.2	15.1
41071	Yamhill County, Oregon.............	108,239	8.0	21.1	10.9	25.3	24.1	18.6	39.9	87.0	2.3	4.1	3.4	-	16.2
42000	**PENNSYLVANIA**	12,964,056	0.8	20.6	8.7	25.5	26.1	19.0	40.9	81.1	12.8	1.2	4.4	0.1	7.9
42001	Adams County, Pennsylvania.......	104,127	1.6	19.3	9.5	22.0	27.2	21.9	43.9	93.7	3.1	1.2	1.2	-	5.4
42003	Allegheny County, Pennsylvania..	1,238,090	-0.6	18.8	8.4	28.1	25.1	19.7	40.6	82.2	15.0	1.1	5.2	0.1	3.3
42005	Armstrong County, Pennsylvania.	65,093	-6.1	18.8	6.5	22.1	29.1	23.5	47.3	98.4	1.1	0.9	0.5	-	1.4
42007	Beaver County, Pennsylvania......	166,624	-3.9	19.4	6.7	24.3	27.4	22.2	44.7	92.5	7.0	1.9	0.9	-	3.3
42011	Berks County, Pennsylvania	429,342	2.4	22.2	9.2	24.8	26.1	17.7	39.8	79.3	7.4	1.6	1.9	-	20.7
42013	Blair County, Pennsylvania..........	121,767	-4.1	20.3	7.6	24.1	26.6	21.4	43.6	97.4	1.4	2.1	1.1	-	2.3
42017	Bucks County, Pennsylvania	646,098	0.5	20.1	7.7	23.4	29.0	19.8	44.1	88.0	5.5	0.7	6.0	0.2	6.0
42019	Butler County, Pennsylvania	194,273	2.2	19.6	8.5	23.3	28.6	20.0	43.5	96.4	1.9	1.3	1.3	-	2.9
42021	Cambria County, Pennsylvania....	132,167	-9.4	19.3	8.8	21.0	27.4	23.6	46.0	96.0	4.1	1.5	0.8	0.1	1.3
42025	Carbon County, Pennsylvania......	65,412	-1.6	19.9	7.9	21.8	28.8	21.6	45.2	98.0	3.4	2.5	-	-	4.1
42027	Centre County, Pennsylvania.......	157,527	5.5	14.7	23.5	23.5	22.7	15.6	34.2	90.2	4.6	1.2	6.3	-	4.1
42029	Chester County, Pennsylvania	538,649	5.2	22.3	8.9	24.5	27.2	17.2	40.7	84.6	7.4	1.1	7.5	0.1	8.3
42033	Clearfield County, Pennsylvania..	80,082	-2.9	18.5	6.8	24.1	28.7	21.9	45.5	95.7	3.3	1.6	0.4	-	3.1
42039	Crawford County, Pennsylvania...	83,351	-4.7	20.1	9.2	22.0	27.0	21.7	43.9	96.3	2.7	0.7	0.9	-	2.1
42041	Cumberland County, Pennsylvania............................	262,919	7.6	20.6	9.3	26.0	25.1	19.1	40.4	89.2	6.8	1.8	5.5	-	3.3
42043	Dauphin County, Pennsylvania ...	287,400	3.8	22.6	7.6	26.6	25.5	17.7	39.8	71.8	20.7	1.2	7.0	0.3	7.5
42045	Delaware County, Pennsylvania ..	573,849	1.4	22.0	9.4	25.8	25.7	17.1	39.2	68.6	24.1	0.7	7.3	-	5.0
42049	Erie County, Pennsylvania...........	269,011	-3.9	21.0	9.4	24.2	26.3	19.1	40.6	88.3	9.7	1.0	2.5	-	5.0
42051	Fayette County, Pennsylvania......	126,931	-5.4	19.1	6.4	23.7	28.7	22.0	45.6	95.0	5.1	2.2	0.6	-	3.3
42055	Franklin County, Pennsylvania	156,289	3.6	22.0	7.7	23.7	26.6	20.1	42.1	92.1	5.3	1.1	1.4	-	5.8

STATE County code	STATE County	Two or more races (percent)	Hispanic or Latino (percent)	Native, born in state of residence (percent)	Foreign born (percent)	Non-citizens (percent)	Total house-holds	Family households Total	Married couple	Male house-holder	Female house-holder	Nonfamily households Total	One-person house-holds	Percent of households with people age 60 years and over
	ACS table number:	B02001	B03003	B05002	B05002	B05002	B11001	B11001	B11001	B11001	B11001	B11001	B11001	B11006
	Column number:	15	16	17	18	19	20	21	22	23	24	25	26	27
	OHIO—Cont.													
39151	Stark County, Ohio	7.0	2.4	83.5	2.2	1.2	156,111	63.9	45.1	5.2	13.6	36.1	29.2	43.8
39153	Summit County, Ohio	8.1	2.5	76.5	6.1	2.5	229,060	60.1	42.9	4.7	12.5	39.9	32.7	43.4
39155	Trumbull County, Ohio...............	5.9	2.1	76.9	1.1	0.2	84,911	62.8	44.9	5.1	12.8	37.2	31.3	48.8
39157	Tuscarawas County, Ohio...........	4.7	3.6	87.0	0.8	0.4	38,684	66.8	49.1	7.6	10.2	33.2	28.6	44.8
39165	Warren County, Ohio.................	4.6	3.2	66.9	8.2	4.4	89,396	74.0	61.0	4.0	9.0	26.0	20.2	37.4
39169	Wayne County, Ohio..................	2.9	2.2	82.4	2.8	1.9	44,215	67.3	53.4	4.7	9.2	32.7	29.0	44.9
39173	Wood County, Ohio...................	6.8	6.1	79.3	3.4	1.6	54,012	58.2	44.4	5.8	8.0	41.8	32.8	35.0
40000	**OKLAHOMA**	14.0	11.7	60.6	5.8	3.6	1,547,967	64.6	47.3	5.2	12.1	35.4	29.3	39.8
40017	Canadian County, Oklahoma	10.9	11.0	62.9	5.3	2.8	57,753	70.0	55.2	4.2	10.6	30.0	22.4	36.5
40027	Cleveland County, Oklahoma	13.5	9.9	58.3	6.2	3.1	116,142	64.7	49.7	4.9	10.1	35.3	27.2	33.9
40031	Comanche County, Oklahoma	15.6	14.3	43.9	5.0	2.2	44,822	64.1	45.3	4.3	14.5	35.9	29.2	33.8
40037	Creek County, Oklahoma............	10.2	5.1	72.1	2.1	0.8	28,339	69.2	51.1	6.6	11.5	30.8	26.4	44.5
40101	Muskogee County, Oklahoma	12.0	7.2	70.3	3.4	2.2	25,965	65.3	45.4	4.1	15.7	34.7	30.8	42.8
40109	Oklahoma County, Oklahoma	14.0	18.5	57.2	9.9	6.4	324,819	62.0	43.5	5.1	13.4	38.0	31.1	35.6
40119	Payne County, Oklahoma............	9.3	5.0	58.6	6.1	4.1	31,537	57.1	36.4	6.9	13.8	42.9	33.3	30.2
40125	Pottawatomie County, Oklahoma	11.9	5.8	68.4	2.5	1.3	26,650	62.7	47.8	4.2	10.7	37.3	33.0	44.5
40131	Rogers County, Oklahoma	12.8	5.5	60.3	3.0	1.5	35,815	73.3	58.4	4.7	10.3	26.7	21.8	43.1
40143	Tulsa County, Oklahoma	15.7	13.9	57.1	8.8	5.3	270,263	61.5	43.2	5.8	12.4	38.5	31.8	37.3
40145	Wagoner County, Oklahoma.......	16.6	7.6	63.5	4.2	2.1	30,502	73.3	57.7	5.3	10.3	26.7	20.4	41.7
41000	**OREGON**	11.8	14.0	45.6	9.7	5.1	1,702,599	61.9	47.4	4.8	9.7	38.1	28.1	41.9
41003	Benton County, Oregon..............	8.7	8.2	43.4	9.0	5.7	39,350	54.2	41.3	4.5	8.4	45.8	27.5	36.0
41005	Clackamas County, Oregon.........	11.1	9.5	51.7	8.8	3.1	161,945	70.1	57.4	3.8	8.8	29.9	22.3	44.2
41017	Deschutes County, Oregon	6.7	8.6	42.3	6.5	4.2	83,763	65.0	51.4	3.8	9.8	35.0	23.4	45.1
41019	Douglas County, Oregon.............	10.4	6.5	48.4	3.0	0.5	45,981	60.9	46.1	5.3	9.5	39.1	33.7	56.6
41029	Jackson County, Oregon.............	12.3	14.3	40.2	6.9	2.9	90,817	61.1	45.7	6.8	8.7	38.9	30.6	50.5
41033	Josephine County, Oregon	10.8	8.3	38.1	3.4	1.3	36,755	58.8	39.9	5.5	13.4	41.2	32.0	57.0
41035	Klamath County, Oregon	11.3	14.5	49.9	3.6	1.7	28,888	57.8	42.6	4.7	10.5	42.2	30.0	48.7
41039	Lane County, Oregon..................	10.7	9.8	47.3	5.6	2.6	160,158	59.6	44.9	3.9	10.9	40.4	27.9	42.9
41043	Linn County, Oregon...................	9.7	10.2	58.9	4.2	3.0	51,347	65.8	51.0	5.5	9.3	34.2	26.7	45.8
41047	Marion County, Oregon...............	16.8	28.2	53.3	13.5	8.3	124,719	67.2	49.8	6.1	11.2	32.8	26.3	41.1
41051	Multnomah County, Oregon.......	12.1	12.7	41.0	13.1	5.4	348,216	51.8	38.4	4.5	9.0	48.2	34.5	31.4
41053	Polk County, Oregon...................	9.0	15.3	55.3	6.0	3.5	33,425	68.1	56.0	4.4	7.7	31.9	24.4	42.6
41059	Umatilla County, Oregon	11.1	28.6	41.7	9.2	6.0	27,247	71.1	43.3	7.9	19.9	28.9	22.0	41.6
41067	Washington County, Oregon.......	12.2	17.6	42.0	17.0	8.1	233,615	65.9	51.8	4.9	9.3	34.1	25.0	35.3
41071	Yamhill County, Oregon..............	11.2	16.8	52.1	7.4	4.4	38,988	72.4	55.6	5.1	11.6	27.6	22.2	44.1
42000	**PENNSYLVANIA**	7.0	8.4	71.4	7.2	3.1	5,228,956	63.1	46.9	4.6	11.6	36.9	30.2	44.4
42001	Adams County, Pennsylvania.......	4.5	7.4	60.8	2.9	1.7	39,986	67.0	50.8	7.6	8.6	33.0	26.7	50.4
42003	Allegheny County, Pennsylvania..	6.3	2.4	74.5	6.4	3.1	545,892	56.3	42.0	3.6	10.6	43.7	35.5	42.4
42005	Armstrong County, Pennsylvania.	2.3	0.9	91.6	0.3	0.1	27,796	64.7	50.8	5.9	8.0	35.3	30.9	52.2
42007	Beaver County, Pennsylvania.......	5.5	2.0	84.2	1.6	0.5	71,450	62.6	48.0	4.6	10.0	37.4	33.1	50.0
42011	Berks County, Pennsylvania........	10.2	23.9	70.4	9.1	3.9	164,312	65.9	48.4	5.6	11.9	34.1	27.6	43.8
42013	Blair County, Pennsylvania...........	4.3	1.4	89.0	1.3	0.7	49,795	64.7	49.4	3.7	11.7	35.3	30.4	48.5
42017	Bucks County, Pennsylvania	6.0	6.1	63.2	10.0	3.3	248,122	69.9	55.9	4.9	9.1	30.1	25.3	48.4
42019	Butler County, Pennsylvania	3.6	1.8	83.2	1.4	0.7	81,220	66.9	56.3	2.9	7.7	33.1	27.6	44.9
42021	Cambria County, Pennsylvania	3.9	1.9	87.8	0.7	0.2	55,283	60.9	47.7	3.7	9.4	39.1	33.3	50.3
42025	Carbon County, Pennsylvania......	6.2	6.4	74.4	2.4	0.9	26,810	63.2	44.8	4.3	14.2	36.8	29.4	47.0
42027	Centre County, Pennsylvania.......	6.3	3.1	68.2	7.7	4.3	57,518	57.1	47.7	2.8	6.6	42.9	34.1	39.0
42029	Chester County, Pennsylvania	8.0	7.7	63.0	8.9	4.5	204,047	70.6	59.0	3.0	8.5	29.4	22.7	41.7
42033	Clearfield County, Pennsylvania...	4.1	3.3	88.4	1.3	0.4	31,570	62.1	49.9	4.2	8.0	37.9	32.6	48.7
42039	Crawford County, Pennsylvania...	2.7	1.6	82.6	1.7	0.9	32,896	65.6	48.6	5.4	11.6	34.4	29.4	50.7
42041	Cumberland County, Pennsylvania	6.0	4.8	69.9	6.4	2.7	104,768	65.7	52.5	4.7	8.4	34.3	27.8	40.7
42043	Dauphin County, Pennsylvania ...	7.9	10.7	69.1	9.2	4.2	120,423	59.3	43.9	3.9	11.6	40.7	33.7	42.4
42045	Delaware County, Pennsylvania...	5.2	4.5	71.1	11.1	4.5	218,280	64.8	46.5	4.6	13.7	35.2	30.3	43.4
42049	Erie County, Pennsylvania............	6.1	4.8	78.7	4.8	1.7	110,561	58.6	42.0	4.4	12.2	41.4	34.2	44.9
42051	Fayette County, Pennsylvania......	6.0	1.4	83.0	1.2	0.3	55,986	62.2	45.0	5.1	12.1	37.8	32.1	48.8
42055	Franklin County, Pennsylvania	5.4	6.7	67.6	3.1	1.3	62,081	65.7	53.3	3.0	9.5	34.3	29.1	46.5

Table A-2. Counties — Who: Age, Race/Ethnicity, and Household Structure, 2021—*Continued*

STATE County code	STATE County	Total population	Percent change, 2010–2019	Under 18 years	18 to 24 years	25 to 44 years	45 to 64 years	65 years and over	Median age	White	Black or African American	American Indian and Alaska Native	Asian	Native Hawaiian or Other Pacific Islander	Some other race
	ACS table number:	B01003	Population Estimates	B01001	B01001	B01001	B01001	B01001	B01002	B02008	B02009	B02010	B02011	B02012	B02013
	Column number:	1	2	3	4	5	6	7	8	9	10	11	12	13	14
	PENNSYLVANIA—Cont.														
42063	Indiana County, Pennsylvania......	82,886	-5.4	18.4	15.3	20.5	25.2	20.6	40.8	95.5	3.3	0.6	1.4	-	2.4
42069	Lackawanna County, Pennsylvania	215,663	-2.2	20.6	8.3	24.8	26.0	20.2	42.1	91.7	5.1	2.4	3.7	-	8.5
42071	Lancaster County, Pennsylvania...	553,652	5.1	23.3	8.7	24.9	24.1	19.0	39.3	88.5	6.4	0.9	3.2	0.1	8.8
42073	Lawrence County, Pennsylvania....	85,497	-6.1	19.8	7.8	22.5	27.0	22.9	44.9	94.3	6.3	1.1	0.8	0.2	2.9
42075	Lebanon County, Pennsylvania......	143,493	6.2	22.6	8.2	23.6	25.5	20.1	40.5	87.3	3.5	2.2	2.2	-	14.3
42077	Lehigh County, Pennsylvania......	375,539	5.7	22.8	9.0	26.1	25.1	17.1	39.1	75.7	11.1	1.6	4.1	0.4	25.3
42079	Luzerne County, Pennsylvania.....	326,053	-1.1	20.2	8.3	25.2	26.5	19.8	41.9	84.8	7.0	2.1	1.6	0.3	15.4
42081	Lycoming County, Pennsylvania...	113,605	-2.4	20.6	8.5	25.1	25.6	20.2	40.8	92.4	5.9	1.5	1.2	0.2	2.8
42085	Mercer County, Pennsylvania	109,972	-6.2	19.2	9.1	21.8	27.2	22.6	44.8	92.7	6.2	1.6	1.0	-	4.2
42089	Monroe County, Pennsylvania	169,273	0.3	19.4	9.1	23.3	29.7	18.5	43.7	77.0	15.8	2.0	3.1	-	16.5
42091	Montgomery County, Pennsylvania	860,578	3.9	21.4	7.8	25.8	26.7	18.3	41.2	80.2	11.4	0.8	9.3	0.1	5.5
42095	Northampton County, Pennsylvania	313,628	2.5	19.6	9.8	24.0	26.8	19.7	41.8	83.1	8.3	1.0	3.8	-	13.2
42097	Northumberland County, Pennsylvania	91,266	-3.9	19.7	7.6	23.0	27.7	22.0	44.6	93.9	3.3	1.1	0.5	-	5.2
42101	Philadelphia County, Pennsylvania	1,576,251	3.8	21.6	9.2	32.3	22.5	14.4	35.2	41.5	43.0	1.4	8.8	0.2	14.6
42107	Schuylkill County, Pennsylvania...	143,264	-4.7	20.1	6.8	23.9	28.6	20.7	43.9	94.7	4.2	1.8	0.9	-	5.8
42111	Somerset County, Pennsylvania...	73,627	-5.5	18.1	6.6	23.1	28.9	23.4	46.8	96.6	2.9	1.5	-	-	2.2
42125	Washington County, Pennsylvania	209,470	-0.5	19.7	8.4	23.0	27.9	21.0	44.0	94.3	4.0	1.1	1.7	-	4.0
42129	Westmoreland County, Pennsylvania	353,057	-4.5	18.2	7.2	22.2	28.9	23.6	47.3	95.7	3.8	0.9	1.4	-	2.8
42133	York County, Pennsylvania	458,696	3.2	21.9	8.2	24.7	26.9	18.3	40.9	87.7	8.4	0.9	2.0	0.1	7.8
44000	**RHODE ISLAND**......................	1,095,610	0.6	19.0	10.4	26.0	26.4	18.3	40.6	80.6	8.8	1.5	4.1	0.3	17.7
44003	Kent County, Rhode Island..........	170,715	-1.1	18.3	7.8	25.8	28.4	19.7	43.4	92.6	3.9	1.1	3.3	-	7.3
44005	Newport County, Rhode Island....	85,264	-1.0	15.9	8.4	23.8	27.1	24.8	46.7	93.3	6.7	1.0	2.9	-	5.7
44007	Providence County, Rhode Island	658,221	2.0	20.3	10.6	27.9	25.2	16.0	37.9	71.8	12.2	1.5	4.8	0.3	25.9
44009	Washington County, Rhode Island	130,592	-1.1	15.8	13.0	20.2	28.3	22.7	46.2	95.5	2.4	2.3	2.9	-	3.6
45000	**SOUTH CAROLINA**....................	5,190,705	8.6	21.5	9.2	25.3	25.4	18.6	40.2	69.7	26.9	1.9	2.3	0.2	5.9
45003	Aiken County, South Carolina	170,776	6.7	21.6	7.6	25.1	25.0	20.8	41.3	74.0	26.4	1.2	1.3	-	7.2
45007	Anderson County, South Carolina	206,908	8.2	22.7	7.8	25.2	26.0	18.3	41.0	83.3	14.8	4.0	1.6	-	4.3
45013	Beaufort County, South Carolina.	191,748	18.4	17.8	9.9	19.8	23.7	28.8	47.6	75.7	16.8	2.5	1.8	-	10.1
45015	Berkeley County, South Carolina.	236,701	28.2	23.8	9.1	28.1	24.4	14.6	37.0	70.8	26.1	1.4	4.0	0.3	7.0
45019	Charleston County, South Carolina	413,024	17.5	19.3	8.7	30.2	24.1	17.6	39.1	70.4	25.7	1.7	2.5	0.3	4.4
45035	Dorchester County, South Carolina	163,327	19.2	24.1	8.1	27.4	25.5	14.8	38.3	67.6	27.6	1.5	3.2		5.4
45041	Florence County, South Carolina.	136,504	1.0	23.6	8.5	25.0	24.9	17.9	40.0	52.8	44.1	0.7	1.8	-	3.4
45045	Greenville County, South Carolina	533,834	16.0	22.8	8.6	27.0	25.1	16.5	38.5	75.5	17.6	2.8	3.2	-	9.8
45047	Greenwood County, South Carolina	69,241	1.7	22.8	10.3	24.2	23.2	19.6	39.3	66.5	31.6	3.3	1.4	-	3.3
45051	Horry County, South Carolina	365,579	31.5	17.3	6.9	22.0	27.8	26.1	49.1	84.1	13.5	1.1	2.3	0.2	6.3
45055	Kershaw County, South Carolina.	66,130	7.9	22.9	7.7	23.7	26.9	18.8	41.3	71.9	26.3	0.7	1.4	-	5.5
45057	Lancaster County, South Carolina	100,336	27.9	21.5	7.6	25.2	24.3	21.3	40.3	77.1	18.4	3.0	2.4	-	5.1
45059	Laurens County, South Carolina..	67,803	1.4	21.9	8.7	24.5	26.2	18.7	41.3	71.8	26.1	0.6	-	-	6.4
45063	Lexington County, South Carolina	300,137	13.9	22.9	7.6	26.3	26.7	16.5	39.6	79.7	17.4	1.1	2.9	-	7.0
45073	Oconee County, South Carolina..	79,203	7.1	18.8	6.5	21.9	28.6	24.2	47.2	91.6	6.5	4.5	-	-	4.0
45075	Orangeburg County, South Carolina	82,962	-6.8	21.9	10.0	21.7	25.3	21.1	41.1	NA	NA	NA	NA	NA	NA
45077	Pickens County, South Carolina...	132,229	6.4	18.7	17.2	23.5	23.7	17.0	35.9	92.0	5.9	2.7	2.3	0.3	3.7
45079	Richland County, South Carolina.	418,307	8.1	21.5	15.0	26.8	23.1	13.6	34.2	45.8	49.9	1.3	3.6	0.1	5.6
45083	Spartanburg County, South Carolina	335,864	12.5	23.3	9.0	26.2	25.3	16.3	38.1	74.1	20.5	2.4	3.2	0.1	7.6

Table A-2. Counties — Who: Age, Race/Ethnicity, and Household Structure, 2021—Continued

STATE County	Two or more races (percent)	Hispanic or Latino (percent)	Native, born in state of residence (percent)	Foreign born (percent)	Non-citizens (percent)	Total households	Family households Total	Married couple	Male house-holder	Female house-holder	Nonfamily households Total	One-person house-holds	Percent of households with people age 60 years and over
ACS table number:	B02001	B03003	B05002	B05002	B05002	B11001	B11001	B11001	B11001	B11001	B11001	B11001	B11006
Column number:	15	16	17	18	19	20	21	22	23	24	25	26	27
PENNSYLVANIA—Cont.													
42063 Indiana County, Pennsylvania......	3.2	1.5	85.2	1.8	0.8	32,956	60.8	46.4	3.8	10.6	39.2	33.2	49.2
42069 Lackawanna County, Pennsylvania	9.8	9.5	77.7	4.9	2.2	88,294	61.2	44.2	5.1	11.9	38.8	31.7	47.3
42071 Lancaster County, Pennsylvania...	7.4	11.5	74.5	5.9	2.2	210,063	70.1	57.1	4.3	8.7	29.9	23.4	44.3
42073 Lawrence County, Pennsylvania...	4.7	1.8	84.2	1.8	0.7	36,286	64.8	47.6	5.8	11.4	35.2	29.3	52.6
42075 Lebanon County, Pennsylvania....	8.9	14.9	76.5	4.1	1.6	54,906	67.3	53.3	4.8	9.1	32.7	26.3	48.8
42077 Lehigh County, Pennsylvania.......	16.7	28.0	59.7	13.1	6.3	141,505	66.3	46.5	5.4	14.4	33.7	28.1	42.0
42079 Luzerne County, Pennsylvania.....	10.2	16.0	71.4	8.9	5.3	134,132	61.2	42.3	6.5	12.4	38.8	31.7	44.7
42081 Lycoming County, Pennsylvania...	4.0	2.3	83.6	1.9	0.9	47,022	63.6	49.0	3.9	10.7	36.4	29.4	44.5
42085 Mercer County, Pennsylvania	5.8	1.7	81.4	2.1	0.4	46,701	64.8	48.5	2.9	13.5	35.2	31.3	49.7
42089 Monroe County, Pennsylvania.....	13.9	18.3	42.8	9.7	3.3	65,907	72.3	53.9	6.1	12.3	27.7	21.9	47.8
42091 Montgomery County, Pennsylvania	6.9	5.8	69.0	10.8	4.3	335,248	67.9	54.2	3.8	9.9	32.1	25.9	43.6
42095 Northampton County, Pennsylvania	8.7	15.3	57.8	7.9	2.7	122,615	68.6	51.4	6.0	11.1	31.4	24.6	46.5
42097 Northumberland County, Pennsylvania	4.0	4.5	85.6	0.7	0.2	37,823	63.0	47.1	6.1	9.9	37.0	30.9	50.1
42101 Philadelphia County, Pennsylvania	8.4	15.9	63.7	15.0	7.5	660,921	53.3	28.1	5.2	20.0	46.7	37.1	36.4
42107 Schuylkill County, Pennsylvania ...	6.9	6.7	83.9	2.4	1.2	58,212	60.2	41.3	7.4	11.4	39.8	33.3	47.8
42111 Somerset County, Pennsylvania ...	3.3	1.7	84.5	0.6	0.4	29,115	67.3	55.1	4.4	7.8	32.7	28.7	53.4
42125 Washington County, Pennsylvania	4.9	1.9	82.0	1.7	0.6	88,544	61.6	47.7	3.9	10.0	38.4	33.1	46.7
42129 Westmoreland County, Pennsylvania	4.4	1.4	86.6	1.8	0.7	154,810	63.3	49.8	4.2	9.3	36.7	31.4	49.3
42133 York County, Pennsylvania	6.4	8.9	64.5	4.0	1.7	178,898	69.3	52.8	6.1	10.4	30.7	24.4	44.2
44000 **RHODE ISLAND**.........................	11.9	17.1	56.6	14.5	6.0	440,170	61.0	44.2	4.8	12.0	39.0	30.4	44.3
44003 Kent County, Rhode Island..........	7.9	6.7	70.8	6.4	2.3	73,182	60.6	45.3	4.4	10.9	39.4	31.0	44.6
44005 Newport County, Rhode Island....	8.6	6.2	40.2	6.6	1.6	38,311	57.4	47.8	3.2	6.4	42.6	32.2	52.9
44007 Providence County, Rhode Island	15.2	25.0	54.6	19.9	8.9	254,178	60.9	40.8	5.9	14.2	39.1	31.0	41.5
44009 Washington County, Rhode Island	5.5	3.7	54.1	5.9	2.5	54,044	63.8	54.3	1.4	8.1	36.2	24.9	48.8
45000 **SOUTH CAROLINA**....................	6.6	6.3	55.0	5.2	3.2	2,049,972	65.2	47.0	4.5	13.7	34.8	29.1	43.5
45003 Aiken County, South Carolina.....	9.8	6.3	35.9	4.3	2.3	67,224	67.9	48.6	4.7	14.5	32.1	26.6	49.0
45007 Anderson County, South Carolina	7.6	4.4	60.1	4.3	2.6	82,203	68.3	48.1	5.0	15.1	31.7	27.9	44.6
45013 Beaufort County, South Carolina.	6.8	11.2	26.0	7.8	5.6	76,249	65.5	54.8	2.4	8.3	34.5	28.1	56.3
45015 Berkeley County, South Carolina.	9.0	7.5	48.6	5.0	1.7	88,092	70.4	51.7	5.2	13.6	29.6	23.7	39.8
45019 Charleston County, South Carolina	4.6	5.5	47.4	5.9	3.3	169,851	59.6	44.4	4.3	10.9	40.4	31.0	39.5
45035 Dorchester County, South Carolina	5.0	6.3	45.8	4.4	2.6	58,435	70.5	54.1	3.1	13.3	29.5	25.5	39.7
45041 Florence County, South Carolina.	2.8	3.0	77.2	1.8	1.1	51,484	62.6	43.8	4.2	14.5	37.4	32.5	43.9
45045 Greenville County, South Carolina	8.8	10.0	49.3	9.3	5.2	212,333	66.4	49.2	5.0	12.2	33.6	28.1	38.8
45047 Greenwood County, South Carolina	6.1	6.7	75.2	3.3	2.7	26,577	63.3	46.8	3.4	13.1	36.7	30.6	43.7
45051 Horry County, South Carolina	7.4	6.3	32.9	5.4	2.4	145,335	64.0	48.9	3.5	11.6	36.0	30.7	55.2
45055 Kershaw County, South Carolina.	5.6	5.4	61.4	4.6	3.4	25,412	66.6	50.1	1.2	15.2	33.4	32.0	48.2
45057 Lancaster County, South Carolina	6.2	6.6	47.5	4.2	2.5	38,570	72.0	56.5	3.0	12.5	28.0	25.8	45.8
45059 Laurens County, South Carolina ..	5.4	5.7	71.5	4.4	3.0	26,580	71.2	48.4	7.8	14.9	28.8	24.7	46.6
45063 Lexington County, South Carolina	7.9	6.6	57.9	5.0	2.6	120,968	65.9	48.9	6.0	11.1	34.1	28.8	39.1
45073 Oconee County, South Carolina..	6.8	5.9	58.9	4.2	3.5	34,023	68.5	50.1	4.8	13.7	31.5	26.0	48.1
45075 Orangeburg County, South Carolina	NA	NA	82.5	1.6	0.1	32,017	58.9	32.8	4.4	21.6	41.1	37.7	51.5
45077 Pickens County, South Carolina...	6.8	4.3	61.3	4.0	2.8	51,996	61.6	49.4	4.9	7.3	38.4	30.6	40.6
45079 Richland County, South Carolina.	5.6	5.6	57.0	5.7	2.6	166,515	58.2	39.1	4.2	14.9	41.8	33.5	34.6
45083 Spartanburg County, South Carolina	7.7	7.9	58.4	7.4	3.5	128,437	70.4	50.4	5.2	14.8	29.6	25.0	38.8

STATE County	Total population	Percent change, 2010–2019	Population by age (percent)					Median age	Race alone or in combination (percent)					
			Under 18 years	18 to 24 years	25 to 44 years	45 to 64 years	65 years and over		White	Black or African American	American Indian and Alaska Native	Asian	Native Hawaiian or Other Pacific Islander	Some other race
ACS table number:	B01003	Population Estimates	B01001	B01001	B01001	B01001	B01001	B01002	B02008	B02009	B02010	B02011	B02012	B02013
Column number:	1	2	3	4	5	6	7	8	9	10	11	12	13	14
SOUTH CAROLINA—Cont.														
45085 Sumter County, South Carolina...	104,758	-0.7	23.8	9.7	25.5	23.8	17.3	36.8	51.1	47.6	1.1	2.1	-	3.9
45091 York County, South Carolina.......	288,595	24.3	23.8	8.0	26.5	26.7	14.9	39.5	76.2	20.5	1.6	3.5	-	5.7
46000 **SOUTH DAKOTA**...................	895,376	6.8	24.6	9.4	24.9	23.4	17.6	37.6	86.6	2.9	10.5	2.3	0.2	3.9
46083 Lincoln County, South Dakota.....	67,870	36.4	28.1	7.3	29.1	21.5	14.0	35.6	94.4	0.0	1.2	4.4	-	3.7
46099 Minnehaha County, South Dakota	199,685	14.0	25.3	8.4	29.5	22.9	13.9	35.9	87.4	7.8	3.9	2.7	-	5.5
46103 Pennington County, South Dakota	111,806	12.7	22.8	8.2	24.3	25.1	19.6	40.0	88.1	2.9	12.7	1.9	-	4.6
47000 **TENNESSEE**	6,975,218	5.8	22.0	8.9	26.4	25.6	17.0	39.2	79.4	17.4	2.0	2.4	0.2	5.8
47001 Anderson County, Tennessee	77,576	2.5	21.2	7.5	24.5	26.1	20.7	41.1	93.3	5.4	3.4	0.5	-	4.5
47009 Blount County, Tennessee..........	137,605	8.2	19.9	8.2	24.0	27.0	20.9	42.7	96.7	2.1	3.2	1.2	-	4.1
47011 Bradley County, Tennessee.........	110,162	9.2	21.7	9.3	24.8	27.0	17.2	39.6	92.0	4.6	2.4	1.4	-	5.6
47037 Davidson County, Tennessee	703,953	10.8	20.2	9.6	34.6	22.4	13.2	35.0	64.6	28.0	1.2	4.6	0.1	10.6
47059 Greene County, Tennessee.........	70,621	0.3	18.8	7.9	22.3	28.9	22.2	45.8	97.4	2.3	2.1	0.5	-	3.5
47065 Hamilton County, Tennessee......	369,135	9.3	20.8	9.1	26.6	25.3	18.1	39.4	76.7	19.8	1.0	2.7	0.1	6.5
47093 Knox County, Tennessee	486,677	8.8	20.9	11.5	26.8	24.5	16.3	37.7	88.7	8.7	2.8	3.0	0.2	5.3
47113 Madison County, Tennessee........	98,775	12.3	22.3	10.4	25.0	24.7	17.6	38.5	58.4	38.9	0.9	1.6	-	5.0
47119 Maury County, Tennessee	104,760	-1.5	23.2	6.7	27.3	26.0	16.8	39.9	86.8	14.3	1.2	1.3	-	5.0
47125 Montgomery County, Tennessee .	227,900	21.3	27.1	10.6	31.6	21.0	9.7	31.9	74.5	25.7	4.0	4.3	1.5	6.7
47141 Putnam County, Tennessee	81,188	11.0	20.2	14.5	23.9	24.2	17.2	37.9	92.5	3.5	0.9	1.8	-	5.6
47147 Robertson County, Tennessee.....	74,098	8.3	23.6	7.3	26.4	26.9	15.8	39.9	87.6	7.4	2.3	1.0	-	7.5
47149 Rutherford County, Tennessee.....	352,182	26.5	24.5	11.4	29.0	23.9	11.2	34.6	76.0	18.1	1.4	4.9	0.8	7.9
47155 Sevier County, Tennessee	99,517	9.3	20.4	8.0	23.3	28.2	20.1	43.5	93.2	0.6	2.4	1.6	-	8.0
47157 Shelby County, Tennessee..........	924,454	1.0	25.1	8.8	27.7	23.9	14.5	35.8	39.1	54.7	0.9	3.5	0.5	6.7
47163 Sullivan County, Tennessee........	159,265	1.0	18.9	7.3	23.5	27.9	22.4	45.2	97.5	1.9	2.2	1.1	-	2.3
47165 Sumner County, Tennessee.........	200,557	19.1	23.3	7.0	26.2	27.1	16.4	40.5	87.3	9.5	0.8	2.4	0.3	5.7
47179 Washington County, Tennessee...	134,236	5.2	18.9	11.3	24.5	26.3	19.0	41.1	94.3	3.8	2.5	2.0	0.4	4.2
47187 Williamson County, Tennessee	255,735	30.2	26.2	8.2	23.4	28.0	14.3	40.2	90.5	5.0	3.0	4.3	-	5.2
47189 Wilson County, Tennessee..........	151,917	26.9	23.3	7.5	26.3	26.8	16.1	40.8	90.1	7.2	3.6	2.5	-	4.6
48000 **TEXAS**	29,527,941	12.6	25.3	9.6	28.4	23.5	13.2	35.5	70.9	13.7	2.4	6.3	0.2	31.4
48005 Angelina County, Texas...............	86,506	-0.1	25.4	8.0	24.4	23.9	18.2	37.7	81.8	11.8	6.3	1.3	-	20.1
48021 Bastrop County, Texas................	102,058	19.6	24.4	5.8	25.1	27.8	16.8	40.6	76.1	5.7	4.6	3.1	-	31.0
48027 Bell County, Texas.....................	379,617	17.0	27.6	11.2	29.4	20.4	11.4	31.7	65.4	28.0	3.1	4.6	0.5	16.8
48029 Bexar County, Texas...................	2,028,236	16.8	25.1	10.1	29.8	22.5	12.5	34.4	75.1	9.7	3.0	4.5	0.4	45.0
48037 Bowie County, Texas..................	92,581	0.7	23.7	9.2	26.3	24.0	16.8	38.1	72.6	26.8	1.5	1.6	-	2.4
48039 Brazoria County, Texas...............	379,689	19.5	25.9	8.5	28.7	24.4	12.5	36.2	68.4	17.2	1.7	7.7	0.4	25.7
48041 Brazos County, Texas..................	237,032	17.6	20.7	24.8	26.6	17.7	10.1	28.2	77.0	11.9	1.9	6.7	0.2	14.4
48061 Cameron County, Texas..............	423,029	4.2	29.1	10.7	24.7	21.5	14.0	32.6	87.6	0.7	1.0	0.9	-	64.0
48085 Collin County, Texas..................	1,109,462	32.3	25.1	8.3	28.8	26.4	11.3	37.6	66.1	12.5	1.8	18.9	0.3	12.7
48091 Comal County, Texas..................	174,986	44.0	22.1	7.9	24.3	27.5	18.2	41.9	89.7	3.2	2.4	2.2	-	25.7
48099 Coryell County, Texas.................	84,232	0.7	22.3	15.0	31.6	20.7	10.5	32.7	72.9	20.0	5.5	3.5	1.4	13.8
48113 Dallas County, Texas..................	2,586,050	11.3	25.5	9.5	30.2	23.3	11.5	34.0	54.7	24.3	2.7	7.7	0.2	33.2
48121 Denton County, Texas	941,647	33.9	23.7	9.2	30.0	26.0	11.1	36.8	71.1	13.1	2.8	11.5	0.2	17.2
48135 Ector County, Texas....................	161,091	21.2	30.7	9.9	29.5	19.8	10.2	31.9	67.2	6.6	1.8	1.5	-	50.3
48139 Ellis County, Texas.....................	202,678	4.8	26.5	8.6	26.3	25.3	13.2	36.3	73.1	14.7	2.7	1.2	-	24.4
48141 El Paso County, Texas.................	867,947	23.5	26.5	11.0	28.0	21.8	12.8	33.0	75.1	4.6	2.5	2.4	0.4	64.0
48157 Fort Bend County, Texas.............	858,527	38.7	26.9	7.8	27.7	25.5	12.1	36.9	46.6	22.1	1.4	22.9	0.2	21.9
48167 Galveston County, Texas............	355,062	17.4	23.9	8.2	26.9	25.9	15.1	38.2	77.9	14.2	1.6	4.4	0.6	21.2
48181 Grayson County, Texas...............	139,336	12.7	23.9	8.1	23.3	26.2	18.5	40.7	89.7	7.8	3.5	1.9	-	10.4
48183 Gregg County, Texas..................	124,201	1.8	25.6	10.1	25.8	23.0	15.5	36.2	77.1	20.7	4.1	2.0	-	17.9
48187 Guadalupe County, Texas...........	177,036	26.8	24.4	8.5	28.0	24.5	14.6	37.6	82.1	9.8	1.6	3.9	-	30.9
48201 Harris County, Texas..................	4,728,030	15.2	26.2	9.2	30.0	23.2	11.4	34.4	56.4	20.7	2.3	8.3	0.2	37.6
48203 Harrison County, Texas..............	69,150	1.4	24.7	9.3	23.7	24.2	18.1	39.4	71.1	21.4	2.5	1.0	-	12.7
48209 Hays County, Texas	255,397	46.5	22.8	15.7	28.1	21.6	11.7	33.6	87.2	5.1	4.6	2.7	-	32.4
48213 Henderson County, Texas...........	83,667	5.4	21.8	7.9	22.0	25.9	22.5	42.9	92.0	7.3	1.6	0.9	-	12.6
48215 Hidalgo County, Texas...............	880,356	12.1	31.6	11.1	25.8	20.1	11.3	30.1	86.6	1.2	1.0	1.0	0.1	71.4
48231 Hunt County, Texas...................	103,394	14.5	24.0	8.7	26.3	25.0	16.0	37.2	84.7	9.9	1.9	1.7	-	13.3

Table A-2. Counties — Who: Age, Race/Ethnicity, and Household Structure, 2021—*Continued*

STATE County	Two or more races (percent)	Hispanic or Latino (percent)	Native, born in state of residence (percent)	Foreign born (percent)	Non-citizens (percent)	Total households	Household type (percent of all households) Family households Total	Married couple	Male householder	Female householder	Nonfamily households Total	One-person households	Percent of households with people age 60 years and over
ACS table number:	B02001	B03003	B05002	B05002	B05002	B11001	B11001	B11001	B11001	B11001	B11001	B11001	B11006
Column number:	15	16	17	18	19	20	21	22	23	24	25	26	27
SOUTH CAROLINA—Cont.													
45085 Sumter County, South Carolina...	6.5	4.5	63.5	3.1	1.1	43,191	62.9	42.9	3.6	16.3	37.1	34.2	39.8
45091 York County, South Carolina......	7.1	6.6	36.0	5.1	2.5	113,195	70.1	51.4	4.6	14.2	29.9	23.4	36.5
46000 **SOUTH DAKOTA**.....................	6.0	4.2	63.6	3.5	2.2	356,887	62.0	49.0	4.6	8.3	38.0	30.2	41.1
46083 Lincoln County, South Dakota.....	4.7	2.8	61.1	6.0	1.5	26,565	71.1	56.9	5.1	9.1	28.9	22.5	33.0
46099 Minnehaha County, South Dakota ...	6.9	5.6	59.1	6.2	3.2	82,289	63.2	49.4	5.0	8.8	36.8	28.0	32.7
46103 Pennington County, South Dakota ...	10.0	5.8	57.4	1.9	1.0	46,296	59.7	48.4	4.1	7.2	40.3	31.3	44.0
47000 **TENNESSEE**	6.8	6.0	59.1	5.3	3.1	2,770,395	64.4	47.1	4.8	12.5	35.6	29.2	41.1
47001 Anderson County, Tennessee	6.1	3.5	57.7	3.1	1.9	31,735	63.0	43.6	7.1	12.3	37.0	32.1	45.7
47009 Blount County, Tennessee	7.0	4.0	59.7	2.5	1.6	55,446	65.9	52.9	3.2	9.8	34.1	29.4	44.2
47011 Bradley County, Tennessee..........	5.9	7.1	56.7	5.5	1.9	43,025	70.0	52.0	8.1	9.9	30.0	27.3	45.2
47037 Davidson County, Tennessee	9.0	10.6	46.6	13.3	8.1	316,273	52.4	35.4	4.7	12.4	47.6	34.7	29.8
47059 Greene County, Tennessee..........	5.7	3.3	66.6	1.6	0.7	28,585	69.5	54.0	4.1	11.5	30.5	26.1	51.3
47065 Hamilton County, Tennessee	6.6	6.4	54.7	5.6	3.9	151,676	63.0	45.5	6.1	11.4	37.0	31.0	42.1
47093 Knox County, Tennessee	8.2	4.9	58.3	5.0	2.8	198,914	58.9	44.8	3.9	10.2	41.1	32.3	38.9
47113 Madison County, Tennessee	4.4	4.4	71.3	2.6	1.2	39,730	62.2	38.2	5.2	18.8	37.8	33.1	45.0
47119 Maury County, Tennessee	7.8	6.8	56.6	2.6	1.3	41,309	72.6	58.3	3.2	11.1	27.4	24.0	40.2
47125 Montgomery County, Tennessee .	14.9	11.0	36.4	7.1	3.5	84,145	72.3	52.4	5.8	14.0	27.7	19.8	28.4
47141 Putnam County, Tennessee	4.2	6.9	54.8	4.5	3.0	33,652	60.0	45.5	6.6	8.0	40.0	29.6	40.5
47147 Robertson County, Tennessee......	5.5	7.9	64.3	4.8	2.7	27,233	72.1	55.0	5.5	11.6	27.9	21.9	40.8
47149 Rutherford County, Tennessee.....	8.4	9.5	51.4	9.7	5.4	121,944	69.4	55.2	3.7	10.6	30.6	23.1	32.4
47155 Sevier County, Tennessee	5.8	7.1	54.0	4.2	3.1	36,670	67.1	51.0	4.6	11.5	32.9	27.0	49.4
47157 Shelby County, Tennessee	4.9	6.9	61.9	7.1	4.6	366,593	60.7	36.3	4.6	19.7	39.3	33.6	38.1
47163 Sullivan County, Tennessee..........	4.8	2.3	58.2	1.7	0.7	68,804	61.5	44.9	5.3	11.4	38.5	34.4	48.6
47165 Sumner County, Tennessee..........	5.4	5.9	53.8	4.1	2.4	77,760	69.5	54.3	4.4	10.8	30.5	25.0	39.8
47179 Washington County, Tennessee ...	6.9	4.0	56.4	3.3	0.9	56,752	58.3	47.1	3.8	7.4	41.7	32.0	43.6
47187 Williamson County, Tennessee ...	7.9	5.2	38.0	7.0	2.8	91,406	79.7	69.2	1.8	8.7	20.3	16.9	36.3
47189 Wilson County, Tennessee...........	7.7	5.3	56.7	4.9	3.5	55,047	69.1	57.0	3.2	9.0	30.9	23.8	40.8
48000 **TEXAS**	23.9	40.2	59.5	17.2	10.3	10,796,247	68.3	49.5	5.3	13.5	31.7	25.6	35.5
48005 Angelina County, Texas................	20.3	23.4	75.9	8.4	5.5	32,538	62.3	42.0	5.6	14.8	37.7	31.0	44.2
48021 Bastrop County, Texas.................	20.3	42.3	64.1	13.6	7.9	36,341	74.4	55.8	8.9	9.8	25.6	21.1	44.9
48027 Bell County, Texas.....................	16.7	26.5	47.2	7.0	3.5	139,582	67.3	47.2	4.9	15.1	32.7	27.9	30.9
48029 Bexar County, Texas....................	35.9	61.3	62.6	13.6	7.6	742,836	67.6	44.5	6.7	16.5	32.4	25.7	33.4
48037 Bowie County, Texas...................	4.7	8.4	64.7	4.3	2.9	34,038	66.8	44.7	5.0	17.0	33.2	30.2	43.2
48039 Brazoria County, Texas................	20.2	32.3	64.6	13.9	5.9	130,734	74.9	56.8	5.0	13.1	25.1	21.2	35.2
48041 Brazos County, Texas..................	11.7	27.0	65.8	11.3	7.0	86,154	54.5	40.4	4.4	9.6	45.5	30.8	28.2
48061 Cameron County, Texas	53.8	90.0	67.8	22.9	13.9	135,734	76.7	49.6	7.9	19.2	23.3	20.0	41.3
48085 Collin County, Texas....................	11.5	15.8	43.5	22.0	10.6	399,810	73.7	61.8	3.2	8.6	26.3	21.0	30.8
48091 Comal County, Texas...................	22.5	29.2	57.9	8.4	5.5	67,392	72.2	62.1	5.3	4.8	27.8	22.7	43.6
48099 Coryell County, Texas..................	16.4	20.0	43.5	5.2	2.7	26,980	74.4	54.5	3.1	16.9	25.6	21.6	32.4
48113 Dallas County, Texas...................	22.0	41.4	54.2	25.1	16.5	975,062	62.6	41.9	5.7	15.1	37.4	31.0	31.9
48121 Denton County, Texas	14.6	20.0	47.7	15.2	7.2	350,081	71.9	58.9	4.4	8.6	28.1	22.0	30.1
48135 Ector County, Texas....................	26.5	64.7	60.1	21.3	12.3	64,169	73.3	52.8	4.7	15.7	26.7	21.9	30.0
48139 Ellis County, Texas.....................	15.1	28.1	69.1	8.8	2.5	69,223	81.5	62.2	5.9	13.4	18.5	16.5	37.4
48141 El Paso County, Texas.................	47.5	82.9	58.2	22.9	11.2	298,059	72.8	46.5	6.8	19.5	27.2	22.8	37.3
48157 Fort Bend County, Texas.............	14.7	25.5	46.0	32.1	13.7	283,446	80.7	65.8	5.3	9.6	19.3	15.4	37.7
48167 Galveston County, Texas	19.3	26.4	62.4	10.1	4.4	144,182	69.5	54.3	4.3	11.0	30.5	24.9	37.7
48181 Grayson County, Texas................	12.4	15.0	65.0	6.0	3.8	56,005	70.3	50.2	6.3	13.8	29.7	24.9	45.3
48183 Gregg County, Texas...................	19.9	20.1	66.4	9.9	6.6	46,766	66.4	45.0	4.9	16.6	33.6	27.9	39.0
48187 Guadalupe County, Texas............	27.5	39.4	61.3	7.5	4.7	61,414	76.5	55.0	5.7	15.8	23.5	19.2	35.4
48201 Harris County, Texas...................	24.5	44.4	53.0	26.3	15.9	1,735,020	66.7	45.2	6.1	15.4	33.3	26.7	32.8
48203 Harrison County, Texas...............	8.3	14.3	66.1	5.4	2.2	25,866	73.4	49.0	2.5	22.0	26.6	22.7	47.6
48209 Hays County, Texas	30.3	40.6	62.2	8.9	5.6	94,205	63.7	47.1	4.6	12.0	36.3	23.2	32.0
48213 Henderson County, Texas...........	14.4	14.3	70.9	4.1	2.5	32,576	66.9	55.0	3.6	8.3	33.1	28.7	51.9
48215 Hidalgo County, Texas................	60.9	92.6	64.3	25.6	17.3	268,598	78.3	51.4	4.8	22.2	21.7	18.6	35.5
48231 Hunt County, Texas....................	11.3	19.5	67.3	6.2	3.7	37,206	71.3	50.1	5.5	15.6	28.7	22.6	43.8

Table A-2. Counties — Who: Age, Race/Ethnicity, and Household Structure, 2021—*Continued*

STATE County	Total population	Percent change, 2010–2019	Population by age (percent)					Median age	Race alone or in combination (percent)					
			Under 18 years	18 to 24 years	25 to 44 years	45 to 64 years	65 years and over		White	Black or African American	American Indian and Alaska Native	Asian	Native Hawaiian or Other Pacific Islander	Some other race
ACS table number:	B01003	Population Estimates	B01001	B01001	B01001	B01001	B01001	B01002	B02008	B02009	B02010	B02011	B02012	B02013
Column number:	1	2	3	4	5	6	7	8	9	10	11	12	13	14
TEXAS—Cont.														
48245 Jefferson County, Texas	253,704	-0.5	24.4	9.2	27.6	23.5	15.3	36.3	57.4	33.0	3.0	4.4	-	19.1
48251 Johnson County, Texas	187,280	-0.9	25.8	8.5	26.8	25.4	13.5	37.2	87.8	5.9	1.6	2.4	0.3	17.0
48257 Kaufman County, Texas	157,768	-0.6	28.3	8.8	28.1	23.3	11.5	34.5	77.1	18.7	2.6	2.3	-	20.9
48291 Liberty County, Texas	97,621	4.6	28.6	9.3	26.6	21.0	14.5	35.6	79.5	9.2	0.8	-	-	30.7
48303 Lubbock County, Texas	314,451	12.9	23.7	16.6	26.9	20.0	12.9	31.6	80.9	8.8	2.0	3.0	0.1	26.5
48309 McLennan County, Texas	263,115	11.4	24.4	14.0	24.8	21.8	14.9	34.1	77.9	15.8	1.6	2.3	-	23.6
48329 Midland County, Texas	167,969	12.1	28.2	8.1	33.7	20.0	10.1	32.8	79.7	7.5	3.1	3.2	-	32.3
48339 Montgomery County, Texas	648,886	0.3	26.0	8.5	26.5	25.3	13.7	37.6	84.5	7.3	1.3	4.5	0.5	19.2
48355 Nueces County, Texas	353,079	5.0	24.2	10.1	27.0	23.3	15.4	36.4	87.3	4.1	1.4	2.6	0.1	53.4
48361 Orange County, Texas	84,742	6.5	25.2	7.3	24.0	24.6	15.9	38.0	89.7	9.4	1.8	1.4	-	7.8
48367 Parker County, Texas	156,764	-2.5	24.8	6.9	26.5	26.1	15.8	39.3	94.4	1.1	3.7	1.2	0.2	12.8
48375 Potter County, Texas	116,547	-3.0	26.8	9.1	28.3	22.8	13.0	35.3	75.1	11.9	3.4	6.0	-	25.2
48381 Randall County, Texas	143,854	14.1	23.6	10.8	27.4	23.0	15.2	36.0	89.8	4.9	1.6	2.3	-	18.1
48397 Rockwall County, Texas	116,381	33.9	26.7	6.6	27.6	25.4	13.7	37.5	81.4	9.8	1.6	4.7	-	18.1
48409 San Patricio County, Texas	69,699	3.0	26.3	8.8	26.8	23.2	14.9	35.7	88.4	1.3	0.9	1.6	-	43.3
48423 Smith County, Texas	237,186	11.0	24.3	9.6	25.7	23.2	17.1	37.4	78.4	18.2	1.7	2.0	-	8.0
48427 Starr County, Texas	66,049	6.0	33.5	11.4	25.7	18.8	10.6	28.4	NA	NA	NA	NA	NA	NA
48439 Tarrant County, Texas	2,126,477	16.2	25.7	9.4	28.7	24.2	12.0	35.1	63.1	19.6	2.0	7.1	0.3	25.1
48441 Taylor County, Texas	143,326	5.0	24.6	13.9	26.7	20.2	14.6	33.3	84.3	9.8	1.5	2.9	-	19.3
48451 Tom Green County, Texas	119,411	8.1	24.0	12.1	26.3	21.5	16.1	35.3	86.8	4.6	3.8	2.1	-	25.7
48453 Travis County, Texas	1,305,154	24.4	20.7	8.9	36.4	23.5	10.6	35.5	73.1	9.6	2.7	9.3	0.1	25.1
48469 Victoria County, Texas	90,964	6.1	25.3	10.2	26.4	21.6	16.5	36.3	85.4	7.0	1.4	1.5	-	33.7
48471 Walker County, Texas	77,977	7.5	14.7	23.3	27.2	20.6	14.2	33.3	73.0	22.3	3.2	1.3	-	15.4
48479 Webb County, Texas	267,945	10.5	31.7	11.6	25.8	20.8	10.1	29.7	88.6	0.4	0.6	0.7	-	78.3
48485 Wichita County, Texas	130,069	0.6	22.7	13.4	26.6	22.2	15.0	34.6	81.7	12.1	2.8	3.1	-	14.0
48491 Williamson County, Texas	643,026	39.7	24.5	7.9	30.9	24.1	12.6	36.9	76.3	8.6	2.3	10.2	0.3	20.1
48497 Wise County, Texas	71,714	18.4	24.6	7.0	26.9	26.0	15.4	39.0	85.9	1.2	1.9	1.6	-	18.2
49000 **UTAH**	3,337,975	12.2	28.3	11.4	28.5	20.1	11.6	31.8	88.4	2.1	2.5	4.0	1.6	11.8
49005 Cache County, Utah	137,417	13.9	29.6	18.5	25.8	16.0	10.0	25.9	93.3	0.4	2.8	3.8	0.6	8.6
49011 Davis County, Utah	367,285	16.0	30.8	9.5	28.8	20.3	10.6	32.3	92.0	2.4	1.5	3.7	1.2	8.4
49035 Salt Lake County, Utah	1,186,421	12.7	25.9	9.7	31.1	21.7	11.6	33.8	82.5	3.1	2.8	6.0	2.4	16.1
49045 Tooele County, Utah	76,640	24.1	31.3	9.0	30.1	20.2	9.4	32.5	94.8	1.7	2.7	1.0	1.3	7.8
49049 Utah County, Utah	684,986	23.2	32.2	16.2	27.7	15.9	7.9	25.9	91.6	1.6	1.8	3.4	1.9	10.7
49053 Washington County, Utah	191,226	28.6	24.8	9.8	22.1	21.4	21.9	39.2	92.6	1.1	2.1	3.2	-	8.1
49057 Weber County, Utah	267,066	12.5	27.0	9.8	29.9	21.1	12.2	33.5	87.7	2.0	2.8	2.6	0.6	12.9
50000 **VERMONT**	645,570	-0.3	18.1	10.2	24.0	27.1	20.6	42.9	95.9	2.0	1.9	2.5	0.1	3.1
50007 Chittenden County, Vermont	168,865	4.6	17.5	15.2	27.0	24.1	16.2	37.4	92.3	3.5	1.4	5.5	-	3.0
51000 **VIRGINIA**	8,642,274	5.9	21.8	9.5	27.0	25.5	16.3	38.8	69.4	21.2	2.0	8.5	0.3	9.1
51003 Albemarle County, Virginia	113,535	10.5	19.7	11.9	23.7	25.0	19.8	40.8	81.3	11.4	0.9	6.9	-	6.0
51013 Arlington County, Virginia	232,965	14.1	18.1	8.3	38.5	23.2	11.9	35.9	74.1	12.0	2.0	13.3	-	14.0
51015 Augusta County, Virginia	77,563	2.5	19.1	8.5	23.0	28.0	21.4	44.6	NA	NA	NA	NA	NA	NA
51019 Bedford County, Virginia	80,131	15.0	19.3	7.6	21.0	29.6	22.5	47.1	90.9	6.7	1.7	1.8	-	4.4
51041 Chesterfield County, Virginia	370,688	11.6	23.7	8.5	26.1	25.9	15.8	39.2	64.6	26.5	2.0	4.4	0.7	8.9
51059 Fairfax County, Virginia	1,139,720	6.1	23.1	8.3	27.6	26.5	14.5	38.8	62.1	12.0	2.0	23.4	0.3	15.1
51061 Fauquier County, Virginia	73,815	9.2	22.2	9.0	24.0	27.8	17.0	40.4	89.5	9.0	2.3	2.4	-	7.8
51069 Frederick County, Virginia	93,717	14.1	22.8	7.3	25.9	26.0	18.0	40.2	84.8	4.6	1.5	2.6	-	11.1
51085 Hanover County, Virginia	111,603	7.9	21.5	7.9	23.0	28.2	19.3	43.1	88.0	10.5	1.6	2.9	-	4.7
51087 Henrico County, Virginia	333,554	7.8	22.2	7.6	28.2	25.6	16.4	39.3	56.7	32.2	1.5	10.7	0.2	6.5
51095 James City County, Virginia	79,882	14.2	19.6	8.0	19.5	26.2	26.8	47.1	82.9	14.9	1.3	3.9	-	4.6
51107 Loudoun County, Virginia	427,592	32.4	27.1	7.8	28.0	26.9	10.1	37.6	64.8	9.8	1.5	24.1	0.1	13.3
51121 Montgomery County, Virginia	98,473	4.4	15.3	28.1	23.9	19.2	13.6	30.2	88.1	5.7	1.1	7.2	-	2.9
51153 Prince William County, Virginia	484,472	17.0	26.7	8.9	28.0	25.6	10.8	36.1	59.1	24.3	3.1	12.4	0.4	19.2
51161 Roanoke County, Virginia	96,589	2.0	19.7	7.1	23.1	27.4	22.8	45.1	88.4	6.6	2.1	4.2	-	3.8
51165 Rockingham County, Virginia	84,394	7.4	22.1	8.3	24.5	25.5	19.7	39.9	95.5	5.0	2.0	1.7	-	7.5
51177 Spotsylvania County, Virginia	143,676	11.3	24.4	8.1	25.9	26.7	14.9	38.3	72.3	20.5	1.0	4.2	-	10.4
51179 Stafford County, Virginia	160,877	18.5	26.0	9.8	27.7	26.0	10.5	36.6	66.8	23.8	1.7	6.4	0.3	13.1

Table A-2. Counties — Who: Age, Race/Ethnicity, and Household Structure, 2021—*Continued*

STATE County	Two or more races (percent)	Hispanic or Latino (percent)	Native, born in state of residence (percent)	Foreign born (percent)	Non-citizens (percent)	Total house-holds	Family households Total	Family households Married couple	Family households Male house-holder	Family households Female house-holder	Nonfamily households Total	Nonfamily households One-person house-holds	Percent of households with people age 60 years and over
ACS table number:	B02001	B03003	B05002	B05002	B05002	B11001	B11001	B11001	B11001	B11001	B11001	B11001	B11006
Column number:	15	16	17	18	19	20	21	22	23	24	25	26	27
TEXAS—Cont.													
48245 Jefferson County, Texas..............	16.6	23.1	69.3	11.1	6.5	94,828	63.8	41.8	4.0	17.9	36.2	30.5	40.2
48251 Johnson County, Texas	14.4	24.2	72.9	6.6	4.0	64,338	80.4	63.3	5.2	11.9	19.6	16.6	40.2
48257 Kaufman County, Texas..............	20.0	25.9	64.3	9.2	4.1	50,212	76.0	59.7	4.2	12.1	24.0	18.4	33.2
48291 Liberty County, Texas	20.8	34.3	70.6	13.1	11.1	29,290	73.7	57.4	4.7	11.7	26.3	20.4	39.9
48303 Lubbock County, Texas...............	20.5	37.3	77.0	5.0	2.2	124,689	61.9	43.1	5.3	13.5	38.1	29.2	31.7
48309 McLennan County, Texas............	20.3	27.6	69.3	8.1	4.8	97,065	63.8	45.0	5.6	13.2	36.2	28.1	37.3
48329 Midland County, Texas...............	25.2	48.2	67.6	13.4	7.6	66,052	70.9	56.6	6.0	8.4	29.1	23.7	26.6
48339 Montgomery County, Texas........	16.8	26.4	53.0	14.7	8.9	232,095	74.4	60.5	4.9	9.0	25.6	21.5	37.6
48355 Nueces County, Texas.................	48.0	65.2	75.0	8.8	5.7	127,624	69.1	47.1	6.4	15.7	30.9	24.2	39.1
48361 Orange County, Texas	9.6	9.3	72.8	2.7	1.2	31,323	71.7	57.1	4.2	10.4	28.3	24.1	38.8
48367 Parker County, Texas.................	12.3	14.0	64.5	4.6	3.6	55,525	74.4	65.0	2.1	7.2	25.6	22.5	41.1
48375 Potter County, Texas.................	19.9	40.1	66.5	14.0	7.8	44,472	61.1	39.6	7.9	13.7	38.9	31.6	33.1
48381 Randall County, Texas................	16.6	24.9	69.2	5.7	3.3	56,509	65.5	53.8	3.3	8.4	34.5	27.6	37.7
48397 Rockwall County, Texas..............	14.0	20.2	54.0	13.2	6.9	39,329	80.3	69.9	1.8	8.5	19.7	16.2	36.6
48409 San Patricio County, Texas........	36.2	58.7	76.2	5.2	2.7	25,495	71.7	47.7	5.4	18.6	28.3	23.5	39.7
48423 Smith County, Texas..................	8.0	20.7	70.2	8.2	5.5	81,175	69.7	54.1	3.5	12.0	30.3	25.3	42.1
48427 Starr County, Texas	NA	NA	65.4	29.0	20.0	19,460	75.1	45.1	3.2	26.9	24.9	22.3	39.5
48439 Tarrant County, Texas...............	16.3	30.2	54.4	17.2	10.0	771,657	67.8	48.4	5.2	14.2	32.2	25.9	32.9
48441 Taylor County, Texas..................	17.3	26.0	66.8	6.0	3.4	55,974	62.3	43.7	4.3	14.2	37.7	27.8	36.3
48451 Tom Green County, Texas..........	22.7	42.0	71.4	5.0	2.7	45,516	60.9	44.9	5.9	10.1	39.1	31.0	41.0
48453 Travis County, Texas..................	19.1	33.4	48.8	17.6	10.3	567,627	53.5	41.5	3.3	8.7	46.5	34.1	26.0
48469 Victoria County, Texas...............	28.3	49.1	82.0	6.9	4.5	36,753	64.9	44.7	7.9	12.3	35.1	25.9	37.7
48471 Walker County, Texas................	15.1	18.7	70.4	5.5	3.1	24,704	55.6	36.2	4.3	15.0	44.4	34.5	38.4
48479 Webb County, Texas	68.6	95.4	68.1	25.8	16.5	78,730	78.6	48.2	6.7	23.7	21.4	18.3	36.4
48485 Wichita County, Texas...............	12.7	20.7	62.5	5.2	3.1	49,071	61.6	43.7	5.3	12.6	38.4	32.8	40.6
48491 Williamson County, Texas...........	16.6	25.4	49.9	15.2	8.1	241,836	70.9	57.9	4.0	8.9	29.1	22.8	31.4
48497 Wise County, Texas	8.6	20.8	67.0	7.4	4.1	24,449	77.9	57.5	8.1	12.4	22.1	18.9	44.7
49000 **UTAH**	9.5	14.8	61.7	8.3	4.8	1,101,499	72.5	59.3	4.6	8.6	27.5	20.6	32.8
49005 Cache County, Utah....................	9.0	11.2	64.2	5.9	3.0	43,099	77.3	64.5	4.0	8.8	22.7	16.0	27.4
49011 Davis County, Utah....................	8.6	10.7	66.3	5.1	2.2	114,119	76.2	62.7	4.4	9.1	23.8	19.5	32.1
49035 Salt Lake County, Utah...............	11.5	19.3	59.0	12.8	7.2	420,303	66.3	50.7	5.3	10.3	33.7	24.8	31.7
49045 Tooele County, Utah	8.0	14.2	71.4	2.5	1.2	23,495	81.6	68.6	4.1	8.9	18.4	14.5	32.3
49049 Utah County, Utah.....................	9.9	12.7	59.7	7.3	4.3	194,258	80.0	70.2	3.7	6.1	20.0	12.5	26.0
49053 Washington County, Utah...........	7.2	11.3	52.4	6.7	3.5	68,090	73.4	67.3	1.9	4.2	26.6	21.1	47.9
49057 Weber County, Utah	8.0	18.8	65.9	6.3	3.4	92,869	72.9	57.0	6.2	9.8	27.1	22.3	34.3
50000 **VERMONT**	5.1	2.0	48.8	4.2	2.2	270,163	61.1	48.4	4.0	8.7	38.9	27.9	44.9
50007 Chittenden County, Vermont......	5.5	2.6	41.8	8.0	3.8	70,730	56.8	46.5	3.4	6.9	43.2	27.0	37.7
51000 **VIRGINIA**	9.5	10.2	49.5	12.4	5.9	3,331,461	65.0	48.9	4.6	11.5	35.0	28.3	40.4
51003 Albemarle County, Virginia	6.6	5.9	44.7	9.3	5.7	45,195	60.4	47.8	5.1	7.5	39.6	31.5	43.9
51013 Arlington County, Virginia	13.7	15.6	22.4	22.1	11.5	108,396	44.8	37.1	2.6	5.1	55.2	41.7	24.9
51015 Augusta County, Virginia	NA	NA	69.9	2.7	0.8	30,186	70.0	52.2	4.5	13.4	30.0	25.5	48.7
51019 Bedford County, Virginia............	5.6	2.7	61.0	3.5	1.8	33,397	71.5	59.1	4.1	8.3	28.5	24.5	49.2
51041 Chesterfield County, Virginia	6.4	10.2	56.2	8.9	4.4	136,070	72.0	56.4	3.3	12.3	28.0	23.8	41.5
51059 Fairfax County, Virginia.............	13.4	16.6	29.6	29.9	11.1	410,660	69.6	57.1	3.9	8.5	30.4	23.8	38.3
51061 Fauquier County, Virginia...........	10.7	10.4	50.9	7.1	3.3	26,887	70.2	60.1	2.5	7.6	29.8	24.4	47.0
51069 Frederick County, Virginia	5.1	10.6	52.5	7.9	5.4	34,581	73.1	54.0	6.4	12.6	26.9	20.2	43.1
51085 Hanover County, Virginia	7.4	3.5	69.2	4.0	1.6	42,274	73.9	59.4	4.5	10.0	26.1	21.6	46.3
51087 Henrico County, Virginia............	6.9	6.3	59.0	12.7	5.8	137,035	61.8	44.4	3.7	13.7	38.2	31.0	39.5
51095 James City County, Virginia........	7.2	6.6	41.5	5.4	1.5	31,060	74.5	61.1	2.9	10.4	25.5	22.7	52.9
51107 Loudoun County, Virginia	12.4	13.9	33.4	25.6	9.9	141,935	78.4	66.4	4.7	7.3	21.6	16.7	30.4
51121 Montgomery County, Virginia.....	5.1	3.7	53.7	6.3	3.7	37,796	49.5	39.2	2.9	7.5	50.5	30.3	32.6
51153 Prince William County, Virginia ...	17.0	25.4	35.6	26.2	10.4	154,619	75.0	56.6	6.2	12.1	25.0	21.0	35.6
51161 Roanoke County, Virginia...........	4.9	3.6	63.0	6.0	2.3	39,093	67.1	51.1	6.1	10.0	32.9	30.8	48.4
51165 Rockingham County, Virginia......	8.6	8.2	65.1	6.3	3.8	32,551	70.9	59.4	5.6	6.0	29.1	24.6	47.6
51177 Spotsylvania County, Virginia	8.1	11.8	50.0	8.8	4.6	51,179	76.7	59.2	6.3	11.3	23.3	18.9	40.4
51179 Stafford County, Virginia............	11.0	15.5	37.7	12.7	4.0	51,007	78.2	62.7	5.5	10.0	21.8	18.9	32.8

Table A-2. Counties — Who: Age, Race/Ethnicity, and Household Structure, 2021—*Continued*

STATE County	Total population	Percent change, 2010–2019	Population by age (percent)					Median age	Race alone or in combination (percent)					
			Under 18 years	18 to 24 years	25 to 44 years	45 to 64 years	65 years and over		White	Black or African American	American Indian and Alaska Native	Asian	Native Hawaiian or Other Pacific Islander	Some other race
ACS table number:	B01003	Population Estimates	B01001	B01001	B01001	B01001	B01001	B01002	B02008	B02009	B02010	B02011	B02012	B02013
Column number:	1	2	3	4	5	6	7	8	9	10	11	12	13	14
VIRGINIA—Cont.														
51199 York County, Virginia	70,915	4.3	22.8	8.1	26.6	25.1	17.4	39.8	80.4	13.0	4.1	8.3	1.5	7.0
51510 Alexandria city, Virginia.............	154,706	13.9	18.3	5.3	39.5	24.2	12.8	37.2	66.2	24.3	1.3	7.7	0.2	15.6
51550 Chesapeake city, Virginia	251,269	10.2	24.3	8.9	27.9	24.8	14.1	37.8	65.0	30.2	3.4	5.4	0.7	6.7
51650 Hampton city, Virginia	137,746	-2.1	21.4	11.8	28.5	22.8	15.5	36.0	45.3	53.2	4.0	3.4	-	5.4
51680 Lynchburg city, Virginia	79,009	8.7	17.9	26.9	23.6	16.7	14.8	27.6	65.7	30.1	2.8	4.0	-	4.8
51700 Newport News city, Virginia	184,587	-0.8	23.3	11.8	29.0	22.3	13.5	34.5	50.1	44.0	1.6	5.2	-	10.3
51710 Norfolk city, Virginia	235,089	-0.0	19.4	17.4	31.6	19.8	11.8	31.3	50.8	43.5	1.4	5.0	-	7.8
51740 Portsmouth city, Virginia	97,840	-1.2	23.2	9.2	30.5	21.4	15.6	35.6	43.2	56.5	4.4	3.0	-	4.4
51760 Richmond city, Virginia	226,604	12.8	17.1	11.4	35.9	21.4	14.2	34.8	48.4	46.3	1.3	3.1	0.3	8.8
51770 Roanoke city, Virginia	98,865	2.2	22.4	7.6	28.3	24.2	17.5	37.6	66.5	31.8	0.9	3.9	-	5.6
51800 Suffolk city, Virginia	96,194	8.9	23.7	8.0	26.8	26.7	14.9	39.0	55.0	42.8	3.3	2.9	-	4.4
51810 Virginia Beach city, Virginia	457,672	2.7	22.0	8.8	29.8	24.2	15.1	37.1	69.9	22.2	1.5	10.4	0.9	7.4
WASHINGTON	7,738,692	10.1	21.7	8.6	29.3	24.3	16.2	38.2	78.1	5.9	3.5	12.3	1.4	12.3
53005 Benton County, Washington	210,025	16.7	26.3	8.3	27.0	22.7	15.7	36.4	84.0	2.6	2.6	5.0	0.4	21.4
53007 Chelan County, Washington	79,646	6.6	23.0	9.4	25.0	21.6	21.1	39.3	77.5	0.9	2.8	1.7	0.4	27.6
53009 Clallam County, Washington	78,209	8.3	17.1	5.7	21.4	24.3	31.4	51.5	91.7	1.9	7.0	3.0	0.2	7.8
53011 Clark County, Washington	511,404	14.8	23.0	8.1	27.0	25.7	16.3	39.2	86.1	4.1	3.0	7.1	1.6	9.5
53015 Cowlitz County, Washington	111,524	8.0	22.7	6.5	25.7	25.6	19.5	41.6	92.5	1.6	4.1	2.5	0.3	8.5
53021 Franklin County, Washington	98,268	21.8	31.4	11.3	26.8	21.6	8.9	30.7	68.9	2.4	1.9	1.7	2.2	46.3
53025 Grant County, Washington	100,297	9.7	28.6	8.9	26.6	22.7	13.1	33.9	72.0	0.7	5.8	2.0	-	35.7
53027 Grays Harbor County, Washington	76,841	3.1	20.0	7.0	23.9	26.1	22.9	44.5	89.9	1.1	7.4	2.9	1.4	10.1
53029 Island County, Washington	87,432	8.5	17.5	10.6	22.6	24.0	25.2	44.2	85.9	4.8	3.1	7.6	-	6.4
53033 King County, Washington	2,252,305	16.6	19.8	7.8	34.1	24.6	13.7	37.4	66.3	8.6	2.3	23.7	1.4	9.8
53035 Kitsap County, Washington........	274,314	8.1	19.9	8.7	27.6	24.4	19.3	40.0	86.4	5.2	3.4	9.1	2.0	7.0
53041 Lewis County, Washington	84,398	7.0	21.7	6.6	24.9	26.1	20.7	42.3	92.2	1.8	4.2	3.0	-	9.3
53045 Mason County, Washington	67,615	10.0	19.5	7.0	24.2	26.2	23.1	44.4	90.5	0.9	9.6	2.9	2.0	11.5
53053 Pierce County, Washington	925,708	13.8	23.2	8.7	29.7	23.9	14.4	36.9	78.1	11.1	4.4	10.9	2.9	10.0
53057 Skagit County, Washington	130,696	10.5	21.3	7.4	24.9	24.4	22.1	41.6	84.1	2.0	4.4	3.7	0.4	17.5
53061 Snohomish County, Washington .	833,540	15.2	22.3	7.3	30.2	25.8	14.4	38.3	77.3	5.6	3.0	15.8	1.4	10.4
53063 Spokane County, Washington	546,040	10.9	21.8	9.2	28.4	24.0	16.8	37.9	91.2	4.0	3.2	4.0	1.2	6.4
53067 Thurston County, Washington	297,977	15.2	21.1	8.5	28.1	24.0	18.2	39.3	85.2	5.8	3.8	8.9	1.9	9.1
53073 Whatcom County, Washington ...	228,831	14.0	18.7	13.5	25.9	23.3	18.6	38.8	87.7	2.0	4.5	6.8	0.6	8.2
53077 Yakima County, Washington	256,035	3.1	29.4	9.5	26.1	21.0	14.1	32.8	72.0	1.6	6.0	2.3	0.5	46.6
WEST VIRGINIA	1,782,959	-2.0	20.3	8.8	23.8	26.5	20.7	42.8	95.6	4.3	1.8	1.2	0.1	2.4
54003 Berkeley County, West Virginia ...	126,069	14.4	22.9	8.3	26.8	27.2	14.8	38.5	89.8	10.4	1.4	1.7	-	6.5
54011 Cabell County, West Virginia.......	93,418	-4.5	20.0	12.4	25.1	23.7	18.8	39.7	94.3	4.9	2.8	1.6	-	1.6
54033 Harrison County, West Virginia ...	65,158	-2.7	21.6	7.3	24.4	27.1	19.7	42.4	98.2	1.3	2.4	0.9	-	3.5
54039 Kanawha County, West Virginia..	177,952	-7.7	20.2	6.7	25.0	26.4	21.7	43.7	91.7	9.4	0.6	1.8	-	1.2
54061 Monongalia County, West Virginia..............	106,387	9.8	17.2	20.3	28.0	21.0	13.5	33.0	93.2	4.2	3.1	4.1	-	1.3
54081 Raleigh County, West Virginia	73,771	-7.0	21.6	7.3	23.7	25.6	21.8	43.1	NA	NA	NA	NA	NA	NA
54107 Wood County, West Virginia.......	83,624	-4.0	21.1	7.2	23.4	27.4	20.8	43.4	98.3	2.8	1.2	0.4	0.5	1.3
WISCONSIN	5,895,908	1.9	21.6	9.2	25.2	26.1	17.9	40.1	87.4	7.6	2.0	3.7	0.1	7.0
55009 Brown County, Wisconsin	269,591	6.7	23.3	9.0	26.6	25.4	15.7	38.3	87.8	4.5	3.5	4.0	-	10.0
55017 Chippewa County, Wisconsin	66,865	3.6	21.6	7.2	23.8	27.6	19.7	42.9	96.2	2.1	1.0	1.8	-	3.4
55025 Dane County, Wisconsin	563,951	12.0	20.0	13.5	29.3	22.8	14.5	35.9	86.2	7.4	1.0	7.4	0.1	7.1
55027 Dodge County, Wisconsin...........	89,313	-1.0	19.7	7.9	25.5	28.4	18.5	42.4	95.4	4.2	1.5	1.0	-	5.8
55035 Eau Claire County, Wisconsin......	106,452	6.0	20.2	15.8	26.0	21.5	16.5	35.5	93.5	2.5	0.9	5.2	-	3.3
55039 Fond du Lac County, Wisconsin ..	104,362	1.7	21.2	8.3	24.4	27.2	18.9	41.8	92.1	3.4	1.2	2.2	-	6.5
55055 Jefferson County, Wisconsin.......	84,943	1.3	20.0	9.6	23.4	28.8	18.3	42.9	94.3	1.6	0.7	1.3	-	7.4
55059 Kenosha County, Wisconsin........	168,732	1.9	22.0	9.7	25.9	27.6	14.9	39.9	88.2	7.3	4.6	2.6	-	12.5
55063 La Crosse County, Wisconsin	120,433	2.9	20.2	15.1	24.1	23.4	17.2	36.5	92.8	2.9	0.9	5.4	-	2.5
55071 Manitowoc County, Wisconsin....	81,505	-3.0	20.2	7.8	22.3	28.0	21.7	44.6	95.7	1.9	1.2	3.2	0.6	3.8
55073 Marathon County, Wisconsin	137,648	1.2	22.7	7.4	24.3	26.9	18.7	41.4	90.8	1.5	1.1	7.0	-	2.6
55079 Milwaukee County, Wisconsin ...	928,059	-0.2	23.9	9.4	29.4	22.9	14.3	35.4	61.8	28.9	1.9	5.6	0.2	14.0
55087 Outagamie County, Wisconsin	191,545	6.3	23.2	8.1	26.6	26.4	15.7	38.2	91.8	2.4	2.2	4.4	-	5.0

Table A-2. Counties — Who: Age, Race/Ethnicity, and Household Structure, 2021—*Continued*

STATE County code	STATE County	Two or more races (percent)	Hispanic or Latino (percent)	Native, born in state of residence (percent)	Foreign born (percent)	Non-citizens (percent)	Total households	Family households Total	Married couple	Male householder	Female householder	Nonfamily households Total	One-person households	Percent of households with people age 60 years and over
	ACS table number:	B02001	B03003	B05002	B05002	B05002	B11001	B11001	B11001	B11001	B11001	B11001	B11001	B11006
	Column number:	15	16	17	18	19	20	21	22	23	24	25	26	27
	VIRGINIA—Cont.													
51199	York County, Virginia	12.1	7.5	37.6	7.9	1.5	26,641	79.1	65.3	4.1	9.7	20.9	16.7	43.2
51510	Alexandria city, Virginia	14.4	16.5	23.7	23.7	13.7	72,024	43.4	33.0	2.3	8.1	56.6	46.5	28.7
51550	Chesapeake city, Virginia	10.6	7.3	51.4	5.5	1.7	93,849	73.8	53.4	5.3	15.2	26.2	20.4	37.2
51650	Hampton city, Virginia	9.5	6.7	50.1	5.1	0.9	58,181	63.7	38.8	6.5	18.4	36.3	32.2	40.3
51680	Lynchburg city, Virginia	6.0	4.8	55.9	5.5	3.6	28,346	57.4	38.0	3.5	15.8	42.6	33.3	35.5
51700	Newport News city, Virginia	10.6	10.0	51.8	7.0	2.8	77,489	55.3	34.7	4.1	16.5	44.7	36.9	34.5
51710	Norfolk city, Virginia	7.9	9.1	46.1	9.2	4.6	97,596	53.7	33.1	6.2	14.4	46.3	36.0	31.4
51740	Portsmouth city, Virginia	10.4	5.2	64.4	2.9	1.0	40,827	62.2	32.6	5.1	24.5	37.8	30.5	38.2
51760	Richmond city, Virginia	7.0	7.8	60.2	7.1	4.4	99,929	41.1	22.1	5.2	13.9	58.9	46.2	34.5
51770	Roanoke city, Virginia	8.4	7.1	65.9	5.6	3.2	42,455	50.1	30.3	5.9	14.0	49.9	39.8	39.8
51800	Suffolk city, Virginia	8.2	4.9	60.5	3.2	1.3	37,383	72.8	50.1	6.8	16.0	27.2	21.5	37.8
51810	Virginia Beach city, Virginia	10.5	8.9	44.2	8.4	3.4	182,775	66.4	48.2	5.7	12.5	33.6	26.4	37.3
53000	**WASHINGTON**	12.4	13.7	46.4	14.8	7.9	3,022,255	64.1	49.8	4.6	9.7	35.9	27.1	39.0
53005	Benton County, Washington	15.4	24.0	50.6	11.9	7.4	76,855	66.9	49.9	4.6	12.3	33.1	27.2	41.5
53007	Chelan County, Washington	10.3	28.7	57.0	12.2	8.5	32,050	65.7	48.4	4.7	12.7	34.3	27.7	45.6
53009	Clallam County, Washington	11.5	7.4	48.8	4.5	1.8	34,773	66.3	52.8	4.7	8.8	33.7	26.0	57.7
53011	Clark County, Washington	10.3	11.0	37.0	11.8	4.6	193,919	67.1	50.4	5.4	11.3	32.9	24.5	40.9
53015	Cowlitz County, Washington	9.2	9.9	48.7	3.4	1.6	43,204	62.0	47.6	4.4	10.0	38.0	30.4	44.4
53021	Franklin County, Washington	22.6	54.1	54.7	20.2	13.9	28,989	81.4	54.7	6.9	19.8	18.6	12.7	28.2
53025	Grant County, Washington	15.5	43.1	58.9	17.1	12.1	35,572	67.4	46.8	9.4	11.2	32.6	22.9	35.7
53027	Grays Harbor County, Washington...............................	12.1	10.9	61.1	5.7	3.3	30,500	60.9	41.9	5.4	13.5	39.1	32.2	54.3
53029	Island County, Washington	7.5	8.7	36.7	8.0	3.2	35,976	64.4	53.7	0.9	9.8	35.6	28.9	52.3
53033	King County, Washington	10.9	10.3	39.3	25.0	13.0	924,763	59.3	48.1	3.5	7.6	40.7	29.7	32.3
53035	Kitsap County, Washington........	11.4	8.5	41.9	7.0	2.4	106,399	68.2	54.6	5.5	8.1	31.8	24.2	43.4
53041	Lewis County, Washington..........	9.9	11.4	62.5	4.9	2.8	32,304	66.7	47.8	6.3	12.6	33.3	23.7	50.4
53045	Mason County, Washington	14.3	11.3	53.3	6.3	3.2	25,036	71.9	57.3	7.4	7.2	28.1	21.8	53.3
53053	Pierce County, Washington.........	15.2	12.2	49.7	10.3	4.1	347,668	67.9	51.5	5.1	11.3	32.1	24.0	38.2
53057	Skagit County, Washington........	10.7	19.5	55.5	9.5	4.9	51,971	67.5	50.4	6.0	11.1	32.5	25.4	49.2
53061	Snohomish County, Washington .	12.2	11.2	51.2	17.4	8.6	312,365	68.9	54.9	4.7	9.3	31.1	24.3	38.4
53063	Spokane County, Washington......	9.4	6.6	55.3	4.9	2.0	217,920	61.5	45.8	5.6	10.2	38.5	30.1	40.1
53067	Thurston County, Washington	13.7	10.1	45.7	8.5	3.7	117,186	66.7	50.7	4.7	11.4	33.3	25.9	41.9
53073	Whatcom County, Washington ...	9.3	10.3	51.0	8.6	4.0	92,219	60.2	47.6	3.6	9.0	39.8	25.9	41.1
53077	Yakima County, Washington	28.0	51.8	61.4	17.5	12.1	86,992	69.4	45.5	8.9	15.0	30.6	25.4	39.1
54000	**WEST VIRGINIA**	5.0	1.7	68.5	1.6	0.8	722,201	64.0	47.8	5.0	11.2	36.0	29.9	46.4
54003	Berkeley County, West Virginia	9.1	5.4	34.4	3.6	1.4	50,841	66.8	48.9	4.9	13.0	33.2	23.7	37.3
54011	Cabell County, West Virginia.......	4.9	1.5	72.9	1.8	0.6	39,631	59.4	42.4	3.9	13.2	40.6	33.6	41.0
54033	Harrison County, West Virginia ...	6.2	1.9	78.4	0.9	0.1	26,143	59.1	43.6	5.8	9.7	40.9	34.7	43.6
54039	Kanawha County, West Virginia..	4.3	1.2	79.8	1.4	0.2	77,634	60.8	45.3	3.8	11.6	39.2	33.8	45.5
54061	Monongalia County, West Virginia...............................	5.5	2.3	56.3	4.4	2.7	42,710	52.1	42.8	2.8	6.6	47.9	34.0	29.6
54081	Raleigh County, West Virginia	NA	NA	71.9	2.0	1.3	29,505	63.6	46.4	5.3	11.9	36.4	30.0	44.8
54107	Wood County, West Virginia.......	3.6	1.3	74.4	0.9	0.4	35,756	63.7	48.0	5.6	10.2	36.3	30.8	45.5
55000	**WISCONSIN**	7.4	7.5	70.9	5.1	2.7	2,449,970	61.8	47.5	4.7	9.7	38.2	30.3	40.9
55009	Brown County, Wisconsin	9.8	9.7	73.9	5.0	2.9	110,225	60.9	46.7	5.2	9.1	39.1	31.9	37.1
55017	Chippewa County, Wisconsin	4.6	2.0	81.8	2.3	0.5	26,791	60.3	48.7	4.0	7.5	39.7	33.7	45.4
55025	Dane County, Wisconsin............	8.7	6.9	60.2	9.9	5.8	243,924	53.5	43.0	3.1	7.5	46.5	34.0	31.8
55027	Dodge County, Wisconsin..........	7.3	5.8	82.4	3.6	2.5	36,286	60.3	49.0	4.0	7.4	39.7	33.0	45.0
55035	Eau Claire County, Wisconsin......	5.3	2.9	70.6	3.0	1.1	43,253	63.2	49.6	7.1	6.5	36.8	27.1	38.3
55039	Fond du Lac County, Wisconsin ..	4.8	6.0	82.3	3.7	2.4	42,758	66.5	53.5	3.5	9.5	33.5	28.5	42.6
55055	Jefferson County, Wisconsin	5.3	7.8	73.0	4.1	3.0	35,088	65.1	51.5	2.8	10.7	34.9	28.7	41.8
55059	Kenosha County, Wisconsin	13.4	14.4	52.4	7.4	3.3	67,810	65.8	50.4	4.8	10.7	34.2	29.3	38.3
55063	La Crosse County, Wisconsin	4.9	2.3	71.1	3.2	0.5	50,217	53.6	43.0	3.6	7.0	46.4	33.4	40.4
55071	Manitowoc County, Wisconsin....	6.0	4.9	80.4	2.3	1.1	35,716	60.0	45.5	4.7	9.7	40.0	34.1	46.3
55073	Marathon County, Wisconsin......	2.9	3.1	76.8	4.6	1.5	57,566	64.8	51.9	4.9	8.0	35.2	26.7	41.2
55079	Milwaukee County, Wisconsin ...	11.8	16.4	68.4	9.2	5.0	389,434	55.5	33.2	5.8	16.5	44.5	35.4	34.6
55087	Outagamie County, Wisconsin	5.7	4.9	77.8	3.6	1.5	77,071	62.4	52.1	3.8	6.5	37.6	29.9	37.0

Table A-2. Counties — Who: Age, Race/Ethnicity, and Household Structure, 2021—*Continued*

STATE County	Total population	Percent change, 2010–2019	Population by age (percent)						Median age	Race alone or in combination (percent)					
			Under 18 years	18 to 24 years	25 to 44 years	45 to 64 years	65 years and over			White	Black or African American	American Indian and Alaska Native	Asian	Native Hawaiian or Other Pacific Islander	Some other race
ACS table number:	B01003	Population Estimates	B01001	B01001	B01001	B01001	B01001		B01002	B02008	B02009	B02010	B02011	B02012	B02013
STATE County code / Column number:	1	2	3	4	5	6	7		8	9	10	11	12	13	14
WISCONSIN—Cont.															
55089 Ozaukee County, Wisconsin........	92,497	3.3	21.2	7.9	21.9	27.9	21.1		43.7	94.9	2.8	1.1	3.4	-	3.8
55097 Portage County, Wisconsin	70,468	1.1	19.0	14.7	24.1	24.3	18.0		38.5	94.4	1.9	2.0	3.0	-	3.8
55101 Racine County, Wisconsin	196,896	0.5	22.7	7.8	25.5	26.5	17.6		40.4	83.0	13.9	2.4	1.8	0.1	12.5
55105 Rock County, Wisconsin..............	164,381	1.9	22.8	7.9	25.4	27.1	16.8		39.9	91.9	6.8	1.3	1.8	-	8.3
55109 St. Croix County, Wisconsin	95,044	7.5	24.1	7.3	25.4	27.8	15.4		40.7	97.2	1.5	2.3	1.1	-	4.1
55111 Sauk County, Wisconsin.............	65,697	4.0	22.6	6.9	25.2	25.9	19.3		41.0	95.0	1.9	2.1	-	-	7.9
55117 Sheboygan County, Wisconsin	117,747	-0.1	21.9	7.7	24.4	27.0	19.0		41.6	90.0	3.2	0.9	6.6	-	6.0
55127 Walworth County, Wisconsin	106,799	1.6	20.0	12.8	21.3	26.4	19.5		41.3	93.7	1.6	0.7	1.1	-	10.9
55131 Washington County, Wisconsin...	137,175	3.1	21.1	7.5	23.2	29.3	18.9		43.4	96.4	2.3	1.2	2.2	-	3.9
55133 Waukesha County, Wisconsin	408,756	3.7	21.2	7.6	23.5	28.1	19.7		43.5	92.6	2.6	0.9	4.9	-	4.8
55139 Winnebago County, Wisconsin ...	171,623	2.9	20.3	11.8	25.4	25.7	16.9		38.4	91.3	4.6	2.0	3.9	-	4.0
55141 Wood County, Wisconsin............	74,070	-2.3	21.4	7.0	23.1	27.5	21.1		43.0	94.6	1.6	1.3	2.3	-	4.2
56000 **WYOMING**	578,803	2.8	22.7	9.0	26.0	24.3	17.9		39.0	92.6	1.6	4.2	1.6	0.1	8.5
56021 Laramie County, Wyoming..........	100,863	8.5	22.4	9.0	26.2	25.3	17.1		38.8	89.1	4.3	1.9	2.3	-	9.8
56025 Natrona County, Wyoming	79,555	5.8	24.1	7.2	27.8	24.0	16.8		37.5	96.8	0.7	4.2	1.3	0.6	7.2
72000 **PUERTO RICO**..........................	3,263,584	-14.3	16.7	9.7	24.6	26.3	22.7		44.1	60.3	13.4	2.2	0.3	0.0	64.3
72013 Arecibo Municipio, Puerto Rico ...	87,053	-15.0	16.4	9.1	24.4	26.7	23.4		45.1	61.1	6.3	0.8	1.7	-	88.1
72021 Bayamón Municipio, Puerto Rico.	182,673	-18.7	15.8	9.2	26.1	25.1	23.8		43.8	54.8	9.0	0.3	0.3	-	85.3
72025 Caguas Municipio, Puerto Rico ...	126,756	-12.8	16.5	9.1	25.9	26.5	22.0		44.2	59.3	15.8	1.8	-	-	47.3
72031 Carolina Municipio, Puerto Rico ..	152,993	-16.8	15.9	9.1	25.1	25.7	24.1		44.8	43.6	20.4	1.1	0.4	-	63.6
72061 Guaynabo Municipio, Puerto Rico	89,195	-14.5	14.3	8.2	25.6	27.1	24.9		47.0	65.4	10.5	1.0	-	-	79.9
72097 Mayagüez Municipio, Puerto Rico	71,939	-19.7	15.7	15.5	20.9	21.9	26.0		42.6	16.3	4.7	1.3	-	-	90.2
72113 Ponce Municipio, Puerto Rico......	135,084	-20.7	17.6	9.5	24.0	24.4	24.5		43.9	83.0	7.8	0.6	-	-	61.7
72127 San Juan Municipio, Puerto Rico .	337,300	-19.4	15.8	9.4	24.4	25.6	24.8		45.3	53.8	16.8	1.4	0.3	-	60.8
72135 Toa Alta Municipio, Puerto Rico ..	67,569	-2.8	17.4	10.7	27.4	28.4	16.2		40.4	67.2	10.2	-	-	-	76.3
72137 Toa Baja Municipio, Puerto Rico ..	74,368	-17.1	16.7	9.5	26.5	25.8	21.5		42.8	33.5	10.3	1.3	-	-	79.5
72139 Trujillo Alto Municipio, Puerto Rico	67,211	-14.9	16.6	9.2	26.4	26.4	21.4		43.5	65.4	20.2	-	-	-	33.5

NA = Not available.

X= Not applicable.

- = Indicates that either no sample observations or too few sample observations were available to compute an estimate, or a ratio of medians cannot be calculated because one or both of the median estimates falls in the lowest interval or upper interval of an open-ended distribution, or the margin of error associated with a median was larger than the median itself.

STATE County code	STATE County	Two or more races (percent)	Hispanic or Latino (percent)	Native, born in state of residence (percent)	Foreign born (percent)	Non-citizens (percent)	Total house-holds	Household type (percent of all households)						Percent of households with people age 60 years and over
								Family households				Nonfamily households		
								Total	Married couple	Male house-holder	Female house-holder	Total	One-person house-holds	
	ACS table number:	B02001	B03003	B05002	B05002	B05002	B11001	B11001	B11001	B11001	B11001	B11001	B11001	B11006
	Column number:	15	16	17	18	19	20	21	22	23	24	25	26	27
	WISCONSIN—Cont.													
55089	Ozaukee County, Wisconsin.......	5.5	3.5	70.6	4.9	1.6	36,144	68.3	60.6	3.2	4.5	31.7	27.6	50.9
55097	Portage County, Wisconsin	5.4	3.8	78.3	2.7	0.8	29,937	62.0	47.9	5.3	8.8	38.0	28.1	38.9
55101	Racine County, Wisconsin	12.4	14.8	71.1	5.8	3.1	79,068	65.1	45.9	5.1	14.1	34.9	26.9	41.9
55105	Rock County, Wisconsin..............	10.1	9.7	72.3	4.3	2.9	67,876	64.6	46.9	6.0	11.6	35.4	28.6	41.5
55109	St. Croix County, Wisconsin	5.8	2.8	44.5	2.6	1.5	36,873	68.6	57.3	5.0	6.4	31.4	25.5	37.7
55111	Sauk County, Wisconsin..............	7.3	5.9	78.0	1.6	1.2	27,524	68.0	51.6	4.5	12.0	32.0	25.4	44.1
55117	Sheboygan County, Wisconsin	6.5	7.2	77.2	5.7	2.7	49,416	60.0	48.4	4.4	7.2	40.0	34.2	44.1
55127	Walworth County, Wisconsin......	8.1	11.6	57.7	5.5	2.6	43,086	63.2	48.2	6.0	9.1	36.8	28.8	46.2
55131	Washington County, Wisconsin...	5.6	3.5	82.7	2.9	1.2	56,636	69.2	56.6	6.2	6.4	30.8	24.8	41.3
55133	Waukesha County, Wisconsin	5.7	5.3	75.8	5.6	2.0	167,089	70.3	59.2	3.4	7.7	29.7	23.9	43.4
55139	Winnebago County, Wisconsin ...	4.9	4.7	78.3	3.7	1.5	72,794	60.1	47.0	4.8	8.4	39.9	28.9	38.5
55141	Wood County, Wisconsin............	3.8	3.6	80.3	2.1	1.4	31,890	67.2	48.6	5.7	12.9	32.8	28.5	46.5
56000	**WYOMING**	8.1	10.6	43.0	3.4	1.8	242,763	62.1	49.8	4.6	7.7	37.9	30.9	40.0
56021	Laramie County, Wyoming.........	7.3	15.5	35.8	3.5	1.6	43,728	60.5	48.0	4.3	8.3	39.5	34.3	36.9
56025	Natrona County, Wyoming	9.9	9.3	49.9	1.7	0.5	33,203	57.2	43.3	5.0	8.8	42.8	38.6	38.4
72000	**PUERTO RICO............................**	35.8	99.2	NA	2.7	NA	1,165,982	63.4	34.5	6.6	22.3	36.6	31.3	53.2
72013	Arecibo Municipio, Puerto Rico ...	57.2	99.5	NA	NA	NA	28,742	60.5	29.5	7.3	23.8	39.5	35.7	50.6
72021	Bayamón Municipio, Puerto Rico.	49.0	99.5	X	4.4	1.7	66,385	65.1	34.8	5.8	24.5	34.9	30.3	53.4
72025	Caguas Municipio, Puerto Rico ...	22.1	98.9	X	2.2	1.4	47,586	62.0	32.2	9.3	20.5	38.0	32.7	50.3
72031	Carolina Municipio, Puerto Rico ..	27.4	99.5	X	5.8	2.7	58,930	61.6	27.7	6.0	27.9	38.4	31.0	49.8
72061	Guaynabo Municipio, Puerto Rico..	53.8	98.8	X	6.6	3.6	32,826	65.3	42.7	5.8	16.8	34.7	30.8	55.1
72097	Mayagüez Municipio, Puerto Rico..	10.2	99.7	X	2.3	1.8	27,447	57.0	31.9	4.3	20.8	43.0	37.0	54.9
72113	Ponce Municipio, Puerto Rico......	52.2	99.6	X	1.4	0.9	50,007	59.6	32.3	5.7	21.6	40.4	36.2	56.2
72127	San Juan Municipio, Puerto Rico .	31.0	98.2	X	10.8	6.2	135,865	54.5	25.1	5.0	24.4	45.5	39.6	50.4
72135	Toa Alta Municipio, Puerto Rico ..	51.5	99.7	NA	NA	NA	20,918	69.3	36.8	7.1	25.4	30.7	25.9	45.2
72137	Toa Baja Municipio, Puerto Rico ..	23.9	99.7	NA	NA	NA	28,276	64.3	33.9	8.2	22.2	35.7	29.2	51.4
72139	Trujillo Alto Municipio, Puerto Rico..	18.7	99.3	NA	NA	NA	24,898	69.9	42.1	7.2	20.7	30.1	25.4	52.9

NA = Not available.
X= Not applicable.
- = Indicates that either no sample observations or too few sample observations were available to compute an estimate, or a ratio of medians cannot be calculated because one or both of the median estimates falls in the lowest interval or upper interval of an open-ended distribution, or the margin of error associated with a median was larger than the median itself.

Table A-3. Metropolitan Areas — Who: Age, Race/Ethnicity, and Household Structure, 2021

Metropolitan area / division code	Metropolitan area / division	Total population	Percent change, 2010–2019	Under 18 years	18 to 24 years	25 to 44 years	45 to 64 years	65 years and over	Median age	White	Black or African American	Asian + Native Hawaiian or Other Pacific Islander	American Indian and Alaska Native + Some other race	Hispanic or Latino (percent)
	ACS table number:	B01003	Population Estimates	B01001	B01001	B01001	B01001	B01001	B01002	B02008	B02009	B02011 + B02012	B02010 + B02013	B03003
	column number:	1	2	3	4	5	6	7	8	9	10	11	12	13
10180	Abilene, TX	178,608	4.1	23.9	12.7	27.7	21.1	14.6	34.4	85.4	9.2	2.5	20.0	24.4
10380	Aguadilla-Isabela, PR	309,515	NA	16.3	9.4	23.7	27.5	23.1	45.3	84.7	17.6	0.3	52.7	98.5
10420	Akron, OH	700,015	0.0	20.3	9.7	24.9	26.4	18.7	41.1	84.4	13.1	4.4	6.4	2.4
10500	Albany, GA	146,961	-4.6	23.5	10.7	25.0	23.8	17.0	38.4	45.4	53.4	1.3	4.7	3.2
10540	Albany-Lebanon, OR	129,839	11.2	22.4	8.2	24.9	25.3	19.2	40.3	93.1	1.5	2.3	13.1	10.2
10580	Albany-Schenectady-Troy, NY	899,286	1.1	19.2	10.4	25.8	26.2	18.4	40.7	84.4	10.1	5.7	8.0	5.7
10740	Albuquerque, NM	921,311	3.5	21.4	8.7	27.7	24.4	17.9	39.4	76.0	4.5	4.6	47.8	50.1
10780	Alexandria, LA	150,890	-1.2	23.8	8.5	26.1	25.0	16.5	39.1	67.3	30.1	1.9	5.9	3.9
10900	Allentown-Bethlehem-Easton, PA-NJ	865,310	2.8	20.9	9.0	24.6	26.8	18.6	41.2	81.6	9.0	3.9	18.8	19.6
11020	Altoona, PA	121,767	-4.1	20.3	7.6	24.1	26.6	21.4	43.6	97.4	1.4	1.1	4.4	1.4
11100	Amarillo, TX	270,119	5.2	25.3	9.9	27.8	22.8	14.2	35.8	83.7	7.8	4.0	23.2	31.3
11180	Ames, IA	126,195	6.5	17.3	26.1	22.3	19.8	14.5	30.1	92.4	3.2	5.7	5.6	3.5
11260	Anchorage, AK	398,807	4.1	24.5	9.0	30.4	23.2	12.9	35.5	75.0	6.7	14.1	19.7	8.5
11460	Ann Arbor, MI	369,390	6.6	18.4	17.8	26.0	22.7	15.0	34.8	77.6	13.9	10.8	6.3	5.2
11500	Anniston-Oxford, AL	115,972	-4.2	21.6	10.4	24.3	25.4	18.2	40.2	75.4	20.3	1.7	8.4	4.2
11540	Appleton, WI	244,084	5.5	23.2	8.1	26.0	26.8	15.8	38.9	92.2	2.0	4.3	7.1	4.9
11640	Arecibo, PR	182,014	NA	16.6	8.4	25.2	27.2	22.6	44.8	74.6	4.8	0.8	55.8	99.7
11700	Asheville, NC	472,341	-12.5	18.0	7.4	24.8	26.6	23.2	44.8	93.2	5.5	1.8	8.9	7.7
12020	Athens-Clarke County, GA	217,382	8.9	20.3	18.3	26.0	20.7	14.6	33.0	74.4	18.6	4.0	12.0	8.8
12060	Atlanta-Sandy Springs-Alpharetta, GA	6,144,970	11.0	23.7	9.0	28.1	26.0	13.1	37.2	53.9	36.4	7.7	12.4	11.2
12100	Atlantic City-Hammonton, NJ	274,966	13.9	20.9	8.7	23.7	27.5	19.2	42.2	67.1	17.1	9.2	19.6	19.9
12220	Auburn-Opelika, AL	177,218	-4.0	21.0	16.6	26.5	22.9	12.9	33.3	72.4	23.8	4.8	4.9	3.9
12260	Augusta-Richmond County, GA-SC	616,395	17.3	23.0	9.7	26.2	24.4	16.8	38.1	60.5	37.9	3.2	7.8	5.9
12420	Austin-Round Rock-Georgetown, TX	2,352,426	7.8	22.2	9.2	33.3	23.7	11.7	35.9	75.9	8.6	8.7	28.0	32.8
12540	Bakersfield, CA	917,673	29.8	28.7	10.0	28.6	21.3	11.4	32.5	69.9	6.7	6.8	43.5	56.1
12580	Baltimore-Columbia-Towson, MD	2,838,327	7.2	21.9	8.6	27.4	25.8	16.3	38.9	60.6	31.5	7.5	7.9	6.7
12620	Bangor, ME	152,765	3.3	17.8	10.6	24.5	27.8	19.4	42.2	96.0	1.7	1.6	5.8	1.7
12700	Barnstable Town, MA	232,411	-1.2	14.5	6.2	18.7	28.4	32.3	54.6	90.8	4.3	2.2	9.7	3.6
12940	Baton Rouge, LA	871,905	-1.3	23.4	10.7	27.6	23.1	15.2	36.3	60.4	36.2	2.3	7.1	4.9
12980	Battle Creek, MI	133,819	3.5	22.7	9.1	24.1	26.0	18.2	40.3	85.0	12.6	3.3	8.6	5.8
13020	Bay City, MI	102,985	-1.5	19.0	8.2	23.7	27.3	21.7	43.9	96.6	4.2	1.1	6.8	5.8
13140	Beaumont-Port Arthur, TX	395,419	-4.3	24.6	8.5	27.1	24.0	15.8	37.1	69.2	24.0	3.4	17.8	17.8
13220	Beckley, WV	113,698	1.0	20.5	7.3	23.2	26.7	22.3	44.2	92.4	7.7	0.9	2.8	1.1
13380	Bellingham, WA	228,831	-7.3	18.7	13.5	25.9	23.3	18.6	38.8	87.7	2.0	7.4	12.7	10.3
13460	Bend, OR	204,801	14.0	19.3	6.1	27.7	26.2	20.7	42.6	93.7	1.1	3.1	9.6	8.6
13740	Billings, MT	187,037	25.3	22.8	7.5	26.2	24.7	18.8	39.3	92.6	1.3	1.7	10.8	5.8
13780	Binghamton, NY	245,220	8.7	19.4	12.1	22.4	26.0	20.0	41.4	89.2	7.3	4.5	4.5	4.3
13820	Birmingham-Hoover, AL	1,114,262	-5.2	22.8	8.6	26.2	25.6	16.7	39.4	65.2	31.1	2.1	6.2	4.7
13900	Bismarck, ND	134,028	2.8	22.5	9.2	26.7	24.3	17.2	38.7	91.1	3.3	1.5	8.1	2.8
13980	Blacksburg-Christiansburg, VA	168,404	16.6	16.3	23.0	23.0	21.4	16.3	33.9	89.9	6.0	5.0	3.9	3.0
14010	Bloomington, IL	170,889	2.8	21.2	11.7	24.8	21.8	14.5	33.9	85.2	9.3	5.7	5.6	5.4
14020	Bloomington, IN	161,321	1.1	16.5	24.3	24.4	20.7	14.2	31.6	90.7	4.4	5.9	5.2	3.6
14100	Bloomsburg-Berwick, PA	82,959	6.1	18.6	11.9	22.8	26.0	20.7	43.1	97.1	2.1	1.3	4.9	3.5
14260	Boise City, ID	801,470	-2.8	23.9	8.5	28.2	24.0	15.5	37.4	89.0	1.8	4.0	15.9	14.2
14460	Boston-Cambridge-Newton, MA-NH	4,899,932	21.5	19.4	9.9	28.0	26.2	16.5	39.2	77.0	10.5	10.0	14.8	12.0
1446014454	Boston, MA Metro Division	2,028,753	7.6	19.0	10.5	29.0	25.4	16.1	38.3	72.2	16.7	9.5	15.8	9.5
1446015764	Cambridge-Newton-Framingham, MA Metro Division	2,421,816	6.9	20.0	9.3	27.7	26.4	16.6	39.4	77.6	6.8	11.7	15.4	11.7
1446040484	Rockingham County-Strafford County, NH Metro Division	449,363	5.3	18.4	9.8	24.6	29.0	18.2	42.7	95.4	1.7	4.8	6.8	4.8
14500	Boulder, CO	329,543	10.7	18.1	14.1	26.8	25.1	15.9	38.2	91.5	2.0	7.1	13.9	14.1
14540	Bowling Green, KY	186,107	13.0	23.0	13.7	25.8	23.1	14.3	34.7	87.1	7.5	4.3	6.7	5.0
14740	Bremerton-Silverdale-Port Orchard, WA	274,314	8.1	19.9	8.7	27.6	24.4	19.3	40.0	86.4	5.2	11.1	10.4	8.5
14860	Bridgeport-Stamford-Norwalk, CT	959,768	2.9	21.9	9.0	24.5	28.1	16.5	41.2	71.2	14.2	6.9	21.8	21.3
15180	Brownsville-Harlingen, TX	423,029	4.2	29.1	10.7	24.7	21.5	14.0	32.6	87.6	0.7	0.9	64.9	90.0
15260	Brunswick, GA	115,033	5.7	21.2	8.2	22.8	26.7	21.1	41.4	74.4	21.9	1.5	7.7	5.2

Metropolitan area / division code	Metropolitan area / division	Born in state of residence (percent)	Foreign born (percent)	Total households	Household type (percent of all households)						Percent of households with people age 60 years and over
					Family households				Nonfamily households		
					Total	Married-couple	Male householder	Female householder	Total	One-person households	
	ACS table number:	B05002	B05002	B11001	B11001	B11001	B11001	B11001	B11001	B11001	B11006
	column number:	14	15	16	17	18	19	20	21	22	23
10180	Abilene, TX	68.9	5.3	66,816	63.9	46.3	4.2	13.5	36.1	27.4	37.0
10380	Aguadilla-Isabela, PR	NA	1.3	107,572	61.4	36.5	5.5	19.4	38.6	32.5	55.8
10420	Akron, OH	77.2	5.3	292,156	60.6	43.3	5.1	12.2	39.4	32.2	43.9
10500	Albany, GA	79.5	1.4	57,880	61.4	35.9	5.2	20.2	38.6	34.6	43.2
10540	Albany-Lebanon, OR	58.9	4.2	51,347	65.8	51.0	5.5	9.3	34.2	26.7	45.8
10580	Albany-Schenectady-Troy, NY	74.6	7.8	378,258	59.0	44.2	4.0	10.8	41.0	31.7	42.7
10740	Albuquerque, NM	53.6	8.7	376,596	61.9	42.5	5.7	13.8	38.1	31.6	41.9
10780	Alexandria, LA	78.2	3.7	55,249	66.1	45.8	4.7	15.6	33.9	28.9	43.2
10900	Allentown-Bethlehem-Easton, PA-NJ .	60.7	10.2	337,283	66.9	48.9	5.5	12.6	33.1	26.8	44.5
11020	Altoona, PA	89.0	1.3	49,795	64.7	49.4	3.7	11.7	35.3	30.4	48.5
11100	Amarillo, TX	68.2	9.2	104,421	63.5	47.8	5.2	10.5	36.5	29.5	36.0
11180	Ames, IA	67.5	5.2	49,702	51.0	43.2	1.4	6.5	49.0	33.4	34.5
11260	Anchorage, AK	40.4	8.9	150,581	65.0	48.6	6.1	10.4	35.0	27.7	33.8
11460	Ann Arbor, MI	60.6	12.2	149,133	57.0	44.3	3.3	9.4	43.0	29.7	36.1
11500	Anniston-Oxford, AL	68.3	2.9	44,631	62.5	41.9	4.9	15.7	37.5	33.3	43.0
11540	Appleton, WI	78.2	3.9	98,164	65.2	53.8	4.2	7.2	34.8	28.1	37.5
11640	Arecibo, PR	NA	0.9	61,581	64.6	36.7	5.2	22.8	35.4	31.9	50.3
11700	Asheville, NC	48.7	5.2	185,423	61.2	47.2	3.0	11.0	38.8	32.3	48.4
12020	Athens-Clarke County, GA	60.4	7.7	87,263	58.2	45.7	3.9	8.5	41.8	27.2	35.2
12060	Atlanta-Sandy Springs-Alpharetta, GA	46.7	13.8	2,277,482	67.3	48.2	4.6	14.4	32.7	26.0	35.1
12100	Atlantic City-Hammonton, NJ	56.7	16.0	112,299	62.9	42.3	6.6	14.0	37.1	30.2	50.2
12220	Auburn-Opelika, AL	49.0	6.3	67,358	63.9	48.1	5.7	10.1	36.1	27.5	32.3
12260	Augusta-Richmond County, GA-SC ...	51.3	4.4	222,266	66.5	45.5	4.1	16.8	33.5	28.4	44.1
12420	Austin-Round Rock-Georgetown, TX	51.6	15.7	955,207	59.9	46.9	3.8	9.2	40.1	29.5	29.0
12540	Bakersfield, CA	68.5	19.7	282,963	73.3	48.7	8.0	16.5	26.7	21.5	37.7
12580	Baltimore-Columbia-Towson, MD	59.1	11.0	1,117,510	64.6	46.1	4.5	14.0	35.4	28.8	40.7
12620	Bangor, ME	67.3	3.6	65,441	59.4	47.1	2.9	9.3	40.6	30.7	41.3
12700	Barnstable Town, MA	58.3	10.2	104,733	63.7	48.7	3.4	11.6	36.3	30.0	62.8
12940	Baton Rouge, LA	79.8	4.7	328,816	65.4	44.2	5.1	16.0	34.6	28.1	38.8
12980	Battle Creek, MI	78.1	3.6	53,482	64.3	45.6	7.5	11.2	35.7	30.6	43.0
13020	Bay City, MI	88.8	1.3	45,487	57.0	44.1	4.4	8.5	43.0	35.2	47.4
13140	Beaumont-Port Arthur, TX	71.4	8.0	148,489	66.3	46.8	4.2	15.3	33.7	28.9	40.0
13220	Beckley, WV	73.8	1.3	46,282	63.3	46.9	5.4	11.0	36.7	31.8	48.8
13380	Bellingham, WA	51.0	8.6	92,219	60.2	47.6	3.6	9.0	39.8	25.9	41.1
13460	Bend, OR	42.3	6.5	83,763	65.0	51.4	3.8	9.8	35.0	23.4	45.1
13740	Billings, MT	57.6	2.0	77,868	64.6	49.4	6.5	8.7	35.4	27.4	42.2
13780	Binghamton, NY	71.9	6.1	105,514	57.5	41.8	5.9	9.7	42.5	33.7	45.4
13820	Birmingham-Hoover, AL	73.9	3.6	436,615	64.0	45.0	4.6	14.4	36.0	31.1	40.6
13900	Bismarck, ND	72.2	1.9	52,921	59.4	47.6	6.2	5.6	40.6	33.8	40.6
13980	Blacksburg-Christiansburg, VA	60.9	4.6	66,952	53.0	40.2	3.5	9.3	47.0	31.4	37.6
14010	Bloomington, IL	73.3	7.6	69,263	55.7	44.7	1.7	9.2	44.3	33.2	33.2
14020	Bloomington, IN	61.4	6.3	65,340	50.9	38.6	3.2	9.1	49.1	35.6	33.6
14100	Bloomsburg-Berwick, PA	83.6	2.8	33,496	62.2	49.7	3.7	8.9	37.8	28.9	45.6
14260	Boise City, ID	42.0	7.5	294,959	69.4	55.6	4.5	9.3	30.6	21.9	37.7
14460	Boston-Cambridge-Newton, MA-NH .	54.5	19.5	1,920,160	62.2	47.1	4.2	10.9	37.8	28.0	40.9
1446014454	Boston, MA Metro Division	57.2	20.8	797,408	58.8	42.9	4.3	11.6	41.2	30.2	40.0
1446015764	Cambridge-Newton-Framingham, MA Metro Division	55.9	21.2	942,803	63.9	49.0	4.2	10.7	36.1	27.1	41.0
1446040484	Rockingham County-Strafford County, NH Metro Division	34.9	4.8	179,949	68.3	55.4	4.2	8.7	31.7	23.5	44.1
14500	Boulder, CO	33.3	10.2	135,607	56.2	44.5	4.9	6.8	43.8	29.8	36.5
14540	Bowling Green, KY	64.1	6.5	71,929	66.8	46.6	7.2	13.0	33.2	27.9	36.0
14740	Bremerton-Silverdale-Port Orchard, WA	41.9	7.0	106,399	68.2	54.6	5.5	8.1	31.8	24.2	43.4
14860	Bridgeport-Stamford-Norwalk, CT	42.2	22.6	357,271	67.2	51.2	3.6	12.4	32.8	26.6	43.8
15180	Brownsville-Harlingen, TX	67.8	22.9	135,734	76.7	49.6	7.9	19.2	23.3	20.0	41.3
15260	Brunswick, GA	59.3	5.0	46,763	62.2	42.0	4.4	15.9	37.8	32.4	49.5

Metropolitan area / division code	Metropolitan area / division	Total population	Percent change, 2010–2019	Population by age (percent)					Median age	Race alone or in combination (percent)				Hispanic or Latino (percent)
				Under 18 years	18 to 24 years	25 to 44 years	45 to 64 years	65 years and over		White	Black or African American	Asian + Native Hawaiian or Other Pacific Islander	American Indian and Alaska Native + Some other race	
	ACS table number:	B01003	Population Estimates	B01001	B01001	B01001	B01001	B01001	B01002	B02008	B02009	B02011 + B02012	B02010 + B02013	B03003
	column number:	1	2	3	4	5	6	7	8	9	10	11	12	13
15380	Buffalo-Cheektowaga, NY	1,162,336	-0.7	20.1	8.7	25.9	26.2	19.1	40.8	81.8	13.7	4.5	6.5	5.5
15500	Burlington, NC	173,877	12.2	22.2	11.3	23.1	26.5	16.9	39.6	71.0	21.8	3.0	14.4	13.7
15540	Burlington-South Burlington, VT	226,715	4.3	18.4	13.3	26.6	25.1	16.5	38.5	93.5	2.8	4.3	5.0	2.2
15680	California-Lexington Park, MD	114,468	7.9	23.8	8.9	27.1	26.5	13.8	37.2	81.1	16.5	4.1	9.2	5.7
15940	Canton-Massillon, OH	400,525	-1.7	21.4	8.3	23.6	26.3	20.4	41.8	91.9	9.6	1.5	4.3	2.3
15980	Cape Coral-Fort Myers, FL	787,976	24.5	17.3	6.8	21.2	25.7	29.0	49.5	85.3	9.6	2.6	21.3	23.8
16020	Cape Girardeau, MO-IL	96,456	0.5	21.2	12.9	24.7	23.3	17.9	37.6	91.4	7.3	2.0	8.2	2.6
16060	Carbondale-Marion, IL	133,006	-2.4	19.6	12.6	25.3	23.6	18.9	38.9	87.8	10.5	1.6	6.7	3.8
16180	Carson City, NV	58,993	1.2	20.1	7.6	24.5	26.9	20.9	43.3	85.6	2.6	5.4	27.0	25.6
16220	Casper, WY	79,555	5.8	24.1	7.2	27.8	24.0	16.8	37.5	96.8	0.7	2.0	11.4	9.3
16300	Cedar Rapids, IA	275,435	5.9	22.8	8.9	25.7	25.4	17.3	39.8	90.5	7.9	3.2	4.7	3.4
16540	Chambersburg-Waynesboro, PA	156,289	3.6	22.0	7.7	23.7	26.6	20.1	42.1	92.1	5.3	1.4	6.9	6.7
16580	Champaign-Urbana, IL	222,696	3.8	19.4	21.5	24.9	20.3	13.9	31.9	75.4	14.5	11.0	8.0	6.3
16620	Charleston, WV	252,942	-7.5	21.4	6.7	24.2	25.9	21.8	43.4	93.9	7.1	1.5	1.5	0.9
16700	Charleston-North Charleston, SC	813,052	20.7	21.6	8.7	29.0	24.5	16.2	38.3	69.9	26.2	3.3	6.9	6.2
16740	Charlotte-Concord-Gastonia, NC-SC	2,701,046	17.5	23.2	8.6	27.8	26.2	14.3	38.1	67.0	24.2	5.1	12.1	11.1
16820	Charlottesville, VA	220,569	8.5	18.6	12.6	25.6	24.3	18.9	38.9	81.7	13.1	6.1	7.3	6.3
16860	Chattanooga, TN-GA	567,395	7.0	21.0	8.6	26.3	25.5	18.6	40.3	83.5	14.3	2.2	6.8	5.1
16940	Cheyenne, WY	100,863	8.5	22.4	9.0	26.2	25.3	17.1	38.8	89.1	4.3	2.3	11.7	15.5
16980	Chicago-Naperville-Elgin, IL-IN-WI	9,510,390	-0.0	22.3	8.8	27.7	25.7	15.6	38.5	65.7	17.5	8.3	22.3	23.1
1698016984	Chicago-Naperville-Evanston, IL Metro Division	7,159,394	-0.4	21.9	8.5	28.5	25.4	15.6	38.3	61.9	19.7	9.2	22.3	9.2
1698020994	Elgin, IL Metro Division	750,869	4.2	24.6	10.0	25.5	26.0	13.9	37.5	78.9	6.6	5.0	28.5	5.0
1698023844	Gary, IN Metro Division	720,156	-0.7	22.8	8.6	25.4	25.7	17.5	40.1	74.8	17.9	2.0	17.2	2.0
1698029404	Lake County-Kenosha County, IL-WI Metro Division	879,971	-0.4	23.2	10.0	24.4	27.1	15.3	39.1	77.8	8.2	9.3	21.2	9.3
17020	Chico, CA	208,309	-0.4	20.4	14.2	25.0	22.0	18.4	36.8	85.3	3.3	7.5	18.9	18.4
17140	Cincinnati, OH-KY-IN	2,261,665	3.9	23.3	9.2	26.3	25.3	15.9	38.1	83.4	13.4	3.7	5.7	3.7
17300	Clarksville, TN-KY	329,864	12.4	26.7	11.4	29.9	20.6	11.4	32.1	76.0	23.4	4.7	9.7	9.9
17420	Cleveland, TN	129,855	7.9	21.1	8.6	24.6	27.9	17.9	41.3	92.8	4.1	1.5	7.6	6.1
17460	Cleveland-Elyria, OH	2,075,662	-1.4	20.8	8.2	25.2	26.4	19.4	41.3	75.3	21.7	3.4	7.6	6.5
17660	Coeur d'Alene, ID	179,789	19.6	22.7	7.6	25.2	24.9	19.5	40.5	96.1	0.8	2.1	9.5	5.4
17780	College Station-Bryan, TX	271,026	15.8	20.8	22.4	26.8	18.8	11.2	29.7	77.1	12.6	6.1	17.5	26.9
17820	Colorado Springs, CO	762,792	15.5	23.2	10.4	29.5	23.2	13.7	35.4	85.5	8.7	6.3	16.8	18.1
17860	Columbia, MO	212,796	9.3	20.5	16.9	26.7	21.5	14.4	34.1	85.4	11.4	5.2	3.7	3.3
17900	Columbia, SC	836,324	9.2	22.0	11.5	25.9	25.0	15.7	37.2	60.7	35.8	3.1	7.5	6.1
17980	Columbus, GA-AL	326,491	4.3	24.2	10.0	27.5	23.7	14.7	36.0	50.5	45.8	3.2	8.4	7.9
18020	Columbus, IN	82,475	9.1	24.2	7.2	28.1	24.3	16.3	37.0	85.7	3.2	8.4	7.7	8.0
18140	Columbus, OH	2,151,017	11.6	23.4	9.1	29.3	24.3	13.9	36.6	76.8	18.3	6.2	6.6	4.7
18580	Corpus Christi, TX	422,778	5.9	24.6	9.9	27.0	23.3	15.3	36.3	87.5	3.6	2.4	53.0	64.1
18700	Corvallis, OR	96,017	8.7	15.7	22.8	23.5	20.2	17.9	33.5	88.2	2.1	10.1	9.2	8.2
18880	Crestview-Fort Walton Beach-Destin, FL	293,324	20.8	21.9	7.7	27.1	25.9	17.3	39.5	84.9	10.1	5.3	11.2	9.3
19060	Cumberland, MD-WV	94,586	-5.8	17.5	11.4	24.0	26.1	21.0	42.4	91.5	7.6	1.2	3.4	1.6
19100	Dallas-Fort Worth-Arlington, TX	7,759,615	19.0	25.4	9.1	29.1	24.6	11.9	35.6	64.3	18.1	9.1	26.5	29.6
1910019124	Dallas-Plano-Irving, TX Division	5,217,380	20.1	25.2	9.1	29.5	24.6	11.6	35.5	62.7	18.6	10.3	27.0	10.3
1910023104	Fort Worth-Arlington-Grapevine, TX Division	2,542,235	16.6	25.6	9.1	28.4	24.4	12.4	35.7	67.5	17.0	6.3	25.7	6.3
19140	Dalton, GA	142,799	1.8	24.7	10.0	26.0	24.3	15.0	36.5	84.8	3.8	1.4	19.0	31.3
19180	Danville, IL	73,095	-7.2	23.4	6.7	24.3	25.7	19.9	41.0	83.5	15.6	1.2	5.3	5.6
19300	Daphne-Fairhope-Foley, AL	239,294	22.5	21.2	6.6	23.4	27.5	21.4	43.9	87.6	9.7	1.5	6.3	4.8
19340	Davenport-Moline-Rock Island, IA-IL	381,447	-0.1	22.7	8.5	24.4	25.2	19.2	40.6	86.9	8.7	3.3	10.7	9.5
19380	Dayton-Kettering, OH	813,516	1.0	22.0	9.4	25.4	24.7	18.6	39.3	80.4	17.8	3.6	4.6	3.3
19460	Decatur, AL	156,758	-0.8	22.9	7.7	24.7	26.5	18.2	41.0	81.0	12.9	0.0	13.4	8.6
19500	Decatur, IL	102,432	-6.1	22.2	8.7	23.4	25.0	20.6	41.5	81.8	18.3	1.5	6.0	2.6
19660	Deltona-Daytona Beach-Ormond Beach, FL	685,344	13.2	17.4	7.7	21.4	27.3	26.1	48.3	78.4	12.3	2.6	14.5	15.3

Table A-3. Metropolitan Areas — Who: Age, Race/Ethnicity, and Household Structure, 2021—*Continued*

					Household type (percent of all households)						Percent of households with people age 60 years and over
					Family households				Nonfamily households		
Metropolitan area / division	Metropolitan area / division	Born in state of residence (percent)	Foreign born (percent)	Total households	Total	Married-couple	Male householder	Female householder	Total	One-person households	
	ACS table number:	B05002	B05002	B11001	B11001	B11001	B11001	B11001	B11001	B11001	B11006
code	column number:	14	15	16	17	18	19	20	21	22	23
15380	Buffalo-Cheektowaga, NY	81.2	6.3	503,845	58.3	40.4	4.9	13.1	41.7	34.3	43.6
15500	Burlington, NC	64.8	8.4	69,343	65.1	46.6	4.4	14.1	34.9	30.7	41.0
15540	Burlington-South Burlington, VT	49.3	6.4	93,290	59.6	48.0	3.4	8.1	40.4	25.7	39.1
15680	California-Lexington Park, MD	45.2	5.6	42,078	69.3	54.7	3.8	10.8	30.7	24.4	36.6
15940	Canton-Massillon, OH	83.9	2.0	168,332	64.3	45.7	5.1	13.6	35.7	28.8	43.7
15980	Cape Coral-Fort Myers, FL	26.7	18.0	320,466	65.5	52.3	3.9	9.3	34.5	28.3	56.6
16020	Cape Girardeau, MO-IL	73.0	1.8	37,991	63.1	47.9	5.6	9.6	36.9	29.7	43.5
16060	Carbondale-Marion, IL	76.6	2.7	55,292	55.8	40.8	4.4	10.7	44.2	35.4	41.7
16180	Carson City, NV	31.4	13.7	23,930	55.5	41.5	3.3	10.7	44.5	35.2	46.9
16220	Casper, WY	49.9	1.7	33,203	57.2	43.3	5.0	8.8	42.8	38.6	38.4
16300	Cedar Rapids, IA	75.8	4.5	112,468	63.1	48.9	4.5	9.7	36.9	29.8	40.6
16540	Chambersburg-Waynesboro, PA	67.6	3.1	62,081	65.7	53.3	3.0	9.5	34.3	29.1	46.5
16580	Champaign-Urbana, IL	68.9	11.0	91,044	53.7	40.1	3.0	10.7	46.3	34.5	33.2
16620	Charleston, WV	80.8	1.3	106,310	63.9	47.9	4.4	11.6	36.1	31.0	47.3
16700	Charleston-North Charleston, SC	47.4	5.3	316,378	64.6	48.2	4.3	12.1	35.4	28.0	39.6
16740	Charlotte-Concord-Gastonia, NC-SC	46.3	10.6	1,048,452	65.6	48.3	4.4	12.8	34.4	28.1	35.6
16820	Charlottesville, VA	45.8	8.4	88,339	56.2	44.2	4.1	7.9	43.8	33.7	41.8
16860	Chattanooga, TN-GA	50.8	4.2	228,853	64.9	47.6	5.3	12.0	35.1	29.2	43.1
16940	Cheyenne, WY	35.8	3.5	43,728	60.5	48.0	4.3	8.3	39.5	34.3	36.9
16980	Chicago-Naperville-Elgin, IL-IN-WI	62.7	17.8	3,670,416	63.7	46.3	5.0	12.5	36.3	29.7	39.4
1698016984	Chicago-Naperville-Evanston, IL Metro Division	63.2	19.5	2,802,657	61.7	44.4	4.8	12.5	38.3	31.5	39.0
1698020994	Elgin, IL Metro Division	68.7	14.5	266,551	72.4	54.6	6.7	11.2	27.6	20.5	38.2
1698023844	Gary, IN Metro Division	57.6	6.1	278,654	67.6	46.8	5.6	15.2	32.4	27.1	43.3
1698029404	Lake County-Kenosha County, IL-WI Metro Division	57.7	16.8	322,554	70.6	55.6	4.4	10.6	29.4	24.5	39.9
17020	Chico, CA	74.0	8.2	81,353	60.2	41.2	6.6	12.5	39.8	26.8	40.7
17140	Cincinnati, OH-KY-IN	67.2	5.2	903,245	62.3	46.2	4.5	11.7	37.7	29.9	38.8
17300	Clarksville, TN-KY	41.2	5.7	121,468	70.1	51.3	5.3	13.4	29.9	22.8	31.3
17420	Cleveland, TN	57.8	4.9	50,236	70.3	53.5	7.3	9.5	29.7	26.9	46.3
17460	Cleveland-Elyria, OH	75.4	5.9	890,105	58.3	41.2	4.2	12.9	41.7	35.2	44.4
17660	Coeur d'Alene, ID	29.3	2.1	67,771	68.5	57.2	3.5	7.8	31.5	23.6	45.9
17780	College Station-Bryan, TX	67.1	10.7	99,917	56.4	41.6	4.5	10.3	43.6	30.2	31.1
17820	Colorado Springs, CO	30.6	6.9	294,814	67.4	52.0	5.3	10.2	32.6	24.0	34.7
17860	Columbia, MO	62.1	5.6	84,946	56.5	45.0	2.7	8.8	43.5	32.7	34.9
17900	Columbia, SC	58.9	5.2	334,313	61.5	43.2	4.8	13.5	38.5	32.0	38.8
17980	Columbus, GA-AL	53.7	4.2	127,247	64.7	40.6	5.2	18.9	35.3	30.8	37.0
18020	Columbus, IN	69.7	10.2	32,518	67.5	53.8	3.8	10.0	32.5	25.9	36.9
18140	Columbus, OH	69.4	9.6	856,193	63.8	45.9	5.0	13.0	36.2	27.6	34.7
18580	Corpus Christi, TX	75.2	8.2	153,119	69.6	47.2	6.2	16.2	30.4	24.1	39.2
18700	Corvallis, OR	43.4	9.0	39,350	54.2	41.3	4.5	8.4	45.8	27.5	36.0
18880	Crestview-Fort Walton Beach-Destin, FL	30.5	7.3	118,438	66.4	53.3	3.1	10.0	33.6	28.1	43.7
19060	Cumberland, MD-WV	59.4	1.9	40,079	56.9	42.4	3.5	11.0	43.1	36.8	43.6
19100	Dallas-Fort Worth-Arlington, TX	53.4	19.1	2,836,892	68.6	50.9	4.9	12.7	31.4	25.6	32.7
1910019124	Dallas-Plano-Irving, TX Division	51.9	20.9	1,920,923	68.2	51.0	4.8	12.3	31.8	26.0	31.9
1910023104	Fort Worth-Arlington-Grapevine, TX Division	56.7	15.4	915,969	69.4	50.7	5.1	13.6	30.6	24.9	34.2
19140	Dalton, GA	64.8	14.4	50,580	73.4	53.2	6.6	13.6	26.6	23.2	42.0
19180	Danville, IL	83.1	3.0	29,007	57.6	41.0	4.3	12.4	42.4	35.3	45.6
19300	Daphne-Fairhope-Foley, AL	54.3	3.3	94,105	65.6	53.8	4.3	7.6	34.4	30.2	48.6
19340	Davenport-Moline-Rock Island, IA-IL	63.2	5.6	159,133	61.2	46.0	4.4	10.8	38.8	31.5	42.6
19380	Dayton-Kettering, OH	69.8	5.0	338,505	60.3	43.7	4.6	11.9	39.7	32.3	42.5
19460	Decatur, AL	71.0	4.1	60,796	65.9	52.5	4.0	9.5	34.1	31.1	44.9
19500	Decatur, IL	80.1	2.4	43,914	58.1	42.7	3.5	12.0	41.9	36.4	46.4
19660	Deltona-Daytona Beach-Ormond Beach, FL	33.3	8.8	291,531	62.8	46.4	5.1	11.3	37.2	29.2	55.7

Metropolitan area / division code	Metropolitan area / division	Total population	Percent change, 2010–2019	Population by age (percent)					Median age	Race alone or in combination (percent)				
				Under 18 years	18 to 24 years	25 to 44 years	45 to 64 years	65 years and over		White	Black or African American	Asian + Native Hawaiian or Other Pacific Islander	American Indian and Alaska Native + Some other race	Hispanic or Latino (percent)
	ACS table number:	B01003	Population Estimates	B01001	B01001	B01001	B01001	B01001	B01002	B02008	B02009	B02011 + B02012	B02010 + B02013	B03003
	column number:	1	2	3	4	5	6	7	8	9	10	11	12	13
19740	Denver-Aurora-Lakewood, CO	2,972,567	16.7	21.5	7.9	32.4	24.5	13.8	37.3	80.6	7.4	6.3	22.1	23.6
19780	Des Moines-West Des Moines, IA	719,146	15.3	24.6	8.5	28.9	23.7	14.2	36.7	87.0	7.2	5.2	7.9	7.8
19820	Detroit-Warren-Dearborn, MI	4,365,205	0.5	21.8	8.0	25.9	27.0	17.3	40.3	71.1	23.6	5.9	6.6	4.9
1982019804	Detroit-Dearborn-Livonia, MI Division	1,774,816	-3.9	23.7	8.3	26.4	25.4	16.2	37.9	55.7	39.6	4.6	7.6	4.6
1982047664	Warren-Troy-Farmington Hills, MI Division	2,590,389	3.8	20.6	7.8	25.5	28.0	18.1	41.9	81.6	12.6	7.5	5.9	7.5
20020	Dothan, AL	151,618	2.6	22.5	7.8	24.3	25.9	19.5	41.0	73.1	24.6	1.8	5.3	3.7
20100	Dover, DE	184,149	11.4	23.0	9.6	25.7	23.9	17.8	38.8	66.0	30.9	3.3	9.6	7.8
20220	Dubuque, IA	98,718	3.9	22.7	9.9	24.1	24.5	18.9	39.4	94.4	4.6	2.6	3.1	2.9
20260	Duluth, MN-WI	292,285	-0.7	19.4	11.1	23.4	25.8	20.3	41.8	94.7	2.3	1.7	6.4	1.9
20500	Durham-Chapel Hill, NC	654,012	14.2	19.7	11.5	27.0	25.0	16.7	38.8	63.2	27.3	6.1	13.1	11.5
20700	East Stroudsburg, PA	169,273	0.3	19.4	9.1	23.3	29.7	18.5	43.7	77.0	15.8	3.1	18.5	18.3
20740	Eau Claire, WI	173,317	5.1	20.7	12.5	25.2	23.9	17.7	37.9	94.5	2.4	3.9	4.2	2.6
20940	El Centro, CA	179,851	3.8	28.3	9.8	27.3	20.9	13.6	32.8	42.8	5.8	2.1	79.4	85.8
21060	Elizabethtown-Fort Knox, KY	157,318	3.8	25.9	7.9	27.1	24.1	15.1	37.1	87.7	11.4	3.1	6.6	5.4
21140	Elkhart-Goshen, IN	206,921	4.4	27.3	9.1	24.8	23.3	15.5	36.0	84.5	7.3	1.7	16.5	17.6
21300	Elmira, NY	83,045	-6.0	20.5	7.4	25.6	27.1	19.4	42.1	90.8	8.7	2.1	4.6	3.6
21340	El Paso, TX	871,727	5.0	26.4	11.0	28.0	21.8	12.8	33.1	75.1	4.6	2.7	66.5	82.9
21420	Enid, OK	61,926	0.8	25.7	8.4	25.7	23.0	17.2	37.3	87.2	1.9	2.0	21.9	14.2
21500	Erie, PA	269,011	-3.9	21.0	9.4	24.2	26.3	19.1	40.6	88.3	9.7	2.5	6.0	4.8
21660	Eugene-Springfield, OR	383,189	8.6	17.9	11.6	26.3	23.7	20.5	40.5	91.9	2.5	5.5	11.9	9.8
21780	Evansville, IN-KY	313,946	1.1	22.3	8.9	25.5	25.0	18.3	39.7	91.0	8.6	1.9	5.1	2.5
21820	Fairbanks, AK	95,593	-0.8	23.5	12.3	30.4	21.2	12.6	32.0	82.5	7.0	7.1	19.6	8.4
22020	Fargo, ND-MN	252,136	17.9	23.2	13.3	29.3	21.0	13.2	33.8	89.2	6.5	3.2	6.5	3.6
22140	Farmington, NM	120,993	-4.7	25.4	9.0	25.3	24.2	16.1	36.9	44.6	0.9	0.9	61.0	21.8
22180	Fayetteville, NC	524,588	9.5	24.5	11.3	29.3	21.4	12.7	33.0	56.6	36.3	4.0	14.6	13.2
22220	Fayetteville-Springdale-Rogers, AR	558,507	21.5	24.8	10.9	28.6	22.5	13.1	34.8	87.6	3.7	6.7	28.4	17.2
22380	Flagstaff, AZ	145,052	6.7	20.0	19.7	24.6	21.6	14.0	33.0	62.7	2.2	3.3	41.4	14.9
22420	Flint, MI	404,208	-4.7	22.3	8.2	24.6	26.6	18.3	40.3	77.7	22.1	1.5	4.1	3.9
22500	Florence, SC	199,259	-0.3	23.1	8.6	24.5	25.1	18.8	40.9	53.8	43.6	1.5	3.7	2.9
22520	Florence-Muscle Shoals, AL	151,517	0.6	20.4	9.5	23.1	26.6	20.4	41.0	86.9	11.4	1.1	6.2	3.2
22540	Fond du Lac, WI	104,362	1.7	21.2	8.3	24.4	27.2	18.9	41.8	92.1	3.4	2.2	7.7	6.0
22660	Fort Collins, CO	362,533	19.1	18.7	13.8	28.0	22.7	16.8	36.4	92.7	2.6	3.3	12.9	12.4
22900	Fort Smith, AR-OK	247,661	0.9	23.7	9.3	23.9	25.9	17.2	38.7	82.7	5.5	4.0	18.5	11.5
23060	Fort Wayne, IN	423,038	6.3	25.4	8.8	26.8	23.7	15.4	36.4	82.6	11.4	5.3	10.4	7.7
23420	Fresno, CA	1,013,581	7.4	28.2	9.6	28.4	21.3	12.6	33.1	60.5	6.3	12.9	50.1	54.7
23460	Gadsden, AL	103,162	-2.1	21.6	8.6	23.8	26.9	19.1	41.5	81.6	17.2	1.0	6.2	4.6
23540	Gainesville, FL	344,881	7.9	18.6	17.4	25.5	22.1	16.4	34.7	74.6	19.0	6.5	10.3	10.6
23580	Gainesville, GA	207,369	13.8	24.3	9.0	25.1	26.1	15.4	38.2	83.4	8.9	2.8	26.6	29.5
23900	Gettysburg, PA	104,127	1.6	19.3	9.5	22.0	27.2	21.9	43.9	93.7	3.1	1.2	6.6	7.4
24020	Glens Falls, NY	126,574	-2.9	18.2	6.5	23.8	29.1	22.4	46.2	95.2	3.7	1.2	4.7	2.2
24140	Goldsboro, NC	116,835	0.4	23.9	9.4	26.0	23.8	16.9	38.1	61.3	30.9	3.0	16.7	13.3
24220	Grand Forks, ND-MN	103,462	2.4	22.5	15.9	26.2	20.4	15.0	33.0	91.1	4.7	4.0	9.1	5.5
24260	Grand Island, NE	76,175	3.9	26.1	6.7	25.5	24.3	17.3	37.9	80.2	3.0	1.8	23.5	25.8
24300	Grand Junction, CO	157,335	5.1	20.9	9.0	25.3	24.1	20.6	41.1	95.4	1.5	1.7	16.0	15.3
24340	Grand Rapids-Kentwood, MI	1,091,620	8.4	23.5	10.1	27.4	23.8	15.1	36.5	86.3	8.9	3.8	10.4	10.2
24420	Grants Pass, OR	88,346	5.8	18.9	5.8	22.2	26.0	27.1	48.5	96.7	0.0	1.8	12.9	8.3
24500	Great Falls, MT	84,511	0.0	22.7	8.5	26.0	23.6	19.3	38.6	90.5	2.9	1.9	13.3	5.2
24540	Greeley, CO	340,036	28.3	25.7	9.1	29.5	23.1	12.5	35.2	85.8	2.7	3.1	24.5	30.6
24580	Green Bay, WI	329,490	5.4	22.7	8.5	25.8	26.1	16.9	39.7	89.7	3.8	3.5	11.9	8.4
24660	Greensboro-High Point, NC	778,848	6.6	22.0	9.7	25.2	26.2	16.9	39.5	63.7	29.3	5.0	11.0	9.3
24780	Greenville, NC	172,169	7.5	20.9	18.1	25.7	21.0	14.3	33.0	57.0	37.3	2.6	7.3	6.9
24860	Greenville-Anderson, SC	940,774	11.7	22.2	9.6	25.9	25.2	17.1	38.9	79.2	15.9	2.7	10.4	7.7
25020	Guayama, PR	67,526	NA	16.0	7.0	26.0	28.4	22.6	46.0	55.9	16.0	0.0	65.7	99.7
25060	Gulfport-Biloxi, MS	418,082	7.5	23.2	7.9	25.9	26.0	17.0	39.1	76.0	20.6	4.4	9.0	5.8
25180	Hagerstown-Martinsburg, MD-WV	300,820	7.0	21.8	8.3	26.5	26.6	16.8	39.9	87.9	11.7	2.1	7.8	5.6

Metropolitan area / division code	Metropolitan area / division	Born in state of residence (percent)	Foreign born (percent)	Total households	Household type (percent of all households)							Percent of households with people age 60 years and over
					Family households				Nonfamily households			
					Total	Married-couple	Male householder	Female householder	Total	One-person households		
	ACS table number:	B05002	B05002	B11001	B11001	B11001	B11001	B11001	B11001	B11001		B11006
	column number:	14	15	16	17	18	19	20	21	22		23
19740	Denver-Aurora-Lakewood, CO	42.2	12.3	1,192,117	61.3	47.0	4.6	9.7	38.7	29.0		33.9
19780	Des Moines-West Des Moines, IA	68.9	8.3	291,147	62.9	49.0	4.4	9.4	37.1	29.3		35.8
19820	Detroit-Warren-Dearborn, MI	75.6	10.0	1,759,573	63.2	44.3	5.4	13.5	36.8	30.8		42.3
1982019804	Detroit-Dearborn-Livonia, MI Division.....	75.9	9.6	695,038	60.5	36.4	6.2	17.8	39.5	33.8		42.0
1982047664	Warren-Troy-Farmington Hills, MI Division	75.4	10.2	1,064,535	65.0	49.4	4.8	10.7	35.0	28.8		42.5
20020	Dothan, AL	64.9	2.0	61,173	64.9	44.8	5.0	15.1	35.1	30.9		46.1
20100	Dover, DE	48.8	7.5	70,167	67.3	50.7	3.2	13.4	32.7	26.7		45.6
20220	Dubuque, IA	76.8	2.7	40,482	64.8	52.7	4.2	7.9	35.2	27.5		40.6
20260	Duluth, MN-WI	71.9	2.1	124,996	57.3	42.8	5.0	9.6	42.7	32.9		43.6
20500	Durham-Chapel Hill, NC	48.6	11.8	263,996	59.9	44.8	3.7	11.3	40.1	31.6		39.2
20700	East Stroudsburg, PA	42.8	9.7	65,907	72.3	53.9	6.1	12.3	27.7	21.9		47.8
20740	Eau Claire, WI	74.9	2.7	70,044	62.1	49.3	5.9	6.9	37.9	29.6		41.0
20940	El Centro, CA	62.4	29.2	47,849	77.0	48.5	7.9	20.7	23.0	20.2		47.5
21060	Elizabethtown-Fort Knox, KY	60.2	3.1	58,210	65.9	48.1	5.2	12.6	34.1	28.4		39.3
21140	Elkhart-Goshen, IN	67.5	8.7	69,015	72.5	54.9	5.4	12.2	27.5	24.1		40.9
21300	Elmira, NY	76.6	3.1	35,407	59.2	45.2	3.6	10.4	40.8	32.0		45.4
21340	El Paso, TX	58.0	23.0	299,177	72.8	46.5	6.8	19.5	27.2	22.8		37.4
21420	Enid, OK	59.1	4.9	23,016	69.6	53.8	7.0	8.8	30.4	26.5		44.7
21500	Erie, PA	78.7	4.8	110,561	58.6	42.0	4.4	12.2	41.4	34.2		44.9
21660	Eugene-Springfield, OR	47.3	5.6	160,158	59.6	44.9	3.9	10.9	40.4	27.9		42.9
21780	Evansville, IN-KY	71.8	2.0	132,942	61.2	46.2	4.6	10.4	38.8	32.8		41.6
21820	Fairbanks, AK	34.8	6.7	36,426	61.9	51.7	2.2	8.1	38.1	30.4		28.8
22020	Fargo, ND-MN	52.4	6.8	109,997	56.1	41.6	5.0	9.5	43.9	36.3		30.3
22140	Farmington, NM	63.7	3.8	40,844	68.5	40.4	9.1	19.0	31.5	25.7		46.4
22180	Fayetteville, NC	46.6	6.2	198,062	64.7	44.7	4.2	15.8	35.3	30.6		33.2
22220	Fayetteville-Springdale-Rogers, AR	46.7	10.7	206,712	69.7	53.2	5.3	11.2	30.3	23.8		32.5
22380	Flagstaff, AZ	56.1	5.0	55,145	60.1	45.0	3.9	11.2	39.9	24.5		37.9
22420	Flint, MI	83.1	3.0	167,895	60.7	41.6	4.2	14.9	39.3	32.6		44.1
22500	Florence, SC	78.2	1.7	77,918	62.7	42.3	4.2	16.2	37.3	33.0		43.7
22520	Florence-Muscle Shoals, AL	73.4	2.1	61,492	64.0	46.1	5.6	12.3	36.0	30.7		45.9
22540	Fond du Lac, WI	82.3	3.7	42,758	66.5	53.5	3.5	9.5	33.5	28.5		42.6
22660	Fort Collins, CO	38.1	6.0	152,123	59.3	49.9	2.4	7.1	40.7	26.3		36.6
22900	Fort Smith, AR-OK	56.4	6.0	97,188	66.6	47.8	6.2	12.7	33.4	26.9		43.3
23060	Fort Wayne, IN	66.9	7.3	168,833	63.5	47.3	4.7	11.4	36.5	29.1		38.3
23420	Fresno, CA	69.9	19.7	322,646	71.7	46.4	8.6	16.7	28.3	22.5		38.0
23460	Gadsden, AL	77.9	1.6	38,006	64.2	44.6	5.5	14.1	35.8	31.2		47.2
23540	Gainesville, FL	53.5	9.5	134,946	56.7	40.9	4.7	11.2	43.3	31.9		40.5
23580	Gainesville, GA	53.0	16.2	72,454	69.9	52.7	5.1	12.1	30.1	24.1		41.4
23900	Gettysburg, PA	60.8	2.9	39,986	67.0	50.8	7.6	8.6	33.0	26.7		50.4
24020	Glens Falls, NY	76.5	3.3	54,582	60.7	46.7	4.7	9.3	39.3	31.3		46.1
24140	Goldsboro, NC	61.2	8.0	46,932	65.5	42.3	7.3	15.9	34.5	28.3		42.0
24220	Grand Forks, ND-MN	53.3	5.3	43,220	55.7	41.4	4.4	9.9	44.3	30.6		31.5
24260	Grand Island, NE	67.7	14.2	30,478	67.0	50.8	5.8	10.5	33.0	26.4		40.1
24300	Grand Junction, CO	52.0	3.3	63,796	64.3	48.4	5.2	10.8	35.7	29.5		47.1
24340	Grand Rapids-Kentwood, MI	77.4	6.8	410,413	66.9	52.4	4.7	9.9	33.1	25.4		37.1
24420	Grants Pass, OR	38.1	3.4	36,755	58.8	39.9	5.5	13.4	41.2	32.0		57.0
24500	Great Falls, MT	55.7	1.7	34,303	61.2	51.7	3.3	6.2	38.8	33.3		43.3
24540	Greeley, CO	49.9	8.9	119,502	72.8	58.0	5.1	9.7	27.2	20.0		34.8
24580	Green Bay, WI	75.7	4.3	135,686	62.7	48.8	5.3	8.5	37.3	30.3		39.6
24660	Greensboro-High Point, NC	59.7	8.8	307,003	63.5	44.9	4.0	14.7	36.5	30.5		41.9
24780	Greenville, NC	66.9	4.7	75,578	50.4	30.2	6.0	14.2	49.6	38.4		33.0
24860	Greenville-Anderson, SC	55.0	7.1	373,112	66.5	49.0	5.2	12.3	33.5	28.2		40.9
25020	Guayama, PR	55.4	3.5	25,902	64.8	41.6	3.1	20.0	35.2	31.9		53.9
25060	Gulfport-Biloxi, MS	NA	NA	162,594	66.4	46.6	4.7	15.1	33.6	28.2		43.2
25180	Hagerstown-Martinsburg, MD-WV ...	49.6	4.4	117,803	65.6	47.8	5.3	12.6	34.4	26.2		41.7

Metropolitan area / division code	Metropolitan area / division	Total population	Percent change, 2010–2019	Population by age (percent)					Median age	Race alone or in combination (percent)				Hispanic or Latino (percent)
				Under 18 years	18 to 24 years	25 to 44 years	45 to 64 years	65 years and over		White	Black or African American	Asian + Native Hawaiian or Other Pacific Islander	American Indian and Alaska Native + Some other race	
	ACS table number:	B01003	Population Estimates	B01001	B01001	B01001	B01001	B01001	B01002	B02008	B02009	B02011 + B02012	B02010 + B02013	B03003
	column number:	1	2	3	4	5	6	7	8	9	10	11	12	13
25220	Hammond, LA	135,217	11.3	24.6	11.6	25.8	21.9	16.1	35.6	67.7	31.0	1.6	5.1	4.7
25260	Hanford-Corcoran, CA	153,443	-0.0	27.0	10.2	32.2	19.9	10.7	32.2	59.3	8.3	6.2	51.1	56.6
25420	Harrisburg-Carlisle, PA	596,305	5.2	21.6	8.3	26.1	25.6	18.5	40.3	81.5	13.1	6.0	6.7	7.5
25500	Harrisonburg, VA	135,824	7.8	19.6	18.1	25.6	21.0	15.6	34.3	89.0	8.0	3.1	14.4	13.0
25540	Hartford-East Hartford-Middletown, CT	1,211,906	-0.6	19.7	10.2	25.2	26.7	18.2	40.6	75.6	15.1	6.7	14.4	16.2
25620	Hattiesburg, MS	172,507	4.0	24.3	13.1	23.7	24.6	14.2	35.8	70.2	29.7	2.3	4.9	2.6
25860	Hickory-Lenoir-Morganton, NC	366,441	1.2	20.4	8.4	23.0	28.0	20.2	43.2	87.5	7.2	4.1	10.1	7.7
25940	Hilton Head Island-Bluffton, SC	222,072	18.8	17.2	9.6	20.9	23.9	28.4	47.2	72.9	18.9	1.7	13.2	11.9
25980	Hinesville, GA	79,371	3.9	28.0	14.1	30.5	17.4	10.0	29.3	53.0	46.9	4.3	10.6	11.2
26140	Homosassa Springs, FL	158,083	6.0	14.5	5.0	17.8	26.0	36.7	57.8	93.9	3.6	2.2	6.8	6.7
26300	Hot Springs, AR	100,330	3.5	19.8	6.9	22.6	26.7	24.0	45.5	90.2	9.8	1.1	4.8	6.4
26380	Houma-Thibodaux, LA	206,212	-0.0	24.0	8.1	25.9	25.3	16.8	38.7	76.8	18.3	1.8	11.0	5.1
26420	Houston-The Woodlands-Sugar Land, TX	7,206,841	19.4	26.2	8.9	29.0	23.8	12.1	35.3	60.1	18.9	9.5	34.3	38.5
26580	Huntington-Ashland, WV-KY-OH	356,581	-4.1	20.8	8.5	23.9	26.4	20.5	42.4	96.8	3.1	0.9	4.0	1.0
26620	Huntsville, AL	502,728	13.0	21.7	8.8	27.1	26.7	15.7	39.8	74.4	23.0	4.0	8.1	5.7
26820	Idaho Falls, ID	163,293	13.7	30.4	7.7	27.1	21.5	13.3	33.6	92.3	1.3	2.1	13.1	13.3
26900	Indianapolis-Carmel-Anderson, IN	2,129,479	9.9	24.4	8.6	28.1	24.7	14.3	37.0	77.4	17.0	4.7	8.3	7.4
26980	Iowa City, IA	177,239	13.4	20.4	18.7	27.4	19.7	13.8	32.0	85.6	8.4	6.5	8.2	6.2
27060	Ithaca, NY	105,162	0.6	12.0	31.2	20.1	21.4	15.3	31.4	81.0	5.9	11.6	6.6	5.5
27100	Jackson, MI	160,050	-1.1	21.4	7.6	25.9	26.6	18.5	40.9	90.1	10.4	1.3	6.1	3.9
27140	Jackson, MS	586,758	1.4	23.4	9.2	26.6	24.8	16.0	38.4	49.2	49.4	1.4	4.0	2.4
27180	Jackson, TN	180,799	-0.6	23.0	9.8	24.9	24.4	17.9	38.6	69.1	28.9	1.1	5.9	4.5
27260	Jacksonville, FL	1,637,666	15.9	22.3	8.1	27.0	25.8	16.8	39.5	71.2	22.6	5.7	11.5	10.3
27340	Jacksonville, NC	206,160	11.3	24.3	21.9	27.7	16.6	9.6	27.3	80.0	16.7	5.0	13.2	13.4
27500	Janesville-Beloit, WI	164,381	1.9	22.8	7.9	25.4	27.1	16.8	39.9	91.9	6.8	1.8	9.7	9.7
27620	Jefferson City, MO	151,698	1.0	22.7	9.3	26.4	25.0	16.6	39.1	90.8	8.7	1.7	5.9	3.1
27740	Johnson City, TN	205,972	2.5	18.3	10.5	23.2	27.4	20.6	42.7	95.7	3.0	1.8	6.5	3.5
27780	Johnstown, PA	132,167	-9.4	19.3	8.8	21.0	27.4	23.6	46.0	96.0	4.1	0.9	2.9	1.9
27860	Jonesboro, AR	134,878	10.6	25.1	9.9	28.4	22.1	14.5	34.5	81.7	15.3	1.6	9.3	5.2
27900	Joplin, MO	182,541	2.3	24.4	8.7	25.8	24.3	16.8	38.0	93.2	2.1	3.1	12.8	7.9
27980	Kahului-Wailuku-Lahaina, HI	164,268	8.1	21.5	6.0	25.7	26.9	19.8	42.9	50.6	1.8	71.7	9.6	12.1
28020	Kalamazoo-Portage, MI	261,108	5.9	21.5	15.6	25.3	22.1	15.6	34.7	83.2	13.9	3.7	7.0	5.6
28100	Kankakee, IL	106,601	-3.2	22.4	11.0	23.7	24.6	18.4	39.3	81.4	16.0	2.1	7.6	11.6
28140	Kansas City, MO-KS	2,199,544	7.4	23.8	8.0	27.7	24.8	15.7	37.9	80.2	14.2	4.2	11.0	9.7
28420	Kennewick-Richland, WA	308,293	18.3	27.9	9.3	26.9	22.3	13.5	34.6	79.2	2.5	4.9	31.7	33.6
28660	Killeen-Temple, TX	486,416	13.6	26.3	11.6	29.6	20.8	11.7	32.3	67.9	25.7	4.9	19.7	24.9
28700	Kingsport-Bristol, TN-VA	307,318	-0.8	18.8	7.3	23.1	28.2	22.6	45.7	97.2	2.2	0.8	4.4	2.1
28740	Kingston, NY	182,951	-2.7	17.2	8.0	25.3	28.9	20.7	44.5	87.2	8.4	3.2	16.2	11.1
28940	Knoxville, TN	893,002	6.6	20.4	9.6	25.1	26.0	18.9	40.4	92.0	6.1	2.2	7.7	4.6
29020	Kokomo, IN	83,687	-0.3	21.9	8.3	24.0	26.4	19.4	41.5	90.6	7.7	2.1	8.6	3.9
29100	La Crosse-Onalaska, WI-MN	139,211	2.2	20.4	14.0	23.8	23.9	18.0	37.4	93.7	2.6	4.7	3.0	2.0
29180	Lafayette, LA	479,212	4.8	24.5	8.9	27.1	24.4	15.2	37.5	72.0	26.5	2.4	6.2	4.0
29200	Lafayette-West Lafayette, IN	224,253	10.8	20.3	20.6	24.7	20.5	13.9	32.0	86.1	6.3	6.9	9.7	8.2
29340	Lake Charles, LA	208,680	5.4	24.6	8.4	26.6	24.7	15.8	37.6	72.6	25.6	1.7	6.2	4.2
29420	Lake Havasu City-Kingman, AZ	217,692	6.0	16.4	5.6	18.6	28.0	31.3	53.4	90.0	2.1	2.5	17.1	17.7
29460	Lakeland-Winter Haven, FL	753,520	20.4	22.1	8.3	25.9	23.9	19.8	39.9	66.6	17.2	2.4	26.6	27.4
29540	Lancaster, PA	553,652	5.1	23.3	8.7	24.9	24.1	19.0	39.3	88.5	6.4	3.3	9.7	11.5
29620	Lansing-East Lansing, MI	540,281	2.9	20.3	13.5	25.9	23.6	16.8	37.1	86.0	10.3	5.3	7.6	6.6
29700	Laredo, TX	267,945	10.5	31.7	11.6	25.8	20.8	10.1	29.7	88.6	0.4	0.7	78.9	95.4
29740	Las Cruces, NM	221,508	4.3	23.5	13.8	25.4	20.9	16.3	33.6	64.0	2.8	1.6	60.2	69.3
29820	Las Vegas-Henderson-Paradise, NV	2,292,476	16.2	22.7	8.1	28.8	25.0	15.4	38.1	60.3	15.2	15.2	29.4	32.3
29940	Lawrence, KS	119,363	10.3	17.5	21.3	27.9	19.5	13.7	32.3	89.1	6.4	5.9	9.3	6.7
30020	Lawton, OK	127,078	-3.0	24.1	12.3	29.4	20.5	13.7	33.3	71.0	19.0	5.2	21.5	14.2
30140	Lebanon, PA	143,493	6.2	22.6	8.2	23.6	25.5	20.1	40.5	87.3	3.5	2.2	16.5	14.9

Metropolitan area / division code	Metropolitan area / division	Born in state of residence (percent)	Foreign born (percent)	Total households	Family households Total	Married-couple	Male householder	Female householder	Nonfamily households Total	One-person households	Percent of households with people age 60 years and over
	ACS table number:	B05002	B05002	B11001	B11001	B11001	B11001	B11001	B11001	B11001	B11006
	column number:	14	15	16	17	18	19	20	21	22	23
25220	Hammond, LA	80.5	0.8	49,915	61.3	39.6	5.6	16.1	38.7	32.9	38.9
25260	Hanford-Corcoran, CA	65.6	18.1	43,143	80.0	50.5	6.6	22.9	20.0	15.3	34.7
25420	Harrisburg-Carlisle, PA	70.9	7.4	243,253	63.1	48.8	4.4	10.0	36.9	30.2	42.0
25500	Harrisonburg, VA	59.6	8.4	50,478	65.2	49.3	5.7	10.2	34.8	23.4	39.2
25540	Hartford-East Hartford-Middletown, CT	57.0	13.4	488,173	62.8	45.7	4.2	12.9	37.2	29.6	43.5
25620	Hattiesburg, MS	72.9	2.0	66,682	68.1	47.6	5.2	15.3	31.9	26.5	35.5
25860	Hickory-Lenoir-Morganton, NC	68.7	4.5	146,600	66.4	49.1	4.6	12.6	33.6	28.4	48.0
25940	Hilton Head Island-Bluffton, SC	28.9	7.9	89,701	65.8	54.4	2.8	8.6	34.2	27.7	54.8
25980	Hinesville, GA	38.6	6.0	29,290	71.1	48.0	5.9	17.2	28.9	24.8	27.7
26140	Homosassa Springs, FL	32.2	4.4	68,269	60.4	47.2	4.2	8.9	39.6	33.8	69.7
26300	Hot Springs, AR	54.0	2.6	42,077	62.5	43.3	7.9	11.3	37.5	31.1	50.4
26380	Houma-Thibodaux, LA	87.8	2.3	82,107	67.4	48.1	5.6	13.8	32.6	27.6	41.8
26420	Houston-The Woodlands-Sugar Land, TX	53.7	24.1	2,601,401	69.8	50.4	5.7	13.6	30.2	24.4	34.4
26580	Huntington-Ashland, WV-KY-OH	65.8	1.2	144,383	65.0	47.9	4.6	12.4	35.0	29.3	46.8
26620	Huntsville, AL	54.4	5.3	205,178	66.0	50.4	4.3	11.3	34.0	28.8	38.5
26820	Idaho Falls, ID	56.2	3.7	54,348	71.1	59.7	3.6	7.8	28.9	24.9	37.5
26900	Indianapolis-Carmel-Anderson, IN	66.7	7.8	834,540	64.3	48.3	4.5	11.6	35.7	28.5	36.6
26980	Iowa City, IA	62.4	7.9	69,788	54.4	46.0	1.7	6.7	45.6	30.4	33.1
27060	Ithaca, NY	54.7	11.2	44,469	48.4	36.9	3.4	8.1	51.6	36.3	34.8
27100	Jackson, MI	84.3	1.3	61,937	62.3	44.9	6.5	10.9	37.7	32.7	45.1
27140	Jackson, MS	77.8	2.5	228,001	66.6	42.4	5.2	19.0	33.4	28.5	39.8
27180	Jackson, TN	72.7	2.3	71,462	65.6	43.7	4.6	17.3	34.4	29.3	45.4
27260	Jacksonville, FL	44.4	10.0	644,887	65.3	47.2	4.4	13.7	34.7	27.4	40.5
27340	Jacksonville, NC	34.3	4.7	73,121	70.6	55.4	3.2	12.0	29.4	25.6	26.6
27500	Janesville-Beloit, WI	72.3	4.3	67,876	64.6	46.9	6.0	11.6	35.4	28.6	41.5
27620	Jefferson City, MO	78.3	1.5	55,812	64.2	47.9	4.6	11.7	35.8	30.7	41.9
27740	Johnson City, TN	58.5	2.7	86,767	59.4	48.0	3.6	7.8	40.6	32.5	47.4
27780	Johnstown, PA	87.8	0.7	55,283	60.9	47.7	3.7	9.4	39.1	33.3	50.3
27860	Jonesboro, AR	71.3	1.6	51,155	66.4	46.4	5.8	14.1	33.6	28.2	34.9
27900	Joplin, MO	58.6	4.1	69,646	68.0	51.4	4.2	12.3	32.0	24.6	43.1
27980	Kahului-Wailuku-Lahaina, HI	48.7	19.2	56,319	66.0	48.1	6.2	11.7	34.0	26.5	54.7
28020	Kalamazoo-Portage, MI	75.9	5.0	105,642	56.4	42.1	4.4	9.9	43.6	32.6	36.7
28100	Kankakee, IL	81.8	4.0	41,020	64.5	45.8	5.2	13.5	35.5	26.5	43.5
28140	Kansas City, MO-KS	54.0	6.9	883,621	64.6	49.5	4.2	10.8	35.4	28.2	37.4
28420	Kennewick-Richland, WA	51.9	14.5	105,844	70.9	51.2	5.2	14.4	29.1	23.3	37.9
28660	Killeen-Temple, TX	47.1	6.6	174,498	68.7	49.2	4.7	14.9	31.3	26.6	32.1
28700	Kingsport-Bristol, TN-VA	57.6	1.5	128,312	63.6	46.6	5.2	11.8	36.4	32.3	48.8
28740	Kingston, NY	73.3	7.2	75,053	60.1	44.5	4.7	10.8	39.9	30.4	49.4
28940	Knoxville, TN	59.4	3.8	361,646	62.7	47.7	3.9	11.0	37.3	30.5	43.2
29020	Kokomo, IN	75.0	2.9	36,530	68.6	47.2	9.0	12.4	31.4	25.7	40.5
29100	La Crosse-Onalaska, WI-MN	65.7	2.9	58,000	54.2	43.8	3.4	7.0	45.8	33.5	42.3
29180	Lafayette, LA	85.2	3.1	187,662	65.1	45.5	5.6	14.0	34.9	29.5	38.3
29200	Lafayette-West Lafayette, IN	61.5	8.4	88,853	54.2	42.4	3.6	8.2	45.8	32.5	33.0
29340	Lake Charles, LA	80.4	4.1	72,746	68.9	50.8	4.1	14.1	31.1	26.2	43.6
29420	Lake Havasu City-Kingman, AZ	17.2	7.9	102,398	64.0	47.0	4.6	12.4	36.0	29.2	61.1
29460	Lakeland-Winter Haven, FL	44.0	10.4	276,469	67.7	47.7	5.2	14.9	32.3	24.5	47.2
29540	Lancaster, PA	74.5	5.9	210,063	70.1	57.1	4.3	8.7	29.9	23.4	44.3
29620	Lansing-East Lansing, MI	78.2	6.2	220,067	58.4	43.4	4.9	10.1	41.6	31.9	38.5
29700	Laredo, TX	68.1	25.8	78,730	78.6	48.2	6.7	23.7	21.4	18.3	36.4
29740	Las Cruces, NM	46.2	15.0	85,021	63.7	42.3	8.0	13.5	36.3	29.7	39.8
29820	Las Vegas-Henderson-Paradise, NV	25.0	21.3	854,289	63.4	42.6	6.8	14.0	36.6	28.2	39.8
29940	Lawrence, KS	52.5	5.5	49,759	49.7	37.6	3.2	8.8	50.3	41.9	30.3
30020	Lawton, OK	44.6	4.9	46,916	64.3	45.2	4.6	14.5	35.7	29.3	34.3
30140	Lebanon, PA	76.5	4.1	54,906	67.3	53.3	4.8	9.1	32.7	26.3	48.8

Metropolitan area / division code	Metropolitan area / division	Total population	Percent change, 2010–2019	Population by age (percent)					Median age	Race alone or in combination (percent)				
				Under 18 years	18 to 24 years	25 to 44 years	45 to 64 years	65 years and over		White	Black or African American	Asian + Native Hawaiian or Other Pacific Islander	American Indian and Alaska Native + Some other race	Hispanic or Latino (percent)
	ACS table number:	B01003	Population Estimates	B01001	B01001	B01001	B01001	B01001	B01002	B02008	B02009	B02011 + B02012	B02010 + B02013	B03003
	column number:	1	2	3	4	5	6	7	8	9	10	11	12	13
30300	Lewiston, ID-WA	64,851	3.5	20.0	10.3	21.6	25.5	22.6	42.5	93.4	2.1	0.7	10.0	4.5
30340	Lewiston-Auburn, ME	111,034	0.5	21.0	8.8	24.9	26.8	18.5	40.8	94.1	4.8	1.7	6.1	2.1
30460	Lexington-Fayette, KY	517,846	9.5	21.8	11.8	27.0	24.2	15.2	36.7	84.2	11.6	3.6	8.7	6.5
30620	Lima, OH	101,670	-3.7	23.0	10.1	24.1	24.0	18.8	39.9	85.6	13.3	1.2	7.0	3.7
30700	Lincoln, NE	343,035	11.3	22.6	15.1	26.1	21.5	14.8	34.2	89.2	5.6	5.5	8.0	7.6
30780	Little Rock-North Little Rock-Conway, AR	749,673	6.1	23.3	9.4	27.2	24.2	16.0	37.4	71.2	25.6	2.4	6.3	5.7
30860	Logan, UT-ID	152,492	13.3	29.7	17.4	26.2	16.2	10.5	26.8	93.6	0.4	4.0	11.0	10.6
30980	Longview, TX	287,868	2.4	24.5	9.5	25.1	24.1	16.7	38.3	78.5	18.0	1.5	18.5	16.8
31020	Longview, WA	111,524	8.0	22.7	6.5	25.7	25.6	19.5	41.6	92.5	1.6	2.8	12.6	9.9
31080	Los Angeles-Long Beach-Anaheim, CA	12,997,353	3.0	21.2	8.9	29.3	25.8	14.9	38.1	50.8	7.7	19.6	42.4	45.4
3108011244	Anaheim-Santa Ana-Irvine, CA Division	3,167,809	5.5	21.4	8.7	27.4	26.7	15.7	39.2	58.4	2.8	27.0	30.4	27.0
3108031084	Los Angeles-Long Beach-Glendale, CA Division	9,829,544	2.2	21.1	8.9	29.9	25.5	14.6	37.8	48.4	9.3	17.0	46.3	17.0
31140	Louisville/Jefferson County, KY-IN	1,284,826	5.2	22.2	8.3	26.8	25.9	16.8	39.5	82.0	16.4	3.2	8.4	5.7
31180	Lubbock, TX	326,546	10.8	23.7	16.3	26.8	20.2	12.9	31.7	81.0	8.6	3.0	28.7	37.7
31340	Lynchburg, VA	263,571	4.3	19.7	14.1	22.4	24.7	19.1	40.0	77.9	18.8	2.5	6.9	3.3
31420	Macon-Bibb County, GA	232,775	-1.0	23.2	9.8	25.0	24.8	17.1	38.1	51.6	45.5	2.2	4.7	3.4
31460	Madera, CA	159,410	4.3	27.6	9.3	26.2	22.0	14.9	35.1	58.9	4.0	4.0	56.6	60.2
31540	Madison, WI	683,183	9.8	20.2	12.3	28.5	23.7	15.3	37.1	88.0	6.4	6.4	7.5	6.3
31700	Manchester-Nashua, NH	424,079	4.1	19.9	8.4	26.9	27.9	16.9	41.0	90.1	4.6	5.6	9.1	7.9
31740	Manhattan, KS	133,932	2.5	22.8	20.3	29.3	16.9	10.8	27.8	84.7	10.1	6.3	10.1	10.3
31860	Mankato, MN	103,612	5.4	20.4	18.2	25.2	20.4	15.8	34.0	92.7	4.3	2.7	7.1	4.6
31900	Mansfield, OH	125,195	-2.7	21.9	8.2	24.6	25.3	20.1	40.7	90.4	9.2	1.3	6.8	2.2
32420	Mayagüez, PR	96,503	NA	16.0	14.1	20.4	23.5	26.1	44.4	23.6	3.5	0.0	84.2	99.1
32580	McAllen-Edinburg-Mission, TX	880,356	12.1	31.6	11.1	25.8	20.1	11.3	30.1	86.6	1.2	1.1	72.4	92.6
32780	Medford, OR	223,734	8.7	20.5	7.2	25.3	24.1	22.9	42.1	91.0	1.7	3.1	17.3	14.3
32820	Memphis, TN-MS-AR	1,336,438	2.3	24.6	8.9	27.1	24.5	14.9	36.6	46.8	48.4	3.1	7.3	6.1
32900	Merced, CA	286,461	8.6	29.1	11.2	27.4	20.6	11.7	31.8	41.9	4.6	8.9	58.5	62.5
33100	Miami-Fort Lauderdale-Pompano Beach, FL	6,091,747	10.8	20.1	7.7	26.1	27.2	19.0	42.0	68.3	22.9	3.4	39.6	46.2
3310022744	Fort Lauderdale-Pompano Beach-Sunrise, FL Division	1,930,983	11.7	21.0	7.5	26.6	27.5	17.5	41.3	60.6	32.0	4.8	26.9	4.8
3310033124	Miami-Miami Beach-Kendall, FL Division	2,662,777	8.8	20.2	8.1	27.2	27.7	16.9	40.9	73.1	17.4	2.2	58.0	2.2
3310048424	West Palm Beach-Boca Raton-Boynton Beach, FL Division	1,497,987	13.4	19.0	7.2	23.4	25.9	24.5	45.4	69.6	20.7	3.8	23.5	3.8
33140	Michigan City-La Porte, IN	112,390	-1.4	21.5	8.2	25.6	26.3	18.4	40.7	86.5	12.1	1.0	10.2	7.3
33220	Midland, MI	83,457	-0.6	20.9	8.2	25.4	26.0	19.5	41.1	94.0	2.0	2.8	6.5	3.3
33260	Midland, TX	172,231	28.9	28.3	7.9	33.4	20.2	10.2	32.8	79.5	7.3	3.1	36.0	48.1
33340	Milwaukee-Waukesha, WI	1,566,487	1.2	22.8	8.7	26.9	25.1	16.5	38.5	74.8	18.2	5.1	11.6	11.6
33460	Minneapolis-St. Paul-Bloomington, MN-WI	3,690,512	9.2	23.3	8.2	28.2	25.2	15.0	38.0	80.3	11.1	8.4	8.2	6.2
33540	Missoula, MT	119,533	9.4	18.4	12.7	30.1	22.2	16.6	37.4	93.2	1.0	2.9	7.7	3.8
33660	Mobile, AL	430,714	-0.2	23.4	8.9	25.7	25.0	17.0	38.9	59.3	37.2	2.5	4.9	3.0
33700	Modesto, CA	552,999	7.0	26.9	9.2	27.5	22.7	13.5	34.7	69.3	4.4	8.8	47.5	49.5
33740	Monroe, LA	204,884	-2.0	23.1	9.9	24.8	24.5	17.7	38.7	61.3	36.6	1.1	4.8	2.7
33780	Monroe, MI	155,274	-1.0	21.1	8.1	23.2	27.9	19.8	42.8	96.3	3.7	1.0	6.1	4.0
33860	Montgomery, AL	386,814	-0.3	23.2	9.1	26.3	25.1	16.3	38.5	50.7	47.0	2.5	4.3	3.5
34060	Morgantown, WV	140,745	7.2	17.7	16.9	27.5	22.5	15.4	35.3	93.4	4.5	3.2	4.2	2.2
34100	Morristown, TN	143,855	4.5	21.8	7.4	24.3	27.1	19.4	41.0	95.0	3.2	0.6	10.0	7.1
34580	Mount Vernon-Anacortes, WA	130,696	10.5	21.3	7.4	24.9	24.4	22.1	41.6	84.1	2.0	4.1	22.0	19.5
34620	Muncie, IN	111,871	-3.0	18.3	20.4	21.2	22.8	17.2	35.2	93.1	6.8	2.0	5.2	2.8
34740	Muskegon, MI	176,511	0.8	22.8	8.5	25.3	24.9	18.5	39.8	83.6	15.7	1.2	8.1	6.2
34820	Myrtle Beach-Conway-North Myrtle Beach, SC-NC	509,794	31.9	16.4	6.7	20.7	28.0	28.3	50.7	85.1	12.6	2.1	7.2	6.0
34900	Napa, CA	136,207	0.9	19.7	8.7	24.9	26.4	20.4	42.7	72.7	3.2	11.2	31.2	35.6

Metropolitan area / division code	Metropolitan area / division	Born in state of residence (percent)	Foreign born (percent)	Total households	Household type (percent of all households)							Percent of households with people age 60 years and over
					Family households				Nonfamily households			
					Total	Married-couple	Male householder	Female householder	Total	One-person households		
	ACS table number:	B05002	B05002	B11001	B11001	B11001	B11001	B11001	B11001	B11001		B11006
	column number:	14	15	16	17	18	19	20	21	22		23
30300	Lewiston, ID-WA	43.6	1.2	27,019	58.4	42.9	6.5	9.1	41.6	34.8		46.5
30340	Lewiston-Auburn, ME	71.3	4.2	46,323	59.0	47.4	3.1	8.5	41.0	34.7		43.0
30460	Lexington-Fayette, KY	63.1	7.1	215,613	59.6	43.7	4.2	11.7	40.4	31.0		35.7
30620	Lima, OH	81.6	2.5	41,021	62.7	45.1	5.1	12.4	37.3	30.1		43.7
30700	Lincoln, NE	65.9	7.2	138,209	59.0	46.5	3.8	8.7	41.0	31.9		34.3
30780	Little Rock-North Little Rock-Conway, AR	68.1	3.9	308,436	65.6	48.1	4.3	13.2	34.4	28.0		36.7
30860	Logan, UT-ID	60.8	5.6	48,180	77.7	64.8	3.8	9.1	22.3	15.6		28.1
30980	Longview, TX	68.4	7.2	106,151	69.4	47.0	4.4	18.0	30.6	25.9		43.6
31020	Longview, WA	48.7	3.4	43,204	62.0	47.6	4.4	10.0	38.0	30.4		44.4
31080	Los Angeles-Long Beach-Anaheim, CA	52.6	32.6	4,452,780	66.9	45.9	7.0	14.0	33.1	24.8		40.9
3108011244	Anaheim-Santa Ana-Irvine, CA Division	52.8	30.4	1,077,193	70.8	53.5	5.6	11.7	29.2	21.4		42.4
3108031084	Los Angeles-Long Beach-Glendale, CA Division	52.5	33.3	3,375,587	65.7	43.4	7.5	14.8	34.3	25.9		40.4
31140	Louisville/Jefferson County, KY-IN	63.8	6.9	522,921	62.9	45.5	5.2	12.3	37.1	30.2		39.7
31180	Lubbock, TX	77.1	5.1	129,092	62.2	43.3	5.4	13.5	37.8	28.9		31.9
31340	Lynchburg, VA	65.5	3.5	103,894	64.6	48.6	4.1	11.9	35.4	29.8		44.4
31420	Macon-Bibb County, GA	76.4	2.5	85,760	61.9	39.1	3.5	19.3	38.1	32.5		44.2
31460	Madera, CA	69.5	17.8	44,048	74.7	48.1	8.7	17.9	25.3	19.8		48.5
31540	Madison, WI	63.3	8.5	292,919	55.8	44.7	3.4	7.7	44.2	32.5		33.8
31700	Manchester-Nashua, NH	40.4	9.8	167,899	66.0	51.6	5.4	8.9	34.0	25.1		41.7
31740	Manhattan, KS	46.2	6.7	51,018	60.0	50.5	1.6	7.9	40.0	30.7		28.0
31860	Mankato, MN	77.9	5.1	40,715	59.1	46.3	4.4	8.5	40.9	27.4		36.2
31900	Mansfield, OH	80.6	1.9	49,536	61.9	48.7	3.2	10.0	38.1	33.2		46.6
32420	Mayagüez, PR	NA	2.3	36,278	58.5	33.5	4.1	20.9	41.5	35.5		55.3
32580	McAllen-Edinburg-Mission, TX	64.3	25.6	268,598	78.3	51.4	4.8	22.2	21.7	18.6		35.5
32780	Medford, OR	40.2	6.9	90,817	61.1	45.7	6.8	8.7	38.9	30.6		50.5
32820	Memphis, TN-MS-AR	58.2	5.6	520,309	63.4	40.4	4.7	18.3	36.6	31.4		39.4
32900	Merced, CA	66.4	25.5	84,967	75.8	47.7	7.5	20.6	24.2	19.7		37.6
33100	Miami-Fort Lauderdale-Pompano Beach, FL	33.1	41.5	2,306,639	64.9	43.6	6.2	15.1	35.1	28.1		45.9
3310022744	Fort Lauderdale-Pompano Beach-Sunrise, FL Division	36.0	35.6	747,715	63.2	42.9	5.8	14.5	36.8	29.0		43.6
3310033124	Miami-Miami Beach-Kendall, FL Division	32.8	53.6	963,477	67.7	42.9	7.1	17.6	32.3	25.8		43.8
3310048424	West Palm Beach-Boca Raton-Boynton Beach, FL Division	30.1	27.3	595,447	62.5	45.5	5.2	11.9	37.5	30.5		52.5
33140	Michigan City-La Porte, IN	73.2	2.2	43,445	64.9	45.4	5.0	14.5	35.1	28.0		47.0
33220	Midland, MI	78.7	3.7	35,453	64.8	50.3	3.5	11.1	35.2	29.7		42.3
33260	Midland, TX	67.4	13.6	68,042	70.7	55.6	6.1	9.0	29.3	24.0		27.7
33340	Milwaukee-Waukesha, WI	71.7	7.4	649,303	61.3	43.5	5.1	12.7	38.7	31.1		38.4
33460	Minneapolis-St. Paul-Bloomington, MN-WI	63.1	10.8	1,453,400	62.6	49.1	4.4	9.1	37.4	28.5		37.3
33540	Missoula, MT	45.2	2.9	51,957	56.5	42.2	4.4	9.9	43.5	28.8		37.5
33660	Mobile, AL	74.2	3.2	168,977	64.0	41.9	4.4	17.6	36.0	31.7		41.0
33700	Modesto, CA	67.7	21.8	174,209	75.3	51.2	8.3	15.8	24.7	19.7		38.6
33740	Monroe, LA	79.4	1.5	80,334	62.1	38.3	4.9	18.9	37.9	33.2		42.3
33780	Monroe, MI	62.0	2.1	61,574	65.2	50.8	5.8	8.7	34.8	29.2		47.0
33860	Montgomery, AL	72.1	4.2	150,996	64.0	39.2	4.3	20.5	36.0	32.0		39.5
34060	Morgantown, WV	58.5	3.6	56,020	58.2	47.5	3.2	7.5	41.8	30.5		34.3
34100	Morristown, TN	64.2	4.3	53,925	67.3	51.4	4.6	11.3	32.7	29.4		47.9
34580	Mount Vernon-Anacortes, WA	55.5	9.5	51,971	67.5	50.4	6.0	11.1	32.5	25.4		49.2
34620	Muncie, IN	76.6	1.3	45,977	59.0	42.3	5.2	11.4	41.0	32.2		39.0
34740	Muskegon, MI	85.7	1.4	67,707	67.4	47.1	5.8	14.4	32.6	25.5		44.5
34820	Myrtle Beach-Conway-North Myrtle Beach, SC-NC	35.5	4.9	210,672	65.3	50.8	4.0	10.5	34.7	29.2		57.9
34900	Napa, CA	57.1	23.0	49,979	67.9	52.3	7.3	8.3	32.1	24.9		47.6

Metropolitan area / division code	Metropolitan area / division	Total population	Percent change, 2010–2019	Population by age (percent)					Median age	Race alone or in combination (percent)				Hispanic or Latino (percent)
				Under 18 years	18 to 24 years	25 to 44 years	45 to 64 years	65 years and over		White	Black or African American	Asian + Native Hawaiian or Other Pacific Islander	American Indian and Alaska Native + Some other race	
	ACS table number:	B01003	Population Estimates	B01001	B01001	B01001	B01001	B01001	B01002	B02008	B02009	B02011 + B02012	B02010 + B02013	B03003
	column number:	1	2	3	4	5	6	7	8	9	10	11	12	13
34940	Naples-Marco Island, FL	385,980	19.7	16.5	6.3	19.0	25.2	33.0	52.7	84.3	7.7	2.4	27.2	29.0
34980	Nashville-Davidson--Murfreesboro--Franklin, TN	2,013,506	17.5	22.7	8.9	29.4	24.9	14.1	37.2	78.7	16.4	3.8	9.2	8.0
35100	New Bern, NC	120,508	-2.0	19.8	11.2	22.9	24.2	21.8	41.2	74.4	22.2	3.5	5.7	8.0
35300	New Haven-Milford, CT	863,700	-0.9	19.9	9.6	25.8	26.5	18.1	40.5	72.0	16.5	5.4	18.7	20.2
35380	New Orleans-Metairie, LA	1,261,726	6.8	22.2	7.8	27.4	25.4	17.3	39.4	59.2	35.7	3.8	11.3	9.3
35620	New York-Newark-Jersey City, NY-NJ-PA	19,768,458	1.7	21.4	8.2	27.6	26.2	16.7	39.5	56.4	19.2	13.2	25.0	25.3
3562035004	Nassau County-Suffolk County, NY Division	2,917,251	0.0	21.1	8.5	24.1	28.3	18.0	41.8	73.2	11.2	8.8	18.4	8.8
3562035084	Newark, NJ-PA Division	2,273,431	0.9	22.2	8.2	25.9	27.8	16.0	40.3	58.3	22.8	7.7	23.3	7.7
3562035154	New Brunswick-Lakewood, NJ Metro Division	2,500,806	1.7	22.1	8.4	24.0	27.2	18.4	41.3	70.7	9.1	15.3	15.1	15.3
3562035614	New York-Jersey City-White Plains, NY-NJ Division	12,076,970	2.2	21.1	8.0	29.4	25.1	16.3	38.5	49.0	22.6	14.8	28.9	14.8
35660	Niles, MI	153,101	-2.2	21.6	8.1	23.0	26.4	20.9	42.9	80.2	15.8	2.7	7.9	6.1
35840	North Port-Sarasota-Bradenton, FL	859,760	19.2	15.7	6.1	19.0	26.4	32.8	53.9	87.3	7.5	2.8	13.6	13.4
35980	Norwich-New London, CT	268,805	-3.2	19.1	9.8	24.9	26.9	19.2	41.6	84.2	9.9	5.5	14.0	12.0
36100	Ocala, FL	385,915	10.3	18.6	6.5	20.9	25.4	28.7	48.5	82.6	14.8	2.8	13.7	15.5
36140	Ocean City, NJ	95,661	-5.4	16.9	5.7	20.8	29.0	27.6	51.6	90.9	6.1	1.4	8.4	8.4
36220	Odessa, TX	161,091	21.2	30.7	9.9	29.5	19.8	10.2	31.9	67.2	6.6	1.5	52.2	64.7
36260	Ogden-Clearfield, UT	708,543	14.5	29.5	9.6	28.9	20.7	11.3	32.8	90.8	2.1	4.0	11.9	13.8
36420	Oklahoma City, OK	1,441,647	12.4	24.2	10.1	28.1	22.9	14.7	36.1	78.2	12.9	4.6	18.7	14.4
36500	Olympia-Lacey-Tumwater, WA	297,977	15.2	21.1	8.5	28.1	24.0	18.2	39.3	85.2	5.8	10.8	12.9	10.1
36540	Omaha-Council Bluffs, NE-IA	972,195	9.7	25.2	8.7	27.9	23.7	14.5	36.7	84.3	9.3	4.3	11.5	11.4
36740	Orlando-Kissimmee-Sanford, FL	2,691,925	22.2	21.5	9.0	29.0	25.0	15.5	38.5	67.2	19.0	5.8	30.3	32.6
36780	Oshkosh-Neenah, WI	171,623	2.9	20.3	11.8	25.4	25.7	16.9	38.4	91.3	4.6	3.9	6.0	4.7
36980	Owensboro, KY	122,696	4.1	23.5	8.8	24.7	25.2	17.9	39.5	93.2	4.5	2.0	5.6	3.2
37100	Oxnard-Thousand Oaks-Ventura, CA	839,784	2.8	22.2	8.8	26.2	26.1	16.7	39.0	76.7	3.1	10.2	36.5	44.1
37340	Palm Bay-Melbourne-Titusville, FL	616,628	10.8	18.2	6.8	22.8	28.0	24.2	47.0	82.3	12.4	4.3	11.9	11.6
37460	Panama City, FL	179,168	3.5	20.7	7.0	26.2	28.2	17.9	41.1	84.2	12.2	4.1	8.0	7.4
37620	Parkersburg-Vienna, WV	88,181	-3.6	21.1	7.4	22.9	28.1	20.6	43.7	98.4	2.6	0.8	2.4	1.3
37860	Pensacola-Ferry Pass-Brent, FL	516,388	11.9	21.4	9.5	26.4	25.5	17.1	39.5	79.1	18.2	4.9	8.3	6.4
37900	Peoria, IL	398,473	-3.8	23.0	8.1	25.0	25.0	19.0	40.2	88.1	10.0	3.1	6.0	3.9
37980	Philadelphia-Camden-Wilmington, PA-NJ-DE-MD	6,228,601	2.3	21.5	8.6	27.2	25.9	16.8	39.3	67.0	22.6	7.7	11.0	10.4
3798015804	Camden, NJ Division	1,292,517	-0.6	21.7	8.2	26.2	27.1	16.9	40.3	70.1	19.0	6.7	12.9	6.7
3798033874	Montgomery County-Bucks County-Chester County, PA Division	2,045,325	3.1	21.2	8.0	24.7	27.6	18.5	42.0	83.8	8.5	8.0	7.3	8.0
3798037964	Philadelphia, PA Division	2,150,100	3.2	21.7	9.3	30.5	23.4	15.1	36.1	48.7	38.0	8.5	13.2	8.5
3798048864	Wilmington, DE-MD-NJ Division	740,659	2.6	21.4	8.8	26.5	26.5	16.8	39.8	68.6	23.7	11.0	11.9	11.0
38060	Phoenix-Mesa-Chandler, AZ	4,946,145	18.0	23.0	9.1	27.7	24.0	16.3	37.6	77.6	7.4	6.1	29.7	31.9
38220	Pine Bluff, AR	86,747	-12.4	20.9	8.7	25.8	25.5	19.0	40.2	50.0	49.5	0.0	4.2	2.8
38300	Pittsburgh, PA	2,353,538	-1.6	18.9	7.9	25.7	26.6	20.8	42.8	88.3	9.8	3.4	4.4	2.0
38340	Pittsfield, MA	128,657	-4.8	16.2	9.1	21.6	28.6	24.6	47.8	94.1	5.1	2.3	5.8	5.5
38540	Pocatello, ID	97,645	5.3	26.5	10.1	28.1	20.7	14.6	34.1	90.7	1.3	2.2	13.0	11.7
38660	Ponce, PR	219,010	NA	18.0	9.9	24.2	24.8	23.0	43.0	81.0	9.7	0.0	65.9	99.7
38860	Portland-South Portland, ME	556,893	4.7	18.2	7.6	25.9	27.7	20.6	43.5	94.7	3.1	2.6	6.6	2.1
38900	Portland-Vancouver-Hillsboro, OR-WA	2,510,696	12.0	20.6	7.9	30.3	25.3	15.9	39.1	82.4	4.8	10.8	14.8	13.0
38940	Port St. Lucie, FL	503,521	15.4	18.7	6.9	21.2	26.3	26.8	48.3	77.3	17.8	2.4	15.7	19.1
39100	Poughkeepsie-Newburgh-Middletown, NY	701,637	1.3	22.6	10.2	24.3	26.7	16.2	39.4	75.3	14.2	4.4	18.1	18.9
39140	Prescott Valley-Prescott, AZ	242,253	11.4	15.6	6.2	18.0	26.4	33.8	55.3	91.9	1.5	2.5	17.3	15.3
39300	Providence-Warwick, RI-MA	1,675,774	1.5	19.5	9.8	25.9	26.8	18.0	40.8	82.2	8.5	4.0	17.7	14.4
39340	Provo-Orem, UT	696,699	23.1	32.2	16.1	27.7	15.9	8.0	25.9	91.7	1.6	5.2	12.4	12.5
39380	Pueblo, CO	169,622	5.9	22.1	8.7	25.4	24.5	19.2	40.0	88.9	2.8	1.8	24.9	43.7
39460	Punta Gorda, FL	194,843	18.1	11.9	4.9	15.5	27.1	40.7	60.4	89.9	6.6	1.8	8.1	8.2
39540	Racine, WI	196,896	0.5	22.7	7.8	25.5	26.5	17.6	40.4	83.0	13.9	1.9	14.8	14.8

Metropolitan area / division code	Metropolitan area / division	Born in state of residence (percent)	Foreign born (percent)	Total households	Household type (percent of all households)							Percent of households with people age 60 years and over
					Family households				Nonfamily households			
					Total	Married-couple	Male householder	Female householder	Total	One-person households		
	ACS table number:	B05002	B05002	B11001	B11001	B11001	B11001	B11001	B11001	B11001		B11006
	column number:	14	15	16	17	18	19	20	21	22		23
34940	Naples-Marco Island, FL	21.9	25.0	163,943	68.2	55.5	3.9	8.8	31.8	26.2		60.4
34980	Nashville-Davidson--Murfreesboro--Franklin, TN	50.9	8.5	794,373	64.1	49.0	4.1	11.0	35.9	27.4		34.6
35100	New Bern, NC	53.6	3.2	51,021	62.2	45.8	4.8	11.6	37.8	31.5		49.7
35300	New Haven-Milford, CT	58.5	14.8	349,089	62.4	42.2	5.4	14.8	37.6	30.5		43.7
35380	New Orleans-Metairie, LA	72.2	7.8	507,992	60.7	40.2	5.1	15.5	39.3	33.7		42.4
35620	New York-Newark-Jersey City, NY-NJ-PA	53.5	29.4	7,347,700	64.7	45.1	5.2	14.4	35.3	28.7		43.8
3562035004	Nassau County-Suffolk County, NY Division	73.0	19.3	971,403	73.9	58.1	4.8	11.0	26.1	21.4		51.1
3562035084	Newark, NJ-PA Division	51.1	25.0	851,554	68.7	49.8	5.2	13.7	31.3	26.3		42.0
3562035154	New Brunswick-Lakewood, NJ Metro Division	54.3	21.3	930,244	69.9	55.3	4.4	10.1	30.1	24.9		46.3
3562035614	New York-Jersey City-White Plains, NY-NJ Division	49.1	34.4	4,594,499	60.9	39.5	5.4	16.0	39.1	31.5		42.0
35660	Niles, MI	58.4	5.3	65,764	61.6	45.9	4.3	11.4	38.4	32.1		48.4
35840	North Port-Sarasota-Bradenton, FL	27.4	12.3	367,538	61.8	50.9	2.8	8.1	38.2	30.8		62.2
35980	Norwich-New London, CT	53.5	7.8	110,950	63.0	45.2	5.4	12.4	37.0	30.0		43.3
36100	Ocala, FL	39.4	9.5	157,348	67.2	48.7	5.5	13.0	32.8	27.8		57.4
36140	Ocean City, NJ	48.6	5.0	48,860	65.4	53.0	4.5	7.9	34.6	29.4		51.7
36220	Odessa, TX	60.1	21.3	64,169	73.3	52.8	4.7	15.7	26.7	21.9		30.0
36260	Ogden-Clearfield, UT	66.9	5.4	230,356	75.1	60.6	5.2	9.4	24.9	20.5		33.1
36420	Oklahoma City, OK	59.8	7.7	565,309	64.6	47.9	4.9	11.8	35.4	28.5		36.2
36500	Olympia-Lacey-Tumwater, WA	45.7	8.5	117,186	66.7	50.7	4.7	11.4	33.3	25.9		41.9
36540	Omaha-Council Bluffs, NE-IA	59.2	7.6	385,487	63.5	48.9	4.4	10.2	36.5	30.0		35.5
36740	Orlando-Kissimmee-Sanford, FL	34.0	20.1	990,500	68.1	48.2	5.1	14.9	31.9	24.4		39.2
36780	Oshkosh-Neenah, WI	78.3	3.7	72,794	60.1	47.0	4.8	8.4	39.9	28.9		38.5
36980	Owensboro, KY	74.0	3.3	48,574	65.9	48.5	5.1	12.3	34.1	28.3		41.4
37100	Oxnard-Thousand Oaks-Ventura, CA	60.1	21.8	279,168	70.7	53.6	5.3	11.7	29.3	22.4		47.6
37340	Palm Bay-Melbourne-Titusville, FL	31.8	9.7	254,314	63.2	47.6	4.6	11.0	36.8	30.8		51.6
37460	Panama City, FL	40.6	8.9	79,532	66.2	47.4	5.7	13.1	33.8	24.5		41.5
37620	Parkersburg-Vienna, WV	75.2	0.9	37,656	64.3	47.1	6.3	10.9	35.7	30.3		46.0
37860	Pensacola-Ferry Pass-Brent, FL	42.5	5.3	198,702	66.6	47.5	5.6	13.6	33.4	27.6		43.3
37900	Peoria, IL	80.3	4.7	171,067	62.5	46.9	4.5	11.1	37.5	32.0		40.5
37980	Philadelphia-Camden-Wilmington, PA-NJ-DE-MD	61.0	11.3	2,442,868	63.5	45.0	4.8	13.8	36.5	29.5		41.8
3798015804	Camden, NJ Division	54.6	9.7	489,519	68.0	49.8	5.3	12.9	32.0	25.4		43.2
3798033874	Montgomery County-Bucks County-Chester County, PA Division	65.6	10.0	787,417	69.2	56.0	3.9	9.3	30.8	24.9		44.6
3798037964	Philadelphia, PA Division	65.7	13.9	879,201	56.2	32.7	5.0	18.5	43.8	35.4		38.2
3798048864	Wilmington, DE-MD-NJ Division	45.8	10.1	286,731	62.6	44.2	5.3	13.0	37.4	30.7		42.8
38060	Phoenix-Mesa-Chandler, AZ	38.9	13.4	1,863,195	66.4	48.5	6.0	11.9	33.6	25.2		39.8
38220	Pine Bluff, AR	78.7	2.9	30,092	64.5	42.6	6.7	15.1	35.5	32.2		50.3
38300	Pittsburgh, PA	79.3	4.1	1,025,698	59.6	45.6	3.9	10.1	40.4	33.5		45.2
38340	Pittsfield, MA	62.5	5.9	57,765	58.9	45.7	4.7	8.5	41.1	33.1		51.7
38540	Pocatello, ID	61.4	3.9	36,438	66.5	48.7	5.7	12.0	33.5	27.4		38.9
38660	Ponce, PR	NA	0.9	75,345	63.5	34.8	7.0	21.7	36.5	32.2		56.1
38860	Portland-South Portland, ME	51.5	5.3	237,186	61.6	49.1	4.0	8.5	38.4	29.6		45.3
38900	Portland-Vancouver-Hillsboro, OR-WA	43.0	12.5	1,001,984	62.2	48.0	4.7	9.6	37.8	27.6		37.1
38940	Port St. Lucie, FL	32.7	16.0	200,954	65.1	48.6	5.1	11.4	34.9	29.2		58.2
39100	Poughkeepsie-Newburgh-Middletown, NY	70.1	11.0	255,736	67.7	53.3	4.6	9.8	32.3	26.4		44.2
39140	Prescott Valley-Prescott, AZ	30.5	7.8	112,075	62.8	50.3	4.9	7.6	37.2	29.3		61.6
39300	Providence-Warwick, RI-MA	58.7	14.2	673,701	62.3	44.3	5.0	13.0	37.7	29.7		43.8
39340	Provo-Orem, UT	60.1	7.2	197,599	80.1	70.2	3.8	6.1	19.9	12.5		26.1
39380	Pueblo, CO	61.3	4.2	69,078	62.8	43.1	6.3	13.4	37.2	31.6		45.2
39460	Punta Gorda, FL	19.3	9.9	88,988	65.9	54.6	4.3	7.0	34.1	27.3		69.7
39540	Racine, WI	71.1	5.8	79,068	65.1	45.9	5.1	14.1	34.9	26.9		41.9

Metropolitan area / division code	Metropolitan area / division	Total population	Percent change, 2010–2019	Under 18 years	18 to 24 years	25 to 44 years	45 to 64 years	65 years and over	Median age	White	Black or African American	Asian + Native Hawaiian or Other Pacific Islander	American Indian and Alaska Native + Some other race	Hispanic or Latino (percent)
	ACS table number:	B01003	Population Estimates	B01001	B01001	B01001	B01001	B01001	B01002	B02008	B02009	B02011 + B02012	B02010 + B02013	B03003
	column number:	1	2	3	4	5	6	7	8	9	10	11	12	13
39580	Raleigh-Cary, NC	1,448,411	23.0	23.4	8.8	28.9	25.9	12.9	37.7	68.1	21.3	7.7	12.2	11.1
39660	Rapid City, SD	141,190	12.4	22.8	8.9	23.9	25.4	18.9	39.7	88.8	2.8	2.0	15.8	5.5
39740	Reading, PA	429,342	2.4	22.2	9.2	24.8	26.1	17.7	39.8	79.3	7.4	1.9	22.3	23.9
39820	Redding, CA	182,139	1.6	21.8	7.6	24.5	25.2	21.0	41.8	90.1	2.6	5.6	15.6	11.4
39900	Reno, NV	496,997	11.8	21.1	8.6	28.2	24.7	17.4	38.9	76.3	3.5	8.9	26.7	25.7
40060	Richmond, VA	1,317,525	8.9	21.4	8.5	27.9	25.6	16.6	39.2	62.0	31.3	5.5	8.6	7.1
40140	Riverside-San Bernardino-Ontario, CA	4,653,105	10.1	25.3	9.6	28.0	23.6	13.6	35.4	54.0	9.2	10.1	49.0	53.6
40220	Roanoke, VA	315,442	1.5	20.2	7.5	23.9	27.0	21.3	43.6	82.3	15.0	3.0	5.6	4.5
40340	Rochester, MN	227,151	7.3	24.2	8.3	26.3	24.4	16.8	38.5	87.7	6.4	5.5	5.8	4.9
40380	Rochester, NY	1,084,973	-0.9	20.2	9.5	25.1	26.2	19.0	40.7	82.3	13.1	3.8	8.5	7.9
40420	Rockford, IL	336,278	-3.8	23.5	8.5	24.6	25.2	18.1	39.1	78.8	14.2	3.0	16.0	15.9
40580	Rocky Mount, NC	143,535	-4.3	21.5	9.0	22.8	27.0	19.8	42.1	47.5	45.5	1.3	11.1	7.0
40660	Rome, GA	98,771	2.3	22.6	11.3	23.9	25.5	16.7	38.5	79.1	14.9	1.8	15.2	12.1
40900	Sacramento-Roseville-Folsom, CA	2,411,428	10.0	22.5	9.0	27.8	24.6	16.2	38.2	64.9	9.7	19.6	22.1	22.7
40980	Saginaw, MI	189,591	-4.8	21.6	9.3	23.8	25.5	19.7	40.9	75.6	21.1	1.6	8.7	9.2
41060	St. Cloud, MN	200,406	6.8	23.8	13.7	24.5	22.9	15.1	35.1	87.7	9.4	3.1	4.5	3.8
41100	St. George, UT	191,226	28.6	24.8	9.8	22.1	21.4	21.9	39.2	92.6	1.1	3.2	10.3	11.3
41140	St. Joseph, MO-KS	120,274	-1.7	22.5	8.5	25.9	25.5	17.6	39.4	90.5	7.0	2.2	7.8	5.9
41180	St. Louis, MO-IL	2,806,615	0.6	22.0	8.0	26.5	26.0	17.6	40.0	78.4	18.8	3.7	7.2	3.3
41420	Salem, OR	436,283	11.0	23.6	9.7	26.8	23.1	16.8	37.2	82.5	2.1	5.4	28.5	25.6
41500	Salinas, CA	437,325	4.6	25.9	9.7	27.3	22.7	14.5	35.4	45.2	3.4	9.0	57.8	60.4
41540	Salisbury, MD-DE	429,223	11.2	19.0	8.7	20.5	26.1	25.6	46.7	78.1	17.9	2.5	9.9	7.8
41620	Salt Lake City, UT	1,263,061	13.3	26.2	9.7	31.1	21.6	11.5	33.6	83.2	3.0	8.0	18.4	19.0
41660	San Angelo, TX	122,066	8.0	24.2	11.9	26.3	21.5	16.2	35.4	86.8	4.5	2.1	29.6	41.8
41700	San Antonio-New Braunfels, TX	2,601,788	19.1	24.6	9.6	28.9	23.3	13.6	35.7	77.7	8.6	4.4	44.7	56.2
41740	San Diego-Chula Vista-Carlsbad, CA	3,286,069	7.9	21.3	9.8	30.2	23.9	14.9	36.9	68.6	6.7	16.1	31.8	34.8
41860	San Francisco-Oakland-Berkeley, CA	4,623,264	9.1	19.5	7.4	30.1	26.3	16.7	40.2	50.2	9.0	33.1	21.9	22.3
4186036084	Oakland-Berkeley-Livermore, CA Division	2,809,969	10.4	21.0	7.9	29.4	26.1	15.7	39.4	47.1	11.6	31.4	23.7	31.4
4186041884	San Francisco-San Mateo-Redwood City, CA Division	1,553,089	8.2	16.8	6.7	32.8	26.1	17.5	40.6	50.6	5.2	37.7	19.3	37.7
4186042034	San Rafael, CA Division	260,206	2.5	19.2	6.7	21.0	29.4	23.7	46.9	80.3	4.1	25.3	17.9	25.3
41900	San Germán, PR	119,361	NA	15.9	11.8	20.4	26.0	25.9	47.0	77.6	6.7	0.0	27.7	99.6
41940	San Jose-Sunnyvale-Santa Clara, CA	1,952,185	8.4	21.3	8.2	30.3	25.8	14.4	38.1	46.4	3.4	42.4	25.6	26.3
41980	San Juan-Bayamón-Caguas, PR	2,070,305	NA	16.7	9.7	25.1	26.2	22.3	43.8	53.1	14.3	0.4	72.2	99.3
42020	San Luis Obispo-Paso Robles, CA	283,159	5.0	17.5	14.8	23.2	22.9	21.5	40.2	87.5	2.9	6.6	22.2	23.8
42100	Santa Cruz-Watsonville, CA	267,792	4.1	18.6	14.4	23.9	24.7	18.3	39.0	73.4	2.1	7.3	34.2	34.4
42140	Santa Fe, NM	155,201	4.3	16.8	7.0	23.2	26.3	26.7	47.9	77.3	1.6	2.3	46.9	50.5
42200	Santa Maria-Santa Barbara, CA	446,475	5.3	22.1	15.0	25.0	21.8	16.0	34.6	72.7	2.9	8.1	43.2	47.2
42220	Santa Rosa-Petaluma, CA	485,887	2.2	19.1	7.9	25.7	26.2	21.1	42.7	76.6	2.8	8.0	28.0	28.3
42340	Savannah, GA	410,008	13.2	22.3	9.9	28.6	23.7	15.5	36.9	61.3	35.7	3.7	7.9	7.3
42540	Scranton--Wilkes-Barre, PA	567,750	-1.7	20.3	8.3	24.9	26.4	20.1	42.1	88.0	6.0	2.6	14.4	12.9
42660	Seattle-Tacoma-Bellevue, WA	4,011,553	15.7	21.1	7.9	32.3	24.7	14.0	37.5	71.3	8.6	20.8	12.9	10.9
4266042644	Seattle-Bellevue-Kent, WA Division	3,085,845	16.3	20.5	7.7	33.0	24.9	13.9	37.7	69.3	7.8	22.4	12.4	22.4
4266045104	Tacoma-Lakewood, WA Division	925,708	13.8	23.2	8.7	29.7	23.9	14.4	36.9	78.1	11.1	11.2	14.4	11.2
42680	Sebastian-Vero Beach, FL	163,662	15.9	15.4	6.8	16.8	26.5	34.5	55.1	84.7	10.2	2.0	14.3	13.3
42700	Sebring-Avon Park, FL	103,296	7.5	16.6	5.6	17.9	23.7	36.1	54.4	80.6	12.4	1.8	18.2	22.1
43100	Sheboygan, WI	117,747	-0.1	21.9	7.7	24.4	27.0	19.0	41.6	90.0	3.2	6.6	6.9	7.2
43300	Sherman-Denison, TX	139,336	12.7	23.9	8.1	23.3	26.2	18.5	40.7	89.7	7.8	1.9	13.9	15.0
43340	Shreveport-Bossier City, LA	389,155	-1.0	24.0	8.8	26.4	23.5	17.4	38.3	57.1	41.6	2.0	4.9	4.4
43420	Sierra Vista-Douglas, AZ	126,050	-4.1	21.2	8.1	23.2	23.8	23.8	43.2	85.7	6.0	4.0	30.1	35.9
43580	Sioux City, IA-NE-SD	149,400	0.8	27.1	9.3	25.1	23.3	15.3	36.9	84.5	7.4	2.9	21.6	20.1
43620	Sioux Falls, SD	282,557	17.5	26.0	8.1	29.0	22.6	14.3	36.0	89.6	5.7	2.9	8.1	4.8
43780	South Bend-Mishawaka, IN-MI	323,695	1.4	22.9	10.4	24.6	24.6	17.5	38.8	83.5	14.5	3.2	9.6	8.9
43900	Spartanburg, SC	335,864	12.5	23.3	9.0	26.2	25.3	16.3	38.1	74.1	20.5	3.3	10.0	7.9
44060	Spokane-Spokane Valley, WA	593,466	10.4	21.7	9.0	27.7	24.3	17.4	38.6	91.2	3.7	5.1	9.9	6.4
44100	Springfield, IL	207,245	-1.6	22.3	7.6	24.8	26.3	18.9	40.8	85.5	13.2	2.7	4.5	2.5
44140	Springfield, MA	695,305	0.6	19.1	12.9	24.2	25.2	18.6	39.9	83.8	9.7	4.1	18.4	20.2

Metropolitan area / division code	Metropolitan area / division	Born in state of residence (percent)	Foreign born (percent)	Total households	Family households Total	Married-couple	Male householder	Female householder	Nonfamily households Total	One-person households	Percent of households with people age 60 years and over
	ACS table number:	B05002	B05002	B11001	B11001	B11001	B11001	B11001	B11001	B11001	B11006
	column number:	14	15	16	17	18	19	20	21	22	23
39580	Raleigh-Cary, NC	45.5	12.6	548,713	67.3	52.4	4.0	10.9	32.7	25.3	33.1
39660	Rapid City, SD	56.5	2.1	57,532	61.4	49.0	4.7	7.7	38.6	29.7	44.3
39740	Reading, PA	70.4	9.1	164,312	65.9	48.4	5.6	11.9	34.1	27.6	43.8
39820	Redding, CA	72.3	4.3	71,506	60.2	43.3	4.8	12.1	39.8	27.7	47.6
39900	Reno, NV	34.5	13.3	199,715	60.2	43.5	6.6	10.1	39.8	28.1	41.2
40060	Richmond, VA	60.7	7.8	521,067	62.8	45.4	4.2	13.3	37.2	30.3	41.0
40140	Riverside-San Bernardino-Ontario, CA	63.7	21.7	1,441,602	75.2	52.4	7.5	15.3	24.8	19.2	41.9
40220	Roanoke, VA	66.1	4.8	131,211	62.6	46.4	5.4	10.8	37.4	32.2	47.0
40340	Rochester, MN	64.7	8.0	90,956	64.7	53.6	3.5	7.5	35.3	28.4	37.5
40380	Rochester, NY	75.9	7.0	454,044	59.7	43.1	4.7	11.9	40.3	31.7	43.5
40420	Rockford, IL	70.2	8.8	134,008	64.7	44.5	5.9	14.2	35.3	28.5	43.1
40580	Rocky Mount, NC	73.2	4.0	56,840	62.7	40.1	3.7	18.9	37.3	32.1	48.6
40660	Rome, GA	75.2	5.4	35,417	68.2	47.9	4.7	15.7	31.8	25.7	41.9
40900	Sacramento-Roseville-Folsom, CA	62.7	18.8	879,647	66.2	49.1	5.7	11.4	33.8	24.9	41.3
40980	Saginaw, MI	84.8	2.1	80,146	60.2	41.3	3.5	15.4	39.8	32.1	44.6
41060	St. Cloud, MN	77.3	6.4	79,091	62.9	48.4	5.7	8.7	37.1	27.5	35.1
41100	St. George, UT	52.4	6.7	68,090	73.4	67.3	1.9	4.2	26.6	21.1	47.9
41140	St. Joseph, MO-KS	69.5	2.9	46,798	59.6	43.8	4.5	11.3	40.4	31.8	41.4
41180	St. Louis, MO-IL	68.8	4.7	1,144,111	62.8	46.3	4.8	11.7	37.2	30.9	41.5
41420	Salem, OR	53.7	12.0	158,144	67.4	51.1	5.8	10.5	32.6	25.9	41.4
41500	Salinas, CA	55.2	29.0	133,224	71.9	49.7	7.4	14.8	28.1	20.9	43.8
41540	Salisbury, MD-DE	45.9	7.7	177,002	67.0	49.6	4.6	12.8	33.0	27.1	55.0
41620	Salt Lake City, UT	59.7	12.2	443,798	67.1	51.7	5.3	10.2	32.9	24.3	31.7
41660	San Angelo, TX	71.7	5.0	46,604	61.0	45.2	5.8	10.0	39.0	31.0	41.1
41700	San Antonio-New Braunfels, TX	62.9	12.1	948,519	69.2	47.9	6.3	15.0	30.8	24.7	35.5
41740	San Diego-Chula Vista-Carlsbad, CA	51.3	22.4	1,162,896	65.6	48.8	5.3	11.5	34.4	24.9	39.0
41860	San Francisco-Oakland-Berkeley, CA	49.4	31.2	1,719,049	63.9	48.9	4.5	10.4	36.1	27.1	41.0
4186036084	Oakland-Berkeley-Livermore, CA Division	51.6	30.5	1,000,740	68.2	51.6	4.9	11.7	31.8	24.0	41.1
4186041884	San Francisco-San Mateo-Redwood City, CA Division	45.5	34.4	614,931	57.2	44.6	4.0	8.6	42.8	31.7	39.0
4186042034	San Rafael, CA Division	50.0	19.5	103,378	61.8	49.4	4.1	8.4	38.2	29.7	52.0
41900	San Germán, PR	NA	NA	43,263	61.8	31.6	9.7	20.5	38.2	34.0	59.2
41940	San Jose-Sunnyvale-Santa Clara, CA	46.3	39.6	670,900	70.4	54.4	5.5	10.5	29.6	21.9	37.9
41980	San Juan-Bayamón-Caguas, PR	NA	3.7	747,507	63.7	33.8	6.9	23.1	36.3	30.9	52.2
42020	San Luis Obispo-Paso Robles, CA	67.2	9.9	107,571	63.9	50.1	5.2	8.6	36.1	26.2	50.4
42100	Santa Cruz-Watsonville, CA	61.2	18.2	97,353	64.9	49.8	4.7	10.4	35.1	23.9	48.9
42140	Santa Fe, NM	47.6	9.8	70,152	58.8	43.2	4.4	11.2	41.2	33.5	52.2
42200	Santa Maria-Santa Barbara, CA	57.7	22.1	150,550	64.9	46.6	6.3	12.1	35.1	24.2	43.5
42220	Santa Rosa-Petaluma, CA	63.5	17.1	190,586	64.2	49.7	4.9	9.6	35.8	26.2	48.1
42340	Savannah, GA	53.6	5.8	160,666	66.4	46.3	4.7	15.4	33.6	25.5	39.1
42540	Scranton--Wilkes-Barre, PA	74.2	7.0	233,473	61.5	43.5	5.9	12.2	38.5	31.5	46.0
42660	Seattle-Tacoma-Bellevue, WA	44.2	20.0	1,584,796	63.1	50.2	4.1	8.8	36.9	27.4	34.8
4266042644	Seattle-Bellevue-Kent, WA Division	42.5	22.9	1,237,128	61.8	49.9	3.8	8.1	38.2	28.3	33.8
4266045104	Tacoma-Lakewood, WA Division	49.7	10.3	347,668	67.9	51.5	5.1	11.3	32.1	24.0	38.2
42680	Sebastian-Vero Beach, FL	33.7	8.1	69,974	61.6	46.8	3.9	10.8	38.4	34.3	63.7
42700	Sebring-Avon Park, FL	36.8	12.8	46,166	66.1	50.6	3.9	11.6	33.9	28.9	62.2
43100	Sheboygan, WI	77.2	5.7	49,416	60.0	48.4	4.4	7.2	40.0	34.2	44.1
43300	Sherman-Denison, TX	65.0	6.0	56,005	70.3	50.2	6.3	13.8	29.7	24.9	45.3
43340	Shreveport-Bossier City, LA	73.1	2.1	155,848	63.3	39.5	6.6	17.3	36.7	32.4	41.7
43420	Sierra Vista-Douglas, AZ	37.0	12.6	49,952	59.7	46.0	4.2	9.4	40.3	35.7	52.5
43580	Sioux City, IA-NE-SD	52.2	12.9	57,421	69.5	50.8	6.4	12.3	30.5	23.6	38.6
43620	Sioux Falls, SD	60.6	5.9	114,967	65.3	51.4	5.1	8.7	34.7	26.6	33.3
43780	South Bend-Mishawaka, IN-MI	60.1	5.8	128,774	62.2	46.3	4.6	11.3	37.8	31.4	42.3
43900	Spartanburg, SC	58.4	7.4	128,437	70.4	50.4	5.2	14.8	29.6	25.0	38.8
44060	Spokane-Spokane Valley, WA	55.7	4.6	237,024	61.7	46.5	5.4	9.7	38.3	30.2	41.2
44100	Springfield, IL	81.6	3.3	89,340	58.3	41.8	4.0	12.5	41.7	36.0	42.3
44140	Springfield, MA	63.3	8.9	275,788	60.9	41.0	5.2	14.7	39.1	30.0	45.2

Table A-3. Metropolitan Areas — Who: Age, Race/Ethnicity, and Household Structure, 2021—Continued

Metropolitan area / division code	Metropolitan area / division	Total population	Percent change, 2010–2019	Population by age (percent)					Median age	Race alone or in combination (percent)				
				Under 18 years	18 to 24 years	25 to 44 years	45 to 64 years	65 years and over		White	Black or African American	Asian + Native Hawaiian or Other Pacific Islander	American Indian and Alaska Native + Some other race	Hispanic or Latino (percent)
	ACS table number:	B01003	Population Estimates	B01001	B01001	B01001	B01001	B01001	B01002	B02008	B02009	B02011 + B02012	B02010 + B02013	B03003
	column number:	1	2	3	4	5	6	7	8	9	10	11	12	13
44180	Springfield, MO	479,598	7.7	22.3	11.3	25.5	23.7	17.1	37.4	95.4	2.3	2.4	6.8	3.5
44220	Springfield, OH	135,633	-3.1	22.5	8.6	23.3	25.9	19.7	41.1	90.1	11.2	1.1	5.1	3.8
44300	State College, PA	157,527	5.5	14.7	23.5	23.5	22.7	15.6	34.2	90.2	4.6	6.3	5.3	3.1
44420	Staunton, VA	125,774	3.9	18.8	8.8	25.1	27.1	20.3	42.9	93.7	6.6	0.8	6.6	4.8
44700	Stockton, CA	789,410	11.2	26.7	9.4	27.7	23.0	13.2	35.0	52.3	9.2	22.6	44.9	43.0
44940	Sumter, SC	135,782	-1.4	22.3	9.8	24.7	24.3	19.0	39.1	51.7	47.1	1.9	5.3	4.2
45060	Syracuse, NY	658,281	-2.1	20.8	10.6	24.3	26.2	18.1	39.9	86.2	10.4	3.9	7.3	4.7
45220	Tallahassee, FL	387,127	5.4	18.9	17.8	25.2	22.5	15.6	35.4	62.8	33.6	3.8	8.8	7.3
45300	Tampa-St. Petersburg-Clearwater, FL	3,219,514	14.8	19.7	7.5	26.1	26.6	20.2	42.3	77.2	14.4	4.9	19.3	21.3
45460	Terre Haute, IN	186,369	-1.8	21.3	11.2	25.1	24.8	17.6	38.5	93.3	5.8	1.9	3.9	2.3
45500	Texarkana, TX-AR	146,424	-0.3	23.6	8.9	25.6	24.1	17.8	38.4	72.9	25.7	1.1	4.4	6.5
45540	The Villages, FL	135,638	41.7	7.0	2.4	11.9	20.4	58.3	68.4	90.4	5.8	1.5	8.1	6.2
45780	Toledo, OH	644,217	-1.5	22.2	9.9	25.1	25.3	17.5	38.8	83.0	14.6	2.5	8.5	7.4
45820	Topeka, KS	232,670	-0.8	23.4	7.8	25.0	24.3	19.6	39.1	87.3	8.8	1.9	11.5	11.2
45940	Trenton-Princeton, NJ	385,898	0.3	21.2	11.1	25.1	26.7	16.0	39.8	58.8	22.1	14.0	16.0	19.4
46060	Tucson, AZ	1,052,030	6.8	20.3	11.4	24.9	22.7	20.7	39.1	77.6	5.7	4.9	34.0	38.5
46140	Tulsa, OK	1,024,191	6.5	24.4	8.6	26.7	24.3	16.1	37.7	77.8	10.1	3.7	24.3	11.0
46220	Tuscaloosa, AL	266,638	5.4	21.2	14.3	26.1	22.8	15.5	35.9	62.6	35.9	2.0	4.1	3.8
46300	Twin Falls, ID	118,253	11.7	27.3	8.9	26.2	21.4	16.3	35.9	88.8	0.6	2.5	22.9	22.1
46340	Tyler, TX	237,186	11.0	24.3	9.6	25.7	23.2	17.1	37.4	78.4	18.2	2.0	9.7	20.7
46520	Urban Honolulu, HI	1,000,890	2.2	21.0	8.8	27.8	23.7	18.8	39.0	38.3	4.3	85.6	8.3	10.4
46540	Utica-Rome, NY	290,211	-3.1	21.0	8.9	23.7	26.5	19.9	41.6	91.0	5.8	3.9	8.5	5.8
46660	Valdosta, GA	147,916	5.5	25.7	14.7	26.7	19.8	13.1	31.9	60.3	37.5	2.9	5.4	5.8
46700	Vallejo, CA	451,716	8.3	21.9	8.3	27.8	25.0	16.9	38.9	52.6	17.3	22.2	26.3	28.6
47020	Victoria, TX	100,796	6.1	25.3	9.7	26.6	22.5	16.0	36.5	85.9	6.8	1.3	33.5	48.5
47220	Vineland-Bridgeton, NJ	153,627	-4.7	24.2	8.2	26.7	25.0	15.9	37.7	66.3	23.6	2.0	31.0	33.0
47260	Virginia Beach-Norfolk-Newport News, VA-NC	1,806,423	3.2	22.0	10.5	28.1	23.9	15.5	37.1	62.8	32.4	6.4	9.3	7.6
47300	Visalia, CA	477,054	5.4	30.2	10.2	27.1	20.9	11.7	31.7	65.3	2.5	4.8	57.6	66.7
47380	Waco, TX	280,485	8.4	24.5	13.6	24.9	22.1	14.9	34.4	76.9	16.2	2.9	24.8	27.6
47460	Walla Walla, WA	62,682	3.4	18.8	12.7	27.7	21.4	19.5	38.2	83.9	2.2	5.4	23.4	22.6
47580	Warner Robins, GA	195,246	10.6	24.0	9.8	26.6	25.3	14.3	38.2	60.0	35.4	5.0	5.8	7.3
47900	Washington-Arlington-Alexandria, DC-VA-MD-WV	6,358,652	11.2	22.8	8.5	28.9	25.8	14.0	37.9	54.6	27.6	13.1	17.2	16.7
4790023224	Frederick-Gaithersburg-Rockville, MD Division	1,334,662	8.7	23.0	7.8	26.2	26.9	16.2	39.8	57.8	19.0	16.3	19.2	16.3
4790047894	Washington-Arlington-Alexandria, DC-VA-MD-WV Division	5,023,990	11.8	22.7	8.7	29.7	25.5	13.4	37.5	53.8	29.9	12.1	16.7	12.1
47940	Waterloo-Cedar Falls, IA	167,796	0.4	22.3	12.9	24.9	21.7	18.2	36.6	87.3	9.2	3.0	6.6	4.2
48060	Watertown-Fort Drum, NY	116,295	-5.5	23.5	11.3	29.1	21.7	14.5	34.7	88.7	8.2	4.0	8.1	7.7
48140	Wausau-Weston, WI	166,189	0.3	22.0	7.2	23.7	27.7	19.4	42.3	91.9	1.7	6.0	3.7	3.0
48260	Weirton-Steubenville, WV-OH	113,798	-6.7	19.0	8.0	23.4	26.4	23.3	44.8	95.7	4.4	1.1	4.4	1.7
48300	Wenatchee, WA	123,342	8.8	23.7	9.0	25.6	22.0	19.7	38.7	75.9	0.9	2.4	31.0	30.4
48540	Wheeling, WV-OH	137,740	-6.1	19.3	8.1	23.5	26.7	22.3	43.9	96.1	3.8	0.7	3.6	1.2
48620	Wichita, KS	647,919	2.8	25.2	9.0	26.3	23.5	16.0	36.4	83.2	9.4	4.8	15.4	14.1
48660	Wichita Falls, TX	149,013	-0.0	22.5	12.6	26.0	22.9	16.0	36.0	83.6	10.8	2.8	15.8	19.1
48700	Williamsport, PA	113,605	-2.4	20.6	8.5	25.1	25.6	20.2	40.8	92.4	5.9	1.4	4.4	2.3
48900	Wilmington, NC	291,833	16.7	18.8	10.5	26.1	25.9	18.7	40.9	85.1	11.6	2.0	11.7	6.6
49020	Winchester, VA-WV	142,562	9.4	23.1	8.1	23.7	27.1	18.0	40.3	85.5	6.7	2.1	12.1	9.5
49180	Winston-Salem, NC	681,438	5.5	21.9	9.0	23.8	27.1	18.2	41.3	75.2	19.6	2.3	11.8	11.2
49340	Worcester, MA-CT	978,447	3.3	20.5	9.4	25.7	27.7	16.7	40.1	84.2	7.2	5.6	14.8	12.8
49420	Yakima, WA	256,035	3.1	29.4	9.5	26.1	21.0	14.1	32.8	72.0	1.6	2.8	52.7	51.8
49500	Yauco, PR	88,542	NA	18.0	7.0	25.2	26.5	23.3	44.7	80.3	5.1	0.0	25.6	99.2
49620	York-Hanover, PA	458,696	3.2	21.9	8.2	24.7	26.9	18.3	40.9	87.7	8.4	2.1	8.7	8.9
49660	Youngstown-Warren-Boardman, OH-PA	538,069	-5.2	20.1	8.4	22.6	26.8	22.1	44.0	87.4	12.7	1.1	5.9	4.1
49700	Yuba City, CA	182,484	5.2	26.0	9.0	27.5	22.6	14.8	35.7	64.3	5.0	16.4	34.8	31.8
49740	Yuma, AZ	206,990	9.2	25.1	10.2	25.4	19.9	19.4	35.4	79.4	3.2	2.2	62.4	65.5

NA = Not available.

Metropolitan area / division code	Metropolitan area / division	Born in state of residence (percent)	Foreign born (percent)	Total households	Household type (percent of all households)							Percent of households with people age 60 years and over
					Family households				Nonfamily households			
					Total	Married-couple	Male householder	Female householder	Total	One-person households		
	ACS table number:	B05002	B05002	B11001	B11001	B11001	B11001	B11001	B11001	B11001		B11006
	column number:	14	15	16	17	18	19	20	21	22		23
44180	Springfield, MO	61.5	2.8	195,260	62.1	49.4	3.1	9.6	37.9	28.9		38.1
44220	Springfield, OH	79.9	2.1	57,013	62.3	42.2	7.3	12.8	37.7	31.4		45.4
44300	State College, PA	68.2	7.7	57,518	57.1	47.7	2.8	6.6	42.9	34.1		39.0
44420	Staunton, VA	66.9	3.6	51,802	63.9	46.9	4.3	12.6	36.1	30.5		46.1
44700	Stockton, CA	64.7	23.8	241,760	75.2	51.4	9.0	14.8	24.8	19.9		41.2
44940	Sumter, SC	66.5	3.0	54,669	62.6	41.8	3.8	16.9	37.4	33.9		44.0
45060	Syracuse, NY	77.9	6.0	270,350	60.1	42.8	5.3	11.9	39.9	31.9		43.4
45220	Tallahassee, FL	61.2	6.4	155,921	57.0	38.3	5.0	13.7	43.0	30.0		37.0
45300	Tampa-St. Petersburg-Clearwater, FL .	36.2	14.8	1,309,614	60.7	44.5	4.6	11.6	39.3	31.5		45.3
45460	Terre Haute, IN	75.3	1.7	73,024	59.5	43.6	5.3	10.7	40.5	32.9		44.4
45500	Texarkana, TX-AR	51.9	2.9	55,179	64.6	43.0	5.0	16.6	35.4	31.4		42.5
45540	The Villages, FL	20.8	5.3	68,792	61.7	57.2	0.7	3.8	38.3	31.6		81.4
45780	Toledo, OH	77.3	3.9	273,165	58.1	40.8	5.3	11.9	41.9	34.4		40.2
45820	Topeka, KS	71.2	3.7	95,988	59.6	45.5	4.5	9.7	40.4	34.4		44.8
45940	Trenton-Princeton, NJ	51.1	22.5	143,970	64.5	48.6	3.4	12.5	35.5	29.9		43.5
46060	Tucson, AZ	43.3	11.4	433,148	61.8	44.0	5.9	11.9	38.2	29.7		45.1
46140	Tulsa, OK	60.6	6.6	403,034	64.3	46.7	5.7	11.9	35.7	29.6		39.7
46220	Tuscaloosa, AL	73.2	3.3	101,825	64.5	46.3	3.9	14.3	35.5	30.2		39.3
46300	Twin Falls, ID	50.7	10.7	42,906	69.2	55.1	5.5	8.6	30.8	26.7		41.1
46340	Tyler, TX	70.2	8.2	81,175	69.7	54.1	3.5	12.0	30.3	25.3		42.1
46520	Urban Honolulu, HI	51.5	20.4	338,093	68.7	51.7	4.9	12.0	31.3	24.4		47.8
46540	Utica-Rome, NY	80.6	6.8	118,513	58.7	42.1	5.1	11.4	41.3	34.3		47.1
46660	Valdosta, GA	59.6	3.2	55,279	60.4	39.7	3.8	16.9	39.6	33.8		33.7
46700	Vallejo, CA	57.7	20.3	157,617	69.7	49.1	6.9	13.7	30.3	24.1		45.7
47020	Victoria, TX	82.7	6.9	41,036	66.4	47.3	7.5	11.7	33.6	25.3		39.1
47220	Vineland-Bridgeton, NJ	68.2	10.9	53,883	67.2	42.9	7.2	17.0	32.8	24.6		42.5
47260	Virginia Beach-Norfolk-Newport News, VA-NC	49.1	6.4	721,212	65.9	46.2	5.2	14.4	34.1	27.4		38.5
47300	Visalia, CA	67.8	23.4	143,541	78.4	49.9	9.3	19.2	21.6	16.6		37.1
47380	Waco, TX	69.2	8.0	102,138	63.5	45.1	5.5	12.9	36.5	28.8		38.2
47460	Walla Walla, WA	51.6	7.2	23,444	61.8	49.5	2.4	9.9	38.2	32.3		48.1
47580	Warner Robins, GA	55.8	6.3	70,357	71.5	47.9	8.6	15.0	28.5	25.6		37.4
47900	Washington-Arlington-Alexandria, DC-VA-MD-WV	32.4	23.0	2,384,977	64.1	48.1	4.6	11.4	35.9	28.9		36.9
4790023224	Frederick-Gaithersburg-Rockville, MD Division	31.0	28.4	492,081	69.4	53.8	4.6	11.0	30.6	25.1		41.8
4790047894	Washington-Arlington-Alexandria, DC-VA-MD-WV Division	32.8	21.6	1,892,896	62.8	46.6	4.6	11.5	37.2	29.9		35.6
47940	Waterloo-Cedar Falls, IA	76.1	5.5	68,479	58.4	47.0	3.7	7.7	41.6	32.4		40.2
48060	Watertown-Fort Drum, NY	66.1	4.4	48,628	63.8	49.6	4.9	9.3	36.2	27.4		34.4
48140	Wausau-Weston, WI	77.5	4.1	69,891	64.9	52.2	4.6	8.1	35.1	27.3		43.0
48260	Weirton-Steubenville, WV-OH	62.5	1.3	49,145	60.5	43.5	6.1	10.9	39.5	33.8		50.9
48300	Wenatchee, WA	57.5	12.6	47,559	66.2	47.4	4.7	14.1	33.8	26.8		45.8
48540	Wheeling, WV-OH	63.3	0.8	57,332	58.4	43.0	3.7	11.8	41.6	34.6		47.5
48620	Wichita, KS	65.1	6.7	250,146	64.7	47.4	5.7	11.6	35.3	30.1		39.8
48660	Wichita Falls, TX	64.0	4.9	56,846	63.6	46.1	5.1	12.4	36.4	31.4		42.2
48700	Williamsport, PA	83.6	1.9	47,022	63.6	49.0	3.9	10.7	36.4	29.4		44.5
48900	Wilmington, NC	48.4	4.6	127,095	57.5	47.9	3.2	6.4	42.5	32.6		39.6
49020	Winchester, VA-WV	49.1	6.9	52,949	67.2	48.9	5.6	12.7	32.8	25.4		41.2
49180	Winston-Salem, NC	61.3	7.1	273,913	64.0	47.6	4.4	12.0	36.0	30.7		43.6
49340	Worcester, MA-CT	63.8	12.4	379,159	65.9	48.3	5.0	12.6	34.1	26.5		41.6
49420	Yakima, WA	61.4	17.5	86,992	69.4	45.5	8.9	15.0	30.6	25.4		39.1
49500	Yauco, PR	NA	NA	29,142	66.0	38.6	6.2	21.2	34.0	26.7		57.9
49620	York-Hanover, PA	64.5	4.0	178,898	69.3	52.8	6.1	10.4	30.7	24.4		44.2
49660	Youngstown-Warren-Boardman, OH-PA	78.8	1.7	230,536	61.6	43.3	4.8	13.5	38.4	33.0		48.2
49700	Yuba City, CA	63.9	19.0	61,597	73.5	47.7	10.1	15.7	26.5	21.1		45.4
49740	Yuma, AZ	39.3	23.0	74,981	74.7	52.6	5.1	16.9	25.3	19.2		45.3

NA = Not available.

Table A-4. Cities — Who: Age, Race/Ethnicity, and Household Structure, 2021

STATE and place code	STATE Place	Total popula-tion	Percent change, 2014–2019	Population by age (percent)					Median age	Race alone or in combination (percent)					
				Under 18 years	18 to 24 years	25 to 44 years	45 to 64 years	65 years and over		White	Black	American Indian and Alaska Native	Asian	Native Hawaiian or Other Pacific Islander	Some other race
	ACS table number:	B01003	Population Estimates	B01001	B01001	B01001	B01001	B01001	B01002	B02008	B02009	B02010	B02011	B02012	B02013
FIPS	column number:	1	2	3	4	5	6	7	8	9	10	11	12	13	·14
00000	UNITED STATES......................	331,893,745	6.3	22.1	9.1	26.8	25.2	16.8	38.8	72.9	14.2	2.6	7.1	0.5	16.2
01000	ALABAMA.................................	5,039,877	2.0	22.2	9.3	25.2	25.7	17.6	39.8	69.6	27.3	2.1	1.9	0.2	4.3
0103076	Auburn city, Alabama	78,552	9.9	20.7	24.7	26.6	16.6	11.4	27.8	71.0	20.7	0.0	9.5	0.0	3.4
0107000	Birmingham city, Alabama	196,410	-1.2	19.9	11.8	28.9	22.3	17.1	37.2	23.6	72.2	0.8	1.8	0.0	4.7
0121184	Dothan city, Alabama	71,283	-1.3	22.4	8.1	25.3	25.1	19.0	40.5	61.0	37.7	1.7	2.1	0.0	3.1
0135896	Hoover city, Alabama	92,588	1.7	23.8	5.3	30.1	24.9	16.0	38.9	71.8	18.7	1.9	7.7	0.0	3.1
0137000	Huntsville city, Alabama	215,482	7.5	19.4	11.0	29.6	23.2	16.8	38.0	70.0	28.0	3.3	4.7	0.5	5.5
0150000	Mobile city, Alabama	184,960	-3.1	22.5	9.5	26.3	24.3	17.4	37.8	43.6	54.4	0.7	2.8	0.0	2.1
0151000	Montgomery city, Alabama.........	198,659	-1.0	24.4	9.9	27.2	22.6	15.9	36.1	30.9	65.4	0.8	3.3	0.0	3.4
0177256	Tuscaloosa city, Alabama............	100,606	5.2	18.5	24.9	25.7	19.0	11.9	29.4	49.3	46.7	0.8	4.1	0.0	4.1
02000	ALASKA	732,673	4.2	24.5	9.2	29.4	23.5	13.4	35.6	71.3	5.3	20.7	9.0	2.5	6.0
0203000	Anchorage municipality, Alaska...	288,121	-4.3	23.9	9.5	31.2	22.7	12.7	35.2	70.2	8.3	13.5	13.3	4.4	6.8
04000	ARIZONA..................................	7,276,316	9.8	22.2	9.4	26.3	23.8	18.3	38.6	77.6	6.3	6.0	4.8	0.4	25.9
0404720	Avondale city, Arizona	90,562	10.4	31.3	11.5	27.7	21.6	7.8	30.2	66.1	14.3	3.0	4.9	0.0	47.5
0407940	Buckeye city, Arizona.................	101,314	33.9	28.6	5.3	27.9	23.6	14.6	35.1	72.3	7.7	2.9	2.8	0.0	34.1
0410670	Casas Adobes CDP, Arizona	73,450	-2.8	16.5	13.0	24.5	24.1	21.9	41.4	85.1	3.8	3.0	5.4	0.0	16.2
0412000	Chandler city, Arizona................	279,445	2.7	23.1	8.5	30.6	25.7	12.1	36.6	74.3	7.4	3.3	12.4	0.4	18.3
0423620	Flagstaff city, Arizona	76,984	9.1	16.9	30.4	26.3	19.4	7.1	26.7	71.5	2.3	17.8	3.1	0.6	17.7
0427400	Gilbert town, Arizona	273,138	6.2	29.7	8.0	29.3	22.4	10.6	35.3	82.8	6.1	1.4	8.9	0.5	15.9
0427820	Glendale city, Arizona	249,627	6.3	23.4	10.8	27.7	24.2	13.8	36.1	75.4	9.5	3.1	6.8	0.5	33.7
0428380	Goodyear city, Arizona...............	101,744		25.1	8.2	27.3	23.6	15.8	38.7	76.6	9.8	5.8	4.0	0.0	27.8
0446000	Mesa city, Arizona.....................	509,492	11.5	22.6	8.7	27.7	23.3	17.8	37.7	80.8	6.1	3.9	4.6	0.4	21.3
0454050	Peoria city, Arizona	194,910	5.4	22.0	6.1	24.7	28.6	18.6	42.7	83.1	7.9	3.9	7.1	0.1	16.5
0455000	Phoenix city, Arizona..................	1,624,539	9.4	24.7	9.7	30.3	23.6	11.7	34.5	71.7	9.2	4.3	5.4	0.4	35.7
0458150	Queen Creek town, Arizona	69,311	57.6	32.2	8.4	22.1	27.0	10.3	37.0	89.1	6.6	0.0	3.2	0.0	8.5
0464210	San Tan Valley CDP, Arizona.......	103,399	6.7	29.3	7.0	33.3	19.0	11.4	33.3	85.6	4.7	2.7	4.7	1.0	21.0
0465000	Scottsdale city, Arizona..............	242,754	12.0	13.4	6.0	25.7	28.4	26.5	49.5	89.7	3.1	1.0	5.8	0.5	9.8
0471510	Surprise city, Arizona.................	149,191	12.2	23.0	9.0	22.3	23.6	22.1	40.6	86.2	6.1	1.4	3.9	0.9	17.5
0473000	Tempe city, Arizona...................	184,109	13.3	14.2	22.7	37.3	16.7	9.2	29.0	73.9	7.2	4.6	9.7	1.0	19.5
0477000	Tucson city, Arizona..................	543,215	3.8	20.6	14.9	28.3	20.9	15.2	33.6	73.3	7.4	5.7	4.8	0.5	33.3
0485540	Yuma city, Arizona.....................	97,097	5.2	27.0	12.4	27.5	16.1	16.9	30.7	76.1	4.4	2.8	3.3	0.4	54.4
05000	ARKANSAS	3,025,891	3.0	23.3	9.4	25.4	24.6	17.4	38.5	79.5	16.2	2.8	2.2	0.5	9.2
0515190	Conway city, Arkansas	65,126	4.9	21.0	23.3	27.4	18.4	9.9	29.1	75.6	20.6	1.8	3.0	0.0	6.4
0523290	Fayetteville city, Arkansas...........	95,231	8.6	20.4	23.0	29.7	18.1	8.8	28.4	89.9	7.3	2.2	3.6	0.0	10.3
0524550	Fort Smith city, Arkansas............	89,574	0.6	22.5	11.2	26.3	23.8	16.2	36.7	71.4	10.5	4.7	8.3	0.0	15.8
0535710	Jonesboro city, Arkansas	79,330	8.5	24.9	12.2	28.7	19.6	14.6	32.8	72.2	23.2	3.3	2.4	0.0	6.2
0541000	Little Rock city, Arkansas............	201,984	-0.2	23.4	8.3	27.5	24.5	16.3	37.9	50.0	44.6	1.1	3.3	0.0	6.7
0560410	Rogers city, Arkansas	71,114	11.7	25.3	8.5	31.7	22.7	11.9	33.5	85.9	1.4	2.4	3.0	0.5	36.9
0566080	Springdale city, Arkansas............	87,255	3.0	27.6	10.3	27.6	22.1	12.4	34.0	76.6	5.5	6.3	5.7	10.0	37.3
06000	CALIFORNIA..............................	39,237,836	6.1	22.4	9.1	28.7	24.7	15.2	37.6	57.1	7.3	3.3	17.8	0.8	34.2
0600562	Alameda city, California	76,352	0.0	20.8	4.8	32.0	26.4	16.0	40.6	55.2	7.8	2.4	37.0	2.2	11.9
0600884	Alhambra city, California.............	81,219	-2.2	17.9	6.5	33.7	24.2	17.8	39.5	28.7	3.9	3.7	48.7	1.5	34.2
0602000	Anaheim city, California..............	345,935	1.0	22.1	8.8	29.7	25.4	14.0	37.2	58.4	3.7	2.4	20.3	0.7	38.5
0602252	Antioch city, California...............	114,801	2.3	25.3	8.1	27.2	26.1	13.3	36.9	39.6	23.5	4.4	17.7	2.4	28.6
0602364	Apple Valley town, California......	76,217	2.6	31.4	6.6	22.6	20.3	19.1	36.8	77.2	10.4	4.4	5.9	0.0	29.6
0602553	Arden-Arcade CDP, California	100,613	8.3	23.8	7.7	30.2	24.9	13.4	34.7	59.8	16.9	5.5	13.7	0.0	17.7
0603526	Bakersfield city, California	407,581	4.2	28.7	10.5	28.7	20.8	11.3	32.1	67.3	6.9	3.1	10.2	0.4	36.7
0603666	Baldwin Park city, California	70,634	-2.5	18.7	12.2	26.2	29.2	13.7	39.3	39.6	1.4	12.9	19.3	0.0	64.9
0604982	Bellflower city, California	77,407	-2.3	25.6	7.5	31.1	24.4	11.5	35.6	39.3	11.6	4.4	11.7	0.0	55.6
0606000	Berkeley city, California	117,147	2.1	12.6	23.1	28.8	20.4	15.1	33.0	64.5	10.1	2.2	23.3	0.3	11.4
0608786	Buena Park city, California	83,017	-1.6	22.1	10.7	27.8	26.5	12.9	38.1	47.2	3.3	5.5	37.4	1.7	30.9
0608954	Burbank city, California...............	105,407	-2.7	17.2	6.3	30.9	25.3	20.2	42.4	72.7	5.2	2.4	17.3	0.5	16.4
0610046	Camarillo city, California.............	70,838	4.4	19.9	9.3	23.0	25.4	22.5	43.1	73.8	3.4	2.9	15.3	1.2	17.7
0611194	Carlsbad city, California...............	115,291	2.7	19.3	5.1	24.4	29.0	22.2	46.3	82.6	2.1	1.4	12.0	1.2	15.3
0611390	Carmichael CDP, California	81,039	0.5	21.5	9.0	26.0	24.5	19.0	39.7	77.6	10.1	2.1	11.1	0.0	12.9
0611530	Carson city, California.................	93,526	-2.0	22.2	8.3	27.3	24.5	17.8	40.6	25.5	24.1	1.6	37.1	1.3	31.7
0611964	Castro Valley CDP, California.......	66,408	-1.5	21.6	4.8	25.3	27.0	21.2	42.8	45.1	10.8	0.5	42.7	0.0	12.2

STATE and place code	STATE Place	Two or more races (percent)	Hispanic or Latino (percent)	Native, born in state of residence (percent)	Foreign born (percent)	Non-citizens (percent)	Total house-holds	Household type (percent of all households)						Percent of house-holds with people age 60 years and over
								Family households				Nonfamily households		
								Total	Married-couple	Male house-holder	Female house-holder	Total	One-person house-holds	
	ACS table number:	B02001	B03003	B05002	B05002	B05002	B11001	B11001	B11001	B11001	B11001	B11001	B11001	B11006
FIPS	column number:	15	16	17	18	19	20	21	22	23	24	25	26	27
00000	UNITED STATES.........................	12.6	18.8	58.0	13.6	6.6	127,544,730	64.7	47.3	5.0	12.3	35.3	28.3	41.5
01000	ALABAMA.............................	5.0	4.7	69.2	3.5	2.0	1,967,559	64.6	46.0	4.6	14.1	35.4	30.9	42.6
0103076	Auburn city, Alabama	3.9	4.7	48.0	9.4	5.8	29,136	59.7	47.7	3.5	8.5	40.3	26.7	28.9
0107000	Birmingham city, Alabama	3.0	4.6	78.7	3.9	2.3	87,570	48.8	21.6	5.0	22.2	51.2	44.6	38.1
0121184	Dothan city, Alabama.................	5.0	3.4	62.8	2.0	0.9	30,301	62.8	39.6	4.0	19.2	37.2	32.5	41.4
0135896	Hoover city, Alabama	3.1	2.8	57.9	8.7	3.6	36,721	68.7	59.0	4.1	5.6	31.3	27.4	39.4
0137000	Huntsville city, Alabama	10.0	6.0	50.5	6.2	2.9	96,551	56.3	41.1	4.4	10.9	43.7	36.9	35.8
0150000	Mobile city, Alabama	3.5	2.1	75.0	3.4	1.2	77,991	55.6	33.3	3.4	19.0	44.4	38.9	39.1
0151000	Montgomery city, Alabama	3.7	4.1	71.1	5.2	3.5	81,529	60.5	31.0	4.9	24.6	39.5	34.4	36.0
0177256	Tuscaloosa city, Alabama.............	4.5	5.6	70.8	5.1	3.1	39,266	55.9	32.9	6.0	17.1	44.1	34.4	33.5
02000	ALASKA	13.3	7.1	42.9	8.1	2.9	271,311	63.5	47.9	5.5	10.1	36.5	28.6	36.3
0203000	Anchorage municipality, Alaska...	14.9	9.7	39.5	11.0	3.8	109,584	62.6	46.1	5.7	10.8	37.4	30.1	33.1
04000	ARIZONA.............................	20.1	32.3	39.9	12.6	7.4	2,817,723	65.5	47.7	5.8	12.0	34.5	26.3	43.2
0404720	Avondale city, Arizona	36.4	52.6	45.7	15.3	7.4	26,611	79.6	53.4	5.5	20.7	20.4	11.0	30.6
0407940	Buckeye city, Arizona.................	19.6	43.0	39.9	8.5	3.5	30,913	79.0	67.3	2.3	9.4	21.0	15.4	38.3
0410670	Casas Adobes CDP, Arizona........	13.2	27.1	40.8	10.1	5.7	31,869	63.1	46.5	4.5	12.1	36.9	27.8	45.7
0412000	Chandler city, Arizona.................	15.3	25.9	36.4	15.1	6.7	107,668	68.4	52.5	4.9	11.0	31.6	23.5	30.5
0423620	Flagstaff city, Arizona.................	11.8	18.9	52.2	5.6	3.5	29,435	49.5	39.7	1.7	8.1	50.5	27.3	25.5
0427400	Gilbert town, Arizona	14.8	18.9	39.3	8.5	3.1	93,472	76.4	62.5	4.7	9.2	23.6	18.4	28.9
0427820	Glendale city, Arizona	28.1	40.2	39.0	20.3	10.6	90,604	68.1	47.9	6.3	14.0	31.9	24.7	37.8
0428380	Goodyear city, Arizona................	23.2	32.5	37.1	8.1	3.9	33,130	81.0	67.6	4.0	9.3	19.0	12.9	42.1
0446000	Mesa city, Arizona....................	16.2	27.3	40.0	11.0	6.1	199,112	63.6	46.2	5.8	11.7	36.4	27.7	41.4
0454050	Peoria city, Arizona	16.1	21.2	39.8	10.5	4.1	75,479	68.3	53.5	4.2	10.6	31.7	24.7	44.8
0455000	Phoenix city, Arizona.................	25.8	42.7	42.4	18.5	11.4	602,039	64.0	41.7	7.8	14.5	36.0	27.1	33.5
0458150	Queen Creek town, Arizona	10.0	10.9	40.6	3.8	0.9	20,981	88.5	73.3	4.7	10.6	11.5	8.3	31.8
0464210	San Tan Valley CDP, Arizona........	19.4	27.6	40.9	7.8	3.0	31,781	80.7	60.3	7.4	13.0	19.3	15.6	35.2
0465000	Scottsdale city, Arizona	9.7	11.8	22.2	10.8	3.6	119,122	55.2	45.5	2.9	6.7	44.8	33.8	47.3
0471510	Surprise city, Arizona..................	14.8	22.0	33.7	6.5	1.8	55,339	76.2	57.4	7.1	11.7	23.8	19.3	48.3
0473000	Tempe city, Arizona...................	14.3	25.1	39.2	11.5	6.1	77,306	45.0	29.3	6.1	9.6	55.0	31.2	23.0
0477000	Tucson city, Arizona..................	23.5	45.7	47.6	13.1	5.9	223,068	56.7	35.3	6.7	14.7	43.3	33.0	36.2
0485540	Yuma city, Arizona....................	40.2	61.6	39.9	18.0	9.6	36,530	73.7	46.6	6.6	20.6	26.3	19.0	37.2
05000	ARKANSAS	9.9	8.2	60.5	4.7	3.2	1,183,675	65.7	47.8	5.1	12.8	34.3	28.7	41.3
0515190	Conway city, Arkansas	7.1	7.2	70.8	5.1	2.1	25,251	59.1	41.3	4.4	13.4	40.9	30.7	24.1
0523290	Fayetteville city, Arkansas............	13.0	5.1	51.1	5.2	4.2	40,104	52.1	36.0	6.4	9.7	47.9	34.5	22.6
0524550	Fort Smith city, Arkansas..............	9.8	18.2	50.8	11.5	4.7	36,390	64.3	41.6	6.5	16.2	35.7	26.6	41.9
0535710	Jonesboro city, Arkansas..............	6.4	5.9	68.2	1.4	1.2	30,432	65.0	44.5	5.3	15.3	35.0	31.2	33.8
0541000	Little Rock city, Arkansas.............	5.4	7.9	69.9	6.3	4.0	89,422	59.0	38.0	4.2	16.8	41.0	35.1	37.1
0560410	Rogers city, Arkansas	29.8	33.6	38.5	18.9	15.8	25,872	76.0	56.9	5.9	13.2	24.0	19.7	32.2
0566080	Springdale city, Arkansas.............	38.7	41.4	46.5	24.4	18.3	28,942	67.8	46.0	7.5	14.4	32.2	24.3	32.4
06000	CALIFORNIA.............................	19.0	40.2	56.1	26.6	12.4	13,429,063	68.1	48.5	6.4	13.1	31.9	24.0	41.4
0600562	Alameda city, California..............	15.3	13.6	48.4	24.1	5.3	30,281	61.3	47.2	3.1	11.1	38.7	30.9	38.0
0600884	Alhambra city, California..............	16.8	39.2	48.8	42.1	12.4	29,022	70.5	46.8	8.3	15.4	29.5	21.8	46.4
0602000	Anaheim city, California..............	23.1	52.0	52.2	36.8	18.1	105,608	72.5	50.4	7.8	14.3	27.5	20.0	42.0
0602252	Antioch city, California.................	14.7	35.2	59.0	24.0	11.4	37,081	76.8	52.8	5.7	18.3	23.2	18.1	42.5
0602364	Apple Valley town, California......	25.0	42.7	68.9	12.7	5.6	24,657	71.4	54.2	5.9	11.3	28.6	24.8	50.2
0602553	Arden-Arcade CDP, California	12.8	22.3	68.2	16.1	10.4	40,688	57.9	36.9	7.5	13.4	42.1	28.6	33.0
0603526	Bakersfield city, California	23.2	53.0	69.9	19.1	9.2	128,007	72.7	49.4	7.9	15.4	27.3	22.1	36.9
0603666	Baldwin Park city, California.......	37.4	75.4	51.1	45.3	17.1	19,112	83.0	48.7	13.2	21.2	17.0	12.3	48.4
0604982	Bellflower city, California...........	22.9	67.1	61.5	28.8	13.2	24,327	75.1	43.9	11.4	19.8	24.9	19.4	38.1
0606000	Berkeley city, California..............	10.8	12.8	49.1	21.0	10.3	43,893	43.0	32.9	3.6	6.4	57.0	36.2	38.4
0608786	Buena Park city, California	22.6	40.2	57.3	32.8	12.3	24,306	81.8	56.3	8.3	17.2	18.2	12.1	41.5
0608954	Burbank city, California..............	12.4	21.3	46.5	32.4	7.8	44,471	56.4	40.9	6.6	8.8	43.6	33.6	43.9
0610046	Camarillo city, California.............	13.3	31.5	61.7	15.6	4.4	27,588	64.2	51.7	3.9	8.5	35.8	27.3	50.4
0611194	Carlsbad city, California..............	13.7	17.2	49.9	13.6	5.2	48,098	63.0	50.4	3.4	9.2	37.0	26.9	46.3
0611390	Carmichael CDP, California..........	12.3	17.9	62.0	17.5	8.3	32,172	61.7	43.1	3.9	14.7	38.3	28.3	44.2
0611530	Carson city, California.................	19.0	35.8	51.6	35.3	12.5	25,743	78.1	49.0	11.1	18.0	21.9	18.4	55.3
0611964	Castro Valley CDP, California.......	12.0	14.4	55.3	30.4	10.1	23,103	73.5	56.3	4.1	13.1	26.5	20.2	51.5

Table A-4. Cities — Who: Age, Race/Ethnicity, and Household Structure, 2021—*Continued*

STATE and place code	STATE Place	Total population	Percent change, 2014–2019	Under 18 years	18 to 24 years	25 to 44 years	45 to 64 years	65 years and over	Median age	White	Black	American Indian and Alaska Native	Asian	Native Hawaiian or Other Pacific Islander	Some other race
						Population by age (percent)						Race alone or in combination (percent)			
	ACS table number:	B01003	Population Estimates	B01001	B01001	B01001	B01001	B01001	B01002	B02008	B02009	B02010	B02011	B02012	B02013
FIPS	column number:	1	2	3	4	5	6	7	8	9	10	11	12	13	14
	CALIFORNIA—Cont.														
0613014	Chico city, California.................	102,340	15.8	19.9	20.5	26.4	19.0	14.2	31.7	83.2	3.6	4.6	7.0	0.6	15.2
0613210	Chino city, California.................	92,988	11.3	25.2	7.3	29.4	26.6	11.5	37.7	43.2	7.6	2.4	23.0	0.0	47.9
0613214	Chino Hills city, California	78,675	8.9	20.4	8.3	29.8	29.9	11.7	38.0	38.1	5.4	1.2	47.0	0.0	26.4
0613392	Chula Vista city, California	277,211	5.2	23.8	8.6	29.7	24.4	13.4	36.7	60.8	6.7	3.4	18.1	0.6	53.4
0613588	Citrus Heights city, California	87,411	1.9	18.2	8.6	29.1	26.7	17.5	40.1	79.7	5.3	2.9	9.6	0.8	12.4
0614218	Clovis city, California.................	122,985	12.1	31.2	7.6	27.4	21.7	12.1	33.7	69.4	5.3	3.5	14.8	0.6	28.6
0615044	Compton city, California..............	93,584	-3.0	22.9	10.6	27.0	26.3	13.2	37.3	44.6	28.5	1.1	0.9	0.0	64.7
0616000	Concord city, California..............	124,091		20.7	7.0	31.7	24.0	16.7	39.1	63.0	6.5	3.3	18.4	0.0	27.6
0616350	Corona city, California...............	159,749	5.2	23.7	10.3	25.4	28.1	12.5	38.3	54.5	4.3	4.3	14.5	0.5	43.0
0616532	Costa Mesa city, California..........	110,750	0.2	19.2	7.5	34.7	24.3	14.4	37.1	66.3	3.3	1.9	13.0	1.4	34.3
0617918	Daly City city, California.............	101,221	0.2	13.4	10.5	27.0	26.6	22.5	44.4	26.3	4.2	1.7	61.4	1.1	17.1
0618100	Davis city, California.................	66,798	4.0	14.6	33.0	23.3	17.9	11.2	26.0	66.6	3.7	2.5	29.9	0.0	10.7
0619766	Downey city, California	111,637	-2.7	20.0	9.0	26.8	27.3	16.9	40.3	52.6	4.3	4.0	10.3	0.0	62.5
0620018	Dublin city, California.................	71,680	18.5	26.8	4.6	35.3	23.0	10.4	37.8	37.0	3.5	0.7	61.4	0.0	7.8
0620802	East Los Angeles CDP, California .	115,803	2.2	23.8	10.1	28.8	26.9	10.3	35.5	28.9	0.5	5.1	1.1	0.0	83.7
0621230	Eastvale city, California.............	71,374	12.5	26.0	9.0	30.5	24.4	10.2	37.2	34.7	10.6	0.7	31.4	1.1	32.7
0621712	El Cajon city, California.............	105,431	-0.4	25.0	9.4	29.7	22.3	13.6	34.4	69.0	12.5	2.8	6.1	1.9	21.9
0622020	Elk Grove city, California............	178,988	6.9	28.6	6.9	25.7	25.4	13.3	38.2	47.3	15.1	3.0	36.5	1.8	14.7
0622230	El Monte city, California.............	106,913	-1.0	22.9	9.6	27.9	25.2	14.3	38.1	27.1	1.4	6.6	28.6	0.0	57.2
0622804	Escondido city, California............	150,656	0.9	25.7	7.4	29.5	24.9	12.5	36.7	63.3	3.3	5.1	10.3	0.4	44.0
0623182	Fairfield city, California..............	119,710	5.4	27.1	8.1	28.6	22.8	13.4	35.3	44.3	17.8	2.8	27.0	3.9	24.4
0624638	Folsom city, California	81,212	7.9	21.9	8.0	26.4	31.1	12.6	40.7	68.0	6.6	2.0	23.4	0.6	14.0
0624680	Fontana city, California	210,786		27.1	9.8	30.9	23.2	9.0	33.0	29.8	10.0	3.5	8.2	0.5	63.8
0626000	Fremont city, California..............	227,523	5.4	23.6	5.6	33.1	24.5	13.3	38.3	25.5	3.0	0.9	66.2	2.1	10.2
0627000	Fresno city, California................	544,500	3.0	27.5	10.0	29.0	20.9	12.6	32.9	60.3	9.3	3.0	16.7	0.6	42.6
0628000	Fullerton city, California..............	141,875	-0.7	21.8	10.2	28.2	25.7	14.1	35.1	52.3	4.6	1.8	25.9	1.0	36.8
0629000	Garden Grove city, California	170,492	-2.0	21.1	8.5	25.9	29.5	14.9	40.3	38.4	1.8	1.7	45.6	0.0	25.8
0630000	Glendale city, California.............	192,376	-0.4	19.4	7.1	30.5	24.1	18.8	40.0	67.7	3.1	2.0	16.7	0.0	17.2
0632548	Hawthorne city, California	86,093	-1.7	22.3	10.1	33.4	23.4	10.8	33.7	40.4	23.8	5.6	7.0	0.0	52.6
0633000	Hayward city, California..............	159,839	3.0	21.4	7.2	31.9	25.3	14.2	37.8	28.8	10.7	2.1	32.0	3.4	37.2
0633182	Hemet city, California................	90,446	2.8	21.9	5.1	24.0	24.9	24.1	44.3	59.2	13.6	2.5	4.3	0.6	42.0
0633434	Hesperia city, California	100,959	3.2	30.2	10.4	27.3	22.2	9.8	32.0	73.8	5.6	4.6	1.5	0.0	37.6
0636000	Huntington Beach city, California	196,650	-0.8	17.8	7.0	26.3	29.2	19.6	44.0	77.8	1.7	1.9	17.0	0.7	17.1
0636448	Indio city, California...................	90,421	7.1	19.1	6.7	26.3	24.4	23.6	42.9	62.0	2.6	2.6	3.9	1.8	62.2
0636546	Inglewood city, California	105,179	-3.3	21.2	7.8	32.0	25.4	13.5	36.9	25.8	45.4	3.9	2.7	0.2	43.2
0636770	Irvine city, California	309,014	15.6	24.4	10.9	31.3	23.1	10.3	34.2	47.1	4.0	1.5	48.3	1.5	11.4
0637692	Jurupa Valley city, California........	106,937	10.8	27.7	10.6	30.1	22.0	9.7	32.9	31.6	5.9	2.6	5.3	0.0	67.7
0639486	Lake Elsinore city, California.......	71,573	15.4	30.8	7.3	29.5	24.8	7.5	34.0	61.0	14.0	7.1	5.8	0.0	39.5
0639496	Lake Forest city, California	85,732	6.7	19.3	9.2	26.5	29.5	15.5	42.1	63.4	3.3	2.1	25.5	0.0	23.8
0639892	Lakewood city, California............	80,607	-2.9	22.6	6.4	31.0	27.1	12.9	37.3	52.1	9.7	3.3	22.2	1.1	29.0
0640130	Lancaster city, California............	170,134	-2.1	28.3	10.2	30.1	21.4	10.0	31.8	50.2	24.1	3.7	4.6	0.0	41.8
0641992	Livermore city, California............	86,812	3.8	20.9	7.6	26.4	30.5	14.6	40.5	70.9	2.8	2.9	20.8	1.4	19.9
0642202	Lodi city, California	67,020	5.7	21.6	12.9	22.4	25.3	17.8	39.1	69.9	3.2	11.8	9.0	0.0	39.6
0643000	Long Beach city, California..........	456,063	-2.3	19.9	8.9	32.4	24.9	13.9	36.5	51.9	14.2	4.0	17.3	0.7	29.0
0644000	Los Angeles city, California	3,849,306	1.3	19.7	9.5	32.3	24.9	13.7	37.0	49.3	10.0	3.2	13.7	0.5	43.1
0644574	Lynwood city, California..............	65,502	-2.7	25.4	11.1	28.4	24.5	10.5	33.7	35.7	10.9	5.7	1.3	0.0	74.0
0645022	Madera city, California................	67,956	3.6	29.2	8.4	27.8	22.6	12.1	33.6	47.8	3.1	6.3	3.2	0.0	68.1
0645484	Manteca city, California..............	85,799	13.0	24.8	5.7	29.8	26.0	13.7	38.8	61.1	2.3	4.2	26.2	2.2	27.9
0646842	Menifee city, California	106,396	11.2	24.9	7.3	26.6	24.3	16.9	38.0	68.9	12.9	2.4	6.9	0.0	38.2
0646898	Merced city, California................	89,292	2.4	30.9	11.5	27.9	19.2	10.5	30.0	39.3	8.4	3.7	13.7	0.0	47.5
0647766	Milpitas city, California...............	79,074	14.3	21.7	6.0	35.0	23.8	13.5	37.1	18.3	3.5	1.2	74.4	1.0	10.9
0648256	Mission Viejo city, California	92,449	-2.9	18.6	6.0	23.0	29.5	22.9	46.9	83.7	1.6	1.2	13.7	0.7	13.5
0648354	Modesto city, California	218,782	2.8	25.3	8.1	28.5	24.1	14.0	35.6	71.0	6.2	3.3	8.4	1.7	37.0
0649270	Moreno Valley city, California......	211,607	5.0	26.4	10.7	31.3	21.5	10.1	32.3	33.6	19.5	3.6	6.4	1.2	58.1
0649670	Mountain View city, California	81,517	4.2	21.4	6.1	40.5	20.4	11.5	35.7	51.7	6.1	1.8	39.8	0.0	15.7
0650076	Murrieta city, California	112,984	7.2	28.0	10.5	26.0	21.5	14.0	34.7	67.4	7.8	1.2	15.1	0.7	25.8
0650258	Napa city, California....................	78,824	-2.3	20.8	8.4	26.9	25.6	18.3	41.4	79.7	1.8	3.7	4.4	0.4	32.9

STATE Place	Two or more races (percent)	Hispanic or Latino (percent)	Native, born in state of residence (percent)	Foreign born (percent)	Non-citizens (percent)	Total house-holds	Family households				Nonfamily households		Percent of house-holds with people age 60 years and over
							Total	Married-couple	Male house-holder	Female house-holder	Total	One-person house-holds	
ACS table number:	B02001	B03003	B05002	B05002	B05002	B11001	B11001	B11001	B11001	B11001	B11001	B11001	B11006
FIPS column number:	15	16	17	18	19	20	21	22	23	24	25	26	27
CALIFORNIA—Cont.													
0613014 Chico city, California..................	13.1	20.1	72.8	9.5	4.4	40,956	54.0	34.7	6.7	12.6	46.0	27.1	31.1
0613210 Chino city, California..................	21.8	54.9	63.3	26.2	11.7	26,774	81.2	61.1	6.6	13.5	18.8	15.1	40.2
0613214 Chino Hills city, California	17.7	31.4	55.2	34.8	12.2	25,703	85.5	70.9	7.0	7.6	14.5	9.4	36.0
0613392 Chula Vista city, California	40.2	64.1	53.9	31.4	12.1	83,451	79.9	55.6	7.6	16.7	20.1	16.3	40.3
0613588 Citrus Heights city, California	9.3	14.7	64.7	16.8	5.5	34,140	59.3	43.7	4.1	11.5	40.7	27.8	42.5
0614218 Clovis city, California	21.0	35.7	74.6	10.8	3.5	38,762	77.0	59.9	7.7	9.4	23.0	17.9	37.5
0615044 Compton city, California	39.6	70.4	61.7	28.0	13.6	28,820	70.5	36.6	11.2	22.7	29.5	25.1	42.3
0616000 Concord city, California...............	18.1	31.8	60.0	24.8	10.6	46,375	66.8	48.3	5.1	13.5	33.2	24.8	40.1
0616350 Corona city, California	19.7	50.0	61.3	26.2	10.7	48,905	79.1	60.1	5.3	13.7	20.9	15.9	37.7
0616532 Costa Mesa city, California	19.0	34.6	59.6	23.1	11.1	43,711	58.9	40.5	6.0	12.4	41.1	27.7	37.2
0617918 Daly City city, California.............	10.1	20.8	41.5	49.8	13.7	32,887	69.2	48.9	7.7	12.7	30.8	22.6	54.9
0618100 Davis city, California..................	12.9	14.8	57.6	18.1	8.5	25,316	46.7	37.9	1.7	7.0	53.3	23.7	26.2
0619766 Downey city, California	32.8	71.3	59.0	33.5	12.7	36,008	75.6	48.5	9.1	18.0	24.4	19.0	47.3
0620018 Dublin city, California.................	10.5	9.7	44.2	42.2	20.3	23,688	79.6	67.9	2.8	8.8	20.4	17.0	27.2
0620802 East Los Angeles CDP, California .	18.9	96.8	55.8	40.6	24.3	31,072	78.9	44.6	12.6	21.7	21.1	16.0	43.8
0621230 Eastvale city, California	10.8	36.3	66.6	23.3	7.2	18,470	90.6	76.0	3.3	11.3	9.4	6.8	37.0
0621712 El Cajon city, California	13.3	30.2	55.4	24.7	9.1	34,443	70.2	39.5	6.1	24.7	29.8	22.8	40.5
0622020 Elk Grove city, California	15.4	17.8	62.2	25.1	6.3	53,724	81.8	65.6	6.4	9.8	18.2	12.8	40.9
0622230 El Monte city, California.............	20.2	67.7	49.4	46.8	21.5	29,036	81.2	43.8	13.6	23.9	18.8	11.8	46.9
0622804 Escondido city, California............	25.6	50.4	50.3	28.8	13.7	50,171	69.9	51.7	6.1	12.1	30.1	24.4	37.4
0623182 Fairfield city, California..............	18.0	27.8	55.1	23.0	11.4	38,097	73.3	48.6	8.5	16.3	26.7	22.1	42.7
0624638 Folsom city, California...............	12.5	14.3	60.9	18.0	8.5	28,441	70.3	59.5	4.1	6.6	29.7	25.5	35.7
0624680 Fontana city, California..............	14.8	71.3	64.1	26.8	12.9	57,836	85.2	56.8	10.8	17.6	14.8	11.1	35.2
0626000 Fremont city, California.............	7.2	10.6	41.3	49.1	21.5	75,716	77.4	66.1	3.4	7.9	22.6	16.6	36.7
0627000 Fresno city, California...............	30.7	49.7	70.3	19.2	8.3	181,841	66.0	39.9	8.5	17.7	34.0	26.9	36.4
0628000 Fullerton city, California.............	21.4	43.6	58.8	27.8	10.9	48,423	69.2	51.3	7.7	10.2	30.8	19.2	36.4
0629000 Garden Grove city, California	13.2	35.2	43.6	47.7	17.5	48,769	75.6	49.6	8.4	17.5	24.4	17.6	49.5
0630000 Glendale city, California.............	6.6	19.9	38.1	50.7	15.0	70,831	68.0	50.3	6.1	11.6	32.0	24.0	44.2
0632548 Hawthorne city, California	28.8	60.7	54.2	35.8	19.6	30,039	64.7	35.1	8.2	21.4	35.3	26.5	33.6
0633000 Hayward city, California.............	13.1	40.1	47.4	41.4	18.8	48,619	72.7	51.4	6.6	14.7	27.3	19.0	43.0
0633182 Hemet city, California...............	20.6	46.0	61.4	20.2	10.7	33,486	67.6	40.1	9.7	17.8	32.4	27.4	62.0
0633434 Hesperia city, California.............	20.3	62.3	69.2	18.1	9.6	29,237	79.0	54.5	9.8	14.8	21.0	16.2	34.1
0636000 Huntington Beach city, California	15.3	18.9	57.7	18.6	6.0	79,930	63.7	48.8	4.9	10.0	36.3	27.6	44.9
0636448 Indio city, California...................	33.6	69.0	59.1	25.1	12.5	34,673	65.2	48.5	8.1	8.6	34.8	30.9	51.4
0636546 Inglewood city, California	18.6	47.2	59.6	24.6	12.3	37,972	61.8	29.8	11.6	20.4	38.2	30.6	38.8
0636770 Irvine city, California..................	12.3	13.6	40.1	40.4	20.6	111,648	63.0	52.0	2.5	8.6	37.0	24.4	27.3
0637692 Jurupa Valley city, California........	12.6	74.7	67.8	25.9	15.2	27,454	80.3	50.4	11.0	18.8	19.7	14.4	41.8
0639486 Lake Elsinore city, California........	24.0	46.7	62.1	17.2	6.7	21,422	79.7	55.8	5.1	18.9	20.3	14.0	27.0
0639496 Lake Forest city, California..........	17.7	26.9	51.2	28.1	12.2	30,962	72.4	58.4	4.7	9.2	27.6	20.1	40.5
0639892 Lakewood city, California............	17.0	36.0	65.5	18.2	4.5	26,533	74.8	58.2	5.0	11.5	25.2	18.3	42.8
0640130 Lancaster city, California............	23.8	47.6	74.0	14.6	6.1	51,333	71.1	41.5	7.0	22.5	28.9	22.6	33.0
0641992 Livermore city, California............	16.4	24.9	59.5	20.6	11.3	31,472	72.6	58.1	5.5	9.1	27.4	23.3	39.5
0642202 Lodi city, California....................	27.4	46.4	64.2	22.0	12.7	24,245	68.0	51.7	5.1	11.2	32.0	24.7	42.7
0643000 Long Beach city, California..........	15.6	42.3	58.6	24.2	11.8	172,599	57.9	36.1	6.7	15.1	42.1	30.2	35.5
0644000 Los Angeles city, California..........	18.4	48.1	47.3	35.9	17.6	1,410,594	58.7	37.4	7.3	13.9	41.3	31.0	36.5
0644574 Lynwood city, California..............	27.1	84.3	56.9	37.1	23.9	16,079	82.6	44.5	14.1	24.0	17.4	14.5	42.5
0645022 Madera city, California................	27.8	80.3	66.7	22.6	15.0	18,595	75.3	37.9	14.3	23.1	24.7	19.2	40.7
0645484 Manteca city, California..............	19.0	32.2	62.0	24.7	6.2	27,310	76.8	54.6	8.6	13.7	23.2	20.0	46.4
0646842 Menifee city, California...............	26.4	43.0	69.5	12.3	4.3	35,601	70.1	52.0	7.1	11.0	29.9	25.3	46.6
0646898 Merced city, California................	11.1	55.5	71.0	21.4	10.2	28,358	71.7	37.4	5.8	28.6	28.3	21.9	35.4
0647766 Milpitas city, California...............	8.6	12.9	37.2	51.9	23.1	23,632	78.1	64.7	7.3	6.1	21.9	13.2	40.5
0648256 Mission Viejo city, California	13.6	15.9	53.6	19.3	4.3	34,168	75.6	65.6	4.3	5.7	24.4	20.0	49.8
0648354 Modesto city, California...............	26.6	43.5	69.0	18.7	8.7	71,775	71.8	45.9	7.7	18.2	28.2	21.5	37.2
0649270 Moreno Valley city, California......	20.4	62.9	64.1	23.9	12.0	54,104	84.0	52.8	9.2	22.0	16.0	12.6	38.7
0649670 Mountain View city, California	14.1	17.4	35.5	42.2	24.4	34,637	54.1	43.9	4.0	6.2	45.9	35.8	27.1
0650076 Murrieta city, California	17.4	29.4	60.8	16.1	4.3	34,414	81.0	61.7	8.4	10.8	19.0	14.9	42.1
0650258 Napa city, California...................	21.7	42.1	58.3	22.7	12.1	30,418	66.1	50.3	8.5	7.2	33.9	26.8	41.7

Table A-4. Cities — Who: Age, Race/Ethnicity, and Household Structure, 2021—*Continued*

STATE and place code	STATE Place	Total popula-tion	Percent change, 2014–2019	Population by age (percent) Under 18 years	18 to 24 years	25 to 44 years	45 to 64 years	65 years and over	Median age	Race alone or in combination (percent) White	Black	American Indian and Alaska Native	Asian	Native Hawaiian or Other Pacific Islander	Some other race
	ACS table number:	B01003	Population Estimates	B01001	B01001	B01001	B01001	B01001	B01002	B02008	B02009	B02010	B02011	B02012	B02013
FIPS	column number:	1	2	3	4	5	6	7	8	9	10	11	12	13	14
	CALIFORNIA—Cont.														
0651182	Newport Beach city, California	84,784	-3.1	17.1	5.6	23.7	32.9	20.7	48.4	86.3	0.5	0.0	13.9	0.0	8.4
0652526	Norwalk city, California	100,369	-3.0	23.7	8.6	28.3	24.5	14.8	36.5	32.9	3.2	10.2	11.9	0.4	64.4
0653000	Oakland city, California	433,797	4.7	19.3	7.3	34.0	24.8	14.6	38.2	39.7	24.3	3.0	21.1	0.9	24.5
0653322	Oceanside city, California	172,990	0.7	21.7	8.4	29.4	25.7	14.8	37.9	70.1	7.5	3.9	10.9	1.0	36.0
0653896	Ontario city, California	177,961	9.4	24.2	10.1	31.7	23.7	10.3	33.4	51.2	9.0	4.3	11.8	0.0	58.4
0653980	Orange city, California	137,287	-0.8	21.9	10.3	31.4	23.1	13.3	35.6	64.3	3.7	2.4	15.9	0.7	32.3
0654652	Oxnard city, California	201,898	1.7	27.0	9.1	30.1	22.7	11.2	33.9	67.5	3.0	6.9	9.4	0.6	57.5
0655156	Palmdale city, California	165,795	-2.0	28.3	8.4	28.6	23.3	11.4	33.5	53.4	12.5	2.9	5.0	0.7	52.9
0655282	Palo Alto city, California	66,666	-2.4	25.2	6.8	23.3	27.5	17.2	41.1	54.8	2.9	0.9	36.7	0.0	14.0
0656000	Pasadena city, California	135,745	0.1	17.6	7.2	33.5	26.5	15.2	40.1	50.5	10.6	2.0	21.5	0.4	29.9
0656700	Perris city, California	79,831	7.5	27.0	12.2	29.3	24.7	6.7	30.3	30.6	7.3	2.6	5.4	0.0	75.1
0657456	Pittsburg city, California	76,551	6.5	20.8	11.4	30.0	25.8	12.0	35.1	35.8	14.8	3.4	21.7	1.5	44.9
0657792	Pleasanton city, California	78,250	5.3	20.3	7.2	23.9	31.4	17.2	44.2	48.8	3.0	1.1	42.0	1.5	10.8
0658072	Pomona city, California	148,339	-1.1	25.8	10.9	28.4	23.9	11.0	32.9	41.8	8.0	5.9	10.9	0.3	65.8
0659444	Rancho Cordova city, California ..	80,423	7.7	25.6	8.2	31.2	23.0	11.9	36.4	57.5	14.0	5.1	21.4	3.3	18.0
0659451	Rancho Cucamonga city, Califor-nia.	175,138	1.9	25.2	8.4	28.5	24.7	13.3	35.8	57.5	12.9	3.7	17.0	0.0	27.9
0659920	Redding city, California	93,466	1.1	22.6	9.3	26.2	23.4	18.6	38.9	88.8	3.6	3.9	7.2	0.0	11.1
0659962	Redlands city, California	73,280	1.3	28.7	9.7	26.8	18.4	16.4	31.5	60.0	7.2	2.9	10.9	0.0	34.2
0660018	Redondo Beach city, California....	69,779	-2.0	22.4	5.5	24.1	31.3	16.5	44.0	74.0	3.4	2.2	22.6	1.8	14.7
0660102	Redwood City city, California	81,653	3.7	19.7	6.3	32.7	29.1	12.3	37.6	57.5	4.9	5.7	22.2	1.8	27.7
0660466	Rialto city, California	104,380	0.8	30.0	8.3	31.5	20.6	9.5	31.7	28.0	15.9	2.9	2.6	0.0	69.7
0660620	Richmond city, California	115,642	1.9	22.2	7.7	30.3	24.1	15.6	37.5	35.7	23.5	5.7	16.8	0.8	35.1
0662000	Riverside city, California	317,257	3.7	22.1	15.1	30.0	21.9	10.9	32.9	46.7	9.1	3.5	10.0	1.0	49.3
0662364	Rocklin city, California	72,986	14.0	25.6	9.6	25.8	25.5	13.6	38.0	81.6	2.7	3.3	15.9	1.9	13.4
0662938	Roseville city, California	151,902	10.0	23.4	6.8	28.8	24.5	16.4	39.0	78.9	4.7	1.4	17.1	1.5	12.7
0664000	Sacramento city, California	525,028	5.9	19.9	9.3	32.7	23.0	15.0	36.3	47.4	15.3	5.2	23.3	3.0	24.1
0664224	Salinas city, California	162,780	-0.8	30.3	10.7	28.2	19.8	11.0	31.5	25.5	1.8	2.3	4.4	0.3	80.4
0665000	San Bernardino city, California	222,194	0.3	26.8	11.2	30.7	21.8	9.6	32.4	35.8	15.2	4.7	4.8	0.5	59.5
0665042	San Buenaventura (Ventura) city, California.	109,938	-0.3	20.1	7.8	25.8	28.1	18.2	41.5	83.2	3.8	5.9	6.7	0.8	22.6
0666000	San Diego city, California	1,381,600	3.1	18.8	11.2	32.5	23.6	13.8	35.9	63.4	7.9	2.4	20.5	0.9	24.1
0667000	San Francisco city, California	815,201	3.4	14.0	6.5	36.4	25.6	17.5	40.4	49.9	6.7	1.7	39.8	0.9	14.2
0668000	San Jose city, California	983,530	0.6	21.2	8.4	30.1	26.2	14.0	38.4	42.4	4.1	2.5	42.0	0.9	27.3
0668084	San Leandro city, California	88,878	-0.6	16.0	8.5	28.0	31.0	16.6	43.3	33.4	14.4	3.5	37.3	1.0	22.6
0668196	San Marcos city, California	94,927	4.1	27.7	7.8	28.8	21.7	14.0	37.6	77.9	3.9	4.2	13.3	0.0	25.5
0668252	San Mateo city, California	102,175	1.5	20.1	6.5	33.0	23.9	16.5	38.0	54.9	2.2	2.8	31.2	2.6	20.9
0668378	San Ramon city, California	86,939	0.9	29.1	5.7	24.4	28.4	12.4	40.2	41.6	4.1	0.8	54.0	0.5	7.7
0669000	Santa Ana city, California	309,468	-0.8	23.5	11.3	30.8	23.8	10.6	34.0	32.8	0.9	2.7	15.7	0.1	65.4
0669070	Santa Barbara city, California	88,252	0.2	16.4	11.8	30.0	26.0	15.9	37.1	73.6	3.3	3.2	5.5	0.6	36.6
0669084	Santa Clara city, California	127,155	6.7	19.0	9.6	37.5	22.6	11.4	34.5	44.0	4.2	1.3	48.6	0.6	12.7
0669088	Santa Clarita city, California	224,588	17.3	24.0	8.1	26.9	27.7	13.3	38.4	68.1	6.7	2.1	14.0	0.7	34.2
0669196	Santa Maria city, California	109,709	3.7	31.3	12.4	26.0	18.6	11.6	29.9	68.6	1.9	4.9	7.8	0.0	65.3
0670000	Santa Monica city, California......	91,103	-2.8	14.7	5.3	35.1	28.4	16.5	41.3	76.5	7.6	2.1	14.2	0.0	17.6
0670098	Santa Rosa city, California	176,942	1.5	20.0	9.1	26.8	25.9	18.1	40.4	69.3	2.7	6.0	9.1	1.4	28.0
0672016	Simi Valley city, California	125,967	-1.0	17.5	10.2	25.1	31.6	15.7	43.0	76.5	4.1	2.6	12.2	0.4	23.5
0673080	South Gate city, California	91,148	-3.0	23.6	9.2	29.1	25.1	13.0	36.3	46.7	2.2	5.4	0.8	0.0	84.4
0675000	Stockton city, California	322,107	3.4	27.1	11.0	28.0	21.7	12.2	32.4	39.8	15.2	9.0	25.9	1.8	39.4
0677000	Sunnyvale city, California	152,258	1.8	19.5	6.3	38.1	22.5	13.6	35.2	38.0	1.8	2.2	51.2	0.0	15.7
0678120	Temecula city, California	110,863		29.4	6.8	27.4	24.9	11.4	35.6	72.5	7.4	4.8	14.8	1.5	25.8
0678582	Thousand Oaks city, California	125,766	-2.0	21.1	8.1	22.7	27.7	20.4	43.5	82.0	3.2	3.9	12.1	0.3	21.1
0680000	Torrance city, California	143,589	-3.3	20.8	5.1	25.3	30.6	18.2	44.1	53.0	4.9	2.7	41.0	0.9	17.3
0680238	Tracy city, California	95,384	10.4	29.3	7.9	28.4	22.0	12.4	35.2	50.3	8.3	4.6	22.5	2.0	35.4
0680644	Tulare city, California	70,724	5.9	33.6	9.5	26.6	20.3	9.9	29.6	67.5	5.0	3.1	2.1	0.0	52.0
0680812	Turlock city, California	72,673	3.3	28.4	10.0	27.0	19.2	15.3	35.0	54.4	4.5	1.9	8.8	1.6	44.9
0680854	Tustin city, California	79,428	-1.6	24.9	9.8	29.2	25.2	10.9	35.9	49.8	4.2	2.0	30.2	0.0	33.4
0681204	Union City city, California	68,668	0.7	17.0	7.2	28.6	29.5	17.7	43.5	25.2	5.0	2.4	57.6	1.3	20.3
0681344	Upland city, California	79,264	1.4	21.5	10.7	25.9	28.1	13.8	38.4	61.2	6.8	4.0	12.3	0.0	38.9

Table A-4. Cities — Who: Age, Race/Ethnicity, and Household Structure, 2021—*Continued*

									Household type (percent of all households)						Percent of house-holds with people age 60 years and over
									Family households				Nonfamily households		
STATE and place code	STATE Place	Two or more races (percent)	Hispanic or Latino (percent)	Native, born in state of residence (percent)	Foreign born (percent)	Non-citizens (percent)	Total house-holds	Total	Married-couple	Male house-holder	Female house-holder	Total	One-person house-holds	
	ACS table number:	B02001	B03003	B05002	B05002	B05002	B11001	B11001	B11001	B11001	B11001	B11001	B11001	B11006
FIPS	column number:	15	16	17	18	19	20	21	22	23	24	25	26	27
	CALIFORNIA—Cont.													
0651182	Newport Beach city, California	9.9	9.2	54.9	16.6	5.7	39,131	58.1	48.2	3.0	7.0	41.9	33.8	44.3
0652526	Norwalk city, California	22.1	78.6	59.1	35.7	13.1	26,506	81.9	60.3	8.6	13.0	18.1	14.3	47.7
0653000	Oakland city, California	11.9	27.0	49.3	28.3	14.3	170,366	55.2	36.3	5.5	13.4	44.8	34.0	36.0
0653322	Oceanside city, California	27.1	40.4	51.6	21.2	9.3	59,683	66.9	49.7	6.5	10.6	33.1	22.3	44.0
0653896	Ontario city, California	34.2	65.1	64.8	28.0	12.9	55,819	77.9	49.6	10.3	17.9	22.1	16.1	36.1
0653980	Orange city, California	18.3	41.3	62.6	21.8	10.2	43,291	73.2	48.9	7.8	16.5	26.8	18.0	38.9
0654652	Oxnard city, California	43.2	75.9	56.4	34.5	19.4	50,611	79.9	52.3	9.4	18.2	20.1	12.3	41.0
0655156	Palmdale city, California	26.6	62.6	64.6	25.0	11.2	46,650	82.9	56.8	8.9	17.2	17.1	15.1	42.1
0655282	Palo Alto city, California	8.9	12.9	35.7	35.9	16.3	24,501	70.9	60.9	3.7	6.4	29.1	23.1	40.6
0656000	Pasadena city, California	14.0	35.3	48.7	30.8	13.4	56,992	53.1	38.9	5.2	9.0	46.9	34.8	36.4
0656700	Perris city, California	21.0	80.9	61.4	32.9	16.5	19,923	87.5	61.7	11.4	14.4	12.5	9.7	31.6
0657456	Pittsburg city, California	20.3	48.9	57.5	34.1	18.0	23,827	77.0	47.5	12.8	16.7	23.0	16.2	40.8
0657792	Pleasanton city, California	7.0	14.3	47.8	34.0	15.8	29,330	75.2	61.9	5.0	8.4	24.8	19.9	42.3
0658072	Pomona city, California	30.1	74.3	61.2	31.6	16.7	40,142	77.1	48.6	9.4	19.1	22.9	16.3	37.1
0659444	Rancho Cordova city, California ..	16.3	23.4	61.0	23.3	7.9	28,428	67.5	49.2	8.8	9.5	32.5	25.3	33.7
0659451	Rancho Cucamonga city, Califor-nia................	17.6	36.6	64.2	20.1	6.1	57,290	74.5	53.3	6.9	14.3	25.5	21.5	39.3
0659920	Redding city, California	12.7	14.2	71.0	5.6	2.3	37,302	54.9	36.6	4.8	13.5	45.1	31.9	43.5
0659962	Redlands city, California	15.5	44.5	65.5	17.8	8.6	24,452	66.4	46.0	8.0	12.4	33.6	24.8	43.5
0660018	Redondo Beach city, California....	18.0	15.7	54.0	20.4	7.7	26,986	65.8	53.0	2.8	10.0	34.2	27.6	38.2
0660102	Redwood City city, California	18.7	30.2	48.1	31.5	15.3	29,450	67.7	56.2	4.1	7.3	32.3	21.4	32.8
0660466	Rialto city, California	17.7	76.5	68.6	24.0	11.6	29,043	80.2	53.1	8.9	18.2	19.8	14.6	36.1
0660620	Richmond city, California	15.4	40.4	52.0	31.1	16.8	40,019	71.7	43.4	5.5	22.8	28.3	23.6	43.6
0662000	Riverside city, California	18.3	55.9	65.7	22.7	10.1	91,110	73.1	48.4	7.3	17.4	26.9	18.9	37.5
0662364	Rocklin city, California	15.9	13.7	65.4	12.1	4.3	25,528	73.9	59.8	5.7	8.3	26.1	20.5	37.5
0662938	Roseville city, California	14.0	14.8	64.3	13.9	5.2	57,569	70.3	56.6	4.3	9.4	29.7	23.9	38.5
0664000	Sacramento city, California	16.1	29.3	60.7	22.0	8.0	202,093	57.5	39.4	5.9	12.2	42.5	31.2	38.5
0664224	Salinas city, California	13.9	86.0	54.2	39.4	32.6	41,871	81.2	46.9	14.2	20.1	18.8	13.3	36.0
0665000	San Bernardino city, California	19.3	70.1	67.6	22.4	13.6	63,331	73.5	44.2	9.5	19.8	26.5	19.5	36.6
0665042	San Buenaventura (Ventura) city, California................	20.9	35.9	66.1	12.5	5.6	42,288	65.0	49.7	4.8	10.5	35.0	27.3	45.5
0666000	San Diego city, California	18.2	29.0	47.5	24.1	9.7	521,000	58.4	43.6	4.6	10.2	41.6	29.1	34.7
0667000	San Francisco city, California	11.7	15.7	41.6	34.3	13.4	350,796	48.5	37.4	3.3	7.9	51.5	37.0	36.4
0668000	San Jose city, California	18.1	30.6	47.8	40.8	17.8	322,881	71.2	52.4	5.8	12.9	28.8	20.9	38.6
0668084	San Leandro city, California.........	11.1	27.3	51.1	38.3	14.8	30,977	64.7	43.7	7.0	14.0	35.3	26.9	50.1
0668196	San Marcos city, California	24.6	38.4	51.3	20.8	8.2	34,037	73.2	56.1	2.8	14.3	26.8	22.0	36.0
0668252	San Mateo city, California	12.9	24.6	51.1	33.6	15.6	39,340	62.4	48.9	3.9	9.5	37.6	29.5	37.8
0668378	San Ramon city, California	8.2	8.8	46.7	36.0	13.2	29,662	79.3	66.4	5.2	7.7	20.7	13.7	34.7
0669000	Santa Ana city, California...........	17.1	75.7	51.0	41.5	22.0	78,674	81.4	56.9	8.5	16.0	18.6	12.8	37.6
0669070	Santa Barbara city, California	21.9	40.9	54.7	22.9	14.1	35,676	52.3	38.5	3.5	10.3	47.7	31.3	38.5
0669084	Santa Clara city, California	10.7	14.2	42.1	43.2	26.5	49,011	62.4	50.4	4.6	7.4	37.6	26.3	29.3
0669088	Santa Clarita city, California	23.8	37.9	60.5	22.1	7.2	73,509	76.1	57.3	6.5	12.3	23.9	18.1	40.6
0669196	Santa Maria city, California	48.3	77.5	54.4	34.1	24.0	30,316	73.6	47.8	9.1	16.7	26.4	22.3	40.0
0670000	Santa Monica city, California.......	17.8	20.7	41.6	25.3	7.9	45,541	40.8	30.7	2.5	7.6	59.2	45.3	37.0
0670098	Santa Rosa city, California	14.6	34.7	59.9	21.8	11.9	68,686	63.0	44.9	5.2	12.9	37.0	27.5	43.3
0672016	Simi Valley city, California	17.8	27.8	65.1	17.3	6.4	45,308	68.3	54.0	4.8	9.5	31.7	24.5	47.6
0673080	South Gate city, California	37.5	95.0	54.4	42.7	23.6	24,891	82.6	44.1	17.1	21.4	17.4	14.6	44.8
0675000	Stockton city, California	22.8	44.4	64.7	23.7	10.7	97,447	72.7	41.2	12.2	19.3	27.3	21.7	39.5
0677000	Sunnyvale city, California	8.8	17.7	36.2	49.9	29.5	59,567	65.1	53.3	4.9	6.8	34.9	25.1	31.3
0678120	Temecula city, California	23.1	28.0	56.1	18.1	7.2	34,958	82.6	63.6	6.6	12.4	17.4	15.9	35.3
0678582	Thousand Oaks city, California	21.0	24.6	55.6	20.1	7.3	45,081	68.5	55.6	3.4	9.4	31.5	25.0	51.6
0680000	Torrance city, California..............	18.0	19.5	49.8	30.0	12.0	57,584	66.1	53.1	4.5	8.5	33.9	27.7	44.3
0680238	Tracy city, California	19.9	43.4	62.5	26.7	8.1	28,353	83.3	68.6	3.9	10.8	16.7	12.9	40.8
0680644	Tulare city, California.................	27.6	60.7	72.6	17.2	9.8	20,974	77.2	50.7	8.4	18.1	22.8	19.4	36.8
0680812	Turlock city, California................	14.6	48.5	63.6	26.7	14.7	24,885	72.4	51.4	5.2	15.9	27.6	25.2	41.2
0680854	Tustin city, California.................	19.4	36.9	51.4	34.6	12.2	26,762	75.1	50.1	8.1	16.9	24.9	18.4	33.1
0681204	Union City city, California	10.9	23.5	41.4	50.0	17.6	21,637	79.0	64.4	6.7	7.9	21.0	16.6	47.8
0681344	Upland city, California.................	23.7	47.1	64.4	21.7	8.5	26,052	76.8	50.3	8.6	17.9	23.2	16.0	42.7

Table A-4. Cities — Who: Age, Race/Ethnicity, and Household Structure, 2021—*Continued*

STATE and place code	STATE Place	Total population	Percent change, 2014–2019	Population by age (percent)					Median age	Race alone or in combination (percent)					
				Under 18 years	18 to 24 years	25 to 44 years	45 to 64 years	65 years and over		White	Black	American Indian and Alaska Native	Asian	Native Hawaiian or Other Pacific Islander	Some other race
	ACS table number:	B01003	Population Estimates	B01001	B01001	B01001	B01001	B01001	B01002	B02008	B02009	B02010	B02011	B02012	B02013
FIPS	column number:	1	2	3	4	5	6	7	8	9	10	11	12	13	14
	CALIFORNIA—Cont.														
0681554	Vacaville city, California..............	103,092	5.0	20.1	8.8	30.6	25.1	15.4	38.1	66.2	13.7	2.3	14.8	0.7	17.9
0681666	Vallejo city, California................	124,869	1.2	20.0	9.0	28.8	23.1	19.1	40.0	37.9	24.8	2.8	22.8	2.9	27.0
0682590	Victorville city, California.............	135,952	0.4	27.0	12.0	27.8	22.8	10.4	32.6	55.5	16.7	3.6	7.9	0.0	35.1
0682954	Visalia city, California.................	142,976	4.1	27.3	10.3	28.6	21.4	12.4	33.6	67.9	4.1	7.0	7.5	0.0	40.8
0682996	Vista city, California	98,671	3.6	22.3	10.9	35.0	20.5	11.3	33.5	75.7	5.8	4.3	9.7	1.1	43.9
0683346	Walnut Creek city, California........	69,705	3.7	18.4	7.2	24.5	23.3	26.5	44.9	78.0	1.8	1.1	22.1	0.0	9.2
0684200	West Covina city, California	107,031	-3.1	19.9	9.1	27.7	24.6	18.7	40.1	37.5	5.1	2.7	31.3	0.1	43.8
0684550	Westminster city, California..........	90,213	-1.5	20.5	9.2	23.5	29.4	17.4	41.9	28.1	1.3	2.0	49.7	1.4	26.4
0685292	Whittier city, California	85,306	-2.6	20.3	11.3	25.9	29.2	13.3	38.7	49.3	1.8	3.9	7.3	1.4	57.8
0686832	Yorba Linda city, California..........	67,992	-0.3	19.2	5.4	25.0	29.7	20.7	45.4	64.0	2.4	0.9	31.7	0.8	18.5
0686972	Yuba City city, California............	69,544	1.9	23.9	9.7	27.0	24.2	15.2	36.5	57.3	5.5	5.3	22.3	0.8	28.5
08000	COLORADO........................	5,812,069	11.5	21.4	9.0	30.1	24.3	15.1	37.6	84.8	5.7	3.3	4.8	0.4	17.1
0803455	Arvada city, Colorado.................	123,829	6.4	21.5	6.3	29.9	23.7	18.5	39.7	91.4	2.4	2.7	3.0	0.0	13.4
0804000	Aurora city, Colorado.................	389,675	7.3	24.0	9.2	31.4	23.2	12.1	35.6	62.3	18.8	3.0	8.4	0.6	26.6
0807850	Boulder city, Colorado................	104,178	0.5	11.7	30.6	27.0	18.4	12.4	29.2	90.5	2.1	1.3	6.7	0.0	10.7
0809280	Broomfield city, Colorado...........	75,325	13.4	21.0	8.0	29.9	26.0	15.0	38.9	86.2	2.3	1.9	8.1	0.0	11.6
0812415	Castle Rock town, Colorado	76,366	22.9	28.9	7.3	28.8	26.2	8.8	35.6	95.0	1.8	1.7	3.5	0.0	12.6
0812815	Centennial city, Colorado............	106,957	3.5	23.8	6.7	24.9	27.0	17.6	41.0	89.7	4.4	1.9	7.0	0.0	10.2
0816000	Colorado Springs city, Colorado........................	483,969	7.3	21.8	10.1	30.8	22.5	14.8	35.6	84.4	8.5	3.4	5.7	1.0	14.0
0820000	Denver city, Colorado.................	711,463	9.5	18.6	8.1	40.0	21.1	12.1	35.1	75.8	11.1	3.2	5.4	0.3	23.3
0827425	Fort Collins city, Colorado...........	168,535	8.8	17.1	21.1	31.7	18.9	11.1	30.4	90.9	3.5	2.8	4.5	0.4	10.9
0831660	Grand Junction city, Colorado.....	66,951	5.6	17.3	13.1	27.9	21.0	20.8	39.0	93.5	2.2	3.8	1.3	0.0	11.7
0832155	Greeley city, Colorado................	109,340	10.2	26.0	12.9	28.7	21.0	11.4	31.7	80.7	4.3	4.6	2.8	0.0	27.0
0836410	Highlands Ranch CDP, Colorado..	98,239	-0.4	22.2	8.5	22.6	32.6	14.0	43.1	87.2	3.1	2.2	10.0	0.0	7.6
0843000	Lakewood city, Colorado.............	156,612	5.5	16.3	7.4	33.3	25.1	17.8	39.4	86.4	2.9	4.1	6.8	0.2	17.1
0845970	Longmont city, Colorado.............	100,427	7.2	18.6	7.2	30.1	25.0	19.0	40.9	91.7	1.5	1.6	5.1	0.3	18.6
0846465	Loveland city, Colorado..............	77,185	8.6	18.7	7.5	24.6	24.8	24.4	43.8	95.0	2.5	3.9	1.0	0.0	8.0
0862000	Pueblo city, Colorado.................	112,358	3.6	21.8	10.1	25.4	24.0	18.7	38.6	85.7	3.4	5.4	2.1	0.0	23.4
0877290	Thornton city, Colorado..............	142,599	8.6	25.8	9.9	31.0	22.6	10.7	34.7	79.1	3.5	5.2	6.7	0.0	28.5
0883835	Westminster city, Colorado	114,573	1.0	18.4	9.4	33.6	23.4	15.3	36.4	85.8	2.7	5.2	6.2	0.5	19.0
09000	CONNECTICUT	3,605,597	0.4	20.2	9.5	25.0	27.3	18.0	41.1	75.7	13.8	1.5	5.8	0.2	15.6
0908000	Bridgeport city, Connecticut........	148,345	-2.2	20.3	10.2	28.5	25.8	15.3	38.1	32.6	39.7	1.1	4.9	0.5	36.9
0918430	Danbury city, Connecticut...........	86,749	1.1	19.5	10.5	27.6	26.4	16.0	41.7	65.1	7.9	2.2	7.9	0.0	34.7
0937000	Hartford city, Connecticut...........	120,593	-2.1	23.8	15.0	29.1	20.7	11.4	32.3	40.2	49.1	1.0	1.9	0.0	27.9
0950370	New Britain city, Connecticut	73,835	-0.5	23.6	10.6	29.8	21.8	14.2	34.0	65.1	17.9	1.9	2.1	0.0	34.9
0952000	New Haven city, Connecticut	135,076	-0.0	20.5	15.8	32.9	18.6	12.2	31.6	41.8	37.3	1.3	5.5	0.0	27.0
0955990	Norwalk city, Connecticut	91,203	0.8	21.5	6.0	30.9	26.2	15.4	38.3	69.4	13.9	0.9	7.6	0.0	28.0
0973000	Stamford city, Connecticut..........	136,312	1.1	18.7	9.2	31.5	25.3	15.4	38.3	65.4	18.6	2.9	9.4	0.0	24.6
0980000	Waterbury city, Connecticut.........	113,820	-1.6	22.4	9.6	25.2	27.8	15.1	37.9	60.8	23.9	2.5	4.0	0.0	29.9
10000	DELAWARE	1,003,384	7.1	20.8	8.3	25.0	25.8	20.1	41.6	68.9	24.3	2.4	5.1	0.3	9.5
1077580	Wilmington city, Delaware	70,750	-2.3	18.2	5.7	30.7	27.7	17.6	41.0	40.2	52.0	3.9	2.6	0.0	11.3
11000	DISTRICT OF COLUMBIA	670,050	15.3	18.8	9.8	38.3	20.4	12.8	34.8	45.8	47.1	1.5	5.8	0.1	10.3
1150000	Washington city, District of Columbia.................	670,050	17.3	18.8	9.8	38.3	20.4	12.8	34.8	45.8	47.1	1.5	5.8	0.1	10.3
12000	FLORIDA.................................	21,781,128	11.6	19.7	7.9	25.1	26.1	21.1	42.8	74.1	17.7	1.4	3.8	0.2	22.9
1200410	Alafaya CDP, Florida..................	95,779	14.1	18.3	13.9	25.1	32.1	10.6	37.0	77.9	10.3	3.1	9.9	0.0	32.4
1207300	Boca Raton city, Florida.............	95,785	9.3	15.8	12.1	19.4	27.7	25.0	48.0	87.5	6.0	1.6	4.0	0.0	12.6
1207875	Boynton Beach city, Florida	80,083	7.6	18.6	7.4	25.0	24.8	24.2	44.4	56.6	36.9	1.2	3.5	0.0	18.9
1208150	Brandon CDP, Florida.................	116,994	11.1	21.8	6.5	34.5	23.3	13.9	36.8	63.9	21.9	1.3	5.7	0.0	26.9
1210275	Cape Coral city, Florida..............	204,519	14.5	15.9	7.3	21.1	30.5	25.1	49.7	89.4	4.5	0.6	1.2	0.0	25.5
1212875	Clearwater city, Florida...............	116,667	5.6	12.1	9.9	24.0	28.7	25.4	49.0	81.5	12.5	1.4	4.0	0.0	14.3
1214400	Coral Springs city, Florida...........	132,822	4.5	24.6	8.4	26.6	27.6	12.7	37.4	61.4	29.7	1.2	6.6	0.0	28.9
1216475	Davie town, Florida....................	104,873	7.5	22.5	8.2	30.8	25.7	12.8	37.5	80.6	9.3	0.0	8.3	0.0	33.5
1216525	Daytona Beach city, Florida........	74,435	9.8	13.4	15.1	25.1	24.3	22.1	42.1	64.6	29.2	1.1	1.8	0.0	11.0
1216725	Deerfield Beach city, Florida	86,355	2.8	14.8	7.3	27.0	29.0	22.0	46.0	67.2	25.8	2.1	2.9	0.0	26.6

Table A-4. Cities — Who: Age, Race/Ethnicity, and Household Structure, 2021—*Continued*

STATE and place code	STATE Place	Two or more races (percent)	Hispanic or Latino (percent)	Native, born in state of residence (percent)	Foreign born (percent)	Non-citizens (percent)	Total households	Family households				Nonfamily households		Percent of households with people age 60 years and over
								Total	Married-couple	Male householder	Female householder	Total	One-person households	
	ACS table number:	B02001	B03003	B05002	B05002	B05002	B11001	B11001	B11001	B11001	B11001	B11001	B11001	B11006
FIPS	column number:	15	16	17	18	19	20	21	22	23	24	25	26	27
	CALIFORNIA—Cont.													
0681554	Vacaville city, California.............	14.7	26.1	64.2	12.7	4.8	33,777	74.1	56.4	5.2	12.5	25.9	18.1	39.6
0681666	Vallejo city, California.................	15.5	31.4	56.0	26.4	10.5	43,906	66.0	41.7	6.5	17.8	34.0	26.7	48.7
0682590	Victorville city, California............	19.9	55.9	67.9	17.8	9.4	38,400	79.8	45.0	9.2	25.6	20.2	16.2	38.0
0682954	Visalia city, California	24.7	54.4	71.6	15.1	7.1	47,660	71.8	46.6	8.7	16.5	28.2	20.7	35.6
0682996	Vista city, California	39.3	53.1	59.6	21.3	10.7	30,614	68.0	46.7	7.3	14.0	32.0	19.5	34.0
0683346	Walnut Creek city, California.......	12.2	9.8	45.4	24.9	10.0	31,035	58.8	50.0	3.8	4.9	41.2	34.8	49.9
0684200	West Covina city, California	19.7	51.9	55.1	37.9	11.3	32,012	82.4	53.9	8.6	19.9	17.6	12.7	50.8
0684550	Westminster city, California.........	8.3	29.0	45.4	44.3	14.9	27,935	78.4	54.9	7.3	16.1	21.6	18.0	51.1
0685292	Whittier city, California...............	20.2	66.2	73.1	17.1	4.9	27,773	75.3	53.4	7.4	14.5	24.7	19.1	38.3
0686832	Yorba Linda city, California..........	16.8	20.5	57.3	23.8	7.5	24,098	75.7	65.0	3.1	7.6	24.3	17.7	53.0
0686972	Yuba City city, California.............	18.3	30.0	59.2	25.0	12.8	24,176	68.2	44.6	7.6	16.0	31.8	24.5	47.0
08000	**COLORADO**..............................	14.9	22.3	42.2	9.8	4.8	2,313,042	62.6	48.6	4.6	9.4	37.4	27.9	36.6
0803455	Arvada city, Colorado..................	12.7	16.0	51.4	4.8	2.1	50,678	65.2	53.0	4.1	8.1	34.8	25.9	41.4
0804000	Aurora city, Colorado..................	18.1	30.8	38.9	22.3	13.0	140,003	63.6	43.6	6.5	13.6	36.4	28.1	34.4
0807850	Boulder city, Colorado................	11.2	11.8	27.1	12.7	6.9	42,376	43.6	33.8	4.4	5.5	56.4	31.8	26.1
0809280	Broomfield city, Colorado............	9.7	13.5	38.6	9.9	4.4	30,161	65.6	50.7	4.1	10.9	34.4	25.4	36.8
0812415	Castle Rock town, Colorado	14.2	11.6	38.0	4.8	1.4	27,249	76.1	65.7	3.6	6.8	23.9	18.4	27.3
0812815	Centennial city, Colorado............	12.0	10.6	42.0	8.7	2.3	39,660	75.0	58.9	5.1	11.0	25.0	19.7	41.9
0816000	Colorado Springs city, Colorado	15.3	19.0	30.7	7.6	3.0	197,542	63.9	47.3	5.7	11.0	36.1	26.9	34.2
0820000	Denver city, Colorado..................	17.7	29.0	38.4	14.2	7.7	326,634	46.8	33.8	3.5	9.5	53.2	38.9	27.0
0827425	Fort Collins city, Colorado	12.1	12.5	37.2	7.3	3.0	70,686	50.4	40.9	1.9	7.6	49.6	27.4	26.5
0831660	Grand Junction city, Colorado.....	12.7	16.5	46.5	4.0	2.5	28,352	54.2	41.0	3.1	10.0	45.8	36.6	44.9
0832155	Greeley city, Colorado.................	17.3	43.8	50.8	12.9	7.3	38,381	68.9	49.5	6.3	13.1	31.1	23.3	33.1
0836410	Highlands Ranch CDP, Colorado..	8.4	8.7	34.7	11.6	3.3	38,117	73.5	59.9	5.6	8.0	26.5	20.3	37.4
0843000	Lakewood city, Colorado.............	16.2	22.5	44.7	9.4	3.9	70,751	54.3	40.7	4.2	9.3	45.7	34.9	37.7
0845970	Longmont city, Colorado.............	18.0	22.3	38.6	8.9	3.5	43,519	55.5	40.7	6.3	8.5	44.5	33.3	42.6
0846465	Loveland city, Colorado...............	8.5	16.1	38.4	5.0	1.1	35,803	59.8	48.8	4.1	6.9	40.2	32.1	46.8
0862000	Pueblo city, Colorado..................	19.3	52.0	64.4	4.6	2.5	47,901	57.3	34.0	7.1	16.2	42.7	36.9	44.4
0877290	Thornton city, Colorado...............	21.4	39.3	52.2	15.7	10.5	48,263	72.6	56.0	5.9	10.7	27.4	19.0	29.6
0883835	Westminster city, Colorado	16.0	24.2	47.2	7.6	3.5	47,797	60.0	44.7	4.1	11.2	40.0	30.0	36.2
09000	**CONNECTICUT**	11.6	17.7	53.8	15.2	6.8	1,428,313	64.2	46.5	4.5	13.1	35.8	28.8	44.1
0908000	Bridgeport city, Connecticut.......	14.3	42.2	39.8	32.3	15.9	57,732	59.4	33.5	4.9	21.1	40.6	33.8	43.4
0918430	Danbury city, Connecticut...........	17.7	30.3	36.1	32.4	18.0	33,024	59.1	45.8	2.9	10.4	40.9	33.4	41.7
0937000	Hartford city, Connecticut...........	19.6	49.9	46.1	21.3	12.2	45,491	60.2	22.2	9.8	28.2	39.8	34.6	33.2
0950370	New Britain city, Connecticut	21.7	43.6	56.6	15.8	6.1	28,450	59.3	29.4	4.3	25.6	40.7	33.0	38.0
0952000	New Haven city, Connecticut	12.6	30.5	46.4	19.7	13.4	56,373	49.3	22.2	5.7	21.4	50.7	38.8	30.9
0955990	Norwalk city, Connecticut...........	18.5	30.7	44.0	27.9	13.7	36,847	59.8	45.9	2.5	11.4	40.2	31.8	40.2
0973000	Stamford city, Connecticut..........	18.2	28.0	37.8	31.4	16.3	52,816	60.9	43.2	5.1	12.7	39.1	27.7	36.5
0980000	Waterbury city, Connecticut........	20.4	37.7	51.4	21.8	8.3	45,008	63.6	30.9	6.9	25.8	36.4	30.7	43.0
10000	**DELAWARE**	9.4	10.1	44.0	10.1	5.1	395,656	64.8	47.1	4.8	12.9	35.2	29.0	47.5
1077580	Wilmington city, Delaware	8.7	10.2	51.7	6.7	3.4	32,049	47.2	25.0	5.4	16.8	52.8	46.0	42.5
11000	**DISTRICT OF COLUMBIA**	9.6	11.5	37.2	13.3	6.2	319,565	40.3	24.2	3.1	13.0	59.7	48.2	30.2
1150000	Washington city, District of Columbia..................	9.6	11.5	35.0	13.3	6.6	319,565	40.3	24.2	3.1	13.0	59.7	48.2	30.2
12000	**FLORIDA**.................................	19.1	26.8	35.8	21.2	9.0	8,565,329	64.3	46.4	5.0	12.9	35.7	28.4	47.8
1200410	Alafaya CDP, Florida....................	31.5	40.3	33.7	18.4	6.9	32,823	67.1	50.5	3.2	13.4	32.9	20.6	28.9
1207300	Boca Raton city, Florida..............	11.3	14.2	24.8	21.2	6.8	41,318	58.4	45.1	3.7	9.6	41.6	33.2	49.4
1207875	Boynton Beach city, Florida	16.0	19.6	32.1	28.9	10.3	33,201	56.2	37.4	5.3	13.6	43.8	35.9	48.6
1208150	Brandon CDP, Florida...................	19.9	32.3	38.6	16.6	6.1	46,925	63.0	41.3	6.8	14.9	37.0	31.6	30.4
1210275	Cape Coral city, Florida	21.1	29.0	25.4	19.1	3.9	79,845	67.9	53.5	4.6	9.7	32.1	26.0	55.5
1212875	Clearwater city, Florida...............	13.5	16.7	28.4	17.2	6.2	49,486	54.0	39.0	4.1	11.0	46.0	36.2	51.1
1214400	Coral Springs city, Florida............	26.1	32.0	38.3	32.6	11.0	44,417	77.9	54.6	7.4	15.8	22.1	18.9	39.0
1216475	Davie town, Florida.....................	31.5	43.6	37.9	33.8	13.4	39,061	69.1	51.8	4.7	12.5	30.9	22.2	38.5
1216525	Daytona Beach city, Florida.........	7.5	11.2	36.0	8.2	3.7	34,721	45.6	27.6	5.8	12.2	54.4	38.9	48.7
1216725	Deerfield Beach city, Florida	21.7	25.6	29.6	35.8	14.3	39,934	51.5	34.5	4.3	12.7	48.5	41.0	46.9

Table A-4. Cities — Who: Age, Race/Ethnicity, and Household Structure, 2021—*Continued*

STATE and place code	STATE Place	Total popula-tion	Percent change, 2014–2019	Population by age (percent)					Median age	Race alone or in combination (percent)					
				Under 18 years	18 to 24 years	25 to 44 years	45 to 64 years	65 years and over		White	Black	American Indian and Alaska Native	Asian	Native Hawaiian or Other Pacific Islander	Some other race
	ACS table number:	B01003	Population Estimates	B01001	B01001	B01001	B01001	B01001	B01002	B02008	B02009	B02010	B02011	B02012	B02013
FIPS	column number:	1	2	3	4	5	6	7	8	9	10	11	12	13	14
	FLORIDA—Cont.														
1217100	Delray Beach city, Florida............	66,579	6.8	16.3	4.7	21.9	27.6	29.5	51.0	69.4	26.2	0.4	4.3	0.0	13.0
1217200	Deltona city, Florida	95,771	6.7	20.3	8.6	28.5	26.6	16.0	39.0	59.6	16.3	1.4	1.7	0.0	32.2
1217935	Doral city, Florida	75,954	21.5	24.2	9.1	32.6	27.2	6.9	36.6	86.0	3.0	0.0	1.8	0.0	48.8
1224000	Fort Lauderdale city, Florida........	181,666	3.6	16.3	7.4	26.2	29.5	20.7	45.1	70.0	28.1	1.4	2.1	0.0	20.2
1224125	Fort Myers city, Florida	92,244	22.8	20.7	5.5	29.5	20.9	23.4	41.0	68.8	25.9	1.8	2.9	0.0	25.2
1225175	Gainesville city, Florida	140,406	4.3	14.5	29.1	29.7	13.7	13.0	27.7	66.7	24.9	1.0	8.3	0.0	10.5
1230000	Hialeah city, Florida.................	220,479	-0.9	18.0	7.9	22.3	31.7	20.2	46.1	85.3	2.4	0.0	0.9	0.0	82.2
1232000	Hollywood city, Florida..............	152,139		21.3	7.0	27.0	25.2	19.6	41.4	74.3	18.3	1.5	2.4	0.6	29.7
1232275	Homestead city, Florida.............	80,523	6.1	27.4	7.9	30.7	23.5	10.5	34.8	64.2	29.2	0.0	2.3	0.0	48.6
1232610	Horizon West CDP, Florida	72,283	85.9	NA	NA	NA	NA	NA	35.4	83.7	11.5	0.0	5.4	0.0	21.4
1235000	Jacksonville city, Florida............	954,624	6.8	22.8	8.5	29.5	24.6	14.6	36.6	59.7	32.8	1.7	6.3	0.2	10.7
1236100	Kendall CDP, Florida.................	81,524	1.6	21.3	5.9	24.3	28.1	20.3	43.4	84.7	9.8	0.0	2.6	0.0	47.0
1236950	Kissimmee city, Florida..............	79,440	8.9	28.4	10.0	29.2	21.2	11.3	33.4	46.2	13.3	0.0	4.2	0.0	56.3
1238250	Lakeland city, Florida................	115,401	9.6	20.1	10.9	24.4	22.3	22.2	40.8	64.6	24.9	2.0	2.9	0.0	15.2
1239425	Largo city, Florida...................	82,333		15.5	6.5	26.6	26.9	24.6	46.3	79.5	12.9	0.9	5.0	0.0	13.4
1239550	Lauderhill city, Florida...............	73,461		22.3	7.8	23.9	27.0	19.0	41.5	9.8	84.5	1.0	2.8	0.0	10.3
1239925	Lehigh Acres CDP, Florida...........	126,557	20.9	27.5	8.5	25.8	22.9	15.3	34.9	71.2	21.3	0.6	1.2	0.3	33.9
1243975	Melbourne city, Florida..............	85,091	5.8	19.2	8.2	26.5	24.5	21.6	42.7	81.4	11.9	1.7	4.5	0.6	13.0
1245000	Miami city, Florida...................	439,906	8.7	15.1	7.4	33.4	26.3	17.8	40.4	75.6	14.6	1.5	1.7	0.0	63.7
1245025	Miami Beach city, Florida............	80,673	-3.1	16.0	5.8	31.3	27.8	19.1	42.7	83.1	5.0	1.0	2.7	0.0	42.1
1245060	Miami Gardens city, Florida	110,881	-2.0	24.2	6.7	27.8	25.9	15.4	38.5	32.3	66.7	0.0	0.0	0.4	27.6
1245975	Miramar city, Florida	135,066	4.6	22.5	6.1	31.9	27.0	12.6	39.8	42.6	47.7	1.4	5.1	0.0	18.2
1249675	North Port city, Florida..............	80,027	17.1	16.7	8.1	17.1	30.5	27.6	50.6	88.6	5.3	0.0	3.3	0.0	7.8
1253000	Orlando city, Florida.................	309,193	9.5	18.6	8.3	37.2	23.4	12.4	35.7	60.3	27.9	0.7	5.1	0.1	32.1
1254000	Palm Bay city, Florida...............	122,932	9.2	23.6	8.0	22.9	25.9	19.6	41.2	71.8	23.1	0.7	4.1	0.0	17.4
1254200	Palm Coast city, Florida.............	93,845	9.0	17.6	6.5	18.7	27.4	29.8	50.8	80.1	13.2	0.8	4.2	0.0	11.1
1255775	Pembroke Pines city, Florida	169,388	5.4	17.1	8.0	25.1	30.6	19.2	44.8	64.1	27.2	1.5	6.8	0.0	29.6
1256825	Pine Hills CDP, Florida...............	85,927	24.7	30.2	9.5	24.1	24.2	11.9	34.2	20.1	72.6	0.9	4.1	0.0	14.1
1257425	Plantation city, Florida..............	92,981	3.4	24.9	5.2	29.6	24.3	16.1	39.6	65.4	25.8	2.9	4.4	0.0	25.8
1257900	Poinciana CDP, Florida...............	65,257	29.9	20.5	12.3	26.0	20.5	20.7	39.9	44.0	30.0	0.0	0.0	0.0	52.0
1258050	Pompano Beach city, Florida........	111,356	5.7	17.4	6.0	29.8	27.7	19.2	41.8	59.0	36.4	0.7	2.4	0.0	20.2
1258350	Port Charlotte CDP, Florida.........	65,671	17.8	13.5	6.6	17.1	29.4	33.3	56.3	87.3	9.4	0.8	2.7	0.0	10.7
1258715	Port St. Lucie city, Florida	217,535	15.9	19.8	7.3	26.2	26.6	20.0	43.1	73.2	22.7	1.6	1.7	0.0	17.2
1260950	Riverview CDP, Florida...............	114,560	19.5	25.4	6.7	31.9	24.9	11.2	35.6	65.9	27.2	1.6	3.9	0.0	19.8
1263000	St. Petersburg city, Florida..........	258,214	4.6	18.3	6.4	29.1	26.0	20.2	41.9	73.6	23.3	1.1	4.2	0.1	8.1
1268350	Spring Hill CDP, Florida..............	123,509	15.0	19.3	7.0	24.5	26.0	23.3	44.5	82.0	9.4	1.1	2.7	0.0	21.3
1269700	Sunrise city, Florida..................	96,031	4.3	22.6	8.2	25.7	25.4	18.1	39.6	52.4	38.2	0.8	6.4	0.0	31.4
1270600	Tallahassee city, Florida.............	197,103	3.4	16.2	26.5	28.3	16.6	12.4	29.6	57.3	38.3	1.9	5.0	0.2	7.2
1270675	Tamarac city, Florida.................	71,522	4.6	21.3	7.2	23.3	26.9	21.3	43.7	50.3	39.6	0.0	4.6	0.0	28.3
1271000	Tampa city, Florida	387,037	11.4	21.0	9.6	32.6	22.7	14.2	35.8	67.7	24.0	1.4	6.0	0.3	20.8
1271625	The Villages CDP, Florida............	80,691	NA	NA	NA	NA	NA	NA	74.1	98.0	0.7	0.9	1.1	0.0	2.0
1272145	Town 'n' Country CDP, Florida.....	87,862	12.1	21.2	6.9	28.3	30.8	12.8	40.7	75.2	11.8	0.7	5.9	0.0	44.7
1275875	Wesley Chapel CDP, Florida........	77,319	26.6	30.2	10.0	25.4	24.1	10.3	34.9	70.5	16.0	2.5	9.4	0.7	18.3
1276582	Weston city, Florida..................	67,322	3.0	29.3	9.3	18.7	31.4	11.4	40.0	77.5	5.5	0.0	13.5	0.0	37.1
1276600	West Palm Beach city, Florida	117,253	7.6	17.5	8.2	28.0	24.9	21.3	42.2	56.5	37.9	0.7	3.5	0.0	21.3
13000	**GEORGIA**..............................	10,799,566	7.6	23.4	9.7	27.0	25.3	14.7	37.5	59.5	33.4	2.4	5.3	0.2	8.7
1301052	Albany city, Georgia.................	67,146	-3.2	24.1	12.2	25.9	22.0	15.9	36.3	25.0	75.9	1.5	0.8	0.0	0.0
1301696	Alpharetta city, Georgia	66,108	6.6	24.6	7.8	23.5	32.2	12.0	40.6	69.6	10.4	2.0	20.6	0.0	9.5
1303440	Athens-Clarke County unified government (balance), Georgia...	126,006	5.7	16.4	26.8	27.2	17.8	11.8	29.0	64.3	26.9	3.0	4.7	0.0	10.3
1304000	Atlanta city, Georgia	496,480	11.1	16.9	13.7	35.5	20.9	13.0	34.3	47.1	47.3	1.7	6.8	0.1	5.5
1304204	Augusta-Richmond County con-solidated government (balance), Georgia	200,032	-0.1	22.9	11.1	28.2	22.6	15.2	35.2	39.9	60.3	1.5	3.2	0.0	5.1
1319000	Columbus city, Georgia..............	205,617	-2.5	24.8	9.6	29.2	22.2	14.1	34.7	45.0	49.9	1.5	3.7	0.7	7.8
1342425	Johns Creek city, Georgia...........	82,078	1.8	28.9	5.3	23.0	31.1	11.7	39.5	58.3	13.7	3.5	26.8	0.0	8.4
1349008	Macon-Bibb County, Georgia......	156,762	-0.3	24.2	10.7	25.8	23.3	16.0	35.7	39.3	57.2	0.8	2.6	0.0	3.8
1367284	Roswell city, Georgia.................	92,532	0.7	26.4	6.3	27.9	27.7	11.7	37.5	77.1	15.7	3.3	6.0	0.0	10.9
1368516	Sandy Springs city, Georgia.........	107,179	7.4	18.2	7.0	33.3	27.1	14.4	37.2	65.6	22.9	2.3	11.2	0.0	7.3

Table A-4. Cities — Who: Age, Race/Ethnicity, and Household Structure, 2021—*Continued*

								Household type (percent of all households)						Percent of house-holds with people age 60 years and over
								Family households				Nonfamily households		
STATE and place code	STATE Place	Two or more races (percent)	Hispanic or Latino (percent)	Native, born in state of residence (percent)	Foreign born (percent)	Non-citizens (percent)	Total house-holds	Total	Married-couple	Male house-holder	Female house-holder	Total	One-person house-holds	
	ACS table number:	B02001	B03003	B05002	B05002	B05002	B11001	B11001	B11001	B11001	B11001	B11001	B11001	B11006
FIPS	column number:	15	16	17	18	19	20	21	22	23	24	25	26	27
	FLORIDA—Cont.													
1217100	Delray Beach city, Florida............	13.4	11.0	28.2	25.3	9.2	30,472	46.7	33.1	4.0	9.6	53.3	40.1	56.1
1217200	Deltona city, Florida....................	9.6	37.8	35.4	13.1	7.0	35,384	72.7	53.9	6.0	12.8	27.3	22.8	42.4
1217935	Doral city, Florida.........................	39.6	84.1	21.2	65.6	37.3	25,419	81.4	60.0	6.3	15.1	18.6	13.4	23.0
1224000	Fort Lauderdale city, Florida.........	19.9	23.5	34.3	26.7	13.7	83,021	49.2	34.6	4.2	10.5	50.8	40.8	42.2
1224125	Fort Myers city, Florida	22.5	25.9	36.1	20.2	10.9	37,323	60.0	39.1	4.0	16.9	40.0	33.9	45.7
1225175	Gainesville city, Florida	10.7	12.2	55.7	10.3	5.9	56,513	37.6	25.0	3.8	8.8	62.4	41.1	29.9
1230000	Hialeah city, Florida....................	70.7	94.6	23.6	71.7	27.5	75,692	74.0	41.9	9.0	23.2	26.0	20.1	53.2
1232000	Hollywood city, Florida................	24.6	44.3	31.7	39.0	14.7	61,598	60.3	44.0	6.7	9.6	39.7	31.7	41.4
1232275	Homestead city, Florida...............	44.7	58.5	43.2	35.9	14.0	27,094	69.8	37.8	12.6	19.3	30.2	28.9	29.3
1232610	Horizon West CDP, Florida	26.9	26.9	27.7	20.6	16.2	21,444	86.6	74.7	3.4	8.4	13.4	10.2	0.0
1235000	Jacksonville city, Florida.............	10.4	11.6	46.9	12.3	5.1	386,283	60.3	39.7	4.9	15.7	39.7	31.7	36.8
1236100	Kendall CDP, Florida....................	43.6	62.6	43.4	38.3	8.7	33,184	65.1	48.0	2.9	14.1	34.9	30.1	46.0
1236950	Kissimmee city, Florida................	19.0	68.2	29.2	34.5	23.7	25,999	74.6	42.0	4.5	28.1	25.4	20.7	35.2
1238250	Lakeland city, Florida..................	8.6	17.7	47.0	9.1	3.9	45,548	61.7	42.0	4.7	15.0	38.3	30.5	46.5
1239425	Largo city, Florida.......................	11.7	12.2	32.0	13.2	4.4	36,493	50.9	35.6	2.8	12.6	49.1	41.7	50.1
1239550	Lauderhill city, Florida.................	7.7	8.8	43.7	39.0	16.9	26,555	67.1	32.6	6.2	28.2	32.9	28.6	46.3
1239925	Lehigh Acres CDP, Florida............	28.1	44.5	36.1	28.5	13.1	40,295	75.4	55.4	5.9	14.1	24.6	19.3	41.3
1243975	Melbourne city, Florida	11.4	13.1	34.5	10.8	5.1	36,651	54.3	38.1	4.0	12.2	45.7	37.9	45.4
1245000	Miami city, Florida......................	56.4	71.8	25.4	57.5	27.1	192,219	51.2	31.3	6.0	13.8	48.8	38.2	39.4
1245025	Miami Beach city, Florida.............	33.1	50.0	22.4	52.9	23.7	40,788	40.8	31.7	3.3	5.8	59.2	48.7	36.7
1245060	Miami Gardens city, Florida.........	27.2	35.6	47.9	39.1	10.5	34,332	74.4	42.7	8.0	23.8	25.6	22.2	50.8
1245975	Miramar city, Florida....................	14.1	36.8	46.5	38.6	10.6	42,707	74.7	47.4	7.7	19.5	25.3	14.3	42.9
1249675	North Port city, Florida................	5.2	7.6	25.2	11.5	1.7	30,622	73.0	57.0	4.6	11.4	27.0	21.4	60.0
1253000	Orlando city, Florida....................	25.4	34.5	34.0	22.0	13.2	130,037	54.0	33.2	6.0	14.8	46.0	33.5	28.8
1254000	Palm Bay city, Florida..................	16.8	19.7	33.9	14.4	4.1	45,145	70.3	42.3	8.6	19.3	29.7	25.9	48.2
1254200	Palm Coast city, Florida...............	9.3	12.5	28.0	13.3	4.0	36,896	73.6	58.0	5.0	10.7	26.4	20.2	61.2
1255775	Pembroke Pines city, Florida	26.5	45.7	38.9	36.6	9.6	64,378	65.9	46.4	7.1	12.3	34.1	23.7	48.6
1256825	Pine Hills CDP, Florida.................	9.7	21.2	48.0	30.5	17.8	25,752	80.6	34.5	9.9	36.1	19.4	13.9	39.5
1257425	Plantation city, Florida.................	23.3	27.9	41.3	25.1	10.3	36,564	65.3	45.0	5.6	14.7	34.7	27.1	38.4
1257900	Poinciana CDP, Florida.................	26.8	54.2	19.3	26.9	9.9	21,402	74.4	49.6	6.8	18.0	25.6	21.1	54.2
1258050	Pompano Beach city, Florida........	18.2	18.4	35.1	30.7	15.6	48,363	53.1	32.0	7.7	13.4	46.9	37.6	45.5
1258350	Port Charlotte CDP, Florida...........	10.8	11.8	21.3	14.3	8.3	29,120	65.2	52.1	3.7	9.4	34.8	26.2	61.6
1258715	Port St. Lucie city, Florida	15.0	24.9	31.1	22.1	5.8	77,190	73.3	54.9	4.5	13.9	26.7	21.2	51.3
1260950	Riverview CDP, Florida.................	16.7	23.4	31.6	14.4	5.8	40,114	74.3	53.1	5.8	15.3	25.7	19.3	30.6
1263000	St. Petersburg city, Florida...........	9.5	8.4	41.6	10.6	2.9	111,349	50.6	36.1	4.1	10.5	49.4	38.7	43.3
1268350	Spring Hill CDP, Florida................	15.9	20.6	30.3	8.0	1.9	46,360	72.9	51.5	7.0	14.4	27.1	20.5	55.1
1269700	Sunrise city, Florida.....................	26.6	36.9	32.6	39.3	12.6	35,166	69.2	43.3	6.3	19.6	30.8	24.8	42.9
1270600	Tallahassee city, Florida...............	8.9	8.4	59.9	8.3	3.1	84,920	45.2	27.3	5.5	12.4	54.8	33.9	28.9
1270675	Tamarac city, Florida...................	22.6	36.7	30.8	42.9	9.8	29,065	63.1	44.4	5.1	13.5	36.9	33.5	47.7
1271000	Tampa city, Florida	18.9	25.7	42.6	17.7	7.9	159,925	53.2	36.5	4.7	12.0	46.8	36.9	33.0
1271625	The Villages CDP, Florida.............	0.0	1.9	4.2	5.5	0.8	47,527	63.4	61.0	0.2	2.2	36.6	32.3	96.2
1272145	Town 'n' Country CDP, Florida.....	35.9	54.8	28.6	39.3	16.8	35,155	67.0	40.1	5.0	21.9	33.0	24.5	37.1
1275875	Wesley Chapel CDP, Florida.........	15.1	24.9	33.4	15.9	4.7	23,868	76.8	54.7	3.9	18.3	23.2	16.6	30.3
1276582	Weston city, Florida....................	33.3	45.5	26.0	51.7	23.0	20,227	88.9	68.1	4.3	16.4	11.1	9.8	38.8
1276600	West Palm Beach city, Florida	19.2	24.6	35.2	29.2	13.6	50,409	54.0	32.6	7.8	13.5	46.0	38.7	42.7
13000	**GEORGIA**..............................	8.8	10.0	54.4	10.0	5.5	4,001,109	66.9	47.0	4.8	15.0	33.1	26.8	38.2
1301052	Albany city, Georgia....................	4.6	2.0	80.8	0.8	0.2	27,357	53.6	24.6	4.3	24.7	46.4	43.2	41.5
1301696	Alpharetta city, Georgia	11.8	11.0	32.0	25.0	10.3	25,457	72.0	60.1	1.9	10.1	28.0	22.1	35.0
1303440	Athens-Clarke County unified government (balance), Georgia...	9.1	10.7	53.9	9.8	5.5	54,438	46.4	33.6	3.9	8.9	53.6	32.5	29.1
1304000	Atlanta city, Georgia	7.7	5.8	46.6	8.4	4.7	232,720	40.6	25.6	3.0	11.9	59.4	44.5	28.4
1304204	Augusta-Richmond County con-solidated government (balance), Georgia	8.5	5.5	61.0	3.3	0.9	72,760	58.3	31.6	3.7	23.0	41.7	35.2	42.2
1319000	Columbus city, Georgia...............	7.9	8.2	56.1	4.8	2.2	82,663	62.5	35.0	6.2	21.3	37.5	32.6	35.0
1342425	Johns Creek city, Georgia............	10.3	8.5	24.1	29.0	12.6	29,256	80.5	70.6	3.5	6.4	19.5	17.5	33.0
1349008	Macon-Bibb County, Georgia......	3.6	3.9	75.1	2.8	1.3	57,677	59.1	33.7	4.1	21.3	40.9	34.8	41.1
1367284	Roswell city, Georgia...................	12.3	15.3	32.1	18.0	10.5	37,044	66.6	54.7	3.0	8.9	33.4	22.8	29.5
1368516	Sandy Springs city, Georgia.........	8.6	7.1	29.8	16.9	10.1	52,487	53.1	42.4	1.5	9.3	46.9	36.9	28.1

STATE and place code	STATE Place	Total popula-tion	Percent change, 2014–2019	Under 18 years	18 to 24 years	25 to 44 years	45 to 64 years	65 years and over	Median age	White	Black	American Indian and Alaska Native	Asian	Native Hawaiian or Other Pacific Islander	Some other race
				Population by age (percent)						Race alone or in combination (percent)					
	ACS table number:	B01003	Population Estimates	B01001	B01001	B01001	B01001	B01001	B01002	B02008	B02009	B02010	B02011	B02012	B02013
FIPS	column number:	1	2	3	4	5	6	7	8	9	10	11	12	13	14
	GEORGIA—Cont.														
1369000	Savannah city, Georgia..............	147,087	0.1	21.5	14.4	29.8	20.1	14.1	33.1	46.6	51.5	1.7	3.9	0.0	6.8
1372122	South Fulton city, Georgia..........	108,573	NA	28.0	6.2	29.7	25.2	10.8	35.4	5.2	92.5	1.3	1.7	0.0	2.5
1380508	Warner Robins city, Georgia........	82,252	6.0	25.2	10.5	29.2	25.0	10.0	33.5	49.1	43.7	2.0	7.2	0.0	3.5
15000	**HAWAII**	1,441,553	4.9	21.1	8.0	27.0	24.3	19.6	40.2	42.9	3.7	2.8	56.5	26.4	6.0
1571550	Urban Honolulu CDP, Hawaii.......	345,532	-1.5	15.2	8.0	28.5	25.4	22.8	43.7	33.5	3.6	1.9	64.6	19.1	4.0
16000	**IDAHO**	1,900,923	9.5	24.7	9.1	26.3	23.3	16.5	37.3	90.5	1.3	3.2	2.5	0.4	12.0
1608830	Boise City city, Idaho..................	237,457	5.9	21.6	9.4	30.6	24.1	14.3	37.2	89.5	3.2	2.1	6.3	0.5	8.1
1639700	Idaho Falls city, Idaho................	66,895	7.2	25.3	10.1	26.4	21.9	16.3	35.0	89.5	1.0	1.5	2.1	0.0	14.6
1652120	Meridian city, Idaho	125,959	30.1	22.5	7.5	27.4	25.9	16.7	39.7	91.0	1.5	3.7	2.2	0.0	11.0
1656260	Nampa city, Idaho......................	106,186	12.5	24.7	9.5	31.3	20.3	14.2	34.5	87.8	2.0	3.2	0.8	0.0	20.0
17000	**ILLINOIS**	12,671,469	-0.2	22.1	9.0	26.8	25.5	16.6	39.0	71.8	15.2	2.1	6.8	0.1	15.8
1702154	Arlington Heights village, Illinois .	75,579	-3.5	20.2	5.9	25.3	28.8	19.7	43.5	86.0	3.4	0.4	11.6	0.0	6.3
1703012	Aurora city, Illinois.....................	183,491	-0.9	26.0	9.4	27.6	25.6	11.4	36.5	64.4	10.3	3.2	12.5	0.0	40.2
1706587	Bloomington city, Illinois	78,283	25.1	22.5	14.2	28.8	21.9	12.6	34.1	82.2	10.2	1.6	8.6	0.0	6.0
1707133	Bolingbrook village, Illinois.........	74,526	-0.1	20.0	13.4	26.9	28.7	11.1	37.0	50.8	26.5	1.7	15.8	0.0	20.7
1712385	Champaign city, Illinois	89,116	5.2	18.0	29.9	24.3	16.4	11.4	26.2	65.1	19.4	0.4	16.6	0.0	5.6
1714000	Chicago city, Illinois....................	2,696,561	-1.0	20.0	9.2	34.1	22.7	13.8	35.8	49.2	30.3	2.5	8.0	0.2	25.1
1714351	Cicero town, Illinois....................	83,167	-4.2	25.2	14.1	26.2	22.7	11.7	35.7	35.1	4.6	2.8	0.0	0.0	78.6
1718823	Decatur city, Illinois...................	70,676	-4.8	19.8	9.8	24.2	25.1	21.2	42.3	74.1	25.6	4.6	2.2	0.0	3.2
1723074	Elgin city, Illinois.......................	117,850	-4.9	23.1	10.4	26.5	28.2	11.8	36.8	61.1	7.3	3.7	9.7	0.5	40.7
1724582	Evanston city, Illinois..................	77,532	-2.9	17.1	17.0	23.6	23.3	18.9	36.8	69.5	15.3	0.9	12.7	0.0	12.3
1738570	Joliet city, Illinois	152,563	1.5	24.7	11.1	27.5	26.0	10.7	34.9	64.9	16.9	3.0	2.6	0.3	27.5
1751622	Naperville city, Illinois	148,863	2.9	24.9	6.6	24.1	30.2	14.2	40.9	71.9	6.3	0.6	22.0	0.0	6.1
1757225	Palatine village, Illinois	66,272	-2.8	24.3	5.6	26.7	28.2	15.2	38.1	66.2	8.2	0.0	19.7	0.6	10.5
1759000	Peoria city, Illinois......................	110,915	-6.3	23.6	10.5	25.0	23.0	17.9	37.5	66.9	29.7	3.6	6.5	0.0	6.3
1765000	Rockford city, Illinois..................	148,539	-3.5	25.2	8.1	27.1	22.1	17.5	36.5	65.9	25.3	2.7	3.5	0.0	18.0
1768003	Schaumburg village, Illinois........	75,913	-3.2	24.6	6.7	28.1	25.4	15.2	39.2	65.8	4.4	1.0	26.4	0.0	14.7
1770122	Skokie village, Illinois.................	66,410		22.3	6.1	23.1	27.9	20.6	43.7	60.7	8.4	1.3	27.9	0.0	10.1
1772000	Springfield city, Illinois...............	114,340	-2.1	21.9	8.1	26.2	25.6	18.3	39.7	76.7	21.0	1.8	4.1	0.0	3.4
1779293	Waukegan city, Illinois................	85,791	-3.1	19.6	11.6	30.3	26.4	12.1	36.3	52.6	18.9	6.9	8.4	0.0	49.9
18000	**INDIANA**	6,805,985	2.8	23.3	9.7	25.8	24.8	16.4	38.2	85.0	10.8	2.0	3.0	0.1	6.9
1805860	Bloomington city, Indiana...........	78,988	3.8	10.4	42.5	22.5	14.3	10.2	23.8						
1810342	Carmel city, Indiana	100,780	17.1	22.1	7.8	24.0	28.1	18.0	41.6	83.6	2.5	1.5	13.7	0.0	6.7
1822000	Evansville city, Indiana................	117,273	-3.1	21.4	10.4	26.5	24.2	17.4	38.8	84.1	13.8	3.7	1.6	0.4	4.0
1823278	Fishers city, Indiana	103,081	13.3	28.2	9.5	27.2	25.7	9.4	35.9	90.7	3.5	1.2	7.4	0.0	3.6
1825000	Fort Wayne city, Indiana..............	263,814	2.7	24.2	10.1	28.0	22.9	14.8	34.9	76.1	16.0	2.8	6.6	0.0	9.6
1831000	Hammond city, Indiana	76,991	-3.7	20.7	10.1	29.7	26.3	13.3	37.4	49.6	24.0	2.4	1.4	0.0	36.2
1836003	Indianapolis city (balance), Indi-ana.	882,327	2.2	24.6	9.4	30.2	22.9	12.9	34.5	60.9	31.5	1.6	5.1	0.2	9.9
1840788	Lafayette city, Indiana	72,041	8.4	23.8	11.4	29.8	19.8	15.1	33.9	85.0	9.4	2.6	2.7	0.0	9.6
1854180	Noblesville city, Indiana	71,810	6.1	26.0	9.6	29.9	22.6	12.0	35.8	81.5	14.2	1.0	4.8	0.0	4.3
1871000	South Bend city, Indiana..............	104,523	-0.4	25.0	10.1	25.5	22.3	17.0	36.7	68.9	28.6	1.4	2.9	0.2	14.7
19000	**IOWA**......................................	3,193,079	3.2	23.1	10.0	25.0	24.1	17.8	38.5	90.9	5.1	1.8	3.1	0.3	6.0
1901855	Ames city, Iowa..........................	66,422	4.7	11.5	43.6	18.9	13.3	12.7	22.8	88.3	3.6	2.8	9.2	0.0	3.4
1902305	Ankeny city, Iowa.......................	70,289	25.2	27.0	8.4	29.2	24.6	10.8	36.7	93.1	1.5	0.0	5.2	0.0	5.4
1912000	Cedar Rapids city, Iowa...............	136,464	3.4	20.8	12.4	27.3	23.8	15.7	36.6	85.7	12.7	1.2	3.6	0.0	4.9
1919000	Davenport city, Iowa...................	101,010	-0.8	19.9	9.8	27.7	23.3	19.2	39.2	87.7	13.4	2.6	1.8	0.0	6.3
1921000	Des Moines city, Iowa..................	212,333	2.5	22.4	10.8	30.1	23.8	13.0	35.1	77.1	12.0	1.3	8.8	0.2	11.9
1938595	Iowa City city, Iowa....................	74,582	2.3	15.9	29.4	24.1	19.2	11.4	28.2	82.7	11.4	1.7	8.8	0.0	4.2
1973335	Sioux City city, Iowa...................	86,369	2.3	25.9	10.0	25.5	23.4	15.3	37.0	84.2	9.1	3.8	4.2	0.0	19.1
1982425	Waterloo city, Iowa	66,934	-1.5	24.1	8.3	26.2	21.0	20.4	37.8	75.6	18.9	2.9	4.1	0.0	6.9
1983910	West Des Moines city, Iowa.........	69,951	5.3	17.5	9.8	32.9	21.3	18.5	37.6	89.2	6.9	2.1	5.2	0.0	5.5
20000	**KANSAS**	2,934,582	2.1	23.9	9.9	25.7	23.7	16.7	37.3	86.1	7.5	3.1	3.8	0.2	10.5
2036000	Kansas City city, Kansas	154,804	3.0	27.5	9.2	27.7	22.3	13.3	34.7	55.0	24.3	3.3	6.3	0.0	26.9
2038900	Lawrence city, Kansas	95,251	7.6	16.0	23.7	29.3	19.2	11.8	31.3	87.6	7.6	4.3	6.7	0.0	5.6
2052575	Olathe city, Kansas.....................	143,006	5.6	24.0	9.0	26.4	26.9	13.6	39.5	85.2	8.6	1.4	5.1	0.1	10.7

STATE and place code	STATE Place	Two or more races (percent)	Hispanic or Latino (percent)	Native, born in state of residence (percent)	Foreign born (percent)	Non-citizens (percent)	Total house-holds	Family households				Nonfamily households		Percent of house-holds with people age 60 years and over
								Total	Married-couple	Male house-holder	Female house-holder	Total	One-person house-holds	
	ACS table number:	B02001	B03003	B05002	B05002	B05002	B11001	B11001	B11001	B11001	B11001	B11001	B11001	B11006
FIPS	column number:	15	16	17	18	19	20	21	22	23	24	25	26	27
	GEORGIA—Cont.													
1369000	Savannah city, Georgia................	10.2	8.7	53.9	5.9	2.5	59,612	56.2	31.5	5.5	19.2	43.8	33.0	37.3
1372122	South Fulton city, Georgia...........	0.0	5.3	55.1	8.2	3.7	41,405	65.0	34.9	6.1	24.0	35.0	28.5	34.9
1380508	Warner Robins city, Georgia........	5.5	9.0	56.2	9.3	6.8	30,701	67.1	37.5	11.9	17.8	32.9	28.0	30.4
15000	**HAWAII**	26.3	11.1	52.3	18.8	7.9	490,080	68.3	50.6	5.4	12.3	31.7	24.6	50.2
1571550	Urban Honolulu CDP, Hawaii.......	19.2	7.2	45.1	26.5	10.9	138,398	56.8	40.4	4.5	11.8	43.2	34.1	49.4
16000	**IDAHO**....................................	9.4	13.3	46.1	6.1	3.3	693,882	68.7	55.6	4.5	8.6	31.3	24.2	41.2
1608830	Boise City city, Idaho..................	8.9	9.5	40.7	8.6	4.1	99,250	59.3	46.4	4.0	8.9	40.7	28.6	33.9
1639700	Idaho Falls city, Idaho.................	8.8	17.6	57.2	4.4	3.3	24,257	62.3	48.6	3.6	10.2	37.7	32.1	38.8
1652120	Meridian city, Idaho....................	8.0	10.6	37.7	6.9	5.0	47,825	69.7	61.5	3.5	4.8	30.3	20.1	37.2
1656260	Nampa city, Idaho.......................	14.1	23.2	43.4	9.9	4.1	37,666	70.3	54.7	5.5	10.1	29.7	18.6	32.0
17000	**ILLINOIS**	11.1	18.0	67.4	14.2	6.4	4,991,641	62.8	46.1	4.8	11.9	37.2	30.6	40.5
1702154	Arlington Heights village, Illinois .	7.6	7.0	64.0	19.9	9.0	31,415	68.1	57.9	2.7	7.4	31.9	27.4	41.9
1703012	Aurora city, Illinois.....................	30.0	43.5	55.5	25.5	14.4	62,379	74.8	50.6	7.8	16.4	25.2	18.0	31.5
1706587	Bloomington city, Illinois	8.5	5.7	69.5	9.8	6.3	33,803	51.6	41.2	1.1	9.4	48.4	37.8	28.9
1707133	Bolingbrook village, Illinois	14.0	22.9	59.9	20.4	9.3	24,600	78.6	56.1	8.8	13.8	21.4	16.9	33.9
1712385	Champaign city, Illinois	7.2	5.1	65.4	14.6	10.6	37,423	47.3	31.0	1.5	14.8	52.7	37.0	27.0
1714000	Chicago city, Illinois...................	14.2	28.8	59.0	20.4	10.3	1,139,537	50.9	32.0	4.8	14.1	49.1	39.2	33.4
1714351	Cicero town, Illinois	21.8	85.9	50.8	42.8	27.2	24,737	72.9	43.5	10.0	19.4	27.1	20.6	37.9
1718823	Decatur city, Illinois...................	9.2	3.2	77.4	3.2	2.4	32,087	51.8	34.8	3.7	13.3	48.2	42.0	46.1
1723074	Elgin city, Illinois.......................	21.4	45.1	58.1	27.3	13.4	40,585	72.1	54.1	7.8	10.3	27.9	20.6	38.2
1724582	Evanston city, Illinois..................	10.1	13.5	49.7	14.5	8.8	31,157	54.8	42.7	2.4	9.7	45.2	33.7	41.5
1738570	Joliet city, Illinois	13.7	33.2	71.6	15.4	7.1	51,263	68.3	46.5	6.8	14.9	31.7	24.4	31.8
1751622	Naperville city, Illinois................	6.9	5.9	54.8	21.0	8.0	54,377	74.0	62.0	3.7	8.3	26.0	21.1	37.3
1757225	Palatine village, Illinois...............	5.3	13.5	62.3	24.7	10.3	26,402	67.9	50.7	2.0	15.2	32.1	25.8	36.5
1759000	Peoria city, Illinois.....................	11.1	6.6	67.7	12.7	8.2	50,176	55.0	35.9	4.3	14.9	45.0	38.7	37.6
1765000	Rockford city, Illinois..................	14.8	21.9	69.8	10.7	5.2	59,909	56.8	34.4	6.5	15.8	43.2	35.4	41.1
1768003	Schaumburg village, Illinois	11.8	14.4	55.1	30.1	12.9	31,569	60.9	49.7	2.4	8.9	39.1	32.9	36.3
1770122	Skokie village, Illinois	8.4	12.2	52.5	33.8	7.1	23,599	70.7	55.6	6.4	8.6	29.3	24.1	49.7
1772000	Springfield city, Illinois...............	6.5	2.6	79.7	5.1	2.5	51,317	50.6	32.7	5.1	12.8	49.4	42.8	41.0
1779293	Waukegan city, Illinois................	34.8	58.4	49.6	34.3	22.4	30,068	67.6	42.2	9.6	15.8	32.4	27.8	34.2
18000	**INDIANA**	7.4	7.6	67.7	5.6	3.1	2,680,694	64.1	48.0	4.9	11.2	35.9	29.1	40.0
1805860	Bloomington city, Indiana............			52.7	11.7	8.5	31,711	34.9	24.4	3.4	7.1	65.1	46.7	25.4
1810342	Carmel city, Indiana....................	7.6	5.8	48.7	14.7	5.2	39,994	67.7	62.3	1.7	3.7	32.3	25.9	40.3
1822000	Evansville city, Indiana................	7.3	3.6	69.8	3.3	2.2	53,896	51.6	31.8	5.5	14.3	48.4	41.2	39.7
1823278	Fishers city, Indiana....................	6.1	3.7	58.8	7.4	4.8	35,466	78.1	70.8	3.7	3.6	21.9	18.8	24.3
1825000	Fort Wayne city, Indiana.............	10.7	10.2	63.5	9.2	5.0	109,640	59.0	40.4	4.7	13.8	41.0	32.6	35.7
1831000	Hammond city, Indiana	13.4	42.6	42.8	10.0	5.7	30,737	63.4	35.2	8.3	19.9	36.6	30.9	36.7
1836003	Indianapolis city (balance), Indi-ana.	8.6	11.2	65.4	10.9	7.7	358,150	56.3	37.2	4.1	15.0	43.7	34.4	34.1
1840788	Lafayette city, Indiana	7.9	12.0	67.7	5.8	2.7	31,585	53.6	37.1	4.3	12.2	46.4	38.8	33.3
1854180	Noblesville city, Indiana	5.8	4.8	61.0	11.4	8.8	25,035	79.3	56.8	7.9	14.6	20.7	18.7	33.7
1871000	South Bend city, Indiana..............	15.6	16.6	59.6	8.5	5.4	42,707	57.2	35.8	6.1	15.3	42.8	34.8	42.5
19000	**IOWA**.....................................	6.8	6.6	69.7	5.4	3.0	1,300,467	62.1	49.1	4.2	8.8	37.9	30.2	41.0
1901855	Ames city, Iowa..........................	7.1	4.1	57.4	7.9	5.1	25,901	36.0	30.7	0.5	4.8	64.0	38.2	29.1
1902305	Ankeny city, Iowa.......................	5.1	5.5	66.5	6.0	3.6	27,720	68.1	56.3	2.2	9.7	31.9	24.3	28.3
1912000	Cedar Rapids city, Iowa..............	8.2	5.6	71.5	7.0	4.0	59,107	55.1	38.9	5.1	11.1	44.9	36.3	36.9
1919000	Davenport city, Iowa	11.7	8.9	58.0	3.4	1.5	44,958	53.5	36.7	4.2	12.6	46.5	36.4	39.8
1921000	Des Moines city, Iowa	10.7	15.1	64.8	13.6	7.1	90,416	54.4	37.2	6.1	11.1	45.6	36.5	35.8
1938595	Iowa City city, Iowa....................	8.2	5.5	52.6	11.0	5.3	30,270	45.3	37.6	1.1	6.6	54.7	34.3	27.3
1973335	Sioux City city, Iowa...................	20.4	22.1	59.4	14.4	7.2	33,659	66.7	47.3	6.6	12.9	33.3	25.6	39.2
1982425	Waterloo city, Iowa	6.6	6.9	70.7	9.6	3.8	29,948	53.5	39.4	4.4	9.7	46.5	38.3	40.0
1983910	West Des Moines city, Iowa........	8.7	4.4	65.5	6.9	2.8	36,066	43.7	35.0	3.8	5.0	56.3	45.1	34.2
20000	**KANSAS**	10.6	12.7	59.2	6.9	4.2	1,159,026	63.9	49.5	4.7	9.7	36.1	30.0	39.7
2036000	Kansas City city, Kansas	15.3	32.4	52.1	18.0	12.1	57,819	63.6	41.1	6.6	15.9	36.4	29.4	37.3
2038900	Lawrence city, Kansas.................	11.4	7.0	48.8	6.5	4.4	41,041	44.6	32.3	3.4	8.9	55.4	45.8	27.3
2052575	Olathe city, Kansas.....................	10.6	10.8	42.3	9.6	3.8	53,285	74.3	62.4	4.2	7.7	25.7	20.1	33.5

STATE and place code	STATE Place	Total population	Percent change, 2014–2019	Population by age (percent)					Median age	Race alone or in combination (percent)					
				Under 18 years	18 to 24 years	25 to 44 years	45 to 64 years	65 years and over		White	Black	American Indian and Alaska Native	Asian	Native Hawaiian or Other Pacific Islander	Some other race
	ACS table number:	B01003	Population Estimates	B01001	B01001	B01001	B01001	B01001	B01002	B02008	B02009	B02010	B02011	B02012	B02013
FIPS	column number:	1	2	3	4	5	6	7	8	9	10	11	12	13	14
	KANSAS—Cont.														
2053775	Overland Park city, Kansas..........	197,113	5.9	23.1	7.9	30.4	22.6	16.1	37.1	83.0	6.2	0.5	10.9	0.0	7.5
2064500	Shawnee city, Kansas..................	67,521	1.8	23.4	7.4	26.0	27.1	16.1	38.4	85.8	9.5	1.6	4.7	0.0	7.7
2071000	Topeka city, Kansas.....................	125,969	-1.5	21.8	9.2	26.6	22.7	19.8	37.8	80.7	13.2	3.7	3.0	0.0	12.5
2079000	Wichita city, Kansas	395,707	0.4	24.4	9.8	27.5	22.4	15.8	35.6	77.2	13.3	3.8	5.9	0.1	15.2
21000	**KENTUCKY**	4,509,394	2.6	22.5	9.2	25.6	25.6	17.0	39.1	89.3	9.0	2.3	2.1	0.2	3.9
2108902	Bowling Green city, Kentucky........	73,513	12.9	22.1	22.2	28.4	17.5	9.8	28.5	75.3	12.1	2.3	9.3	0.0	6.6
2146027	Lexington-Fayette urban county, Kentucky	321,793	4.0	20.7	14.0	28.0	22.9	14.3	35.3	79.0	15.1	3.1	5.2	0.0	7.2
2148006	Louisville/Jefferson County metro government (balance), Kentucky.	628,577	0.8	22.3	9.1	27.6	25.0	16.0	37.9	72.6	25.7	3.2	4.3	0.2	6.5
22000	**LOUISIANA**	4,624,047	3.3	23.4	9.2	26.7	24.2	16.6	38.0	63.9	33.2	2.2	2.3	0.1	5.6
2205000	Baton Rouge city, Louisiana........	222,177	-3.8	21.9	16.6	27.5	19.9	14.1	31.6	39.9	53.9	1.2	5.2	0.0	5.1
2239475	Kenner city, Louisiana	65,376	-1.0	25.9	6.7	24.8	23.8	18.8	38.4	67.7	21.2	0.0	2.6	0.0	27.6
2240735	Lafayette city, Louisiana	121,763	0.1	21.3	11.9	29.4	21.6	15.7	36.2	64.5	32.2	1.2	3.2	0.0	8.3
2241155	Lake Charles city, Louisiana........	81,102	4.7	21.2	10.8	26.8	24.7	16.5	37.5	53.2	41.7	0.5	3.1	0.0	9.3
2250115	Metairie CDP, Louisiana...............	144,999	-9.6	20.8	6.9	28.5	22.6	21.3	40.0	80.4	13.9	2.7	4.4	0.0	13.4
2255000	New Orleans city, Louisiana........	376,971	1.5	19.8	8.2	30.9	24.5	16.6	38.3	37.1	59.6	1.7	3.6	0.1	5.3
2270000	Shreveport city, Louisiana............	183,489	-5.6	24.6	8.3	26.3	23.1	17.7	38.3	38.7	59.5	0.9	1.8	0.0	2.8
23000	**MAINE**	1,372,247	0.6	18.2	7.8	24.3	28.0	21.7	44.7	95.9	2.2	1.7	1.9	0.1	3.9
2360545	Portland city, Maine	68,329	-0.7	16.3	6.0	38.6	22.4	16.8	37.8	82.1	11.7	0.6	6.6	0.0	3.1
24000	**MARYLAND**	6,165,129	4.8	22.1	8.6	26.7	26.3	16.3	39.3	55.8	32.3	1.7	8.0	0.2	10.8
2404000	Baltimore city, Maryland.............	576,498	-4.7	20.3	9.3	32.1	23.5	14.8	36.1	32.3	63.2	1.8	3.5	0.2	5.8
2407125	Bethesda CDP, Maryland..............	68,014	-1.7	21.9	7.2	23.0	28.3	19.6	43.9	81.3	4.7	1.2	16.1	0.0	11.0
2419125	Columbia CDP, Maryland..............	104,043	7.2	21.5	8.0	31.3	22.0	17.2	37.9	58.0	31.3	0.5	13.7	0.0	6.0
2426000	Ellicott City CDP, Maryland..........	76,286	0.4	25.9	7.8	21.8	26.9	17.7	42.4	53.9	8.7	0.9	34.6	0.0	7.9
2430325	Frederick city, Maryland	79,588	5.6	22.3	8.1	27.3	26.2	16.1	37.9	72.2	17.4	2.7	6.9	0.0	14.3
2431175	Gaithersburg city, Maryland........	69,109	1.8	22.6	8.6	32.5	24.2	12.1	35.9	39.9	20.6	1.5	22.1	0.0	26.3
2432025	Germantown CDP, Maryland.......	85,247	-1.5	24.0	9.3	29.1	26.7	11.0	37.0	32.6	32.4	1.8	24.1	0.0	20.0
2432650	Glen Burnie CDP, Maryland..........	71,019	7.2	24.3	6.7	28.7	26.9	13.4	36.6	59.5	26.0	3.0	8.6	0.0	13.6
2467675	Rockville city, Maryland...............	67,133	3.3	22.1	5.3	30.5	23.8	18.2	39.7	52.1	11.8	1.9	24.4	0.0	19.2
2472450	Silver Spring CDP, Maryland	80,265	7.1	23.8	9.7	32.4	20.6	13.5	35.9	43.7	38.8	1.7	11.3	0.0	16.7
2481175	Waldorf CDP, Maryland................	80,123	12.4	22.0	8.3	28.4	30.1	11.3	39.0	27.2	67.2	3.9	6.4	0.0	5.1
25000	**MASSACHUSETTS**	6,984,723	4.8	19.5	9.9	26.9	26.3	17.4	39.9	78.7	10.1	1.1	8.3	0.1	14.2
2507000	Boston city, Massachusetts..........	654,281	5.8	15.4	15.1	36.3	20.5	12.7	33.0	58.0	28.8	1.5	11.0	0.1	21.3
2509000	Brockton city, Massachusetts.......	105,455	1.0	25.2	9.8	25.5	23.3	16.3	36.6	39.3	49.4	0.5	2.1	0.0	31.0
2511000	Cambridge city, Massachusetts ...	117,097	8.4	10.8	21.4	41.8	14.6	11.4	30.6	66.3	11.8	0.7	24.6	0.0	7.8
2523000	Fall River city, Massachusetts.......	93,883	0.9	21.8	8.5	25.6	28.1	15.9	39.1	78.7	14.8	0.8	3.1	0.0	20.2
2524960	Framingham city, Massachusetts.	71,260	5.2	25.0	8.6	31.0	23.2	12.1	36.6	68.8	8.9	0.8	11.9	0.0	28.0
2529405	Haverhill city, Massachusetts.......	67,356	2.4	23.7	8.4	26.3	28.1	13.5	37.0	84.8	8.6	1.2	4.6	0.0	21.6
2534550	Lawrence city, Massachusetts.......	88,511	2.4	27.1	11.9	29.0	21.3	10.6	31.0	42.6	8.3	1.7	0.0	0.0	75.5
2537000	Lowell city, Massachusetts...........	114,005	1.0	21.3	12.3	26.5	26.1	13.7	36.3	65.5	11.1	1.0	19.1	0.0	11.0
2537490	Lynn city, Massachusetts	100,831	2.3	23.3	8.9	28.8	25.2	13.8	37.8	54.6	18.1	2.0	5.2	0.0	37.4
2537875	Malden city, Massachusetts........	65,057	-0.6	18.3	8.1	38.1	22.8	12.7	36.4	48.8	20.2	0.5	29.7	0.0	17.8
2545000	New Bedford city, Massachusetts	100,947	0.5	22.5	9.5	26.9	24.4	16.7	38.5	68.0	12.8	2.7	3.2	0.0	35.1
2545560	Newton city, Massachusetts	87,455	0.1	22.0	13.3	22.8	25.1	16.8	39.2	78.0	4.3	0.5	20.3	0.0	8.8
2555745	Quincy city, Massachusetts..........	101,131	1.2	15.6	7.9	35.6	25.4	15.5	37.6	61.2	9.3	0.9	28.7	0.0	8.6
2562535	Somerville city, Massachusetts.....	79,819	3.1	9.7	13.6	45.6	18.6	12.6	33.2	74.5	6.5	1.2	15.4	0.0	16.4
2567000	Springfield city, Massachusetts....	154,788	-0.3	24.8	13.0	26.7	22.3	13.2	33.3	62.3	27.0	2.2	2.3	0.0	39.4
2582000	Worcester city, Massachusetts.....	205,917	1.3	19.2	16.0	29.7	22.6	12.6	33.6	67.8	19.6	1.7	6.8	0.2	24.7
26000	**MICHIGAN**	10,050,811	0.8	21.4	9.2	25.2	26.1	18.1	40.2	80.6	15.4	1.8	4.1	0.1	5.5
2603000	Ann Arbor city, Michigan	121,541	1.9	12.9	29.9	28.4	15.2	13.5	28.2	76.9	8.3	1.3	17.8	0.0	2.9
2621000	Dearborn city, Michigan..............	108,419	-1.7	27.8	10.1	27.0	23.3	11.8	32.6	92.2	4.5	0.7	3.9	0.0	4.9
2622000	Detroit city, Michigan..................	632,589	-1.5	24.9	8.8	27.6	23.8	14.8	35.3	15.8	79.7	1.5	1.8	0.1	7.4
2627440	Farmington Hills city, Michigan....	83,289	-1.0	18.2	8.0	29.9	25.5	18.5	40.5	68.1	19.5	0.5	13.3	0.0	2.5
2629000	Flint city, Michigan......................	80,628	-3.5	24.3	9.4	26.7	26.5	13.0	36.9	41.1	60.3	2.2	0.9	0.0	2.8
2634000	Grand Rapids city, Michigan........	197,423	3.7	21.3	11.8	33.9	20.2	12.7	32.8	70.4	24.1	1.4	4.7	0.0	13.4

Table A-4. Cities — Who: Age, Race/Ethnicity, and Household Structure, 2021—*Continued*

STATE and place code	STATE Place	Two or more races (percent)	Hispanic or Latino (percent)	Native, born in state of residence (percent)	Foreign born (percent)	Non-citizens (percent)	Total households	Family households				Nonfamily households		Percent of households with people age 60 years and over
								Total	Married-couple	Male householder	Female householder	Total	One-person households	
	ACS table number:	B02001	B03003	B05002	B05002	B05002	B11001	B11001	B11001	B11001	B11001	B11001	B11001	B11006
FIPS	column number:	15	16	17	18	19	20	21	22	23	24	25	26	27
	KANSAS—Cont.													
2053775	Overland Park city, Kansas...........	7.9	7.6	39.5	12.8	6.1	82,593	62.4	51.3	4.1	7.0	37.6	29.0	34.9
2064500	Shawnee city, Kansas..................	9.0	8.6	49.5	5.5	2.6	27,114	67.4	55.8	4.3	7.3	32.6	25.7	37.6
2071000	Topeka city, Kansas....................	12.3	17.7	65.8	5.6	3.7	55,844	52.2	35.0	5.1	12.2	47.8	41.0	43.5
2079000	Wichita city, Kansas...................	14.3	18.4	61.9	9.3	5.0	156,668	61.4	42.3	6.5	12.6	38.6	33.0	37.6
21000	**KENTUCKY**.............................	6.3	3.9	68.3	4.0	2.5	1,785,682	64.9	47.6	5.1	12.2	35.1	28.5	41.3
2108902	Bowling Green city, Kentucky......	7.2	9.3	55.0	12.2	8.5	28,947	58.6	35.3	5.9	17.4	41.4	33.7	28.1
2146027	Lexington-Fayette urban county, Kentucky.....	9.3	7.5	57.9	9.8	6.2	139,303	53.8	38.6	4.3	10.9	46.2	34.9	33.5
2148006	Louisville/Jefferson County metro government (balance), Kentucky.	11.0	7.1	66.2	9.9	5.8	264,336	59.5	39.5	5.3	14.7	40.5	32.7	38.8
22000	**LOUISIANA**	6.7	5.5	77.6	4.3	2.5	1,783,924	63.8	42.4	5.4	16.0	36.2	30.7	41.5
2205000	Baton Rouge city, Louisiana.........	5.0	3.7	74.6	8.1	4.6	87,440	50.8	27.3	5.2	18.2	49.2	37.7	35.0
2239475	Kenner city, Louisiana	20.0	24.3	68.0	17.5	9.6	25,267	63.8	43.9	6.6	13.2	36.2	32.9	48.3
2240735	Lafayette city, Louisiana	8.8	7.1	80.3	6.3	4.8	51,150	54.4	36.0	3.5	14.9	45.6	36.2	33.4
2241155	Lake Charles city, Louisiana........	7.8	7.8	76.5	9.3	7.9	28,683	62.1	43.1	3.8	15.2	37.9	29.9	41.4
2250115	Metairie CDP, Louisiana..............	14.3	13.5	65.2	14.3	6.5	62,315	64.4	46.3	6.1	12.0	35.6	31.0	44.2
2255000	New Orleans city, Louisiana.........	6.3	5.7	68.9	5.7	2.8	158,827	46.8	27.3	3.8	15.8	53.2	45.1	39.4
2270000	Shreveport city, Louisiana............	3.7	2.9	79.2	1.5	0.9	76,167	59.5	32.4	6.6	20.5	40.5	36.3	40.3
23000	**MAINE**...................................	5.5	1.9	61.6	4.1	1.6	593,626	61.5	48.5	3.9	9.1	38.5	29.9	46.9
2360545	Portland city, Maine	3.9	2.0	43.7	13.1	7.1	32,523	44.0	33.0	2.4	8.5	56.0	40.1	33.0
24000	**MARYLAND**	8.0	11.1	47.4	15.9	7.4	2,355,652	65.8	47.1	4.9	13.8	34.2	27.9	41.5
2404000	Baltimore city, Maryland..............	6.2	6.0	65.8	8.0	3.8	254,370	48.2	23.9	4.4	19.9	51.8	42.4	36.8
2407125	Bethesda CDP, Maryland..............	13.3	9.7	12.3	23.4	12.4	27,748	64.8	55.1	3.2	6.5	35.2	29.3	43.2
2419125	Columbia CDP, Maryland	8.9	6.6	37.7	22.8	7.8	42,050	67.4	47.6	5.2	14.5	32.6	25.1	37.2
2426000	Ellicott City CDP, Maryland..........	5.5	7.3	37.8	28.8	10.4	27,318	81.3	67.4	4.8	9.1	18.7	16.3	45.2
2430325	Frederick city, Maryland	14.8	17.8	46.3	16.2	6.1	33,907	59.9	41.4	5.3	13.2	40.1	32.7	37.2
2431175	Gaithersburg city, Maryland	9.9	25.4	27.9	38.9	21.2	26,764	61.6	46.8	4.7	10.1	38.4	32.0	31.0
2432025	Germantown CDP, Maryland.......	10.3	21.6	30.7	39.9	15.9	30,985	72.6	51.0	4.2	17.4	27.4	24.5	32.9
2432650	Glen Burnie CDP, Maryland........	10.9	14.4	61.1	15.9	8.4	27,700	65.0	45.5	6.4	13.1	35.0	30.2	39.2
2467675	Rockville city, Maryland...............	9.3	20.2	25.6	36.2	18.2	25,537	66.8	54.3	4.7	7.7	33.2	25.8	40.2
2472450	Silver Spring CDP, Maryland	11.2	16.5	19.1	34.8	19.1	33,307	55.3	37.1	4.4	13.8	44.7	37.8	31.1
2481175	Waldorf CDP, Maryland...............	8.3	5.0	36.4	10.5	3.5	29,701	69.1	46.0	5.3	17.8	30.9	25.9	37.7
25000	**MASSACHUSETTS**	11.2	12.8	59.4	17.6	7.8	2,759,018	62.3	46.0	4.5	11.9	37.7	28.5	42.4
2507000	Boston city, Massachusetts..........	17.0	20.5	42.1	27.5	13.0	271,941	44.7	27.4	3.8	13.4	55.3	38.3	31.5
2509000	Brockton city, Massachusetts.......	21.2	10.9	62.1	28.5	9.3	37,554	70.4	35.1	9.8	25.5	29.6	26.9	45.6
2511000	Cambridge city, Massachusetts ...	10.8	7.1	26.5	29.8	18.2	52,487	36.2	29.6	1.0	5.6	63.8	40.5	25.2
2523000	Fall River city, Massachusetts.......	15.7	13.8	57.2	24.4	12.2	40,521	61.7	34.6	7.0	20.1	38.3	31.9	38.1
2524960	Framingham city, Massachusetts.	17.8	19.3	50.2	29.0	17.2	26,320	68.0	54.8	5.3	7.9	32.0	25.1	30.5
2529405	Haverhill city, Massachusetts.......	20.2	24.7	69.8	10.1	3.8	25,293	69.0	45.2	6.2	17.5	31.0	22.4	38.9
2534550	Lawrence city, Massachusetts......	28.1	83.9	39.5	44.7	26.5	30,366	72.1	30.2	10.3	31.6	27.9	23.9	35.1
2537000	Lowell city, Massachusetts...........	7.1	15.6	55.2	27.0	13.0	42,577	61.2	35.7	8.2	17.3	38.8	29.8	42.6
2537490	Lynn city, Massachusetts	15.6	41.0	56.2	33.2	16.1	37,304	65.0	36.9	9.3	18.8	35.0	30.1	41.0
2537875	Malden city, Massachusetts........	14.5	11.9	42.7	41.9	19.9	26,386	59.4	41.9	5.9	11.6	40.6	30.3	31.9
2545000	New Bedford city, Massachusetts	17.8	25.5	61.4	22.5	12.4	42,743	56.8	31.7	9.5	15.7	43.2	36.0	36.0
2545560	Newton city, Massachusetts........	11.7	4.7	43.3	23.4	8.9	29,961	73.5	65.0	2.4	6.1	26.5	19.4	42.3
2555745	Quincy city, Massachusetts..........	8.4	7.4	53.1	31.4	13.7	44,051	53.3	38.2	6.2	8.9	46.7	33.6	36.3
2562535	Somerville city, Massachusetts.....	11.2	15.4	38.3	26.8	14.3	35,015	42.1	32.4	3.2	6.5	57.9	31.5	29.6
2567000	Springfield city, Massachusetts.....	29.6	49.0	55.0	11.1	4.0	57,806	61.8	28.4	6.0	27.4	38.2	30.1	38.7
2582000	Worcester city, Massachusetts.....	18.8	26.6	51.8	22.4	11.1	76,065	59.2	37.9	5.2	16.2	40.8	30.5	34.4
26000	**MICHIGAN**	7.0	5.6	76.2	6.8	3.2	4,051,798	62.9	46.3	5.0	11.6	37.1	30.2	42.9
2603000	Ann Arbor city, Michigan	6.5	4.0	47.7	16.8	8.9	51,238	42.8	33.3	1.9	7.7	57.2	36.1	30.3
2621000	Dearborn city, Michigan..............	5.9	3.7	59.2	28.1	6.4	35,209	71.5	53.9	5.5	12.1	28.5	22.9	39.5
2622000	Detroit city, Michigan..................	5.7	7.7	78.2	5.3	3.0	251,729	52.6	19.2	7.3	26.1	47.4	41.2	40.7
2627440	Farmington Hills city, Michigan....	3.8	2.1	64.9	19.9	8.2	35,224	62.1	52.7	2.2	7.2	37.9	31.9	42.5
2629000	Flint city, Michigan.....................	6.8	4.7	79.9	4.1	1.5	32,837	53.0	23.4	6.5	23.0	47.0	39.4	37.8
2634000	Grand Rapids city, Michigan........	13.1	13.8	70.2	9.7	5.3	79,486	53.4	34.5	5.1	13.8	46.6	33.7	30.4

Table A-4. Cities — Who: Age, Race/Ethnicity, and Household Structure, 2021—*Continued*

STATE and place code	STATE Place	Total population	Percent change, 2014–2019	Population by age (percent)					Median age	Race alone or in combination (percent)					
				Under 18 years	18 to 24 years	25 to 44 years	45 to 64 years	65 years and over		White	Black	American Indian and Alaska Native	Asian	Native Hawaiian or Other Pacific Islander	Some other race
	ACS table number:	B01003	Population Estimates	B01001	B01001	B01001	B01001	B01001	B01002	B02008	B02009	B02010	B02011	B02012	B02013
FIPS	column number:	1	2	3	4	5	6	7	8	9	10	11	12	13	14
	MICHIGAN—Cont.														
2642160	Kalamazoo city, Michigan	73,255	0.4	19.3	28.3	27.5	15.7	9.2	25.8	70.0	24.6	0.9	2.8	0.0	8.8
2646000	Lansing city, Michigan................	111,833	2.7	19.3	14.4	31.1	21.4	13.8	34.5	66.6	30.3	3.4	5.4	0.0	9.0
2649000	Livonia city, Michigan.................	94,407	-1.4	18.0	5.4	24.4	28.9	23.4	47.3	90.9	6.4	1.4	3.9	0.0	2.8
2659440	Novi city, Michigan.....................	66,575	4.3	21.9	7.6	25.8	28.9	15.8	42.6	62.4	10.0	0.2	29.6	0.0	3.6
2669035	Rochester Hills city, Michigan	76,021	1.9	22.9	9.5	26.4	26.3	14.9	38.7	78.7	5.1	1.4	17.0	0.0	6.3
2674900	Southfield city, Michigan.............	75,901	-0.4	18.7	8.3	23.3	24.7	25.0	44.7	32.7	67.8	1.2	2.4	0.0	1.7
2676460	Sterling Heights city, Michigan	133,256	0.5	19.9	7.9	25.3	26.6	20.3	41.6	83.1	7.3	0.6	10.5	0.0	3.2
2680700	Troy city, Michigan	86,837	1.2	20.7	8.8	22.1	28.7	19.7	43.9	67.5	6.6	2.5	28.8	0.0	4.8
2684000	Warren city, Michigan	138,142	-0.9	18.5	6.5	30.4	26.5	18.1	40.9	67.8	22.3	1.7	11.3	0.0	2.6
2686000	Westland city, Michigan.............	84,528	-1.0	18.2	7.9	28.6	28.1	17.3	41.9	74.0	20.7	2.9	4.3	0.0	3.3
2688940	Wyoming city, Michigan.............	76,747	1.1	28.9	8.5	27.9	22.8	11.9	31.8	76.2	12.8	0.0	2.6	0.0	26.1
27000	**MINNESOTA**............................	5,707,390	5.1	22.9	8.8	26.5	25.0	16.8	38.8	84.3	8.5	2.3	6.2	0.1	5.9
2706382	Blaine city, Minnesota	70,953	7.2	28.6	7.1	25.7	25.4	13.1	36.4	78.4	11.6	1.1	10.3	0.0	5.2
2706616	Bloomington city, Minnesota.......	89,308	-1.6	20.0	6.1	26.6	25.3	22.1	42.3	74.8	15.1	1.4	8.1	0.0	9.8
2707966	Brooklyn Park city, Minnesota	84,533	2.1	25.8	5.1	33.5	24.1	11.4	35.5	52.4	31.3	3.0	16.4	0.7	10.3
2717000	Duluth city, Minnesota	86,373	-0.7	17.9	21.4	24.7	20.3	15.7	32.9	93.6	3.5	3.2	2.5	0.0	3.0
2717288	Eagan city, Minnesota	68,646	0.4	24.8	5.8	29.7	26.7	12.9	36.5	76.4	11.6	1.0	11.3	0.0	4.6
2735180	Lakeville city, Minnesota.............	72,805	12.4	27.6	7.6	26.8	27.9	10.0	36.8	82.5	11.6	1.7	7.9	0.0	6.9
2740166	Maple Grove city, Minnesota.......	70,730	8.5	22.5	5.9	27.1	30.2	14.4	40.3	85.6	7.6	1.6	6.2	0.0	3.7
2743000	Minneapolis city, Minnesota........	425,338	5.5	18.3	13.7	36.6	20.6	10.9	33.5	71.8	19.9	2.8	7.3	0.1	9.2
2751730	Plymouth city, Minnesota............	79,833	6.3	24.1	6.4	27.1	27.2	15.2	40.7	78.0	9.7	0.8	12.9	0.0	4.7
2754880	Rochester city, Minnesota	121,471	6.8	23.1	10.4	27.3	23.1	16.1	37.0	80.1	11.4	0.7	8.5	0.0	5.0
2756896	St. Cloud city, Minnesota	69,809	3.9	18.9	19.7	25.2	21.8	14.4	32.6	80.0	14.7	2.5	4.2	0.0	4.7
2758000	St. Paul city, Minnesota	307,176	3.5	24.1	10.3	32.2	20.9	12.5	33.2	60.0	18.9	2.1	20.4	0.2	7.9
2771428	Woodbury city, Minnesota	76,994	9.0	26.0	8.2	29.8	21.9	14.1	36.3	79.0	4.1	0.4	16.6	0.0	4.2
28000	**MISSISSIPPI**.............................	2,949,965	0.5	23.5	9.8	25.1	24.8	16.8	38.6	60.8	37.7	2.3	1.6	0.2	3.1
2829700	Gulfport city, Mississippi............	72,096	-0.1	23.0	9.6	27.8	25.0	14.6	36.7	61.8	38.4	3.3	4.1	0.0	2.5
2836000	Jackson city, Mississippi..............	149,813	-6.2	23.5	11.4	27.7	22.6	14.8	34.0	16.6	83.7	2.0	0.3	0.0	1.1
29000	**MISSOURI**	6,168,187	2.1	22.4	9.0	25.9	25.0	17.6	39.2	84.7	12.4	2.2	2.8	0.3	5.6
2915670	Columbia city, Missouri	126,850	5.4	20.5	22.6	31.2	15.1	10.6	29.4	79.3	14.1	1.1	8.3	0.0	2.9
2935000	Independence city, Missouri	122,083	-0.7	21.3	7.5	22.3	28.9	20.0	43.7	80.3	16.4	2.4	1.3	0.0	10.8
2938000	Kansas City city, Missouri	508,415	5.2	22.3	8.8	32.8	22.3	13.9	35.1	66.6	27.2	2.2	3.8	0.3	9.6
2941348	Lee's Summit city, Missouri..........	102,506	4.9	29.0	6.8	25.2	24.9	14.1	38.0	83.3	12.9	1.1	3.4	0.0	4.0
2954074	O'Fallon city, Missouri	93,651	5.5	25.6	7.9	28.3	26.2	12.0	35.8	90.3	3.6	2.3	5.6	0.0	8.6
2964082	St. Charles city, Missouri	70,832	4.3	18.7	10.7	29.5	22.5	18.6	37.0	87.8	8.2	2.5	4.4	0.0	4.1
2964550	St. Joseph city, Missouri	75,763	-1.9	22.7	9.9	28.1	23.5	15.9	37.6	87.5	8.8	2.6	2.6	0.0	6.3
2965000	St. Louis city, Missouri	293,310	-5.3	18.4	8.5	34.4	23.7	15.0	36.8	50.7	45.4	1.2	4.2	0.0	4.7
2970000	Springfield city, Missouri	169,850	1.5	18.0	18.3	28.4	19.1	16.2	32.8	93.4	3.8	4.1	2.8	0.0	4.4
30000	**MONTANA**	1,104,271	6.2	21.3	9.3	25.4	24.4	19.7	40.1	91.3	1.0	8.3	1.5	0.2	4.3
3006550	Billings city, Montana.................	117,453	0.6	22.8	8.0	27.4	22.8	19.1	37.5	90.2	1.5	6.7	2.2	0.3	6.0
3050200	Missoula city, Montana	74,834	8.2	17.2	15.1	33.2	19.4	15.0	34.7	92.7	0.5	5.2	2.3	0.0	4.8
31000	**NEBRASKA**..............................	1,963,692	5.1	24.6	9.6	26.0	23.4	16.4	37.2	86.8	6.3	2.4	3.4	0.2	10.1
3128000	Lincoln city, Nebraska.................	292,648	5.9	22.0	16.1	26.6	20.7	14.6	33.3	87.7	6.4	2.2	6.0	0.0	6.8
3137000	Omaha city, Nebraska	487,299	7.1	24.0	9.9	28.7	23.2	14.2	35.6	77.0	14.1	2.1	5.1	0.2	12.7
32000	**NEVADA**.................................	3,143,991	11.0	22.2	8.1	28.2	25.1	16.5	38.7	65.7	11.9	3.2	11.3	1.5	25.2
3223770	Enterprise CDP, Nevada...............	245,286	51.8	23.2	8.7	33.2	23.7	11.1	35.7	54.6	15.1	2.1	26.6	3.5	15.7
3231900	Henderson city, Nevada..............	322,202	15.4	23.7	5.6	26.5	25.0	19.3	40.7	73.7	8.1	2.5	12.0	1.4	15.8
3240000	Las Vegas city, Nevada	646,776	6.1	21.5	8.0	27.5	26.7	16.4	39.6	63.5	13.9	3.2	10.0	1.7	29.1
3251800	North Las Vegas city, Nevada.......	274,146	9.2	26.0	9.6	30.7	22.7	11.1	33.7	49.3	26.9	2.3	9.2	2.5	36.2
3254600	Paradise CDP, Nevada	185,849	0.2	19.0	10.1	30.4	26.4	14.1	38.1	56.1	16.4	2.4	12.2	0.8	31.1
3260600	Reno city, Nevada	268,843	7.9	20.7	10.4	30.7	21.7	16.5	36.3	71.9	5.2	2.7	9.3	1.5	24.0
3268400	Sparks city, Nevada	109,788	10.9	21.7	8.0	27.3	26.0	17.1	39.7	79.9	1.5	5.4	9.1	0.5	25.0
3268585	Spring Valley CDP, Nevada	213,552	15.8	20.4	7.2	32.6	24.6	15.1	37.9	54.9	16.0	2.6	26.8	1.8	15.2
3271400	Sunrise Manor CDP, Nevada........	196,147	2.0	26.9	10.5	26.6	24.2	11.8	33.1	48.4	17.7	3.4	6.8	1.4	46.1

STATE and place code	STATE Place	Two or more races (percent)	Hispanic or Latino (percent)	Native, born in state of residence (percent)	Foreign born (percent)	Non-citizens (percent)	Total house-holds	Family households Total	Family households Married-couple	Family households Male house-holder	Family households Female house-holder	Nonfamily households Total	Nonfamily households One-person house-holds	Percent of house-holds with people age 60 years and over
	ACS table number:	B02001	B03003	B05002	B05002	B05002	B11001	B11001	B11001	B11001	B11001	B11001	B11001	B11006
FIPS	column number:	15	16	17	18	19	20	21	22	23	24	25	26	27
	MICHIGAN—Cont.													
2642160	Kalamazoo city, Michigan	7.0	10.4	68.8	6.6	4.3	29,853	37.1	21.9	5.0	10.2	62.9	45.0	23.4
2646000	Lansing city, Michigan.................	12.9	10.1	73.9	9.4	5.1	50,590	48.5	27.4	6.0	15.1	51.5	39.3	32.7
2649000	Livonia city, Michigan..................	5.1	3.6	78.0	7.4	1.9	38,329	65.8	54.4	3.0	8.4	34.2	28.0	50.6
2659440	Novi city, Michigan......................	5.8	3.4	56.7	25.5	15.5	28,217	69.1	55.9	3.8	9.4	30.9	29.1	33.3
2669035	Rochester Hills city, Michigan	7.6	4.6	62.1	21.5	11.4	28,831	68.9	60.3	3.6	5.0	31.1	25.4	37.5
2674900	Southfield city, Michigan..............	5.1	1.6	74.7	5.4	2.7	35,649	53.5	27.8	3.3	22.4	46.5	44.3	49.5
2676460	Sterling Heights city, Michigan	4.7	2.4	59.6	29.3	6.9	51,805	72.3	53.6	7.0	11.8	27.7	24.1	49.0
2680700	Troy city, Michigan......................	9.1	3.5	54.7	29.8	12.7	33,822	71.8	60.2	3.4	8.3	28.2	23.2	43.9
2684000	Warren city, Michigan	4.9	2.5	74.7	13.5	3.2	57,632	60.4	37.2	6.3	16.8	39.6	33.6	44.5
2686000	Westland city, Michigan...............	5.1	5.5	75.7	12.4	6.3	37,870	51.1	33.4	5.2	12.5	48.9	41.9	40.1
2688940	Wyoming city, Michigan...............	18.3	30.2	72.7	13.7	7.9	28,253	62.4	43.0	6.7	12.7	37.6	32.1	34.4
27000	**MINNESOTA**.............................	6.9	5.8	67.7	8.5	3.7	2,281,033	62.6	49.2	4.5	8.9	37.4	29.1	39.7
2706382	Blaine city, Minnesota	6.4	4.6	68.2	14.4	4.7	25,869	71.5	57.4	4.2	9.8	28.5	21.2	36.1
2706616	Bloomington city, Minnesota.......	8.2	9.5	57.4	18.6	9.1	38,725	57.4	42.4	4.1	10.8	42.6	35.0	47.8
2707966	Brooklyn Park city, Minnesota	12.3	11.3	53.5	23.7	9.0	30,074	64.8	44.1	5.3	15.4	35.2	28.4	33.9
2717000	Duluth city, Minnesota................	5.7	2.4	74.8	2.9	1.8	36,310	48.6	35.6	3.2	9.7	51.4	36.4	35.0
2717288	Eagan city, Minnesota.................	4.4	4.5	57.2	14.6	4.8	27,069	66.6	53.6	5.5	7.5	33.4	23.8	35.6
2735180	Lakeville city, Minnesota.............	9.2	6.7	61.5	10.6	2.9	23,868	85.3	71.9	4.6	8.8	14.7	10.2	32.2
2740166	Maple Grove city, Minnesota.......	4.3	3.2	58.8	9.8	3.6	28,026	68.2	61.7	3.1	3.4	31.8	23.1	36.9
2743000	Minneapolis city, Minnesota........	10.2	9.8	52.3	13.7	6.4	188,681	40.7	28.8	5.5	6.4	59.3	41.2	25.3
2751730	Plymouth city, Minnesota	6.0	3.1	56.0	13.7	5.6	32,923	65.7	53.0	2.2	10.5	34.3	28.0	39.3
2754880	Rochester city, Minnesota	5.6	5.4	56.2	12.4	4.1	49,984	58.7	47.2	3.0	8.5	41.3	33.2	33.4
2756896	St. Cloud city, Minnesota	6.0	6.2	66.4	9.9	5.2	30,029	53.4	34.1	7.6	11.8	46.6	32.1	28.5
2758000	St. Paul city, Minnesota...............	8.2	8.5	54.8	18.4	5.8	121,964	53.3	34.8	4.9	13.6	46.7	35.9	32.9
2771428	Woodbury city, Minnesota	4.3	2.9	54.7	12.9	2.5	28,751	73.1	56.2	4.6	12.4	26.9	18.9	34.2
28000	**MISSISSIPPI**.............................	5.1	3.2	71.5	2.1	1.2	1,129,611	65.8	44.2	4.7	16.9	34.2	29.7	43.1
2829700	Gulfport city, Mississippi..............	9.1	3.2	58.5	2.3	1.2	29,385	59.5	32.4	6.8	20.3	40.5	34.3	40.0
2836000	Jackson city, Mississippi...............	2.7	1.8	81.6	1.8	1.4	62,140	56.8	23.7	6.4	26.7	43.2	37.4	37.7
29000	**MISSOURI**	7.6	4.6	65.9	4.1	2.1	2,468,726	63.0	47.7	4.4	11.0	37.0	30.1	41.5
2915670	Columbia city, Missouri..............	5.5	4.0	56.8	8.0	4.2	50,572	49.7	38.1	2.5	9.1	50.3	36.1	24.1
2935000	Independence city, Missouri........	10.7	10.7	67.5	5.1	3.4	53,057	60.8	42.7	4.3	13.8	39.2	32.3	47.3
2938000	Kansas City city, Missouri	9.1	11.1	53.6	8.0	4.4	219,020	54.5	37.9	3.8	12.8	45.5	35.4	32.6
2941348	Lee's Summit city, Missouri..........	5.6	3.9	59.4	3.3	1.1	37,795	75.7	60.2	3.1	12.4	24.3	20.1	37.8
2954074	O'Fallon city, Missouri	10.5	8.4	66.5	7.7	2.8	34,412	74.7	60.1	5.5	9.2	25.3	20.1	32.7
2964082	St. Charles city, Missouri	6.9	3.4	65.1	4.7	3.0	29,992	62.0	46.5	3.9	11.6	38.0	30.7	38.2
2964550	St. Joseph city, Missouri	6.9	7.7	69.9	3.9	2.7	29,750	54.6	37.1	4.1	13.3	45.4	34.4	38.3
2965000	St. Louis city, Missouri................	5.8	4.4	67.7	6.2	2.8	139,736	42.2	22.6	4.4	15.2	57.8	47.5	34.0
2970000	Springfield city, Missouri	8.0	4.8	59.5	3.9	2.3	79,232	47.8	32.8	3.1	11.9	52.2	39.5	32.4
30000	**MONTANA**.............................	6.3	4.3	53.4	2.2	1.0	448,949	61.4	48.8	4.5	8.1	38.6	29.2	44.3
3006550	Billings city, Montana.................	6.7	7.5	58.4	2.4	1.6	50,365	59.9	45.0	6.7	8.2	40.1	30.2	41.9
3050200	Missoula city, Montana	5.5	5.2	42.3	3.3	1.8	33,744	48.8	34.5	3.5	10.8	51.2	32.9	31.7
31000	**NEBRASKA**.............................	8.7	11.9	64.7	7.4	4.3	785,982	63.0	49.8	4.3	8.9	37.0	30.4	38.6
3128000	Lincoln city, Nebraska.................	8.9	8.5	64.3	8.2	4.6	120,407	56.3	43.5	3.9	8.9	43.7	34.1	33.6
3137000	Omaha city, Nebraska	10.7	15.0	59.0	10.7	6.4	201,469	57.3	41.0	4.8	11.6	42.7	34.9	34.4
32000	**NEVADA**.................................	17.5	29.9	27.2	18.4	9.8	1,191,380	63.3	43.8	6.7	12.7	36.7	28.0	41.3
3223770	Enterprise CDP, Nevada..............	16.3	18.8	23.8	23.4	6.5	83,983	67.9	46.1	8.0	13.8	32.1	22.6	34.5
3231900	Henderson city, Nevada..............	12.6	22.2	22.8	13.8	4.6	124,470	68.4	50.8	5.1	12.5	31.6	24.4	44.4
3240000	Las Vegas city, Nevada...............	19.5	34.5	25.8	21.5	10.9	250,350	61.0	41.2	7.0	12.8	39.0	31.8	40.9
3251800	North Las Vegas city, Nevada.......	24.9	43.3	29.9	20.7	10.7	85,966	72.8	44.8	9.1	18.8	27.2	19.1	35.4
3254600	Paradise CDP, Nevada	18.2	37.2	21.1	24.4	12.3	78,005	53.2	32.6	6.9	13.7	46.8	35.8	36.8
3260600	Reno city, Nevada	13.4	25.8	33.9	14.8	8.0	110,993	54.7	37.6	6.1	11.1	45.3	32.1	38.4
3268400	Sparks city, Nevada	20.5	30.0	36.4	14.2	6.6	43,392	63.2	42.7	9.4	11.1	36.8	25.7	41.4
3268585	Spring Valley CDP, Nevada	15.7	21.2	22.4	26.5	9.2	88,063	54.0	34.8	5.7	13.5	46.0	34.0	34.8
3271400	Sunrise Manor CDP, Nevada........	21.8	55.2	29.4	26.4	16.5	62,737	70.9	41.8	9.0	20.1	29.1	21.6	37.3

STATE and place code	STATE Place	Total population	Percent change, 2014–2019	Population by age (percent) Under 18 years	18 to 24 years	25 to 44 years	45 to 64 years	65 years and over	Median age	Race alone or in combination (percent) White	Black	American Indian and Alaska Native	Asian	Native Hawaiian or Other Pacific Islander	Some other race
	ACS table number:	B01003	Population Estimates	B01001	B01001	B01001	B01001	B01001	B01002	B02008	B02009	B02010	B02011	B02012	B02013
FIPS	column number:	1	2	3	4	5	6	7	8	9	10	11	12	13	14
33000	NEW HAMPSHIRE..................	1,388,992	2.0	18.4	9.0	24.8	28.5	19.3	43.1	94.1	2.7	1.2	3.5	0.1	5.2
3345140	Manchester city, New Hampshire	115,470	2.0	18.6	9.1	34.2	24.4	13.8	36.6	85.0	10.4	1.1	4.2	0.0	12.8
3350260	Nashua city, New Hampshire.......	91,122	2.4	19.2	9.5	28.1	25.2	18.0	40.6	83.6	4.7	1.1	10.4	0.0	13.8
34000	NEW JERSEY	9,267,130	2.4	21.8	8.3	26.0	27.0	16.9	40.3	65.2	15.5	1.3	11.1	0.2	19.7
3403580	Bayonne city, New Jersey	69,195	-1.6	23.6	5.4	29.7	25.6	15.7	38.3	68.3	14.3	1.4	11.9	0.0	30.1
3410000	Camden city, New Jersey.............	71,771	-4.9	29.8	10.9	26.6	21.5	11.2	32.2	11.7	41.3	2.9	2.3	0.0	51.5
3413690	Clifton city, New Jersey	89,382	-1.0	17.1	9.6	26.9	27.4	18.9	42.3	62.7	10.2	0.8	10.6	0.0	34.8
3419390	East Orange city, New Jersey.......	68,893	-1.1	25.1	5.2	28.5	27.0	14.3	37.5	3.0	88.5	1.4	1.0	0.0	16.1
3421000	Elizabeth city, New Jersey...........	135,405	0.4	26.6	9.0	29.3	24.3	10.8	36.0	35.7	19.1	1.8	2.3	0.0	59.1
3436000	Jersey City city, New Jersey.........	283,943	-0.0	20.1	6.8	39.6	20.8	12.6	35.4	39.8	25.0	1.2	26.5	0.0	26.5
3438580	Lakewood CDP, New Jersey.........	66,405	9.9	51.4	10.1	22.5	10.3	5.7	17.3	93.5	5.3	0.0	0.0	0.0	7.3
3451000	Newark city, New Jersey.............	307,216	0.5	24.4	10.3	30.1	23.8	11.3	35.1	18.0	50.9	1.0	3.0	0.0	39.7
3456550	Passaic city, New Jersey.............	69,637	-2.5	30.8	12.3	27.1	23.0	6.8	30.8	73.3	9.5	2.4	4.4	0.0	66.5
3457000	Paterson city, New Jersey	157,783		27.2	8.8	29.2	23.2	11.7	33.6	31.9	26.3	1.5	5.2	0.0	61.5
3473110	Toms River CDP, New Jersey	93,947	2.6	22.1	8.2	25.2	26.1	18.4	40.8	87.2	5.8	0.4	3.4	0.0	8.6
3474000	Trenton city, New Jersey.............	90,458	-1.0	24.7	6.7	28.9	26.1	13.6	38.3	22.8	53.8	0.0	0.0	0.0	32.3
3474630	Union City city, New Jersey.........	65,639	-1.0	23.2	11.4	28.5	26.4	10.4	35.8	49.2	16.0	0.0	5.4	0.0	68.4
35000	NEW MEXICO	2,115,877	1.4	22.3	9.1	26.2	23.9	18.5	39.1	71.4	3.5	12.8	2.7	0.3	38.5
3502000	Albuquerque city, New Mexico....	562,591	0.6	20.5	9.5	28.9	24.2	16.9	38.9	75.1	5.4	9.0	5.4	0.6	36.9
3539380	Las Cruces city, New Mexico	112,907	2.0	24.3	13.5	28.9	19.2	14.2	32.4	68.8	4.2	5.5	2.3	0.0	48.3
3563460	Rio Rancho city, New Mexico	105,839	6.6	23.6	7.3	27.3	25.0	16.8	39.0	79.5	5.0	8.8	4.0	0.0	29.0
3570500	Santa Fe city, New Mexico.........	88,196	20.5	19.1	7.7	26.8	23.2	23.2	42.5	76.5	2.0	4.7	2.9	0.0	42.7
36000	NEW YORK	19,835,913	2.4	20.7	8.8	27.0	26.0	17.5	39.8	64.0	17.6	1.8	9.9	0.2	18.2
3601000	Albany city, New York	98,624	-2.1	14.6	21.3	29.1	19.9	15.0	33.4	60.4	29.1	1.4	8.3	0.0	8.3
3611000	Buffalo city, New York...............	276,804	-1.3	22.4	11.0	30.3	23.0	13.3	34.5	53.2	36.1	1.7	8.6	0.0	9.6
3615000	Cheektowaga CDP, New York	76,676	0.7	20.9	7.4	28.2	25.3	18.2	39.2	78.2	17.8	0.7	3.7	0.0	4.3
3649121	Mount Vernon city, New York	72,584	-1.6	20.2	7.8	26.5	30.1	15.3	41.4	22.3	62.1	1.0	2.9	0.0	22.9
3650617	New Rochelle city, New York.......	81,590	-1.3	17.1	9.6	25.1	29.8	18.3	44.0	63.5	20.1	2.4	7.1	0.0	25.8
3651000	New York city, New York.............	8,467,513	-1.8	20.7	7.9	30.4	24.7	16.3	38.1	42.5	26.5	2.1	16.0	0.3	27.1
3663000	Rochester city, New York............	210,594	-2.0	20.9	11.6	29.8	23.6	14.1	34.6	49.4	42.1	1.1	3.6	0.0	13.3
3665508	Schenectady city, New York	66,985	-1.0	20.3	11.3	27.5	26.4	14.5	37.8	63.7	26.1	4.6	8.5	0.7	16.0
3673000	Syracuse city, New York	146,124	-1.4	20.5	15.5	27.7	20.7	15.6	33.2	62.4	31.7	2.2	6.5	0.0	8.0
3684000	Yonkers city, New York...............	209,506	-0.2	22.2	8.8	26.5	25.3	17.2	38.5	53.9	25.0	3.0	5.7	0.0	34.1
37000	NORTH CAROLINA	10,551,162	7.7	21.8	9.5	25.9	25.8	17.0	39.4	70.1	22.6	3.0	3.9	0.2	9.2
3702140	Asheville city, North Carolina......	94,070	5.7	14.5	8.3	30.1	23.9	23.2	41.6	88.8	8.7	1.0	3.0	0.0	8.4
3710740	Cary town, North Carolina..........	178,508	9.9	24.3	9.5	26.1	28.4	11.6	38.7	66.1	10.4	1.1	22.8	0.0	10.4
3712000	Charlotte city, North Carolina.....	879,697	9.4	22.2	9.6	32.9	23.9	11.3	34.8	49.3	37.3	1.5	7.6	0.1	14.1
3714100	Concord city, North Carolina	107,688	12.6	26.6	9.8	27.9	22.8	12.9	36.0	63.4	29.4	1.0	5.9	0.0	11.4
3719000	Durham city, North Carolina	285,439	10.9	20.4	10.8	33.3	22.6	12.9	35.3	49.4	39.4	1.9	6.9	0.0	11.9
3722920	Fayetteville city, North Carolina ..	208,792	3.8	23.9	13.8	31.4	18.4	12.6	30.8	46.7	46.9	3.3	4.7	0.9	10.4
3725580	Gastonia city, North Carolina	81,159	4.9	23.6	7.7	28.0	25.2	15.5	38.8	65.6	31.3	0.0	1.7	0.0	7.5
3728000	Greensboro city, North Carolina ..	298,250	5.0	20.6	12.7	27.3	23.4	16.0	36.3	45.8	46.3	1.5	6.1	0.0	7.4
3728080	Greenville city, North Carolina.....	88,733	3.9	17.8	28.6	25.4	17.9	10.3	26.6	52.7	43.8	0.8	2.9	0.0	3.6
3731400	High Point city, North Carolina	115,287	3.5	23.8	11.5	24.9	24.7	15.1	37.5	53.9	36.6	1.8	8.0	0.0	8.8
3734200	Jacksonville city, North Carolina ..	72,881	4.9	16.7	40.2	27.1	10.5	5.6	22.8	77.6	17.9	5.0	3.8	0.5	11.6
3755000	Raleigh city, North Carolina........	469,502	7.9	20.3	11.2	33.1	23.2	12.2	35.0	60.2	29.9	1.6	5.4	0.2	11.9
3774440	Wilmington city, North Carolina ..	117,642	8.8	12.5	16.5	24.0	26.8	20.2	42.0	84.1	12.2	6.3	3.6	0.0	4.8
3775000	Winston-Salem city, North Carolina	250,337	3.6	22.2	11.5	27.2	23.5	15.7	36.4	55.6	33.6	3.0	3.2	0.2	16.1
38000	NORTH DAKOTA......................	774,948	12.3	23.6	11.0	27.2	22.2	16.0	35.8	89.0	4.1	7.1	2.1	0.5	3.9
3807200	Bismarck city, North Dakota	74,141	10.3	21.4	8.5	27.4	24.4	18.2	39.3	89.6	3.9	5.1	2.0	0.0	4.2
3825700	Fargo city, North Dakota	124,843	6.1	21.1	16.2	30.2	19.8	12.7	31.8	86.5	9.9	2.6	3.6	0.0	3.0
39000	OHIO	11,780,017	1.1	22.1	9.0	25.5	25.6	17.8	39.6	83.4	14.3	1.6	3.1	0.2	4.4
3901000	Akron city, Ohio........................	189,343	-0.1	20.2	10.1	27.1	24.6	17.9	39.5	66.9	33.2	4.3	5.7	0.1	4.2
3912000	Canton city, Ohio......................	70,438	-2.5	22.4	7.9	25.5	27.3	17.0	40.9	77.4	27.3	3.6	0.7	0.0	5.3

Table A-4. Cities — Who: Age, Race/Ethnicity, and Household Structure, 2021—*Continued*

STATE and place code	STATE Place	Two or more races (percent)	Hispanic or Latino (percent)	Native, born in state of residence (percent)	Foreign born (percent)	Non-citizens (percent)	Total households	Family households Total	Married-couple	Male householder	Female householder	Nonfamily households Total	One-person households	Percent of households with people age 60 years and over
	ACS table number:	B02001	B03003	B05002	B05002	B05002	B11001	B11001	B11001	B11001	B11001	B11001	B11001	B11006
FIPS	column number:	15	16	17	18	19	20	21	22	23	24	25	26	27
33000	**NEW HAMPSHIRE**....................	6.4	4.3	40.6	5.9	2.7	548,026	65.9	52.3	4.7	8.9	34.1	25.9	45.8
3345140	Manchester city, New Hampshire	12.6	11.9	46.0	14.5	5.9	48,649	55.0	37.9	7.3	9.8	45.0	31.7	35.3
3350260	Nashua city, New Hampshire.......	13.6	13.6	34.0	14.4	6.1	36,986	61.3	44.2	5.6	11.5	38.7	28.1	41.0
34000	**NEW JERSEY**	12.1	21.5	51.5	23.0	9.7	3,497,945	68.0	50.4	4.9	12.7	32.0	26.2	43.4
3403580	Bayonne city, New Jersey	25.4	33.5	51.9	29.9	9.3	28,375	61.6	40.9	5.4	15.3	38.4	32.8	36.1
3410000	Camden city, New Jersey.............	9.6	59.0	51.9	16.0	10.6	24,276	66.0	18.1	7.1	40.8	34.0	28.3	39.5
3413690	Clifton city, New Jersey	17.0	39.5	43.3	37.3	9.3	32,408	70.4	51.0	6.5	12.9	29.6	24.1	50.0
3419390	East Orange city, New Jersey	9.5	12.1	50.9	30.9	11.8	28,318	56.1	22.1	6.3	27.8	43.9	39.1	42.0
3421000	Elizabeth city, New Jersey............	18.3	67.0	42.2	48.3	28.1	46,107	70.0	37.8	7.1	25.1	30.0	25.2	34.9
3436000	Jersey City city, New Jersey..........	18.2	27.7	34.5	40.2	20.7	119,158	56.2	39.0	3.7	13.5	43.8	32.5	30.1
3438580	Lakewood CDP, New Jersey..........	0.0	8.4	64.2	7.8	2.6	13,701	83.9	72.1	9.8	2.1	16.1	15.5	19.9
3451000	Newark city, New Jersey...............	11.5	36.2	47.2	35.4	21.0	115,145	61.6	27.8	8.8	25.0	38.4	32.6	34.2
3456550	Passaic city, New Jersey..............	55.4	73.1	43.0	41.3	27.3	20,446	75.3	36.9	4.0	34.3	24.7	22.3	30.6
3457000	Paterson city, New Jersey	24.4	64.1	41.4	43.0	22.4	51,612	72.2	36.1	9.0	27.2	27.8	23.3	38.6
3473110	Toms River CDP, New Jersey	5.3	10.3	66.8	10.7	3.8	35,128	68.6	50.8	6.0	11.8	31.4	25.7	46.5
3474000	Trenton city, New Jersey..............	9.4	37.0	52.7	23.5	15.2	34,116	56.1	28.2	6.6	21.3	43.9	37.8	43.7
3474630	Union City city, New Jersey	38.7	82.9	28.8	57.9	32.0	24,041	65.2	33.1	9.1	23.0	34.8	25.4	28.2
35000	**NEW MEXICO**	27.5	50.1	53.8	9.1	5.1	834,007	62.7	42.9	6.1	13.6	37.3	30.9	44.3
3502000	Albuquerque city, New Mexico....	30.2	50.6	51.9	9.9	4.7	243,582	57.1	37.2	5.4	14.5	42.9	35.6	39.1
3539380	Las Cruces city, New Mexico	28.6	63.4	52.7	9.8	4.5	45,991	57.0	33.9	9.5	13.7	43.0	35.2	35.4
3563460	Rio Rancho city, New Mexico	24.5	42.5	48.3	3.9	1.3	40,013	72.6	56.3	5.4	11.0	27.4	21.7	41.0
3570500	Santa Fe city, New Mexico...........	27.0	50.2	47.6	11.2	5.2	40,641	54.8	37.1	5.2	12.6	45.2	38.2	45.6
36000	**NEW YORK**	10.7	19.5	63.1	22.3	9.1	7,652,666	61.6	42.7	5.2	13.7	38.4	30.9	44.3
3601000	Albany city, New York	7.6	10.3	66.0	10.7	5.8	44,279	36.8	21.5	1.2	14.2	63.2	47.2	34.7
3611000	Buffalo city, New York.................	8.3	11.5	74.2	10.6	4.2	122,569	49.6	25.1	4.9	19.6	50.4	40.1	35.5
3615000	Cheektowaga CDP, New York	4.4	4.6	82.8	7.8	3.1	33,247	58.8	42.0	5.0	11.8	41.2	33.4	45.2
3649121	Mount Vernon city, New York	11.4	21.4	49.1	37.9	17.1	26,465	70.7	39.4	8.1	23.1	29.3	26.5	46.3
3650617	New Rochelle city, New York.......	17.9	30.7	53.5	28.1	11.9	32,877	59.3	46.2	3.3	9.7	40.7	35.9	48.6
3651000	New York city, New York..............	13.1	29.1	48.7	36.4	14.9	3,263,895	58.0	35.0	5.7	17.3	42.0	33.6	41.7
3663000	Rochester city, New York.............	9.1	17.8	67.2	9.1	4.1	93,263	47.2	20.6	4.6	22.0	52.8	41.5	33.4
3665508	Schenectady city, New York	17.6	12.6	64.7	14.8	5.1	28,965	51.9	31.5	6.3	14.1	48.1	37.0	39.6
3673000	Syracuse city, New York...............	10.0	9.1	66.5	10.7	5.7	62,663	47.0	24.0	5.1	17.9	53.0	43.3	39.5
3684000	Yonkers city, New York................	18.1	40.5	58.8	29.2	10.5	81,397	63.4	38.2	7.6	17.6	36.6	33.0	44.7
37000	**NORTH CAROLINA**	8.4	10.1	56.0	8.2	4.9	4,179,632	64.3	47.3	4.3	12.6	35.7	29.4	40.6
3702140	Asheville city, North Carolina.......	10.1	6.8	44.3	6.9	2.9	38,131	48.9	39.2	1.4	8.3	51.1	41.0	46.5
3710740	Cary town, North Carolina..........	9.5	9.7	29.8	24.1	11.5	65,254	73.1	62.2	1.7	9.2	26.9	19.3	32.5
3712000	Charlotte city, North Carolina......	9.2	14.8	40.7	17.1	10.5	365,269	56.1	37.8	4.4	13.9	43.9	35.1	27.2
3714100	Concord city, North Carolina.......	11.0	13.8	47.5	12.0	7.6	33,859	75.9	58.3	3.5	14.2	24.1	21.5	34.7
3719000	Durham city, North Carolina.......	8.9	12.0	45.6	14.0	7.8	122,412	54.3	37.6	3.8	12.8	45.7	35.6	29.8
3722920	Fayetteville city, North Carolina ...	11.6	12.3	38.9	7.9	2.9	83,147	58.3	38.6	3.9	15.8	41.7	36.4	30.8
3725580	Gastonia city, North Carolina	7.6	11.8	60.2	6.5	3.9	33,292	57.7	34.8	4.8	18.1	42.3	30.2	39.1
3728000	Greensboro city, North Carolina ..	6.3	8.5	55.1	11.7	5.4	123,955	55.4	34.4	3.4	17.6	44.6	36.9	37.9
3728080	Greenville city, North Carolina.....	3.5	4.6	64.3	3.2	1.4	41,575	38.6	19.1	5.8	13.8	61.4	46.4	24.4
3731400	High Point city, North Carolina ...	7.9	10.9	55.3	13.7	7.3	42,738	65.4	43.3	4.1	18.1	34.6	26.6	41.5
3734200	Jacksonville city, North Carolina ..	14.7	20.0	22.3	7.0	2.0	22,024	65.1	52.4	1.9	10.8	34.9	30.1	19.7
3755000	Raleigh city, North Carolina.........	8.3	12.1	45.9	13.8	7.9	194,917	55.0	39.3	3.3	12.4	45.0	35.0	29.8
3774440	Wilmington city, North Carolina..	8.9	6.0	46.3	4.7	2.4	59,341	45.3	37.1	2.3	5.9	54.7	40.9	37.2
3775000	Winston-Salem city, North Carolina.................	10.5	18.5	54.2	11.1	7.4	101,551	57.7	37.8	4.7	15.2	42.3	36.3	37.9
38000	**NORTH DAKOTA**......................	6.1	4.1	61.8	4.4	2.6	322,511	59.1	46.1	5.4	7.6	40.9	33.2	35.9
3807200	Bismarck city, North Dakota	5.3	2.8	70.5	2.3	1.0	31,426	52.6	39.8	6.0	6.7	47.4	41.4	41.2
3825700	Fargo city, North Dakota	5.2	3.7	49.1	9.4	5.3	58,269	49.4	34.6	5.8	9.0	50.6	41.7	30.2
39000	**OHIO**	6.4	4.3	74.7	5.0	2.3	4,832,922	61.8	44.7	4.8	12.3	38.2	31.1	41.8
3901000	Akron city, Ohio.........................	12.9	3.9	77.4	6.4	2.9	84,914	51.1	27.4	5.7	18.0	48.9	40.5	39.0
3912000	Canton city, Ohio.......................	12.6	4.9	81.3	1.8	1.3	31,168	58.7	30.0	8.5	20.1	41.3	34.7	40.9

STATE and place code	STATE Place	Total popula-tion	Percent change, 2014–2019	Population by age (percent)					Median age	Race alone or in combination (percent)					
				Under 18 years	18 to 24 years	25 to 44 years	45 to 64 years	65 years and over		White	Black	American Indian and Alaska Native	Asian	Native Hawaiian or Other Pacific Islander	Some other race
	ACS table number:	B01003	Population Estimates	B01001	B01001	B01001	B01001	B01001	B01002	B02008	B02009	B02010	B02011	B02012	B02013
FIPS	column number:	1	2	3	4	5	6	7	8	9	10	11	12	13	14
	OHIO—Cont.														
3915000	Cincinnati city, Ohio	308,913	1.9	21.3	13.4	31.8	20.0	13.4	32.5	56.0	42.0	1.9	3.4	0.2	4.4
3916000	Cleveland city, Ohio	368,006	-2.2	20.3	10.3	29.3	25.1	15.0	36.3	42.5	52.6	1.7	3.3	0.0	10.2
3918000	Columbus city, Ohio	907,310	7.9	21.5	11.7	33.7	21.9	11.2	33.1	60.9	32.4	1.4	7.3	0.2	6.9
3921000	Dayton city, Ohio	137,581	-0.4	24.2	14.9	27.4	19.7	13.8	31.9	57.4	42.3	1.4	2.9	0.0	4.7
3944856	Lorain city, Ohio	65,440	0.1	22.7	8.1	20.5	29.1	19.6	42.5	70.3	22.7	1.6	1.1	0.0	24.0
3961000	Parma city, Ohio	79,984	-2.4	20.3	8.0	25.7	26.2	19.8	40.4	89.3	9.2	1.9	1.5	0.0	8.3
3977000	Toledo city, Ohio	268,504	-2.9	21.8	10.2	27.4	24.5	16.2	36.4	68.1	30.5	3.8	1.7	0.0	6.3
40000	**OKLAHOMA**	3,986,639	4.8	24.0	9.8	26.5	23.5	16.2	37.2	78.8	9.6	14.6	3.2	0.3	8.7
4009050	Broken Arrow city, Oklahoma	117,775	4.2	24.4	7.1	26.5	26.7	15.3	38.6	81.3	7.5	11.9	5.4	0.2	9.6
4023200	Edmond city, Oklahoma	95,334	6.2	26.3	8.8	23.8	25.7	15.2	38.2	90.0	6.7	6.8	4.4	0.0	4.8
4041850	Lawton city, Oklahoma	91,058	-4.1	22.7	14.5	30.5	19.2	13.1	31.6	65.9	23.8	12.2	5.3	0.9	10.3
4052500	Norman city, Oklahoma	128,087	5.8	16.3	21.7	26.9	20.6	14.4	32.5	82.2	8.3	8.5	6.1	0.0	7.4
4055000	Oklahoma City city, Oklahoma	687,691		24.9	9.5	29.5	22.6	13.5	35.0	71.5	17.3	8.1	5.6	0.2	12.7
4075000	Tulsa city, Oklahoma	411,905	0.6	24.2	9.5	28.0	22.9	15.4	35.9	70.3	18.0	10.4	4.1	0.3	14.1
41000	**OREGON**	4,246,155	8.1	20.2	8.4	28.0	24.7	18.6	40.1	85.9	3.2	4.2	6.6	0.8	12.4
4105350	Beaverton city, Oregon	98,204	4.1	19.0	8.5	33.0	24.9	14.5	39.0	76.1	6.0	3.3	12.2	1.1	18.5
4105800	Bend city, Oregon	102,079	19.5	19.6	6.3	30.7	23.4	20.1	41.2	95.1	1.8	1.4	3.3	0.0	5.8
4123850	Eugene city, Oregon	175,102	7.5	16.2	17.9	29.5	20.5	16.0	34.8	90.5	3.5	3.2	6.7	0.3	8.5
4131250	Gresham city, Oregon	113,106	-0.5	23.7	7.8	28.1	24.8	15.6	38.7	82.1	7.8	3.1	6.8	2.5	12.8
4134100	Hillsboro city, Oregon	106,651	9.8	19.9	10.3	35.7	23.1	11.0	34.8	70.6	3.0	3.4	16.3	2.2	19.7
4147000	Medford city, Oregon	86,374	5.8	17.8	8.7	26.5	24.8	22.2	41.6	89.2	2.8	5.2	3.7	0.0	17.7
4159000	Portland city, Oregon	642,218	5.5	16.7	7.9	37.0	24.5	13.9	38.3	79.8	7.8	3.4	11.7	0.9	9.8
4164900	Salem city, Oregon	177,727	7.9	24.2	10.6	29.8	20.5	15.0	34.4	82.4	2.7	7.2	6.7	2.7	21.0
42000	**PENNSYLVANIA**	12,964,056	0.8	20.6	8.7	25.5	26.1	19.0	40.9	81.1	12.8	1.2	4.4	0.1	7.9
4202000	Allentown city, Pennsylvania	125,934	2.0	22.2	11.7	29.2	22.7	14.2	34.6	51.3	22.7	1.7	1.9	0.0	49.6
4206088	Bethlehem city, Pennsylvania	75,134	-3.4	16.6	17.0	25.8	21.1	19.5	37.6	70.4	14.1	1.9	3.8	0.0	25.0
4224000	Erie city, Pennsylvania	94,013	-4.0	22.2	11.8	24.0	25.8	16.2	38.0	74.6	21.9	2.0	3.3	0.0	7.6
4260000	Philadelphia city, Pennsylvania	1,576,251	1.5	21.6	9.2	32.3	22.5	14.4	35.2	41.5	43.0	1.4	8.8	0.2	14.6
4261000	Pittsburgh city, Pennsylvania	300,454	-1.7	14.2	16.9	32.0	21.1	15.8	34.2	71.3	24.8	1.6	6.5	0.2	4.3
4263624	Reading city, Pennsylvania	94,834	0.6	30.7	11.1	25.9	22.0	10.3	32.1	45.2	16.1	3.5	0.7	0.0	60.9
4269000	Scranton city, Pennsylvania	75,867	1.8	20.6	12.5	25.2	23.0	18.7	37.5	83.5	8.5	2.4	6.4	0.0	15.3
44000	**RHODE ISLAND**	1,095,610	0.6	19.0	10.4	26.0	26.4	18.3	40.6	80.6	8.8	1.5	4.1	0.3	17.7
4419180	Cranston city, Rhode Island	82,568	0.5	18.5	7.3	28.9	29.4	15.9	41.3	83.5	8.3	0.6	5.5	0.0	16.0
4454640	Pawtucket city, Rhode Island	75,379	0.9	22.2	9.5	32.0	23.5	12.8	35.6	57.6	26.5	2.5	3.5	0.0	35.3
4459000	Providence city, Rhode Island	189,697	0.4	21.2	15.5	31.8	20.9	10.6	32.7	52.5	15.1	2.3	7.8	0.7	43.1
4474300	Warwick city, Rhode Island	83,014	-1.2	17.9	9.3	25.6	26.7	20.5	42.0	91.1	5.7	0.7	2.8	0.0	7.2
45000	**SOUTH CAROLINA**	5,190,705	8.6	21.5	9.2	25.3	25.4	18.6	40.2	69.7	26.9	1.9	2.3	0.2	5.9
4513330	Charleston city, South Carolina	152,046	9.5	17.0	13.9	32.3	20.5	16.2	35.7	74.0	21.2	2.6	2.3	0.0	4.7
4516000	Columbia city, South Carolina	137,960	-0.3	19.7	25.3	28.1	16.7	10.2	27.5	51.3	45.1	1.2	3.9	0.0	4.3
4530850	Greenville city, South Carolina	72,103	13.5	17.0	15.3	30.7	23.1	13.9	33.9	73.7	24.9	3.1	1.6	0.0	5.3
4548535	Mount Pleasant town, South Carolina	92,398	17.8	22.8	3.3	28.0	28.0	17.9	43.0	95.1	3.0	0.0	2.2	0.0	2.0
4550875	North Charleston city, South Carolina	117,463	13.4	21.5	10.2	34.1	21.8	12.5	34.6	46.0	45.7	1.3	5.3	0.0	8.5
4561405	Rock Hill city, South Carolina	74,107	7.3	24.2	12.4	26.8	24.4	12.1	34.8	58.2	38.7	1.1	4.0	0.0	3.0
46000	**SOUTH DAKOTA**	895,376	6.8	24.6	9.4	24.9	23.4	17.6	37.6	86.6	2.9	10.5	2.3	0.2	3.9
4652980	Rapid City city, South Dakota	76,173	6.7	23.1	9.8	24.9	23.2	19.0	38.3	86.6	3.9	13.4	1.9	0.0	5.0
4659020	Sioux Falls city, South Dakota	196,528	9.0	25.1	9.1	29.7	22.4	13.7	35.9	85.9	8.1	3.9	4.0	0.0	5.3
47000	**TENNESSEE**	6,975,218	5.8	22.0	8.9	26.4	25.6	17.0	39.2	79.4	17.4	2.0	2.4	0.2	5.8
4714000	Chattanooga city, Tennessee	182,111	5.2	20.6	10.7	27.9	22.9	17.9	37.0	62.8	33.4	1.0	2.8	0.0	7.0
4715160	Clarksville city, Tennessee	170,966	7.7	28.2	11.9	31.4	19.6	8.9	29.9	69.6	29.3	4.3	5.5	1.9	7.2
4727740	Franklin city, Tennessee	85,473	17.7	22.9	10.7	26.6	25.2	14.6	39.5	84.9	8.6	2.4	6.7	0.0	5.4
4737640	Jackson city, Tennessee	68,114	-0.2	24.9	12.7	25.9	20.1	16.5	34.7	48.0	48.4	0.8	2.0	0.0	6.1
4738320	Johnson City city, Tennessee	70,889	3.1	18.5	15.5	26.8	21.6	17.6	35.6	91.5	5.9	1.8	3.4	0.8	4.1
4740000	Knoxville city, Tennessee	192,657	1.8	18.3	17.2	28.8	22.1	13.6	33.6	82.0	16.2	3.2	2.4	0.0	6.8
4748000	Memphis city, Tennessee	628,118	-0.9	25.1	9.5	29.1	22.2	14.1	34.3	28.4	65.4	1.0	2.3	0.0	8.1

STATE and place code	STATE Place	Two or more races (percent)	Hispanic or Latino (percent)	Native, born in state of residence (percent)	Foreign born (percent)	Non-citizens (percent)	Total house-holds	Household type (percent of all households)						Percent of house-holds with people age 60 years and over
								Family households				Nonfamily households		
							Total	Total	Married-couple	Male house-holder	Female house-holder	Total	One-person house-holds	
	ACS table number:	B02001	B03003	B05002	B05002	B05002	B11001	B11001	B11001	B11001	B11001	B11001	B11001	B11006
FIPS	column number:	15	16	17	18	19	20	21	22	23	24	25	26	27
	OHIO—Cont.													
3915000	Cincinnati city, Ohio..................	7.3	5.6	68.1	6.9	4.6	144,929	42.2	22.7	2.9	16.6	57.8	46.2	29.1
3916000	Cleveland city, Ohio	9.8	12.2	72.0	5.7	3.3	171,321	44.6	19.2	4.6	20.8	55.4	46.2	37.7
3918000	Columbus city, Ohio..................	8.1	6.9	62.5	15.1	7.5	390,605	53.0	32.3	5.0	15.6	47.0	34.4	29.5
3921000	Dayton city, Ohio......................	8.1	6.2	70.6	4.7	2.5	55,114	51.5	21.9	6.1	23.5	48.5	39.5	40.9
3944856	Lorain city, Ohio.......................	19.3	27.0	71.8	1.9	0.3	27,852	55.7	32.2	7.6	15.9	44.3	38.5	45.4
3961000	Parma city, Ohio.......................	9.1	8.5	80.8	8.2	2.4	33,401	63.4	40.5	8.8	14.2	36.6	30.4	46.5
3977000	Toledo city, Ohio......................	9.8	9.2	75.4	4.2	1.9	120,895	50.0	29.0	4.5	16.5	50.0	41.2	38.8
40000	**OKLAHOMA**	14.0	11.7	60.6	5.8	3.6	1,547,967	64.6	47.3	5.2	12.1	35.4	29.3	39.8
4009050	Broken Arrow city, Oklahoma	15.0	10.9	54.8	8.1	3.8	45,138	71.2	54.2	6.4	10.6	28.8	24.4	40.7
4023200	Edmond city, Oklahoma..............	12.3	6.4	51.0	5.1	2.8	36,530	72.5	61.4	4.4	6.8	27.5	20.7	37.7
4041850	Lawton city, Oklahoma..............	16.6	16.4	40.7	5.7	2.5	33,921	60.1	39.1	5.4	15.6	39.9	32.2	32.4
4052500	Norman city, Oklahoma..............	12.1	9.2	52.5	8.4	5.1	53,446	55.2	42.1	4.0	9.1	44.8	33.1	32.1
4055000	Oklahoma City city, Oklahoma....	14.1	19.6	57.7	10.8	6.7	275,285	61.9	43.4	4.8	13.7	38.1	30.9	34.2
4075000	Tulsa city, Oklahoma	16.2	17.1	56.6	10.5	6.8	173,943	55.5	36.1	5.8	13.6	44.5	36.6	36.5
41000	**OREGON**	11.8	14.0	45.6	9.7	5.1	1,702,599	61.9	47.4	4.8	9.7	38.1	28.1	41.9
4105350	Beaverton city, Oregon................	16.2	20.3	40.2	16.5	8.8	42,858	55.4	37.5	4.7	13.2	44.6	31.5	35.2
4105800	Bend city, Oregon......................	7.4	7.0	35.0	5.6	2.7	44,620	62.9	46.2	5.3	11.4	37.1	24.9	38.9
4123850	Eugene city, Oregon....................	11.9	10.2	42.8	7.6	3.4	74,740	50.7	36.8	3.9	10.0	49.3	32.7	34.1
4131250	Gresham city, Oregon	14.1	18.8	56.7	15.4	7.3	43,487	67.5	43.1	9.1	15.3	32.5	25.9	39.8
4134100	Hillsboro city, Oregon.................	13.7	24.8	40.9	18.2	8.8	40,891	63.3	50.6	4.9	7.7	36.7	25.8	29.0
4147000	Medford city, Oregon.................	17.6	20.1	41.3	7.9	3.4	36,525	55.6	38.6	6.8	10.2	44.4	34.7	50.2
4159000	Portland city, Oregon	11.9	11.4	37.7	12.7	4.9	286,734	48.4	36.8	3.7	8.0	51.6	36.8	29.3
4164900	Salem city, Oregon.....................	17.9	23.4	51.2	13.1	7.9	64,959	64.1	47.3	4.6	12.1	35.9	28.8	37.7
42000	**PENNSYLVANIA**	7.0	8.4	71.4	7.2	3.1	5,228,956	63.1	46.9	4.6	11.6	36.9	30.2	44.4
4202000	Allentown city, Pennsylvania	25.6	56.2	39.5	23.7	13.2	47,204	57.7	32.3	7.6	17.9	42.3	35.7	39.4
4206088	Bethlehem city, Pennsylvania.......	13.3	29.9	52.0	10.6	6.3	30,099	56.9	31.4	7.1	18.4	43.1	31.2	44.6
4224000	Erie city, Pennsylvania................	9.2	8.3	75.2	8.7	3.9	38,636	53.0	32.7	4.3	16.0	47.0	38.2	43.0
4260000	Philadelphia city, Pennsylvania.....	8.4	15.9	63.7	15.0	7.5	660,921	53.3	28.1	5.2	20.0	46.7	37.1	36.4
4261000	Pittsburgh city, Pennsylvania.......	7.6	3.5	65.3	8.6	4.9	136,747	43.5	27.7	3.2	12.6	56.5	42.2	34.4
4263624	Reading city, Pennsylvania...........	24.3	69.9	43.9	24.6	12.0	32,504	61.6	24.5	9.1	27.9	38.4	30.2	32.6
4269000	Scranton city, Pennsylvania..........	14.1	16.7	69.1	9.1	4.0	30,096	59.1	40.6	4.2	14.3	40.9	34.1	44.1
44000	**RHODE ISLAND**.......................	11.9	17.1	56.6	14.5	6.0	440,170	61.0	44.2	4.8	12.0	39.0	30.4	44.3
4419180	Cranston city, Rhode Island........	12.7	14.9	64.9	13.7	6.3	33,049	62.1	43.1	4.9	14.1	37.9	29.7	43.5
4454640	Pawtucket city, Rhode Island.......	23.9	26.7	52.3	22.3	8.4	29,735	57.7	30.6	6.2	20.9	42.3	33.8	35.9
4459000	Providence city, Rhode Island	20.2	44.6	35.0	33.6	16.0	68,179	55.4	33.4	6.5	15.4	44.6	32.6	31.0
4474300	Warwick city, Rhode Island..........	8.1	7.0	68.0	6.5	2.7	36,595	58.0	42.2	3.9	11.9	42.0	33.5	48.4
45000	**SOUTH CAROLINA**....................	6.6	6.3	55.0	5.2	3.2	2,049,972	65.2	47.0	4.5	13.7	34.8	29.1	43.5
4513330	Charleston city, South Carolina ...	4.9	6.9	42.4	6.1	2.3	63,391	54.1	41.1	4.9	8.1	45.9	34.4	35.2
4516000	Columbia city, South Carolina.....	5.5	5.1	52.2	5.6	2.9	51,455	48.9	31.0	2.5	15.3	51.1	39.1	29.5
4530850	Greenville city, South Carolina.....	8.2	5.3	50.1	5.9	3.8	34,154	48.6	32.7	1.0	14.8	51.4	41.5	27.3
4548535	Mount Pleasant town, South Carolina................	3.2	2.0	34.6	5.6	3.3	37,983	63.3	54.3	2.6	6.3	36.7	28.1	39.5
4550875	North Charleston city, South Carolina................	6.9	7.8	56.8	8.1	5.9	47,324	57.6	34.1	3.8	19.6	42.4	32.8	30.0
4561405	Rock Hill city, South Carolina.......	4.6	3.3	49.8	3.0	1.4	29,268	62.0	38.4	4.3	19.3	38.0	28.3	30.8
46000	**SOUTH DAKOTA**......................	6.0	4.2	63.6	3.5	2.2	356,887	62.0	49.0	4.6	8.3	38.0	30.2	41.1
4652980	Rapid City city, South Dakota	10.7	6.4	59.4	1.3	0.7	32,471	55.4	43.4	4.1	7.9	44.6	35.4	42.1
4659020	Sioux Falls city, South Dakota	6.9	5.8	56.9	7.9	3.6	83,498	60.5	45.9	5.4	9.3	39.5	30.5	32.5
47000	**TENNESSEE**	6.8	6.0	59.1	5.3	3.1	2,770,395	64.4	47.1	4.8	12.5	35.6	29.2	41.1
4714000	Chattanooga city, Tennessee.......	6.9	8.2	57.2	7.1	5.3	77,299	54.5	34.3	6.8	13.5	45.5	37.5	42.1
4715160	Clarksville city, Tennessee............	16.2	12.0	34.9	7.6	3.4	63,787	72.2	49.8	6.5	15.9	27.8	20.7	26.9
4727740	Franklin city, Tennessee...............	7.9	4.7	34.9	8.6	4.8	33,275	70.0	60.1	2.2	7.8	30.0	23.7	32.4
4737640	Jackson city, Tennessee...............	4.9	5.6	69.2	3.1	1.5	26,505	57.4	31.1	4.2	22.1	42.6	37.8	41.9
4738320	Johnson City city, Tennessee.......	7.2	4.0	53.4	4.5	1.1	30,806	52.7	39.4	4.2	9.2	47.3	36.4	40.0
4740000	Knoxville city, Tennessee.............	10.4	6.7	58.8	6.2	4.1	85,151	46.1	28.8	4.8	12.4	53.9	40.3	33.4
4748000	Memphis city, Tennessee.............	4.8	8.5	65.2	6.7	4.9	256,968	55.4	27.2	5.4	22.9	44.6	37.8	36.8

STATE and place code	STATE Place	Total popula-tion	Percent change, 2014–2019	Population by age (percent)					Median age	Race alone or in combination (percent)					
				Under 18 years	18 to 24 years	25 to 44 years	45 to 64 years	65 years and over		White	Black	American Indian and Alaska Native	Asian	Native Hawaiian or Other Pacific Islander	Some other race
	ACS table number:	B01003	Population Estimates	B01001	B01001	B01001	B01001	B01001	B01002	B02008	B02009	B02010	B02011	B02012	B02013
FIPS	column number:	1	2	3	4	5	6	7	8	9	10	11	12	13	14
	TENNESSEE—Cont.														
4751560	Murfreesboro city, Tennessee	157,509	21.5	21.5	14.9	29.0	23.8	10.8	32.6	76.2	20.9	1.0	4.6	0.0	4.8
4752006	Nashville-Davidson metropolitan government (balance), Tennessee	678,845	3.8	20.1	9.8	34.9	22.1	13.1	34.9	63.6	28.7	1.2	4.7	0.1	10.9
48000	**TEXAS**	29,527,941	12.6	25.3	9.6	28.4	23.5	13.2	35.5	70.9	13.7	2.4	6.3	0.2	31.4
4801000	Abilene city, Texas....................	129,601	2.5	23.9	14.6	28.4	19.5	13.6	32.6	81.3	11.8	1.4	3.1	0.0	21.4
4801924	Allen city, Texas.......................	106,868	12.2	25.3	7.2	23.9	29.6	14.1	40.8	66.2	9.2	1.5	24.0	0.0	10.0
4803000	Amarillo city, Texas..................	198,781	-1.4	26.3	10.0	27.5	22.0	14.3	34.7	81.7	8.8	2.9	4.6	0.2	21.5
4804000	Arlington city, Texas.................	392,802	4.1	24.0	10.0	30.1	23.4	12.5	34.7	59.0	23.9	2.5	7.4	0.3	28.8
4804462	Atascocita CDP, Texas...............	85,808	13.1	26.0	6.8	34.3	22.0	10.9	34.8	53.5	28.5	4.2	6.3	0.0	29.6
4805000	Austin city, Texas.....................	964,000	7.3	19.0	9.8	40.0	21.5	9.7	34.4	73.2	9.0	2.2	10.4	0.2	23.6
4806128	Baytown city, Texas..................	79,676	1.6	31.3	8.4	27.3	20.8	12.2	31.8	52.5	19.7	0.9	3.6	0.6	51.4
4807000	Beaumont city, Texas................	112,559	-0.6	24.7	10.8	26.0	22.3	16.3	35.3	44.7	47.5	1.5	4.1	0.0	16.2
4810768	Brownsville city, Texas..............	187,840	-0.1	29.3	12.7	25.2	20.7	12.0	29.9	87.1	0.0	1.5	0.7	0.0	71.4
4810912	Bryan city, Texas......................	86,851		22.7	15.8	30.4	18.6	12.4	31.2	71.9	18.9	1.1	4.2	0.0	18.3
4813024	Carrollton city, Texas................	132,569	8.5	21.5	7.6	32.2	26.1	12.6	37.4	64.8	10.6	2.4	16.7	0.0	21.2
4813552	Cedar Park city, Texas...............	78,326	22.4	23.8	7.5	31.7	24.5	12.5	37.0	72.1	6.0	1.3	19.1	0.0	12.6
4815976	College Station city, Texas..........	120,032	13.9	19.3	36.3	24.3	13.4	6.7	22.9	77.3	8.8	2.3	10.1	0.4	11.7
4816432	Conroe city, Texas....................	94,401	38.3	23.8	12.4	30.3	19.0	14.5	33.8	76.3	11.8	1.6	5.9	0.0	18.3
4817000	Corpus Christi city, Texas............	317,768	1.9	23.6	10.4	27.5	23.2	15.4	36.4	87.0	4.5	1.4	2.5	0.1	53.0
4819000	Dallas city, Texas.....................	1,288,441	4.9	23.9	9.4	32.7	22.6	11.4	33.7	54.7	25.8	2.8	4.3	0.2	34.3
4819972	Denton city, Texas....................	148,139		16.0	21.7	27.6	22.6	12.1	31.1	75.5	14.4	2.2	4.4	0.2	16.8
4822660	Edinburg city, Texas..................	102,477	21.9	27.5	10.2	29.2	21.0	12.1	31.8	91.1	2.6	1.9	3.1	0.0	65.1
4824000	El Paso city, Texas....................	678,422	0.4	25.2	10.6	27.9	22.2	14.1	34.3	75.7	4.9	2.6	2.5	0.3	63.5
4826232	Flower Mound town, Texas........	78,375	19.9	23.9	10.1	20.1	34.8	11.1	42.6	77.1	5.6	1.4	18.8	0.0	8.5
4827000	Fort Worth city, Texas...............	940,437	12.4	27.3	9.9	30.1	22.4	10.3	32.9	57.5	22.7	2.1	6.0	0.2	28.9
4827684	Frisco city, Texas.....................	210,735	38.2	28.7	7.3	29.1	25.6	9.4	37.1	62.2	10.0	1.5	28.0	0.4	12.9
4829000	Garland city, Texas	241,870	1.7	27.7	9.6	26.4	24.0	12.3	33.1	63.1	18.3	3.0	11.3	0.2	38.5
4829336	Georgetown city, Texas..............	75,407	34.7	21.2	7.4	24.4	20.5	26.5	41.1	85.9	5.6	1.9	2.4	0.0	24.5
4830464	Grand Prairie city, Texas............	197,338	4.9	27.8	9.9	26.8	25.4	10.0	34.1	44.2	28.8	2.3	9.0	0.0	36.8
4832372	Harlingen city, Texas................	71,928	-1.3	28.6	5.3	26.1	21.2	18.7	36.7	87.1	1.7	0.0	2.4	0.0	47.7
4835000	Houston city, Texas...................	2,287,047	3.4	23.3	10.0	32.3	22.3	12.2	34.8	51.8	24.2	2.1	8.0	0.2	37.9
4837000	Irving city, Texas.....................	254,190	3.2	27.0	9.4	35.2	20.1	8.3	32.0	45.6	13.3	2.5	25.2	0.0	30.5
4839148	Killeen city, Texas	156,260	9.8	31.9	10.6	32.7	18.2	6.5	29.5	47.5	44.1	2.7	4.2	0.6	19.1
4841464	Laredo city, Texas	258,014	4.1	31.5	11.6	26.1	21.0	9.9	29.8	88.3	0.4	0.7	0.7	0.0	78.3
4841980	League City city, Texas..............	114,664	13.2	26.1	6.1	28.6	25.5	13.7	38.2	81.4	10.3	1.2	8.4	0.0	13.4
4842016	Leander city, Texas...................	68,993	100.8	28.7	6.2	27.1	32.4	5.6	38.2	78.5	9.3	1.7	12.7	0.0	18.6
4842508	Lewisville city, Texas................	112,853	6.1	20.3	8.7	36.2	23.6	11.2	34.6	57.2	19.2	2.5	13.5	0.0	24.7
4843888	Longview city, Texas.................	81,877	-2.2	25.6	11.9	26.3	22.2	14.0	34.5	75.4	21.7	2.6	1.9	0.0	19.1
4845000	Lubbock city, Texas..................	260,990		23.4	18.7	26.6	18.7	12.6	30.0	78.4	10.1	2.4	3.2	0.1	27.4
4845384	McAllen city, Texas...................	143,922	3.4	27.4	10.0	28.1	21.4	13.2	33.9	75.9	2.0	1.2	2.4	0.0	53.7
4845744	McKinney city, Texas.................	202,680	27.1	27.0	7.4	30.4	25.1	10.1	37.0	66.4	16.5	2.5	15.3	0.0	12.4
4846452	Mansfield city, Texas................	74,106	18.8	25.7	7.7	27.0	26.6	13.0	38.6	66.4	23.3	1.8	9.1	0.0	14.6
4847892	Mesquite city, Texas.................	148,087	-2.4	27.7	10.6	27.6	23.1	11.1	32.8	55.0	31.3	3.1	4.3	0.0	39.8
4848072	Midland city, Texas...................	131,292	14.1	27.6	8.9	35.5	18.2	9.8	31.9	79.5	7.9	3.0	2.9	0.0	34.7
4848768	Mission city, Texas...................	86,215	2.3	26.8	12.2	26.7	22.0	12.2	33.1	83.8	0.0	1.4	1.9	0.0	69.9
4848804	Missouri City city, Texas.............	76,462	0.6	21.6	7.3	24.8	29.3	17.0	42.0	25.5	50.9	0.0	17.8	0.0	16.8
4850820	New Braunfels city, Texas...........	96,630	38.0	23.4	10.2	30.4	21.7	14.3	37.0	91.4	4.7	2.2	1.6	0.0	27.9
4852356	North Richland Hills city, Texas.....	70,212	3.1	20.7	7.7	25.5	27.8	18.2	41.2	84.1	6.8	4.4	4.9	0.0	14.9
4853388	Odessa city, Texas....................	116,436	5.8	28.0	10.9	30.7	20.3	10.1	32.0	67.8	9.2	2.4	0.0	0.0	46.1
4856000	Pasadena city, Texas.................	148,629	-1.7	26.0	9.1	28.0	23.4	13.5	34.7	74.2	6.5	1.6	2.5	0.0	58.5
4856348	Pearland city, Texas..................	120,694	25.5	26.8	6.7	29.0	22.9	14.5	36.1	56.6	20.4	0.6	19.8	0.0	14.3
4857176	Pflugerville city, Texas..............	66,700	19.6	27.5	5.5	30.2	27.9	8.8	38.0	63.4	16.9	1.0	8.1	0.0	26.9
4857200	Pharr city, Texas......................	79,697	5.0	32.7	12.0	25.6	16.8	12.9	30.1	86.5	0.0	0.0	0.0	0.0	58.9
4858016	Plano city, Texas......................	287,037	2.9	22.0	9.5	29.1	27.2	12.3	38.3	60.6	10.3	1.2	24.0	0.3	15.3
4861796	Richardson city, Texas...............	116,369	11.7	21.2	12.0	28.1	24.3	14.4	35.7	66.5	11.8	1.0	15.8	0.0	16.1
4863500	Round Rock city, Texas..............	127,130	18.9	25.2	10.1	30.9	22.6	11.3	35.3	70.9	15.6	3.0	8.8	0.0	22.9
4864472	San Angelo city, Texas..............	101,063	1.0	23.8	12.5	27.3	20.9	15.5	34.8	85.5	5.1	4.0	2.5	0.0	27.2

STATE and place code	STATE Place	Two or more races (percent)	Hispanic or Latino (percent)	Native, born in state of residence (percent)	Foreign born (percent)	Non-citizens (percent)	Total house-holds	Household type (percent of all households)						Percent of house-holds with people age 60 years and over
								Family households				Nonfamily households		
								Total	Married-couple	Male house-holder	Female house-holder	Total	One-person house-holds	
	ACS table number:	B02001	B03003	B05002	B05002	B05002	B11001	B11001	B11001	B11001	B11001	B11001	B11001	B11006
FIPS	column number:	15	16	17	18	19	20	21	22	23	24	25	26	27
	TENNESSEE—Cont.													
4751560	Murfreesboro city, Tennessee	8.0	7.3	51.2	6.4	2.9	58,371	62.9	49.5	3.2	10.3	37.1	27.7	30.3
4752006	Nashville-Davidson metropolitan government (balance), Tennessee	9.0	10.9	46.6	13.6	8.3	305,247	52.0	34.8	4.8	12.4	48.0	34.9	29.5
48000	**TEXAS**	23.9	40.2	59.5	17.2	10.3	10,796,247	68.3	49.5	5.3	13.5	31.7	25.6	35.5
4801000	Abilene city, Texas........................	18.6	28.0	66.8	6.5	3.9	48,398	60.5	40.1	4.5	15.8	39.5	28.4	36.0
4801924	Allen city, Texas............................	10.6	11.0	44.0	19.6	8.9	37,461	80.4	69.7	3.0	7.8	19.6	17.3	35.9
4803000	Amarillo city, Texas.......................	18.6	33.6	66.0	10.6	5.7	82,129	61.7	44.5	5.3	12.0	38.3	30.8	33.8
4804000	Arlington city, Texas......................	21.0	34.5	51.7	21.9	12.7	146,888	67.4	45.2	5.4	16.8	32.6	26.6	32.5
4804462	Atascocita CDP, Texas...................	20.3	31.6	64.1	11.3	4.1	29,579	74.8	61.8	1.6	11.3	25.2	15.6	30.3
4805000	Austin city, Texas..........................	17.7	32.0	47.2	18.2	11.5	449,399	46.8	35.9	3.2	7.7	53.2	39.1	22.7
4806128	Baytown city, Texas.......................	27.3	60.5	60.0	22.1	13.6	28,264	69.0	46.3	4.1	18.6	31.0	26.9	32.4
4807000	Beaumont city, Texas.....................	14.1	18.1	72.1	9.3	5.9	46,375	58.0	32.7	5.6	19.6	42.0	36.6	39.7
4810768	Brownsville city, Texas...................	60.5	95.2	67.9	25.9	15.6	56,522	80.4	50.9	7.4	22.0	19.6	18.1	37.9
4810912	Bryan city, Texas...........................	14.0	40.9	68.1	10.7	7.5	32,910	52.8	34.6	4.5	13.6	47.2	34.7	32.4
4813024	Carrollton city, Texas....................	15.1	35.5	46.8	27.5	14.8	50,308	70.4	54.1	5.2	11.2	29.6	21.7	34.8
4813552	Cedar Park city, Texas...................	11.4	15.2	42.8	22.0	11.7	30,407	65.4	56.7	1.6	7.2	34.6	24.1	31.3
4815976	College Station city, Texas	10.2	17.5	63.6	12.4	7.8	41,586	49.9	38.3	3.8	7.7	50.1	31.1	21.1
4816432	Conroe city, Texas.........................	15.2	22.8	50.1	14.2	7.2	37,297	60.9	47.2	5.5	8.2	39.1	33.0	32.9
4817000	Corpus Christi city, Texas..............	47.9	65.4	74.5	9.0	5.9	117,366	67.3	44.7	6.3	16.2	32.7	25.7	38.6
4819000	Dallas city, Texas...........................	21.4	42.0	54.8	23.3	16.4	536,008	53.7	33.9	5.8	14.0	46.3	38.7	29.8
4819972	Denton city, Texas.........................	12.6	21.5	55.5	10.6	6.6	57,963	55.2	44.4	2.4	8.4	44.8	30.5	29.0
4822660	Edinburg city, Texas.......................	62.5	87.7	70.3	19.6	11.3	37,541	70.2	41.5	4.3	24.5	29.8	25.2	30.2
4824000	El Paso city, Texas.........................	48.2	82.0	58.7	22.4	10.9	242,529	71.7	44.5	7.0	20.2	28.3	23.9	38.5
4826232	Flower Mound town, Texas...........	10.3	11.6	40.5	15.5	4.9	27,696	81.8	73.2	3.0	5.7	18.2	13.1	33.2
4827000	Fort Worth city, Texas...................	16.3	34.0	55.1	17.6	10.9	334,286	65.6	46.5	5.0	14.2	34.4	27.9	29.9
4827684	Frisco city, Texas...........................	13.8	13.5	35.5	27.4	12.2	72,282	77.5	68.8	2.8	5.9	22.5	17.6	24.3
4829000	Garland city, Texas........................	33.5	44.1	51.9	29.5	17.5	77,777	80.1	49.9	7.8	22.4	19.9	14.8	37.6
4829336	Georgetown city, Texas	19.6	32.7	53.3	9.7	5.5	30,207	66.4	56.1	3.0	7.3	33.6	27.5	51.3
4830464	Grand Prairie city, Texas...............	20.6	42.8	55.4	24.0	12.8	64,208	74.3	50.3	7.0	17.0	25.7	20.3	33.4
4832372	Harlingen city, Texas.....................	39.4	82.5	71.6	16.3	9.8	27,051	68.2	41.3	11.6	15.3	31.8	26.3	46.3
4835000	Houston city, Texas.......................	23.4	44.0	51.1	28.8	19.6	924,981	58.6	35.8	6.4	16.4	41.4	33.0	31.9
4837000	Irving city, Texas...........................	16.4	44.0	40.0	42.3	29.0	95,309	64.3	47.8	4.9	11.7	35.7	29.2	23.6
4839148	Killeen city, Texas	16.4	32.6	38.1	9.1	4.7	57,875	65.3	40.6	5.4	19.3	34.7	29.7	21.8
4841464	Laredo city, Texas	68.4	95.3	68.1	25.9	16.5	76,095	78.4	47.8	6.8	23.8	21.6	18.3	35.8
4841980	League City city, Texas.................	14.5	18.1	53.6	10.8	4.3	44,419	73.8	65.1	2.1	6.6	26.2	22.5	32.4
4842016	Leander city, Texas.......................	20.2	23.6	45.1	18.3	11.9	24,031	79.1	68.5	2.5	8.1	20.9	15.7	24.6
4842508	Lewisville city, Texas.....................	16.5	28.1	45.5	20.0	11.7	46,897	62.6	41.7	6.1	14.8	37.4	29.9	26.8
4843888	Longview city, Texas.....................	20.4	22.1	66.3	10.3	7.5	31,072	63.0	38.6	6.4	18.0	37.0	30.6	34.6
4845000	Lubbock city, Texas.......................	20.7	38.4	76.2	5.0	2.5	104,426	59.2	39.6	5.3	14.3	40.8	31.2	30.4
4845384	McAllen city, Texas........................	34.8	88.2	60.7	24.5	15.0	48,438	75.9	52.7	3.7	19.5	24.1	22.0	36.6
4845744	McKinney city, Texas	12.3	17.2	45.1	17.5	9.7	73,357	73.4	61.2	1.9	10.3	26.6	20.9	26.4
4846452	Mansfield city, Texas.....................	14.3	15.6	51.7	13.5	5.5	25,327	78.7	55.8	7.1	15.8	21.3	17.0	33.4
4847892	Mesquite city, Texas	32.4	44.0	59.0	22.6	13.9	52,023	72.2	42.0	6.2	24.0	27.8	25.2	33.3
4848072	Midland city, Texas.......................	27.1	50.2	69.2	12.5	6.8	52,898	69.6	54.6	6.8	8.2	30.4	25.0	25.5
4848768	Mission city, Texas........................	58.4	86.9	60.7	26.7	15.4	28,128	74.3	50.1	5.4	18.7	25.7	22.4	37.4
4848804	Missouri City city, Texas..............	11.4	17.3	46.3	25.9	7.2	29,801	73.3	54.5	5.0	13.8	26.7	21.4	52.7
4850820	New Braunfels city, Texas	27.1	33.2	61.4	9.0	7.5	37,815	65.4	51.6	5.5	8.3	34.6	27.6	31.6
4852356	North Richland Hills city, Texas.....	12.3	22.2	54.8	11.5	5.9	26,937	65.9	50.0	4.2	11.7	34.1	24.7	41.6
4853388	Odessa city, Texas.........................	25.6	63.7	63.1	17.3	8.7	48,530	66.0	49.1	3.4	13.4	34.0	26.7	27.3
4856000	Pasadena city, Texas.....................	43.2	70.9	59.0	26.9	17.2	50,598	72.5	47.8	7.6	17.1	27.5	22.2	40.7
4856348	Pearland city, Texas......................	11.6	20.3	60.5	17.9	4.8	43,012	74.5	58.5	3.4	12.6	25.5	22.2	40.2
4857176	Pflugerville city, Texas..................	16.3	37.0	60.1	11.0	4.2	23,875	70.3	56.7	3.1	10.5	29.7	22.6	27.2
4857200	Pharr city, Texas............................	0.0	93.2	54.5	33.3	23.4	24,797	77.4	46.6	2.9	27.8	22.6	18.5	35.7
4858016	Plano city, Texas............................	10.8	17.9	38.8	29.3	15.8	108,472	70.6	57.1	3.5	10.1	29.4	23.8	34.7
4861796	Richardson city, Texas...................	10.9	20.3	49.4	22.1	10.3	45,148	63.9	50.8	4.2	8.8	36.1	27.0	37.0
4863500	Round Rock city, Texas..................	19.3	26.5	51.1	17.3	7.7	49,740	69.6	49.1	6.0	14.4	30.4	26.4	29.2
4864472	San Angelo city, Texas..................	24.1	44.1	70.7	5.2	3.0	39,065	58.6	42.0	5.7	10.9	41.4	32.8	38.8

Table A-4. Cities — Who: Age, Race/Ethnicity, and Household Structure, 2021—*Continued*

STATE and place code	STATE Place	Total popula-tion	Percent change, 2014–2019	Population by age (percent)					Median age	Race alone or in combination (percent)					
				Under 18 years	18 to 24 years	25 to 44 years	45 to 64 years	65 years and over		White	Black	American Indian and Alaska Native	Asian	Native Hawaiian or Other Pacific Islander	Some other race
	ACS table number:	B01003	Population Estimates	B01001	B01001	B01001	B01001	B01001	B01002	B02008	B02009	B02010	B02011	B02012	B02013
FIPS	column number:	1	2	3	4	5	6	7	8	9	10	11	12	13	14
	TEXAS—Cont.														
4865000	San Antonio city, Texas...............	1,451,863		24.4	10.5	30.1	21.9	13.1	34.1	76.1	8.1	3.2	4.1	0.4	48.3
4865600	San Marcos city, Texas................	68,578	10.0	17.0	35.6	27.1	11.9	8.4	24.3	81.9	10.9	7.7	1.8	0.0	29.6
4869596	Spring CDP, Texas.......................	71,893	18.0	26.3	9.9	30.2	24.0	9.5	31.3	68.9	25.1	1.4	0.0	0.0	32.7
4870808	Sugar Land city, Texas.................	109,337	36.6	26.3	6.3	21.6	27.7	18.1	41.6	50.2	7.9	1.6	42.1	0.0	8.0
4872176	Temple city, Texas.......................	85,428	10.8	24.7	10.0	27.7	22.3	15.3	34.9	84.3	11.7	2.3	4.6	0.0	19.6
4872656	The Woodlands CDP, Texas	116,251	14.1	26.5	4.9	21.6	30.9	16.0	42.5	84.4	5.7	0.7	8.2	0.0	20.3
4874144	Tyler city, Texas..........................	107,199	5.5	22.7	12.7	27.6	21.2	15.7	33.9	65.9	29.0	2.3	2.6	0.0	7.7
4875428	Victoria city, Texas......................	65,384	1.2	26.9	10.3	28.9	19.4	14.4	33.3	81.7	9.0	1.3	1.7	0.0	39.2
4876000	Waco city, Texas.........................	139,601	7.0	23.7	18.4	25.3	19.6	12.9	29.5	70.9	24.8	1.6	2.7	0.0	26.2
4879000	Wichita Falls city, Texas	102,986	-0.4	23.1	15.1	27.9	19.8	14.1	32.7	78.1	14.4	2.2	3.7	0.0	16.4
49000	**UTAH**...................................	3,337,975	12.2	28.3	11.4	28.5	20.1	11.6	31.8	88.4	2.1	2.5	4.0	1.6	11.8
4943660	Layton city, Utah........................	83,299	8.0	29.9	10.2	29.7	19.8	10.3	31.9	92.5	3.6	1.1	2.7	0.8	9.6
4944320	Lehi city, Utah...........................	79,979	23.9	40.4	9.4	33.1	12.7	4.4	25.2	96.1	0.5	0.3	3.8	1.8	5.5
4955980	Ogden city, Utah........................	86,800	4.1	23.5	10.9	33.5	20.5	11.7	33.2	80.8	3.4	4.2	2.3	0.0	19.2
4957300	Orem city, Utah..........................	97,872	6.6	24.6	17.0	30.4	17.2	10.8	28.8	86.7	2.6	1.9	3.3	1.9	17.7
4962470	Provo city, Utah..........................	114,085	1.6	21.1	38.3	22.3	12.8	5.6	23.5	87.9	2.6	3.1	6.3	2.4	14.1
4965330	St. George city, Utah...................	99,965	14.1	24.6	13.0	19.4	22.2	20.7	38.7	90.0	1.2	2.0	4.0	0.0	7.9
4967000	Salt Lake City city, Utah..............	200,475	5.1	17.8	13.8	36.7	20.6	11.1	32.5	80.8	4.7	2.8	6.8	2.8	13.6
4967440	Sandy city, Utah.........................	95,038	5.8	26.5	6.6	27.8	23.9	15.2	37.4	91.9	0.8	2.0	5.4	1.3	6.2
4970850	South Jordan city, Utah	80,142	22.0	31.3	5.6	28.0	21.4	13.5	34.4	89.0	1.1	0.8	8.7	1.3	8.1
4982950	West Jordan city, Utah................	116,544	5.0	29.7	9.2	31.6	19.4	10.1	32.5	81.6	3.1	3.8	5.0	0.0	22.6
4983470	West Valley City city, Utah..........	139,094	0.6	28.6	11.7	27.7	22.9	9.0	31.3	60.1	3.6	4.0	6.8	4.4	38.1
50000	**VERMONT**...........................	645,570	-0.3	18.1	10.2	24.0	27.1	20.6	42.9	95.9	2.0	1.9	2.5	0.1	3.1
51000	**VIRGINIA**............................	8,642,274	5.9	21.8	9.5	27.0	25.5	16.3	38.8	69.4	21.2	2.0	8.5	0.3	9.1
5101000	Alexandria city, Virginia..............	154,706	5.9	18.3	5.3	39.5	24.2	12.8	37.2	66.2	24.3	1.3	7.7	0.2	15.6
5103000	Arlington CDP, Virginia	232,965	4.4	18.1	8.3	38.5	23.2	11.9	35.9	74.1	12.0	2.0	13.3	0.0	14.0
5114440	Centreville CDP, Virginia.............	75,010	-14.4	24.5	10.4	27.9	24.4	12.8	37.1	56.5	10.2	2.1	33.8	0.0	14.8
5116000	Chesapeake city, Virginia............	251,269	4.9	24.3	8.9	27.9	24.8	14.1	37.8	65.0	30.2	3.4	5.4	0.7	6.7
5121088	Dale City CDP, Virginia................	79,782	0.1	28.5	8.5	29.0	24.7	9.3	35.8	48.1	29.0	5.3	14.1	0.7	28.9
5135000	Hampton city, Virginia................	137,746	-1.7	21.4	11.8	28.5	22.8	15.5	36.0	45.3	53.2	4.0	3.4	0.0	5.4
5147672	Lynchburg city, Virginia	79,009	3.9	17.9	26.9	23.6	16.7	14.8	27.6	65.7	30.1	2.8	4.0	0.0	4.8
5156000	Newport News city, Virginia	184,587	-2.0	23.3	11.8	29.0	22.3	13.5	34.5	50.1	44.0	1.6	5.2	0.0	10.3
5157000	Norfolk city, Virginia...................	235,089	-1.1	19.4	17.4	31.6	19.8	11.8	31.3	50.8	43.5	1.4	5.0	0.0	7.8
5164000	Portsmouth city, Virginia............	97,840	-1.7	23.2	9.2	30.5	21.4	15.6	35.6	43.2	56.5	4.4	3.0	0.0	4.4
5167000	Richmond city, Virginia	226,604	5.8	17.1	11.4	35.9	21.4	14.2	34.8	48.4	46.3	1.3	3.1	0.3	8.8
5168000	Roanoke city, Virginia	98,865	-0.3	22.4	7.6	28.3	24.2	17.5	37.6	66.5	31.8	0.9	3.9	0.0	5.6
5176432	Suffolk city, Virginia	96,194	6.1	23.7	8.0	26.8	26.7	14.9	39.0	55.0	42.8	3.3	2.9	0.0	4.4
5182000	Virginia Beach city, Virginia	457,672	-0.2	22.0	8.8	29.8	24.2	15.1	37.1	69.9	22.2	1.5	10.4	0.9	7.4
53000	**WASHINGTON**.......................	7,738,692	10.1	21.7	8.6	29.3	24.3	16.2	38.2	78.1	5.9	3.5	12.3	1.4	12.3
5303180	Auburn city, Washington	87,061	4.1	23.2	10.3	30.1	25.1	11.4	35.5	63.5	10.3	3.5	16.8	3.0	16.7
5305210	Bellevue city, Washington	149,429	8.6	20.3	6.2	32.7	25.8	15.0	38.5	49.5	5.0	1.0	45.1	1.8	6.4
5305280	Bellingham city, Washington	92,290	10.8	14.0	22.4	30.4	18.7	14.6	32.9	89.5	2.5	3.3	6.7	0.7	7.9
5322640	Everett city, Washington.............	110,820	4.4	20.1	8.4	32.0	25.4	14.1	38.4	75.3	7.9	3.9	13.7	1.2	15.8
5323515	Federal Way city, Washington	99,028	3.1	24.9	6.7	28.4	24.7	15.2	37.4	45.9	25.4	3.9	19.3	3.4	16.9
5335275	Kennewick city, Washington	84,478	9.0	25.6	9.6	27.2	21.7	15.9	34.3	80.1	3.8	3.2	2.1	0.0	29.8
5335415	Kent city, Washington................	134,837	5.4	26.6	7.2	31.9	22.9	11.4	35.2	45.1	17.3	1.9	25.5	3.5	17.3
5335940	Kirkland city, Washington	92,105	8.5	20.7	7.0	34.9	22.3	15.1	38.4	77.7	1.9	2.2	20.4	0.4	7.2
5343955	Marysville city, Washington	71,151	8.0	23.1	8.1	31.6	23.5	13.8	36.6	82.8	4.9	3.0	10.4	0.0	13.1
5353545	Pasco city, Washington	84,190	7.2	32.5	11.0	26.7	21.7	8.2	30.2	69.2	2.7	2.2	1.9	2.4	46.6
5357535	Redmond city, Washington	76,360	21.4	22.3	8.2	41.9	16.8	10.8	33.5	51.5	4.3	0.5	46.7	0.0	3.2
5357745	Renton city, Washington............	105,200	3.4	21.8	6.9	33.7	23.7	13.9	37.0	54.2	10.9	4.0	30.5	2.0	17.2
5361115	Sammamish city, Washington	66,630	28.6	29.5	6.0	25.1	32.8	6.5	39.8	58.5	4.6	0.6	41.4	0.0	4.1
5363000	Seattle city, Washington.............	733,904	12.8	13.5	10.4	41.6	21.9	12.5	35.5	72.6	8.4	2.5	21.6	0.8	7.2
5365922	South Hill CDP, Washington	66,875	15.4	28.6	7.7	27.7	25.8	10.2	35.6	81.7	13.8	5.7	11.0	1.4	11.3
5367000	Spokane city, Washington...........	229,065	4.7	22.4	9.1	30.9	22.2	15.3	35.7	88.9	4.7	3.5	5.3	1.9	6.2
5367167	Spokane Valley city, Washington.	105,912	10.2	20.6	9.2	29.2	24.2	16.9	37.9	91.9	3.8	3.1	3.9	0.4	5.9

STATE and place code	STATE Place	Two or more races (percent)	Hispanic or Latino (percent)	Native, born in state of residence (percent)	Foreign born (percent)	Non-citizens (percent)	Total house-holds	Household type (percent of all households)						Percent of house-holds with people age 60 years and over
								Family households				Nonfamily households		
								Total	Married-couple	Male house-holder	Female house-holder	Total	One-person house-holds	
	ACS table number:	B02001	B03003	B05002	B05002	B05002	B11001	B11001	B11001	B11001	B11001	B11001	B11001	B11006
FIPS	column number:	15	16	17	18	19	20	21	22	23	24	25	26	27
	TEXAS—Cont.													
4865000	San Antonio city, Texas...............	38.5	66.4	65.4	14.6	8.6	549,245	64.7	40.2	6.6	17.9	35.3	28.1	33.4
4865600	San Marcos city, Texas.................	27.5	43.8	68.6	5.3	3.3	27,015	41.6	22.9	5.0	13.6	58.4	31.2	22.7
4869596	Spring CDP, Texas.......................	28.8	45.1	61.5	14.3	9.3	23,096	80.7	51.4	10.7	18.6	19.3	15.4	29.4
4870808	Sugar Land city, Texas	9.1	7.6	40.3	35.9	12.9	37,008	78.3	70.8	1.8	5.7	21.7	19.2	48.2
4872176	Temple city, Texas......................	21.0	23.9	60.8	3.8	1.5	34,371	57.3	41.1	4.4	11.7	42.7	34.4	36.9
4872656	The Woodlands CDP, Texas	19.2	23.4	31.2	26.2	12.9	43,992	76.5	63.6	3.9	8.9	23.5	21.4	39.5
4874144	Tyler city, Texas.........................	7.6	24.1	68.0	9.2	6.3	36,169	63.9	46.7	4.3	12.9	36.1	30.6	38.1
4875428	Victoria city, Texas.....................	32.0	59.1	80.4	8.6	5.8	25,410	64.9	41.2	8.1	15.6	35.1	24.6	36.1
4876000	Waco city, Texas.........................	24.1	29.3	66.3	8.6	5.8	53,286	52.9	34.9	4.7	13.3	47.1	34.7	32.2
4879000	Wichita Falls city, Texas	14.0	23.5	63.4	5.2	3.4	38,051	60.6	41.0	6.2	13.3	39.4	33.2	39.2
49000	**UTAH**	9.5	14.8	61.7	8.3	4.8	1,101,499	72.5	59.3	4.6	8.6	27.5	20.6	32.8
4943660	Layton city, Utah........................	9.4	15.5	59.5	6.8	1.9	27,176	73.7	60.7	4.1	8.9	26.3	22.0	31.1
4944320	Lehi city, Utah............................	7.2	5.9	66.7	4.7	3.1	22,067	83.2	75.5	2.9	4.8	16.8	10.5	18.0
4955980	Ogden city, Utah........................	9.4	25.3	57.3	8.7	4.7	32,631	63.2	43.8	7.7	11.7	36.8	29.6	30.3
4957300	Orem city, Utah..........................	13.1	16.1	53.3	11.8	8.6	32,398	73.0	60.4	5.1	7.5	27.0	18.3	29.4
4962470	Provo city, Utah..........................	13.5	17.4	42.7	12.5	8.3	32,518	69.3	58.6	4.4	6.3	30.7	11.3	19.4
4965330	St. George city, Utah...................	5.5	13.8	53.2	9.0	4.2	35,656	71.5	64.0	1.6	5.8	28.5	22.6	43.7
4967000	Salt Lake City city, Utah..............	10.7	19.4	49.8	13.2	7.6	89,839	43.4	29.8	5.7	7.9	56.6	40.1	24.8
4967440	Sandy city, Utah.........................	7.0	9.7	57.2	11.7	5.1	33,587	72.6	61.0	4.4	7.2	27.4	21.1	41.1
4970850	South Jordan city, Utah...............	8.8	9.0	64.3	7.7	4.0	25,502	80.0	69.5	2.7	7.8	20.0	17.3	35.3
4982950	West Jordan city, Utah................	15.9	25.6	64.3	12.1	6.7	36,309	83.0	64.4	6.2	12.5	17.0	13.0	31.7
4983470	West Valley City city, Utah..........	15.7	42.8	52.8	25.2	16.0	42,003	75.9	52.1	8.3	15.5	24.1	16.8	34.5
50000	**VERMONT**	5.1	2.0	48.8	4.2	2.2	270,163	61.1	48.4	4.0	8.7	38.9	27.9	44.9
51000	**VIRGINIA**	9.5	10.2	49.5	12.4	5.9	3,331,461	65.0	48.9	4.6	11.5	35.0	28.3	40.4
5101000	Alexandria city, Virginia..............	14.4	16.5	23.7	23.7	13.7	72,024	43.4	33.0	2.3	8.1	56.6	46.5	28.7
5103000	Arlington CDP, Virginia	13.7	15.6	22.4	22.1	11.5	108,396	44.8	37.1	2.6	5.1	55.2	41.7	24.9
5114440	Centreville CDP, Virginia.............	15.2	15.6	33.5	36.7	14.1	24,957	77.0	59.0	6.5	11.6	23.0	18.4	38.6
5116000	Chesapeake city, Virginia............	10.6	7.3	51.4	5.5	1.7	93,849	73.8	53.4	5.3	15.2	26.2	20.4	37.2
5121088	Dale City CDP, Virginia................	24.7	36.1	37.6	35.7	14.1	22,465	78.7	58.5	5.9	14.4	21.3	17.6	38.6
5135000	Hampton city, Virginia................	9.5	6.7	50.1	5.1	0.9	58,181	63.7	38.8	6.5	18.4	36.3	32.2	40.3
5147672	Lynchburg city, Virginia..............	6.0	4.8	55.9	5.5	3.6	28,346	57.4	38.0	3.5	15.8	42.6	33.3	35.5
5156000	Newport News city, Virginia	10.6	10.0	51.8	7.0	2.8	77,489	55.3	34.7	4.1	16.5	44.7	36.9	34.5
5157000	Norfolk city, Virginia..................	7.9	9.1	46.1	9.2	4.6	97,596	53.7	33.1	6.2	14.4	46.3	36.0	31.4
5164000	Portsmouth city, Virginia	10.4	5.2	64.4	2.9	1.0	40,827	62.2	32.6	5.1	24.5	37.8	30.5	38.2
5167000	Richmond city, Virginia	7.0	7.8	60.2	7.1	4.4	99,929	41.1	22.1	5.2	13.9	58.9	46.2	34.5
5168000	Roanoke city, Virginia	8.4	7.1	65.9	5.6	3.2	42,455	50.1	30.3	5.9	14.0	49.9	39.8	39.8
5176432	Suffolk city, Virginia	8.2	4.9	60.5	3.2	1.3	37,383	72.8	50.1	6.8	16.0	27.2	21.5	37.8
5182000	Virginia Beach city, Virginia	10.5	8.9	44.2	8.4	3.4	182,775	66.4	48.2	5.7	12.5	33.6	26.4	37.3
53000	**WASHINGTON**	12.4	13.7	46.4	14.8	7.9	3,022,255	64.1	49.8	4.6	9.7	35.9	27.1	39.0
5303180	Auburn city, Washington	12.8	18.0	46.2	25.1	13.0	31,836	65.5	46.8	5.7	13.0	34.5	22.6	35.8
5305210	Bellevue city, Washington	8.0	6.8	30.6	42.0	23.1	61,440	63.8	54.0	2.2	7.6	36.2	27.9	30.7
5305280	Bellingham city, Washington	10.3	10.7	48.7	7.2	4.2	40,653	46.6	36.6	3.5	6.6	53.4	32.6	31.1
5322640	Everett city, Washington.............	15.5	17.1	50.9	19.6	9.2	45,029	54.5	38.7	4.6	11.1	45.5	35.8	35.8
5323515	Federal Way city, Washington	12.1	19.1	43.2	29.5	14.5	35,047	70.5	46.2	5.9	18.4	29.5	22.9	41.3
5335275	Kennewick city, Washington	17.8	33.4	48.2	15.7	10.4	30,679	63.6	42.7	3.6	17.3	36.4	30.9	41.7
5335415	Kent city, Washington.................	9.9	18.3	43.7	33.4	16.6	46,036	69.6	50.8	4.4	14.4	30.4	21.2	35.9
5335940	Kirkland city, Washington	9.1	7.5	44.0	21.9	11.4	37,746	62.4	53.9	3.1	5.4	37.6	28.3	35.7
5343955	Marysville city, Washington	14.5	13.6	57.4	12.7	6.0	25,906	70.4	55.0	5.8	9.6	29.6	20.6	36.9
5353545	Pasco city, Washington	24.0	55.9	53.5	21.0	14.5	25,084	81.0	54.1	5.7	21.2	19.0	13.0	27.5
5357535	Redmond city, Washington	5.8	3.6	23.2	48.2	33.1	31,181	65.1	56.5	3.7	5.0	34.9	26.9	21.6
5357745	Renton city, Washington	16.4	20.2	41.4	28.7	13.4	41,997	60.5	43.0	5.8	11.8	39.5	29.4	33.4
5361115	Sammamish city, Washington	9.3	3.6	31.0	36.3	19.9	22,090	87.1	80.8	0.8	5.5	12.9	8.5	25.2
5363000	Seattle city, Washington..............	12.0	7.4	34.9	19.5	11.0	351,650	44.0	35.8	2.5	5.6	56.0	40.0	25.4
5365922	South Hill CDP, Washington	22.3	13.4	52.5	9.1	3.1	22,379	79.8	57.2	5.9	16.7	20.2	16.4	33.6
5367000	Spokane city, Washington...........	9.8	7.4	55.4	5.8	2.1	94,748	55.0	37.5	5.8	11.8	45.0	35.5	36.6
5367167	Spokane Valley city, Washington .	8.5	7.8	56.3	4.2	2.1	44,047	59.3	42.8	6.7	9.8	40.7	30.1	38.9

Table A-4. Cities — Who: Age, Race/Ethnicity, and Household Structure, 2021—*Continued*

STATE and place code	STATE Place	Total popula-tion	Percent change, 2014–2019	Population by age (percent)					Median age	Race alone or in combination (percent)					
				Under 18 years	18 to 24 years	25 to 44 years	45 to 64 years	65 years and over		White	Black	American Indian and Alaska Native	Asian	Native Hawaiian or Other Pacific Islander	Some other race
	ACS table number:	B01003	Population Estimates	B01001	B01001	B01001	B01001	B01001	B01002	B02008	B02009	B02010	B02011	B02012	B02013
FIPS	column number:	1	2	3	4	5	6	7	8	9	10	11	12	13	14
	WASHINGTON—Cont.														
5370000	Tacoma city, Washington	219,203	6.2	20.7	8.2	33.2	23.3	14.7	37.1	71.9	14.3	5.1	13.9	2.5	9.6
5374060	Vancouver city, Washington	192,176	8.9	18.4	8.8	30.2	24.1	18.5	39.4	81.7	5.8	4.0	8.7	2.8	11.1
5380010	Yakima city, Washington	96,565	0.3	25.0	9.1	26.5	21.8	17.5	36.2	73.5	1.1	3.8	2.0	0.0	43.1
54000	**WEST VIRGINIA**	1,782,959	-2.0	20.3	8.8	23.8	26.5	20.7	42.8	95.6	4.3	1.8	1.2	0.1	2.4
55000	**WISCONSIN**	5,895,908	1.9	21.6	9.2	25.2	26.1	17.9	40.1	87.4	7.6	2.0	3.7	0.1	7.0
5502375	Appleton city, Wisconsin	72,951	3.8	24.8	8.9	26.1	24.8	15.4	36.6	86.4	5.0	1.7	8.5	0.0	7.9
5522300	Eau Claire city, Wisconsin	69,196	1.1	20.3	21.4	25.5	19.4	13.4	31.2	91.1	2.0	0.7	8.0	0.0	4.4
5531000	Green Bay city, Wisconsin	107,020	-0.3	20.7	9.8	29.2	24.8	15.5	38.1	84.7	5.5	5.1	3.6	0.0	13.9
5537825	Janesville city, Wisconsin	65,953	0.9	22.2	7.7	26.4	28.8	14.9	41.5	92.8	4.8	0.8	3.4	0.0	7.6
5539225	Kenosha city, Wisconsin	99,285	0.0	24.7	10.9	28.3	23.8	12.3	36.2	84.1	10.6	6.2	3.2	0.0	15.8
5548000	Madison city, Wisconsin	269,162	5.7	16.2	20.2	30.7	19.4	13.5	32.3	81.7	10.0	0.9	9.9	0.2	8.1
5553000	Milwaukee city, Wisconsin	569,326	-1.6	25.9	11.5	30.5	20.5	11.6	32.3	47.6	41.8	1.7	5.4	0.2	17.5
5560500	Oshkosh city, Wisconsin	66,594	0.6	15.5	18.2	24.6	24.8	16.8	35.3	87.7	7.3	1.9	5.2	0.0	2.0
5566000	Racine city, Wisconsin	77,131	-1.7	26.6	9.6	28.5	22.4	13.0	34.6	70.7	25.7	4.7	0.0	0.0	22.7
5584250	Waukesha city, Wisconsin	71,254	1.2	18.5	11.7	29.8	24.6	15.3	36.2	92.9	3.7	2.4	3.3	0.0	8.1
56000	**WYOMING**	578,803	2.8	22.7	9.0	26.0	24.3	17.9	39.0	92.6	1.6	4.2	1.6	0.1	8.5
5613900	Cheyenne city, Wyoming	65,048	2.2	22.5	8.8	27.7	24.3	16.7	39.3	87.3	5.6	1.9	2.0	0.0	10.5
72000	**PUERTO RICO**	3,263,584	-14.3	16.7	9.7	24.6	26.3	22.7	44.1	60.3	13.4	2.2	0.3	0.0	64.3
7206593	Bayamón zona urbana, Puerto Rico	168,592	NA	15.2	9.5	26.9	24.6	23.8	43.4	53.7	9.2	0.4	0.3	0.0	85.5
7210334	Caguas zona urbana, Puerto Rico	76,577	NA	16.4	8.8	26.2	25.1	23.5	44.2	58.6	17.6	1.8	0.0	0.0	46.2
7214290	Carolina zona urbana, Puerto Rico	141,050	NA	16.6	9.5	25.5	25.9	22.5	43.4	42.9	20.7	1.1	0.4	0.0	63.2
7232522	Guaynabo zona urbana, Puerto Rico	72,088	NA	14.8	8.9	24.4	27.6	24.2	46.9	66.9	8.7	0.9	0.0	0.0	78.3
7263820	Ponce zona urbana, Puerto Rico..	112,005	NA	17.9	9.9	23.2	23.5	25.4	43.8	81.1	8.6	0.7	0.0	0.0	60.1
7276770	San Juan zona urbana, Puerto Rico	320,456	NA	15.9	9.2	24.5	25.2	25.3	45.4	54.1	16.7	1.2	0.3	0.0	60.8

NA = Not available.

STATE and place code	STATE Place	Two or more races (percent)	Hispanic or Latino (percent)	Native, born in state of residence (percent)	Foreign born (percent)	Non-citizens (percent)	Total households	Household type (percent of all households)						Percent of households with people age 60 years and over
								Family households				Nonfamily households		
								Total	Married-couple	Male house-holder	Female house-holder	Total	One-person house-holds	
	ACS table number:	B02001	B03003	B05002	B05002	B05002	B11001	B11001	B11001	B11001	B11001	B11001	B11001	B11006
FIPS	column number:	15	16	17	18	19	20	21	22	23	24	25	26	27
	WASHINGTON—Cont.													
5370000	Tacoma city, Washington	14.8	12.9	50.6	12.3	4.8	88,819	60.1	42.5	5.3	12.3	39.9	30.7	35.4
5374060	Vancouver city, Washington	12.2	14.4	33.5	14.4	6.6	81,814	57.2	39.5	5.3	12.3	42.8	32.4	42.8
5380010	Yakima city, Washington	23.4	46.5	58.1	15.5	10.7	37,282	60.5	37.5	6.0	17.0	39.5	33.1	42.6
54000	**WEST VIRGINIA**	5.0	1.7	68.5	1.6	0.8	722,201	64.0	47.8	5.0	11.2	36.0	29.9	46.4
55000	**WISCONSIN**..............................	7.4	7.5	70.9	5.1	2.7	2,449,970	61.8	47.5	4.7	9.7	38.2	30.3	40.9
5502375	Appleton city, Wisconsin.............	9.6	9.6	67.4	7.5	2.8	29,204	61.3	45.7	4.9	10.7	38.7	32.9	38.3
5522300	Eau Claire city, Wisconsin...........	6.2	3.4	69.8	3.2	1.4	28,218	59.4	43.0	9.1	7.3	40.6	29.9	33.8
5531000	Green Bay city, Wisconsin	12.5	16.4	69.8	7.0	4.4	46,857	53.6	36.6	5.5	11.5	46.4	38.9	35.9
5537825	Janesville city, Wisconsin	9.3	7.9	76.5	3.8	2.9	28,236	62.0	42.3	5.9	13.7	38.0	30.5	38.9
5539225	Kenosha city, Wisconsin.............	17.2	18.9	56.2	8.6	4.3	38,438	65.7	46.5	6.1	13.1	34.3	29.0	35.1
5548000	Madison city, Wisconsin.............	10.2	8.3	53.9	12.5	7.4	123,938	42.4	32.2	2.6	7.6	57.6	41.3	28.8
5553000	Milwaukee city, Wisconsin..........	13.5	20.3	66.9	10.1	6.1	232,362	54.1	25.1	7.2	21.8	45.9	35.6	29.9
5560500	Oshkosh city, Wisconsin.............	3.7	3.7	78.0	4.4	1.5	28,532	49.9	36.6	5.5	7.8	50.1	33.1	37.9
5566000	Racine city, Wisconsin	21.8	26.1	69.6	6.9	4.5	30,885	59.5	29.0	5.8	24.7	40.5	32.0	37.5
5584250	Waukesha city, Wisconsin	10.2	13.6	70.3	6.9	3.9	31,139	58.6	42.2	4.5	11.9	41.4	32.2	34.7
56000	**WYOMING**..............................	8.1	10.6	43.0	3.4	1.8	242,763	62.1	49.8	4.6	7.7	37.9	30.9	40.0
5613900	Cheyenne city, Wyoming	7.2	16.5	38.1	3.5	2.0	28,727	56.7	44.4	4.1	8.2	43.3	37.7	35.0
72000	**PUERTO RICO**..........................	35.8	99.2	NA	2.7	NA	1,165,982	63.4	34.5	6.6	22.3	36.6	31.3	53.2
7206593	Bayamón zona urbana, Puerto Rico....	48.1	99.5	0.0	4.7	1.9	61,688	64.4	34.3	5.8	24.3	35.6	31.2	52.8
7210334	Caguas zona urbana, Puerto Rico	22.7	98.5	NA	NA	NA	29,970	58.4	22.7	8.9	26.9	41.6	36.2	48.4
7214290	Carolina zona urbana, Puerto Rico....	26.6	99.6	0.0	6.2	2.9	54,012	61.7	26.5	6.0	29.2	38.3	30.6	47.3
7232522	Guaynabo zona urbana, Puerto Rico....	52.9	98.9	0.0	7.0	3.6	26,979	65.5	44.6	5.5	15.4	34.5	31.0	53.8
7263820	Ponce zona urbana, Puerto Rico..	49.4	99.5	0.0	1.6	1.1	42,404	58.9	32.0	5.2	21.7	41.1	36.4	56.4
7276770	San Juan zona urbana, Puerto Rico....	31.3	98.1	0.0	10.5	6.1	129,554	54.7	25.3	4.8	24.6	45.3	39.2	50.7

NA = Not available.

What
Education, Employment, and Income

What: Education, Employment, and Income

What do Americans do? In 2021, over 168 million Americans were in the labor force, and nearly 80 million were enrolled in school. Many people were in both groups at the same time. Americans' employment and income potential are closely related to their educational attainment. Educational differences among states, cities, and metropolitan areas can influence location decisions of both workers and employers. Employers with low-wage jobs might seek locations with lower education levels, while locations with highly educated work forces might be sought out by other employers.

Education

About 35 percent of Americans (age 25 years and over) held bachelor's degrees and/or advanced degrees, and another 28.1 percent had attended some college or held associate degrees. Nearly two-thirds (63.0 percent) of residents of the District of Columbia held bachelor's and/or advanced degrees, while Massachusetts had the highest level of the 50 states (46.6 percent). In Vermont, Colorado, New Jersey, Maryland, Connecticut, Virginia, and New Hampshire, more than 40 percent of the population held bachelor's and/or advanced degrees, while less than 25 percent of people in West Virginia and Mississippi were college educated. More than half of the seven metropolitan areas with the highest proportions of college-educated residents—more than half of their populations—Boulder, Colorado; Corvallis, Oregon; Ithaca, New York; and Ann Arbor, Michigan—were relatively small metropolitan areas with large universities. More than half of the population held bachelor's degrees or higher in fore of the largest metropolitan areas: Washington-Arlington-Alexandria, DC-MD-VA-WV; San Jose-Sunnyvale-Santa Clara and San Francisco-Oakland-Berkey, CA; and Boston-Cambridge-Newton, MA-NH. In 19 more metropolitan areas, more than 45 percent of the residents had college degrees. In 67 of the counties surveyed 2021, more than half of residents had bachelor's or advanced degrees, with five of the top ten counties being suburbs of Washington, DC. More than three-quarters of the people in 46 cities were college

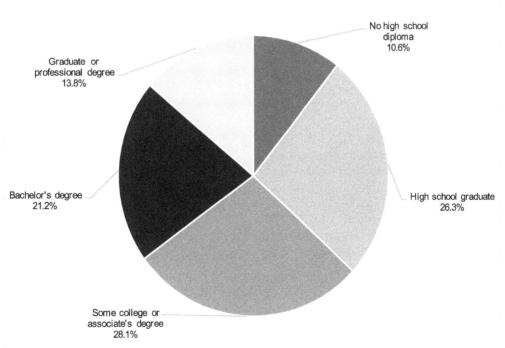

Figure B-1. Educational Attainment in the United States, Percent Distribution, 2021

- No high school diploma 10.6%
- High school graduate 26.3%
- Some college or associate's degree 28.1%
- Bachelor's degree 21.2%
- Graduate or professional degree 13.8%

educated. Some were university cities; some were suburbs of large metropolitan areas; and many had fewer than 100,000 people.

(The number of counties and cities in this book is limited due to the fact that the 2021 supplemental tables were not available at the time this edition went to press. The population threshold consequently was raised from 20,000 to 65,000.)

In addition to those who have earned bachelor's or advanced degrees, 28.1 percent of Americans have received associate degrees or attended college but did not graduate. This group includes more than one-third of residents of five states—Wyoming, North Dakota, Utah, Idaho, and Oregon—where more than a third have attained this level of education. The ACS measure of educational attainment specifically excludes vocational programs, but many adults have earned non-degree credentials such as certificates and licenses.

In the United States, 10.6 percent of adults had not graduated from high school. Another 26.3 percent had a high school diploma but no further education in regular 2-year or 4-year colleges. Thus, almost 40 percent of the American people were in the group with a high school diploma or less. In West Virginia, just over half of the people had not attended college, and nearly half of residents in Louisiana, Arkansas, and Kentucky had completed their education with a high school diploma or less. In three metropolitan areas, more than 57 percent of residents had not attended college: Dalton, Georgia; Merced, California; and Vineland-Bridgeton, New Jersey. In seven small cities—including three in California—more than 75 percent of the people had a high school education or less, while 5 cities had levels below 8 percent. In five counties, more than 60 percent of residents had a high school diploma or less: Starr County, Texas; Putnam County, Florida; Iberia Parish, Louisiana; Somerset County, Pennsylvania; and Belmont County, Ohio.

Among 16- to 19-year-olds in the United States, 2.0 percent were not enrolled in school, not high school graduates, and not in the labor force. This measure provides one way to use ACS data to identify unemployed high school dropouts. Twenty-two states and Puerto Rico exceeded the national level, led by New Mexico (3.9 percent) and North Dakota (3.8 percent) in this high-risk category. Puerto Rico, Alaska, and Arizona had 3.0 percent or higher in this group, while Nebraska and Rhode Island had the lowest levels, with both under 1.0 percent.

Of the nearly million people enrolled in school in the United States in 2021, 68.2 were in kindergarten through 12th grade, 26.7 percent were in college or graduate school, and the remaining 5.2 percent were in preschool. Overall, 18.1 percent of the students were in private schools, but this varied by level of school and by location. Approximately 40 percent of both preschoolers and graduate students were in private schools, but private schools enrolled only about 11 percent of high school students and 23 percent of undergraduate college students. The proportion of high school students in private schools ranged from 22.1 percent in Hawaii to 5.5 percent in Nevada. In some states with large numbers of private colleges, higher education attracts many students from other states. Over three-quarters of the college undergraduates in the District of Columbia were in private schools, as were more than 40 percent in Massachusetts, Pennsylvania, and Rhode Island. Private school proportions were even higher for medical, law, and graduate school enrollment, with nearly 70 percent in private schools in Massachusetts and the District of Columbia, and over 50 percent in private schools in Connecticut, New York, Rhode Island, Pennsylvania, New Jersey, Illinois, and New Hampshire.

Employment

Nearly 63 percent of adults (age 16 years and over) in the United States were in the labor force—the civilian labor force or the armed forces. Those who were not in the labor force might be retired, in school, disabled, homemakers, or formerly employed individuals who have become discouraged from seeking work. Labor force participation was highest in the District of Columbia, where more than 70 percent of adults were in the labor force, with just under 70 percent participating in Utah, Nebraska, Minnesota, North Dakota, and Colorado. In nine states and Puerto Rico, labor force participation was below 60 percent, with the lowest levels in West Virginia, at only 52.6 percent, and Puerto Rico, with only 44.8 percent. But labor force participation does not mean full-time permanent work. Only 65.1 percent of adults age 16 and over worked 35 hours or more per week for 50 to 52 weeks—full-year, full-time workers—in the past 12 months. These full-year, full-time workers included 56.3 percent of men and 43.7 percent of women. Arkansas, Nebraska, and the District of Columbia had the highest levels at more than 69 percent. Hawaii, Alaska, and Puerto Rico had the lowest levels of full-year, full-time workers—all below 60 percent. At least 56 percent of men worked full-year, full-time jobs in 27 states, with the highest levels—over 60 percent—in Utah and Wyoming and the lowest level in the District of Columbia at 47.7 percent. Full-year, full-time work among women was lower, with the highest level of 52.3 in the District of Columbia, followed by Mississippi, Hawaii, Puerto Rico, Vermont, Delaware, Maryland, and Louisiana, where 46

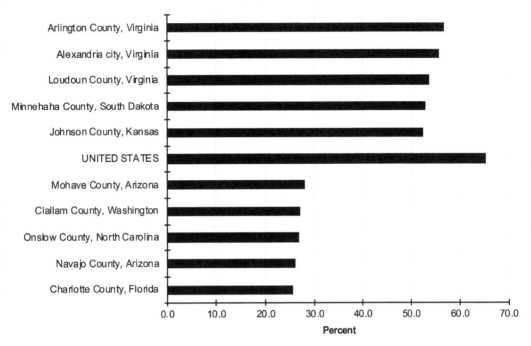

Figure B-2. Highest and Lowest Proportions of Persons, Age 16 Years and Over, Who Worked Year-Round, Full-Time, by County, 2021

percent or more of women worked full-year, full-time. In Utah, Wyoming, and North Dakota, less than 41 percent of women were employed at full-year, full-time jobs.

In 2021, in nine metropolitan areas, less than 30 percent of the population age 16 years and old had full-year, full-time employment. At the county level in 2021, Arlington County, Virginia, had the highest proportion of full-year, full-time workers age 16 years and over at 56.5 percent. In Navajo County, Arizona, less than 24 percent of adults age 16 years and over worked full time and year round. Among cities, Miramar, Florida, had the highest level at 57.1 percent. These levels are not comparable to those presented in previous editions of this volume, as previous editions only measured the population age 16 to 64 years.

In 2021, the national unemployment rate, as measured in the ACS, was 5.5 percent, but 15 states, Puerto Rico, and the District of Columbia had higher levels. Puerto Rico, Nevada, New York, California, New Mexico, and New Jersey had unemployment rates at or above seven percent and five more states and the District of Columbia had rates over six percent. Nebraska's unemployment rate was 2.2 percent and nine other states had rates below 3.5 percent. Three metropolitan areas had unemployment rates over 12 percent: Merced, California (14.5 percent); El Centro, California (14.3 percent); and Madera, California (12.1 percent). Nineteen metropolitan areas

had unemployment rates below three percent, the lowest being Sioux Falls, South Dakota, at 1.6 percent. Five cities had unemployment rates over 15 percent, topped Detroit, Michigan, at 17.4 percent. Bronx County, New York (16.1 percent), was the only surveyed county with an unemployment rate over 15 percent.

In the United States, there were just under 70 million children under the age of 18, with nearly two-thirds of them living in families with two parents. Both parents were in the labor force for 42.5 percent of children. Another 22.3 percent lived with both parents but only one parent was in the labor force. About 27.3 percent lived with a single parent who was in the labor force. In eight states, at least half of the children had two parents in the labor force, with the highest levels in South Dakota, Minnesota, Iowa, and Vermont, all over 54 percent.

Nearly four out of five employed civilians age 16 years and over worked for private employers in 2021. Twenty-two states had higher levels of private employment, led by Indiana, Michigan, and Pennsylvania, all above 83 percent. Alaska had the lowest level of private sector employment, with only 67.8 percent of its labor force employed in the private sector. Nationally, 14.6 percent worked for federal, state, or local government agencies, but in Alaska and the District of Columbia, government employment provided more than 25 percent of jobs. New Mexico, Hawaii,

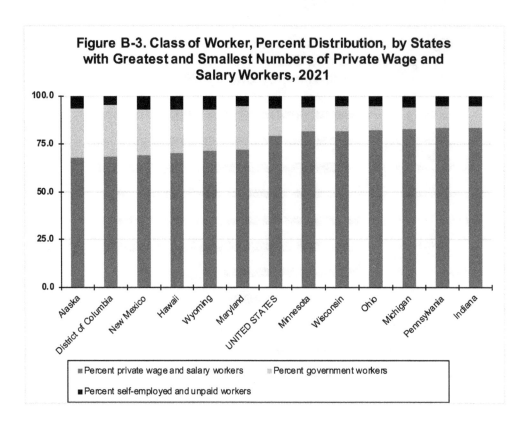

Figure B-3. Class of Worker, Percent Distribution, by States with Greatest and Smallest Numbers of Private Wage and Salary Workers, 2021

Legend:
- ■ Percent private wage and salary workers
- ■ Percent government workers
- ■ Percent self-employed and unpaid workers

Maryland, Wyoming, and Virginia also had high levels of government employment, all over 20 percent. Government employment was lowest—under 12 percent—in Michigan, Pennsylvania, Florida, and Indiana. At the national level, 6.3 percent of workers were self-employed or unpaid family workers. In Puerto Rico, Montana, Maine, Vermont, South Dakota, Idaho, and North Dakota, the proportion was over eight percent. Delaware had the lowest levels of self-employment, at 4.7 percent.

Income

The median income for all American households in 2021 inflation-adjusted dollars was $69,717, ranging from a high of $90.203 in Maryland to lows of $48,716 in Mississippi and $22,237 in Puerto Rico. The San Jose-Sunnyvale-Santa Clara, California, metropolitan area had the highest median income, at $139,892. Six other metropolitan areas had median household incomes above $110,000—San Francisco-Oakland-Berkley, California, and Washington-Arlington-Alexandria, DC-VA-MD-WV. Excluding Puerto Rico, Beckley, West Virginia, had the lowest median income, at $38,737. Five other metropolitan areas among the states had median incomes below $45,000, mainly concentrated in the South: Valdosta, Georgia; Sumter, South Carolina; Morristown, Tennessee; Greenville, North Carolina; and McAllen-Edinburg-Mission, Texas. Fifty-six of the surveyed counties had 2021 median incomes over $100,000, topped by Loudoun County, Virginia, with a median income of $153,506 and Santa Clara County, California, with a median income of $141,562. Starr County, Texas, ($33,367) and Putnam County, Florida, ($33,370) had the lowest median incomes. In 12 of the 634 cities surveyed, the median household income was over $150,000, topped by Dublin, California; Sammamish, Washington; and Palo Alto, California. Cities at the lower end of the income spectrum among the states included Pharr, Texas; Jackson, Mississippi; and Cleveland, Ohio, all under $36,000.

In the United States in 2021, households headed by 45- to 64-year-olds had higher incomes than other households. Among households of different race and Hispanic origin groups, Asian-headed households had the highest median incomes, followed by non-Hispanic White households. Among household types, married-couple families with children under 18 years old had the highest median incomes. Among individuals, the median income for men was higher than the median income for women. Per capita income is the total aggregate income in the geographic area, divided by the population of the area, resulting in a measure of the income for every man, woman, and child. The per capita income for the United States was $38,332. The District of Columbia had the highest per capita income, at $65,808 (partly because it has a very high proportion of one-person households, and a high proportion of prime working-age residents), followed by Massachusetts, Connecticut, New

Figure B-4. Top and Bottom Median Household Incomes, by City, 2021

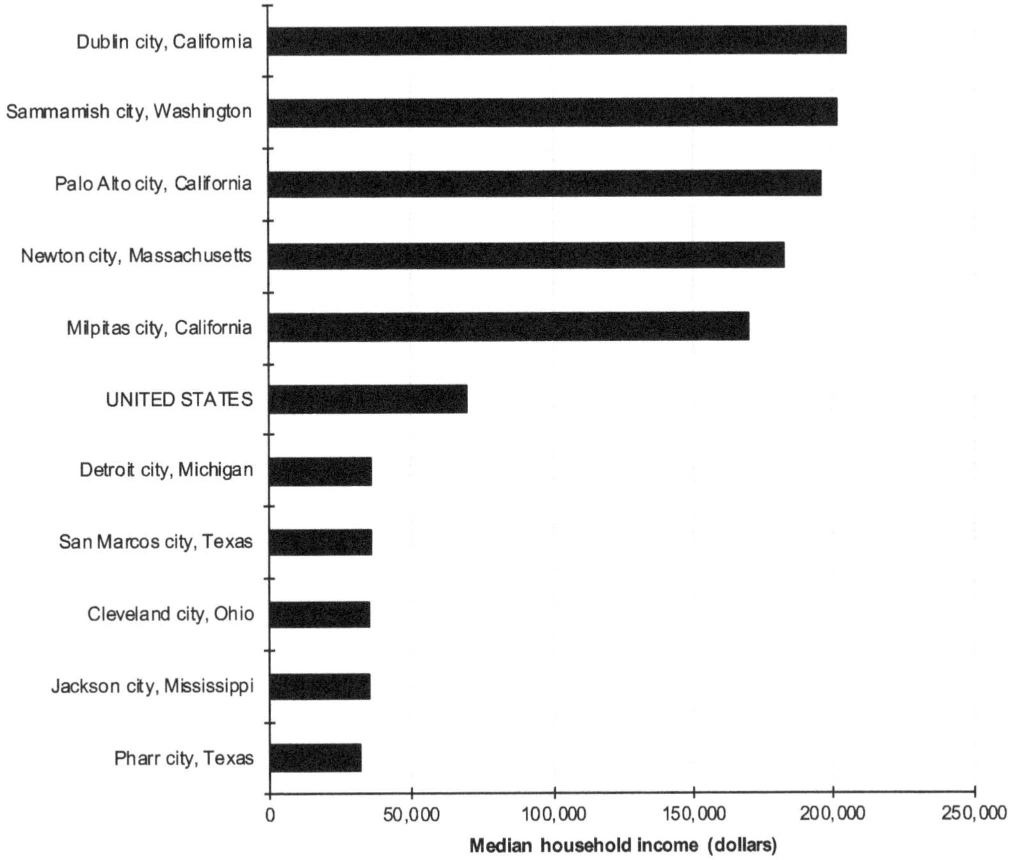

Median household income (dollars)

Jersey, Maryland, Washington, New Hampshire, Colorado, Virginia, and New York, all over $43,000. The lowest per capita incomes were in Puerto Rico, Mississippi, Arkansas, and Oklahoma, all under $30,000.

Most American households (74.3 percent) had some wage and salary income in 2021, ranging from 81.8 percent of Utah's households to 64.8 percent of West Virginia's households and 49.5 percent of Puerto Rico's households. Social Security income was reported by 31.2 percent of households. West Virginia had the highest level among states at 41.0 percent, while more than 35 percent of households in 10 other states and Puerto Rico collected Social Security. With younger populations, less than 25 percent of households in the District of Columbia, Alaska, and Utah had income from Social Security.

In 2021, 14.1 percent of households reported income from cash public assistance or SNAP (Supplemental Assistance Nutrition Program, or Food Stamps.) Puerto Rico had a rate of 49.9 percent, while New Mexico and Louisiana had the highest proportions of households in this

group among states—at or over 20 percent. West Virginia, Oregon, New York, Rhode Island, Massachusetts, and the District of Columbia all had levels above 16 percent. The lowest levels were in Wyoming, Utah, North Dakota, and New Hampshire, all under 8 percent. Interest, dividend, and net rental income were reported by 19.1 percent of households. The highest level, by far, was 41.3 percent of households in Alaska, where most residents receive an annual dividend payment from the state. The lowest level among states was in Mississippi where only 11.7 percent of households had any income in this category.

About 9.8 percent of American households had incomes over $200,000 in 2021. In the District of Columbia, Massachusetts, New Jersey, California, and Maryland, the proportion in this income bracket was 15 percent or higher. West Virginia, Arkansas, Puerto Rico, and Mississippi had levels below four percent.

In the United States, 17.7 percent of households had incomes over $150,000. In 19 metropolitan areas, more than 25 percent of households had incomes of $150,000 or more, topped by the San Jose-Sunnyvale-Santa Clara, California, metropolitan area at 47.2 percent and the San Francisco-Oakland-Berkeley, California, metropolitan area at 39.8 percent. In the Gadsden, Alabama, metropolitan area, less than five percent of households had incomes in that range. In 34 of the counties supplying 2021 data, more than one-third of all households had incomes of $150,000 or more. In 74 additional counties, the proportion of $150,000 households was more than 25 percent. In 25 counties, less than 6 percent of households had incomes in this high range. In 12 cities, more than half of households had incomes of $150,000 or more, with the highest proportion—about 70 percent—in Sammamish, Washington. Eight of the remaining eleven cities were located in California. In 8 cities, less than 4 percent of households had these high incomes.

Poverty status is determined by a standard national definition that includes a household or family's income and number of household or family members. In the 2021 ACS, an estimated 12.8 percent of households were below the poverty level. The poverty measure does not vary from state to state despite variations in the cost of living. In Mississippi and Louisiana, nearly 20 percent of households had incomes below the poverty level, as did more than 17 percent of households in New Mexico and West Virginia. Less than 11 percent of households in Vermont, Alaska, New Jersey, Connecticut, Maryland, Virginia, Colorado, Washington, Minnesota, Utah, and New Hampshire were below the poverty level. In Puerto Rico, 42.7 percent of households were below the poverty level. In all states, poverty rates were higher for female-headed family households.

About 17.4 percent of American households had incomes under $25,000, below the weighted average poverty level for a family of four. The proportion was over 25 percent in Mississippi, West Virginia, and Louisiana, and under 14 percent in Minnesota, Maryland, Washington, Colorado, Utah, and New Hampshire. There were 11 cities where more than 35 percent of all households had incomes below $25,000. San Marcos, Texas, had the highest level at nearly 40 percent. In 11 cities, this low-income proportion was less than 5 percent of households. In Starr County, Texas; McKinley County, New Mexico; Orangeburg County, South Carolina; Putnam County, Florida; Scioto County, Ohio, Apache County, Arizona; and St. Landry Parish, Louisiana, over 35 percent of households had incomes below $25,000.

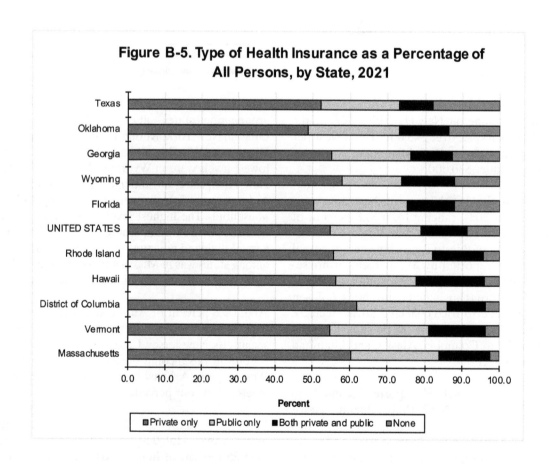

Figure B-5. Type of Health Insurance as a Percentage of All Persons, by State, 2021

Health Care Coverage

More than 90 percent of Americans had some type of health care coverage (public, private, or both), while 8.6 percent of all Americans had no health care coverage. Massachusetts had the highest percentage of residents with some type of health care coverage, at 97.5 percent. More than 90 percent of residents in 37 other states, Puerto Rico, and the District of Columbia had some health insurance coverage. Texas had the highest percentage of residents with no health care coverage, at 18.0 percent, while about 14 percent of residents in Oklahoma and around 13 percent in Georgia had no health insurance.

A little more than half of all Americans (54.6 percent) had only private health care coverage, while 24.4 percent had only public coverage, and 12.4 percent had both private and public health care coverage. Private insurance is most often employment related but also includes insurance purchased directly by individuals, while public health insurance includes Medicare (primarily for persons age 65 and older), and Medicaid (mainly for low-income persons). Utah and North Dakota had the highest proportions of private health insurance, both over 63 percent, while New Mexico and Puerto Rico had the lowest proportion of private health insurance, at 39.2 percent and 31.6 percent, respectively. New Mexico had the highest proportion of public-only health care coverage among the states, at 36.8 percent. Hawaii had the highest proportion of residents carrying both private and public health care coverage (18.2 percent). Many Medicare recipients carry supplemental private insurance, and several states with large older populations had high proportions with both public and private insurance. The lowest proportions were in Texas, Utah, and Puerto Rico, all under 10 percent.

State Rankings, 2021

Selected Rankings

High school diploma or less rank	State	Percent with a high school diploma or less [B-1, cols. 2 + 3]	Bachelor's degree or more rank	State	Percent with a bachelor's degree or more [B-1, cols. 5 + 6]	Labor force participation rate rank	State	Labor force participation rate [B-1, col. 20]
	UNITED STATES.......................	36.9		UNITED STATES.......................	35.0		UNITED STATES.......................	63.0
1	West Virginia................	50.3	1	District of Columbia................	63.0	1	District of Columbia................	70.7
2	Louisiana............	46.2	2	Massachusetts............	46.6	2	Utah............	68.7
3	Arkansas............	45.4	3	Vermont............	44.4	3	Nebraska............	68.6
4	Kentucky............	44.8	3	Colorado............	44.4	4	Minnesota............	68.4
5	Alabama............	43.3	5	New Jersey............	43.1	5	North Dakota............	68.1
5	Mississippi............	43.3	6	Maryland............	42.5	5	Colorado............	68.1
7	Indiana............	42.7	7	Connecticut............	42.1	7	Massachusetts............	66.8
8	Oklahoma............	42.0	8	Virginia............	41.8	8	New Hampshire............	66.7
9	Tennessee............	41.5	9	New Hampshire............	40.2	9	South Dakota............	66.6
10	Pennsylvania............	41.4	10	New York............	39.9	9	Maryland............	66.6
11	Ohio............	41.1	11	Washington............	39.0	11	Iowa............	66.1
12	Nevada............	40.1	12	Minnesota............	38.9	12	Alaska............	65.9
13	Missouri............	39.3	13	Illinois............	37.1	13	Kansas............	65.7
14	Texas............	39.2	14	Utah............	36.8	14	Connecticut............	65.6
15	South Carolina............	38.9	15	Rhode Island............	36.5	14	New Jersey............	65.6
16	Rhode Island............	38.6	16	Oregon............	36.3	16	Wyoming............	65.3
17	New Mexico............	38.2	17	California............	36.2	17	Virginia............	65.2
18	Florida............	37.9	18	Maine............	36.0	18	Rhode Island............	65.1
19	Georgia............	37.7	19	Delaware............	35.6	18	Wisconsin............	65.1
20	Delaware............	37.0	20	Kansas............	35.4	20	Texas............	64.6
21	Iowa............	36.9	21	Hawaii............	35.3	21	Illinois............	64.5
22	Michigan............	36.8	22	North Carolina............	34.9	22	Vermont............	64.3
23	Wisconsin............	36.7	23	Montana............	34.8	23	Washington............	63.9
24	New York............	36.3	24	Georgia............	34.6	24	Indiana............	63.4
24	California............	36.3	25	Pennsylvania............	34.5	24	Hawaii............	63.4
26	South Dakota............	36.2	26	Nebraska............	34.4	24	California............	63.4
27	Idaho............	35.6	27	Florida............	33.2	27	Idaho............	63.1
28	North Carolina............	35.2	28	Texas............	33.1	28	Nevada............	63.0
28	Maine............	35.1	29	Alaska............	32.8	29	Georgia............	62.9
30	Illinois............	35.0	30	Wisconsin............	32.5	30	Missouri............	62.8
31	Alaska............	34.6	31	Arizona............	32.4	31	Ohio............	62.6
32	New Jersey............	34.5	32	North Dakota............	31.7	32	New York............	62.5
32	Arizona............	34.5	32	Missouri............	31.7	33	Pennsylvania............	62.4
34	Connecticut............	34.4	32	Michigan............	31.7	34	North Carolina............	62.2
35	Wyoming............	33.7	32	South Dakota............	31.7	35	Montana............	61.8
36	Kansas............	33.5	36	South Carolina............	31.5	36	Oregon............	61.6
37	Hawaii............	33.4	37	Ohio............	30.7	37	Maine............	61.3
38	Nebraska............	33.0	37	Idaho............	30.7	38	Tennessee............	61.2
39	Maryland............	32.8	39	Iowa............	30.5	39	Oklahoma............	61.0
40	North Dakota............	32.7	39	Tennessee............	30.5	40	Michigan............	60.9
41	Virginia............	32.5	41	New Mexico............	30.1	41	Arizona............	60.6
41	Montana............	32.5	42	Wyoming............	29.2	42	Delaware............	60.1
43	New Hampshire............	32.1	43	Indiana............	28.9	43	South Carolina............	59.6
44	Massachusetts............	31.7	43	Oklahoma............	27.9	44	Florida............	59.1
45	Vermont............	31.6	45	Nevada............	27.6	45	Kentucky............	58.8
46	Oregon............	30.1	46	Alabama............	27.4	46	Arkansas............	58.6
47	Washington............	29.3	47	Kentucky............	27.0	47	Louisiana............	58.5
48	Minnesota............	29.2	48	Louisiana............	26.4	48	Alabama............	57.7
49	Utah............	29.0	49	Arkansas............	25.3	48	New Mexico............	56.9
50	Colorado............	27.7	50	Mississippi............	24.8	50	Mississippi............	56.6
51	District of Columbia............	22.0	51	West Virginia............	24.1	51	West Virginia............	52.6

State Rankings, 2021

Selected Rankings

Unemployment rate rank	State	Unemployment rate [B-1, col. 23]	Veterans rank	State	Veterans as a percent of population 18 years and over [B-1, col. 84]	Families with income below poverty rank	State	Percent of households with income below poverty [B-1, col. 138]
	UNITED STATES..................	6.3		UNITED STATES.....................	6.4		UNITED STATES.....................	12.8
1	Nevada..............................	9.6	1	Alaska	11.0	1	Louisiana	19.4
2	New York............................	8.7	2	Virginia	9.7	2	Mississippi	19.2
3	California............................	8.3	3	Montana	9.4	3	New Mexico	17.8
4	District of Columbia...............	8.1	4	Wyoming..............................	9.2	4	West Virginia	17.6
5	New Jersey	8.0	5	Maine	8.8	5	Kentucky	16.7
6	New Mexico	7.7	6	South Carolina	8.7	6	Arkansas.............................	16.4
7	Rhode Island........................	7.6	7	Idaho	8.6	7	Alabama	16.1
8	Louisiana	7.5	8	Washington	8.2	8	Oklahoma............................	15.3
9	Illinois................................	7.3	9	South Dakota	8.1	9	District of Columbia................	14.7
10	Hawaii................................	7.2	9	Alabama	8.1	10	South Carolina	14.4
11	Michigan	6.9	11	Arizona................................	8.1	11	New York.............................	14.2
12	Connecticut.........................	6.6	12	Hawaii.................................	8.0	12	Tennessee...........................	13.8
12	Massachusetts	6.6	12	Oklahoma............................	8.0	12	Nevada...............................	13.8
14	Alaska	6.5	14	Nevada................................	7.9	14	Texas	13.7
15	Pennsylvania........................	6.4	14	New Mexico	7.9	15	Georgia	13.5
16	Oregon...............................	6.3	16	Florida	7.8	15	Ohio	13.5
16	Mississippi	6.3	16	New Hampshire	7.8	17	North Carolina	13.4
18	West Virginia	6.2	18	Colorado	7.7	18	Florida	13.1
19	Texas	6.1	18	Oregon...............................	7.7	18	Michigan	13.1
20	Oklahoma............................	5.9	18	Arkansas.............................	7.7	20	Missouri..............................	13.0
21	Maryland	5.8	21	North Carolina	7.6	21	Illinois................................	12.5
21	Washington	5.8	21	West Virginia	7.6	22	Maine	12.3
23	Arizona...............................	5.7	23	Missouri..............................	7.5	22	California............................	12.3
23	North Carolina	5.7	24	Nebraska	7.4	24	Pennsylvania........................	12.2
25	South Carolina	5.6	25	Tennessee...........................	7.3	24	Kansas................................	12.2
25	Florida	5.6	25	Georgia	7.3	26	Rhode Island........................	12.1
27	Delaware	5.5	27	Delaware	7.0	26	Arizona...............................	12.1
27	Arkansas.............................	5.5	27	Maryland	7.0	26	Indiana...............................	12.1
27	Georgia	5.5	29	Mississippi	6.9	29	Oregon...............................	12.0
30	Ohio	5.4	29	North Dakota........................	6.9	30	Montana	11.8
30	Kentucky	5.4	30	Kentucky	6.8	30	Wyoming.............................	11.8
32	Alabama	5.3	30	Ohio	6.8	32	Hawaii................................	11.7
32	Tennessee...........................	5.3	33	Kansas................................	6.7	32	North Dakota........................	11.7
34	Colorado	5.2	34	Iowa...................................	6.6	34	Delaware	11.5
35	Minnesota	4.9	34	Wisconsin............................	6.6	34	Massachusetts	11.5
35	Maine	4.9	36	Indiana...............................	6.4	36	Iowa...................................	11.4
37	Indiana...............................	4.7	36	Texas	6.4	37	Nebraska	11.3
38	Virginia	4.6	38	Louisiana	6.3	37	South Dakota	11.3
38	Missouri..............................	4.6	39	Pennsylvania........................	6.2	39	Idaho	11.1
40	Kansas................................	4.3	40	Vermont	6.1	40	Wisconsin............................	11.0
41	Vermont	4.2	40	Minnesota	6.1	41	Vermont	10.8
42	Montana	3.9	42	Michigan	6.0	42	Alaska	10.7
43	Wyoming.............................	3.7	43	Rhode Island........................	5.6	43	New Jersey	10.5
44	New Hampshire	3.6	44	Illinois................................	5.0	43	Connecticut.........................	10.5
44	Iowa...................................	3.6	45	Connecticut.........................	4.9	45	Maryland	10.4
46	Wisconsin............................	3.5	46	Utah...................................	4.8	45	Virginia	10.4
46	Utah...................................	3.5	47	California............................	4.4	47	Colorado	10.0
48	Idaho	3.3	48	Massachusetts	4.2	48	Washington	9.9
49	North Dakota........................	2.8	49	New Jersey	3.9	49	Minnesota	9.6
49	South Dakota	2.8	49	New York.............................	3.9	50	Utah...................................	9.5
51	Nebraska	2.6	51	District of Columbia................	3.6	51	New Hampshire	7.6

State Rankings, 2021

Selected Rankings

Median household income rank	State	Median household income (dollars) [B-1. col. 85]	Households with income of less than $25,000 rank	State	Percent of households with income of less than $25,000 [B-1, cols. 123 + 124 + 125]	Households with income of $100,000 or more rank	State	Percent of households with income of $100,000 or more [B-1, col. 130+131+132]
	UNITED STATES...............	$69,717		**UNITED STATES**...............	17.4		**UNITED STATES**...............	34.0
1	Maryland	90,203	1	Mississippi	26.6	1	District of Columbia	46.2
2	District of Columbia	90,088	2	Louisiana	25.6	2	Massachusetts	45.6
3	Massachusetts	89,645	3	West Virginia	25.2	3	New Jersey	45.3
4	New Jersey	89,296	4	Alabama	23.7	4	California	43.1
5	New Hampshire	88,465	5	New Mexico	23.6	5	Maryland	45.3
6	California	84,907	6	Arkansas	23.4	6	Connecticut	42.6
7	Hawaii	84,857	7	Kentucky	22.9	6	Washington	42.6
8	Washington	84,247	8	Oklahoma	21.3	8	Virginia	40.9
9	Connecticut	83,771	9	South Carolina	20.5	9	Hawaii	41.9
10	Colorado	82,254	10	Tennessee	19.8	10	New York	37.7
11	Virginia	80,963	11	North Carolina	19.3	11	Colorado	40.9
12	Utah	79,449	12	Ohio	19.1	12	New Hampshire	44.2
13	Alaska	77,845	13	Missouri	18.6	13	Rhode Island	37.0
14	Minnesota	77,720	14	New York	18.5	14	Alaska	38.5
15	New York	74,314	15	Florida	18.4	15	Illinois	35.4
16	Rhode Island	74,008	16	Michigan	18.3	16	Minnesota	38.0
17	Vermont	72,431	17	Maine	18.1	17	Utah	38.3
18	Illinois	72,205	18	Georgia	17.9	18	Oregon	34.4
19	Oregon	71,562	18	District of Columbia	17.9	19	Texas	32.5
20	Delaware	71,091	18	Wyoming	17.9	20	Vermont	33.8
21	Arizona	69,056	18	Rhode Island	17.9	21	Pennsylvania	33.0
22	Pennsylvania	68,957	22	Pennsylvania	17.8	22	Georgia	31.4
23	Wisconsin	67,125	23	Nevada	17.7	23	Delaware	34.2
24	Texas	66,963	24	Montana	17.6	24	Arizona	32.5
25	Nebraska	66,817	25	Texas	17.5	25	Florida	29.2
26	Georgia	66,559	25	North Dakota	17.5	26	Nevada	30.9
27	North Dakota	66,519	27	Kansas	17.4	27	North Carolina	28.7
28	Idaho	66,474	28	Indiana	17.3	28	Montana	28.4
29	Nevada	66,274	29	Illinois	17.2	29	Nebraska	30.8
30	South Dakota	66,143	30	Iowa	16.6	30	Michigan	29.1
31	Iowa	65,600	30	South Dakota	16.6	31	Maine	29.5
32	Wyoming	65,204	32	Nebraska	16.5	32	Wisconsin	30.7
33	Maine	64,767	33	Oregon	16.2	32	Idaho	29.7
34	Kansas	64,124	34	Arizona	15.9	34	Kansas	29.3
35	Michigan	63,498	34	Idaho	15.9	34	Ohio	28.3
36	Montana	63,249	34	Vermont	15.9	36	Missouri	27.6
37	Florida	63,062	37	Wisconsin	15.8	37	Tennessee	26.7
38	Indiana	62,743	38	Massachusetts	15.7	38	Iowa	29.3
39	Ohio	62,262	39	Delaware	15.6	39	North Dakota	30.4
40	North Carolina	61,972	40	Connecticut	15.2	40	South Carolina	26.6
41	Missouri	61,847	41	California	14.8	41	Wyoming	29.1
42	Tennessee	59,695	42	Alaska	14.7	42	New Mexico	25.2
43	South Carolina	59,318	43	Virginia	14.5	43	Indiana	27.6
44	Oklahoma	55,826	44	Hawaii	14.3	44	South Dakota	28.1
45	Kentucky	55,573	45	New Jersey	14.0	45	Louisiana	24.2
46	New Mexico	53,992	46	Minnesota	13.3	45	Alabama	24.2
47	Alabama	53,913	47	Maryland	13.2	45	Kentucky	24.2
48	Arkansas	52,528	48	Washington	13.1	48	Oklahoma	24.3
49	Louisiana	52,087	49	Colorado	13.0	49	Arkansas	22.2
50	West Virginia	51,248	50	Utah	11.6	49	West Virginia	22.2
51	Mississippi	48,716	51	New Hampshire	11.5	51	Mississippi	20.7

County Rankings, 2021

Selected Rankings

High school diploma or less rank	County	Percent with a high school diploma or less [B-2, col. 2]	Bachelor's degree or more rank	County	Percent with a bachelor's degree or more [B-2, col. 3]	Unemployment rate rank	County	Unemployment rate [B-2, col. 6]
	UNITED STATES	36.9		**UNITED STATES**	35.0		**UNITED STATES**	6.3
1	Starr County, Texas	69.5	1	Arlington County, Virginia	76.6	1	Bronx County, New York	16.1
2	Putnam County, Florida	62.9	2	Alexandria city, Virginia	65.4	2	Lea County, New Mexico	15.0
3	Iberia Parish, Louisiana	62.0	3	Loudoun County, Virginia	65.3	3	Starr County, Texas	14.8
4	Somerset County, Pennsylvania	60.2	4	Fairfax County, Virginia	64.9	4	Merced County, California	14.7
5	Belmont County, Ohio	60.1	5	Howard County, Maryland	64.6	5	Imperial County, California	14.5
6	Liberty County, Texas	58.8	6	Orange County, North Carolina	63.1	6	Walker County, Texas	13.9
6	Lea County, New Mexico	58.8	7	District of Columbia	63.0	7	Madera County, California	13.8
8	Whitfield County, Georgia	58.3	8	New York County, New York	62.5	8	Putnam County, Florida	13.7
9	Fayette County, Pennsylvania	58.0	8	Boulder County, Colorado	62.5	9	Carbon County, Pennsylvania	12.6
10	Merced County, California	57.9	10	Hamilton County, Indiana	62.3	10	Queens County, New York	11.8
11	DeKalb County, Alabama	57.7	11	Williamson County, Tennessee	62.0	11	Lake County, California	11.7
12	Cumberland County, New Jersey	57.1	12	San Francisco County, California	60.9	12	Navajo County, Arizona	11.4
13	Hidalgo County, Texas	57.0	12	Montgomery County, Maryland	60.9	13	Kings County, California	11.2
13	Lafourche Parish, Louisiana	57.0	14	Marin County, California	59.5	13	Kings County, New York	11.2
13	Ross County, Ohio	57.0	15	Fulton County, Georgia	59.4	13	Sutter County, California	11.2
13	St. Landry Parish, Louisiana	57.0	16	Middlesex County, Massachusetts	58.9	13	Otero County, New Mexico	11.2
17	Schuylkill County, Pennsylvania	56.7	16	Broomfield County, Colorado	58.9	17	Macon County, Illinois	11.1
17	Northumberland County, Pennsylvania	56.7	18	Tompkins County, New York	58.5	18	Caddo Parish, Louisiana	11.0
17	Scioto County, Ohio	56.7	19	Douglas County, Colorado	58.4	19	Essex County, New Jersey	10.9
20	Ector County, Texas	56.6	19	Chittenden County, Vermont	58.4	19	Clark County, Nevada	10.9
21	Ashtabula County, Ohio	56.4	21	Somerset County, New Jersey	58.2	19	Wayne County, Michigan	10.9
22	Terrebonne Parish, Louisiana	56.2	22	Albemarle County, Virginia	57.4	19	Ector County, Texas	10.9
22	Robeson County, North Carolina	56.2	22	Delaware County, Ohio	57.4	23	Passaic County, New Jersey	10.8
24	Armstrong County, Pennsylvania	56.1	24	Washtenaw County, Michigan	57.3	24	Klamath County, Oregon	10.7
25	Walker County, Texas	55.7	24	Johnson County, Kansas	57.3	25	Wicomico County, Maryland	10.6
26	Mayagüez Municipio, Puerto Rico	55.6	26	Norfolk County, Massachusetts	57.1	25	New York County, New York	10.6
27	Columbiana County, Ohio	55.3	27	Morris County, New Jersey	57.0	27	San Juan County, New Mexico	10.5
28	Potter County, Texas	55.1	28	Wake County, North Carolina	56.8	27	Hawaii County, Hawaii	10.5
28	Spalding County, Georgia	55.1	29	King County, Washington	56.3	27	St. Landry Parish, Louisiana	10.5
30	Carbon County, Pennsylvania	55.0	29	Chester County, Pennsylvania	56.3	27	Philadelphia County, Pennsylvania	10.5
30	Cameron County, Texas	55.0	31	Forsyth County, Georgia	56.2	27	Iberia Parish, Louisiana	10.5
32	Tuscarawas County, Ohio	54.7	31	Gallatin County, Montana	56.2	32	Citrus County, Florida	10.4
33	Marion County, Ohio	54.4	33	Travis County, Texas	55.7	33	Atlantic County, New Jersey	10.2
33	Pulaski County, Kentucky	54.4	34	Santa Clara County, California	55.1	33	Genesee County, Michigan	10.2
35	Wayne County, Ohio	54.3	35	Denver County, Colorado	55.0	33	Jefferson County, Arkansas	10.2
36	Wilkes County, North Carolina	53.6	36	Benton County, Oregon	54.9	36	Tulare County, California	10.1
36	St. Clair County, Alabama	53.6	37	Collin County, Texas	54.7	36	Valencia County, New Mexico	10.1
38	Crawford County, Pennsylvania	53.5	38	Westchester County, New York	54.4	38	Kern County, California	9.9
38	Laurens County, South Carolina	53.5	39	Hunterdon County, New Jersey	54.3	38	Winnebago County, Illinois	9.9
38	Elkhart County, Indiana	53.5	40	Dane County, Wisconsin	54.1	40	Wilkes County, North Carolina	9.8
38	Blair County, Pennsylvania	53.5	41	Durham County, North Carolina	53.9	41	Kauai County, Hawaii	9.7
38	McKinley County, New Mexico	53.5	42	Hampshire County, Massachusetts	53.2	41	Josephine County, Oregon	9.7
43	Tulare County, California	53.4	42	Hennepin County, Minnesota	53.2	43	DeKalb County, Illinois	9.6
43	Clearfield County, Pennsylvania	53.4	44	Carver County, Minnesota	53.1	44	Yakima County, Washington	9.5
43	Trumbull County, Ohio	53.4	44	Newport County, Rhode Island	53.1	45	East Baton Rouge Parish, Louisiana	9.4
46	Madera County, California	53.3	46	Bergen County, New Jersey	53.0	46	Stanislaus County, California	9.3
46	Wilson County, North Carolina	53.3	47	Montgomery County, Pennsylvania	52.9	46	Orleans Parish, Louisiana	9.3
48	Kings County, California	53.2	48	Douglas County, Kansas	52.5	46	Highlands County, Florida	9.3
48	Marshall County, Alabama	53.1	48	Johnson County, Iowa	52.5	46	Los Angeles County, California	9.3
50	Montcalm County, Michigan	53.0	50	Lincoln County, South Dakota	52.3	50	Pitt County, North Carolina	9.2
51	Ionia County, Michigan	52.9	51	Cumberland County, Maine	52.2	50	Hunt County, Texas	9.2
52	Yakima County, Washington	52.7	52	San Mateo County, California	51.8	50	Bulloch County, Georgia	9.2
53	Muskingum County, Ohio	52.6	53	Larimer County, Colorado	51.7	50	Mendocino County, California	9.2
53	Imperial County, California	52.6	54	James City County, Virginia	51.4	54	Pulaski County, Kentucky	9.1
55	Richland County, Ohio	52.3	55	DuPage County, Illinois	51.1	54	Fresno County, California	9.1
56	Highlands County, Florida	52.1	55	Riley County, Kansas	51.1	56	Hidalgo County, Texas	9.0
57	Henderson County, Texas	52.0	57	Cobb County, Georgia	50.6	56	San Joaquin County, California	9.0
58	Washington County, Maryland	51.8	57	Washington County, Rhode Island	50.6	58	Salem County, New Jersey	8.9
58	Adams County, Pennsylvania	51.8	59	Fort Bend County, Texas	50.5	58	Providence County, Rhode Island	8.9
58	Franklin County, Washington	51.8	59	Fairfield County, Connecticut	50.5	58	Grant County, Indiana	8.9
61	Walker County, Georgia	51.7	59	Oakland County, Michigan	50.5	58	Richmond County, Georgia	8.9
62	Yuma County, Arizona	51.6	62	Ozaukee County, Wisconsin	50.4	62	Apache County, Arizona	8.8
62	Raleigh County, West Virginia	51.6	62	Guaynabo Municipio, Puerto Rico	50.4	62	Hinds County, Mississippi	8.8
64	Greene County, Tennessee	51.5	64	Dallas County, Iowa	50.2	62	Fayette County, Pennsylvania	8.8
64	Kern County, California	51.5	64	Monmouth County, New Jersey	50.2	62	Cook County, Illinois	8.8
66	Bronx County, New York	51.4	66	Chatham County, North Carolina	50.1	62	Harrison County, Texas	8.8
67	Rapides Parish, Louisiana	51.3	66	Alameda County, California	50.1	67	Talladega County, Alabama	8.7
67	Sutter County, California	51.3	68	Story County, Iowa	49.8	67	San Bernardino County, California	8.7
67	Cattaraugus County, New York	51.3	68	Mecklenburg County, North Carolina	49.8	67	Shasta County, California	8.7
70	Etowah County, Alabama	51.2	70	Nassau County, New York	49.7	67	Oswego County, New York	8.7
70	Orangeburg County, South Carolina	51.2	71	Monongalia County, West Virginia	49.6	67	Butte County, California	8.7
70	Kosciusko County, Indiana	51.2	72	Boone County, Missouri	49.5	67	Delaware County, Indiana	8.7
70	Tangipahoa Parish, Louisiana	51.2	73	Jefferson County, Colorado	49.3	73	Mohave County, Arizona	8.6
74	Allen County, Ohio	51.0	74	Monroe County, Indiana	49.2	73	Riverside County, California	8.6
74	Talladega County, Alabama	51.0	75	Multnomah County, Oregon	49.1	73	Camden County, New Jersey	8.6
			75	Clarke County, Georgia	49.1	73	Dougherty County, Georgia	8.6
						73	Whitfield County, Georgia	8.6
						73	Yuma County, Arizona	8.6
						73	Delaware County, Pennsylvania	8.6
						73	Rock Island County, Illinois	8.6

County Rankings, 2021

Households who received cash public assistance or food stamps/ SNAP rank	County	Percent of households who received cash public assistance or food stamps/ SNAP [B-2, col. 12]	Households with income of less than $25,000 rank	County	Percent of households with income of less than $25,000 [B-2, col. 10]	Households with income of $150,000 or more rank	County	Percent of households with income of $150,000 or more [B-2, col. 11]
	UNITED STATES	14.1		UNITED STATES	17.4		UNITED STATES	17.7
1	Starr County, Texas	50.2	1	Starr County, Texas	42.4	1	Loudoun County, Virginia	52.0
2	McKinley County, New Mexico	40.7	2	McKinley County, New Mexico	38.1	2	Santa Clara County, California	47.7
3	Bronx County, New York	38.7	3	Orangeburg County, South Carolina	38.0	3	Fairfax County, Virginia	44.8
4	Robeson County, North Carolina	34.4	4	Putnam County, Florida	35.8	4	San Mateo County, California	44.6
5	Hidalgo County, Texas	31.9	5	Scioto County, Ohio	35.7	5	Howard County, Maryland	43.8
6	Putnam County, Florida	29.8	5	Apache County, Arizona	35.7	6	San Francisco County, California	42.3
7	San Juan County, New Mexico	29.7	7	St. Landry Parish, Louisiana	35.6	7	Marin County, California	42.0
8	Apache County, Arizona	29.7	8	Pulaski County, Kentucky	34.3	8	Douglas County, Colorado	41.7
9	St. Landry Parish, Louisiana	29.0	8	Robeson County, North Carolina	34.3	9	Nassau County, New York	41.6
10	Cameron County, Texas	28.8	10	Walker County, Georgia	34.1	10	Somerset County, New Jersey	40.9
11	Philadelphia County, Pennsylvania	28.7	11	Lowndes County, Georgia	33.9	10	Arlington County, Virginia	40.9
12	Yuba County, California	28.3	11	Jones County, Mississippi	33.9	12	Morris County, New Jersey	40.7
13	Baltimore city, Maryland	28.3	13	Rockingham County, North Carolina	33.1	13	Williamson County, Tennessee	40.5
14	Dougherty County, Georgia	27.7	14	Caldwell County, North Carolina	32.8	14	Hunterdon County, New Jersey	39.1
15	Miami-Dade County, Florida	27.3	15	Bronx County, New York	32.5	15	Norfolk County, Massachusetts	38.1
16	Webb County, Texas	27.2	15	Ouachita Parish, Louisiana	32.5	16	Forsyth County, Georgia	37.8
17	Valencia County, New Mexico	26.9	17	Calhoun County, Alabama	31.9	17	Westchester County, New York	37.7
18	Imperial County, California	26.8	17	Sumter County, South Carolina	31.9	17	Alameda County, California	37.6
18	Wayne County, North Carolina	26.8	19	DeKalb County, Alabama	31.7	18	Middlesex County, Massachusetts	37.6
20	Doña Ana County, New Mexico	26.7	20	Talladega County, Alabama	31.6	18	Montgomery County, Maryland	37.6
21	Scioto County, Ohio	26.5	21	Orleans Parish, Louisiana	31.5	21	Contra Costa County, California	37.1
22	Hampden County, Massachusetts	26.2	22	Hinds County, Mississippi	31.1	22	King County, Washington	36.5
23	Umatilla County, Oregon	26.0	22	Lauderdale County, Mississippi	31.1	23	Monmouth County, New Jersey	36.3
24	Tulare County, California	25.9	22	Raleigh County, West Virginia	31.1	24	Calvert County, Maryland	36.2
25	Josephine County, Oregon	25.8	25	Hidalgo County, Texas	30.4	24	Suffolk County, New York	36.2
26	Klamath County, Oregon	25.6	26	Caddo Parish, Louisiana	30.2	26	Fauquier County, Virginia	36.1
27	Yakima County, Washington	25.5	27	Florence County, South Carolina	29.8	27	Prince William County, Virginia	35.3
17	Otero County, New Mexico	25.5	28	Dougherty County, Georgia	29.7	28	Delaware County, Ohio	34.7
29	Kings County, New York	25.1	29	Montgomery County, Virginia	29.6	29	Chester County, Pennsylvania	34.6
30	Wayne County, Michigan	24.8	30	Pitt County, North Carolina	29.4	29	Stafford County, Virginia	34.6
31	Iberia Parish, Louisiana	24.1	30	Cameron County, Texas	29.4	31	Bergen County, New Jersey	34.3
32	Calcasieu Parish, Louisiana	24.0	32	St. Francois County, Missouri	29.3	32	Fairfield County, Connecticut	34.1
33	Franklin County, Washington	23.9	32	San Juan County, New Mexico	29.3	33	Putnam County, New York	34.0
34	Merced County, California	23.8	34	Wilson County, North Carolina	29.2	34	Broomfield County, Colorado	33.5
35	Bibb County, Georgia	23.3	35	Payne County, Oklahoma	28.8	35	Anne Arundel County, Maryland	33.3
36	Laurens County, South Carolina	23.2	35	Cabell County, West Virginia	28.8	36	Washington County, Minnesota	32.5
36	Fayette County, Pennsylvania	23.2	37	Columbiana County, Ohio	28.6	37	Hamilton County, Indiana	32.4
36	Tangipahoa Parish, Louisiana	23.2	38	Pickens County, South Carolina	28.3	37	Carver County, Minnesota	32.4
36	El Paso County, Texas	23.2	39	Doña Ana County, New Mexico	28.2	39	Oldham County, Kentucky	32.3
40	Milwaukee County, Wisconsin	23.1	40	Saginaw County, Michigan	28.1	40	Montgomery County, Pennsylvania	32.1
41	Yuma County, Arizona	23.0	41	Etowah County, Alabama	28.0	40	Scott County, Minnesota	32.1
41	Orleans Parish, Louisiana	23.0	41	Ross County, Ohio	28.0	42	Alexandria city, Virginia	32.0
43	Marion County, Oregon	22.9	43	Tehama County, California	27.9	43	New York County, New York	31.8
43	Caddo Parish, Louisiana	22.9	44	Mohave County, Arizona	27.8	43	Placer County, California	31.8
45	Fresno County, California	22.7	45	St. Louis city, Missouri	27.7	45	Boone County, Indiana	31.7
46	Wilson County, North Carolina	22.5	46	Craighead County, Arkansas	27.6	46	Orange County, California	31.6
47	Suffolk County, Massachusetts	22.4	47	Sullivan County, Tennessee	27.4	47	Carroll County, Maryland	31.5
47	Allegany County, Maryland	22.4	48	Wilkes County, North Carolina	27.3	47	Collin County, Texas	31.5
49	Polk County, Oregon	22.2	48	Wayne County, Indiana	27.3	49	Santa Cruz County, California	31.4
49	Navajo County, Arizona	22.2	48	Lafourche Parish, Louisiana	27.3	50	Rockwall County, Texas	31.2
51	Lea County, New Mexico	22.1	51	Iberia Parish, Louisiana	27.2	51	District of Columbia, District of Columbia	31.1
51	Rapides Parish, Louisiana	22.1	51	Monroe County, Indiana	27.2	51	Plymouth County, Massachusetts	31.1
53	Osceola County, Florida	22.0	53	Philadelphia County, Pennsylvania	27.1	53	Napa County, California	31.0
53	Muscogee County, Georgia	22.0	53	Henderson County, Texas	27.1	54	San Benito County, California	30.7
53	Hawaii County, Hawaii	22.0	53	Lea County, New Mexico	27.1	55	Frederick County, Maryland	30.5
56	Liberty County, Georgia	21.9	56	Jefferson County, Arkansas	26.8	56	Rockland County, New York	30.0
56	Linn County, Oregon	21.9	57	Tangipahoa Parish, Louisiana	26.7	57	St. Mary's County, Maryland	29.9
56	Raleigh County, West Virginia	21.9	57	Montgomery County, Alabama	26.7	48	Boulder County, Colorado	29.7
59	Winnebago County, Illinois	21.8	57	Navajo County, Arizona	26.7	59	Lake County, Illinois	29.4
60	Florence County, South Carolina	21.7	60	Richmond County, Georgia	26.6	59	DuPage County, Illinois	29.4
60	Lane County, Oregon	21.7	61	Chautauqua County, New York	26.5	61	St. Johns County, Florida	29.2
62	Mahoning County, Ohio	21.6	61	Potter County, Texas	26.5	62	Albemarle County, Virginia	29.1
62	Madera County, California	21.6	63	Bibb County, Georgia	26.4	62	Bucks County, Pennsylvania	29.1
62	Grant County, Washington	21.6	63	Baltimore city, Maryland	26.4	64	Rockingham County, New Hampshire	29.0
62	Richmond County, Georgia	21.6	65	Forrest County, Mississippi	26.3	64	Charles County, Maryland	29.0
66	Grays Harbor County, Washington	21.5	66	Kershaw County, South Carolina	26.2	66	Chatham County, North Carolina	28.8
66	East Baton Rouge Parish, Louisiana	21.5	67	Brazos County, Texas	26.1	67	Middlesex County, New Jersey	28.6
66	Aroostook County, Maine	21.5	68	Roanoke city, Virginia	26.0	68	Sonoma County, California	28.5
69	Douglas County, Oregon	21.4	68	Marshall County, Alabama	26.0	69	Snohomish County, Washington	28.3
70	Peoria County, Illinois	21.3	68	Mahoning County, Ohio	26.0	70	Sussex County, New Jersey	28.2
70	Lawrence County, Pennsylvania	21.3	71	Valencia County, New Mexico	25.9	71	El Dorado County, California	28.0
72	Washington County, Maryland	21.2	72	Vigo County, Indiana	25.7	71	Cherokee County, Georgia	28.0
72	Saginaw County, Michigan	21.2	72	Fayette County, Pennsylvania	25.7	73	Denton County, Texas	27.9
74	Macon County, Illinois	21.1	74	Houston County, Alabama	25.6	73	Fort Bend County, Texas	27.9
74	Wilkes County, North Carolina	21.1	74	Kanawha County, West Virginia	25.6	75	Union County, New Jersey	27.8
74	Passaic County, New Jersey	21.1	74	Richmond County, Virginia	25.6			
			74	Delaware County, Indiana	25.6			
			74	Portsmouth city, Virginia	25.6			

Metropolitan Area Rankings, 2021

Selected Rankings

High school diploma or less rank	Area name	Percent with a high school diploma or less [B-3, col. 2]	Bachelor's degree or more rank	Area name	Percent with a bachelor's degree or more [B-3, col. 3]
	UNITED STATES..	36.9		UNITED STATES..	35.0
1	Dalton, GA	58.3	1	Boulder, CO	64.8
2	Merced, CA	57.9	2	Corvallis, OR	57.9
3	Vineland-Bridgeton, NJ	57.1	2	Ithaca, NY	56.9
4	McAllen-Edinburg-Mission, TX	57.0	2	Ann Arbor, MI	55.9
5	Houma-Thibodaux, LA	56.6	5	San Jose-Sunnyvale-Santa Clara, CA	52.7
5	Odessa, TX	56.6	6	Washington-Arlington-Alexandria, DC-VA-MD-WV	51.4
7	Brownsville-Harlingen, TX	55.0	6	San Francisco-Oakland-Berkeley, CA	51.4
8	Beckley, WV	54.6	8	Boston-Cambridge-Newton, MA-NH	49.3
9	Elkhart-Goshen, IN	53.5	9	Charlottesville, VA	49.2
9	Altoona, PA	53.5	10	Bridgeport-Stamford-Norwalk, CT	49.1
11	Visalia, CA	53.4	11	Fort Collins, CO	49.0
12	Madera, CA	53.3	12	Iowa City, IA	48.8
13	Hanford-Corcoran, CA	53.2	13	Madison, WI	48.6
14	Yakima, WA	52.7	14	Raleigh-Cary, NC	48.0
14	Alexandria, LA	52.7	15	Barnstable Town, MA	47.1
16	Pine Bluff, AR	52.6	15	Lawrence, KS	47.1
16	El Centro, CA	52.6	17	Durham-Chapel Hill, NC	46.3
18	Mansfield, OH	52.3	18	Austin-Round Rock-Georgetown, TX	46.2
19	Sebring-Avon Park, FL	52.1	19	Bloomington, IL	45.8
20	Gettysburg, PA	51.8	19	Denver-Aurora-Lakewood, CO	45.8
21	Yuma, AZ	51.6	21	Burlington-South Burlington, VT	44.6
22	Bakersfield, CA	51.5	21	Ames, IA	44.6
23	Morristown, TN	51.4	23	Trenton-Princeton, NJ	44.5
24	Bloomsburg-Berwick, PA	51.3	23	Champaign-Urbana, IL	44.5
25	Gadsden, AL	51.2	25	Missoula, MT	44.4
25	Hammond, LA	51.2	26	Seattle-Tacoma-Bellevue, WA	44.1
27	Wheeling, WV-OH	51.1	27	Columbia, MO	44.0
28	Lima, OH	51.0	28	Santa Cruz-Watsonville, CA	43.8
29	St. Joseph, MO-KS	50.8	28	State College, PA	43.8
30	Victoria, TX	50.7	30	Minneapolis-St. Paul-Bloomington, MN-WI	43.2
31	Chambersburg-Waynesboro, PA	50.5	31	Athens-Clarke County, GA	42.4
32	Terre Haute, IN	50.4	32	Portland-South Portland, ME	42.3
32	Modesto, CA	50.4	33	Baltimore-Columbia-Towson, MD	41.9
34	Texarkana, TX-AR	50.2	34	New York-Newark-Jersey City, NY-NJ-PA	41.8
35	Laredo, TX	50.1	35	Auburn-Opelika, AL	41.4
35	Lebanon, PA	50.1	36	Rochester, MN	41.2
35	Danville, IL	50.1	37	Bloomington, IN	41.0
35	Reading, PA	50.1	38	Provo-Orem, UT	40.6
35	Enid, OK	50.1	39	Fargo, ND-MN	40.4
40	Johnstown, PA	49.7	40	Portland-Vancouver-Hillsboro, OR-WA	40.3
41	Lafayette, LA	49.5	41	Huntsville, AL	40.2
42	Charleston, WV	49.4	42	Santa Fe, NM	40.1
42	Hagerstown-Martinsburg, MD-WV	49.4	43	Atlanta-Sandy Springs-Alpharetta, GA	39.9
44	Michigan City-La Porte, IN	49.2	43	San Diego-Chula Vista-Carlsbad, CA	39.9
45	Cumberland, MD-WV	49.1	45	Hartford-East Hartford-Middletown, CT	39.7
45	Grand Island, NE	49.1	45	Lincoln, NE	39.7
47	Kingsport-Bristol, TN-VA	49.0	47	Flagstaff, AZ	39.6
48	Youngstown-Warren-Boardman, OH-PA	48.8	48	Albany-Schenectady-Troy, NY	39.5
49	Lakeland-Winter Haven, FL	48.4	49	Wilmington, NC	39.3
50	Albany, GA	48.1	50	Chicago-Naperville-Elgin, IL-IN-WI	39.2
50	Decatur, IL	48.1	51	Colorado Springs, CO	39.2
52	Fort Smith, AR-OK	48.0	52	Philadelphia-Camden-Wilmington, PA-NJ-DE-MD	39.0
53	Williamsport, PA	47.9	53	Gainesville, FL	38.9
53	Homosassa Springs, FL	47.9	54	Bend, OR	38.7
55	Anniston-Oxford, AL	47.8	54	Tallahassee, FL	38.7
56	Farmington, NM	47.5	56	Nashville-Davidson--Murfreesboro--Franklin, TN	38.5
56	Huntington-Ashland, WV-KY-OH	47.5	57	Lexington-Fayette, KY	38.3
58	Weirton-Steubenville, WV-OH	47.3	57	Kalamazoo-Portage, MI	38.3
58	Florence-Muscle Shoals, AL	47.3	59	Hilton Head Island-Bluffton, SC	38.0
60	Wichita Falls, TX	47.2	59	Des Moines-West Des Moines, IA	38.0
60	Yuba City, CA	47.2	59	College Station-Bryan, TX	38.0
62	Lake Havasu City-Kingman, AZ	47.1	62	Morgantown, WV	37.9
62	Stockton, CA	47.1	62	Columbus, OH	37.9
62	Monroe, LA	47.1	64	Manchester-Nashua, NH	37.8
62	Lancaster, PA	47.1	65	Kansas City, MO-KS	37.7
66	Springfield, OH	47.0	65	Omaha-Council Bluffs, NE-IA	37.7
67	Salinas, CA	46.8	67	Richmond, VA	37.6
67	Sumter, SC	46.8	68	Charleston-North Charleston, SC	37.5
67	Sioux City, IA-NE-SD	46.8	69	Santa Rosa-Petaluma, CA	37.4
70	Canton-Massillon, OH	46.6	69	Manhattan, KS	37.4
70	Hickory-Lenoir-Morganton, NC	46.6	71	Mankato, MN	37.2
70	Mobile, AL	46.6	71	San Luis Obispo-Paso Robles, CA	37.2
70	Florence, SC	46.6	73	Rochester, NY	37.1
74	Dothan, AL	46.5	74	Salt Lake City, UT	36.5
74	York-Hanover, PA	46.5	74	Columbus, IN	36.5

Metropolitan Area Rankings, 2021

Selected Rankings

Unemploy-ment rate rank	Area name	Unemployment rate [B-3, col. 6]	Households who received cash public assistance or food stamps/SNAP rank	Area name	Percent of households who received cash public assistance or food stamps/SNAP [B-2, col. 12]
	UNITED STATES............	6.3		UNITED STATES............	14.1
1	Merced, CA	14.5	1	McAllen-Edinburg-Mission, TX	31.9
2	El Centro, CA	14.3	2	Farmington, NM	29.7
3	Madera, CA	12.1	3	Brownsville-Harlingen, TX	28.8
4	Hanford-Corcoran, CA	11.1	4	Laredo, TX	27.2
5	Decatur, IL	10.9	5	El Centro, CA	26.8
5	Las Vegas-Henderson-Paradise, NV	10.9	5	Goldsboro, NC	26.8
7	Odessa, TX	10.8	7	Las Cruces, NM	26.7
8	Rockford, IL	10.5	8	Visalia, CA	25.9
8	Farmington, NM	10.4	9	Grants Pass, OR	25.8
10	Homosassa Springs, FL	10.2	10	Yakima, WA	25.5
10	Atlantic City-Hammonton, NJ	10.2	11	Merced, CA	23.8
12	Flint, MI	10.1	12	Lake Charles, LA	23.7
13	Visalia, CA	10.0	13	Rocky Mount, NC	23.4
14	Monroe, LA	9.9	14	Hammond, LA	23.2
15	Bakersfield, CA	9.7	15	Beckley, WV	23.1
16	Grants Pass, OR	9.5	15	El Paso, TX	23.1
17	Yakima, WA	9.3	17	Yuma, AZ	23.0
17	New York-Newark-Jersey City, NY-NJ-PA	9.3	18	Salem, OR	22.8
17	Modesto, CA	9.3	19	Fresno, CA	22.7
20	Sebring-Avon Park, FL	9.2	20	Springfield, MA	22.5
21	Greenville, NC	9.1	21	Columbus, GA-AL	22.4
22	Fresno, CA	9.0	22	Albany, GA	22.1
22	McAllen-Edinburg-Mission, TX	9.0	23	Albany-Lebanon, OR	21.9
24	Stockton, CA	8.9	24	Eugene-Springfield, OR	21.7
25	Shreveport-Bossier City, LA	8.8	25	Florence, SC	21.6
26	Los Angeles-Long Beach-Anaheim, CA	8.7	25	Madera, CA	21.6
26	Redding, CA	8.7	25	Yuba City, CA	21.6
26	Chico, CA	8.7	28	Rockford, IL	21.5
26	Riverside-San Bernardino-Ontario, CA	8.7	29	Macon-Bibb County, GA	21.3
30	Muncie, IN	8.6	30	Saginaw, MI	21.2
30	Lake Havasu City-Kingman, AZ	8.6	31	Decatur, IL	21.1
30	Yuba City, CA	8.6	32	Alexandria, LA	21.0
30	Sumter, SC	8.6	32	Longview, WA	21.0
34	Yuma, AZ	8.5	32	Springfield, OH	21.0
34	Pine Bluff, AR	8.5	32	Hinesville, GA	21.0
36	New Orleans-Metairie, LA	8.2	36	Pueblo, CO	20.8
37	Lima, OH	8.1	36	Monroe, LA	20.8
37	Brownsville-Harlingen, TX	8.1	36	Charleston, WV	20.8
37	Saginaw, MI	8.1	39	Lima, OH	20.6
40	San Diego-Chula Vista-Carlsbad, CA	8.0	39	Sumter, SC	20.6
40	New Haven-Milford, CT	8.0	41	Erie, PA	20.5
42	Detroit-Warren-Dearborn, MI	7.9	42	Albuquerque, NM	20.4
42	El Paso, TX	7.9	42	Miami-Fort Lauderdale-Pompano Beach, FL	20.4
44	Walla Walla, WA	7.8	44	Valdosta, GA	20.3
44	Worcester, MA-CT	7.8	44	Mobile, AL	20.3
44	Sierra Vista-Douglas, AZ	7.8	46	Huntington-Ashland, WV-KY-OH	20.2
44	Battle Creek, MI	7.8	47	Bakersfield, CA	20.1
48	Baton Rouge, LA	7.7	48	Kennewick-Richland, WA	20.0
48	Weirton-Steubenville, WV-OH	7.7	49	Baton Rouge, LA	19.9
48	Flagstaff, AZ	7.7	50	Elmira, NY	19.6
48	Carbondale-Marion, IL	7.7	51	Hanford-Corcoran, CA	19.5
48	Medford, OR	7.7	51	Corpus Christi, TX	19.5
48	Springfield, MA	7.7	51	Danville, IL	19.5
54	Santa Cruz-Watsonville, CA	7.6	54	Fayetteville, NC	19.4
54	Dalton, GA	7.6	54	Shreveport-Bossier City, LA	19.4
54	Albany, GA	7.6	56	Greenville, NC	19.1
54	Memphis, TN-MS-AR	7.6	57	Sierra Vista-Douglas, AZ	19.0
54	Muskegon, MI	7.6	58	Cumberland, MD-WV	18.9
54	Trenton-Princeton, NJ	7.6	59	Johnstown, PA	18.8
54	Chicago-Naperville-Elgin, IL-IN-WI	7.6	59	Houma-Thibodaux, LA	18.8
61	Erie, PA	7.5	61	Flint, MI	18.8
61	Macon-Bibb County, GA	7.5	62	Anniston-Oxford, AL	18.7
61	Lawton, OK	7.5	63	Spokane-Spokane Valley, WA	18.6
61	Santa Fe, NM	7.5	63	Scranton--Wilkes-Barre, PA	18.6
65	Gadsden, AL	7.4	65	Parkersburg-Vienna, WV	18.5
65	San Luis Obispo-Paso Robles, CA	7.4	66	Youngstown-Warren-Boardman, OH-PA	18.4
65	Oxnard-Thousand Oaks-Ventura, CA	7.4	67	Lafayette, LA	18.3
68	Providence-Warwick, RI-MA	7.3	68	Providence-Warwick, RI-MA	18.2
68	Houston-The Woodlands-Sugar Land, TX	7.3	68	Pittsfield, MA	18.2
68	Philadelphia-Camden-Wilmington, PA-NJ-DE-MD	7.3	68	Muskegon, MI	18.2
68	Augusta-Richmond County, GA-SC	7.3	68	Medford, OR	18.2
68	Gulfport-Biloxi, MS	7.3	72	Stockton, CA	18.1
73	Kokomo, IN	7.2	73	Carbondale-Marion, IL	18.0
73	Lansing-East Lansing, MI	7.2	73	Montgomery, AL	17.8
73	San Francisco-Oakland-Berkeley, CA	7.2	73	Greensboro-High Point, NC	17.8
73	Santa Maria-Santa Barbara, CA	7.2	75	Greensboro-High Point, NC	17.8
73	Eugene-Springfield, OR	7.2	75	Vineland-Bridgeton, NJ	17.7
73	Las Cruces, NM	7.2	75	Bowling Green, KY	17.7
73	Cleveland, TN	7.2			

Metropolitan Area Rankings, 2021

Selected Rankings

Households with income of less than $25,000 rank	Area name	Percent of households with income of less than $25,000 [B-3, col. 10]	Households with income of $150,000 or more rank	Area name	Percent of households with income of $150,000 or more [B-3, col. 11]
	UNITED STATES..	17.4		UNITED STATES..	17.7
1	Monroe, LA	33.5	1	San Jose-Sunnyvale-Santa Clara, CA	47.2
2	Valdosta, GA	33.4	2	San Francisco-Oakland-Berkeley, CA	39.8
3	Sumter, SC	32.3	3	Washington-Arlington-Alexandria, DC-VA-MD-WV	35.3
4	Beckley, WV	32.1	4	Bridgeport-Stamford-Norwalk, CT	34.1
5	Anniston-Oxford, AL	31.9	5	Boston-Cambridge-Newton, MA-NH	32.2
6	Florence, SC	30.6	6	Seattle-Tacoma-Bellevue, WA	31.7
7	McAllen-Edinburg-Mission, TX	30.4	7	Santa Cruz-Watsonville, CA	31.4
7	Greenville, NC	29.4	8	Napa, CA	31.0
7	Brownsville-Harlingen, TX	29.4	8	California-Lexington Park, MD	29.9
7	Jonesboro, AR	29.4	10	Boulder, CO	29.7
11	Farmington, NM	29.3	11	Santa Rosa-Petaluma, CA	28.5
12	Morristown, TN	28.8	12	Oxnard-Thousand Oaks-Ventura, CA	27.4
13	Las Cruces, NM	28.2	13	New York-Newark-Jersey City, NY-NJ-PA	27.2
14	Saginaw, MI	28.1	14	San Diego-Chula Vista-Carlsbad, CA	26.3
15	Gadsden, AL	28.0	15	Trenton-Princeton, NJ	25.7
16	Lake Havasu City-Kingman, AZ	27.8	16	Denver-Aurora-Lakewood, CO	25.6
17	Pine Bluff, AR	27.4	16	Baltimore-Columbia-Towson, MD	25.6
18	Kingsport-Bristol, TN-VA	27.3	18	Santa Maria-Santa Barbara, CA	25.5
19	Shreveport-Bossier City, LA	27.2	18	Urban Honolulu, HI	25.5
20	Blacksburg-Christiansburg, VA	26.8	20	Barnstable Town, MA	24.8
21	Hammond, LA	26.7	20	Poughkeepsie-Newburgh-Middletown, NY	24.8
22	Dothan, AL	26.6	22	Los Angeles-Long Beach-Anaheim, CA	24.4
23	Charleston, WV	26.2	23	Austin-Round Rock-Georgetown, TX	24.3
23	Huntington-Ashland, WV-KY-OH	26.2	24	Minneapolis-St. Paul-Bloomington, MN-WI	23.9
25	Weirton-Steubenville, WV-OH	25.8	25	Kahului-Wailuku-Lahaina, HI	23.7
26	Muncie, IN	25.6	26	Raleigh-Cary, NC	23.7
27	Lafayette, LA	25.5	26	Manchester-Nashua, NH	23.7
28	Bloomsburg-Berwick, PA	25.4	26	Kingston, NY	23.3
29	Bloomington, IN	25.3	29	Bremerton-Silverdale-Port Orchard, WA	23.1
29	College Station-Bryan, TX	25.3	29	Hartford-East Hartford-Middletown, CT	23.1
31	El Paso, TX	25.2	31	Philadelphia-Camden-Wilmington, PA-NJ-DE-MD	22.9
31	Danville, IL	25.2	31	Sacramento-Roseville-Folsom, CA	22.9
33	Texarkana, TX-AR	25.1	33	San Luis Obispo-Paso Robles, CA	22.7
33	Parkersburg-Vienna, WV	25.1	34	Worcester, MA-CT	22.6
35	Homosassa Springs, FL	25.0	35	Charlottesville, VA	22.3
35	Laredo, TX	25.0	35	Anchorage, AK	22.3
35	Hot Springs, AR	25.0	37	Midland, TX	22.2
38	Auburn-Opelika, AL	24.9	38	Portland-Vancouver-Hillsboro, OR-WA	22.1
38	Merced, CA	24.9	38	Naples-Marco Island, FL	22.1
38	Alexandria, LA	24.9	40	Vallejo, CA	22.0
48	El Centro, CA	24.9	41	Burlington-South Burlington, VT	21.9
42	Decatur, IL	24.8	42	Fort Collins, CO	21.8
42	Columbus, GA-AL	24.8	43	Ann Arbor, MI	21.6
42	Jackson, TN	24.8	44	Provo-Orem, UT	21.4
45	Goldsboro, NC	24.7	45	Chicago-Naperville-Elgin, IL-IN-WI	21.3
46	Pueblo, CO	24.6	45	Salinas, CA	21.3
46	Florence-Muscle Shoals, AL	24.6	47	Huntsville, AL	20.6
48	Tuscaloosa, AL	24.6	48	New Haven-Milford, CT	20.5
49	Wheeling, WV-OH	24.5	49	Stockton, CA	20.3
49	Carbondale-Marion, IL	24.5	49	Atlanta-Sandy Springs-Alpharetta, GA	20.3
51	Mobile, AL	24.4	51	Bend, OR	20.2
52	Fort Smith, AR-OK	24.3	52	Dallas-Fort Worth-Arlington, TX	20.0
53	Youngstown-Warren-Boardman, OH-PA	24.1	53	Durham-Chapel Hill, NC	19.9
54	Mansfield, OH	24.0	53	Norwich-New London, CT	19.9
54	Brunswick, GA	24.0	55	Rochester, MN	19.7
54	Johnson City, TN	24.0	55	Madison, WI	19.7
57	Sebring-Avon Park, FL	23.9	55	Ogden-Clearfield, UT	19.7
58	Albany, GA	23.8	58	Greeley, CO	19.5
58	Jackson, MS	23.8	59	Kennewick-Richland, WA	19.3
58	Lubbock, TX	23.8	60	Houston-The Woodlands-Sugar Land, TX	19.2
58	Lawton, OK	23.8	61	Salt Lake City, UT	19.1
62	Grants Pass, OR	23.7	62	Richmond, VA	19.0
62	Montgomery, AL	23.7	63	Colorado Springs, CO	18.8
64	Gainesville, FL	23.6	63	Providence-Warwick, RI-MA	18.8
64	New Orleans-Metairie, LA	23.6	65	Portland-South Portland, ME	18.7
64	Houma-Thibodaux, LA	23.6	66	Albany-Schenectady-Troy, NY	18.4
67	Terre Haute, IN	23.5	66	Olympia-Lacey-Tumwater, WA	18.4
68	Rocky Mount, NC	23.3	66	Ocean City, NJ	18.4
68	Sierra Vista-Douglas, AZ	23.2	69	Santa Fe, NM	18.3
69	Madera, CA	23.2	69	Nashville-Davidson--Murfreesboro--Franklin, TN	18.3
71	Macon-Bibb County, GA	23.1	71	Charlotte-Concord-Gastonia, NC-SC	18.0
72	Bangor, ME	23.0	71	Reno, NV	18.0
72	Lawrence, KS	23.0	73	Phoenix-Mesa-Chandler, AZ	17.7
74	Erie, PA	22.9	73	Omaha-Council Bluffs, NE-IA	17.7
74	Hickory-Lenoir-Morganton, NC	22.9	75	Riverside-San Bernardino-Ontario, CA	17.6
			75	Corvallis, OR	17.6

City Rankings, 2021

Selected Rankings

High school diploma or less rank	City	Percent with a high school diploma or less [B-4, col. 2]	Bachelor's degree or more rank	City	Percent with a bachelor's degree or more [B-4, col. 3]	Unemployment rate rank	City	Unemployment rate [B-4, col. 6]
	UNITED STATES	36.9		**UNITED STATES**	35.0		**UNITED STATES**	6.3
1	Cicero town, Illinois	73.1	1	Bethesda CDP, Maryland	87.3	1	Detroit city, Michigan	17.4
2	East Los Angeles CDP, California	71.8	2	Newton city, Massachusetts	84.4	2	Paterson city, New Jersey	15.8
3	Passaic city, New Jersey	69.0	3	Cambridge city, Massachusetts	81.4	3	Flint city, Michigan	15.7
4	Reading city, Pennsylvania	68.4	4	Davis city, California	80.9	3	Pine Hills CDP, Florida	15.7
5	South Gate city, California	67.8	5	Palo Alto city, California	80.6	5	Newark city, New Jersey	15.3
6	Lynwood city, California	67.0	6	Redmond city, Washington	80.2	6	Mount Vernon city, New York	14.7
7	Camden city, New Jersey	66.8	7	Sammamish city, Washington	78.7	6	Merced city, California	14.7
8	Salinas city, California	66.5	8	Arlington CDP, Virginia	76.6	8	Baytown city, Texas	14.5
9	Perris city, California	64.8	8	Boulder city, Colorado	75.6	9	Reading city, Pennsylvania	14.4
10	El Monte city, California	64.3	10	Ann Arbor city, Michigan	75.5	10	Decatur city, Illinois	14.3
11	Paterson city, New Jersey	63.7	11	Mountain View city, California	74.4	10	Passaic city, New Jersey	14.3
12	Lawrence city, Massachusetts	62.8	12	Carmel city, Indiana	73.7	12	Paradise CDP, Nevada	14.2
13	Elizabeth city, New Jersey	62.5	12	Berkeley city, California	73.7	13	Madera city, California	13.6
14	Sunrise Manor CDP, Nevada	62.1	14	Newport Beach city, California	73.3	14	El Cajon city, California	13.3
14	San Bernardino city, California	62.1	15	Johns Creek city, Georgia	72.1	15	Spring Valley CDP, Nevada	13.2
16	Compton city, California	61.9	16	Naperville city, Illinois	71.7	16	Victorville city, California	13.1
17	Pine Hills CDP, Florida	60.9	17	Evanston city, Illinois	71.2	17	Yakima city, Washington	13.0
18	Hartford city, Connecticut	60.8	18	Santa Monica city, California	71.0	17	Trenton city, New Jersey	13.0
18	Madera city, California	60.8	19	Alpharetta city, Georgia	70.9	17	Union City city, New Jersey	13.0
20	Trenton city, New Jersey	60.5	20	Bellevue city, Washington	70.7	20	Turlock city, California	12.9
21	Newark city, New Jersey	60.5	21	Ellicott City CDP, Maryland	70.5	21	Rockford city, Illinois	12.8
22	Hammond city, Indiana	59.5	22	Sandy Springs city, Georgia	70.3	21	Springfield city, Massachusetts	12.8
22	Pharr city, Texas	59.5	23	Cary town, North Carolina	70.2	23	East Orange city, New Jersey	12.7
24	Baldwin Park city, California	59.4	24	Walnut Creek city, California	69.9	24	Greenville city, North Carolina	12.3
24	Union City city, New Jersey	59.4	25	San Ramon city, California	69.2	24	Cleveland city, Ohio	12.3
26	Hialeah city, Florida	59.1	26	Roswell city, Georgia	68.8	26	Gulfport city, Mississippi	11.9
27	West Valley City city, Utah	58.8	27	Seattle city, Washington	68.3	26	Hartford city, Connecticut	11.9
27	Jurupa Valley city, California	58.8	27	Irvine city, California	68.3	28	New York city, New York	11.8
29	Rialto city, California	58.6	29	Weston city, Florida	67.8	29	Sunrise Manor CDP, Nevada	11.7
30	New Bedford city, Massachusetts	58.2	30	Dublin city, California	67.6	29	Pasadena city, Texas	11.7
31	Fall River city, Massachusetts	57.5	31	Sunnyvale city, California	67.4	31	Shreveport city, Louisiana	11.4
32	Tulare city, California	57.4	32	Frisco city, Texas	67.2	32	Waterbury city, Connecticut	11.3
33	Allentown city, Pennsylvania	57.3	33	Rockville city, Maryland	66.1	33	Camden city, New Jersey	11.1
33	Santa Maria city, California	57.3	34	Santa Clara city, California	65.9	33	Warren city, Michigan	11.1
35	Santa Ana city, California	57.2	35	Hoover city, Alabama	65.8	33	Hesperia city, California	11.1
36	Waukegan city, Illinois	57.1	36	Columbia CDP, Maryland	65.7	33	North Las Vegas city, Nevada	11.1
37	Indio city, California	56.7	37	Mount Pleasant town, South Carolina	65.5	37	Pittsburg city, California	11.0
38	Brownsville city, Texas	56.6	38	Franklin city, Tennessee	65.4	37	Hawthorne city, California	11.0
38	Springdale city, Arkansas	55.9	38	Alexandria city, Virginia	65.4	37	Rochester city, New York	11.0
40	Lauderhill city, Florida	55.7	40	Sugar Land city, Texas	65.3	40	Baton Rouge city, Louisiana	10.9
41	Pasadena city, Texas	55.4	41	Novi city, Michigan	65.2	41	Jackson city, Mississippi	10.8
41	New Britain city, Connecticut	55.4	42	Flower Mound town, Texas	64.8	41	Las Vegas city, Nevada	10.8
43	Springfield city, Massachusetts	55.0	43	Woodbury city, Minnesota	64.6	41	Westminster city, California	10.8
44	Hesperia city, California	54.3	44	Overland Park city, Kansas	63.9	44	Hemet city, California	10.7
45	Pawtucket city, Rhode Island	54.1	45	Pleasanton city, California	63.7	44	Los Angeles city, California	10.7
46	Palmdale city, California	53.8	45	Fremont city, California	63.7	46	Inglewood city, California	10.6
47	Pomona city, California	53.5	47	The Woodlands CDP, Texas	63.6	47	Temecula city, California	10.5
48	Oxnard city, California	53.4	47	Plymouth city, Minnesota	63.6	47	Philadelphia city, Pennsylvania	10.5
49	Lehigh Acres CDP, Florida	53.2	49	Highlands Ranch CDP, Colorado	63.3	49	Yuba City city, California	10.4
50	Baytown city, Texas	53.0	50	Washington city, District of Columbia	63.0	49	Stockton city, California	10.4
51	Homestead city, Florida	52.8	50	Auburn city, Alabama	63.0	49	Perris city, California	10.4
51	Pasco city, Washington	52.8	52	Somerville city, Massachusetts	62.6	49	Canton city, Ohio	10.4
53	Canton city, Ohio	52.6	53	Ames city, Iowa	62.5	53	New Bedford city, Massachusetts	10.3
54	Waterbury city, Connecticut	52.5	54	Kirkland city, Washington	62.3	53	Worcester city, Massachusetts	10.3
54	Decatur city, Illinois	52.5	55	Redondo Beach city, California	62.2	55	Buffalo city, New York	10.2
56	Victoria city, Texas	52.4	56	Rochester Hills city, Michigan	61.6	56	Chicago city, Illinois	10.1
57	Lynn city, Massachusetts	52.3	57	Centreville CDP, Virginia	60.9	56	Pomona city, California	10.1
58	Mission city, Texas	52.2	57	San Francisco city, California	60.9	56	Lawrence city, Massachusetts	10.1
58	Norwalk city, California	52.2	59	Bloomington city, Indiana	60.8	56	Allentown city, Pennsylvania	10.1
60	Kansas City city, Kansas	51.6	60	Alameda city, California	60.7	60	Vallejo city, California	9.9
60	Lorain city, Ohio	51.6	61	Scottsdale city, Arizona	60.4	60	Albany city, New York	9.9
62	Ontario city, California	51.5	61	Carlsbad city, California	60.4	62	Dayton city, Ohio	9.8
63	Miami Gardens city, Florida	51.4	61	Centennial city, Colorado	60.4	62	Chino Hills city, California	9.8
64	Flint city, Michigan	51.2	64	Guaynabo zona urbana, Puerto Rico	60.3	62	Memphis city, Tennessee	9.8
64	Westminster city, California	51.2	65	Iowa City city, Iowa	59.9	62	Yonkers city, New York	9.8
64	North Las Vegas city, Nevada	51.2	65	Troy city, Michigan	59.9	62	Enterprise CDP, Nevada	9.8
67	Yuba City city, California	50.9	65	Austin city, Texas	59.9	62	Flagstaff city, Arizona	9.8
68	Fontana city, California	50.8	68	Atlanta city, Georgia	59.8	68	Fullerton city, California	9.6
69	Moreno Valley city, California	50.6	69	Arlington Heights village, Illinois	59.7	68	Carson city, California	9.6
69	Scranton city, Pennsylvania	50.6	70	Plano city, Texas	59.1	68	Vista city, California	9.6
71	St. Joseph city, Missouri	50.4	71	Madison city, Wisconsin	58.9	68	Southfield city, Michigan	9.6
71	Sioux City city, Iowa	50.4	71	Broomfield city, Colorado	58.9	68	Cranston city, Rhode Island	9.6
73	Victorville city, California	50.2	73	Silver Spring CDP, Maryland	58.6	73	West Covina city, California	9.5
74	Brockton city, Massachusetts	50.0	74	Fort Collins city, Colorado	58.5	70	Lansing city, Michigan	9.5
74	Cleveland city, Ohio	50.0	75	Cedar Park city, Texas	58.3	70	Murrieta city, California	9.5
						70	Richmond city, California	9.5
						70	Schenectady city, New York	9.5

City Rankings, 2021

Selected Rankings

Households who received cash public assistance or food stamps/ SNAP	City	Percent of households who received cash public assistance or food stamps/ SNAP [B-2, col. 12]	Households with income of less than $25,000 rank	City	Percent of households with income of less than $25,000 [B-4, col. 10]	Households with income of $150,000 or more rank	City	Percent of households with income of $150,000 or more [B-4, col. 11]
	UNITED STATES	14.1		UNITED STATES	17.4		UNITED STATES	17.7
1	Lawrence city, Massachusetts	57.4	1	San Marcos city, Texas	38.9	1	Sammamish city, Washington	70.1
2	Reading city, Pennsylvania	48.5	2	Kalamazoo city, Michigan	37.8	2	Dublin city, California	65.6
3	Hialeah city, Florida	47.5	2	Bloomington city, Indiana	37.8	3	Palo Alto city, California	57.6
4	Pine Hills CDP, Florida	44.4	4	Pharr city, Texas	37.7	4	Newton city, Massachusetts	57.5
5	Camden city, New Jersey	43.2	5	Detroit city, Michigan	36.7	5	Milpitas city, California	56.7
6	Passaic city, New Jersey	41.3	6	Jackson city, Mississippi	36.6	6	San Ramon city, California	55.9
7	Detroit city, Michigan	40.8	7	Flint city, Michigan	36.3	7	Bethesda CDP, Maryland	55.2
8	Springfield city, Massachusetts	39.4	7	Cleveland city, Ohio	36.3	8	Redmond city, Washington	52.6
9	Pharr city, Texas	37.7	9	Greenville city, North Carolina	35.9	9	Fremont city, California	52.5
10	Kissimmee city, Florida	37.5	10	Camden city, New Jersey	35.7	10	Mountain View city, California	52.4
11	Miami Gardens city, Florida	37.4	11	Reading city, Pennsylvania	35.2	11	Sunnyvale city, California	51.6
12	Paterson city, New Jersey	37.3	12	Syracuse city, New York	34.9	11	Santa Clara city, California	51.6
13	Homestead city, Florida	35.0	13	Birmingham city, Alabama	34.8	13	Bellevue city, Washington	48.5
14	Hartford city, Connecticut	34.8	14	Springfield city, Massachusetts	33.3	14	Flower Mound town, Texas	48.3
15	Flint city, Michigan	34.6	15	Buffalo city, New York	33.1	14	Pleasanton city, California	48.3
16	Fall River city, Massachusetts	34.3	16	Albany city, Georgia	32.9	16	Redwood City city, California	47.6
17	Buffalo city, New York	33.9	17	Cincinnati city, Ohio	32.7	17	Newport Beach city, California	46.3
18	Cleveland city, Ohio	33.8	18	Newark city, New Jersey	32.4	18	Ellicott City CDP, Maryland	46.1
19	New Bedford city, Massachusetts	33.2	19	Madera city, California	32.1	19	Highlands Ranch CDP, Colorado	45.0
20	Brownsville city, Texas	33.1	19	Rochester city, New York	32.1	20	Johns Creek city, Georgia	44.9
21	Akron city, Ohio	32.6	21	Baton Rouge city, Louisiana	32.0	21	Yorba Linda city, California	44.3
22	Brockton city, Massachusetts	32.4	21	Shreveport city, Louisiana	32.0	22	Kirkland city, Washington	44.2
23	Haverhill city, Massachusetts	32.2	23	Erie city, Pennsylvania	31.8	23	Naperville city, Illinois	43.8
24	New Britain city, Connecticut	31.7	24	Decatur city, Illinois	31.7	23	Livermore city, California	43.8
25	Trenton city, New Jersey	31.6	24	Harlingen city, Texas	31.7	25	Alpharetta city, Georgia	43.4
26	Lynn city, Massachusetts	31.5	26	New Orleans city, Louisiana	31.5	26	San Mateo city, California	43.1
27	Rochester city, New York	31.1	27	Auburn city, Alabama	31.3	27	San Jose city, California	42.7
27	Merced city, California	31.1	28	Trenton city, New Jersey	31.2	28	Redondo Beach city, California	42.5
29	Rockford city, Illinois	31.0	28	Daytona Beach city, Florida	31.2	29	Frisco city, Texas	42.4
30	Worcester city, Massachusetts	30.7	30	Tuscaloosa city, Alabama	30.9	30	San Francisco city, California	42.3
30	Poinciana CDP, Florida	30.7	30	Kissimmee city, Florida	30.9	31	Castro Valley CDP, California	41.6
32	Milwaukee city, Wisconsin	30.6	32	Dayton city, Ohio	30.5	32	Mission Viejo city, California	41.4
32	Albany city, Georgia	30.6	32	Toledo city, Ohio	30.5	33	Folsom city, California	40.9
34	Madera city, California	30.5	34	Pueblo city, Colorado	30.2	33	Arlington CDP, Virginia	40.9
35	Erie city, Pennsylvania	30.3	34	Brownsville city, Texas	30.2	35	Alameda city, California	40.2
36	Syracuse city, New York	30.2	34	Gainesville city, Florida	30.2	35	Fishers city, Indiana	40.2
37	Lauderhill city, Florida	29.9	34	Jonesboro city, Arkansas	30.2	37	Lakeville city, Minnesota	40.0
38	Lakewood CDP, New Jersey	29.7	34	Bryan city, Texas	30.2	38	Union City city, California	39.3
39	Providence city, Rhode Island	29.5	39	Merced city, California	30.0	39	Rockville city, Maryland	39.2
39	Canton city, Ohio	29.5	40	Paterson city, New Jersey	29.9	40	Woodbury city, Minnesota	39.1
41	Philadelphia city, Pennsylvania	28.7	41	Las Cruces city, New Mexico	29.8	40	Weston city, Florida	39.1
41	El Monte city, California	28.7	42	Fall River city, Massachusetts	29.7	42	Carlsbad city, California	39.0
43	Victorville city, California	28.6	43	Akron city, Ohio	29.6	43	Thousand Oaks city, California	38.6
44	Dayton city, Ohio	28.5	44	Hartford city, Connecticut	29.5	44	Chino Hills city, California	38.5
45	Bridgeport city, Connecticut	28.3	45	Canton city, Ohio	29.3	45	Cary town, North Carolina	38.2
45	Baltimore city, Maryland	28.3	46	Pine Hills CDP, Florida	29.1	45	The Woodlands CDP, Texas	38.2
47	Allentown city, Pennsylvania	28.2	46	Miami city, Florida	29.1	47	Sugar Land city, Texas	37.7
47	Lowell city, Massachusetts	28.2	48	Columbia city, South Carolina	28.8	48	Seattle city, Washington	37.6
47	Waterbury city, Connecticut	28.2	49	Bowling Green city, Kentucky	28.7	49	Walnut Creek city, California	37.5
50	Miami city, Florida	28.1	49	Lake Charles city, Louisiana	28.7	50	Castle Rock town, Colorado	37.4
51	El Cajon city, California	28.0	51	Schenectady city, New York	28.6	51	Irvine city, California	37.2
52	New Haven city, Connecticut	27.7	51	Edinburg city, Texas	28.6	52	Allen city, Texas	36.8
53	Scranton city, Pennsylvania	27.3	51	Montgomery city, Alabama	28.6	53	Franklin city, Tennessee	36.4
54	Las Cruces city, New Mexico	27.2	54	Allentown city, Pennsylvania	28.4	54	Somerville city, Massachusetts	36.3
55	Lake Charles city, Louisiana	26.9	55	Mobile city, Alabama	28.2	55	Carmel city, Indiana	36.0
56	Birmingham city, Alabama	26.8	55	Albany city, New York	28.2	55	Plymouth city, Minnesota	36.0
56	Laredo city, Texas	26.8	57	Lorain city, Ohio	28.0	57	Berkeley city, California	35.9
58	Baton Rouge city, Louisiana	26.5	58	Gulfport city, Mississippi	27.8	58	New Rochelle city, New York	35.8
58	Pasco city, Washington	26.5	59	St. Louis city, Missouri	27.7	59	Centreville CDP, Virginia	35.6
60	Cicero town, Illinois	26.4	60	Knoxville city, Tennessee	27.5	59	Lake Forest city, California	35.6
61	Sunrise Manor CDP, Nevada	26.3	61	Jackson city, Tennessee	27.4	59	Roswell city, Georgia	35.6
62	Fresno city, California	26.1	62	Memphis city, Tennessee	27.2	62	Lehi city, Utah	35.5
62	Kennewick city, Washington	26.1	63	New Haven city, Connecticut	27.1	63	Centennial city, Colorado	35.1
62	Yakima city, Washington	26.1	63	Philadelphia city, Pennsylvania	27.1	64	Santa Monica city, California	34.8
65	Decatur city, Illinois	26.0	63	Lauderhill city, Florida	27.1	65	Cedar Park city, Texas	34.7
66	Stockton city, California	25.7	66	Rockford city, Illinois	27.0	66	Leander city, Texas	34.6
66	Racine city, Wisconsin	25.7	66	Hialeah city, Florida	27.0	67	Cambridge city, Massachusetts	34.3
66	Peoria city, Illinois	25.7	68	New Bedford city, Massachusetts	26.8	68	Roseville city, California	34.1
69	Pueblo city, Colorado	25.4	68	Milwaukee city, Wisconsin	26.8	69	Rocklin city, California	34.0
70	Union City city, New Jersey	25.2	70	Peoria city, Illinois	26.7	70	Santa Clarita city, California	33.8
71	Deerfield Beach city, Florida	25.0	70	New Britain city, Connecticut	26.7	71	Columbia CDP, Maryland	33.6
71	San Bernardino city, California	25.0	70	Bridgeport city, Connecticut	26.7	72	Broomfield city, Colorado	33.5
73	Mission city, Texas	24.9	70	Dothan city, Alabama	26.7	73	Maple Grove city, Minnesota	33.2
74	Newark city, New Jersey	24.8	70	Augusta-Richmond County consolidated government (balance), Georgia	26.7	74	Sandy Springs city, Georgia	33.1
74	Compton city, California	24.8	75	Lawton city, Oklahoma	26.5	75	Huntington Beach city, California	32.8

Table B-1. States — What: Education, Employment, and Income, 2021

	STATE	Total population 25 years and over	Educational attainment (percent)					Total enrolled in school	School enrollment by level of school (percent)		
			No high school diploma	High school graduate	Some college or associate's degree	Bachelor's degree	Graduate or professional degree		Enrolled in preschool	Enrolled in grades K–12	Enrolled in college or graduate school
State code	ACS table number:	C15003	C15003	C15003	C15003	C15003	C15003	C14002	C14002	C14002	C14002
	Column number:	1	2	3	4	5	6	7	8	9	10

Table B-1. States — What: Education, Employment, and Income, 2021—*Continued*

	STATE	Percent enrolled in private schools by level of school							Total population 16 years and over	Total labor force
		All levels	Preschool, nursery school	Kinder garten	Grades 1–8	Grades 9–12	College, under-graduate	Graduate or professional school		
State code	ACS table number:	C14002	C14002	C14002	C14002	C14002	C14002	C14002	C23001	C23001
	Column number:	11	12	13	14	15	16	17	18	19

Table B-1. States — What: Education, Employment, and Income, 2021—*Continued*

	STATE	Labor force participation (percent)			Unemployment rates by age (percent unemployed)				Total labor force 25 to 64 years
		Total	Men	Women	Total labor force	16 to 24 years	25 to 64 years	65 years and over	
State code	ACS table number:	C23001	C23001	C23001	C23001	C23001	C23001	C23001	B23006
	Column number:	20	21	22	23	24	25	26	27

Table B-1. States — What: Education, Employment, and Income, 2021—*Continued*

	STATE	Unemployment rates for the labor force age 25 to 64 by educational attainment					Total population 16 to 19 years	16 to 19 years, not enrolled in school, not high school graduate, not in labor force	Total labor force
		Unemployment rate (percent unemployed)							
		Total 25 to 64 years	No high school diploma	High school graduate	Some college or associate's degree	Bachelor's degree or higher			
State code	ACS table number:	B23006	B23006	B23006	B23006	B23006	C14005	C14005	C23001
	Column number:	28	29	30	31	32	33	34	35

Table B-1. States — What: Education, Employment, and Income, 2021—*Continued*

	STATE	Percent of population 16 to 64 years who worked full-time, year-round in the past 12 months			Total households	Percent of households with no workers	Family status of children under 18 years, by employment status of parents and age of children			
							Children under 18 years in families			
								Percent living with two parents		Percent living with one parent who is in labor force
		Total	Male	Female			Number	Both in labor force	One parent in labor force	
State code	ACS table number:	S2402	S2402	S2402	B08202	B08202	C23008	C23008	C23008	C23008
	Column number:	36	37	38	39	40	41	42	43	44

Table B-1. States — What: Education, Employment, and Income, 2021—*Continued*

		Family status of children under 18 years, by employment status of parents and age of children							
		Children under 6 years in families				Children 6–17 years in families			
			Percent living with two parents		Percent living with one parent who is in labor force		Percent living with two parents		Percent living with one parent who is in labor force
	STATE	Number	Both in labor force	One parent in labor force		Number	Both in labor force	One parent in labor force	
State code	ACS table number:	C23008	C23008	C23008	C23008	C23008	C23008	C23008	C23008
	Column number:	45	46	47	48	49	50	51	52

Table B-1. States — What: Education, Employment, and Income, 2021—*Continued*

		Employment status of family householders					Women 20 to 64 years in households, by presence of children and labor force status		
			Opposite-sex married-couple families		Families maintained by women and men with no spouse				
	STATE	Total families with children under 18	Total	Both in labor force (percent)	Total	Householder in labor force (percent)	Total women 20 to 64 years in households	Percent with children under 18 years	Percent in labor force with children under 18 years
State code	ACS table number:	C23007	C23007	C23007	C23007	C23007	B23003	B23003	B23003
	Column number:	53	54	55	56	57	58	59	60

Table B-1. States — What: Education, Employment, and Income, 2021—*Continued*

		Class of worker for employed civilians 16 years and over					Occupation (percent)				
	STATE	Civilian employed population 16 years and over	Percent private wage and salary workers	Percent government workers	Percent self-employed and unpaid workers	Civilian employed population 16 years and over	Management, business, science, and arts	Service	Sales and office	Natural resources, construction, and maintenance	Production, transportation, and material moving
State code	ACS table number:	C24080	C24080	C24080	C24080	C24060	C24060	C24060	C24060	C24060	C24060
	Column number:	61	62	63	64	65	66	67	68	69	70

Table B-1. States — What: Education, Employment, and Income, 2021—*Continued*

		Industry (percent)							
	STATE	Agriculture, forestry, fishing and hunting, and mining	Construction	Manufacturing	Wholesale trade	Retail trade	Transportation and warehousing, and utilities	Information	Finance and insurance, real estate, and rental and leasing
State code	ACS table number:	C24070	C24070	C24070	C24070	C24070	C24070	C24070	C24070
	Column number:	71	72	73	74	75	76	77	78

Table B-1. States — What: Education, Employment, and Income, 2021—*Continued*

		Industry (percent)						Median income in the past 12 months (in 2021 inflation-adjusted dollars)				
									Median household income by age of householder			
	STATE	Professional, scientific, and management, and administrative and waste management services	Educational services, and health care and social assistance	Arts, entertainment, and recreation, and accommodation and food services	Other services, except public administration	Public administration	Veterans as a percent of the civilian population 18 years and over	All households	Householder under 25 years	Householder 25 to 44 years	Householder 45 to 64 years	Householder 65 years and over
State code	ACS table number:	C24070	C24070	C24070	C24070	C24070	B21001	B19049	B19049	B19049	B19049	B19049
	Column number:	79	80	81	82	83	84	85	86	87	88	89

Table B-1. States — What: Education, Employment, and Income, 2021—*Continued*

		Median income in the past 12 months (in 2021 inflation-adjusted dollars)								
		Median household income by race and Hispanic origin of householder								
	STATE	White alone	Black alone	American Indian, Alaska Native alone	Asian alone	Native Hawaiian and other Pacific Islander alone	Some other race alone	Two or more races	White alone, not Hispanic or Latino	Hispanic or Latino
State code	ACS table number:	B19013A	B19013B	B19013C	B19013D	B19013E	B19013F	B19013G	B19013H	B19013I
	Column number:	90	91	92	93	94	95	96	97	98

Table B-1. States — What: Education, Employment, and Income, 2021—*Continued*

		Median income in the past 12 months (in 2021 inflation-adjusted dollars)											
		Median family income by type of family							Median nonfamily household income			Median individual income	
	STATE	All families	Married-couple families with children under 18	Married-couple families, no children under 18	Male householder with children under 18	Male householder, no children under 18	Female householder with children under 18	Female householder, no children under 18	All nonfamily households	Living alone, 65 years and over		Persons 15 years and over who worked full-time, year-round	
										Male	Female	Male	Female
State code	ACS table number:	B19126	B19126	B19126	B19126	B19126	B19126	B19126	B19215	B19215	B19215	B19326	B19326
	Column number:	99	100	101	102	103	104	105	106	107	108	109	110

Table B-1. States — What: Education, Employment, and Income, 2021—*Continued*

		Per capita income in the past 12 months (in 2021 inflation-adjusted dollars)		Households, by type of income (percent)									
	STATE		Total number of households	With wage or salary income	With self-employment income	With interest, dividends, or net rental income	With Social Security	With Supplemental Security Income (SSI)	With public assistance income	With cash public assistance or food stamps/ SNAP	With retirement income	With other types of income
State code	ACS table number:	B19301	B19052	B19052	B19053	B19054	B19055	B19056	B19057	B19058	B19059	B19060
	Column number:	111	112	113	114	115	116	117	118	119	120	121

Table B-1. States — What: Education, Employment, and Income, 2021—*Continued*

		Household income in the past 12 months (in 2021 inflation-adjusted dollars)										
		Total number of households	Households by income group (percent)									
	STATE		Less than $10,000	$10,000 to $14,999	$15,000 to $24,999	$25,000 to $34,999	$35,000 to $49,999	$50,000 to $74,999	$75,000 to $99,999	$100,000 to $149,999	$150,000 to $199,999	$200,000 or more
State code	ACS table number:	B19001	B19001	B19001	B19001	B19001	B19001	B19001	B19001	B19001	B19001	B19001
	Column number:	122	123	124	125	126	127	128	129	130	131	132

Table B-1. States — What: Education, Employment, and Income, 2021—*Continued*

		Households with income over $100,000, by age of householder (as a percent of all households in age group)					Households with income below poverty (as a percent of all households in household-type group)						
	STATE	All households	Householder under 25 years	Householder 25 to 44 years	Householder 45 to 64 years	Householder 65 years and over	All households	Family households	Married-couple family households	Male householder family households	Female householder family households	Male householder nonfamily households	Female householder nonfamily households
State code	ACS table number:	B19001	B19037	B19037	B19037	B19037	C17017	C17017	C17017	C17017	C17017	C17017	C17017
	Column number:	133	134	135	136	137	138	139	140	141	142	143	144

Table B-1. States — What: Education, Employment, and Income, 2021—*Continued*

			Persons with income below poverty by age (as a percent of all persons in age group)				Persons with income below poverty by selected race and Hispanic origin groups (as a percent of all persons in race/Hispanic group)			
	STATE	Population for whom poverty status is determined	All ages	Under 18 years	18 to 64 years	65 years and over	White alone, not Hispanic or Latino	Black or African American alone	Asian alone	Hispanic or Latino
State code	ACS table number:	C17001	C17001	C17001	C17001	C17001	C17001H	C17001B	C17001D	C17001I
	Column number:	145	146	147	148	149	150	151	152	153

Table B-1. States — What: Education, Employment, and Income, 2021—*Continued*

		Total civilian non-institutionalized population	Type of health insurance (as a percent of all persons)			
	STATE		Private only	Public only	Both private and public	None
	ACS table number:	C27010	C27010	C27010	C27010	C27010
State code	Column number:	154	155	156	157	158

Table B-2. Counties — What: Education, Employment, and Income, 2021

		Educational attainment			Employment status				Household income and benefits			
	STATE County	Total population 25 years and over	Percent with a high school diploma or less	Percent with a bachelor's degree or more	Total population 16 years and over	Labor force participation (percent)	Percent unemployed	Percent age 16 years and over who worked full-time year-round in the past 12 months	Total households	Median household income in the past 12 months (in 2021 inflation-adjusted dollars)	Income less than $25,000 (percent)	Income greater than $150,000 (percent)	Percent who received cash public assistance or food stamps/ SNAP
STATE County code	ACS table number:	C15003	C15003	C15003	C23001	C23001	C23001	S2402	B19001	B19049	B19001	B19001	B19058
	Column number:	1	2	3	4	5	6	7	8	9	10	11	12

Table B-3. Metropolitan Areas — What: Education, Employment, and Income, 2021

		Educational attainment			Employment status				Household income and benefits			
	Metropolitan area / division	Total population 25 years and over	Percent with a high school diploma or less	Percent with a bachelor's degree or more	Total population 16 years and over	Labor force participation (percent)	Percent unemployed	Percent age 16 years and over who worked full-time year-round in the past 12 months	Total households	Median household income in the past 12 months (in 2021 inflation-adjusted dollars)	Income less than $25,000 (percent)	Income greater than $150,000 (percent)	Percent who received cash public assistance or food stamps/ SNAP
Metropolitan area / division code	ACS table number:	C15003	C15003	C15003	C23001	C23001	C23001	S2402	B19001	B19049	B19001	B19001	B19058
	Column number:	1	2	3	4	5	6	7	8	9	10	11	12

Table B-4. Cities — What: Education, Employment, and Income, 2021

		Educational attainment			Employment status				Household income and benefits			
	STATE Place	Total population 25 years and over	Percent with a high school diploma or less	Percent with a bachelor's degree or more	Total population 16 years and over	Labor force participation (percent)	Percent unemployed	Percent age 16 years and over who worked full-time year-round in the past 12 months	Total households	Median household income in the past 12 months (in 2021 inflation-adjusted dollars)	Income less than $25,000 (percent)	Income greater than $150,000 (percent)	Percent who received cash public assistance or food stamps/ SNAP
STATE and place code	ACS table number:	C15003	C15003	C15003	C23001	C23001	C23001	S2402	B19001	B19049	B19001	B19001	B19058
	column number:	1	2	3	4	5	6	7	8	9	10	11	12

Table B-1. States — What: Education, Employment, and Income, 2021

State code	STATE	Total population 25 years and over	Educational attainment (percent)					School enrollment by level of school (percent)			
			No high school diploma	High school graduate	Some college or associate's degree	Bachelor's degree	Graduate or professional degree	Total enrolled in school	Enrolled in preschool	Enrolled in grades K–12	Enrolled in college or graduate school
	ACS table number:	C15003	C15003	C15003	C15003	C15003	C15003	C14002	C14002	C14002	C14002
	Column number:	1	2	3	4	5	6	7	8	9	10
00	UNITED STATES..............	228,193,464	10.6	26.3	28.1	21.2	13.8	79,453,524	5.2	68.2	26.7
01	Alabama........................	3,451,208	12.1	31.3	29.2	16.6	10.9	1,177,441	5.4	69.7	24.9
02	Alaska	485,779	6.7	27.9	32.6	20.9	11.9	174,378	5.8	72.5	21.7
04	Arizona.........................	4,980,297	11.0	23.5	33.1	19.8	12.6	1,712,924	3.8	70.1	26.2
05	Arkansas.......................	2,037,763	11.3	34.1	29.3	15.9	9.4	700,877	5.5	72.3	22.2
06	California......................	26,909,869	15.6	20.7	27.5	22.1	14.0	9,874,004	4.4	65.7	29.9
08	Colorado.......................	4,044,182	7.6	20.1	27.9	27.4	17.0	1,383,214	5.5	67.4	27.0
09	Connecticut...................	2,534,376	8.9	25.5	23.5	23.2	18.9	874,560	5.4	63.6	30.9
10	Delaware.......................	711,104	8.6	28.3	27.4	20.6	15.0	234,867	5.6	64.6	29.8
11	District of Columbia........	478,774	7.2	14.8	14.9	25.2	37.8	158,721	8.5	51.7	39.8
12	Florida..........................	15,762,122	10.2	27.7	29.0	20.6	12.6	4,730,466	5.3	67.5	27.2
13	Georgia	7,234,271	11.0	26.7	27.7	20.9	13.7	2,746,549	5.5	69.0	25.5
15	Hawaii..........................	1,021,687	7.1	26.3	31.3	22.2	13.1	333,721	5.1	65.7	29.1
16	Idaho...........................	1,257,566	8.7	26.9	33.6	20.2	10.5	481,832	5.0	72.6	22.4
17	Illinois..........................	8,730,697	9.8	25.1	27.9	22.1	15.0	3,049,269	5.9	67.9	26.2
18	Indiana.........................	4,559,631	9.4	33.3	28.5	18.5	10.4	1,645,886	5.6	69.7	24.7
19	Iowa............................	2,137,261	6.7	30.3	32.5	20.7	9.9	789,863	5.9	68.8	25.3
20	Kansas..........................	1,942,133	8.1	25.4	31.1	22.0	13.4	753,828	6.0	69.5	24.6
21	Kentucky.......................	3,077,867	12.0	32.7	28.3	15.9	11.1	1,033,023	5.3	70.7	24.0
22	Louisiana.......................	3,117,186	13.3	32.8	27.4	16.8	9.7	1,119,445	6.1	70.5	23.5
23	Maine...........................	1,015,078	5.5	29.6	28.9	22.2	13.8	274,439	4.4	68.1	27.5
24	Maryland.......................	4,273,260	8.9	23.8	24.7	22.4	20.2	1,516,189	4.8	65.6	29.6
25	Massachusetts	4,934,755	8.9	22.8	21.7	25.3	21.3	1,669,642	5.2	61.2	33.5
26	Michigan	6,971,895	8.0	28.7	31.6	19.2	12.5	2,313,566	5.1	68.2	26.7
27	Minnesota	3,898,742	5.9	23.3	31.9	25.5	13.4	1,385,795	5.9	69.4	24.7
28	Mississippi	1,968,167	13.5	29.8	31.9	15.4	9.3	728,376	4.9	70.8	24.3
29	Missouri........................	4,226,634	8.4	30.8	29.0	19.5	12.2	1,456,311	6.0	69.5	24.5
30	Montana	766,758	5.6	26.8	32.7	22.4	12.4	247,237	5.8	70.0	24.2
31	Nebraska.......................	1,292,536	7.8	25.2	32.6	22.2	12.3	514,905	7.0	68.1	24.9
32	Nevada.........................	2,192,826	12.8	27.2	32.3	17.9	9.6	709,413	3.6	71.9	24.5
33	New Hampshire	1,008,318	5.6	26.6	27.6	24.5	15.7	293,741	4.8	65.6	29.6
34	New Jersey	6,474,427	9.0	25.5	22.4	25.7	17.4	2,240,670	6.3	66.9	26.8
35	New Mexico	1,450,549	12.5	25.7	31.7	16.0	14.1	495,428	3.7	70.9	25.4
36	New York.......................	13,987,094	12.0	24.4	23.7	22.2	17.7	4,624,625	5.7	64.6	29.7
37	North Carolina...............	7,245,632	10.3	24.9	29.9	21.7	13.2	2,522,354	4.9	67.5	27.6
38	North Dakota.................	506,739	6.4	26.3	35.6	22.4	9.4	190,174	5.4	66.2	28.4
39	Ohio............................	8,117,973	8.3	32.8	28.2	18.9	11.8	2,724,429	5.7	69.6	24.7
40	Oklahoma......................	2,639,889	11.3	30.7	30.0	18.3	9.6	985,616	5.8	72.0	22.2
41	Oregon.........................	3,030,635	8.1	21.9	33.6	22.4	13.9	913,400	4.5	68.9	26.7
42	Pennsylvania..................	9,161,945	8.1	33.3	24.1	20.6	13.9	2,878,255	5.1	68.2	26.7
72	Puerto Rico	2,401,409	20.4	28.0	23.2	20.5	7.9	707,157	4.0	62.1	33.9
44	Rhode Island..................	773,464	10.9	27.7	24.9	20.9	15.6	260,253	4.6	60.0	35.4
45	South Carolina...............	3,598,398	10.4	28.5	29.5	19.6	11.9	1,175,906	4.7	71.1	24.2
46	South Dakota	590,377	6.9	29.3	32.1	21.6	10.1	217,810	7.0	71.5	21.4
47	Tennessee......................	4,814,533	10.3	31.2	28.1	19.2	11.3	1,571,789	4.9	70.9	24.2
48	Texas...........................	19,224,688	14.6	24.6	27.7	21.2	11.9	7,690,444	4.8	71.7	23.5
49	Utah............................	2,010,727	6.8	22.1	34.2	24.1	12.7	1,022,486	5.1	68.3	26.6
50	Vermont........................	462,705	5.5	26.2	23.9	26.0	18.4	143,264	5.6	60.6	33.8
51	Virginia.........................	5,942,672	8.6	23.9	25.7	23.5	18.3	2,087,185	4.8	66.1	29.1
53	Washington....................	5,401,149	7.7	21.6	31.7	23.8	15.1	1,761,985	5.1	69.4	25.5
54	West Virginia.................	1,265,439	11.2	39.1	25.6	14.2	9.9	356,283	4.2	72.3	23.6
55	Wisconsin......................	4,076,339	6.7	30.0	30.8	21.5	11.0	1,365,700	4.7	70.0	25.3
56	Wyoming.......................	395,348	6.4	27.3	37.1	18.5	10.7	140,986	5.6	71.9	22.5

NA = Not available.

'- = Indicates that either no sample observations or too few sample observations were available to compute an estimate, or a ratio of medians cannot be calculated because one or both of the median estimates falls in the lowest interval or upper interval of an open-ended distribution, or the margin of error associated with a median was larger than the median itself.

Table B-1. States — What: Education, Employment, and Income, 2021—*Continued*

State code	STATE	Percent enrolled in private schools by level of school							Total population 16 years and over	Total labor force
		All levels	Preschool, nursery school	Kinder garten	Grades 1–8	Grades 9–12	College, under-graduate	Graduate or professional school		
	ACS table number:	C14002	C14002	C14002	C14002	C14002	C14002	C14002	C23001	C23001
	Column number:	11	12	13	14	15	16	17	18	19
00	UNITED STATES.....................	18.1	42.6	15.9	13.3	11.2	23.2	40.1	267,057,693	168,236,937
01	Alabama.............................	15.2	39.2	17.3	12.7	11.7	14.9	25.0	4,046,627	2,335,486
02	Alaska................................	21.6	46.5	18.9	21.0	17.4	20.2	24.0	571,832	376,965
04	Arizona..............................	14.3	35.5	14.1	11.2	9.4	17.1	33.3	5,852,913	3,544,778
05	Arkansas.............................	13.1	28.2	9.9	10.6	9.8	18.4	19.3	2,405,035	1,408,602
06	California............................	15.1	47.4	13.2	10.8	8.9	15.6	43.1	31,507,237	19,961,610
08	Colorado	14.2	38.4	13.5	11.4	8.6	13.1	32.7	4,720,626	3,212,836
09	Connecticut........................	21.2	41.2	10.8	9.2	13.4	33.3	57.3	2,971,314	1,950,159
10	Delaware	20.9	57.7	14.5	15.4	19.2	18.3	40.6	819,868	492,382
11	District of Columbia...............	38.0	18.6	4.6	13.8	17.4	75.9	69.7	553,437	391,439
12	Florida	19.7	46.2	18.0	16.0	12.9	21.7	41.0	18,010,659	10,652,489
13	Georgia	16.0	35.3	14.6	11.7	11.7	19.6	34.8	8,575,918	5,394,701
15	Hawaii	25.8	70.3	24.9	21.1	22.1	24.5	35.1	1,166,220	739,336
16	Idaho	17.6	56.0	17.9	13.1	10.2	27.0	19.6	1,484,932	937,369
17	Illinois	20.5	40.6	18.8	14.1	10.6	28.8	51.4	10,203,044	6,584,794
18	Indiana	19.4	42.7	14.0	17.2	12.8	23.5	29.4	5,401,077	3,426,897
19	Iowa	15.9	28.3	14.5	11.9	7.4	24.9	38.7	2,543,525	1,681,087
20	Kansas	14.3	33.1	17.7	11.6	10.4	15.3	23.7	2,315,379	1,520,362
21	Kentucky	19.2	43.8	15.4	15.8	16.3	23.1	25.6	3,612,858	2,125,669
22	Louisiana	20.4	37.5	18.0	19.5	17.5	18.2	32.7	3,663,069	2,143,567
23	Maine	20.1	47.5	15.2	13.7	10.2	32.4	40.4	1,155,699	708,906
24	Maryland	20.5	50.4	18.3	15.2	15.5	21.1	41.6	4,964,751	3,304,168
25	Massachusetts	29.1	53.6	13.7	11.0	11.9	54.3	65.7	5,790,261	3,865,417
26	Michigan	15.9	41.2	16.1	13.9	10.9	17.1	23.6	8,156,411	4,966,693
27	Minnesota	16.7	36.7	15.3	12.6	9.3	22.9	36.2	4,554,126	3,114,145
28	Mississippi	16.0	31.1	14.4	15.7	16.0	9.6	29.4	2,340,485	1,325,864
29	Missouri	19.3	38.1	18.9	15.3	11.0	25.4	40.2	4,949,628	3,107,007
30	Montana	14.7	57.5	9.0	13.8	9.5	9.8	20.7	895,986	554,118
31	Nebraska	17.4	37.3	12.6	12.9	12.3	23.8	28.4	1,534,896	1,053,466
32	Nevada	14.4	41.7	17.0	11.4	8.9	16.9	32.9	2,526,328	1,590,604
33	New Hampshire	23.3	60.4	16.6	12.2	10.8	40.0	50.9	1,164,253	776,061
34	New Jersey	22.0	47.3	19.7	12.5	13.1	33.5	51.6	7,489,289	4,914,835
35	New Mexico	12.1	25.2	10.4	10.7	9.5	14.3	19.7	1,700,082	967,832
36	New York............................	26.0	40.3	19.6	16.6	16.0	39.3	56.9	16,210,453	10,138,385
37	North Carolina......................	17.3	49.4	14.9	14.3	11.4	17.5	35.8	8,524,268	5,301,767
38	North Dakota.......................	12.5	26.2	13.8	10.5	8.7	14.1	19.3	610,714	415,807
39	Ohio.................................	19.3	41.4	18.9	16.7	12.8	22.2	31.9	9,480,334	5,936,933
40	Oklahoma...........................	14.4	23.2	11.9	13.2	11.2	15.8	28.7	3,140,799	1,917,143
41	Oregon..............................	17.0	58.0	18.3	13.8	9.2	18.3	33.8	3,487,919	2,147,998
42	Pennsylvania........................	25.2	52.3	20.3	16.6	13.6	41.1	52.7	10,602,171	6,618,867
72	Puerto Rico.........................	36.9	29.1	24.6	26.5	23.6	57.0	68.9	2,794,959	1,252,484
44	Rhode Island........................	27.2	29.7	17.0	15.0	15.4	45.3	55.2	913,136	594,888
45	South Carolina......................	16.4	45.9	15.1	12.9	11.2	20.7	27.0	4,207,365	2,507,997
46	South Dakota	14.2	32.5	13.5	12.8	7.9	17.1	21.3	699,893	466,270
47	Tennessee...........................	20.1	42.8	16.0	15.7	15.5	25.2	41.0	5,616,708	3,439,821
48	Texas	13.1	37.7	12.4	9.1	8.0	17.8	31.2	22,934,023	14,826,344
49	Utah.................................	14.6	41.2	11.2	7.8	5.5	28.2	30.1	2,507,029	1,721,142
50	Vermont............................	21.8	32.4	3.6	13.2	13.6	35.0	43.2	542,827	349,096
51	Virginia..............................	18.3	55.7	21.7	13.4	10.1	20.0	37.9	6,980,718	4,553,835
53	Washington.........................	17.3	53.1	21.6	13.3	7.8	19.7	39.9	6,250,868	3,993,077
54	West Virginia.......................	14.0	26.6	8.1	14.7	9.0	15.7	21.5	1,465,755	771,429
55	Wisconsin...........................	18.2	33.0	19.9	17.2	11.4	20.5	33.6	4,773,326	3,105,191
56	Wyoming............................	12.8	35.4	14.1	13.4	7.5	7.6	26.1	461,622	301,303

NA = Not available.
'– = Indicates that either no sample observations or too few sample observations were available to compute an estimate, or a ratio of medians cannot be calculated because one or both of the median estimates falls in the lowest interval or upper interval of an open-ended distribution, or the margin of error associated with a median was larger than the median itself.

Table B-1. States — What: Education, Employment, and Income, 2019—*Continued*

State code	STATE	Labor force participation (percent)			Unemployment rates by age (percent unemployed)				Total labor force 25 to 64 years
		Total	Men	Women	Total labor force	16 to 24 years	25 to 64 years	65 years and over	
	ACS table number:	C23001	C23001	C23001	C23001	C23001	C23001	C23001	B23006
	Column number:	20	21	22	23	24	25	26	27
00	UNITED STATES..............	63.0	67.8	58.4	6.3	10.9	5.5	5.8	172,301,450
01	Alabama.........................	57.7	62.8	53.0	5.3	10.5	4.5	3.4	2,565,399
02	Alaska	65.9	69.5	62.0	6.5	10.7	5.8	6.4	387,369
04	Arizona..........................	60.6	65.8	55.4	5.7	9.7	5.0	5.5	3,646,312
05	Arkansas........................	58.6	63.0	54.3	5.5	9.9	4.7	5.0	1,512,610
06	California.......................	63.4	69.0	57.8	8.3	13.7	7.4	8.9	20,945,343
08	Colorado........................	68.1	73.0	63.0	5.2	9.1	4.6	5.0	3,164,015
09	Connecticut....................	65.6	70.1	61.4	6.6	11.5	5.7	8.0	1,885,204
10	Delaware	60.1	63.3	57.0	5.5	6.9	5.3	5.3	509,553
11	District of Columbia.........	70.7	73.6	68.2	8.1	19.3	6.9	5.7	393,159
12	Florida	59.1	63.9	54.6	5.6	9.5	5.1	4.6	11,163,126
13	Georgia	62.9	67.4	58.7	5.5	10.5	4.7	4.5	5,648,584
15	Hawaii...........................	63.4	67.0	59.8	7.2	12.1	6.6	6.2	739,120
16	Idaho............................	63.1	68.8	57.5	3.3	5.8	2.8	3.5	943,556
17	Illinois...........................	64.5	68.9	60.3	7.3	13.3	6.4	6.6	6,627,388
18	Indiana..........................	63.4	68.5	58.6	4.7	8.8	4.0	2.9	3,444,052
19	Iowa.............................	66.1	70.3	61.9	3.6	5.5	3.2	3.2	1,569,680
20	Kansas...........................	65.7	70.2	61.2	4.3	9.4	3.4	2.4	1,452,457
21	Kentucky	58.8	63.2	54.7	5.4	10.7	4.5	3.7	2,309,451
22	Louisiana	58.5	62.0	55.2	7.5	14.4	6.5	5.5	2,350,856
23	Maine............................	61.3	65.0	57.9	4.9	6.4	4.3	8.1	717,977
24	Maryland........................	66.6	70.9	62.5	5.8	12.7	4.9	4.7	3,269,877
25	Massachusetts	66.8	70.6	63.1	6.6	11.0	5.7	8.3	3,718,308
26	Michigan	60.9	65.4	56.5	6.9	11.6	6.1	5.5	5,148,611
27	Minnesota	68.4	71.8	65.0	4.9	8.3	4.2	5.4	2,939,470
28	Mississippi.....................	56.6	59.9	53.6	6.3	11.0	5.6	4.9	1,471,222
29	Missouri.........................	62.8	66.9	58.8	4.6	7.8	4.0	3.9	3,141,866
30	Montana	61.8	65.4	58.2	3.9	5.9	3.5	4.7	549,460
31	Nebraska	68.6	73.1	64.2	2.6	5.4	2.2	1.0	969,703
32	Nevada	63.0	67.3	58.6	9.6	13.3	8.8	13.0	1,673,258
33	New Hampshire	66.7	71.3	62.1	3.6	5.7	3.2	3.6	740,577
34	New Jersey	65.6	70.8	60.7	8.0	14.0	7.0	10.8	4,910,806
35	New Mexico	56.9	60.6	53.4	7.7	11.6	7.1	6.5	1,058,752
36	New York........................	62.5	66.4	59.0	8.7	15.6	7.8	8.0	10,509,757
37	North Carolina................	62.2	67.5	57.3	5.7	10.6	4.9	3.8	5,449,263
38	North Dakota..................	68.1	73.0	62.9	2.8	3.1	2.8	2.1	382,899
39	Ohio.............................	62.6	66.8	58.7	5.4	9.3	4.8	4.3	6,015,404
40	Oklahoma.......................	61.0	65.6	56.6	5.9	10.1	5.2	3.6	1,994,715
41	Oregon...........................	61.6	65.8	57.5	6.3	12.1	5.5	5.6	2,240,739
42	Pennsylvania	62.4	66.6	58.4	6.4	11.6	5.6	5.6	6,697,042
72	Puerto Rico	44.8	49.5	40.7	13.0	28.1	11.2	4.4	1,660,923
44	Rhode Island...................	65.1	69.2	61.4	7.6	13.0	6.5	8.7	573,263
45	South Carolina.................	59.6	64.3	55.3	5.6	10.2	4.8	5.0	2,631,175
46	South Dakota	66.6	70.2	63.0	2.8	5.2	2.4	1.7	432,494
47	Tennessee......................	61.2	66.5	56.3	5.3	10.2	4.5	3.8	3,627,179
48	Texas............................	64.6	71.0	58.4	6.1	10.7	5.4	5.3	15,332,277
49	Utah.............................	68.7	76.1	61.1	3.5	5.8	2.9	2.7	1,622,607
50	Vermont	64.3	67.1	61.6	4.2	7.1	3.7	3.7	329,532
51	Virginia..........................	65.2	70.2	60.5	4.6	8.8	4.0	4.0	4,536,192
53	Washington	63.9	68.9	58.8	5.8	11.5	4.9	5.5	4,149,509
54	West Virginia	52.6	56.1	49.2	6.2	13.7	5.2	2.3	896,664
55	Wisconsin.......................	65.1	68.6	61.6	3.5	6.9	3.0	2.2	3,022,092
56	Wyoming........................	65.3	70.3	60.0	3.7	7.1	3.0	3.5	291,526

NA = Not available.
'- = Indicates that either no sample observations or too few sample observations were available to compute an estimate, or a ratio of medians cannot be calculated because one or both of the median estimates falls in the lowest interval or upper interval of an open-ended distribution, or the margin of error associated with a median was larger than the median itself.

	STATE	Unemployment rates for the labor force age 25 to 64 by educational attainment					Total population 16 to 19 years	16 to 19 years, not enrolled in school, not high school graduate, not in labor force	Total labor force
		Unemployment rate (percent unemployed)							
		Total 25 to 64 years	No high school diploma	High school graduate	Some college or associate's degree	Bachelor's degree or higher			
	ACS table number:	B23006	B23006	B23006	B23006	B23006	C14005	C14005	C23001
State code	Column number:	28	29	30	31	32	33	34	35
00	UNITED STATES...............	5.5	9.5	7.3	6.0	3.4	17,481,586	2.0	168,236,937
01	Alabama........................	4.5	11.0	6.0	4.4	1.8	271,458	2.4	2,335,486
02	Alaska	5.8	17.0	8.7	5.2	2.8	40,198	3.0	376,965
04	Arizona.........................	5.0	8.5	6.5	5.4	2.9	384,404	3.0	3,544,778
05	Arkansas.......................	4.7	8.8	6.1	5.0	2.0	166,792	2.2	1,408,602
06	California.......................	7.4	9.4	9.3	8.7	5.1	2,065,676	1.6	19,961,610
08	Colorado	4.6	8.2	6.6	5.5	3.0	302,724	1.8	3,212,836
09	Connecticut...................	5.7	10.9	8.0	5.2	4.2	197,465	1.0	1,950,159
10	Delaware	5.3	4.3	8.2	5.1	3.8	51,129	2.0	492,382
11	District of Columbia.........	6.9	21.1	21.7	15.9	2.6	NA	NA	391,439
12	Florida	5.1	8.5	6.3	5.2	3.4	1,004,117	2.6	10,652,489
13	Georgia	4.7	7.2	6.6	4.9	2.9	615,838	2.4	5,394,701
15	Hawaii	6.6	12.2	8.6	7.2	4.2	58,318	2.3	739,336
16	Idaho...........................	2.8	2.1	3.5	4.0	1.1	107,530	2.6	937,369
17	Illinois..........................	6.4	10.9	9.4	7.3	3.6	669,675	1.4	6,584,794
18	Indiana.........................	4.0	7.3	5.5	4.5	1.8	373,166	2.2	3,426,897
19	Iowa............................	3.2	7.5	4.7	3.4	1.3	181,373	1.3	1,681,087
20	Kansas..........................	3.4	8.2	5.5	3.2	1.7	170,309	1.2	1,520,362
21	Kentucky	4.5	8.2	5.9	4.6	2.5	246,047	2.5	2,125,669
22	Louisiana	6.5	13.7	8.8	6.6	2.6	239,298	2.9	2,143,567
23	Maine...........................	4.3	11.8	5.7	4.0	3.0	63,037	2.0	708,906
24	Maryland	4.9	10.1	6.8	5.1	3.2	312,864	2.0	3,304,168
25	Massachusetts................	5.7	12.0	8.6	7.3	3.4	379,358	1.0	3,865,417
26	Michigan	6.1	14.3	8.9	6.2	3.2	525,239	2.2	4,966,693
27	Minnesota	4.2	9.3	5.5	4.8	2.7	301,792	1.6	3,114,145
28	Mississippi	5.6	15.9	6.6	5.5	2.0	173,049	2.1	1,325,864
29	Missouri........................	4.0	9.0	5.9	4.2	2.0	334,109	2.7	3,107,007
30	Montana	3.5	13.4	3.1	4.0	2.2	54,270	1.4	554,118
31	Nebraska.......................	2.2	5.2	3.1	2.1	1.4	108,882	0.8	1,053,466
32	Nevada.........................	8.8	10.1	10.7	10.4	5.0	148,123	2.6	1,590,604
33	New Hampshire...............	3.2	6.9	3.3	3.5	2.7	69,479	1.3	776,061
34	New Jersey	7.0	11.0	9.8	8.4	4.7	462,704	1.5	4,914,835
35	New Mexico	7.1	11.7	9.1	8.2	3.5	117,622	3.9	967,832
36	New York.......................	7.8	12.8	10.8	9.0	5.0	983,272	1.7	10,138,385
37	North Carolina...............	4.9	9.8	6.9	5.3	2.7	573,105	1.8	5,301,767
38	North Dakota.................	2.8	6.9	2.8	3.5	1.6	43,052	3.8	415,807
39	Ohio............................	4.8	11.0	6.5	5.0	2.5	614,828	1.8	5,936,933
40	Oklahoma......................	5.2	9.8	6.5	5.8	2.2	222,732	2.7	1,917,143
41	Oregon.........................	5.5	9.8	7.2	6.1	3.4	202,768	2.3	2,147,998
42	Pennsylvania..................	5.6	10.9	7.8	6.1	3.1	655,409	2.0	6,618,867
72	Puerto Rico....................	11.2	21.8	13.9	12.8	6.6	167,669	3.2	1,252,484
44	Rhode Island..................	6.5	17.5	8.1	6.7	3.6	62,526	0.3	594,888
45	South Carolina................	4.8	9.7	6.6	4.8	2.5	282,486	2.1	2,507,997
46	South Dakota	2.4	6.2	4.0	2.0	1.1	51,192	2.2	466,270
47	Tennessee......................	4.5	10.3	6.2	4.6	2.1	358,791	1.7	3,439,821
48	Texas	5.4	7.0	6.8	6.4	3.4	1,696,415	2.6	14,826,344
49	Utah............................	2.9	3.5	3.8	3.3	2.0	216,002	1.8	1,721,142
50	Vermont........................	3.7	8.6	4.1	5.1	2.5	34,361	2.0	349,096
51	Virginia.........................	4.0	7.6	5.9	5.0	2.2	463,500	1.3	4,553,835
53	Washington....................	4.9	7.7	6.2	5.6	3.5	368,064	1.8	3,993,077
54	West Virginia..................	5.2	12.7	6.3	5.6	2.2	87,786	1.2	771,429
55	Wisconsin......................	3.0	6.8	4.0	3.1	1.7	309,415	1.5	3,105,191
56	Wyoming.......................	3.0	9.2	5.0	2.0	1.5	30,557	1.9	301,303

NA = Not available.
'- = Indicates that either no sample observations or too few sample observations were available to compute an estimate, or a ratio of medians cannot be calculated because one or both of the median estimates falls in the lowest interval or upper interval of an open-ended distribution, or the margin of error associated with a median was larger than the median itself.

Table B-1. States — What: Education, Employment, and Income, 2021—*Continued*

	STATE	Percent of population 16 to 64 years who worked full-time, year-round in the past 12 months			Total households	Percent of households with no workers	Family status of children under 18 years, by employment status of parents and age of children			
							Children under 18 years in families			
							Number	Percent living with two parents		Percent living with one parent who is in labor force
		Total	Male	Female				Both in labor force	One parent in labor force	
	ACS table number:	S2402	S2402	S2402	B08202	B08202	C23008	C23008	C23008	C23008
State code	Column number:	36	37	38	39	40	41	42	43	44
00	**UNITED STATES**...............	65.1	56.3	43.7	127,544,730	27.4	69,660,788	42.5	22.3	27.3
01	Alabama......................	68.1	56.2	43.8	1,967,559	32.2	1,035,443	38.0	21.4	30.4
02	Alaska	55.9	55.1	44.9	271,311	25.3	169,043	39.1	27.4	26.8
04	Arizona.......................	66.1	57.3	42.7	2,817,723	28.8	1,526,776	37.2	25.5	29.2
05	Arkansas.....................	69.4	54.9	45.1	1,183,675	31.6	651,479	40.9	20.1	29.5
06	California....................	61.8	58.3	41.7	13,429,063	24.6	8,339,945	39.5	24.9	27.2
08	Colorado.....................	65.7	57.8	42.2	2,313,042	22.9	1,192,764	47.7	23.3	23.5
09	Connecticut.................	63.4	55.3	44.7	1,428,313	26.6	697,108	46.6	19.2	28.7
10	Delaware	65.6	53.7	46.3	395,656	31.1	196,998	42.0	20.9	29.5
11	District of Columbia..........	69.2	47.7	52.3	319,565	24.9	116,148	38.7	10.8	36.6
12	Florida	66.9	55.4	44.6	8,565,329	31.2	4,052,565	39.5	20.7	31.3
13	Georgia	67.5	54.6	45.4	4,001,109	25.2	2,371,032	39.3	21.4	29.7
15	Hawaii........................	57.0	53.0	47.0	490,080	26.3	280,855	44.8	22.7	24.3
16	Idaho.........................	64.0	59.0	41.0	693,882	26.4	449,177	42.5	31.8	20.8
17	Illinois	65.0	55.8	44.2	4,991,641	27.3	2,682,097	44.9	20.8	27.5
18	Indiana.......................	66.7	57.2	42.8	2,680,694	26.8	1,496,367	43.1	22.8	26.8
19	Iowa..........................	67.5	57.1	42.9	1,300,467	26.9	708,669	54.6	17.1	24.0
20	Kansas........................	67.7	56.8	43.2	1,159,026	25.4	667,909	48.3	21.0	25.8
21	Kentucky	64.9	55.4	44.6	1,785,682	32.1	933,125	41.7	23.2	25.2
22	Louisiana	64.9	54.0	46.0	1,783,924	31.8	1,018,038	36.2	17.1	34.5
23	Maine	65.4	54.8	45.2	593,626	32.0	236,991	49.6	19.0	23.6
24	Maryland	68.2	53.8	46.2	2,355,652	23.6	1,295,521	46.5	18.3	28.2
25	Massachusetts	63.3	55.6	44.4	2,759,018	26.0	1,305,132	50.6	16.9	25.4
26	Michigan	61.0	57.2	42.8	4,051,798	31.6	2,055,474	42.4	22.4	26.6
27	Minnesota	64.6	56.9	43.1	2,281,033	25.4	1,255,094	54.6	16.3	24.3
28	Mississippi	68.6	52.9	47.1	1,129,611	33.4	644,756	35.7	18.0	33.3
29	Missouri......................	67.1	55.2	44.8	2,468,726	28.1	1,301,513	46.3	20.2	27.2
30	Montana	62.0	58.3	41.7	448,949	30.2	220,788	48.4	21.4	24.7
31	Nebraska	69.3	56.9	43.1	785,982	23.5	461,743	52.0	18.9	24.7
32	Nevada	60.8	56.3	43.7	1,191,380	29.5	658,140	36.0	22.5	32.2
33	New Hampshire	67.0	57.8	42.2	548,026	25.7	245,217	51.3	19.4	23.0
34	New Jersey	64.4	56.5	43.5	3,497,945	25.0	1,940,455	47.7	22.8	23.6
35	New Mexico	62.8	56.0	44.0	834,007	33.2	441,105	33.2	21.3	35.3
36	New York	62.0	54.2	45.8	7,652,666	29.2	3,893,765	43.1	21.1	27.1
37	North Carolina................	65.6	55.3	44.7	4,179,632	28.7	2,168,346	41.2	22.0	29.1
38	North Dakota.................	65.2	59.2	40.8	322,511	24.1	175,172	52.4	19.1	22.0
39	Ohio..........................	65.6	56.1	43.9	4,832,922	29.8	2,453,395	43.6	19.3	28.8
40	Oklahoma....................	66.7	55.7	44.3	1,547,967	28.9	895,900	39.7	24.2	27.8
41	Oregon.......................	62.0	57.5	42.5	1,702,599	29.9	808,257	42.5	24.5	25.3
42	Pennsylvania..................	65.6	56.0	44.0	5,228,956	29.7	2,550,943	44.8	20.2	26.7
72	Puerto Rico	54.9	53.1	46.9	1,165,982	48.8	521,330	21.9	11.6	46.3
44	Rhode Island.................	63.2	56.2	43.8	440,170	28.5	196,915	47.3	14.6	30.3
45	South Carolina................	66.8	54.8	45.2	2,049,972	30.9	1,044,487	37.9	21.2	32.3
46	South Dakota	68.5	56.9	43.1	356,887	24.4	205,422	55.3	15.7	22.6
47	Tennessee	67.8	55.8	44.2	2,770,395	28.8	1,429,023	40.7	22.7	27.6
48	Texas	67.8	57.3	42.7	10,796,247	22.4	7,109,152	39.0	25.9	26.8
49	Utah..........................	63.4	62.4	37.6	1,101,499	19.1	913,106	45.2	35.6	15.5
50	Vermont......................	63.4	53.6	46.4	270,163	28.6	112,908	54.3	12.7	24.8
51	Virginia.......................	67.2	56.1	43.9	3,331,461	24.6	1,786,124	46.2	21.7	25.9
53	Washington...................	63.2	58.2	41.8	3,022,255	26.3	1,596,811	43.1	27.2	22.2
54	West Virginia.................	67.0	55.9	44.1	722,201	38.0	325,283	38.4	24.6	25.2
55	Wisconsin....................	66.9	57.1	42.9	2,449,970	27.9	1,222,906	49.3	17.6	27.3
56	Wyoming......................	62.5	60.5	39.5	242,763	27.1	125,406	49.9	23.0	22.8

NA = Not available.

'- = Indicates that either no sample observations or too few sample observations were available to compute an estimate, or a ratio of medians cannot be calculated because one or both of the median estimates falls in the lowest interval or upper interval of an open-ended distribution, or the margin of error associated with a median was larger than the median itself.

Table B-1. States — What: Education, Employment, and Income, 2021—*Continued*

State code	STATE	Family status of children under 18 years, by employment status of parents and age of children							
		Children under 6 years in families				Children 6–17 years in families			
		Number	Percent living with two parents		Percent living with one parent who is in labor force	Number	Percent living with two parents		Percent living with one parent who is in labor force
			Both in labor force	One parent in labor force			Both in labor force	One parent in labor force	
	ACS table number:	C23008	C23008	C23008	C23008	C23008	C23008	C23008	C23008
	Column number:	45	46	47	48	49	50	51	52
00	UNITED STATES...............	21,632,850	41.1	24.5	25.6	48,027,938	18.5	11.0	11.6
01	Alabama..........................	326,228	34.1	24.2	31.4	709,215	15.7	11.2	14.4
02	Alaska............................	55,651	35.2	32.8	25.1	113,392	17.3	16.1	12.3
04	Arizona...........................	461,443	34.9	26.4	29.6	1,065,333	15.1	11.4	12.8
05	Arkansas.........................	206,155	37.9	21.7	29.0	445,324	17.5	10.0	13.4
06	California........................	2,557,977	39.3	26.1	25.4	5,781,968	17.4	11.5	11.2
08	Colorado.........................	357,662	46.0	28.6	18.8	835,102	19.7	12.3	8.1
09	Connecticut.....................	208,227	47.0	21.4	25.8	488,881	20.0	9.1	11.0
10	Delaware.........................	62,294	36.8	23.7	30.9	134,704	17.0	11.0	14.3
11	District of Columbia..........	45,818	47.0	11.9	31.0	70,330	30.6	7.7	20.2
12	Florida............................	1,258,465	38.7	22.2	29.5	2,794,100	17.4	10.0	13.3
13	Georgia	728,314	37.3	23.8	27.5	1,642,718	16.6	10.5	12.2
15	Hawaii............................	88,914	41.2	27.4	22.8	191,941	19.1	12.7	10.6
16	Idaho..............................	135,261	38.8	37.7	17.7	313,916	16.7	16.3	7.6
17	Illinois............................	823,325	43.4	22.4	26.3	1,858,772	19.2	9.9	11.7
18	Indiana...........................	472,948	40.2	27.0	24.9	1,023,419	18.6	12.5	11.5
19	Iowa...............................	222,490	50.9	20.5	23.6	486,179	23.3	9.4	10.8
20	Kansas............................	207,075	46.8	23.2	24.9	460,834	21.0	10.4	11.2
21	Kentucky.........................	297,816	39.7	25.0	24.3	635,309	18.6	11.7	11.4
22	Louisiana	328,860	34.5	17.9	33.1	689,178	16.4	8.5	15.8
23	Maine.............................	71,872	47.7	23.2	21.5	165,119	20.8	10.1	9.4
24	Maryland.........................	409,065	46.3	21.2	25.0	886,456	21.4	9.8	11.5
25	Massachusetts..................	401,199	52.4	17.3	22.9	903,933	23.3	7.7	10.2
26	Michigan	637,249	40.3	25.4	25.1	1,418,225	18.1	11.4	11.3
27	Minnesota	391,189	53.6	18.9	22.0	863,905	24.3	8.6	10.0
28	Mississippi	197,558	35.8	17.6	33.1	447,198	15.8	7.8	14.6
29	Missouri..........................	410,464	45.0	22.1	25.5	891,049	20.7	10.2	11.8
30	Montana	65,791	48.5	24.5	21.4	154,997	20.6	10.4	9.1
31	Nebraska	148,088	50.3	22.3	22.0	313,655	23.7	10.5	10.4
32	Nevada...........................	205,243	34.9	23.1	30.8	452,897	15.8	10.5	14.0
33	New Hampshire................	71,583	51.9	23.3	19.9	173,634	21.4	9.6	8.2
34	New Jersey	605,567	46.4	24.5	22.9	1,334,888	21.1	11.1	10.4
35	New Mexico	135,891	29.2	23.5	34.7	305,214	13.0	10.5	15.5
36	New York.........................	1,239,638	43.3	22.5	24.8	2,654,127	20.2	10.5	11.6
37	North Carolina.................	667,514	38.2	24.5	28.0	1,500,832	17.0	10.9	12.5
38	North Dakota...................	59,811	51.1	24.1	19.5	115,361	26.5	12.5	10.1
39	Ohio...............................	765,975	41.9	22.0	26.8	1,687,420	19.0	10.0	12.2
40	Oklahoma........................	282,971	35.1	27.6	28.1	612,929	16.2	12.7	13.0
41	Oregon............................	241,649	42.6	27.9	22.2	566,608	18.2	11.9	9.5
42	Pennsylvania....................	788,253	43.3	22.5	24.9	1,762,690	19.4	10.0	11.1
72	Puerto Rico	130,043	19.4	10.1	47.1	391,287	6.4	3.4	15.7
44	Rhode Island....................	61,129	45.4	15.4	30.8	135,786	20.4	6.9	13.9
45	South Carolina..................	316,454	36.3	22.9	31.7	728,033	15.8	10.0	13.8
46	South Dakota	66,821	54.5	18.5	19.4	138,601	26.3	8.9	9.3
47	Tennessee........................	456,131	38.1	26.0	26.7	972,892	17.9	12.2	12.5
48	Texas	2,217,200	36.8	28.2	25.6	4,891,952	16.7	12.8	11.6
49	Utah...............................	277,837	40.9	41.3	12.8	635,269	17.9	18.0	5.6
50	Vermont..........................	31,570	54.5	14.4	22.4	81,338	21.2	5.6	8.7
51	Virginia...........................	559,186	44.4	25.1	23.8	1,226,938	20.2	11.4	10.9
53	Washington......................	501,643	41.8	30.5	19.7	1,095,168	19.1	14.0	9.0
54	West Virginia	98,871	34.4	26.5	25.5	226,412	15.0	11.6	11.1
55	Wisconsin........................	369,671	48.4	20.7	24.4	853,235	21.0	9.0	10.6
56	Wyoming.........................	34,844	46.4	26.4	22.4	90,562	17.9	10.2	8.6

NA = Not available.
'- = Indicates that either no sample observations or too few sample observations were available to compute an estimate, or a ratio of medians cannot be calculated because one or both of the median estimates falls in the lowest interval or upper interval of an open-ended distribution, or the margin of error associated with a median was larger than the median itself.

Table B-1. States — What: Education, Employment, and Income, 2021—*Continued*

State code	STATE	Employment status of family householders					Women 20 to 64 years in households, by presence of children and labor force status		
		Total families with children under 18	Opposite-sex married-couple families			Families maintained by women and men with no spouse		Total women 20 to 64 years in households	Percent with children under 18 years	Percent in labor force with children under 18 years
			Total	Both in labor force (percent)	Total	Householder in labor force (percent)			
	ACS table number:	C23007	C23007	C23007	C23007	C23007	B23003	B23003	B23003
	Column number:	53	54	55	56	57	58	59	60
00	UNITED STATES..............	33,470,951	22,721,720	67.4	10,749,231	84.6	95,557,930	34.5	24.2
01	Alabama.....................	489,167	313,578	65.7	175,589	82.4	1,453,316	34.3	22.9
02	Alaska	76,712	54,015	61.3	22,697	84.6	202,314	36.6	24.7
04	Arizona....................	724,865	478,702	61.6	246,163	85.2	2,025,823	34.7	23.2
05	Arkansas..................	322,538	209,700	68.1	112,838	83.0	848,072	37.3	24.0
06	California.................	3,806,811	2,656,451	62.6	1,150,360	84.7	11,433,017	33.6	22.5
08	Colorado..................	596,344	433,391	69.1	162,953	87.8	1,706,660	33.8	23.7
09	Connecticut..............	366,836	247,213	72.8	119,623	88.4	1,049,320	34.0	24.9
10	Delaware	91,327	59,069	69.1	32,258	84.4	285,922	32.0	24.0
11	District of Columbia.........	50,434	28,958	75.9	21,476	72.6	218,849	23.9	34.3
12	Florida	1,948,025	1,246,772	65.9	701,253	85.1	6,183,234	31.5	23.3
13	Georgia	1,113,010	719,397	66.8	393,613	83.5	3,223,306	35.6	23.6
15	Hawaii	120,094	89,108	65.5	30,986	83.2	397,629	33.1	23.9
16	Idaho......................	205,442	154,517	62.9	50,925	90.8	521,748	39.2	22.9
17	Illinois.....................	1,297,886	893,563	69.6	404,323	86.8	3,671,170	34.7	24.9
18	Indiana	712,273	482,080	67.8	230,193	85.3	1,925,244	36.1	24.7
19	Iowa.......................	348,231	244,298	77.4	103,933	88.1	871,398	37.6	27.3
20	Kansas.....................	322,527	227,414	71.1	95,113	87.9	803,758	37.7	27.3
21	Kentucky	460,455	308,491	68.0	151,964	79.3	1,278,385	35.6	24.2
22	Louisiana	468,285	272,640	67.9	195,645	81.5	1,333,707	35.6	25.2
23	Maine......................	129,617	89,711	72.4	39,906	83.2	393,533	31.5	25.7
24	Maryland	636,517	433,435	73.9	203,082	86.5	1,838,053	34.6	26.3
25	Massachusetts	697,438	483,811	75.7	213,627	83.6	2,072,101	32.7	26.2
26	Michigan	993,296	658,093	67.6	335,203	82.2	2,868,822	33.4	24.4
27	Minnesota	607,084	438,460	79.0	168,624	88.6	1,604,893	35.6	28.2
28	Mississippi	291,954	174,933	68.6	117,021	79.5	846,898	36.7	25.3
29	Missouri	625,218	421,631	71.5	203,587	87.2	1,750,855	34.8	26.2
30	Montana	102,231	72,779	70.9	29,452	89.1	299,441	32.2	26.0
31	Nebraska	215,607	154,585	75.6	61,022	90.0	535,293	37.3	28.4
32	Nevada	312,668	196,630	62.7	116,038	86.8	909,525	32.9	23.0
33	New Hampshire	131,080	94,849	74.8	36,231	83.7	402,739	32.3	25.4
34	New Jersey	993,837	725,061	68.9	268,776	85.7	2,712,592	35.7	24.2
35	New Mexico	207,471	121,335	59.9	86,136	85.0	584,399	35.1	23.0
36	New York...................	1,828,519	1,222,538	68.6	605,981	82.3	5,832,567	31.0	24.6
37	North Carolina..............	1,059,044	706,521	67.3	352,523	84.5	3,093,128	34.1	23.7
38	North Dakota................	79,561	56,087	74.4	23,474	87.9	204,518	35.2	29.0
39	Ohio.......................	1,215,310	776,173	71.8	439,137	83.8	3,347,855	34.9	25.3
40	Oklahoma..................	424,359	280,304	64.3	144,055	83.5	1,113,576	37.0	23.1
41	Oregon.....................	418,153	290,450	65.2	127,703	84.1	1,226,350	32.7	23.6
42	Pennsylvania.................	1,266,818	854,849	71.3	411,969	83.4	3,673,433	33.3	25.0
72	Puerto Rico.................	232,735	89,849	62.1	142,886	74.3	980,853	26.6	18.3
44	Rhode Island...............	100,803	65,796	76.7	35,007	84.2	321,408	31.0	28.4
45	South Carolina.................	505,801	321,734	66.3	184,067	83.9	1,497,485	34.2	24.9
46	South Dakota	93,088	66,353	80.2	26,735	86.0	233,576	37.8	27.4
47	Tennessee..................	690,328	459,896	66.0	230,432	83.3	2,037,690	34.1	23.9
48	Texas......................	3,345,095	2,312,990	61.6	1,032,105	84.8	8,541,134	38.9	22.8
49	Utah.......................	381,819	311,172	59.5	70,647	91.0	923,040	41.6	21.4
50	Vermont	61,163	41,680	79.4	19,483	77.5	183,953	30.6	25.9
51	Virginia....................	896,775	635,026	70.0	261,749	86.4	2,519,858	35.0	24.4
53	Washington.................	797,302	572,481	63.9	224,821	81.9	2,241,863	34.0	23.4
54	West Virginia	160,430	105,844	62.3	54,586	79.7	494,485	31.9	23.4
55	Wisconsin..................	616,056	410,140	75.7	205,916	87.3	1,664,355	34.6	26.4
56	Wyoming...................	65,247	47,016	71.2	18,231	92.1	155,640	38.7	24.9

NA = Not available.
'– = Indicates that either no sample observations or too few sample observations were available to compute an estimate, or a ratio of medians cannot be calculated because one or both of the median estimates falls in the lowest interval or upper interval of an open-ended distribution, or the margin of error associated with a median was larger than the median itself.

Table B-1. States — What: Education, Employment, and Income, 2021—*Continued*

	STATE	Class of worker for employed civilians 16 years and over				Occupation (percent)					
		Civilian employed population 16 years and over	Percent private wage and salary workers	Percent government workers	Percent self-employed and unpaid workers	Civilian employed population 16 years and over	Management, business, science, and arts	Service	Sales and office	Natural resources, construction, and maintenance	Production, transportation, and material moving
	ACS table number:	C24080	C24080	C24080	C24080	C24060	C24060	C24060	C24060	C24060	C24060
State code	Column number:	61	62	63	64	65	66	67	68	69	70
00	UNITED STATES..............	156,380,433	79.1	14.6	6.3	156,380,433	42.2	16.1	20.0	8.5	13.1
01	Alabama.........................	2,190,915	78.2	16.2	5.6	2,190,915	37.3	15.8	20.3	9.6	17.0
02	Alaska	327,953	67.8	25.8	6.4	327,953	39.9	17.2	18.4	10.7	13.7
04	Arizona..........................	3,314,799	79.6	14.2	6.2	3,314,799	41.0	16.7	22.5	8.8	11.0
05	Arkansas........................	1,323,511	77.4	15.5	7.1	1,323,511	37.0	15.8	20.2	10.4	16.7
06	California.......................	18,156,051	77.8	14.7	7.6	18,156,051	42.9	16.8	19.5	8.8	12.1
08	Colorado........................	3,002,106	79.4	13.9	6.7	3,002,106	46.9	14.7	19.8	8.7	10.0
09	Connecticut....................	1,810,942	80.1	13.3	6.5	1,810,942	46.8	15.8	19.5	6.9	11.0
10	Delaware	461,096	79.6	15.7	4.7	461,096	42.1	17.3	20.2	8.6	11.7
11	District of Columbia.........	355,398	68.5	26.7	4.8	355,398	72.3	10.2	11.8	2.0	3.7
12	Florida	9,983,261	81.0	11.9	7.0	9,983,261	39.0	18.0	23.0	9.1	10.9
13	Georgia..........................	5,032,459	79.5	14.7	5.8	5,032,459	41.5	15.0	20.5	8.2	14.8
15	Hawaii	636,963	70.4	22.7	6.9	636,963	39.5	20.8	21.8	9.4	8.5
16	Idaho............................	901,819	76.1	15.3	8.5	901,819	37.9	17.0	20.1	11.4	13.6
17	Illinois...........................	6,079,192	81.7	13.3	5.1	6,079,192	43.1	15.7	19.8	7.0	14.5
18	Indiana	3,259,178	83.3	11.8	4.9	3,259,178	37.9	15.2	19.0	8.9	19.1
19	Iowa..............................	1,616,533	79.1	14.4	6.5	1,616,533	39.0	14.8	19.7	9.7	16.8
20	Kansas...........................	1,437,472	76.8	16.9	6.3	1,437,472	41.8	15.4	20.2	9.0	13.5
21	Kentucky	1,992,331	80.1	14.3	5.6	1,992,331	37.1	14.8	20.4	8.5	19.3
22	Louisiana	1,957,790	77.6	15.9	6.5	1,957,790	38.6	17.9	20.4	10.4	12.6
23	Maine............................	672,480	76.7	14.4	8.9	672,480	42.6	15.3	19.9	9.9	12.2
24	Maryland	3,070,750	72.0	22.6	5.4	3,070,750	50.0	14.9	18.4	7.4	9.3
25	Massachusetts	3,604,672	81.6	12.8	5.6	3,604,672	51.3	15.2	17.9	6.6	9.0
26	Michigan	4,617,618	83.1	11.4	5.5	4,617,618	39.8	15.5	19.7	8.2	16.7
27	Minnesota	2,957,951	81.8	12.7	5.6	2,957,951	44.8	14.8	19.1	7.8	13.4
28	Mississippi	1,227,616	75.5	18.5	6.0	1,227,616	35.5	16.0	20.8	9.7	18.0
29	Missouri.........................	2,939,431	81.1	12.9	6.0	2,939,431	40.8	15.2	20.7	8.4	14.9
30	Montana	527,565	72.7	17.5	9.8	527,565	41.5	17.6	18.4	11.8	10.7
31	Nebraska	1,019,100	78.4	15.1	6.5	1,019,100	40.3	15.5	19.9	9.7	14.6
32	Nevada	1,424,693	81.2	13.4	5.4	1,424,693	33.9	22.1	22.3	9.2	12.5
33	New Hampshire	745,750	80.3	13.7	6.0	745,750	44.4	13.9	20.6	8.7	12.4
34	New Jersey	4,508,519	80.3	14.6	5.1	4,508,519	47.9	13.7	20.3	6.9	11.2
35	New Mexico	878,606	69.1	24.0	6.9	878,606	41.5	18.9	18.6	10.3	10.7
36	New York........................	9,226,373	77.5	16.8	5.8	9,226,373	46.2	18.1	19.5	6.7	9.5
37	North Carolina	4,889,866	79.6	14.1	6.3	4,889,866	42.1	14.9	20.0	8.9	14.1
38	North Dakota..................	394,601	74.1	17.6	8.3	394,601	40.2	17.0	19.3	11.2	12.3
39	Ohio..............................	5,600,209	82.2	12.6	5.2	5,600,209	40.0	15.8	19.9	7.5	16.8
40	Oklahoma.......................	1,780,086	75.2	17.8	7.0	1,780,086	38.0	16.9	20.4	10.6	14.1
41	Oregon...........................	2,007,468	78.3	14.2	7.5	2,007,468	42.5	16.6	20.0	8.5	12.5
42	Pennsylvania...................	6,190,796	83.2	11.7	5.0	6,190,796	42.6	15.8	19.5	7.8	14.3
72	Puerto Rico.....................	1,085,614	68.9	18.6	12.5	1,085,614	29.9	20.9	26.7	10.0	12.6
44	Rhode Island...................	546,249	81.1	13.4	5.4	546,249	43.1	17.8	20.4	7.5	11.2
45	South Carolina................	2,335,354	78.4	15.5	6.1	2,335,354	38.4	16.7	20.3	9.3	15.4
46	South Dakota	449,435	76.3	15.0	8.7	449,435	39.8	15.9	20.2	10.7	13.5
47	Tennessee......................	3,239,311	78.7	13.8	7.5	3,239,311	38.7	15.3	20.7	8.3	16.9
48	Texas	13,796,229	78.5	14.4	7.1	13,796,229	40.1	16.2	20.6	10.2	12.9
49	Utah..............................	1,653,768	79.6	15.0	5.4	1,653,768	42.2	13.7	22.0	8.7	13.4
50	Vermont.........................	333,135	76.1	15.1	8.8	333,135	47.1	13.8	17.8	10.3	11.1
51	Virginia..........................	4,206,422	74.3	20.5	5.2	4,206,422	48.3	15.4	18.3	7.5	10.6
53	Washington.....................	3,696,564	78.3	15.9	5.8	3,696,564	45.4	15.0	18.3	9.3	12.0
54	West Virginia	721,479	75.3	19.9	4.8	721,479	37.2	18.3	20.3	10.2	14.0
55	Wisconsin.......................	2,991,136	81.9	12.7	5.4	2,991,136	39.5	14.8	19.0	8.9	17.8
56	Wyoming........................	287,432	71.7	21.1	7.2	287,432	37.3	16.8	18.2	14.1	13.6

NA = Not available.
'- = Indicates that either no sample observations or too few sample observations were available to compute an estimate, or a ratio of medians cannot be calculated because one or both of the median estimates falls in the lowest interval or upper interval of an open-ended distribution, or the margin of error associated with a median was larger than the median itself.

Table B-1. States — What: Education, Employment, and Income, 2021—*Continued*

		Industry (percent)							
	STATE	Agriculture, forestry, fishing and hunting, and mining	Construction	Manufacturing	Wholesale trade	Retail trade	Transportation and warehousing, and utilities	Information	Finance and insurance, real estate, and rental and leasing
	ACS table number:	C24070	C24070	C24070	C24070	C24070	C24070	C24070	C24070
State code	Column number:	71	72	73	74	75	76	77	78
00	UNITED STATES...............	1.6	6.9	10.1	2.3	11.1	5.9	1.9	6.8
01	Alabama........................	1.2	7.0	13.8	2.2	12.0	5.9	1.2	5.7
02	Alaska	4.3	6.8	4.9	1.2	10.1	9.4	1.8	3.9
04	Arizona........................	1.2	7.6	7.8	2.1	12.2	5.6	1.6	8.8
05	Arkansas......................	2.4	7.3	12.6	2.3	13.3	6.3	1.2	5.4
06	California......................	2.1	6.8	9.0	2.6	10.2	6.2	2.9	5.8
08	Colorado......................	1.8	8.1	7.0	2.4	10.8	5.1	2.5	7.5
09	Connecticut..................	0.4	6.1	11.1	2.1	11.2	4.4	1.9	9.0
10	Delaware......................	0.9	7.2	6.6	1.4	13.0	5.6	1.2	9.7
11	District of Columbia........	0.1	2.3	1.3	0.6	4.8	3.3	3.3	7.3
12	Florida.........................	0.8	8.1	5.4	2.4	12.4	6.2	1.6	8.3
13	Georgia	0.9	6.8	10.3	2.5	11.6	7.5	2.1	6.0
15	Hawaii.........................	1.1	7.7	2.7	2.3	10.7	6.4	1.3	7.0
16	Idaho..........................	4.5	8.9	10.0	2.5	11.1	5.3	1.4	5.7
17	Illinois.........................	1.0	5.4	11.9	2.7	10.3	6.9	1.7	7.6
18	Indiana........................	1.3	6.5	18.2	2.2	10.9	6.3	1.3	5.6
19	Iowa...........................	3.8	6.8	15.0	2.6	11.9	5.0	1.4	7.9
20	Kansas.........................	3.2	6.3	11.8	2.2	10.6	5.6	1.6	6.6
21	Kentucky......................	1.7	6.2	14.4	2.0	12.3	7.0	1.3	5.8
22	Louisiana	3.1	7.9	7.2	2.3	11.7	5.8	1.2	5.2
23	Maine..........................	2.4	7.9	9.8	1.9	11.8	4.3	1.6	7.1
24	Maryland......................	0.6	7.3	4.9	1.7	9.3	5.2	1.7	6.0
25	Massachusetts	0.5	5.9	8.9	1.8	10.1	4.2	1.9	7.6
26	Michigan......................	1.1	5.9	18.6	2.0	11.0	4.9	1.2	6.2
27	Minnesota	2.2	6.4	13.3	2.6	11.0	5.0	1.3	7.2
28	Mississippi	2.2	7.1	12.9	1.9	11.7	7.3	1.1	4.9
29	Missouri.......................	1.7	6.4	11.6	2.4	11.7	5.8	1.5	7.2
30	Montana	6.1	9.4	4.1	2.0	11.4	5.1	1.9	5.1
31	Nebraska......................	4.1	6.9	10.6	2.4	10.3	6.0	1.3	8.2
32	Nevada........................	1.3	7.5	5.4	1.6	11.7	7.1	1.6	6.6
33	New Hampshire..............	0.6	7.2	12.5	2.2	12.0	4.1	2.1	6.4
34	New Jersey	0.3	6.2	8.2	2.9	11.1	6.5	2.7	8.9
35	New Mexico	3.9	7.2	4.0	1.8	10.4	5.2	1.2	4.7
36	New York......................	0.6	5.7	5.8	2.0	9.8	5.5	2.8	8.2
37	North Carolina...............	1.1	7.5	11.9	2.2	11.4	5.5	1.5	7.3
38	North Dakota.................	7.2	8.3	6.5	2.9	10.5	5.5	1.1	6.2
39	Ohio...........................	1.0	5.9	14.9	2.4	11.2	6.1	1.3	6.9
40	Oklahoma.....................	3.5	7.0	9.1	2.1	12.3	5.9	1.8	5.6
41	Oregon........................	2.4	6.8	10.8	2.8	11.9	5.0	1.2	5.3
42	Pennsylvania	1.2	5.9	11.8	2.4	11.2	6.0	1.6	6.7
72	Puerto Rico	1.4	6.5	9.4	3.1	13.9	3.4	1.6	5.3
44	Rhode Island.................	0.4	5.8	10.2	2.5	11.3	5.2	1.4	7.7
45	South Carolina...............	0.9	7.0	13.5	2.1	11.4	5.5	1.5	6.2
46	South Dakota	6.0	7.6	9.9	2.4	12.2	4.8	1.4	7.6
47	Tennessee.....................	0.8	6.7	13.0	2.4	11.8	7.1	1.5	6.1
48	Texas...........................	2.2	8.5	8.7	2.5	11.2	6.6	1.6	7.1
49	Utah...........................	1.4	8.1	10.9	2.4	11.6	5.2	1.8	7.5
50	Vermont.......................	2.7	8.5	10.1	1.6	11.4	3.4	2.0	4.9
51	Virginia........................	0.9	6.4	7.1	1.7	9.7	4.8	1.8	6.4
53	Washington...................	2.5	7.2	9.4	2.2	11.9	6.0	2.6	5.3
54	West Virginia	3.0	6.6	8.1	1.9	12.0	5.9	1.5	4.6
55	Wisconsin.....................	2.1	6.4	18.0	2.5	11.4	5.2	1.5	6.3
56	Wyoming......................	8.7	8.4	4.6	1.7	11.8	6.3	1.6	4.0

NA = Not available.

'- = Indicates that either no sample observations or too few sample observations were available to compute an estimate, or a ratio of medians cannot be calculated because one or both of the median estimates falls in the lowest interval or upper interval of an open-ended distribution, or the margin of error associated with a median was larger than the median itself.

Table B-1. States — What: Education, Employment, and Income, 2021—*Continued*

	STATE	Industry (percent)					Veterans as a percent of the civilian population 18 years and over	Median income in the past 12 months (in 2021 inflation-adjusted dollars)				
								Median household income by age of householder				
		Professional, scientific, and management, and administrative and waste management services	Educational services, and health care and social assistance	Arts, entertainment, and recreation, and accommodation and food services	Other services, except public administration	Public administration		All households	Householder under 25 years	Householder 25 to 44 years	Householder 45 to 64 years	Householder 65 years and over
	ACS table number:	C24070	C24070	C24070	C24070	C24070	B21001	B19049	B19049	B19049	B19049	B19049
State code	Column number:	79	80	81	82	83	84	85	86	87	88	89
00	UNITED STATES..............	12.4	23.5	8.2	4.6	4.8	6.4	69,717	38,164	77,338	83,812	50,969
01	Alabama.........................	10.1	23.0	7.9	4.7	5.3	8.1	53,913	31,213	60,535	64,925	41,927
02	Alaska...........................	9.4	23.0	9.1	3.9	12.2	11.0	77,845	39,965	82,206	88,273	63,567
04	Arizona.........................	12.5	22.0	9.5	4.4	4.8	8.1	69,056	42,911	76,238	82,112	54,411
05	Arkansas........................	7.9	24.6	7.4	4.6	4.5	7.7	52,528	34,595	61,101	60,855	40,247
06	California.......................	14.3	22.0	8.7	4.6	4.8	4.4	84,907	45,964	92,837	99,571	62,083
08	Colorado........................	15.1	21.8	8.4	5.0	4.6	7.7	82,254	46,765	90,246	98,801	59,069
09	Connecticut....................	11.8	27.1	7.0	4.3	3.5	4.9	83,771	38,768	89,933	104,504	60,217
10	Delaware.......................	12.4	24.4	7.9	3.6	6.1	7.0	71,091	40,408	73,868	83,771	60,707
11	District of Columbia..........	26.8	16.5	6.2	9.1	18.5	3.6	90,088	42,297	110,168	89,183	60,159
12	Florida..........................	14.1	20.9	10.4	5.0	4.4	7.8	63,062	38,820	68,353	75,155	50,014
13	Georgia.........................	13.6	21.4	8.2	4.3	4.9	7.3	66,559	37,348	69,826	81,588	48,559
15	Hawaii..........................	10.7	24.5	13.7	3.8	8.2	8.0	84,857	58,114	86,755	100,030	74,606
16	Idaho...........................	10.4	22.1	8.8	4.3	5.1	8.6	66,474	41,765	74,717	81,069	49,731
17	Illinois..........................	12.8	23.7	7.8	4.3	4.0	5.0	72,205	33,574	80,297	87,347	51,393
18	Indiana.........................	8.8	23.0	7.8	4.5	3.7	6.4	62,743	36,058	71,219	75,350	46,803
19	Iowa............................	7.5	23.9	6.6	4.2	3.4	6.6	65,600	40,094	74,745	80,526	48,171
20	Kansas..........................	10.2	25.1	7.5	4.3	5.0	6.7	64,124	33,772	72,088	79,005	47,612
21	Kentucky.......................	9.1	23.8	7.5	4.7	4.3	6.8	55,573	36,323	64,543	65,350	42,134
22	Louisiana.......................	9.7	25.7	9.2	5.1	5.8	6.3	52,087	29,059	58,725	63,719	39,946
23	Maine...........................	10.6	27.3	6.6	4.1	4.7	8.8	64,767	42,270	78,795	77,148	46,314
24	Maryland.......................	16.5	23.6	6.9	4.9	11.2	7.0	90,203	46,384	94,336	108,299	66,528
25	Massachusetts.................	15.9	28.1	7.0	3.9	4.2	4.2	89,645	50,138	103,351	109,842	57,075
26	Michigan.......................	10.1	23.0	8.1	4.5	3.5	6.0	63,498	35,552	70,947	77,491	48,534
27	Minnesota......................	10.4	25.7	6.7	4.4	3.8	6.1	77,720	44,761	89,633	95,668	53,323
28	Mississippi......................	7.1	24.7	8.7	4.7	5.8	6.9	48,716	31,878	52,777	57,567	38,527
29	Missouri........................	10.2	24.5	8.1	4.8	4.1	7.5	61,847	33,181	69,912	74,591	46,550
30	Montana........................	9.9	24.1	9.9	4.9	6.0	9.4	63,249	39,524	70,863	78,994	47,180
31	Nebraska.......................	9.5	24.4	7.2	4.4	4.7	7.4	66,817	39,745	76,366	82,469	48,587
32	Nevada.........................	11.7	18.0	18.5	4.4	4.8	7.9	66,274	41,119	69,586	77,843	51,777
33	New Hampshire................	12.3	25.3	7.3	3.7	4.4	7.8	88,465	55,960	100,750	106,087	59,123
34	New Jersey.....................	14.2	24.1	6.5	4.1	4.4	3.9	89,296	44,749	96,324	108,515	61,139
35	New Mexico....................	13.5	25.8	9.2	4.5	8.4	7.9	53,992	29,551	59,107	63,405	47,049
36	New York.......................	13.1	29.7	7.4	4.5	4.8	3.9	74,314	40,445	84,149	87,878	52,702
37	North Carolina.................	12.0	22.7	8.1	4.7	4.2	7.6	61,972	35,286	70,049	73,385	45,982
38	North Dakota...................	6.9	26.3	9.0	4.7	5.0	6.9	66,519	31,206	77,852	84,110	47,170
39	Ohio............................	9.9	24.1	8.3	4.2	3.8	6.8	62,262	36,833	70,390	76,062	46,269
40	Oklahoma......................	9.1	23.5	8.9	4.9	6.3	8.0	55,826	33,519	62,634	66,149	43,065
41	Oregon.........................	12.4	22.9	8.7	5.0	4.9	7.7	71,562	38,592	81,572	83,627	53,732
42	Pennsylvania...................	11.0	26.4	7.1	4.5	4.3	6.2	68,957	36,797	79,012	85,000	48,257
72	Puerto Rico.....................	11.0	21.1	8.9	6.3	8.0	2.4	22,237	9,635	26,363	26,180	18,682
44	Rhode Island...................	11.4	27.4	8.4	4.1	4.3	5.6	74,008	31,979	80,230	92,518	52,485
45	South Carolina.................	11.4	22.1	8.9	4.9	4.6	8.7	59,318	32,294	63,883	68,592	47,463
46	South Dakota	6.6	24.9	7.8	4.6	4.2	8.1	66,143	39,607	72,598	80,387	47,737
47	Tennessee......................	10.3	22.4	8.6	5.0	4.1	7.3	59,695	36,032	66,890	70,790	44,943
48	Texas	12.5	21.8	8.3	4.9	4.3	6.4	66,963	36,667	72,568	80,760	48,825
49	Utah............................	12.8	21.8	7.6	4.2	4.7	4.8	79,449	44,852	84,419	99,914	59,711
50	Vermont........................	9.6	28.8	7.8	4.6	4.7	6.1	72,431	31,714	80,818	85,727	53,579
51	Virginia.........................	17.0	22.4	8.0	5.2	8.7	9.7	80,963	40,527	87,736	101,402	58,282
53	Washington.....................	14.5	21.3	7.8	4.1	5.2	8.2	84,247	46,587	97,432	102,079	58,752
54	West Virginia...................	7.9	28.8	8.6	4.6	6.6	7.6	51,248	30,792	59,538	62,084	41,438
55	Wisconsin.......................	9.0	23.2	6.9	4.0	3.6	6.6	67,125	37,218	77,203	82,293	47,407
56	Wyoming........................	7.9	24.3	8.7	5.0	6.9	9.2	65,204	35,231	72,661	75,220	53,974

NA = Not available.
'- = Indicates that either no sample observations or too few sample observations were available to compute an estimate, or a ratio of medians cannot be calculated because one or both of the median estimates falls in the lowest interval or upper interval of an open-ended distribution, or the margin of error associated with a median was larger than the median itself.

	Median income in the past 12 months (in 2021 inflation-adjusted dollars)								
	Median household income by race and Hispanic origin of householder								
STATE	White alone	Black alone	American Indian, Alaska Native alone	Asian alone	Native Hawaiian and other Pacific Islander alone	Some other race alone	Two or more races	White alone, not Hispanic or Latino	Hispanic or Latino
ACS table number:	B19013A	B19013B	B19013C	B19013D	B19013E	B19013F	B19013G	B19013H	B19013I
State code / Column number:	90	91	92	93	94	95	96	97	98
00 **UNITED STATES**...............	74,932	46,774	53,149	100,572	69,973	57,671	63,854	75,412	60,566
01 Alabama......................	62,496	36,058	48,139	84,745	58,696	40,722	52,917	62,545	44,747
02 Alaska	82,051	61,411	50,892	80,106	66,513	64,187	87,839	83,864	61,216
04 Arizona......................	73,604	54,765	42,397	91,289	89,655	59,089	60,630	75,017	59,561
05 Arkansas....................	56,707	36,292	48,188	85,380	47,838	46,382	54,916	56,847	51,613
06 California...................	93,981	58,936	68,988	109,675	78,988	66,120	77,353	96,566	70,081
08 Colorado	87,052	58,655	55,016	94,467	63,504	61,156	69,739	88,715	63,547
09 Connecticut................	93,318	58,565	83,504	112,170	18,148	51,535	66,287	94,548	54,754
10 Delaware	76,648	55,604	NA	111,860	-	56,900	56,382	76,655	56,472
11 District of Columbia..........	146,265	52,812	NA	110,029	-	59,997	106,059	145,975	89,612
12 Florida	68,415	47,028	56,386	81,024	66,875	53,753	59,845	68,839	58,126
13 Georgia	76,809	51,590	56,752	90,137	83,810	53,854	65,157	77,047	59,633
15 Hawaii	81,090	64,676	71,083	90,519	77,970	65,159	85,534	81,554	75,809
16 Idaho........................	69,120	58,393	62,380	78,422	NA	55,926	58,649	69,391	59,663
17 Illinois	79,304	42,118	63,926	97,831	81,512	61,895	67,311	79,694	65,075
18 Indiana	65,569	42,775	46,864	80,948	NA	56,257	59,917	65,642	57,653
19 Iowa.........................	67,389	41,436	42,941	84,495	62,608	53,964	50,624	67,652	52,082
20 Kansas	66,666	45,527	47,955	87,945	60,617	50,936	56,510	66,969	54,102
21 Kentucky....................	58,040	39,247	23,910	71,005	NA	51,862	42,188	58,081	47,848
22 Louisiana	64,597	33,576	62,550	60,352	NA	48,894	49,455	64,728	54,249
23 Maine	65,080	33,952	55,285	70,055	114,468	65,539	66,603	65,064	66,030
24 Maryland	100,980	71,790	60,714	113,117	146,213	72,160	90,113	101,178	81,032
25 Massachusetts	96,869	66,792	60,275	113,919	43,961	57,147	62,559	97,665	54,226
26 Michigan	67,746	39,488	48,757	99,438	NA	53,933	59,282	67,867	57,617
27 Minnesota	80,862	47,739	48,354	92,688	NA	64,664	69,328	80,923	64,102
28 Mississippi	61,340	33,377	42,264	56,386	-	33,329	47,509	61,318	42,941
29 Missouri.....................	65,668	41,132	53,856	83,431	83,261	60,412	50,804	65,820	53,178
30 Montana	64,608	44,492	36,501	59,204	-	63,525	64,491	64,833	57,253
31 Nebraska....................	69,017	43,139	53,298	68,339	NA	61,354	61,309	69,319	57,636
32 Nevada	72,808	41,828	51,902	72,994	57,328	57,386	67,465	72,941	62,401
33 New Hampshire	88,378	82,455	64,908	106,393	-	73,846	80,081	88,306	72,727
34 New Jersey	99,514	61,029	62,834	138,278	64,208	59,782	73,435	100,584	63,608
35 New Mexico	62,477	42,295	41,920	75,276	2,500-	48,521	48,401	64,539	48,685
36 New York...................	82,802	54,443	53,265	81,411	37,297	51,230	67,768	83,392	55,245
37 North Carolina.............	69,522	42,961	39,932	103,348	67,456	52,545	57,619	69,704	53,880
38 North Dakota..............	68,951	45,023	42,875	70,370	250,000+	36,680	57,416	69,004	51,546
39 Ohio.........................	66,881	37,860	44,636	83,133	NA	47,179	52,711	66,987	52,154
40 Oklahoma...................	59,946	39,099	50,027	69,106	52,432	50,628	51,009	60,323	50,990
41 Oregon......................	72,853	60,927	64,484	93,857	56,377	64,620	63,291	73,077	63,296
42 Pennsylvania...............	73,603	42,199	58,829	89,308	39,867	45,524	61,415	73,738	53,229
72 Puerto Rico.................	21,782	22,156	24,438	NA	-	20,954	24,110	31,963	22,190
44 Rhode Island...............	81,390	57,881	NA	93,809	NA	47,365	52,770	82,358	48,922
45 South Carolina.............	67,300	40,310	42,615	77,989	NA	51,643	55,127	67,329	54,297
46 South Dakota	69,690	39,986	27,011	76,693	93,635	51,341	52,617	69,702	57,045
47 Tennessee...................	63,577	42,413	49,324	79,923	68,316	53,691	55,440	63,701	53,917
48 Texas	77,631	49,767	61,896	100,417	63,582	51,283	57,583	81,384	54,857
49 Utah.........................	82,306	55,182	53,268	83,084	61,250	64,996	72,184	82,932	67,777
50 Vermont	72,634	NA	39,361	69,400	-	47,336	77,187	72,803	83,641
51 Virginia......................	86,719	55,345	73,529	120,536	78,922	71,570	83,150	86,830	79,845
53 Washington.................	85,698	62,356	64,044	123,382	84,490	61,959	76,525	86,105	65,248
54 West Virginia...............	52,028	40,155	NA	57,206	-	45,010	41,804	52,032	44,917
55 Wisconsin...................	70,320	36,379	58,112	81,378	NA	51,969	57,571	70,353	53,186
56 Wyoming....................	67,124	45,376	65,876	NA	-	62,333	56,732	68,091	47,780

NA = Not available.

'- = Indicates that either no sample observations or too few sample observations were available to compute an estimate, or a ratio of medians cannot be calculated because one or both of the median estimates falls in the lowest interval or upper interval of an open-ended distribution, or the margin of error associated with a median was larger than the median itself.

Table B-1. States — What: Education, Employment, and Income, 2021—*Continued*

		Median income in the past 12 months (in 2021 inflation-adjusted dollars)											
		Median family income by type of family							Median nonfamily household income			Median individual income	
	STATE	All families	Married-couple families with children under 18	Married-couple families, no children under 18	Male householder with children under 18	Male householder, no children under 18	Female householder with children under 18	Female householder, no children under 18	All nonfamily households	Living alone, 65 years and over — Male	Living alone, 65 years and over — Female	Persons 15 years and over who worked full-time, year-round — Male	Persons 15 years and over who worked full-time, year-round — Female
	ACS table number:	B19126	B19126	B19126	B19126	B19126	B19126	B19126	B19215	B19215	B19215	B19326	B19326
State code	Column number:	99	100	101	102	103	104	105	106	107	108	109	110
00	UNITED STATES...............	85,806	112,461	96,393	51,255	67,439	32,990	57,584	41,549	31,238	26,529	61,957	50,654
01	Alabama............................	71,006	97,695	81,456	46,571	54,579	23,975	46,544	30,575	27,469	22,577	54,731	40,576
02	Alaska	95,344	115,261	104,758	73,505	59,922	43,276	65,575	48,081	29,116	33,296	64,715	57,955
04	Arizona.............................	81,622	103,821	91,158	49,334	65,778	34,174	58,702	43,690	32,089	28,214	57,569	48,048
05	Arkansas...........................	66,148	86,329	75,217	42,287	55,475	27,438	44,429	29,499	22,154	21,648	50,098	40,577
06	California..........................	97,388	122,034	113,452	56,558	76,741	38,969	69,090	54,015	35,591	29,512	67,463	60,041
08	Colorado...........................	102,073	125,839	111,510	63,870	77,541	42,125	66,593	51,542	36,116	29,625	67,400	56,552
09	Connecticut......................	106,576	141,991	122,826	61,661	83,200	40,133	70,172	45,211	33,923	29,005	75,940	62,295
10	Delaware	87,132	116,012	96,570	56,851	77,273	34,966	61,756	45,456	43,126	31,202	62,244	54,384
11	District of Columbia..........	136,184	235,944	201,337	93,102	59,196	31,949	77,313	76,236	40,210	39,582	104,331	89,551
12	Florida	76,199	98,222	86,498	48,677	64,375	32,911	54,668	39,766	30,542	26,008	52,135	43,947
13	Georgia	80,731	107,333	93,523	50,551	61,854	31,302	54,652	41,300	27,540	26,576	56,696	46,598
15	Hawaii..............................	100,890	109,762	116,166	66,371	81,962	38,535	82,067	49,452	43,367	34,229	63,819	51,455
16	Idaho................................	79,993	95,437	84,735	51,593	67,854	33,518	54,171	38,607	31,609	24,252	54,282	41,761
17	Illinois..............................	90,861	119,382	101,831	50,948	70,234	34,216	59,048	43,121	30,850	28,008	65,834	52,123
18	Indiana.............................	79,243	101,088	86,492	48,830	63,616	31,811	53,836	36,751	30,958	25,556	57,053	44,713
19	Iowa.................................	84,908	108,576	89,374	50,795	63,870	33,723	54,147	38,979	31,536	26,400	59,051	46,072
20	Kansas..............................	82,637	105,889	88,360	52,466	59,974	32,428	58,002	36,685	31,175	26,848	57,070	45,772
21	Kentucky	70,060	93,766	78,316	41,165	54,615	26,208	42,178	32,452	27,544	22,686	53,677	41,984
22	Louisiana..........................	67,045	99,719	80,668	51,115	53,509	23,593	41,551	30,626	24,332	21,392	57,377	41,207
23	Maine...............................	82,842	109,002	87,912	53,626	64,432	35,827	55,123	38,143	28,230	23,965	60,586	49,515
24	Maryland...........................	110,978	145,809	127,388	62,314	79,624	43,800	73,808	54,348	41,032	35,378	74,531	64,120
25	Massachusetts	113,822	157,418	123,919	62,413	81,563	37,974	74,373	52,250	31,385	26,398	80,454	68,564
26	Michigan...........................	80,523	108,023	88,656	47,415	65,975	31,041	54,494	37,666	33,132	27,353	61,675	49,239
27	Minnesota.........................	99,567	131,047	102,821	55,607	69,446	40,865	66,809	46,436	35,526	29,918	66,299	54,370
28	Mississippi........................	64,035	90,542	77,654	42,472	45,518	24,661	40,530	26,954	22,706	20,504	50,291	38,212
29	Missouri............................	79,084	103,979	85,734	51,272	62,314	31,729	51,304	36,036	30,016	25,222	56,549	44,766
30	Montana	79,958	104,208	84,764	49,583	62,807	30,789	51,375	38,707	27,474	27,051	57,644	42,748
31	Nebraska	88,484	109,819	92,858	54,429	64,061	37,310	55,983	37,749	31,295	25,164	59,069	45,842
32	Nevada	78,526	95,997	89,758	43,759	67,458	36,384	62,054	42,026	30,700	26,681	55,431	46,408
33	New Hampshire	108,208	138,988	109,959	68,072	90,699	37,405	71,279	48,469	33,433	30,517	70,931	53,702
34	New Jersey	110,102	144,964	123,709	60,716	86,315	39,109	72,994	50,424	35,686	29,054	77,665	63,426
35	New Mexico	67,786	89,357	84,746	43,462	51,858	26,778	46,099	35,517	27,179	26,317	52,082	44,979
36	New York..........................	92,454	125,251	106,959	52,933	72,626	35,486	62,829	45,740	33,106	26,253	70,253	61,246
37	North Carolina..................	77,601	106,344	86,764	48,846	55,755	30,882	50,211	36,966	27,074	24,011	55,334	45,746
38	North Dakota....................	89,504	114,605	93,938	60,192	62,810	32,232	56,713	38,264	29,391	27,587	59,685	46,079
39	Ohio.................................	80,760	112,307	89,371	49,217	60,513	29,381	52,251	37,034	30,390	25,665	60,045	47,605
40	Oklahoma.........................	69,967	89,335	81,886	43,561	56,144	27,325	46,282	32,980	27,000	24,568	52,406	40,763
41	Oregon.............................	88,085	109,661	95,639	50,569	71,391	35,757	57,405	44,491	34,501	29,226	62,709	52,258
42	Pennsylvania.....................	87,500	119,089	95,732	50,659	70,330	31,826	58,789	39,969	31,355	24,882	64,176	51,418
72	Puerto Rico	27,669	45,930	33,900	18,885	26,809	10,921	23,371	13,535	12,253	11,034	26,113	25,725
44	Rhode Island.....................	97,304	122,141	113,683	46,426	70,887	29,236	65,304	43,210	29,420	23,326	65,955	56,432
45	South Carolina..................	73,901	100,018	84,154	44,289	54,316	30,444	49,495	35,847	27,390	24,305	55,169	41,732
46	South Dakota	82,562	102,004	86,775	49,142	62,179	31,645	49,464	40,405	32,411	25,376	55,702	42,748
47	Tennessee.........................	74,709	97,552	84,555	42,358	56,315	30,544	47,838	35,951	27,851	23,970	52,995	42,974
48	Texas	80,304	103,155	94,092	50,396	61,343	31,558	52,568	41,190	29,789	25,162	58,495	46,749
49	Utah.................................	92,192	103,704	96,526	61,090	75,482	40,003	70,670	45,487	37,096	28,137	62,151	45,837
50	Vermont	90,556	117,166	95,165	50,770	62,008	31,702	65,763	40,968	32,978	25,584	57,734	54,216
51	Virginia.............................	100,763	129,909	111,373	52,429	79,122	39,637	62,619	47,745	35,523	30,625	69,967	55,351
53	Washington.......................	102,178	130,077	110,665	59,242	81,853	38,320	63,944	52,055	36,548	31,810	76,953	60,350
54	West Virginia	66,669	91,052	74,149	37,352	47,218	24,931	42,214	28,989	26,795	22,191	54,279	40,838
55	Wisconsin.........................	85,810	113,617	90,937	51,930	70,941	36,462	55,810	40,664	31,012	27,259	60,114	48,238
56	Wyoming..........................	83,789	99,339	89,418	57,044	53,218	32,290	61,179	36,982	30,576	26,975	61,567	42,405

NA = Not available.

'– = Indicates that either no sample observations or too few sample observations were available to compute an estimate, or a ratio of medians cannot be calculated because one or both of the median estimates falls in the lowest interval or upper interval of an open-ended distribution, or the margin of error associated with a median was larger than the median itself.

Table B-1. States — What: Education, Employment, and Income, 2021—*Continued*

State code	STATE	Per capita income in the past 12 months (in 2021 inflation-adjusted dollars)	Total number of households	Households, by type of income (percent)								
				With wage or salary income	With self-employment income	With interest, dividends, or net rental income	With Social Security	With Supplemental Security Income (SSI)	With public assistance income	With cash public assistance or food stamps/SNAP	With retirement income	With other types of income
	ACS table number:	B19301	B19052	B19052	B19053	B19054	B19055	B19056	B19057	B19058	B19059	B19060
	Column number:	111	112	113	114	115	116	117	118	119	120	121
00	UNITED STATES...............	38,332	127,544,730	74.3	10.8	19.1	31.2	5.2	3.4	14.1	24.0	13.7
01	Alabama.........................	30,608	1,967,559	69.5	8.4	14.3	35.6	6.5	1.9	14.9	26.0	12.1
02	Alaska	39,509	271,311	78.4	12.2	41.3	24.2	4.9	7.4	14.3	24.0	35.6
04	Arizona..........................	36,295	2,817,723	72.7	10.4	18.5	33.5	4.2	3.0	12.9	26.1	12.3
05	Arkansas........................	29,252	1,183,675	69.4	10.4	14.8	35.0	6.4	1.8	11.7	22.9	11.4
06	California.......................	42,396	13,429,063	76.3	13.0	20.8	28.1	6.0	4.9	14.7	21.5	16.0
08	Colorado........................	44,617	2,313,042	78.4	13.0	23.0	25.3	3.4	3.2	10.3	21.9	13.2
09	Connecticut....................	48,146	1,428,313	74.5	11.2	22.5	31.8	4.6	3.2	13.4	25.5	15.0
10	Delaware........................	38,797	395,656	71.4	7.5	21.9	35.4	4.9	2.4	11.6	32.5	12.8
11	District of Columbia..........	65,808	319,565	78.3	9.7	23.7	19.1	4.7	5.0	16.2	16.1	9.8
12	Florida...........................	36,196	8,565,329	69.8	10.9	18.8	36.7	5.0	3.2	15.6	25.6	11.9
13	Georgia..........................	35,086	4,001,109	76.2	10.5	15.6	29.4	5.1	2.4	13.7	22.2	13.5
15	Hawaii...........................	38,614	490,080	75.6	13.2	27.6	37.2	4.1	5.4	15.2	30.7	18.7
16	Idaho............................	33,841	693,882	73.4	14.7	19.6	32.8	4.8	4.0	10.5	25.1	13.5
17	Illinois...........................	39,794	4,991,641	74.9	9.3	19.7	29.2	4.5	3.4	15.7	23.6	11.7
18	Indiana..........................	33,054	2,680,694	75.7	9.2	16.2	31.8	4.8	2.4	10.7	24.9	11.8
19	Iowa.............................	35,715	1,300,467	74.8	12.5	20.7	31.6	4.4	2.6	11.1	23.8	12.7
20	Kansas...........................	35,028	1,159,026	75.8	11.8	20.2	30.2	4.0	2.1	8.5	23.7	11.1
21	Kentucky........................	30,728	1,785,682	70.3	9.4	15.0	34.4	7.4	2.2	15.4	25.7	12.7
22	Louisiana........................	30,117	1,783,924	70.2	9.5	14.7	31.7	7.6	2.0	20.0	21.9	11.8
23	Maine............................	38,483	593,626	68.7	14.0	21.8	36.6	5.6	3.2	13.0	26.0	14.8
24	Maryland........................	46,500	2,355,652	77.9	10.9	20.8	27.9	4.4	3.5	14.2	26.4	13.2
25	Massachusetts	49,746	2,759,018	75.8	11.0	22.8	29.8	5.6	4.4	16.7	22.2	14.7
26	Michigan........................	35,353	4,051,798	71.1	9.5	18.1	34.5	5.8	3.7	15.3	27.9	17.6
27	Minnesota	41,753	2,281,033	76.5	11.6	21.8	29.8	4.1	4.1	9.8	23.9	16.0
28	Mississippi	26,941	1,129,611	68.9	8.8	11.7	35.8	8.5	2.1	14.5	24.0	11.8
29	Missouri.........................	34,593	2,468,726	73.6	10.6	17.7	32.9	4.9	2.2	11.2	25.6	12.0
30	Montana	36,020	448,949	70.7	15.6	27.5	35.3	3.8	3.1	10.5	25.5	14.3
31	Nebraska........................	36,227	785,982	77.1	13.1	19.4	29.2	4.1	2.0	9.5	21.0	12.2
32	Nevada..........................	34,933	1,191,380	73.2	9.2	15.2	30.4	4.3	4.2	15.7	23.5	16.9
33	New Hampshire................	45,365	548,026	76.1	11.2	24.6	33.6	4.5	3.0	7.6	26.1	12.5
34	New Jersey......................	47,338	3,497,945	77.0	9.8	22.4	31.6	4.5	3.0	10.9	24.3	15.0
35	New Mexico	31,043	834,007	68.2	9.5	17.4	35.2	5.6	4.6	22.4	26.2	13.7
36	New York........................	43,078	7,652,666	73.4	10.3	19.7	32.1	6.1	4.8	17.1	24.9	14.8
37	North Carolina.................	35,254	4,179,632	73.3	10.3	17.4	32.2	4.6	2.2	15.0	24.0	12.2
38	North Dakota...................	36,497	322,511	76.6	14.3	22.5	27.0	2.7	2.0	7.3	19.2	12.4
39	Ohio..............................	35,119	4,832,922	72.7	9.2	17.2	31.8	5.6	3.1	14.5	26.2	12.9
40	Oklahoma.......................	29,969	1,547,967	72.3	10.8	16.7	32.1	5.3	3.3	15.1	22.5	13.6
41	Oregon..........................	38,975	1,702,599	71.7	12.7	22.7	32.6	4.5	4.9	18.1	25.3	16.4
42	Pennsylvania	38,315	5,228,956	72.6	9.0	20.9	35.0	5.5	3.8	15.6	27.4	14.1
72	Puerto Rico	14,468	1,165,982	49.5	10.4	4.2	47.3	0.4	3.9	49.9	17.4	13.4
44	Rhode Island....................	40,382	440,170	74.3	9.4	19.8	32.6	6.7	5.5	16.8	25.7	14.1
45	South Carolina.................	33,339	2,049,972	70.6	9.2	15.7	35.3	5.2	1.8	12.1	27.0	12.5
46	South Dakota	35,135	356,887	76.2	15.4	22.0	30.6	3.7	2.3	9.1	20.3	12.2
47	Tennessee.......................	33,904	2,770,395	72.4	11.3	16.4	32.8	5.6	2.4	13.0	23.4	11.6
48	Texas.............................	34,717	10,796,247	78.7	12.0	15.7	25.4	4.6	2.8	13.8	19.2	13.1
49	Utah..............................	35,220	1,101,499	81.8	12.9	19.6	23.9	3.3	2.1	7.0	20.1	10.6
50	Vermont.........................	40,016	270,163	72.6	16.2	26.6	35.5	5.4	4.2	12.8	24.8	15.5
51	Virginia..........................	43,756	3,331,461	76.9	10.1	21.3	29.5	4.1	2.7	10.1	26.7	13.4
53	Washington.....................	46,177	3,022,255	76.1	10.8	23.8	28.7	4.5	4.1	14.2	24.0	16.2
54	West Virginia	30,195	722,201	64.8	7.0	15.7	41.0	7.4	4.1	19.5	29.3	14.2
55	Wisconsin.......................	37,221	2,449,970	74.1	9.7	21.6	31.9	4.4	2.5	12.9	26.2	11.7
56	Wyoming........................	37,156	242,763	75.1	13.4	23.2	31.0	3.4	2.2	7.1	25.5	15.9

NA = Not available.
'- = Indicates that either no sample observations or too few sample observations were available to compute an estimate, or a ratio of medians cannot be calculated because one or both of the median estimates falls in the lowest interval or upper interval of an open-ended distribution, or the margin of error associated with a median was larger than the median itself.

	STATE	Total number of households	Household income in the past 12 months (in 2021 inflation-adjusted dollars)										
			Households by income group (percent)										
			Less than $10,000	$10,000 to $14,999	$15,000 to $24,999	$25,000 to $34,999	$35,000 to $49,999	$50,000 to $74,999	$75,000 to $99,999	$100,000 to $149,999	$150,000 to $199,999	$200,000 or more
	ACS table number:	B19001	B19001	B19001	B19001	B19001	B19001	B19001	B19001	B19001	B19001	B19001
State code	Column number:	122	123	124	125	126	127	128	129	130	131	132
00	UNITED STATES...............	127,544,730	6.0	3.9	7.5	7.8	11.3	16.8	12.8	16.3	7.9	9.8
01	Alabama............................	1,967,559	7.7	5.6	10.4	9.4	13.3	17.3	12.1	13.2	5.8	5.2
02	Alaska...............................	271,311	5.4	3.0	6.3	6.2	10.3	16.7	13.6	18.6	9.7	10.2
04	Arizona.............................	2,817,723	5.6	3.2	7.1	7.8	12.4	17.8	13.6	17.1	7.2	8.1
05	Arkansas...........................	1,183,675	7.6	5.4	10.4	10.0	13.9	18.1	12.3	12.5	4.9	4.7
06	California..........................	13,429,063	5.3	3.5	6.0	6.2	9.0	14.7	12.2	17.6	10.0	15.5
08	Colorado...........................	2,313,042	4.8	2.7	5.4	6.3	10.2	16.3	13.3	18.6	10.3	12.0
09	Connecticut.......................	1,428,313	5.2	3.3	6.7	6.5	9.3	14.6	11.8	17.9	10.1	14.6
10	Delaware	395,656	5.2	3.1	7.2	7.0	11.8	18.0	13.5	16.2	9.6	8.3
11	District of Columbia..........	319,565	9.6	2.8	5.5	5.3	6.2	12.9	11.4	15.2	9.5	21.6
12	Florida..............................	8,565,329	6.3	3.8	8.3	8.9	12.4	18.2	12.9	15.1	6.4	7.8
13	Georgia.............................	4,001,109	6.3	3.7	7.9	8.5	11.4	17.4	13.3	15.7	7.3	8.4
15	Hawaii...............................	490,080	5.4	3.0	5.9	5.0	9.2	15.8	13.6	18.2	10.5	13.3
16	Idaho................................	693,882	4.5	3.7	7.7	8.0	12.2	19.9	14.3	16.6	6.6	6.5
17	Illinois...............................	4,991,641	6.4	3.4	7.3	7.4	10.7	16.4	12.8	17.1	8.3	10.1
18	Indiana..............................	2,680,694	5.7	3.8	7.8	9.5	12.6	19.3	13.9	15.5	6.3	5.7
19	Iowa..................................	1,300,467	4.9	3.8	7.9	8.3	12.7	18.7	14.4	16.6	6.5	6.2
20	Kansas...............................	1,159,026	5.7	3.8	7.9	8.5	12.7	18.6	13.4	16.1	6.7	6.5
21	Kentucky...........................	1,785,682	8.1	5.2	9.7	9.3	13.0	18.0	12.6	13.8	5.2	5.2
22	Louisiana	1,783,924	9.2	5.9	10.5	9.7	12.6	16.8	11.1	12.7	5.8	5.7
23	Maine................................	593,626	5.4	4.5	8.2	8.4	12.2	17.5	14.4	16.2	6.5	6.7
24	Maryland...........................	2,355,652	5.2	2.6	5.3	5.6	8.7	14.7	12.6	18.8	11.4	15.1
25	Massachusetts	2,759,018	5.4	3.8	6.4	5.7	8.2	13.4	11.4	17.5	11.0	17.1
26	Michigan	4,051,798	6.3	3.9	8.1	8.6	12.7	18.1	13.2	15.5	6.9	6.7
27	Minnesota	2,281,033	4.2	3.1	5.9	6.9	10.7	17.4	13.7	18.6	9.4	9.9
28	Mississippi	1,129,611	9.3	6.3	10.9	11.0	13.3	16.6	11.9	12.5	4.6	3.5
29	Missouri.............................	2,468,726	5.9	4.3	8.4	9.1	13.0	18.3	13.4	14.7	6.6	6.4
30	Montana	448,949	5.2	4.2	8.3	9.1	13.1	18.7	13.1	15.0	6.6	6.9
31	Nebraska	785,982	5.2	3.8	7.5	8.2	12.5	18.0	14.1	16.8	7.2	6.8
32	Nevada..............................	1,191,380	7.2	3.2	7.3	8.7	11.6	17.7	13.3	16.0	7.3	7.5
33	New Hampshire	548,026	3.1	2.8	5.5	6.5	9.6	15.5	12.8	21.3	11.5	11.3
34	New Jersey	3,497,945	4.9	3.2	5.9	6.0	8.6	14.1	11.9	17.9	10.7	16.7
35	New Mexico	834,007	9.0	5.0	9.6	9.3	13.2	17.3	11.3	13.8	5.6	5.8
36	New York...........................	7,652,666	7.0	4.3	7.3	7.0	9.8	15.0	12.0	16.0	8.8	12.9
37	North Carolina...................	4,179,632	6.4	4.4	8.6	8.9	12.5	17.8	12.7	14.7	6.5	7.4
38	North Dakota.....................	322,511	5.6	4.0	7.9	8.8	11.8	17.4	14.1	16.8	7.6	6.0
39	Ohio..................................	4,832,922	6.6	4.3	8.3	8.7	12.8	17.9	13.2	15.4	6.4	6.5
40	Oklahoma..........................	1,547,967	6.8	5.0	9.4	9.9	13.5	18.8	12.2	14.2	5.1	5.0
41	Oregon..............................	1,702,599	5.3	3.8	7.0	7.5	11.5	17.1	13.5	17.4	8.0	9.0
42	Pennsylvania......................	5,228,956	5.9	4.1	7.8	7.8	11.5	16.8	13.2	16.5	7.9	8.7
72	Puerto Rico........................	1,165,982	24.6	11.3	18.4	12.8	12.0	10.7	4.5	3.3	1.0	1.4
44	Rhode Island......................	440,170	5.8	4.4	7.6	6.7	10.0	16.0	12.4	18.4	8.3	10.3
45	South Carolina...................	2,049,972	7.1	4.5	8.9	8.9	13.2	18.3	12.5	14.6	6.0	6.0
46	South Dakota	356,887	4.8	3.9	7.9	8.5	12.5	19.0	15.3	16.7	5.7	5.7
47	Tennessee..........................	2,770,395	6.6	4.5	8.8	9.2	13.2	18.3	12.8	14.2	6.1	6.3
48	Texas.................................	10,796,247	6.1	3.7	7.8	8.3	11.8	17.4	12.5	16.0	7.6	8.9
49	Utah..................................	1,101,499	4.3	2.6	4.7	6.7	10.5	18.4	14.5	19.8	8.7	9.8
50	Vermont	270,163	4.1	4.3	7.5	7.5	11.1	17.1	14.7	17.3	7.7	8.7
51	Virginia..............................	3,331,461	5.0	3.1	6.4	6.8	9.9	15.5	12.3	17.8	9.8	13.4
53	Washington	3,022,255	4.8	2.8	5.4	6.0	9.9	15.7	12.9	18.5	10.1	14.0
54	West Virginia.....................	722,201	8.4	5.9	10.9	9.8	13.9	17.1	11.8	13.0	4.9	4.4
55	Wisconsin..........................	2,449,970	4.8	3.9	7.2	8.3	12.4	18.8	14.0	17.2	7.0	6.6
56	Wyoming...........................	242,763	6.0	3.7	8.1	8.9	11.1	18.4	14.5	16.4	6.9	5.8

NA = Not available.

'- = Indicates that either no sample observations or too few sample observations were available to compute an estimate, or a ratio of medians cannot be calculated because one or both of the median estimates falls in the lowest interval or upper interval of an open-ended distribution, or the margin of error associated with a median was larger than the median itself.

Table B-1. States — What: Education, Employment, and Income, 2021—*Continued*

	STATE	Households with income over $100,000, by age of householder (as a percent of all households in age group)					Households with income below poverty (as a percent of all households in household-type group)						
		All households	Householder under 25 years	Householder 25 to 44 years	Householder 45 to 64 years	Householder 65 years and over	All households	Family households	Married-couple family households	Male householder family households	Female householder family households	Male householder nonfamily households	Female householder nonfamily households
	ACS table number:	B19001	B19037	B19037	B19037	B19037	C17017	C17017	C17017	C17017	C17017	C17017	C17017
State code	Column number:	133	134	135	136	137	138	139	140	141	142	143	144
00	UNITED STATES............	34.0	9.2	37.2	42.2	22.3	12.8	5.9	37.9	11.2	50.9	41.8	58.2
01	Alabama......................	24.2	5.2	25.9	31.3	15.6	16.1	7.6	30.9	8.8	60.3	39.6	60.4
02	Alaska	38.5	14.7	41.0	44.5	30.0	10.7	4.5	37.1	16.7	46.3	49.8	50.2
04	Arizona......................	32.5	10.4	34.9	41.2	22.7	12.1	6.0	39.4	12.6	48.0	44.9	55.1
05	Arkansas.....................	22.2	5.2	24.8	28.3	14.4	16.4	7.6	38.0	10.6	51.3	41.8	58.2
06	California....................	43.1	15.4	46.7	49.8	31.0	12.3	6.1	43.0	12.7	44.3	41.8	58.2
08	Colorado....................	40.9	13.9	44.7	49.5	27.3	10.0	3.9	39.8	10.7	49.5	44.2	55.8
09	Connecticut................	42.6	12.3	44.8	52.6	29.2	10.5	4.3	30.6	13.9	55.5	43.1	56.9
10	Delaware....................	34.2	6.3	36.2	41.9	25.9	11.5	5.6	35.5	6.7	57.8	36.3	63.7
11	District of Columbia.......	46.2	17.6	53.9	45.8	34.9	14.7	5.1	14.9	9.8	75.3	39.4	60.6
12	Florida	29.2	8.4	30.6	36.5	21.3	13.1	6.0	42.6	10.2	47.2	41.2	58.8
13	Georgia......................	31.4	7.4	32.1	40.2	20.6	13.5	7.1	34.9	10.5	54.6	40.5	59.5
15	Hawaii	41.9	15.7	41.8	50.0	35.5	11.7	5.4	49.7	10.8	39.5	43.5	56.5
16	Idaho........................	29.7	6.7	33.0	39.0	17.9	11.1	5.3	52.1	10.5	37.4	42.4	57.6
17	Illinois.......................	35.4	9.4	38.7	44.2	22.9	12.5	5.4	37.3	11.7	51.0	42.1	57.9
18	Indiana	27.6	5.5	30.0	36.7	15.8	12.1	5.3	33.9	12.3	53.8	40.9	59.1
19	Iowa.........................	29.3	9.0	32.9	38.9	17.4	11.4	4.3	39.1	9.9	51.0	40.0	60.0
20	Kansas.......................	29.3	4.5	32.9	38.4	18.2	12.2	5.1	39.8	12.5	47.6	45.0	55.0
21	Kentucky....................	24.2	4.4	27.6	30.9	14.7	16.7	7.9	37.2	11.9	51.0	41.4	58.6
22	Louisiana....................	24.2	5.1	26.0	31.2	15.7	19.4	9.7	29.3	10.5	60.2	42.3	57.7
23	Maine........................	29.5	14.8	34.0	37.0	17.6	12.3	4.4	40.5	11.0	48.6	44.5	55.5
24	Maryland....................	45.3	14.9	47.2	54.3	32.5	10.4	4.8	34.6	11.5	53.9	37.4	62.6
25	Massachusetts	45.6	21.0	51.7	54.4	28.5	11.5	4.4	35.0	11.1	54.0	38.2	61.8
26	Michigan	29.1	6.0	32.0	38.3	17.3	13.1	5.7	35.6	12.4	52.0	43.4	56.6
27	Minnesota	38.0	11.6	43.9	48.1	20.9	9.6	3.4	38.4	15.1	46.5	41.6	58.4
28	Mississippi..................	20.7	3.5	21.2	26.4	14.9	19.2	9.5	29.0	8.8	62.2	42.5	57.5
29	Missouri.....................	27.6	5.0	30.4	36.4	16.9	13.0	5.3	36.4	9.9	53.7	39.9	60.1
30	Montana	28.4	6.7	31.6	38.4	17.8	11.8	4.4	41.6	12.4	46.0	45.8	54.2
31	Nebraska....................	30.8	6.6	34.6	39.7	19.8	11.3	4.2	42.3	12.1	45.6	41.8	58.2
32	Nevada	30.9	10.7	32.0	37.6	22.6	13.8	6.7	43.7	14.5	41.8	46.5	53.5
33	New Hampshire............	44.2	15.5	50.5	54.1	26.9	7.6	3.1	37.3	16.6	46.1	38.6	61.4
34	New Jersey	45.3	14.4	48.5	54.2	30.4	10.5	5.0	40.4	9.3	50.4	40.7	59.3
35	New Mexico	25.2	4.8	25.7	32.5	19.0	17.8	9.0	38.6	13.0	48.4	46.5	53.5
36	New York....................	37.7	14.3	42.4	44.7	25.2	14.2	6.2	38.5	10.9	50.5	42.1	57.9
37	North Carolina..............	28.7	6.7	31.7	36.0	18.4	13.4	6.0	35.5	10.5	54.1	40.3	59.7
38	North Dakota...............	30.4	5.9	35.1	41.8	17.6	11.7	3.7	33.6	9.4	57.0	50.7	49.3
39	Ohio.........................	28.3	6.9	31.6	36.8	16.6	13.5	5.8	28.7	11.4	59.9	43.6	56.4
40	Oklahoma...................	24.3	4.1	25.8	31.9	16.6	15.3	7.4	36.2	12.2	51.6	42.1	57.9
41	Oregon......................	34.4	9.3	38.7	42.2	23.3	12.0	4.7	43.9	13.7	42.4	42.3	57.7
42	Pennsylvania................	33.0	9.0	37.7	42.2	19.4	12.2	5.3	32.5	11.3	56.3	40.7	59.3
72	Puerto Rico.................	5.7	0.0	5.5	8.2	3.7	42.7	23.3	35.5	12.4	52.0	38.5	61.5
44	Rhode Island................	37.0	8.1	38.7	46.4	25.5	12.1	4.3	34.1	12.3	53.6	39.6	60.4
45	South Carolina..............	26.6	6.9	27.7	33.5	19.2	14.4	7.1	33.2	9.9	56.9	40.8	59.2
46	South Dakota	28.1	8.8	30.8	37.8	17.9	11.3	4.9	37.3	12.6	50.1	40.7	59.3
47	Tennessee...................	26.7	5.6	28.5	34.7	17.0	13.8	6.2	36.8	11.2	52.1	39.3	60.7
48	Texas........................	32.5	7.4	34.7	40.5	21.3	13.7	7.5	41.6	9.5	48.9	42.1	57.9
49	Utah.........................	38.3	9.8	40.2	49.9	25.9	9.5	4.3	52.9	8.8	38.3	43.7	56.3
50	Vermont.....................	33.8	8.8	36.6	42.3	23.5	10.8	3.9	34.1	13.6	52.3	41.1	58.9
51	Virginia......................	40.9	10.6	43.6	50.7	27.8	10.4	4.5	35.7	11.5	52.8	39.7	60.3
53	Washington.................	42.6	16.0	48.6	51.2	26.1	9.9	4.2	37.5	11.8	50.7	45.7	54.3
54	West Virginia...............	22.2	2.9	26.4	28.8	13.8	17.6	7.9	39.5	13.0	47.5	42.2	57.8
55	Wisconsin...................	30.7	7.6	35.3	40.3	16.6	11.0	4.2	34.2	13.8	52.0	43.7	56.3
56	Wyoming....................	29.1	7.3	31.2	36.2	22.7	11.8	4.8	47.0	14.5	38.4	42.4	57.6

NA = Not available.

'- = Indicates that either no sample observations or too few sample observations were available to compute an estimate, or a ratio of medians cannot be calculated because one or both of the median estimates falls in the lowest interval or upper interval of an open-ended distribution, or the margin of error associated with a median was larger than the median itself.

State code	STATE	Population for whom poverty status is determined	Persons with income below poverty by age (as a percent of all persons in age group)				Persons with income below poverty by selected race and Hispanic origin groups (as a percent of all persons in race/Hispanic group)			
			All ages	Under 18 years	18 to 64 years	65 years and over	White alone, not Hispanic or Latino	Black or African American alone	Asian alone	Hispanic or Latino
	ACS table number:	C17001	C17001	C17001	C17001	C17001	C17001H	C17001B	C17001D	C17001I
	Column number:	145	146	147	148	149	150	151	152	153
00	UNITED STATES..................	324,173,084	12.8	16.9	11.9	10.3	9.5	21.8	10.2	17.5
01	Alabama...........................	4,920,613	16.1	22.2	15.3	11.4	11.6	26.0	11.6	24.5
02	Alaska	716,769	10.5	12.4	10.2	8.5	7.6	16.7	7.9	8.8
04	Arizona............................	7,126,930	12.8	17.3	12.0	9.6	8.8	16.7	10.6	17.2
05	Arkansas..........................	2,944,289	16.3	22.4	15.2	11.7	13.3	29.0	10.6	21.3
06	California.........................	38,481,790	12.3	15.8	11.3	11.1	9.0	19.9	10.1	15.1
08	Colorado..........................	5,696,140	9.7	11.8	9.5	7.7	7.4	17.7	8.3	15.0
09	Connecticut......................	3,506,226	10.1	12.7	9.7	8.6	6.8	15.8	7.4	20.1
10	Delaware	978,675	11.6	16.8	11.3	6.9	7.8	16.1	10.1	21.2
11	District of Columbia..............	637,491	16.5	23.9	14.9	13.8	5.1	27.7	16.1	10.5
12	Florida.............................	21,368,535	13.1	17.8	12.3	11.0	9.9	20.4	10.0	15.7
13	Georgia	10,529,506	14.0	20.2	12.6	10.0	9.5	20.1	8.8	19.3
15	Hawaii	1,402,392	11.2	13.6	10.9	9.4	11.7	14.3	7.6	13.5
16	Idaho	1,868,374	11.0	13.1	10.6	9.5	10.2	27.6	12.1	12.4
17	Illinois.............................	12,380,582	12.1	16.0	11.2	10.0	8.5	24.8	10.5	14.8
18	Indiana............................	6,608,427	12.2	16.0	11.6	8.6	10.1	20.6	16.2	19.1
19	Iowa................................	3,100,317	11.1	12.5	11.4	8.4	9.4	28.3	12.8	19.4
20	Kansas.............................	2,854,624	11.7	13.4	11.7	9.1	9.7	23.1	8.6	17.7
21	Kentucky	4,379,845	16.5	22.1	15.7	11.7	15.3	24.1	8.7	25.1
22	Louisiana	4,501,071	19.6	26.9	18.3	14.1	12.4	31.9	18.8	21.6
23	Maine..............................	1,338,019	11.5	15.1	11.3	9.2	11.2	27.8	15.8	9.3
24	Maryland	6,023,847	10.3	14.0	9.2	9.1	6.6	14.5	8.8	15.3
25	Massachusetts	6,748,410	10.4	12.6	9.6	10.6	7.4	15.3	10.9	23.6
26	Michigan	9,847,403	13.1	17.8	12.5	9.3	10.2	26.2	10.9	18.5
27	Minnesota........................	5,587,189	9.3	10.8	9.0	8.5	7.4	20.9	11.6	14.5
28	Mississippi	2,861,627	19.4	27.7	17.6	13.8	11.5	31.2	12.9	23.8
29	Missouri...........................	5,999,824	12.7	16.2	12.3	9.5	10.5	22.9	12.7	18.9
30	Montana	1,079,864	11.9	14.1	12.1	8.8	10.0	#DIV/0!	20.9	15.0
31	Nebraska	1,914,212	10.8	12.5	10.6	8.7	8.7	20.6	13.8	17.5
32	Nevada	3,103,176	14.1	18.8	13.2	11.3	11.1	25.7	11.4	16.0
33	New Hampshire	1,348,892	7.2	9.2	6.7	6.9	6.9	6.4	6.4	14.1
34	New Jersey	9,093,135	10.2	14.2	9.0	9.4	6.5	16.5	6.0	18.2
35	New Mexico	2,076,524	18.4	23.9	18.2	12.8	13.2	24.8	12.0	20.3
36	New York..........................	19,329,338	13.9	18.5	12.8	12.2	9.6	20.3	14.7	20.9
37	North Carolina...................	10,285,053	13.4	18.1	12.6	10.2	9.5	20.6	8.5	22.9
38	North Dakota.....................	752,033	11.1	10.5	11.8	9.4	9.2	21.3	14.9	16.4
39	Ohio................................	11,470,517	13.4	18.6	12.6	9.5	10.5	27.5	11.4	20.5
40	Oklahoma.........................	3,877,776	15.6	21.2	14.8	10.6	12.6	26.1	15.6	23.4
41	Oregon............................	4,166,362	12.2	13.5	12.6	9.3	11.2	20.0	11.8	15.4
42	Pennsylvania.....................	12,571,365	12.1	16.9	11.2	9.6	8.9	24.8	11.9	22.5
72	Puerto Rico.......................	3,235,303	40.5	54.9	37.5	38.0	35.8	39.8	NA	40.6
44	Rhode Island......................	1,052,091	11.4	15.0	10.8	9.8	7.5	20.2	13.8	23.2
45	South Carolina...................	5,063,148	14.6	20.1	13.9	10.7	10.0	23.8	13.9	21.7
46	South Dakota	867,039	12.3	14.6	11.7	11.0	8.2	19.0	8.5	21.5
47	Tennessee.........................	6,811,613	13.6	18.1	13.0	10.2	11.1	22.2	11.1	20.2
48	Texas...............................	28,933,638	14.2	19.6	12.6	11.8	8.4	19.5	8.3	19.4
49	Utah................................	3,290,444	8.6	8.1	8.9	7.7	7.6	22.7	6.3	11.7
50	Vermont...........................	621,338	10.3	10.4	10.6	9.1	9.6	23.0	13.5	13.5
51	Virginia............................	8,401,227	10.2	13.1	9.7	9.3	7.7	16.5	7.5	14.7
53	Washington.......................	7,599,960	9.9	12.0	9.6	8.2	8.3	19.2	8.2	15.5
54	West Virginia.....................	1,734,876	16.8	20.7	17.4	11.5	16.0	28.3	7.6	20.1
55	Wisconsin.........................	5,754,788	10.8	13.4	10.5	8.7	8.4	29.5	13.2	18.0
56	Wyoming..........................	565,760	11.4	13.4	12.0	6.7	9.9	53.1	19.1	15.7

NA = Not available.
'- = Indicates that either no sample observations or too few sample observations were available to compute an estimate, or a ratio of medians cannot be calculated because one or both of the median estimates falls in the lowest interval or upper interval of an open-ended distribution, or the margin of error associated with a median was larger than the median itself.

State code	STATE	Total civilian non-institutionalized population	Type of health insurance (as a percent of all persons)			
			Private only	Public only	Both private and public	None
	ACS table number:	C27010	C27010	C27010	C27010	C27010
	Column number:	154	155	156	157	158
00	UNITED STATES............................	326,912,547	54.6	24.4	12.4	8.6
01	Alabama................................	4,957,633	52.8	23.7	13.6	9.9
02	Alaska	702,154	51.0	24.4	13.1	11.4
04	Arizona..................................	7,174,053	50.3	26.1	12.9	10.7
05	Arkansas................................	2,974,701	46.4	31.8	12.7	9.2
06	California...............................	38,724,294	53.7	29.3	10.0	7.0
08	Colorado................................	5,715,497	58.7	22.0	11.3	8.0
09	Connecticut.............................	3,557,526	57.2	25.6	12.0	5.2
10	Delaware	987,964	54.2	23.0	17.1	5.7
11	District of Columbia...................	659,979	61.8	24.4	10.1	3.7
12	Florida..................................	21,465,883	50.5	24.7	12.6	12.1
13	Georgia	10,600,385	54.9	21.3	11.2	12.6
15	Hawaii	1,381,713	56.3	21.6	18.2	3.9
16	Idaho...................................	1,879,248	54.4	23.1	13.7	8.8
17	Illinois..................................	12,495,329	58.0	23.6	11.4	7.0
18	Indiana	6,707,875	56.6	23.5	12.5	7.5
19	Iowa	3,151,182	58.2	22.9	14.2	4.8
20	Kansas..................................	2,878,792	59.7	18.2	13.0	9.2
21	Kentucky	4,428,392	48.9	31.5	13.9	5.7
22	Louisiana...............................	4,518,319	45.4	35.2	11.7	7.6
23	Maine...................................	1,357,120	54.5	23.7	16.1	5.7
24	Maryland................................	6,059,298	58.5	20.9	14.4	6.1
25	Massachusetts	6,916,106	60.2	23.6	13.7	2.5
26	Michigan	9,949,959	54.6	24.5	15.9	5.0
27	Minnesota	5,651,958	61.3	19.7	14.6	4.5
28	Mississippi..............................	2,885,936	47.9	28.4	11.9	11.9
29	Missouri.................................	6,063,301	57.7	20.8	12.1	9.4
30	Montana	1,088,496	52.0	24.9	15.0	8.2
31	Nebraska	1,936,190	62.4	18.1	12.4	7.1
32	Nevada	3,105,760	51.8	25.7	10.9	11.6
33	New Hampshire	1,372,918	62.2	18.3	14.3	5.1
34	New Jersey	9,163,640	59.7	21.6	11.6	7.2
35	New Mexico	2,077,326	39.2	36.8	14.1	10.0
36	New York................................	19,599,048	52.9	28.9	13.0	5.2
37	North Carolina..........................	10,345,935	53.8	22.7	13.1	10.4
38	North Dakota	756,440	63.8	14.9	13.5	7.9
39	Ohio.....................................	11,611,229	54.9	25.9	12.7	6.5
40	Oklahoma...............................	3,905,272	48.9	24.0	13.3	13.8
41	Oregon..................................	4,206,414	52.6	26.9	14.4	6.1
42	Pennsylvania............................	12,767,386	56.3	22.8	15.4	5.5
72	Puerto Rico	3,237,924	31.6	56.2	6.5	5.7
44	Rhode Island............................	1,080,438	55.6	26.5	13.6	4.3
45	South Carolina..........................	5,099,812	51.1	24.5	14.4	10.0
46	South Dakota	877,855	59.5	18.0	13.0	9.5
47	Tennessee	6,872,677	53.6	23.3	13.2	10.0
48	Texas....................................	29,066,872	52.3	20.6	9.1	18.0
49	Utah.....................................	3,309,594	68.7	13.2	9.1	9.0
50	Vermont.................................	639,228	54.7	26.4	15.3	3.7
51	Virginia	8,412,758	60.5	19.3	13.4	6.8
53	Washington	7,618,375	57.1	23.0	13.4	6.4
54	West Virginia	1,755,887	45.1	31.2	17.6	6.1
55	Wisconsin	5,828,354	59.5	21.1	14.0	5.4
56	Wyoming................................	570,046	57.7	16.0	14.1	12.2

NA = Not available.
'– = Indicates that either no sample observations or too few sample observations were available to compute an estimate, or a ratio of medians cannot be calculated because one or both of the median estimates falls in the lowest interval or upper interval of an open-ended distribution, or the margin of error associated with a median was larger than the median itself.

Table B-2. Counties — What: Education, Employment, and Income, 2021

STATE County / STATE County code		Educational attainment			Employment status				Household income and benefits				
		Total population 25 years and over	Percent with a high school diploma or less	Percent with a bachelor's degree or more	Total population 16 years and over	Labor force participation (percent)	Percent unemployed	Percent age 16 years and over who worked full-time year-round in the past 12 months	Total households	Median household income in the past 12 months (in 2021 inflation-adjusted dollars)	Income less than $25,000 (percent)	Income greater than $150,000 (percent)	Percent who received cash public assistance or food stamps/SNAP
ACS table number:		C15003	C15003	C15003	C23001	C23001	C23001	S2402	B19001	B19049	B19001	B19001	B19058
Column number:		1	2	3	4	5	6	7	8	9	10	11	12
00000	UNITED STATES	228,193,464	36.9	35.0	267,057,693	63.0	6.3	65.1	127,544,730	69,717	17.4	17.7	14.1
01000	ALABAMA	3,451,208	43.3	27.4	4,046,627	57.7	5.3	68.1	1,967,559	53,913	23.7	10.9	14.9
01003	Baldwin County, Alabama	172,896	33.8	34.5	194,430	58.9	2.8	41.4	94,105	63,866	15.6	13.8	8.2
01015	Calhoun County, Alabama	78,876	47.8	19.4	93,742	54.8	5.8	35.9	44,631	46,524	31.9	5.3	18.7
01043	Cullman County, Alabama	62,372	44.9	20.6	72,182	60.4	2.5	42.7	35,131	55,517	19.9	9.3	10.3
01049	DeKalb County, Alabama	48,798	57.7	13.6	55,909	55.3	2.3	NA	24,979	41,800	31.7	8.0	15.7
01051	Elmore County, Alabama	62,483	47.7	20.1	71,833	57.7	8.2	NA	32,108	59,032	18.3	8.0	12.3
01055	Etowah County, Alabama	72,023	51.2	18.2	83,219	53.9	7.5	NA	38,006	45,298	28.0	4.5	12.9
01069	Houston County, Alabama	74,673	43.5	21.0	86,003	56.5	5.0	38.2	44,058	46,931	25.6	8.5	16.7
01073	Jefferson County, Alabama	456,323	36.8	35.8	532,974	61.0	5.6	41.5	270,147	55,006	23.2	13.0	16.1
01077	Lauderdale County, Alabama	64,884	47.2	26.5	76,414	58.2	3.5	38.6	38,250	50,218	23.7	9.1	10.2
01081	Lee County, Alabama	110,446	30.9	40.6	143,890	60.5	3.0	39.2	67,358	52,424	24.9	10.8	11.1
01083	Limestone County, Alabama	75,512	42.8	28.0	87,600	59.5	3.5	NA	40,685	66,796	17.5	18.5	7.2
01089	Madison County, Alabama	273,575	25.0	46.9	318,816	63.7	3.4	44.0	164,493	78,525	13.8	21.1	8.0
01095	Marshall County, Alabama	64,901	53.1	19.9	75,680	59.1	7.1	41.3	36,003	50,191	26.0	10.6	15.5
01097	Mobile County, Alabama	280,014	46.1	22.8	327,793	58.6	7.2	40.9	162,963	49,721	24.0	8.3	20.3
01101	Montgomery County, Alabama	152,015	40.0	33.9	179,508	60.2	7.5	38.5	92,407	50,385	26.7	8.9	20.9
01103	Morgan County, Alabama	85,594	44.1	24.8	99,040	54.9	3.8	40.6	47,558	55,286	24.1	10.4	14.0
01115	St. Clair County, Alabama	65,186	53.6	18.9	NA	NA	NA	NA	33,093	60,433	18.1	8.7	14.4
01117	Shelby County, Alabama	156,281	25.6	47.3	181,947	66.2	2.3	48.4	86,970	84,260	13.8	21.5	5.4
01121	Talladega County, Alabama	57,900	51.0	17.2	66,804	48.9	8.7	NA	33,775	45,063	31.6	6.7	17.1
01125	Tuscaloosa County, Alabama	143,738	39.4	29.2	183,968	61.0	5.6	41.3	86,694	56,559	23.2	12.8	12.0
02000	ALASKA	485,779	34.6	32.8	571,832	65.9	6.5	55.9	271,311	77,845	14.7	19.9	14.3
02020	Anchorage Municipality, Alaska	191,999	28.0	38.3	225,620	70.2	6.2	40.1	109,584	86,654	12.5	23.4	13.3
02090	Fairbanks North Star Borough, Alaska	61,318	30.5	38.1	75,513	67.1	3.8	NA	36,426	72,149	14.9	17.5	8.3
02170	Matanuska-Susitna Borough, Alaska	73,187	40.2	23.6	85,254	60.0	5.8	34.9	40,997	78,856	14.3	19.2	11.2
04000	ARIZONA	4,980,297	34.5	32.4	5,852,913	60.6	5.7	66.1	2,817,723	69,056	15.9	15.3	12.9
04001	Apache County, Arizona	42,467	44.7	16.2	50,798	41.6	8.8	28.3	19,875	40,628	35.7	6.0	29.7
04003	Cochise County, Arizona	89,149	38.3	26.2	102,096	50.9	7.8	30.5	49,952	56,600	23.2	8.9	19.0
04005	Coconino County, Arizona	87,394	31.6	39.5	118,934	62.4	7.7	37.3	55,145	64,533	21.4	17.5	14.2
04013	Maricopa County, Arizona	3,045,558	32.4	36.1	3,581,935	64.6	5.2	43.9	1,708,034	76,247	13.1	18.2	11.2
04015	Mohave County, Arizona	169,737	47.1	15.1	186,723	45.6	8.6	28.0	102,398	46,616	27.8	7.3	14.0
04017	Navajo County, Arizona	72,372	44.1	18.2	84,024	46.4	11.4	25.9	40,087	49,449	26.7	6.5	22.2
04019	Pima County, Arizona	718,288	31.9	34.9	864,266	58.9	5.9	36.7	433,148	60,667	19.1	12.6	14.4
04021	Pinal County, Arizona	315,517	39.3	20.1	361,301	52.7	5.5	36.3	155,161	70,993	13.5	11.6	13.7
04025	Yavapai County, Arizona	189,526	33.4	28.9	210,145	48.7	4.3	28.8	112,075	57,230	19.0	10.0	10.3
04027	Yuma County, Arizona	133,866	51.6	17.3	160,561	54.9	8.6	34.7	74,981	57,304	19.2	7.9	23.0
05000	ARKANSAS	2,037,763	45.4	25.3	2,405,035	58.6	5.5	69.4	1,183,675	52,528	23.4	9.7	11.7
05007	Benton County, Arkansas	193,678	40.0	34.8	227,075	67.2	3.8	52.5	106,553	78,691	10.1	20.1	5.2
05031	Craighead County, Arkansas	72,159	37.9	32.3	87,027	61.7	6.1	42.8	42,186	50,186	27.6	13.9	14.1
05045	Faulkner County, Arkansas	77,893	32.1	34.6	99,645	61.7	2.4	45.2	48,497	55,635	21.5	10.6	8.4
05051	Garland County, Arkansas	73,615	42.7	23.8	83,602	55.1	6.8	35.7	42,077	47,694	25.0	7.1	12.3
05069	Jefferson County, Arkansas	45,337	48.6	26.9	53,334	53.1	10.2	NA	24,319	48,499	26.8	7.7	14.9
05085	Lonoke County, Arkansas	50,215	44.6	20.0	58,658	61.9	5.6	41.0	27,880	63,641	16.9	12.1	9.9
05119	Pulaski County, Arkansas	271,852	32.9	38.1	314,360	63.5	6.1	43.9	172,100	52,479	23.2	11.7	12.1
05125	Saline County, Arkansas	86,589	37.9	27.5	100,079	64.9	3.0	48.8	49,768	67,345	13.4	11.0	5.2
05131	Sebastian County, Arkansas	85,086	43.4	24.5	101,900	57.8	5.7	38.6	51,472	47,874	24.6	10.0	16.0
05143	Washington County, Arkansas	155,106	43.6	32.3	197,495	64.8	3.1	47.5	94,220	65,125	17.2	13.2	6.3
05145	White County, Arkansas	50,581	49.7	22.6	61,744	58.2	6.9	NA	29,359	51,402	21.6	7.3	12.1
06000	CALIFORNIA	26,909,869	36.3	36.2	31,507,237	63.4	8.3	61.8	13,429,063	84,907	14.8	25.5	14.7
06001	Alameda County, California	1,187,688	27.5	50.1	1,354,894	66.4	6.6	44.3	589,180	109,729	12.5	37.6	13.4
06007	Butte County, California	136,280	32.6	32.3	170,370	59.8	8.7	31.9	81,353	64,738	18.9	14.8	15.0
06013	Contra Costa County, California	812,075	28.3	45.1	935,414	65.1	7.6	40.5	411,560	111,080	10.5	37.1	12.1
06017	El Dorado County, California	141,938	25.6	39.4	159,055	60.0	6.2	38.0	74,909	87,491	12.9	28.0	8.0

	STATE County	Educational attainment			Employment status				Household income and benefits				
		Total popula-tion 25 years and over	Percent with a high school diploma or less	Percent with a bachelor's degree or more	Total popula-tion 16 years and over	Labor force participation (percent)	Percent unem-ployed	Percent age 16 years and over who worked full-time year-round in the past 12 months	Total house-holds	Median household income in the past 12 months (in 2021 inflation-adjusted dollars)	Income less than $25,000 (percent)	Income greater than $150,000 (percent)	Percent who received cash public assistance or food stamps/ SNAP
STATE County code	ACS table number:	C15003	C15003	C15003	C23001	C23001	C23001	S2402	B19001	B19049	B19001	B19001	B19058
	Column number:	1	2	3	4	5	6	7	8	9	10	11	12
	CALIFORNIA—Cont.												
06019	Fresno County, California............	630,729	45.5	24.0	761,696	60.8	9.1	37.1	322,646	63,656	20.1	15.5	22.7
06023	Humboldt County, California	94,056	32.6	29.9	113,209	56.6	8.3	31.2	55,184	54,752	20.9	9.8	20.5
06025	Imperial County, California	111,355	52.6	13.5	133,162	52.5	14.5	28.3	47,849	51,809	24.9	7.5	26.8
06029	Kern County, California	562,716	51.5	18.6	685,864	57.9	9.9	30.7	282,963	58,217	20.6	12.8	20.1
06031	Kings County, California	96,368	53.2	11.2	117,290	53.8	11.2	29.6	43,143	62,155	17.4	12.5	19.5
06033	Lake County, California..............	49,279	38.4	23.2	55,773	51.2	11.7	NA	27,472	61,221	20.0	12.1	19.3
06037	Los Angeles County, California ...	6,883,696	40.2	35.1	8,002,494	64.3	9.3	39.0	3,375,587	77,456	17.6	22.1	17.1
06039	Madera County, California.........	100,667	53.3	17.7	120,503	55.0	13.8	30.5	44,048	63,454	23.2	17.2	21.6
06041	Marin County, California............	192,747	17.0	59.5	216,956	62.6	7.5	37.5	103,378	118,209	11.5	42.0	8.5
06045	Mendocino County, California	65,672	42.1	25.0	73,781	56.4	9.2	NA	34,273	59,444	22.3	12.6	17.9
06047	Merced County, California	170,994	57.9	14.4	213,398	57.4	14.7	31.5	84,967	53,992	24.9	9.2	23.8
06053	Monterey County, California	281,950	46.8	27.2	337,011	59.5	6.6	36.5	133,224	82,163	11.1	21.3	10.5
06055	Napa County, California.............	97,626	33.8	37.7	113,324	63.9	6.4	41.2	49,979	97,213	10.7	31.0	10.3
06057	Nevada County, California	80,366	26.0	42.3	87,925	55.3	6.1	33.3	42,679	79,519	17.0	24.4	7.5
06059	Orange County, California..........	2,212,457	30.1	43.1	2,573,809	65.4	7.5	40.3	1,077,193	100,559	11.9	31.6	11.2
06061	Placer County, California............	291,736	23.0	43.9	332,095	60.1	4.8	38.7	155,945	103,659	9.6	31.8	8.5
06065	Riverside County, California	1,623,431	44.1	24.0	1,927,625	60.5	8.6	38.1	765,673	79,024	13.9	18.8	13.9
06067	Sacramento County, California ...	1,088,807	34.0	33.1	1,261,294	63.1	7.6	40.3	571,949	80,063	15.1	19.9	16.2
06069	San Benito County, California	43,868	43.0	21.6	51,031	68.8	4.1	45.0	20,307	101,923	8.3	30.7	11.5
06071	San Bernardino County, California.................	1,408,059	46.4	23.3	1,692,156	61.4	8.7	39.1	675,929	74,846	15.5	16.3	16.7
06073	San Diego County, California	2,265,902	29.6	42.0	2,668,188	66.4	8.1	39.7	1,162,896	91,003	13.4	26.3	12.8
06075	San Francisco County, California .	647,880	22.3	60.9	713,617	68.6	8.4	45.4	350,796	121,826	15.8	42.3	14.9
06077	San Joaquin County, California ...	504,631	47.1	20.1	602,505	60.3	9.0	37.7	241,760	80,681	14.4	20.3	18.1
06079	San Luis Obispo County, California.................	191,488	25.8	39.4	239,898	57.6	7.4	32.4	107,571	80,615	14.2	22.7	8.3
06081	San Mateo County, California	539,718	24.9	51.8	609,864	66.7	6.5	45.0	264,135	131,796	8.7	44.6	7.9
06083	Santa Barbara County, California	280,575	35.1	36.3	359,531	62.0	7.2	35.7	150,550	84,846	15.3	25.5	14.0
06085	Santa Clara County, California	1,331,753	24.1	55.1	1,535,714	66.6	6.0	46.7	650,593	141,562	8.8	47.7	9.0
06087	Santa Cruz County, California.....	179,402	27.2	42.8	224,521	63.3	7.7	36.4	97,353	93,933	11.5	31.4	13.0
06089	Shasta County, California............	128,739	35.5	23.6	146,930	55.3	8.7	33.4	71,506	61,125	19.6	12.3	15.6
06095	Solano County, California............	315,084	34.6	29.4	363,577	62.3	7.1	36.7	157,617	87,770	12.9	22.0	12.8
06097	Sonoma County, California..........	354,563	29.7	38.3	403,841	64.0	6.8	38.1	190,586	94,295	11.3	28.5	10.7
06099	Stanislaus County, California.......	352,947	50.4	19.3	420,902	62.2	9.3	36.9	174,209	73,982	15.1	15.9	16.1
06101	Sutter County, California	65,770	51.3	17.3	76,677	60.6	11.2	36.2	33,655	64,251	16.7	12.6	16.0
06103	Tehama County, California.........	43,837	44.1	14.4	51,838	53.2	7.5	NA	23,950	48,810	27.9	6.9	13.4
06107	Tulare County, California...........	284,391	53.4	16.2	350,237	58.8	10.1	35.6	143,541	58,209	19.4	11.3	25.9
06111	Ventura County, California.........	579,194	35.0	34.7	676,606	64.6	7.4	39.8	279,168	96,454	10.3	27.4	11.3
06113	Yolo County, California..............	129,833	31.2	43.5	178,655	61.2	6.5	38.3	76,844	78,146	17.5	21.6	13.8
06115	Yuba County, California..............	52,695	42.0	19.1	62,816	58.4	5.5	NA	27,942	63,303	18.3	12.1	28.3
08000	**COLORADO**.........................	4,044,182	27.7	44.4	4,720,626	68.1	5.2	65.7	2,313,042	82,254	13.0	22.3	10.3
08001	Adams County, Colorado............	343,417	44.4	28.6	406,724	71.5	5.8	48.1	183,023	81,258	12.0	17.3	13.1
08005	Arapahoe County, Colorado	452,832	26.7	46.1	523,894	70.8	5.4	47.1	250,041	84,386	11.9	24.4	9.6
08013	Boulder County, Colorado..........	223,309	16.8	62.5	277,373	67.1	5.5	40.0	135,607	90,168	13.5	29.7	9.5
08014	Broomfield County, Colorado......	53,433	17.7	58.9	61,651	69.4	3.7	49.5	30,161	107,638	6.5	33.5	4.4
08031	Denver County, Colorado...........	521,474	24.4	55.0	592,643	74.2	6.2	51.3	326,634	81,630	15.0	23.3	10.8
08035	Douglas County, Colorado..........	252,300	14.8	58.4	292,314	73.4	4.0	52.3	136,238	129,299	4.5	41.7	2.9
08041	El Paso County, Colorado...........	486,985	24.0	41.7	585,651	67.7	5.7	40.7	282,904	79,427	10.6	18.9	11.1
08059	Jefferson County, Colorado........	427,770	23.8	49.3	483,395	68.8	5.4	47.3	239,823	94,549	9.9	26.1	7.2
08069	Larimer County, Colorado..........	244,592	21.1	51.7	304,449	66.2	4.4	42.0	152,123	78,109	12.7	21.8	8.3
08077	Mesa County, Colorado	110,190	35.4	31.2	128,269	60.1	5.7	35.7	63,796	64,055	16.8	13.3	13.1
08101	Pueblo County, Colorado...........	117,286	38.0	26.6	136,889	55.3	6.5	34.9	69,078	56,689	24.6	9.8	20.8
08123	Weld County, Colorado	221,613	34.7	31.7	262,320	69.2	4.7	47.4	119,502	85,290	12.9	19.5	11.5
09000	**CONNECTICUT**	2,534,376	34.4	42.1	2,971,314	65.6	6.6	63.4	1,428,313	83,771	15.2	24.7	13.4
09001	Fairfield County, Connecticut......	663,240	29.9	50.5	775,819	67.7	6.2	43.3	357,271	100,810	13.8	34.1	11.5
09003	Hartford County, Connecticut......	631,153	35.3	40.3	733,746	65.2	6.7	42.3	360,140	80,069	16.1	22.2	14.9

Table B-2. Counties — What: Education, Employment, and Income, 2021—*Continued*

		Educational attainment			Employment status				Household income and benefits				
	STATE County	Total popula-tion 25 years and over	Percent with a high school diploma or less	Percent with a bachelor's degree or more	Total popula-tion 16 years and over	Labor force participation (percent)	Percent unem-ployed	Percent age 16 years and over who worked full-time year-round in the past 12 months	Total house-holds	Median household income in the past 12 months (in 2021 inflation-adjusted dollars)	Income less than $25,000 (percent)	Income greater than $150,000 (percent)	Percent who received cash public assistance or food stamps/ SNAP
STATE County code	ACS table number:	C15003	C15003	C15003	C23001	C23001	C23001	S2402	B19001	B19049	B19001	B19001	B19058
	Column number:	1	2	3	4	5	6	7	8	9	10	11	12
	CONNECTICUT—Cont.												
09005	Litchfield County, Connecticut	139,619	35.2	38.0	157,185	63.5	6.4	42.2	77,106	84,978	13.2	22.8	9.6
09007	Middlesex County, Connecticut...	122,993	31.1	45.0	142,203	66.1	5.1	43.5	69,789	94,887	9.9	26.9	6.7
09009	New Haven County, Connecticut......	608,407	37.6	39.5	713,029	65.3	8.0	41.1	349,089	75,295	17.0	20.5	16.1
09011	New London County, Connecticut......	190,962	36.2	34.5	222,922	63.8	4.9	37.2	110,950	78,828	13.1	19.9	13.9
09013	Tolland County, Connecticut.......	95,471	29.9	43.6	129,671	63.1	5.7	36.6	58,244	82,778	18.0	23.9	8.9
09015	Windham County, Connecticut...	82,531	44.9	26.5	96,739	64.8	7.5	39.6	45,724	72,068	17.1	14.6	17.8
10000	**DELAWARE**	711,104	37.0	35.6	819,868	60.1	5.5	65.6	395,656	71,091	15.6	18.0	11.6
10001	Kent County, Delaware	124,208	42.8	27.0	146,872	58.1	5.0	39.0	70,167	64,308	16.8	10.2	14.4
10003	New Castle County, Delaware.....	398,664	33.4	39.7	464,161	64.4	5.8	42.5	220,758	73,854	15.1	20.5	10.5
10005	Sussex County, Delaware	188,232	40.7	32.6	208,835	51.7	5.0	32.8	104,731	70,556	15.7	17.7	11.8
11000	**DISTRICT** OF COLUMBIA............	478,774	22.0	63.0	553,437	70.7	8.1	69.2	319,565	90,088	17.9	31.1	16.2
11001	District of Columbia....................	478,774	22.0	63.0	553,437	70.7	8.1	49.0	319,565	90,088	17.9	31.1	16.2
12000	**FLORIDA**..................................	15,762,122	37.9	33.2	18,010,659	59.1	5.6	66.9	8,565,329	63,062	18.4	14.1	15.6
12001	Alachua County, Florida	172,799	27.3	46.5	233,698	60.3	3.9	36.5	108,189	56,445	22.9	14.0	8.6
12005	Bay County, Florida....................	129,450	35.7	29.9	147,141	63.4	4.3	42.0	79,532	60,557	16.1	11.0	11.4
12009	Brevard County, Florida...............	462,336	33.7	33.1	519,483	56.3	4.9	38.6	254,314	65,333	18.3	14.3	11.4
12011	Broward County, Florida	1,382,208	37.1	35.9	1,574,220	66.2	6.3	44.2	747,715	65,747	18.0	15.5	17.0
12015	Charlotte County, Florida............	162,234	42.0	25.9	175,973	42.1	6.2	25.4	88,988	59,285	18.2	10.1	11.0
12017	Citrus County, Florida	127,256	47.9	20.8	137,704	36.8	10.4	NA	68,269	47,197	25.0	5.3	12.9
12019	Clay County, Florida	152,462	36.8	27.8	175,723	62.1	2.1	43.9	80,459	76,679	11.5	13.3	11.1
12021	Collier County, Florida.................	297,766	36.6	40.3	330,215	51.6	4.8	32.2	163,943	74,215	12.6	22.1	8.6
12023	Columbia County, Florida............	48,804	46.6	18.3	57,006	54.4	5.9	NA	27,545	54,077	19.2	7.5	20.2
12031	Duval County, Florida..................	688,860	35.8	33.6	797,130	65.2	4.4	44.5	406,301	59,980	18.8	11.4	17.2
12033	Escambia County, Florida	218,891	37.7	27.9	261,978	62.0	6.2	37.7	126,980	54,228	21.7	9.6	19.0
12035	Flagler County, Florida	93,556	35.9	31.0	104,262	48.0	5.7	NA	48,187	62,618	16.6	13.1	8.3
12053	Hernando County, Florida	151,076	42.7	21.8	167,972	51.7	5.1	33.3	81,497	56,868	18.3	8.1	16.6
12055	Highlands County, Florida	80,311	52.1	18.3	88,081	44.5	9.3	NA	46,166	48,564	23.9	4.4	16.9
12057	Hillsborough County, Florida	1,024,586	35.5	37.1	1,189,374	65.6	5.2	45.6	578,259	65,905	18.2	16.4	15.4
12061	Indian River County, Florida........	127,374	33.3	33.9	140,566	48.6	5.5	30.8	69,974	58,972	17.1	13.2	12.8
12069	Lake County, Florida	293,018	39.4	27.3	328,319	52.3	6.7	35.1	156,435	64,795	16.4	11.1	11.4
12071	Lee County, Florida.....................	598,375	40.0	30.9	668,245	53.4	5.2	34.7	320,466	66,256	17.4	13.5	11.4
12073	Leon County, Florida	176,607	24.8	48.2	244,469	66.8	5.2	43.0	121,423	58,118	20.0	12.9	13.8
12081	Manatee County, Florida..............	312,839	35.7	35.6	349,131	55.0	5.5	34.7	163,520	68,172	15.3	16.0	9.2
12083	Marion County, Florida	289,018	46.4	23.1	323,475	49.2	5.7	34.5	157,348	55,161	19.5	8.8	15.5
12085	Martin County, Florida	123,061	30.9	35.7	136,834	51.5	5.7	32.9	69,719	64,625	17.0	18.0	9.7
12086	Miami-Dade County, Florida........	1,911,144	43.8	32.3	2,191,172	63.2	6.0	43.4	963,477	59,044	21.8	14.3	27.3
12087	Monroe County, Florida	64,801	33.2	37.0	71,352	63.4	3.1	41.5	36,078	68,563	15.5	19.6	11.3
12089	Nassau County, Florida................	69,435	28.9	35.0	NA	NA	NA	NA	40,276	75,981	14.6	17.5	11.1
12091	Okaloosa County, Florida	146,604	31.3	35.2	170,555	63.1	3.2	38.1	84,497	69,823	12.2	16.2	10.2
12095	Orange County, Florida	974,593	33.5	36.7	1,150,270	65.7	7.3	42.4	512,496	64,833	18.1	16.3	19.2
12097	Osceola County, Florida	268,650	39.9	27.9	320,763	65.2	6.3	41.2	133,330	60,585	18.0	10.4	22.0
12099	Palm Beach County, Florida.........	1,105,948	33.8	39.7	1,246,914	59.4	6.6	38.6	595,447	70,002	17.2	18.9	13.5
12101	Pasco County, Florida..................	424,021	41.6	28.5	479,815	57.1	5.1	39.2	230,060	59,470	19.5	13.0	14.1
12103	Pinellas County, Florida...............	746,325	32.9	36.9	826,278	58.3	5.0	39.2	419,798	61,947	19.1	14.3	10.6
12105	Polk County, Florida....................	524,102	48.4	21.1	606,637	55.9	5.1	39.5	276,469	56,379	20.1	9.2	15.8
12107	Putnam County, Florida...............	53,529	62.9	10.9	59,695	42.1	13.7	NA	29,765	33,370	35.8	3.9	29.8
12109	St. Johns County, Florida.............	208,441	24.6	48.3	237,054	60.5	3.5	42.7	109,147	91,602	8.2	29.2	5.5
12111	St. Lucie County, Florida..............	251,598	40.0	27.3	284,169	56.1	6.5	40.2	131,235	62,797	16.7	8.7	15.5
12113	Santa Rosa County, Florida.........	137,773	31.7	34.4	156,565	58.5	2.5	37.5	71,722	82,059	9.9	16.8	11.5
12115	Sarasota County, Florida.............	359,536	30.5	39.0	393,312	50.2	3.4	33.5	204,018	71,761	15.5	17.3	7.1
12117	Seminole County, Florida.............	335,194	28.4	43.4	384,876	66.3	4.1	45.6	188,239	70,236	13.1	17.4	12.7
12119	Sumter County, Florida................	122,943	36.0	35.0	127,313	24.6	6.9	NA	68,792	64,608	15.8	11.6	6.2
12127	Volusia County, Florida...............	419,497	39.8	26.1	477,010	53.2	4.3	37.0	243,344	58,380	20.8	8.4	14.9
12131	Walton County, Florida...............	59,769	31.7	38.1	65,672	58.6	3.5	NA	33,941	61,787	17.4	15.8	8.1

Table B-2. Counties — What: Education, Employment, and Income, 2021—*Continued*

	STATE County	Educational attainment			Employment status				Household income and benefits				
		Total population 25 years and over	Percent with a high school diploma or less	Percent with a bachelor's degree or more	Total population 16 years and over	Labor force participation (percent)	Percent unemployed	Percent age 16 years and over who worked full-time year-round in the past 12 months	Total households	Median household income in the past 12 months (in 2021 inflation-adjusted dollars)	Income less than $25,000 (percent)	Income greater than $150,000 (percent)	Percent who received cash public assistance or food stamps/SNAP
	ACS table number:	C15003	C15003	C15003	C23001	C23001	C23001	S2402	B19001	B19049	B19001	B19001	B19058
STATE County code	Column number:	1	2	3	4	5	6	7	8	9	10	11	12
13000	**GEORGIA**.................................	7,234,271	37.7	34.6	8,575,918	62.9	5.5	67.5	4,001,109	66,559	17.9	15.8	13.7
13013	Barrow County, Georgia	57,544	46.1	21.2	67,183	64.0	3.0	47.3	30,194	65,273	12.0	10.9	12.7
13015	Bartow County, Georgia	75,612	48.1	25.6	89,534	60.7	5.3	NA	38,903	71,523	15.5	10.2	10.1
13021	Bibb County, Georgia.................	102,096	43.0	25.3	122,337	58.5	8.2	37.9	57,677	48,176	26.4	8.6	23.3
13031	Bulloch County, Georgia	45,284	38.9	32.3	69,541	60.3	9.2	NA	29,318	57,656	20.6	9.0	17.6
13045	Carroll County, Georgia	78,856	49.9	22.2	96,544	61.8	6.5	NA	43,859	58,473	21.1	8.7	16.3
13047	Catoosa County, Georgia............	47,966	44.3	21.7	54,964	65.4	3.8	NA	26,864	65,576	15.9	12.8	11.8
13051	Chatham County, Georgia	202,993	30.2	37.6	241,566	63.5	6.1	40.6	121,028	61,843	17.9	13.3	15.4
13057	Cherokee County, Georgia..........	186,889	29.3	42.0	218,046	70.1	4.0	48.1	100,023	96,267	9.8	28.0	6.8
13059	Clarke County, Georgia	73,573	28.1	49.1	108,932	64.9	4.2	36.9	55,332	50,447	22.8	8.5	9.1
13063	Clayton County, Georgia	187,852	46.6	24.7	225,117	64.8	7.4	42.4	106,249	51,233	21.9	7.0	20.0
13067	Cobb County, Georgia	524,650	23.9	50.6	616,010	70.1	5.4	47.7	292,841	88,029	11.7	25.2	8.1
13073	Columbia County, Georgia	103,662	26.2	41.6	124,800	63.9	6.9	38.0	51,178	84,220	13.3	23.2	9.3
13077	Coweta County, Georgia	103,351	36.3	32.5	120,274	65.5	3.7	46.1	55,729	84,788	10.8	21.6	10.3
13089	DeKalb County, Georgia	523,708	28.3	47.0	603,312	68.1	6.4	45.1	273,981	70,985	14.6	19.2	14.0
13095	Dougherty County, Georgia	54,748	49.6	23.3	67,801	54.9	8.6	37.5	34,835	42,067	29.7	7.5	27.7
13097	Douglas County, Georgia............	95,251	35.1	33.0	114,738	64.3	6.9	42.1	51,441	65,046	14.8	15.0	14.5
13103	Effingham County, Georgia.........	44,467	42.5	25.3	NA	NA	NA	NA	23,373	74,460	18.1	12.8	8.5
13113	Fayette County, Georgia	81,731	24.7	46.3	97,006	57.5	4.9	39.2	43,689	90,806	12.7	25.3	6.6
13115	Floyd County, Georgia	65,299	46.0	22.9	78,949	58.1	3.1	42.6	35,417	60,825	18.2	10.4	12.7
13117	Forsyth County, Georgia	171,590	19.6	56.2	200,894	69.9	4.9	47.5	86,475	118,814	7.4	37.8	5.2
13121	Fulton County, Georgia..............	735,014	21.2	59.4	869,628	68.8	4.8	48.2	467,735	83,192	15.9	25.6	12.2
13127	Glynn County, Georgia	59,841	35.1	30.3	NA	NA	NA	NA	34,137	61,984	19.3	9.8	13.4
13135	Gwinnett County, Georgia..........	622,377	35.3	38.4	742,013	66.7	4.5	46.9	323,014	74,622	12.8	17.7	9.7
13139	Hall County, Georgia..................	138,144	46.3	25.0	162,282	64.6	4.0	45.5	72,454	66,719	18.4	14.6	11.9
13151	Henry County, Georgia	161,386	37.0	30.3	191,448	63.6	7.4	43.5	84,978	74,614	12.7	12.5	11.1
13153	Houston County, Georgia	109,549	35.7	30.3	130,086	65.1	5.7	44.5	60,815	72,848	15.2	13.7	15.6
13157	Jackson County, Georgia............	53,127	48.5	27.9	NA	NA	NA	NA	25,272	72,116	16.9	15.4	12.1
13179	Liberty County, Georgia	37,042	41.7	22.7	48,512	59.1	5.5	NA	23,883	48,624	21.9	5.4	21.9
13185	Lowndes County, Georgia..........	70,468	42.4	24.5	93,173	57.8	7.2	34.7	45,139	42,242	33.9	6.8	19.5
13215	Muscogee County, Georgia.........	134,716	37.6	31.3	159,069	59.7	6.7	39.2	82,663	52,734	23.5	10.5	22.0
13217	Newton County, Georgia	75,746	42.7	23.8	88,834	67.0	6.7	45.7	41,515	75,589	13.4	12.1	14.0
13223	Paulding County, Georgia	114,641	37.8	31.4	133,744	65.2	3.7	45.2	58,025	93,815	11.0	16.8	7.9
13245	Richmond County, Georgia.........	136,111	42.3	24.1	163,422	63.5	8.9	34.0	74,476	48,048	26.6	7.7	21.6
13247	Rockdale County, Georgia..........	63,708	42.5	30.9	73,802	63.8	5.1	NA	33,141	66,267	10.6	15.9	15.5
13255	Spalding County, Georgia	46,828	55.1	17.1	NA	NA	NA	NA	25,696	54,585	25.4	4.6	18.1
13285	Troup County, Georgia...............	49,663	49.5	19.2	NA	NA	NA	NA	26,768	49,187	22.4	7.3	12.3
13295	Walker County, Georgia..............	49,052	51.7	16.1	55,438	57.1	4.6	NA	26,315	43,672	22.7	6.1	12.1
13297	Walton County, Georgia.............	66,674	44.0	21.8	79,031	60.8	6.5	42.0	35,628	73,151	18.2	15.5	15.4
13313	Whitfield County, Georgia	66,749	58.3	18.8	79,838	62.8	8.6	NA	35,746	55,519	19.6	9.8	12.2
15000	**HAWAII**.....................................	1,021,687	33.4	35.3	1,166,220	63.4	7.2	57.0	490,080	84,857	14.3	23.8	15.2
15001	Hawaii County, Hawaii...............	147,497	36.1	30.7	164,053	57.3	10.5	32.2	72,194	69,473	20.5	17.1	22.0
15003	Honolulu County, Hawaii............	702,553	32.3	37.1	810,934	64.5	6.5	37.3	338,093	90,704	12.9	25.5	13.8
15007	Kauai County, Hawaii..................	52,526	33.5	36.2	59,072	64.1	9.7	32.5	23,464	80,582	14.4	19.7	16.6
15009	Maui County, Hawaii	119,076	36.7	30.0	132,126	64.0	6.7	35.7	56,319	76,273	15.2	23.7	14.7
16000	**IDAHO**......................................	1,257,566	35.6	30.7	1,484,932	63.1	3.3	64.0	693,882	66,474	15.9	13.1	10.5
16001	Ada County, Idaho......................	354,052	26.8	43.2	410,228	64.8	2.9	44.2	196,255	79,279	12.4	18.8	9.0
16005	Bannock County, Idaho...............	56,252	30.4	31.6	68,780	60.4	4.1	37.9	33,557	60,736	20.7	9.1	18.0
16019	Bonneville County, Idaho	79,331	31.2	32.6	92,970	64.7	4.0	40.6	42,905	68,614	12.4	16.2	7.9
16027	Canyon County, Idaho	155,157	44.1	20.9	183,918	64.0	4.3	42.9	82,667	64,314	16.9	10.0	12.8
16055	Kootenai County, Idaho	125,181	33.6	26.6	143,384	61.7	2.6	38.9	67,771	67,593	14.3	13.2	7.4
16083	Twin Falls County, Idaho	58,634	41.2	24.3	70,048	62.9	6.4	NA	34,311	52,880	22.4	10.6	13.0
17000	**ILLINOIS**	8,730,697	35.0	37.1	10,203,044	64.5	7.3	65.0	4,991,641	72,205	17.2	18.4	15.7
17019	Champaign County, Illinois	119,676	24.8	47.7	170,059	62.7	4.5	38.8	84,248	56,847	22.2	13.0	10.2
17031	Cook County, Illinois..................	3,622,494	33.8	41.9	4,187,374	65.6	8.8	42.9	2,072,143	72,092	18.9	19.6	18.0
17037	DeKalb County, Illinois	63,143	33.5	33.8	81,202	69.9	9.6	39.5	38,916	65,615	17.0	12.5	16.9

Table B-2. Counties — What: Education, Employment, and Income, 2021—*Continued*

STATE County code	STATE County	Educational attainment			Employment status				Household income and benefits				
		Total population 25 years and over	Percent with a high school diploma or less	Percent with a bachelor's degree or more	Total population 16 years and over	Labor force participation (percent)	Percent unemployed	Percent age 16 years and over who worked full-time year-round in the past 12 months	Total house-holds	Median household income in the past 12 months (in 2021 inflation-adjusted dollars)	Income less than $25,000 (percent)	Income greater than $150,000 (percent)	Percent who received cash public assistance or food stamps/SNAP
	ACS table number:	C15003	C15003	C15003	C23001	C23001	C23001	S2402	B19001	B19049	B19001	B19001	B19058
	Column number:	1	2	3	4	5	6	7	8	9	10	11	12
	ILLINOIS—Cont.												
17043	DuPage County, Illinois	641,066	24.7	51.1	743,605	68.1	6.1	45.6	350,639	99,577	10.7	29.4	9.3
17089	Kane County, Illinois	343,222	36.1	37.9	404,583	69.6	6.2	45.1	183,427	91,336	10.0	25.1	13.5
17091	Kankakee County, Illinois	71,036	42.1	21.5	85,581	61.6	5.0	38.9	41,020	63,364	17.6	12.0	15.8
17093	Kendall County, Illinois	84,423	33.2	29.8	102,325	70.6	3.9	NA	44,208	91,560	6.2	21.7	14.5
17097	Lake County, Illinois	472,440	29.5	46.9	566,193	67.4	6.3	42.8	254,744	95,796	11.6	29.4	11.4
17099	LaSalle County, Illinois	77,662	42.0	20.5	89,527	61.5	7.2	36.9	44,972	64,673	21.0	11.9	15.4
17111	McHenry County, Illinois	215,133	32.5	35.0	248,395	70.1	6.2	46.2	116,768	91,887	10.0	23.5	7.3
17113	McLean County, Illinois	104,443	26.7	47.4	138,324	65.1	3.7	43.2	69,263	69,612	18.8	16.8	10.9
17115	Macon County, Illinois	70,757	48.1	19.0	82,176	56.8	11.1	34.1	43,914	46,807	24.8	7.5	21.1
17119	Madison County, Illinois	184,762	35.4	29.8	214,065	61.9	5.7	41.7	109,818	65,663	16.5	14.2	14.8
17143	Peoria County, Illinois................	120,639	32.4	35.4	140,811	61.5	6.8	40.5	79,307	55,949	21.5	11.7	21.3
17161	Rock Island County, Illinois..........	98,000	41.3	23.3	114,139	59.4	8.6	34.7	60,187	57,895	22.2	8.0	19.7
17163	St. Clair County, Illinois	175,589	33.2	30.7	201,796	63.8	6.5	39.4	98,926	67,530	17.2	13.3	18.4
17167	Sangamon County, Illinois...........	136,862	32.6	37.1	157,405	60.5	7.2	41.6	84,414	68,466	19.0	15.0	17.0
17179	Tazewell County, Illinois	91,792	34.3	29.4	104,568	62.9	4.3	40.9	55,208	63,621	16.1	12.7	11.6
17183	Vermilion County, Illinois	51,090	50.1	15.9	58,110	51.4	6.6	33.5	29,007	49,091	25.2	6.5	19.5
17197	Will County, Illinois	466,633	33.4	37.4	552,893	68.3	6.6	44.5	242,530	93,752	9.8	24.6	11.6
17199	Williamson County, Illinois	48,048	36.4	25.8	54,991	51.1	5.9	NA	27,361	54,859	20.3	11.7	19.7
17201	Winnebago County, Illinois	193,485	42.0	25.5	225,003	61.1	9.9	37.7	115,282	56,132	21.1	10.5	21.8
18000	**INDIANA**	4,559,631	42.7	28.9	5,401,077	63.4	4.7	66.7	2,680,694	62,743	17.3	12.0	10.7
18003	Allen County, Indiana.................	254,546	38.1	30.6	299,468	65.8	5.0	43.7	154,866	62,542	16.2	10.7	10.7
18005	Bartholomew County, Indiana.....	56,650	35.5	36.2	65,164	67.8	4.0	45.5	32,518	73,564	12.2	16.7	9.3
18011	Boone County, Indiana................	49,511	26.5	48.1	NA	NA	NA	NA	28,048	98,867	8.0	31.7	4.9
18019	Clark County, Indiana.................	86,392	42.0	25.9	98,736	63.7	4.8	42.9	50,153	62,231	18.1	9.9	11.5
18035	Delaware County, Indiana..........	68,558	43.4	24.5	93,555	58.5	8.7	35.2	45,977	50,497	25.6	6.5	15.1
18039	Elkhart County, Indiana..............	131,567	53.5	21.8	156,722	63.0	5.0	41.3	69,015	60,143	16.3	9.9	7.5
18043	Floyd County, Indiana.................	56,241	41.0	29.1	64,608	65.1	4.3	45.6	30,846	66,596	13.6	13.3	10.5
18053	Grant County, Indiana.................	44,256	47.8	22.2	53,659	58.0	8.9	35.7	26,342	49,401	23.0	5.0	17.6
18057	Hamilton County, Indiana	236,892	16.2	62.3	275,346	72.0	3.3	50.3	132,255	102,452	6.2	32.4	3.5
18059	Hancock County, Indiana	57,049	35.1	32.2	64,942	69.9	2.7	NA	32,661	79,182	6.8	14.7	4.7
18063	Hendricks County, Indiana	120,832	31.0	40.0	140,158	68.2	2.0	49.2	65,751	89,228	6.7	20.2	5.3
18067	Howard County, Indiana.............	58,410	45.6	20.5	67,299	60.6	7.3	NA	36,530	55,088	17.4	8.6	14.8
18081	Johnson County, Indiana............	110,640	38.9	34.9	128,901	67.2	2.8	45.8	62,116	78,697	10.4	18.1	6.4
18085	Kosciusko County, Indiana..........	54,023	51.2	22.7	63,828	63.1	2.5	43.2	31,523	65,540	14.5	10.5	8.6
18089	Lake County, Indiana	339,934	47.0	23.4	395,853	60.7	7.1	39.4	192,256	61,443	19.9	11.6	15.2
18091	LaPorte County, Indiana..............	79,010	49.2	21.2	91,635	55.3	4.4	37.3	43,445	63,714	17.8	10.5	9.8
18095	Madison County, Indiana	92,361	48.3	21.3	106,004	58.8	6.6	37.7	53,910	53,785	21.6	8.6	15.3
18097	Marion County, Indiana	640,404	39.4	34.4	755,923	67.8	5.8	46.0	394,717	58,560	18.5	11.5	14.4
18105	Monroe County, Indiana	80,703	28.3	49.2	120,310	57.2	4.6	32.4	56,714	51,945	27.2	11.3	6.4
18109	Morgan County, Indiana	50,825	50.2	18.7	58,932	54.6	1.0	NA	26,821	67,848	13.4	13.1	12.9
18127	Porter County, Indiana	122,045	39.6	31.7	142,012	61.4	3.0	42.0	68,266	80,547	14.5	17.3	6.1
18141	St. Joseph County, Indiana..........	178,037	38.9	31.9	214,834	63.0	5.3	40.9	107,076	59,189	19.9	10.7	11.4
18157	Tippecanoe County, Indiana........	105,209	31.3	42.0	152,933	63.1	3.0	37.3	73,525	52,617	23.6	8.9	8.3
18163	Vanderburgh County, Indiana	122,910	39.1	26.9	145,431	64.1	4.7	42.5	79,215	53,171	18.4	7.7	14.2
18167	Vigo County, Indiana	68,486	49.8	23.0	87,233	58.6	6.8	34.5	42,140	46,802	25.7	7.2	17.6
18177	Wayne County, Indiana...............	44,889	47.9	17.7	53,595	55.6	4.5	36.3	26,452	50,138	27.3	6.0	16.0
19000	**IOWA**.....................................	2,137,261	36.9	30.5	2,543,525	66.1	3.6	67.5	1,300,467	65,600	16.6	12.7	11.1
19013	Black Hawk County, Iowa	83,052	38.5	29.9	105,186	65.8	3.3	40.2	53,951	60,264	20.1	8.3	12.4
19049	Dallas County, Iowa	68,406	22.0	50.2	NA	NA	NA	NA	41,681	90,750	10.2	21.7	9.5
19061	Dubuque County, Iowa...............	66,573	37.0	32.6	79,814	67.9	4.1	44.1	40,482	75,590	14.2	14.9	6.2
19103	Johnson County, Iowa.................	92,873	17.3	52.5	128,241	72.4	2.7	43.0	61,301	67,134	15.8	18.3	7.4
19113	Linn County, Iowa......................	155,088	28.7	36.2	182,774	66.9	4.2	45.1	94,884	69,420	15.4	13.2	11.1
19153	Polk County, Iowa......................	331,392	32.6	38.4	388,394	70.3	4.0	49.3	203,390	73,292	13.5	16.5	11.0
19155	Pottawattamie County, Iowa.......	63,487	41.7	26.8	74,954	62.0	4.2	44.2	37,930	66,542	18.5	11.7	12.8
19163	Scott County, Iowa	118,440	32.8	34.9	137,821	66.4	4.6	43.1	72,128	65,566	17.6	16.1	16.7
19169	Story County, Iowa	52,373	19.3	49.8	85,059	63.9	3.9	36.3	38,868	63,774	21.1	11.1	6.3
19193	Woodbury County, Iowa	67,458	48.6	21.9	81,710	68.3	3.4	45.5	41,327	59,376	17.7	10.9	13.3

Table B-2. Counties — What: Education, Employment, and Income, 2021—*Continued*

	STATE County	Educational attainment			Employment status			Percent age 16 years and over who worked full-time year-round in the past 12 months	Household income and benefits				
		Total population 25 years and over	Percent with a high school diploma or less	Percent with a bachelor's degree or more	Total population 16 years and over	Labor force participation (percent)	Percent unemployed		Total households	Median household income in the past 12 months (in 2021 inflation-adjusted dollars)	Income less than $25,000 (percent)	Income greater than $150,000 (percent)	Percent who received cash public assistance or food stamps/ SNAP
STATE County code	ACS table number:	C15003	C15003	C15003	C23001	C23001	C23001	S2402	B19001	B19049	B19001	B19001	B19058
	Column number:	1	2	3	4	5	6	7	8	9	10	11	12
20000	**KANSAS**	1,942,133	33.5	35.4	2,315,379	65.7	4.3	67.7	1,159,026	64,124	17.4	13.2	8.5
20015	Butler County, Kansas.................	45,031	30.7	34.5	52,818	62.6	1.3	42.4	24,545	71,274	16.9	12.2	7.7
20045	Douglas County, Kansas.............	72,974	21.9	52.5	100,916	65.9	5.5	39.7	49,759	56,576	23.0	12.5	8.6
20091	Johnson County, Kansas	419,511	17.6	57.3	484,757	71.3	2.8	52.6	245,646	92,945	9.3	27.0	3.3
20103	Leavenworth County, Kansas......	55,907	33.7	37.1	65,061	60.0	2.3	39.9	29,963	83,028	11.5	18.6	5.7
20161	Riley County, Kansas.................	38,889	19.5	51.1	61,575	70.6	4.9	NA	27,866	57,335	23.3	12.3	4.9
20173	Sedgwick County, Kansas	343,232	36.8	31.2	407,206	66.1	6.7	41.8	203,656	60,364	17.9	10.4	12.4
20177	Shawnee County, Kansas............	122,369	36.0	33.6	142,152	61.3	2.8	44.6	74,908	55,499	20.8	9.7	8.7
20209	Wyandotte County, Kansas.........	105,801	50.9	21.3	125,992	64.9	6.3	42.2	62,538	55,605	20.4	7.4	16.4
21000	**KENTUCKY**	3,077,867	44.8	27.0	3,612,858	58.8	5.4	64.9	1,785,682	55,573	22.9	10.4	15.4
21015	Boone County, Kentucky.............	91,609	37.9	34.1	105,412	70.6	3.8	50.0	50,728	83,877	8.4	18.0	7.8
21029	Bullitt County, Kentucky.............	59,070	50.6	16.3	67,963	62.5	3.5	NA	30,979	68,269	16.6	10.0	12.0
21037	Campbell County, Kentucky........	65,369	29.7	40.9	76,222	67.3	5.1	44.2	39,048	71,701	17.1	18.6	6.7
21047	Christian County, Kentucky.........	41,066	50.5	16.2	53,521	58.7	3.3	NA	25,317	47,754	23.5	3.0	13.1
21059	Daviess County, Kentucky...........	69,689	39.6	27.2	81,139	59.7	5.1	42.6	41,246	59,307	19.7	11.5	12.4
21067	Fayette County, Kentucky...........	209,898	27.3	46.3	263,438	67.5	5.4	42.0	139,303	60,942	21.1	13.0	10.0
21093	Hardin County, Kentucky............	74,447	39.9	27.0	87,300	64.5	5.2	36.7	42,714	61,089	17.6	12.8	13.6
21111	Jefferson County, Kentucky........	540,154	36.2	36.7	626,024	64.4	4.9	41.8	331,104	60,561	18.1	13.5	12.7
21117	Kenton County, Kentucky............	117,154	34.9	38.2	135,098	66.6	4.7	43.1	68,073	70,171	16.1	14.5	8.8
21145	McCracken County, Kentucky.....	47,255	37.8	30.6	53,795	54.6	4.5	NA	25,531	64,082	21.7	14.3	11.5
21151	Madison County, Kentucky	58,406	41.5	31.6	77,280	61.5	4.2	38.4	36,052	52,425	23.7	8.7	15.9
21185	Oldham County, Kentucky	46,129	27.6	48.7	NA	NA	NA	NA	22,895	110,041	7.4	32.3	3.8
21199	Pulaski County, Kentucky...........	46,275	54.4	16.0	52,641	51.9	9.1	NA	25,509	44,561	34.3	7.4	18.0
21227	Warren County, Kentucky	83,302	39.2	34.3	108,542	66.1	4.3	39.6	53,093	59,752	22.1	9.8	16.8
22000	**LOUISIANA**	3,117,186	46.2	26.4	3,663,069	58.5	7.5	64.9	1,783,924	52,087	25.6	11.5	20.0
22005	Ascension Parish, Louisiana........	84,580	41.3	28.0	98,181	66.8	4.4	NA	48,129	72,662	13.3	20.6	16.6
22015	Bossier Parish, Louisiana.............	85,392	38.8	32.8	100,707	59.2	5.0	34.2	49,418	59,041	20.7	11.7	11.8
22017	Caddo Parish, Louisiana.............	159,189	46.8	23.5	184,662	55.8	11.0	36.1	96,369	44,022	30.2	8.8	22.9
22019	Calcasieu Parish, Louisiana.........	137,147	43.4	26.0	159,395	59.8	4.1	38.7	71,511	58,020	21.2	13.0	24.0
22033	East Baton Rouge Parish, Louisiana	290,229	35.9	36.6	362,497	61.7	9.4	38.9	175,731	51,432	24.2	14.9	21.5
22045	Iberia Parish, Louisiana..............	45,259	62.0	11.1	52,889	53.9	10.5	NA	25,440	49,447	27.2	6.0	24.1
22051	Jefferson Parish, Louisiana.........	305,607	43.1	28.4	347,383	62.2	8.0	40.6	179,775	56,282	22.0	11.3	16.5
22055	Lafayette Parish, Louisiana.........	163,185	40.1	34.4	192,450	64.4	5.8	40.9	97,877	59,093	23.1	15.3	13.8
22057	Lafourche Parish, Louisiana........	66,762	57.0	19.7	77,902	55.1	6.2	NA	38,111	59,637	27.3	9.5	20.1
22063	Livingston Parish, Louisiana........	95,733	42.0	23.4	112,369	60.8	3.9	NA	51,960	75,682	13.7	16.7	16.3
22071	Orleans Parish, Louisiana............	271,452	32.1	41.5	310,676	59.9	9.3	37.8	158,827	46,942	31.5	13.8	23.0
22073	Ouachita Parish, Louisiana.........	104,073	43.0	26.7	125,267	59.3	8.2	39.6	61,594	47,400	32.5	9.4	20.9
22079	Rapides Parish, Louisiana...........	86,159	51.3	22.9	100,642	55.7	7.8	38.6	48,405	45,183	25.5	9.5	22.1
22097	St. Landry Parish, Louisiana	53,091	57.0	15.8	62,931	55.6	10.5	NA	32,213	38,599	35.6	5.4	29.0
22103	St. Tammany Parish, Louisiana.....	185,599	33.0	39.7	212,826	62.0	6.7	40.6	103,543	66,582	16.8	17.2	9.3
22105	Tangipahoa Parish, Louisiana.......	86,266	51.2	20.5	106,063	61.0	5.0	NA	49,915	52,872	26.7	8.3	23.2
22109	Terrebonne Parish, Louisiana	73,202	56.2	21.5	84,076	57.6	5.2	NA	43,996	63,100	20.4	10.3	17.8
23000	**MAINE**	1,015,078	35.1	36.0	1,155,699	61.3	4.9	65.4	593,626	64,767	18.1	13.2	13.0
23001	Androscoggin County, Maine......	77,917	42.6	24.7	91,270	63.6	4.8	41.0	46,323	62,958	19.0	8.5	14.9
23003	Aroostook County, Maine..........	49,740	45.2	22.4	56,521	56.7	7.6	36.1	30,220	52,849	21.6	6.9	21.5
23005	Cumberland County, Maine........	224,854	22.0	52.2	256,719	67.0	3.9	45.4	129,977	80,982	13.2	21.7	8.6
23011	Kennebec County, Maine............	90,553	41.2	31.3	103,920	59.0	4.5	41.3	53,803	60,528	19.4	10.2	13.7
23019	Penobscot County, Maine...........	109,464	36.0	31.3	129,888	61.0	5.4	38.9	65,441	56,250	23.0	10.7	14.9
23031	York County, Maine..................	160,616	34.6	35.3	180,618	63.7	5.3	42.4	90,907	73,875	13.6	15.5	9.9
24000	**MARYLAND**	4,273,260	32.8	42.5	4,964,751	66.6	5.8	68.2	2,355,652	90,203	13.2	26.4	14.2
24001	Allegany County, Maryland........	47,636	49.6	21.8	57,810	49.3	5.5	33.5	28,535	48,888	24.7	7.5	22.4
24003	Anne Arundel County, Maryland.	409,290	28.2	43.1	473,881	69.1	4.4	47.8	225,064	107,823	7.6	33.3	9.3
24005	Baltimore County, Maryland.......	589,564	33.6	40.4	686,282	65.6	5.8	44.5	332,529	80,453	13.4	22.1	15.1
24009	Calvert County, Maryland	64,805	35.8	34.4	74,722	66.7	2.2	48.4	33,994	122,266	7.5	36.2	6.7
24013	Carroll County, Maryland............	121,642	32.2	39.9	140,888	67.6	2.6	47.3	64,161	102,476	7.8	31.5	6.9

Table B-2. Counties — What: Education, Employment, and Income, 2021—*Continued*

		Educational attainment			Employment status				Household income and benefits				
STATE County code	STATE County	Total population 25 years and over	Percent with a high school diploma or less	Percent with a bachelor's degree or more	Total population 16 years and over	Labor force participation (percent)	Percent unemployed	Percent age 16 years and over who worked full-time year-round in the past 12 months	Total households	Median household income in the past 12 months (in 2021 inflation-adjusted dollars)	Income less than $25,000 (percent)	Income greater than $150,000 (percent)	Percent who received cash public assistance or food stamps/ SNAP
	ACS table number:	C15003	C15003	C15003	C23001	C23001	C23001	S2402	B19001	B19049	B19001	B19001	B19058
	Column number:	1	2	3	4	5	6	7	8	9	10	11	12
	MARYLAND—Cont.												
24015	Cecil County, Maryland..............	72,911	47.9	26.3	84,450	61.2	6.7	43.3	41,000	75,692	16.2	15.8	14.8
24017	Charles County, Maryland...........	114,590	32.8	33.1	133,635	68.2	5.2	48.3	59,481	105,493	10.7	29.0	11.7
24021	Frederick County, Maryland	191,943	30.5	44.9	222,590	69.6	4.3	46.8	103,685	104,780	9.2	30.5	7.2
24025	Harford County, Maryland	183,122	32.9	37.8	210,287	68.4	3.8	47.9	101,196	96,328	10.4	25.7	10.6
24027	Howard County, Maryland.........	227,684	17.1	64.6	263,819	68.3	3.5	49.7	120,546	133,267	7.4	43.8	7.1
24031	Montgomery County, Maryland ..	732,659	21.7	60.9	843,210	69.5	6.0	46.5	388,396	112,854	9.6	37.6	10.2
24033	Prince George's County, Maryland......................................	656,295	39.9	34.8	766,786	68.4	7.7	46.6	346,127	90,182	13.0	23.7	15.7
24037	St. Mary's County, Maryland	77,108	34.3	36.0	90,184	69.3	6.2	45.9	42,078	108,397	10.1	29.9	11.0
24043	Washington County, Maryland....	108,974	51.8	22.5	125,340	55.6	4.0	37.1	60,215	65,367	19.6	13.1	21.2
24045	Wicomico County, Maryland........	64,960	40.8	29.2	84,309	64.8	10.6	39.1	40,577	63,333	18.9	11.4	20.5
24510	Baltimore city, Maryland..............	405,797	37.7	37.7	472,136	62.3	7.9	42.8	254,370	54,652	26.4	13.0	28.3
25000	**MASSACHUSETTS**	4,934,755	31.7	46.6	5,790,261	66.8	6.6	63.3	2,759,018	89,645	15.7	28.1	16.7
25001	Barnstable County, Massachusetts.........................	184,483	25.3	46.4	202,830	59.9	5.9	33.6	104,733	83,537	14.3	24.8	10.5
25003	Berkshire County, Massachusetts	96,128	35.5	38.4	110,107	61.8	6.9	37.2	57,765	60,749	20.0	16.6	18.2
25005	Bristol County, Massachusetts.....	410,415	44.4	29.5	475,547	65.1	7.0	40.0	233,531	73,102	18.8	19.3	21.0
25009	Essex County, Massachusetts	566,988	34.8	42.0	659,916	67.6	6.6	42.0	309,972	87,433	15.8	26.9	20.8
25011	Franklin County, Massachusetts ..	53,948	32.3	41.9	60,471	62.2	6.2	36.7	30,374	69,771	17.6	14.0	18.5
25013	Hampden County, Massachusetts	319,087	43.8	30.8	378,119	57.9	8.1	36.7	184,544	61,747	23.1	14.1	26.2
25015	Hampshire County, Massachusetts.........................	99,542	24.1	53.2	141,317	60.2	7.3	30.4	60,870	77,495	16.9	21.2	13.3
25017	Middlesex County, Massachusetts	1,144,028	24.4	58.9	1,337,101	69.7	5.2	46.7	632,831	112,764	11.5	37.6	12.1
25021	Norfolk County, Massachusetts ...	512,751	23.5	57.1	593,416	68.3	7.0	45.5	280,067	115,357	12.1	38.1	10.6
25023	Plymouth County, Massachusetts	377,735	32.8	42.7	436,265	66.8	4.9	42.6	202,084	100,082	12.1	31.1	13.5
25025	Suffolk County, Massachusetts....	539,971	34.2	48.4	659,095	69.2	7.9	42.0	315,257	78,155	22.1	24.6	22.4
25027	Worcester County, Massachusetts.........................	603,326	34.5	40.0	706,816	67.0	7.9	41.9	333,435	84,952	15.7	23.6	17.6
26000	**MICHIGAN**	6,971,895	36.8	31.7	8,156,411	60.9	6.9	61.0	4,051,798	63,498	18.3	13.6	15.3
26005	Allegan County, Michigan...........	83,378	42.7	24.7	95,158	62.5	3.4	41.2	44,479	74,371	13.5	12.4	10.9
26017	Bay County, Michigan..................	74,942	41.8	19.9	86,297	60.5	5.2	38.0	45,487	56,911	19.7	9.4	12.8
26021	Berrien County, Michigan............	107,677	35.7	33.2	124,028	60.1	5.6	37.8	65,764	57,535	22.1	14.1	14.7
26025	Calhoun County, Michigan	91,332	43.9	23.9	107,126	59.4	7.8	35.7	53,482	55,192	21.2	10.9	13.4
26037	Clinton County, Michigan...........	55,748	30.0	32.5	64,308	61.7	3.7	40.3	30,952	76,534	11.7	13.4	8.0
26045	Eaton County, Michigan..............	77,908	33.4	29.9	88,516	62.1	7.0	40.0	45,137	70,133	14.0	13.3	11.1
26049	Genesee County, Michigan	280,947	39.7	23.8	324,886	57.9	10.2	32.1	167,895	52,025	22.2	9.2	18.8
26055	Grand Traverse County, Michigan	69,990	27.9	38.0	78,603	62.0	5.4	37.6	40,083	65,651	13.7	8.0	10.7
26065	Ingham County, Michigan...........	176,118	28.1	42.0	234,153	62.6	8.4	36.1	115,752	57,226	21.3	10.7	15.3
26067	Ionia County, Michigan...............	46,091	52.9	15.4	53,577	55.5	3.8	35.9	23,531	65,729	16.4	7.9	14.6
26075	Jackson County, Michigan...........	113,648	43.5	21.9	129,947	56.6	4.2	36.7	61,937	58,254	17.2	11.4	15.4
26077	Kalamazoo County, Michigan	164,236	26.9	39.5	210,748	65.5	5.6	38.8	105,642	62,128	20.5	12.4	12.9
26081	Kent County, Michigan	441,547	32.2	39.9	518,821	69.0	4.8	43.7	253,092	72,021	14.2	15.3	12.9
26087	Lapeer County, Michigan............	63,836	45.2	20.2	73,278	61.0	6.2	38.1	34,447	71,479	15.5	11.8	11.1
26091	Lenawee County, Michigan..........	69,784	43.5	24.4	80,884	55.7	5.9	34.6	38,963	61,257	20.5	8.0	15.7
26093	Livingston County, Michigan.......	139,909	26.2	41.5	159,901	65.1	5.3	41.3	75,370	91,344	9.0	24.0	6.2
26099	Macomb County, Michigan.........	625,976	40.1	26.4	719,101	63.8	7.6	38.8	358,011	67,527	15.7	13.8	15.2
26103	Marquette County, Michigan.......	44,816	31.9	32.7	55,887	57.2	4.9	32.3	27,290	55,301	21.3	7.0	9.1
26111	Midland County, Michigan..........	59,204	28.8	38.5	68,067	58.6	6.0	36.4	35,453	67,707	17.1	17.4	12.3
26115	Monroe County, Michigan	109,946	41.0	22.6	126,068	57.9	5.7	36.7	61,574	65,512	15.9	13.4	11.9
26117	Montcalm County, Michigan.......	47,083	53.0	13.6	53,967	54.5	3.6	34.9	23,745	55,832	19.2	5.8	13.3
26121	Muskegon County, Michigan	121,226	46.0	19.6	140,578	56.9	7.6	36.1	67,707	55,462	19.7	7.1	18.2
26125	Oakland County, Michigan..........	910,122	22.8	50.5	1,043,160	66.1	5.6	42.8	530,383	86,523	12.6	25.1	10.5
26139	Ottawa County, Michigan...........	189,606	33.0	36.9	238,474	66.5	3.9	39.7	110,045	79,116	12.1	17.4	9.3
26145	Saginaw County, Michigan..........	130,970	42.8	22.5	153,337	55.9	8.1	33.5	80,146	50,606	28.1	8.5	21.2
26147	St. Clair County, Michigan	115,594	43.7	18.7	131,394	60.5	6.4	36.4	66,324	60,992	15.1	10.3	16.2
26155	Shiawassee County, Michigan......	48,292	43.8	19.0	55,486	58.9	6.8	35.1	28,226	51,959	18.1	6.1	15.2

Table B-2. Counties — What: Education, Employment, and Income, 2021—*Continued*

STATE County code	STATE County	Educational attainment			Employment status				Household income and benefits				
		Total population 25 years and over	Percent with a high school diploma or less	Percent with a bachelor's degree or more	Total population 16 years and over	Labor force participation (percent)	Percent unemployed	Percent age 16 years and over who worked full-time year-round in the past 12 months	Total households	Median household income in the past 12 months (in 2021 inflation-adjusted dollars)	Income less than $25,000 (percent)	Income greater than $150,000 (percent)	Percent who received cash public assistance or food stamps/SNAP
	ACS table number:	C15003	C15003	C15003	C23001	C23001	C23001	S2402	B19001	B19049	B19001	B19001	B19058
	Column number:	1	2	3	4	5	6	7	8	9	10	11	12
	MICHIGAN—Cont.												
26159	Van Buren County, Michigan.......	52,528	44.7	22.4	60,278	56.5	6.1	35.1	28,457	59,081	20.6	11.0	14.9
26161	Washtenaw County, Michigan	235,544	19.0	57.3	310,111	64.0	4.8	37.6	149,133	76,918	15.1	21.6	9.6
26163	Wayne County, Michigan...........	1,207,427	42.0	27.2	1,402,749	58.8	10.9	34.5	695,038	52,605	23.9	11.4	24.8
27000	**MINNESOTA**.............................	3,898,742	29.2	38.9	4,554,126	68.4	4.9	64.6	2,281,033	77,720	13.3	19.4	9.8
27003	Anoka County, Minnesota	251,490	32.9	32.3	289,879	69.8	4.4	48.9	135,265	88,410	9.0	21.6	9.8
27013	Blue Earth County, Minnesota.....	41,148	29.5	34.6	57,530	71.4	4.8	42.5	27,604	69,858	15.1	15.1	8.6
27019	Carver County, Minnesota	70,844	21.2	53.1	84,023	70.7	4.1	49.1	40,141	102,694	6.8	32.4	5.7
27027	Clay County, Minnesota............	40,979	23.6	46.6	51,279	68.9	5.2	42.4	26,236	67,539	18.7	14.4	9.2
27035	Crow Wing County, Minnesota...	48,629	32.7	28.1	54,964	57.6	6.9	35.6	27,753	63,921	16.6	10.0	9.8
27037	Dakota County, Minnesota.........	301,686	24.5	43.6	348,430	72.2	5.0	47.0	170,696	93,786	8.3	25.1	6.6
27053	Hennepin County, Minnesota......	886,834	20.8	53.2	1,022,868	71.7	6.0	45.7	532,149	84,244	13.2	24.8	11.1
27109	Olmsted County, Minnesota.......	109,130	23.1	47.7	128,171	70.6	4.4	45.3	65,122	83,070	13.2	22.4	9.0
27123	Ramsey County, Minnesota........	365,869	29.3	44.5	430,603	68.5	6.1	43.0	218,817	70,518	13.7	18.1	14.6
27131	Rice County, Minnesota	43,368	42.0	30.6	54,935	64.9	3.9	38.1	23,779	67,267	13.1	16.4	10.5
27137	St. Louis County, Minnesota.......	136,095	28.1	33.4	166,470	59.6	4.5	33.7	85,576	64,959	17.4	11.5	10.7
27139	Scott County, Minnesota............	101,015	25.5	45.3	118,377	76.5	4.0	52.2	55,327	106,987	7.7	32.1	6.6
27141	Sherburne County, Minnesota	65,739	30.4	25.8	NA	NA	NA	NA	34,738	90,638	10.7	24.9	5.5
27145	Stearns County, Minnesota	97,700	32.1	28.0	126,396	71.1	4.9	40.0	62,168	65,742	17.8	12.1	9.7
27163	Washington County, Minnesota..	185,021	21.9	48.8	214,078	69.3	3.7	47.4	102,421	104,935	8.0	32.5	6.0
27171	Wright County, Minnesota..........	95,272	31.2	34.9	110,629	71.1	2.1	48.3	52,260	99,964	8.1	21.2	7.0
28000	**MISSISSIPPI**............................	1,968,167	43.3	24.8	2,340,485	56.6	6.3	68.6	1,129,611	48,716	26.6	8.2	14.5
28033	DeSoto County, Mississippi	124,942	40.1	27.4	147,150	66.1	4.3	47.2	68,966	70,490	16.6	12.9	10.4
28035	Forrest County, Mississippi........	46,194	34.0	30.5	61,607	63.9	6.7	NA	30,600	46,226	26.3	8.8	17.7
28047	Harrison County, Mississippi.......	140,911	36.7	27.9	166,048	58.5	8.2	35.1	81,224	55,702	21.6	8.0	14.5
28049	Hinds County, Mississippi...........	146,808	34.6	31.3	175,815	58.2	8.8	36.3	91,067	40,658	31.1	6.4	16.3
28059	Jackson County, Mississippi........	100,698	36.1	27.6	116,164	62.5	7.0	42.8	56,984	57,383	20.0	10.2	12.1
28067	Jones County, Mississippi...........	43,740	47.0	19.8	52,756	49.9	6.4	NA	23,506	40,116	33.9	4.0	16.1
28073	Lamar County, Mississippi..........	43,961	33.8	30.8	NA	NA	NA	NA	25,688	65,334	13.4	11.7	9.4
28075	Lauderdale County, Mississippi....	49,681	42.9	21.0	57,139	55.7	6.9	NA	28,212	41,174	31.1	4.6	16.5
28081	Lee County, Mississippi	55,411	38.1	30.1	64,791	61.0	4.8	NA	32,722	59,274	24.0	11.9	15.8
28089	Madison County, Mississippi	74,092	26.1	46.7	87,064	66.6	3.6	48.1	42,558	75,678	11.1	19.0	8.4
28121	Rankin County, Mississippi	109,672	33.3	34.5	126,777	63.2	2.7	46.8	59,894	71,241	14.4	12.6	5.3
29000	**MISSOURI**	4,226,634	39.3	31.7	4,949,628	62.8	4.6	67.1	2,468,726	61,847	18.6	13.0	11.2
29019	Boone County, Missouri.............	114,508	26.4	49.5	151,673	67.4	5.0	39.6	75,036	62,296	21.0	12.6	8.2
29021	Buchanan County, Missouri.........	57,346	50.7	24.1	66,543	59.7	4.3	40.2	33,334	50,113	24.6	9.3	15.0
29031	Cape Girardeau County, Missouri	53,330	43.2	33.3	66,439	63.8	2.4	40.9	32,800	61,330	19.2	9.3	10.9
29037	Cass County, Missouri	74,982	35.5	26.8	85,868	67.7	3.7	49.3	42,361	79,554	10.5	17.4	8.2
29043	Christian County, Missouri	61,895	38.8	32.6	71,522	65.0	3.5	46.1	34,116	71,343	13.1	13.4	6.3
29047	Clay County, Missouri	175,351	32.8	35.3	202,329	70.5	5.8	48.0	100,737	74,728	12.4	15.4	7.4
29051	Cole County, Missouri................	53,452	40.1	34.8	61,983	62.7	1.6	40.6	29,522	63,326	16.7	12.2	11.4
29071	Franklin County, Missouri...........	73,794	43.0	23.2	84,698	62.1	3.3	NA	41,301	68,410	16.8	14.2	9.3
29077	Greene County, Missouri............	198,487	33.5	34.1	245,634	63.9	3.6	42.4	130,986	53,127	19.4	9.8	10.5
29095	Jackson County, Missouri...........	490,994	36.4	33.8	569,116	66.7	5.3	46.0	302,965	63,459	17.2	13.2	11.6
29097	Jasper County, Missouri	81,273	44.0	25.3	95,978	61.8	3.4	41.8	47,864	52,221	23.6	8.8	13.2
29099	Jefferson County, Missouri	159,156	39.5	23.3	182,102	66.6	3.5	46.3	88,806	67,955	11.9	12.2	8.3
29165	Platte County, Missouri..............	74,605	21.0	47.3	86,232	71.1	5.4	47.5	43,201	85,157	12.5	19.6	6.2
29183	St. Charles County, Missouri	283,227	28.3	42.5	328,382	69.9	3.9	48.4	157,907	91,601	7.7	23.9	4.9
29187	St. Francois County, Missouri......	48,270	50.8	15.7	NA	NA	NA	NA	25,030	47,682	29.3	8.3	14.2
29189	St. Louis County, Missouri..........	694,679	27.5	46.4	802,412	64.2	5.0	42.6	412,833	72,378	16.0	20.2	10.0
29510	St. Louis city, Missouri................	214,271	34.6	38.9	245,307	64.7	6.3	42.5	139,736	49,965	27.7	9.1	20.4
30000	**MONTANA**	766,758	32.5	34.8	895,986	61.8	3.9	62.0	448,949	63,249	17.6	13.4	10.5
30013	Cascade County, Montana.........	58,183	37.4	27.4	67,823	61.1	3.2	34.6	34,303	57,706	21.2	9.5	13.1
30029	Flathead County, Montana.........	78,071	29.8	36.5	88,259	63.6	2.4	41.0	42,900	66,126	14.0	15.2	6.4
30031	Gallatin County, Montana.........	79,821	19.1	56.2	101,145	67.9	0.9	43.0	48,796	80,763	14.4	25.4	5.4
30049	Lewis and Clark County, Montana.	51,485	29.2	40.0	59,015	62.6	3.9	43.4	31,208	66,686	12.7	14.0	11.1

STATE County code	STATE County	Educational attainment			Employment status				Household income and benefits				
		Total population 25 years and over	Percent with a high school diploma or less	Percent with a bachelor's degree or more	Total population 16 years and over	Labor force participation (percent)	Percent unemployed	Percent age 16 years and over who worked full-time year-round in the past 12 months	Total households	Median household income in the past 12 months (in 2021 inflation-adjusted dollars)	Income less than $25,000 (percent)	Income greater than $150,000 (percent)	Percent who received cash public assistance or food stamps/ SNAP
	ACS table number:	C15003	C15003	C15003	C23001	C23001	C23001	S2402	B19001	B19049	B19001	B19001	B19058
	Column number:	1	2	3	4	5	6	7	8	9	10	11	12
	MONTANA—Cont.												
30063	Missoula County, Montana	82,368	23.2	45.6	99,414	69.5	5.1	40.0	51,957	66,803	17.0	17.1	13.8
30111	Yellowstone County, Montana	115,251	29.8	35.6	132,760	63.8	4.4	40.9	69,001	69,882	16.4	13.7	10.5
31000	**NEBRASKA**.............................	1,292,536	33.0	34.4	1,534,896	68.6	2.6	69.3	785,982	66,817	16.5	14.0	9.5
31055	Douglas County, Nebraska..........	383,565	29.0	40.9	452,360	70.3	3.5	48.4	236,106	69,290	16.5	17.4	12.1
31109	Lancaster County, Nebraska........	202,642	26.5	43.4	259,943	71.1	2.8	46.0	131,417	64,980	16.3	13.4	8.7
31153	Sarpy County, Nebraska.............	125,891	23.6	43.4	147,916	72.1	1.7	50.3	72,428	87,979	9.7	21.8	7.2
32000	**NEVADA**.................................	2,192,826	40.1	27.6	2,526,328	63.0	9.6	60.8	1,191,380	66,274	17.7	14.9	15.7
32003	Clark County, Nevada	1,586,157	40.7	27.3	1,831,711	63.5	10.9	37.5	854,289	63,677	18.6	14.4	16.8
32031	Washoe County, Nevada.............	346,385	35.4	34.5	400,493	65.5	5.1	43.5	198,018	76,220	13.8	18.1	13.4
33000	**NEW HAMPSHIRE**....................	1,008,318	32.1	40.2	1,164,253	66.7	3.6	67.0	548,026	88,465	11.5	22.9	7.6
33005	Cheshire County, New Hampshire...................................	54,988	41.2	28.7	64,872	62.3	3.2	39.1	28,266	67,344	15.8	15.8	7.9
33009	Grafton County, New Hampshire...................................	65,399	31.6	46.0	78,867	61.8	3.1	40.8	35,199	80,866	12.7	20.9	6.9
33011	Hillsborough County, New Hampshire...................................	304,324	30.9	41.4	349,991	70.5	3.6	48.8	167,899	91,627	10.0	23.7	7.5
33013	Merrimack County, New Hampshire...................................	112,957	35.9	37.7	130,743	64.6	4.3	41.0	58,733	80,918	13.5	19.2	8.6
33015	Rockingham County, New Hampshire...................................	234,036	27.6	45.5	265,176	69.7	4.0	47.8	127,882	104,664	7.7	29.0	6.1
33017	Strafford County, New Hampshire...................................	88,832	28.2	42.1	112,236	68.0	3.2	44.7	52,067	95,733	11.0	24.6	7.3
34000	**NEW JERSEY**	6,474,427	34.5	43.1	7,489,289	65.6	8.0	64.4	3,497,945	89,296	14.0	27.4	10.9
34001	Atlantic County, New Jersey........	193,469	43.4	32.3	224,620	61.9	10.2	35.0	112,299	66,388	18.0	15.2	15.5
34003	Bergen County, New Jersey.........	677,243	26.1	53.0	777,161	67.5	8.3	43.5	352,030	105,171	10.8	34.3	6.9
34005	Burlington County, New Jersey....	331,265	30.7	43.2	381,560	65.9	6.6	42.3	175,859	94,397	10.3	27.4	7.0
34007	Camden County, New Jersey.......	363,076	38.7	36.1	418,498	65.6	8.6	41.2	201,158	78,347	16.8	20.1	14.1
34009	Cape May County, New Jersey	74,047	33.6	40.8	81,385	56.6	6.2	NA	48,860	78,657	14.0	18.4	10.8
34011	Cumberland County, New Jersey	103,800	57.1	18.3	121,314	54.2	5.8	38.5	53,883	58,389	20.7	10.9	17.7
34013	Essex County, New Jersey............	580,052	39.6	38.5	675,799	64.8	10.9	41.0	322,453	66,198	22.0	21.7	15.9
34015	Gloucester County, New Jersey ...	212,360	36.9	36.6	247,169	65.0	6.8	41.8	112,502	94,412	11.1	27.3	8.4
34017	Hudson County, New Jersey........	509,351	35.6	47.6	574,228	69.2	7.6	47.3	292,000	80,329	18.6	25.1	16.0
34019	Hunterdon County, New Jersey	95,892	25.2	54.3	110,125	64.1	5.3	44.5	51,292	121,982	8.0	39.1	3.9
34021	Mercer County, New Jersey.........	261,325	33.0	45.9	313,405	63.6	7.6	40.1	143,970	87,662	14.9	25.7	12.7
34023	Middlesex County, New Jersey	596,637	33.6	45.1	698,337	66.8	7.6	42.9	307,831	99,427	11.8	28.6	9.4
34025	Monmouth County, New Jersey ..	457,330	25.5	50.2	528,640	66.4	7.2	42.6	250,738	108,000	12.1	36.3	6.9
34027	Morris County, New Jersey..........	363,623	23.9	57.0	419,619	67.9	7.0	44.7	192,847	122,962	7.9	40.7	6.0
34029	Ocean County, New Jersey..........	440,359	40.4	32.4	505,122	59.7	7.3	35.8	240,736	75,719	14.2	21.1	8.5
34031	Passaic County, New Jersey.........	346,696	47.4	30.6	408,372	66.0	10.8	41.2	177,063	75,430	17.6	21.5	21.1
34033	Salem County, New Jersey	45,591	47.4	25.8	52,240	60.3	8.9	35.4	24,973	69,886	15.6	15.1	13.4
34035	Somerset County, New Jersey	244,001	23.0	58.2	282,578	69.3	7.0	48.4	130,939	124,764	7.5	40.9	5.3
34037	Sussex County, New Jersey..........	106,411	31.9	40.3	121,424	67.5	6.4	45.3	58,767	99,904	8.6	28.2	4.7
34039	Union County, New Jersey	391,116	40.0	38.2	454,808	67.5	8.2	44.8	201,392	86,764	12.5	27.8	10.1
34041	Warren County, New Jersey	80,783	39.0	36.5	92,885	62.8	6.2	40.1	46,353	81,159	15.4	20.1	12.8
35000	**NEW MEXICO**	1,450,549	38.2	30.1	1,700,082	56.9	7.7	62.8	834,007	53,992	23.6	11.4	22.4
35001	Bernalillo County, New Mexico ...	472,615	31.8	37.9	551,453	62.3	5.9	40.0	285,185	59,640	20.7	13.8	20.4
35013	Doña Ana County, New Mexico ..	138,777	41.9	30.1	176,124	57.4	7.2	32.3	85,021	45,178	28.2	8.7	26.7
35025	Lea County, New Mexico	44,720	58.8	16.5	52,730	57.6	15.0	NA	24,390	50,725	27.1	8.6	22.1
35031	McKinley County, New Mexico....	45,876	53.5	13.7	54,936	46.8	8.5	34.2	20,949	41,643	38.1	6.1	40.7
35035	Otero County, New Mexico.........	46,071	49.2	21.1	55,095	51.6	11.2	NA	24,034	51,214	22.8	7.6	25.5
35043	Sandoval County, New Mexico....	106,509	28.7	33.8	122,123	58.5	7.9	39.1	56,655	72,151	10.9	15.5	17.7
35045	San Juan County, New Mexico....	79,371	47.5	15.6	94,363	51.6	10.5	30.9	40,844	47,819	29.3	8.5	29.7
35049	Santa Fe County, New Mexico.....	118,349	24.6	46.2	132,192	57.9	7.5	35.1	70,152	67,341	17.2	18.3	13.6
35061	Valencia County, New Mexico	53,279	48.6	16.9	61,845	48.6	10.1	NA	28,875	48,188	25.9	6.0	26.9

Table B-2. Counties — What: Education, Employment, and Income, 2021—*Continued*

STATE County	Educational attainment			Employment status				Household income and benefits				
	Total population 25 years and over	Percent with a high school diploma or less	Percent with a bachelor's degree or more	Total population 16 years and over	Labor force participation (percent)	Percent unemployed	Percent age 16 years and over who worked full-time year-round in the past 12 months	Total households	Median household income in the past 12 months (in 2021 inflation-adjusted dollars)	Income less than $25,000 (percent)	Income greater than $150,000 (percent)	Percent who received cash public assistance or food stamps/ SNAP
ACS table number:	C15003	C15003	C15003	C23001	C23001	C23001	S2402	B19001	B19049	B19001	B19001	B19058
STATE County code — Column number:	1	2	3	4	5	6	7	8	9	10	11	12
36000 **NEW YORK**	13,987,094	36.3	39.9	16,210,453	62.5	8.7	62.0	7,652,666	74,314	18.5	21.7	17.1
36001 Albany County, New York	213,786	27.1	45.9	263,455	63.2	6.7	40.2	132,171	75,232	15.7	18.0	13.5
36005 Bronx County, New York	941,302	51.4	23.0	1,114,497	58.1	16.1	31.8	533,004	43,011	32.5	8.1	38.7
36007 Broome County, New York	133,043	35.7	31.2	164,528	60.2	6.9	36.4	84,452	55,591	21.9	11.1	14.3
36009 Cattaraugus County, New York ...	52,748	51.3	20.2	62,103	55.7	4.8	33.8	32,562	55,153	23.8	5.7	17.7
36011 Cayuga County, New York	56,124	43.0	23.5	63,373	54.5	4.0	34.9	32,392	63,511	20.8	11.1	20.6
36013 Chautauqua County, New York...	90,332	45.6	24.4	104,454	49.4	6.0	30.3	53,309	46,661	26.5	5.7	20.4
36015 Chemung County, New York	59,845	44.6	27.8	68,241	54.1	6.9	36.7	35,407	60,219	21.9	8.8	19.6
36019 Clinton County, New York	55,390	45.6	26.3	67,323	56.3	4.8	36.4	33,860	60,285	21.8	7.8	16.7
36027 Dutchess County, New York........	211,594	31.4	42.1	251,369	62.4	6.4	39.9	118,175	88,051	13.5	24.6	10.3
36029 Erie County, New York	674,510	32.0	38.9	781,093	62.8	6.8	38.8	412,870	63,035	19.9	14.0	18.1
36045 Jefferson County, New York........	75,886	37.6	29.6	91,946	63.7	5.4	34.3	48,628	60,398	14.7	8.1	14.4
36047 Kings County, New York	1,842,478	39.1	41.8	2,102,166	63.8	11.2	37.3	1,001,868	67,567	22.5	19.9	25.1
36053 Madison County, New York	46,143	38.5	30.7	56,092	55.9	5.4	35.3	25,294	67,495	18.7	15.3	11.8
36055 Monroe County, New York	527,832	32.3	40.4	618,384	64.0	6.6	40.6	318,883	65,957	17.8	14.8	15.4
36059 Nassau County, New York	976,200	29.7	49.7	1,128,864	66.0	6.6	44.1	459,452	125,696	9.0	41.6	6.9
36061 New York County, New York.......	1,213,339	22.8	62.5	1,368,422	66.0	10.6	41.4	737,575	84,435	21.1	31.8	17.1
36063 Niagara County, New York.........	152,572	39.7	27.9	174,470	62.1	7.5	37.3	90,975	61,340	18.8	12.4	15.5
36065 Oneida County, New York..........	160,158	41.0	27.1	186,321	56.7	5.6	36.8	93,373	60,215	19.5	10.5	17.6
36067 Onondaga County, New York	325,594	33.4	37.9	384,636	61.7	5.8	38.8	198,132	65,541	19.9	14.8	16.9
36069 Ontario County, New York	81,003	32.3	39.7	93,528	62.3	5.6	39.4	47,607	77,972	12.2	17.8	9.2
36071 Orange County, New York	259,965	37.5	33.8	313,357	64.3	6.6	39.5	137,561	90,405	13.7	24.9	10.4
36075 Oswego County, New York	80,236	48.4	20.4	96,025	59.9	8.7	35.7	46,924	59,423	22.7	9.3	18.4
36079 Putnam County, New York	71,760	32.6	44.6	81,567	60.4	5.1	41.6	35,166	106,891	12.0	34.0	5.5
36081 Queens County, New York	1,698,378	43.3	35.3	1,917,787	61.9	11.8	36.3	820,686	73,262	17.7	19.0	17.6
36083 Rensselaer County, New York.....	114,196	35.0	35.5	132,595	62.5	6.2	40.8	66,431	75,676	17.9	17.9	11.4
36085 Richmond County, New York	346,022	40.0	37.4	399,911	58.4	7.5	40.4	170,762	86,054	15.1	26.1	14.7
36087 Rockland County, New York........	209,076	33.6	41.9	250,039	62.7	8.5	36.8	102,609	99,087	13.3	30.0	13.8
36089 St. Lawrence County, New York..	72,219	47.0	23.9	89,097	52.3	7.5	30.7	42,298	55,775	22.7	6.4	15.1
36091 Saratoga County, New York	173,344	29.6	43.8	197,574	65.4	3.9	44.3	100,226	86,804	12.9	23.0	9.4
36093 Schenectady County, New York ..	109,871	32.7	34.7	129,371	61.6	6.6	41.5	66,910	75,284	17.7	14.3	13.0
36101 Steuben County, New York	66,268	41.7	26.4	75,454	58.9	7.3	37.0	39,500	57,378	20.2	11.1	13.5
36103 Suffolk County, New York..........	1,076,738	34.1	40.6	1,253,053	66.4	5.7	43.3	511,951	113,683	9.6	36.2	7.9
36105 Sullivan County, New York.........	56,295	42.6	29.7	65,018	58.5	6.5	NA	32,529	54,276	22.2	16.4	15.5
36109 Tompkins County, New York	59,716	21.8	58.5	94,552	58.0	7.1	32.7	44,469	66,441	17.1	17.1	10.9
36111 Ulster County, New York............	136,944	31.6	41.1	155,741	60.0	6.5	38.6	75,053	78,938	16.0	23.3	8.5
36113 Warren County, New York	49,775	35.0	35.5	55,249	60.0	4.7	39.3	29,729	73,028	14.0	16.5	12.5
36117 Wayne County, New York	65,397	40.2	26.0	74,338	63.6	5.3	43.0	38,634	64,993	15.2	9.4	14.0
36119 Westchester County, New York...	698,730	26.3	54.4	809,402	65.3	7.9	42.1	371,736	110,705	13.4	37.7	11.5
37000 **NORTH CAROLINA**	7,245,632	35.2	34.9	8,524,268	62.2	5.7	65.6	4,179,632	61,972	19.3	13.9	15.0
37001 Alamance County, North Carolina.............	115,642	40.1	28.9	139,425	61.9	5.7	41.9	69,343	58,400	17.8	7.4	13.1
37019 Brunswick County, North Carolina.............	115,401	30.3	35.4	126,504	49.7	5.1	29.6	65,337	65,374	16.5	12.4	11.8
37021 Buncombe County, North Carolina.............	201,458	30.0	45.4	229,261	59.0	6.3	38.1	97,345	64,532	17.4	15.0	12.2
37023 Burke County, North Carolina	64,289	44.1	21.8	73,862	57.4	5.6	NA	35,709	55,529	21.0	6.4	19.7
37025 Cabarrus County, North Carolina	151,852	34.7	35.3	180,305	68.4	5.6	43.7	73,486	79,672	13.5	16.8	10.2
37027 Caldwell County, North Carolina.	57,514	50.2	19.2	66,415	58.0	8.3	NA	32,600	41,210	32.8	7.5	13.3
37031 Carteret County, North Carolina .	52,535	30.8	32.5	58,565	55.3	5.7	34.9	30,589	62,907	18.1	13.5	12.3
37035 Catawba County, North Carolina	113,032	44.0	24.9	131,617	59.4	6.3	40.5	64,302	59,603	20.3	9.6	15.7
37037 Chatham County, North Carolina	56,858	29.3	50.1	65,103	53.3	3.0	NA	31,474	84,555	20.7	28.8	10.3
37045 Cleveland County, North Carolina	69,249	45.9	17.7	80,702	59.7	6.3	NA	40,296	47,150	24.4	6.5	20.0
37049 Craven County, North Carolina ...	67,073	32.2	28.9	81,621	59.9	4.3	34.5	42,139	57,359	19.8	7.7	13.2
37051 Cumberland County, North Carolina.............	209,143	31.5	28.8	260,059	65.9	7.4	34.3	129,898	52,372	22.1	7.5	20.3

STATE County code	STATE County	Educational attainment			Employment status				Household income and benefits				
		Total population 25 years and over	Percent with a high school diploma or less	Percent with a bachelor's degree or more	Total population 16 years and over	Labor force participation (percent)	Percent unemployed	Percent age 16 years and over who worked full-time year-round in the past 12 months	Total households	Median household income in the past 12 months (in 2021 inflation-adjusted dollars)	Income less than $25,000 (percent)	Income greater than $150,000 (percent)	Percent who received cash public assistance or food stamps/SNAP
	ACS table number:	C15003	C15003	C15003	C23001	C23001	C23001	S2402	B19001	B19049	B19001	B19001	B19058
	Column number:	1	2	3	4	5	6	7	8	9	10	11	12
	NORTH CAROLINA—Cont.												
37057	Davidson County, North Carolina	121,048	47.7	19.9	138,626	55.6	5.0	39.9	66,245	52,205	21.6	8.1	15.9
37063	Durham County, North Carolina..	228,446	25.1	53.9	268,419	65.6	5.5	46.0	138,497	71,403	14.3	17.7	12.1
37067	Forsyth County, North Carolina ...	260,296	35.0	36.7	308,984	61.8	6.0	40.9	155,985	59,879	21.4	12.7	18.4
37069	Franklin County, North Carolina..	49,846	42.6	27.2	58,010	60.9	6.1	NA	26,689	64,064	19.6	9.2	16.7
37071	Gaston County, North Carolina ...	160,733	41.3	24.4	185,621	61.8	5.8	42.6	93,913	54,734	22.7	10.4	19.9
37081	Guilford County, North Carolina .	363,677	31.5	38.8	437,091	64.5	5.5	42.2	212,574	60,734	19.2	12.4	18.1
37085	Harnett County, North Carolina ..	89,793	40.3	24.2	105,315	59.1	5.0	35.7	49,555	62,478	18.1	8.6	15.8
37089	Henderson County, North Carolina............	88,200	31.7	38.2	97,855	55.5	4.5	36.7	50,136	59,669	16.6	11.4	12.7
37097	Iredell County, North Carolina.....	134,015	37.2	33.2	154,477	64.7	6.0	42.9	73,434	69,410	15.4	17.1	9.2
37101	Johnston County, North Carolina	151,189	40.8	27.5	174,263	65.3	3.3	46.2	82,113	69,394	18.6	12.2	17.5
37109	Lincoln County, North Carolina ...	64,818	41.8	28.5	73,125	60.7	4.5	45.2	36,361	74,201	14.1	17.2	11.5
37119	Mecklenburg County, North Carolina............	765,685	25.7	49.8	893,307	71.7	4.7	50.8	458,344	74,890	12.9	20.4	10.5
37125	Moore County, North Carolina....	74,066	25.1	40.8	82,526	58.2	5.6	NA	43,554	67,160	16.4	19.3	10.4
37127	Nash County, North Carolina	65,795	41.6	23.0	76,893	62.8	5.7	43.1	38,029	56,560	19.3	10.6	19.1
37129	New Hanover County, North Carolina............	161,448	26.2	43.4	192,552	64.6	5.6	40.9	103,762	66,097	17.0	16.2	10.4
37133	Onslow County, North Carolina ..	111,047	42.1	23.8	161,136	68.2	4.2	26.7	73,121	55,534	19.8	8.8	13.2
37135	Orange County, North Carolina...	93,928	17.7	63.1	124,857	62.1	5.0	39.3	56,263	80,294	18.8	26.4	6.5
37147	Pitt County, North Carolina.........	105,102	33.7	33.6	141,122	61.4	9.2	39.8	75,578	44,450	29.4	9.5	19.1
37151	Randolph County, North Carolina	100,414	47.8	16.4	115,873	60.1	4.3	41.7	55,948	57,367	18.7	7.6	16.3
37155	Robeson County, North Carolina.	75,132	56.2	14.3	90,274	52.4	5.2	35.7	43,529	37,008	34.3	4.3	34.4
37157	Rockingham County, North Carolina............	67,637	49.1	14.5	74,969	54.3	7.9	NA	38,481	42,901	33.1	6.0	18.4
37159	Rowan County, North Carolina ...	102,730	43.7	20.0	117,722	59.0	7.1	38.1	57,024	56,408	22.8	9.3	18.3
37171	Surry County, North Carolina	51,341	45.1	20.1	58,245	56.6	5.0	39.7	30,317	51,950	22.4	6.1	18.8
37179	Union County, North Carolina.....	157,452	32.9	39.5	189,055	67.4	5.1	45.0	83,407	86,606	8.7	25.1	9.5
37183	Wake County, North Carolina	779,711	20.0	56.8	915,995	69.2	5.3	48.0	439,911	91,299	12.5	26.7	8.2
37191	Wayne County, North Carolina....	77,954	45.8	20.3	92,465	60.4	4.6	38.7	46,932	47,595	24.7	7.5	26.8
37193	Wilkes County, North Carolina....	47,913	53.6	19.5	54,147	52.0	9.8	NA	26,770	43,933	27.3	5.0	21.1
37195	Wilson County, North Carolina ...	54,675	53.3	17.8	62,609	56.0	5.0	NA	32,868	47,201	29.2	6.6	22.5
38000	**NORTH DAKOTA**.....................	506,739	32.7	31.7	610,714	68.1	2.8	65.2	322,511	66,519	17.5	13.6	7.3
38015	Burleigh County, North Dakota ...	67,599	29.7	37.9	78,982	67.9	2.5	46.0	39,295	68,424	14.4	15.9	8.1
38017	Cass County, North Dakota.........	118,968	23.9	42.7	147,939	75.9	3.0	47.8	83,761	66,009	16.3	16.0	6.7
38035	Grand Forks County, North Dakota	42,845	26.0	37.9	58,498	71.2	2.4	40.5	31,152	65,184	21.9	10.4	6.4
38101	Ward County, North Dakota........	43,082	34.0	31.6	54,368	70.0	3.3	NA	28,795	71,061	14.8	11.9	6.4
39000	**OHIO**	8,117,973	41.1	30.7	9,480,334	62.6	5.4	65.6	4,832,922	62,262	19.1	12.9	14.5
39003	Allen County, Ohio	68,062	51.0	18.5	80,529	57.8	8.2	35.3	41,021	51,497	21.8	7.8	20.6
39007	Ashtabula County, Ohio..............	68,750	56.4	15.8	78,527	57.4	7.8	36.2	39,915	46,771	23.4	5.1	19.7
39013	Belmont County, Ohio	48,674	60.1	17.3	55,035	50.6	4.9	32.4	26,949	50,993	24.9	5.6	15.4
39017	Butler County, Ohio	250,046	40.8	33.1	309,966	63.6	6.3	41.3	146,057	72,820	16.5	17.5	10.8
39023	Clark County, Ohio	93,487	47.0	18.9	108,294	62.1	6.1	39.1	57,013	59,431	21.7	9.6	21.0
39025	Clermont County, Ohio...............	145,276	40.4	30.5	168,838	63.7	5.3	43.4	84,219	69,489	14.6	16.9	10.6
39029	Columbiana County, Ohio...........	73,040	55.3	18.0	83,908	57.4	5.9	36.7	41,047	49,265	28.6	8.6	16.4
39035	Cuyahoga County, Ohio..............	887,374	36.2	35.5	1,021,604	63.1	7.6	40.3	557,572	55,132	23.1	12.1	19.0
39041	Delaware County, Ohio...............	147,423	19.6	57.4	171,265	71.6	3.7	50.0	80,640	117,224	6.6	34.7	5.0
39043	Erie County, Ohio.......................	54,660	46.9	26.1	60,924	58.4	6.6	37.7	32,926	58,403	24.2	9.6	15.3
39045	Fairfield County, Ohio	109,339	38.2	31.2	126,863	62.7	4.3	43.6	59,818	81,226	12.4	16.8	10.7
39049	Franklin County, Ohio	887,388	31.8	41.8	1,046,269	69.0	5.6	46.1	549,475	65,988	16.4	14.3	13.1
39055	Geauga County, Ohio	66,658	34.8	39.8	76,923	62.1	4.7	41.8	35,431	91,305	10.0	27.2	6.4
39057	Greene County, Ohio	114,524	27.4	43.1	137,925	61.8	2.7	40.5	67,822	79,271	15.2	18.5	8.0
39061	Hamilton County, Ohio	559,932	32.9	41.3	656,834	66.2	5.2	43.7	353,674	64,065	21.2	15.6	14.9
39063	Hancock County, Ohio................	52,123	38.9	28.5	NA	NA	NA	NA	31,951	64,024	12.2	13.8	12.6
39085	Lake County, Ohio	168,998	36.7	31.4	191,981	66.6	4.5	46.9	99,990	74,273	12.1	15.5	7.5
39089	Licking County, Ohio..................	121,661	41.3	28.3	144,868	61.7	3.8	43.5	67,761	73,325	15.3	14.8	12.3

Table B-2. Counties — What: Education, Employment, and Income, 2021—*Continued*

STATE County code	STATE County	Educational attainment			Employment status				Household income and benefits				
		Total population 25 years and over	Percent with a high school diploma or less	Percent with a bachelor's degree or more	Total population 16 years and over	Labor force participation (percent)	Percent unemployed	Percent age 16 years and over who worked full-time year-round in the past 12 months	Total households	Median household income in the past 12 months (in 2021 inflation-adjusted dollars)	Income less than $25,000 (percent)	Income greater than $150,000 (percent)	Percent who received cash public assistance or food stamps/ SNAP
	ACS table number:	C15003	C15003	C15003	C23001	C23001	C23001	S2402	B19001	B19049	B19001	B19001	B19058
	Column number:	1	2	3	4	5	6	7	8	9	10	11	12
	OHIO—Cont.												
39093	Lorain County, Ohio..................	220,715	40.9	26.6	254,456	61.4	6.3	41.1	124,879	62,448	17.8	13.2	11.3
39095	Lucas County, Ohio...................	293,578	39.2	29.0	340,578	64.3	7.4	40.0	184,315	52,687	23.9	9.9	16.8
39099	Mahoning County, Ohio	162,231	44.7	27.2	186,232	57.6	7.3	32.6	98,924	49,520	26.0	7.4	21.6
39101	Marion County, Ohio................	46,570	54.4	13.8	52,809	51.2	5.8	NA	24,692	48,919	23.7	5.5	18.8
39103	Medina County, Ohio................	129,434	34.1	37.2	148,510	66.5	2.9	45.3	72,233	86,646	10.5	20.3	8.3
39109	Miami County, Ohio.................	76,440	44.3	25.7	87,499	64.2	4.2	42.2	43,896	64,345	16.4	14.3	9.8
39113	Montgomery County, Ohio	367,358	35.5	29.8	430,283	62.6	5.9	39.6	226,787	56,471	19.9	10.9	15.0
39119	Muskingum County, Ohio..........	59,029	52.6	13.7	69,006	59.6	5.2	39.8	33,876	51,173	24.8	9.3	21.0
39133	Portage County, Ohio...............	107,653	45.7	29.4	135,676	62.8	5.5	38.5	63,096	64,471	21.3	15.1	10.7
39139	Richland County, Ohio..............	87,623	52.3	17.4	101,247	58.1	5.2	35.5	49,536	51,158	24.0	7.8	15.4
39141	Ross County, Ohio	54,883	57.0	16.7	63,053	55.4	6.2	NA	30,550	50,395	28.0	10.1	20.9
39145	Scioto County, Ohio.................	50,855	56.7	18.8	59,201	44.6	8.2	NA	27,496	40,522	35.7	7.1	26.5
39151	Stark County, Ohio..................	262,169	45.8	24.9	302,176	61.6	4.7	40.1	156,111	59,127	17.4	10.9	16.4
39153	Summit County, Ohio...............	382,242	37.0	35.6	438,939	63.2	5.2	41.1	229,060	63,117	19.5	14.1	19.2
39155	Trumbull County, Ohio..............	143,611	53.4	21.7	164,902	54.1	4.8	35.4	84,911	51,057	23.7	5.7	16.2
39157	Tuscarawas County, Ohio..........	64,323	54.7	17.6	74,320	59.4	3.8	37.7	38,684	58,060	17.1	9.8	14.4
39165	Warren County, Ohio................	168,199	33.4	41.9	195,928	63.7	3.8	45.2	89,396	95,817	7.3	26.2	5.3
39169	Wayne County, Ohio................	76,801	54.3	24.0	92,759	60.4	4.5	37.6	44,215	59,666	16.1	9.1	9.0
39173	Wood County, Ohio..................	83,693	34.4	38.6	108,933	64.7	6.5	40.9	54,012	63,620	17.4	12.7	8.5
40000	**OKLAHOMA**	2,639,889	42.0	27.9	3,140,799	61.0	5.9	66.7	1,547,967	55,826	21.3	10.1	15.1
40017	Canadian County, Oklahoma	106,103	36.2	32.8	125,879	68.5	4.7	45.9	57,753	74,768	13.0	12.5	9.9
40027	Cleveland County, Oklahoma	194,014	33.9	35.7	243,995	64.2	5.5	41.8	116,142	67,172	15.8	11.2	12.7
40031	Comanche County, Oklahoma	77,411	41.7	24.3	95,871	61.0	7.5	34.3	44,822	49,325	23.5	7.1	14.6
40037	Creek County, Oklahoma	49,564	48.4	19.8	57,021	57.7	4.1	41.1	28,339	52,818	22.2	8.5	14.0
40101	Muskogee County, Oklahoma.....	43,926	50.7	19.5	51,656	55.5	6.6	36.4	25,965	43,437	25.1	5.2	19.7
40109	Oklahoma County, Oklahoma.....	523,019	36.1	34.0	618,729	66.0	5.9	44.2	324,819	57,764	20.3	12.3	17.1
40119	Payne County, Oklahoma..........	45,724	28.0	44.3	68,138	58.7	4.9	NA	31,537	49,348	28.8	6.8	12.5
40125	Pottawatomie County, Oklahoma	48,748	45.1	19.1	58,256	56.4	4.4	38.4	26,650	51,451	22.5	7.1	16.3
40131	Rogers County, Oklahoma	66,577	41.4	26.6	76,812	62.1	6.4	43.3	35,815	68,777	13.8	14.6	11.7
40143	Tulsa County, Oklahoma	444,632	36.0	34.6	523,177	64.7	6.5	43.2	270,263	58,954	19.8	12.7	13.7
40145	Wagoner County, Oklahoma.......	56,954	38.2	29.8	66,114	63.1	5.1	44.5	30,502	70,313	14.8	14.8	9.6
41000	**OREGON**	3,030,635	30.1	36.3	3,487,919	61.6	6.3	62.0	1,702,599	71,562	16.2	17.0	18.1
41003	Benton County, Oregon.............	59,125	18.8	54.9	82,376	58.4	6.7	30.1	39,350	64,163	21.8	17.6	14.4
41005	Clackamas County, Oregon........	303,395	24.9	40.0	344,306	62.7	5.9	40.6	161,945	91,329	12.2	24.3	12.5
41017	Deschutes County, Oregon	152,916	26.2	41.2	169,974	62.0	4.8	39.4	83,763	79,796	13.2	20.2	11.5
41019	Douglas County, Oregon...........	83,831	40.3	18.2	93,245	49.4	6.5	28.1	45,981	51,166	23.5	7.7	21.4
41029	Jackson County, Oregon............	161,605	32.5	33.1	182,687	56.3	7.7	32.7	90,817	64,249	17.8	11.0	18.2
41033	Josephine County, Oregon.........	66,489	39.0	21.0	74,299	49.5	9.7	NA	36,755	48,785	23.7	9.2	25.8
41035	Klamath County, Oregon...........	49,292	43.6	19.8	56,375	52.4	10.7	NA	28,888	46,721	24.8	7.0	25.6
41039	Lane County, Oregon.................	270,064	28.9	32.4	322,719	59.8	7.2	33.9	160,158	61,712	18.3	11.6	21.7
41043	Linn County, Oregon.................	90,157	35.5	23.5	103,634	60.6	6.9	36.9	51,347	65,196	16.4	9.5	21.9
41047	Marion County, Oregon	232,221	38.6	25.3	273,996	60.0	5.9	38.6	124,719	64,406	15.4	11.6	22.9
41051	Multnomah County, Oregon	596,677	23.3	49.1	674,147	69.3	7.0	42.9	348,216	78,319	15.5	20.8	19.1
41053	Polk County, Oregon.................	58,715	28.5	33.1	71,839	61.2	3.7	NA	33,425	71,532	14.3	17.6	22.2
41059	Umatilla County, Oregon	53,157	46.5	17.3	61,919	56.5	6.9	NA	27,247	58,329	16.1	9.0	26.0
41067	Washington County, Oregon.......	420,656	23.4	47.0	485,618	67.0	5.4	45.0	233,615	92,147	11.2	26.9	13.4
41071	Yamhill County, Oregon.............	73,657	36.5	29.1	88,384	62.7	5.9	39.0	38,988	77,256	16.1	14.5	13.4
42000	**PENNSYLVANIA**	9,161,945	41.4	34.5	10,602,171	62.4	6.4	65.6	5,228,956	68,957	17.8	16.6	15.6
42001	Adams County, Pennsylvania.......	74,093	51.8	28.7	87,049	62.6	4.3	41.6	39,986	72,985	12.4	15.2	7.7
42003	Allegheny County, Pennsylvania..	901,520	30.1	45.2	1,033,672	64.4	6.2	42.4	545,892	69,091	18.5	17.8	14.5
42005	Armstrong County, Pennsylvania..	48,597	56.1	17.5	54,550	57.7	8.3	38.2	27,796	54,039	19.9	9.1	15.0
42007	Beaver County, Pennsylvania......	123,035	40.2	28.7	137,915	61.9	5.4	39.4	71,450	65,003	19.9	10.2	16.1
42011	Berks County, Pennsylvania........	294,555	50.1	26.2	345,128	62.9	6.2	40.1	164,312	68,658	17.6	15.9	17.6
42013	Blair County, Pennsylvania..........	87,847	53.5	24.4	99,740	57.6	5.5	38.3	49,795	57,361	19.0	8.6	16.3
42017	Bucks County, Pennsylvania	466,800	32.5	44.3	532,982	65.7	5.7	44.8	248,122	100,144	10.6	29.1	9.4
42019	Butler County, Pennsylvania	139,735	36.0	39.5	161,366	62.2	4.2	42.6	81,220	78,146	14.9	18.6	9.7

STATE / County	Educational attainment			Employment status				Household income and benefits				
	Total popula-tion 25 years and over	Percent with a high school diploma or less	Percent with a bachelor's degree or more	Total popula-tion 16 years and over	Labor force participation (percent)	Percent unem-ployed	Percent age 16 years and over who worked full-time year-round in the past 12 months	Total house-holds	Median household income in the past 12 months (in 2021 inflation-adjusted dollars)	Income less than $25,000 (percent)	Income greater than $150,000 (percent)	Percent who received cash public assistance or food stamps/ SNAP
ACS table number:	C15003	C15003	C15003	C23001	C23001	C23001	S2402	B19001	B19049	B19001	B19001	B19058
STATE County code — Column number:	1	2	3	4	5	6	7	8	9	10	11	12
PENNSYLVANIA—Cont.												
42021 Cambria County, Pennsylvania	95,014	49.7	23.4	110,309	53.4	6.6	34.5	55,283	52,995	22.2	8.5	18.8
42025 Carbon County, Pennsylvania......	47,220	55.0	16.4	53,858	62.6	12.6	NA	26,810	57,262	24.4	8.1	19.5
42027 Centre County, Pennsylvania.......	97,255	37.4	45.3	136,930	57.5	5.7	33.5	57,518	66,789	19.8	17.4	8.6
42029 Chester County, Pennsylvania	370,783	24.4	56.3	433,230	68.8	4.4	47.1	204,047	109,601	9.5	34.6	6.8
42033 Clearfield County, Pennsylvania...	59,844	53.4	22.9	67,306	51.3	4.8	33.9	31,570	55,193	21.8	7.2	16.7
42039 Crawford County, Pennsylvania...	58,957	53.5	22.5	68,151	52.7	7.0	34.8	32,896	55,593	22.0	9.9	18.5
42041 Cumberland County, Pennsylvania................................	184,521	37.2	38.8	214,837	64.4	4.7	41.5	104,768	82,691	11.0	18.7	8.9
42043 Dauphin County, Pennsylvania...	200,530	45.0	31.8	229,596	63.8	5.3	44.2	120,423	66,454	17.3	13.3	12.8
42045 Delaware County, Pennsylvania...	393,553	32.0	42.9	459,604	66.2	8.6	43.3	218,280	78,220	14.3	23.4	14.4
42049 Erie County, Pennsylvania............	187,160	43.2	29.2	219,172	59.1	7.6	37.5	110,561	56,851	22.9	8.8	20.5
42051 Fayette County, Pennsylvania	94,495	58.0	18.2	105,711	53.9	8.8	34.2	55,986	47,981	25.7	7.7	23.2
42055 Franklin County, Pennsylvania	109,934	50.5	25.1	126,008	61.9	4.4	40.2	62,081	66,715	14.7	13.7	11.1
42063 Indiana County, Pennsylvania.......	54,976	48.4	24.7	69,422	58.1	5.4	36.3	32,956	52,023	22.9	8.6	16.5
42069 Lackawanna County, Pennsylvania................................	153,170	43.1	30.5	177,091	60.4	7.0	40.2	88,294	62,136	21.0	11.8	18.7
42071 Lancaster County, Pennsylvania...	376,040	47.1	29.7	437,874	65.8	3.8	42.7	210,063	75,688	12.8	16.4	11.1
42073 Lawrence County, Pennsylvania...	61,894	50.1	19.1	70,589	59.5	7.7	41.3	36,286	59,536	21.0	9.0	21.3
42075 Lebanon County, Pennsylvania....	99,281	50.1	24.9	114,959	62.9	5.0	41.0	54,906	72,732	15.3	14.0	15.7
42077 Lehigh County, Pennsylvania.......	256,466	42.3	32.6	299,217	64.0	6.4	42.5	141,505	68,738	17.7	17.0	15.5
42079 Luzerne County, Pennsylvania	233,076	46.4	26.0	268,525	59.9	6.9	39.7	134,132	60,020	19.9	10.0	18.6
42081 Lycoming County, Pennsylvania...	80,539	47.9	26.1	92,609	59.5	5.2	36.8	47,022	60,494	17.5	8.4	17.2
42085 Mercer County, Pennsylvania	78,794	48.9	26.5	91,836	54.0	5.7	33.1	46,701	54,067	20.5	9.0	15.7
42089 Monroe County, Pennsylvania	121,060	42.4	29.0	140,933	61.8	6.7	42.9	65,907	78,575	15.3	14.8	16.4
42091 Montgomery County, Pennsylvania................................	609,268	26.3	52.9	696,814	68.3	5.0	46.9	335,248	102,896	11.2	32.1	8.5
42095 Northampton County, Pennsylvania................................	221,352	39.6	33.6	259,410	63.5	5.5	41.8	122,615	79,578	12.0	18.0	11.5
42097 Northumberland County, Pennsylvania................................	66,350	56.7	19.9	75,833	58.9	5.3	38.7	37,823	50,751	20.9	6.6	18.6
42101 Philadelphia County, Pennsylvania................................	1,090,520	43.1	34.8	1,270,642	62.9	10.5	39.1	660,921	52,899	27.1	12.6	28.7
42107 Schuylkill County, Pennsylvania ...	104,826	56.7	19.8	118,279	54.8	7.5	36.7	58,212	58,614	19.2	9.5	18.3
42111 Somerset County, Pennsylvania...	55,442	60.2	16.0	61,704	54.7	7.4	36.4	29,115	54,352	21.2	6.3	14.3
42125 Washington County, Pennsylvania................................	150,693	41.1	33.1	172,337	62.9	4.2	42.3	88,544	68,408	16.2	16.1	13.8
42129 Westmoreland County, Pennsylvania................................	263,356	41.2	30.9	296,839	59.9	6.1	38.9	154,810	63,064	19.1	13.2	15.3
42133 York County, Pennsylvania	320,624	46.5	27.5	371,013	65.3	4.5	43.2	178,898	72,949	13.3	16.3	11.9
44000 **RHODE ISLAND**.........................	773,464	38.6	36.5	913,136	65.1	7.6	63.2	440,170	74,008	17.9	18.6	16.8
44003 Kent County, Rhode Island..........	126,158	35.0	35.0	142,869	66.5	5.5	44.2	73,182	73,159	16.4	19.3	14.4
44005 Newport County, Rhode Island....	64,518	27.5	53.1	73,275	63.0	6.7	38.4	38,311	88,090	17.3	24.2	12.2
44007 Providence County, Rhode Island	454,914	45.1	30.4	541,070	65.7	8.9	41.4	254,178	67,368	19.7	15.5	21.0
44009 Washington County, Rhode Island................................	92,883	24.8	50.6	112,417	62.9	6.0	38.7	54,044	90,427	13.8	25.0	6.6
45000 **SOUTH CAROLINA**...................	3,598,398	38.9	31.5	4,207,365	59.6	5.6	66.8	2,049,972	59,318	20.5	12.0	12.1
45003 Aiken County, South Carolina.....	121,057	42.5	27.9	137,807	57.2	7.1	38.2	67,224	55,138	20.0	11.1	12.0
45007 Anderson County, South Carolina	143,926	43.6	28.1	165,264	57.9	5.2	39.0	82,203	59,037	20.8	8.9	12.7
45013 Beaufort County, South Carolina.	138,647	28.0	45.2	162,344	53.2	3.0	29.8	76,249	70,501	14.4	18.8	6.7
45015 Berkeley County, South Carolina.	158,888	37.1	30.2	186,302	65.7	3.8	44.9	88,092	75,004	12.7	14.1	9.4
45019 Charleston County, South Carolina................................	297,184	26.5	48.2	340,963	65.4	5.3	45.3	169,851	72,147	18.4	19.1	8.8
45035 Dorchester County, South Carolina................................	110,619	34.3	34.6	129,474	63.9	6.5	45.7	58,435	70,009	14.4	18.0	8.1
45041 Florence County, South Carolina.	92,616	46.2	23.0	108,589	55.6	4.8	40.9	51,484	51,860	29.8	10.1	21.7
45045 Greenville County, South Carolina................................	365,917	31.4	41.7	426,485	64.2	5.0	43.2	212,333	68,540	15.2	16.1	9.3

Table B-2. Counties — What: Education, Employment, and Income, 2021—*Continued*

STATE County code	STATE County	Educational attainment			Employment status				Household income and benefits				
		Total population 25 years and over	Percent with a high school diploma or less	Percent with a bachelor's degree or more	Total population 16 years and over	Labor force participation (percent)	Percent unemployed	Percent age 16 years and over who worked full-time year-round in the past 12 months	Total households	Median household income in the past 12 months (in 2021 inflation-adjusted dollars)	Income less than $25,000 (percent)	Income greater than $150,000 (percent)	Percent who received cash public assistance or food stamps/ SNAP
	ACS table number:	C15003	C15003	C15003	C23001	C23001	C23001	S2402	B19001	B19049	B19001	B19001	B19058
	Column number:	1	2	3	4	5	6	7	8	9	10	11	12
	SOUTH CAROLINA—Cont.												
45047	Greenwood County, South Carolina................	46,341	43.7	23.5	55,620	55.9	4.4	41.7	26,577	52,636	22.9	6.2	13.8
45051	Horry County, South Carolina	277,044	39.6	25.5	308,854	52.3	6.9	31.3	145,335	55,819	19.2	8.9	8.7
45055	Kershaw County, South Carolina................	45,903	45.0	21.3	NA	NA	NA	NA	25,412	47,995	26.2	7.8	11.2
45057	Lancaster County, South Carolina................	71,147	37.9	35.5	81,821	57.5	2.3	NA	38,570	69,796	16.1	15.2	7.6
45059	Laurens County, South Carolina..	47,076	53.5	17.3	54,419	58.1	4.6	NA	26,580	56,624	22.4	5.0	23.2
45063	Lexington County, South Carolina................	208,590	34.4	33.8	238,994	63.7	5.0	45.3	120,968	64,800	15.6	11.6	9.9
45073	Oconee County, South Carolina....	59,152	44.3	24.6	66,460	51.3	8.1	NA	34,023	50,393	24.4	8.3	13.2
45075	Orangeburg County, South Carolina................	56,478	51.2	18.3	66,215	52.5	7.4	NA	32,017	34,685	38.0	3.5	19.7
45077	Pickens County, South Carolina...	84,827	42.8	30.0	110,756	56.0	4.0	35.6	51,996	48,489	28.3	9.7	10.6
45079	Richland County, South Carolina.	265,553	30.2	40.7	340,007	64.9	7.4	39.8	166,515	56,439	22.0	11.7	12.1
45083	Spartanburg County, South Carolina................	227,599	44.0	24.8	267,295	62.3	4.4	43.1	128,437	60,472	19.2	10.3	12.5
45085	Sumter County, South Carolina...	69,743	43.2	24.0	82,637	59.9	7.9	38.0	43,191	46,003	31.9	7.0	19.9
45091	York County, South Carolina.......	196,661	30.1	38.5	228,372	64.9	5.4	45.5	113,195	72,772	14.5	18.2	7.6
46000	**SOUTH DAKOTA**.....................	590,377	36.2	31.7	699,893	66.6	2.8	68.5	356,887	66,143	16.6	11.4	9.1
46083	Lincoln County, South Dakota.....	43,872	21.9	52.3	NA	NA	NA	NA	26,565	82,898	6.7	22.3	2.7
46099	Minnehaha County, South Dakota................	132,335	31.5	32.6	153,906	74.0	1.7	53.0	82,289	72,748	13.0	14.4	8.9
46103	Pennington County, South Dakota................	77,123	30.2	36.1	89,219	64.3	3.0	39.3	46,296	64,057	17.2	12.3	11.0
47000	**TENNESSEE**	4,814,533	41.5	30.5	5,616,708	61.2	5.3	67.8	2,770,395	59,695	19.8	12.4	13.0
47001	Anderson County, Tennessee	55,319	37.8	27.6	63,376	58.5	7.1	41.6	31,735	60,364	20.7	10.1	14.0
47009	Blount County, Tennessee	98,969	46.9	25.2	113,281	60.6	2.5	43.6	55,446	62,102	14.3	7.9	6.1
47011	Bradley County, Tennessee...........	76,012	44.5	21.4	88,593	58.4	8.1	39.5	43,025	56,139	18.3	7.3	14.2
47037	Davidson County, Tennessee.......	493,869	30.9	46.6	577,612	69.3	4.2	48.2	316,273	65,348	16.5	16.7	11.8
47059	Greene County, Tennessee..........	51,797	51.5	21.0	59,248	55.3	5.9	NA	28,585	56,488	22.5	8.5	14.1
47065	Hamilton County, Tennessee	258,674	33.8	36.1	300,665	63.7	5.0	42.6	151,676	66,096	19.1	13.8	11.2
47093	Knox County, Tennessee.............	329,006	32.0	40.5	396,600	63.8	4.5	43.5	198,914	64,894	19.0	15.2	10.3
47113	Madison County, Tennessee.........	66,458	41.4	29.3	79,343	59.2	5.5	39.5	39,730	53,720	24.2	9.2	15.8
47119	Maury County, Tennessee	73,477	35.4	26.5	NA	NA	NA	NA	41,309	68,840	12.6	15.6	9.8
47125	Montgomery County, Tennessee................	141,983	35.0	28.2	171,680	65.5	3.9	36.9	84,145	63,331	13.9	10.0	11.8
47141	Putnam County, Tennessee	52,990	39.5	30.0	67,245	65.6	4.4	39.2	33,652	52,278	22.3	10.9	12.7
47147	Robertson County, Tennessee......	51,207	50.4	21.1	58,902	59.9	5.1	40.5	27,233	65,139	14.5	11.2	11.4
47149	Rutherford County, Tennessee.....	225,679	34.9	37.7	274,420	70.4	3.7	50.1	121,944	78,201	11.1	15.0	8.3
47155	Sevier County, Tennessee	71,242	46.3	19.2	81,631	57.3	4.9	36.1	36,670	50,239	19.4	9.4	13.0
47157	Shelby County, Tennessee...........	611,379	37.3	34.3	718,319	64.6	8.1	43.6	366,593	54,841	22.1	13.2	17.3
47163	Sullivan County, Tennessee.........	117,538	44.7	24.6	132,773	55.0	7.1	35.2	68,804	48,063	27.4	9.7	16.0
47165	Sumner County, Tennessee.........	139,733	39.0	29.9	160,130	65.6	4.9	44.3	77,760	70,092	12.8	13.3	9.8
47179	Washington County, Tennessee................	93,674	35.0	34.9	112,364	60.1	5.8	40.1	56,752	56,009	20.1	13.2	11.1
47187	Williamson County, Tennessee	167,804	16.4	62.0	197,815	68.6	2.6	48.0	91,406	117,927	5.2	40.5	2.3
47189	Wilson County, Tennessee...........	105,153	35.2	37.4	121,169	65.3	5.2	46.0	55,047	80,960	12.5	19.4	6.9
48000	**TEXAS**	19,224,688	39.2	33.1	22,934,023	64.6	6.1	67.8	10,796,247	66,963	17.5	16.5	13.8
48005	Angelina County, Texas..............	57,616	45.5	18.3	67,332	54.9	5.9	NA	32,538	50,045	23.7	7.5	18.0
48021	Bastrop County, Texas................	71,262	46.2	26.0	NA	NA	NA	NA	36,341	80,423	13.7	22.5	9.9
48027	Bell County, Texas.....................	232,413	34.0	28.3	286,451	64.6	6.9	36.2	139,582	58,542	20.7	9.0	13.5
48029	Bexar County, Texas...................	1,314,267	38.8	30.9	1,576,383	65.7	6.4	42.1	742,826	63,057	18.1	13.3	17.4
48037	Bowie County, Texas..................	62,113	49.4	23.6	73,271	54.8	3.8	39.9	34,038	54,154	24.4	10.9	9.6
48039	Brazoria County, Texas...............	249,035	36.1	33.4	293,230	63.8	5.7	48.0	130,734	82,460	10.4	22.6	10.8
48041	Brazos County, Texas..................	129,137	32.9	42.2	193,444	60.7	5.4	36.1	86,154	49,362	26.1	12.5	8.8
48061	Cameron County, Texas..............	254,651	55.0	20.6	314,947	58.0	8.1	37.3	135,734	48,115	29.4	7.6	28.8

STATE County code	STATE County	Educational attainment			Employment status				Household income and benefits				
		Total population 25 years and over	Percent with a high school diploma or less	Percent with a bachelor's degree or more	Total population 16 years and over	Labor force participation (percent)	Percent unemployed	Percent age 16 years and over who worked full-time year-round in the past 12 months	Total households	Median household income in the past 12 months (in 2021 inflation-adjusted dollars)	Income less than $25,000 (percent)	Income greater than $150,000 (percent)	Percent who received cash public assistance or food stamps/SNAP
	ACS table number:	C15003	C15003	C15003	C23001	C23001	C23001	S2402	B19001	B19049	B19001	B19001	B19058
	Column number:	1	2	3	4	5	6	7	8	9	10	11	12
	TEXAS—Cont.												
48085	Collin County, Texas..............	738,091	20.4	54.7	865,710	69.4	5.2	50.6	399,810	101,494	8.7	31.5	4.6
48091	Comal County, Texas..................	122,483	28.6	40.6	141,236	63.6	3.5	43.1	67,392	93,829	8.8	26.3	6.0
48099	Coryell County, Texas................	52,838	38.5	18.9	67,793	56.4	4.5	NA	26,980	62,737	13.8	9.4	11.2
48113	Dallas County, Texas..................	1,681,026	41.6	34.4	1,999,019	68.3	5.6	47.3	975,062	63,494	17.9	15.3	12.8
48121	Denton County, Texas................	631,822	22.7	48.7	743,888	72.5	5.4	51.6	350,081	97,671	9.5	27.9	7.4
48135	Ector County, Texas..................	95,780	56.6	16.2	117,856	66.4	10.9	46.1	64,169	57,473	19.4	7.4	14.0
48139	Ellis County, Texas......................	131,498	38.4	26.9	155,311	67.4	5.4	49.4	69,223	89,799	9.2	19.4	6.7
48141	El Paso County, Texas................	542,747	44.3	26.1	664,584	62.9	8.0	37.6	298,059	51,044	25.2	8.6	23.2
48157	Fort Bend County, Texas............	560,448	27.9	50.5	654,759	65.2	5.9	46.2	283,446	96,468	9.4	27.9	9.9
48167	Galveston County, Texas............	241,001	32.9	34.9	279,752	64.1	6.4	44.9	144,182	78,336	15.1	19.6	12.5
48181	Grayson County, Texas..............	94,750	37.1	26.6	109,970	61.5	3.3	44.3	56,005	62,919	16.3	14.5	9.4
48183	Gregg County, Texas..................	79,868	42.5	22.3	95,971	61.4	4.8	40.6	46,766	59,869	20.2	8.1	15.2
48187	Guadalupe County, Texas............	118,836	39.1	32.6	139,816	62.5	4.0	43.5	61,414	80,464	11.4	17.9	11.0
48201	Harris County, Texas..................	3,051,418	41.2	33.5	3,628,715	67.1	8.2	43.9	1,735,020	63,498	18.3	16.7	16.8
48203	Harrison County, Texas..............	45,617	44.0	22.4	54,526	56.2	8.8	NA	25,866	59,405	23.9	9.2	11.4
48209	Hays County, Texas	156,995	31.9	38.8	203,585	65.9	4.3	44.8	94,205	76,842	19.6	19.0	7.8
48213	Henderson County, Texas............	58,835	52.0	18.7	68,229	49.6	6.2	NA	32,576	49,830	27.1	6.9	16.9
48215	Hidalgo County, Texas................	504,147	57.0	20.0	633,534	57.1	9.0	35.2	268,598	44,818	30.4	6.5	31.9
48231	Hunt County, Texas..................	69,510	43.7	22.9	81,568	60.9	9.2	40.6	37,206	56,761	18.5	13.9	14.2
48245	Jefferson County, Texas..............	168,581	43.9	19.2	196,386	58.1	5.6	40.9	94,828	56,904	21.9	11.0	15.1
48251	Johnson County, Texas..............	123,020	47.1	24.5	145,162	63.3	3.5	48.2	64,338	77,933	13.1	14.0	7.9
48257	Kaufman County, Texas..............	99,272	35.8	27.7	117,669	64.0	4.4	47.1	50,212	72,175	12.0	13.9	10.1
48291	Liberty County, Texas	60,623	58.8	12.0	72,417	53.0	6.7	NA	29,290	55,697	17.5	10.9	16.8
48303	Lubbock County, Texas..............	187,893	36.2	33.7	249,539	66.4	5.3	44.8	124,689	57,798	24.0	12.8	12.5
48309	McLennan County, Texas............	161,943	36.9	28.2	206,359	62.8	4.9	42.6	97,065	60,437	19.7	14.1	11.5
48329	Midland County, Texas..............	107,121	33.4	34.8	126,585	73.4	4.8	NA	66,052	82,248	13.8	22.7	9.1
48339	Montgomery County, Texas........	425,252	32.7	40.7	498,672	63.1	4.7	46.0	232,095	86,903	13.1	26.7	10.4
48355	Nueces County, Texas..............	231,959	42.5	24.6	277,431	60.8	5.7	42.2	127,624	59,983	21.0	10.9	19.3
48361	Orange County, Texas................	57,164	48.9	15.9	65,578	59.4	7.3	NA	31,323	71,022	15.9	18.6	13.4
48367	Parker County, Texas..................	107,156	38.0	32.9	122,033	64.1	4.4	44.6	55,525	85,641	11.4	22.1	6.9
48375	Potter County, Texas	74,656	55.1	19.9	89,055	57.2	4.0	40.4	44,472	44,721	26.5	6.3	15.1
48381	Randall County, Texas..................	94,431	28.5	33.4	113,436	67.2	2.8	48.7	56,509	70,322	14.8	15.3	5.9
48397	Rockwall County, Texas............	77,646	27.0	46.0	NA	NA	NA	NA	39,329	121,568	8.9	31.2	6.2
48409	San Patricio County, Texas..........	45,232	46.5	16.8	NA	NA	NA	NA	25,495	59,276	19.5	10.6	20.7
48423	Smith County, Texas..................	156,651	38.8	27.7	186,104	61.3	5.1	42.6	81,175	63,115	14.9	13.3	12.9
48427	Starr County, Texas	36,389	69.5	12.7	45,995	52.6	14.8	NA	19,460	33,367	42.4	6.9	50.2
48439	Tarrant County, Texas................	1,379,726	37.1	34.2	1,646,118	68.2	5.2	47.4	771,657	71,346	13.7	16.9	11.0
48441	Taylor County, Texas..................	88,086	43.9	27.3	111,051	63.2	2.1	42.4	55,974	53,315	20.5	9.4	14.5
48451	Tom Green County, Texas..........	76,254	45.0	23.8	93,583	63.4	3.7	42.4	45,516	61,649	20.5	7.8	8.0
48453	Travis County, Texas	919,819	23.5	55.7	1,065,381	73.1	5.0	51.2	567,627	84,531	13.1	25.1	7.9
48469	Victoria County, Texas..............	58,677	50.7	20.1	70,233	63.5	6.0	42.0	36,753	54,596	21.7	10.1	17.1
48471	Walker County, Texas................	48,403	55.7	18.2	67,574	43.4	13.9	NA	24,704	41,470	34.1	5.1	16.0
48479	Webb County, Texas	152,011	50.1	20.6	192,237	59.5	6.4	39.7	78,730	51,867	25.0	9.1	27.2
48485	Wichita County, Texas..............	83,133	47.6	23.3	103,820	63.0	3.3	42.4	49,071	53,465	22.7	10.0	14.5
48491	Williamson County, Texas............	434,704	24.4	48.1	504,455	71.1	4.8	50.3	241,836	96,073	8.1	25.7	6.2
48497	Wise County, Texas....................	49,028	45.4	18.5	56,462	64.9	7.8	NA	24,449	81,400	14.2	21.6	12.8
49000	**UTAH**........................	2,010,727	29.0	36.8	2,507,029	68.7	3.5	63.4	1,101,499	79,449	11.6	18.6	7.0
49005	Cache County, Utah..................	71,197	23.1	41.0	101,047	70.2	1.6	41.5	43,099	69,154	12.5	13.2	6.2
49011	Davis County, Utah	219,193	25.0	37.9	267,223	70.2	2.9	45.3	114,119	93,182	9.0	24.3	7.0
49035	Salt Lake County, Utah..............	764,172	30.6	37.2	916,909	71.1	4.1	46.7	420,303	80,712	11.9	19.3	7.1
49045	Tooele County, Utah	45,754	39.8	19.8	NA	NA	NA	NA	23,495	93,908	6.9	15.5	6.9
49049	Utah County, Utah..................	353,155	21.2	46.0	489,506	71.3	2.9	41.4	194,258	86,781	9.0	21.6	6.4
49053	Washington County, Utah..........	125,129	26.7	34.3	150,518	55.8	4.4	34.5	68,090	61,186	14.3	11.2	5.9
49057	Weber County, Utah..................	168,747	36.6	28.9	203,103	68.4	3.3	45.1	92,869	72,087	13.8	15.9	7.9
50000	**VERMONT**........................	462,705	31.6	44.4	542,827	64.3	4.2	63.4	270,163	72,431	15.9	16.4	12.8
50007	Chittenden County, Vermont	113,671	20.3	58.4	143,035	67.9	3.3	42.6	70,730	85,213	14.9	23.9	9.9

Table B-2. Counties — What: Education, Employment, and Income, 2021—*Continued*

STATE County code / STATE County / ACS table number / Column number	Educational attainment			Employment status				Household income and benefits				
	Total population 25 years and over	Percent with a high school diploma or less	Percent with a bachelor's degree or more	Total population 16 years and over	Labor force participation (percent)	Percent unemployed	Percent age 16 years and over who worked full-time year-round in the past 12 months	Total households	Median household income in the past 12 months (in 2021 inflation-adjusted dollars)	Income less than $25,000 (percent)	Income greater than $150,000 (percent)	Percent who received cash public assistance or food stamps/ SNAP
ACS table number:	C15003	C15003	C15003	C23001	C23001	C23001	S2402	B19001	B19049	B19001	B19001	B19058
Column number:	1	2	3	4	5	6	7	8	9	10	11	12
51000 VIRGINIA	5,942,672	32.5	41.8	6,980,718	65.2	4.6	67.2	3,331,461	80,963	14.5	23.2	10.1
51003 Albemarle County, Virginia	77,671	22.4	57.4	93,914	60.6	2.9	43.6	45,195	92,568	9.0	29.1	3.0
51013 Arlington County, Virginia	171,343	12.1	76.6	195,525	76.3	3.3	56.6	108,396	125,651	8.2	40.9	4.3
51015 Augusta County, Virginia	56,195	48.0	26.9	64,798	60.5	3.1	43.9	30,186	68,584	12.7	13.7	5.5
51019 Bedford County, Virginia	58,575	35.0	30.3	67,131	57.8	2.7	NA	33,397	66,415	13.4	15.3	8.4
51041 Chesterfield County, Virginia	251,241	30.0	44.0	293,816	67.6	5.8	45.9	136,070	85,796	11.0	23.0	7.2
51059 Fairfax County, Virginia	781,818	17.8	64.9	907,409	70.2	5.0	48.3	410,660	134,115	7.1	44.8	6.0
51061 Fauquier County, Virginia	50,758	34.4	41.8	59,425	67.3	2.7	NA	26,887	108,497	12.1	36.1	5.9
51069 Frederick County, Virginia	65,540	42.5	31.4	75,197	65.2	6.5	43.7	34,581	86,044	10.1	17.5	7.5
51085 Hanover County, Virginia	78,718	31.3	39.3	90,407	65.2	2.8	46.7	42,274	94,381	9.8	25.6	6.5
51087 Henrico County, Virginia	234,035	29.1	46.1	268,819	67.5	4.5	49.0	137,035	78,868	12.0	21.9	9.7
51095 James City County, Virginia........	57,829	26.1	51.4	66,474	58.1	4.3	35.8	31,060	88,604	9.3	23.0	8.3
51107 Loudoun County, Virginia	278,210	15.7	65.3	326,204	73.2	2.9	53.8	141,935	153,506	4.5	52.0	5.0
51121 Montgomery County, Virginia	55,769	26.9	47.9	85,319	54.3	4.2	34.0	37,796	55,210	29.6	10.0	6.4
51153 Prince William County, Virginia ...	312,284	31.7	43.1	370,057	72.0	4.9	49.3	154,619	118,117	7.0	35.3	6.5
51161 Roanoke County, Virginia	70,767	33.9	37.4	79,973	60.4	3.9	40.4	39,093	72,231	19.1	16.2	8.4
51165 Rockingham County, Virginia......	58,776	47.2	31.1	68,370	68.2	3.9	47.0	32,551	73,163	11.5	15.0	6.3
51177 Spotsylvania County, Virginia	96,937	35.6	34.6	112,705	67.5	4.9	47.1	51,179	101,289	10.2	26.6	7.1
51179 Stafford County, Virginia............	103,289	26.8	45.2	124,161	69.5	4.8	46.4	51,007	117,251	6.4	34.6	4.4
51199 York County, Virginia	49,016	20.5	47.7	56,375	65.6	3.2	NA	26,641	97,758	7.7	22.9	4.7
51510 Alexandria city, Virginia.............	118,235	17.2	65.4	128,797	78.7	4.2	55.8	72,024	101,162	12.3	32.0	7.5
51550 Chesapeake city, Virginia	167,938	30.9	38.0	197,892	68.5	4.3	43.5	93,849	88,815	11.5	23.5	8.5
51650 Hampton city, Virginia	92,008	35.4	28.3	111,814	66.8	5.3	40.7	58,181	57,647	17.0	11.4	18.2
51680 Lynchburg city, Virginia	43,640	31.9	44.7	66,455	62.3	6.9	37.9	28,346	56,110	22.9	12.0	12.2
51700 Newport News city, Virginia	119,715	37.4	27.9	144,914	68.6	6.4	40.8	77,489	58,937	17.9	8.9	16.8
51710 Norfolk city, Virginia	148,436	33.2	35.2	194,344	70.0	3.6	35.1	97,596	58,591	18.1	11.4	14.9
51740 Portsmouth city, Virginia	66,099	39.7	25.6	76,958	64.7	6.8	39.0	40,827	54,429	25.6	7.4	19.3
51760 Richmond city, Virginia	162,072	32.7	43.7	191,729	65.9	7.3	42.7	99,929	51,770	25.6	12.4	17.8
51770 Roanoke city, Virginia	69,168	44.0	29.8	78,700	63.2	5.7	41.4	42,455	47,202	26.0	6.4	18.4
51800 Suffolk city, Virginia	65,767	36.0	32.1	76,772	65.4	5.3	42.4	37,383	79,556	13.6	19.3	11.9
51810 Virginia Beach city, Virginia	316,512	26.9	42.2	367,769	69.5	3.7	44.0	182,775	81,634	11.8	19.0	8.3
53000 WASHINGTON	5,401,149	29.3	39.0	6,250,868	63.9	5.8	63.2	3,022,255	84,247	13.1	24.1	14.2
53005 Benton County, Washington	137,407	33.7	32.8	161,865	59.5	4.9	39.4	76,855	77,059	14.1	19.5	18.6
53007 Chelan County, Washington	53,916	36.3	34.1	63,437	59.8	4.9	38.8	32,050	65,847	16.3	18.5	15.2
53009 Clallam County, Washington.......	60,363	32.7	26.6	66,194	49.4	7.4	26.9	34,773	62,695	14.5	11.4	13.9
53011 Clark County, Washington	352,410	33.4	31.9	407,416	62.3	6.2	39.8	193,919	83,837	12.5	19.0	15.7
53015 Cowlitz County, Washington	78,862	43.7	18.0	88,891	55.0	5.2	35.5	43,204	71,194	18.0	13.4	21.0
53021 Franklin County, Washington	56,248	51.8	19.5	70,952	67.4	2.8	48.9	28,989	81,940	8.8	18.8	23.9
53025 Grant County, Washington	62,647	44.5	18.8	75,456	62.6	4.9	NA	35,572	62,227	15.5	10.2	21.6
53027 Grays Harbor County, Washington	56,049	42.7	17.5	63,329	49.4	7.7	30.9	30,500	54,631	20.7	10.6	21.5
53029 Island County, Washington	62,812	26.5	38.8	73,373	56.3	4.9	NA	35,976	76,505	13.9	19.9	10.5
53033 King County, Washington	1,630,500	20.3	56.3	1,856,727	68.9	5.7	45.4	924,763	110,586	11.4	36.5	11.1
53035 Kitsap County, Washington........	195,935	25.4	37.0	225,953	60.3	5.4	34.2	106,399	87,314	12.3	23.1	12.7
53041 Lewis County, Washington.........	60,504	40.7	17.4	68,165	57.4	7.5	34.5	32,304	65,047	18.4	12.6	19.5
53045 Mason County, Washington.......	49,674	37.5	23.9	56,080	53.7	6.1	NA	25,036	77,070	16.8	17.1	17.5
53053 Pierce County, Washington	630,128	33.4	30.8	733,221	66.9	5.3	41.7	347,668	85,866	10.8	22.1	14.5
53057 Skagit County, Washington	93,248	35.1	28.6	106,116	56.3	6.2	33.7	51,971	72,648	15.3	16.0	16.9
53061 Snohomish County, Washington .	586,700	29.1	37.7	668,236	66.4	5.3	43.7	312,365	100,042	9.6	28.3	10.6
53063 Spokane County, Washington	377,237	29.3	31.4	438,864	61.8	6.2	37.9	217,920	65,722	16.5	12.9	18.8
53067 Thurston County, Washington	209,608	25.3	37.7	242,143	60.7	6.2	38.3	117,186	81,659	12.7	18.4	15.0
53073 Whatcom County, Washington ...	155,017	28.4	38.3	190,879	62.6	6.2	34.1	92,219	72,055	13.7	16.5	15.3
53077 Yakima County, Washington	156,443	52.7	18.4	189,619	61.6	9.5	37.3	86,992	61,012	16.9	8.5	25.5

		Educational attainment			Employment status				Household income and benefits				
	STATE County	Total population 25 years and over	Percent with a high school diploma or less	Percent with a bachelor's degree or more	Total population 16 years and over	Labor force participation (percent)	Percent unemployed	Percent age 16 years and over who worked full-time year-round in the past 12 months	Total households	Median household income in the past 12 months (in 2021 inflation-adjusted dollars)	Income less than $25,000 (percent)	Income greater than $150,000 (percent)	Percent who received cash public assistance or food stamps/ SNAP
STATE County code	ACS table number:	C15003	C15003	C15003	C23001	C23001	C23001	S2402	B19001	B19049	B19001	B19001	B19058
	Column number:	1	2	3	4	5	6	7	8	9	10	11	12
54000	**WEST VIRGINIA**	1,265,439	50.3	24.1	1,465,755	52.6	6.2	67.0	722,201	51,248	25.2	9.3	19.5
54003	Berkeley County, West Virginia	86,789	45.0	24.7	101,294	63.6	3.5	44.8	50,841	71,733	14.8	10.9	11.5
54011	Cabell County, West Virginia	63,136	38.7	32.9	76,838	57.5	6.6	35.1	39,631	47,020	28.8	11.3	20.8
54033	Harrison County, West Virginia	46,336	43.5	27.8	52,461	55.8	5.6	40.6	26,143	51,533	18.7	10.1	15.2
54039	Kanawha County, West Virginia	130,046	44.2	30.9	146,314	55.5	5.9	38.5	77,634	56,122	25.6	10.1	20.6
54061	Monongalia County, West Virginia	66,497	32.5	49.6	89,944	61.2	6.1	39.1	42,710	56,347	23.8	16.1	10.6
54081	Raleigh County, West Virginia	52,459	51.6	22.3	59,161	48.5	7.4	NA	29,505	38,687	31.1	8.1	21.9
54107	Wood County, West Virginia	59,924	45.3	25.2	68,194	57.0	6.9	35.4	35,756	54,153	25.4	8.6	18.1
55000	**WISCONSIN**	4,076,339	36.7	32.5	4,773,326	65.1	3.5	66.9	2,449,970	67,125	15.8	13.5	12.9
55009	Brown County, Wisconsin	182,524	36.7	34.7	214,218	67.3	4.0	42.8	110,225	66,191	15.1	11.4	11.4
55017	Chippewa County, Wisconsin	47,584	42.5	23.0	54,175	59.8	3.5	37.5	26,791	60,533	18.2	7.4	14.1
55025	Dane County, Wisconsin	375,350	21.8	54.1	464,086	69.9	2.8	49.0	243,924	77,221	14.3	20.9	9.1
55027	Dodge County, Wisconsin	64,671	49.9	19.0	74,025	66.2	3.7	44.8	36,286	65,773	13.8	8.6	11.3
55035	Eau Claire County, Wisconsin	68,125	30.4	33.9	87,144	68.5	2.6	43.6	43,253	62,445	15.9	11.8	13.8
55039	Fond du Lac County, Wisconsin	73,527	42.9	25.2	85,127	65.6	2.3	45.2	42,758	69,068	13.2	11.0	9.7
55055	Jefferson County, Wisconsin	59,823	39.6	28.6	70,579	67.9	4.7	47.0	35,088	68,319	12.1	8.9	11.9
55059	Kenosha County, Wisconsin	115,316	36.0	31.5	136,254	65.3	4.4	43.5	67,810	70,971	16.0	15.2	14.6
55063	La Crosse County, Wisconsin	77,999	28.7	32.6	98,745	66.6	2.4	44.4	50,217	60,382	17.9	11.5	13.7
55071	Manitowoc County, Wisconsin	58,681	49.3	20.7	67,162	60.1	1.9	41.7	35,716	57,918	18.8	8.1	11.3
55073	Marathon County, Wisconsin	96,193	38.6	28.2	110,119	68.1	3.7	48.9	57,566	74,494	14.5	12.3	9.4
55079	Milwaukee County, Wisconsin	618,414	38.5	34.5	728,614	64.9	5.4	42.6	389,434	56,347	21.9	11.5	23.1
55087	Outagamie County, Wisconsin	131,497	36.4	31.2	151,833	68.7	3.2	48.6	77,071	73,057	12.5	14.5	8.8
55089	Ozaukee County, Wisconsin	65,592	24.0	50.4	75,973	63.1	3.4	39.4	36,144	85,402	9.8	25.0	7.4
55097	Portage County, Wisconsin	46,736	36.3	29.7	58,640	67.6	3.4	42.1	29,937	65,928	15.3	10.0	9.5
55101	Racine County, Wisconsin	136,852	40.6	24.6	157,976	62.7	4.6	42.1	79,068	68,758	15.3	13.1	14.7
55105	Rock County, Wisconsin	113,903	39.0	24.9	132,147	65.0	3.9	44.2	67,876	66,090	15.4	8.3	15.3
55109	St. Croix County, Wisconsin	65,199	29.7	37.5	75,089	69.8	2.6	48.1	36,873	93,547	7.8	24.4	7.3
55111	Sauk County, Wisconsin	46,272	35.1	29.8	52,707	66.9	2.9	44.3	27,524	70,914	13.0	11.7	12.6
55117	Sheboygan County, Wisconsin	82,869	39.5	27.0	95,172	65.2	2.7	42.7	49,416	62,188	16.0	11.8	10.1
55127	Walworth County, Wisconsin	71,775	35.6	31.9	87,814	63.8	5.5	39.7	43,086	69,996	16.7	12.4	9.8
55131	Washington County, Wisconsin	97,930	35.4	32.6	111,627	69.1	2.2	48.1	56,636	83,384	9.8	16.8	5.9
55133	Waukesha County, Wisconsin	291,147	23.4	48.9	332,976	66.6	2.5	45.2	167,089	94,171	9.2	24.9	6.9
55139	Winnebago County, Wisconsin	116,688	36.8	29.6	141,220	66.9	2.2	43.4	72,794	64,095	15.4	10.7	12.5
55141	Wood County, Wisconsin	53,047	44.9	18.4	59,684	59.6	4.5	37.4	31,890	52,627	19.5	11.8	15.5
56000	**WYOMING**	395,348	33.7	29.2	461,622	65.3	3.7	62.5	242,763	65,204	17.9	12.8	7.1
56021	Laramie County, Wyoming	69,242	29.1	30.7	80,473	64.2	2.4	40.5	43,728	61,381	17.5	10.0	9.2
56025	Natrona County, Wyoming	54,603	36.9	27.7	62,292	65.0	3.7	40.0	33,203	63,605	17.8	10.5	9.1
72000	**PUERTO RICO**	2,401,409	48.3	28.5	2,794,959	44.8	13.0	54.9	1,165,982	22,237	54.3	2.4	49.9
72013	Arecibo Municipio, Puerto Rico	64,832	50.8	26.4	74,289	39.0	14.8	NA	28,742	18,341	60.3	0.9	55.1
72021	Bayamón Municipio, Puerto Rico	136,945	38.8	30.7	157,838	43.7	8.6	26.1	66,385	26,014	48.4	1.6	39.2
72025	Caguas Municipio, Puerto Rico	94,261	46.3	33.9	108,144	48.6	8.2	NA	47,586	26,473	48.4	4.5	46.7
72031	Carolina Municipio, Puerto Rico	114,608	41.2	33.3	132,202	52.8	13.9	32.2	58,930	30,734	42.5	2.4	39.3
72061	Guaynabo Municipio, Puerto Rico	69,145	32.1	50.4	78,785	48.7	7.9	NA	32,826	44,673	34.4	10.4	27.7
72097	Mayagüez Municipio, Puerto Rico	49,514	55.6	24.5	62,384	42.4	22.7	NA	27,447	15,941	70.4	1.9	57.3
72113	Ponce Municipio, Puerto Rico	98,553	46.6	31.9	114,078	41.7	15.9	NA	50,007	17,876	60.1	2.1	53.3
72127	San Juan Municipio, Puerto Rico	252,577	38.4	39.8	291,763	52.2	14.6	25.2	135,865	22,175	53.4	5.1	39.6
72135	Toa Alta Municipio, Puerto Rico	48,622	37.9	30.3	NA	NA	NA	NA	20,918	26,292	48.5	1.1	45.9
72137	Toa Baja Municipio, Puerto Rico	54,916	42.0	27.6	64,041	54.9	10.4	NA	28,276	30,561	44.8	2.0	39.9
72139	Trujillo Alto Municipio, Puerto Rico	49,903	34.3	36.3	57,408	57.6	12.7	NA	24,898	36,349	34.9	4.8	41.2

NA = Not available.

Table B-3. Metropolitan Areas — What: Education, Employment, and Income, 2021

Metropolitan area / division code	Metropolitan area / division	Educational attainment			Employment status				Household income and benefits				
		Total population 25 years and over	Percent with a high school diploma or less	Percent with a bachelor's degree or more	Total population 16 years and over	Labor force participation (percent)	Percent unemployed	Percent age 16 years and over who worked full-time year-round in the past 12 months	Total households	Median household income in the past 12 months (in 2021 inflation-adjusted dollars)	Income less than $25,000 (percent)	Income greater than $150,000 (percent)	Percent who received cash public assistance or food stamps/ SNAP
	ACS table number:	C15003	C15003	C15003	C23001	C23001	C23001	S2402	B19001	B19049	B19001	B19001	B19058
	Column number:	1	2	3	4	5	6	7	8	9	10	11	12
10180	Abilene, TX	113,152	44.9	24.7	139,631	60.4	2.7	40.6	66,816	54,037	19.8	8.7	14.4
10380	Aguadilla-Isabela, PR	230,101	51.4	25.0	266,599	41.8	17.6	19.6	107,572	17,926	61.8	0.7	56.7
10420	Akron, OH	489,895	38.9	34.2	574,615	63.1	5.3	40.5	292,156	63,367	19.9	14.3	17.4
10500	Albany, GA	96,691	48.1	23.0	117,435	56.0	7.6	39.3	57,880	48,659	23.8	6.5	22.1
10540	Albany-Lebanon, OR	90,157	35.5	23.5	103,634	60.6	6.9	36.9	51,347	65,196	16.4	9.5	21.9
10580	Albany-Schenectady-Troy, NY	632,631	30.9	40.6	748,175	63.1	5.8	41.4	378,258	78,272	15.9	18.4	12.0
10740	Albuquerque, NM	644,343	33.1	35.1	749,735	60.4	6.7	38.8	376,596	60,070	19.8	13.3	20.4
10780	Alexandria, LA	102,081	52.7	21.6	119,271	53.7	7.0	37.8	55,249	47,032	24.9	9.2	21.0
10900	Allentown-Bethlehem-Easton, PA-NJ	605,821	41.9	32.2	705,370	63.6	6.5	41.7	337,283	72,058	15.8	17.1	14.0
11020	Altoona, PA	87,847	53.5	24.4	99,740	57.6	5.5	38.3	49,795	57,361	19.0	8.6	16.3
11100	Amarillo, TX	175,133	40.6	27.3	209,375	62.9	3.2	45.3	104,421	58,354	20.1	11.5	9.8
11180	Ames, IA	71,342	23.7	44.7	107,022	64.0	3.4	37.8	49,702	64,569	20.3	12.6	7.4
11260	Anchorage, AK	265,186	31.4	34.2	310,874	67.4	6.1	38.7	150,581	84,476	13.0	22.3	12.7
11460	Ann Arbor, MI	235,544	19.0	57.3	310,111	64.0	4.8	37.6	149,133	76,918	15.1	21.6	9.6
11500	Anniston-Oxford, AL	78,876	47.8	19.4	93,742	54.8	5.8	35.9	44,631	46,524	31.9	5.3	18.7
11540	Appleton, WI	167,737	36.3	31.7	194,341	69.2	3.0	48.6	98,164	74,331	12.0	15.3	9.0
11640	Arecibo, PR	136,554	52.2	25.8	156,084	40.7	10.8	NA	61,581	20,297	58.4	0.7	56.9
11700	Asheville, NC	352,272	31.7	40.5	398,602	57.2	5.4	37.3	185,423	60,261	18.5	12.3	12.5
12020	Athens-Clarke County, GA	133,374	30.4	45.4	177,768	62.7	3.9	37.2	87,263	59,628	20.5	13.5	9.3
12060	Atlanta-Sandy Springs-Alpharetta, GA	4,134,448	31.8	42.2	4,865,041	66.6	5.3	45.7	2,277,482	77,589	14.1	20.3	11.4
12100	Atlantic City-Hammonton, NJ	193,469	43.4	32.3	224,620	61.9	10.2	35.0	112,299	66,388	18.0	15.2	15.5
12220	Auburn-Opelika, AL	110,446	30.9	40.6	143,890	60.5	3.0	39.2	67,358	52,424	24.9	10.8	11.1
12260	Augusta-Richmond County, GA-SC	415,155	39.9	28.2	491,081	60.9	7.3	36.6	222,266	56,515	21.5	12.3	15.0
12420	Austin-Round Rock-Georgetown, TX	1,613,795	26.2	50.0	1,892,801	70.9	4.9	49.7	955,207	86,530	12.4	24.3	7.6
12540	Bakersfield, CA	562,716	51.5	18.6	685,864	57.9	9.9	30.7	282,963	58,217	20.6	12.8	20.1
12580	Baltimore-Columbia-Towson, MD	1,973,442	31.3	42.9	2,288,285	66.5	5.3	45.9	1,117,510	86,302	14.0	25.6	15.1
12620	Bangor, ME	109,464	36.0	31.3	129,888	61.0	5.4	38.9	65,441	56,250	23.0	10.7	14.9
12700	Barnstable Town, MA	184,483	25.3	46.4	202,830	59.9	5.9	33.6	104,733	83,537	14.3	24.8	10.5
12940	Baton Rouge, LA	574,862	41.8	29.3	691,117	60.5	7.8	39.8	328,816	58,276	21.3	15.3	19.9
12980	Battle Creek, MI	91,332	43.9	23.9	107,126	59.4	7.8	35.7	53,482	55,192	21.2	10.9	13.4
13020	Bay City, MI	74,942	41.8	19.9	86,297	60.5	5.2	38.0	45,487	56,911	19.7	9.4	12.8
13140	Beaumont-Port Arthur, TX	264,491	45.6	18.3	306,966	57.9	5.7	41.4	148,489	61,429	19.9	13.3	14.4
13220	Beckley, WV	82,012	54.6	20.4	92,676	45.4	7.0	NA	46,282	38,737	32.1	5.6	23.1
13380	Bellingham, WA	155,017	28.4	38.3	190,879	62.6	6.2	34.1	92,219	72,055	13.7	16.5	15.3
13460	Bend, OR	152,916	26.2	41.2	169,974	62.0	4.8	39.4	83,763	79,796	13.2	20.2	11.5
13740	Billings, MT	130,403	30.5	35.0	149,547	63.5	4.4	40.1	77,868	70,018	16.6	14.2	10.5
13780	Binghamton, NY	167,904	36.6	30.0	204,541	60.4	6.8	37.2	105,514	56,968	21.4	11.0	14.7
13820	Birmingham-Hoover, AL	764,151	38.1	34.4	890,312	61.0	4.9	42.2	436,615	60,725	20.6	13.9	14.0
13900	Bismarck, ND	91,483	30.8	34.6	107,310	67.2	2.9	45.9	52,921	67,793	15.0	14.9	7.1
13980	Blacksburg-Christiansburg, VA	102,204	34.4	36.2	144,528	55.4	3.8	35.9	66,952	54,737	26.8	8.9	7.8
14010	Bloomington, IL	104,443	26.7	47.4	138,324	65.1	3.7	43.2	69,263	69,612	18.8	16.8	10.9
14020	Bloomington, IN	95,598	33.6	43.9	137,425	58.2	4.5	34.6	65,340	52,588	25.3	10.9	7.6
14100	Bloomsburg-Berwick, PA	57,580	51.3	27.9	70,077	55.2	5.2	35.9	33,496	57,046	25.4	11.1	8.7
14260	Boise City, ID	542,026	33.0	35.5	632,898	64.2	3.2	43.4	294,959	73,343	14.0	15.7	10.3
14460	Boston-Cambridge-Newton, MA-NH	3,464,341	28.7	51.1	4,063,205	68.7	6.0	44.6	1,920,160	100,750	13.8	32.2	14.6
1446014454	Boston, MA Metro Division	1,430,457	30.0	50.0	1,688,776	68.3	8.2	51.2	797,408	96,332	16.1	31.0	16.0
1446015764	Cambridge-Newton-Framingham, MA Metro Division	1,711,016	27.8	53.3	1,997,017	69.0	6.8	52.7	942,803	103,510	13.0	34.1	15.0
1446040484	Rockingham County-Strafford County, NH Metro Division	322,868	27.8	44.6	377,412	69.2	4.9	54.8	179,949	103,025	8.6	27.7	6.4
14500	Boulder, CO	223,309	16.8	62.5	277,373	67.1	5.5	40.0	135,607	90,168	13.5	29.7	9.5
14540	Bowling Green, KY	117,707	45.1	28.2	147,253	62.6	5.1	38.1	71,929	57,057	22.8	8.3	17.7
14740	Bremerton-Silverdale-Port Orchard, WA	195,935	25.4	37.0	225,953	60.3	5.4	34.2	106,399	87,314	12.3	23.1	12.7
14860	Bridgeport-Stamford-Norwalk, CT	663,240	29.9	50.5	775,819	67.7	6.2	43.3	357,271	100,810	13.8	34.1	11.5
15180	Brownsville-Harlingen, TX	254,651	55.0	20.6	314,947	58.0	8.1	37.3	135,734	48,115	29.4	7.6	28.8
15260	Brunswick, GA	81,228	40.7	25.6	93,017	55.9	3.7	37.2	46,763	54,561	24.0	9.3	15.9

Metropolitan area / division code	Metropolitan area / division	Educational attainment			Employment status				Household income and benefits				
		Total population 25 years and over	Percent with a high school diploma or less	Percent with a bachelor's degree or more	Total population 16 years and over	Labor force participation (percent)	Percent unemployed	Percent age 16 years and over who worked full-time year-round in the past 12 months	Total households	Median household income in the past 12 months (in 2021 inflation-adjusted dollars)	Income less than $25,000 (percent)	Income greater than $150,000 (percent)	Percent who received cash public assistance or food stamps/SNAP
	ACS table number:	C15003	C15003	C15003	C23001	C23001	C23001	S2402	B19001	B19049	B19001	B19001	B19058
	Column number:	1	2	3	4	5	6	7	8	9	10	11	12
15380	Buffalo-Cheektowaga, NY	827,082	33.4	36.9	955,563	62.7	6.9	38.5	503,845	62,794	19.7	13.7	17.6
15500	Burlington, NC	115,642	40.1	28.9	139,425	61.9	5.7	41.9	69,343	58,400	17.8	7.4	13.1
15540	Burlington-South Burlington, VT	154,750	26.0	51.0	189,660	67.6	3.0	43.6	93,290	81,852	14.9	21.9	11.8
15680	California-Lexington Park, MD	77,108	34.3	36.0	90,184	69.3	6.2	45.9	42,078	108,397	10.1	29.9	11.0
15940	Canton-Massillon, OH	281,499	46.6	24.2	324,035	61.7	4.5	40.3	168,332	58,810	17.5	10.9	16.2
15980	Cape Coral-Fort Myers, FL	598,375	40.0	30.9	668,245	53.4	5.2	34.7	320,466	66,256	17.4	13.5	11.4
16020	Cape Girardeau, MO-IL	63,566	45.1	30.2	78,114	62.4	3.1	40.3	37,991	60,726	19.9	8.7	11.3
16060	Carbondale-Marion, IL	90,189	33.9	28.9	110,711	52.6	7.7	33.3	55,292	50,953	24.5	8.8	18.0
16180	Carson City, NV	42,671	39.1	25.5	NA	NA	NA	NA	23,930	65,330	18.5	11.8	12.1
16220	Casper, WY	54,603	36.9	27.7	62,292	65.0	3.7	40.0	33,203	63,605	17.8	10.5	9.1
16300	Cedar Rapids, IA	188,241	30.7	33.9	219,582	65.4	3.9	44.7	112,468	69,923	15.8	13.5	10.7
16540	Chambersburg-Waynesboro, PA	109,934	50.5	25.1	126,008	61.9	4.4	40.2	62,081	66,715	14.7	13.7	11.1
16580	Champaign-Urbana, IL	131,525	25.8	46.6	183,232	62.9	4.4	39.5	91,044	59,189	21.3	13.2	10.3
16620	Charleston, WV	181,748	49.4	25.4	205,995	50.8	6.2	35.6	106,310	53,549	26.2	8.5	20.8
16700	Charleston-North Charleston, SC	566,691	31.0	40.5	656,739	65.2	5.1	45.3	316,378	72,719	16.1	17.5	8.8
16740	Charlotte-Concord-Gastonia, NC-SC	1,842,756	32.4	39.3	2,148,547	67.0	5.1	46.3	1,048,452	71,041	14.9	18.0	11.4
16820	Charlottesville, VA	151,753	24.8	50.8	184,358	61.0	4.0	40.5	88,339	78,819	14.9	22.3	7.0
16860	Chattanooga, TN-GA	399,271	39.4	29.8	461,577	61.7	4.8	41.8	228,853	62,385	19.5	12.1	11.6
16940	Cheyenne, WY	69,242	29.1	30.7	80,473	64.2	2.4	40.5	43,728	61,381	17.5	10.0	9.2
16980	Chicago-Naperville-Elgin, IL-IN-WI	6,553,947	33.6	40.6	7,639,907	66.3	7.6	43.3	3,670,416	78,166	15.9	21.3	15.1
1698016984	Chicago-Naperville-Evanston, IL Metro Division	4,981,215	32.6	42.2	5,773,416	66.4	8.9	50.5	2,802,657	77,381	16.6	21.4	15.8
1698020994	Elgin, IL Metro Division	490,788	35.3	36.0	588,110	69.8	6.8	53.4	266,551	86,464	10.3	22.7	14.2
1698023844	Gary, IN Metro Division	494,188	45.5	25.4	575,934	61.0	6.7	46.8	278,654	65,774	18.2	12.7	12.4
1698029404	Lake County-Kenosha County, IL-WI Metro Division	587,756	30.7	43.8	702,447	67.0	6.7	51.3	322,554	88,522	12.5	26.4	12.1
17020	Chico, CA	136,280	32.6	32.3	170,370	59.8	8.7	31.9	81,353	64,738	18.9	14.8	15.0
17140	Cincinnati, OH-KY-IN	1,527,139	37.1	36.5	1,797,484	65.1	5.0	43.4	903,245	70,818	17.0	16.8	11.6
17300	Clarksville, TN-KY	203,998	39.3	24.7	248,834	62.5	3.8	35.5	121,468	59,255	17.2	8.5	12.0
17420	Cleveland, TN	91,397	45.4	20.8	105,166	56.8	7.2	38.3	50,236	56,350	19.0	8.4	14.4
17460	Cleveland-Elyria, OH	1,473,179	36.7	34.1	1,693,474	63.5	6.5	41.7	890,105	62,315	19.6	13.9	15.3
17660	Coeur d'Alene, ID	125,181	33.6	26.6	143,384	61.7	2.6	38.9	67,771	67,593	14.3	13.2	7.4
17780	College Station-Bryan, TX	153,997	36.1	38.1	221,691	60.4	5.8	36.6	99,917	49,927	25.3	11.8	9.8
17820	Colorado Springs, CO	506,459	24.0	41.5	607,070	67.3	5.7	40.6	294,814	79,014	10.6	18.8	11.3
17860	Columbia, MO	133,199	29.8	45.7	173,558	65.4	4.8	38.8	84,946	61,781	20.9	11.8	7.9
17900	Columbia, SC	556,347	34.7	34.9	675,200	62.9	6.0	41.2	334,313	58,213	20.6	11.0	11.8
17980	Columbus, GA-AL	214,945	40.2	27.5	254,901	58.0	6.3	36.8	127,247	52,802	24.8	9.5	22.4
18020	Columbus, IN	56,650	35.5	36.2	65,164	67.8	4.0	45.5	32,518	73,564	12.2	16.7	9.3
18140	Columbus, OH	1,453,545	34.2	39.0	1,705,276	67.1	5.0	45.7	856,193	71,839	14.9	16.6	12.1
18580	Corpus Christi, TX	277,191	43.2	23.4	330,379	60.9	5.4	42.6	153,119	59,853	20.7	10.9	19.5
18700	Corvallis, OR	59,125	18.8	54.9	82,376	58.4	6.7	30.1	39,350	64,163	21.8	17.6	14.4
18880	Crestview-Fort Walton Beach-Destin, FL	206,373	31.4	36.1	236,227	61.9	3.3	37.9	118,438	67,029	13.7	16.1	9.6
19060	Cumberland, MD-WV	67,225	49.1	22.8	79,875	50.7	5.3	35.3	40,079	51,440	22.3	9.2	18.9
19100	Dallas-Fort Worth-Arlington, TX	5,087,795	34.7	38.3	6,023,260	68.5	5.3	48.3	2,836,892	75,975	13.7	20.0	10.0
1910019124	Dallas-Plano-Irving, TX Division	3,428,865	33.0	40.9	4,053,485	69.0	6.2	57.7	1,920,923	77,527	13.8	21.4	9.7
1910023104	Fort Worth-Arlington-Grapevine, TX Division	1,658,930	38.2	32.9	1,969,775	67.5	6.1	56.1	915,969	72,492	13.5	17.2	10.6
19140	Dalton, GA	93,314	58.3	16.8	111,281	61.3	7.6	42.3	50,580	54,289	20.6	8.2	12.6
19180	Danville, IL	51,090	50.1	15.9	58,110	51.4	6.6	33.5	29,007	49,091	25.2	6.5	19.5
19300	Daphne-Fairhope-Foley, AL	172,896	33.8	34.5	194,430	58.9	2.8	41.4	94,105	63,866	15.6	13.8	8.2
19340	Davenport-Moline-Rock Island, IA-IL	262,437	38.0	28.4	304,126	62.6	6.4	39.2	159,133	61,166	19.7	12.3	17.1
19380	Dayton-Kettering, OH	558,322	35.0	32.0	655,707	62.6	5.0	40.2	338,505	61,986	18.5	12.9	12.9
19460	Decatur, AL	108,815	46.0	22.1	125,619	55.1	3.1	40.2	60,796	57,041	21.8	9.6	13.9
19500	Decatur, IL	70,757	48.1	19.0	82,176	56.8	11.1	34.1	43,914	46,807	24.8	7.5	21.1
19660	Deltona-Daytona Beach-Ormond Beach, FL	513,053	39.1	27.0	581,272	52.3	4.5	36.2	291,531	59,171	20.1	9.2	13.8

Table B-3. Metropolitan Areas — What: Education, Employment, and Income, 2021—*Continued*

Metropolitan area / division code	Metropolitan area / division	Educational attainment			Employment status				Household income and benefits				
		Total population 25 years and over	Percent with a high school diploma or less	Percent with a bachelor's degree or more	Total population 16 years and over	Labor force participation (percent)	Percent unemployed	Percent age 16 years and over who worked full-time year-round in the past 12 months	Total households	Median household income in the past 12 months (in 2021 inflation-adjusted dollars)	Income less than $25,000 (percent)	Income greater than $150,000 (percent)	Percent who received cash public assistance or food stamps/ SNAP
ACS table number:		C15003	C15003	C15003	C23001	C23001	C23001	S2402	B19001	B19049	B19001	B19001	B19058
Column number:		1	2	3	4	5	6	7	8	9	10	11	12
19740	Denver-Aurora-Lakewood, CO	2,098,660	26.7	47.8	2,412,295	71.5	5.4	48.9	1,192,117	90,716	11.3	25.6	9.0
19780	Des Moines-West Des Moines, IA	480,787	31.8	38.2	560,245	70.7	3.6	50.2	291,147	74,208	12.8	17.2	11.0
19820	Detroit-Warren-Dearborn, MI	3,062,864	35.3	34.2	3,529,583	62.4	8.0	38.3	1,759,573	67,153	17.7	16.5	17.1
1982019804	Detroit-Dearborn-Livonia, MI Division	1,207,427	42.0	27.2	1,402,749	58.8	11.5	40.1	695,038	52,605	23.9	11.4	24.8
1982047664	Warren-Troy-Farmington Hills, MI Division	1,855,437	31.0	38.7	2,126,834	64.7	6.8	46.8	1,064,535	77,754	13.6	19.9	12.2
20020	Dothan, AL	105,698	46.5	20.5	121,236	55.2	4.6	37.3	61,173	47,665	26.6	8.0	16.6
20100	Dover, DE	124,208	42.8	27.0	146,872	58.1	5.0	39.0	70,167	64,308	16.8	10.2	14.4
20220	Dubuque, IA	66,573	37.0	32.6	79,814	67.9	4.1	44.1	40,482	75,590	14.2	14.9	6.2
20260	Duluth, MN-WI	203,172	31.5	30.9	242,532	60.0	4.3	35.3	124,996	64,960	17.8	10.9	10.7
20500	Durham-Chapel Hill, NC	449,650	26.6	50.8	540,830	61.8	5.6	42.2	263,996	71,601	17.6	19.9	12.2
20700	East Stroudsburg, PA	121,060	42.4	29.0	140,933	61.8	6.7	42.9	65,907	78,575	15.3	14.8	16.4
20740	Eau Claire, WI	115,709	35.4	29.4	141,319	65.2	2.9	41.3	70,044	61,684	16.8	10.2	13.9
20940	El Centro, CA	111,355	52.6	13.5	133,162	52.5	14.5	28.3	47,849	51,809	24.9	7.5	26.8
21060	Elizabethtown-Fort Knox, KY	104,259	44.1	24.5	121,452	62.3	5.0	36.0	58,210	60,025	18.9	11.4	15.5
21140	Elkhart-Goshen, IN	131,567	53.5	21.8	156,722	63.0	5.0	41.3	69,015	60,143	16.3	9.9	7.5
21300	Elmira, NY	59,845	44.6	27.8	68,241	54.1	6.9	36.7	35,407	60,219	21.9	8.8	19.6
21340	El Paso, TX	545,787	44.4	26.0	668,097	62.7	7.9	37.5	299,177	51,002	25.2	8.6	23.1
21420	Enid, OK	40,829	50.1	23.8	47,716	62.7	2.8	NA	23,016	60,721	18.8	7.2	13.4
21500	Erie, PA	187,160	43.2	29.2	219,172	59.1	7.6	37.5	110,561	56,851	22.9	8.8	20.5
21660	Eugene-Springfield, OR	270,064	28.9	32.4	322,719	59.8	7.2	33.9	160,158	61,712	18.3	11.6	21.7
21780	Evansville, IN-KY	215,958	39.0	27.6	252,378	63.4	3.5	43.2	132,942	59,153	17.3	10.9	11.4
21820	Fairbanks, AK	61,318	30.5	38.1	75,513	67.1	3.8	NA	36,426	72,149	14.9	17.5	8.3
22020	Fargo, ND-MN	159,947	23.8	43.7	199,218	74.1	3.6	46.4	109,997	66,216	16.8	15.6	7.3
22140	Farmington, NM	79,371	47.5	15.6	94,363	51.6	10.5	30.9	40,844	47,819	29.3	8.5	29.7
22180	Fayetteville, NC	332,195	34.1	26.6	405,557	63.1	7.0	34.2	198,062	55,027	21.3	7.9	19.4
22220	Fayetteville-Springdale-Rogers, AR	359,159	42.4	33.1	436,497	65.8	3.4	50.0	206,712	71,767	13.6	16.9	5.9
22380	Flagstaff, AZ	87,394	31.6	39.5	118,934	62.4	7.7	37.3	55,145	64,533	21.4	17.5	14.2
22420	Flint, MI	280,947	39.7	23.8	324,886	57.9	10.2	32.1	167,895	52,025	22.2	9.2	18.8
22500	Florence, SC	136,222	46.6	21.4	159,195	54.8	5.1	40.2	77,918	49,724	30.6	8.3	21.6
22520	Florence-Muscle Shoals, AL	106,173	47.3	24.8	123,399	57.5	3.8	39.9	61,492	51,639	24.6	7.4	11.8
22540	Fond du Lac, WI	73,527	42.9	25.2	85,127	65.6	2.3	45.2	42,758	69,068	13.2	11.0	9.7
22660	Fort Collins, CO	244,592	21.1	51.7	304,449	66.2	4.4	42.0	152,123	78,109	12.7	21.8	8.3
22900	Fort Smith, AR-OK	165,932	48.0	20.3	195,664	55.7	5.8	37.2	97,188	49,065	24.3	7.2	15.8
23060	Fort Wayne, IN	278,535	39.0	29.7	326,681	65.5	4.9	43.7	168,833	62,155	16.3	10.7	10.2
23420	Fresno, CA	630,729	45.5	24.0	761,696	60.8	9.1	37.1	322,646	63,656	20.1	15.5	22.7
23460	Gadsden, AL	72,023	51.2	18.2	83,219	53.9	7.5	NA	38,006	45,298	28.0	4.5	12.9
23540	Gainesville, FL	220,870	33.2	40.1	287,420	58.3	3.9	36.5	134,946	53,728	23.6	12.4	10.9
23580	Gainesville, GA	138,144	46.3	25.0	162,282	64.6	4.0	45.5	72,454	66,719	18.4	14.6	11.9
23900	Gettysburg, PA	74,093	51.8	28.7	87,049	62.6	4.3	41.6	39,986	72,985	12.4	15.2	7.7
24020	Glens Falls, NY	95,280	41.7	27.9	106,558	59.5	4.7	38.6	54,582	65,557	16.0	12.2	11.6
24140	Goldsboro, NC	77,954	45.8	20.3	92,465	60.4	4.6	38.7	46,932	47,595	24.7	7.5	26.8
24220	Grand Forks, ND-MN	63,766	29.3	33.1	82,659	69.4	3.3	40.4	43,220	62,568	21.2	11.1	8.4
24260	Grand Island, NE	51,142	49.1	21.2	NA	NA	NA	NA	30,478	61,749	17.4	10.4	10.1
24300	Grand Junction, CO	110,190	35.4	31.2	128,269	60.1	5.7	35.7	63,796	64,055	16.8	13.3	13.1
24340	Grand Rapids-Kentwood, MI	724,327	35.1	35.8	864,839	66.5	4.4	41.6	410,413	72,014	14.1	14.9	12.1
24420	Grants Pass, OR	66,489	39.0	21.0	74,299	49.5	9.7	NA	36,755	48,785	23.7	9.2	25.8
24500	Great Falls, MT	58,183	37.4	27.4	67,823	61.1	3.2	34.6	34,303	57,706	21.2	9.5	13.1
24540	Greeley, CO	221,613	34.7	31.7	262,320	69.2	4.7	47.4	119,502	85,290	12.9	19.5	11.5
24580	Green Bay, WI	226,592	39.1	31.5	263,424	66.4	3.5	43.0	135,686	66,652	14.9	11.5	10.7
24660	Greensboro-High Point, NC	531,728	36.8	31.5	627,933	62.4	5.6	41.0	307,003	57,908	20.9	10.7	17.8
24780	Greenville, NC	105,102	33.7	33.6	141,122	61.4	9.2	39.8	75,578	44,450	29.4	9.5	19.1
24860	Greenville-Anderson, SC	641,746	37.3	35.3	756,924	61.2	4.9	41.0	373,112	62,265	18.8	12.8	11.2
25020	Guayama, PR	51,994	54.0	18.9	NA	NA	NA	NA	25,902	16,373	64.6	2.6	60.6
25060	Gulfport-Biloxi, MS	287,790	37.4	26.8	334,518	58.7	7.3	37.5	162,594	56,348	21.1	8.2	13.8

Metropolitan area / division code	Metropolitan area / division	Educational attainment			Employment status				Household income and benefits				
		Total population 25 years and over	Percent with a high school diploma or less	Percent with a bachelor's degree or more	Total population 16 years and over	Labor force participation (percent)	Percent unemployed	Percent age 16 years and over who worked full-time year-round in the past 12 months	Total households	Median household income in the past 12 months (in 2021 inflation-adjusted dollars)	Income less than $25,000 (percent)	Income greater than $150,000 (percent)	Percent who received cash public assistance or food stamps/ SNAP
	ACS table number:	C15003	C15003	C15003	C23001	C23001	C23001	S2402	B19001	B19049	B19001	B19001	B19058
	Column number:	1	2	3	4	5	6	7	8	9	10	11	12
25180	Hagerstown-Martinsburg, MD-WV	210,285	49.4	23.5	243,418	59.0	4.0	40.3	117,803	67,372	17.3	12.0	16.4
25220	Hammond, LA	86,266	51.2	20.5	106,063	61.0	5.0	NA	49,915	52,872	26.7	8.3	23.2
25260	Hanford-Corcoran, CA	96,368	53.2	11.2	117,290	53.8	11.2	29.6	43,143	62,155	17.4	12.5	19.5
25420	Harrisburg-Carlisle, PA	418,309	42.6	33.7	481,763	63.9	4.8	43.2	243,253	73,559	14.1	15.5	11.0
25500	Harrisonburg, VA	84,588	45.4	31.4	112,804	66.3	4.7	42.4	50,478	66,564	18.6	13.9	9.3
25540	Hartford-East Hartford-Middletown, CT	849,617	34.1	41.4	1,005,620	65.0	6.4	41.8	488,173	82,258	15.5	23.1	13.0
25620	Hattiesburg, MS	107,871	36.3	28.5	134,178	62.3	5.5	40.9	66,682	55,444	21.3	9.9	13.6
25860	Hickory-Lenoir-Morganton, NC	260,973	46.6	21.5	302,397	57.8	6.2	37.9	146,600	52,737	22.9	7.9	15.6
25940	Hilton Head Island-Bluffton, SC	162,612	30.2	43.3	189,040	54.0	2.9	31.5	89,701	67,779	14.9	17.0	7.0
25980	Hinesville, GA	45,922	41.8	20.8	58,927	60.0	5.5	NA	29,290	49,733	21.2	4.8	21.0
26140	Homosassa Springs, FL	127,256	47.9	20.8	137,704	36.8	10.4	NA	68,269	47,197	25.0	5.3	12.9
26300	Hot Springs, AR	73,615	42.7	23.8	83,602	55.1	6.8	35.7	42,077	47,694	25.0	7.1	12.3
26380	Houma-Thibodaux, LA	139,964	56.6	20.6	161,978	56.4	5.7	38.3	82,107	61,478	23.6	9.9	18.8
26420	Houston-The Woodlands-Sugar Land, TX	4,675,062	38.4	35.8	5,536,798	65.8	7.3	44.5	2,601,401	70,893	16.2	19.2	14.9
26580	Huntington-Ashland, WV-KY-OH	252,137	47.5	22.7	291,253	53.3	6.7	34.7	144,383	50,456	26.2	9.3	20.2
26620	Huntsville, AL	349,087	28.8	42.8	406,416	62.8	3.4	43.8	205,178	76,963	14.6	20.6	7.8
26820	Idaho Falls, ID	101,160	32.2	31.0	118,393	64.4	4.0	40.5	54,348	70,559	12.5	14.1	8.6
26900	Indianapolis-Carmel-Anderson, IN	1,428,725	35.7	37.8	1,669,051	67.1	4.4	46.0	834,540	70,224	14.1	16.6	10.5
26980	Iowa City, IA	107,985	20.7	48.7	145,555	71.4	2.7	43.2	69,788	66,216	16.0	17.5	7.7
27060	Ithaca, NY	59,716	21.8	58.5	94,552	58.0	7.1	32.7	44,469	66,441	17.1	17.1	10.9
27100	Jackson, MI	113,648	43.5	21.9	129,947	56.6	4.2	36.7	61,937	58,254	17.2	11.4	15.4
27140	Jackson, MS	395,536	35.5	33.0	466,584	58.9	5.4	40.7	228,001	54,123	23.8	10.5	12.2
27180	Jackson, TN	121,519	46.2	25.6	143,710	58.4	5.0	40.7	71,462	52,186	24.8	8.5	16.1
27260	Jacksonville, FL	1,139,561	33.9	35.3	1,311,572	63.3	3.8	43.9	644,887	68,394	15.8	15.2	14.1
27340	Jacksonville, NC	111,047	42.1	23.8	161,136	68.2	4.2	26.7	73,121	55,534	19.8	8.8	13.2
27500	Janesville-Beloit, WI	113,903	39.0	24.9	132,147	65.0	3.9	44.2	67,876	66,090	15.4	8.3	15.3
27620	Jefferson City, MO	103,252	45.5	28.6	121,607	62.1	2.1	43.2	55,812	63,942	17.1	11.0	8.7
27740	Johnson City, TN	146,522	40.0	29.8	172,792	57.1	5.9	37.9	86,767	51,119	24.0	10.6	12.8
27780	Johnstown, PA	95,014	49.7	23.4	110,309	53.4	6.6	34.5	55,283	52,995	22.2	8.5	18.8
27860	Jonesboro, AR	87,650	42.1	28.7	104,825	61.5	6.2	42.9	51,155	47,935	29.4	12.0	15.4
27900	Joplin, MO	122,197	44.0	24.3	143,004	61.6	3.7	40.5	69,646	55,045	21.0	9.6	12.5
27980	Kahului-Wailuku-Lahaina, HI	119,076	36.7	30.0	132,126	64.0	6.7	35.7	56,319	76,273	15.2	23.7	14.7
28020	Kalamazoo-Portage, MI	164,236	26.9	39.5	210,748	65.5	5.6	38.8	105,642	62,128	20.5	12.4	12.9
28100	Kankakee, IL	71,036	42.1	21.5	85,581	61.6	5.0	38.9	41,020	63,364	17.6	12.0	15.8
28140	Kansas City, MO-KS	1,498,921	31.4	39.5	1,736,407	67.9	4.5	47.6	883,621	73,900	13.9	17.5	8.4
28420	Kennewick-Richland, WA	193,655	39.0	29.0	232,817	61.9	4.2	42.3	105,844	78,367	12.6	19.3	20.0
28660	Killeen-Temple, TX	302,040	35.0	26.5	372,803	62.5	6.3	34.9	174,498	59,753	19.3	9.0	12.9
28700	Kingsport-Bristol, TN-VA	227,180	49.0	21.9	256,709	52.3	6.6	34.3	128,312	48,771	27.3	8.0	16.1
28740	Kingston, NY	136,944	31.6	41.1	155,741	60.0	5.6	38.6	75,053	78,938	16.0	23.3	8.5
28940	Knoxville, TN	624,887	39.8	32.3	731,743	60.4	4.6	41.3	361,646	62,592	18.7	12.3	11.2
29020	Kokomo, IN	58,410	45.6	20.5	67,299	60.6	7.3	NA	36,530	55,088	17.4	8.6	14.8
29100	La Crosse-Onalaska, WI-MN	91,353	29.4	31.7	114,037	66.9	2.4	44.8	58,000	61,342	17.4	11.5	12.7
29180	Lafayette, LA	319,525	49.5	24.4	375,069	61.6	5.6	39.8	187,662	53,931	25.5	10.8	18.3
29200	Lafayette-West Lafayette, IN	132,560	36.1	36.4	183,513	62.6	3.3	37.6	88,853	53,559	22.3	8.1	8.2
29340	Lake Charles, LA	139,857	43.7	25.9	162,203	59.8	4.0	38.8	72,746	58,736	21.2	13.0	23.7
29420	Lake Havasu City-Kingman, AZ	169,737	47.1	15.1	186,723	45.6	8.6	28.0	102,398	46,616	27.8	7.3	14.0
29460	Lakeland-Winter Haven, FL	524,102	48.4	21.1	606,637	55.9	5.1	39.5	276,469	56,379	20.1	9.2	15.8
29540	Lancaster, PA	376,040	47.1	29.7	437,874	65.8	3.8	42.7	210,063	75,688	12.8	16.4	11.1
29620	Lansing-East Lansing, MI	358,066	31.7	34.8	442,463	61.9	7.2	37.3	220,067	61,980	18.0	11.0	13.4
29700	Laredo, TX	152,011	50.1	20.6	192,237	59.5	6.4	39.7	78,730	51,867	25.0	9.1	27.2
29740	Las Cruces, NM	138,777	41.9	30.1	176,124	57.4	7.2	32.3	85,021	45,178	28.2	8.7	26.7
29820	Las Vegas-Henderson-Paradise, NV	1,586,157	40.7	27.3	1,831,711	63.5	10.9	37.5	854,289	63,677	18.6	14.4	16.8
29940	Lawrence, KS	72,974	21.9	52.5	100,916	65.9	5.5	39.7	49,759	56,576	23.0	12.5	8.6
30020	Lawton, OK	80,894	41.6	24.3	99,940	60.9	7.5	34.4	46,916	49,422	23.8	7.2	14.5

Metropolitan area / division code	Metropolitan area / division	Educational attainment			Employment status				Household income and benefits				
		Total population 25 years and over	Percent with a high school diploma or less	Percent with a bachelor's degree or more	Total population 16 years and over	Labor force participation (percent)	Percent unemployed	Percent age 16 years and over who worked full-time year-round in the past 12 months	Total households	Median household income in the past 12 months (in 2021 inflation-adjusted dollars)	Income less than $25,000 (percent)	Income greater than $150,000 (percent)	Percent who received cash public assistance or food stamps/ SNAP
	ACS table number:	C15003	C15003	C15003	C23001	C23001	C23001	S2402	B19001	B19049	B19001	B19001	B19058
	Column number:	1	2	3	4	5	6	7	8	9	10	11	12
30140	Lebanon, PA	99,281	50.1	24.9	114,959	62.9	5.0	41.0	54,906	72,732	15.3	14.0	15.7
30300	Lewiston, ID-WA	45,199	39.5	23.9	NA	NA	NA	NA	27,019	57,610	21.8	12.0	12.5
30340	Lewiston-Auburn, ME	77,917	42.6	24.7	91,270	63.6	4.8	41.0	46,323	62,958	19.0	8.5	14.9
30460	Lexington-Fayette, KY	343,764	31.8	40.1	418,706	65.5	4.8	42.2	215,613	62,612	19.3	13.5	11.1
30620	Lima, OH	68,062	51.0	18.5	80,529	57.8	8.2	35.3	41,021	51,497	21.8	7.8	20.6
30700	Lincoln, NE	213,689	27.0	42.7	274,656	71.1	2.8	46.1	138,209	65,229	16.2	13.5	8.6
30780	Little Rock-North Little Rock-Conway, AR	504,900	35.4	33.3	594,252	63.0	4.8	44.6	308,436	58,357	20.7	11.4	10.2
30860	Logan, UT-ID	80,657	26.8	37.9	112,319	69.7	1.6	41.7	48,180	67,022	13.2	12.4	6.6
30980	Longview, TX	190,016	44.1	21.2	226,826	57.7	5.9	39.5	106,151	56,777	22.5	8.9	13.6
31020	Longview, WA	78,862	43.7	18.0	88,891	55.0	5.2	35.5	43,204	71,194	18.0	13.4	21.0
31080	Los Angeles-Long Beach-Anaheim, CA	9,096,153	37.8	37.1	10,576,303	64.6	8.8	39.3	4,452,780	82,503	16.2	24.4	15.7
3108011244	Anaheim-Santa Ana-Irvine, CA Division	2,212,457	30.1	43.1	2,573,809	65.4	8.8	46.9	1,077,193	100,559	11.9	31.6	11.2
3108031084	Los Angeles-Long Beach-Glendale, CA Division	6,883,696	40.2	35.1	8,002,494	64.3	10.5	45.3	3,375,587	77,456	17.6	22.1	17.1
31140	Louisville/Jefferson County, KY-IN	892,649	39.1	32.8	1,033,895	63.7	4.8	42.0	522,921	64,029	17.2	13.6	12.0
31180	Lubbock, TX	195,767	37.0	33.1	259,088	66.3	5.3	44.7	129,092	57,634	23.8	12.6	12.7
31340	Lynchburg, VA	174,719	39.2	30.7	218,071	61.1	5.0	40.5	103,894	58,617	17.9	11.7	11.2
31420	Macon-Bibb County, GA	155,864	46.2	24.4	184,193	57.4	7.5	38.4	85,760	53,397	23.1	9.4	21.3
31460	Madera, CA	100,667	53.3	17.7	120,503	55.0	13.8	30.5	44,048	63,454	23.2	17.2	21.6
31540	Madison, WI	461,251	25.0	48.8	561,764	69.2	2.8	48.3	292,919	76,731	13.8	19.7	9.3
31700	Manchester-Nashua, NH	304,324	30.9	41.4	349,991	70.5	3.6	48.8	167,899	91,627	10.0	23.7	7.5
31740	Manhattan, KS	76,234	28.5	40.8	106,187	70.2	4.4	37.5	51,018	57,835	21.2	10.6	7.2
31860	Mankato, MN	63,671	29.6	35.0	85,361	70.8	3.8	42.0	40,715	70,130	13.8	15.1	8.0
31900	Mansfield, OH	87,623	52.3	17.4	101,247	58.1	5.2	35.5	49,536	51,158	24.0	7.8	15.4
32420	Mayagüez, PR	67,517	55.9	24.7	83,416	41.2	21.6	NA	36,278	16,618	68.6	1.6	57.0
32580	McAllen-Edinburg-Mission, TX	504,147	57.0	20.0	633,534	57.1	9.0	35.2	268,598	44,818	30.4	6.5	31.9
32780	Medford, OR	161,605	32.5	33.1	182,687	56.3	7.7	32.7	90,817	64,249	17.8	11.0	18.2
32820	Memphis, TN-MS-AR	888,410	39.6	31.0	1,043,878	63.7	7.6	43.1	520,309	55,840	21.6	12.6	16.0
32900	Merced, CA	170,994	57.9	14.4	213,398	57.4	14.7	31.5	84,967	53,992	24.9	9.2	23.8
33100	Miami-Fort Lauderdale-Pompano Beach, FL	4,399,300	39.2	35.3	5,012,306	63.2	6.3	42.5	2,306,639	63,814	19.4	15.9	20.4
3310022744	Fort Lauderdale-Pompano Beach-Sunrise, FL Division	1,382,208	37.1	35.9	1,574,220	66.2	6.9	50.3	747,715	65,747	18.0	15.5	17.0
3310033124	Miami-Miami Beach-Kendall, FL Division	1,911,144	43.8	32.3	2,191,172	63.2	7.8	49.8	963,477	59,044	21.8	14.3	27.3
3310048424	West Palm Beach-Boca Raton-Boynton Beach, FL Division	1,105,948	33.8	39.7	1,246,914	59.4	7.2	43.6	595,447	70,002	17.2	18.9	13.5
33140	Michigan City-La Porte, IN	79,010	49.2	21.2	91,635	55.3	4.4	37.3	43,445	63,714	17.8	10.5	9.8
33220	Midland, MI	59,204	28.8	38.5	68,067	58.6	6.0	36.4	35,453	67,707	17.1	17.4	12.3
33260	Midland, TX	109,882	33.8	34.1	130,043	72.9	5.4	51.2	68,042	80,478	14.2	22.2	9.8
33340	Milwaukee-Waukesha, WI	1,073,083	33.2	39.2	1,249,190	65.6	4.2	43.6	649,303	68,449	16.9	16.2	16.5
33460	Minneapolis-St. Paul-Bloomington, MN-WI	2,525,349	25.7	44.7	2,930,197	70.8	5.0	46.5	1,453,400	87,433	11.1	23.9	9.8
33540	Missoula, MT	82,368	23.2	45.6	99,414	69.5	5.1	40.0	51,957	66,803	17.0	17.1	13.8
33660	Mobile, AL	291,740	46.6	22.3	341,703	58.0	7.0	40.5	168,977	49,691	24.4	8.4	20.3
33700	Modesto, CA	352,947	50.4	19.3	420,902	62.2	9.3	36.9	174,209	73,982	15.1	15.9	16.1
33740	Monroe, LA	137,348	47.1	23.9	163,858	56.9	10.0	37.4	80,334	45,001	33.5	8.9	20.8
33780	Monroe, MI	109,946	41.0	22.6	126,068	57.9	5.7	36.7	61,574	65,512	15.9	13.4	11.9
33860	Montgomery, AL	261,916	43.7	29.1	307,081	59.4	6.7	38.7	150,996	52,677	23.7	9.3	17.8
34060	Morgantown, WV	92,081	38.6	40.5	118,601	58.9	6.1	37.6	56,020	58,274	22.5	14.0	11.6
34100	Morristown, TN	101,742	51.4	18.2	115,490	54.9	6.8	38.0	53,925	43,213	28.8	5.6	13.4
34580	Mount Vernon-Anacortes, WA	93,248	35.1	28.6	106,116	56.3	6.2	33.7	51,971	72,648	15.3	16.0	16.9
34620	Muncie, IN	68,558	43.4	24.5	93,555	58.5	8.7	35.2	45,977	50,497	25.6	6.5	15.1
34740	Muskegon, MI	121,226	46.0	19.6	140,578	56.9	7.6	36.1	67,707	55,462	19.7	7.1	18.2
34820	Myrtle Beach-Conway-North Myrtle Beach, SC-NC	392,445	36.9	28.4	435,358	51.5	6.4	30.8	210,672	59,073	18.3	10.0	9.6

Table B-3. Metropolitan Areas — What: Education, Employment, and Income, 2021—*Continued*

Metropolitan area / division code	Metropolitan area / division	Educational attainment: Total population 25 years and over	Percent with a high school diploma or less	Percent with a bachelor's degree or more	Employment status: Total population 16 years and over	Labor force participation (percent)	Percent unemployed	Percent age 16 years and over who worked full-time year-round in the past 12 months	Household income and benefits: Total households	Median household income in the past 12 months (in 2021 inflation-adjusted dollars)	Income less than $25,000 (percent)	Income greater than $150,000 (percent)	Percent who received cash public assistance or food stamps/SNAP
	ACS table number:	C15003	C15003	C15003	C23001	C23001	C23001	S2402	B19001	B19049	B19001	B19001	B19058
	Column number:	1	2	3	4	5	6	7	8	9	10	11	12
34900	Napa, CA	97,626	33.8	37.7	113,324	63.9	6.4	41.2	49,979	97,213	10.7	31.0	10.3
34940	Naples-Marco Island, FL	297,766	36.6	40.3	330,215	51.6	4.8	32.2	163,943	74,215	12.6	22.1	8.6
34980	Nashville-Davidson--Murfreesboro--Franklin, TN	1,377,272	33.7	40.2	1,611,166	67.5	4.0	47.2	794,373	72,725	13.7	18.3	9.5
35100	New Bern, NC	83,134	34.5	27.7	99,463	58.0	4.9	34.8	51,021	55,390	21.0	7.7	13.3
35300	New Haven-Milford, CT	608,407	37.6	39.5	713,029	65.3	8.0	41.1	349,089	75,295	17.0	20.5	16.1
35380	New Orleans-Metairie, LA	883,996	38.5	33.6	1,014,149	61.5	8.5	39.8	507,992	56,837	23.6	13.5	17.3
35620	New York-Newark-Jersey City, NY-NJ-PA	13,928,619	35.3	43.6	16,032,587	64.5	9.3	40.4	7,347,700	84,409	16.9	27.2	15.8
3562035004	Nassau County-Suffolk County, NY Division	2,052,938	32.0	44.9	2,381,917	66.2	7.0	50.7	971,403	120,124	9.3	38.7	7.5
3562035084	Newark, NJ-PA Division	1,582,979	34.8	43.5	1,832,441	66.0	9.8	49.9	851,554	87,988	14.6	28.7	10.7
3562035154	New Brunswick-Lakewood, NJ Metro Division	1,738,327	31.7	45.1	2,014,677	65.2	8.3	48.5	930,244	97,484	11.9	30.5	7.9
3562035614	New York-Jersey City-White Plains, NY-NJ Division	8,554,375	36.9	43.0	9,803,552	63.6	11.9	44.5	4,594,499	75,228	20.0	23.8	20.0
35660	Niles, MI	107,677	35.7	33.2	124,028	60.1	5.6	37.8	65,764	57,535	22.1	14.1	14.7
35840	North Port-Sarasota-Bradenton, FL	672,375	32.9	37.4	742,443	52.5	4.5	34.1	367,538	70,095	15.4	16.8	8.0
35980	Norwich-New London, CT	190,962	36.2	34.5	222,922	63.8	4.9	37.2	110,950	78,828	13.1	19.9	13.9
36100	Ocala, FL	289,018	46.4	23.1	323,475	49.2	5.7	34.5	157,348	55,161	19.5	8.8	15.5
36140	Ocean City, NJ	74,047	33.6	40.8	81,385	56.6	6.2	NA	48,860	78,657	14.0	18.4	10.8
36220	Odessa, TX	95,780	56.6	16.2	117,856	66.4	10.9	46.1	64,169	57,473	19.4	7.4	14.0
36260	Ogden-Clearfield, UT	431,549	30.9	33.4	524,687	69.1	3.0	44.9	230,356	81,364	11.4	19.7	7.1
36420	Oklahoma City, OK	946,808	37.0	33.2	1,133,958	64.9	5.5	43.3	565,309	61,815	18.5	12.0	14.7
36500	Olympia-Lacey-Tumwater, WA	209,608	25.3	37.7	242,143	60.7	6.2	38.3	117,186	81,659	12.7	18.4	15.0
36540	Omaha-Council Bluffs, NE-IA	642,524	29.6	38.9	754,463	69.5	3.1	48.3	385,487	73,720	15.2	17.7	10.5
36740	Orlando-Kissimmee-Sanford, FL	1,871,455	34.5	35.2	2,184,228	63.7	6.5	41.7	990,500	64,936	16.9	14.9	17.1
36780	Oshkosh-Neenah, WI	116,688	36.8	29.6	141,220	66.9	2.2	43.4	72,794	64,095	15.4	10.7	12.5
36980	Owensboro, KY	83,149	39.5	26.4	97,155	59.6	5.8	41.7	48,574	60,189	18.8	11.6	12.5
37100	Oxnard-Thousand Oaks-Ventura, CA ...	579,194	35.0	34.7	676,606	64.6	7.4	39.8	279,168	96,454	10.3	27.4	11.3
37340	Palm Bay-Melbourne-Titusville, FL	462,336	33.7	33.1	519,483	56.3	4.9	38.6	254,314	65,333	18.3	14.3	11.4
37460	Panama City, FL	129,450	35.7	29.9	147,141	63.4	4.3	42.0	79,532	60,557	16.1	11.0	14.0
37620	Parkersburg-Vienna, WV	63,116	46.2	24.6	72,057	57.1	6.5	35.0	37,656	54,284	25.1	8.5	18.5
37860	Pensacola-Ferry Pass-Brent, FL	356,664	35.4	30.4	418,543	60.7	4.9	37.6	198,702	64,877	17.4	12.2	16.3
37900	Peoria, IL	274,771	35.2	30.9	316,778	61.1	5.7	40.0	171,067	59,760	18.7	12.3	16.4
37980	Philadelphia-Camden-Wilmington, PA-NJ-DE-MD	4,354,791	34.7	41.9	5,041,350	65.4	7.3	42.7	2,442,868	80,007	16.5	22.9	15.1
3798015804	Camden, NJ Division	906,701	35.4	38.8	1,047,227	65.6	7.9	48.2	489,519	87,634	13.1	24.4	10.3
3798033874	Montgomery County-Bucks County-Chester County, PA Division	1,446,851	27.8	51.0	1,663,026	67.6	5.8	53.2	787,417	103,717	10.6	31.8	8.3
3798037964	Philadelphia, PA Division..................	1,484,073	40.2	36.9	1,730,246	63.8	11.3	46.9	879,201	58,921	23.9	15.3	25.2
3798048864	Wilmington, DE-MD-NJ Division	517,166	36.7	36.6	600,851	63.6	7.6	48.8	286,731	73,711	15.3	19.4	11.4
38060	Phoenix-Mesa-Chandler, AZ	3,361,075	33.0	34.6	3,943,236	63.6	5.2	43.2	1,863,195	75,731	13.2	17.7	11.4
38220	Pine Bluff, AR	61,026	52.6	23.3	70,913	48.2	8.5	32.9	30,092	46,826	27.4	8.7	13.4
38300	Pittsburgh, PA	1,721,431	36.2	38.1	1,962,390	62.5	6.0	41.1	1,025,698	66,609	18.6	15.7	14.8
38340	Pittsfield, MA	96,128	35.5	38.4	110,107	61.8	6.9	37.2	57,765	60,749	20.0	16.6	18.2
38540	Pocatello, ID	61,858	31.2	30.3	74,782	60.1	4.0	38.2	36,438	60,475	19.3	8.6	17.5
38660	Ponce, PR	157,855	49.8	29.4	183,717	42.8	16.8	21.9	75,345	19,006	60.0	1.7	55.5
38860	Portland-South Portland, ME	413,081	27.2	45.0	467,802	65.3	4.4	43.6	237,186	78,558	13.4	18.7	9.2
38900	Portland-Vancouver-Hillsboro, OR-WA ..	1,794,958	26.5	42.2	2,053,829	65.7	6.1	42.1	1,001,984	83,943	13.4	22.1	15.7
38940	Port St. Lucie, FL	374,659	37.0	30.1	421,003	54.6	6.2	37.8	200,954	63,771	16.8	12.0	13.5
39100	Poughkeepsie-Newburgh-Middletown, NY	471,559	34.8	37.5	564,726	63.5	6.5	39.7	255,736	89,033	13.6	24.8	10.4
39140	Prescott Valley-Prescott, AZ	189,526	33.4	28.9	210,145	48.7	4.3	28.8	112,075	57,230	19.0	10.0	10.3
39300	Providence-Warwick, RI-MA	1,183,879	40.6	34.1	1,388,683	65.1	7.4	40.8	673,701	73,788	18.2	18.8	18.2
39340	Provo-Orem, UT	359,760	21.5	45.5	497,799	71.3	3.0	41.4	197,599	86,629	9.1	21.4	6.4

Table B-3. Metropolitan Areas — What: Education, Employment, and Income, 2021—*Continued*

Metropolitan area / division code	Metropolitan area / division	Educational attainment			Employment status				Household income and benefits				
		Total population 25 years and over	Percent with a high school diploma or less	Percent with a bachelor's degree or more	Total population 16 years and over	Labor force participation (percent)	Percent unemployed	Percent age 16 years and over who worked full-time year-round in the past 12 months	Total households	Median household income in the past 12 months (in 2021 inflation-adjusted dollars)	Income less than $25,000 (percent)	Income greater than $150,000 (percent)	Percent who received cash public assistance or food stamps/ SNAP
	ACS table number:	C15003	C15003	C15003	C23001	C23001	C23001	S2402	B19001	B19049	B19001	B19001	B19058
	Column number:	1	2	3	4	5	6	7	8	9	10	11	12
39380	Pueblo, CO	117,286	38.0	26.6	136,889	55.3	6.5	34.9	69,078	56,689	24.6	9.8	20.8
39460	Punta Gorda, FL	162,234	42.0	25.9	175,973	42.1	6.2	25.4	88,988	59,285	18.2	10.1	11.0
39540	Racine, WI	136,852	40.6	24.6	157,976	62.7	4.6	42.1	79,068	68,758	15.3	13.1	14.7
39580	Raleigh-Cary, NC	980,746	24.4	50.7	1,148,268	68.2	5.0	47.4	548,713	85,303	13.7	23.7	10.0
39660	Rapid City, SD	96,311	31.8	34.6	112,660	65.3	2.9	40.2	57,532	63,342	16.6	11.1	9.5
39740	Reading, PA	294,555	50.1	26.2	345,128	62.9	6.2	40.1	164,312	68,658	17.6	15.9	17.6
39820	Redding, CA	128,739	35.5	23.6	146,930	55.3	8.7	33.4	71,506	61,125	19.6	12.3	15.6
39900	Reno, NV	349,273	35.3	34.3	403,687	65.5	5.2	43.4	199,715	76,182	13.9	18.0	13.4
40060	Richmond, VA	924,313	33.2	40.2	1,068,574	65.1	5.4	45.2	521,067	74,151	15.5	19.0	11.3
40140	Riverside-San Bernardino-Ontario, CA	3,031,490	45.2	23.7	3,619,781	60.9	8.7	38.6	1,441,602	77,018	14.7	17.6	15.2
40220	Roanoke, VA	227,781	40.4	30.8	259,097	59.3	4.0	39.9	131,211	59,630	20.9	11.2	11.7
40340	Rochester, MN	153,221	27.2	42.1	178,776	70.0	4.4	45.5	90,956	80,434	13.8	19.7	8.5
40380	Rochester, NY	762,590	34.5	37.5	892,192	62.9	6.4	39.9	454,044	66,516	17.1	14.1	14.3
40420	Rockford, IL	228,436	42.6	24.6	266,628	61.4	10.6	37.9	134,008	56,746	20.3	10.6	21.5
40580	Rocky Mount, NC	99,759	44.8	21.2	116,462	59.4	5.7	40.4	56,840	51,769	23.3	9.0	23.4
40660	Rome, GA	65,299	46.0	22.9	78,949	58.1	3.1	42.6	35,417	60,825	18.2	10.4	12.7
40900	Sacramento-Roseville-Folsom, CA	1,652,314	31.1	36.4	1,931,099	62.2	6.9	39.7	879,647	84,421	14.1	22.9	13.9
40980	Saginaw, MI	130,970	42.8	22.5	153,337	55.9	8.1	33.5	80,146	50,606	28.1	8.5	21.2
41060	St. Cloud, MN	125,230	33.1	27.1	158,613	71.5	5.0	41.7	79,091	65,641	16.9	11.2	9.2
41100	St. George, UT	125,129	26.7	34.3	150,518	55.8	4.4	34.5	68,090	61,186	14.3	11.2	5.9
41140	St. Joseph, MO-KS	83,016	50.8	22.9	95,740	58.3	4.4	39.7	46,798	54,702	22.5	9.6	13.1
41180	St. Louis, MO-IL	1,964,659	32.9	37.1	2,264,687	64.7	5.0	43.4	1,144,111	70,189	16.1	16.8	11.7
41420	Salem, OR	290,936	36.6	26.8	345,835	60.2	5.4	38.6	158,144	65,665	15.2	12.9	22.8
41500	Salinas, CA	281,950	46.8	27.2	337,011	59.5	6.6	36.5	133,224	82,163	11.1	21.3	10.5
41540	Salisbury, MD-DE	310,073	40.7	31.6	358,360	55.1	7.1	34.1	177,002	68,470	17.4	16.0	14.6
41620	Salt Lake City, UT	809,926	31.1	36.2	972,894	71.2	4.0	47.1	443,798	81,307	11.6	19.1	7.1
41660	San Angelo, TX	78,104	44.7	23.9	95,433	63.1	3.7	42.3	46,604	61,302	20.4	7.7	7.9
41700	San Antonio-New Braunfels, TX	1,709,986	38.4	31.4	2,034,700	64.5	5.9	41.8	948,519	66,775	16.8	14.8	15.7
41740	San Diego-Chula Vista-Carlsbad, CA	2,265,902	29.6	42.0	2,668,188	66.4	8.1	39.7	1,162,896	91,003	13.4	26.3	12.8
41860	San Francisco-Oakland-Berkeley, CA	3,380,108	25.7	51.8	3,830,745	66.3	7.2	43.3	1,719,049	116,005	12.1	39.8	12.3
4186036084	Oakland-Berkeley-Livermore, CA Division	1,999,763	27.8	48.0	2,290,308	65.9	8.3	49.0	1,000,740	110,350	11.7	37.4	12.9
4186041884	San Francisco-San Mateo-Redwood City, CA Division	1,187,598	23.5	56.8	1,323,481	67.7	8.4	50.4	614,931	127,097	12.8	43.3	11.9
4186042034	San Rafael, CA Division	192,747	17.0	59.5	216,956	62.6	7.2	42.2	103,378	118,209	11.5	42.0	8.5
41900	San Germán, PR	86,303	54.6	25.0	102,725	39.2	16.4	NA	43,263	18,454	62.9	1.6	53.3
41940	San Jose-Sunnyvale-Santa Clara, CA	1,375,621	24.7	54.0	1,586,745	66.7	6.0	46.6	670,900	139,892	8.7	47.2	9.1
41980	San Juan-Bayamón-Caguas, PR	1,523,855	45.7	30.3	1,773,577	47.3	12.1	26.8	747,507	25,042	49.9	3.1	46.3
42020	San Luis Obispo-Paso Robles, CA	191,488	25.8	39.4	239,898	57.6	7.4	32.4	107,571	80,615	14.2	22.7	8.3
42100	Santa Cruz-Watsonville, CA	179,402	27.2	42.8	224,521	63.3	7.7	36.4	97,353	93,933	11.5	31.4	13.0
42140	Santa Fe, NM	118,349	24.6	46.2	132,192	57.9	7.5	35.1	70,152	67,341	17.2	18.3	13.6
42200	Santa Maria-Santa Barbara, CA	280,575	35.1	36.3	359,531	62.0	7.2	35.7	150,550	84,846	15.3	25.5	14.0
42220	Santa Rosa-Petaluma, CA	354,563	29.7	38.3	403,841	64.0	6.8	38.1	190,586	94,295	11.3	28.5	10.7
42340	Savannah, GA	277,937	33.0	35.5	328,167	63.8	5.4	41.7	160,666	66,245	17.4	13.8	13.8
42540	Scranton--Wilkes-Barre, PA	405,140	45.3	27.5	467,393	59.9	6.9	39.7	233,473	61,174	20.1	10.6	18.6
42660	Seattle-Tacoma-Bellevue, WA	2,847,328	25.0	46.8	3,258,184	67.9	5.6	44.2	1,584,796	101,721	10.9	31.7	11.8
4266042644	Seattle-Bellevue-Kent, WA Division	2,217,200	22.6	51.4	2,524,963	68.2	6.4	51.2	1,237,128	106,715	10.9	34.4	11.0
4266045104	Tacoma-Lakewood, WA Division	630,128	33.4	30.8	733,221	66.9	6.2	48.5	347,668	85,866	10.8	22.1	14.5
42680	Sebastian-Vero Beach, FL	127,374	33.3	33.9	140,566	48.6	5.5	30.8	69,974	58,972	17.1	13.2	12.8
42700	Sebring-Avon Park, FL	80,311	52.1	18.3	88,081	44.5	9.3	NA	46,166	48,564	23.9	4.4	16.9
43100	Sheboygan, WI	82,869	39.5	27.0	95,172	65.2	2.7	42.7	49,416	62,188	16.0	11.8	10.1
43300	Sherman-Denison, TX	94,750	37.1	26.6	109,970	61.5	3.3	44.3	56,005	62,919	16.3	14.5	9.4
43340	Shreveport-Bossier City, LA	261,751	45.0	25.8	306,513	56.3	8.9	35.0	155,848	48,164	27.2	9.8	19.4
43420	Sierra Vista-Douglas, AZ	89,149	38.3	26.2	102,096	50.9	7.8	30.5	49,952	56,600	23.2	8.9	19.0
43580	Sioux City, IA-NE-SD	95,004	46.8	23.8	113,804	68.8	3.4	46.8	57,421	64,232	16.6	11.0	12.8

Metropolitan area / division code	Metropolitan area / division	Educational attainment			Employment status				Household income and benefits				
		Total population 25 years and over	Percent with a high school diploma or less	Percent with a bachelor's degree or more	Total population 16 years and over	Labor force participation (percent)	Percent unemployed	Percent age 16 years and over who worked full-time year-round in the past 12 months	Total households	Median household income in the past 12 months (in 2021 inflation-adjusted dollars)	Income less than $25,000 (percent)	Income greater than $150,000 (percent)	Percent who received cash public assistance or food stamps/SNAP
	ACS table number:	C15003	C15003	C15003	C23001	C23001	C23001	S2402	B19001	B19049	B19001	B19001	B19058
	Column number:	1	2	3	4	5	6	7	8	9	10	11	12
43620	Sioux Falls, SD	186,236	30.0	37.0	216,201	74.7	1.8	55.2	114,967	75,946	11.7	15.9	7.6
43780	South Bend-Mishawaka, IN-MI	215,827	39.8	30.2	257,357	62.5	5.1	40.4	128,774	59,416	19.9	11.0	12.1
43900	Spartanburg, SC	227,599	44.0	24.8	267,295	62.3	4.4	43.1	128,437	60,472	19.2	10.3	12.5
44060	Spokane-Spokane Valley, WA	411,288	30.4	30.5	477,404	60.6	6.2	37.4	237,024	65,283	16.6	12.6	18.6
44100	Springfield, IL	145,130	32.9	36.4	166,947	60.5	7.2	41.7	89,340	68,796	18.8	14.7	17.0
44140	Springfield, MA	472,577	38.3	36.8	579,907	58.9	7.7	35.2	275,788	65,520	21.1	15.7	22.5
44180	Springfield, MO	318,066	38.1	31.2	385,663	62.7	3.9	41.9	195,260	56,896	18.8	10.3	9.9
44220	Springfield, OH	93,487	47.0	18.9	108,294	62.1	6.1	39.1	57,013	59,431	21.7	9.6	21.0
44300	State College, PA	97,255	37.4	45.3	136,930	57.5	5.7	33.5	57,518	66,789	19.8	17.4	8.6
44420	Staunton, VA	91,118	45.5	28.0	104,891	61.3	4.6	42.0	51,802	60,488	16.8	11.5	9.6
44700	Stockton, CA	504,631	47.1	20.1	602,505	60.3	9.0	37.7	241,760	80,681	14.4	20.3	18.1
44940	Sumter, SC	92,260	46.8	22.0	109,453	56.5	8.6	36.3	54,669	43,210	32.3	6.6	20.6
45060	Syracuse, NY	451,973	36.6	34.1	536,753	60.8	6.3	37.9	270,350	64,296	20.3	13.9	16.7
45220	Tallahassee, FL	245,067	31.5	40.4	323,155	63.1	5.4	41.1	155,921	58,945	19.8	12.3	16.2
45300	Tampa-St. Petersburg-Clearwater, FL	2,346,008	36.2	34.5	2,663,439	60.9	5.1	41.7	1,309,614	62,951	18.7	14.6	13.7
45460	Terre Haute, IN	125,739	50.4	19.7	151,040	57.1	6.3	36.4	73,024	50,440	23.5	8.4	14.4
45500	Texarkana, TX-AR	98,828	50.2	20.9	115,211	54.3	5.1	39.4	55,179	50,070	25.1	9.8	11.4
45540	The Villages, FL	122,943	36.0	35.0	127,313	24.6	6.9	NA	68,792	64,608	15.8	11.6	6.2
45780	Toledo, OH	437,599	39.1	30.2	517,313	63.7	6.7	39.8	273,165	58,191	21.4	10.7	14.2
45820	Topeka, KS	160,146	37.9	31.4	184,977	61.8	3.1	44.0	95,988	57,474	19.5	9.0	8.2
45940	Trenton-Princeton, NJ	261,325	33.0	45.9	313,405	63.6	7.6	40.1	143,970	87,662	14.9	25.7	12.7
46060	Tucson, AZ	718,288	31.9	34.9	864,266	58.9	5.9	36.7	433,148	60,667	19.1	12.6	14.4
46140	Tulsa, OK	686,657	38.8	30.7	802,858	62.8	6.2	42.6	403,034	59,696	19.5	12.3	13.5
46220	Tuscaloosa, AL	171,953	43.7	26.4	215,687	58.5	5.2	39.9	101,825	53,998	24.6	12.1	13.7
46300	Twin Falls, ID	75,530	45.1	21.4	89,779	62.5	5.6	39.8	42,906	55,519	20.6	10.3	12.8
46340	Tyler, TX	156,651	38.8	27.7	186,104	61.3	5.1	42.6	81,175	63,115	14.9	13.3	12.9
46520	Urban Honolulu, HI	702,553	32.3	37.1	810,934	64.5	6.5	37.3	338,093	90,704	12.9	25.5	13.8
46540	Utica-Rome, NY	203,350	41.0	26.3	235,624	57.2	5.6	37.0	118,513	60,313	19.9	9.9	16.5
46660	Valdosta, GA	88,106	46.2	22.3	114,199	56.7	7.1	34.5	55,279	42,233	33.4	6.5	20.3
46700	Vallejo, CA	315,084	34.6	29.4	363,577	62.3	7.1	36.7	157,617	87,770	12.9	22.0	12.8
47020	Victoria, TX	65,539	50.7	20.1	77,711	63.2	5.6	42.9	41,036	54,333	20.6	10.8	16.5
47220	Vineland-Bridgeton, NJ	103,800	57.1	18.3	121,314	54.2	5.8	38.5	53,883	58,389	20.7	10.9	17.7
47260	Virginia Beach-Norfolk-Newport News, VA-NC	1,219,244	32.0	36.1	1,452,061	67.2	4.6	41.2	721,212	72,686	14.7	16.4	11.8
47300	Visalia, CA	284,391	53.4	16.2	350,237	58.8	10.1	35.6	143,541	58,209	19.4	11.3	25.9
47380	Waco, TX	173,636	37.4	27.3	219,682	61.8	4.8	41.8	102,138	60,070	19.8	13.8	11.9
47460	Walla Walla, WA	42,966	32.6	29.5	52,115	59.5	7.9	NA	23,444	65,271	14.3	14.5	11.8
47580	Warner Robins, GA	129,087	39.0	28.8	154,603	62.8	5.5	42.4	70,357	70,552	16.1	12.7	14.9
47900	Washington-Arlington-Alexandria, DC-VA-MD-WV	4,369,426	25.9	53.4	5,075,249	70.3	5.5	48.5	2,384,977	110,355	10.4	35.3	9.7
4790023224	Frederick-Gaithersburg-Rockville, MD Division	924,602	23.5	57.6	1,065,800	69.5	6.5	53.7	492,081	111,159	9.5	36.1	9.6
4790047894	Washington-Arlington-Alexandria, DC-VA-MD-WV Division	3,444,824	26.5	52.3	4,009,449	70.5	6.4	57.0	1,892,896	110,131	10.6	35.1	9.8
47940	Waterloo-Cedar Falls, IA	108,717	38.0	29.5	134,965	65.4	3.4	40.5	68,479	61,833	19.2	8.6	11.4
48060	Watertown-Fort Drum, NY	75,886	37.6	29.6	91,946	63.7	5.4	34.3	48,628	60,398	14.7	8.1	14.4
48140	Wausau-Weston, WI	117,692	40.5	26.4	133,935	66.8	3.7	47.3	69,891	71,486	15.5	11.4	10.4
48260	Weirton-Steubenville, WV-OH	83,102	47.3	22.5	94,965	56.1	7.7	35.1	49,145	49,362	25.8	6.8	16.7
48300	Wenatchee, WA	82,988	41.0	29.2	97,445	59.9	4.2	38.2	47,559	65,006	15.2	16.3	16.6
48540	Wheeling, WV-OH	99,986	51.1	23.1	114,855	55.1	5.1	36.5	57,332	52,728	24.5	7.8	16.6
48620	Wichita, KS	426,603	35.9	30.9	503,699	65.2	6.2	41.7	250,146	61,131	17.7	10.3	11.7
48660	Wichita Falls, TX	96,707	47.2	23.7	119,251	62.3	3.2	42.2	56,846	55,107	22.0	10.6	13.8
48700	Williamsport, PA	80,539	47.9	26.1	92,609	59.5	5.2	36.8	47,022	60,494	17.5	8.4	17.2
48900	Wilmington, NC	206,473	28.6	39.7	243,382	63.5	5.4	41.1	127,095	66,939	16.3	15.6	10.7

Table B-3. Metropolitan Areas — What: Education, Employment, and Income, 2021—*Continued*

Metropolitan area / division code	Metropolitan area / division	Educational attainment			Employment status				Household income and benefits				
		Total population 25 years and over	Percent with a high school diploma or less	Percent with a bachelor's degree or more	Total population 16 years and over	Labor force participation (percent)	Percent unemployed	Percent age 16 years and over who worked full-time year-round in the past 12 months	Total households	Median household income in the past 12 months (in 2021 inflation-adjusted dollars)	Income less than $25,000 (percent)	Income greater than $150,000 (percent)	Percent who received cash public assistance or food stamps/ SNAP
	ACS table number:	C15003	C15003	C15003	C23001	C23001	C23001	S2402	B19001	B19049	B19001	B19001	B19058
	Column number:	1	2	3	4	5	6	7	8	9	10	11	12
49020	Winchester, VA-WV	98,028	45.2	29.8	114,621	62.6	6.2	42.3	52,949	72,798	13.9	15.2	10.9
49180	Winston-Salem, NC	470,590	40.3	30.1	550,952	59.4	5.4	40.1	273,913	57,392	21.1	11.2	16.9
49340	Worcester, MA-CT	685,857	35.7	38.4	803,555	66.7	7.8	41.6	379,159	83,195	15.9	22.6	17.6
49420	Yakima, WA	156,443	52.7	18.4	189,619	61.6	9.5	37.3	86,992	61,012	16.9	8.5	25.5
49500	Yauco, PR	66,397	54.2	24.2	75,063	37.6	14.3	NA	29,142	17,728	62.1	0.3	56.3
49620	York-Hanover, PA	320,624	46.5	27.5	371,013	65.3	4.5	43.2	178,898	72,949	13.3	16.3	11.9
49660	Youngstown-Warren-Boardman, OH-PA	384,636	48.8	25.0	442,970	55.6	6.0	33.8	230,536	51,194	24.1	7.1	18.4
49700	Yuba City, CA	118,465	47.2	18.1	139,493	59.6	8.6	34.6	61,597	63,678	17.4	12.4	21.6
49740	Yuma, AZ	133,866	51.6	17.3	160,561	54.9	8.6	34.7	74,981	57,304	19.2	7.9	23.0

NA = Not available.

Table B-4. Cities — What: Education, Employment, and Income, 2021

STATE Place / ACS table number / column number	Educational attainment			Employment status				Household income and benefits				
	Total population 25 years and over	Percent with a high school diploma or less	Percent with a bachelor's degree or more	Total population 16 years and over	Labor force participation (percent)	Percent unemployed	Percent age 16 years and over who worked full-time year-round in the past 12 months	Total households	Median household income in the past 12 months (in 2021 inflation-adjusted dollars)	Income less than $25,000 (percent)	Income greater than $150,000 (percent)	Percent who received cash public assistance or food stamps/ SNAP
STATE and place code	C15003	C15003	C15003	C23001	C23001	C23001	S2402	B19001	B19049	B19001	B19001	B19058
	1	2	3	4	5	6	7	8	9	10	11	12
00000 **UNITED STATES**..................	228,193,464	36.9	35.0	267,057,693	63.0	6.3	65.1	127,544,730	69,717	17.4	17.7	14.1
01000 **ALABAMA**..........................	3,451,208	43.3	27.4	4,046,627	57.7	5.3	68.1	1,967,559	53,913	23.7	10.9	14.9
0103076 Auburn city, Alabama	42,899	17.9	63.0	NA	NA	NA	NA	29,136	48,531	31.3	17.7	8.0
0107000 Birmingham city, Alabama	134,181	41.7	29.2	162,461	58.9	7.3	36.8	87,570	36,614	34.8	6.6	26.8
0121184 Dothan city, Alabama	49,536	41.3	25.2	57,160	56.6	5.3	37.6	30,301	45,088	26.7	9.9	16.9
0135896 Hoover city, Alabama	65,696	13.2	65.8	73,403	68.9	3.5	48.8	36,721	99,276	12.7	27.7	3.9
0137000 Huntsville city, Alabama	150,060	24.3	48.9	177,146	62.2	3.9	42.1	96,551	70,757	15.7	17.8	9.5
0150000 Mobile city, Alabama	125,812	40.9	27.7	147,671	58.7	7.8	41.8	77,991	43,786	28.2	8.3	23.3
0151000 Montgomery city, Alabama	130,448	41.5	32.8	155,597	59.6	8.4	37.6	81,529	46,957	28.6	7.1	22.4
0177256 Tuscaloosa city, Alabama	56,962	38.2	38.5	83,826	58.9	6.4	36.7	39,266	41,770	30.9	11.2	14.3
02000 **ALASKA**	485,779	34.6	32.8	571,832	65.9	6.5	55.9	271,311	77,845	14.7	19.9	14.3
0203000 Anchorage municipality, Alaska....	191,999	28.0	38.3	225,620	70.2	6.2	40.1	109,584	86,654	12.5	23.4	13.3
04000 **ARIZONA**............................	4,980,297	34.5	32.4	5,852,913	60.6	5.7	66.1	2,817,723	69,056	15.9	15.3	12.9
0404720 Avondale city, Arizona	51,756	45.7	22.0	65,382	70.5	7.3	NA	26,611	71,423	14.3	13.0	17.0
0407940 Buckeye city, Arizona	66,949	38.2	23.0	NA	NA	NA	NA	30,913	75,417	7.4	15.0	7.4
0410670 Casas Adobes CDP, Arizona	51,767	25.9	39.4	62,665	64.1	4.6	39.1	31,869	71,547	9.9	12.3	8.1
0412000 Chandler city, Arizona.................	191,101	23.5	47.3	223,189	71.2	3.3	52.3	107,668	94,613	9.0	24.4	8.0
0423620 Flagstaff city, Arizona	40,608	24.9	47.7	64,986	68.3	9.8	NA	29,435	61,386	24.3	13.9	12.4
0427400 Gilbert town, Arizona	170,153	20.0	47.4	200,934	72.6	4.2	50.1	93,472	104,802	5.2	30.8	5.7
0427820 Glendale city, Arizona	164,077	44.1	23.1	198,646	65.2	6.7	41.5	90,604	62,910	18.5	11.3	16.2
0428380 Goodyear city, Arizona................	67,881	28.8	33.2	79,785	56.2	3.3	NA	33,130	90,577	5.7	19.2	14.5
0446000 Mesa city, Arizona.....................	350,239	33.1	32.3	406,200	64.0	4.2	42.6	199,112	69,266	14.0	14.2	10.8
0454050 Peoria city, Arizona	140,143	29.5	35.7	158,505	62.2	4.6	45.7	75,479	92,566	9.7	23.8	7.4
0455000 Phoenix city, Arizona..................	1,065,082	38.4	32.8	1,270,317	67.6	5.9	45.8	602,039	68,435	15.7	15.5	15.3
0458150 Queen Creek town, Arizona	41,193	20.6	46.8	NA	NA	NA	NA	20,981	121,262	3.8	31.9	1.4
0464210 San Tan Valley CDP, Arizona.........	65,896	30.5	21.6	75,604	65.8	3.8	NA	31,781	81,956	7.6	11.6	12.5
0465000 Scottsdale city, Arizona..............	195,691	13.9	60.4	213,895	62.9	4.3	44.4	119,122	99,097	10.5	30.5	3.9
0471510 Surprise city, Arizona.................	101,429	27.7	32.2	118,550	57.5	4.3	40.6	55,339	78,411	9.3	12.3	6.3
0473000 Tempe city, Arizona	116,182	21.9	49.1	160,795	72.0	6.5	46.0	77,306	68,662	15.1	15.6	10.2
0477000 Tucson city, Arizona	350,124	35.6	29.1	445,020	62.7	6.8	37.9	223,068	50,306	23.8	7.9	18.2
0485540 Yuma city, Arizona.....................	58,776	45.7	21.2	73,289	61.1	7.6	37.7	36,530	54,260	18.2	7.1	24.1
05000 **ARKANSAS**	2,037,763	45.4	25.3	2,405,035	58.6	5.5	69.4	1,183,675	52,528	23.4	9.7	11.7
0515190 Conway city, Arkansas	36,296	25.3	42.0	NA	NA	NA	NA	25,251	53,029	20.5	13.0	7.2
0523290 Fayetteville city, Arkansas............	53,920	27.8	48.0	77,789	68.4	3.6	43.6	40,104	61,428	22.0	14.4	7.0
0524550 Fort Smith city, Arkansas..............	59,415	45.9	23.5	71,964	59.0	7.3	NA	36,390	44,718	25.4	9.7	18.2
0535710 Jonesboro city, Arkansas	49,908	34.5	34.3	61,522	59.3	7.4	NA	30,432	45,497	30.2	13.0	15.4
0541000 Little Rock city, Arkansas.............	137,931	28.8	45.1	158,248	64.8	5.0	47.0	89,422	53,565	24.5	14.6	11.8
0560410 Rogers city, Arkansas.................	47,130	45.7	34.9	54,133	72.8	6.2	54.4	25,872	67,408	9.9	19.3	3.8
0566080 Springdale city, Arkansas.............	54,155	55.9	22.1	65,984	66.4	1.9	NA	28,942	63,396	13.4	11.9	6.3
06000 **CALIFORNIA**.........................	26,909,869	36.3	36.2	31,507,237	63.4	8.3	61.8	13,429,063	84,907	14.8	25.5	14.7
0600562 Alameda city, California	56,820	17.6	60.7	62,106	67.5	6.4	46.6	30,281	115,468	9.6	40.2	11.6
0600884 Alhambra city, California..............	61,446	36.0	39.2	67,773	62.2	9.3	36.9	29,022	72,222	19.5	16.0	15.7
0602000 Anaheim city, California..............	238,905	44.2	29.4	278,757	65.0	7.7	39.7	105,608	81,747	14.5	21.9	16.9
0602252 Antioch city, California.................	76,519	38.9	25.5	89,692	62.9	8.6	39.2	37,081	81,008	14.1	26.4	20.8
0602364 Apple Valley town, California.......	47,240	42.7	17.0	NA	NA	NA	NA	24,657	63,031	11.8	11.0	16.1
0602553 Arden-Arcade CDP, California	68,903	35.6	32.1	78,629	67.9	8.3	41.9	40,688	62,145	17.5	17.6	21.3
0603526 Bakersfield city, California...........	247,870	43.0	24.8	304,281	62.4	8.3	33.4	128,007	66,666	16.8	16.6	19.2
0603666 Baldwin Park city, California.........	48,793	59.4	14.0	59,548	61.1	7.9	37.9	19,112	69,854	14.5	13.8	14.5
0604982 Bellflower city, California	51,828	48.9	22.2	59,873	65.2	8.2	41.1	24,327	67,909	13.5	12.8	21.9
0606000 Berkeley city, California...............	75,318	10.3	73.7	104,883	62.5	9.4	34.6	43,893	101,048	14.6	35.9	9.7
0608786 Buena Park city, California............	55,779	37.5	33.8	66,473	68.8	8.6	41.9	24,306	101,346	6.7	27.3	12.9
0608954 Burbank city, California...............	80,582	24.9	43.4	89,562	65.0	9.2	40.3	44,471	81,177	19.1	24.5	15.4
0610046 Camarillo city, California.............	50,206	26.4	40.2	58,302	60.4	7.0	39.2	27,588	100,238	13.8	28.8	9.3
0611194 Carlsbad city, California	87,183	14.0	60.4	96,035	61.5	5.5	37.5	48,098	124,669	11.9	39.0	5.9
0611390 Carmichael CDP, California	56,322	29.4	33.5	65,227	60.9	8.4	35.4	32,172	71,656	16.3	19.1	16.3

STATE and place code	STATE Place	Educational attainment			Employment status				Household income and benefits				
		Total population 25 years and over	Percent with a high school diploma or less	Percent with a bachelor's degree or more	Total population 16 years and over	Labor force participation (percent)	Percent unemployed	Percent age 16 years and over who worked full-time year-round in the past 12 months	Total households	Median household income in the past 12 months (in 2021 inflation-adjusted dollars)	Income less than $25,000 (percent)	Income greater than $150,000 (percent)	Percent who received cash public assistance or food stamps/ SNAP
	ACS table number:	C15003	C15003	C15003	C23001	C23001	C23001	S2402	B19001	B19049	B19001	B19001	B19058
	column number:	1	2	3	4	5	6	7	8	9	10	11	12
	CALIFORNIA—Cont.												
0611530	Carson city, California................	65,028	40.3	26.6	76,374	59.8	9.6	37.2	25,743	92,609	13.7	23.1	16.5
0611964	Castro Valley CDP, California........	48,881	27.4	40.3	NA	NA	NA	NA	23,103	121,384	8.6	41.6	11.9
0613014	Chico city, California..................	60,966	23.5	43.0	84,178	63.9	8.3	31.1	40,956	61,850	23.2	13.9	15.6
0613210	Chino city, California	62,819	36.3	31.9	72,201	65.8	8.3	41.5	26,774	97,473	11.3	27.6	10.6
0613214	Chino Hills city, California	56,133	21.8	53.1	64,474	66.5	9.8	44.1	25,703	113,811	10.8	38.5	9.7
0613392	Chula Vista city, California	187,274	38.3	33.0	218,876	67.4	9.4	39.7	83,451	91,949	13.2	22.2	17.0
0613588	Citrus Heights city, California	64,014	35.8	25.8	73,313	63.3	8.4	39.6	34,140	66,607	15.0	13.2	18.5
0614218	Clovis city, California.................	75,223	25.4	36.3	89,132	67.1	7.1	43.3	38,762	84,837	9.2	25.6	12.2
0615044	Compton city, California	62,225	61.9	11.9	74,624	60.3	6.6	41.3	28,820	62,050	22.8	9.2	24.8
0616000	Concord city, California..............	89,720	33.4	36.5	101,576	65.3	6.7	41.6	46,375	96,961	9.9	29.0	12.0
0616350	Corona city, California	105,364	40.4	29.5	126,487	66.9	7.0	43.9	48,905	92,606	9.2	20.9	11.0
0616532	Costa Mesa city, California	81,247	29.8	43.3	91,763	73.7	5.5	45.5	43,711	97,904	10.5	28.3	10.9
0617918	Daly City city, California	77,014	35.2	36.2	89,217	67.4	8.8	42.1	32,887	95,424	12.7	27.0	13.9
0618100	Davis city, California.................	35,002	6.3	80.9	58,424	58.4	4.9	NA	25,316	84,074	20.3	30.9	14.1
0619766	Downey city, California	79,255	48.0	26.1	91,408	63.9	6.8	39.9	36,008	72,556	14.2	20.4	14.2
0620018	Dublin city, California.................	49,204	14.1	67.6	NA	NA	NA	NA	23,688	205,219	4.2	65.6	9.6
0620802	East Los Angeles CDP, California..	76,477	71.8	9.2	92,537	63.3	7.1	36.6	31,072	65,971	18.8	10.4	20.9
0621230	Eastvale city, California	46,433	29.9	40.9	NA	NA	NA	NA	NA	136,834	NA	NA	8.4
0621712	El Cajon city, California..............	69,215	43.6	25.1	81,291	63.0	13.3	31.5	34,443	61,356	18.3	13.5	18.0
0622020	Elk Grove city, California............	115,424	29.4	37.9	133,449	66.3	8.3	44.2	53,724	109,242	5.5	31.5	11.0
0622230	El Monte city, California.............	72,132	64.3	14.0	85,202	60.1	8.4	32.9	29,036	55,609	22.5	9.7	28.7
0622804	Escondido city, California...........	100,771	41.7	27.8	116,697	65.4	5.9	44.1	50,171	80,749	16.1	18.1	14.8
0623182	Fairfield city, California..............	77,589	37.4	28.0	90,943	62.0	7.3	36.1	38,097	90,346	12.4	21.0	16.6
0624638	Folsom city, California...............	56,942	22.7	55.3	65,709	56.9	4.4	NA	28,441	125,010	11.0	40.9	3.6
0624680	Fontana city, California..............	133,136	50.8	20.8	160,818	68.6	9.0	46.7	57,836	93,851	9.9	19.7	13.2
0626000	Fremont city, California..............	161,130	21.0	63.7	180,103	66.8	4.4	50.9	75,716	155,968	8.0	52.5	9.3
0627000	Fresno city, California................	340,182	43.7	26.1	410,825	62.1	9.3	37.7	181,841	61,250	22.6	14.0	26.1
0628000	Fullerton city, California.............	96,535	26.4	41.9	114,719	65.7	9.6	41.2	48,423	95,431	10.7	31.2	12.3
0629000	Garden Grove city, California	119,898	48.6	24.0	139,086	63.1	8.4	36.7	48,769	74,109	17.4	19.1	20.1
0630000	Glendale city, California.............	141,319	29.6	48.1	159,720	62.3	8.8	39.8	70,831	79,633	19.2	22.8	21.1
0632548	Hawthorne city, California	58,259	47.3	23.4	69,122	71.4	11.0	42.3	30,039	70,122	17.1	12.3	24.6
0633000	Hayward city, California	114,163	44.5	32.0	129,071	65.9	7.3	44.6	48,619	96,386	13.2	27.9	17.5
0633182	Hemet city, California................	66,037	48.1	13.7	72,473	49.5	10.7	NA	33,486	45,042	25.4	8.8	22.4
0633434	Hesperia city, California	59,976	54.3	13.7	75,144	59.8	11.1	NA	29,237	67,950	17.5	8.6	15.2
0636000	Huntington Beach city, California.	147,759	21.9	47.8	165,763	66.1	7.3	41.9	79,930	107,808	11.3	32.8	10.5
0636448	Indio city, California	67,095	56.7	18.0	75,928	56.7	6.8	39.0	34,673	66,841	16.0	13.4	17.3
0636546	Inglewood city, California............	74,585	45.6	25.3	84,793	68.0	10.6	41.1	37,972	68,135	21.8	12.6	20.9
0636770	Irvine city, California..................	199,921	11.7	68.3	240,593	67.7	6.8	43.2	111,648	105,774	14.2	37.2	9.2
0637692	Jurupa Valley city, California........	66,016	58.8	15.4	81,569	63.7	7.8	43.0	27,454	81,052	12.0	17.2	12.9
0639486	Lake Elsinore city, California........	44,265	38.4	26.4	NA	NA	NA	NA	21,422	76,707	12.4	18.2	17.1
0639496	Lake Forest city, California...........	61,333	24.5	48.4	71,965	65.3	6.3	43.0	30,962	108,838	10.0	35.6	8.0
0639892	Lakewood city, California............	57,220	32.8	33.6	64,310	70.4	6.2	47.6	26,533	104,534	10.0	25.6	11.3
0640130	Lancaster city, California............	104,615	47.1	19.7	128,224	55.2	9.1	38.8	51,333	64,242	22.8	14.2	21.2
0641992	Livermore city, California............	62,087	23.5	44.3	70,155	68.7	7.0	43.8	31,472	130,111	10.2	43.8	9.1
0642202	Lodi city, California	43,860	44.5	24.3	54,727	61.6	8.3	NA	24,245	76,874	12.7	14.5	10.6
0643000	Long Beach city, California	325,010	34.9	37.0	375,508	66.7	7.7	42.1	172,599	73,905	17.2	18.0	17.5
0644000	Los Angeles city, California	2,727,338	40.3	37.3	3,178,578	66.0	10.7	38.0	1,410,594	70,372	20.7	20.5	19.1
0644574	Lynwood city, California..............	41,575	67.0	9.1	50,250	58.1	8.9	NA	16,079	61,695	22.0	11.6	23.3
0645022	Madera city, California................	42,447	60.8	11.6	50,103	59.2	13.6	NA	18,595	49,358	32.1	14.7	30.5
0645484	Manteca city, California	59,625	45.2	20.5	66,618	58.5	5.7	40.6	27,310	82,068	10.5	27.3	10.8
0646842	Menifee city, California	72,152	35.4	21.3	83,641	58.8	8.1	NA	35,601	85,175	13.4	24.4	12.1
0646898	Merced city, California................	51,405	45.3	19.5	65,357	59.7	14.7	32.7	28,358	52,127	30.0	12.1	31.1
0647766	Milpitas city, California...............	57,169	25.8	54.7	63,857	66.6	7.1	48.4	23,632	169,460	10.3	56.7	8.2
0648256	Mission Viejo city, California........	69,743	17.4	55.9	77,009	64.6	8.0	41.1	34,168	124,971	8.0	41.4	7.7
0648354	Modesto city, California..............	145,736	45.0	21.5	168,929	62.6	7.9	38.2	71,775	70,469	15.2	16.4	18.4
0649270	Moreno Valley city, California	133,047	50.6	17.6	160,907	62.7	8.2	38.5	54,104	79,840	9.8	16.1	13.9
0649670	Mountain View city, California......	59,044	14.4	74.4	66,078	72.1	3.2	56.9	34,637	157,243	4.9	52.4	5.4

Table B-4. Cities — What: Education, Employment, and Income, 2021—*Continued*

STATE and place code	STATE Place	Educational attainment			Employment status				Household income and benefits				
		Total population 25 years and over	Percent with a high school diploma or less	Percent with a bachelor's degree or more	Total population 16 years and over	Labor force participation (percent)	Percent unemployed	Percent age 16 years and over who worked full-time year-round in the past 12 months	Total households	Median household income in the past 12 months (in 2021 inflation-adjusted dollars)	Income less than $25,000 (percent)	Income greater than $150,000 (percent)	Percent who received cash public assistance or food stamps/SNAP
	ACS table number:	C15003	C15003	C15003	C23001	C23001	C23001	S2402	B19001	B19049	B19001	B19001	B19058
	column number:	1	2	3	4	5	6	7	8	9	10	11	12
	CALIFORNIA—Cont.												
0650076	Murrieta city, California	69,548	25.4	33.5	86,654	61.2	9.5	36.5	34,414	104,708	8.2	26.1	6.7
0650258	Napa city, California....................	55,826	35.4	35.5	65,060	65.8	6.7	42.7	30,418	92,878	12.5	28.6	10.2
0651182	Newport Beach city, California	65,578	9.1	73.3	71,611	64.0	8.2	NA	39,131	136,588	8.9	46.3	4.8
0652526	Norwalk city, California................	67,923	52.2	19.5	80,696	60.6	8.3	38.8	26,506	79,850	16.4	19.4	18.6
0653000	Oakland city, California...............	318,281	31.4	46.8	359,568	67.1	7.7	42.8	170,366	82,236	17.4	28.8	18.2
0653322	Oceanside city, California............	121,012	35.8	33.6	139,608	64.7	9.2	38.1	59,683	78,125	12.8	20.6	11.1
0653896	Ontario city, California	116,918	51.5	20.2	140,790	63.5	7.0	42.1	55,819	73,872	14.8	15.6	13.7
0653980	Orange city, California	93,060	31.3	35.7	111,311	66.3	6.4	41.3	43,291	103,045	11.8	31.0	10.7
0654652	Oxnard city, California..................	129,156	53.4	20.2	153,506	68.0	7.5	43.2	50,611	88,268	8.8	19.6	19.4
0655156	Palmdale city, California...............	104,958	53.8	17.0	124,008	60.7	8.3	38.9	46,650	73,417	15.1	13.0	21.4
0655282	Palo Alto city, California..............	45,327	8.9	80.6	52,307	62.6	4.5	NA	24,501	195,781	8.0	57.6	6.2
0656000	Pasadena city, California	102,061	24.7	55.6	114,617	68.3	6.5	46.4	56,992	86,677	15.2	31.1	11.5
0656700	Perris city, California	48,474	64.8	9.9	61,051	64.2	10.4	NA	19,923	69,843	10.6	9.3	16.8
0657456	Pittsburg city, California..............	51,908	49.2	20.7	62,848	68.5	11.0	39.8	23,827	92,800	16.6	19.4	23.2
0657792	Pleasanton city, California...........	56,702	13.0	63.7	64,676	65.5	6.2	NA	29,330	145,263	5.6	48.3	7.4
0658072	Pomona city, California	93,916	53.5	20.1	114,384	64.1	10.1	39.1	40,142	70,494	17.9	16.8	19.3
0659444	Rancho Cordova city, California ...	53,235	33.7	28.9	62,151	64.5	7.7	44.7	28,428	84,037	13.9	20.1	15.6
0659451	Rancho Cucamonga city, California.....................................	116,400	29.5	36.9	136,143	61.5	6.3	40.1	57,290	83,850	12.1	21.5	9.2
0659920	Redding city, California	63,703	34.2	25.5	74,757	59.4	6.2	37.3	37,302	58,702	19.5	11.5	16.8
0659962	Redlands city, California	45,152	34.3	38.3	54,225	61.6	6.9	41.9	24,452	87,634	10.5	19.7	11.7
0660018	Redondo Beach city, California.....	50,248	19.0	62.2	55,838	63.9	7.7	NA	26,986	121,445	10.3	42.5	11.2
0660102	Redwood City city, California	60,453	27.2	54.2	67,578	70.8	6.6	50.4	29,450	145,128	5.6	47.6	9.2
0660466	Rialto city, California....................	64,319	58.6	13.5	77,069	63.2	9.1	44.8	29,043	69,982	14.3	12.2	21.7
0660620	Richmond city, California	81,025	37.9	36.2	92,405	67.8	9.5	40.4	40,019	85,754	18.3	26.2	20.4
0662000	Riverside city, California	199,160	46.2	23.4	254,549	66.9	8.8	41.0	91,110	76,558	12.7	17.3	12.9
0662364	Rocklin city, California..................	47,353	18.9	48.3	57,462	63.8	4.6	40.6	25,528	107,520	8.4	34.0	6.9
0662938	Roseville city, California...............	105,905	20.6	44.7	119,610	66.7	4.2	43.7	57,569	107,714	8.3	34.1	9.9
0664000	Sacramento city, California	371,474	33.7	36.9	434,705	63.0	7.5	40.2	202,093	75,311	18.1	17.0	17.7
0664224	Salinas city, California	96,003	66.5	12.5	118,724	60.9	5.0	38.8	41,871	80,154	11.3	15.1	11.1
0665000	San Bernardino city, California	137,842	62.1	14.0	169,897	59.3	7.0	38.9	63,331	65,311	19.7	9.5	25.0
0665042	San Buenaventura (Ventura) city, California...................................	79,273	27.0	39.7	91,710	63.8	7.7	37.3	42,288	97,816	10.3	24.1	10.8
0666000	San Diego city, California	966,483	25.8	48.8	1,150,367	68.9	7.7	41.6	521,000	93,042	13.0	27.6	12.7
0667000	San Francisco city, California	647,880	22.3	60.9	713,617	68.6	8.4	45.4	350,796	121,826	15.8	42.3	14.9
0668000	San Jose city, California................	691,752	30.4	45.8	799,912	67.4	6.6	45.6	322,881	126,377	9.4	42.7	11.8
0668084	San Leandro city, California..........	67,147	39.9	30.2	75,968	66.7	8.5	41.2	30,977	84,017	18.2	23.4	15.1
0668196	San Marcos city, California...........	61,237	24.3	48.0	71,440	64.3	8.9	41.5	34,037	89,239	17.9	31.3	9.3
0668252	San Mateo city, California	75,078	22.7	57.9	83,845	68.8	6.6	48.1	39,340	129,957	9.0	43.1	5.9
0668378	San Ramon city, California	56,663	12.4	69.2	64,637	69.0	4.0	NA	29,662	162,388	4.9	55.9	5.1
0669000	Santa Ana city, California	201,627	57.2	18.5	247,234	65.5	7.0	38.6	78,674	80,265	11.7	18.6	15.9
0669070	Santa Barbara city, California	63,359	24.3	49.7	75,782	66.6	6.3	39.8	35,676	90,711	14.5	30.1	11.7
0669084	Santa Clara city, California	90,840	15.1	65.9	105,706	70.9	6.2	51.0	49,011	155,238	12.2	51.6	7.9
0669088	Santa Clarita city, California	152,516	26.7	37.8	176,763	67.0	7.5	41.3	73,509	109,336	9.6	33.8	13.5
0669196	Santa Maria city, California	61,773	57.3	15.8	80,113	65.2	7.1	40.1	30,316	69,714	18.4	15.3	20.9
0670000	Santa Monica city, California........	72,865	9.7	71.0	79,124	69.4	7.7	45.5	45,541	94,906	18.7	34.8	11.1
0670098	Santa Rosa city, California............	125,328	34.3	35.1	145,676	64.5	7.4	38.6	68,686	86,459	12.2	24.5	11.9
0672016	Simi Valley city, California............	91,134	30.7	35.4	106,850	67.8	6.2	43.7	45,308	101,621	9.7	30.0	7.1
0673080	South Gate city, California	61,286	67.8	11.0	72,447	64.4	7.8	38.4	24,891	65,351	16.9	12.8	22.4
0675000	Stockton city, California	199,370	49.7	15.9	244,427	60.8	10.4	35.9	97,447	69,844	18.3	12.7	25.7
0677000	Sunnyvale city, California	112,990	17.4	67.4	126,032	70.2	6.2	51.8	59,567	156,059	7.3	51.6	5.1
0678120	Temecula city, California	70,694	26.6	37.7	81,560	64.6	10.5	39.6	34,958	99,805	10.0	25.4	12.9
0678582	Thousand Oaks city, California	89,056	25.8	48.3	102,051	61.9	6.2	37.4	45,081	114,791	8.7	38.6	10.5
0680000	Torrance city, California	106,391	20.2	55.1	116,828	64.2	6.9	42.0	57,584	100,392	11.4	30.7	7.3
0680238	Tracy city, California	59,968	39.5	27.2	70,183	59.9	5.8	NA	28,353	102,263	10.7	28.1	11.6
0680644	Tulare city, California....................	40,214	57.4	11.6	50,189	57.1	8.0	NA	20,974	63,668	15.3	9.4	24.6
0680812	Turlock city, California..................	44,772	43.4	23.3	54,283	63.2	12.9	NA	24,885	74,032	14.8	14.9	16.8
0680854	Tustin city, California....................	51,863	25.5	48.4	62,363	71.7	9.1	43.0	26,762	98,092	11.0	30.7	14.0

STATE and place code	STATE Place	Educational attainment			Employment status				Household income and benefits				
		Total population 25 years and over	Percent with a high school diploma or less	Percent with a bachelor's degree or more	Total population 16 years and over	Labor force participation (percent)	Percent unemployed	Percent age 16 years and over who worked full-time year-round in the past 12 months	Total households	Median household income in the past 12 months (in 2021 inflation-adjusted dollars)	Income less than $25,000 (percent)	Income greater than $150,000 (percent)	Percent who received cash public assistance or food stamps/ SNAP
	ACS table number:	C15003	C15003	C15003	C23001	C23001	C23001	S2402	B19001	B19049	B19001	B19001	B19058
	column number:	1	2	3	4	5	6	7	8	9	10	11	12
	CALIFORNIA—Cont.												
0681204	Union City city, California	52,066	33.8	40.7	58,774	63.5	5.6	43.7	21,637	114,700	7.9	39.3	11.5
0681344	Upland city, California..................	53,764	33.8	31.8	64,667	63.5	7.4	39.2	26,052	88,346	16.0	19.7	13.5
0681554	Vacaville city, California...............	73,268	33.9	26.5	84,593	62.5	5.1	34.8	33,777	97,777	9.2	25.3	9.5
0681666	Vallejo city, California..................	88,669	37.8	28.1	102,270	61.7	9.9	37.0	43,906	77,711	17.7	19.1	16.4
0682590	Victorville city, California.............	82,987	50.2	15.2	103,413	56.6	13.1	NA	38,400	65,478	19.4	9.6	28.6
0682954	Visalia city, California..................	89,182	38.6	26.3	107,351	61.1	8.3	36.9	47,660	64,165	18.3	17.9	23.8
0682996	Vista city, California....................	65,890	41.4	25.6	79,077	71.8	9.6	45.3	30,614	84,262	10.6	23.1	10.0
0683346	Walnut Creek city, California........	51,851	13.5	69.9	57,993	59.4	3.0	NA	31,035	118,483	9.3	37.5	5.2
0684200	West Covina city, California	75,958	39.0	32.4	88,889	61.8	9.5	37.9	32,012	88,476	12.6	22.3	15.8
0684550	Westminster city, California........	63,437	51.2	24.9	74,785	58.6	10.8	30.9	27,935	66,862	24.5	20.3	17.7
0685292	Whittier city, California	58,355	38.4	31.8	70,554	63.1	7.0	40.5	27,773	84,320	12.7	29.6	9.3
0686832	Yorba Linda city, California..........	51,294	16.6	53.8	56,752	59.1	8.0	NA	24,098	133,365	12.6	44.3	8.9
0686972	Yuba City city, California..............	46,192	50.9	17.5	54,208	60.7	10.4	NA	24,176	61,443	16.2	9.6	16.2
08000	**COLORADO**...............................	4,044,182	27.7	44.4	4,720,626	68.1	5.2	65.7	2,313,042	82,254	13.0	22.3	10.3
0803455	Arvada city, Colorado..................	89,381	25.9	46.7	100,012	70.5	4.5	50.5	50,678	92,647	9.6	24.5	6.2
0804000	Aurora city, Colorado..................	260,054	36.7	33.8	306,401	71.1	5.8	45.8	140,003	71,647	14.0	16.8	13.1
0807850	Boulder city, Colorado.................	60,169	11.5	75.6	94,422	63.3	5.5	32.1	42,376	84,167	21.5	28.1	10.1
0809280	Broomfield city, Colorado.............	53,433	17.7	58.9	61,651	69.4	3.7	49.5	30,161	107,638	6.5	33.5	4.4
0812415	Castle Rock town, Colorado	48,682	16.3	54.4	56,465	75.0	5.0	NA	27,249	125,657	7.1	37.4	3.4
0812815	Centennial city, Colorado.............	74,353	17.4	60.4	85,147	68.2	5.2	45.7	39,660	108,531	7.8	35.1	4.2
0816000	Colorado Springs city, Colorado...	329,454	24.8	42.8	390,552	67.9	6.0	41.8	197,542	74,579	11.6	17.2	12.5
0820000	Denver city, Colorado..................	521,474	24.4	55.0	592,643	74.2	6.2	51.3	326,634	81,630	15.0	23.3	10.8
0827425	Fort Collins city, Colorado	104,081	16.9	58.5	143,735	71.4	4.1	42.8	70,686	73,945	13.4	19.9	7.9
0831660	Grand Junction city, Colorado......	46,645	32.7	32.3	56,261	59.9	3.7	NA	28,352	59,201	19.8	10.3	12.8
0832155	Greeley city, Colorado.................	66,800	40.6	26.0	84,090	65.2	6.3	42.7	38,381	64,853	19.1	13.0	16.3
0836410	Highlands Ranch CDP, Colorado...	68,100	12.1	63.3	79,536	72.4	4.0	51.3	38,117	137,241	3.7	45.0	3.0
0843000	Lakewood city, Colorado..............	119,369	26.0	45.6	134,164	66.2	5.9	46.6	70,751	77,122	13.0	19.8	9.8
0845970	Longmont city, Colorado..............	74,520	25.9	46.6	83,965	68.8	6.9	45.1	43,519	72,911	11.8	20.6	11.8
0846465	Loveland city, Colorado...............	56,949	26.9	40.3	64,956	58.2	7.2	NA	35,803	66,535	14.5	15.2	10.4
0862000	Pueblo city, Colorado..................	76,546	40.9	24.2	90,585	55.2	7.5	33.2	47,901	49,598	30.2	7.0	25.4
0877290	Thornton city, Colorado	91,640	39.7	31.6	109,180	74.1	6.6	51.1	48,263	93,873	7.9	20.5	12.8
0883835	Westminster city, Colorado	82,754	27.4	41.1	96,285	72.8	4.6	50.3	47,797	86,688	9.3	21.4	9.9
09000	**CONNECTICUT**	2,534,376	34.4	42.1	2,971,314	65.6	6.6	63.4	1,428,313	83,771	15.2	24.7	13.4
0908000	Bridgeport city, Connecticut........	103,066	49.9	23.7	122,308	67.5	8.2	39.0	57,732	46,445	26.7	10.5	28.3
0918430	Danbury city, Connecticut............	60,733	40.2	36.6	71,359	71.3	7.4	45.7	33,024	79,079	13.2	22.6	8.6
0937000	Hartford city, Connecticut............	73,884	60.8	17.0	95,075	61.3	11.9	34.1	45,491	42,468	29.5	7.2	34.8
0950370	New Britain city, Connecticut	48,570	55.4	20.2	58,230	67.8	8.7	41.6	28,450	51,586	26.7	8.9	31.7
0952000	New Haven city, Connecticut	86,033	41.7	39.6	112,634	60.8	8.0	34.9	56,373	50,569	27.1	8.7	27.7
0955990	Norwalk city, Connecticut............	66,104	31.7	47.2	73,424	69.0	7.2	43.4	36,847	89,047	16.2	30.0	13.4
0973000	Stamford city, Connecticut..........	98,268	32.6	50.5	112,984	71.7	4.4	48.0	52,816	100,543	11.3	30.2	11.9
0980000	Waterbury city, Connecticut........	77,479	52.5	20.0	90,668	63.4	11.3	35.1	45,008	48,793	26.2	9.5	28.2
10000	**DELAWARE**	711,104	37.0	35.6	819,868	60.1	5.5	65.6	395,656	$71,091	15.6	18.0	11.6
1077580	Wilmington city, Delaware	53,835	41.4	35.1	59,070	62.5	8.4	41.0	32,049	55,136	25.8	12.6	21.3
11000	**DISTRICT OF** COLUMBIA	478,774	22.0	63.0	553,437	70.7	8.1	69.2	319,565	90,088	17.9	31.1	16.2
1150000	Washington city, District of Columbia................................	478,774	22.0	63.0	553,437	70.7	8.1	49.0	319,565	90,088	17.9	31.1	16.2
12000	**FLORIDA**....................................	15,762,122	37.9	33.2	18,010,659	59.1	5.6	66.9	8,565,329	63,062	18.4	14.1	15.6
1200410	Alafaya CDP, Florida....................	64,991	24.5	42.1	NA	NA	NA	NA	32,823	74,796	12.3	15.9	14.2
1207300	Boca Raton city, Florida...............	69,057	18.9	57.1	82,579	60.6	7.2	37.5	41,318	85,194	14.7	28.5	6.6
1207875	Boynton Beach city, Florida	59,249	39.5	33.2	66,474	62.1	3.7	42.2	33,201	61,293	19.8	10.3	19.1
1208150	Brandon CDP, Florida...................	83,861	36.6	31.3	94,374	67.4	5.7	51.7	46,925	64,357	15.5	14.5	12.6
1210275	Cape Coral city, Florida...............	156,983	43.5	24.6	174,998	59.4	5.1	40.5	79,845	66,425	15.1	11.9	12.1
1212875	Clearwater city, Florida...............	91,079	38.2	34.5	104,364	56.4	5.1	37.2	49,486	56,626	22.8	15.8	14.0
1214400	Coral Springs city, Florida............	88,920	34.0	36.2	103,922	70.2	5.7	46.1	44,417	81,067	9.4	18.5	14.5
1216475	Davie town, Florida.....................	72,651	30.2	43.7	82,553	66.7	5.1	43.9	39,061	73,332	13.0	17.6	9.4

Table B-4. Cities — What: Education, Employment, and Income, 2021—*Continued*

STATE and place code	STATE Place	Educational attainment — Total population 25 years and over	Percent with a high school diploma or less	Percent with a bachelor's degree or more	Employment status — Total population 16 years and over	Labor force participation (percent)	Percent unemployed	Percent age 16 years and over who worked full-time year-round in the past 12 months	Household income and benefits — Total households	Median household income in the past 12 months (in 2021 inflation-adjusted dollars)	Income less than $25,000 (percent)	Income greater than $150,000 (percent)	Percent who received cash public assistance or food stamps/ SNAP
	ACS table number:	C15003	C15003	C15003	C23001	C23001	C23001	S2402	B19001	B19049	B19001	B19001	B19058
	column number:	1	2	3	4	5	6	7	8	9	10	11	12
	FLORIDA—Cont.												
1216525	Daytona Beach city, Florida	53,229	42.7	25.6	65,532	52.8	3.3	NA	34,721	43,864	31.2	5.0	19.3
1216725	Deerfield Beach city, Florida	67,253	41.6	28.6	74,777	63.7	8.3	NA	39,934	49,865	22.0	8.7	25.0
1217100	Delray Beach city, Florida.............	52,587	31.8	44.8	NA	NA	NA	NA	30,472	64,730	16.1	21.9	12.7
1217200	Deltona city, Florida	68,115	43.8	18.9	79,214	61.7	4.3	47.2	35,384	63,727	18.0	8.3	19.7
1217935	Doral city, Florida	50,673	19.1	57.4	61,093	70.0	3.8	NA	25,419	84,956	10.0	20.6	14.4
1224000	Fort Lauderdale city, Florida..........	138,716	31.3	41.6	156,138	66.2	6.9	44.1	83,021	64,912	20.7	19.0	15.4
1224125	Fort Myers city, Florida	68,133	48.9	29.8	75,375	51.4	6.3	33.3	37,323	53,583	25.5	11.5	18.1
1225175	Gainesville city, Florida	79,107	26.6	47.8	121,565	58.9	4.0	32.0	56,513	40,822	30.2	7.0	9.7
1230000	Hialeah city, Florida	163,516	59.1	18.3	186,771	60.9	4.9	36.8	75,692	46,674	27.0	7.5	47.5
1232000	Hollywood city, Florida	109,186	34.7	34.5	123,058	66.5	5.9	42.3	61,598	60,490	17.6	12.1	16.5
1232275	Homestead city, Florida................	52,137	52.8	21.3	59,874	63.9	7.8	NA	27,094	52,365	26.2	7.3	35.0
1232610	Horizon West CDP, Florida	NA	NA	NA	NA	NA	NA	NA	NA	121,007	NA	NA	2.9
1235000	Jacksonville city, Florida...............	655,734	36.6	32.3	759,046	64.9	4.5	44.4	386,283	58,621	19.3	10.4	17.7
1236100	Kendall CDP, Florida....................	59,279	25.6	45.7	66,003	63.8	4.3	NA	33,184	76,255	14.7	21.8	14.4
1236950	Kissimmee city, Florida	49,013	43.4	23.9	59,246	67.3	7.0	NA	25,999	42,615	30.9	4.7	37.5
1238250	Lakeland city, Florida...................	79,555	44.1	26.8	95,205	56.7	5.6	38.6	45,548	55,029	22.2	8.1	16.3
1239425	Largo city, Florida.......................	64,262	40.6	29.2	71,022	58.7	5.2	NA	36,493	55,228	20.0	5.3	13.8
1239550	Lauderhill city, Florida..................	51,366	55.7	17.9	59,106	61.0	8.3	NA	26,555	44,975	27.1	7.0	29.9
1239925	Lehigh Acres CDP, Florida.............	81,054	53.2	17.6	95,985	60.8	5.3	42.8	40,295	58,422	19.6	3.9	16.1
1243975	Melbourne city, Florida	61,810	31.0	32.0	70,791	59.8	4.9	41.7	36,651	57,132	18.1	8.9	12.3
1245000	Miami city, Florida......................	340,917	44.1	35.9	381,863	64.5	5.9	45.0	192,219	48,789	29.1	12.6	28.1
1245025	Miami Beach city, Florida..............	63,033	25.1	51.5	69,484	65.6	6.4	44.8	40,788	55,512	25.7	20.0	20.9
1245060	Miami Gardens city, Florida	76,618	51.4	20.2	86,370	59.1	8.9	42.2	34,332	54,276	22.2	9.1	37.4
1245975	Miramar city, Florida...................	96,465	45.4	31.0	107,068	74.6	4.6	57.1	42,707	79,282	9.9	20.3	17.7
1249675	North Port city, Florida	60,195	35.8	29.1	NA	NA	NA	NA	30,622	68,583	18.4	12.4	11.1
1253000	Orlando city, Florida	225,813	32.1	39.7	258,748	69.3	7.7	45.1	130,037	54,167	21.1	13.4	21.5
1254000	Palm Bay city, Florida..................	84,101	41.1	22.0	99,653	60.3	5.0	42.1	45,145	54,746	20.3	9.1	18.8
1254200	Palm Coast city, Florida................	71,224	35.9	29.8	80,084	50.6	5.7	NA	36,896	60,648	17.3	11.9	9.1
1255775	Pembroke Pines city, Florida	126,830	39.8	36.7	145,070	64.4	4.8	47.3	64,378	76,439	18.4	18.7	13.2
1256825	Pine Hills CDP, Florida..................	51,780	60.9	11.6	62,593	70.6	15.7	NA	25,752	42,153	29.1	3.5	44.4
1257425	Plantation city, Florida..................	65,054	28.0	43.7	72,238	66.5	3.9	46.5	36,564	72,955	13.7	19.9	14.0
1257900	Poinciana CDP, Florida..................	43,873	45.9	19.1	NA	NA	NA	NA	21,402	57,296	17.5	3.6	30.7
1258050	Pompano Beach city, Florida........	85,302	41.7	32.1	94,860	62.0	9.0	38.3	48,363	53,737	19.0	8.7	18.3
1258350	Port Charlotte CDP, Florida..........	52,486	48.0	19.6	58,527	47.2	6.4	NA	29,120	54,814	19.5	6.4	16.5
1258715	Port St. Lucie city, Florida	158,506	37.6	28.8	179,892	60.3	6.8	44.0	77,190	71,381	12.7	9.7	13.9
1260950	Riverview CDP, Florida..................	77,803	31.4	35.5	88,037	72.8	6.2	53.1	40,114	81,195	8.5	17.0	11.3
1263000	St. Petersburg city, Florida............	194,476	29.4	40.7	216,896	64.7	5.2	43.0	111,349	64,141	18.9	13.7	10.9
1268350	Spring Hill CDP, Florida.................	91,034	41.5	20.7	102,506	55.2	5.9	NA	46,360	59,363	16.5	7.6	17.7
1269700	Sunrise city, Florida.....................	66,458	35.0	34.4	77,156	66.8	6.5	46.0	35,166	66,184	20.6	11.8	19.2
1270600	Tallahassee city, Florida................	112,948	21.7	51.6	169,439	68.6	6.0	41.7	84,920	51,224	22.4	10.2	15.3
1270675	Tamarac city, Florida....................	51,114	39.7	28.0	NA	NA	NA	NA	29,065	59,885	18.3	8.0	15.3
1271000	Tampa city, Florida	268,691	31.9	45.6	313,221	66.2	5.2	45.5	159,925	63,404	21.2	19.6	18.8
1271625	The Villages CDP, Florida.............	80,639	28.7	42.4	NA	NA	NA	NA	47,527	65,117	13.0	10.8	2.6
1272145	Town 'n' Country CDP, Florida.....	63,171	40.9	31.0	71,357	69.7	6.8	47.1	35,155	58,140	18.8	9.9	21.6
1275875	Wesley Chapel CDP, Florida..........	46,254	23.4	48.4	NA	NA	NA	NA	23,868	90,878	13.1	28.3	11.1
1276582	Weston city, Florida.....................	41,362	12.8	67.8	50,697	63.0	3.7	NA	20,227	122,774	7.0	39.1	11.9
1276600	West Palm Beach city, Florida	87,003	34.4	38.9	99,576	61.1	5.6	40.8	50,409	59,400	22.4	13.1	17.3
13000	**GEORGIA**..............................	7,234,271	37.7	34.6	8,575,918	62.9	5.5	67.5	4,001,109	66,559	17.9	15.8	13.7
1301052	Albany city, Georgia....................	42,799	49.4	20.9	53,098	52.0	8.1	NA	27,357	38,999	32.9	6.3	30.6
1301696	Alpharetta city, Georgia	44,721	9.7	70.9	NA	NA	NA	NA	25,457	122,326	8.2	43.4	4.8
1303440	Athens-Clarke County unified government (balance), Georgia....	71,633	27.9	49.6	106,888	64.8	4.2	36.4	54,438	50,299	22.8	8.2	9.2
1304000	Atlanta city, Georgia....................	344,635	21.8	59.8	419,538	66.4	5.2	45.5	232,720	74,107	20.5	21.8	15.2
1304204	Augusta-Richmond County consolidated government (balance), Georgia	132,111	42.3	24.4	158,765	63.3	8.8	33.6	72,760	47,921	26.7	7.6	21.4

Table B-4. Cities — What: Education, Employment, and Income, 2021—*Continued*

STATE and place code	STATE Place	Educational attainment			Employment status				Household income and benefits				
		Total population 25 years and over	Percent with a high school diploma or less	Percent with a bachelor's degree or more	Total population 16 years and over	Labor force participation (percent)	Percent unemployed	Percent age 16 years and over who worked full-time year-round in the past 12 months	Total households	Median household income in the past 12 months (in 2021 inflation-adjusted dollars)	Income less than $25,000 (percent)	Income greater than $150,000 (percent)	Percent who received cash public assistance or food stamps/ SNAP
	ACS table number:	C15003	C15003	C15003	C23001	C23001	C23001	S2402	B19001	B19049	B19001	B19001	B19058
	column number:	1	2	3	4	5	6	7	8	9	10	11	12
	GEORGIA—Cont.												
1319000	Columbus city, Georgia...............	134,716	37.6	31.3	159,069	59.7	6.7	39.2	82,663	52,734	23.5	10.5	22.0
1342425	Johns Creek city, Georgia............	54,031	12.6	72.1	61,190	64.5	3.7	NA	29,256	132,870	7.3	44.9	4.3
1349008	Macon-Bibb County, Georgia.......	102,096	43.0	25.3	122,337	58.5	8.2	37.9	57,677	48,176	26.4	8.6	23.3
1367284	Roswell city, Georgia..................	62,264	15.7	68.8	NA	NA	NA	NA	37,044	104,825	7.3	35.6	4.6
1368516	Sandy Springs city, Georgia.........	80,196	13.6	70.3	91,332	72.4	3.3	52.9	52,487	94,456	9.7	33.1	5.8
1369000	Savannah city, Georgia................	94,196	37.5	32.7	117,972	63.1	7.3	36.6	59,612	49,612	25.7	6.0	21.3
1372122	South Fulton city, Georgia...........	71,368	30.8	42.6	NA	NA	NA	NA	41,405	73,958	16.9	18.1	14.5
1380508	Warner Robins city, Georgia.........	52,857	38.3	25.4	64,037	66.5	7.4	NA	30,701	58,864	16.9	11.0	22.8
15000	**HAWAII**	1,021,687	33.4	35.3	1,166,220	63.4	7.2	57.0	490,080	84,857	14.3	23.8	15.2
1571550	Urban Honolulu CDP, Hawaii.......	265,184	31.4	39.9	299,015	62.8	7.6	36.1	138,398	73,434	17.1	20.1	12.4
16000	**IDAHO**	1,257,566	35.6	30.7	1,484,932	63.1	3.3	64.0	693,882	66,474	15.9	13.1	10.5
1608830	Boise City city, Idaho..................	163,909	24.5	48.0	191,700	67.5	2.8	44.9	99,250	70,217	14.3	16.7	10.0
1639700	Idaho Falls city, Idaho................	43,241	33.9	31.4	51,745	62.9	4.2	38.5	24,257	61,833	18.0	15.1	8.8
1652120	Meridian city, Idaho	88,143	28.6	40.1	NA	NA	NA	NA	47,825	88,088	10.4	19.0	7.0
1656260	Nampa city, Idaho	69,854	42.1	22.4	NA	NA	NA	NA	37,666	63,471	14.3	11.5	11.3
17000	**ILLINOIS**	8,730,697	35.0	37.1	10,203,044	64.5	7.3	65.0	4,991,641	72,205	17.2	18.4	15.7
1702154	Arlington Heights village, Illinois ..	55,810	18.3	59.7	61,927	69.1	4.4	46.6	31,415	102,237	9.0	31.1	7.6
1703012	Aurora city, Illinois.....................	118,625	38.7	37.7	141,905	71.9	6.0	47.8	62,379	83,996	12.6	18.2	18.1
1706587	Bloomington city, Illinois	49,552	22.7	49.8	62,712	68.1	3.0	47.6	33,803	71,700	18.0	16.3	13.0
1707133	Bolingbrook village, Illinois	49,679	29.2	40.9	62,269	72.3	4.9	48.7	24,600	94,040	7.7	21.8	16.8
1712385	Champaign city, Illinois	46,420	17.8	56.5	74,678	64.8	4.8	36.6	37,423	53,410	25.5	12.4	10.0
1714000	Chicago city, Illinois...................	1,907,020	33.7	43.7	2,212,422	67.2	10.1	43.5	1,139,537	66,576	22.0	18.7	21.7
1714351	Cicero town, Illinois....................	50,449	73.1	10.4	66,176	59.4	4.4	NA	24,737	57,495	20.9	10.5	26.4
1718823	Decatur city, Illinois...................	49,795	52.5	16.4	58,136	55.1	14.3	NA	32,087	40,368	31.7	5.0	26.0
1723074	Elgin city, Illinois.......................	78,375	46.1	24.9	93,858	69.5	5.7	45.2	40,585	79,120	11.0	18.3	15.5
1724582	Evanston city, Illinois	51,102	13.1	71.2	65,901	61.4	6.6	37.4	31,157	82,154	15.9	29.9	9.3
1738570	Joliet city, Illinois	97,974	42.8	26.0	120,356	68.9	7.9	43.2	51,263	76,495	13.3	16.0	20.2
1751622	Naperville city, Illinois	101,859	10.8	71.7	116,746	67.2	5.4	46.4	54,377	129,664	8.5	43.8	7.8
1757225	Palatine village, Illinois	46,438	27.9	47.7	51,761	69.4	4.8	48.5	26,402	75,479	14.8	27.1	10.2
1759000	Peoria city, Illinois.....................	73,070	33.0	38.7	87,480	60.0	9.4	37.3	50,176	47,287	26.7	12.4	25.7
1765000	Rockford city, Illinois..................	98,989	46.0	24.2	115,148	58.7	12.8	33.2	59,909	44,525	27.0	6.7	31.0
1768003	Schaumburg village, Illinois	52,142	23.8	46.0	59,652	67.3	5.5	47.2	31,569	79,308	12.9	15.7	7.5
1770122	Skokie village, Illinois	47,541	26.4	50.8	54,584	61.9	7.4	NA	23,599	88,618	13.8	26.4	13.9
1772000	Springfield city, Illinois...............	80,051	33.3	38.5	92,121	59.8	8.9	41.0	51,317	62,505	22.4	12.5	21.3
1779293	Waukegan city, Illinois................	58,982	57.1	21.2	71,856	69.8	8.1	45.7	30,068	64,178	17.6	12.1	23.0
18000	**INDIANA**	4,559,631	42.7	28.9	5,401,077	63.4	4.7	66.7	2,680,694	62,743	17.3	12.0	10.7
1805860	Bloomington city, Indiana...........	37,163	22.0	60.8	71,752	53.6	4.9	25.2	31,711	37,734	37.8	10.7	7.2
1810342	Carmel city, Indiana	70,585	9.2	73.7	81,702	69.2	2.1	46.6	39,994	106,990	6.1	36.0	2.7
1822000	Evansville city, Indiana................	79,920	43.7	21.8	94,593	62.3	5.5	39.9	53,896	46,662	22.0	3.4	19.0
1823278	Fishers city, Indiana	NA	NA	NA	NA	NA	NA	NA	35,466	121,501	6.1	40.2	1.4
1825000	Fort Wayne city, Indiana.............	173,358	39.9	27.8	206,445	64.9	5.9	41.6	109,640	54,737	19.5	7.3	12.7
1831000	Hammond city, Indiana...............	53,323	59.5	11.4	62,593	61.7	8.4	41.4	30,737	46,248	22.8	5.4	22.1
1836003	Indianapolis city (balance), Indiana	582,418	39.2	34.7	687,369	67.8	6.0	46.0	358,150	58,479	18.6	11.5	14.3
1840788	Lafayette city, Indiana	46,651	40.7	29.8	56,542	65.2	4.3	43.9	31,585	47,456	22.0	3.7	9.6
1854180	Noblesville city, Indiana..............	46,289	23.5	49.5	NA	NA	NA	NA	25,035	81,849	6.3	19.3	5.6
1871000	South Bend city, Indiana.............	67,784	43.2	27.5	80,611	59.6	5.6	40.2	42,707	50,248	24.9	7.3	17.2
19000	**IOWA**............................	2,137,261	36.9	30.5	2,543,525	66.1	3.6	67.5	1,300,467	$65,600	16.6	12.7	11.1
1901855	Ames city, Iowa.........................	29,822	14.4	62.5	60,072	60.6	4.6	NA	25,901	52,005	26.3	9.5	5.0
1902305	Ankeny city, Iowa.......................	45,386	20.8	49.9	NA	NA	NA	NA	27,720	94,508	8.0	22.0	3.6
1912000	Cedar Rapids city, Iowa..............	91,163	28.0	36.2	110,621	69.1	4.9	47.2	59,107	60,977	16.4	11.9	12.6
1919000	Davenport city, Iowa	70,938	38.2	27.4	82,916	64.4	5.9	40.7	44,958	53,914	20.5	10.3	21.2
1921000	Des Moines city, Iowa	141,934	42.0	27.7	169,315	70.1	5.3	46.7	90,416	60,693	17.0	9.7	18.2
1938595	Iowa City city, Iowa....................	40,813	12.5	59.9	64,383	73.2	3.9	36.3	30,270	61,301	23.0	13.6	11.8
1973335	Sioux City city, Iowa...................	55,413	50.4	20.6	67,028	66.8	3.9	NA	33,659	55,622	18.7	10.3	13.8

Table B-4. Cities — What: Education, Employment, and Income, 2021—*Continued*

STATE and place code	STATE Place	Educational attainment			Employment status				Household income and benefits				
		Total population 25 years and over	Percent with a high school diploma or less	Percent with a bachelor's degree or more	Total population 16 years and over	Labor force participation (percent)	Percent unemployed	Percent age 16 years and over who worked full-time year-round in the past 12 months	Total households	Median household income in the past 12 months (in 2021 inflation-adjusted dollars)	Income less than $25,000 (percent)	Income greater than $150,000 (percent)	Percent who received cash public assistance or food stamps/ SNAP
	ACS table number:	C15003	C15003	C15003	C23001	C23001	C23001	S2402	B19001	B19049	B19001	B19001	B19058
	column number:	1	2	3	4	5	6	7	8	9	10	11	12
	IOWA—Cont.												
1982425	Waterloo city, Iowa	45,234	46.3	20.6	52,820	64.4	3.8	40.4	29,948	50,549	23.7	4.3	14.4
1983910	West Des Moines city, Iowa..........	50,854	21.3	49.8	NA	NA	NA	NA	36,066	62,073	15.3	15.6	8.1
20000	**KANSAS**	1,942,133	33.5	35.4	2,315,379	65.7	4.3	67.7	1,159,026	64,124	17.4	13.2	8.5
2036000	Kansas City city, Kansas	97,885	51.6	21.3	116,860	64.6	6.7	41.8	57,819	53,884	21.3	6.8	16.7
2038900	Lawrence city, Kansas	57,431	20.3	54.3	81,488	66.6	5.5	38.6	41,041	52,475	25.7	10.4	9.5
2052575	Olathe city, Kansas......................	95,744	21.2	50.0	114,185	71.6	2.1	51.2	53,285	99,631	10.5	25.5	4.1
2053775	Overland Park city, Kansas............	136,060	14.1	63.9	156,748	72.6	3.5	54.6	82,593	89,280	9.4	26.0	3.1
2064500	Shawnee city, Kansas	46,734	19.7	54.6	NA	NA	NA	NA	27,114	92,844	9.8	26.8	4.3
2071000	Topeka city, Kansas	86,996	38.7	30.1	102,020	60.6	3.4	44.4	55,844	49,040	24.9	7.5	10.3
2079000	Wichita city, Kansas	260,354	38.8	29.9	309,615	65.9	7.2	41.8	156,668	56,293	20.2	9.8	14.4
21000	**KENTUCKY**	3,077,867	44.8	27.0	3,612,858	58.8	5.4	64.9	1,785,682	55,573	22.9	10.4	15.4
2108902	Bowling Green city, Kentucky.......	40,992	42.3	32.4	59,017	67.2	4.4	NA	28,947	43,443	28.7	9.4	21.9
2146027	Lexington-Fayette urban county, Kentucky	209,898	27.3	46.3	263,438	67.5	5.4	42.0	139,303	60,942	21.1	13.0	10.0
2148006	Louisville/Jefferson County metro government (balance), Kentucky..	431,054	39.6	33.2	504,444	64.4	5.3	41.4	264,336	57,182	19.5	12.2	14.2
22000	**LOUISIANA**	3,117,186	46.2	26.4	3,663,069	58.5	7.5	64.9	1,783,924	52,087	25.6	11.5	20.0
2205000	Baton Rouge city, Louisiana..........	136,594	39.9	35.3	178,891	59.7	10.9	35.9	87,440	41,257	32.0	11.2	26.5
2239475	Kenner city, Louisiana	44,111	44.5	26.2	50,438	61.7	8.1	NA	25,267	55,753	25.5	11.8	17.2
2240735	Lafayette city, Louisiana	81,369	36.2	39.1	99,438	64.7	4.3	40.6	51,150	57,953	24.3	16.0	14.5
2241155	Lake Charles city, Louisiana	55,109	42.3	27.5	NA	NA	NA	NA	28,683	45,995	28.7	8.3	26.9
2250115	Metairie CDP, Louisiana................	104,896	33.5	40.0	117,623	64.4	4.1	44.8	62,315	66,074	15.5	16.8	11.9
2255000	New Orleans city, Louisiana..........	271,452	32.1	41.5	310,676	59.9	9.3	37.8	158,827	46,942	31.5	13.8	23.0
2270000	Shreveport city, Louisiana.............	123,087	43.8	26.6	143,517	56.9	11.4	36.7	76,167	42,034	32.0	8.4	23.9
23000	**MAINE**	1,015,078	35.1	36.0	1,155,699	61.3	4.9	65.4	593,626	64,767	18.1	13.2	13.0
2360545	Portland city, Maine	53,102	19.2	57.2	57,985	70.1	5.6	48.3	32,523	70,244	19.1	19.2	12.3
24000	**MARYLAND**	4,273,260	32.8	42.5	4,964,751	66.6	5.8	68.2	2,355,652	90,203	13.2	26.4	14.2
2404000	Baltimore city, Maryland..............	405,797	37.7	37.7	472,136	62.3	7.9	42.8	254,370	54,652	26.4	13.0	28.3
2407125	Bethesda CDP, Maryland..............	48,191	5.0	87.3	55,086	66.1	3.8	NA	27,748	167,162	6.7	55.2	4.1
2419125	Columbia CDP, Maryland..............	73,376	15.4	65.7	83,577	69.0	2.8	49.2	42,050	110,002	10.4	33.6	9.0
2426000	Ellicott City CDP, Maryland...........	50,554	12.8	70.5	59,383	65.4	6.1	46.1	27,318	141,110	6.6	46.1	6.6
2430325	Frederick city, Maryland...............	55,421	32.6	42.3	63,457	69.6	5.8	NA	33,907	81,411	12.0	19.2	9.8
2431175	Gaithersburg city, Maryland	47,522	25.0	53.0	54,668	72.2	4.7	47.3	26,764	99,429	13.1	27.4	16.0
2432025	Germantown CDP, Maryland.......	56,878	28.5	48.3	67,501	73.2	6.1	48.2	30,985	91,931	10.3	26.2	13.9
2432650	Glen Burnie CDP, Maryland..........	48,955	39.7	23.6	55,881	69.4	5.0	51.3	27,700	83,577	9.4	16.6	15.5
2467675	Rockville city, Maryland................	48,740	20.7	66.1	53,699	66.6	3.6	47.0	25,537	118,903	11.2	39.2	8.2
2472450	Silver Spring CDP, Maryland	53,372	26.0	58.6	63,047	76.0	7.0	46.5	33,307	84,223	12.0	23.2	15.3
2481175	Waldorf CDP, Maryland................	55,878	30.1	36.7	64,745	74.1	7.1	52.5	29,701	103,784	11.7	26.8	14.3
25000	**MASSACHUSETTS**	4,934,755	31.7	46.6	5,790,261	66.8	6.6	63.3	2,759,018	89,645	15.7	28.1	16.7
2507000	Boston city, Massachusetts..........	454,669	30.6	52.5	564,064	69.3	8.0	42.7	271,941	79,283	22.1	25.7	22.1
2509000	Brockton city, Massachusetts.......	68,610	50.0	24.9	81,857	68.4	7.9	38.9	37,554	68,581	18.7	17.4	32.4
2511000	Cambridge city, Massachusetts	79,413	10.2	81.4	106,121	69.6	3.7	46.6	52,487	104,746	16.5	34.3	10.7
2523000	Fall River city, Massachusetts........	65,372	57.5	15.8	75,691	59.6	8.9	35.7	40,521	46,672	29.7	8.3	34.3
2524960	Framingham city, Massachusetts ..	47,324	28.1	51.6	55,532	72.2	2.7	47.6	26,320	94,023	15.2	30.6	20.4
2529405	Haverhill city, Massachusetts	45,746	43.4	28.2	53,302	71.7	8.1	43.9	25,293	80,388	17.1	21.1	32.2
2534550	Lawrence city, Massachusetts.......	53,939	62.8	14.4	67,261	66.2	10.1	35.6	30,366	49,087	25.3	5.5	57.4
2537000	Lowell city, Massachusetts...........	75,626	49.7	28.6	92,421	65.5	4.8	39.8	42,577	64,221	19.1	11.4	28.2
2537490	Lynn city, Massachusetts	68,449	52.3	22.5	80,691	65.1	5.2	42.0	37,304	64,986	23.5	14.1	31.5
2537875	Malden city, Massachusetts..........	47,864	38.4	45.5	NA	NA	NA	NA	26,386	86,410	13.2	21.4	23.3
2545000	New Bedford city, Massachusetts .	68,613	58.2	17.6	80,888	63.3	10.3	34.1	42,743	49,237	26.8	5.3	33.2
2545560	Newton city, Massachusetts	56,582	7.7	84.4	70,890	67.8	3.9	44.5	29,961	183,208	7.0	57.5	7.0
2555745	Quincy city, Massachusetts..........	77,334	33.0	45.9	87,211	72.1	8.4	45.1	44,051	81,748	16.4	22.9	19.5
2562535	Somerville city, Massachusetts......	61,244	22.5	62.6	72,757	74.7	3.6	53.0	35,015	107,651	12.4	36.3	9.9
2567000	Springfield city, Massachusetts.....	96,251	55.0	22.3	121,502	53.5	12.8	30.2	57,806	42,498	33.3	6.0	39.4
2582000	Worcester city, Massachusetts.......	133,480	41.3	34.4	171,081	64.9	10.3	37.9	76,065	63,194	23.6	14.3	30.7

STATE and place code	STATE Place	Educational attainment			Employment status				Household income and benefits				
		Total population 25 years and over	Percent with a high school diploma or less	Percent with a bachelor's degree or more	Total population 16 years and over	Labor force participation (percent)	Percent unemployed	Percent age 16 years and over who worked full-time year-round in the past 12 months	Total households	Median household income in the past 12 months (in 2021 inflation-adjusted dollars)	Income less than $25,000 (percent)	Income greater than $150,000 (percent)	Percent who received cash public assistance or food stamps/ SNAP
	ACS table number:	C15003	C15003	C15003	C23001	C23001	C23001	S2402	B19001	B19049	B19001	B19001	B19058
	column number:	1	2	3	4	5	6	7	8	9	10	11	12
26000	**MICHIGAN**	6,971,895	36.8	31.7	8,156,411	60.9	6.9	61.0	4,051,798	63,498	18.3	13.6	15.3
2603000	Ann Arbor city, Michigan	69,418	10.9	75.5	107,211	63.0	4.3	32.7	51,238	68,864	20.1	20.4	6.0
2621000	Dearborn city, Michigan	67,288	40.1	34.9	82,553	52.8	7.8	29.8	35,209	61,079	21.7	11.8	22.1
2622000	Detroit city, Michigan	419,011	49.7	18.1	491,793	54.9	17.4	28.2	251,729	36,140	36.7	4.9	40.8
2627440	Farmington Hills city, Michigan	61,523	19.1	55.7	70,646	68.3	4.0	46.7	35,224	95,960	11.6	23.1	7.3
2629000	Flint city, Michigan	53,438	51.2	14.8	63,236	54.7	15.7	NA	32,837	37,102	36.3	4.4	34.6
2634000	Grand Rapids city, Michigan	131,954	32.3	40.3	159,622	69.3	6.6	42.3	79,486	59,596	20.7	9.2	17.4
2642160	Kalamazoo city, Michigan	38,406	32.6	37.2	60,120	64.6	7.8	32.5	29,853	40,227	37.8	8.4	18.5
2646000	Lansing city, Michigan	74,175	36.6	31.6	92,536	64.3	9.5	38.0	50,590	48,818	23.1	5.9	22.5
2649000	Livonia city, Michigan	72,342	26.1	43.4	79,492	59.9	5.1	39.9	38,329	87,332	9.3	22.8	7.4
2659440	Novi city, Michigan	46,909	16.8	65.2	NA	NA	NA	NA	28,217	104,597	10.2	31.9	7.6
2669035	Rochester Hills city, Michigan	51,385	19.9	61.6	61,206	65.5	4.9	42.4	28,831	103,023	10.2	31.9	5.2
2674900	Southfield city, Michigan	55,365	23.0	38.2	63,261	60.4	9.6	NA	35,649	55,463	21.7	15.3	16.7
2676460	Sterling Heights city, Michigan	96,253	40.8	30.5	109,930	60.8	8.4	35.1	51,805	69,104	17.0	13.5	20.6
2680700	Troy city, Michigan	61,232	19.5	59.9	71,415	61.5	4.0	42.3	33,822	98,170	11.3	31.8	10.6
2684000	Warren city, Michigan	103,508	48.4	20.0	115,283	63.9	11.1	37.3	57,632	60,042	18.9	10.2	21.6
2686000	Westland city, Michigan	62,499	46.5	19.8	70,827	62.2	5.9	39.6	37,870	56,191	18.2	6.6	17.4
2688940	Wyoming city, Michigan	48,042	47.9	22.2	56,718	71.0	5.8	NA	28,253	61,583	19.0	4.7	21.0
27000	**MINNESOTA**	3,898,742	29.2	38.9	4,554,126	68.4	4.9	64.6	2,281,033	77,720	13.3	19.4	9.8
2706382	Blaine city, Minnesota	45,596	31.5	37.9	53,128	71.2	5.3	49.6	25,869	89,533	6.7	23.7	7.6
2706616	Bloomington city, Minnesota	66,059	24.1	45.2	73,670	65.7	6.9	41.1	38,725	80,577	13.0	19.7	8.8
2707966	Brooklyn Park city, Minnesota	58,363	28.8	34.6	NA	NA	NA	NA	30,074	74,807	12.3	19.6	12.2
2717000	Duluth city, Minnesota	52,434	21.7	45.3	72,363	65.2	6.1	33.6	36,310	61,944	18.3	11.8	11.3
2717288	Eagan city, Minnesota	47,588	13.9	57.3	54,301	76.4	4.1	51.8	27,069	100,490	7.1	32.2	6.6
2735180	Lakeville city, Minnesota	47,167	22.2	46.4	54,386	74.8	4.1	51.8	23,868	131,125	2.0	40.0	8.6
2740166	Maple Grove city, Minnesota	50,711	16.6	57.0	NA	NA	NA	NA	28,026	117,442	6.6	33.2	2.9
2743000	Minneapolis city, Minnesota	289,530	22.1	53.6	356,026	73.8	8.4	42.7	188,681	69,397	18.2	17.9	15.9
2751730	Plymouth city, Minnesota	55,505	13.4	63.6	NA	NA	NA	NA	32,923	106,962	6.5	36.0	6.3
2754880	Rochester city, Minnesota	80,830	23.4	49.3	96,762	70.3	4.2	44.2	49,984	75,902	14.3	19.2	9.4
2756896	St. Cloud city, Minnesota	42,835	28.2	27.4	58,592	70.9	8.0	35.3	30,029	53,036	22.8	8.6	12.5
2758000	St. Paul city, Minnesota	201,457	32.5	42.0	242,177	70.0	6.3	43.4	121,964	66,098	15.7	15.7	18.8
2771428	Woodbury city, Minnesota	50,679	9.8	64.6	NA	NA	NA	NA	28,751	114,592	6.8	39.1	2.7
28000	**MISSISSIPPI**	1,968,167	43.3	24.8	2,340,485	56.6	6.3	68.6	1,129,611	48,716	26.6	8.2	14.5
2829700	Gulfport city, Mississippi	48,584	43.1	25.0	57,884	57.3	11.9	NA	29,385	43,066	27.8	5.6	22.3
2836000	Jackson city, Mississippi	97,401	38.0	29.0	118,207	59.2	10.8	34.2	62,140	35,070	36.6	4.1	20.3
29000	**MISSOURI**	4,226,634	39.3	31.7	4,949,628	62.8	4.6	67.1	2,468,726	61,847	18.6	13.0	11.2
2915670	Columbia city, Missouri	72,139	22.0	56.1	102,554	68.7	5.5	37.5	50,572	60,662	23.6	11.7	8.0
2935000	Independence city, Missouri	86,843	49.8	19.5	99,495	58.2	5.9	38.3	53,057	52,919	19.5	7.5	13.7
2938000	Kansas City city, Missouri	350,305	32.3	38.7	406,818	70.1	6.2	48.4	219,020	63,396	18.8	12.3	11.4
2941348	Lee's Summit city, Missouri	65,768	20.7	47.2	77,033	71.0	4.2	49.7	37,795	100,246	5.8	27.0	4.3
2954074	O'Fallon city, Missouri	62,228	27.3	44.6	73,382	74.7	2.4	51.2	34,412	97,868	6.3	23.2	8.1
2964082	St. Charles city, Missouri	50,025	25.3	45.5	59,179	66.9	2.6	47.5	29,992	76,340	11.2	19.5	4.3
2964550	St. Joseph city, Missouri	51,112	50.4	24.0	59,992	59.6	4.6	39.5	29,750	46,089	26.0	8.8	15.9
2965000	St. Louis city, Missouri	214,271	34.6	38.9	245,307	64.7	6.3	42.5	139,736	49,965	27.7	9.1	20.4
2970000	Springfield city, Missouri	108,128	35.3	32.4	142,675	63.8	4.8	38.7	79,232	41,808	25.3	6.1	13.1
30000	**MONTANA**	766,758	32.5	34.8	895,986	61.8	3.9	62.0	448,949	63,249	17.6	13.4	10.5
3006550	Billings city, Montana	81,307	28.9	37.5	93,390	64.2	5.0	39.4	50,365	65,818	17.1	12.3	9.8
3050200	Missoula city, Montana	50,625	21.4	48.9	62,540	72.3	5.5	39.7	33,744	63,270	18.6	16.3	14.7
3128000	Lincoln city, Nebraska	181,191	26.5	43.0	235,804	71.1	2.8	45.6	120,407	62,294	17.2	11.9	9.1
31000	**NEBRASKA**	1,292,536	33.0	34.4	1,534,896	68.6	2.6	69.3	785,982	66,817	16.5	14.0	9.5
3137000	Omaha city, Nebraska	322,158	31.4	38.1	382,774	69.1	4.1	46.1	201,469	62,948	18.4	14.7	13.6
32000	**NEVADA**	2,192,826	40.1	27.6	2,526,328	63.0	9.6	60.8	1,191,380	66,274	17.7	14.9	15.7
3223770	Enterprise CDP, Nevada	166,915	30.3	36.5	193,980	71.9	9.8	42.4	83,983	84,902	11.9	21.7	11.2
3231900	Henderson city, Nevada	227,779	29.5	35.2	255,102	63.1	8.4	40.3	124,470	77,924	12.4	21.1	8.6

Table B-4. Cities — What: Education, Employment, and Income, 2021—*Continued*

STATE and place code	STATE Place	Educational attainment			Employment status				Household income and benefits				
		Total population 25 years and over	Percent with a high school diploma or less	Percent with a bachelor's degree or more	Total population 16 years and over	Labor force participation (percent)	Percent unemployed	Percent age 16 years and over who worked full-time year-round in the past 12 months	Total households	Median household income in the past 12 months (in 2021 inflation-adjusted dollars)	Income less than $25,000 (percent)	Income greater than $150,000 (percent)	Percent who received cash public assistance or food stamps/SNAP
	ACS table number:	C15003	C15003	C15003	C23001	C23001	C23001	S2402	B19001	B19049	B19001	B19001	B19058
	column number:	1	2	3	4	5	6	7	8	9	10	11	12
	NEVADA—Cont.												
3240000	Las Vegas city, Nevada	456,127	41.4	27.6	523,043	62.0	10.8	35.9	250,350	59,746	20.6	14.3	17.8
3251800	North Las Vegas city, Nevada	176,739	51.2	17.0	214,223	64.0	11.1	39.4	85,966	67,035	15.8	9.7	20.6
3254600	Paradise CDP, Nevada	131,746	45.4	23.7	153,400	65.9	14.2	35.8	78,005	50,096	24.6	8.6	23.8
3260600	Reno city, Nevada	185,320	36.0	35.9	219,436	65.6	4.7	43.8	110,993	67,478	17.7	15.4	16.8
3268400	Sparks city, Nevada	77,248	37.0	32.0	88,542	68.4	7.6	45.1	43,392	78,778	8.4	15.3	7.9
3268585	Spring Valley CDP, Nevada	154,428	33.3	34.0	173,478	68.2	13.2	38.6	88,063	61,179	21.8	11.9	15.8
3271400	Sunrise Manor CDP, Nevada	122,855	62.1	10.4	149,673	60.9	11.7	35.6	62,737	51,287	22.2	4.8	26.3
33000	**NEW HAMPSHIRE**	1,008,318	32.1	40.2	1,164,253	66.7	3.6	67.0	548,026	88,465	11.5	22.9	7.6
3345140	Manchester city, New Hampshire	83,473	37.5	33.5	95,871	74.6	3.8	51.8	48,649	73,639	12.7	11.4	10.6
3350260	Nashua city, New Hampshire	64,995	28.9	44.2	75,784	69.6	4.6	47.4	36,986	85,870	13.3	19.2	11.3
34000	**NEW JERSEY**	6,474,427	34.5	43.1	7,489,289	65.6	8.0	64.4	3,497,945	89,296	14.0	27.4	10.9
3403580	Bayonne city, New Jersey	49,084	39.9	40.2	54,389	63.6	6.8	NA	28,375	73,110	17.1	15.1	14.7
3410000	Camden city, New Jersey	42,562	66.8	9.9	52,899	53.6	11.1	NA	24,276	39,654	35.7	4.8	43.2
3413690	Clifton city, New Jersey	65,453	43.8	34.6	75,083	65.6	7.7	44.5	32,408	81,857	13.9	23.1	14.2
3419390	East Orange city, New Jersey	48,037	44.8	22.2	53,088	64.6	12.7	NA	28,318	51,368	25.2	5.5	24.6
3421000	Elizabeth city, New Jersey	87,169	62.5	14.5	103,700	64.7	6.6	45.1	46,107	51,549	20.8	11.0	18.7
3436000	Jersey City, New Jersey	207,393	31.4	51.9	232,176	67.3	8.6	48.3	119,158	81,958	20.7	27.2	17.7
3438580	Lakewood CDP, New Jersey	25,565	42.5	33.1	NA	NA	NA	NA	13,701	40,338	24.8	15.1	29.7
3451000	Newark city, New Jersey	200,579	60.5	17.6	240,399	59.5	15.3	35.6	115,145	43,242	32.4	6.1	24.8
3456550	Passaic city, New Jersey	39,632	69.0	18.8	50,319	68.0	14.3	35.5	20,446	51,806	25.1	12.2	41.3
3457000	Paterson city, New Jersey	100,985	63.7	14.0	119,685	63.7	15.8	37.9	51,612	46,451	29.9	8.7	37.3
3473110	Toms River CDP, New Jersey	65,437	36.6	38.6	76,145	64.4	6.4	43.7	35,128	87,797	16.1	26.7	7.9
3474000	Trenton city, New Jersey	62,083	60.5	17.5	70,160	59.0	13.0	NA	34,116	41,715	31.2	5.9	31.6
3474630	Union City city, New Jersey	42,877	59.4	27.7	52,464	68.3	13.0	NA	24,041	59,393	20.2	9.8	25.2
35000	**NEW MEXICO**	1,450,549	38.2	30.1	1,700,082	56.9	7.7	62.8	834,007	53,992	23.6	11.4	22.4
3502000	Albuquerque city, New Mexico	393,957	31.3	38.5	462,194	64.0	6.0	40.8	243,582	58,512	20.8	12.7	20.8
3539380	Las Cruces city, New Mexico	70,251	34.7	33.6	88,307	60.0	7.3	NA	45,991	42,058	29.8	8.8	27.2
3563460	Rio Rancho city, New Mexico	73,104	24.4	34.3	84,131	61.0	7.8	42.1	40,013	76,096	8.9	14.3	17.0
3570500	Santa Fe city, New Mexico	64,505	24.5	48.7	72,844	63.7	8.5	36.9	40,641	60,517	18.5	15.2	15.0
36000	**NEW YORK**	13,987,094	36.3	39.9	16,210,453	62.5	8.7	62.0	7,652,666	74,314	18.5	21.7	17.1
3601000	Albany city, New York	63,166	30.3	42.0	85,930	62.1	9.9	34.2	44,279	49,763	28.2	10.5	23.7
3611000	Buffalo city, New York	184,416	39.1	32.8	221,386	59.7	10.2	31.4	122,569	40,669	33.1	7.7	33.9
3615000	Cheektowaga CDP, New York	54,969	41.8	28.7	62,395	67.2	6.2	44.6	33,247	64,106	15.4	8.3	14.2
3649121	Mount Vernon city, New York	52,228	39.5	35.8	60,121	64.9	14.7	NA	26,465	78,562	18.9	21.3	23.9
3650617	New Rochelle city, New York	59,793	28.6	56.6	69,054	67.6	7.0	NA	32,877	106,386	14.4	35.8	15.3
3651000	New York city, New York	6,041,519	39.0	41.0	6,902,783	62.5	11.8	37.1	3,263,895	67,997	22.2	20.8	23.1
3663000	Rochester city, New York	142,044	46.4	28.1	172,160	61.6	11.0	35.4	93,263	41,980	32.1	6.5	31.1
3665508	Schenectady city, New York	45,822	40.3	25.7	55,229	59.2	9.5	NA	28,965	53,316	28.6	8.3	24.7
3673000	Syracuse city, New York	93,514	42.1	30.9	119,472	53.7	6.9	29.7	62,663	40,076	34.9	5.2	30.2
3684000	Yonkers city, New York	144,615	36.3	36.6	168,631	63.0	9.8	37.7	81,397	66,395	23.1	20.4	19.3
37000	**NORTH CAROLINA**	7,245,632	35.2	34.9	8,524,268	62.2	5.7	65.6	4,179,632	61,972	19.3	13.9	15.0
3702140	Asheville city, North Carolina	72,579	23.4	53.0	82,277	58.8	7.9	NA	38,131	59,758	22.7	13.4	16.5
3710740	Cary town, North Carolina	118,111	12.6	70.2	141,875	69.1	5.3	50.0	65,254	123,857	9.1	38.2	4.1
3712000	Charlotte city, North Carolina	599,527	26.8	48.8	704,784	72.2	5.0	51.3	365,269	70,869	13.9	18.9	11.9
3714100	Concord city, North Carolina	68,499	31.0	41.3	82,971	71.6	5.2	NA	33,859	79,329	12.6	15.4	11.6
3719000	Durham city, North Carolina	196,538	22.9	56.9	234,030	67.2	5.2	47.2	122,412	71,343	14.5	17.9	13.0
3722920	Fayetteville city, North Carolina	130,060	29.9	29.3	163,632	67.3	7.2	32.7	83,147	51,629	22.3	6.6	19.7
3725580	Gastonia city, North Carolina	55,735	42.4	22.3	63,677	65.0	5.8	44.6	33,292	53,424	22.9	7.5	24.1
3728000	Greensboro city, North Carolina	198,941	31.5	38.1	243,836	64.4	6.4	40.1	123,955	51,825	21.0	9.5	20.4
3728080	Greenville city, North Carolina	47,558	28.1	38.9	74,651	63.3	12.3	NA	41,575	36,687	35.9	7.9	20.0
3731400	High Point city, North Carolina	74,573	34.8	36.2	90,765	61.7	6.7	41.0	42,738	57,698	22.4	8.5	23.2
3734200	Jacksonville city, North Carolina	31,421	39.3	24.5	61,639	75.2	2.7	NA	22,024	44,497	22.9	6.5	13.5
3755000	Raleigh city, North Carolina	321,562	23.0	53.9	384,856	68.6	5.5	47.1	194,917	74,612	16.3	20.0	11.2
3774440	Wilmington city, North Carolina	83,531	28.9	42.5	105,299	63.5	7.2	38.5	59,341	53,186	23.5	14.6	12.2
3775000	Winston-Salem city, North Carolina	166,146	37.4	35.6	202,207	61.0	6.2	39.5	101,551	54,228	24.6	12.2	23.3

STATE Place	Educational attainment			Employment status				Household income and benefits				
	Total population 25 years and over	Percent with a high school diploma or less	Percent with a bachelor's degree or more	Total population 16 years and over	Labor force participation (percent)	Percent unemployed	Percent age 16 years and over who worked full-time year-round in the past 12 months	Total households	Median household income in the past 12 months (in 2021 inflation-adjusted dollars)	Income less than $25,000 (percent)	Income greater than $150,000 (percent)	Percent who received cash public assistance or food stamps/ SNAP
ACS table number:	C15003	C15003	C15003	C23001	C23001	C23001	S2402	B19001	B19049	B19001	B19001	B19058
column number:	1	2	3	4	5	6	7	8	9	10	11	12
38000 **NORTH DAKOTA**..........	506,739	32.7	31.7	610,714	68.1	2.8	65.2	322,511	66,519	17.5	13.6	7.3
3807200 Bismarck city, North Dakota........	51,945	29.6	37.9	60,156	66.3	2.2	45.8	31,426	61,861	15.4	13.2	8.1
3825700 Fargo city, North Dakota.............	78,318	25.2	43.5	100,455	74.6	4.1	46.0	58,269	59,089	18.7	14.9	7.6
39000 **OHIO**..........	8,117,973	41.1	30.7	9,480,334	62.6	5.4	65.6	4,832,922	62,262	19.1	12.9	14.5
3901000 Akron city, Ohio..........	131,899	47.5	23.0	155,107	59.9	8.2	34.6	84,914	41,628	29.6	4.2	32.6
3912000 Canton city, Ohio..........	49,113	52.6	16.1	56,665	56.2	10.4	NA	31,168	40,934	29.3	3.7	29.5
3915000 Cincinnati city, Ohio..........	201,459	33.9	41.1	249,792	64.4	7.5	39.9	144,929	42,733	32.7	10.4	22.6
3916000 Cleveland city, Ohio..........	255,254	50.0	21.7	299,643	59.8	12.3	35.6	171,321	35,562	36.3	4.3	33.8
3918000 Columbus city, Ohio..........	605,747	34.1	38.4	731,827	69.7	6.2	45.4	390,605	58,202	19.2	9.0	15.2
3921000 Dayton city, Ohio..........	83,787	45.3	20.0	107,339	55.9	9.8	31.5	55,114	39,315	30.5	4.1	28.5
3944856 Lorain city, Ohio..........	45,237	51.6	13.3	51,640	56.4	6.9	NA	27,852	43,410	28.0	4.5	18.8
3961000 Parma city, Ohio..........	57,304	42.5	22.4	65,475	65.3	5.8	41.3	33,401	57,444	16.3	6.5	17.3
3977000 Toledo city, Ohio..........	182,651	44.4	23.0	214,639	63.2	9.2	37.0	120,895	44,150	30.5	4.0	21.1
40000 **OKLAHOMA**	2,639,889	42.0	27.9	3,140,799	61.0	5.9	66.7	1,547,967	55,826	21.3	10.1	15.1
4009050 Broken Arrow city, Oklahoma	80,743	32.1	34.3	92,715	67.5	5.1	46.5	45,138	73,628	12.1	14.2	6.7
4023200 Edmond city, Oklahoma..............	61,785	16.0	55.5	73,894	64.8	3.6	44.6	36,530	90,384	10.4	25.5	6.4
4041850 Lawton city, Oklahoma..............	57,213	42.8	23.2	72,527	61.1	8.5	31.8	33,921	44,751	26.5	4.7	16.1
4052500 Norman city, Oklahoma..............	79,364	25.5	46.1	109,954	64.1	6.7	38.4	53,446	57,786	22.3	11.6	12.6
4055000 Oklahoma City city, Oklahoma.....	450,933	37.6	33.2	535,782	67.0	5.8	44.2	275,285	59,214	19.5	11.2	17.0
4075000 Tulsa city, Oklahoma..................	273,027	37.3	35.3	322,290	63.4	7.0	41.2	173,943	51,008	24.0	10.8	17.0
41000 **OREGON**	3,030,635	30.1	36.3	3,487,919	61.6	6.3	62.0	1,702,599	71,562	16.2	17.0	18.1
4105350 Beaverton city, Oregon..........	71,213	20.5	49.8	81,869	69.4	4.5	45.6	42,858	76,520	17.1	19.8	16.6
4105800 Bend city, Oregon..........	75,713	18.7	50.8	NA	NA	NA	NA	44,620	82,102	10.7	20.9	10.3
4123850 Eugene city, Oregon..........	115,474	22.4	44.5	150,773	63.1	7.9	35.2	74,740	59,338	20.2	13.9	21.2
4131250 Gresham city, Oregon	77,452	38.9	23.2	89,369	63.3	7.4	40.1	43,487	66,129	18.2	11.2	23.0
4134100 Hillsboro city, Oregon..........	74,445	24.8	44.4	88,418	68.0	5.6	46.7	40,891	97,436	8.9	24.0	11.7
4147000 Medford city, Oregon..........	63,449	37.7	31.1	72,238	59.2	7.5	NA	36,525	63,703	19.3	10.4	19.3
4159000 Portland city, Oregon..........	484,685	20.4	54.3	546,399	70.7	7.1	43.5	286,734	79,057	15.7	22.3	18.8
4164900 Salem city, Oregon..........	115,980	36.9	28.9	139,835	60.1	5.6	38.9	64,959	63,927	16.6	13.1	24.6
42000 **PENNSYLVANIA**	9,161,945	41.4	34.5	10,602,171	62.4	6.4	65.6	5,228,956	68,957	17.8	16.6	15.6
4202000 Allentown city, Pennsylvania........	83,233	57.3	15.7	100,079	58.8	10.1	39.2	47,204	46,745	28.4	5.4	28.2
4206088 Bethlehem city, Pennsylvania........	49,863	42.1	33.0	64,256	60.9	6.7	35.5	30,099	57,320	21.0	12.0	21.4
4224000 Erie city, Pennsylvania..........	62,102	49.7	22.7	74,897	58.4	8.5	33.7	38,636	43,186	31.8	3.4	30.3
4260000 Philadelphia city, Pennsylvania......	1,090,520	43.1	34.8	1,270,642	62.9	10.5	39.1	660,921	52,899	27.1	12.6	28.7
4261000 Pittsburgh city, Pennsylvania........	207,183	30.1	47.6	262,349	63.2	7.2	38.9	136,747	57,821	25.9	13.6	19.8
4263624 Reading city, Pennsylvania..........	55,150	68.4	11.4	68,868	58.5	14.4	NA	32,504	37,107	35.2	4.5	48.5
4269000 Scranton city, Pennsylvania..........	50,713	50.6	24.3	62,305	58.2	7.0	39.1	30,096	54,279	25.0	7.2	27.3
44000 **RHODE ISLAND**..........	773,464	38.6	36.5	913,136	65.1	7.6	63.2	440,170	74,008	17.9	18.6	16.8
4419180 Cranston city, Rhode Island..........	61,265	38.3	34.9	69,330	65.8	9.6	45.3	33,049	80,564	14.5	20.0	15.5
4454640 Pawtucket city, Rhode Island........	51,482	54.1	17.9	60,761	70.2	7.0	42.8	29,735	51,817	23.6	8.0	24.3
4459000 Providence city, Rhode Island........	119,983	45.8	33.9	153,374	66.5	9.4	39.9	68,179	60,970	24.3	14.5	29.5
4474300 Warwick city, Rhode Island..........	60,428	33.1	35.0	69,923	63.8	5.8	42.2	36,595	72,025	15.5	13.4	12.7
45000 **SOUTH CAROLINA**..........	3,598,398	38.9	31.5	4,207,365	59.6	5.6	66.8	2,049,972	59,318	20.5	12.0	12.1
4513330 Charleston city, South Carolina..........	105,056	21.6	54.6	128,193	66.1	4.2	46.0	63,391	74,139	16.8	19.2	7.6
4516000 Columbia city, South Carolina.....	75,889	31.8	44.6	114,499	64.4	9.4	32.9	51,455	47,524	28.8	12.1	14.4
4530850 Greenville city, South Carolina......	48,816	22.5	55.6	61,371	68.8	5.1	43.3	34,154	57,253	21.2	18.7	14.4
4548535 Mount Pleasant town, South Carolina..........	68,320	14.4	65.5	NA	NA	NA	NA	37,983	99,298	13.0	29.8	2.2
4550875 North Charleston city, South Carolina..........	80,213	35.3	31.4	94,018	71.2	5.8	48.4	47,324	55,864	22.8	10.2	14.3
4561405 Rock Hill city, South Carolina.......	46,951	29.9	36.1	58,604	68.6	6.0	NA	29,268	60,237	17.2	10.4	11.3
46000 **SOUTH DAKOTA**..........	590,377	36.2	31.7	699,893	66.6	2.8	68.5	356,887	66,143	16.6	11.4	9.1
4652980 Rapid City city, South Dakota.......	51,144	30.8	37.9	60,706	65.0	3.0	39.4	32,471	61,495	19.2	11.9	11.5
4659020 Sioux Falls city, South Dakota.......	129,261	28.5	39.1	152,198	74.4	1.8	55.0	83,498	73,273	12.8	14.9	8.7

Table B-4. Cities — What: Education, Employment, and Income, 2021—*Continued*

STATE and place code	STATE Place	Educational attainment			Employment status				Household income and benefits				
		Total population 25 years and over	Percent with a high school diploma or less	Percent with a bachelor's degree or more	Total population 16 years and over	Labor force participation (percent)	Percent unemployed	Percent age 16 years and over who worked full-time year-round in the past 12 months	Total households	Median household income in the past 12 months (in 2021 inflation-adjusted dollars)	Income less than $25,000 (percent)	Income greater than $150,000 (percent)	Percent who received cash public assistance or food stamps/ SNAP
	ACS table number:	C15003	C15003	C15003	C23001	C23001	C23001	S2402	B19001	B19049	B19001	B19001	B19058
	column number:	1	2	3	4	5	6	7	8	9	10	11	12
47000	**TENNESSEE**	4,814,533	41.5	30.5	5,616,708	61.2	5.3	67.8	2,770,395	59,695	19.8	12.4	13.0
4714000	Chattanooga city, Tennessee.......	125,155	36.9	34.3	147,712	62.8	6.0	41.0	77,299	55,065	24.4	10.5	14.6
4715160	Clarksville city, Tennessee	102,427	34.7	28.1	126,915	65.5	3.6	35.8	63,787	60,686	14.6	7.4	13.0
4727740	Franklin city, Tennessee	56,741	13.2	65.4	NA	NA	NA	NA	33,275	104,515	4.4	36.4	2.8
4737640	Jackson city, Tennessee	42,521	40.9	29.0	53,165	59.0	7.3	NA	26,505	45,651	27.4	7.5	20.6
4738320	Johnson City city, Tennessee........	46,754	29.5	41.5	59,433	60.7	8.6	NA	30,806	56,248	23.9	12.3	14.0
4740000	Knoxville city, Tennessee..............	124,268	35.1	35.2	161,269	63.3	5.4	40.4	85,151	45,700	27.5	9.1	14.8
4748000	Memphis city, Tennessee..............	410,799	42.8	28.3	486,563	64.0	9.8	41.5	256,968	44,317	27.2	8.1	21.1
4751560	Murfreesboro city, Tennessee	100,258	28.3	45.9	127,554	73.7	4.2	51.3	58,371	77,584	12.5	16.9	7.9
4752006	Nashville-Davidson metropolitan government (balance), Tennessee	475,979	31.0	46.1	557,684	69.5	4.2	48.2	305,247	64,857	16.5	16.2	12.0
48000	**TEXAS**	19,224,688	39.2	33.1	22,934,023	64.6	6.1	67.8	10,796,247	66,963	17.5	16.5	13.8
4801000	Abilene city, Texas......................	79,667	46.3	26.1	101,229	60.3	2.1	40.5	48,398	51,931	21.5	9.4	15.4
4801924	Allen city, Texas	72,222	17.4	54.1	NA	NA	NA	NA	37,461	107,438	6.4	36.8	3.9
4803000	Amarillo city, Texas......................	126,695	39.3	27.6	152,535	66.0	3.5	47.3	82,129	55,572	21.0	10.0	11.2
4804000	Arlington city, Texas	259,066	40.0	30.5	309,051	69.0	6.4	47.2	146,888	59,889	16.6	12.7	10.0
4804462	Atascocita CDP, Texas.................	57,696	25.6	39.3	65,639	73.4	5.3	NA	29,579	101,686	4.6	29.7	6.1
4805000	Austin city, Texas........................	687,073	21.6	59.9	801,564	75.3	5.3	52.5	449,399	79,542	14.6	24.3	8.2
4806128	Baytown city, Texas.....................	48,021	53.0	16.1	57,052	63.6	14.5	NA	28,264	48,287	19.4	8.7	22.9
4807000	Beaumont city, Texas...................	72,600	40.5	25.5	86,197	65.4	4.6	45.5	46,375	51,361	24.3	7.9	17.1
4810768	Brownsville city, Texas	108,783	56.6	20.9	138,686	58.7	9.0	36.6	56,522	47,435	30.2	7.9	33.1
4810912	Bryan city, Texas.........................	53,397	46.6	31.2	69,752	59.4	6.2	NA	32,910	44,017	30.2	7.5	11.6
4813024	Carrollton city, Texas	93,939	29.8	42.6	107,819	73.7	3.8	54.8	50,308	86,647	11.3	18.8	5.6
4813552	Cedar Park city, Texas..................	53,809	18.2	58.3	NA	NA	NA	NA	30,407	114,450	7.2	34.7	5.3
4815976	College Station city, Texas	53,351	20.0	52.3	99,251	63.4	5.0	33.5	41,586	49,215	26.3	12.6	7.2
4816432	Conroe city, Texas	60,215	29.0	39.0	NA	NA	NA	NA	37,297	68,428	14.6	16.7	12.7
4817000	Corpus Christi city, Texas.............	209,826	42.3	24.6	251,782	60.8	5.2	42.6	117,366	59,812	21.0	10.2	19.1
4819000	Dallas city, Texas........................	858,890	40.8	37.1	1,013,782	68.2	6.0	47.0	536,008	57,995	21.1	15.0	14.5
4819972	Denton city, Texas.......................	92,278	28.2	42.4	128,401	68.5	6.4	41.7	57,963	64,873	20.5	15.1	10.3
4822660	Edinburg city, Texas.....................	63,814	44.8	28.7	NA	NA	NA	NA	37,541	47,596	28.6	4.8	23.6
4824000	El Paso city, Texas.......................	435,120	42.7	27.9	527,673	62.3	7.6	38.1	242,529	51,241	25.2	9.3	22.3
4826232	Flower Mound town, Texas..........	51,730	12.4	64.8	62,072	73.2	4.3	52.3	27,696	144,642	5.4	48.3	2.4
4827000	Fort Worth city, Texas..................	590,796	40.4	31.6	712,123	68.1	5.1	47.6	334,286	68,235	14.8	15.9	13.9
4827684	Frisco city, Texas........................	134,941	14.9	67.2	160,303	72.5	5.0	52.5	72,282	130,118	3.7	42.4	4.7
4829000	Garland city, Texas	151,667	49.6	22.7	181,476	65.6	5.2	45.7	77,777	61,607	15.1	11.2	13.7
4829336	Georgetown city, Texas	53,795	24.9	43.4	60,164	57.4	4.8	NA	30,207	79,601	9.6	20.3	7.7
4830464	Grand Prairie city, Texas	122,811	44.8	27.7	150,048	67.4	4.6	45.9	64,208	68,473	14.7	13.7	12.9
4832372	Harlingen city, Texas....................	47,509	49.1	23.4	NA	NA	NA	NA	27,051	50,861	31.7	4.9	20.5
4835000	Houston city, Texas......................	1,526,340	42.2	36.3	1,816,331	67.3	8.4	43.7	924,981	55,499	21.9	14.8	18.2
4837000	Irving city, Texas.........................	161,663	38.2	43.2	192,072	72.8	5.1	53.7	95,309	70,340	11.9	16.1	8.1
4839148	Killeen city, Texas	89,807	35.9	21.6	111,134	67.5	8.8	37.0	57,875	51,619	23.6	5.3	20.3
4841464	Laredo city, Texas	147,006	49.5	21.2	185,708	59.9	6.5	39.7	76,095	52,438	24.6	9.3	26.8
4841980	League City city, Texas.................	77,784	23.7	47.6	88,048	69.9	4.6	NA	44,419	101,382	8.7	30.1	6.2
4842016	Leander city, Texas	44,948	21.9	48.9	NA	NA	NA	NA	24,031	120,165	10.4	34.6	5.3
4842508	Lewisville city, Texas	80,182	28.0	37.4	91,947	74.9	6.9	52.0	46,897	75,915	9.6	17.0	10.1
4843888	Longview city, Texas	51,111	45.0	21.2	63,444	62.9	5.2	41.6	31,072	51,209	22.5	5.7	16.7
4845000	Lubbock city, Texas	151,115	34.0	34.2	207,548	66.8	5.4	43.2	104,426	54,747	26.2	10.9	13.4
4845384	McAllen city, Texas	90,083	41.5	32.5	109,901	62.7	6.8	39.1	48,438	57,359	23.0	10.1	21.2
4845744	McKinney city, Texas	132,992	19.0	53.3	153,362	69.5	3.6	52.8	73,357	98,317	9.0	31.7	3.4
4846452	Mansfield city, Texas	49,353	27.8	40.6	NA	NA	NA	NA	25,327	91,255	5.7	23.2	4.1
4847892	Mesquite city, Texas	91,498	47.7	19.1	112,418	71.1	6.9	45.9	52,023	60,957	19.3	8.0	13.8
4848072	Midland city, Texas	83,330	34.9	33.7	99,350	73.4	5.2	NA	52,898	72,038	16.8	20.7	9.0
4848768	Mission city, Texas......................	52,550	52.2	26.2	65,416	57.8	7.9	NA	28,128	57,749	26.4	9.8	24.9
4848804	Missouri City city, Texas...............	54,423	29.2	43.5	NA	NA	NA	NA	29,801	81,451	7.1	16.7	6.5
4850820	New Braunfels city, Texas	64,192	31.4	35.7	NA	NA	NA	NA	37,815	89,073	9.5	12.3	6.9
4852356	North Richland Hills city, Texas......	50,261	30.2	38.1	57,731	64.8	3.5	NA	26,937	78,496	14.0	18.3	8.4
4853388	Odessa city, Texas.......................	71,194	48.2	22.8	87,843	70.6	6.2	51.0	48,530	61,964	17.8	8.8	13.2

Table B-4. Cities — What: Education, Employment, and Income, 2021—*Continued*

STATE and place code	STATE Place	Educational attainment			Employment status				Household income and benefits				
		Total population 25 years and over	Percent with a high school diploma or less	Percent with a bachelor's degree or more	Total population 16 years and over	Labor force participation (percent)	Percent unemployed	Percent age 16 years and over who worked full-time year-round in the past 12 months	Total households	Median household income in the past 12 months (in 2021 inflation-adjusted dollars)	Income less than $25,000 (percent)	Income greater than $150,000 (percent)	Percent who received cash public assistance or food stamps/SNAP
	ACS table number:	C15003	C15003	C15003	C23001	C23001	C23001	S2402	B19001	B19049	B19001	B19001	B19058
	column number:	1	2	3	4	5	6	7	8	9	10	11	12
	TEXAS—Cont.												
4856000	Pasadena city, Texas	96,426	55.4	15.9	114,531	62.8	11.7	NA	50,598	60,939	18.5	9.4	18.9
4856348	Pearland city, Texas	80,221	24.9	48.2	NA	NA	NA	NA	43,012	103,227	7.9	28.0	8.0
4857176	Pflugerville city, Texas	44,657	26.0	43.7	NA	NA	NA	NA	23,875	103,687	6.1	23.6	8.7
4857200	Pharr city, Texas	44,043	59.5	18.4	NA	NA	NA	NA	24,797	32,217	37.7	6.4	37.7
4858016	Plano city, Texas	196,763	19.4	59.1	231,608	68.8	5.1	50.0	108,472	95,002	11.4	29.3	5.5
4861796	Richardson city, Texas	77,718	20.0	55.5	94,122	70.0	7.0	43.8	45,148	85,580	13.3	25.6	5.8
4863500	Round Rock city, Texas	82,318	26.8	43.1	100,568	72.4	5.3	51.4	49,740	79,649	11.1	18.5	5.1
4864472	San Angelo city, Texas	64,328	46.0	23.2	79,426	63.9	4.0	42.4	39,065	60,030	22.1	7.0	7.5
4865000	San Antonio city, Texas	943,969	41.8	28.3	1,135,774	65.6	7.1	41.2	549,245	54,923	20.9	10.3	19.7
4865600	San Marcos city, Texas	32,499	35.9	30.5	58,190	66.3	8.6	NA	27,015	36,080	38.9	6.7	11.1
4869596	Spring CDP, Texas	45,810	45.0	26.7	NA	NA	NA	NA	23,096	79,884	7.0	9.7	23.6
4870808	Sugar Land city, Texas	73,710	17.8	65.3	84,478	63.2	6.7	NA	37,008	112,868	8.7	37.7	9.2
4872176	Temple city, Texas	55,801	35.0	31.5	67,602	64.9	7.1	41.6	34,371	58,284	17.1	10.4	9.2
4872656	The Woodlands CDP, Texas	79,676	13.4	63.6	NA	NA	NA	NA	43,992	104,787	11.4	38.2	6.8
4874144	Tyler city, Texas	69,170	37.3	28.6	85,145	62.7	6.3	42.0	36,169	54,998	15.7	14.6	15.4
4875428	Victoria city, Texas	41,059	52.4	18.8	49,844	66.3	7.5	NA	25,410	54,786	22.7	9.4	20.1
4876000	Waco city, Texas	80,764	38.7	28.5	110,131	61.8	5.5	41.1	53,286	49,952	25.9	10.7	13.1
4879000	Wichita Falls city, Texas	63,670	47.6	22.8	82,013	62.6	3.6	40.1	38,051	50,786	24.7	7.7	14.4
49000	**UTAH**	2,010,727	29.0	36.8	2,507,029	68.7	3.5	63.4	1,101,499	79,449	11.6	18.6	7.0
4943660	Layton city, Utah	49,817	27.5	34.7	61,885	72.9	1.3	48.7	27,176	81,011	10.7	23.3	5.8
4944320	Lehi city, Utah	40,098	18.3	54.3	NA	NA	NA	NA	22,067	114,136	4.4	35.5	4.7
4955980	Ogden city, Utah	56,995	40.8	27.6	68,835	67.5	4.6	42.5	32,631	56,501	20.9	12.4	14.5
4957300	Orem city, Utah	57,170	21.1	42.3	77,235	71.8	2.3	40.4	32,398	72,449	10.8	14.2	6.9
4962470	Provo city, Utah	46,371	19.3	49.0	93,082	73.3	3.8	31.0	32,518	57,659	19.6	12.0	8.7
4965330	St. George city, Utah	62,326	29.4	31.6	79,350	57.9	4.7	NA	35,656	59,365	14.9	11.9	5.8
4967000	Salt Lake City city, Utah	137,219	23.2	50.9	169,555	74.2	3.9	47.6	89,839	66,658	17.0	16.4	10.1
4967440	Sandy city, Utah	63,583	23.6	46.2	73,449	67.5	2.4	46.6	33,587	100,153	10.3	26.8	3.1
4970850	South Jordan city, Utah	50,521	17.0	46.4	NA	NA	NA	NA	25,502	104,170	6.5	30.8	2.8
4982950	West Jordan city, Utah	71,176	35.9	26.3	86,023	71.7	4.7	46.8	36,309	86,252	9.6	18.7	6.1
4983470	West Valley City city, Utah	82,978	58.8	13.7	104,188	73.5	4.1	49.1	42,003	74,348	9.9	10.0	9.5
50000	**VERMONT**	462,705	31.6	44.4	542,827	64.3	4.2	63.4	270,163	72,431	15.9	16.4	12.8
51000	**VIRGINIA**	5,942,672	32.5	41.8	6,980,718	65.2	4.6	67.2	3,331,461	80,963	14.5	23.2	10.1
5101000	Alexandria city, Virginia	118,235	17.2	65.4	128,797	78.7	4.2	55.8	72,024	101,162	12.3	32.0	7.5
5103000	Arlington CDP, Virginia	171,343	12.1	76.6	195,525	76.3	3.3	56.6	108,396	125,651	8.2	40.9	4.3
5114440	Centreville CDP, Virginia	48,804	17.2	60.9	58,971	73.8	4.9	45.9	24,957	113,518	8.0	35.6	6.2
5116000	Chesapeake city, Virginia	167,983	30.9	38.0	197,892	68.5	4.3	43.5	93,849	88,815	11.5	23.5	8.5
5121088	Dale City CDP, Virginia	50,272	43.7	30.5	59,096	73.3	6.1	48.6	22,465	107,272	8.3	31.5	12.0
5135000	Hampton city, Virginia	92,008	35.4	28.3	111,814	66.8	5.3	40.7	58,181	57,647	17.0	11.4	18.2
5147672	Lynchburg city, Virginia	43,640	31.9	44.7	66,455	62.3	6.9	37.9	28,346	56,110	22.9	12.0	12.2
5156000	Newport News city, Virginia	119,715	37.4	27.9	144,914	68.6	6.4	40.8	77,489	58,937	17.9	8.9	16.8
5157000	Norfolk city, Virginia	148,436	33.2	35.2	194,344	70.0	3.6	35.1	97,596	58,591	18.1	11.4	14.9
5164000	Portsmouth city, Virginia	66,099	39.7	25.6	76,958	64.7	6.8	39.0	40,827	54,429	25.6	7.4	19.3
5167000	Richmond city, Virginia	162,072	32.7	43.7	191,729	65.9	7.3	42.7	99,929	51,770	25.6	12.4	17.8
5168000	Roanoke city, Virginia	69,168	44.0	29.8	78,700	63.2	5.7	41.4	42,455	47,202	26.0	6.4	18.4
5176432	Suffolk city, Virginia	65,767	36.0	32.1	76,772	65.4	5.3	42.4	37,383	79,556	13.6	19.3	11.9
5182000	Virginia Beach city, Virginia	316,512	26.9	42.2	367,769	69.5	3.7	44.0	182,775	81,634	11.8	19.0	8.3
53000	**WASHINGTON**	5,401,149	29.3	39.0	6,250,868	63.9	5.8	63.2	3,022,255	84,247	13.1	24.1	14.2
5303180	Auburn city, Washington	57,928	39.8	23.5	69,638	68.2	6.9	42.1	31,836	79,368	16.7	17.0	19.7
5305210	Bellevue city, Washington	109,738	12.9	70.7	122,386	65.2	5.8	45.7	61,440	144,274	10.3	48.5	7.3
5305280	Bellingham city, Washington	58,731	23.6	47.3	81,123	66.7	6.9	33.9	40,653	58,597	16.2	14.7	15.4
5322640	Everett city, Washington	79,266	35.8	28.2	90,807	66.1	4.8	42.8	45,029	70,023	14.1	16.4	15.0
5323515	Federal Way city, Washington	67,659	37.2	27.2	76,998	63.9	7.2	35.6	35,047	78,734	14.3	17.7	21.1
5335275	Kennewick city, Washington	54,742	42.6	26.2	64,877	56.9	4.9	NA	30,679	56,041	20.0	13.2	26.1
5335415	Kent city, Washington	89,253	38.9	29.5	102,309	69.8	7.6	43.4	46,036	81,373	11.2	20.4	21.8
5335940	Kirkland city, Washington	66,617	13.3	62.3	74,193	68.5	5.5	47.0	37,746	130,397	8.0	44.2	6.0

STATE and place code	STATE Place	Educational attainment			Employment status				Household income and benefits				
		Total population 25 years and over	Percent with a high school diploma or less	Percent with a bachelor's degree or more	Total population 16 years and over	Labor force participation (percent)	Percent unemployed	Percent age 16 years and over who worked full-time year-round in the past 12 months	Total households	Median household income in the past 12 months (in 2021 inflation-adjusted dollars)	Income less than $25,000 (percent)	Income greater than $150,000 (percent)	Percent who received cash public assistance or food stamps/ SNAP
	ACS table number:	C15003	C15003	C15003	C23001	C23001	C23001	S2402	B19001	B19049	B19001	B19001	B19058
	column number:	1	2	3	4	5	6	7	8	9	10	11	12
	WASHINGTON—Cont.												
5343955	Marysville city, Washington	48,960	37.9	22.9	55,895	67.1	4.3	44.4	25,906	92,347	10.4	20.3	13.7
5353545	Pasco city, Washington	47,644	52.8	17.7	60,101	69.1	3.3	49.5	25,084	82,561	8.8	18.0	26.5
5357535	Redmond city, Washington	53,129	7.0	80.2	NA	NA	NA	NA	31,181	155,426	8.7	52.6	4.2
5357745	Renton city, Washington	75,017	31.1	39.1	85,029	68.3	6.4	42.5	41,997	83,699	13.0	22.8	14.6
5361115	Sammamish city, Washington	42,932	6.8	78.7	NA	NA	NA	NA	22,090	201,370	3.9	70.1	4.5
5363000	Seattle city, Washington	558,105	14.2	68.3	643,854	73.3	5.3	48.8	351,650	110,781	13.5	37.6	10.9
5365922	South Hill CDP, Washington	42,628	34.9	27.6	50,400	69.3	4.0	NA	22,379	97,622	8.6	26.0	12.0
5367000	Spokane city, Washington	156,822	29.6	32.7	182,624	62.3	7.0	38.1	94,748	58,714	20.0	10.8	21.5
5367167	Spokane Valley city, Washington	74,429	36.2	24.7	85,781	65.8	4.8	39.9	44,047	58,904	17.0	7.4	23.3
5370000	Tacoma city, Washington	155,967	33.5	34.9	178,283	66.6	5.2	42.2	88,819	77,141	14.5	18.7	19.6
5374060	Vancouver city, Washington	139,888	35.2	29.9	159,927	62.5	7.6	39.6	81,814	69,993	17.5	14.1	19.3
5380010	Yakima city, Washington	63,616	48.6	20.6	75,497	57.1	13.0	NA	37,282	52,689	21.4	6.7	26.1
54000	**WEST VIRGINIA**	1,265,439	50.3	24.1	1,465,755	52.6	6.2	67.0	722,201	51,248	25.2	9.3	19.5
55000	**WISCONSIN**	4,076,339	36.7	32.5	4,773,326	65.1	3.5	66.9	2,449,970	67,125	15.8	13.5	12.9
5502375	Appleton city, Wisconsin	48,349	32.7	34.9	56,497	65.5	3.8	41.9	29,204	66,449	15.1	11.4	16.6
5522300	Eau Claire city, Wisconsin	40,364	27.2	34.9	56,628	69.8	3.1	41.3	28,218	57,732	18.8	9.4	17.2
5531000	Green Bay city, Wisconsin	74,331	43.1	27.1	88,157	65.7	5.1	39.8	46,857	51,908	19.3	5.8	19.0
5537825	Janesville city, Wisconsin	46,231	40.3	24.7	NA	NA	NA	NA	28,236	63,435	17.0	6.7	16.3
5539225	Kenosha city, Wisconsin	63,966	38.7	26.9	78,043	66.0	5.4	43.2	38,438	67,223	17.8	11.5	19.9
5548000	Madison city, Wisconsin	171,208	19.4	58.9	229,022	69.2	3.2	46.5	123,938	67,270	19.1	17.0	10.5
5553000	Milwaukee city, Wisconsin	356,426	45.2	27.3	436,763	64.1	6.9	39.5	232,362	46,637	26.8	7.1	30.6
5560500	Oshkosh city, Wisconsin	44,107	39.1	28.7	57,198	62.6	2.8	37.7	28,532	55,446	20.9	5.6	15.8
5566000	Racine city, Wisconsin	49,263	49.5	17.5	59,341	63.1	6.4	NA	30,885	47,861	23.4	3.8	25.7
5584250	Waukesha city, Wisconsin	49,721	29.0	40.7	NA	NA	NA	NA	31,139	69,533	13.0	11.6	13.5
56000	**WYOMING**	395,348	33.7	29.2	461,622	65.3	3.7	62.5	242,763	65,204	17.9	12.8	7.1
5613900	Cheyenne city, Wyoming	44,666	28.8	30.7	52,124	66.7	2.0	NA	28,727	60,893	16.5	7.6	7.3
72000	**PUERTO RICO**	2,401,409	48.3	28.5	2,794,959	44.8	13.0	54.9	1,165,982	22,237	54.3	2.4	49.9
7206593	Bayamón zona urbana, Puerto Rico	126,847	37.0	32.1	146,523	44.5	9.1	26.4	61,688	26,540	47.7	1.7	37.8
7210334	Caguas zona urbana, Puerto Rico	57,315	47.1	29.9	65,149	46.4	8.6	NA	29,970	22,125	54.4	1.3	48.3
7214290	Carolina zona urbana, Puerto Rico	104,201	39.3	34.7	121,133	54.0	14.0	32.7	54,012	31,597	40.8	2.4	38.4
7232522	Guaynabo zona urbana, Puerto Rico	54,955	22.6	60.3	63,354	50.7	7.7	NA	26,979	53,479	28.3	11.9	19.6
7263820	Ponce zona urbana, Puerto Rico	80,835	44.3	33.8	93,878	41.0	15.1	NA	42,404	17,207	60.1	2.3	53.2
7276770	San Juan zona urbana, Puerto Rico	240,199	37.3	40.8	276,505	52.1	14.8	25.6	129,554	22,556	52.7	5.0	39.3

NA = Not available.

Where
Migration, Housing, and Transportation

Where: Migration, Housing, and Transportation

Migration

An important question that the ACS can help to answer is how many people have moved recently, and from where to where. Nationally, 87.2 percent of Americans lived in the same home in 2021 as they did one year earlier. However, there was much variation among the smaller geographic areas.

Among the states, Colorado (16.7 percent) had the highest proportion of movers and New York and West Virginia had the lowest proportion (10.4 percent each). The District of Columbia had an even higher proportion of movers at 20.3 percent, as well as the highest percentage of residents who moved from abroad—1.1 percent. Hawaii and Massachusetts had the next-highest proportions of residents who moved from abroad, at 0.9 and 0.7 percent, respectively.

In 47 metropolitan areas, 90 percent or more of the residents had not moved in the past year. The uptick in this number is likely to the quarantines experienced during the COVID-19 pandemic. Most of these were smaller metropolitan areas, but among them was New York-Newark-Jersey City, NY-NJ-PA—the metropolitan area with the largest population. In 25 metropolitan areas (a substantial uptick once more, likely due to the same circumstances), 80 percent or less of the population had lived in the same house—most with large student or military populations: Ithaca, New York; College Station-Bryan, Texas; Munice, Indiana; Ames, Iowa; Panama City, Florida; Jacksonville, North Carolina; Lawrence, Kansas; and Bloomington, Indiana.

In two of the limited number of counties surveyed in 2021, more than 20 percent of the population moved into the county within a year or less. The highest proportion

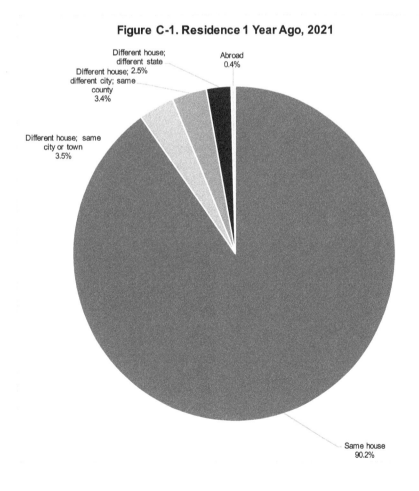

Figure C-1. Residence 1 Year Ago, 2021

Different house; different state 2.5%

Different house; different city; same county 3.4%

Abroad 0.4%

Different house; same city or town 3.5%

Same house 90.2%

was Tompkins County, New York (21.8 percent). Among larger counties, 10.5 percent of the residents of Fulton County, Georgia (where Atlanta is located), moved into the county within the past year, and 9.8 percent of the population were new residents in 2021 in Travis County, Texas (Austin). New York County (Manhattan) had a rate of nearly 8 percent.

In 20 of the 634 cities surveyed in 2021, more than 93 percent of the residents lived in the same house they had lived in one year earlier. With a few exceptions, they were relatively small cities. At the other extreme, less than 60 percent of the population in three cities lived in the same house a year earlier. These were also small cities, all with universities.

(The number of counties and cities in this book is limited due to the fact that the 2021 supplemental tables were not available at the time this edition went to press. The population threshold consequently was raised from 20,000 to 65,000.)

Owning and Renting

Homeownership in the United States reached record high levels in the last decade before beginning to decline in 2008. In 2021, owners occupied 65.4 percent of American housing units, after hovering around 63.1 percent for much of the latter 2010s. West Virginia and Maine had the highest rates of ownership, with both states near or just above 75 percent, followed by 10 states in which more than 70 percent of households owned their homes: Michigan, Minnesota, Vermont, Delaware, New Hampshire, Iowa, Idaho, Wyoming, and Indiana. The states with the smallest proportion of owner-occupied units were New York and California, both under 56 percent. The District of Columbia (41.6 percent) had a lower rate than any of the states. However, the District of Columbia's homeownership rate was higher than cities like Los Angeles, San Francisco, Boston, New York, and Miami. New York City's relatively low homeownership rate of 33.3 percent brought down the state's overall rate.

Homeownership rates vary considerably by race of householder. Nationally, 73.3 percent of non-Hispanic White households lived in a home they owned, while fewer than half of Black householders were homeowners. Six states—led by South Carolina with 51.2 percent—had 50 percent or more of Black householders residing in owner-occupied units. More than 50 percent of Latino households were homeowners in 31 states—including Texas, Arizona, and Florida, which have large Latino populations. Just under two-thirds of Asian and Native Hawaiian and Other Pacific Islander–headed households were homeowners.

Homeownership varied even more by age of householder. For all householders age 25 to 44 years, 51.9 percent owned their own homes, compared with 72.8 percent of 45- to 64-year-olds and 78.7 percent of householders 65 years old and over. Iowa, Minnesota, Maine, and West Virginia had the highest proportions of younger homeowners, with more than 63 percent of 25- to 44-year-olds owning homes in these states, while Wyoming, West Virginia, and South Carolina had the highest homeownership rates among householders 65 years old and older, all over 85 percent.

Nearly 82 percent of married-couple family households were homeowners, while only 49 percent of female-headed family households owned their homes. The homeownership rate of nonfamily households was slightly higher, at 50.4 percent. In West Virginia, 61.9 percent of nonfamily households owned their homes. More than 88 percent of married-couple families in 6 states owned their homes, topped by Maine, which was just over 90 percent. The lowest homeownership rate for married-couple families was about 69 percent in the District of Columbia, while California and Hawaii had rates below 71 percent.

In The Villages, Florida metropolitan area, 89.1 percent of housing units were owner occupied. Homosassa Springs, Florida, and Punta Gorda, Florida, also had homeownership rates above 80 percent, as did Barnstable Town, Massachusetts; East Stroudsburg, Pennsylvania; and Monroe, Michigan. Greenville, North Carolina; Los Angeles-Long Beach-Anaheim, California; and Hinesville, Georgia, had the lowest homeownership rate of the metropolitan areas, with less than half of households owning their homes.

Seventy-five of the counties surveyed in 2021 had homeownership rates higher than 80 percent, most of them counties with populations under 100,000, but New York's Nassau and Suffolk counties, with nearly half a million households each, were in this group. The three lowest homeownership rates in the country were in the New York City boroughs of Bronx County at 19.6 percent, New York County (Manhattan) at 25.0 percent, and Kings County (Brooklyn) at 30.3 percent.

Twenty-two small cities—many of them suburban—had homeownership rates higher than 80 percent, and 20 had rates below 35 percent (of the limited number of 634 cities for which data were provided in 2021). Many of these were university towns, but they included Miami, Florida, with a homeownership rate of 30.4 percent, and Newark, New Jersey, at 20.81 percent. New York City's overall homeownership rate was 33.3 percent. Very few of the largest cities exceeded homeownership rates of 60 percent.

Figure C-2. Counties with the Most and Least Owner-Occupied Housing Units, 2021

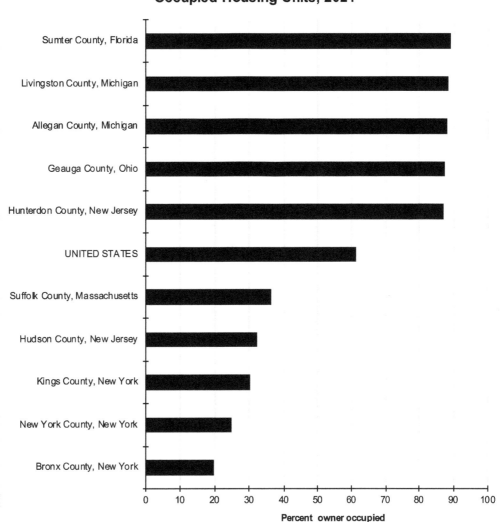

Percent owner occupied

Housing Characteristics

In 2021, American households had an average size of 2.54 persons per household. Owner-occupied households tended to be slightly larger (2.65) than renter-occupied households (2.33). Utah had the largest size households, with an average of 2.99 person per household. Maine and Vermont had the smallest households at just under 2.30 persons each, while the District of Columbia had small households with an average of 1.98 persons per household.

Housing quality is sometimes measured by crowding (more than one person per room is considered crowded) and/or lack of complete plumbing (which consists of hot and cold piped water, a flush toilet, and a bathtub or shower). Nationally, 3.6 percent of housing units were considered substandard by this definition, but 10.0 percent

of housing units in Alaska did not meet these standards. Hawaii and California also had high levels of substandard housing at 9.4 and 8.6 percent respectively.

Over 9 in 10 American households had access to the Internet in 2021 through subscriptions and desktop, laptop, or handheld computers. In 22 metropolitan areas, 95 percent or more of the households have internet access, topped by the San Jose-Sunnyvale-Santa Clara, California; Colorado Springs, Colorado; and Boulder, Colorado, metropolitan areas at nearly 96 percent. Among the states, two metropolitan areas have levels below 70 percent: Farmington, New Mexico, and Beckley, West Virginia. In 460 of the counties surveyed in 2021, more than 90 percent of the households have Internet subscriptions, topped by Forsyth County, Georgia, at 98 percent. In four of the 841 counties surveyed in 2021, less than three-quarters of

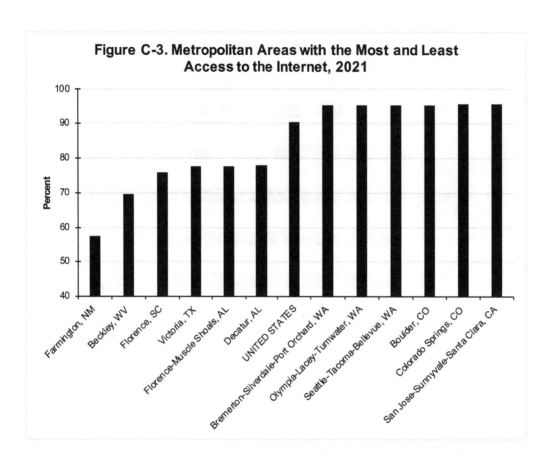

Figure C-3. Metropolitan Areas with the Most and Least Access to the Internet, 2021

households had Internet access: Apache County, Arizona; San Juan County; New Mexico; McKinley County, New Mexico; and Raleigh County, West Virginia. In over two-thirds of the limited number of cities surveyed in 2021, more than 90 percent of households had Internet access. The lowest level of Internet availability was 52.3 percent in Lakewood CDP, New Jersey, which has a large Orthodox Jewish community.

Housing Value and Costs

The median value of owner-occupied housing units in the United States was $281,400. Hawaii and the District of Columbia had median housing values over $665,000, with California at $648,100. The median value was about $145,000 in Mississippi and West Virginia. Twenty-five metropolitan areas had median housing values over $500,000—two each in Hawaii, Colorado, Washington, and Massachusetts; one each in New York and Oregon; and the remainder in California—with the highest median value in the San Jose-Sunnyvale-Santa Clara, California, metropolitan area at $1.24 million. At the other extreme, 12 metropolitan areas and all of the municipos in Puerto Rico had median housing values below $125,000. Three areas could be found in West Virginia (with one having some of its area located in Ohio);

two each could be found in Illinois, Indiana, and Texas; and one each could be found in Pennsylvania, Michigan, and Arkansas. Two California cities had median housing values of $2,000,000 or more, and 28 additional cities had median values over $1,000,000. Most of these were also in California. Flint, Michigan, had a median value of less than $50,000, while the median value in Detroit was just under $70,000.

Just over 61 percent of owner-occupants held mortgages on their homes. More than 70 percent of homeowners in the District of Columbia and Maryland held mortgages, while less than 50 percent of Mississippi and West Virginia's homeowners did. Just over seven and a half percent of all owner-occupants held a second mortgage and/or a home equity loan, but 10 percent or more held these mortgages in Wisconsin, Maryland, the District of Columbia, Ohio, Connecticut, Vermont, Maine, Rhode Island, Massachusetts, and Hawaii. Fewer than four percent had them in Alaska, Oklahoma, Arkansas, and Texas.

For all Americans, the median monthly housing cost was $1,182. For owners, this included mortgages, real estate taxes, insurance, utilities, fuel, and condominium fees, where appropriate. For renters, this included the contract rent, utilities, and fuels if paid by the renter. Median housing costs were highest in the District of Columbia,

Figure C-4. Median Gross Rent for Renter-Occupied Units, by State, 2021

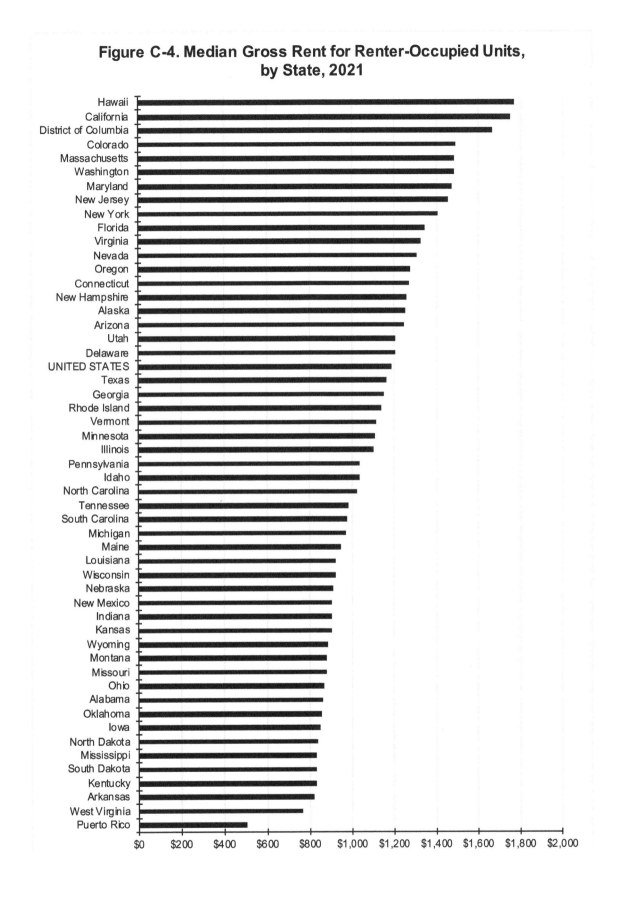

California, Hawaii, Massachusetts, New Jersey, Maryland, Washington, and Colorado (more than $1,500) and lowest in West Virginia ($645) and Puerto Rico ($343).

On average, renters devoted a relatively high share of their monthly income to rent: a median of 30.6 percent. Even owners with a mortgage spent relatively less on their housing—20.8 percent of monthly household income. (Those with no mortgage spent 11.0 percent.) Homeowners with mortgages in Hawaii paid more than 25 percent of their incomes for owner costs, while those in West Virginia paid only 17.4 percent.

Among the states, renters in Florida, Hawaii, Vermont, Louisiana, Nevada, New York, and California, paid the highest proportion of their incomes for their rental costs—between 30 and 33 percent—while renters in North Dakota paid only 24.1 percent of their incomes. Median gross rents were highest in Hawaii, California, and the District of Columbia—all $1,650 or more. The lowest median

gross rents were in West Virginia—$767—and Puerto Rico—$504.

Property taxes vary widely from the national annual median of $2,795. New Jersey residents pay a median of $8,796 per year, with New Hampshire, Connecticut, New York, and Massachusetts all paying more than $5,000. The median is below $1,000 in three states and Puerto Rico, with Alabama households paying only $674 per year.

Transportation

More than 90 percent of households had at least one vehicle. More than half of households had two or more vehicles, and the share of housing units with three or more vehicles was more than double the share without any at all. In the District of Columbia, 36.0 percent of households had no vehicles. New York had the highest level among the

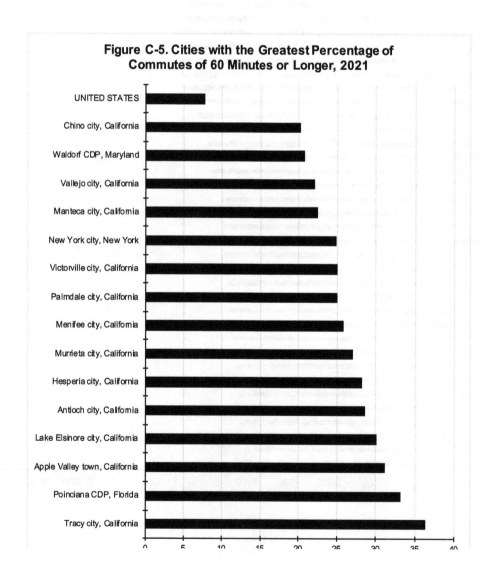

Figure C-5. Cities with the Greatest Percentage of Commutes of 60 Minutes or Longer, 2021

states—28.1 percent. In Idaho, Utah, Montana, Wyoming, and South Dakota, more than 30 percent of households had three or more vehicles.

Commuting patterns have changed due to the global pandemic, with workers working at home roughly tripling between 2019 and 2021. For those who commute, more than two out of three drove their cars to work alone, and less than one in ten carpooled. Two and a half percent took public transportation, while 4.1 percent walked, bicycled, or used "other means." Americans' average commute (excluding those who worked at home) was 25.6 minutes. This ranged from about 17 and a half minutes in North Dakota and South Dakota to nearly 31 and a half minutes in New York. Nationally, commuting by public transportation averaged about one and a half times as long as commuting by car, but car trips ranged from an average of 17 and a half minutes in North Dakota and South Dakota to nearly 30 minutes in Maryland. Public transportation ranged from 24 minutes in Arkansas to more than 55 minutes in Connecticut, New Jersey, and Nevada.

Commuting patterns are influenced by local conditions, so broad national averages are not very revealing. Walking or biking are generally more popular in a climate with good weather, and the presence or absence of public transport obviously determines how many people use it. For instance, more people take public transportation in states with cities containing well-developed systems (such as New York, the District of Columbia, and New Jersey)—not many other Americans have this option. Public transportation usage has also decreased due to the conditions of the pandemic.

Lived in the same house one year ago rank	State	Percent who lived in the same house one year ago [C-1, col. 2]	Did not live in the state one year ago rank	State	Percent who did not live in the state one year ago [C-1, cols. 6 + 7]	Owner-occupied housing unit rank	State	Percent of owner-occupied housing units [C-1, col. 9]
	UNITED STATES...............	87.2		UNITED STATES...............	2.8		UNITED STATES..............	65.4
1	West Virginia..................	89.6	1	District of Columbia...........	9.9	1	West Virginia..................	75.2
1	New York.......................	89.6	2	Hawaii...........................	5.9	2	Maine............................	74.8
3	Delaware.......................	89.4	3	Idaho............................	5.4	3	Michigan........................	73.2
3	New Jersey	89.4	4	Vermont........................	5.3	4	Minnesota	73.0
5	Mississippi....................	89.3	5	North Dakota..................	5.2	5	Vermont........................	72.7
6	Pennsylvania..................	89.2	6	Wyoming.......................	5.1	6	Delaware.......................	72.6
7	New Hampshire...............	88.8	7	Alaska...........................	4.9	7	New Hampshire...............	72.5
8	California.......................	88.7	8	Colorado........................	4.8	8	Iowa.............................	71.9
8	Connecticut...................	88.7	8	Delaware........................	4.8	8	Idaho............................	71.9
8	Michigan	88.7	10	Nevada..........................	4.6	10	South Carolina................	71.8
11	Maine	88.5	11	Rhode Island...................	4.5	11	Wyoming.......................	71.4
11	Illinois	88.5	11	Montana	4.5	12	Indiana	71.1
13	Rhode Island..................	88.4	13	Arizona.........................	4.2	13	Alabama........................	70.0
14	Maryland	88.3	13	South Carolina.................	4.2	14	Pennsylvania..................	69.9
15	Vermont	88.1	15	New Hampshire	4.1	15	Utah.............................	69.7
16	Alabama........................	88.0	16	Kansas..........................	4.0	15	Mississippi	69.7
17	Wisconsin......................	87.7	17	Florida..........................	3.8	17	New Mexico	69.5
18	Ohio............................	87.6	18	Virginia.........................	3.7	17	Montana........................	69.5
19	New Mexico	87.4	19	North Carolina.................	3.6	19	South Dakota..................	69.4
19	Massachusetts................	87.4	19	Utah............................	3.6	20	Missouri........................	68.8
21	Minnesota	87.3	19	New Mexico	3.6	21	Kentucky.......................	68.7
22	Louisiana.......................	87.2	19	Washington	3.6	22	Wisconsin......................	68.1
23	Kentucky.......................	86.9	23	Oregon..........................	3.5	23	Maryland	67.8
24	Arkansas.......................	86.8	23	Tennessee......................	3.5	23	Nebraska	67.8
25	Indiana.........................	86.7	23	Connecticut....................	3.5	25	Arizona.........................	67.6
26	Missouri........................	86.6	26	Maine	3.4	25	Virginia.........................	67.6
27	Georgia.........................	86.5	27	South Dakota	3.3	27	Illinois	67.5
27	North Carolina.................	86.5	28	Maryland	3.2	27	Tennessee......................	67.5
27	Nebraska	86.5	28	Georgia.........................	3.2	29	Florida..........................	67.4
30	South Carolina.................	86.4	30	Oklahoma......................	3.1	30	Louisiana	67.3
31	Alaska	86.3	31	Massachusetts.................	3.0	31	Ohio............................	67.2
31	Montana	86.3	31	Missouri........................	3.0	32	Kansas..........................	67.0
31	Tennessee......................	86.3	33	Nebraska	2.8	32	Arkansas.......................	67.0
31	Virginia.........................	86.3	34	Iowa............................	2.7	34	North Carolina.................	66.9
31	Hawaii..........................	86.3	34	Arkansas.......................	2.7	35	Colorado........................	66.8
31	Iowa............................	86.3	34	New Jersey	2.7	35	Alaska...........................	66.8
37	Florida..........................	86.0	34	Kentucky.......................	2.7	37	Connecticut....................	66.6
37	Texas...........................	86.0	34	Indiana	2.7	38	Georgia	66.0
39	South Dakota	85.9	39	Texas...........................	2.6	39	Oklahoma......................	65.5
40	Oregon..........................	85.6	39	West Virginia...................	2.6	40	New Jersey	64.4
41	Nevada.........................	85.5	39	Alabama........................	2.6	41	Washington	64.0
41	Utah............................	85.5	42	Pennsylvania...................	2.4	42	Oregon..........................	63.8
43	Arizona.........................	85.3	42	Mississippi	2.4	43	Rhode Island...................	63.3
44	Idaho...........................	85.2	44	Wisconsin......................	2.3	44	Massachusetts	63.2
45	Oklahoma......................	84.9	45	Louisiana	2.2	45	North Dakota..................	63.1
45	Kansas..........................	84.9	46	Illinois	2.0	46	Texas...........................	62.6
47	Washington....................	84.6	47	Minnesota	1.9	46	Hawaii..........................	62.6
48	Wyoming.......................	83.9	47	New York.......................	1.9	48	Nevada.........................	59.1
49	North Dakota..................	83.8	47	Ohio............................	1.9	49	California.......................	55.9
50	Colorado........................	83.3	50	Michigan	1.7	50	New York.......................	55.4
51	District of Columbia...........	79.7	51	California.......................	1.6	51	District of Columbia.........	41.6

State Rankings, 2021

Selected Rankings

Median value of owner-occupied housing units rank	State	Median value of owner-occupied housing units (dollars) [C-1, col. 45]	Mean travel time to work rank	State	Mean travel time to work (minutes) [C-1, col. 78]	Median selected monthly owner (with a mortgage) costs as a percentage of household income rank	State	Median selected monthly owner (with a mortgage) costs as a percentage of household income [C-1, col. 59]
	UNITED STATES....................	$281,400		UNITED STATES....................	25.6		UNITED STATES....................	20.8
1	Hawaii................................	722,500	1	New York..............................	31.4	1	Hawaii................................	26.1
2	District of Columbia...............	669,900	2	Maryland..............................	29.3	2	California............................	24.7
3	California............................	648,100	3	New Jersey	28.6	3	New Jersey	23.4
4	Washington..........................	485,700	4	District of Columbia...............	28.3	4	Florida................................	22.8
5	Massachusetts	480,600	5	California............................	27.6	5	Oregon...............................	22.5
6	Colorado.............................	466,200	6	Massachusetts	27.5	5	New York............................	22.5
7	Oregon...............................	422,700	7	Florida................................	27.1	7	Rhode Island........................	22.3
8	Utah...................................	421,700	7	Georgia	27.1	8	Washington..........................	22.2
9	New Jersey	389,800	9	Illinois................................	26.8	9	Colorado.............................	21.9
10	Nevada	373,000	10	Virginia...............................	26.4	9	Nevada	21.9
11	Maryland..............................	370,800	11	Washington..........................	26.0	11	Connecticut..........................	21.8
12	Idaho..................................	369,300	12	Texas	25.9	11	Massachusetts	21.8
13	New York.............................	368,800	13	Pennsylvania........................	25.7	11	Alaska	21.8
14	Rhode Island........................	348,100	13	West Virginia........................	25.7	14	Vermont	21.7
15	New Hampshire	345,200	13	New Hampshire	25.7	15	Texas	21.5
16	Arizona...............................	336,300	16	Connecticut..........................	25.6	16	New Hampshire	21.3
17	Virginia...............................	330,600	16	South Carolina......................	25.6	16	Montana..............................	21.3
18	Montana..............................	322,800	18	Louisiana.............................	25.5	18	Wyoming..............................	21.1
19	Connecticut..........................	311,500	19	Delaware	25.4	19	New Mexico	20.8
20	Alaska	304,900	20	Hawaii................................	25.3	20	Illinois................................	20.7
21	Delaware	300,500	20	Alabama..............................	25.3	21	Arizona...............................	20.6
22	Florida................................	290,700	22	Tennessee	25.2	22	District of Columbia...............	20.5
23	Minnesota	285,400	22	Mississippi	25.2	22	Delaware	20.5
24	Vermont	271,500	24	Colorado.............................	25.0	22	South Dakota	20.5
25	Wyoming..............................	266,400	25	Arizona...............................	24.8	25	Idaho..................................	20.4
26	Maine..................................	252,100	25	Rhode Island........................	24.8	26	Maryland..............................	20.3
27	Georgia	249,700	27	Nevada	24.6	27	Utah...................................	20.2
28	Texas	237,400	28	North Carolina......................	24.5	27	Louisiana.............................	20.2
29	North Carolina......................	236,900	29	Maine..................................	24.2	29	Virginia...............................	20.1
30	Tennessee	235,200	30	Indiana	23.8	30	Maine..................................	20.0
31	Illinois................................	231,500	30	Michigan	23.8	31	Mississippi	19.7
32	Wisconsin............................	230,700	32	Kentucky	23.6	32	Minnesota	19.6
33	North Dakota........................	224,400	33	New Mexico	23.2	32	Georgia	19.6
34	Pennsylvania........................	222,300	34	Missouri..............................	23.1	32	Tennessee	19.6
35	South Dakota	219,900	34	Ohio...................................	23.1	35	Wisconsin............................	19.5
36	New Mexico	214,000	36	Vermont	23.0	35	Nebraska.............................	19.5
37	South Carolina......................	213,500	37	Oregon...............................	22.6	37	South Carolina......................	19.4
38	Nebraska.............................	204,900	38	Arkansas.............................	22.2	37	Oklahoma............................	19.4
39	Michigan	199,100	38	Minnesota	22.2	39	Kansas................................	19.3
40	Missouri..............................	198,300	40	Oklahoma............................	22.0	39	North Carolina......................	19.3
41	Louisiana.............................	192,800	41	Wisconsin............................	21.9	39	North Dakota........................	19.3
42	Kansas................................	183,800	42	Idaho..................................	21.6	42	Michigan	19.2
43	Indiana	182,400	43	Utah...................................	21.4	43	Pennsylvania........................	19.0
44	Ohio...................................	180,200	44	Alaska	19.8	43	Kentucky	19.0
45	Iowa...................................	174,400	45	Iowa...................................	19.7	45	Missouri..............................	18.9
46	Kentucky	173,300	46	Kansas................................	19.6	45	Alabama..............................	18.9
47	Alabama..............................	172,800	47	Nebraska.............................	19.3	47	Iowa...................................	18.7
48	Oklahoma............................	168,500	47	Montana..............................	19.1	47	Arkansas.............................	18.7
49	Arkansas.............................	162,300	49	Wyoming..............................	18.3	49	Ohio...................................	18.5
50	Mississippi	145,600	50	North Dakota........................	17.5	50	Indiana	18.0
51	West Virginia	143,200	50	South Dakota	17.4	51	West Virginia	17.4

County Rankings, 2021

Selected Rankings

Lived in the same house one year ago rank	County	Percent who lived in the same house one year ago [C-2, col. 2]	Did not live in the county one year ago rank	County	Percent who did not live in the county one year ago [C-2, col. 3]
	UNITED STATES............	87.2		UNITED STATES............	6.0
1	McKinley County, New Mexico............	95.4	1	Tompkins County, New York	21.8
2	Robeson County, North Carolina............	94.6	2	Coryell County, Texas	21.6
3	Kendall County, Illinois............	94.5	3	Clarke County, Georgia............	18.2
3	Apache County, Arizona............	94.5	4	Hampshire County, Massachusetts	17.5
5	Armstrong County, Pennsylvania............	94.2	5	Grand Forks County, North Dakota	17.2
6	Cameron County, Texas............	94.1	6	Story County, Iowa	16.7
6	Umatilla County, Oregon............	94.1	7	Walker County, Texas	16.5
8	Monroe County, Pennsylvania............	93.9	8	Albemarle County, Virginia	16.1
9	Harrison County, Texas............	93.8	9	Monroe County, Indiana	15.8
9	Richmond County, New York	93.8	9	Benton County, Oregon	15.8
11	Clearfield County, Pennsylvania............	93.7	11	Liberty County, Georgia	15.5
11	Mason County, Washington............	93.7	12	Onslow County, North Carolina	15.3
11	Bullitt County, Kentucky............	93.7	13	Arlington County, Virginia	14.8
14	Fayette County, Pennsylvania............	93.6	14	Lynchburg city, Virginia	14.5
14	Fauquier County, Virginia............	93.6	15	Broomfield County, Colorado	13.7
14	Somerset County, Pennsylvania............	93.6	15	Monongalia County, West Virginia	13.7
17	Sevier County, Tennessee............	93.4	15	Bulloch County, Georgia	13.7
17	Wayne County, New York	93.4	18	Kaufman County, Texas	13.2
19	Greene County, Tennessee............	93.2	18	Orange County, North Carolina	13.2
19	Hanover County, Virginia............	93.2	18	Richland County, South Carolina	13.2
19	Bronx County, New York............	93.2	18	Alexandria city, Virginia	13.2
22	Medina County, Ohio............	93.1	22	Boulder County, Colorado	13.1
22	Carroll County, Maryland............	93.1	23	York County, Virginia	13.0
22	Jones County, Mississippi............	93.1	23	Riley County, Kansas	13.0
25	Carbon County, Pennsylvania............	93.0	25	Norfolk city, Virginia	12.9
26	Greenwood County, South Carolina............	92.9	25	Centre County, Pennsylvania	12.9
26	Nassau County, New York	92.9	27	Montgomery County, Tennessee	12.8
26	Madera County, California............	92.9	28	Harnett County, North Carolina	12.7
26	Jackson County, Georgia............	92.9	29	Montgomery County, Virginia	12.5
30	Northumberland County, Pennsylvania............	92.8	29	DeKalb County, Illinois	12.5
30	Allegan County, Michigan............	92.8	29	Leavenworth County, Kansas	12.5
32	Belmont County, Ohio............	92.7	32	Douglas County, Kansas	12.5
33	Garland County, Arkansas............	92.6	33	Campbell County, Kentucky	12.4
34	Kankakee County, Illinois............	92.5	34	St. Johns County, Florida	12.3
34	DeSoto County, Mississippi............	92.5	34	Stafford County, Virginia	12.3
34	Cattaraugus County, New York............	92.5	36	Bay County, Florida	12.1
37	Johnston County, North Carolina............	92.4	36	Richmond city, Virginia	12.1
37	Tulare County, California............	92.4	36	Alachua County, Florida	12.1
37	Imperial County, California............	92.4	36	Chesapeake city, Virginia	12.1
40	Walker County, Georgia............	92.3	36	Douglas County, Colorado	12.1
40	Robertson County, Tennessee............	92.3	41	Brazos County, Texas............	12.0
40	Clinton County, Michigan............	92.3	42	Washtenaw County, Michigan	11.9
43	Carver County, Minnesota............	92.2	42	Pickens County, South Carolina	11.9
43	Queens County, New York............	92.2	42	Ward County, North Dakota	11.9
43	Augusta County, Virginia............	92.2	42	LaPorte County, Indiana	11.9
43	Harrison County, West Virginia............	92.2	46	Coconino County, Arizona	11.8
43	St. Croix County, Wisconsin............	92.2	47	Ingham County, Michigan	11.7
48	Salem County, New Jersey............	92.1	48	Denver County, Colorado	11.6
48	Guadalupe County, Texas............	92.1	49	Hays County, Texas	11.5
48	Trumbull County, Ohio............	92.1	49	Dorchester County, South Carolina	11.5
48	Lee County, Mississippi............	92.1	51	Clay County, Minnesota	11.4
52	Kern County, California............	92.0	51	Madison County, Kentucky	11.4
52	Maury County, Tennessee............	92.0	53	Yolo County, California	11.2
52	Sherburne County, Minnesota............	92.0	54	Anderson County, Tennessee	11.1
55	Johnson County, Texas............	91.9	54	Tippecanoe County, Indiana	11.1
55	Woodbury County, Iowa............	91.9	54	Citrus County, Florida	11.1
55	Lebanon County, Pennsylvania............	91.9	57	Dallas County, Iowa	11.0
55	St. Lucie County, Florida............	91.9	57	Larimer County, Colorado	11.0
59	Whitfield County, Georgia............	91.8	59	Lamar County, Mississippi	10.9
59	Geauga County, Ohio............	91.8	59	Muscogee County, Georgia	10.9
59	Oneida County, New York............	91.8	61	New Hanover County, North Carolina	10.8
59	Sullivan County, New York............	91.8	61	Okaloosa County, Florida	10.8
59	Elkhart County, Indiana............	91.8	63	El Paso County, Colorado	10.7
64	Davidson County, North Carolina............	91.7	63	Columbia County, Florida	10.7
64	Stanislaus County, California............	91.7	65	Lancaster County, South Carolina	10.6
64	Nevada County, California............	91.7	66	Newport County, Rhode Island	10.5
64	Ventura County, California............	91.7	66	Houston County, Georgia	10.5
64	Caldwell County, North Carolina............	91.7	66	Davidson County, Tennessee	10.5
69	Warren County, New York............	91.6	66	Pitt County, North Carolina	10.5
69	Burke County, North Carolina............	91.6	66	Fulton County, Georgia	10.5
71	Passaic County, New Jersey............	91.6	71	Collier County, Florida	10.4
71	Rockland County, New York............	91.6	71	Walton County, Florida	10.4
73	Steuben County, New York............	91.5	73	Hampton city, Virginia	10.3
73	Manitowoc County, Wisconsin............	91.5	73	Johnson County, Iowa	10.3
73	Hampden County, Massachusetts............	91.5	73	Pinal County, Arizona	10.3
73	Bucks County, Pennsylvania............	91.5			
73	Cecil County, Maryland............	91.5			
73	Bowie County, Texas............	91.5			

County Rankings, 2021

Selected Rankings

Percent with a commute to work of less than 10 minutes rank	County	Percent with a commute to work of less than 10 minutes [C-2. col. 11]	Percent owner-occupied housing units rank	County	Percent owner-occupied housing units [C-2, col. 5]
	UNITED STATES..	13.2		UNITED STATES..	65.4
1	Aroostook County, Maine	37.1	1	Sumter County, Florida	89.1
2	Lea County, New Mexico	35.0	2	Livingston County, Michigan	88.2
3	Mendocino County, California	32.2	3	Allegan County, Michigan	88.0
4	Story County, Iowa	32.1	4	Geauga County, Ohio	87.3
5	Grand Forks County, North Dakota	31.3	5	Hunterdon County, New Jersey	86.9
6	Wichita County, Texas	31.0	6	Sussex County, New Jersey	86.7
7	Buchanan County, Missouri	30.9	6	Calvert County, Maryland	86.7
8	Twin Falls County, Idaho	30.7	8	Sherburne County, Minnesota	86.5
9	Grant County, Washington	30.0	9	Rockwall County, Texas	86.0
10	Rice County, Minnesota	29.7	10	Tooele County, Utah	85.9
11	Riley County, Kansas	29.5	10	Bullitt County, Kentucky	85.9
12	Island County, Washington	29.3	12	Lapeer County, Michigan	85.4
13	Blue Earth County, Minnesota	29.0	12	Kendall County, Illinois	85.4
13	Umatilla County, Oregon	29.0	14	Paulding County, Georgia	85.3
15	Christian County, Kentucky	28.9	14	Morgan County, Indiana	85.3
16	Cache County, Utah	28.6	16	Carroll County, Maryland	85.2
17	Chautauqua County, New York	28.3	16	Oldham County, Kentucky	85.2
18	Cascade County, Montana	28.1	18	Forsyth County, Georgia	84.7
19	Marquette County, Michigan	27.9	19	Flagler County, Florida	84.4
20	Portage County, Wisconsin	27.8	20	Brunswick County, North Carolina	84.1
21	Payne County, Oklahoma	27.7	21	Wise County, Texas	84.0
22	St. Lawrence County, New York	27.6	21	Citrus County, Florida	84.0
23	Monroe County, Florida	27.5	23	Nassau County, New York	83.9
24	Marion County, Ohio	27.4	24	McHenry County, Illinois	83.5
25	White County, Arkansas	27.2	25	Sandoval County, New Mexico	83.4
26	Navajo County, Arizona	27.1	25	Will County, Illinois	83.4
27	St. Francois County, Missouri	27.0	27	Toa Alta Municipio, Puerto Rico	83.3
28	Clallam County, Washington	26.8	28	Trujillo Alto Municipio, Puerto Rico	83.2
28	Bannock County, Idaho	26.8	29	Hanover County, Virginia	82.9
30	Sauk County, Wisconsin	26.5	29	Putnam County, New York	82.9
31	Cattaraugus County, New York	26.4	29	Kershaw County, South Carolina	82.9
32	Starr County, Texas	26.1	29	Suffolk County, New York	82.9
33	Wood County, Wisconsin	26.0	33	Charlotte County, Florida	82.7
34	Dubuque County, Iowa	25.9	33	St. Croix County, Wisconsin	82.7
34	Jefferson County, New York	25.9	33	Mason County, Washington	82.7
36	Sheboygan County, Wisconsin	25.8	36	Bedford County, Virginia	82.5
37	Glynn County, Georgia	25.6	37	Williamson County, Tennessee	82.4
38	LaSalle County, Illinois	25.5	37	Medina County, Ohio	82.4
39	Montgomery County, Virginia	25.4	39	Montcalm County, Michigan	82.3
40	Ward County, North Dakota	25.3	39	Barnstable County, Massachusetts	82.3
41	Kosciusko County, Indiana	25.3	41	Lancaster County, South Carolina	82.2
42	Wayne County, Ohio	25.1	41	Liberty County, Texas	82.2
43	Josephine County, Oregon	24.7	41	Bartow County, Georgia	82.2
43	Bartholomew County, Indiana	24.7	44	Spotsylvania County, Virginia	82.1
45	Cayuga County, New York	24.6	45	Sussex County, Delaware	81.8
46	Otero County, New Mexico	24.6	45	Washington County, Minnesota	81.8
47	Missoula County, Montana	24.5	45	Hernando County, Florida	81.8
47	Blair County, Pennsylvania	24.5	48	Union County, North Carolina	81.6
47	Humboldt County, California	24.5	49	Scott County, Minnesota	81.5
50	Deschutes County, Oregon	24.4	49	Carver County, Minnesota	81.5
51	Grant County, Indiana	24.2	49	Monroe County, Pennsylvania	81.5
51	Grays Harbor County, Washington	24.2	49	Wright County, Minnesota	81.5
53	Daviess County, Kentucky	24.1	53	Clinton County, Michigan	81.4
53	Black Hawk County, Iowa	24.1	53	Monroe County, Michigan	81.4
55	Delaware County, Indiana	24.0	55	Pinal County, Arizona	81.3
56	Scioto County, Ohio	23.9	56	Warren County, Ohio	81.2
56	Steuben County, New York	23.9	56	Shelby County, Alabama	81.2
58	Indiana County, Pennsylvania	23.7	56	Jefferson County, Missouri	81.2
58	Eau Claire County, Wisconsin	23.7	59	Hancock County, Indiana	81.1
60	Lycoming County, Pennsylvania	23.6	60	Columbia County, Georgia	80.9
60	Harrison County, Texas	23.6	61	Lenawee County, Michigan	80.8
62	Lynchburg city, Virginia	23.5	61	Santa Rosa County, Florida	80.8
62	Cochise County, Arizona	23.5	61	Terrebonne Parish, Louisiana	80.8
62	Coryell County, Texas	23.5	61	Parker County, Texas	80.8
65	Chemung County, New York	23.4	65	St. Charles County, Missouri	80.7
65	Taylor County, Texas	23.4	65	Van Buren County, Michigan	80.7
65	Lenawee County, Michigan	23.4	65	Fayette County, Georgia	80.7
68	Clinton County, New York	23.3	68	Gloucester County, New Jersey	80.6
68	Erie County, Ohio	23.3	68	Cass County, Missouri	80.6
70	Benton County, Oregon	23.2	70	Lincoln County, North Carolina	80.5
70	Wayne County, Indiana	23.2	70	Ocean County, New Jersey	80.5
70	McLean County, Illinois	23.2	72	Valencia County, New Mexico	80.3
70	Nevada County, California	23.2	72	Chatham County, North Carolina	80.3
74	Cole County, Missouri	23.1	74	St. Johns County, Florida	80.2
74	Kings County, California	23.1	75	Boone County, Indiana	80.1
74	Mercer County, Pennsylvania	23.1			

County Rankings, 2021

Selected Rankings

Percent owner-occupied housing units with a mortgage, contract to purchase, or similar debt rank	County	Percent owner-occupied housing units with a mortgage, contract to purchase, or similar debt [C-2, col. 6]	Percent of households with Internet access rank	County	Percent who did not live in the county one year ago [C-2, col. 3]	Percent of households with Internet access [C-2, col. 9]	County	Median value of owner-occupied housing units [C-4, col. 7]
	UNITED STATES	61.3		UNITED STATES		90.3	UNITED STATES	$281,400
1	Charles County, Maryland	81.6	1	Forsyth County, Georgia		98.0	San Mateo County, California	1,411,000
2	Loudoun County, Virginia	80.9	2	Douglas County, Colorado		97.5	Marin County, California	1,314,100
3	Tooele County, Utah	80.5	3	Delaware County, Ohio		97.4	San Francisco County, California	1,306,400
4	Prince William County, Virginia	79.6	4	Loudoun County, Virginia		97.3	Santa Clara County, California	1,270,200
5	Prince George's County, Maryland	79.5	5	Spotsylvania County, Virginia		97.2	Alameda County, California	960,900
6	Alexandria city, Virginia	77.8	6	Howard County, Maryland		97.0	New York County, New York	940,900
6	Stafford County, Virginia	77.8	6	Stafford County, Virginia		97.0	Santa Cruz County, California	922,300
8	Kendall County, Illinois	77.7	8	Arlington County, Virginia		96.7	Orange County, California	832,300
9	Calvert County, Maryland	77.6	8	Oldham County, Kentucky		96.7	Kings County, New York	793,300
10	Suffolk city, Virginia	77.5	10	Prince William County, Virginia		96.5	Honolulu County, Hawaii	781,600
11	Douglas County, Colorado	77.4	10	Williamson County, Tennessee		96.5	Contra Costa County, California	780,500
12	Paulding County, Georgia	77.3	12	Fayette County, Georgia		96.4	Arlington County, Virginia	779,400
13	Boone County, Indiana	76.8	12	Boone County, Indiana		96.4	King County, Washington	750,100
14	Spotsylvania County, Virginia	76.0	14	Collin County, Texas		96.2	Napa County, California	749,700
15	Chesapeake city, Virginia	75.6	14	Cobb County, Georgia		96.2	Maui County, Hawaii	744,400
15	Forsyth County, Georgia	75.6	16	Lincoln County, South Dakota		96.1	San Diego County, California	722,200
17	District of Columbia, District of Columbia	75.3	16	Paulding County, Georgia		96.1	Los Angeles County, California	720,300
18	Denver County, Colorado	75.2	16	Fairfax County, Virginia		96.1	Sonoma County, California	718,500
19	Hancock County, Indiana	75.1	19	Montgomery County, Maryland		96.0	San Luis Obispo County, California	695,500
19	Henry County, Georgia	75.1	20	Johnson County, Kansas		95.9	Kauai County, Hawaii	695,100
21	Wake County, North Carolina	75.0	20	Santa Clara County, California		95.9	Ventura County, California	691,000
21	Arlington County, Virginia	75.0	20	Anne Arundel County, Maryland		95.9	Monterey County, California	683,200
23	Hendricks County, Indiana	74.9	23	Livingston Parish, Louisiana		95.8	San Benito County, California	681,500
23	Oldham County, Kentucky	74.9	23	Scott County, Minnesota		95.8	District of Columbia, District of Columbia	669,900
25	Henrico County, Virginia	74.8	25	Hamilton County, Indiana		95.7	Santa Barbara County, California	669,000
26	Norfolk city, Virginia	74.6	25	Somerset County, New Jersey		95.7	Monroe County, Florida	661,400
27	Mecklenburg County, North Carolina	74.5	27	King County, Washington		95.6	Boulder County, Colorado	654,500
27	Virginia Beach city, Virginia	74.5	27	Comal County, Texas		95.6	Loudoun County, Virginia	648,400
29	Weld County, Colorado	74.4	27	Morris County, New Jersey		95.6	Fairfax County, Virginia	646,800
30	Hamilton County, Indiana	74.3	27	Rockwall County, Texas		95.6	Queens County, New York	642,000
31	Frederick County, Maryland	74.0	31	Boulder County, Colorado		95.5	Middlesex County, Massachusetts	640,500
31	Snohomish County, Washington	74.0	31	San Mateo County, California		95.5	Suffolk County, Massachusetts	636,800
31	Utah County, Utah	74.0	31	Cherokee County, Georgia		95.5	Alexandria city, Virginia	630,500
34	Anne Arundel County, Maryland	73.8	31	El Paso County, Colorado		95.5	Douglas County, Colorado	630,400
35	Scott County, Minnesota	73.6	31	Denton County, Texas		95.5	Placer County, California	627,500
35	St. Mary's County, Maryland	73.6	36	James City County, Virginia		95.4	Nassau County, New York	619,800
37	Williamson County, Tennessee	73.4	36	Williamson County, Texas		95.4	Williamson County, Tennessee	617,400
37	Solano County, California	73.4	38	McHenry County, Illinois		95.3	Snohomish County, Washington	612,400
39	Sherburne County, Minnesota	73.4	38	Santa Rosa County, Florida		95.3	El Dorado County, California	609,100
40	Cobb County, Georgia	73.3	38	Broomfield County, Colorado		95.3	Richmond County, New York	605,500
40	Durham County, North Carolina	73.3	41	Weber County, Utah		95.2	Norfolk County, Massachusetts	602,600
42	Adams County, Colorado	73.2	41	Thurston County, Washington		95.2	Westchester County, New York	592,900
43	Fairfax County, Virginia	73.1	41	Kitsap County, Washington		95.2	Gallatin County, Montana	584,500
43	Denton County, Texas	73.1	41	Seminole County, Florida		95.2	Broomfield County, Colorado	576,200
45	Arapahoe County, Colorado	73.0	45	Nassau County, Florida		95.1	Nevada County, California	575,300
46	Union County, North Carolina	72.9	45	Kendall County, Illinois		95.1	Montgomery County, Maryland	572,600
47	Delaware County, Ohio	72.7	45	St. Charles County, Missouri		95.1	Jefferson County, Colorado	548,200
48	Davis County, Utah	72.5	45	Clark County, Washington		95.1	Bergen County, New Jersey	548,200
49	San Benito County, California	72.4	45	Wright County, Minnesota		95.1	Deschutes County, Oregon	543,900
49	Broomfield County, Colorado	72.4	45	Contra Costa County, California		95.1	Solano County, California	543,100
49	Pierce County, Washington	72.4	45	Washington County, Rhode Island		95.1	Denver County, Colorado	541,500
49	Newport News city, Virginia	72.4	45	Virginia Beach city, Virginia		95.1	Yolo County, California	534,900
49	El Paso County, Colorado	72.4	53	Sussex County, New Jersey		95.0	Clackamas County, Oregon	533,100
54	Cherokee County, Georgia	72.3	53	Wake County, North Carolina		95.0	Essex County, Massachusetts	529,400
55	Cecil County, Maryland	72.2	53	Rockingham County, New Hampshire		95.0	Howard County, Maryland	529,300
55	Contra Costa County, California	72.2	53	Clackamas County, Oregon		95.0	Whatcom County, Washington	506,200
57	Sarpy County, Nebraska	72.1	53	Jefferson County, Colorado		95.0	Monmouth County, New Jersey	505,500
57	Howard County, Maryland	72.1	58	San Diego County, California		94.9	Newport County, Rhode Island	504,900
59	Yamhill County, Oregon	72.0	58	Snohomish County, Washington		94.9	Morris County, New Jersey	504,300
60	Chesterfield County, Virginia	71.8	58	Washington County, Oregon		94.9	Rockland County, New York	503,000
61	Williamson County, Texas	71.7	58	Island County, Washington		94.9	Barnstable County, Massachusetts	500,800
62	Fulton County, Georgia	71.6	62	Warren County, Ohio		94.8	Washington County, Oregon	498,800
62	St. Charles County, Missouri	71.6	62	Fort Bend County, Texas		94.8	Suffolk County, New York	488,200
64	Johnson County, Iowa	71.5	62	Washington County, Minnesota		94.8	Larimer County, Colorado	487,700
65	Boone County, Kentucky	71.4	62	Kauai County, Hawaii		94.8	Multnomah County, Oregon	487,300

County Rankings, 2021—*Continued*

Selected Rankings

Percent owner-occupied housing units with a mortgage, contract to purchase, or similar debt rank	County	Percent owner-occupied housing units with a mortgage, contract to purchase, or similar debt [C-2, col. 6]	Percent of households with Internet access rank	County	Percent who did not live in the county one year ago [C-2, col. 3]	Percent of households with Internet access [C-2, col. 9]	County	Median value of owner-occupied housing units [C-4, col. 7]
65	Hanover County, Virginia	71.4	62	Putnam County, New York	94.8	66	Arapahoe County, Colorado	481,500
67	Suffolk County, Massachusetts	71.3	67	Iredell County, North Carolina	94.7	67	Fauquier County, Virginia	480,100
68	McHenry County, Illinois	71.2	67	Sonoma County, California	94.7	68	Kitsap County, Washington	473,900
68	Fauquier County, Virginia	71.2	67	Clay County, Florida	94.7	69	Hawaii County, Hawaii	472,800
68	Anchorage Municipality, Alaska	71.2	67	Madison County, Mississippi	94.7	70	Skagit County, Washington	471,500
71	Salt Lake County, Utah	71.1	71	DuPage County, Illinois	94.6	71	Plymouth County, Massachusetts	470,500
72	Portsmouth city, Virginia	71.0	72	Orange County, California	94.5	71	Somerset County, New Jersey	470,500
73	Multnomah County, Oregon	70.9	72	Middlesex County, Massachusetts	94.5	73	Island County, Washington	470,400
74	Collin County, Texas	70.8	72	Marin County, California	94.5	74	Fairfield County, Connecticut	469,600
74	Washington County, Oregon	70.8	75	Anchorage Municipality, Alaska	94.4	75	Hudson County, New Jersey	468,100
74	Franklin County, Ohio	70.8	75	Ada County, Idaho	94.4			
			75	Oakland County, Michigan	94.4			
			75	Montgomery County, Pennsylvania	94.4			
			75	Franklin County, Washington	94.4			
			75	Union County, North Carolina	94.4			
			75	Nassau County, New York	94.4			
			75	Pierce County, Washington	94.4			

Metropolitan Area Rankings, 2021

Selected Rankings

Lived in the same house one year ago rank	Area name	Percent who lived in the same house one year ago [C-3, col. 2]
	UNITED STATES..	87.2
1	Brownsville-Harlingen, TX..	94.1
2	East Stroudsburg, PA..	93.9
3	Madera, CA..	92.9
4	Hot Springs, AR...	92.6
4	Dalton, GA...	92.6
6	Kankakee, IL..	92.5
7	Visalia, CA...	92.4
7	El Centro, CA...	92.4
9	Utica-Rome, NY..	92.1
10	Bakersfield, CA...	92.0
11	Lebanon, PA...	91.9
12	Elkhart-Goshen, IN...	91.8
13	Modesto, CA..	91.7
13	Oxnard-Thousand Oaks-Ventura, CA........................	91.7
15	Morristown, TN..	91.6
16	Rocky Mount, NC...	91.4
16	Weirton-Steubenville, WV-OH..................................	91.4
18	Bloomsburg-Berwick, PA..	91.3
18	Wheeling, WV-OH..	91.3
18	Dover, DE..	91.3
21	Hickory-Lenoir-Morganton, NC................................	91.2
22	Kingston, NY..	91.0
23	Port St. Lucie, FL..	90.8
23	Atlantic City-Hammonton, NJ...................................	90.8
23	Altoona, PA...	90.8
26	Vineland-Bridgeton, NJ..	90.7
26	Parkersburg-Vienna, WV...	90.7
26	Bay City, MI...	90.7
29	Muskegon, MI..	90.6
30	Charleston, WV..	90.5
30	Danville, IL...	90.5
32	Youngstown-Warren-Boardman, OH-PA....................	90.4
32	Merced, CA..	90.4
32	Elmira, NY...	90.4
32	Detroit-Warren-Dearborn, MI...................................	90.4
32	Burlington, NC...	90.4
32	Barnstable Town, MA...	90.4
38	Fresno, CA...	90.3
38	Johnstown, PA...	90.3
38	Houma-Thibodaux, LA..	90.3
41	Sioux City, IA-NE-SD..	90.1
41	Chambersburg-Waynesboro, PA................................	90.1
41	Riverside-San Bernardino-Ontario, CA......................	90.1
41	Battle Creek, MI...	90.1
45	York-Hanover, PA...	90.0
45	New York-Newark-Jersey City, NY-NJ-PA..................	90.0
45	Enid, OK..	90.0
48	Dubuque, IA...	89.9
48	Cedar Rapids, IA..	89.9
48	Monroe, MI..	89.9
48	McAllen-Edinburg-Mission, TX..................................	89.9
52	Allentown-Bethlehem-Easton, PA-NJ........................	89.8
53	Los Angeles-Long Beach-Anaheim, CA......................	89.7
54	Salinas, CA..	89.6
54	Yuba City, CA...	89.6
54	Napa, CA...	89.6
54	Huntington-Ashland, WV-KY-OH..............................	89.6
58	Yakima, WA...	89.5
58	Buffalo-Cheektowaga, NY..	89.5
58	Lancaster, PA...	89.5
58	Hartford-East Hartford-Middletown, CT....................	89.5
62	Beaumont-Port Arthur, TX..	89.4
62	Sebring-Avon Park, FL..	89.4
64	Appleton, WI..	89.3
64	Pine Bluff, AR..	89.3
64	Janesville-Beloit, WI..	89.3
64	Stockton, CA..	89.3
64	Poughkeepsie-Newburgh-Middletown, NY................	89.3
64	Glens Falls, NY..	89.3
64	Dothan, AL..	89.3
71	Laredo, TX...	89.2
71	Portland-South Portland, ME....................................	89.2
71	Hagerstown-Martinsburg, MD-WV...........................	89.2
71	Williamsport, PA..	89.2
71	Tyler, TX..	89.2
71	Decatur, AL..	89.2
71	Springfield, IL...	89.2

Metropolitan Area Rankings, 2021

Selected Rankings

Percent with commute less than 10 minutes rank	Area name	Percent with commute less than 10 minutes [C-3, col. 11]	Median value of owner-occupied units rank	Area name	Median value of owner-occupied housing units [C-3, col. 7]
	UNITED STATES..	13.2		UNITED STATES..	$281,400
1	Walla Walla, WA	35.6	1	San Jose-Sunnyvale-Santa Clara, CA	1,237,800
2	Grand Forks, ND-MN	31.4	2	San Francisco-Oakland-Berkeley, CA	1,042,300
3	Lewiston, ID-WA	30.8	3	Santa Cruz-Watsonville, CA	922,300
4	Ames, IA	29.7	4	Urban Honolulu, HI	781,600
5	Mankato, MN	29.2	5	Napa, CA	749,700
6	Wichita Falls, TX	28.8	6	Los Angeles-Long Beach-Anaheim, CA	748,700
7	Great Falls, MT	28.1	7	Kahului-Wailuku-Lahaina, HI	744,400
8	St. Joseph, MO-KS	27.5	8	San Diego-Chula Vista-Carlsbad, CA	722,200
9	Enid, OK	27.3	9	Santa Rosa-Petaluma, CA	718,500
10	Logan, UT-ID	27.2	10	San Luis Obispo-Paso Robles, CA	695,500
11	Twin Falls, ID	27.1	11	Oxnard-Thousand Oaks-Ventura, CA	691,000
12	Pocatello, ID	26.4	12	Salinas, CA	683,200
13	Manhattan, KS	26.0	13	Santa Maria-Santa Barbara, CA	669,000
14	Dubuque, IA	25.9	14	Boulder, CO	654,500
14	Watertown-Fort Drum, NY	25.9	15	Seattle-Tacoma-Bellevue, WA	638,400
16	Sheboygan, WI	25.8	16	Boston-Cambridge-Newton, MA-NH	561,500
17	Grants Pass, OR	24.7	17	Bend, OR	543,900
17	Waterloo-Cedar Falls, IA	24.7	18	Vallejo, CA	543,100
17	Columbus, IN	24.7	19	New York-Newark-Jersey City, NY-NJ-PA	533,700
17	Carson City, NV	24.7	20	Denver-Aurora-Lakewood, CO	519,600
21	Missoula, MT	24.5	21	Sacramento-Roseville-Folsom, CA	513,600
21	Altoona, PA	24.5	22	Bellingham, WA	506,200
23	Bend, OR	24.4	23	Barnstable Town, MA	500,800
24	Grand Island, NE	24.0	24	Washington-Arlington-Alexandria, DC-VA-MD-WV	497,800
24	Muncie, IN	24.0	25	Fort Collins, CO	487,700
26	Owensboro, KY	23.8	26	Portland-Vancouver-Hillsboro, OR-WA	483,000
27	Williamsport, PA	23.6	27	Bremerton-Silverdale-Port Orchard, WA	473,900
28	Sierra Vista-Douglas, AZ	23.5	28	Mount Vernon-Anacortes, WA	471,500
29	Elmira, NY	23.4	29	Bridgeport-Stamford-Norwalk, CT	469,600
29	Lawton, OK	23.4	30	Provo-Orem, UT	459,500
31	Corvallis, OR	23.2	31	Stockton, CA	457,600
31	Bloomington, IL	23.2	32	Reno, NV	457,500
33	Hanford-Corcoran, CA	23.1	33	Riverside-San Bernardino-Ontario, CA	453,000
33	Duluth, MN-WI	23.1	34	Coeur d'Alene, ID	444,900
35	Abilene, TX	22.9	35	Salt Lake City, UT	444,200
35	Fond du Lac, WI	22.9	36	St. George, UT	443,200
37	Hot Springs, AR	22.8	37	Corvallis, OR	443,100
38	Lawrence, KS	22.7	38	Boise City, ID	426,800
39	Chico, CA	22.6	39	Greeley, CO	416,700
40	Sioux City, IA-NE-SD	22.5	40	Naples-Marco Island, FL	416,200
41	Brunswick, GA	22.4	41	Olympia-Lacey-Tumwater, WA	412,800
42	Jacksonville, NC	22.3	42	Wenatchee, WA	406,200
43	Flagstaff, AZ	22.1	43	Missoula, MT	405,300
44	Carbondale-Marion, IL	22.0	44	Colorado Springs, CO	397,900
45	Harrisonburg, VA	21.9	45	Modesto, CA	397,200
46	Blacksburg-Christiansburg, VA	21.8	46	Austin-Round Rock-Georgetown, TX	397,100
47	Yuma, AZ	21.7	47	Ogden-Clearfield, UT	395,400
47	San Angelo, TX	21.7	48	Flagstaff, AZ	393,900
47	Bismarck, ND	21.7	49	Carson City, NV	393,500
50	Houma-Thibodaux, LA	21.6	50	Phoenix-Mesa-Chandler, AZ	374,100
50	Kokomo, IN	21.6	51	Grants Pass, OR	371,600
52	Redding, CA	21.5	52	Chico, CA	370,700
52	Lubbock, TX	21.5	53	Medford, OR	368,700
54	Eau Claire, WI	21.4	54	Yuba City, CA	366,600
55	Niles, MI	21.2	55	Hilton Head Island-Bluffton, SC	365,800
55	Bay City, MI	21.2	55	Las Vegas-Henderson-Paradise, NV	365,800
57	Pittsfield, MA	21.0	57	Eugene-Springfield, OR	365,700
58	Cheyenne, WY	20.9	58	Ocean City, NJ	365,100
59	Bloomsburg-Berwick, PA	20.7	59	Providence-Warwick, RI-MA	364,000
59	San Luis Obispo-Paso Robles, CA	20.7	60	Miami-Fort Lauderdale-Pompano Beach, FL	362,500
59	Johnstown, PA	20.7	61	Santa Fe, NM	362,200
62	Wausau-Weston, WI	20.5	62	Prescott Valley-Prescott, AZ	361,900
62	Albany-Lebanon, OR	20.5	63	Manchester-Nashua, NH	361,000
64	Mansfield, OH	20.4	64	Salem, OR	360,300
65	Idaho Falls, ID	20.3	65	Logan, UT-ID	358,500
66	Bangor, ME	20.2	65	Longview, WA	358,500
67	Santa Maria-Santa Barbara, CA	19.9	67	Portland-South Portland, ME	356,800
68	Erie, PA	19.6	68	California-Lexington Park, MD	356,400
68	Cape Girardeau, MO-IL	19.6	69	Spokane-Spokane Valley, WA	351,600
70	Kankakee, IL	19.5	70	Baltimore-Columbia-Towson, MD	351,200
70	Lake Havasu City-Kingman, AZ	19.5	71	Charlottesville, VA	350,000
72	Vineland-Bridgeton, NJ	19.4	72	Worcester, MA-CT	349,500
72	Goldsboro, NC	19.4	72	Madera, CA	348,500
72	Saginaw, MI	19.4	74	Burlington-South Burlington, VT	347,900
75	Lima, OH	19.3	75	Walla Walla, WA	347,200
75	Rapid City, SD	19.3			
75	Midland, MI	19.3			

Metropolitan Area Rankings, 2021

Selected Rankings

Percent of owners with a mortgage, contract to purchase, or similar debt rank	Area name	Percent of owners with a mortgage, contract to purchase, or similar debt [C-3, col. 6]	Percent of households with access to the Internet rank	Area name	Percent of households with access to the Internet [C-3, col. 9]
	UNITED STATES............	61.3		UNITED STATES............	90.3
1	Washington-Arlington-Alexandria, DC-VA-MD-WV	75.5	1	San Jose-Sunnyvale-Santa Clara, CA	95.8
2	Greeley, CO	74.4	2	Colorado Springs, CO	95.5
3	Provo-Orem, UT	73.9	2	Boulder, CO	95.5
4	California-Lexington Park, MD	73.6	4	Seattle-Tacoma-Bellevue, WA	95.2
5	Vallejo, CA	73.4	4	Olympia-Lacey-Tumwater, WA	95.2
6	Denver-Aurora-Lakewood, CO	73.2	4	Bremerton-Silverdale-Port Orchard, WA	95.2
7	Raleigh-Cary, NC	73.0	7	San Diego-Chula Vista-Carlsbad, CA	94.9
8	Virginia Beach-Norfolk-Newport News, VA-NC	72.8	8	Santa Rosa-Petaluma, CA	94.7
9	Colorado Springs, CO	72.3	9	Washington-Arlington-Alexandria, DC-VA-MD-WV	94.5
10	Salt Lake City, UT	71.7	10	Ogden-Clearfield, UT	94.4
11	Seattle-Tacoma-Bellevue, WA	71.5	11	Napa, CA	94.3
12	Richmond, VA	71.2	11	Bellingham, WA	94.3
13	Ogden-Clearfield, UT	70.8	11	Barnstable Town, MA	94.3
14	Baltimore-Columbia-Towson, MD	70.5	11	Austin-Round Rock-Georgetown, TX	94.3
15	Riverside-San Bernardino-Ontario, CA	70.3	15	Manchester-Nashua, NH	94.2
16	Atlanta-Sandy Springs-Alpharetta, GA	70.0	16	Provo-Orem, UT	94.1
17	Anchorage, AK	69.8	16	Portland-Vancouver-Hillsboro, OR-WA	94.1
17	Indianapolis-Carmel-Anderson, IN	69.8	16	Salt Lake City, UT	94.1
19	San Diego-Chula Vista-Carlsbad, CA	69.7	19	Anchorage, AK	94.0
19	Portland-Vancouver-Hillsboro, OR-WA	69.5	19	Ann Arbor, MI	94.0
19	Iowa City, IA	69.5	19	San Francisco-Oakland-Berkeley, CA	94.0
22	Worcester, MA-CT	69.4	19	Salinas, CA	94.0
23	Columbus, OH	69.3	23	Oxnard-Thousand Oaks-Ventura, CA	93.8
24	Bremerton-Silverdale-Port Orchard, WA	69.2	24	Denver-Aurora-Lakewood, CO	93.7
24	Las Vegas-Henderson-Paradise, NV	69.2	24	Sacramento-Roseville-Folsom, CA	93.7
26	Des Moines-West Des Moines, IA	69.1	26	Santa Cruz-Watsonville, CA	93.6
27	San Francisco-Oakland-Berkeley, CA	68.9	27	Logan, UT-ID	93.5
28	Oxnard-Thousand Oaks-Ventura, CA	68.8	27	Raleigh-Cary, NC	93.5
28	Minneapolis-St. Paul-Bloomington, MN-WI	68.8	27	Vallejo, CA	93.5
30	Boston-Cambridge-Newton, MA-NH	68.7	30	Bridgeport-Stamford-Norwalk, CT	93.4
30	Sacramento-Roseville-Folsom, CA	68.7	30	Port St. Lucie, FL	93.4
32	Stockton, CA	68.6	30	Atlanta-Sandy Springs-Alpharetta, GA	93.4
32	Charlotte-Concord-Gastonia, NC-SC	68.6	33	Minneapolis-St. Paul-Bloomington, MN-WI	93.3
34	Omaha-Council Bluffs, NE-IA	68.5	33	Grand Junction, CO	93.3
34	Boise City, ID	68.5	33	Boston-Cambridge-Newton, MA-NH	93.3
36	Los Angeles-Long Beach-Anaheim, CA	68.4	33	Boise City, ID	93.3
37	Bridgeport-Stamford-Norwalk, CT	68.2	37	Los Angeles-Long Beach-Anaheim, CA	93.2
38	Providence-Warwick, RI-MA	68.1	37	Mount Vernon-Anacortes, WA	93.2
39	Phoenix-Mesa-Chandler, AZ	68.0	37	Phoenix-Mesa-Chandler, AZ	93.2
40	Cheyenne, WY	67.9	37	Prescott Valley-Prescott, AZ	93.2
41	Madison, WI	67.8	37	Bend, OR	93.2
42	Urban Honolulu, HI	67.7	42	Modesto, CA	93.0
42	San Jose-Sunnyvale-Santa Clara, CA	67.7	42	Columbus, OH	93.0
44	Salinas, CA	67.3	44	Nashville-Davidson--Murfreesboro--Franklin, TN	92.9
44	Lexington-Fayette, KY	67.3	44	Urban Honolulu, HI	92.9
46	Grand Junction, CO	67.2	46	Burlington-South Burlington, VT	92.8
46	Santa Rosa-Petaluma, CA	67.2	46	Dallas-Fort Worth-Arlington, TX	92.8
46	Nashville-Davidson--Murfreesboro--Franklin, TN	67.2	46	Riverside-San Bernardino-Ontario, CA	92.8
46	Austin-Round Rock-Georgetown, TX	67.2	46	Eugene-Springfield, OR	92.8
50	Bakersfield, CA	67.1	50	Fort Collins, CO	92.7
50	Fort Collins, CO	67.1	50	Oshkosh-Neenah, WI	92.7
52	Reno, NV	66.8	50	Orlando-Kissimmee-Sanford, FL	92.7
52	Savannah, GA	66.8	53	Idaho Falls, ID	92.6
54	Greenville, NC	66.7	53	East Stroudsburg, PA	92.6
54	Lewiston-Auburn, ME	66.7	53	Fayetteville-Springdale-Rogers, AR	92.6
54	Fayetteville, NC	66.7	56	Midland, TX	92.5
57	Lawrence, KS	66.6	57	Sioux Falls, SD	92.4
57	Bend, OR	66.6	57	New Haven-Milford, CT	92.4
59	Columbus, IN	66.5	57	Carson City, NV	92.4
60	Boulder, CO	66.4	57	St. George, UT	92.4
61	Portland-South Portland, ME	66.3	57	Madison, WI	92.4
62	Hanford-Corcoran, CA	66.2	57	Savannah, GA	92.4
62	Kokomo, IN	66.2	63	Kingston, NY	92.3
62	Cincinnati, OH-KY-IN	66.2	63	Portland-South Portland, ME	92.3
62	Burlington-South Burlington, VT	66.2	63	Myrtle Beach-Conway-North Myrtle Beach, SC-NC	92.3
62	Manchester-Nashua, NH	66.2	63	Dubuque, IA	92.3
62	Salem, OR	66.2	63	Worcester, MA-CT	92.3
62	Orlando-Kissimmee-Sanford, FL	66.0	68	Columbus, IN	92.2
69	Louisville/Jefferson County, KY-IN	66.0	68	Fort Wayne, IN	92.2
69	Cedar Rapids, IA	66.0	68	San Luis Obispo-Paso Robles, CA	92.2
69	Olympia-Lacey-Tumwater, WA	66.0	71	Virginia Beach-Norfolk-Newport News, VA-NC	92.1
72	Janesville-Beloit, WI	65.9	71	Greeley, CO	92.1
72	Coeur d'Alene, ID	65.9	71	Indianapolis-Carmel-Anderson, IN	92.1
72	Yuba City, CA	65.9	71	Salem, OR	92.1
75	Savannah, GA	66.6	71	Missoula, MT	92.1
			71	Charlotte-Concord-Gastonia, NC-SC	92.1
			71	North Port-Sarasota-Bradenton, FL	92.1

City Rankings, 2021

Selected Rankings

Lived in the same house one year ago rank	City	Percent who lived in the same house one year ago [C-4, col. 2]	Percent with commute less than 10 minutes to work rank	City	Percent with commute less than 10 minutes to work [C-4. col. 11]	Percent owner-occupied housing units rank	City	Percent owner-occupied housing units [C-4, col. 5]
	UNITED STATES	87.2		**UNITED STATES**	13.2		**UNITED STATES**	65.4
1	El Monte city, California	96.7	1	Jacksonville city, North Carolina	40.7	1	The Villages CDP, Florida	93.4
1	Jurupa Valley city, California	96.7	2	Ames city, Iowa	37.4	2	Buckeye city, Arizona	92.4
3	Norwalk city, California	96.5	3	Bend city, Oregon	33.8	3	Lakeville city, Minnesota	90.5
4	Whittier city, California	95.4	4	St. Joseph city, Missouri	33.5	4	Queen Creek town, Arizona	88.5
5	Passaic city, New Jersey	94.6	5	Missoula city, Montana	33.2	5	Livonia city, Michigan	87.2
6	Union City city, New Jersey	94.5	6	Wichita Falls city, Texas	30.5	6	Maple Grove city, Minnesota	84.9
7	Garden Grove city, California	93.9	7	Columbia city, South Carolina	29.7	7	Blaine city, Minnesota	84.3
8	Dearborn city, Michigan	93.7	8	Chico city, California	29.1	8	Atascocita CDP, Texas	83.8
9	East Los Angeles CDP, California	93.6	9	Bloomington city, Indiana	28.0	8	San Tan Valley CDP, Arizona	83.6
9	Visalia city, California	93.6	10	Bowling Green city, Kentucky	27.7	10	Port St. Lucie city, Florida	83.5
9	Lakewood city, California	93.6	11	Bloomington city, Illinois	27.1	11	Sammamish city, Washington	83.3
12	Salinas city, California	93.5	12	Idaho Falls city, Idaho	26.2	12	Flower Mound town, Texas	82.5
12	Miami Gardens city, Florida	93.5	13	Lawton city, Oklahoma	26.1	13	Palm Coast city, Florida	82.4
12	Palmdale city, California	93.5	14	Bismarck city, North Dakota	25.9	14	Dale City CDP, Virginia	82.2
12	Lake Elsinore city, California	93.5	15	Yuma city, Arizona	25.8	15	South Jordan city, Utah	82.0
16	Mount Vernon city, New York	93.3	15	Eau Claire city, Wisconsin	25.8	16	Sugar Land city, Texas	81.5
16	Oxnard city, California	93.3	17	Yakima city, Washington	25.4	17	Port Charlotte CDP, Florida	81.3
18	Inglewood city, California	93.2	18	Flagstaff city, Arizona	25.0	18	Highlands Ranch CDP, Colorado	81.2
18	Dale City CDP, Virginia	93.2	19	Abilene city, Texas	24.8	19	Rio Rancho city, New Mexico	81.0
20	Harlingen city, Texas	93.1	20	Lawrence city, Kansas	24.5	20	Spring Hill CDP, Florida	80.2
21	West Covina city, California	93.0	21	Redding city, California	24.4	21	O'Fallon city, Missouri	80.1
21	Brownsville city, Texas	93.0	22	Edinburg city, Texas	24.3	21	Yorba Linda city, California	80.1
21	Downey city, California	93.0	23	San Angelo city, Texas	23.6	23	Toms River CDP, New Jersey	79.6
24	Paterson city, New Jersey	92.9	24	Grand Junction city, Colorado	23.5	24	South Hill CDP, Washington	79.3
24	Miramar city, Florida	92.9	24	Lynchburg city, Virginia	23.5	25	Castle Rock town, Colorado	79.1
26	Chula Vista city, California	92.7	26	Duluth city, Minnesota	23.4	25	Centennial city, Colorado	79.1
27	Bellflower city, California	92.6	27	Rapid City city, South Dakota	23.1	27	Deltona city, Florida	79.0
28	Pembroke Pines city, Florida	92.5	28	Harlingen city, Texas	23.0	28	Bolingbrook village, Illinois	78.7
29	Kenner city, Louisiana	92.4	29	Fayetteville city, North Carolina	22.9	29	Eastvale city, California	78.6
30	Simi Valley city, California	92.3	29	Lubbock city, Texas	22.9	30	Menifee city, California	78.3
31	San Tan Valley CDP, Arizona	92.3	29	Provo city, Utah	22.9	31	Mission Viejo city, California	78.0
31	Cheektowaga CDP, New York	92.3	32	Appleton city, Wisconsin	22.7	32	Surprise city, Arizona	77.8
31	Springdale city, Arkansas	92.3	32	Athens-Clarke County unified government (balance), Georgia	22.7	33	Goodyear city, Arizona	77.6
34	Garland city, Texas	92.3	34	Santa Barbara city, California	22.4	33	Fishers city, Indiana	77.6
35	Lancaster city, California	92.2	35	Columbia city, Missouri	22.0	35	Sandy city, Utah	77.4
35	Sioux City city, Iowa	92.2	35	Davis city, California	22.0	35	Cape Coral city, Florida	77.4
35	Fontana city, California	92.2	37	Oshkosh city, Wisconsin	21.8	35	Johns Creek city, Georgia	77.4
38	Bakersfield city, California	92.1	37	Bellingham city, Washington	21.8	38	Lehi city, Utah	77.3
38	Hayward city, California	92.1	39	Conway city, Arkansas	21.6	38	Peoria city, Arizona	77.3
38	Westland city, Michigan	92.1	40	Temple city, Texas	21.5	40	Meridian city, Idaho	77.2
41	Antioch city, California	92.0	41	Janesville city, Wisconsin	21.2	41	Palm Bay city, Florida	77.1
41	Moreno Valley city, California	92.0	41	Canton city, Ohio	21.2	41	North Port city, Florida	77.1
41	Indio city, California	92.0	41	Santa Fe city, New Mexico	21.2	43	Sterling Heights city, Michigan	77.0
41	New Rochelle city, New York	92.0	44	Kalamazoo city, Michigan	21.1	44	Poinciana CDP, Florida	76.7
41	Elizabeth city, New Jersey	92.0	44	Erie city, Pennsylvania	21.1	45	Thornton city, Colorado	76.6
41	Richmond city, California	92.0	46	Cheyenne city, Wyoming	20.9	46	Missouri City city, Texas	76.4
47	Lorain city, Ohio	91.9	47	St. Cloud city, Minnesota	20.2	47	Leander city, Texas	76.1
48	Ontario city, California	91.8	48	Longview city, Texas	20.1	47	Ellicott City CDP, Maryland	76.1
48	Livonia city, Michigan	91.8	48	Lodi city, California	20.1	49	Olathe city, Kansas	76.0
48	Thousand Oaks city, California	91.8	50	Melbourne city, Florida	20.0	50	Woodbury city, Minnesota	75.8
48	Santa Maria city, California	91.8	51	Las Cruces city, New Mexico	19.9	51	Brooklyn Park city, Minnesota	75.7
48	Corona city, California	91.8	52	Greenville city, North Carolina	19.8	51	West Jordan city, Utah	75.7
53	West Jordan city, Utah	91.7	52	Fargo city, North Dakota	19.8	53	Arvada city, Colorado	75.6
53	Daly City city, California	91.7	54	Dothan city, Alabama	19.7	54	The Woodlands CDP, Texas	75.5
53	Bolingbrook village, Illinois	91.7	55	Springdale city, Arkansas	19.5	54	Lee's Summit city, Missouri	75.5
56	Carmichael CDP, California	91.6	55	Waterloo city, Iowa	19.5	56	Naperville city, Illinois	75.3
56	Alafaya CDP, Florida	91.6	55	St. George city, Utah	19.5	57	Spring CDP, Texas	75.2
56	Lauderhill city, Florida	91.6	58	Springfield city, Missouri	19.4	57	Guaynabo zona urbana, Puerto Rico	75.2
59	Brooklyn Park city, Minnesota	91.5	58	Lake Charles city, Louisiana	19.4	59	Murrieta city, California	75.1
59	Pomona city, California	91.5	58	Boulder city, Colorado	19.4	60	Gilbert town, Arizona	74.9
59	Kendall CDP, Florida	91.5	61	Evansville city, Indiana	19.3	61	Chino Hills city, California	74.8
62	Merced city, California	91.4	62	Iowa City city, Iowa	19.0	62	Joliet city, Illinois	74.7
62	Hesperia city, California	91.4	62	Wilmington city, North Carolina	19.0	62	League City city, Texas	74.7
62	Napa city, California	91.4	62	Kenosha city, Wisconsin	19.0	62	Parma city, Ohio	74.7
65	Waukegan city, Illinois	91.2	65	Decatur city, Illinois	18.9	65	Pasco city, Washington	74.3
65	Clovis city, California	91.2	65	Salt Lake City city, Utah	18.9	66	Centreville CDP, Virginia	74.2
65	Gastonia city, North Carolina	91.2	67	Savannah city, Georgia	18.8	66	Eagan city, Minnesota	74.2
68	Modesto city, California	91.1	67	Champaign city, Illinois	18.8	68	Rochester Hills city, Michigan	74.1
68	Waterbury city, Connecticut	91.1	69	Auburn city, Alabama	18.7	68	Mount Pleasant town, South Carolina	74.1
68	Pearland city, Texas	91.1	70	Topeka city, Kansas	18.6	70	Pearland city, Texas	74.0
71	Upland city, California	90.9	71	Ann Arbor city, Michigan	18.4	70	Troy city, Michigan	74.0
71	Elk Grove city, California	90.9	72	College Station city, Texas	18.3	72	Warwick city, Rhode Island	73.7
71	Port St. Lucie city, Florida	90.9	72	Sioux Falls city, South Dakota	18.3	72	Weston city, Florida	73.7
71	Danbury city, Connecticut	90.9	74	Scranton city, Pennsylvania	18.2	72	Chesapeake city, Virginia	73.7
71	Westminster city, California	90.9	75	Waukesha city, Wisconsin	18.1	72	Elk Grove city, California	73.7
71	Alhambra city, California	90.9	75	Fort Smith city, Arkansas	18.1	72	Arlington Heights village, Illinois	73.7
			75	Cedar Rapids city, Iowa	18.1			

City Rankings, 2019

Percent of owners with a mortgage, contract to purchase, or similar debt rank	City	Percent of owners with a mortgage, contract to purchase, or similar debt [C-4, col. 6]	Median value of owner-occupied units rank	City	Median value of owner-occupied housing units [C-4, col. 7]
	UNITED STATES............	61.3		UNITED STATES............	$281,400
1	Silver Spring CDP, Maryland	85.2	1	Newport Beach city, California	2,000,000+
2	Phoenix city, Arizona	84.2	1	Palo Alto city, California	2,000,000+
3	Layton city, Utah	83.3	3	Mountain View city, California	1,636,100
4	Sunnyvale city, California	82.6	4	Santa Monica city, California	1,582,300
5	Jurupa Valley city, California	82.5	5	Sunnyvale city, California	1,575,200
5	Folsom city, California	82.5	6	Redwood City city, California	1,567,400
7	Washington city, District of Columbia	81.9	7	San Mateo city, California	1,518,800
8	Omaha city, Nebraska	81.8	8	Santa Barbara city, California	1,476,800
9	Evansville city, Indiana	81.4	9	Santa Clara city, California	1,382,300
10	Broomfield city, Colorado	81.3	10	San Francisco city, California	1,306,400
11	Seattle city, Washington	80.8	11	Berkeley city, California	1,270,000
12	Savannah city, Georgia	80.6	12	San Ramon city, California	1,233,100
13	Torrance city, California	80.3	13	Pleasanton city, California	1,230,600
14	Lee's Summit city, Missouri	79.7	14	Fremont city, California	1,175,600
15	Flagstaff city, Arizona	79.2	15	Sammamish city, Washington	1,158,000
16	Anaheim city, California	79.1	16	Newton city, Massachusetts	1,147,300
17	Arlington CDP, Virginia	79.0	17	Milpitas city, California	1,146,600
18	South Jordan city, Utah	78.9	18	Redmond city, Washington	1,120,300
18	Modesto city, California	78.9	19	San Jose city, California	1,119,500
20	Ames city, Iowa	78.8	20	Dublin city, California	1,114,800
21	Mountain View city, California	78.3	21	Redondo Beach city, California	1,110,800
22	Port St. Lucie city, Florida	78.2	22	Bellevue city, Washington	1,107,200
23	Queen Creek town, Arizona	78.1	23	Alameda city, California	1,077,900
24	Corona city, California	78.0	24	Daly City city, California	1,052,800
25	Compton city, California	77.8	25	Carlsbad city, California	1,042,900
25	West Valley City city, Utah	77.8	26	Bethesda CDP, Maryland	1,023,800
25	Bloomington city, Illinois	77.8	27	Yorba Linda city, California	1,012,900
28	Manteca city, California	77.7	28	Cambridge city, Massachusetts	1,006,100
29	Renton city, Washington	77.6	29	Castro Valley CDP, California	1,004,800
29	Richmond city, California	77.6	29	Walnut Creek city, California	1,004,800
29	Rockville city, Maryland	77.6	31	Glendale city, California	995,700
29	Greeley city, Colorado	77.6	32	Union City city, California	995,200
33	Roanoke city, Virginia	77.5	33	Irvine city, California	970,500
34	Fall River city, Massachusetts	77.3	34	Livermore city, California	942,300
34	Glendale city, Arizona	77.3	35	Boulder city, Colorado	941,100
34	Avondale city, Arizona	77.3	36	Burbank city, California	940,400
34	McAllen city, Texas	77.3	37	Kirkland city, Washington	939,900
38	Pasco city, Washington	77.2	38	Huntington Beach city, California	937,200
39	Riverside city, California	77.1	39	Costa Mesa city, California	930,900
40	Casas Adobes CDP, Arizona	77.0	39	Torrance city, California	930,500
41	North Charleston city, South Carolina	76.8	41	Pasadena city, California	905,900
41	Chesapeake city, Virginia	76.8	42	Mission Viejo city, California	859,500
43	Lafayette city, Indiana	76.5	43	Thousand Oaks city, California	858,200
44	San Mateo city, California	76.4	44	Oakland city, California	848,600
44	Fairfield city, California	76.4	45	Seattle city, Washington	848,100
44	Jacksonville city, North Carolina	76.4	46	Orange city, California	827,200
47	Fort Worth city, Texas	76.3	47	Somerville city, Massachusetts	818,100
47	Concord city, California	76.2	48	Los Angeles city, California	812,800
49	Las Vegas city, Nevada	76.0	49	Lake Forest city, California	804,400
49	Concord city, North Carolina	76.0	50	Fullerton city, California	790,900
49	Ellicott City CDP, Maryland	76.0	51	Chino Hills city, California	787,400
52	Pembroke Pines city, Florida	75.8	52	Arlington CDP, Virginia	779,400
52	Clovis city, California	75.8	53	San Leandro city, California	775,000
52	Oceanside city, California	75.8	54	San Diego city, California	768,800
52	Santa Clara city, California	75.8	55	Westminster city, California	762,300
56	Irvine city, California	75.7	56	Davis city, California	752,300
57	Centreville CDP, Virginia	75.6	57	Hawthorne city, California	738,000
57	Santa Rosa city, California	75.6	58	Hayward city, California	735,000
59	Boston city, Massachusetts	75.5	59	Urban Honolulu CDP, Hawaii	733,000
60	Spokane Valley city, Washington	75.4	60	Tustin city, California	727,000
61	Wilmington city, Delaware	75.3	61	Concord city, California	719,000
61	Kirkland city, Washington	75.3	62	Napa city, California	718,700
61	El Cajon city, California	75.3	63	Whittier city, California	718,300
64	Colorado Springs city, Colorado	75.2	64	Alhambra city, California	718,100
64	Thornton city, Colorado	75.2	65	San Marcos city, California	710,500
66	Clarksville city, Tennessee	75.0	66	Lakewood city, California	704,700
66	Alexandria city, Virginia	75.0	67	San Buenaventura (Ventura) city, California	702,500
68	Bethesda CDP, Maryland	74.8	68	Camarillo city, California	694,200
68	Lowell city, Massachusetts	74.8	69	Long Beach city, California	693,600
68	Westminster city, California	74.8	70	Anaheim city, California	688,400
71	Lawrence city, Kansas	74.7	71	Eastvale city, California	686,100
71	Germantown CDP, Maryland	74.7	72	Downey city, California	686,000
71	Eagan city, Minnesota	74.7	73	New York city, New York	685,700
71	Chico city, California	74.7	74	Simi Valley city, California	685,500
75	Lake Elsinore city, California	74.6	75	Inglewood city, California	684,500
75	Newport News city, Virginia	74.6			

Table C-1. States — Where: Migration, Housing, and Transportation, 2021

State code	STATE	Total population 1 year and over	Residence 1 year ago (percent)							Total occupied housing units (households)	Percent owner occupied
			Same house	Different house; same city or town	Different house; different city; same county	Different house; diferent county; same state	Different house; different state	Abroad			
	ACS table number:	C07204	C07204	C07204	C07204	C07204	C07204	C07204	B25003	B25003
	Column number	1	2	3	4	5	6	7	8	9

Table C-1. States — Where: Migration, Housing, and Transportation, 2021—*Continued*

State code	STATE	Homeownership by race and Hispanic origin of householder									
		White alone, not of Hispanic or Latino origin		Black or African American alone		American Indian and Alaska Native alone		Asian, Native Hawaiian, and Other Pacific Islander alone		Hispanic or Latino	
		Number of householders	Percent owners	Number of householders	Percent owners	Number of householders	Percent owners	Number of householders	Percent owners	Number of householders	Percent owners
	ACS table number:	B25003H	B25003H	B25003B	B25003B	B25003C	B25003C	B25003D+ B25003E	B25003D + B25003E	B25003I	B25003I
	Column number	10	11	12	13	14	15	16	17	18	19

Table C-1. States — Where: Migration, Housing, and Transportation, 2021—*Continued*

State code	STATE	Homeownership by age of householder							
		Householder 15 to 24 years		Householder 25 to 44 years		Householder 45 to 64 years		Householder 65 years and over	
		Number of householders	Percent owners	Number of householders	Percent owners	Number of householders	Percent owners	Number of householders	Percent owners
	ACS table number:	B25007	B25007	B25007	B25007	B25007	B25007	B25007	B25007
	Column number	20	21	22	23	24	25	26	27

Table C-1. States — Where: Migration, Housing, and Transportation, 2021—*Continued*

State code	STATE	Homeownership by household type								Average household size			Percent of housing units that are crowded or lacking complete plumbing
		Married-couple family households		Male householder families, no spouse present		Female householder families, no spouse present		Nonfamily households		All households	Owner-occupied households	Renter-occupied households	
		Number of householders	Percent owners	Number of householders	Percent owners	Number of householders	Percent owners	Number of householders	Percent owners				
	ACS table number:	B25115	B25115	B25115	B25115	B25115	B25115	B25115	B25115	B25010	B25010	B25010	C25016
	Column number	28	29	30	31	32	33	34	35	36	37	38	39

Table C-1. States — Where: Migration, Housing, and Transportation, 2021—*Continued*

State code	STATE	Median household income in the past 12 months (in 2019 inflation-adjusted dollars)					Median housinng value (owner estimated)		
		All households	Owner-occupied households			Renter-occupied households	All owner-occupied households	Households with a mortgage	Households without a mortgage
			All owner-occupied households	Households with a mortgage	Households without a mortgage				
	ACS table number:	B25119	B25099	B25099	B25099	B25119	B25097	B25097	B25097
	Column number	40	41	42	43	44	45	46	47

Table C-1. States — Where: Migration, Housing, and Transportation, 2021—*Continued*

State code	STATE	Owner occupied housing units			Median monthly housing costs for all housing units with costs (dollars)	Gross rent for renter-occupied housing units		Median selected monthly owner costs for owner-occupied housing units			Median annual real estate taxes paid by owner-occupied housing units (dollars)
		Total owner-occupied housing units	Percent with a mortgage	Percent with a second mortgage, or a home equity loan, or both		Median gross rent (dollars)	As a percentage of household income	All owner-occupied households	Households with a mortgage	Households without a mortgage	
	ACS table number:	B25081	B25081	B25081	B25105	B25064	B25071	B25088	B25088	B25088	B25103
	Column number	48	49	50	51	52	53	54	55	56	57

Table C-1. States — Where: Migration, Housing, and Transportation, 2021—*Continued*

		Median selected monthly owner costs as a percentage of household income			Households who pay 30 percent or more of income for housing expenses by tenure and age of householder (percent)							
					Owner-occupied households				Renter-occupied households			
	STATE	All owner-occupied households	Households with a mortgage	Households without a mortgage1	Householder 15 to 24 years	Householder 25 to 34 years	Householder 35 to 64 years	Householder 65 years and over	Householder 15 to 24 years	Householder 25 to 34 years	Householder 35 to 64 years	Householder 65 years and over
State code	ACS table number:	B25092	B25092	B25092	C25093	C25093	C25093	C25093	B25072	B25072	B25072	B25072
	Column number	58	59	60	61	62	63	64	65	66	67	68

Table C-1. States — Where: Migration, Housing, and Transportation, 2021—*Continued*

			Means of transportation to work (percent)						
			Car, truck, or van		Public transportation (excluding taxicab)	Bicycle	Walked	Taxicab, motorcycle, or other means	Worked at home
	STATE	Total number of workers 16 years and over	Drove alone	Car-pooled					
	ACS table number:	B08301	B08301	B08301	B08301	B08301	B08301	B08301	B08301
State code	Column number	69	70	71	72	73	74	75	76

Table C-1. States — Where: Migration, Housing, and Transportation, 2021—*Continued*

			Mean travel time to work (minutes)					Vehicles available (percent of households)					
	STATE	Number of workers who did not work at home	All workers who did not work at home	By car, truck, or van	Public transportation	Taxicab, motorcycle, bicycle, walked, or by other means	Number of households	No vehicles	One vehicle	Two vehicles	Three or more vehicles	Average vehicles per household
	ACS table number:	B08301	C08136/C08301	C08136/C08301	C08136/C08301	C08136/C08301	B08201	B08201	B08201	B08201	B08201	B25046/B08201
State code	Column number	77	78	79	80	81	82	83	84	85	86	87

Table C-2. Counties — Where: Migration, Housing, and Transportation, 2021

		Total population 1 year and over	Lived in the same house 1 year ago (percent)	Did not live in the same county 1 year ago (percent)	Total occupied housing units	Owner-occupied units (percent)	Percent with a mortgage, contract to purchase, or similar debt	Median value of owner-occupied units (dollars; owner estimated)	Median gross rent of renter-occupied units paying cash rent	Households with Internet access (percent)	Number of workers who commuted to work	Commute of less than 10 minutes (percent)	Commute of 60 minutes or more (percent)
	STATE County												
STATE County code	ACS table number:	C07204	C07204	C07204	B25003	B25003	B25081	B25097	B25064	S2801	B08012	B08012	B08012
	Column number:	1	2	3	4	5	6	7	8	9	10	11	12

Table C-3. Metropolitan Areas — Where: Migration, Housing, and Transportation, 2021

		Total population 1 year and over	Lived in the same house 1 year ago (percent)	Did not live in the same metropolitan area 1 year ago (percent)	Total occupied housing units	Owner-occupied units (percent)	Percent with a mortgage, contract to purchase, or similar debt	Median value of owner-occupied units (dollars; owner estimated)	Median gross rent of renter-occupied units paying cash rent	Households with Internet access (percent)	Number of workers who commuted to work	Commute of less than 10 minutes (percent)	Commute of 60 minutes or more (percent)
	Metropolitan area / division												
Metropolitan area / division code	ACS table number:	C07204	C07204	C07204	B25003	B25003	B25081	B25097	B25064	S2801	B08012	B08012	B08012
	column number:	1	2	3	4	5	6	7	8	9	10	11	12

Table C-4. Cities — Where: Migration, Housing, and Transportation, 2021

		Total population 1 year and over	Lived in the same house 1 year ago (percent)	Did not live in the same city 1 year ago (percent)	Total occupied housing units	Owner-occupied units (percent)	Percent with a mortgage, contract to purchase, or similar debt	Median value of owner-occupied units (dollars; owner estimated)	Median gross rent of renter-occupied units paying cash rent	Households with Internet access (percent)	Number of workers who commuted to work	Commute of less than 10 minutes (percent)	Commute of 60 minutes or more (percent)
STATE and place code	STATE Place												
	ACS table number:	C07204	C07204	C07204	B25003	B25003	B25081	B25097	B25064	S2801	B08012	B08012	B08012
FIPS	column number:	1	2	3	4	5	6	7	8	9	10	11	12

Table C-1. States — Where: Migration, Housing, and Transportation, 2021

State code	STATE	Total population 1 year and over	Residence 1 year ago (percent)						Total occupied housing units (households)	Percent owner occupied
			Same house	Different house; same city or town	Different house; different city; same county	Different house; diferent county; same state	Different house; different state	Abroad		
	ACS table number:	C07204	C07204	C07204	C07204	C07204	C07204	C07204	B25003	B25003
	Column number	1	2	3	4	5	6	7	8	9
00	UNITED STATES....................	328,464,538	87.2	3.4	3.3	3.2	2.4	0.4	127,544,730	65.4
01	Alabama.............................	4,989,797	88.0	2.9	3.7	2.7	2.3	0.3	1,967,559	70.0
02	Alaska................................	723,949	86.3	4.9	2.1	1.8	4.3	0.5	271,311	66.8
04	Arizona..............................	7,202,745	85.3	4.7	4.1	1.7	3.7	0.5	2,817,723	67.6
05	Arkansas............................	2,990,311	86.8	4.1	3.1	3.2	2.5	0.2	1,183,675	67.0
06	California...........................	38,833,197	88.7	3.5	3.2	2.9	1.1	0.5	13,429,063	55.9
08	Colorado............................	5,757,628	83.3	4.5	2.5	4.9	4.3	0.5	2,313,042	66.8
09	Connecticut........................	3,571,470	88.7	2.1	3.8	1.9	3.0	0.5	1,428,313	66.6
10	Delaware............................	994,669	89.4	0.8	4.0	1.0	4.3	0.5	395,656	72.6
11	District of Columbia...............	661,026	79.7	10.4	0.0	0.0	8.7	1.1	319,565	41.6
12	Florida	21,590,684	86.0	2.7	4.4	3.1	3.1	0.6	8,565,329	67.4
13	Georgia..............................	10,688,429	86.5	2.1	3.8	4.5	2.8	0.3	4,001,109	66.0
15	Hawaii................................	1,426,298	86.3	2.7	4.5	0.5	5.0	0.9	490,080	62.6
16	Idaho.................................	1,879,719	85.2	3.5	2.9	3.0	5.1	0.3	693,882	71.9
17	Illinois...............................	12,544,435	88.5	4.0	3.1	2.5	1.6	0.4	4,991,641	67.5
18	Indiana..............................	6,729,771	86.7	3.8	3.0	3.8	2.3	0.3	2,680,694	71.1
19	Iowa..................................	3,159,672	86.3	4.6	2.7	3.7	2.4	0.3	1,300,461	71.9
20	Kansas...............................	2,900,594	84.9	5.5	2.4	3.3	3.5	0.5	1,159,026	67.0
21	Kentucky............................	4,460,646	86.9	3.6	3.2	3.6	2.4	0.3	1,785,682	68.7
22	Louisiana	4,571,302	87.2	3.3	3.8	3.4	1.8	0.4	1,783,924	67.3
23	Maine................................	1,360,264	88.5	1.8	3.7	2.6	3.2	0.2	593,626	74.8
24	Maryland............................	6,099,715	88.3	2.1	3.4	3.0	2.6	0.5	2,355,652	67.8
25	Massachusetts	6,916,314	87.4	2.9	3.4	3.3	2.3	0.7	2,759,018	63.2
26	Michigan............................	9,950,336	88.7	1.9	4.0	3.7	1.4	0.3	4,051,798	73.2
27	Minnesota..........................	5,645,866	87.3	3.4	2.9	4.5	1.7	0.3	2,281,033	73.0
28	Mississippi..........................	2,919,574	89.3	2.8	2.6	2.8	2.0	0.3	1,129,611	69.7
29	Missouri.............................	6,102,443	86.6	3.3	3.3	3.8	2.7	0.3	2,468,726	68.8
30	Montana............................	1,093,888	86.3	3.7	2.6	2.8	4.1	0.4	448,949	69.5
31	Nebraska............................	1,939,700	86.5	5.7	1.8	3.3	2.2	0.5	785,982	67.8
32	Nevada..............................	3,111,722	85.5	4.4	4.7	0.7	4.3	0.4	1,191,380	59.1
33	New Hampshire	1,377,638	88.8	1.8	3.2	2.1	3.9	0.2	548,026	72.5
34	New Jersey..........................	9,174,117	89.4	1.8	3.2	2.9	2.1	0.6	3,497,945	64.4
35	New Mexico........................	2,092,251	87.4	4.7	1.9	2.4	3.3	0.3	834,007	69.5
36	New York............................	19,626,300	89.6	4.2	2.1	2.2	1.5	0.5	7,652,666	55.4
37	North Carolina.....................	10,446,881	86.5	3.1	3.1	3.7	3.2	0.4	4,179,632	66.9
38	North Dakota.......................	764,638	83.8	5.4	2.3	3.2	4.9	0.3	322,511	63.1
39	Ohio..................................	11,660,200	87.6	3.5	3.8	3.2	1.6	0.3	4,832,922	67.2
40	Oklahoma...........................	3,943,443	84.9	5.4	2.9	3.7	2.7	0.3	1,547,967	65.5
41	Oregon..............................	4,207,387	85.6	4.2	3.1	3.6	3.2	0.3	1,702,599	63.8
42	Pennsylvania.......................	12,842,522	89.2	2.1	3.6	2.7	2.0	0.4	5,228,956	69.9
72	Puerto Rico.........................	NA	NA	NA	NA	NA	NA	NA	1,165,982	68.7
44	Rhode Island.......................	1,085,539	88.4	1.9	3.6	1.7	4.0	0.5	440,170	63.3
45	South Carolina.....................	5,142,137	86.4	1.6	4.6	3.2	3.8	0.3	2,049,972	71.8
46	South Dakota	884,616	85.9	5.3	1.8	3.6	3.1	0.2	356,887	69.4
47	Tennessee...........................	6,899,165	86.3	3.9	2.8	3.5	3.2	0.3	2,770,395	67.5
48	Texas	29,170,380	86.0	4.6	3.0	3.8	2.0	0.6	10,796,247	62.6
49	Utah..................................	3,295,561	85.5	3.3	5.0	2.7	3.1	0.5	1,101,499	69.7
50	Vermont.............................	641,007	88.1	1.8	3.0	1.8	5.0	0.3	270,163	72.7
51	Virginia..............................	8,557,020	86.3	2.7	2.3	5.1	3.2	0.5	3,331,461	67.6
53	Washington.........................	7,657,350	84.6	3.9	4.9	3.1	2.9	0.6	3,022,255	64.0
54	West Virginia.......................	1,767,792	89.6	1.7	3.3	2.9	2.5	0.1	722,201	75.2
55	Wisconsin...........................	5,838,954	87.7	3.5	3.1	3.4	2.1	0.2	2,449,970	68.1
56	Wyoming............................	573,476	83.9	4.9	3.7	2.4	4.8	0.4	242,763	71.4

NA = Not available.
'- = The median falls in the lowest interval of an open-ended distribution.
¹A value of 10.0 represents the minimum percentage range--10 percent or less.

State code	STATE	Homeownership by race and Hispanic origin of householder									
		White alone, not of Hispanic or Latino origin		Black or African American alone		American Indian and Alaska Native alone		Asian, Native Hawaiian, and Other Pacific Islander alone		Hispanic or Latino	
		Number of householders	Percent owners	Number of householders	Percent owners	Number of householders	Percent owners	Number of householders	Percent owners	Number of householders	Percent owners
	ACS table number:	B25003H	B25003H	B25003B	B25003B	B25003C	B25003C	B25003D+ B25003E	B25003D + B25003E	B25003I	B25003I
	Column number	10	11	12	13	14	15	16	17	18	19
00	UNITED STATES............................	82,171,862	73.3	15,274,070	44.0	1,005,703	53.9	6,642,755	62.2	18,293,521	50.6
01	Alabama....................................	1,307,851	77.9	511,624	52.5	8,196	66.3	23,426	68.7	62,323	49.3
02	Alaska	181,927	72.1	8,247	27.2	27,623	62.7	15,492	52.3	15,797	44.8
04	Arizona....................................	1,731,825	73.9	117,444	40.8	90,484	56.5	95,579	62.8	696,697	59.4
05	Arkansas..................................	854,896	73.4	176,339	44.6	5,600	59.0	18,457	52.5	63,861	53.2
06	California.................................	5,884,653	64.5	807,471	35.5	159,444	45.3	2,037,785	60.9	4,165,168	45.6
08	Colorado..................................	1,668,162	71.2	83,546	42.2	21,335	48.3	65,168	66.5	393,348	55.1
09	Connecticut..............................	976,539	75.9	140,824	41.6	4,065	41.0	57,292	61.9	206,690	42.0
10	Delaware..................................	262,069	81.1	75,767	54.2	1,221	44.1	14,198	67.3	27,306	54.5
11	District of Columbia..................	129,220	50.3	132,521	35.0	791	46.8	15,120	37.1	29,670	35.5
12	Florida	4,993,684	76.4	1,143,819	49.2	21,911	52.8	209,027	73.0	1,944,262	55.1
13	Georgia	2,180,439	76.4	1,223,502	50.8	16,492	49.1	150,782	67.6	297,078	54.2
15	Hawaii	140,118	59.9	11,033	27.3	1,786	17.6	225,524	68.9	39,821	45.9
16	Idaho.......................................	577,914	74.3	4,178	37.8	6,674	64.8	8,758	60.8	68,206	57.0
17	Illinois.....................................	3,254,690	75.6	674,989	41.2	26,593	61.2	261,348	62.7	652,628	57.5
18	Indiana....................................	2,157,133	75.8	234,497	38.1	6,740	72.0	53,502	61.8	144,116	59.4
19	Iowa..	1,135,711	74.9	36,559	30.8	5,654	38.5	23,766	59.1	59,948	56.6
20	Kansas.....................................	913,765	71.0	60,583	37.6	6,340	50.6	28,876	63.8	103,259	56.1
21	Kentucky..................................	1,516,893	73.0	125,655	40.0	4,375	40.0	20,367	54.5	49,628	36.8
22	Louisiana..................................	1,069,685	78.2	537,083	48.7	7,418	76.4	27,018	59.7	79,539	55.8
23	Maine......................................	547,619	76.0	5,824	27.7	1,896	61.7	5,032	70.3	8,063	59.4
24	Maryland..................................	1,247,155	78.5	696,818	52.2	7,230	63.6	138,733	70.8	180,111	55.9
25	Massachusetts...........................	2,017,855	71.1	163,228	37.4	5,568	43.2	172,790	56.9	281,900	31.9
26	Michigan..................................	3,098,589	79.4	531,274	44.6	18,634	68.5	111,374	64.0	161,615	62.6
27	Minnesota	1,888,783	77.5	128,064	30.5	15,561	49.5	85,420	66.1	88,893	56.6
28	Mississippi	658,587	80.1	395,921	53.8	4,638	62.8	9,417	76.1	25,747	52.2
29	Missouri...................................	1,960,481	73.8	262,645	41.2	7,288	57.5	48,265	55.6	82,095	55.6
30	Montana	395,829	71.0	2,443	41.9	17,420	51.5	3,012	55.4	12,913	57.4
31	Nebraska..................................	646,436	71.8	34,085	30.6	7,039	54.4	14,887	49.5	64,089	54.8
32	Nevada.....................................	645,967	66.7	114,342	31.8	15,191	50.7	99,329	63.8	267,452	52.5
33	New Hampshire..........................	495,949	74.3	5,719	32.8	441	51.7	11,538	61.1	15,924	48.1
34	New Jersey	2,022,003	77.0	443,839	41.7	12,575	26.9	317,107	65.5	621,699	40.1
35	New Mexico	359,824	73.9	18,252	39.7	58,773	63.9	12,657	64.6	365,688	67.3
36	New York..................................	4,560,395	67.8	1,015,210	34.1	38,401	30.9	587,605	52.3	1,240,166	28.6
37	North Carolina...........................	2,738,642	75.2	861,213	46.9	43,529	62.5	107,125	65.4	280,470	51.7
38	North Dakota.............................	280,526	67.1	8,651	15.1	10,189	49.9	4,276	27.8	8,686	27.2
39	Ohio..	3,823,829	73.5	576,291	36.0	8,840	43.9	102,319	58.8	157,366	45.8
40	Oklahoma.................................	1,064,704	70.7	111,593	39.0	100,271	61.7	29,647	61.4	131,330	53.6
41	Oregon.....................................	1,325,666	67.3	27,450	38.8	19,667	41.9	71,197	60.6	171,861	47.1
42	Pennsylvania.............................	4,067,433	75.6	524,637	44.7	7,576	47.7	163,137	63.8	325,947	47.6
72	Puerto Rico...............................	6,520	59.7	70,613	65.1	2,160	57.5	2,239	65.3	1,155,881	68.7
44	Rhode Island.............................	331,749	70.2	19,073	31.8	797	24.0	11,386	54.5	58,346	38.0
45	South Carolina...........................	1,359,420	79.5	504,334	54.8	6,477	51.2	27,392	65.0	88,480	58.5
46	South Dakota	308,557	73.0	4,942	25.3	16,662	38.2	4,492	47.2	11,269	44.4
47	Tennessee.................................	2,082,964	74.2	430,419	44.1	7,103	62.2	39,511	58.8	114,397	45.4
48	Texas.......................................	4,948,038	71.3	1,383,244	41.3	78,870	60.6	537,943	65.2	3,605,939	58.7
49	Utah..	882,688	73.0	10,947	30.9	11,049	57.7	32,828	63.6	130,147	57.4
50	Vermont	249,904	74.1	1,695	31.4	563	63.6	3,749	32.6	4,834	66.0
51	Virginia....................................	2,140,021	74.6	619,327	48.4	10,908	64.1	196,371	72.1	247,632	53.5
53	Washington...............................	2,155,142	68.4	110,305	35.3	30,847	52.6	275,801	63.1	290,209	47.2
54	West Virginia.............................	664,078	76.7	20,701	45.2	791	55.8	4,918	58.2	7,989	67.4
55	Wisconsin.................................	2,059,321	72.9	134,124	28.6	14,724	53.9	53,809	51.5	122,702	45.4
56	Wyoming..................................	206,534	73.4	1,779	52.9	3,443	56.1	1,992	46.2	20,217	53.7

NA = Not available.
'- = The median falls in the lowest interval of an open-ended distribution.
¹A value of 10.0 represents the minimum percentage range--10 percent or less.

		Homeownership by age of householder							
		Householder 15 to 24 years		Householder 25 to 44 years		Householder 45 to 64 years		Householder 65 years and over	
	STATE	Number of householders	Percent owners	Number of householders	Percent owners	Number of householders	Percent owners	Number of householders	Percent owners
	ACS table number:	B25007	B25007	B25007	B25007	B25007	B25007	B25007	B25007
State code	Column number	20	21	22	23	24	25	26	27
00	UNITED STATES............................	4,788,820	16.7	41,929,542	51.9	46,543,977	72.8	34,282,391	78.7
01	Alabama.................................	73,273	22.6	603,219	56.3	727,927	76.1	563,140	83.1
02	Alaska....................................	13,392	14.5	101,782	55.5	96,671	76.0	59,466	82.8
04	Arizona..................................	128,376	16.0	906,459	53.0	968,042	75.1	814,846	83.1
05	Arkansas................................	60,231	15.3	378,288	54.8	417,789	73.5	327,367	82.2
06	California...............................	360,953	11.4	4,633,835	38.8	5,056,673	63.0	3,377,602	73.3
08	Colorado...............................	104,016	13.6	868,716	54.8	797,586	76.9	542,724	81.5
09	Connecticut...........................	36,944	18.5	428,255	52.9	556,729	74.7	406,385	74.4
10	Delaware...............................	11,084	18.0	115,009	59.7	144,691	76.7	124,872	84.5
11	District of Columbia................	14,177	3.6	153,895	32.9	87,260	51.3	64,233	57.8
12	Florida..................................	230,737	17.7	2,477,652	49.2	3,106,913	72.1	2,750,027	82.6
13	Georgia.................................	160,136	14.9	1,369,519	51.5	1,512,396	74.6	959,058	81.8
15	Hawaii...................................	14,263	16.9	142,752	44.6	174,679	67.8	158,386	77.1
16	Idaho....................................	32,654	14.2	229,563	62.8	241,545	79.3	190,120	83.4
17	Illinois...................................	179,566	18.3	1,671,363	55.0	1,816,935	75.5	1,323,777	79.2
18	Indiana..................................	127,331	24.8	890,309	61.8	964,442	77.6	698,612	82.4
19	Iowa......................................	75,324	21.1	424,886	65.4	442,328	79.8	357,929	80.6
20	Kansas...................................	64,297	17.7	391,281	57.5	396,148	75.5	307,300	78.6
21	Kentucky................................	84,717	19.4	559,978	57.2	653,435	75.2	487,552	81.7
22	Louisiana...............................	73,123	21.5	597,342	54.2	624,915	74.1	488,544	81.6
23	Maine....................................	17,080	23.1	168,076	64.7	223,254	80.6	185,216	81.9
24	Maryland...............................	63,638	21.3	758,959	53.8	920,637	75.0	612,418	79.1
25	Massachusetts........................	78,917	9.8	878,641	49.4	1,060,135	71.5	741,325	73.3
26	Michigan...............................	160,559	22.0	1,233,386	62.5	1,497,002	80.1	1,160,851	82.8
27	Minnesota.............................	97,966	21.8	765,584	65.2	819,788	82.1	597,695	78.9
28	Mississippi.............................	40,696	21.7	351,384	55.8	415,751	75.2	321,780	83.7
29	Missouri................................	113,275	19.2	805,668	57.6	871,539	76.4	678,244	80.6
30	Montana................................	22,702	14.1	140,055	56.3	150,792	77.8	135,400	83.1
31	Nebraska................................	46,506	15.1	268,390	59.8	264,919	76.6	206,167	78.6
32	Nevada..................................	38,601	14.8	413,468	45.2	430,835	66.2	308,476	73.5
33	New Hampshire.......................	13,198	11.2	154,815	59.4	218,590	79.4	161,423	80.8
34	New Jersey.............................	60,226	21.3	1,091,939	49.8	1,393,668	70.5	952,112	75.0
35	New Mexico............................	33,818	26.3	263,150	56.7	290,266	74.5	246,773	83.2
36	New York...............................	201,346	14.8	2,389,461	41.2	2,911,618	62.0	2,150,241	66.0
37	North Carolina........................	176,627	15.8	1,332,698	52.8	1,555,576	74.3	1,114,731	81.3
38	North Dakota..........................	28,239	13.2	116,365	55.8	99,800	75.9	78,107	75.7
39	Ohio......................................	201,952	19.8	1,527,328	55.4	1,760,250	74.0	1,343,392	78.8
40	Oklahoma..............................	83,155	17.5	527,464	53.6	529,535	73.2	407,813	80.6
41	Oregon..................................	64,793	8.3	574,159	49.3	577,434	72.1	486,213	78.5
42	Pennsylvania..........................	157,082	17.9	1,596,855	57.6	1,925,168	77.4	1,549,851	78.7
72	Puerto Rico............................	16,307	11.3	269,751	45.2	428,064	72.3	451,860	81.3
44	Rhode Island..........................	11,939	9.5	138,765	49.4	165,432	71.9	124,034	72.4
45	South Carolina........................	73,041	23.5	633,057	58.6	742,405	76.4	601,469	85.7
46	South Dakota	23,317	22.9	114,113	62.6	119,568	78.1	99,889	77.6
47	Tennessee..............................	119,026	16.5	899,300	52.6	1,005,322	75.2	746,747	83.0
48	Texas	530,049	13.6	4,057,366	50.3	3,841,670	72.4	2,367,162	78.9
49	Utah......................................	74,407	20.0	443,677	62.5	354,794	80.0	228,621	83.9
50	Vermont................................	9,528	15.7	79,385	60.0	99,764	81.1	81,486	81.3
51	Virginia.................................	121,134	15.8	1,109,870	53.7	1,234,847	75.7	865,610	81.1
53	Washington............................	119,196	12.1	1,100,204	50.8	1,045,903	73.5	756,952	78.3
54	West Virginia..........................	29,685	21.2	196,894	63.3	261,136	80.6	234,486	85.9
55	Wisconsin..............................	117,581	15.0	773,412	58.2	888,232	76.2	670,745	78.1
56	Wyoming................................	14,947	19.4	81,551	62.5	81,243	78.0	65,022	86.1

NA = Not available.
'- = The median falls in the lowest interval of an open-ended distribution.
¹A value of 10.0 represents the minimum percentage range--10 percent or less.

Table C-1. States — Where: Migration, Housing, and Transportation, 2021—*Continued*

State code	STATE	Homeownership by household type								Average household size			Percent of housing units that are crowded or lacking complete plumbing
		Married-couple family households		Male householder families, no spouse present		Female householder families, no spouse present		Nonfamily households		All households	Owner-occupied households	Renter-occupied households	
		Number of householders	Percent owners	Number of householders	Percent owners	Number of householders	Percent owners	Number of householders	Percent owners				
	ACS table number:	B25115	B25115	B25115	B25115	B25115	B25115	B25115	B25115	B25010	B25010	B25010	C25016
	Column number	28	29	30	31	32	33	34	35	36	37	38	39
00	**UNITED STATES**............	60,360,084	81.7	6,433,318	56.9	15,671,584	49.0	45,079,744	50.4	2.54	2.65	2.33	3.6
01	Alabama......................	904,392	86.1	90,366	63.3	276,625	53.0	696,176	56.7	2.50	2.59	2.30	2.3
02	Alaska........................	129,937	79.0	14,924	62.2	27,515	57.0	98,935	54.1	2.61	2.75	2.32	10.0
04	Arizona.......................	1,344,242	82.2	163,839	56.2	338,277	51.8	971,365	54.9	2.53	2.59	2.41	5.2
05	Arkansas.....................	565,893	82.7	59,813	57.3	151,925	47.9	406,044	53.7	2.49	2.55	2.37	2.9
06	California....................	6,517,082	70.0	864,894	45.8	1,764,642	42.2	4,282,445	42.1	2.86	2.96	2.73	8.6
08	Colorado.....................	1,124,072	83.4	107,081	60.0	217,502	55.3	864,387	49.1	2.46	2.60	2.19	2.9
09	Connecticut.................	664,848	84.6	64,625	58.2	186,889	49.7	511,951	50.5	2.45	2.59	2.17	1.9
10	Delaware.....................	186,477	87.3	18,932	67.6	50,999	54.3	139,248	60.2	2.47	2.54	2.29	2.0
11	District of Columbia..........	77,478	68.8	9,856	36.2	41,399	38.9	190,832	31.4	1.98	2.23	1.81	3.9
12	Florida.......................	3,975,785	80.7	430,783	57.6	1,104,097	51.0	3,054,664	57.4	2.49	2.53	2.43	3.1
13	Georgia......................	1,881,572	83.0	192,141	58.2	601,549	48.1	1,325,847	51.3	2.64	2.74	2.43	2.8
15	Hawaii.......................	248,069	70.1	26,631	62.6	60,199	60.9	155,181	51.2	2.86	2.96	2.67	9.4
16	Idaho........................	385,704	83.8	30,931	56.5	59,835	59.7	217,412	56.2	2.70	2.80	2.44	3.2
17	Illinois.......................	2,300,396	85.0	240,515	59.9	594,689	52.4	1,856,041	51.6	2.48	2.62	2.18	2.8
18	Indiana......................	1,285,451	87.2	130,454	66.5	301,543	54.8	963,246	55.3	2.47	2.59	2.17	2.0
19	Iowa.........................	638,989	89.6	54,496	65.1	114,021	55.7	492,961	53.5	2.38	2.53	2.02	1.8
20	Kansas.......................	574,260	84.1	53,926	53.9	112,843	48.4	417,997	50.3	2.47	2.61	2.18	2.5
21	Kentucky.....................	850,400	84.9	91,550	60.6	217,582	49.4	626,150	54.4	2.46	2.56	2.23	2.1
22	Louisiana....................	756,880	85.7	96,044	62.5	285,207	48.5	645,793	54.7	2.52	2.58	2.40	2.8
23	Maine........................	288,115	90.3	23,378	71.9	53,733	59.9	228,400	59.1	2.25	2.38	1.88	2.4
24	Maryland.....................	1,108,456	83.8	115,941	61.4	324,757	51.7	806,498	53.3	2.56	2.67	2.32	2.2
25	Massachusetts...............	1,268,347	82.4	123,694	57.8	327,491	47.8	1,039,486	45.2	2.44	2.62	2.14	2.0
26	Michigan.....................	1,875,558	89.2	202,365	71.0	471,619	56.0	1,502,256	58.9	2.43	2.54	2.13	1.9
27	Minnesota....................	1,122,121	89.9	101,601	67.0	203,499	59.1	853,812	54.8	2.45	2.59	2.05	2.3
28	Mississippi...................	498,803	85.6	52,635	59.9	191,413	50.8	386,760	59.7	2.54	2.57	2.45	3.2
29	Missouri......................	1,176,418	86.2	108,954	63.1	270,371	49.9	912,983	52.6	2.43	2.57	2.14	2.0
30	Montana......................	219,056	86.2	20,003	58.3	36,564	56.7	173,326	52.3	2.40	2.52	2.13	2.4
31	Nebraska.....................	391,102	85.9	34,063	57.3	69,977	52.5	290,840	48.3	2.44	2.60	2.10	2.2
32	Nevada.......................	522,193	75.2	79,604	46.9	151,899	45.2	437,684	47.0	2.61	2.69	2.49	5.0
33	New Hampshire..............	286,604	87.3	25,947	72.2	48,658	55.5	186,817	54.2	2.46	2.62	2.06	1.6
34	New Jersey...................	1,763,645	79.4	173,007	53.5	442,676	48.1	1,118,617	48.9	2.60	2.73	2.36	3.5
35	New Mexico..................	357,938	83.5	50,975	63.8	113,738	59.0	311,356	58.2	2.49	2.59	2.25	4.1
36	New York.....................	3,268,729	73.9	395,689	49.5	1,051,332	40.2	2,936,916	41.0	2.52	2.68	2.31	5.3
37	North Carolina...............	1,976,957	83.8	181,424	57.4	527,314	48.3	1,493,937	52.2	2.46	2.55	2.28	2.8
38	North Dakota.................	148,550	84.4	17,460	56.6	24,508	46.8	131,993	43.1	2.33	2.54	1.97	1.5
39	Ohio.........................	2,162,168	86.4	230,594	60.7	593,693	47.0	1,846,467	52.0	2.38	2.50	2.12	1.5
40	Oklahoma....................	731,871	82.0	80,753	52.7	187,228	46.6	548,115	51.8	2.51	2.60	2.35	3.1
41	Oregon.......................	806,612	81.6	82,016	53.8	165,404	49.5	648,567	46.5	2.44	2.57	2.21	3.5
42	Pennsylvania.................	2,449,955	87.1	242,449	64.9	606,151	53.5	1,930,401	53.9	2.40	2.53	2.10	1.7
72	Puerto Rico..................	401,781	84.5	76,653	65.3	260,419	57.0	427,129	61.5	2.77	2.83	2.64	NA
44	Rhode Island.................	194,722	84.1	21,138	61.0	52,858	43.8	171,452	45.8	2.39	2.56	2.11	2.0
45	South Carolina...............	964,209	87.0	92,193	57.3	280,887	52.8	712,683	60.5	2.47	2.53	2.33	2.1
46	South Dakota.................	175,003	87.1	16,528	56.2	29,683	51.5	135,673	52.1	2.42	2.56	2.11	2.8
47	Tennessee....................	1,303,575	83.4	131,888	56.9	347,350	49.5	987,582	54.1	2.46	2.54	2.31	2.2
48	Texas........................	5,341,490	79.6	571,198	54.4	1,460,497	48.0	3,423,062	43.8	2.68	2.86	2.38	5.4
49	Utah.........................	652,738	81.5	51,037	62.9	94,270	56.9	303,454	49.5	2.99	3.20	2.51	4.1
50	Vermont......................	130,749	89.6	10,678	66.6	23,612	59.7	105,124	55.2	2.29	2.42	1.96	1.6
51	Virginia......................	1,629,590	83.3	153,061	60.6	382,293	49.5	1,166,517	52.5	2.52	2.64	2.28	2.2
53	Washington..................	1,503,723	80.6	139,845	56.7	293,513	49.4	1,085,174	45.9	2.51	2.66	2.25	3.2
54	West Virginia.................	345,572	88.7	35,843	70.6	80,913	61.9	259,873	61.9	2.41	2.50	2.14	1.9
55	Wisconsin....................	1,162,694	87.7	114,292	59.8	237,670	48.2	935,314	49.8	2.35	2.49	2.04	2.1
56	Wyoming.....................	120,894	87.5	11,264	59.7	18,675	53.7	91,930	55.2	2.33	2.45	2.02	2.5

NA = Not available.
'- = The median falls in the lowest interval of an open-ended distribution.
[1] A value of 10.0 represents the minimum percentage range--10 percent or less.

Table C-1. States — Where: Migration, Housing, and Transportation, 2021—*Continued*

	STATE	Median household income in the past 12 months (in 2019 inflation-adjusted dollars)					Median housinng value (owner estimated)		
		All households	Owner-occupied households			Renter-occupied households	All owner-occupied households	Households with a mortgage	Households without a mortgage
			All owner-occupied households	Households with a mortgage	Households without a mortgage				
	ACS table number:	B25119	B25099	B25099	B25099	B25119	B25097	B25097	B25097
State code	Column number	40	41	42	43	44	45	46	47
00	UNITED STATES............................	69,717	86,236	101,885	62,803	44,913	281,400	309,000	233,600
01	Alabama..	53,913	66,971	83,673	48,918	32,656	172,800	198,700	143,700
02	Alaska...	77,845	98,476	111,511	74,430	50,421	304,900	323,100	262,300
04	Arizona...	69,056	81,852	96,135	59,547	47,467	336,300	360,300	278,000
05	Arkansas.......................................	52,528	65,939	80,393	50,123	34,724	162,300	175,400	137,100
06	California......................................	84,907	109,974	125,821	78,444	60,769	648,100	667,700	598,000
08	Colorado.......................................	82,254	101,183	112,931	73,335	53,626	466,200	476,100	437,200
09	Connecticut...................................	83,771	108,715	121,125	86,182	44,483	311,500	315,800	302,900
10	Delaware.......................................	71,091	83,523	95,262	62,600	45,022	300,500	305,100	290,400
11	District of Columbia......................	90,088	150,878	163,111	108,852	64,150	669,900	666,200	682,500
12	Florida..	63,062	75,169	88,181	57,522	44,720	290,700	309,400	261,800
13	Georgia...	66,559	83,377	97,240	59,081	42,831	249,700	271,000	201,200
15	Hawaii..	84,857	102,536	116,392	76,957	61,905	722,500	729,800	706,700
16	Idaho..	66,474	77,902	88,360	58,850	45,482	369,300	387,200	328,700
17	Illinois..	72,205	89,139	103,775	67,495	42,573	231,500	247,500	203,400
18	Indiana...	62,743	76,001	86,256	57,347	38,099	182,400	194,600	160,300
19	Iowa...	65,600	80,601	92,167	62,057	37,698	174,400	187,600	158,700
20	Kansas..	64,124	79,666	94,440	61,250	40,311	183,800	207,800	154,300
21	Kentucky.......................................	55,573	69,843	84,584	51,023	33,690	173,300	193,800	145,000
22	Louisiana......................................	52,087	67,030	84,006	48,770	30,488	192,800	216,300	161,300
23	Maine...	64,767	78,038	92,405	55,019	37,400	252,100	268,600	225,400
24	Maryland.......................................	90,203	112,839	125,746	81,155	53,062	370,800	379,600	346,000
25	Massachusetts...............................	89,645	117,790	133,816	84,136	51,250	480,600	487,600	465,400
26	Michigan.......................................	63,498	75,792	89,972	57,004	36,548	199,100	219,300	169,200
27	Minnesota.....................................	77,720	93,692	107,022	70,399	44,761	285,400	295,700	265,200
28	Mississippi....................................	48,716	61,012	80,190	43,951	29,577	145,600	177,700	105,900
29	Missouri..	61,847	76,375	89,131	57,294	37,088	198,300	214,400	170,100
30	Montana..	63,249	74,506	92,127	55,393	41,036	322,800	349,300	282,700
31	Nebraska.......................................	66,817	84,509	98,059	64,176	40,330	204,900	220,900	174,500
32	Nevada..	66,274	84,619	93,806	65,817	44,986	373,000	380,300	353,600
33	New Hampshire..............................	88,465	103,743	121,643	75,157	53,114	345,200	353,700	327,100
34	New Jersey.....................................	89,296	115,188	131,170	87,107	52,644	389,800	400,400	370,900
35	New Mexico...................................	53,992	65,720	82,663	50,699	35,289	214,000	240,700	171,100
36	New York.......................................	74,314	99,105	115,791	75,260	49,002	368,800	392,900	331,600
37	North Carolina...............................	61,972	76,454	90,896	54,273	40,508	236,900	261,300	186,200
38	North Dakota.................................	66,519	85,061	100,215	66,845	39,868	224,400	243,400	193,800
39	Ohio...	62,262	78,736	91,272	59,117	36,806	180,200	194,800	160,800
40	Oklahoma......................................	55,826	70,277	84,879	53,704	36,042	168,500	186,100	144,900
41	Oregon..	71,562	89,169	103,145	62,684	48,329	422,700	436,200	391,100
42	Pennsylvania.................................	68,957	84,101	101,122	61,070	40,806	222,300	242,400	190,800
72	Puerto Rico....................................	22,237	27,185	40,665	20,612	13,807	114,100	130,900	100,800
44	Rhode Island.................................	74,008	99,820	107,245	75,150	42,010	348,100	350,000	343,900
45	South Carolina...............................	59,318	70,378	84,653	52,478	37,441	213,500	239,500	168,000
46	South Dakota.................................	66,143	80,033	89,568	64,953	39,971	219,900	240,900	180,400
47	Tennessee......................................	59,695	72,706	87,047	54,171	39,100	235,200	257,700	197,000
48	Texas..	66,963	85,893	103,831	63,903	44,589	237,400	270,600	185,300
49	Utah...	79,449	96,897	103,659	77,336	49,434	421,700	427,700	404,500
50	Vermont..	72,431	85,818	97,846	63,457	40,992	271,500	281,100	254,800
51	Virginia...	80,963	100,476	115,229	68,056	50,821	330,600	357,400	270,900
53	Washington...................................	84,247	103,745	118,975	75,015	55,973	485,700	505,800	441,200
54	West Virginia.................................	51,248	62,096	81,194	47,312	28,353	143,200	170,900	110,300
55	Wisconsin......................................	67,125	82,908	96,125	63,170	41,326	230,700	239,500	215,300
56	Wyoming.......................................	65,204	79,442	89,705	63,285	35,948	266,400	274,200	250,900

NA = Not available.
'- = The median falls in the lowest interval of an open-ended distribution.
¹A value of 10.0 represents the minimum percentage range--10 percent or less.

	STATE	Owner occupied housing units			Median monthly housing costs for all housing units with costs (dollars)	Gross rent for renter-occupied housing units		Median selected monthly owner costs for owner-occupied housing units			Median annual real estate taxes paid by owner-occupied housing units (dollars)
		Total owner-occupied housing units	Percent with a mortgage	Percent with a second mortgage, or a home equity loan, or both		Median gross rent (dollars)	As a percentage of household income	All owner-occupied households	Households with a mortgage	Households without a mortgage	
	ACS table number:	B25081	B25081	B25081	B25105	B25064	B25071	B25088	B25088	B25088	B25103
State code	Column number	48	49	50	51	52	53	54	55	56	57
00	UNITED STATES..............................	83,396,988	61.3	7.6	1,182	1,191	30.6	1,174	1,672	539	2,795
01	Alabama...............................	1,377,932	53.6	5.6	808	861	30.0	760	1,223	379	674
02	Alaska................................	181,145	61.0	3.8	1,332	1,259	29.9	1,403	1,926	619	3,570
04	Arizona...............................	1,905,690	63.3	5.5	1,183	1,253	30.8	1,124	1,544	440	1,707
05	Arkansas..............................	793,038	54.0	3.4	778	820	28.0	737	1,147	372	928
06	California.............................	7,502,706	68.0	7.4	1,810	1,750	33.1	1,912	2,523	694	4,585
08	Colorado..............................	1,546,233	69.7	8.3	1,526	1,491	31.6	1,558	1,962	551	2,259
09	Connecticut...........................	951,516	65.3	10.7	1,487	1,277	31.2	1,660	2,083	926	6,096
10	Delaware..............................	287,111	63.7	8.9	1,190	1,208	30.1	1,175	1,585	463	1,602
11	District of Columbia..................	132,936	75.3	10.2	1,817	1,668	29.1	2,196	2,639	748	3,699
12	Florida................................	5,772,329	56.7	6.1	1,217	1,348	34.6	1,105	1,616	548	2,338
13	Georgia...............................	2,642,126	63.8	6.1	1,131	1,153	30.8	1,112	1,501	457	2,027
15	Hawaii................................	306,653	64.2	13.3	1,765	1,774	33.7	1,790	2,584	596	1,971
16	Idaho.................................	498,872	64.0	9.2	1,043	1,035	28.5	1,048	1,425	419	1,817
17	Illinois...............................	3,370,654	61.3	7.0	1,177	1,106	29.2	1,234	1,717	666	4,800
18	Indiana...............................	1,905,849	64.3	8.9	899	905	28.6	895	1,195	437	1,371
19	Iowa..................................	935,111	60.2	8.2	906	847	27.8	957	1,328	521	2,618
20	Kansas................................	776,740	57.9	6.8	939	904	26.8	969	1,446	534	2,445
21	Kentucky..............................	1,225,996	57.1	8.4	827	830	28.3	825	1,227	405	1,382
22	Louisiana.............................	1,200,910	53.1	4.6	869	924	33.5	807	1,349	372	1,065
23	Maine.................................	444,231	60.3	10.7	998	945	29.1	1,034	1,464	521	2,756
24	Maryland..............................	1,597,663	71.5	10.1	1,559	1,473	31.2	1,631	2,013	638	3,660
25	Massachusetts.........................	1,742,436	67.9	13.2	1,680	1,487	30.8	1,840	2,323	871	5,361
26	Michigan..............................	2,966,347	59.0	7.4	962	969	30.1	958	1,348	521	2,636
27	Minnesota.............................	1,665,101	64.3	8.4	1,192	1,113	29.3	1,246	1,667	590	2,915
28	Mississippi...........................	787,068	48.6	4.5	747	831	31.3	672	1,200	356	1,097
29	Missouri..............................	1,698,595	61.1	6.5	915	882	28.1	946	1,316	465	1,746
30	Montana...............................	311,861	54.8	5.8	919	883	26.2	959	1,558	476	2,390
31	Nebraska..............................	532,582	59.7	7.3	993	912	28.4	1,076	1,491	562	3,091
32	Nevada................................	704,548	67.6	4.9	1,297	1,311	33.0	1,281	1,625	456	1,807
33	New Hampshire.........................	397,225	62.9	9.5	1,433	1,263	28.2	1,535	2,004	860	6,097
34	New Jersey............................	2,252,974	64.3	9.6	1,674	1,457	30.9	1,899	2,458	1,081	8,796
35	New Mexico............................	579,708	52.6	4.6	868	906	29.6	830	1,354	386	1,557
36	New York..............................	4,239,037	58.2	9.6	1,431	1,409	31.8	1,454	2,199	813	5,974
37	North Carolina........................	2,794,211	62.0	8.3	999	1,026	29.4	978	1,387	420	1,668
38	North Dakota..........................	203,549	52.7	5.4	855	839	25.1	874	1,488	494	2,107
39	Ohio..................................	3,246,486	61.4	10.4	914	870	27.7	953	1,293	503	2,534
40	Oklahoma..............................	1,013,837	53.7	3.8	838	855	28.5	817	1,295	431	1,424
41	Oregon................................	1,086,030	65.0	7.7	1,331	1,282	30.9	1,385	1,835	595	3,479
42	Pennsylvania..........................	3,657,478	58.6	11.8	1,037	1,036	29.1	1,038	1,505	544	3,018
72	Puerto Rico...........................	800,555	36.9	0.9	343	504	30.9	259	823	148	649
44	Rhode Island..........................	278,449	67.9	13.0	1,383	1,142	29.4	1,602	1,932	762	4,518
45	South Carolina........................	1,471,296	57.2	6.1	909	976	30.5	855	1,289	382	1,105
46	South Dakota..........................	247,630	54.7	6.1	894	830	25.1	949	1,415	525	2,370
47	Tennessee.............................	1,869,046	58.7	6.5	934	981	29.3	891	1,333	398	1,317
48	Texas.................................	6,761,002	56.6	3.2	1,177	1,167	30.5	1,192	1,765	567	3,797
49	Utah..................................	768,062	69.6	9.7	1,293	1,208	29.3	1,350	1,671	480	2,191
50	Vermont...............................	196,291	60.5	10.7	1,215	1,115	30.0	1,264	1,664	729	4,697
51	Virginia..............................	2,252,170	68.0	9.3	1,348	1,331	29.8	1,361	1,818	494	2,485
53	Washington............................	1,933,901	66.7	8.2	1,551	1,484	29.6	1,613	2,110	667	4,061
54	West Virginia.........................	542,805	46.2	6.4	645	767	29.9	576	1,071	338	785
55	Wisconsin.............................	1,668,575	61.6	10.1	996	921	27.1	1,076	1,464	574	3,484
56	Wyoming...............................	173,247	58.2	5.6	966	889	29.1	1,043	1,490	456	1,452

NA = Not available.
'- = The median falls in the lowest interval of an open-ended distribution.
¹A value of 10.0 represents the minimum percentage range--10 percent or less.

State code	STATE	Median selected monthly owner costs as a percentage of household income			Households who pay 30 percent or more of income for housing expenses by tenure and age of householder (percent)							
					Owner-occupied households				Renter-occupied households			
		All owner-occupied households	Households with a mortgage	Households without a mortgage[1]	Householder 15 to 24 years	Householder 25 to 34 years	Householder 35 to 64 years	Householder 65 years and over	Householder 15 to 24 years	Householder 25 to 34 years	Householder 35 to 64 years	Householder 65 years and over
	ACS table number:	B25092	B25092	B25092	C25093	C25093	C25093	C25093	B25072	B25072	B25072	B25072
	Column number	58	59	60	61	62	63	64	65	66	67	68
00	UNITED STATES............................	17.4	20.8	11.0	33.1	21.9	19.8	25.8	57.1	43.6	44.8	55.5
01	Alabama................................	14.8	18.9	10.0-	28.4	18.3	15.5	20.2	52.7	43.7	40.8	45.2
02	Alaska..................................	17.8	21.8	10.0-	39.5	26.9	22.8	24.0	56.3	42.6	41.2	53.7
04	Arizona.................................	16.9	20.6	10.0-	34.9	23.2	18.3	23.6	57.2	46.6	43.3	56.8
05	Arkansas................................	14.7	18.7	10.0-	27.2	18.3	15.2	20.1	41.3	37.1	38.8	47.0
06	California...............................	21.0	24.7	11.2	45.6	33.4	28.6	33.7	66.2	49.3	50.4	61.8
08	Colorado................................	18.6	21.9	10.0-	40.7	26.2	21.2	27.1	64.1	45.7	47.7	59.1
09	Connecticut............................	19.4	21.8	13.8	46.0	25.0	22.6	33.2	63.7	45.4	45.7	56.4
10	Delaware...............................	16.9	20.5	10.0-	19.2	25.1	19.1	21.8	58.2	55.9	41.0	45.6
11	District of Columbia....................	18.2	20.5	10.0-	63.3	21.8	19.4	31.0	60.0	37.4	46.6	52.1
12	Florida..................................	18.4	22.8	11.9	41.0	25.9	23.6	27.9	63.3	52.9	52.8	60.9
13	Georgia.................................	16.4	19.6	10.0-	34.7	21.1	18.0	23.1	56.4	47.9	44.0	53.7
15	Hawaii..................................	20.5	26.1	10.0-	49.9	46.9	31.2	28.9	70.4	60.5	48.9	52.4
16	Idaho...................................	16.8	20.4	10.0-	23.7	21.1	18.6	22.8	53.0	42.2	36.7	53.3
17	Illinois..................................	17.8	20.7	12.4	31.3	20.1	19.5	26.9	56.0	38.2	41.9	54.8
18	Indiana.................................	15.2	18.0	10.0-	22.0	13.9	13.8	20.0	55.5	37.6	39.5	53.9
19	Iowa....................................	15.9	18.7	10.8	25.0	15.1	14.3	21.1	50.2	34.9	38.5	47.3
20	Kansas..................................	16.3	19.3	11.2	41.1	15.0	15.0	22.0	49.8	34.4	35.2	50.8
21	Kentucky...............................	15.6	19.0	10.3	28.4	19.4	15.9	20.6	48.8	35.3	40.3	43.6
22	Louisiana...............................	15.5	20.2	10.0-	28.1	22.5	19.0	21.3	56.3	48.0	45.5	53.1
23	Maine...................................	17.2	20.0	11.8	18.3	16.5	18.5	25.5	49.0	38.6	41.3	48.6
24	Maryland...............................	17.9	20.3	10.0	38.6	23.2	19.9	26.5	64.4	46.0	45.9	58.3
25	Massachusetts..........................	19.4	21.8	13.3	42.6	25.8	22.2	34.4	61.0	42.3	47.6	54.5
26	Michigan................................	16.5	19.2	11.7	29.3	18.0	17.0	23.1	57.6	41.9	42.9	52.7
27	Minnesota..............................	16.8	19.6	10.4	31.2	17.4	16.3	23.4	55.0	37.8	41.6	57.4
28	Mississippi..............................	15.1	19.7	10.0-	22.8	20.6	18.5	18.4	54.8	43.9	42.4	45.2
29	Missouri................................	15.9	18.9	10.3	26.4	15.0	15.3	21.8	53.9	39.5	38.1	48.8
30	Montana................................	16.9	21.3	10.6	40.2	24.0	18.8	22.6	52.5	36.9	32.2	41.7
31	Nebraska...............................	16.5	19.5	11.3	24.7	16.7	15.7	20.9	52.9	36.1	37.9	54.4
32	Nevada.................................	18.1	21.9	10.0-	26.9	27.4	22.2	26.7	57.3	51.0	48.2	63.6
33	New Hampshire.........................	19.0	21.3	14.0	24.2	19.5	19.9	29.6	51.0	34.7	40.5	53.3
34	New Jersey..............................	20.8	23.4	15.0	43.0	27.5	25.7	36.5	62.3	43.9	47.3	56.7
35	New Mexico.............................	15.8	20.8	10.0-	31.7	24.5	19.2	21.9	59.3	40.7	41.2	49.9
36	New York...............................	18.9	22.5	13.4	37.2	24.9	24.8	31.6	57.4	45.6	48.9	57.1
37	North Carolina..........................	16.2	19.3	10.0-	29.7	17.1	16.6	23.6	56.6	40.7	41.3	52.6
38	North Dakota...........................	15.0	19.3	10.0-	38.2	15.9	15.1	17.8	63.2	21.9	32.2	48.3
39	Ohio....................................	15.8	18.5	11.0	23.2	14.3	14.5	22.6	49.4	36.6	38.1	47.8
40	Oklahoma...............................	15.4	19.4	10.0	31.2	18.3	15.6	20.0	51.1	40.5	37.7	49.8
41	Oregon.................................	19.1	22.5	11.9	26.4	26.1	23.4	28.2	64.2	44.4	43.2	60.8
42	Pennsylvania............................	16.3	19.0	11.4	34.8	16.4	16.1	23.9	52.1	40.1	40.3	54.4
72	Puerto Rico.............................	13.8	24.9	10.0-	34.5	22.4	21.1	17.2	35.6	33.2	26.9	29.5
44	Rhode Island............................	19.8	22.3	13.4	32.1	26.6	25.4	31.9	73.5	39.9	44.5	47.3
45	South Carolina..........................	15.5	19.4	10.0-	22.0	19.8	17.4	21.4	55.9	46.1	40.7	49.8
46	South Dakota...........................	16.4	20.5	10.3	19.8	20.1	14.6	22.8	44.0	34.5	24.6	48.7
47	Tennessee..............................	15.8	19.6	10.0-	25.6	19.4	16.8	19.8	55.0	42.5	40.3	50.0
48	Texas...................................	17.5	21.5	11.4	41.8	25.5	19.8	23.9	58.1	43.2	44.7	58.5
49	Utah....................................	17.1	20.2	10.0-	34.9	24.1	16.1	21.9	56.4	42.1	40.5	54.1
50	Vermont................................	18.9	21.7	13.9	48.2	23.4	20.4	29.3	64.0	39.1	45.2	51.4
51	Virginia.................................	17.2	20.1	10.0-	47.1	21.5	17.6	23.5	57.8	43.8	42.4	54.7
53	Washington.............................	18.9	22.2	11.0	34.6	24.1	21.0	27.6	59.4	38.9	44.5	57.9
54	West Virginia...........................	13.4	17.4	10.0-	26.2	16.9	14.6	14.4	53.7	38.3	38.5	42.1
55	Wisconsin...............................	17.0	19.5	11.6	24.0	15.4	15.5	24.8	51.7	34.9	35.1	53.2
56	Wyoming................................	16.8	21.1	10.0-	20.9	29.5	18.0	19.8	47.0	42.6	39.8	57.3

NA = Not available.
'- = The median falls in the lowest interval of an open-ended distribution.
[1] A value of 10.0 represents the minimum percentage range--10 percent or less.

Table C-1. States — Where: Migration, Housing, and Transportation, 2021—*Continued*

State code	STATE	Total number of workers 16 years and over	Means of transportation to work (percent)						
			Car, truck, or van		Public transportation (excluding taxicab)	Bicycle	Walked	Taxicab, motorcycle, or other means	Worked at home
			Drove alone	Car-pooled					
	ACS table number:	B08301	B08301	B08301	B08301	B08301	B08301	B08301	B08301
	Column number	69	70	71	72	73	74	75	76
00	UNITED STATES.............................	154,314,179	67.8	7.8	2.5	0.4	2.2	1.5	17.9
01	Alabama...............................	2,165,588	80.5	7.6	0.2	0.1	0.9	1.0	9.6
02	Alaska..................................	343,883	66.2	11.1	0.9	0.9	6.8	3.9	10.3
04	Arizona................................	3,280,184	65.8	8.9	0.9	0.4	1.6	1.6	20.7
05	Arkansas..............................	1,307,917	78.9	8.8	0.2	0.1	1.3	0.9	9.7
06	California..............................	17,811,184	63.7	8.4	2.1	0.6	2.1	1.7	21.4
08	Colorado..............................	2,992,582	63.7	7.1	1.3	0.8	2.3	1.2	23.7
09	Connecticut..........................	1,778,730	66.6	7.4	2.5	0.2	2.5	1.3	19.5
10	Delaware..............................	455,993	70.5	6.3	1.6	0.4	1.3	1.4	18.6
11	District of Columbia..............	354,033	25.6	3.0	11.6	2.1	6.7	2.6	48.3
12	Florida.................................	9,859,704	70.5	8.5	1.0	0.4	1.3	1.7	16.6
13	Georgia................................	4,982,073	70.0	8.3	0.7	0.1	1.2	1.5	18.2
15	Hawaii..................................	668,446	65.3	13.9	3.3	0.7	4.0	2.0	10.7
16	Idaho...................................	889,536	74.4	8.2	0.5	0.8	1.9	1.1	13.3
17	Illinois.................................	5,975,117	64.9	7.4	3.8	0.5	2.6	1.5	19.3
18	Indiana................................	3,196,939	76.6	7.8	0.6	0.4	2.0	0.8	11.9
19	Iowa....................................	1,588,122	74.4	7.5	0.5	0.3	2.8	1.1	13.4
20	Kansas.................................	1,429,591	74.4	7.9	0.3	0.3	2.2	1.1	13.8
21	Kentucky..............................	1,962,428	76.4	8.4	0.5	0.2	2.0	1.0	11.5
22	Louisiana..............................	1,939,334	79.3	8.3	0.7	0.4	1.4	1.5	8.4
23	Maine...................................	660,465	69.2	7.7	0.3	0.3	3.8	1.0	17.7
24	Maryland..............................	3,052,346	62.2	7.0	3.0	0.2	1.8	1.8	24.0
25	Massachusetts......................	3,525,906	59.5	6.3	4.5	0.6	3.7	1.7	23.7
26	Michigan..............................	4,526,178	72.5	7.2	0.8	0.3	1.8	1.0	16.4
27	Minnesota............................	2,908,142	66.5	7.1	1.4	0.4	2.5	1.2	20.9
28	Mississippi...........................	1,215,180	83.0	7.8	0.2	0.0	1.0	1.6	6.3
29	Missouri...............................	2,909,996	73.9	7.6	0.8	0.1	1.8	1.0	14.7
30	Montana...............................	522,807	71.3	8.7	0.4	1.2	3.6	0.8	14.0
31	Nebraska..............................	1,009,912	75.0	8.0	0.4	0.3	2.4	1.1	12.8
32	Nevada................................	1,405,397	70.4	10.3	2.0	0.2	1.3	2.9	13.0
33	New Hampshire.....................	733,129	70.0	7.0	0.3	0.1	2.2	1.2	19.3
34	New Jersey...........................	4,414,552	59.9	7.1	5.9	0.3	2.4	2.3	22.1
35	New Mexico..........................	877,399	72.2	8.5	0.4	0.6	1.6	1.5	15.2
36	New York..............................	9,017,848	49.2	5.9	17.3	0.8	5.3	1.9	19.6
37	North Carolina......................	4,887,692	70.4	7.5	0.5	0.1	1.4	1.3	18.8
38	North Dakota........................	397,892	78.5	7.7	0.3	0.2	3.0	1.3	8.9
39	Ohio....................................	5,492,694	73.9	7.2	0.8	0.3	1.8	1.1	14.8
40	Oklahoma.............................	1,773,947	77.2	8.7	0.2	0.2	1.8	1.6	10.4
41	Oregon................................	1,970,090	62.6	7.8	1.7	1.1	3.0	1.2	22.7
42	Pennsylvania.........................	6,072,593	66.8	7.0	2.8	0.4	2.9	1.3	18.7
72	Puerto Rico...........................	1,055,607	81.7	6.3	0.7	0.1	2.5	1.3	7.4
44	Rhode Island.........................	533,088	69.3	7.6	1.2	0.2	2.6	1.5	17.5
45	South Carolina......................	2,320,907	76.6	8.1	0.3	0.2	1.6	1.4	11.7
46	South Dakota........................	445,606	76.1	7.8	0.4	0.3	3.2	1.1	11.1
47	Tennessee.............................	3,194,798	75.8	7.5	0.4	0.1	1.1	1.1	14.0
48	Texas...................................	13,635,342	70.7	9.1	0.8	0.2	1.3	1.6	16.3
49	Utah....................................	1,633,712	66.3	8.8	1.3	0.6	1.9	1.0	20.0
50	Vermont...............................	327,910	67.2	7.4	0.5	0.5	3.9	0.9	19.6
51	Virginia................................	4,262,832	65.6	7.0	1.5	0.2	2.0	1.3	22.3
53	Washington...........................	3,668,157	62.0	7.1	2.1	0.6	2.8	1.3	24.2
54	West Virginia.........................	707,299	77.1	8.8	0.4	0.2	2.1	1.1	10.2
55	Wisconsin.............................	2,945,351	73.4	6.6	0.9	0.5	2.7	1.2	14.8
56	Wyoming..............................	283,628	75.9	9.2	0.8	0.8	3.4	1.0	8.9

NA = Not available.
'- = The median falls in the lowest interval of an open-ended distribution.
¹A value of 10.0 represents the minimum percentage range--10 percent or less.

Table C-1. States — Where: Migration, Housing, and Transportation, 2021—*Continued*

State code	STATE	Number of workers who did not work at home	Mean travel time to work (minutes)				Number of households	Vehicles available (percent of households)				Average vehicles per household
			All workers who did not work at home	By car, truck, or van	Public transportation	Taxicab, motorcycle, bicycle, walked, or by other means		No vehicles	One vehicle	Two vehicles	Three or more vehicles	
	ACS table number:	B08301	C08136/C08301	C08136/C08301	C08136/C08301	C08136/C08301	B08201	B08201	B08201	B08201	B08201	B25046/B08201
	Column number	77	78	79	80	81	82	83	84	85	86	87
00	UNITED STATES..................	126,746,081	25.6	25.3	48.9	18.2	127,544,730	8.0	32.9	37.1	21.9	1.83
01	Alabama..............................	1,956,821	25.3	25.3	31.6	24.1	1,967,559	4.8	31.9	36.6	26.7	1.98
02	Alaska	308,421	19.8	19.3	35.7	21.5	271,311	9.3	31.1	37.8	21.9	1.84
04	Arizona...............................	2,599,725	24.8	24.8	47.0	19.3	2,817,723	5.0	33.3	38.8	22.9	1.90
05	Arkansas.............................	1,180,532	22.2	22.4	24.0	18.3	1,183,675	5.7	32.2	38.5	23.6	1.90
06	California............................	13,999,114	27.6	27.5	48.7	19.0	13,429,063	6.8	30.6	36.7	25.9	1.96
08	Colorado	2,281,922	25.0	24.8	45.2	21.3	2,313,042	5.0	30.1	39.4	25.5	1.98
09	Connecticut.........................	1,432,375	25.6	25.1	58.4	13.7	1,428,313	8.4	33.6	37.5	20.4	1.79
10	Delaware	371,366	25.4	25.6	41.3	12.9	395,656	6.5	34.0	39.2	20.3	1.81
11	District of Columbia..............	183,062	28.3	26.9	41.2	18.6	319,565	36.0	45.6	14.8	3.6	0.87
12	Florida	8,219,409	27.1	27.1	48.9	21.3	8,565,329	5.9	38.9	38.4	16.8	1.72
13	Georgia	4,076,187	27.1	27.2	46.4	20.1	4,001,109	5.3	32.2	38.2	24.3	1.93
15	Hawaii	596,746	25.3	25.3	45.2	16.5	490,080	8.3	33.0	35.3	23.4	1.88
16	Idaho	771,629	21.6	21.7	47.3	16.3	693,882	3.9	23.7	39.0	33.5	2.22
17	Illinois	4,824,560	26.8	26.2	47.5	18.2	4,991,641	10.4	35.5	35.9	18.2	1.69
18	Indiana	2,817,686	23.8	24.0	48.7	14.4	2,680,694	5.6	31.4	39.0	23.9	1.93
19	Iowa	1,374,816	19.7	20.0	34.9	13.0	1,300,467	5.6	30.1	38.0	26.4	1.98
20	Kansas	1,231,975	19.6	19.7	36.4	15.6	1,159,026	5.2	30.5	38.2	26.2	1.99
21	Kentucky	1,737,719	23.6	23.8	35.9	15.8	1,785,682	6.6	31.8	38.2	23.4	1.89
22	Louisiana	1,776,330	25.5	25.5	39.7	22.3	1,783,924	8.4	36.3	37.9	17.3	1.71
23	Maine	543,273	24.2	24.7	43.9	15.6	593,626	6.7	32.7	40.6	19.9	1.82
24	Maryland	2,319,169	29.3	29.0	50.7	18.2	2,355,652	8.2	33.1	36.7	22.0	1.83
25	Massachusetts	2,689,907	27.5	27.0	46.5	18.0	2,759,018	11.7	35.8	35.6	16.8	1.65
26	Michigan	3,784,429	23.8	23.9	43.5	16.2	4,051,798	6.7	34.5	39.0	19.8	1.81
27	Minnesota	2,300,218	22.2	22.3	37.5	15.2	2,281,033	6.4	29.8	40.1	23.7	1.92
28	Mississippi	1,139,216	25.2	25.2	40.4	23.8	1,129,611	6.3	31.8	37.5	24.4	1.90
29	Missouri	2,482,032	23.1	23.1	46.9	18.0	2,468,726	6.3	32.4	38.1	23.2	1.89
30	Montana	449,385	19.1	19.4	46.9	13.7	448,949	3.8	26.2	37.9	32.1	2.16
31	Nebraska	880,415	19.3	19.4	42.8	13.5	785,982	5.2	30.2	37.8	26.7	2.00
32	Nevada	1,223,063	24.6	23.6	62.7	24.3	1,191,380	7.0	35.2	35.7	22.1	1.83
33	New Hampshire	591,321	25.7	25.8	44.9	20.4	548,026	4.3	29.7	42.6	23.3	1.96
34	New Jersey	3,437,038	28.6	27.0	55.3	19.0	3,497,945	11.2	34.8	35.4	18.5	1.69
35	New Mexico	743,745	23.2	23.4	42.7	17.3	834,007	6.1	32.6	35.4	25.9	1.94
36	New York............................	7,246,571	31.4	27.0	51.3	18.6	7,652,666	28.1	34.1	25.8	12.0	1.27
37	North Carolina.....................	3,970,072	24.5	24.6	41.6	18.7	4,179,632	5.4	31.3	38.2	25.2	1.95
38	North Dakota.......................	362,392	17.5	17.9	34.6	9.3	322,511	5.0	28.8	38.2	28.1	2.06
39	Ohio..................................	4,677,145	23.1	23.1	42.8	16.8	4,832,922	7.1	33.6	38.1	21.2	1.83
40	Oklahoma...........................	1,589,401	22.0	22.2	36.7	16.1	1,547,967	5.4	33.0	38.3	23.3	1.90
41	Oregon	1,523,768	22.6	22.6	41.8	17.3	1,702,599	6.6	31.5	38.0	23.9	1.91
42	Pennsylvania	4,938,027	25.7	25.6	43.4	16.2	5,228,956	10.0	34.5	36.7	18.7	1.72
72	Puerto Rico	977,274	27.1	27.4	46.8	16.3	1,165,982	13.4	40.3	31.3	15.0	1.53
44	Rhode Island........................	439,664	24.8	25.0	45.9	15.4	440,170	8.5	36.2	37.2	18.1	1.73
45	South Carolina.....................	2,049,352	25.6	25.8	35.9	20.0	2,049,972	5.2	32.7	38.6	23.5	1.91
46	South Dakota	396,212	17.4	17.5	34.6	14.0	356,887	5.3	26.8	36.4	31.5	2.11
47	Tennessee...........................	2,748,147	25.2	25.3	41.1	17.8	2,770,395	4.9	30.6	38.8	25.8	1.98
48	Texas	11,417,050	25.9	25.9	44.5	19.5	10,796,247	5.2	32.7	39.9	22.2	1.88
49	Utah	1,306,378	21.4	21.3	38.9	16.9	1,101,499	3.8	24.3	39.3	32.5	2.20
50	Vermont.............................	263,683	23.0	23.7	24.3	13.8	270,163	5.4	34.1	41.6	18.9	1.81
51	Virginia..............................	3,312,668	26.4	26.6	44.8	15.3	3,331,461	6.1	30.5	37.6	25.8	1.96
53	Washington	2,780,613	26.0	25.7	47.2	19.8	3,022,255	6.6	30.4	36.5	26.5	1.97
54	West Virginia	635,030	25.7	26.1	36.9	15.4	722,201	7.6	33.7	36.7	22.0	1.82
55	Wisconsin............................	2,508,056	21.9	22.1	36.2	15.3	2,449,970	6.1	32.7	39.9	21.3	1.86
56	Wyoming............................	258,246	18.3	18.4	45.9	12.3	242,763	3.9	27.8	36.5	31.8	2.16

NA = Not available.
'- = The median falls in the lowest interval of an open-ended distribution.
^{1}A value of 10.0 represents the minimum percentage range--10 percent or less.

Table C-2. Counties — Where: Migration, Housing, and Transportation, 2021

STATE County	Total population 1 year and over	Lived in the same house 1 year ago (percent)	Did not live in the same county 1 year ago (percent)	Total occupied housing units	Owner-occupied units (percent)	Percent with a mortgage, contract to purchase, or similar debt	Median value of owner-occupied units (dollars; owner estimated)	Median gross rent of renter-occupied units paying cash rent	Households with Internet access (percent)	Number of workers who commuted to work	Commute of less than 10 minutes (percent)	Commute of 60 minutes or more (percent)
ACS table number:	C07204	C07204	C07204	B25003	B25003	B25081	B25097	B25064	S2801	B08012	B08012	B08012
STATE County code / Column number:	1	2	3	4	5	6	7	8	9	10	11	12
00000 **UNITED STATES**	328,464,538	87.2	6.0	127,544,730	65.4	61.3	281,400	1,191	90.3	126,746,081	13.2	7.7
01000 **ALABAMA**..................	4,989,797	88.0	5.3	1,967,559	70.0	53.6	172,800	861	85.3	1,956,821	12.0	6.9
01003 Baldwin County, Alabama..........	237,039	87.3	6.7	94,105	75.9	58.6	255,800	1,096	92.0	93,834	9.9	8.9
01015 Calhoun County, Alabama.........	115,014	87.8	4.5	44,631	72.8	48.9	139,400	718	84.6	45,414	13.3	6.4
01043 Cullman County, Alabama.........	88,651	85.9	5.6	35,131	76.0	50.6	165,900	799	85.2	39,873	17.3	15.7
01049 DeKalb County, Alabama...........	70,401	88.8	4.4	24,979	78.7	41.2	111,100	623	78.4	27,759	17.1	11.2
01051 Elmore County, Alabama	88,231	89.0	6.9	32,108	71.6	58.8	193,600	882	89.1	33,018	5.3	6.1
01055 Etowah County, Alabama	101,639	88.9	5.4	38,006	73.3	40.2	133,300	717	85.9	38,455	12.8	5.3
01069 Houston County, Alabama.........	106,491	89.0	4.3	44,058	64.1	52.5	155,500	807	86.1	42,702	15.1	6.1
01073 Jefferson County, Alabama........	661,383	87.4	3.8	270,147	64.4	57.6	190,900	976	89.1	260,307	8.8	4.4
01077 Lauderdale County, Alabama	93,017	84.7	6.0	38,250	66.9	42.3	175,300	751	79.7	40,466	14.0	15.3
01081 Lee County, Alabama.................	175,946	83.8	7.5	67,358	64.8	63.0	203,500	895	87.3	73,870	13.7	5.1
01083 Limestone County, Alabama	106,616	91.4	4.5	40,685	74.8	58.4	223,500	803	86.0	42,869	7.7	7.6
01089 Madison County, Alabama.........	390,996	85.4	7.5	164,493	70.4	63.7	254,600	1,014	92.0	156,372	10.3	2.6
01095 Marshall County, Alabama........	96,533	89.4	5.0	36,003	75.0	47.9	156,600	718	87.9	37,874	20.1	10.9
01097 Mobile County, Alabama	407,194	88.1	3.2	162,963	64.1	60.6	159,500	925	85.7	160,167	9.2	6.2
01101 Montgomery County, Alabama...	225,345	84.3	7.1	92,407	59.7	61.5	145,900	953	89.1	90,563	11.2	3.3
01103 Morgan County, Alabama.........	122,430	87.2	4.6	47,558	73.7	51.9	169,900	629	80.8	47,256	11.6	3.4
01115 St. Clair County, Alabama.........	91,940	91.1	4.4	33,093	79.5	NA	193,500	906	91.3	32,642	12.5	6.3
01117 Shelby County, Alabama..........	225,313	88.2	6.1	86,970	81.2	68.4	279,500	1,194	93.9	95,488	11.4	6.0
01121 Talladega County, Alabama........	80,487	86.2	6.4	33,775	72.9	47.7	103,400	709	87.8	27,023	14.6	8.8
01125 Tuscaloosa County, Alabama.......	225,404	85.0	6.7	86,694	61.8	63.5	214,000	917	88.6	96,068	11.0	6.0
02000 **ALASKA**....................	723,949	86.3	6.7	271,311	66.8	61.0	304,900	1,259	90.8	308,421	23.2	5.4
02020 Anchorage Municipality, Alaska ..	285,328	84.6	6.8	109,584	63.6	71.2	346,200	1,335	94.4	127,173	17.3	3.0
02090 Fairbanks North Star Borough, Alaska	94,013	85.5	8.1	36,426	58.5	NA	265,900	1,228	87.8	43,790	12.1	3.9
02170 Matanuska-Susitna Borough, Alaska	108,921	86.8	5.8	40,997	79.0	66.9	288,100	1,221	92.9	42,326	10.4	19.7
04000 **ARIZONA**..................	7,202,745	85.3	5.9	2,817,723	67.6	63.3	336,300	1,253	91.6	2,599,725	12.9	6.1
04001 Apache County, Arizona	65,008	94.5	3.8	19,875	78.5	NA	68,100	641	54.0	17,503	22.4	18.6
04003 Cochise County, Arizona............	125,009	85.7	9.8	49,952	72.5	55.2	175,000	793	84.6	41,598	23.5	11.6
04005 Coconino County, Arizona.........	143,963	80.6	11.8	55,145	58.5	51.7	393,900	1,306	83.9	56,108	22.1	5.2
04013 Maricopa County, Arizona	4,451,026	85.4	4.7	1,708,034	65.8	68.5	383,500	1,389	93.2	1,643,741	11.0	5.6
04015 Mohave County, Arizona	215,753	87.6	7.3	102,398	73.7	50.4	250,300	885	89.3	72,471	19.5	6.2
04017 Navajo County, Arizona	107,208	91.3	5.2	40,087	75.2	32.6	161,100	649	74.9	30,607	27.1	11.4
04019 Pima County, Arizona	1,040,569	84.0	5.7	433,148	64.6	59.4	261,600	1,008	91.4	387,418	11.3	4.0
04021 Pinal County, Arizona...............	444,728	85.5	10.3	155,161	81.3	63.1	304,700	1,177	92.5	143,425	11.3	12.3
04025 Yavapai County, Arizona	241,454	86.1	8.5	112,075	75.6	57.2	361,900	1,101	93.2	81,301	19.1	7.2
04027 Yuma County, Arizona	203,976	82.8	9.6	74,981	70.1	56.2	170,400	906	90.2	71,073	21.7	5.1
05000 **ARKANSAS**	2,990,311	86.8	6.0	1,183,675	67.0	54.0	162,300	820	85.7	1,180,532	18.7	5.4
05007 Benton County, Arkansas............	288,729	87.0	5.9	106,553	68.5	66.7	247,500	1,053	94.0	114,266	13.8	2.7
05031 Craighead County, Arkansas.......	111,170	78.7	6.7	42,186	64.6	NA	177,400	820	88.8	44,444	16.4	5.2
05045 Faulkner County, Arkansas.........	123,457	85.7	6.2	48,497	61.7	59.3	204,500	896	90.9	54,682	16.3	8.1
05051 Garland County, Arkansas...........	99,137	92.6	3.7	42,077	69.4	NA	161,500	801	82.9	39,741	22.8	7.1
05069 Jefferson County, Arkansas.........	65,408	87.6	5.2	24,319	62.4	NA	118,600	785	81.0	22,310	13.4	4.4
05085 Lonoke County, Arkansas............	74,182	81.8	8.5	27,880	75.6	68.2	166,500	892	88.2	31,900	13.5	5.1
05119 Pulaski County, Arkansas............	394,200	85.5	5.2	172,100	58.8	64.0	178,100	927	89.6	158,729	13.9	2.8
05125 Saline County, Arkansas.............	123,139	90.4	4.8	49,768	76.3	62.2	197,800	997	89.3	56,254	11.1	3.1
05131 Sebastian County, Arkansas........	125,657	85.2	8.4	51,472	63.2	51.6	146,700	696	84.5	50,475	17.2	4.3
05143 Washington County, Arkansas	246,131	87.2	5.4	94,220	60.4	61.6	238,800	928	91.3	108,646	15.5	2.3
05145 White County, Arkansas.............	76,510	81.9	5.4	29,359	70.1	49.6	150,800	737	89.7	31,255	27.2	7.6
06000 **CALIFORNIA**.............	38,833,197	88.7	4.5	13,429,063	55.9	68.0	648,100	1,750	93.0	13,999,114	10.1	9.9
06001 Alameda County, California........	1,631,774	87.2	6.2	589,180	54.6	68.7	960,900	2,036	93.1	533,150	8.1	10.7
06007 Butte County, California	206,231	82.7	7.0	81,353	58.4	56.2	370,700	1,238	90.8	79,258	22.6	5.8
06013 Contra Costa County, California .	1,148,769	89.7	5.4	411,560	66.9	72.2	780,500	2,075	95.1	393,238	10.2	16.5
06017 El Dorado County, California.......	191,696	89.1	8.9	74,909	76.3	68.2	609,100	1,589	92.5	65,455	14.4	9.0
06019 Fresno County, California............	1,000,279	90.3	3.1	322,646	55.8	65.4	331,800	1,164	85.8	361,634	12.9	4.2
06023 Humboldt County, California	135,620	83.5	8.5	55,184	57.7	57.2	374,500	1,191	91.6	45,293	24.5	5.9

STATE County	Total population 1 year and over	Lived in the same house 1 year ago (percent)	Did not live in the same county 1 year ago (percent)	Total occupied housing units	Owner-occupied units (percent)	Percent with a mortgage, contract to purchase, or similar debt	Median value of owner-occupied units (dollars; owner estimated)	Median gross rent of renter-occupied units paying cash rent	Households with Internet access (percent)	Number of workers who commuted to work	Commute of less than 10 minutes (percent)	Commute of 60 minutes or more (percent)
ACS table number:	C07204	C07204	C07204	B25003	B25003	B25081	B25097	B25064	S2801	B08012	B08012	B08012
Column number:	1	2	3	4	5	6	7	8	9	10	11	12
CALIFORNIA—Cont.												
06025 Imperial County, California	177,927	92.4	1.7	47,849	57.8	61.6	249,800	913	90.9	53,166	17.9	3.6
06029 Kern County, California	906,932	92.0	2.7	282,963	59.6	67.1	282,100	1,103	90.7	315,610	12.0	6.4
06031 Kings County, California	150,855	86.8	7.3	43,143	53.9	66.2	285,600	1,184	90.1	51,083	23.1	4.8
06033 Lake County, California...............	67,512	89.2	5.3	27,472	67.1	52.6	293,600	1,109	86.0	20,850	22.9	13.8
06037 Los Angeles County, California ...	9,736,069	90.4	2.6	3,375,587	46.5	69.0	720,300	1,711	92.8	3,588,647	7.3	11.0
06039 Madera County, California...........	157,313	92.9	5.3	44,048	63.8	63.2	348,500	1,081	88.1	47,865	16.0	9.1
06041 Marin County, California.............	256,557	87.0	8.9	103,378	64.1	68.1	1,314,100	2,362	94.5	79,276	13.9	6.5
06045 Mendocino County, California	90,576	90.4	5.3	34,273	58.1	56.4	419,600	1,194	89.5	32,522	32.2	4.6
06047 Merced County, California	283,193	90.4	5.1	84,967	51.0	63.4	345,700	1,160	85.7	93,335	15.3	18.4
06053 Monterey County, California.......	432,342	89.6	5.6	133,224	50.9	67.3	683,200	1,767	94.0	161,304	9.9	7.3
06055 Napa County, California..............	135,033	89.6	5.6	49,979	68.1	63.3	749,700	1,862	94.3	53,807	14.1	12.1
06057 Nevada County, California	102,783	91.7	5.0	42,679	74.4	68.2	575,300	1,513	91.2	31,832	23.2	8.2
06059 Orange County, California	3,135,054	87.7	4.7	1,077,193	56.5	67.0	832,300	2,090	94.5	1,184,456	8.9	7.3
06061 Placer County, California.............	407,929	88.0	7.6	155,945	74.0	69.8	627,500	1,823	93.8	139,169	13.7	7.7
06065 Riverside County, California	2,432,550	90.2	5.1	765,673	68.2	70.2	465,400	1,587	92.8	891,612	9.4	16.0
06067 Sacramento County, California ...	1,574,247	88.6	4.3	571,949	58.3	68.7	466,700	1,512	94.1	552,091	9.2	7.0
06069 San Benito County, California	NA	NA	NA	20,307	69.5	72.4	681,500	1,622	94.2	27,319	19.8	23.6
06071 San Bernardino County, California...............	2,170,864	90.0	4.6	675,929	61.8	70.3	436,800	1,518	92.9	802,534	9.6	17.0
06073 San Diego County, California	3,250,645	86.0	5.4	1,162,896	54.3	69.7	722,200	1,908	94.9	1,239,125	8.6	5.2
06075 San Francisco County, California .	806,418	81.5	8.4	350,796	40.1	64.8	1,306,400	2,167	92.8	238,860	7.0	8.9
06077 San Joaquin County, California ...	780,220	89.3	4.7	241,760	61.3	68.6	457,600	1,484	91.3	282,388	10.6	19.5
06079 San Luis Obispo County, California...................	280,454	83.6	9.6	107,571	63.3	64.0	695,500	1,716	92.2	102,110	20.7	4.5
06081 San Mateo County, California	730,894	88.1	5.6	264,135	59.0	67.4	1,411,000	2,502	95.5	249,338	10.3	6.3
06083 Santa Barbara County, California	441,350	82.8	8.4	150,550	51.9	65.2	669,000	1,859	91.9	169,152	19.9	4.9
06085 Santa Clara County, California	1,867,354	85.2	4.5	650,593	55.8	67.5	1,270,200	2,467	95.9	600,637	8.5	4.8
06087 Santa Cruz County, California	265,551	83.7	9.5	97,353	60.4	65.4	922,300	1,960	93.6	96,121	13.7	6.0
06089 Shasta County, California............	180,693	88.9	4.9	71,506	60.9	63.0	334,600	1,105	89.1	63,313	21.5	3.2
06095 Solano County, California	446,949	88.9	5.5	157,617	62.0	73.4	543,100	1,877	93.5	177,381	12.1	17.0
06097 Sonoma County, California.........	481,406	88.4	4.2	190,586	62.8	67.2	718,500	1,900	94.7	184,657	14.0	9.8
06099 Stanislaus County, California.......	546,815	91.7	3.7	174,209	61.6	65.6	397,200	1,358	93.0	210,481	11.3	14.4
06101 Sutter County, California	98,288	91.3	5.3	33,655	57.1	64.5	363,600	1,195	91.3	37,144	13.1	9.6
06103 Tehama County, California	NA	NA	NA	23,950	66.7	NA	272,700	980	84.8	23,276	16.5	2.7
06107 Tulare County, California.............	470,431	92.4	2.5	143,541	57.3	64.0	276,400	1,061	87.4	165,341	17.6	8.3
06111 Ventura County, California..........	830,329	91.7	3.2	279,168	65.2	68.8	691,000	2,032	93.8	318,293	12.3	6.6
06113 Yolo County, California...............	214,778	82.0	11.2	76,844	54.0	66.4	534,900	1,605	91.5	76,415	20.5	5.8
06115 Yuba County, California..............	81,491	87.5	7.2	27,942	58.4	NA	371,100	1,053	90.5	31,516	11.2	9.9
08000 **COLORADO**............................	5,757,628	83.3	9.7	2,313,042	66.8	69.7	466,200	1,491	93.2	2,281,922	13.4	6.4
08001 Adams County, Colorado............	517,440	85.9	7.3	183,023	71.1	73.2	424,600	1,581	92.0	225,240	8.3	9.7
08005 Arapahoe County, Colorado	648,334	84.4	9.5	250,041	65.5	73.0	481,500	1,585	93.4	256,696	8.7	5.2
08013 Boulder County, Colorado..........	327,265	77.9	13.1	135,607	61.7	66.4	654,500	1,732	95.5	110,200	16.0	6.0
08014 Broomfield County, Colorado......	74,621	84.3	13.7	30,161	67.1	72.4	576,200	1,931	95.3	26,610	9.5	4.8
08031 Denver County, Colorado...........	703,702	79.6	11.6	326,634	50.3	75.2	541,500	1,549	92.3	273,410	8.9	4.6
08035 Douglas County, Colorado.........	366,113	82.2	12.1	136,238	79.1	77.4	630,400	1,858	97.5	133,680	12.5	6.0
08041 El Paso County, Colorado...........	728,494	80.8	10.7	282,904	67.1	72.4	397,900	1,451	95.5	301,155	12.2	4.1
08059 Jefferson County, Colorado........	574,687	85.9	8.1	239,823	70.6	69.3	548,200	1,582	95.0	224,178	9.5	5.4
08069 Larimer County, Colorado...........	359,281	78.7	11.0	152,123	64.1	67.1	487,700	1,463	92.7	144,372	16.0	5.5
08077 Mesa County, Colorado	156,323	83.7	7.1	63,796	72.0	67.2	333,400	939	93.3	59,820	18.2	4.0
08101 Pueblo County, Colorado............	168,074	88.6	4.8	69,078	68.3	63.3	253,200	890	88.0	62,975	14.4	4.0
08123 Weld County, Colorado	335,939	85.7	8.6	119,502	74.9	74.4	416,700	1,333	92.1	142,857	12.5	10.7
09000 **CONNECTICUT**	3,571,470	88.7	5.4	1,428,313	66.6	65.3	311,500	1,277	92.3	1,432,375	12.4	7.8
09001 Fairfield County, Connecticut......	949,322	88.4	5.1	357,271	66.9	68.2	469,600	1,644	93.4	366,886	11.1	12.9
09003 Hartford County, Connecticut.....	888,258	89.3	4.1	360,140	66.2	65.6	269,800	1,221	91.1	348,280	11.8	4.2
09005 Litchfield County, Connecticut	183,805	88.8	6.6	77,106	78.0	62.4	300,100	1,110	93.6	76,675	18.3	10.4
09007 Middlesex County, Connecticut...	163,588	90.8	5.6	69,789	75.7	64.0	309,600	1,306	94.2	71,262	14.7	5.1
09009 New Haven County, Connecticut	855,848	89.0	5.5	349,089	61.6	63.3	282,200	1,235	92.4	349,887	11.9	6.6

Table C-2. Counties — Where: Migration, Housing, and Transportation, 2021—*Continued*

STATE County code	STATE County	Total population 1 year and over	Lived in the same house 1 year ago (percent)	Did not live in the same county 1 year ago (percent)	Total occupied housing units	Owner-occupied units (percent)	Percent with a mortgage, contract to purchase, or similar debt	Median value of owner-occupied units (dollars; owner estimated)	Median gross rent of renter-occupied units paying cash rent	Households with Internet access (percent)	Number of workers who commuted to work	Commute of less than 10 minutes (percent)	Commute of 60 minutes or more (percent)
	ACS table number:	C07204	C07204	C07204	B25003	B25003	B25081	B25097	B25064	S2801	B08012	B08012	B08012
	Column number:	1	2	3	4	5	6	7	8	9	10	11	12
	CONNECTICUT—Cont.												
09011	New London County, Connecticut.................	266,345	85.4	7.1	110,950	67.1	61.8	289,400	1,202	91.6	110,049	13.8	5.3
09013	Tolland County, Connecticut.......	148,516	88.9	8.6	58,244	68.8	66.1	282,900	1,225	92.0	60,144	10.2	8.5
09015	Windham County, Connecticut...	115,788	88.7	6.9	45,724	69.2	68.9	239,700	987	88.8	49,192	16.6	8.7
10000	**DELAWARE**	994,669	89.4	5.7	395,656	72.6	63.7	300,500	1,208	92.1	371,366	12.8	6.9
10001	Kent County, Delaware..............	181,919	91.3	3.5	70,167	72.5	62.0	269,900	1,180	90.2	73,268	16.5	8.3
10003	New Castle County, Delaware.....	567,009	88.8	5.7	220,758	68.2	69.7	303,500	1,236	93.3	210,756	11.2	5.9
10005	Sussex County, Delaware	245,741	89.5	7.3	104,731	81.8	54.2	324,000	1,107	90.7	87,342	13.8	8.1
11000	DISTRICT OF COLUMBIA.............	661,026	79.7	9.9	319,565	41.6	75.3	669,900	1,668	90.2	183,062	7.0	7.7
11001	District of Columbia..................	661,026	79.7	9.9	319,565	41.6	75.3	669,900	1,668	90.2	183,062	7.0	7.7
12000	**FLORIDA**...........................	21,590,684	86.0	6.9	8,565,329	67.4	56.7	290,700	1,348	90.6	8,219,409	9.2	7.7
12001	Alachua County, Florida..............	276,743	78.9	12.1	108,189	56.5	55.0	245,300	1,134	88.8	110,857	12.9	4.1
12005	Bay County, Florida....................	176,903	78.0	12.1	79,532	63.3	53.5	243,200	1,244	91.2	78,754	15.8	5.1
12009	Brevard County, Florida..............	611,791	85.0	8.0	254,314	76.9	56.3	269,500	1,197	91.5	229,505	10.2	6.2
12011	Broward County, Florida	1,916,891	87.2	5.0	747,715	63.3	58.5	346,100	1,498	91.6	793,592	6.5	8.2
12015	Charlotte County, Florida...........	193,992	86.6	9.3	88,988	82.7	44.5	267,900	1,207	91.9	57,786	12.4	7.6
12017	Citrus County, Florida.................	157,256	85.9	11.1	68,269	84.0	38.1	206,400	1,036	88.8	38,243	12.1	9.2
12019	Clay County, Florida...................	220,000	87.1	8.7	80,459	75.7	69.4	265,800	1,302	94.7	86,911	8.2	10.2
12021	Collier County, Florida................	384,395	83.0	10.4	163,943	72.9	47.4	416,200	1,503	89.7	137,381	9.0	5.2
12023	Columbia County, Florida............	69,265	83.9	10.7	27,545	71.2	NA	173,800	742	85.8	26,046	10.4	5.2
12031	Duval County, Florida.................	987,152	84.5	6.5	406,301	59.0	66.1	246,900	1,203	90.4	406,036	10.1	3.4
12033	Escambia County, Florida............	318,710	83.2	9.2	126,980	62.9	57.2	212,500	1,096	89.4	129,233	14.6	5.8
12035	Flagler County, Florida................	120,932	89.4	9.2	48,187	84.4	59.6	283,800	1,376	84.4	37,544	5.4	10.8
12053	Hernando County, Florida...........	199,035	86.9	9.0	81,497	81.8	55.3	222,000	1,057	90.0	72,225	14.4	13.5
12055	Highlands County, Florida...........	102,585	89.4	6.0	46,166	78.8	35.0	164,500	917	86.0	30,851	18.4	4.5
12057	Hillsborough County, Florida.......	1,462,378	82.8	6.9	578,259	60.9	64.5	300,200	1,334	93.4	563,007	9.0	6.8
12061	Indian River County, Florida........	162,281	87.3	6.8	69,974	78.6	48.4	279,400	1,159	88.8	55,598	12.9	5.5
12069	Lake County, Florida...................	392,761	88.7	7.0	156,435	77.7	55.1	258,800	1,434	89.1	132,485	9.3	12.2
12071	Lee County, Florida....................	780,540	86.6	7.5	320,466	73.5	54.0	286,000	1,326	91.3	280,020	8.5	8.9
12073	Leon County, Florida...................	289,869	80.6	8.6	121,423	54.2	62.3	249,100	1,131	93.1	122,459	12.7	2.0
12081	Manatee County, Florida.............	410,320	84.9	9.1	163,520	76.3	53.4	313,600	1,309	92.0	149,781	8.3	6.3
12083	Marion County, Florida	383,369	87.2	6.7	157,348	78.5	52.5	193,300	1,072	91.2	129,162	10.4	6.7
12085	Martin County, Florida................	159,015	88.7	7.7	69,719	79.5	46.0	338,100	1,239	92.6	54,630	9.9	6.3
12086	Miami-Dade County, Florida........	2,635,361	87.9	3.5	963,477	52.5	59.6	374,700	1,517	87.6	1,083,772	5.9	9.6
12087	Monroe County, Florida	81,178	81.4	8.5	36,078	60.4	43.4	661,400	1,734	87.9	36,193	27.5	4.5
12089	Nassau County, Florida...............	93,623	89.4	6.6	40,276	79.5	59.2	315,500	1,400	95.1	36,702	10.2	6.9
12091	Okaloosa County, Florida	210,049	80.7	10.8	84,497	66.2	61.7	293,100	1,321	90.3	92,588	16.2	9.3
12095	Orange County, Florida...............	1,411,718	85.2	6.9	512,496	56.8	69.7	320,600	1,428	93.0	553,910	6.9	6.1
12097	Osceola County, Florida..............	399,263	86.6	8.5	133,330	65.5	68.7	285,200	1,402	92.2	166,568	5.2	13.8
12099	Palm Beach County, Florida.........	1,483,763	87.3	5.7	595,447	70.4	53.1	363,000	1,560	90.1	563,290	10.0	6.8
12101	Pasco County, Florida.................	580,581	87.4	7.2	230,060	75.3	55.5	235,200	1,195	90.5	202,234	9.5	11.7
12103	Pinellas County, Florida..............	949,781	86.4	6.2	419,798	70.4	52.9	292,200	1,276	90.0	354,131	12.9	4.3
12105	Polk County, Florida...................	746,832	86.7	6.6	276,469	69.3	56.3	212,500	1,110	88.6	277,040	7.5	9.3
12107	Putnam County, Florida..............	73,152	89.8	6.7	29,765	71.7	37.3	114,200	784	83.0	19,718	15.0	11.1
12109	St. Johns County, Florida............	289,874	81.6	12.3	109,147	80.2	62.7	402,700	1,657	93.2	101,396	11.0	4.7
12111	St. Lucie County, Florida.............	339,696	91.9	5.7	131,235	78.4	54.1	271,300	1,280	93.8	130,258	4.4	10.4
12113	Santa Rosa County, Florida.........	191,160	83.8	9.6	71,722	80.8	64.3	280,100	1,256	95.3	74,663	7.7	8.0
12115	Sarasota County, Florida.............	444,461	84.6	7.7	204,018	75.4	47.0	334,700	1,388	92.1	156,082	11.1	3.9
12117	Seminole County, Florida............	466,392	86.9	7.9	188,239	67.2	66.2	328,000	1,410	95.2	178,933	11.8	6.6
12119	Sumter County, Florida	135,027	87.7	9.3	68,792	89.1	39.8	323,200	1,099	90.5	24,495	8.7	16.1
12127	Volusia County, Florida...............	560,107	87.5	7.5	243,344	73.4	56.1	247,800	1,137	89.6	202,571	10.5	9.4
12131	Walton County, Florida...............	79,601	82.4	10.4	33,941	77.4	57.3	390,200	1,390	90.4	29,258	8.8	7.9
13000	**GEORGIA**...........................	10,688,429	86.5	7.6	4,001,109	66.0	63.8	249,700	1,153	90.1	4,076,187	10.4	8.3
13013	Barrow County, Georgia	85,605	89.0	9.6	30,194	78.7	64.5	233,500	1,053	94.3	37,274	5.1	12.6
13015	Bartow County, Georgia.............	109,740	88.6	8.6	38,903	82.2	62.0	223,100	1,203	85.5	43,809	9.0	10.8
13021	Bibb County, Georgia.................	154,236	83.5	6.2	57,677	55.8	59.9	155,800	896	85.3	57,081	12.3	4.7
13031	Bulloch County, Georgia.............	81,529	71.5	13.7	29,318	52.6	57.0	171,100	946	89.5	32,166	22.1	16.0

STATE County	Total population 1 year and over	Lived in the same house 1 year ago (percent)	Did not live in the same county 1 year ago (percent)	Total occupied housing units	Owner-occupied units (percent)	Percent with a mortgage, contract to purchase, or similar debt	Median value of owner-occupied units (dollars; owner estimated)	Median gross rent of renter-occupied units paying cash rent	Households with Internet access (percent)	Number of workers who commuted to work	Commute of less than 10 minutes (percent)	Commute of 60 minutes or more (percent)
ACS table number:	C07204	C07204	C07204	B25003	B25003	B25081	B25097	B25064	S2801	B08012	B08012	B08012
Column number:	1	2	3	4	5	6	7	8	9	10	11	12
GEORGIA—Cont.												
13045 Carroll County, Georgia	120,231	88.3	6.8	43,859	69.8	61.3	211,600	980	92.2	49,861	15.7	10.1
13047 Catoosa County, Georgia	67,902	84.3	7.5	26,864	72.2	61.7	226,200	885	88.1	30,473	11.4	1.9
13051 Chatham County, Georgia	293,308	81.5	9.8	121,028	58.6	64.2	236,600	1,216	93.4	127,604	13.8	2.5
13057 Cherokee County, Georgia..........	272,098	87.8	8.6	100,023	79.8	72.3	358,300	1,456	95.5	109,822	9.1	8.6
13059 Clarke County, Georgia..............	127,524	73.5	18.2	55,332	40.0	61.6	237,600	1,048	90.9	53,704	22.3	6.7
13063 Clayton County, Georgia............	294,847	89.1	7.9	106,249	57.1	66.8	173,200	1,176	92.5	116,464	2.8	10.5
13067 Cobb County, Georgia	759,619	83.8	8.0	292,841	66.9	73.3	342,200	1,413	96.2	285,362	7.6	7.7
13073 Columbia County, Georgia.........	158,389	90.3	6.6	51,178	80.9	66.4	265,100	1,129	90.0	65,879	6.9	3.6
13077 Coweta County, Georgia	149,088	90.3	4.7	55,729	79.4	68.2	293,800	1,337	93.6	63,863	6.3	10.3
13089 DeKalb County, Georgia............	748,794	87.1	7.1	273,981	60.4	69.0	298,000	1,363	93.4	273,785	5.7	7.1
13095 Dougherty County, Georgia	83,615	85.3	7.4	34,835	46.8	53.6	109,200	809	81.7	29,969	16.5	5.5
13097 Douglas County, Georgia	143,273	84.2	6.8	51,441	65.4	70.6	242,900	1,268	93.8	56,021	6.9	10.2
13103 Effingham County, Georgia.........	65,730	85.5	6.6	23,373	74.4	NA	226,500	985	86.9	29,336	8.0	9.8
13113 Fayette County, Georgia	119,652	87.6	8.7	43,689	80.7	65.0	362,500	1,691	96.4	43,067	15.2	10.3
13115 Floyd County, Georgia	98,145	88.2	6.4	35,417	63.1	55.3	178,900	830	84.7	40,482	16.2	4.0
13117 Forsyth County, Georgia	258,471	83.9	10.1	86,475	84.7	75.6	444,000	1,883	98.0	87,048	6.4	10.9
13121 Fulton County, Georgia..............	1,055,057	80.8	10.5	467,735	54.8	71.6	388,300	1,434	93.4	355,568	7.4	6.3
13127 Glynn County, Georgia	84,208	85.0	8.5	34,137	61.1	60.1	247,500	1,042	89.1	34,565	25.6	3.0
13135 Gwinnett County, Georgia	956,033	89.3	4.9	323,014	67.4	69.6	307,100	1,484	93.5	355,283	6.2	9.8
13139 Hall County, Georgia................	204,579	86.9	6.8	72,454	68.7	58.7	281,400	1,062	91.3	86,725	10.2	10.7
13151 Henry County, Georgia	243,282	88.9	5.9	84,978	76.4	75.1	249,900	1,334	94.3	90,517	4.7	11.5
13153 Houston County, Georgia	164,674	84.5	10.5	60,815	63.6	64.6	169,100	994	91.4	68,444	8.5	3.6
13157 Jackson County, Georgia............	79,744	92.9	5.4	25,272	76.1	64.7	304,300	982	94.1	30,640	10.2	6.0
13179 Liberty County, Georgia.............	63,580	75.0	15.5	23,883	38.8	NA	162,800	1,086	88.6	24,332	17.5	7.8
13185 Lowndes County, Georgia..........	117,347	87.4	6.0	45,139	53.0	60.7	173,300	842	84.8	45,278	18.2	3.1
13215 Muscogee County, Georgia........	202,715	80.9	10.9	82,663	47.6	66.0	170,900	923	87.3	76,658	17.0	3.6
13217 Newton County, Georgia	113,456	89.9	6.1	41,515	77.5	NA	197,100	1,207	92.3	46,276	3.2	14.4
13223 Paulding County, Georgia	171,237	89.7	7.1	58,025	85.3	77.3	259,300	1,462	96.1	68,427	4.6	19.3
13245 Richmond County, Georgia	203,382	84.1	10.2	74,476	51.7	60.4	132,100	942	84.5	84,767	15.7	3.1
13247 Rockdale County, Georgia.........	93,321	87.9	9.9	33,141	68.1	67.7	230,500	1,138	87.7	36,743	9.5	15.3
13255 Spalding County, Georgia.........	67,207	89.7	7.1	25,696	61.0	58.1	173,900	981	83.2	25,636	16.8	10.5
13285 Troup County, Georgia................	69,231	90.3	3.0	26,768	58.6	NA	163,700	842	85.6	29,693	12.5	6.1
13295 Walker County, Georgia..............	67,622	92.3	4.2	26,315	75.9	59.1	147,200	763	90.6	26,587	10.3	7.6
13297 Walton County, Georgia	98,494	89.5	7.0	35,628	74.3	65.5	274,400	1,060	87.8	36,126	8.8	21.8
13313 Whitfield County, Georgia	101,819	91.8	3.1	35,746	65.7	52.9	171,200	830	87.7	43,105	6.7	2.2
15000 **HAWAII**	1,426,298	86.3	6.4	490,080	62.6	64.2	722,500	1,774	91.7	596,746	12.6	7.2
15001 Hawaii County, Hawaii................	201,356	86.2	7.1	72,194	73.4	55.2	472,800	1,328	88.8	71,474	14.6	9.5
15003 Honolulu County, Hawaii............	989,106	86.0	6.6	338,093	59.3	67.7	781,600	1,884	92.9	424,900	10.9	7.0
15007 Kauai County, Hawaii.................	72,912	90.3	4.8	23,464	65.5	59.4	695,100	1,639	94.8	29,639	18.9	4.7
15009 Maui County, Hawaii	162,889	86.6	5.4	56,319	67.1	60.0	744,400	1,592	86.9	70,733	18.1	7.2
16000 **IDAHO**..	1,879,719	85.2	8.4	693,882	71.9	64.0	369,300	1,035	90.8	771,629	19.6	4.7
16001 Ada County, Idaho.....................	506,743	84.7	8.4	196,255	70.5	68.2	463,100	1,292	94.4	203,405	11.1	2.6
16005 Bannock County, Idaho..............	87,123	83.7	7.9	33,557	68.9	61.6	253,000	739	86.3	35,117	26.8	5.3
16019 Bonneville County, Idaho	125,806	81.4	7.9	42,905	73.2	65.7	336,100	907	92.6	49,861	22.8	8.2
16027 Canyon County, Idaho................	240,460	87.9	6.7	82,667	73.8	70.4	355,100	1,134	91.4	100,283	13.1	2.4
16055 Kootenai County, Idaho	177,131	85.2	9.5	67,771	73.7	65.9	444,900	1,176	89.1	72,569	16.8	6.6
16083 Twin Falls County, Idaho	91,388	82.8	7.4	34,311	67.0	62.5	307,900	830	88.0	37,148	30.7	2.9
17000 **ILLINOIS**	12,544,435	88.5	4.5	4,991,641	67.5	61.3	231,500	1,106	89.9	4,824,560	12.9	8.5
17019 Champaign County, Illinois	202,884	79.7	10.0	84,248	53.9	57.4	183,300	915	91.1	80,777	17.3	2.1
17031 Cook County, Illinois	5,119,785	88.2	3.1	2,072,143	58.3	62.8	286,800	1,232	89.6	1,868,800	7.4	10.6
17037 DeKalb County, Illinois...............	99,488	82.8	12.5	38,916	61.6	67.1	212,100	955	92.9	44,519	21.4	9.8
17043 DuPage County, Illinois.............	914,711	89.7	5.4	350,639	73.4	65.0	350,200	1,465	94.6	343,376	11.9	8.8
17089 Kane County, Illinois.................	511,123	87.5	7.6	183,427	76.0	67.6	279,800	1,211	93.8	206,543	10.6	7.6
17091 Kankakee County, Illinois...........	105,751	92.5	3.8	41,020	72.1	57.7	165,700	922	87.6	45,838	19.5	10.5
17093 Kendall County, Illinois..............	133,659	94.5	4.0	44,208	85.4	77.7	275,000	1,191	95.1	54,454	9.0	11.5
17097 Lake County, Illinois..................	705,915	87.5	6.6	254,744	75.3	65.9	298,300	1,274	93.8	274,852	11.4	8.6
17099 LaSalle County, Illinois..............	107,741	90.6	4.2	44,972	70.8	59.0	142,400	738	85.1	47,699	25.5	8.5
17111 McHenry County, Illinois	308,135	90.9	4.1	116,768	83.5	71.2	257,700	1,250	95.3	127,749	13.8	12.1

Table C-2. Counties — Where: Migration, Housing, and Transportation, 2021—*Continued*

STATE County	Total population 1 year and over	Lived in the same house 1 year ago (percent)	Did not live in the same county 1 year ago (percent)	Total occupied housing units	Owner-occupied units (percent)	Percent with a mortgage, contract to purchase, or similar debt	Median value of owner-occupied units (dollars; owner estimated)	Median gross rent of renter-occupied units paying cash rent	Households with Internet access (percent)	Number of workers who commuted to work	Commute of less than 10 minutes (percent)	Commute of 60 minutes or more (percent)
ACS table number:	C07204	C07204	C07204	B25003	B25003	B25081	B25097	B25064	S2801	B08012	B08012	B08012
STATE County code	Column number:	1	2	3	4	5	6	7	8	9	10	11	12
	ILLINOIS—Cont.												
17113	McLean County, Illinois	168,945	84.6	6.3	69,263	64.2	62.1	183,300	858	88.3	65,310	23.2	3.4
17115	Macon County, Illinois................	101,366	84.9	5.7	43,914	68.9	49.2	110,800	719	83.4	36,920	15.3	2.7
17119	Madison County, Illinois.............	262,326	87.0	5.5	109,818	76.5	61.7	151,100	871	90.2	103,453	13.4	3.5
17143	Peoria County, Illinois.................	177,909	86.8	4.4	79,307	67.9	58.7	134,600	813	91.6	66,470	15.6	2.4
17161	Rock Island County, Illinois.........	140,730	86.6	5.1	60,187	69.9	55.3	126,500	807	88.7	55,581	15.9	4.6
17163	St. Clair County, Illinois..............	251,815	88.9	5.1	98,926	69.8	62.0	157,600	931	90.9	98,617	14.8	4.0
17167	Sangamon County, Illinois...........	192,779	88.9	2.3	84,414	71.7	57.6	154,400	859	87.9	77,051	15.3	4.9
17179	Tazewell County, Illinois	129,527	89.6	3.7	55,208	77.8	61.7	152,900	820	87.4	54,002	18.6	3.1
17183	Vermilion County, Illinois............	72,799	90.5	2.6	29,007	69.5	39.2	79,700	741	84.0	25,063	13.0	3.3
17197	Will County, Illinois	689,696	91.3	4.8	242,530	83.4	69.2	272,300	1,284	93.4	283,935	10.2	11.4
17199	Williamson County, Illinois	66,149	90.5	3.1	27,361	72.2	53.2	135,200	815	85.6	24,001	22.0	4.3
17201	Winnebago County, Illinois	279,859	86.1	4.7	115,282	64.6	57.7	142,800	885	88.5	108,331	12.2	6.4
18000	**INDIANA**	6,729,771	86.7	6.5	2,680,694	71.1	64.3	182,400	905	89.5	2,817,686	15.6	5.8
18003	Allen County, Indiana.................	383,168	83.8	4.7	154,866	69.7	64.1	171,500	873	92.8	164,567	12.7	4.1
18005	Bartholomew County, Indiana.....	81,591	85.3	4.8	32,518	71.4	66.5	191,100	1,015	92.2	33,949	24.7	7.1
18011	Boone County, Indiana...............	72,118	86.6	8.8	28,048	80.1	76.8	330,100	1,219	96.4	28,581	18.4	2.4
18019	Clark County, Indiana	121,665	89.4	5.5	50,153	73.2	65.4	188,300	928	90.2	50,354	9.1	5.4
18035	Delaware County, Indiana...........	111,135	77.1	9.1	45,977	66.3	56.6	113,000	753	87.4	44,737	24.0	6.9
18039	Elkhart County, Indiana..............	205,201	91.8	3.5	69,015	74.1	60.7	177,500	903	87.5	85,984	18.9	1.8
18043	Floyd County, Indiana	79,214	88.9	8.0	30,846	73.1	66.0	203,700	918	87.8	33,898	6.9	2.9
18053	Grant County, Indiana................	65,743	85.8	6.8	26,342	72.3	56.7	108,900	723	88.6	25,032	24.2	8.4
18057	Hamilton County, Indiana	352,595	87.2	6.6	132,255	75.6	74.3	336,900	1,375	95.7	136,100	11.8	4.7
18059	Hancock County, Indiana	80,611	90.1	6.4	32,661	81.1	75.1	236,300	1,052	94.2	37,300	7.3	3.3
18063	Hendricks County, Indiana	177,112	86.2	7.5	65,751	79.9	74.9	265,000	1,187	94.3	79,110	11.1	3.4
18067	Howard County, Indiana	83,009	88.4	3.5	36,530	71.6	66.2	151,100	879	90.7	33,910	21.6	8.0
18081	Johnson County, Indiana............	162,172	88.5	8.2	62,116	78.5	68.5	230,200	1,027	91.6	70,002	14.9	4.7
18085	Kosciusko County, Indiana..........	79,674	88.3	6.3	31,523	77.3	62.8	180,200	890	90.4	35,177	25.3	3.6
18089	Lake County, Indiana	493,485	89.5	5.5	192,256	70.6	63.5	201,100	993	89.7	200,050	12.6	9.9
18091	LaPorte County, Indiana.............	110,539	83.0	11.9	43,445	73.7	63.2	168,200	888	92.0	43,733	14.3	6.8
18095	Madison County, Indiana	129,675	84.8	7.8	53,910	70.1	61.9	137,000	776	88.0	49,550	18.7	5.9
18097	Marion County, Indiana	956,865	86.8	5.2	394,717	57.0	68.3	186,500	960	91.7	397,289	10.9	4.0
18105	Monroe County, Indiana	139,297	68.8	15.8	56,714	57.1	63.1	231,500	986	90.8	51,878	19.9	4.8
18109	Morgan County, Indiana	72,067	88.6	7.3	26,821	85.3	61.7	193,300	862	84.6	27,611	9.3	12.5
18127	Porter County, Indiana	173,136	88.4	6.6	68,266	77.7	65.9	257,100	1,096	92.7	73,614	12.3	9.6
18141	St. Joseph County, Indiana..........	268,485	86.2	6.3	107,076	69.9	62.4	161,200	906	90.0	111,637	14.9	4.5
18157	Tippecanoe County, Indiana........	184,835	76.9	11.1	73,525	55.4	69.0	200,400	917	90.4	78,427	15.6	2.0
18163	Vanderburgh County, Indiana	177,935	85.4	7.1	79,215	64.4	61.5	155,100	865	88.1	79,645	16.9	2.0
18167	Vigo County, Indiana	104,840	79.3	10.2	42,140	61.9	61.5	130,900	800	86.3	44,303	18.6	5.7
18177	Wayne County, Indiana...............	65,801	83.2	8.1	26,452	68.7	63.3	120,500	733	88.5	25,701	23.2	5.2
19000	**IOWA**..	3,159,672	86.3	6.5	1,300,467	71.9	60.2	174,400	847	88.6	1,374,816	24.0	4.2
19013	Black Hawk County, Iowa	128,670	81.1	7.2	53,951	66.3	61.3	163,900	839	89.4	59,858	24.1	2.6
19049	Dallas County, Iowa...................	102,766	82.2	11.0	41,681	67.4	67.9	283,100	1,037	91.6	43,126	10.9	3.4
19061	Dubuque County, Iowa...............	98,347	89.9	4.6	40,482	74.8	62.3	200,700	863	92.3	44,648	25.9	5.0
19103	Johnson County, Iowa................	153,605	76.4	10.3	61,301	59.2	71.5	289,400	976	88.4	71,479	16.5	4.7
19113	Linn County, Iowa......................	226,613	90.0	4.1	94,884	75.1	67.5	184,600	854	92.5	93,725	17.8	2.9
19153	Polk County, Iowa......................	491,406	82.9	6.4	203,390	67.4	70.4	226,800	976	91.6	203,521	14.6	2.1
19155	Pottawattamie County, Iowa.......	92,359	88.8	5.5	37,930	69.2	60.5	183,300	861	86.5	39,221	19.8	3.0
19163	Scott County, Iowa	172,463	87.8	4.9	72,128	70.2	64.3	189,400	857	89.4	73,695	13.4	4.5
19169	Story County, Iowa	98,299	68.5	16.7	38,868	55.9	64.3	225,500	887	77.0	40,885	32.1	2.3
19193	Woodbury County, Iowa.............	104,366	91.9	4.2	41,327	71.5	60.4	156,200	828	89.4	49,748	17.9	1.9
20000	**KANSAS**	2,900,594	84.9	7.3	1,159,026	67.0	57.9	183,800	904	90.0	1,231,975	23.0	3.6
20015	Butler County, Kansas................	67,588	85.3	6.5	24,545	77.4	61.9	194,700	854	88.5	29,383	15.8	3.6
20045	Douglas County, Kansas.............	118,571	76.2	12.5	49,759	50.1	66.6	240,900	870	91.2	52,272	22.7	2.7
20091	Johnson County, Kansas	606,030	86.0	7.2	245,646	68.8	68.5	337,700	1,214	95.9	240,286	14.7	2.9
20103	Leavenworth County, Kansas	81,652	81.0	12.5	29,963	69.5	59.4	246,600	957	93.8	33,510	19.4	2.4
20161	Riley County, Kansas..................	71,705	76.1	13.0	27,866	49.5	60.9	225,700	882	92.0	34,764	29.5	3.4
20173	Sedgwick County, Kansas	517,395	83.3	5.3	203,656	63.0	63.0	171,100	868	91.2	224,921	14.7	2.7
20177	Shawnee County, Kansas............	176,507	88.1	3.9	74,908	65.6	60.7	154,700	862	88.2	72,013	15.6	4.2
20209	Wyandotte County, Kansas.........	164,511	86.7	7.6	62,538	60.9	56.1	148,400	984	87.8	64,840	10.0	3.7

STATE County	Total population 1 year and over	Lived in the same house 1 year ago (percent)	Did not live in the same county 1 year ago (percent)	Total occupied housing units	Owner-occupied units (percent)	Percent with a mortgage, contract to purchase, or similar debt	Median value of owner-occupied units (dollars; owner estimated)	Median gross rent of renter-occupied units paying cash rent	Households with Internet access (percent)	Number of workers who commuted to work	Commute of less than 10 minutes (percent)	Commute of 60 minutes or more (percent)
ACS table number:	C07204	C07204	C07204	B25003	B25003	B25081	B25097	B25064	S2801	B08012	B08012	B08012
Column number:	1	2	3	4	5	6	7	8	9	10	11	12
21000 **KENTUCKY**............................	4,460,646	86.9	6.3	1,785,682	68.7	57.1	173,300	830	87.3	1,737,719	15.2	6.2
21015 Boone County, Kentucky............	135,500	86.1	8.3	50,728	77.5	71.4	231,000	1,122	90.2	59,817	7.4	5.5
21029 Bullitt County, Kentucky.............	82,139	93.7	3.5	30,979	85.9	68.0	198,700	903	91.1	36,685	5.6	4.6
21037 Campbell County, Kentucky........	92,046	83.6	12.4	39,048	71.4	63.4	218,000	961	91.0	39,253	14.2	5.3
21047 Christian County, Kentucky........	71,442	84.9	8.3	25,317	46.0	51.2	148,400	904	73.6	28,159	28.9	2.7
21059 Daviess County, Kentucky...........	102,134	85.6	5.8	41,246	73.4	57.3	167,900	748	90.8	40,797	24.1	5.4
21067 Fayette County, Kentucky...........	317,482	80.0	9.2	139,303	53.9	68.1	242,400	968	92.8	141,374	13.5	4.2
21093 Hardin County, Kentucky	110,479	83.7	8.5	42,714	60.3	60.0	183,200	828	90.5	47,024	20.0	7.5
21111 Jefferson County, Kentucky........	766,633	85.5	4.8	331,104	62.7	65.6	222,500	979	90.6	313,046	10.7	2.3
21117 Kenton County, Kentucky...........	167,860	87.7	6.1	68,073	72.8	68.8	215,600	888	91.0	67,606	7.8	3.8
21145 McCracken County, Kentucky.....	67,038	90.0	3.5	25,531	71.9	52.7	176,100	872	87.9	24,359	21.2	0.8
21151 Madison County, Kentucky	93,743	79.4	11.4	36,052	62.2	63.2	206,700	765	87.2	40,647	18.5	6.4
21185 Oldham County, Kentucky..........	67,983	88.8	6.0	22,895	85.2	74.9	342,600	892	96.7	26,226	12.1	1.8
21199 Pulaski County, Kentucky............	NA	NA	NA	25,509	75.2	49.9	146,200	634	81.7	23,392	17.3	6.9
21227 Warren County, Kentucky	136,123	78.9	9.3	53,093	55.8	63.2	229,300	826	90.6	62,089	19.0	6.2
22000 **LOUISIANA**	4,571,302	87.2	5.6	1,783,924	67.3	53.1	192,800	924	85.5	1,776,330	13.0	7.5
22005 Ascension Parish, Louisiana.........	127,723	86.7	6.4	48,129	78.5	63.0	224,600	1,120	90.3	56,632	6.5	4.6
22015 Bossier Parish, Louisiana.............	127,116	84.9	10.0	49,418	63.1	64.1	209,900	1,061	82.5	51,823	14.1	6.3
22017 Caddo Parish, Louisiana	230,768	85.5	5.4	96,369	59.1	52.6	161,200	865	84.1	83,908	11.4	4.0
22019 Calcasieu Parish, Louisiana.........	202,905	84.6	6.2	71,511	75.1	55.0	207,900	988	83.3	85,930	13.8	5.4
22033 East Baton Rouge Parish, Louisiana	447,510	83.4	7.3	175,731	59.4	60.2	224,600	1,020	89.2	176,643	8.3	7.3
22045 Iberia Parish, Louisiana................	NA	NA	NA	25,440	69.4	43.3	140,900	798	84.5	24,186	12.5	6.4
22051 Jefferson Parish, Louisiana	427,964	87.9	4.6	179,775	63.6	54.7	220,300	1,047	87.8	175,735	9.9	5.4
22055 Lafayette Parish, Louisiana.........	241,411	84.2	6.8	97,877	66.6	56.3	205,500	889	91.7	102,941	10.9	6.1
22057 Lafourche Parish, Louisiana........	96,523	91.0	4.7	38,111	78.5	44.5	166,100	786	85.3	37,547	22.9	7.9
22063 Livingston Parish, Louisiana........	144,836	88.1	5.5	51,960	79.0	66.6	217,200	1,070	95.8	61,996	7.5	9.5
22071 Orleans Parish, Louisiana............	372,680	86.5	5.5	158,827	52.6	57.2	279,100	1,082	83.8	135,163	12.1	3.7
22073 Ouachita Parish, Louisiana	157,193	87.6	3.6	61,594	60.2	55.2	179,800	811	84.6	60,448	12.1	7.0
22079 Rapides Parish, Louisiana............	126,403	89.1	3.6	48,405	65.2	52.9	169,800	859	86.4	47,376	14.5	3.7
22097 St. Landry Parish, Louisiana.........	81,190	87.3	3.4	32,213	62.5	NA	130,700	648	74.2	28,365	17.5	12.2
22103 St. Tammany Parish, Louisiana.....	266,165	88.1	5.5	103,543	79.8	64.8	259,800	1,168	92.0	104,466	10.4	13.1
22105 Tangipahoa Parish, Louisiana.......	133,554	84.2	3.2	49,915	71.1	56.8	191,300	846	87.4	55,022	13.8	13.4
22109 Terrebonne Parish, Louisiana	106,739	89.6	1.9	43,996	80.8	52.3	174,900	827	80.9	43,647	20.4	6.6
23000 **MAINE**......................................	1,360,264	88.5	6.0	593,626	74.8	60.3	252,100	945	90.1	543,273	18.6	6.6
23001 Androscoggin County, Maine......	110,139	89.1	5.2	46,323	69.5	66.7	219,800	866	89.9	44,375	17.6	2.8
23003 Aroostook County, Maine...........	66,231	87.9	3.3	30,220	72.4	52.6	124,400	665	84.3	26,056	37.1	4.2
23005 Cumberland County, Maine.........	302,772	88.9	6.4	129,977	70.6	67.4	389,300	1,298	91.4	119,204	16.4	4.9
23011 Kennebec County, Maine............	122,707	88.1	5.4	53,803	74.5	61.0	189,300	856	90.3	47,826	19.4	7.3
23019 Penobscot County, Maine...........	151,683	86.2	6.0	65,441	70.0	58.6	184,700	875	90.1	61,860	20.2	7.0
23031 York County, Maine	212,683	89.8	4.7	90,907	77.8	65.2	334,600	1,117	92.8	87,145	12.9	7.9
24000 **MARYLAND**	6,099,715	88.3	6.2	2,355,652	67.8	71.5	370,800	1,473	91.9	2,319,169	8.9	10.4
24001 Allegany County, Maryland.........	66,996	88.9	5.2	28,535	64.9	56.9	135,400	662	85.1	24,454	17.2	8.3
24003 Anne Arundel County, Maryland.	584,219	88.4	6.2	225,064	74.6	73.8	418,200	1,795	95.9	235,784	9.3	7.8
24005 Baltimore County, Maryland........	839,858	89.2	5.5	332,529	66.7	68.4	313,800	1,371	91.6	336,996	9.4	6.3
24009 Calvert County, Maryland	93,157	90.3	6.2	33,994	86.7	77.6	411,700	1,499	92.5	38,398	8.7	21.4
24013 Carroll County, Maryland............	171,939	93.1	4.4	64,161	85.2	69.5	391,100	1,332	91.4	71,031	12.2	16.8
24015 Cecil County, Maryland...............	103,030	91.5	6.5	41,000	78.1	72.2	305,200	1,142	90.7	39,975	11.1	8.0
24017 Charles County, Maryland...........	166,486	86.0	8.9	59,481	79.7	81.6	371,000	1,715	93.2	67,260	7.5	19.5
24021 Frederick County, Maryland.........	278,217	87.9	7.2	103,685	76.6	74.0	399,700	1,543	93.3	109,286	8.9	16.6
24025 Harford County, Maryland	260,342	90.9	4.3	101,196	80.0	70.0	333,900	1,391	94.3	108,685	8.9	9.1
24027 Howard County, Maryland..........	330,942	88.0	6.6	120,546	74.0	72.1	529,300	1,808	97.0	121,755	8.9	7.7
24031 Montgomery County, Maryland ..	1,044,928	87.3	6.1	388,396	65.7	69.8	572,600	1,821	96.0	340,147	6.9	9.5
24033 Prince George's County, Maryland.....................................	942,895	88.4	5.4	346,127	62.2	79.5	378,800	1,563	93.3	364,552	5.0	13.0
24037 St. Mary's County, Maryland	113,453	87.5	7.3	42,078	75.9	73.6	356,400	1,442	90.5	45,927	10.2	15.8
24043 Washington County, Maryland....	153,026	89.1	5.2	60,215	63.6	63.2	246,500	990	81.8	57,621	11.6	9.6
24045 Wicomico County, Maryland.......	103,349	82.9	9.7	40,577	62.5	65.8	219,500	1,124	85.6	44,159	15.7	7.1
24510 Baltimore city, Maryland.............	568,926	86.8	7.5	254,370	48.5	68.6	193,100	1,167	83.3	200,184	8.9	8.9

STATE County	Total population 1 year and over	Lived in the same house 1 year ago (percent)	Did not live in the same county 1 year ago (percent)	Total occupied housing units	Owner-occupied units (percent)	Percent with a mortgage, contract to purchase, or similar debt	Median value of owner-occupied units (dollars; owner estimated)	Median gross rent of renter-occupied units paying cash rent	Households with Internet access (percent)	Number of workers who commuted to work	Commute of less than 10 minutes (percent)	Commute of 60 minutes or more (percent)
ACS table number:	C07204	C07204	C07204	B25003	B25003	B25081	B25097	B25064	S2801	B08012	B08012	B08012
STATE County code / Column number:	1	2	3	4	5	6	7	8	9	10	11	12
25000 **MASSACHUSETTS**	6,916,314	87.4	6.4	2,759,018	63.2	67.9	480,600	1,487	92.3	2,689,907	11.1	9.5
25001 Barnstable County, Massachusetts	231,205	90.4	6.3	104,733	82.3	61.0	500,800	1,470	94.3	90,703	18.8	7.6
25003 Berkshire County, Massachusetts	127,784	87.3	6.4	57,765	70.1	61.0	260,000	948	90.1	51,887	21.0	3.1
25005 Bristol County, Massachusetts	573,904	90.3	4.5	233,531	61.7	68.3	391,300	1,031	89.1	245,167	10.4	10.0
25009 Essex County, Massachusetts	797,558	89.0	4.5	309,972	65.1	69.6	529,400	1,458	91.9	325,990	11.9	9.2
25011 Franklin County, Massachusetts	70,487	91.0	3.9	30,374	71.5	61.4	286,000	1,048	89.5	28,010	18.7	5.3
25013 Hampden County, Massachusetts	458,096	91.5	3.0	184,544	61.6	66.4	259,100	999	88.1	171,890	12.7	5.7
25015 Hampshire County, Massachusetts	160,331	76.5	17.5	60,870	68.2	61.0	344,000	1,303	90.2	57,700	10.8	5.2
25017 Middlesex County, Massachusetts	1,598,083	85.5	7.1	632,831	62.1	68.6	640,500	1,874	94.5	586,489	10.0	7.9
25021 Norfolk County, Massachusetts	717,955	89.2	6.9	280,067	68.4	67.7	602,600	1,823	94.0	265,729	9.1	11.6
25023 Plymouth County, Massachusetts	529,143	90.2	4.8	202,084	79.2	69.8	470,500	1,433	92.6	213,504	10.3	13.8
25025 Suffolk County, Massachusetts	762,239	81.7	9.7	315,257	36.3	71.3	636,800	1,788	91.3	291,758	8.3	11.3
25027 Worcester County, Massachusetts	854,306	88.1	5.3	333,435	67.0	69.5	365,700	1,197	92.7	345,018	11.8	10.9
26000 **MICHIGAN**	9,950,336	88.7	5.4	4,051,798	73.2	59.0	199,100	969	90.2	3,784,429	14.9	5.6
26005 Allegan County, Michigan	119,626	92.8	4.5	44,479	88.0	59.4	223,100	948	91.0	51,573	13.3	5.0
26017 Bay County, Michigan	102,107	90.7	4.2	45,487	77.5	53.6	115,200	666	89.3	43,040	21.2	4.1
26021 Berrien County, Michigan	151,920	88.1	6.1	65,764	72.2	56.8	194,100	831	88.4	60,298	21.2	5.9
26025 Calhoun County, Michigan	131,724	90.1	5.1	53,482	73.2	60.7	143,400	821	88.7	51,240	17.8	2.1
26037 Clinton County, Michigan	78,659	92.3	5.2	30,952	81.4	61.7	235,900	982	89.9	30,964	15.6	5.3
26045 Eaton County, Michigan	107,882	87.1	7.8	45,137	73.3	68.8	195,100	959	90.7	40,700	11.4	5.1
26049 Genesee County, Michigan	400,105	88.0	4.3	167,895	70.7	56.8	157,400	870	87.2	146,223	13.8	10.9
26055 Grand Traverse County, Michigan	95,593	87.2	7.5	40,083	76.3	59.8	286,400	1,143	91.9	37,523	16.0	5.5
26065 Ingham County, Michigan	282,717	80.0	11.7	115,752	59.7	62.8	166,200	928	90.8	101,160	15.7	4.8
26067 Ionia County, Michigan	66,521	88.1	7.6	23,531	79.8	62.4	163,200	749	84.2	25,480	15.7	7.7
26075 Jackson County, Michigan	158,309	88.4	3.8	61,937	74.9	59.5	169,800	865	90.6	61,056	16.3	6.4
26077 Kalamazoo County, Michigan	258,329	84.2	7.2	105,642	63.6	62.1	208,300	898	89.9	109,442	16.6	5.2
26081 Kent County, Michigan	651,020	88.3	4.8	253,092	70.9	63.7	248,300	1,059	91.4	280,418	13.9	3.3
26087 Lapeer County, Michigan	87,669	90.3	6.2	34,447	85.4	63.9	199,500	867	88.4	36,563	11.3	15.3
26091 Lenawee County, Michigan	98,443	91.0	4.6	38,963	80.8	65.1	172,000	935	90.7	36,642	23.4	12.4
26093 Livingston County, Michigan	192,978	91.0	5.6	75,370	88.2	68.2	313,000	1,237	93.4	77,718	9.8	9.5
26099 Macomb County, Michigan	866,919	91.0	3.9	358,011	75.3	63.5	210,300	1,069	93.3	349,667	10.4	4.6
26103 Marquette County, Michigan	65,923	85.1	6.5	27,290	70.2	61.1	184,000	872	86.0	27,572	27.9	3.8
26111 Midland County, Michigan	82,824	89.1	5.5	35,453	75.4	53.5	172,600	941	90.5	29,902	19.3	5.6
26115 Monroe County, Michigan	154,013	89.9	4.6	61,574	81.4	61.2	205,100	893	87.7	61,160	14.7	8.8
26117 Montcalm County, Michigan	66,394	89.7	6.3	23,745	82.3	57.9	161,300	759	85.7	25,929	12.6	10.0
26121 Muskegon County, Michigan	174,633	90.6	3.9	67,707	75.2	58.4	165,500	869	89.6	66,520	16.1	3.9
26125 Oakland County, Michigan	1,257,456	88.8	4.7	530,383	73.1	66.4	299,800	1,203	94.4	469,223	10.6	4.8
26139 Ottawa County, Michigan	296,677	87.9	7.0	110,045	79.9	62.8	271,100	1,007	91.8	134,021	17.8	3.0
26145 Saginaw County, Michigan	187,556	88.5	5.7	80,146	71.7	51.8	128,600	818	88.2	68,570	19.4	5.6
26147 St. Clair County, Michigan	158,685	90.1	3.6	66,324	78.5	59.0	192,400	906	91.0	66,599	19.0	11.1
26155 Shiawassee County, Michigan	67,271	91.2	4.6	28,226	77.3	58.0	146,400	760	84.8	27,528	23.0	9.2
26159 Van Buren County, Michigan	74,651	90.5	4.9	28,457	80.7	59.6	175,000	711	87.6	28,160	17.0	4.4
26161 Washtenaw County, Michigan	365,442	78.9	11.9	149,133	60.6	65.1	333,000	1,225	94.0	129,418	13.4	4.8
26163 Wayne County, Michigan	1,753,290	91.2	3.3	695,038	65.0	51.9	158,700	975	89.3	585,394	10.8	4.5
27000 **MINNESOTA**	5,645,866	87.3	6.4	2,281,033	73.0	64.3	285,400	1,113	91.6	2,300,218	17.8	4.7
27003 Anoka County, Minnesota	363,533	89.7	6.6	135,265	79.8	70.0	295,900	1,247	93.4	150,239	9.2	4.3
27013 Blue Earth County, Minnesota	68,429	78.6	9.9	27,604	65.0	56.1	219,600	949	87.9	33,749	29.0	2.3
27019 Carver County, Minnesota	107,606	92.2	5.2	40,141	81.5	68.6	393,400	1,344	93.9	41,323	14.6	4.6
27027 Clay County, Minnesota	64,749	83.9	11.4	26,236	68.6	64.1	240,000	829	88.8	28,632	20.6	3.1
27035 Crow Wing County, Minnesota	66,744	88.1	5.9	27,753	77.3	61.5	251,600	840	91.0	25,440	19.5	4.9
27037 Dakota County, Minnesota	437,496	88.2	5.9	170,696	77.1	70.3	333,800	1,296	94.3	178,701	15.3	2.4
27053 Hennepin County, Minnesota	1,252,072	84.4	6.1	532,149	64.0	69.1	349,500	1,318	93.2	464,469	11.1	2.8
27109 Olmsted County, Minnesota	161,758	85.4	6.3	65,122	70.9	61.1	285,500	1,143	91.2	72,480	13.4	3.3
27123 Ramsey County, Minnesota	536,642	86.2	7.1	218,817	61.9	65.3	291,600	1,143	92.3	202,901	11.7	2.6
27131 Rice County, Minnesota	66,636	88.7	6.9	23,779	78.2	66.0	270,700	1,048	92.9	29,068	29.7	6.1

STATE County	Total population 1 year and over	Lived in the same house 1 year ago (percent)	Did not live in the same county 1 year ago (percent)	Total occupied housing units	Owner-occupied units (percent)	Percent with a mortgage, contract to purchase, or similar debt	Median value of owner-occupied units (dollars; owner estimated)	Median gross rent of renter-occupied units paying cash rent	Households with Internet access (percent)	Number of workers who commuted to work	Commute of less than 10 minutes (percent)	Commute of 60 minutes or more (percent)
ACS table number:	C07204	C07204	C07204	B25003	B25003	B25081	B25097	B25064	S2801	B08012	B08012	B08012
Column number:	1	2	3	4	5	6	7	8	9	10	11	12
MINNESOTA—Cont.												
27137 St. Louis County, Minnesota........	196,446	86.0	5.4	85,576	72.7	60.3	187,900	909	89.8	79,285	22.2	4.7
27139 Scott County, Minnesota.............	151,429	89.6	7.6	55,327	81.5	73.6	364,600	1,291	95.8	64,955	17.6	4.6
27141 Sherburne County, Minnesota	98,104	92.0	5.9	34,738	86.5	73.4	324,900	1,075	91.4	47,521	11.4	8.7
27145 Stearns County, Minnesota........	157,398	86.3	8.4	62,168	67.5	57.3	233,900	854	90.0	75,138	19.4	6.6
27163 Washington County, Minnesota..	269,587	87.8	8.5	102,421	81.8	70.0	380,300	1,502	94.8	95,223	14.8	3.2
27171 Wright County, Minnesota.........	142,594	90.3	5.5	52,260	81.5	65.7	306,400	1,038	95.1	61,319	14.4	8.3
28000 **MISSISSIPPI**.............................	2,919,574	89.3	5.2	1,129,611	69.7	48.6	145,600	831	81.9	1,139,216	13.8	7.5
28033 DeSoto County, Mississippi	187,810	92.5	4.1	68,966	78.9	70.2	233,500	1,192	89.3	82,023	10.4	4.6
28035 Forrest County, Mississippi	77,207	82.0	6.4	30,600	53.1	52.0	146,100	868	83.3	33,993	20.1	7.7
28047 Harrison County, Mississippi........	207,132	84.7	9.1	81,224	58.9	56.5	168,400	925	87.2	81,356	13.0	7.4
28049 Hinds County, Mississippi............	219,694	86.1	3.8	91,067	55.7	51.4	135,800	936	86.7	80,882	10.3	3.2
28059 Jackson County, Mississippi.........	141,787	84.4	8.8	56,984	75.9	53.7	158,700	916	88.6	60,210	14.1	5.5
28067 Jones County, Mississippi............	65,810	93.1	4.3	23,506	77.7	34.1	111,200	628	71.3	23,315	11.2	3.4
28073 Lamar County, Mississippi	64,416	83.0	10.9	25,688	69.3	NA	178,700	994	93.4	29,068	14.3	7.4
28075 Lauderdale County, Mississippi....	71,687	83.6	4.5	28,212	64.4	NA	110,000	838	79.2	27,599	7.5	4.3
28081 Lee County, Mississippi...............	82,638	92.1	3.6	32,722	67.7	64.1	176,800	791	82.5	34,710	11.1	3.1
28089 Madison County, Mississippi........	109,343	89.1	5.9	42,558	69.7	69.2	268,900	1,011	94.7	50,727	7.7	5.7
28121 Rankin County, Mississippi..........	156,900	88.9	7.3	59,894	78.1	58.8	199,900	1,001	90.3	70,491	8.1	4.8
29000 **MISSOURI**	6,102,443	86.6	6.8	2,468,726	68.8	61.1	198,300	882	88.7	2,482,032	16.0	5.2
29019 Boone County, Missouri...............	183,611	78.5	10.0	75,036	59.0	67.7	230,000	955	92.0	87,267	18.5	2.2
29021 Buchanan County, Missouri.........	82,234	83.4	8.1	33,334	62.4	54.4	144,400	781	86.8	35,503	30.9,	5.5
29031 Cape Girardeau County, Missouri	80,910	82.0	10.0	32,800	68.8	61.8	183,800	820	91.9	35,624	21.1	4.7
29037 Cass County, Missouri.................	108,549	86.2	8.4	42,361	80.6	64.9	243,800	1,024	90.7	47,380	12.0	6.6
29043 Christian County, Missouri	91,061	90.6	5.8	34,116	77.8	67.7	226,300	844	93.4	38,763	11.4	3.5
29047 Clay County, Missouri.................	252,829	85.1	6.5	100,737	67.5	70.1	237,600	1,034	90.6	109,660	14.1	3.3
29051 Cole County, Missouri.................	75,820	88.9	6.7	29,522	69.2	57.6	188,600	684	87.8	34,785	23.1	1.3
29071 Franklin County, Missouri...........	103,970	90.1	5.0	41,301	79.3	63.3	195,300	749	86.9	44,662	15.1	10.4
29077 Greene County, Missouri.............	298,351	83.6	7.3	130,986	59.5	62.6	187,600	818	88.0	128,500	15.5	3.2
29095 Jackson County, Missouri............	709,694	85.2	5.8	302,965	59.7	66.0	201,500	1,044	91.0	286,551	13.0	3.5
29097 Jasper County, Missouri	121,616	86.7	4.8	47,864	64.9	62.4	148,200	891	89.3	49,462	20.0	3.6
29099 Jefferson County, Missouri..........	225,134	90.5	5.1	88,806	81.2	66.5	208,600	868	89.1	100,563	9.6	8.0
29165 Platte County, Missouri	106,971	86.0	8.6	43,201	67.5	70.2	288,200	1,036	92.4	45,299	12.6	3.1
29183 St. Charles County, Missouri	406,186	88.2	5.9	157,907	80.7	71.6	278,300	1,140	95.1	167,428	9.6	3.9
29187 St. Francois County, Missouri	67,045	86.3	6.6	25,030	66.0	55.6	147,100	692	80.3	24,431	27.0	12.0
29189 St. Louis County, Missouri	987,894	87.7	5.8	412,833	70.3	64.0	245,200	1,018	91.8	372,768	9.4	2.8
29510 St. Louis city, Missouri.................	289,484	85.1	7.6	139,736	45.6	64.4	170,800	843	85.9	117,282	8.7	4.4
30000 **MONTANA**	1,093,888	86.3	7.3	448,949	69.5	54.8	322,800	883	89.2	449,385	26.1	5.1
30013 Cascade County, Montana.........	82,584	85.3	7.6	34,303	65.7	57.6	226,600	760	89.8	36,829	28.1	4.4
30029 Flathead County, Montana.........	107,092	87.2	5.9	42,900	78.5	57.6	444,600	877	92.4	44,569	19.0	6.7
30031 Gallatin County, Montana..........	121,582	80.3	10.2	48,796	63.1	63.0	584,500	1,315	94.3	54,589	21.9	4.1
30049 Lewis and Clark County, Montana	72,012	89.3	4.3	31,208	68.2	60.8	317,000	876	87.2	29,744	18.0	3.0
30063 Missoula County, Montana	118,327	82.5	9.4	51,957	57.5	65.7	405,300	1,034	92.1	53,476	24.5	1.8
30111 Yellowstone County, Montana	165,718	86.1	6.7	69,001	70.7	58.1	302,400	932	92.7	71,750	15.7	3.1
31000 **NEBRASKA**..............................	1,939,700	86.5	6.0	785,982	67.8	59.7	204,900	912	90.0	880,415	23.9	3.7
31055 Douglas County, Nebraska.........	576,567	86.0	5.1	236,106	62.5	70.2	229,000	1,003	91.7	245,474	15.5	3.1
31109 Lancaster County, Nebraska........	321,815	83.1	5.9	131,417	60.8	64.0	237,500	905	92.1	151,896	17.2	3.4
31153 Sarpy County, Nebraska.............	191,751	86.6	7.9	72,428	70.3	72.1	257,100	1,157	94.0	86,280	12.5	2.9
32000 **NEVADA**.................................	3,111,722	85.5	5.4	1,191,380	59.1	67.6	373,000	1,311	90.7	1,223,063	10.2	5.6
32003 Clark County, Nevada	2,266,274	85.3	5.1	854,289	56.7	69.2	365,800	1,325	91.5	876,598	7.9	4.2
32031 Washoe County, Nevada.............	489,861	85.2	5.1	198,018	59.9	66.6	459,400	1,345	87.9	210,576	13.3	3.8
33000 **NEW HAMPSHIRE**...................	1,377,638	88.8	6.2	548,026	72.5	62.9	345,200	1,263	92.5	591,321	14.2	8.0
33005 Cheshire County, New Hampshire	76,190	86.8	6.0	28,266	74.6	56.7	245,000	1,055	90.3	32,947	21.6	6.8
33009 Grafton County, New Hampshire	91,682	89.3	7.7	35,199	70.1	53.7	264,300	1,182	87.9	37,893	16.9	5.8
33011 Hillsborough County, New Hampshire	420,206	87.8	5.9	167,899	67.7	66.2	361,000	1,393	94.2	180,111	12.4	7.6

STATE County	Total population 1 year and over	Lived in the same house 1 year ago (percent)	Did not live in the same county 1 year ago (percent)	Total occupied housing units	Owner-occupied units (percent)	Percent with a mortgage, contract to purchase, or similar debt	Median value of owner-occupied units (dollars; owner estimated)	Median gross rent of renter-occupied units paying cash rent	Households with Internet access (percent)	Number of workers who commuted to work	Commute of less than 10 minutes (percent)	Commute of 60 minutes or more (percent)
STATE County code	ACS table number:	C07204	C07204	C07204	B25003	B25003	B25081	B25097	B25064	S2801	B08012	B08012	B08012
	Column number:	1	2	3	4	5	6	7	8	9	10	11	12

STATE County code	STATE County	1	2	3	4	5	6	7	8	9	10	11	12
	NEW HAMPSHIRE—Cont.												
33013	Merrimack County, New Hampshire	154,206	90.8	6.4	58,733	72.9	63.0	304,900	1,119	92.4	67,249	12.8	6.6
33015	Rockingham County, New Hampshire	314,193	90.5	5.1	127,882	77.2	65.5	427,000	1,451	95.0	137,636	13.1	9.1
33017	Strafford County, New Hampshire	131,455	83.4	9.6	52,067	68.4	66.1	315,400	1,303	93.0	55,777	13.1	7.6
34000	**NEW JERSEY**	9,174,117	89.4	5.7	3,497,945	64.4	64.3	389,800	1,457	92.0	3,437,038	10.6	11.2
34001	Atlantic County, New Jersey	272,618	90.8	4.1	112,299	67.0	63.3	254,200	1,208	91.4	107,131	13.8	8.3
34003	Bergen County, New Jersey	944,044	90.6	4.3	352,030	66.5	61.1	548,200	1,624	94.3	353,993	11.2	12.9
34005	Burlington County, New Jersey	460,338	89.2	6.6	175,859	77.4	65.5	291,600	1,465	94.3	185,667	9.8	7.9
34007	Camden County, New Jersey	518,536	88.6	5.1	201,158	65.3	64.9	240,400	1,209	90.8	196,464	11.7	6.6
34009	Cape May County, New Jersey	94,969	88.0	8.1	48,860	78.1	59.9	365,100	971	90.5	36,356	17.8	6.7
34011	Cumberland County, New Jersey	152,670	90.7	4.7	53,883	65.4	64.5	196,400	1,131	89.9	54,830	19.4	6.6
34013	Essex County, New Jersey	846,839	88.6	5.6	322,453	44.6	69.2	460,600	1,319	87.7	297,112	6.5	13.8
34015	Gloucester County, New Jersey	302,133	89.5	5.5	112,502	80.6	69.6	267,100	1,298	93.0	120,023	14.2	6.9
34017	Hudson County, New Jersey	694,726	86.7	7.0	292,000	32.2	61.9	468,100	1,645	90.8	255,992	6.3	15.3
34019	Hunterdon County, New Jersey	129,101	89.1	6.6	51,292	86.9	68.4	452,000	1,574	94.2	46,984	11.3	13.7
34021	Mercer County, New Jersey	381,778	87.1	7.2	143,970	63.1	62.8	311,900	1,341	90.8	128,137	12.1	7.6
34023	Middlesex County, New Jersey	852,948	87.3	7.4	307,831	64.7	62.3	396,700	1,655	93.4	319,482	10.8	12.7
34025	Monmouth County, New Jersey	639,330	91.0	4.8	250,738	75.7	64.7	505,500	1,616	94.0	239,137	10.8	12.6
34027	Morris County, New Jersey	505,462	90.0	5.5	192,847	75.3	66.4	504,300	1,726	95.6	181,405	11.7	10.5
34029	Ocean County, New Jersey	639,236	90.6	4.5	240,736	80.5	60.6	337,800	1,537	87.8	234,592	14.1	12.7
34031	Passaic County, New Jersey	512,769	91.6	4.5	177,063	52.0	64.6	402,700	1,391	89.3	200,635	7.6	6.4
34033	Salem County, New Jersey	64,553	92.1	4.1	24,973	71.8	55.2	199,700	1,055	90.2	24,309	13.5	6.1
34035	Somerset County, New Jersey	342,997	89.9	7.1	130,939	76.8	66.3	470,500	1,750	95.7	122,749	9.2	11.6
34037	Sussex County, New Jersey	144,316	90.3	6.6	58,767	86.7	67.0	315,000	1,303	95.0	62,172	9.5	16.2
34039	Union County, New Jersey	565,419	89.8	5.3	201,392	57.1	67.2	453,600	1,413	92.7	225,219	10.5	11.6
34041	Warren County, New Jersey	109,335	91.1	6.1	46,353	73.4	60.5	300,700	1,169	91.4	44,649	12.7	16.2
35000	**NEW MEXICO**	2,092,251	87.4	6.0	834,007	69.5	52.6	214,000	906	84.6	743,745	18.0	6.4
35001	Bernalillo County, New Mexico	669,934	85.9	4.9	285,185	63.6	64.8	255,400	946	91.4	259,387	11.4	3.9
35013	Doña Ana County, New Mexico	218,321	88.6	5.1	85,021	63.1	53.4	186,400	751	87.2	83,056	14.6	6.7
35025	Lea County, New Mexico	70,992	88.3	4.0	24,390	69.5	NA	155,600	1,033	83.7	23,668	35.0	9.5
35031	McKinley County, New Mexico	71,497	95.4	2.9	20,949	75.8	NA	59,600	868	58.5	20,463	13.3	6.8
35035	Otero County, New Mexico	67,086	86.7	7.5	24,034	68.0	NA	125,600	866	89.6	23,834	24.6	3.5
35043	Sandoval County, New Mexico	149,341	88.1	7.4	56,655	83.4	63.0	252,200	1,193	90.5	51,055	13.9	12.5
35045	San Juan County, New Mexico	120,129	86.2	7.0	40,844	71.2	NA	154,700	827	57.5	38,763	19.1	7.6
35049	Santa Fe County, New Mexico	154,471	88.1	7.8	70,152	74.4	54.8	362,200	1,166	89.9	52,742	18.7	6.7
35061	Valencia County, New Mexico	75,629	89.9	5.6	28,875	80.3	57.3	171,000	838	79.9	23,130	13.0	9.6
36000	**NEW YORK**	19,626,300	89.6	4.1	7,652,666	55.4	58.2	368,800	1,409	90.6	7,246,571	10.8	15.5
36001	Albany County, New York	310,106	86.3	6.9	132,171	59.5	61.5	253,100	1,140	89.9	120,971	12.3	3.9
36005	Bronx County, New York	1,409,509	93.2	1.3	533,004	19.6	56.4	465,000	1,313	87.7	459,510	4.3	30.4
36007	Broome County, New York	195,437	87.1	5.3	84,452	65.2	54.0	135,900	832	88.8	77,485	18.0	3.8
36009	Cattaraugus County, New York	75,902	92.5	3.2	32,562	76.3	41.7	96,500	680	84.7	29,075	26.4	5.8
36011	Cayuga County, New York	75,190	86.9	3.8	32,392	70.6	55.3	164,500	870	86.6	29,460	24.6	4.2
36013	Chautauqua County, New York	125,218	91.1	3.7	53,309	70.2	46.5	99,900	670	88.2	43,456	28.3	4.8
36015	Chemung County, New York	82,103	90.4	3.9	35,407	68.0	53.7	128,600	873	89.0	30,172	23.4	3.8
36019	Clinton County, New York	78,887	87.4	7.1	33,860	72.1	55.9	148,300	872	90.1	32,213	23.3	4.4
36027	Dutchess County, New York	294,282	88.3	7.3	118,175	72.6	63.1	351,500	1,331	93.1	118,346	12.5	14.3
36029	Erie County, New York	941,888	89.1	3.6	412,870	66.9	57.2	199,200	916	89.6	377,035	14.9	3.2
36045	Jefferson County, New York	114,421	81.6	8.9	48,628	56.2	60.3	177,200	1,056	91.5	49,920	25.9	3.8
36047	Kings County, New York	2,606,266	89.4	2.1	1,001,868	30.3	57.3	793,300	1,628	89.5	828,906	4.4	26.9
36053	Madison County, New York	67,187	88.4	8.5	25,294	79.2	57.0	179,600	775	89.7	25,878	20.4	6.5
36055	Monroe County, New York	747,423	87.1	5.0	318,883	64.8	63.6	174,600	1,001	90.4	300,847	14.4	3.2
36059	Nassau County, New York	1,377,978	92.9	3.9	459,452	83.9	62.8	619,800	1,960	94.4	544,187	9.7	18.1
36061	New York County, New York	1,562,743	81.2	7.9	737,575	25.0	46.0	940,900	1,866	91.4	503,950	7.5	12.1
36063	Niagara County, New York	209,108	91.3	3.8	90,975	71.5	55.2	162,900	768	89.4	87,919	18.6	2.0
36065	Oneida County, New York	227,220	91.8	3.7	93,373	67.2	49.6	157,500	820	87.6	85,525	19.6	4.2
36067	Onondaga County, New York	468,735	85.6	5.5	198,132	65.1	60.8	169,800	924	91.6	188,124	15.0	3.7
36069	Ontario County, New York	111,265	87.4	6.1	47,607	73.0	59.9	192,100	1,008	92.5	46,285	19.5	4.8

STATE County code	STATE County	Total population 1 year and over	Lived in the same house 1 year ago (percent)	Did not live in the same county 1 year ago (percent)	Total occupied housing units	Owner-occupied units (percent)	Percent with a mortgage, contract to purchase, or similar debt	Median value of owner-occupied units (dollars; owner estimated)	Median gross rent of renter-occupied units paying cash rent	Households with Internet access (percent)	Number of workers who commuted to work	Commute of less than 10 minutes (percent)	Commute of 60 minutes or more (percent)
	ACS table number:	C07204	C07204	C07204	B25003	B25003	B25081	B25097	B25064	S2801	B08012	B08012	B08012
	Column number:	1	2	3	4	5	6	7	8	9	10	11	12
	NEW YORK—Cont.												
36071	Orange County, New York	399,906	90.0	5.0	137,561	70.7	68.2	325,100	1,398	90.6	155,080	12.7	15.7
36075	Oswego County, New York	116,323	87.2	5.4	46,924	74.7	54.8	127,800	841	89.4	46,330	19.9	6.6
36079	Putnam County, New York	97,437	91.1	6.3	35,166	82.9	59.4	420,000	1,629	94.8	38,794	7.8	21.7
36081	Queens County, New York	2,306,123	92.2	1.7	820,686	45.6	54.1	642,000	1,717	91.1	836,322	3.7	26.7
36083	Rensselaer County, New York	158,390	85.7	8.6	66,431	63.7	63.5	220,600	997	91.8	60,190	13.7	2.9
36085	Richmond County, New York	487,898	93.8	0.8	170,762	69.8	68.0	605,500	1,442	89.7	174,973	6.2	29.8
36087	Rockland County, New York........	333,016	91.6	3.9	102,609	69.8	60.2	503,000	1,717	87.2	116,551	10.6	13.6
36089	St. Lawrence County, New York ..	107,219	86.0	5.0	42,298	70.8	46.7	99,000	757	88.3	38,718	27.6	5.8
36091	Saratoga County, New York	235,093	90.6	4.7	100,226	73.4	65.4	292,000	1,176	92.0	97,520	13.2	3.9
36093	Schenectady County, New York ..	156,165	87.0	6.0	66,910	65.1	62.7	193,700	1,009	88.9	61,280	12.6	1.9
36101	Steuben County, New York	92,081	91.5	5.3	39,500	74.5	49.6	123,700	815	87.3	37,626	23.9	4.5
36103	Suffolk County, New York	1,511,625	91.4	3.4	511,951	82.9	63.8	488,200	2,020	94.1	647,703	10.3	13.1
36105	Sullivan County, New York	79,024	91.8	6.5	32,529	63.9	46.6	217,000	861	90.3	28,396	11.2	8.9
36109	Tompkins County, New York	104,458	70.3	21.8	44,469	53.5	51.2	261,200	1,272	91.4	38,784	15.8	5.2
36111	Ulster County, New York..............	180,504	91.0	6.7	75,053	74.4	57.9	301,800	1,234	92.3	68,260	11.6	13.3
36113	Warren County, New York	64,994	91.6	5.1	29,729	71.1	54.7	223,200	972	91.3	27,333	21.0	6.8
36117	Wayne County, New York	90,411	93.4	3.2	38,634	78.5	57.5	147,400	816	90.9	39,569	18.9	4.8
36119	Westchester County, New York...	987,077	90.2	5.2	371,736	64.5	61.3	592,900	1,734	93.3	345,503	11.4	17.0
37000	**NORTH CAROLINA**	10,446,881	86.5	7.4	4,179,632	66.9	62.0	236,900	1,026	89.0	3,970,072	13.0	6.0
37001	Alamance County, North Carolina...............	172,052	90.4	4.9	69,343	65.2	63.8	203,000	894	88.4	71,191	11.8	4.3
37019	Brunswick County, North Carolina...............	143,009	87.7	7.0	65,337	84.1	56.7	281,800	1,167	94.0	49,073	9.1	6.9
37021	Buncombe County, North Carolina...............	269,025	88.8	5.9	97,345	65.1	55.4	341,300	1,141	87.9	101,848	8.2	2.8
37023	Burke County, North Carolina	87,219	91.6	5.0	35,709	72.1	45.5	162,100	744	80.7	37,017	11.3	2.9
37025	Cabarrus County, North Carolina	229,402	90.4	6.7	73,486	74.5	69.3	285,000	1,151	92.6	88,711	7.6	6.0
37027	Caldwell County, North Carolina.	79,661	91.7	2.8	32,600	73.6	52.4	163,000	601	83.5	30,960	12.4	3.6
37031	Carteret County, North Carolina .	68,239	85.8	6.4	30,589	76.4	54.9	266,300	871	94.1	25,913	14.9	5.6
37035	Catawba County, North Carolina	160,727	90.0	6.3	64,302	68.9	56.1	194,900	813	86.7	65,068	15.0	6.4
37037	Chatham County, North Carolina	77,188	90.6	7.6	31,474	80.3	57.3	386,700	751	89.6	23,019	10.1	8.7
37045	Cleveland County, North Carolina	99,009	87.9	4.8	40,296	74.6	50.7	142,100	775	81.9	41,278	16.6	7.5
37049	Craven County, North Carolina ...	99,832	86.6	9.3	42,139	65.6	60.2	190,600	1,019	83.1	42,962	17.7	4.8
37051	Cumberland County, North Carolina...............	330,522	83.6	9.0	129,898	52.2	67.0	160,700	1,042	91.5	142,443	17.7	3.9
37057	Davidson County, North Carolina	168,497	91.7	4.6	66,245	73.9	54.5	171,100	766	87.3	63,994	11.6	4.8
37063	Durham County, North Carolina..	323,216	82.5	10.0	138,497	54.7	73.3	316,700	1,194	93.4	113,393	10.5	4.2
37067	Forsyth County, North Carolina ...	382,549	85.7	8.0	155,985	64.7	62.9	212,200	875	90.9	146,235	10.7	5.1
37069	Franklin County, North Carolina..	71,247	87.1	10.0	26,689	79.1	60.9	225,500	913	88.3	28,477	9.3	15.7
37071	Gaston County, North Carolina ...	229,445	90.3	4.5	93,913	66.8	62.5	210,100	962	85.8	89,831	9.8	5.4
37081	Guilford County, North Carolina .	537,023	84.7	7.3	212,574	63.2	65.9	207,100	990	92.1	215,111	13.1	4.5
37085	Harnett County, North Carolina ..	134,645	82.5	12.7	49,555	65.4	66.8	190,000	997	80.3	53,025	10.8	11.6
37089	Henderson County, North Carolina...............	116,063	88.1	8.7	50,136	76.4	54.0	298,500	983	89.4	45,711	12.6	4.9
37097	Iredell County, North Carolina.....	189,709	88.6	8.2	73,434	73.5	64.2	254,000	1,079	94.7	75,323	14.2	5.6
37101	Johnston County, North Carolina	223,860	92.4	3.1	82,113	79.0	67.7	249,300	918	87.2	92,693	7.4	11.1
37109	Lincoln County, North Carolina ...	88,577	90.2	6.5	36,361	80.5	59.7	252,900	836	91.4	35,815	11.4	11.5
37119	Mecklenburg County, North Carolina...............	1,108,721	83.1	7.1	458,344	56.5	74.5	335,100	1,328	93.2	389,009	10.9	4.5
37125	Moore County, North Carolina....	101,465	85.2	9.1	43,554	73.8	59.6	300,000	1,022	87.7	39,414	16.0	8.5
37127	Nash County, North Carolina	94,307	91.0	5.3	38,029	64.7	57.0	162,700	826	85.0	39,363	15.4	5.1
37129	New Hanover County, North Carolina...............	227,221	81.2	10.8	103,762	59.6	67.0	319,600	1,187	92.3	93,337	15.0	5.7
37133	Onslow County, North Carolina ..	201,195	73.4	15.3	73,121	63.0	65.1	190,300	1,002	90.7	90,828	22.3	5.7
37135	Orange County, North Carolina...	147,777	81.8	13.2	56,263	66.5	60.8	364,600	1,239	92.7	46,505	10.2	3.2
37147	Pitt County, North Carolina	170,537	82.9	10.5	75,578	49.5	66.7	171,100	848	83.3	66,843	16.7	4.7
37151	Randolph County, North Carolina	143,498	86.2	6.6	55,948	75.0	60.3	149,200	787	88.4	59,272	10.0	6.7
37155	Robeson County, North Carolina.	114,963	94.6	3.0	43,529	65.5	37.2	88,400	683	75.2	42,283	17.2	6.2
37157	Rockingham County, North Carolina...............	90,358	89.4	6.5	38,481	72.2	52.2	151,000	732	81.2	33,499	19.0	3.4

Table C-2. Counties — Where: Migration, Housing, and Transportation, 2021—*Continued*

STATE County code	STATE County	Total population 1 year and over	Lived in the same house 1 year ago (percent)	Did not live in the same county 1 year ago (percent)	Total occupied housing units	Owner-occupied units (percent)	Percent with a mortgage, contract to purchase, or similar debt	Median value of owner-occupied units (dollars; owner estimated)	Median gross rent of renter-occupied units paying cash rent	Households with Internet access (percent)	Number of workers who commuted to work	Commute of less than 10 minutes (percent)	Commute of 60 minutes or more (percent)
	ACS table number:	C07204	C07204	C07204	B25003	B25003	B25081	B25097	B25064	S2801	B08012	B08012	B08012
	Column number:	1	2	3	4	5	6	7	8	9	10	11	12
	NORTH CAROLINA—Cont.												
37159	Rowan County, North Carolina ...	147,516	90.6	4.5	57,024	72.5	58.5	199,200	818	90.1	57,200	12.4	6.5
37171	Surry County, North Carolina	70,444	90.9	5.8	30,317	74.0	48.1	152,000	677	86.8	29,135	15.8	8.5
37179	Union County, North Carolina.....	240,688	88.7	8.0	83,407	81.6	72.9	338,600	1,142	94.4	90,901	9.1	5.3
37183	Wake County, North Carolina	1,139,389	83.7	7.6	439,911	65.0	75.0	377,800	1,305	95.0	383,672	10.7	4.2
37191	Wayne County, North Carolina....	115,502	82.8	9.6	46,932	58.4	55.3	159,300	829	88.6	49,422	19.4	5.8
37193	Wilkes County, North Carolina ...	NA	NA	NA	26,770	67.5	50.6	150,700	641	85.1	22,196	11.6	10.2
37195	Wilson County, North Carolina ...	77,414	85.3	9.2	32,868	57.3	56.8	141,400	898	82.0	30,117	16.6	9.4
38000	**NORTH DAKOTA**.....................	764,638	83.8	8.5	322,511	63.1	52.7	224,400	839	88.2	362,392	28.4	4.2
38015	Burleigh County, North Dakota ..	97,668	86.6	6.6	39,295	71.2	55.6	272,400	831	89.1	47,779	20.5	3.4
38017	Cass County, North Dakota........	183,692	78.4	10.2	83,761	50.9	63.3	249,000	807	90.3	92,972	18.3	3.6
38035	Grand Forks County, North Dakota	71,929	75.7	17.2	31,152	49.2	60.4	234,200	979	87.8	36,647	31.3	4.1
38101	Ward County, North Dakota.......	67,461	80.2	11.9	28,795	60.7	NA	237,400	1,020	88.3	34,108	25.3	4.9
39000	**OHIO**....................................	11,660,200	87.6	5.1	4,832,922	67.2	61.4	180,200	870	89.1	4,677,145	15.2	4.8
39003	Allen County, Ohio....................	100,459	87.4	5.7	41,021	66.0	60.3	144,100	784	88.7	39,234	19.3	2.3
39007	Ashtabula County, Ohio.............	96,328	88.6	3.6	39,915	71.2	48.2	134,000	742	85.7	38,365	17.4	5.9
39013	Belmont County, Ohio	65,395	92.7	3.3	26,949	72.0	47.4	131,100	627	84.5	24,098	12.5	4.4
39017	Butler County, Ohio..................	385,752	87.0	5.4	146,057	72.6	66.6	216,900	996	91.3	153,544	15.7	3.7
39023	Clark County, Ohio....................	134,317	87.6	3.6	57,013	70.4	60.0	144,500	699	90.1	55,284	17.1	4.8
39025	Clermont County, Ohio..............	207,768	87.8	5.1	84,219	70.3	64.3	225,300	887	90.6	83,678	7.9	4.7
39029	Columbiana County, Ohio..........	99,823	88.7	5.3	41,047	74.2	46.5	117,200	641	85.3	42,863	21.4	5.1
39035	Cuyahoga County, Ohio.............	1,236,275	86.2	4.3	557,572	58.4	58.7	166,000	880	88.3	480,602	11.8	3.5
39041	Delaware County, Ohio..............	218,469	88.5	6.8	80,640	79.4	72.7	379,600	1,191	97.4	79,464	13.4	4.9
39043	Erie County, Ohio......................	74,297	88.6	4.7	32,926	67.3	52.2	168,400	799	83.4	29,873	23.3	4.2
39045	Fairfield County, Ohio...............	159,902	91.3	5.1	59,818	73.8	70.5	254,200	1,019	91.5	61,276	11.9	6.3
39049	Franklin County, Ohio................	1,305,087	82.3	5.7	549,475	53.2	70.8	246,800	1,102	93.3	506,780	11.8	3.0
39055	Geauga County, Ohio................	94,426	91.8	4.0	35,431	87.3	64.4	273,700	994	89.6	36,173	10.3	6.5
39057	Greene County, Ohio.................	167,106	87.2	7.0	67,822	71.4	65.6	220,600	919	91.6	67,020	15.3	3.1
39061	Hamilton County, Ohio..............	817,129	85.2	4.7	353,674	59.5	66.3	199,000	906	91.0	324,937	11.8	2.5
39063	Hancock County, Ohio...............	73,861	87.1	6.2	31,951	74.1	59.8	168,700	835	89.8	33,644	20.6	5.1
39085	Lake County, Ohio.....................	230,489	90.0	5.0	99,990	78.1	61.9	179,300	963	92.5	99,721	11.9	3.2
39089	Licking County, Ohio.................	178,919	88.4	5.8	67,761	76.2	65.8	214,700	871	92.4	69,090	13.4	6.8
39093	Lorain County, Ohio..................	311,707	91.3	3.5	124,879	72.0	62.1	182,700	842	87.5	126,136	12.9	4.8
39095	Lucas County, Ohio....................	423,877	87.8	4.5	184,315	62.8	59.9	138,100	788	88.8	176,584	14.9	3.4
39099	Mahoning County, Ohio	224,722	89.3	4.2	98,924	70.0	51.1	132,000	668	86.0	87,941	14.9	7.2
39101	Marion County, Ohio.................	64,600	86.1	6.3	24,692	69.1	59.7	130,100	807	87.8	23,386	27.4	4.6
39103	Medina County, Ohio.................	181,426	93.1	4.2	72,233	82.4	67.6	245,800	1,080	91.6	78,328	12.2	5.6
39109	Miami County, Ohio...................	107,825	89.3	2.8	43,896	74.1	62.6	198,200	796	89.1	47,492	19.9	3.9
39113	Montgomery County, Ohio	530,981	84.9	6.6	226,787	62.4	62.5	152,200	856	90.7	215,025	12.8	4.6
39119	Muskingum County, Ohio..........	85,466	89.0	4.2	33,876	65.2	61.7	142,300	676	85.6	36,688	13.0	8.1
39133	Portage County, Ohio................	161,371	87.9	7.6	63,096	69.8	61.8	200,900	868	87.1	65,894	14.6	5.4
39139	Richland County, Ohio...............	124,222	87.1	8.8	49,536	68.4	57.8	148,000	718	84.5	50,762	20.4	8.6
39141	Ross County, Ohio.....................	75,949	87.6	5.1	30,550	68.0	58.4	154,700	834	86.3	29,421	13.0	14.2
39145	Scioto County, Ohio...................	72,614	89.2	4.2	27,496	67.2	45.6	107,800	658	87.0	22,070	23.9	6.3
39151	Stark County, Ohio....................	371,060	88.7	3.8	156,111	69.3	60.8	161,500	781	85.3	151,321	17.3	3.7
39153	Summit County, Ohio................	532,800	89.3	4.7	229,060	67.2	63.7	176,800	859	91.1	217,512	14.1	4.5
39155	Trumbull County, Ohio..............	199,430	92.1	3.4	84,911	72.4	51.5	122,600	675	83.9	78,821	19.2	5.9
39157	Tuscarawas County, Ohio...........	91,726	86.8	5.1	38,684	67.0	55.3	158,800	793	85.6	39,291	21.0	6.1
39165	Warren County, Ohio.................	243,520	89.7	7.1	89,396	81.2	68.9	283,000	1,207	94.8	95,340	12.3	4.5
39169	Wayne County, Ohio.................	115,285	88.4	5.9	44,215	73.4	59.4	184,400	718	82.2	46,014	25.1	5.5
39173	Wood County, Ohio...................	130,877	81.1	9.7	54,012	64.1	63.0	202,800	862	92.6	57,237	21.3	3.8
40000	**OKLAHOMA**	3,943,443	84.9	6.8	1,547,967	65.5	53.7	168,500	855	88.0	1,589,401	17.9	4.8
40017	Canadian County, Oklahoma	160,497	81.3	8.6	57,753	76.4	68.9	202,800	1,075	92.3	71,035	10.4	4.4
40027	Cleveland County, Oklahoma......	295,043	80.5	9.4	116,142	64.6	62.0	194,500	956	92.8	126,739	14.1	5.0
40031	Comanche County, Oklahoma	120,620	80.2	9.5	44,822	52.3	56.3	154,600	792	90.2	46,549	22.9	2.4
40037	Creek County, Oklahoma...........	71,354	90.3	7.0	28,339	75.4	49.0	165,400	826	87.4	27,533	11.9	3.9
40101	Muskogee County, Oklahoma.....	65,228	89.7	4.6	25,965	68.4	NA	120,300	719	74.6	24,000	16.0	5.7
40109	Oklahoma County, Oklahoma.....	789,300	82.6	6.5	324,819	58.4	58.1	186,000	930	91.7	331,075	12.1	3.2

STATE County	Total population 1 year and over	Lived in the same house 1 year ago (percent)	Did not live in the same county 1 year ago (percent)	Total occupied housing units	Owner-occupied units (percent)	Percent with a mortgage, contract to purchase, or similar debt	Median value of owner-occupied units (dollars; owner estimated)	Median gross rent of renter-occupied units (dollars) cash rent	Households with Internet access (percent)	Number of workers who commuted to work	Commute of less than 10 minutes (percent)	Commute of 60 minutes or more (percent)
ACS table number:	C07204	C07204	C07204	B25003	B25003	B25081	B25097	B25064	S2801	B08012	B08012	B08012
Column number:	1	2	3	4	5	6	7	8	9	10	11	12
OKLAHOMA—Cont.												
40119 Payne County, Oklahoma............	81,409	79.0	10.1	31,537	51.6	NA	198,700	797	89.9	33,746	27.7	4.4
40125 Pottawatomie County, Oklahoma	72,378	86.6	6.5	26,650	71.4	48.1	145,200	809	88.2	28,381	21.4	6.9
40131 Rogers County, Oklahoma	95,422	85.9	9.2	35,815	78.0	61.1	193,300	891	89.0	39,316	15.4	4.2
40143 Tulsa County, Oklahoma	663,968	83.3	5.6	270,263	59.7	60.0	193,300	921	90.9	267,624	12.9	3.0
40145 Wagoner County, Oklahoma......	82,797	87.1	9.5	30,502	79.9	61.1	204,800	879	91.1	34,478	11.7	2.9
41000 **OREGON**	4,207,387	85.6	7.1	1,702,599	63.8	65.0	422,700	1,282	91.8	1,523,768	17.0	5.6
41003 Benton County, Oregon	94,228	75.2	15.8	39,350	52.3	53.6	443,100	1,190	90.7	32,346	23.2	5.8
41005 Clackamas County, Oregon........	419,000	88.4	6.7	161,945	73.4	68.1	533,100	1,500	95.0	147,668	12.1	6.0
41017 Deschutes County, Oregon	202,972	87.2	7.6	83,763	74.9	66.6	543,900	1,569	93.2	78,616	24.4	2.8
41019 Douglas County, Oregon............	111,468	86.5	4.3	45,981	71.0	52.9	252,600	864	87.3	35,014	21.0	3.3
41029 Jackson County, Oregon	221,207	86.1	5.6	90,817	68.3	60.6	368,700	1,146	88.8	76,535	15.2	3.7
41033 Josephine County, Oregon	87,705	86.4	6.7	36,755	67.3	54.8	371,600	962	89.8	28,792	24.7	6.6
41035 Klamath County, Oregon	69,609	84.3	9.7	28,888	67.7	54.3	246,000	921	85.8	23,090	22.4	3.9
41039 Lane County, Oregon.................	379,789	83.1	6.9	160,158	60.9	63.3	365,700	1,131	92.8	145,637	16.0	4.2
41043 Linn County, Oregon..................	128,823	85.7	8.5	51,347	67.1	65.4	328,900	1,105	90.3	48,960	20.5	7.2
41047 Marion County, Oregon	343,596	84.9	6.5	124,719	62.4	66.7	355,100	1,172	92.3	126,868	14.6	6.8
41051 Multnomah County, Oregon......	797,131	83.0	7.2	348,216	54.8	70.9	487,300	1,386	93.3	289,104	10.0	5.2
41053 Polk County, Oregon..................	88,547	87.0	7.0	33,425	66.0	64.5	378,100	1,137	91.3	32,507	19.7	9.1
41059 Umatilla County, Oregon	78,825	94.1	3.1	27,247	68.7	NA	240,200	878	79.4	29,983	29.0	5.0
41067 Washington County, Oregon......	594,886	86.4	6.5	233,615	58.9	70.8	498,800	1,565	94.9	212,315	12.4	4.5
41071 Yamhill County, Oregon.............	107,006	86.6	8.7	38,988	70.3	72.0	415,800	1,146	91.0	43,972	21.9	10.5
42000 **PENNSYLVANIA**	12,842,522	89.2	5.1	5,228,956	69.9	58.6	222,300	1,036	89.1	4,938,027	13.8	7.5
42001 Adams County, Pennsylvania.......	103,586	88.2	6.2	39,986	79.2	63.3	238,900	888	87.9	44,535	12.2	10.3
42003 Allegheny County, Pennsylvania..	1,225,234	87.1	5.1	545,892	65.9	59.2	200,300	972	90.8	451,430	11.0	5.6
42005 Armstrong County, Pennsylvania.	64,734	94.2	3.1	27,796	78.6	47.0	127,400	672	83.3	25,181	10.3	10.3
42007 Beaver County, Pennsylvania......	165,444	90.8	3.5	71,450	76.2	57.6	169,700	751	87.3	65,246	17.8	5.4
42011 Berks County, Pennsylvania.........	423,545	88.1	5.1	164,312	72.0	60.4	220,900	1,031	88.7	174,110	12.7	7.5
42013 Blair County, Pennsylvania...........	119,935	90.8	3.3	49,795	78.0	56.0	137,400	726	87.4	49,066	24.5	4.3
42017 Bucks County, Pennsylvania........	641,011	91.5	4.2	248,122	76.7	65.7	384,400	1,326	93.9	249,401	11.6	9.2
42019 Butler County, Pennsylvania........	192,974	89.0	5.9	81,220	78.7	57.7	251,700	954	90.3	78,783	13.9	7.4
42021 Cambria County, Pennsylvania	130,952	90.3	3.8	55,283	77.9	45.3	102,200	716	86.0	47,788	20.7	5.5
42025 Carbon County, Pennsylvania......	64,706	93.0	4.1	26,810	73.2	61.5	174,800	806	90.6	25,277	18.3	10.9
42027 Centre County, Pennsylvania.......	156,751	81.3	12.9	57,518	65.7	55.8	273,700	1,021	87.4	57,988	13.5	3.9
42029 Chester County, Pennsylvania......	533,901	88.0	6.6	204,047	74.5	67.9	420,300	1,536	94.0	198,860	13.2	6.5
42033 Clearfield County, Pennsylvania...	79,561	93.7	1.2	31,570	79.5	42.7	114,800	709	83.3	29,247	21.6	8.4
42039 Crawford County, Pennsylvania...	82,212	88.2	5.4	32,896	77.5	48.2	129,400	719	85.0	30,249	20.0	8.7
42041 Cumberland County, Pennsylvania...............	260,341	87.3	6.3	104,768	74.8	63.5	238,300	1,119	92.6	100,905	17.7	4.2
42043 Dauphin County, Pennsylvania...	284,009	87.9	6.3	120,423	65.8	60.8	199,200	1,052	89.6	109,562	12.2	4.3
42045 Delaware County, Pennsylvania...	568,980	90.2	5.3	218,280	69.1	62.5	285,300	1,208	93.8	213,609	13.6	7.6
42049 Erie County, Pennsylvania............	266,438	87.2	4.2	110,561	67.6	55.5	151,500	784	87.0	102,657	19.6	3.8
42051 Fayette County, Pennsylvania	125,795	93.6	2.4	55,986	74.7	46.8	124,500	679	85.2	46,053	14.3	10.7
42055 Franklin County, Pennsylvania	155,299	90.1	4.2	62,081	73.5	60.9	219,400	911	87.8	66,524	14.4	5.5
42063 Indiana County, Pennsylvania......	81,847	89.9	4.8	32,956	72.3	43.8	121,900	690	80.5	32,872	23.7	8.6
42069 Lackawanna County, Pennsylvania...............	214,215	88.9	5.4	88,294	66.6	56.1	172,300	819	87.5	86,252	16.9	4.6
42071 Lancaster County, Pennsylvania...	546,595	89.5	4.7	210,063	69.2	59.6	256,500	1,139	87.7	233,846	15.2	5.6
42073 Lawrence County, Pennsylvania...	84,874	90.8	5.3	36,286	74.6	50.4	141,800	668	86.5	32,683	19.5	4.7
42075 Lebanon County, Pennsylvania....	141,649	91.9	5.5	54,906	70.2	58.5	213,300	893	87.5	60,211	19.2	4.8
42077 Lehigh County, Pennsylvania.......	372,016	88.6	5.2	141,505	64.0	63.8	253,400	1,169	87.8	144,250	11.4	5.1
42079 Luzerne County, Pennsylvania	324,034	88.6	5.5	134,132	68.3	54.4	147,500	866	87.4	129,136	15.2	7.3
42081 Lycoming County, Pennsylvania...	112,813	89.2	3.6	47,022	71.9	58.5	166,500	825	87.3	46,319	23.6	3.5
42085 Mercer County, Pennsylvania	109,040	89.8	4.2	46,701	71.7	47.3	147,400	713	83.8	41,664	23.1	5.7
42089 Monroe County, Pennsylvania	168,367	93.9	4.1	65,907	81.5	64.8	220,900	1,103	92.6	67,768	8.4	18.1
42091 Montgomery County, Pennsylvania...............	852,478	89.5	5.7	335,248	72.3	67.0	373,300	1,428	94.4	316,900	12.7	7.9
42095 Northampton County, Pennsylvania...............	310,770	90.1	6.5	122,615	72.5	60.1	257,700	1,173	90.0	125,701	11.7	8.3

STATE County	Total population 1 year and over	Lived in the same house 1 year ago (percent)	Did not live in the same county 1 year ago (percent)	Total occupied housing units	Owner-occupied units (percent)	Percent with a mortgage, contract to purchase, or similar debt	Median value of owner-occupied units (dollars; owner estimated)	Median gross rent of renter-occupied units paying cash rent	Households with Internet access (percent)	Number of workers who commuted to work	Commute of less than 10 minutes (percent)	Commute of 60 minutes or more (percent)
ACS table number:	C07204	C07204	C07204	B25003	B25003	B25081	B25097	B25064	S2801	B08012	B08012	B08012
STATE County code — Column number:	1	2	3	4	5	6	7	8	9	10	11	12
PENNSYLVANIA—Cont.												
42097 Northumberland County, Pennsylvania	90,327	92.8	4.1	37,823	75.5	51.3	144,500	646	82.5	36,856	16.5	6.6
42101 Philadelphia County, Pennsylvania	1,558,765	87.0	5.4	660,921	52.8	58.1	220,700	1,181	86.9	531,131	6.3	11.2
42107 Schuylkill County, Pennsylvania	142,155	90.2	4.4	58,212	73.8	45.8	120,700	716	84.7	53,799	17.6	9.9
42111 Somerset County, Pennsylvania	73,149	93.6	3.1	29,115	78.9	50.2	115,300	674	80.5	27,577	22.2	6.6
42125 Washington County, Pennsylvania	207,937	91.3	4.2	88,544	80.0	56.6	202,700	789	89.6	82,915	14.4	6.8
42129 Westmoreland County, Pennsylvania	350,341	91.2	5.1	154,810	77.8	56.2	175,100	732	87.7	140,241	14.1	8.5
42133 York County, Pennsylvania	455,017	90.0	4.2	178,898	76.7	64.4	215,900	1,037	90.0	196,881	13.0	8.1
RHODE ISLAND	1,085,539	88.4	6.2	440,170	63.3	67.9	348,100	1,142	90.9	439,664	11.7	6.3
44003 Kent County, Rhode Island	169,510	90.5	6.0	73,182	69.3	68.5	320,500	1,086	90.3	73,864	11.4	5.5
44005 Newport County, Rhode Island	84,318	83.5	10.5	38,311	63.5	61.1	504,900	1,463	93.1	32,297	20.1	8.3
44007 Providence County, Rhode Island	651,027	88.5	5.0	254,178	57.2	69.6	317,000	1,116	90.0	261,871	10.4	6.3
44009 Washington County, Rhode Island	130,317	88.9	7.7	54,044	78.1	65.7	438,400	1,252	95.1	50,315	10.8	5.7
SOUTH CAROLINA	5,142,137	86.4	7.4	2,049,972	71.8	57.2	213,500	976	87.9	2,049,352	11.7	6.5
45003 Aiken County, South Carolina	168,938	89.7	5.0	67,224	77.0	51.4	175,400	868	89.4	63,367	9.1	4.3
45007 Anderson County, South Carolina	204,465	87.0	5.6	82,203	74.1	55.9	187,700	853	90.1	83,282	13.0	6.9
45013 Beaufort County, South Carolina	190,537	86.1	8.3	76,249	74.1	59.8	373,600	1,325	92.3	71,087	17.3	4.5
45015 Berkeley County, South Carolina	234,206	85.7	8.4	88,092	76.0	62.6	271,800	1,332	90.4	97,198	7.3	6.0
45019 Charleston County, South Carolina	408,547	85.9	6.7	169,851	66.4	64.3	398,600	1,346	91.5	170,637	9.8	3.9
45035 Dorchester County, South Carolina	161,499	86.4	11.5	58,435	75.9	65.0	270,700	1,160	90.7	66,244	8.3	8.8
45041 Florence County, South Carolina	135,221	87.3	5.7	51,484	65.9	51.6	150,600	813	77.3	50,280	11.5	4.3
45045 Greenville County, South Carolina	529,286	84.3	7.2	212,333	70.9	62.3	250,000	1,077	91.8	214,311	9.9	5.8
45047 Greenwood County, South Carolina	68,586	92.9	3.2	26,577	64.3	50.5	135,500	741	81.7	28,320	18.7	4.2
45051 Horry County, South Carolina	363,608	86.2	7.2	145,335	74.1	56.1	230,300	1,025	91.5	133,392	11.2	3.8
45055 Kershaw County, South Carolina	65,740	90.2	7.3	25,412	82.9	55.1	159,200	817	90.1	26,488	6.4	7.8
45057 Lancaster County, South Carolina	99,553	86.3	10.6	38,570	82.2	60.2	267,800	746	87.5	35,756	9.7	10.7
45059 Laurens County, South Carolina	66,905	88.3	8.0	26,580	76.8	51.3	144,700	802	86.5	26,409	14.4	7.2
45063 Lexington County, South Carolina	297,157	86.0	6.2	120,968	77.7	63.8	190,200	988	91.5	126,529	8.5	5.1
45073 Oconee County, South Carolina	78,747	89.8	6.3	34,023	76.8	48.0	189,200	755	82.1	28,003	15.6	6.9
45075 Orangeburg County, South Carolina	NA	NA	NA	32,017	63.6	33.9	93,100	719	78.3	28,772	14.0	16.7
45077 Pickens County, South Carolina	130,580	84.1	11.9	51,996	70.3	47.4	188,400	879	86.7	52,509	15.5	5.2
45079 Richland County, South Carolina	415,460	77.9	13.2	166,515	60.9	66.5	200,800	1,009	90.2	176,469	14.8	4.1
45083 Spartanburg County, South Carolina	332,311	87.3	5.0	128,437	74.5	59.4	193,300	900	88.9	140,691	13.2	4.9
45085 Sumter County, South Carolina	103,192	86.8	8.1	43,191	68.1	50.9	150,500	840	84.1	42,874	7.9	13.7
45091 York County, South Carolina	285,595	87.7	6.4	113,195	73.3	68.5	284,800	1,158	93.4	112,101	12.8	7.3
SOUTH DAKOTA	884,616	85.9	7.0	356,887	69.4	54.7	219,900	830	88.3	396,212	29.0	3.3
46083 Lincoln County, South Dakota	67,405	86.4	4.0	26,565	72.0	70.7	287,500	1,020	96.1	33,699	13.6	2.9
46099 Minnehaha County, South Dakota	196,783	82.6	6.8	82,289	64.4	65.6	249,600	858	91.7	93,537	19.8	2.3
46103 Pennington County, South Dakota	110,672	84.6	8.5	46,296	72.1	60.3	259,400	975	89.8	48,287	19.7	3.0
TENNESSEE	6,899,165	86.3	7.0	2,770,395	67.5	58.7	235,200	981	88.1	2,748,147	12.0	6.7
47001 Anderson County, Tennessee	76,778	84.3	11.1	31,735	75.7	57.1	187,500	908	89.2	29,796	13.6	7.1
47009 Blount County, Tennessee	136,603	91.4	4.4	55,446	75.0	56.1	240,300	903	89.9	58,475	8.6	4.8
47011 Bradley County, Tennessee	108,164	81.5	8.1	43,025	68.4	56.5	215,800	874	88.5	41,996	10.8	4.9
47037 Davidson County, Tennessee	693,331	79.0	10.5	316,273	53.7	68.3	350,700	1,316	92.9	290,256	11.6	4.2
47059 Greene County, Tennessee	69,920	93.2	4.3	28,585	79.5	50.9	169,200	633	80.6	28,243	15.6	5.9
47065 Hamilton County, Tennessee	365,094	82.7	5.9	151,676	64.5	60.8	256,300	1,007	90.7	147,468	11.9	3.7

	STATE County	Total population 1 year and over	Lived in the same house 1 year ago (percent)	Did not live in the same county 1 year ago (percent)	Total occupied housing units	Owner-occupied units (percent)	Percent with a mortgage, contract to purchase, or similar debt	Median value of owner-occupied units (dollars; owner estimated)	Median gross rent of renter-occupied units paying cash rent	Households with Internet access (percent)	Number of workers who commuted to work	Commute of less than 10 minutes (percent)	Commute of 60 minutes or more (percent)
STATE County code	ACS table number:	C07204	C07204	C07204	B25003	B25003	B25081	B25097	B25064	S2801	B08012	B08012	B08012
	Column number:	1	2	3	4	5	6	7	8	9	10	11	12
	TENNESSEE—Cont.												
47093	Knox County, Tennessee	481,815	86.2	7.2	198,914	64.2	61.6	256,700	1,023	89.1	203,602	8.9	3.0
47113	Madison County, Tennessee	98,178	87.2	4.1	39,730	63.9	51.0	172,200	934	86.0	40,197	12.1	5.7
47119	Maury County, Tennessee	103,013	92.0	5.3	41,309	71.6	62.3	301,300	1,084	92.5	43,984	7.6	8.4
47125	Montgomery County, Tennessee .	225,185	76.3	12.8	84,145	61.5	66.5	229,800	1,092	91.7	95,775	10.5	11.5
47141	Putnam County, Tennessee	80,455	82.5	9.0	33,652	60.7	53.9	214,600	759	84.0	38,127	17.2	6.8
47147	Robertson County, Tennessee.....	72,659	92.3	5.4	27,233	76.6	65.2	271,600	939	86.4	27,967	16.4	6.4
47149	Rutherford County, Tennessee.....	348,345	84.7	8.1	121,944	70.6	69.5	306,500	1,234	94.3	150,797	11.1	6.2
47155	Sevier County, Tennessee	98,754	93.4	5.1	36,670	74.3	54.3	234,600	870	85.0	39,529	9.7	9.8
47157	Shelby County, Tennessee	913,393	87.7	3.8	366,593	55.4	64.8	213,300	1,043	88.9	364,371	9.6	2.1
47163	Sullivan County, Tennessee.........	158,262	87.5	8.0	68,804	71.0	49.6	167,700	754	86.1	59,919	15.4	3.6
47165	Sumner County, Tennessee	198,381	86.6	8.9	77,760	72.4	64.4	329,600	1,171	92.7	82,690	15.7	8.9
47179	Washington County, Tennessee...	133,062	81.1	10.1	56,752	64.2	56.8	220,600	829	89.5	55,972	10.5	3.8
47187	Williamson County, Tennessee	252,931	84.8	8.9	91,406	82.4	73.4	617,400	1,677	96.5	90,565	9.0	4.1
47189	Wilson County, Tennessee..........	151,095	88.1	7.2	55,047	76.4	64.9	353,500	1,222	94.1	60,309	12.8	9.4
48000	**TEXAS**	29,170,380	86.0	6.4	10,796,247	62.6	56.6	237,400	1,167	90.2	11,417,050	12.0	7.3
48005	Angelina County, Texas	85,533	79.9	7.8	32,538	63.8	NA	136,000	909	89.2	32,361	18.4	10.1
48021	Bastrop County, Texas	NA	NA	NA	36,341	80.0	NA	245,000	1,135	91.3	37,872	5.4	21.1
48027	Bell County, Texas	374,428	80.0	9.4	139,582	54.6	62.6	203,200	1,013	90.0	152,294	14.5	8.3
48029	Bexar County, Texas	2,003,503	84.5	5.6	742,836	59.4	59.6	220,800	1,140	91.8	797,103	10.4	4.8
48037	Bowie County, Texas	91,596	91.5	3.8	34,038	64.5	NA	135,700	845	78.1	35,405	14.3	4.2
48039	Brazoria County, Texas	376,618	89.6	5.1	130,734	73.8	61.6	255,600	1,229	93.7	153,520	8.8	9.1
48041	Brazos County, Texas..................	234,193	76.2	12.0	86,154	48.8	58.9	269,700	1,051	83.8	96,342	15.5	2.1
48061	Cameron County, Texas	418,109	94.1	1.5	135,734	64.7	38.9	103,500	797	81.1	153,332	14.3	3.3
48085	Collin County, Texas	1,098,537	85.5	7.5	399,810	64.7	70.8	395,000	1,559	96.2	378,938	9.4	6.5
48091	Comal County, Texas..................	173,237	83.8	9.7	67,392	73.5	60.3	369,500	1,330	95.6	71,033	7.7	11.5
48099	Coryell County, Texas	83,272	70.6	21.6	26,980	57.4	NA	152,700	1,017	90.6	32,044	23.5	6.3
48113	Dallas County, Texas...................	2,550,755	86.4	5.1	975,062	50.5	57.8	249,800	1,273	90.8	1,030,440	8.2	7.0
48121	Denton County, Texas	933,333	85.9	7.6	350,081	65.2	73.1	361,600	1,361	95.5	364,633	8.7	6.2
48135	Ector County, Texas....................	159,018	80.6	8.2	64,169	67.2	NA	176,500	1,069	88.7	65,103	10.6	5.8
48139	Ellis County, Texas	199,956	89.6	5.7	69,223	76.2	62.8	278,000	1,260	92.7	84,051	9.2	9.6
48141	El Paso County, Texas.................	855,564	87.5	4.9	298,059	65.2	55.1	148,400	906	89.4	336,203	10.1	4.2
48157	Fort Bend County, Texas..............	848,537	87.6	8.0	283,446	78.7	67.1	319,000	1,490	94.8	313,074	5.8	6.4
48167	Galveston County, Texas	349,879	83.1	8.2	144,182	67.6	58.2	270,600	1,191	94.3	141,964	10.8	10.5
48181	Grayson County, Texas	137,755	84.5	8.9	56,005	67.4	54.2	222,900	1,037	90.2	56,339	17.9	9.0
48183	Gregg County, Texas...................	122,771	87.1	5.8	46,766	60.2	NA	171,100	891	89.8	51,496	18.2	6.0
48187	Guadalupe County, Texas............	174,994	92.1	5.9	61,414	78.7	60.6	243,700	1,178	92.4	71,072	9.6	13.9
48201	Harris County, Texas...................	4,661,485	85.2	4.7	1,735,020	54.7	57.8	232,500	1,167	89.9	1,846,598	7.8	8.0
48203	Harrison County, Texas...............	68,435	93.8	3.8	25,866	78.6	NA	159,300	836	81.3	26,031	23.6	8.2
48209	Hays County, Texas	251,895	81.0	11.5	94,205	63.3	67.8	344,000	1,335	93.7	103,606	7.1	10.9
48213	Henderson County, Texas	82,883	87.5	7.6	32,576	75.5	NA	152,200	844	79.1	28,103	19.4	16.3
48215	Hidalgo County, Texas................	865,290	89.9	3.1	268,598	65.1	38.1	107,500	820	86.0	285,978	18.2	3.2
48231	Hunt County, Texas....................	102,519	83.8	9.3	37,206	67.9	NA	194,700	1,027	89.7	37,965	13.9	20.0
48245	Jefferson County, Texas...............	250,796	88.8	5.9	94,828	62.0	43.7	150,800	952	90.8	102,535	14.2	5.3
48251	Johnson County, Texas...............	185,510	91.9	5.0	64,338	77.1	57.2	225,500	1,174	92.3	81,376	9.8	8.7
48257	Kaufman County, Texas...............	155,089	83.0	13.2	50,212	78.3	67.7	265,700	1,246	88.6	57,716	12.4	14.0
48291	Liberty County, Texas	NA	NA	NA	29,290	82.2	NA	152,300	780	91.9	33,560	11.5	23.2
48303	Lubbock County, Texas................	311,570	79.4	9.1	124,689	56.2	56.0	179,800	975	88.3	143,993	21.1	3.4
48309	McLennan County, Texas............	260,226	82.3	6.9	97,065	61.0	54.5	190,600	1,018	89.2	107,038	16.8	4.6
48329	Midland County, Texas...............	164,721	85.8	6.0	66,052	70.1	59.6	279,700	1,027	92.9	80,377	12.5	4.8
48339	Montgomery County, Texas........	643,856	88.5	7.1	232,095	74.2	62.5	293,900	1,288	93.4	243,991	7.8	14.7
48355	Nueces County, Texas.................	349,119	85.4	4.7	127,624	60.0	54.9	169,100	1,112	88.3	148,355	10.2	2.9
48361	Orange County, Texas.................	83,982	88.1	7.3	31,323	78.8	49.8	156,100	1,000	92.4	34,270	14.9	5.9
48367	Parker County, Texas	155,395	87.3	8.4	55,525	80.8	60.8	332,800	1,174	92.9	63,553	12.3	14.6
48375	Potter County, Texas	NA	NA	NA	44,472	57.4	43.6	108,200	896	82.9	44,517	10.0	3.9
48381	Randall County, Texas	142,287	88.5	3.7	56,509	68.2	67.2	201,700	1,023	93.5	64,891	13.7	4.5
48397	Rockwall County, Texas...............	115,298	85.9	9.4	39,329	86.0	70.4	353,700	1,257	95.6	43,288	9.4	13.1
48409	San Patricio County, Texas..........	68,554	85.6	6.0	25,495	64.3	NA	165,800	1,056	80.7	28,950	19.1	6.8
48423	Smith County, Texas...................	234,123	89.2	4.7	81,175	68.9	53.8	202,100	996	89.9	97,883	11.3	5.0

Table C-2. Counties — Where: Migration, Housing, and Transportation, 2021—*Continued*

STATE County code	STATE County	Total population 1 year and over	Lived in the same house 1 year ago (percent)	Did not live in the same county 1 year ago (percent)	Total occupied housing units	Owner-occupied units (percent)	Percent with a mortgage, contract to purchase, or similar debt	Median value of owner-occupied units (dollars; owner estimated)	Median gross rent of renter-occupied units paying cash rent	Households with Internet access (percent)	Number of workers who commuted to work	Commute of less than 10 minutes (percent)	Commute of 60 minutes or more (percent)
	ACS table number:	C07204	C07204	C07204	B25003	B25003	B25081	B25097	B25064	S2801	B08012	B08012	B08012
	Column number:	1	2	3	4	5	6	7	8	9	10	11	12
	TEXAS—Cont.												
48427	Starr County, Texas	NA	NA	NA	19,460	73.2	NA	81,700	635	77.0	18,538	26.1	11.5
48439	Tarrant County, Texas	2,100,995	88.0	4.7	771,657	58.5	62.3	268,300	1,259	92.8	866,004	8.8	6.1
48441	Taylor County, Texas	141,790	84.7	7.5	55,974	59.9	55.7	159,300	981	89.7	61,529	23.4	3.2
48451	Tom Green County, Texas	117,777	85.6	7.8	45,516	68.0	NA	164,500	894	85.6	50,559	21.5	3.7
48453	Travis County, Texas	1,289,908	80.4	9.8	567,627	52.3	66.8	451,000	1,437	94.3	467,017	9.7	5.0
48469	Victoria County, Texas	89,714	85.5	2.6	36,753	62.9	64.0	176,500	991	76.8	37,756	13.4	1.4
48471	Walker County, Texas	77,567	74.8	16.5	24,704	52.4	NA	205,900	868	87.4	23,247	17.6	15.5
48479	Webb County, Texas	263,800	89.2	1.5	78,730	63.8	NA	154,500	860	83.5	100,409	15.2	3.5
48485	Wichita County, Texas	128,906	79.4	9.7	49,071	62.9	47.6	125,600	868	87.3	58,035	31.0	2.7
48491	Williamson County, Texas	635,170	82.8	9.8	241,836	67.9	71.7	385,400	1,486	95.4	228,544	10.5	5.6
48497	Wise County, Texas	70,591	86.1	9.3	24,449	84.0	NA	246,100	1,146	90.4	28,288	11.8	20.2
49000	**UTAH**	3,295,561	85.5	6.3	1,101,499	69.7	69.6	421,700	1,208	93.6	1,306,378	17.2	4.6
49005	Cache County, Utah	135,169	83.2	8.7	43,099	64.8	65.0	368,100	946	93.2	58,551	28.6	3.4
49011	Davis County, Utah	363,615	89.4	4.7	114,119	76.7	72.5	436,100	1,227	94.3	145,607	14.0	4.1
49035	Salt Lake County, Utah	1,171,421	85.3	4.9	420,303	65.9	71.1	450,600	1,315	94.1	469,095	12.4	3.4
49045	Tooele County, Utah	75,749	87.1	7.6	23,495	85.9	80.5	374,100	1,083	94.1	33,925	14.2	10.4
49049	Utah County, Utah	674,271	81.4	7.5	194,258	68.9	74.0	461,700	1,261	94.1	261,175	17.9	4.3
49053	Washington County, Utah	189,653	87.7	6.5	68,090	70.0	60.0	443,200	1,269	92.4	65,210	18.4	3.9
49057	Weber County, Utah	263,264	87.4	6.9	92,869	73.6	70.0	363,000	1,073	95.2	109,490	12.6	6.3
50000	**VERMONT**	641,007	88.1	7.1	270,163	72.7	60.5	271,500	1,115	89.7	263,683	19.3	5.7
50007	Chittenden County, Vermont	167,598	82.7	9.7	70,730	60.6	67.1	378,100	1,537	93.7	67,434	15.7	3.9
51000	**VIRGINIA**	8,557,020	86.3	8.8	3,331,461	67.6	68.0	330,600	1,331	90.8	3,312,668	11.2	7.9
51003	Albemarle County, Virginia	113,052	80.3	16.1	45,195	68.4	63.6	388,900	1,428	92.1	41,887	11.2	3.2
51013	Arlington County, Virginia	230,062	75.8	14.8	108,396	43.9	75.0	779,400	1,975	96.7	73,060	12.7	2.4
51015	Augusta County, Virginia	76,863	92.2	3.5	30,186	77.9	59.4	267,400	919	86.8	34,468	12.3	2.9
51019	Bedford County, Virginia	79,735	89.9	7.8	33,397	82.5	63.6	276,100	812	90.7	31,589	10.9	7.7
51041	Chesterfield County, Virginia	367,729	88.6	7.1	136,070	75.9	71.8	308,400	1,301	93.9	144,067	6.9	4.1
51059	Fairfax County, Virginia	1,127,769	86.3	7.5	410,660	69.3	73.1	646,800	1,964	96.1	373,563	7.2	6.8
51061	Fauquier County, Virginia	73,251	93.6	3.9	26,887	73.4	71.2	480,100	1,249	93.4	29,394	14.2	19.6
51069	Frederick County, Virginia	93,045	88.7	5.8	34,581	75.1	61.7	334,400	1,353	91.4	39,384	7.7	16.7
51085	Hanover County, Virginia	110,061	93.2	4.5	42,274	82.9	71.4	344,400	1,247	92.9	43,588	9.8	4.1
51087	Henrico County, Virginia	331,587	86.8	6.8	137,035	65.6	74.8	295,900	1,308	90.2	121,103	12.5	3.4
51095	James City County, Virginia........	79,090	87.5	9.9	31,060	77.9	66.3	388,300	1,394	95.4	28,156	11.9	6.7
51107	Loudoun County, Virginia	422,168	88.0	8.0	141,935	77.3	80.9	648,400	2,158	97.3	141,929	11.6	11.7
51121	Montgomery County, Virginia.....	97,787	77.9	12.5	37,796	54.5	55.3	258,500	1,096	91.2	35,745	25.4	4.0
51153	Prince William County, Virginia ...	477,078	87.6	7.2	154,619	76.5	79.6	457,400	1,752	96.5	193,243	6.3	14.2
51161	Roanoke County, Virginia	95,865	88.9	8.5	39,093	77.9	64.6	251,900	1,063	90.2	38,166	14.0	3.0
51165	Rockingham County, Virginia	83,669	87.8	5.1	32,551	80.0	55.1	276,300	908	83.9	40,234	16.8	4.6
51177	Spotsylvania County, Virginia......	142,165	86.9	9.1	51,179	82.1	76.0	349,600	1,552	97.2	57,803	8.3	23.3
51179	Stafford County, Virginia............	159,559	85.5	12.3	51,007	78.9	77.8	437,500	1,761	97.0	58,937	9.6	23.0
51199	York County, Virginia	70,371	85.6	13.0	26,641	71.3	70.0	364,600	1,646	93.0	29,531	6.1	5.6
51510	Alexandria city, Virginia............	153,119	82.2	13.2	72,024	43.2	77.8	630,500	1,823	93.9	57,037	6.3	4.7
51550	Chesapeake city, Virginia	249,243	84.3	12.1	93,849	73.7	75.6	320,600	1,294	93.8	107,685	8.6	3.9
51650	Hampton city, Virginia	136,419	83.6	10.3	58,181	54.4	69.4	211,900	1,182	91.2	62,369	10.9	3.3
51680	Lynchburg city, Virginia	78,144	79.4	14.5	28,346	52.1	59.5	175,600	946	93.8	31,631	23.5	2.2
51700	Newport News city, Virginia	182,175	86.3	8.4	77,489	47.1	72.4	227,200	1,125	91.6	80,310	15.3	3.3
51710	Norfolk city, Virginia	232,197	78.8	12.9	97,596	46.0	74.6	250,300	1,108	89.7	112,597	11.5	4.4
51740	Portsmouth city, Virginia	96,664	87.7	9.5	40,827	56.1	71.0	221,500	1,111	87.1	39,852	11.4	3.0
51760	Richmond city, Virginia	224,801	81.1	12.1	99,929	45.0	70.4	311,700	1,144	85.1	86,807	10.7	5.0
51770	Roanoke city, Virginia	98,043	83.4	5.7	42,455	51.8	60.2	160,000	848	85.7	40,413	15.5	3.0
51800	Suffolk city, Virginia	95,138	89.3	7.5	37,383	71.3	77.5	302,200	1,231	91.6	40,938	8.0	9.7
51810	Virginia Beach city, Virginia	452,133	84.9	8.2	182,775	65.2	74.5	328,500	1,431	95.1	203,785	10.9	3.2
53000	**WASHINGTON**	7,657,350	84.6	6.7	3,022,255	64.0	66.7	485,700	1,484	93.6	2,780,613	13.1	8.1
53005	Benton County, Washington	207,684	88.8	4.0	76,855	66.0	63.8	346,300	1,081	89.6	79,356	13.9	5.4
53007	Chelan County, Washington	78,846	87.5	7.1	32,050	60.5	57.3	434,200	1,071	88.7	30,465	19.7	4.6
53009	Clallam County, Washington.......	77,720	88.2	8.4	34,773	75.6	50.0	365,100	960	94.2	25,979	26.8	4.1

STATE County	Total population 1 year and over	Lived in the same house 1 year ago (percent)	Did not live in the same county 1 year ago (percent)	Total occupied housing units	Owner-occupied units (percent)	Percent with a mortgage, contract to purchase, or similar debt	Median value of owner-occupied units (dollars; owner estimated)	Median gross rent of renter-occupied units paying cash rent	Households with Internet access (percent)	Number of workers who commuted to work	Commute of less than 10 minutes (percent)	Commute of 60 minutes or more (percent)
ACS table number:	C07204	C07204	C07204	B25003	B25003	B25081	B25097	B25064	S2801	B08012	B08012	B08012
Column number:	1	2	3	4	5	6	7	8	9	10	11	12
WASHINGTON—Cont.												
53011 Clark County, Washington	506,039	84.9	6.3	193,919	65.4	67.5	452,900	1,456	95.1	182,485	10.9	5.0
53015 Cowlitz County, Washington	110,584	88.3	5.5	43,204	64.9	63.8	358,500	1,022	89.4	39,760	13.3	11.8
53021 Franklin County, Washington	96,431	86.1	7.7	28,989	74.9	69.0	321,900	1,047	94.4	41,118	8.3	4.3
53025 Grant County, Washington	98,380	77.2	9.8	35,572	61.2	NA	274,700	991	92.5	40,466	30.0	5.1
53027 Grays Harbor County, Washington................................	75,913	84.2	9.2	30,500	69.6	55.5	271,100	859	89.3	24,188	24.2	5.5
53029 Island County, Washington	86,573	88.4	6.3	35,976	79.6	59.0	470,400	1,398	94.9	32,031	29.3	11.4
53033 King County, Washington	2,229,689	82.2	6.2	924,763	56.6	70.1	750,100	1,811	95.6	727,357	9.2	7.6
53035 Kitsap County, Washington	271,619	86.2	8.9	106,399	69.6	69.2	473,900	1,484	95.2	101,636	10.9	10.6
53041 Lewis County, Washington..........	83,466	87.1	7.6	32,304	75.4	57.2	330,500	898	90.2	30,927	17.5	12.0
53045 Mason County, Washington	66,611	93.7	3.3	25,036	82.7	67.5	360,700	978	92.0	23,033	13.9	15.4
53053 Pierce County, Washington	915,565	83.4	7.1	347,668	65.4	72.4	464,400	1,546	94.4	379,106	10.3	13.0
53057 Skagit County, Washington........	128,738	87.8	5.8	51,971	71.1	61.8	471,500	1,146	93.2	45,276	17.8	9.8
53061 Snohomish County, Washington .	824,500	85.7	7.1	312,365	69.3	74.0	612,400	1,668	94.9	309,631	8.5	10.1
53063 Spokane County, Washington......	540,753	84.0	5.7	217,920	64.2	65.3	357,200	1,059	91.6	207,147	12.2	4.5
53067 Thurston County, Washington	296,099	84.4	8.5	117,186	66.4	66.0	412,800	1,474	95.2	103,476	13.6	9.3
53073 Whatcom County, Washington ...	227,128	83.4	7.8	92,219	60.5	62.5	506,200	1,347	94.3	91,290	18.9	4.8
53077 Yakima County, Washington	251,971	89.5	2.7	86,992	61.7	59.8	260,200	880	86.5	94,796	18.4	4.0
54000 **WEST VIRGINIA**	1,767,792	89.6	5.5	722,201	75.2	46.2	143,200	767	85.2	635,030	15.3	9.1
54003 Berkeley County, West Virginia ...	124,255	89.2	6.4	50,841	76.8	68.6	225,700	1,079	93.2	52,241	9.1	8.9
54011 Cabell County, West Virginia.......	92,689	85.9	8.4	39,631	66.3	47.6	149,000	819	85.8	36,687	20.7	3.5
54033 Harrison County, West Virginia ...	64,346	92.2	3.3	26,143	74.9	47.7	123,100	768	88.9	24,772	14.4	6.0
54039 Kanawha County, West Virginia..	175,992	89.7	4.7	77,634	69.1	50.2	130,700	854	91.7	66,994	16.2	5.0
54061 Monongalia County, West Virginia................................	105,448	77.1	13.7	42,710	58.3	56.3	240,900	862	91.3	42,538	15.3	7.6
54081 Raleigh County, West Virginia	73,207	88.7	5.5	29,505	74.1	53.1	126,400	750	69.3	23,839	14.4	10.4
54107 Wood County, West Virginia.......	82,423	90.5	2.5	35,756	79.7	54.3	144,200	730	87.9	32,762	13.5	3.5
55000 **WISCONSIN**..............................	5,838,954	87.7	5.7	2,449,970	68.1	61.6	230,700	921	89.9	2,508,056	18.6	4.6
55009 Brown County, Wisconsin	267,029	88.2	4.3	110,225	64.8	63.5	234,800	847	92.7	115,525	15.3	2.5
55017 Chippewa County, Wisconsin	65,908	86.5	8.6	26,791	72.5	53.6	198,400	834	86.9	27,059	17.1	4.2
55025 Dane County, Wisconsin	559,183	81.2	8.3	243,924	57.8	69.5	341,100	1,197	93.4	236,800	15.3	2.6
55027 Dodge County, Wisconsin...........	88,339	91.2	5.0	36,286	73.1	60.0	191,600	805	90.4	43,028	20.7	5.8
55035 Eau Claire County, Wisconsin......	105,428	81.0	9.3	43,253	64.9	58.0	232,600	873	92.6	49,461	23.7	2.4
55039 Fond du Lac County, Wisconsin ..	103,501	87.9	5.6	42,758	74.6	59.0	191,700	846	90.2	48,087	22.9	5.3
55055 Jefferson County, Wisconsin	84,275	89.4	5.1	35,088	75.0	66.6	241,400	900	90.4	38,844	18.9	6.1
55059 Kenosha County, Wisconsin	166,487	87.0	7.1	67,810	66.6	65.9	240,500	1,071	91.7	74,695	15.6	6.8
55063 La Crosse County, Wisconsin	118,971	85.2	7.9	50,217	64.3	58.4	218,900	945	91.6	56,235	18.9	4.0
55071 Manitowoc County, Wisconsin....	80,693	91.5	3.8	35,716	72.5	53.2	163,500	664	86.1	34,973	23.0	4.0
55073 Marathon County, Wisconsin.......	136,457	87.9	4.4	57,566	74.6	62.6	186,700	815	90.2	60,647	18.5	4.6
55079 Milwaukee County, Wisconsin ...	917,197	86.8	4.1	389,434	50.4	63.8	201,000	954	87.8	363,765	12.5	3.0
55087 Outagamie County, Wisconsin	189,594	88.3	6.0	77,071	70.4	58.2	227,100	850	92.3	84,848	18.9	3.9
55089 Ozaukee County, Wisconsin........	91,750	91.3	5.1	36,144	78.4	61.7	339,500	960	93.1	36,040	18.5	3.6
55097 Portage County, Wisconsin	69,758	81.9	8.8	29,937	71.9	57.3	190,100	794	92.8	31,357	27.8	5.0
55101 Racine County, Wisconsin	194,511	87.1	4.7	79,068	67.0	63.7	221,000	908	90.0	82,610	17.5	3.7
55105 Rock County, Wisconsin.............	163,003	89.3	4.9	67,876	70.6	65.9	193,500	883	92.0	74,231	18.3	5.2
55109 St. Croix County, Wisconsin	94,121	92.2	4.3	36,873	82.7	66.0	308,500	1,116	93.1	41,578	16.3	5.5
55111 Sauk County, Wisconsin.............	65,121	91.0	5.2	27,524	74.4	63.1	217,000	866	87.8	30,459	26.5	6.5
55117 Sheboygan County, Wisconsin	116,792	89.1	3.3	49,416	72.3	60.7	197,500	762	89.2	52,629	25.8	4.1
55127 Walworth County, Wisconsin	105,927	84.8	7.2	43,086	71.5	59.4	245,600	980	87.8	44,880	20.7	8.8
55131 Washington County, Wisconsin...	136,103	90.7	6.1	56,636	77.6	70.0	289,300	968	93.4	62,702	14.3	5.1
55133 Waukesha County, Wisconsin	406,368	90.3	5.4	167,089	76.1	66.3	344,000	1,150	94.3	170,701	14.4	3.5
55139 Winnebago County, Wisconsin ...	169,225	85.5	7.8	72,794	65.6	63.7	186,800	807	92.7	78,646	18.6	4.3
55141 Wood County, Wisconsin...........	73,687	90.9	4.2	31,890	72.7	54.8	158,600	728	88.2	30,096	26.0	5.2
56000 **WYOMING**...............................	573,476	83.9	7.5	242,763	71.4	58.2	266,400	889	90.4	258,246	33.3	5.7
56021 Laramie County, Wyoming..........	99,466	86.7	6.6	43,728	66.7	67.9	297,900	945	88.9	43,353	20.9	4.9
56025 Natrona County, Wyoming	78,547	83.8	8.7	33,203	72.9	57.9	243,800	979	89.7	35,907	18.1	6.1

STATE County code	STATE County ACS table number: Column number:	Total population 1 year and over C07204 1	Lived in the same house 1 year ago (percent) C07204 2	Did not live in the same county 1 year ago (percent) C07204 3	Total occupied housing units B25003 4	Owner-occupied units (percent) B25003 5	Percent with a mortgage, contract to purchase, or similar debt B25081 6	Median value of owner-occupied units (dollars; owner estimated) B25097 7	Median gross rent of renter-occupied units paying cash rent B25064 8	Households with Internet access (percent) S2801 9	Number of workers who commuted to work B08012 10	Commute of less than 10 minutes (percent) B08012 11	Commute of 60 minutes or more (percent) B08012 12
72000	**PUERTO RICO...........................**	NA	NA	NA	1,165,982	68.7	36.9	114,100	504	77.6	977,274	9.5	9.9
72013	Arecibo Municipio, Puerto Rico...	NA	NA	NA	28,742	58.4	NA	96,700	438	74.4	21,256	12.6	10.2
72021	Bayamón Municipio, Puerto Rico.	NA	NA	NA	66,385	68.8	45.8	123,400	617	76.6	56,296	7.5	6.4
72025	Caguas Municipio, Puerto Rico ...	NA	NA	NA	47,586	67.0	NA	122,600	602	84.2	41,380	8.0	13.4
72031	Carolina Municipio, Puerto Rico..	NA	NA	NA	58,930	67.4	50.8	135,100	645	89.7	50,624	7.1	7.9
72061	Guaynabo Municipio, ... Puerto Rico.................................	NA	NA	NA	32,826	74.2	44.0	186,600	948	81.6	29,550	4.2	3.8
72097	Mayagüez Municipio, ... Puerto Rico.................................	NA	NA	NA	27,447	49.9	NA	104,600	401	75.1	18,551	11.7	3.5
72113	Ponce Municipio, Puerto Rico......	NA	NA	NA	50,007	71.5	NA	98,500	515	82.8	37,171	7.4	7.4
72127	San Juan Municipio, Puerto Rico .	NA	NA	NA	135,865	51.5	45.9	148,400	524	73.3	113,105	7.4	4.3
72135	Toa Alta Municipio, Puerto Rico ..	NA	NA	NA	20,918	83.3	NA	134,200	555	81.5	24,819	3.7	19.0
72137	Toa Baja Municipio, Puerto Rico ..	NA	NA	NA	28,276	72.9	NA	128,900	692	87.3	26,212	5.6	10.8
72139	Trujillo Alto Municipio, Puerto Rico.................................	NA	NA	NA	24,898	83.2	NA	140,000	566	87.9	25,441	5.8	7.0

NA = Not available.

Table C-3. Metropolitan Areas — Where: Migration, Housing, and Transportation, 2021

Metropolitan area / division code	Metropolitan area / division	Total population 1 year and over	Lived in the same house 1 year ago (percent)	Did not live in the same metropolitan area 1 year ago (percent)	Total occupied housing units	Owner-occupied units (percent)	Percent with a mortgage, contract to purchase, or similar debt	Median value of owner-occupied units (dollars; owner estimated)	Median gross rent of renter-occupied units (dollars)	House-holds with Internet access (percent)	Number of workers who commuted to work	Commute of less than 10 minutes (percent)	Commute of 60 minutes or more (percent)
	ACS table number:	C07204	C07204	C07204	B25003	B25003	B25081	B25097	B25064	S2801	B08012	B08012	B08012
	column number:	1	2	3	4	5	6	7	8	9	10	11	12
10180	Abilene, TX	176,948	84.4	10.0	66,816	63.3	51.4	149,000	972	88.9	73,448	22.9	3.8
10380	Aguadilla-Isabela, PR	NA	NA	NA	107,572	66.1	NA	114,300	431	70.3	83,331	16.9	10.3
10420	Akron, OH	694,171	89.0	8.1	292,156	67.8	63.3	181,700	861	90.2	283,406	14.2	4.7
10500	Albany, GA	145,136	86.2	10.6	57,880	57.4	52.6	143,200	820	80.6	53,458	15.1	4.6
10540	Albany-Lebanon, OR	128,823	85.7	11.9	51,347	67.1	65.4	328,900	1,105	90.3	48,960	20.5	29 pt
10580	Albany-Schenectady-Troy, NY	889,231	87.6	10.0	378,258	65.6	62.6	243,000	1,091	90.6	351,054	12.9	3.8
10740	Albuquerque, NM	913,263	86.6	6.9	376,596	68.2	63.5	246,000	961	90.3	339,364	11.8	5.9
10780	Alexandria, LA	148,523	87.3	10.7	55,249	67.0	52.3	167,900	848	86.0	54,502	14.6	3.6
10900	Allentown-Bethlehem-Easton, PA-NJ	856,827	89.8	8.3	337,283	69.1	61.7	254,600	1,147	89.3	339,877	12.2	8.2
11020	Altoona, PA	119,935	90.8	6.7	49,795	78.0	56.0	137,400	726	87.4	49,066	24.5	4.3
11100	Amarillo, TX	266,689	88.9	5.3	104,421	64.2	57.3	167,000	939	88.6	113,619	12.7	4.3
11180	Ames, IA	124,766	73.7	15.5	49,702	61.3	64.2	213,900	857	79.2	52,524	29.7	3.5
11260	Anchorage, AK	394,249	85.2	8.4	150,581	67.8	69.8	328,100	1,316	94.0	169,499	15.6	7.2
11460	Ann Arbor, MI	365,442	78.9	16.4	149,133	60.6	65.1	333,000	1,225	94.0	129,418	13.4	4.8
11500	Anniston-Oxford, AL	115,014	87.8	9.9	44,631	72.8	48.9	139,400	718	84.6	45,414	13.3	6.4
11540	Appleton, WI	241,639	89.3	9.1	98,164	72.3	59.5	228,300	862	92.0	109,833	18.7	4.4
11640	Arecibo, PR	NA	NA	NA	61,581	65.5	NA	101,700	477	72.8	49,917	6.1	5.9
11700	Asheville, NC	468,750	88.3	10.2	185,423	70.7	53.7	301,400	1,055	87.4	179,600	10.6	4.1
12020	Athens-Clarke County, GA	215,563	79.9	15.1	87,263	55.3	60.5	259,900	1,040	90.0	86,741	18.6	8.6
12060	Atlanta-Sandy Springs-Alpharetta, GA	6,084,305	86.4	12.1	2,277,482	66.9	70.0	300,000	1,370	93.4	2,270,521	7.2	9.7
12100	Atlantic City-Hammonton, NJ	272,618	90.8	7.5	112,299	67.0	63.3	254,200	1,208	91.4	107,131	13.8	8.3
12220	Auburn-Opelika, AL	175,946	83.8	9.5	67,358	64.8	63.0	203,500	895	87.3	73,870	13.7	5.1
12260	Augusta-Richmond County, GA-SC	610,448	88.0	9.7	222,266	68.4	57.7	182,000	915	85.6	246,344	10.9	4.1
12420	Austin-Round Rock-Georgetown, TX	2,325,071	81.9	12.5	955,207	58.8	67.2	397,100	1,427	94.3	856,005	9.7	6.8
12540	Bakersfield, CA	906,932	92.0	5.0	282,963	59.6	67.1	282,100	1,103	90.7	315,610	12.0	6.4
12580	Baltimore-Columbia-Towson, MD	2,806,552	88.8	8.6	1,117,510	67.4	70.5	351,200	1,390	91.4	1,097,176	9.4	8.5
12620	Bangor, ME	151,683	86.2	10.5	65,441	70.0	58.6	184,700	875	90.1	61,860	20.2	7.0
12700	Barnstable Town, MA	231,205	90.4	9.1	104,733	82.3	61.0	500,800	1,470	94.3	90,703	18.8	7.6
12940	Baton Rouge, LA	863,296	86.0	11.1	328,816	68.3	58.4	213,400	1,013	89.4	345,528	9.0	7.8
12980	Battle Creek, MI	131,724	90.1	8.0	53,482	73.2	60.7	143,400	821	88.7	51,240	17.8	2.1
13020	Bay City, MI	102,107	90.7	8.4	45,487	77.5	53.6	115,200	666	89.3	43,040	21.2	4.1
13140	Beaumont-Port Arthur, TX	391,399	89.4	7.5	148,489	68.9	44.4	151,400	953	89.8	159,114	14.1	5.2
13220	Beckley, WV	112,809	88.7	10.0	46,282	73.0	48.6	111,300	692	69.7	35,361	14.4	9.4
13380	Bellingham, WA	227,128	83.4	12.1	92,219	60.5	62.5	506,200	1,347	94.3	91,290	18.9	4.8
13460	Bend, OR	202,972	87.2	9.1	83,763	74.9	66.6	543,900	1,569	93.2	78,616	24.4	2.8
13740	Billings, MT	185,510	87.0	8.8	77,868	71.6	57.5	306,400	925	91.7	80,416	17.3	4.4
13780	Binghamton, NY	243,001	88.2	9.9	105,514	67.6	52.6	135,900	822	88.7	97,597	17.1	4.1
13820	Birmingham-Hoover, AL	1,104,324	87.8	9.2	436,615	70.4	58.3	208,800	972	89.4	436,824	10.0	5.6
13900	Bismarck, ND	132,677	88.8	7.4	52,921	72.8	56.1	264,600	865	88.7	63,027	21.7	3.6
13980	Blacksburg-Christiansburg, VA	166,669	80.2	14.6	66,952	60.5	52.3	194,500	958	87.5	65,639	21.8	4.0
14010	Bloomington, IL	168,945	84.6	10.0	69,263	64.2	62.1	183,300	858	88.3	65,310	23.2	3.4
14020	Bloomington, IN	160,579	71.4	21.6	65,340	60.5	63.0	217,500	973	88.1	62,210	17.4	6.7
14100	Bloomsburg-Berwick, PA	82,736	91.3	7.3	33,496	72.1	46.5	197,800	858	86.7	32,115	20.7	3.3
14260	Boise City, ID	793,454	85.9	11.1	294,959	71.7	68.5	426,800	1,222	93.3	322,249	12.6	3.0
14460	Boston-Cambridge-Newton, MA-NH	4,850,626	86.8	10.0	1,920,160	62.3	68.7	561,500	1,718	93.3	1,876,883	10.3	9.9
1446014454	Boston, MA Metro Division	2,009,337	86.6	9.4	797,408	58.5	69.3	563,600	1,753	92.6	770,991	9.1	7.0
1446015764	Cambridge-Newton-Framingham, MA Metro Division	2,395,641	86.6	10.6	942,803	63.1	68.9	602,100	1,733	93.7	912,479	10.7	5.0
1446040484	Rockingham County-Strafford County, NH Metro Division	445,648	88.4	9.9	179,949	74.6	65.6	394,600	1,406	94.4	193,413	13.1	5.9
14500	Boulder, CO	327,265	77.9	16.4	135,607	61.7	66.4	654,500	1,732	95.5	110,200	16.0	6.0
14540	Bowling Green, KY	184,643	82.7	12.5	71,929	61.2	58.6	193,400	807	88.7	79,131	17.4	7.2
14740	Bremerton-Silverdale-Port Orchard, WA	271,619	86.2	12.3	106,399	69.6	69.2	473,900	1,484	95.2	101,636	10.9	10.6
14860	Bridgeport-Stamford-Norwalk, CT	949,322	88.4	8.8	357,271	66.9	68.2	469,600	1,644	93.4	366,886	11.1	12.9
15180	Brownsville-Harlingen, TX	418,109	94.1	3.2	135,734	64.7	38.9	103,500	797	81.1	153,332	14.3	3.3
15260	Brunswick, GA	114,255	88.0	10.2	46,763	66.2	48.8	180,600	994	87.1	44,427	22.4	4.4
15380	Buffalo-Cheektowaga, NY	1,150,996	89.5	8.0	503,845	67.7	56.8	192,000	888	89.6	464,954	15.6	3.0
15500	Burlington, NC	172,052	90.4	7.9	69,343	65.2	63.8	203,000	894	88.4	71,191	11.8	4.3
15540	Burlington-South Burlington, VT	224,999	85.4	11.8	93,290	64.7	66.2	347,900	1,458	92.8	92,243	15.8	5.0

Table C-3. Metropolitan Areas — Where: Migration, Housing, and Transportation, 2021—*Continued*

Metropolitan area / division code	Metropolitan area / division	Total population 1 year and over	Lived in the same house 1 year ago (percent)	Did not live in the same metropolitan area 1 year ago (percent)	Total occupied housing units	Owner-occupied units (percent)	Percent with a mortgage, contract to purchase, or similar debt	Median value of owner-occupied units (dollars; owner estimated)	Median gross rent of renter-occupied units paying cash rent	House-holds with Internet access (percent)	Number of workers who commuted to work	Commute of less than 10 minutes (percent)	Commute of 60 minutes or more (percent)
ACS table number:		C07204	C07204	C07204	B25003	B25003	B25081	B25097	B25064	S2801	B08012	B08012	B08012
column number:		1	2	3	4	5	6	7	8	9	10	11	12
15680	California-Lexington Park, MD	113,453	87.5	11.8	42,078	75.9	73.6	356,400	1,442	90.5	45,927	10.2	15.8
15940	Canton-Massillon, OH	397,701	88.7	9.0	168,332	69.6	60.5	162,400	780	85.1	163,450	17.2	4.1
15980	Cape Coral-Fort Myers, FL	780,540	86.6	10.7	320,466	73.5	54.0	286,000	1,326	91.3	280,020	8.5	8.9
16020	Cape Girardeau, MO-IL	95,177	82.8	13.4	37,991	70.4	57.7	174,600	794	89.0	40,387	19.6	5.2
16060	Carbondale-Marion, IL	131,458	84.5	11.1	55,292	64.1	50.4	129,400	762	86.8	48,376	22.0	4.6
16180	Carson City, NV	58,397	88.0	7.3	23,930	63.0	58.4	393,500	908	92.4	24,804	24.7	12.3
16220	Casper, WY	78,547	83.8	10.8	33,203	72.9	57.9	243,800	979	89.7	35,907	18.1	6.1
16300	Cedar Rapids, IA	272,558	89.9	7.1	112,468	76.5	66.0	180,700	820	92.0	111,594	18.1	3.0
16540	Chambersburg-Waynesboro, PA	155,299	90.1	8.5	62,081	73.5	60.9	219,400	911	87.8	66,524	14.4	5.5
16580	Champaign-Urbana, IL	219,607	80.1	13.8	91,044	56.0	56.8	182,100	913	90.9	88,493	17.3	2.6
16620	Charleston, WV	250,580	90.5	7.8	106,310	72.0	43.9	124,600	832	88.8	85,969	16.1	7.6
16700	Charleston-North Charleston, SC	804,252	85.9	11.0	316,378	70.8	64.0	315,400	1,308	91.0	334,079	8.8	5.5
16740	Charlotte-Concord-Gastonia, NC-SC	2,672,903	86.6	9.5	1,048,452	66.7	68.6	286,600	1,202	92.1	995,340	10.8	5.9
16820	Charlottesville, VA	218,512	80.3	18.1	88,339	68.1	64.0	350,000	1,356	90.7	81,947	12.2	5.3
16860	Chattanooga, TN-GA	561,737	84.6	11.0	228,853	68.0	59.6	229,500	959	89.4	225,987	11.8	4.9
16940	Cheyenne, WY	99,466	86.7	8.7	43,728	66.7	67.9	297,900	945	88.9	43,353	20.9	4.9
16980	Chicago-Naperville-Elgin, IL-IN-WI	9,415,114	88.7	7.4	3,670,416	65.9	64.9	281,100	1,225	91.3	3,595,239	9.6	10.1
1698016984	Chicago-Naperville-Evanston, IL Metro Division	7,085,033	88.8	6.7	2,802,657	63.5	64.3	290,400	1,256	90.8	2,645,975	8.7	6.3
1698020994	Elgin, IL Metro Division	744,330	88.2	9.5	266,551	75.4	69.5	269,700	1,157	93.9	305,516	11.9	5.9
1698023844	Gary, IN Metro Division	713,349	89.5	8.4	278,654	73.1	64.0	212,900	1,012	90.5	294,201	12.9	6.1
1698029404	Lake County-Kenosha County, IL-WI Metro Division	872,402	87.4	10.7	322,554	73.5	65.9	283,200	1,205	93.4	349,547	12.3	5.8
17020	Chico, CA	206,231	82.7	11.8	81,353	58.4	56.2	370,700	1,238	90.8	79,258	22.6	5.8
17140	Cincinnati, OH-KY-IN	2,236,661	86.9	10.2	903,245	68.9	66.2	217,700	923	90.9	903,252	11.5	4.5
17300	Clarksville, TN-KY	326,173	79.8	13.9	121,468	60.3	62.2	210,100	1,017	87.7	133,132	14.8	9.3
17420	Cleveland, TN	127,464	81.7	12.6	50,236	70.5	56.3	213,100	852	86.8	48,105	10.8	4.9
17460	Cleveland-Elyria, OH	2,054,323	88.3	8.6	890,105	65.6	60.8	184,500	887	89.0	820,960	12.0	4.0
17660	Coeur d'Alene, ID	177,131	85.2	12.4	67,771	73.7	65.9	444,900	1,176	89.1	72,569	16.8	6.6
17780	College Station-Bryan, TX	267,674	78.5	14.5	99,917	52.5	54.9	245,000	1,036	82.7	110,048	15.7	3.3
17820	Colorado Springs, CO	753,303	80.8	13.6	294,814	67.2	72.3	397,900	1,465	95.5	310,510	12.4	4.5
17860	Columbia, MO	210,389	79.7	11.5	84,946	61.5	65.3	217,900	939	91.2	96,950	18.6	2.5
17900	Columbia, SC	829,577	82.6	15.6	334,313	69.7	62.6	185,800	986	89.8	349,199	11.6	5.1
18020	Columbus, IN	81,591	85.3	6.7	32,518	71.4	66.5	191,100	1,015	92.2	33,949	24.7	7.1
18140	Columbus, OH	2,127,269	85.1	8.8	856,193	61.7	69.3	254,700	1,078	93.0	821,007	12.2	4.7
18580	Corpus Christi, TX	417,673	85.5	5.9	153,119	60.7	53.1	168,500	1,105	87.0	177,305	11.6	3.6
18700	Corvallis, OR	94,228	75.2	18.3	39,350	52.3	53.6	443,100	1,190	90.7	32,346	23.2	5.8
18880	Crestview-Fort Walton Beach-Destin, FL	289,650	81.2	17.4	118,438	69.4	60.3	314,300	1,336	90.3	121,846	14.4	9.0
19060	Cumberland, MD-WV	93,718	88.9	9.7	40,079	69.8	52.6	149,500	644	84.3	34,244	15.5	8.2
19100	Dallas-Fort Worth-Arlington, TX	7,667,978	86.8	9.1	2,836,892	59.8	63.6	294,900	1,304	92.8	3,036,252	8.9	7.4
1910019124	Dallas-Plano-Irving, TX Division	5,155,487	86.1	9.7	1,920,923	58.9	64.6	313,300	1,328	92.8	1,997,031	8.8	4.9
1910023104	Fort Worth-Arlington-Grapevine, TX Division	2,512,491	88.2	7.9	915,969	61.8	61.5	268,200	1,249	92.7	1,039,221	9.1	4.7
19140	Dalton, GA	141,213	92.6	5.7	50,580	68.8	51.7	162,100	803	85.9	59,203	7.5	3.1
19180	Danville, IL	72,799	90.5	6.8	29,007	69.5	39.2	79,700	741	84.0	25,063	13.0	3.3
19300	Daphne-Fairhope-Foley, AL	237,039	87.3	10.4	94,105	75.9	58.6	255,800	1,096	92.0	93,834	9.9	8.9
19340	Davenport-Moline-Rock Island, IA-IL	377,183	88.0	8.3	159,133	72.0	58.7	152,000	826	88.9	155,281	16.6	5.2
19380	Dayton-Kettering, OH	805,912	86.0	10.3	338,505	65.7	63.2	169,300	861	90.7	329,537	14.3	4.2
19460	Decatur, AL	155,169	89.2	8.5	60,796	75.1	52.1	165,800	637	78.0	61,392	10.7	4.1
19500	Decatur, IL	101,366	84.9	8.1	43,914	68.9	49.2	110,800	719	83.4	36,920	15.3	2.7
19660	Deltona-Daytona Beach-Ormond Beach, FL	681,039	87.8	10.6	291,531	75.2	56.8	255,900	1,161	88.7	240,115	9.7	9.6
19740	Denver-Aurora-Lakewood, CO	2,944,868	83.7	11.8	1,192,117	65.3	73.2	519,600	1,605	93.7	1,163,472	9.2	6.4
19780	Des Moines-West Des Moines, IA	712,211	83.8	10.9	291,147	69.3	69.1	229,900	971	91.5	295,670	15.1	2.4
19820	Detroit-Warren-Dearborn, MI	4,316,997	90.4	7.7	1,759,573	71.4	60.3	220,900	1,051	91.9	1,585,164	10.9	5.4
1982019804	Detroit-Dearborn-Livonia, MI Division	1,753,290	91.2	6.1	695,038	65.0	51.9	158,700	975	89.3	585,394	10.8	2.7
1982047664	Warren-Troy-Farmington Hills, MI Division	2,563,707	89.8	8.9	1,064,535	75.6	65.0	256,900	1,125	93.5	999,770	11.0	4.1
20020	Dothan, AL	150,333	89.3	6.5	61,173	67.6	52.0	150,300	775	83.8	59,237	14.1	6.4
20100	Dover, DE	181,919	91.3	8.0	70,167	72.5	62.0	269,900	1,180	90.2	73,268	16.5	8.3
20220	Dubuque, IA	98,347	89.9	5.9	40,482	74.8	62.3	200,700	863	92.3	44,648	25.9	5.0

Metropolitan area / division code	Metropolitan area / division	Total population 1 year and over	Lived in the same house 1 year ago (percent)	Did not live in the same metropolitan area 1 year ago (percent)	Total occupied housing units	Owner-occupied units (percent)	Percent with a mortgage, contract to purchase, or similar debt	Median value of owner-occupied units (dollars; owner estimated)	Median gross rent of renter-occupied units paying cash rent	Households with Internet access (percent)	Number of workers who commuted to work	Commute of less than 10 minutes (percent)	Commute of 60 minutes or more (percent)
	ACS table number:	C07204	C07204	C07204	B25003	B25003	B25081	B25097	B25064	S2801	B08012	B08012	B08012
	column number:	1	2	3	4	5	6	7	8	9	10	11	12
20260	Duluth, MN-WI	288,495	87.4	8.3	124,996	73.9	60.5	191,900	873	88.9	118,373	23.1	4.8
20500	Durham-Chapel Hill, NC	648,655	84.4	11.5	263,996	62.8	65.8	314,600	1,147	91.4	217,844	10.5	5.1
20700	East Stroudsburg, PA	168,367	93.9	6.0	65,907	81.5	64.8	220,900	1,103	92.6	67,768	8.4	18.1
20740	Eau Claire, WI	171,336	83.1	12.2	70,044	67.8	56.2	223,000	861	90.4	76,520	21.4	3.0
20940	El Centro, CA	177,927	92.4	4.2	47,849	57.8	61.6	249,800	913	90.9	53,166	17.9	3.6
21060	Elizabethtown-Fort Knox, KY	155,605	84.0	13.5	58,210	63.1	59.4	183,100	820	89.3	63,225	17.4	8.8
21140	Elkhart-Goshen, IN	205,201	91.8	6.8	69,015	74.1	60.7	177,500	903	87.5	85,984	18.9	1.8
21300	Elmira, NY	82,103	90.4	7.2	35,407	68.0	53.7	128,600	873	89.0	30,172	23.4	3.8
21340	El Paso, TX	859,344	87.4	6.0	299,177	65.3	54.9	148,000	905	89.3	337,272	10.2	4.2
21420	Enid, OK	61,613	90.0	6.0	23,016	67.5	NA	143,700	841	84.1	26,469	27.3	6.7
21500	Erie, PA	266,438	87.2	10.3	110,561	67.6	55.5	151,500	784	87.0	102,657	19.6	3.8
21660	Eugene-Springfield, OR	379,789	83.1	11.3	160,158	60.9	63.3	365,700	1,131	92.8	145,637	16.0	4.2
21780	Evansville, IN-KY	310,817	87.3	8.9	132,942	68.8	61.7	168,100	838	88.3	137,532	16.5	2.1
21820	Fairbanks, AK	94,013	85.5	12.5	36,426	58.5	NA	265,900	1,228	87.8	43,790	12.1	3.9
22020	Fargo, ND-MN	248,441	79.8	13.3	109,997	55.1	63.5	246,800	811	90.0	121,604	18.8	3.5
22140	Farmington, NM	120,129	86.2	11.6	40,844	71.2	NA	154,700	827	57.5	38,763	19.1	7.6
22180	Fayetteville, NC	517,535	84.3	12.7	198,062	57.1	66.7	169,900	1,036	88.7	213,695	15.0	6.0
22220	Fayetteville-Springdale-Rogers, AR	549,440	87.4	8.9	206,712	65.0	63.6	242,400	981	92.6	228,245	14.8	2.9
22380	Flagstaff, AZ	143,963	80.6	12.9	55,145	58.5	51.7	393,900	1,306	83.9	56,108	22.1	5.2
22420	Flint, MI	400,105	88.0	10.3	167,895	70.7	56.8	157,400	870	87.2	146,223	13.8	10.9
22500	Florence, SC	197,383	87.8	10.2	77,918	68.3	47.8	135,700	795	76.0	73,753	12.1	5.6
22520	Florence-Muscle Shoals, AL	149,672	86.8	10.8	61,492	71.9	47.0	156,200	755	77.7	64,351	12.9	12.9
22540	Fond du Lac, WI	103,501	87.9	8.3	42,758	74.6	59.0	191,700	846	90.2	48,087	22.9	5.3
22660	Fort Collins, CO	359,281	78.7	14.6	152,123	64.1	67.1	487,700	1,463	92.7	144,372	16.0	5.5
22900	Fort Smith, AR-OK	243,911	86.5	9.2	97,188	67.7	51.1	140,400	698	82.5	95,173	18.7	4.1
23060	Fort Wayne, IN	417,281	84.4	8.5	168,833	71.0	63.4	173,000	871	92.2	179,928	13.3	4.1
23420	Fresno, CA	1,000,279	90.3	5.6	322,646	55.8	65.4	331,800	1,164	85.8	361,634	12.9	4.2
23460	Gadsden, AL	101,639	88.9	8.3	38,006	73.3	40.2	133,300	717	85.9	38,455	12.8	5.3
23540	Gainesville, FL	341,502	80.6	15.4	134,946	61.2	52.4	219,500	1,103	87.5	134,844	13.1	5.5
23580	Gainesville, GA	204,579	86.9	11.3	72,454	68.7	58.7	281,400	1,062	91.3	86,725	10.2	10.7
23900	Gettysburg, PA	103,586	88.2	11.1	39,986	79.2	63.3	238,900	888	87.9	44,535	12.2	10.3
24020	Glens Falls, NY	125,424	89.3	9.0	54,582	73.3	51.5	193,100	954	88.5	53,067	18.3	7.6
24140	Goldsboro, NC	115,502	82.8	15.4	46,932	58.4	55.3	159,300	829	88.6	49,422	19.4	5.8
24220	Grand Forks, ND-MN	102,327	79.8	15.3	43,220	56.3	58.4	221,000	967	88.4	50,140	31.4	4.2
24260	Grand Island, NE	75,285	83.9	6.6	30,478	68.4	49.9	186,600	874	88.9	35,290	24.0	6.0
24300	Grand Junction, CO	156,323	83.7	12.3	63,796	72.0	67.2	333,400	939	93.3	59,820	18.2	4.0
24340	Grand Rapids-Kentwood, MI	1,080,612	88.3	9.8	410,413	74.5	63.0	245,300	1,023	90.8	465,848	15.0	3.9
24420	Grants Pass, OR	87,705	86.4	9.8	36,755	67.3	54.8	371,600	962	89.8	28,792	24.7	6.6
24500	Great Falls, MT	82,584	85.3	9.9	34,303	65.7	57.6	226,600	760	89.8	36,829	28.1	4.4
24540	Greeley, CO	335,939	85.7	11.3	119,502	74.9	74.4	416,700	1,333	92.1	142,857	12.5	10.7
24580	Green Bay, WI	326,534	88.8	8.8	135,686	68.8	61.0	225,300	839	91.9	141,914	15.7	3.2
24660	Greensboro-High Point, NC	770,879	85.5	10.0	307,003	66.4	62.9	180,700	936	90.1	307,882	13.2	4.8
24780	Greenville, NC	170,537	82.9	13.7	75,578	49.5	66.7	171,100	848	83.3	66,843	16.7	4.7
24860	Greenville-Anderson, SC	931,236	85.1	13.3	373,112	71.9	58.0	221,400	978	90.3	376,511	11.7	6.0
25020	Guayama, PR	NA	NA	NA	25,902	76.3	NA	84,400	403	75.9	18,054	6.8	16.9
25060	Gulfport-Biloxi, MS	412,910	86.1	12.0	162,594	67.6	54.6	163,700	906	87.5	163,902	13.0	7.4
25180	Hagerstown-Martinsburg, MD-WV	297,095	89.2	9.7	117,803	70.9	65.5	231,500	1,023	87.2	118,204	10.3	11.0
25220	Hammond, LA	133,554	84.2	11.8	49,915	71.1	56.8	191,300	846	87.4	55,022	13.8	13.4
25260	Hanford-Corcoran, CA	150,855	86.8	10.5	43,143	53.9	66.2	285,600	1,184	90.1	51,083	23.1	4.8
25420	Harrisburg-Carlisle, PA	589,768	88.0	10.9	243,253	71.0	62.2	219,000	1,061	90.6	229,288	14.4	4.5
25500	Harrisonburg, VA	134,882	83.0	14.0	50,478	66.0	58.2	270,000	886	84.9	64,006	21.9	4.1
25540	Hartford-East Hartford-Middletown, CT	1,200,362	89.5	8.7	488,173	67.9	65.4	278,500	1,230	91.6	479,686	12.0	4.9
25620	Hattiesburg, MS	170,751	85.1	10.0	66,682	65.4	50.6	155,800	900	86.7	73,355	17.7	7.7
25860	Hickory-Lenoir-Morganton, NC	363,706	91.2	7.6	146,600	71.5	51.3	174,600	712	83.9	147,627	13.8	4.8
25940	Hilton Head Island-Bluffton, SC	220,596	86.1	11.9	89,701	74.7	60.9	365,800	1,295	90.9	84,279	15.9	4.6
25980	Hinesville, GA	77,221	77.3	18.6	29,290	45.2	NA	161,400	1,084	89.6	29,886	15.8	9.1
26140	Homosassa Springs, FL	157,256	85.9	13.4	68,269	84.0	38.1	206,400	1,036	88.8	38,243	12.1	9.2

Metropolitan area / division code	Metropolitan area / division	Total population 1 year and over	Lived in the same house 1 year ago (percent)	Did not live in the same metropolitan area 1 year ago (percent)	Total occupied housing units	Owner-occupied units (percent)	Percent with a mortgage, contract to purchase, or similar debt	Median value of owner-occupied units (dollars; owner estimated)	Median gross rent of renter-occupied units paying cash rent	Households with Internet access (percent)	Number of workers who commuted to work	Commute of less than 10 minutes (percent)	Commute of 60 minutes or more (percent)
ACS table number:		C07204	C07204	C07204	B25003	B25003	B25081	B25097	B25064	S2801	B08012	B08012	B08012
column number:		1	2	3	4	5	6	7	8	9	10	11	12
26300	Hot Springs, AR	99,137	92.6	6.1	42,077	69.4	NA	161,500	801	82.9	39,741	22.8	7.1
26380	Houma-Thibodaux, LA	203,262	90.3	7.5	82,107	79.7	48.7	171,400	806	82.9	81,194	21.6	7.2
26420	Houston-The Woodlands-Sugar Land, TX	7,114,177	86.0	9.8	2,601,401	61.5	59.5	252,300	1,190	91.0	2,786,418	7.9	8.9
26580	Huntington-Ashland, WV-KY-OH	353,197	89.6	8.3	144,383	73.5	46.4	130,700	779	84.6	130,344	17.9	5.2
26620	Huntsville, AL	497,612	86.7	10.2	205,178	71.2	62.6	246,000	974	90.8	199,241	9.8	3.7
26820	Idaho Falls, ID	161,077	81.8	14.5	54,348	75.8	64.8	324,700	922	92.6	63,978	20.3	8.4
26900	Indianapolis-Carmel-Anderson, IN	2,102,450	87.0	8.2	834,540	67.6	69.8	223,200	989	92.1	865,462	12.1	4.7
26980	Iowa City, IA	175,743	77.6	16.3	69,788	61.5	69.5	270,500	968	88.4	80,964	17.8	4.6
27060	Ithaca, NY	104,458	70.3	28.3	44,469	53.5	51.2	261,200	1,272	91.4	38,784	15.8	5.2
27100	Jackson, MI	158,309	88.4	10.7	61,937	74.9	59.5	169,800	865	90.6	61,056	16.3	6.4
27140	Jackson, MS	581,462	88.5	7.7	228,001	66.4	55.5	178,100	930	87.0	233,362	10.2	5.2
27180	Jackson, TN	179,330	87.8	6.9	71,462	68.2	51.4	158,700	861	86.1	70,637	12.8	6.3
27260	Jacksonville, FL	1,619,174	84.7	9.7	644,887	66.4	65.3	280,600	1,238	91.7	642,652	9.9	4.8
27340	Jacksonville, NC	201,195	73.4	24.1	73,121	63.0	65.1	190,300	1,002	90.7	90,828	22.3	5.7
27500	Janesville-Beloit, WI	163,003	89.3	7.0	67,876	70.6	65.9	193,500	883	92.0	74,231	18.3	5.2
27620	Jefferson City, MO	149,530	88.1	9.1	55,812	73.5	56.5	179,800	672	87.3	65,591	18.6	3.9
27740	Johnson City, TN	204,131	85.1	11.3	86,767	66.9	51.2	184,600	773	86.4	83,001	12.0	4.4
27780	Johnstown, PA	130,952	90.3	8.0	55,283	77.9	45.3	102,200	716	86.0	47,788	20.7	5.5
27860	Jonesboro, AR	133,519	79.4	9.6	51,155	65.6	NA	162,300	801	86.8	53,532	18.4	5.4
27900	Joplin, MO	180,006	86.7	8.6	69,646	70.3	59.3	149,500	868	89.1	74,582	17.3	4.6
27980	Kahului-Wailuku-Lahaina, HI	162,889	86.6	9.7	56,319	67.1	60.0	744,400	1,592	86.9	70,733	18.1	7.2
28020	Kalamazoo-Portage, MI	258,329	84.2	12.5	105,642	63.6	62.1	208,300	898	89.9	109,442	16.6	5.2
28100	Kankakee, IL	105,751	92.5	5.7	41,020	72.1	57.7	165,700	922	87.6	45,838	19.5	10.5
28140	Kansas City, MO-KS	2,174,907	85.6	10.0	883,621	66.0	65.5	247,000	1,075	92.0	886,734	13.8	3.9
28420	Kennewick-Richland, WA	304,115	88.0	8.1	105,844	68.4	65.3	338,400	1,074	90.9	120,474	12.0	5.0
28660	Killeen-Temple, TX	480,162	78.8	15.1	174,498	56.3	61.2	195,300	1,009	90.3	193,425	16.3	8.0
28700	Kingsport-Bristol, TN-VA	304,899	88.9	9.3	128,312	73.1	48.8	164,200	729	84.4	110,197	15.5	5.9
28740	Kingston, NY	180,504	91.0	7.9	75,053	74.4	57.9	301,800	1,234	92.3	68,260	11.6	13.3
28940	Knoxville, TN	884,294	87.7	10.0	361,646	69.8	57.0	232,100	958	88.1	360,479	10.4	5.1
29020	Kokomo, IN	83,009	88.4	6.1	36,530	71.6	66.2	151,100	879	90.7	33,910	21.6	8.0
29100	La Crosse-Onalaska, WI-MN	137,542	85.8	10.7	58,000	67.0	57.2	218,200	938	91.2	65,199	18.5	3.8
29180	Lafayette, LA	473,809	87.9	8.8	187,662	69.5	51.5	181,000	845	87.7	197,384	11.5	7.0
29200	Lafayette-West Lafayette, IN	221,830	78.7	16.9	88,853	60.2	65.3	187,300	907	89.3	94,219	15.7	2.5
29340	Lake Charles, LA	206,217	84.5	11.3	72,746	75.4	54.6	207,500	988	83.2	87,575	14.1	5.3
29420	Lake Havasu City-Kingman, AZ	215,753	87.6	8.9	102,398	73.7	50.4	250,300	885	89.3	72,471	19.5	6.2
29460	Lakeland-Winter Haven, FL	746,832	86.7	11.9	276,469	69.3	56.3	212,500	1,110	88.6	277,040	7.5	9.3
29540	Lancaster, PA	546,595	89.5	9.5	210,063	69.2	59.6	256,500	1,139	87.7	233,846	15.2	5.6
29620	Lansing-East Lansing, MI	536,529	84.6	12.8	220,067	67.8	63.3	179,200	917	89.9	200,352	15.8	5.6
29700	Laredo, TX	263,800	89.2	1.6	78,730	63.8	NA	154,500	860	83.5	100,409	15.2	3.5
29740	Las Cruces, NM	218,321	88.6	6.7	85,021	63.1	53.4	186,400	751	87.2	83,056	14.6	6.7
29820	Las Vegas-Henderson-Paradise, NV	2,266,274	85.3	10.5	854,289	56.7	69.2	365,800	1,325	91.5	876,598	7.9	4.2
29940	Lawrence, KS	118,571	76.2	13.8	49,759	50.1	66.6	240,900	870	91.2	52,272	22.7	2.7
30020	Lawton, OK	125,635	80.6	10.9	46,916	53.5	55.7	150,400	789	89.8	48,643	23.4	2.6
30140	Lebanon, PA	141,649	91.9	7.5	54,906	70.2	58.5	213,300	893	87.5	60,211	19.2	4.8
30300	Lewiston, ID-WA	64,205	86.8	9.5	27,019	69.7	54.7	289,900	835	85.9	28,617	30.8	3.6
30340	Lewiston-Auburn, ME	110,139	89.1	7.7	46,323	69.5	66.7	219,800	866	89.9	44,375	17.6	2.8
30460	Lexington-Fayette, KY	512,392	83.5	8.9	215,613	60.3	67.3	235,900	952	91.6	220,256	15.3	4.6
30620	Lima, OH	100,459	87.4	9.2	41,021	66.0	60.3	144,100	784	88.7	39,234	19.3	2.3
30700	Lincoln, NE	340,176	83.4	6.5	138,209	61.5	64.0	236,000	901	91.9	161,613	17.7	3.4
30780	Little Rock-North Little Rock-Conway, AR	741,479	86.1	9.3	308,436	64.3	63.1	183,700	921	89.5	311,719	14.1	4.4
30860	Logan, UT-ID	150,008	83.8	13.4	48,180	66.0	64.8	358,500	943	93.5	64,403	27.2	3.4
30980	Longview, TX	285,338	87.7	9.6	106,151	71.3	45.8	155,700	878	84.8	112,444	16.6	7.3
31020	Longview, WA	110,584	88.3	10.9	43,204	64.9	63.8	358,500	1,022	89.4	39,760	13.3	11.8
31080	Los Angeles-Long Beach-Anaheim, CA	12,871,123	89.7	6.7	4,452,780	48.9	68.4	748,700	1,786	93.2	4,773,103	7.7	10.1
3108011244	Anaheim-Santa Ana-Irvine, CA Division	3,135,054	87.7	8.8	1,077,193	56.5	67.0	832,300	2,090	94.5	1,184,456	8.9	4.9
3108031084	Los Angeles-Long Beach-Glendale, CA Division	9,736,069	90.4	6.1	3,375,587	46.5	69.0	720,300	1,711	92.8	3,588,647	7.3	6.9
31140	Louisville/Jefferson County, KY-IN	1,268,771	87.5	7.6	522,921	68.6	66.0	220,500	954	90.5	519,735	10.1	3.4

Metropolitan area / division code	Metropolitan area / division	Total population 1 year and over	Lived in the same house 1 year ago (percent)	Did not live in the same metropolitan area 1 year ago (percent)	Total occupied housing units	Owner-occupied units (percent)	Percent with a mortgage, contract to purchase, or similar debt	Median value of owner-occupied units (dollars; owner estimated)	Median gross rent of renter-occupied units paying cash rent	Households with Internet access (percent)	Number of workers who commuted to work	Commute of less than 10 minutes (percent)	Commute of 60 minutes or more (percent)
	ACS table number:	C07204	C07204	C07204	B25003	B25003	B25081	B25097	B25064	S2801	B08012	B08012	B08012
	column number:	1	2	3	4	5	6	7	8	9	10	11	12
31180	Lubbock, TX	323,452	79.9	10.4	129,092	56.8	54.9	175,000	972	88.4	149,501	21.5	3.4
31340	Lynchburg, VA	261,052	86.4	11.3	103,894	72.4	59.7	207,700	874	88.8	106,336	14.1	4.7
31420	Macon-Bibb County, GA	229,299	86.4	6.6	85,760	64.4	54.8	158,000	896	85.8	86,197	11.2	6.8
31460	Madera, CA	157,313	92.9	5.8	44,048	63.8	63.2	348,500	1,081	88.1	47,865	16.0	9.1
31540	Madison, WI	676,909	83.0	11.0	292,919	60.8	67.8	324,300	1,157	92.4	290,258	16.5	3.5
31700	Manchester-Nashua, NH	420,206	87.8	9.3	167,899	67.7	66.2	361,000	1,393	94.2	180,111	12.4	7.6
31740	Manhattan, KS	132,167	75.2	17.5	51,018	53.1	61.0	206,300	925	91.0	61,289	26.0	2.3
31860	Mankato, MN	102,341	79.6	12.9	40,715	68.3	59.2	225,100	898	87.2	49,663	29.2	2.6
31900	Mansfield, OH	124,222	87.1	10.9	49,536	68.4	57.8	148,000	718	84.5	50,762	20.4	8.6
32420	Mayagüez, PR	NA	NA	NA	36,278	54.8	NA	109,900	392	75.2	25,001	9.9	3.8
32580	McAllen-Edinburg-Mission, TX	865,290	89.9	7.3	268,598	65.1	38.1	107,500	820	86.0	285,978	18.2	3.2
32780	Medford, OR	221,207	86.1	10.7	90,817	68.3	60.6	368,700	1,146	88.8	76,535	15.2	3.7
32820	Memphis, TN-MS-AR	1,322,174	88.7	6.3	520,309	61.4	64.1	212,800	1,028	88.3	528,702	10.6	3.8
32900	Merced, CA	283,193	90.4	7.9	84,967	51.0	63.4	345,700	1,160	85.7	93,335	15.3	18.4
33100	Miami-Fort Lauderdale-Pompano Beach, FL	6,036,015	87.5	9.6	2,306,639	60.6	57.3	362,500	1,519	89.5	2,440,654	7.1	8.5
3310022744	Fort Lauderdale-Pompano Beach-Sunrise, FL Division	1,916,891	87.2	10.2	747,715	63.3	58.5	346,100	1,498	91.6	793,592	6.5	5.4
3310033124	Miami-Miami Beach-Kendall, FL Division	2,635,361	87.9	8.6	963,477	52.5	59.6	374,700	1,517	87.6	1,083,772	5.9	5.4
3310048424	West Palm Beach-Boca Raton-Boynton Beach, FL Division	1,483,763	87.3	10.9	595,447	70.4	53.1	363,000	1,560	90.1	563,290	10.0	4.1
33140	Michigan City-La Porte, IN	110,539	83.0	15.2	43,445	73.7	63.2	168,200	888	92.0	43,733	14.3	6.8
33220	Midland, MI	82,824	89.1	8.9	35,453	75.4	53.5	172,600	941	90.5	29,902	19.3	5.6
33260	Midland, TX	168,983	86.0	6.4	68,042	70.7	57.6	275,900	1,018	92.5	81,490	12.8	5.0
33340	Milwaukee-Waukesha, WI	1,551,418	88.3	7.4	649,303	60.9	65.2	266,200	977	90.2	633,208	13.5	3.4
33460	Minneapolis-St. Paul-Bloomington, MN-WI	3,649,201	87.1	9.6	1,453,400	71.7	68.8	330,400	1,246	93.3	1,430,832	12.7	4.1
33540	Missoula, MT	118,327	82.5	12.0	51,957	57.5	65.7	405,300	1,034	92.1	53,476	24.5	1.8
33660	Mobile, AL	424,679	88.2	7.7	168,977	65.0	59.0	159,100	923	84.9	166,040	9.1	6.4
33700	Modesto, CA	546,815	91.7	5.9	174,209	61.6	65.6	397,200	1,358	93.0	210,481	11.3	14.4
33740	Monroe, LA	202,444	88.7	8.7	80,334	64.6	47.7	160,300	794	82.5	75,029	13.3	8.5
33780	Monroe, MI	154,013	89.9	9.2	61,574	81.4	61.2	205,100	893	87.7	61,160	14.7	8.8
33860	Montgomery, AL	382,697	86.9	8.5	150,996	65.1	60.3	160,000	944	88.9	153,012	10.0	5.3
34060	Morgantown, WV	139,776	80.1	17.4	56,020	64.4	54.5	209,500	842	89.6	55,089	14.6	9.2
34100	Morristown, TN	142,373	91.6	7.3	53,925	70.1	53.2	168,500	759	80.9	52,571	11.2	7.8
34580	Mount Vernon-Anacortes, WA	128,738	87.8	10.5	51,971	71.1	61.8	471,500	1,146	93.2	45,276	17.8	9.8
34620	Muncie, IN	111,135	77.1	14.4	45,977	66.3	56.6	113,000	753	87.4	44,737	24.0	6.9
34740	Muskegon, MI	174,633	90.6	7.7	67,707	75.2	58.4	165,500	869	89.6	66,520	16.1	3.9
34820	Myrtle Beach-Conway-North Myrtle Beach, SC-NC	506,617	86.6	12.1	210,672	77.2	56.3	242,800	1,065	92.3	182,465	10.6	4.6
34900	Napa, CA	135,033	89.6	7.8	49,979	68.1	63.3	749,700	1,862	94.3	53,807	14.1	12.1
34940	Naples-Marco Island, FL	384,395	83.0	15.2	163,943	72.9	47.4	416,200	1,503	89.7	137,381	9.0	5.2
34980	Nashville-Davidson--Murfreesboro--Franklin, TN	1,988,442	84.1	11.1	794,373	66.9	67.2	344,900	1,260	92.9	817,727	11.6	6.6
35100	New Bern, NC	119,348	87.4	11.2	51,021	68.2	57.1	185,200	999	82.4	50,174	16.8	5.1
35300	New Haven-Milford, CT	855,848	89.0	8.8	349,089	61.6	63.3	282,200	1,235	92.4	349,887	11.9	6.6
35380	New Orleans-Metairie, LA	1,247,624	88.1	7.9	507,992	65.2	57.5	236,100	1,069	87.5	489,781	11.2	6.8
35620	New York-Newark-Jersey City, NY-NJ-PA	19,556,406	90.0	5.9	7,347,700	52.5	61.2	533,700	1,600	91.5	7,057,098	8.0	18.2
3562035004	Nassau County-Suffolk County, NY Division	2,889,603	92.1	6.9	971,403	83.4	63.3	556,500	1,992	94.2	1,191,890	10.1	9.8
3562035084	Newark, NJ-PA Division	2,250,684	89.3	8.7	851,554	61.1	67.2	442,500	1,397	91.6	834,119	9.3	8.2
3562035154	New Brunswick-Lakewood, NJ Metro Division	2,474,511	89.4	9.3	930,244	73.5	63.1	414,100	1,637	92.5	915,960	11.4	8.4
3562035614	New York-Jersey City-White Plains, NY-NJ Division	11,941,608	89.7	4.4	4,594,499	40.2	57.9	612,000	1,605	90.6	4,115,129	6.4	11.7
35660	Niles, MI	151,920	88.1	10.9	65,764	72.2	56.8	194,100	831	88.4	60,298	21.2	5.9
35840	North Port-Sarasota-Bradenton, FL	854,781	84.7	13.6	367,538	75.8	49.9	326,200	1,362	92.1	305,863	9.7	5.1
35980	Norwich-New London, CT	266,345	85.4	13.5	110,950	67.1	61.8	289,400	1,202	91.6	110,049	13.8	5.3
36100	Ocala, FL	383,369	87.2	11.8	157,348	78.5	52.5	193,300	1,072	91.2	129,162	10.4	6.7
36140	Ocean City, NJ	94,969	88.0	10.5	48,860	78.1	59.9	365,100	971	90.5	36,356	17.8	6.7

Table C-3. Metropolitan Areas — Where: Migration, Housing, and Transportation, 2021—*Continued*

Metropolitan area / division code	Metropolitan area / division	Total population 1 year and over	Lived in the same house 1 year ago (percent)	Did not live in the same metropolitan area 1 year ago (percent)	Total occupied housing units	Owner-occupied units (percent)	Percent with a mortgage, contract to purchase, or similar debt	Median value of owner-occupied units (dollars; owner estimated)	Median gross rent of renter-occupied units paying cash rent	House-holds with Internet access (percent)	Number of workers who commuted to work	Commute of less than 10 minutes (percent)	Commute of 60 minutes or more (percent)
	ACS table number:	C07204	C07204	C07204	B25003	B25003	B25081	B25097	B25064	S2801	B08012	B08012	B08012
	column number:	1	2	3	4	5	6	7	8	9	10	11	12
36220	Odessa, TX	159,018	80.6	12.9	64,169	67.2	NA	176,500	1,069	88.7	65,103	10.6	5.8
36260	Ogden-Clearfield, UT	700,188	88.7	9.2	230,356	75.1	70.8	395,400	1,123	94.4	284,262	14.7	5.0
36420	Oklahoma City, OK	1,426,912	83.0	10.3	565,309	63.9	59.3	190,800	929	91.4	600,256	12.3	4.2
36500	Olympia-Lacey-Tumwater, WA	296,099	84.4	13.6	117,186	66.4	66.0	412,800	1,474	95.2	103,476	13.6	9.3
36540	Omaha-Council Bluffs, NE-IA	960,304	86.8	8.2	385,487	66.8	68.5	231,100	1,007	91.4	416,113	15.4	3.1
36740	Orlando-Kissimmee-Sanford, FL	2,670,134	86.2	11.9	990,500	63.3	66.0	303,300	1,420	92.7	1,031,896	7.8	8.2
36780	Oshkosh-Neenah, WI	169,225	85.5	11.5	72,794	65.6	63.7	186,800	807	92.7	78,646	18.6	4.3
36980	Owensboro, KY	121,702	86.5	7.9	48,574	75.0	56.8	160,700	732	89.9	48,785	23.8	6.3
37100	Oxnard-Thousand Oaks-Ventura, CA	830,329	91.7	5.1	279,168	65.2	68.8	691,000	2,032	93.8	318,293	12.3	6.6
37340	Palm Bay-Melbourne-Titusville, FL	611,791	85.0	12.7	254,314	76.9	56.3	269,500	1,197	91.5	229,505	10.2	6.2
37460	Panama City, FL	176,903	78.0	18.8	79,532	63.3	53.5	243,200	1,244	91.2	78,754	15.8	5.1
37620	Parkersburg-Vienna, WV	86,980	90.7	3.8	37,656	79.9	53.3	139,700	709	87.9	34,935	13.2	3.5
37860	Pensacola-Ferry Pass-Brent, FL	509,870	83.4	14.6	198,702	69.4	60.2	242,900	1,118	91.5	203,896	12.1	6.6
37900	Peoria, IL	395,426	88.2	7.5	171,067	73.7	58.6	141,700	812	88.8	155,388	17.8	3.5
37980	Philadelphia-Camden-Wilmington, PA-NJ-DE-MD	6,170,734	88.9	8.5	2,442,868	67.3	64.7	300,300	1,258	91.7	2,287,095	10.8	8.3
3798015804	Camden, NJ Division	1,281,007	89.0	9.9	489,519	73.2	66.3	266,100	1,294	92.6	502,154	11.6	4.6
3798033874	Montgomery County-Bucks County-Chester County, PA Division	2,027,390	89.7	9.5	787,417	74.3	66.8	388,000	1,426	94.1	765,161	12.5	5.3
3798037964	Philadelphia, PA Division	2,127,745	87.8	6.5	879,201	56.8	59.5	235,700	1,186	88.6	744,740	8.4	6.1
3798048864	Wilmington, DE-MD-NJ Division	734,592	89.4	9.5	286,731	69.9	68.8	294,700	1,216	92.7	275,040	11.4	3.8
38060	Phoenix-Mesa-Chandler, AZ	4,895,754	85.4	9.8	1,863,195	67.1	68.0	374,100	1,384	93.2	1,787,166	11.0	6.2
38220	Pine Bluff, AR	86,234	89.3	8.0	30,092	65.8	NA	115,200	776	80.1	27,667	13.2	4.4
38300	Pittsburgh, PA	2,332,459	89.0	9.4	1,025,698	71.5	57.1	190,000	895	89.5	889,849	12.7	6.7
38340	Pittsfield, MA	127,784	87.3	10.1	57,765	70.1	61.0	260,000	948	90.1	51,887	21.0	3.1
38540	Pocatello, ID	96,418	84.8	9.9	36,438	69.5	62.0	250,400	735	86.9	37,972	26.4	5.1
38660	Ponce, PR	NA	NA	NA	75,345	73.3	NA	97,000	480	84.2	61,473	8.5	6.5
38860	Portland-South Portland, ME	552,324	89.2	9.1	237,186	73.8	66.3	356,800	1,204	92.3	220,301	15.2	6.0
38900	Portland-Vancouver-Hillsboro, OR-WA	2,487,765	85.4	10.3	1,001,984	62.0	69.5	483,000	1,443	94.1	899,350	11.9	5.7
38940	Port St. Lucie, FL	498,711	90.8	8.1	200,954	78.8	51.3	283,300	1,267	93.4	184,888	6.0	9.2
39100	Poughkeepsie-Newburgh-Middletown, NY	694,188	89.3	9.2	255,736	71.6	65.8	337,500	1,369	91.8	273,426	12.6	15.1
39140	Prescott Valley-Prescott, AZ	241,454	86.1	11.8	112,075	75.6	57.2	361,900	1,101	93.2	81,301	19.1	7.2
39300	Providence-Warwick, RI-MA	1,659,443	89.0	8.9	673,701	62.7	68.1	364,000	1,099	90.3	684,831	11.2	7.6
39340	Provo-Orem, UT	685,871	81.5	15.0	197,599	69.0	73.9	459,500	1,253	94.1	265,938	18.2	4.4
39380	Pueblo, CO	168,074	88.6	6.5	69,078	68.3	63.3	253,200	890	88.0	62,975	14.4	4.0
39460	Punta Gorda, FL	193,992	86.6	11.5	88,988	82.7	44.5	267,900	1,207	91.9	57,786	12.4	7.6
39540	Racine, WI	194,511	87.1	7.7	79,068	67.0	63.7	221,000	908	90.0	82,610	17.5	3.7
39580	Raleigh-Cary, NC	1,434,496	85.2	10.8	548,713	67.8	73.0	346,400	1,266	93.5	504,842	10.0	6.1
39660	Rapid City, SD	139,959	84.9	12.5	57,532	72.1	62.6	249,400	1,002	90.9	62,153	19.3	2.8
39740	Reading, PA	423,545	88.1	9.7	164,312	72.0	60.4	220,900	1,031	88.7	174,110	12.7	7.5
39820	Redding, CA	180,693	88.9	8.0	71,506	60.9	63.0	334,600	1,105	89.1	63,313	21.5	3.2
39900	Reno, NV	493,436	85.2	9.1	199,715	60.2	66.8	457,500	1,344	87.9	211,979	13.2	3.8
40060	Richmond, VA	1,306,167	87.3	10.6	521,067	67.0	71.2	299,600	1,202	89.7	498,169	9.4	5.1
40140	Riverside-San Bernardino-Ontario, CA	4,603,414	90.1	7.8	1,441,602	65.2	70.3	453,000	1,552	92.8	1,694,146	9.5	16.5
40220	Roanoke, VA	312,794	88.3	7.9	131,211	69.1	60.4	220,900	863	87.9	124,966	14.0	5.2
40340	Rochester, MN	225,056	87.4	7.9	90,956	75.1	61.2	267,300	1,043	89.8	100,578	16.9	4.2
40380	Rochester, NY	1,074,651	88.0	10.3	454,044	68.2	61.6	171,000	970	90.4	434,068	16.2	4.1
40420	Rockford, IL	332,596	86.8	9.3	134,008	66.6	57.3	149,800	891	89.0	126,372	11.3	6.5
40580	Rocky Mount, NC	142,216	91.4	6.4	56,840	63.7	53.8	151,900	786	81.3	57,043	16.8	5.0
40660	Rome, GA	98,145	88.2	9.7	35,417	63.1	55.3	178,900	830	84.7	40,482	16.2	4.0
40900	Sacramento-Roseville-Folsom, CA	2,388,650	88.0	8.9	879,647	62.3	68.7	513,600	1,556	93.7	833,130	11.4	7.2
40980	Saginaw, MI	187,556	88.5	10.6	80,146	71.7	51.8	128,600	818	88.2	68,570	19.4	5.6
41060	St. Cloud, MN	198,453	85.9	10.0	79,091	68.4	60.5	231,700	857	90.3	95,008	19.0	6.4
41100	St. George, UT	189,653	87.7	8.3	68,090	70.0	60.0	443,200	1,269	92.4	65,210	18.4	3.9
41140	St. Joseph, MO-KS	118,225	85.9	8.3	46,798	66.8	54.1	152,200	790	86.0	49,081	27.5	5.4
41180	St. Louis, MO-IL	2,778,909	88.0	9.6	1,144,111	71.2	64.3	215,700	940	90.7	1,109,252	11.1	4.6
41420	Salem, OR	432,143	85.4	8.9	158,144	63.1	66.2	360,300	1,167	92.1	159,375	15.6	7.2
41500	Salinas, CA	432,342	89.6	8.0	133,224	50.9	67.3	683,200	1,767	94.0	161,304	9.9	7.3

Metropolitan area / division code	Metropolitan area / division	Total population 1 year and over	Lived in the same house 1 year ago (percent)	Did not live in the same metropolitan area 1 year ago (percent)	Total occupied housing units	Owner-occupied units (percent)	Percent with a mortgage, contract to purchase, or similar debt	Median value of owner-occupied units (dollars; owner estimated)	Median gross rent of renter-occupied units paying cash rent	House-holds with Internet access (percent)	Number of workers who commuted to work	Commute of less than 10 minutes (percent)	Commute of 60 minutes or more (percent)
ACS table number:		C07204	C07204	C07204	B25003	B25003	B25081	B25097	B25064	S2801	B08012	B08012	B08012
column number:		1	2	3	4	5	6	7	8	9	10	11	12
41540	Salisbury, MD-DE	426,343	87.8	11.4	177,002	76.1	57.8	293,000	1,092	89.1	159,654	14.8	7.5
41620	Salt Lake City, UT	1,247,170	85.4	10.8	443,798	67.0	71.7	444,200	1,310	94.1	503,020	12.5	3.9
41660	San Angelo, TX	120,389	86.0	8.6	46,604	68.5	NA	163,600	895	85.4	51,303	21.7	4.0
41700	San Antonio-New Braunfels, TX	2,571,428	85.6	8.2	948,519	63.5	58.8	233,500	1,147	91.8	1,019,865	10.4	6.4
41740	San Diego-Chula Vista-Carlsbad, CA	3,250,645	86.0	9.2	1,162,896	54.3	69.7	722,200	1,908	94.9	1,239,125	8.6	5.2
41860	San Francisco-Oakland-Berkeley, CA	4,574,412	87.0	9.0	1,719,049	55.8	68.9	1,042,300	2,156	94.0	1,493,862	9.1	11.0
4186036084	Oakland-Berkeley-Livermore, CA Division	2,780,543	88.2	8.8	1,000,740	59.7	70.3	886,800	2,049	93.9	926,388	9.0	8.6
4186041884	San Francisco-San Mateo-Redwood City, CA Division	1,537,312	84.7	8.9	614,931	48.2	66.2	1,362,400	2,308	94.0	488,198	8.7	4.6
4186042034	San Rafael, CA Division	256,557	87.0	11.8	103,378	64.1	68.1	1,314,100	2,362	94.5	79,276	13.9	3.7
41900	San Germán, PR	NA	NA	NA	43,263	75.4	NA	96,300	469	66.5	30,561	9.4	8.2
41940	San Jose-Sunnyvale-Santa Clara, CA	1,933,548	85.4	9.1	670,900	56.3	67.7	1,237,800	2,454	95.8	627,956	9.0	5.6
41980	San Juan-Bayamón-Caguas, PR	NA	NA	NA	747,507	68.3	42.2	122,100	552	79.5	656,397	9.0	10.7
42020	San Luis Obispo-Paso Robles, CA	280,454	83.6	13.9	107,571	63.3	64.0	695,500	1,716	92.2	102,110	20.7	4.5
42100	Santa Cruz-Watsonville, CA	265,551	83.7	13.0	97,353	60.4	65.4	922,300	1,960	93.6	96,121	13.7	6.0
42140	Santa Fe, NM	154,471	88.1	8.7	70,152	74.4	54.8	362,200	1,166	89.9	52,742	18.7	6.7
42200	Santa Maria-Santa Barbara, CA	441,350	82.8	13.2	150,550	51.9	65.2	669,000	1,859	91.9	169,152	19.9	4.9
42220	Santa Rosa-Petaluma, CA	481,406	88.4	7.8	190,586	62.8	67.2	718,500	1,900	94.7	184,657	14.0	9.8
42340	Savannah, GA	405,439	81.7	15.2	160,666	62.7	66.8	238,200	1,179	92.4	176,429	12.3	4.1
42540	Scranton--Wilkes-Barre, PA	564,026	88.9	9.4	233,473	68.4	55.1	159,100	847	87.4	225,847	15.7	6.1
42660	Seattle-Tacoma-Bellevue, WA	3,969,754	83.2	12.1	1,584,796	61.0	71.5	638,400	1,730	95.2	1,416,094	9.3	9.6
4266042644	Seattle-Bellevue-Kent, WA Division	3,054,189	83.2	11.6	1,237,128	59.8	71.2	699,600	1,781	95.4	1,036,988	9.0	5.4
4266045104	Tacoma-Lakewood, WA Division	915,565	83.4	13.6	347,668	65.4	72.4	464,400	1,546	94.4	379,106	10.3	9.0
42680	Sebastian-Vero Beach, FL	162,281	87.3	9.9	69,974	78.6	48.4	279,400	1,159	88.8	55,598	12.9	5.5
42700	Sebring-Avon Park, FL	102,585	89.4	10.1	46,166	78.8	35.0	164,500	917	86.0	30,851	18.4	4.5
43100	Sheboygan, WI	116,792	89.1	7.6	49,416	72.3	60.7	197,500	762	89.2	52,629	25.8	4.1
43300	Sherman-Denison, TX	137,755	84.5	11.8	56,005	67.4	54.2	222,900	1,037	90.2	56,339	17.9	9.0
43340	Shreveport-Bossier City, LA	384,550	85.7	9.5	155,848	61.5	55.6	175,200	888	83.6	143,795	12.8	5.3
43420	Sierra Vista-Douglas, AZ	125,009	85.7	11.2	49,952	72.5	55.2	175,000	793	84.6	41,598	23.5	11.6
43580	Sioux City, IA-NE-SD	147,675	90.1	6.4	57,421	71.8	57.7	159,300	856	88.7	70,035	22.5	2.0
43620	Sioux Falls, SD	279,113	83.7	7.7	114,967	66.9	65.8	256,700	893	92.4	134,242	18.4	2.8
43780	South Bend-Mishawaka, IN-MI	319,297	86.9	9.8	128,774	71.9	61.1	163,700	889	89.7	133,107	14.9	4.4
43900	Spartanburg, SC	332,311	87.3	11.7	128,437	74.5	59.4	193,300	900	88.9	140,691	13.2	4.9
44060	Spokane-Spokane Valley, WA	587,837	84.3	10.6	237,024	65.7	63.9	351,600	1,044	91.1	221,133	12.7	4.5
44100	Springfield, IL	205,240	89.2	5.6	89,340	72.2	58.1	155,100	855	88.0	81,899	15.0	4.9
44140	Springfield, MA	688,914	88.0	9.6	275,788	64.1	64.5	277,600	1,052	88.7	257,600	12.9	5.5
44180	Springfield, MO	476,113	85.9	10.0	195,260	65.5	62.4	194,100	802	87.9	201,013	14.4	4.2
44220	Springfield, OH	134,317	87.6	7.5	57,013	70.4	60.0	144,500	699	90.1	55,284	17.1	4.8
44300	State College, PA	156,751	81.3	15.3	57,518	65.7	55.8	273,700	1,021	87.4	57,988	13.5	3.9
44420	Staunton, VA	124,541	88.6	9.5	51,802	71.6	63.7	245,200	877	88.0	55,121	14.6	2.8
44700	Stockton, CA	780,220	89.3	6.8	241,760	61.3	68.6	457,600	1,484	91.3	282,388	10.6	19.5
44940	Sumter, SC	134,166	86.5	11.7	54,669	66.6	49.5	146,000	805	83.0	53,129	9.3	14.3
45060	Syracuse, NY	652,245	86.2	11.2	270,350	68.1	59.2	164,000	898	91.0	260,332	16.4	4.5
45220	Tallahassee, FL	384,016	82.8	10.8	155,921	59.1	58.8	223,700	1,111	91.1	156,154	11.8	2.9
45300	Tampa-St. Petersburg-Clearwater, FL	3,191,775	85.0	11.8	1,309,614	67.8	58.2	279,600	1,286	91.6	1,191,597	10.6	7.3
45460	Terre Haute, IN	184,097	83.6	12.6	73,024	68.4	58.4	121,400	770	85.1	76,132	17.5	7.7
45500	Texarkana, TX-AR	144,721	88.1	8.6	55,179	65.1	NA	140,800	803	78.1	55,122	13.3	4.1
45540	The Villages, FL	135,027	87.7	10.5	68,792	89.1	39.8	323,200	1,099	90.5	24,495	8.7	16.1
45780	Toledo, OH	636,646	87.0	8.3	273,165	65.4	60.7	155,900	802	89.7	268,979	16.8	3.9
45820	Topeka, KS	230,463	88.9	6.5	95,988	69.6	58.7	154,800	837	87.6	95,096	15.8	4.8
45940	Trenton-Princeton, NJ	381,778	87.1	10.9	143,970	63.1	62.8	311,900	1,341	90.8	128,137	12.1	7.6
46060	Tucson, AZ	1,040,569	84.0	9.9	433,148	64.6	59.4	261,600	1,008	91.4	387,418	11.3	4.0
46140	Tulsa, OK	1,011,403	85.0	9.3	403,034	65.5	58.1	186,100	903	89.8	406,182	13.8	3.6
46220	Tuscaloosa, AL	264,243	86.2	10.8	101,825	64.1	58.5	195,400	891	86.1	107,718	11.3	7.4
46300	Twin Falls, ID	117,144	84.5	9.3	42,906	69.6	62.8	296,100	815	88.1	48,126	27.1	3.6
46340	Tyler, TX	234,123	89.2	7.7	81,175	68.9	53.8	202,100	996	89.9	97,883	11.3	5.0
46520	Urban Honolulu, HI	989,106	86.0	11.3	338,093	59.3	67.7	781,600	1,884	92.9	424,900	10.9	7.0
46540	Utica-Rome, NY	286,958	92.1	6.0	118,513	68.9	49.2	152,300	793	87.7	109,079	18.8	4.8

Metropolitan area / division code	Metropolitan area / division	Total population 1 year and over	Lived in the same house 1 year ago (percent)	Did not live in the same metropolitan area 1 year ago (percent)	Total occupied housing units	Owner-occupied units (percent)	Percent with a mortgage, contract to purchase, or similar debt	Median value of owner-occupied units (dollars; owner estimated)	Median gross rent of renter-occupied units paying cash rent	House-holds with Internet access (percent)	Number of workers who commuted to work	Commute of less than 10 minutes (percent)	Commute of 60 minutes or more (percent)
ACS table number:		C07204	C07204	C07204	B25003	B25003	B25081	B25097	B25064	S2801	B08012	B08012	B08012
column number:		1	2	3	4	5	6	7	8	9	10	11	12
46660	Valdosta, GA	145,724	87.2	9.1	55,279	55.0	60.9	166,000	828	82.0	55,187	17.8	3.3
46700	Vallejo, CA	446,949	88.9	7.2	157,617	62.0	73.4	543,100	1,877	93.5	177,381	12.1	17.0
47020	Victoria, TX	99,382	86.7	5.1	41,036	63.5	NA	181,400	1,010	77.7	42,080	13.7	1.8
47220	Vineland-Bridgeton, NJ	152,670	90.7	6.9	53,883	65.4	64.5	196,400	1,131	89.9	54,830	19.4	6.6
47260	Virginia Beach-Norfolk-Newport News, VA-NC	1,787,718	84.9	10.3	721,212	62.9	72.8	284,800	1,232	92.1	786,878	10.6	5.1
47300	Visalia, CA	470,431	92.4	4.8	143,541	57.3	64.0	276,400	1,061	87.4	165,341	17.6	8.3
47380	Waco, TX	277,380	82.4	11.6	102,138	61.9	52.8	183,700	1,014	88.9	112,933	16.7	4.7
47460	Walla Walla, WA	62,174	88.6	8.1	23,444	70.8	53.7	347,200	883	87.6	24,379	35.6	3.7
47580	Warner Robins, GA	193,091	85.2	12.3	70,357	66.0	62.9	169,400	987	91.1	79,250	9.0	3.9
47900	Washington-Arlington-Alexandria, DC-VA-MD-WV	6,287,995	85.9	11.1	2,384,977	64.4	75.5	497,800	1,762	94.5	2,217,836	7.6	11.9
4790023224	Frederick-Gaithersburg-Rockville, MD Division	1,323,145	87.4	10.3	492,081	68.0	70.8	514,500	1,784	95.4	449,433	7.4	7.3
4790047894	Washington-Arlington-Alexandria, DC-VA-MD-WV Division	4,964,850	85.5	11.4	1,892,896	63.4	76.8	494,600	1,756	94.2	1,768,403	7.7	7.8
47940	Waterloo-Cedar Falls, IA	165,848	82.0	9.7	68,479	69.9	60.2	167,100	823	89.5	75,671	24.7	3.0
48060	Watertown-Fort Drum, NY	114,421	81.6	16.1	48,628	56.2	60.3	177,200	1,056	91.5	49,920	25.9	3.8
48140	Wausau-Weston, WI	164,661	88.7	9.6	69,891	74.8	62.9	182,700	774	89.3	72,528	20.5	4.6
48260	Weirton-Steubenville, WV-OH	113,063	91.4	6.9	49,145	72.8	44.6	116,100	652	85.3	43,276	18.5	5.8
48300	Wenatchee, WA	122,107	89.1	8.1	47,559	61.5	56.3	406,200	1,107	87.7	48,514	18.2	4.2
48540	Wheeling, WV-OH	136,797	91.3	7.3	57,332	74.0	46.1	131,000	708	86.3	54,386	13.4	7.2
48620	Wichita, KS	640,049	83.6	8.0	250,146	65.1	61.4	170,900	856	90.5	276,502	15.5	2.8
48660	Wichita Falls, TX	147,728	80.9	10.6	56,846	65.2	45.9	127,000	859	86.9	65,941	28.8	3.2
48700	Williamsport, PA	112,813	89.2	9.5	47,022	71.9	58.5	166,500	825	87.3	46,319	23.6	3.5
48900	Wilmington, NC	289,713	81.6	15.2	127,095	64.0	65.8	302,700	1,183	91.5	118,687	13.6	6.2
49020	Winchester, VA-WV	141,527	87.3	12.1	52,949	70.2	61.4	309,400	1,213	89.7	58,133	14.9	14.9
49180	Winston-Salem, NC	675,855	88.7	8.2	273,913	70.1	58.8	193,100	835	89.8	260,441	11.0	6.2
49340	Worcester, MA-CT	970,094	88.2	10.0	379,159	67.3	69.4	349,500	1,168	92.3	394,210	12.4	10.6
49420	Yakima, WA	251,971	89.5	7.9	86,992	61.7	59.8	260,200	880	86.5	94,796	18.4	4.0
49500	Yauco, PR	NA	NA	NA	29,142	75.3	NA	80,200	312	77.4	21,987	6.6	4.1
49620	York-Hanover, PA	455,017	90.0	9.2	178,898	76.7	64.4	215,900	1,037	90.0	196,881	13.0	8.1
49660	Youngstown-Warren-Boardman, OH-PA	533,192	90.4	7.5	230,536	71.2	50.5	131,200	679	84.8	208,426	18.1	6.4
49700	Yuba City, CA	179,779	89.6	7.7	61,597	57.7	65.9	366,600	1,147	90.9	68,660	12.2	9.7
49740	Yuma, AZ	203,976	82.8	13.3	74,981	70.1	56.2	170,400	906	90.2	71,073	21.7	5.1

Table C-4. Cities — Where: Migration, Housing, and Transportation, 2021

STATE and place code	STATE Place	Total population 1 year and over	Lived in the same house 1 year ago (percent)	Did not live in the same city 1 year ago (percent)	Total occupied housing units	Owner-occupied units (percent)	Percent with a mortgage, contract to purchase, or similar debt	Median value of owner-occupied units (dollars; owner estimated)	Median gross rent of renter-occupied units paying cash rent	Households with Internet access (percent)	Number of workers who commuted to work	Commute of less than 10 minutes (percent)	Commute of 60 minutes or more (percent)
	ACS table number:	C07204	C07204	C07204	B25003	B25003	B25081	B25097	B25064	S2801	B08012	B08012	B08012
FIPS	column number:	1	2	3	4	5	6	7	8	9	10	11	12
00000	UNITED STATES..........................	328,464,538	87.2	6.0	127,544,730	65.4	61.3	281,400	1,191	90.3	126,746,081	13.2	7.7
01000	ALABAMA.................................	4,989,797	88.0	5.3	1,967,559	70.0	53.6	172,800	861	85.3	1,956,821	12.0	6.9
0103076	Auburn city, Alabama	78,090	76.1	9.8	29,136	48.1	49.3	319,300	1,009	92.0	30,397	18.7	6.8
0107000	Birmingham city, Alabama	195,149	86.1	6.8	87,570	46.4	54.5	117,600	895	84.5	76,049	10.1	2.7
0121184	Dothan city, Alabama	70,746	87.2	6.0	30,301	55.2	66.1	169,200	832	87.1	27,701	19.7	5.8
0135896	Hoover city, Alabama	91,982	86.6	9.9	36,721	70.8	59.3	363,200	1,212	95.7	39,453	8.7	4.1
0137000	Huntsville city, Alabama	213,007	84.2	9.8	96,551	61.1	56.3	250,400	983	91.7	81,615	13.4	2.3
0150000	Mobile city, Alabama	182,842	85.5	5.7	77,991	53.1	61.1	158,200	932	83.7	70,907	12.7	5.7
0151000	Montgomery city, Alabama	196,797	83.9	7.8	81,529	56.4	60.4	136,800	951	89.5	77,130	12.5	3.2
0177256	Tuscaloosa city, Alabama.............	99,790	83.2	11.2	39,266	41.7	71.2	217,200	934	87.9	41,101	14.1	4.5
02000	ALASKA	723,949	86.3	6.7	271,311	66.8	61.0	304,900	1,259	90.8	308,421	23.2	5.4
0203000	Anchorage municipality, Alaska.....	285,328	84.6	6.8	109,584	63.6	NA	346,200	1,335	94.4	127,173	17.3	3.0
04000	ARIZONA................................	7,202,745	85.3	5.9	2,817,723	67.6	63.3	336,300	1,253	91.6	2,599,725	12.9	6.1
0404720	Avondale city, Arizona	89,033	79.8	16.0	26,611	60.2	77.3	334,900	1,592	93.5	33,699	13.8	9.7
0407940	Buckeye city, Arizona	100,544	85.4	14.0	30,913	92.4	59.2	333,300	1,333	97.9	29,377	7.0	7.5
0410670	Casas Adobes CDP, Arizona	72,604	81.7	14.3	31,869	67.3	77.0	271,900	1,368	94.4	31,561	16.8	5.4
0412000	Chandler city, Arizona.................	276,136	86.7	8.6	107,668	66.0	NA	435,100	1,617	96.3	106,803	12.8	2.1
0423620	Flagstaff city, Arizona.................	76,644	70.2	19.5	29,435	40.6	79.2	457,500	1,413	90.5	33,156	25.0	2.6
0427400	Gilbert town, Arizona.................	270,663	85.9	11.3	93,472	74.9	67.1	484,600	1,742	97.2	94,529	10.9	3.8
0427820	Glendale city, Arizona.................	248,021	89.6	7.9	90,604	57.9	77.3	325,400	1,235	88.7	101,889	10.0	9.8
0428380	Goodyear city, Arizona.................	100,578	84.5	11.6	33,130	77.6	63.9	401,400	1,543	97.5	33,015	10.6	7.8
0446000	Mesa city, Arizona......................	504,304	82.8	10.8	199,112	63.4	72.4	350,100	1,302	92.9	194,557	10.8	5.0
0454050	Peoria city, Arizona	193,168	89.4	9.1	75,479	77.3	69.6	407,600	1,460	95.0	69,017	8.7	8.7
0455000	Phoenix city, Arizona...................	1,604,577	86.4	6.6	602,039	58.8	84.2	352,600	1,293	91.0	614,833	9.6	5.2
0458150	Queen Creek town, Arizona	68,635	86.3	11.1	20,981	88.5	78.1	516,100	2,026	NA	25,467	11.2	7.2
0464210	San Tan Valley CDP, Arizona	102,228	92.3	7.0	31,781	83.6	61.5	347,000	1,692	96.0	36,858	8.1	16.4
0465000	Scottsdale city, Arizona	242,008	82.9	12.0	119,122	67.3	71.3	674,900	1,669	96.7	82,661	15.4	2.8
0471510	Surprise city, Arizona	147,396	86.2	8.9	55,339	77.8	64.3	354,100	1,692	95.0	52,122	13.0	10.2
0473000	Tempe city, Arizona.....................	182,796	71.7	22.1	77,306	41.6	61.1	414,600	1,428	94.7	77,624	14.3	3.9
0477000	Tucson city, Arizona	535,526	81.6	8.7	223,068	51.4	57.4	224,800	956	90.8	211,018	12.5	3.4
0485540	Yuma city, Arizona......................	95,092	75.7	18.4	36,530	58.8	NA	189,000	966	92.5	36,033	25.8	2.1
05000	ARKANSAS	2,990,311	86.8	6.0	1,183,675	67.0	54.0	162,300	820	85.7	1,180,532	18.7	5.4
0515190	Conway city, Arkansas	64,461	82.0	11.7	25,251	44.3	NA	230,900	934	89.9	27,209	21.6	5.9
0523290	Fayetteville city, Arkansas.............	94,034	79.1	12.4	40,104	46.8	NA	272,300	869	94.2	43,255	15.1	3.1
0524550	Fort Smith city, Arkansas..............	87,116	84.0	8.9	36,390	56.8	NA	146,200	677	84.9	36,114	18.1	3.4
0535710	Jonesboro city, Arkansas..............	78,702	74.9	9.1	30,432	57.9	65.3	197,600	819	89.3	28,744	17.1	5.1
0541000	Little Rock city, Arkansas..............	200,063	84.1	7.0	89,422	55.1	64.0	191,700	960	90.1	82,277	15.6	2.8
0560410	Rogers city, Arkansas...................	69,874	84.6	11.3	25,872	58.1	NA	225,300	1,053	93.8	30,926	16.3	2.1
0566080	Springdale city, Arkansas..............	84,697	92.3	4.3	28,942	55.9	68.0	215,900	1,021	91.5	40,448	19.5	2.1
06000	CALIFORNIA.............................	38,833,197	88.7	4.5	13,429,063	55.9	68.0	648,100	1,750	93.0	13,999,114	10.1	9.9
0600562	Alameda city, California	75,721	88.7	8.9	30,281	45.2	56.1	1,077,900	1,981	92.8	24,598	14.2	11.4
0600884	Alhambra city, California...............	80,166	90.9	5.6	29,022	38.6	71.3	718,100	1,702	92.1	30,449	7.7	8.7
0602000	Anaheim city, California	341,397	90.7	5.8	105,608	48.9	79.1	688,400	1,833	92.0	141,816	7.3	7.3
0602252	Antioch city, California.................	113,320	92.0	4.4	37,081	63.8	NA	577,900	1,942	94.4	43,302	7.9	28.6
0602364	Apple Valley town, California........	NA	NA	NA	24,657	65.5	67.1	353,500	1,237	93.8	21,282	11.2	31.1
0602553	Arden-Arcade CDP, California........	100,092	83.3	11.6	40,688	45.2	72.3	480,300	1,280	93.2	37,970	11.5	6.2
0603526	Bakersfield city, California.............	401,763	92.1	3.4	128,007	61.2	72.5	318,600	1,219	93.7	151,120	11.7	6.6
0603666	Baldwin Park city, California..........	NA	NA	NA	19,112	66.7	NA	536,500	1,658	92.0	30,179	8.2	6.6
0604982	Bellflower city, California	75,972	92.6	5.5	24,327	36.8	66.7	595,800	1,621	91.6	29,627	5.8	8.4
0606000	Berkeley city, California.................	116,055	70.3	22.2	43,893	46.0	64.2	1,270,000	1,923	94.5	30,978	9.3	8.5
0608786	Buena Park city, California	NA	NA	NA	24,306	58.7	71.6	666,800	1,893	94.3	35,560	8.6	11.4
0608954	Burbank city, California.................	104,894	90.5	6.8	44,471	44.7	71.5	940,400	1,911	93.9	32,515	8.1	7.8
0610046	Camarillo city, California	70,053	90.8	6.3	27,588	66.0	67.6	694,200	2,288	93.8	25,780	15.6	7.1
0611194	Carlsbad city, California	114,151	83.8	13.6	48,098	61.6	60.5	1,042,900	2,437	96.3	34,394	8.6	7.5
0611390	Carmichael CDP, California...........	80,268	91.6	6.9	32,172	51.6	66.6	495,600	1,410	93.1	27,298	12.2	6.0
0611530	Carson city, California...................	NA	NA	NA	25,743	73.4	64.9	595,900	1,573	94.7	35,341	5.6	11.1
0611964	Castro Valley CDP, California.........	65,885	88.2	10.1	23,103	73.4	62.9	1,004,800	2,211	94.9	21,952	11.0	9.3

Table C-4. Cities — Where: Migration, Housing, and Transportation, 2021—*Continued*

STATE and place code	STATE Place	Total population 1 year and over	Lived in the same house 1 year ago (percent)	Did not live in the same city 1 year ago (percent)	Total occupied housing units	Owner-occupied units (percent)	Percent with a mortgage, contract to purchase, or similar debt	Median value of owner-occupied units (dollars; owner estimated)	Median gross rent of renter-occupied units paying cash rent	Households with Internet access (percent)	Number of workers who commuted to work	Commute of less than 10 minutes (percent)	Commute of 60 minutes or more (percent)
ACS table number:		C07204	C07204	C07204	B25003	B25003	B25081	B25097	B25064	S2801	B08012	B08012	B08012
FIPS	column number:	1	2	3	4	5	6	7	8	9	10	11	12
	CALIFORNIA—Cont.												
0613014	Chico city, California..............	101,515	75.7	14.4	40,956	44.3	74.7	420,100	1,300	92.6	40,611	29.1	4.3
0613210	Chino city, California	92,221	87.4	8.9	26,774	65.1	72.3	589,200	2,015	92.4	32,799	6.3	20.2
0613214	Chino Hills city, California	78,434	89.8	7.9	25,703	74.8	69.3	787,400	2,439	97.5	28,528	6.7	16.5
0613392	Chula Vista city, California	272,591	92.7	4.8	83,451	58.2	64.7	655,100	1,894	95.2	110,943	6.7	6.4
0613588	Citrus Heights city, California	86,455	86.5	9.0	34,140	58.2	72.7	406,500	1,539	91.1	33,767	9.3	8.8
0614218	Clovis city, California..................	121,120	91.2	5.0	38,762	69.0	75.8	418,000	1,410	95.3	47,237	11.6	3.1
0615044	Compton city, California	NA	NA	NA	28,820	62.7	77.8	537,700	1,331	90.1	40,015	0.8	8.5
0616000	Concord city, California	122,634	88.8	7.4	46,375	56.7	76.2	719,000	1,992	94.8	45,343	12.8	14.3
0616350	Corona city, California	158,467	91.8	6.3	48,905	62.3	78.0	620,600	1,810	92.6	63,685	7.5	12.6
0616532	Costa Mesa city, California..........	109,802	83.1	11.2	43,711	40.0	58.6	930,500	2,025	96.1	47,645	12.9	4.2
0617918	Daly City city, California..........	100,732	91.7	5.1	32,887	58.8	63.1	1,052,800	2,245	93.9	43,346	8.9	9.8
0618100	Davis city, California..................	66,482	70.0	21.0	25,316	43.9	63.7	752,300	1,908	94.4	20,262	22.0	4.3
0619766	Downey city, California..............	110,992	93.0	6.9	36,008	52.2	NA	686,000	1,707	93.5	45,330	5.7	9.3
0620018	Dublin city, California..................	70,663	84.4	12.3	23,688	71.0	53.9	1,114,800	2,852	98.0	18,320	12.2	18.7
0620802	East Los Angeles CDP, California ...	115,283	93.6	4.8	31,072	32.0	NA	592,100	1,317	86.0	47,144	7.2	9.7
0621230	Eastvale city, California	NA	NA	NA	18,470	78.6	69.7	686,100	2,638	NA	30,611	13.4	16.5
0621712	El Cajon city, California	103,608	86.9	9.5	34,443	42.6	75.3	591,600	1,574	92.6	38,041	10.5	5.5
0622020	Elk Grove city, California	177,439	90.9	5.9	53,724	73.7	58.6	569,900	2,051	97.1	57,656	7.2	6.3
0622230	El Monte city, California	106,043	96.7	2.2	29,036	37.9	60.0	566,600	1,462	89.9	41,745	8.1	5.5
0622804	Escondido city, California..............	148,966	90.1	6.7	50,171	55.0	71.7	620,200	1,830	93.8	58,621	7.0	6.2
0623182	Fairfield city, California..............	117,491	88.1	6.8	38,097	58.5	76.4	552,300	1,963	92.3	43,536	10.4	16.6
0624638	Folsom city, California..................	80,668	87.2	9.6	28,441	70.3	82.5	671,000	2,003	97.8	20,992	13.4	7.2
0624680	Fontana city, California	208,116	92.2	5.0	57,836	68.3	69.1	511,000	1,576	97.0	81,663	6.8	14.9
0626000	Fremont city, California	225,249	88.7	7.6	75,716	61.3	65.1	1,175,600	2,545	95.5	57,443	5.9	8.4
0627000	Fresno city, California..................	536,835	88.9	5.2	181,841	50.2	63.9	321,300	1,166	85.4	195,615	11.4	4.1
0628000	Fullerton city, California	140,600	88.3	7.9	48,423	48.6	61.1	790,900	1,876	94.6	53,400	8.6	12.8
0629000	Garden Grove city, California	168,358	93.9	5.1	48,769	54.6	69.3	663,900	1,809	91.6	67,560	5.2	8.3
0630000	Glendale city, California..............	191,130	89.4	6.8	70,831	35.6	68.4	995,700	1,900	92.4	69,976	8.8	7.0
0632548	Hawthorne city, California	NA	NA	NA	30,039	27.6	68.2	738,000	1,530	91.9	37,438	7.8	8.9
0633000	Hayward city, California..............	157,356	92.1	6.3	48,619	55.0	NA	735,000	2,109	92.0	60,302	4.7	12.2
0633182	Hemet city, California	90,160	87.1	6.6	33,486	59.7	70.3	266,700	1,381	84.5	28,159	13.2	13.2
0633434	Hesperia city, California	99,555	91.4	7.5	29,237	65.6	62.3	344,000	1,543	92.3	33,733	9.7	28.2
0636000	Huntington Beach city, California..	194,706	85.6	10.0	79,930	56.9	62.7	937,200	2,175	95.5	73,894	11.9	7.2
0636448	Indio city, California..................	89,942	92.0	7.1	34,673	64.2	71.1	381,300	1,255	90.1	35,675	10.1	4.2
0636546	Inglewood city, California	104,152	93.2	5.5	37,972	37.5	64.7	684,500	1,488	91.4	40,452	4.4	10.0
0636770	Irvine city, California	304,798	73.3	16.0	111,648	44.7	75.7	970,500	2,467	95.4	97,525	8.8	5.6
0637692	Jurupa Valley city, California..........	105,940	96.7	2.2	27,454	67.3	82.5	447,500	1,369	94.3	42,626	8.7	12.0
0639486	Lake Elsinore city, California	70,922	93.5	5.3	21,422	68.8	74.6	473,600	1,894	94.0	23,978	9.6	30.0
0639496	Lake Forest city, California..........	85,153	85.8	10.1	30,962	71.0	73.7	804,400	2,280	97.4	30,599	12.0	5.5
0639892	Lakewood city, California..............	79,646	93.6	5.0	26,533	73.0	70.6	704,700	1,875	94.2	33,094	8.5	6.9
0640130	Lancaster city, California	166,234	92.2	5.3	51,333	58.2	67.9	377,200	1,524	91.2	55,624	7.2	15.0
0641992	Livermore city, California	85,683	87.4	10.8	31,472	69.7	65.9	942,300	2,340	95.4	31,264	16.1	12.1
0642202	Lodi city, California	66,677	90.5	5.9	24,245	55.5	71.0	427,900	1,391	90.0	26,353	20.1	7.8
0643000	Long Beach city, California............	452,185	88.9	7.8	172,599	40.2	70.8	693,600	1,634	94.1	179,600	6.6	9.0
0644000	Los Angeles city, California	3,808,901	88.9	4.9	1,410,594	37.0	66.6	812,800	1,703	92.3	1,383,471	6.6	11.7
0644574	Lynwood city, California..............	NA	NA	NA	16,079	49.6	NA	543,800	1,440	91.2	23,975	5.5	10.6
0645022	Madera city, California..............	NA	NA	NA	18,595	47.6	68.0	290,700	1,100	87.0	22,171	16.7	10.5
0645484	Manteca city, California..............	85,385	88.4	6.8	27,310	72.7	77.7	505,500	1,718	93.3	32,059	7.6	22.5
0646842	Menifee city, California..............	105,497	86.4	13.1	35,601	78.3	NA	442,700	1,825	92.2	35,846	4.4	25.8
0646898	Merced city, California..............	88,384	91.4	6.0	28,358	40.6	72.5	325,000	1,154	90.0	28,515	16.1	11.4
0647766	Milpitas city, California..............	78,019	84.8	10.2	23,632	60.5	72.1	1,146,600	2,745	97.5	25,050	4.9	5.7
0648256	Mission Viejo city, California	91,786	88.7	8.0	34,168	78.0	67.1	859,500	2,273	98.0	33,106	9.9	8.1
0648354	Modesto city, California..............	217,009	91.1	4.8	71,775	59.0	78.9	389,500	1,419	92.9	85,775	9.5	14.8
0649270	Moreno Valley city, California........	208,929	92.0	4.6	54,104	61.3	63.8	422,500	1,788	94.8	79,247	6.0	20.1
0649670	Mountain View city, California	80,872	80.0	12.2	34,637	37.7	78.3	1,636,100	2,760	96.0	22,288	10.0	4.7
0650076	Murrieta city, California..............	111,655	87.0	10.1	34,414	75.1	68.0	573,700	2,144	96.7	37,281	11.2	27.0
0650258	Napa city, California..................	78,040	91.4	5.5	30,418	62.3	64.8	718,700	1,851	94.3	31,890	14.2	11.3
0651182	Newport Beach city, California	84,366	79.0	16.3	39,131	54.9	67.7	2,000,000+	2,815	95.9	28,155	9.8	6.7

STATE and place code	STATE Place	Total population 1 year and over	Lived in the same house 1 year ago (percent)	Did not live in the same city 1 year ago (percent)	Total occupied housing units	Owner-occupied units (percent)	Percent with a mortgage, contract to purchase, or similar debt	Median value of owner-occupied units (dollars; owner estimated)	Median gross rent of renter-occupied units paying cash rent	Households with Internet access (percent)	Number of workers who commuted to work	Commute of less than 10 minutes (percent)	Commute of 60 minutes or more (percent)
	ACS table number:	C07204	C07204	C07204	B25003	B25003	B25081	B25097	B25064	S2801	B08012	B08012	B08012
FIPS	column number:	1	2	3	4	5	6	7	8	9	10	11	12
	CALIFORNIA—Cont.												
0652526	Norwalk city, California	99,521	96.5	2.5	26,506	69.2	71.2	585,200	1,694	92.6	39,256	6.4	8.4
0653000	Oakland city, California	429,780	87.3	7.2	170,366	42.6	68.0	848,600	1,737	90.5	145,576	6.2	9.9
0653322	Oceanside city, California	171,352	86.2	9.8	59,683	55.6	75.8	631,300	1,934	94.6	65,770	6.3	10.2
0653896	Ontario city, California	175,019	91.8	6.4	55,819	58.1	70.3	545,200	1,685	94.7	73,952	7.1	16.6
0653980	Orange city, California	136,190	89.6	8.3	43,291	56.0	67.6	827,200	2,038	94.3	51,423	7.7	3.9
0654652	Oxnard city, California	199,015	93.3	3.3	50,611	56.9	73.5	569,700	1,823	93.7	86,031	8.1	4.9
0655156	Palmdale city, California	163,945	93.5	4.7	46,650	67.3	58.9	399,000	1,658	94.2	60,389	7.5	25.0
0655282	Palo Alto city, California	66,269	83.2	12.2	24,501	53.6	72.6	2,000,000+	3,063	95.9	15,881	13.5	2.6
0656000	Pasadena city, California	134,811	88.5	9.1	56,992	43.0	NA	905,900	1,940	93.2	51,525	10.2	9.6
0656700	Perris city, California	NA	NA	NA	19,923	65.8	68.0	415,400	1,536	94.2	32,380	1.4	8.3
0657456	Pittsburg city, California	75,703	89.6	9.6	23,827	54.3	71.8	563,700	1,909	92.6	31,573	5.1	17.3
0657792	Pleasanton city, California	77,860	89.0	8.5	29,330	65.9	69.4	1,230,600	2,430	97.8	22,509	13.9	10.4
0658072	Pomona city, California	147,035	91.5	6.9	40,142	51.3	NA	525,300	1,598	92.0	56,454	8.3	13.9
0659444	Rancho Cordova city, California	79,750	89.8	6.3	28,428	59.2	71.6	438,800	1,413	93.5	26,984	5.4	9.8
0659451	Rancho Cucamonga city, California	173,530	90.4	6.9	57,290	58.8	62.6	632,700	2,047	94.8	65,795	9.9	16.1
0659920	Redding city, California	92,417	85.5	9.0	37,302	49.4	64.4	346,900	1,156	92.6	35,897	24.4	2.9
0659962	Redlands city, California	72,782	86.7	11.1	24,452	56.8	74.3	542,500	1,656	95.3	25,127	15.0	10.3
0660018	Redondo Beach city, California	69,379	86.3	12.4	26,986	55.1	72.4	1,110,800	2,305	97.1	19,746	11.6	7.1
0660102	Redwood City city, California	80,836	85.4	12.2	29,450	54.6	NA	1,567,400	2,950	97.0	26,960	11.3	2.3
0660466	Rialto city, California	103,191	90.8	6.1	29,043	61.9	68.5	431,500	1,526	94.1	38,318	4.9	18.5
0660620	Richmond city, California	113,759	92.0	5.8	40,019	53.6	77.6	641,500	1,737	94.4	43,291	8.6	14.3
0662000	Riverside city, California	314,806	88.6	8.1	91,110	56.2	77.1	483,300	1,586	94.8	133,653	9.4	13.9
0662364	Rocklin city, California	72,318	85.5	11.8	25,528	66.7	73.6	622,100	2,050	96.8	23,414	15.1	7.0
0662938	Roseville city, California	149,902	86.5	9.4	57,569	68.5	67.7	605,300	1,809	94.8	56,189	13.4	7.1
0664000	Sacramento city, California	520,347	87.4	7.4	202,093	51.5	64.9	449,600	1,549	94.8	188,517	10.7	6.0
0664224	Salinas city, California	160,701	93.5	2.3	41,871	40.8	69.0	585,100	1,702	96.7	64,179	7.1	6.7
0665000	San Bernardino city, California	220,367	90.6	8.0	63,331	51.1	63.5	350,000	1,341	87.8	83,525	5.7	10.8
0665042	San Buenaventura (Ventura) city, California	109,355	90.6	5.1	42,288	60.5	70.6	702,500	1,911	94.4	42,614	11.7	5.8
0666000	San Diego city, California	1,368,948	83.3	8.6	521,000	48.3	64.8	768,800	1,962	95.5	530,807	8.4	4.0
0667000	San Francisco city, California	806,418	81.5	8.4	350,796	40.1	69.1	1,306,400	2,167	92.8	238,860	7.0	8.9
0668000	San Jose city, California	974,581	87.3	6.2	322,881	55.7	60.1	1,119,500	2,328	96.0	340,140	6.8	4.7
0668084	San Leandro city, California	88,391	90.8	8.1	30,977	60.2	70.1	775,000	1,746	88.4	37,532	5.0	12.9
0668196	San Marcos city, California	94,191	87.5	6.9	34,037	64.6	69.0	710,500	1,820	98.2	29,707	11.0	2.7
0668252	San Mateo city, California	101,118	85.6	10.1	39,340	53.1	76.4	1,518,800	2,475	94.2	34,450	10.5	5.7
0668378	San Ramon city, California	86,061	86.3	10.1	29,662	69.8	71.9	1,233,100	2,848	96.8	21,776	10.0	15.6
0669000	Santa Ana city, California	306,247	90.8	5.6	78,674	44.9	69.9	623,000	1,760	91.0	126,085	5.8	3.4
0669070	Santa Barbara city, California	87,230	86.3	9.7	35,676	37.2	67.2	1,476,800	2,167	94.0	34,063	22.4	3.0
0669084	Santa Clara city, California	125,438	76.8	16.9	49,011	43.1	75.8	1,382,300	2,600	95.5	41,171	9.6	3.0
0669088	Santa Clarita city, California	221,661	89.1	6.4	73,509	72.7	66.2	656,000	2,198	96.3	84,211	10.5	17.2
0669196	Santa Maria city, California	108,371	91.8	4.3	30,316	49.7	66.1	426,100	1,682	86.4	45,449	17.4	5.1
0670000	Santa Monica city, California	90,522	83.4	11.8	45,541	31.4	69.7	1,582,300	2,157	93.9	27,147	12.0	5.1
0670098	Santa Rosa city, California	175,274	84.8	7.4	68,686	54.3	75.6	638,500	1,936	93.9	70,945	13.8	7.6
0672016	Simi Valley city, California	125,150	92.3	3.9	45,308	72.6	NA	685,500	2,360	92.7	49,617	13.1	6.4
0673080	South Gate city, California	NA	NA	NA	24,891	49.0	69.1	559,900	1,269	92.5	36,947	5.7	12.4
0675000	Stockton city, California	317,458	89.4	5.0	97,447	54.5	63.1	382,900	1,342	89.7	119,008	8.4	17.2
0677000	Sunnyvale city, California	149,997	79.6	12.5	59,567	45.8	82.6	1,575,200	2,618	95.8	43,116	12.4	2.4
0678120	Temecula city, California	109,430	84.5	13.4	34,958	67.6	69.8	613,300	1,937	97.6	36,028	12.0	20.0
0678582	Thousand Oaks city, California	125,086	91.8	5.0	45,081	70.8	64.4	858,200	2,283	94.8	41,887	13.6	8.6
0680000	Torrance city, California	142,863	90.7	6.5	57,584	55.8	80.3	930,500	1,918	93.8	47,830	8.1	6.8
0680238	Tracy city, California	94,334	88.7	8.8	28,353	63.5	NA	643,700	2,126	94.8	29,826	13.2	36.4
0680644	Tulare city, California	NA	NA	NA	20,974	63.2	65.1	280,200	1,107	92.4	24,200	17.3	8.3
0680812	Turlock city, California	72,115	88.8	8.8	24,885	55.4	63.8	401,900	1,345	92.8	26,917	17.0	9.2
0680854	Tustin city, California	78,091	88.6	10.8	26,762	50.6	69.9	727,000	2,126	97.1	32,047	5.1	7.8
0681204	Union City city, California	68,349	89.8	8.7	21,637	66.4	69.3	995,200	2,409	94.5	24,568	9.7	8.5
0681344	Upland city, California	78,922	90.9	7.2	26,052	53.8	73.3	621,700	1,750	96.3	30,608	13.1	11.5
0681554	Vacaville city, California	101,766	88.5	7.0	33,777	64.5	71.2	566,300	2,225	96.3	42,563	17.8	14.5
0681666	Vallejo city, California	124,144	89.4	7.4	43,906	59.0	70.7	505,400	1,667	92.7	48,994	6.7	22.1

Table C-4. Cities — Where: Migration, Housing, and Transportation, 2021—*Continued*

STATE and place code	STATE Place	Total population 1 year and over	Lived in the same house 1 year ago (percent)	Did not live in the same city 1 year ago (percent)	Total occupied housing units	Owner-occupied units (percent)	Percent with a mortgage, contract to purchase, or similar debt	Median value of owner-occupied units (dollars; owner estimated)	Median gross rent of renter-occupied units paying cash rent	Households with Internet access (percent)	Number of workers who commuted to work	Commute of less than 10 minutes (percent)	Commute of 60 minutes or more (percent)
	ACS table number:	C07204	C07204	C07204	B25003	B25003	B25081	B25097	B25064	S2801	B08012	B08012	B08012
FIPS	column number:	1	2	3	4	5	6	7	8	9	10	11	12
	CALIFORNIA—Cont.												
0682590	Victorville city, California..............	134,580	88.0	7.2	38,400	61.1	72.4	323,400	1,337	94.2	44,680	7.9	25.0
0682954	Visalia city, California.................	141,532	93.6	2.9	47,660	54.1	68.6	315,100	1,210	91.4	52,570	15.1	6.1
0682996	Vista city, California..................	97,448	88.1	8.4	30,614	47.0	58.0	634,600	1,896	92.9	42,758	5.0	3.0
0683346	Walnut Creek city, California.........	68,726	82.2	14.8	31,035	65.6	66.4	1,004,800	2,372	97.4	19,702	9.4	11.7
0684200	West Covina city, California..........	105,624	93.0	5.2	32,012	61.7	58.5	636,300	2,040	96.1	40,838	6.1	12.1
0684550	Westminster city, California..........	89,232	90.9	7.1	27,935	48.4	74.8	762,300	1,798	93.2	32,409	7.0	5.2
0685292	Whittier city, California...............	84,670	95.4	3.7	27,773	59.5	64.2	718,300	1,647	91.3	34,209	5.5	12.0
0686832	Yorba Linda city, California...........	67,267	90.3	9.3	24,098	80.1	63.6	1,012,900	1,951	92.9	24,002	6.2	14.6
0686972	Yuba City city, California..............	69,124	90.6	6.3	24,176	55.8	74.2	355,200	1,249	93.7	26,262	13.7	11.2
08000	**COLORADO**.............................	5,757,628	83.3	9.7	2,313,042	66.8	69.7	466,200	1,491	93.2	2,281,922	13.4	6.4
0803455	Arvada city, Colorado..................	122,148	89.4	7.5	50,678	75.6	74.5	537,900	1,592	94.6	49,036	9.1	3.2
0804000	Aurora city, Colorado..................	384,564	82.6	10.5	140,003	64.0	59.9	411,400	1,486	91.8	160,715	6.6	6.8
0807850	Boulder city, Colorado.................	103,586	59.5	28.9	42,376	46.2	72.4	941,100	1,892	94.7	31,763	19.4	4.5
0809280	Broomfield city, Colorado.............	74,621	84.3	13.7	30,161	67.1	81.3	576,200	1,931	95.3	26,610	9.5	4.8
0812415	Castle Rock town, Colorado	74,973	77.2	19.2	27,249	79.1	72.3	577,700	1,863	NA	28,028	13.8	8.3
0812815	Centennial city, Colorado.............	105,852	89.6	9.1	39,660	79.1	71.0	578,200	1,926	97.3	37,314	13.8	3.7
0816000	Colorado Springs city, Colorado....	478,717	79.6	12.0	197,542	62.5	75.2	390,500	1,380	95.4	199,536	12.5	3.3
0820000	Denver city, Colorado.................	703,702	79.6	11.6	326,634	50.3	70.0	541,500	1,549	92.3	273,410	8.9	4.6
0827425	Fort Collins city, Colorado	166,982	72.1	18.4	70,686	52.7	NA	485,500	1,435	92.8	72,989	17.6	4.1
0831660	Grand Junction city, Colorado.......	66,549	75.7	16.8	28,352	58.5	70.1	339,800	931	92.4	28,200	23.5	4.7
0832155	Greeley city, Colorado.................	107,498	84.5	8.9	38,381	61.9	77.6	347,100	1,141	92.7	43,693	17.6	9.6
0836410	Highlands Ranch CDP, Colorado....	97,843	85.0	12.1	38,117	81.2	64.9	629,200	2,143	97.1	34,200	12.9	4.2
0843000	Lakewood city, Colorado..............	155,123	82.5	13.7	70,751	59.5	68.0	483,300	1,488	93.7	59,143	6.6	5.6
0845970	Longmont city, Colorado..............	99,671	84.2	11.2	43,519	63.7	61.1	465,500	1,471	94.4	39,508	13.2	9.2
0846465	Loveland city, Colorado...............	76,671	82.3	11.9	35,803	62.9	61.5	412,300	1,487	90.6	27,188	12.5	9.8
0862000	Pueblo city, Colorado.................	111,513	86.4	6.7	47,901	60.9	74.0	214,500	872	86.9	42,014	17.1	4.0
0877290	Thornton city, Colorado..............	141,277	87.5	8.0	48,263	76.6	75.2	449,200	1,700	96.7	62,251	6.4	13.3
0883835	Westminster city, Colorado	113,695	82.4	12.9	47,797	63.7	69.4	457,500	1,641	93.9	48,629	10.1	4.7
09000	**CONNECTICUT**	3,571,470	88.7	5.4	1,428,313	66.6	65.3	311,500	1,277	92.3	1,432,375	12.4	7.8
0908000	Bridgeport City, Connecticut........	146,769	88.7	7.7	57,732	43.2	72.1	222,800	1,209	85.9	66,444	9.1	11.8
0918430	Danbury city, Connecticut............	86,209	90.9	4.3	33,024	61.1	NA	352,700	1,641	92.9	37,797	10.2	17.7
0937000	Hartford city, Connecticut...........	119,883	84.4	9.7	45,491	28.7	69.4	174,100	1,107	84.3	44,554	10.9	6.6
0950370	New Britain city, Connecticut........	72,115	87.8	7.3	28,450	45.1	66.7	183,300	1,073	85.6	30,868	10.7	3.7
0952000	New Haven city, Connecticut........	133,596	81.2	13.8	56,373	25.6	70.0	205,500	1,273	91.2	51,306	11.4	5.5
0955990	Norwalk city, Connecticut............	89,229	88.1	7.2	36,847	57.5	66.6	478,100	1,825	92.5	33,555	12.0	8.0
0973000	Stamford city, Connecticut...........	134,222	81.9	10.5	52,816	48.9	58.3	576,000	2,045	96.5	58,941	10.3	9.5
0980000	Waterbury city, Connecticut..........	112,690	91.1	5.0	45,008	45.5	64.4	184,300	1,040	87.3	45,396	13.2	8.9
10000	**DELAWARE**	994,669	89.4	5.7	395,656	72.6	63.7	300,500	1,208	92.1	371,366	12.8	6.9
1077580	Wilmington city, Delaware	70,071	87.0	9.0	32,049	51.7	75.3	200,900	1,010	87.8	25,942	15.6	3.9
11000	**DISTRICT OF COLUMBIA**	661,026	79.7	9.9	319,565	41.6	75.3	669,900	1,668	90.2	183,062	7.0	7.7
1150000	Washington city, District of Columbia	661,026	79.7	9.9	319,565	41.6	81.9	669,900	1,668	90.2	183,062	7.0	7.7
12000	**FLORIDA**.................................	21,590,684	86.0	6.9	8,565,329	67.4	56.7	290,700	1,348	90.6	8,219,409	9.2	7.7
1200410	Alafaya CDP, Florida...................	95,519	91.6	5.9	32,823	61.2	49.6	346,300	1,565	94.2	40,769	8.8	13.6
1207300	Boca Raton city, Florida...............	95,132	83.0	14.1	41,318	67.4	48.3	518,200	1,941	90.8	33,782	13.1	6.3
1207875	Boynton Beach city, Florida	78,850	87.0	8.8	33,201	62.4	69.0	284,200	1,604	87.4	35,058	10.0	3.7
1208150	Brandon CDP, Florida..................	115,299	80.0	15.2	46,925	52.2	66.8	276,300	1,409	91.3	43,411	6.8	4.8
1210275	Cape Coral city, Florida...............	202,101	87.6	9.7	79,845	77.4	53.2	291,600	1,482	92.4	85,311	8.8	8.9
1212875	Clearwater city, Florida...............	116,054	81.9	13.5	49,486	59.7	67.5	298,000	1,189	87.1	44,382	8.0	2.0
1214400	Coral Springs city, Florida............	131,688	88.2	9.3	44,417	59.5	57.3	455,000	1,649	94.7	56,449	9.9	7.4
1216475	Davie town, Florida....................	104,504	87.9	10.4	39,061	66.2	45.7	421,300	1,568	93.5	41,484	6.4	12.5
1216525	Daytona Beach city, Florida..........	73,827	82.2	15.2	34,721	51.9	52.0	218,600	1,068	86.7	30,219	15.0	5.8
1216725	Deerfield Beach city, Florida	85,737	84.5	14.7	39,934	62.7	48.1	233,400	1,372	89.1	35,033	10.4	12.2
1217100	Delray Beach city, Florida.............	66,003	85.5	12.1	30,472	65.5	73.4	368,900	1,576	91.6	24,757	13.5	4.0
1217200	Deltona city, Florida	95,224	90.8	8.4	35,384	79.0	NA	229,700	1,355	92.8	39,938	4.4	15.5
1217935	Doral city, Florida......................	74,861	75.2	11.3	25,419	44.5	56.9	462,200	2,175	98.1	31,450	5.1	2.7
1224000	Fort Lauderdale city, Florida..........	179,506	83.1	11.5	83,021	55.0	NA	395,500	1,519	91.9	75,706	12.0	7.7

STATE and place code	STATE Place	Total population 1 year and over	Lived in the same house 1 year ago (percent)	Did not live in the same city 1 year ago (percent)	Total occupied housing units	Owner-occupied units (percent)	Percent with a mortgage, contract to purchase, or similar debt	Median value of owner-occupied units (dollars; owner estimated)	Median gross rent of renter-occupied units paying cash rent	Households with Internet access (percent)	Number of workers who commuted to work	Commute of less than 10 minutes (percent)	Commute of 60 minutes or more (percent)
ACS table number:		C07204	C07204	C07204	B25003	B25003	B25081	B25097	B25064	S2801	B08012	B08012	B08012
FIPS	column number:	1	2	3	4	5	6	7	8	9	10	11	12
	FLORIDA—Cont.												
1224125	Fort Myers city, Florida	91,125	81.2	14.3	37,323	47.1	48.4	334,800	1,156	86.9	29,741	7.6	6.1
1225175	Gainesville city, Florida	139,224	70.6	20.2	56,513	41.3	51.6	195,300	1,103	86.0	56,155	15.3	3.8
1230000	Hialeah city, Florida	217,566	89.8	4.5	75,692	47.1	63.1	324,000	1,368	85.8	91,029	6.5	9.4
1232000	Hollywood city, Florida	151,210	85.3	10.6	61,598	59.1	NA	322,400	1,325	90.6	62,676	6.9	9.6
1232275	Homestead city, Florida	NA	NA	NA	27,094	55.1	NA	275,200	1,401	88.2	32,113	6.1	14.9
1232610	Horizon West CDP, Florida	71,994	81	17	21,444	72.8	66.5	478,100	2,089	NA	NA	NA	NA
1235000	Jacksonville city, Florida	942,505	84.7	6.5	386,283	58.6	59.5	239,400	1,194	90.1	386,542	9.8	3.4
1236100	Kendall CDP, Florida	80,173	91.5	7.3	33,184	65.2	70.0	423,700	1,697	93.3	31,626	4.3	5.8
1236950	Kissimmee city, Florida	77,839	77.0	16.6	25,999	45.8	50.7	258,900	1,361	88.5	30,681	3.4	12.6
1238250	Lakeland city, Florida	114,579	81.9	11.2	45,548	57.0	48.6	186,700	1,124	85.8	42,318	12.4	4.7
1239425	Largo city, Florida	81,895	84.1	12.6	36,493	60.4	NA	201,700	1,214	87.2	33,822	13.5	3.9
1239550	Lauderhill city, Florida	72,721	91.6	7.7	26,555	52.2	72.1	251,700	1,316	86.4	29,869	2.7	12.7
1239925	Lehigh Acres CDP, Florida	125,299	90.3	6.0	40,295	73.1	57.5	235,300	1,279	88.9	49,483	4.5	19.0
1243975	Melbourne city, Florida	84,405	79.5	17.0	36,651	64.8	55.9	234,400	1,167	89.9	33,814	20.0	4.8
1245000	Miami city, Florida	435,517	81.9	9.3	192,219	30.4	48.4	411,300	1,446	79.7	186,515	7.0	7.1
1245025	Miami Beach city, Florida	79,876	79.3	16.4	40,788	35.5	68.8	581,200	1,522	78.6	29,689	11.5	3.5
1245060	Miami Gardens city, Florida	109,919	93.5	4.5	34,332	67.5	54.4	320,600	1,456	83.3	40,786	1.9	11.1
1245975	Miramar city, Florida	134,440	92.9	5.8	42,707	72.7	62.7	374,600	1,580	92.1	61,990	1.8	6.4
1249675	North Port city, Florida	NA	NA	NA	30,622	77.1	67.4	277,100	1,291	93.2	34,118	14.3	6.4
1253000	Orlando city, Florida	306,378	82.1	12.5	130,037	37.7	62.3	319,800	1,415	92.0	130,973	7.3	4.8
1254000	Palm Bay city, Florida	122,172	85.4	10.8	45,145	77.1	63.7	228,400	1,304	90.6	48,044	4.9	6.8
1254200	Palm Coast city, Florida	93,845	89.9	8.7	36,896	82.4	54.1	274,000	1,403	84.8	30,502	5.3	10.4
1255775	Pembroke Pines city, Florida	168,801	92.5	4.9	64,378	69.1	75.8	368,400	1,581	90.6	73,311	3.9	5.3
1256825	Pine Hills CDP, Florida	84,007	77.9	16.6	25,752	51.1	61.4	205,900	1,266	89.2	32,674	3.0	5.1
1257425	Plantation city, Florida	91,963	88.2	9.3	36,564	65.7	NA	409,400	1,763	96.2	35,253	5.8	8.3
1257900	Poinciana CDP, Florida	64,878	86.2	13.8	21,402	76.7	51.7	233,400	1,480	92.0	24,698	4.7	33.1
1258050	Pompano Beach city, Florida	111,001	81.4	13.5	48,363	56.2	48.6	304,000	1,406	89.8	44,599	7.1	8.9
1258350	Port Charlotte CDP, Florida	65,279	88.8	7.4	29,120	81.3	63.3	234,400	1,176	93.6	22,538	13.8	5.6
1258715	Port St. Lucie city, Florida	214,471	90.9	7.3	77,190	83.5	78.2	284,800	1,564	96.6	88,918	4.1	11.0
1260950	Riverview CDP, Florida	113,316	83.6	14.5	40,114	71.7	57.9	291,900	1,727	97.3	43,497	6.4	12.2
1263000	St. Petersburg city, Florida	256,430	85.9	8.3	111,349	63.0	63.3	315,200	1,330	91.6	100,329	13.7	4.7
1268350	Spring Hill CDP, Florida	122,648	85.7	11.3	46,360	80.2	68.3	230,900	1,174	92.1	47,228	12.4	11.8
1269700	Sunrise city, Florida	94,989	89.7	8.7	35,166	66.1	65.5	311,500	1,690	92.5	40,984	6.8	5.9
1270600	Tallahassee city, Florida	194,922	74.3	13.7	84,920	42.0	NA	246,100	1,147	93.5	85,477	15.4	2.0
1270675	Tamarac city, Florida	NA	NA	NA	29,065	71.4	62.7	264,200	1,518	91.5	30,799	2.6	7.1
1271000	Tampa city, Florida	382,531	80.3	12.3	159,925	52.9	34.9	336,200	1,327	93.5	143,707	11.2	5.3
1271625	The Villages CDP, Florida	80,691	89.9	8.0	47,527	93.4	65.8	339,700	1,173	91.9	NA	NA	NA
1272145	Town 'n' Country CDP, Florida	87,053	86.6	7.8	35,155	59.1	70.3	275,200	1,374	95.0	37,840	9.4	5.5
1275875	Wesley Chapel CDP, Florida	77,181	87.1	8.9	23,868	72.8	67.9	335,000	1,847	95.7	28,234	3.4	8.4
1276582	Weston city, Florida	66,520	81.5	14.7	20,227	73.7	51.9	568,600	2,274	95.2	21,701	11.5	6.8
1276600	West Palm Beach city, Florida	116,660	82.1	11.8	50,409	50.4	NA	311,000	1,490	88.3	46,900	9.9	3.2
13000	**GEORGIA**	10,688,429	86.5	7.6	4,001,109	66.0	63.8	249,700	1,153	90.1	4,076,187	10.4	8.3
1301052	Albany city, Georgia	65,917	84.9	8.6	27,357	40.5	72.0	100,800	801	80.6	22,101	17.8	6.3
1301696	Alpharetta city, Georgia	64,969	81.3	17.3	25,457	64.1	61.1	538,400	1,685	97.1	19,547	12.5	2.4
1303440	Athens-Clarke County unified government (balance), Georgia	124,819	73.0	18.5	54,438	39.2	69.2	237,100	1,047	91.0	52,588	22.7	6.6
1304000	Atlanta city, Georgia	491,005	76.4	15.1	232,720	48.6	60.9	375,500	1,446	91.4	158,496	9.3	7.2
1304204	Augusta-Richmond County consolidated government (balance), Georgia	197,785	84.3	10.0	72,760	51.5	66.0	131,900	942	84.6	81,865	16.2	3.0
1319000	Columbus city, Georgia	202,715	80.9	10.9	82,663	47.6	70.3	170,900	923	87.3	76,658	17.0	3.6
1342425	Johns Creek city, Georgia	81,445	76.1	20.5	29,256	77.4	59.9	506,100	1,751	95.6	20,792	6.8	9.5
1349008	Macon-Bibb County, Georgia	154,236	83.5	6.2	57,677	55.8	71.4	155,800	896	85.3	57,081	12.3	4.7
1367284	Roswell city, Georgia	92,095	85.5	9.6	37,044	69.3	70.8	480,800	1,510	97.5	31,434	12.3	7.6
1368516	Sandy Springs city, Georgia	106,231	82.9	13.4	52,487	51.4	63.3	588,300	1,503	95.7	36,331	6.4	2.6
1369000	Savannah city, Georgia	145,245	76.9	16.2	59,612	47.1	80.6	196,900	1,143	91.3	61,890	18.8	2.0
1372122	South Fulton city, Georgia	NA	NA	NA	41,405	67.1	NA	252,500	1,391	96.1	45,787	0.2	9.1
1380508	Warner Robins city, Georgia	80,966	81.3	13.7	30,701	52.2	57.5	147,900	999	92.6	NA	NA	NA

Table C-4. Cities — Where: Migration, Housing, and Transportation, 2021—*Continued*

STATE and place code	STATE Place	Total population 1 year and over (percent)	Lived in the same house 1 year ago (percent)	Did not live in the same city 1 year ago (percent)	Total occupied housing units	Owner-occupied units (percent)	Percent with a mortgage, contract to purchase, or similar debt	Median value of owner-occupied units (dollars; owner estimated)	Median gross rent of renter-occupied units paying cash rent	Households with Internet access (percent)	Number of workers who commuted to work	Commute of less than 10 minutes (percent)	Commute of 60 minutes or more (percent)
ACS table number:		C07204	C07204	C07204	B25003	B25003	B25081	B25097	B25064	S2801	B08012	B08012	B08012
FIPS	column number:	1	2	3	4	5	6	7	8	9	10	11	12
15000	**HAWAII**	1,426,298	86.3	6.4	490,080	62.6	64.2	722,500	1,774	91.7	596,746	12.6	7.2
1571550	Urban Honolulu CDP, Hawaii	342,211	85.3	9.5	138,398	49.5	67.0	733,000	1,659	89.7	147,645	10.4	3.2
16000	**IDAHO**	1,879,719	85.2	8.4	693,882	71.9	64.0	369,300	1,035	90.8	771,629	19.6	4.7
1608830	Boise City city, Idaho	235,797	83.7	9.9	99,250	63.2	59.8	460,200	1,210	93.2	97,360	12.8	3.2
1639700	Idaho Falls city, Idaho	65,870	82.1	9.6	24,257	67.3	73.8	311,100	853	90.0	27,431	26.2	5.9
1652120	Meridian city, Idaho	124,076	88.2	9.7	47,825	77.2	74.1	448,100	1,424	94.8	55,308	9.6	0.7
1656260	Nampa city, Idaho	105,781	85.5	11.5	37,666	70.6	60.3	350,800	1,138	92.7	47,289	16.1	0.9
17000	**ILLINOIS**	12,544,435	88.5	4.5	4,991,641	67.5	61.3	231,500	1,106	89.9	4,824,560	12.9	8.5
1702154	Arlington Heights village, Illinois	74,279	86.4	10.4	31,415	73.7	69.5	376,800	1,452	93.5	28,750	8.8	6.1
1703012	Aurora city, Illinois	181,704	87.5	7.9	62,379	69.5	66.3	232,400	1,332	93.6	74,310	12.7	8.6
1706587	Bloomington city, Illinois	76,922	84.7	9.3	33,803	60.3	77.8	185,400	896	88.6	30,586	27.1	1.7
1707133	Bolingbrook village, Illinois	73,887	91.7	5.2	24,600	78.7	53.9	263,000	1,484	96.9	32,753	16.4	6.7
1712385	Champaign city, Illinois	87,126	72.5	18.0	37,423	46.4	63.9	176,700	1,001	91.2	32,669	18.8	0.7
1714000	Chicago city, Illinois	2,667,710	86.4	4.4	1,139,537	46.6	61.6	297,300	1,240	87.8	955,323	5.6	12.4
1714351	Cicero town, Illinois	NA	NA	NA	24,737	55.5	48.5	220,100	1,021	82.4	33,804	3.4	11.5
1718823	Decatur city, Illinois	69,855	82.5	8.1	32,087	61.7	67.1	87,000	718	80.5	24,115	18.9	2.6
1723074	Elgin city, Illinois	116,344	89.3	6.4	40,585	71.3	62.4	233,200	1,148	93.4	49,898	5.2	6.8
1724582	Evanston city, Illinois	76,953	80.0	16.4	31,157	57.2	73.6	440,100	1,627	91.3	24,857	16.2	6.1
1738570	Joliet city, Illinois	150,825	88.8	8.2	51,263	74.7	69.0	227,500	1,104	91.9	67,698	9.6	11.1
1751622	Naperville city, Illinois	147,509	88.3	9.0	54,377	75.3	69.1	456,400	1,654	96.5	47,655	11.8	10.2
1757225	Palatine village, Illinois	65,536	87.5	10.7	26,402	68.3	57.4	319,400	1,374	96.8	25,073	8.3	6.7
1759000	Peoria city, Illinois	110,050	83.9	8.2	50,176	60.6	51.2	124,500	813	91.3	38,837	14.9	1.2
1765000	Rockford city, Illinois	146,436	84.2	8.5	59,909	52.2	62.9	101,700	853	87.2	51,240	14.0	7.0
1768003	Schaumburg village, Illinois	75,467	90.0	8.3	31,569	63.0	61.6	278,100	1,625	95.3	28,199	10.7	5.3
1770122	Skokie village, Illinois	65,980	90.6	6.3	23,599	70.2	57.2	363,500	1,419	93.7	24,342	14.2	10.9
1772000	Springfield city, Illinois	112,965	85.6	5.2	51,317	65.1	54.6	140,100	858	88.1	42,909	16.0	4.6
1779293	Waukegan city, Illinois	85,333	91.2	6.6	30,068	51.3	58.5	166,500	976	90.8	40,348	7.8	7.7
18000	**INDIANA**	6,729,771	86.7	6.5	2,680,694	71.1	64.3	182,400	905	89.5	2,817,686	15.6	5.8
1805860	Bloomington city, Indiana	78,770	58.7	27.4	31,711	38.0	66.5	249,900	966	89.3	27,630	28.0	3.6
1810342	Carmel city, Indiana	99,709	88.7	8.2	39,994	72.1	61.8	391,300	1,401	96.1	35,164	12.7	2.9
1822000	Evansville city, Indiana	115,737	83.7	8.5	53,896	54.0	81.4	111,800	853	87.9	50,330	19.3	2.3
1823278	Fishers city, Indiana	101,432	85	7	35,466	77.6	64.6	333,300	1,429	97.3	39,091	9.3	4.7
1825000	Fort Wayne city, Indiana	259,383	81.9	7.1	109,640	62.0	58.4	155,600	856	92.2	111,189	14.3	4.1
1831000	Hammond city, Indiana	76,333	88.5	9.7	30,737	58.2	68.9	131,700	959	86.6	32,515	10.9	8.9
1836003	Indianapolis city (balance), Indiana	869,874	86.7	5.5	358,150	56.2	69.1	188,700	963	91.6	358,770	10.9	4.0
1840788	Lafayette city, Indiana	70,796	88.9	6.0	31,585	49.9	76.5	152,400	882	89.5	31,895	16.9	1.6
1854180	Noblesville city, Indiana	70,938	83.9	13.9	25,035	69.7	53.5	266,300	1,244	96.0	30,698	13.3	5.9
1871000	South Bend city, Indiana	102,879	84.2	9.2	42,707	60.8	60.3	114,100	871	87.7	38,927	15.4	4.7
19000	**IOWA**	3,159,672	86.3	6.5	1,300,467	71.9	60.2	174,400	847	88.6	1,374,816	24.0	4.2
1901855	Ames city, Iowa	65,751	59.0	23.4	25,801	43.0	78.8	237,200	902	69.3	26,534	37.4	2.2
1902305	Ankeny city, Iowa	69,903	81.0	14.8	27,720	68.0	70.0	283,900	1,109	93.8	26,605	13.2	1.5
1912000	Cedar Rapids city, Iowa	134,954	87.3	7.6	59,107	71.4	61.3	165,500	880	91.5	58,524	18.1	2.4
1919000	Davenport city, Iowa	99,508	87.4	7.9	44,958	65.4	67.9	146,000	811	87.1	43,409	12.5	4.5
1921000	Des Moines city, Iowa	209,600	80.4	8.1	90,416	63.7	68.8	165,100	916	90.2	90,659	12.9	2.0
1938595	Iowa City city, Iowa	74,012	70.4	16.9	30,270	48.9	60.8	255,000	967	86.9	37,650	19.0	3.9
1973335	Sioux City city, Iowa	85,276	92.2	4.1	33,659	70.6	61.2	153,800	830	88.6	39,863	16.8	1.8
1982425	Waterloo city, Iowa	66,213	84.5	4.5	29,948	62.8	65.2	133,700	801	88.2	29,595	19.5	2.4
1983910	West Des Moines city, Iowa	69,819	73.1	18.5	36,066	52.1	55.1	267,500	981	91.3	32,286	12.1	2.8
20000	**KANSAS**	2,900,594	84.9	7.3	1,159,026	67.0	57.9	183,800	904	90.0	1,231,975	23.0	3.6
2036000	Kansas City city, Kansas	152,542	87.6	6.9	57,819	59.9	65.4	140,200	976	87.2	59,551	10.0	3.2
2038900	Lawrence city, Kansas	94,670	74.0	13.8	41,041	42.9	74.7	229,400	869	90.5	43,032	24.5	2.8
2052575	Olathe city, Kansas	142,086	87.6	8.7	53,285	76.0	66.3	314,300	1,170	95.9	59,172	16.3	2.6
2053775	Overland Park city, Kansas	194,839	81.6	13.6	82,593	61.0	65.4	352,000	1,249	95.8	73,741	13.3	1.8
2064500	Shawnee city, Kansas	66,463	90.2	7.5	27,114	72.3	57.9	312,800	1,068	95.9	26,132	9.8	2.4
2071000	Topeka city, Kansas	124,925	85.6	6.3	55,844	58.4	61.6	123,400	842	86.6	52,052	18.6	3.8
2079000	Wichita city, Kansas	390,384	81.9	6.5	156,668	58.4	NA	165,700	844	90.4	169,365	14.4	2.4

STATE and place code	STATE Place	Total population 1 year and over	Lived in the same house 1 year ago (percent)	Did not live in the same city 1 year ago (percent)	Total occupied housing units	Owner-occupied units (percent)	Percent with a mortgage, contract to purchase, or similar debt	Median value of owner-occupied units (dollars; owner estimated)	Median gross rent of renter-occupied units paying cash rent	Households with Internet access (percent)	Number of workers who commuted to work	Commute of less than 10 minutes (percent)	Commute of 60 minutes or more (percent)
ACS table number:		C07204	C07204	C07204	B25003	B25003	B25081	B25097	B25064	S2801	B08012	B08012	B08012
FIPS	column number:	1	2	3	4	5	6	7	8	9	10	11	12
21000	**KENTUCKY**................................	4,460,646	86.9	6.3	1,785,682	68.7	57.1	173,300	830	87.3	1,737,719	15.2	6.2
2108902	Bowling Green city, Kentucky........	73,107	71.5	17.0	28,947	35.7	68.1	233,500	826	88.9	34,032	27.7	6.7
2146027	Lexington-Fayette urban county, Kentucky	317,482	80.0	9.2	139,303	53.9	66.1	242,400	968	92.8	141,374	13.5	4.2
2148006	Louisville/Jefferson County metro government (balance), Kentucky...	619,473	85.1	6.3	264,336	61.2	56.4	203,900	948	90.3	253,021	10.3	2.2
22000	**LOUISIANA**	4,571,302	87.2	5.6	1,783,924	67.3	53.1	192,800	924	85.5	1,776,330	13.0	7.5
2205000	Baton Rouge city, Louisiana..........	220,109	79.7	11.8	87,440	47.2	49.0	199,600	943	85.6	83,694	12.0	6.3
2239475	Kenner city, Louisiana	64,504	92.4	3.7	25,267	62.7	53.6	214,300	1,092	85.3	26,595	7.1	5.9
2240735	Lafayette city, Louisiana	120,744	80.5	9.5	51,150	53.8	NA	214,800	906	91.0	54,398	15.4	5.9
2241155	Lake Charles city, Louisiana..........	80,664	79.0	12.4	28,683	62.7	57.2	178,800	981	83.0	34,400	19.4	3.5
2250115	Metairie CDP, Louisiana................	142,950	88.4	7.2	62,315	65.8	57.2	283,200	1,048	92.5	62,383	13.7	3.4
2255000	New Orleans city, Louisiana..........	372,680	86.5	5.5	158,827	52.6	55.7	279,100	1,082	83.8	135,163	12.1	3.7
2270000	Shreveport city, Louisiana.............	182,022	86.2	6.1	76,167	53.4	72.0	161,500	868	82.6	66,632	11.7	3.7
23000	**MAINE**.......................................	1,360,264	88.5	6.0	593,626	74.8	60.3	252,100	945	90.1	543,273	18.6	6.6
2360545	Portland city, Maine	67,329	83.8	10.0	32,523	48.1	68.6	443,000	1,305	92.0	27,542	16.4	4.3
24000	**MARYLAND**	6,099,715	88.3	6.2	2,355,652	67.8	71.5	370,800	1,473	91.9	2,319,169	8.9	10.4
2404000	Baltimore city, Maryland...............	568,926	86.8	7.5	254,370	48.5	65.8	193,100	1,167	83.3	200,184	8.9	8.9
2407125	Bethesda CDP, Maryland................	67,743	82.3	13.6	27,748	65.7	74.8	1,023,800	2,222	96.9	15,832	14.1	3.7
2419125	Columbia CDP, Maryland	102,876	87.4	8.8	42,050	65.7	64.6	448,300	1,750	95.0	39,484	8.3	10.3
2426000	Ellicott City CDP, Maryland...........	75,704	90.4	6.6	27,318	76.1	76.0	593,400	1,757	97.6	24,493	6.4	7.3
2430325	Frederick city, Maryland	79,253	83.1	10.0	33,907	59.7	66.8	339,200	1,552	93.3	32,483	9.5	15.4
2431175	Gaithersburg city, Maryland..........	68,043	83.0	13.9	26,764	47.5	74.4	418,000	1,792	95.1	24,262	11.4	3.3
2432025	Germantown CDP, Maryland.........	84,622	89.9	7.7	30,985	65.4	74.7	373,500	1,768	95.6	32,529	6.6	12.0
2432650	Glen Burnie CDP, Maryland...........	70,236	88.9	5.9	27,700	65.6	65.5	316,600	1,436	93.8	30,895	8.9	6.0
2467675	Rockville city, Maryland................	66,657	83.4	14.6	25,537	56.1	77.6	605,600	2,014	95.8	21,257	6.1	11.1
2472450	Silver Spring CDP, Maryland	79,520	80.2	12.8	33,307	40.1	85.2	545,500	1,662	98.3	27,344	6.3	8.0
2481175	Waldorf CDP, Maryland.................	78,803	82.0	13.7	29,701	70.3	71.1	354,000	1,721	94.2	34,322	7.3	20.8
25000	**MASSACHUSETTS**	6,916,314	87.4	6.4	2,759,018	63.2	67.9	480,600	1,487	92.3	2,689,907	11.1	9.5
2507000	Boston city, Massachusetts............	646,938	80.3	10.8	271,941	34.7	75.5	659,700	1,808	91.6	243,731	8.6	10.0
2509000	Brockton city, Massachusetts.........	104,653	90.1	4.0	37,554	59.3	62.5	367,500	1,401	89.6	42,545	9.4	11.6
2511000	Cambridge city, Massachusetts	116,376	72.1	20.9	52,487	30.2	61.8	1,006,100	2,317	94.3	39,193	6.0	4.8
2523000	Fall River city, Massachusetts........	92,711	88.7	4.8	40,521	35.6	77.3	347,600	954	84.1	35,988	11.4	8.1
2524960	Framingham city, Massachusetts	70,603	87.6	9.8	26,320	54.9	72.9	575,400	1,655	94.0	28,395	9.2	10.4
2529405	Haverhill city, Massachusetts.........	66,090	90.5	5.9	25,293	60.3	71.7	420,900	1,426	92.1	28,646	11.5	8.5
2534550	Lawrence city, Massachusetts........	86,848	88.0	5.0	30,366	28.9	72.8	377,500	1,391	83.4	36,753	16.1	4.6
2537000	Lowell city, Massachusetts............	112,652	85.8	9.1	42,577	46.4	74.8	380,400	1,480	89.1	47,953	8.6	7.7
2537490	Lynn city, Massachusetts...............	99,958	89.4	5.3	37,304	53.1	65.2	423,800	1,475	90.6	43,000	9.1	6.5
2537875	Malden city, Massachusetts...........	64,135	80.5	15.1	26,386	43.5	69.5	586,200	1,812	91.7	24,919	10.7	15.4
2545000	New Bedford city, Massachusetts	99,333	89.8	5.2	42,743	39.7	60.7	305,600	969	87.3	42,455	12.7	9.4
2545560	Newton city, Massachusetts..........	86,547	86.4	9.0	29,961	73.3	61.9	1,147,300	2,210	96.6	25,547	12.2	4.3
2555745	Quincy city, Massachusetts...........	100,080	84.6	11.4	44,051	45.2	72.2	563,500	1,779	93.6	42,005	6.3	11.1
2562535	Somerville city, Massachusetts.......	78,731	74.3	20.1	35,015	38.5	70.9	818,100	2,190	91.6	33,140	5.9	7.0
2567000	Springfield city, Massachusetts......	152,873	89.8	5.5	57,806	48.5	67.6	198,200	966	85.3	49,963	14.5	4.9
2582000	Worcester city, Massachusetts.......	203,843	82.9	11.2	76,065	43.0	60.9	317,800	1,253	92.0	84,336	13.4	9.0
26000	**MICHIGAN**	9,950,336	88.7	5.4	4,051,798	73.2	59.0	199,100	969	90.2	3,784,429	14.9	5.6
2603000	Ann Arbor city, Michigan	120,050	63.5	23.8	51,238	45.8	46.7	398,600	1,375	93.6	38,780	18.4	4.0
2621000	Dearborn city, Michigan...............	107,517	93.7	3.6	35,209	70.4	33.8	180,900	1,113	94.9	30,522	12.4	1.4
2622000	Detroit city, Michigan...................	623,360	90.5	4.8	251,729	51.3	67.6	69,300	925	85.3	183,306	8.3	6.2
2627440	Farmington Hills city, Michigan......	82,283	90.8	7.3	35,224	63.7	41.2	301,600	1,264	95.5	33,015	8.5	3.8
2629000	Flint city, Michigan.......................	79,564	89.1	5.7	32,837	55.8	66.5	49,300	794	80.8	25,374	14.8	5.8
2634000	Grand Rapids city, Michigan.........	194,118	83.6	10.6	79,486	56.4	64.7	206,200	1,063	90.1	85,478	14.8	1.7
2642160	Kalamazoo city, Michigan	72,318	76.7	14.8	29,853	44.2	61.5	157,600	833	84.2	31,046	21.1	3.0
2646000	Lansing city, Michigan..................	111,271	82.3	13.2	50,590	55.5	62.1	109,900	863	90.2	41,692	13.7	3.8
2649000	Livonia city, Michigan..................	93,525	91.8	5.8	38,329	87.2	65.4	251,500	1,133	94.7	35,677	12.2	3.3
2659440	Novi city, Michigan.......................	65,959	88.5	8.7	28,217	66.6	64.9	358,400	1,472	98.1	20,897	12.1	2.5

Table C-4. Cities — Where: Migration, Housing, and Transportation, 2021—*Continued*

STATE and place code	STATE Place	Total population 1 year and over	Lived in the same house 1 year ago (percent)	Did not live in the same city 1 year ago (percent)	Total occupied housing units	Owner-occupied units (percent)	Percent with a mortgage, contract to purchase, or similar debt	Median value of owner-occupied units (dollars; owner estimated)	Median gross rent of renter-occupied units paying cash rent	Households with Internet access (percent)	Number of workers who commuted to work	Commute of less than 10 minutes (percent)	Commute of 60 minutes or more (percent)
ACS table number:		C07204	C07204	C07204	B25003	B25003	B25081	B25097	B25064	S2801	B08012	B08012	B08012
FIPS	column number:	1	2	3	4	5	6	7	8	9	10	11	12
	MICHIGAN—Cont.												
2669035	Rochester Hills city, Michigan........	74,834	87.6	9.9	28,831	74.1	67.2	354,000	1,434	94.6	25,029	16.9	7.6
2674900	Southfield city, Michigan..............	75,318	88.4	9.7	35,649	54.9	60.9	208,000	1,174	92.3	25,360	11.4	1.5
2676460	Sterling Heights city, Michigan......	132,038	90.3	7.3	51,805	77.0	60.6	237,300	1,110	95.4	47,740	6.9	4.2
2680700	Troy city, Michigan	86,166	90.6	6.8	33,822	74.0	61.9	375,600	1,426	94.8	28,598	10.6	4.0
2684000	Warren city, Michigan	136,734	88.5	8.5	57,632	70.6	65.7	170,000	1,064	92.2	54,603	7.5	4.5
2686000	Westland city, Michigan................	83,520	92.1	5.9	37,870	61.2	61.6	164,700	957	91.5	33,960	9.8	3.0
2688940	Wyoming city, Michigan................	75,891	88.8	9.0	28,253	63.4	68.7	192,400	1,021	87.7	31,891	10.7	4.4
27000	**MINNESOTA**................	5,645,866	87.3	6.4	2,281,033	73.0	64.3	285,400	1,113	91.6	2,300,218	17.8	4.7
2706382	Blaine city, Minnesota..................	69,846	90.7	6.6	25,869	84.3	63.6	297,300	1,459	94.0	24,923	9.4	7.0
2706616	Bloomington city, Minnesota........	88,243	84.8	12.0	38,725	66.1	67.9	319,600	1,304	91.9	33,108	11.5	1.3
2707966	Brooklyn Park city, Minnesota	82,270	91.5	5.8	30,074	75.7	66.9	297,500	1,192	93.8	35,780	5.1	2.3
2717000	Duluth city, Minnesota.................	84,666	81.4	10.8	36,310	60.4	70.5	211,300	948	91.3	35,331	23.4	1.9
2717288	Eagan city, Minnesota..................	67,992	85.9	11.9	27,069	74.2	74.7	345,500	1,445	96.3	28,290	14.7	2.4
2735180	Lakeville city, Minnesota..............	71,752	86.2	9.9	23,868	90.5	67.1	398,700	1,695	95.3	28,348	16.1	1.3
2740166	Maple Grove city, Minnesota........	68,772	88.3	8.6	28,026	84.9	72.9	373,100	1,767	97.5	28,780	10.9	4.5
2743000	Minneapolis city, Minnesota..........	421,177	78.8	11.8	188,681	49.8	66.4	319,100	1,225	91.4	153,436	10.4	3.4
2751730	Plymouth city, Minnesota.............	79,199	83.1	12.7	32,923	72.3	59.1	439,100	1,459	95.9	28,887	10.4	1.3
2754880	Rochester city, Minnesota............	120,184	84.2	8.0	49,984	65.9	56.1	273,800	1,167	90.8	55,857	13.8	2.8
2756896	St. Cloud city, Minnesota.............	68,822	78.6	12.3	30,029	49.0	69.5	181,700	851	91.7	34,118	20.2	5.1
2758000	St. Paul city, Minnesota...............	303,177	85.7	7.9	121,964	55.5	69.0	267,700	1,115	92.2	115,348	11.2	2.6
2771428	Woodbury city, Minnesota	76,456	82.4	14.6	28,751	75.8	63.8	407,000	1,741	97.1	24,015	15.1	3.1
28000	**MISSISSIPPI**........................	2,919,574	89.3	5.2	1,129,611	69.7	48.6	145,600	831	81.9	1,139,216	13.8	7.5
2829700	Gulfport city, Mississippi..............	71,319	85.4	11.5	29,385	48.9	49.8	141,700	873	86.6	25,997	15.5	11.1
2836000	Jackson city, Mississippi................	147,649	82.5	5.8	62,140	46.5	NA	101,500	930	87.2	55,355	10.8	2.0
29000	**MISSOURI**	6,102,443	86.6	6.8	2,468,726	68.8	61.1	198,300	882	88.7	2,482,032	16.0	5.2
2915670	Columbia city, Missouri................	125,100	72.6	14.1	50,572	49.8	59.7	245,800	955	91.8	58,805	22.0	2.1
2935000	Independence city, Missouri..........	121,426	85.8	10.3	53,057	63.9	65.4	154,700	890	88.7	46,888	12.3	2.8
2938000	Kansas City city, Missouri.............	503,099	82.5	9.0	219,020	54.1	72.9	213,400	1,071	90.0	210,745	13.0	3.6
2941348	Lee's Summit city, Missouri...........	100,421	86.2	10.7	37,795	75.5	79.7	303,700	1,284	96.9	40,213	12.3	2.1
2954074	O'Fallon city, Missouri	92,948	88.3	9.3	34,412	80.1	68.6	281,700	1,200	94.3	40,807	10.2	2.6
2964082	St. Charles city, Missouri	69,931	84.5	11.7	29,992	67.0	56.3	269,200	1,019	93.7	29,130	12.0	1.8
2964550	St. Joseph city, Missouri...............	74,178	82.2	9.1	29,750	58.5	64.4	132,600	781	86.5	31,975	33.5	5.1
2965000	St. Louis city, Missouri.................	289,484	85.1	7.6	139,736	45.6	56.7	170,800	843	85.9	117,282	8.7	4.4
2970000	Springfield city, Missouri..............	168,126	80.0	10.4	79,232	44.4	57.9	154,600	790	84.3	76,944	19.4	2.7
30000	**MONTANA**	1,093,888	86.3	7.3	448,949	69.5	54.8	322,800	883	89.2	449,385	26.1	5.1
3006550	Billings city, Montana	116,521	85.8	7.7	50,365	66.6	68.2	290,000	928	91.9	50,857	16.3	2.9
3050200	Missoula city, Montana.................	74,358	77.9	13.3	33,744	45.1	63.9	406,800	1,058	92.7	33,931	33.2	1.7
31000	**NEBRASKA**	1,939,700	86.5	6.0	785,982	67.8	59.7	204,900	912	90.0	880,415	23.9	3.7
3128000	Lincoln city, Nebraska..................	290,231	82.1	6.3	120,407	58.1	68.6	228,000	904	91.9	137,846	17.9	2.8
3137000	Omaha city, Nebraska..................	481,080	85.4	6.1	201,469	58.3	81.8	211,900	992	91.0	204,548	16.9	3.0
32000	**NEVADA**	3,111,722	85.5	5.4	1,191,380	59.1	67.6	373,000	1,311	90.7	1,223,063	10.2	5.6
3223770	Enterprise CDP, Nevada................	239,696	83.3	11.5	83,983	63.1	69.0	401,900	1,640	97.0	105,277	6.4	2.4
3231900	Henderson city, Nevada................	318,396	87.0	8.5	124,470	64.7	69.2	421,300	1,501	94.4	117,695	8.5	3.7
3240000	Las Vegas city, Nevada.................	641,571	87.0	7.0	250,350	55.4	76.0	362,400	1,249	89.8	244,428	7.4	5.0
3251800	North Las Vegas city, Nevada........	272,439	85.5	11.9	85,966	59.8	68.2	335,200	1,410	95.9	110,229	5.1	4.7
3254600	Paradise CDP, Nevada...................	184,538	83.5	13.7	78,005	43.5	66.1	334,500	1,116	85.9	74,517	8.8	2.9
3260600	Reno city, Nevada.......................	267,627	81.9	9.4	110,993	48.8	69.7	469,100	1,276	85.4	116,997	14.7	3.7
3268400	Sparks city, Nevada	108,354	84.6	11.5	43,392	62.6	63.0	423,400	1,482	92.1	49,474	12.0	2.5
3268585	Spring Valley CDP, Nevada............	210,224	80.2	15.8	88,063	45.7	58.8	382,400	1,444	92.7	82,655	9.0	2.5
3271400	Sunrise Manor CDP, Nevada..........	192,954	86.8	10.1	62,737	54.7	70.2	262,500	1,130	87.6	73,584	6.3	4.8
33000	**NEW HAMPSHIRE**....................	1,377,638	88.8	6.2	548,026	72.5	62.9	345,200	1,263	92.5	591,321	14.2	8.0
3345140	Manchester city, New Hampshire ..	114,540	87.2	7.2	48,649	49.1	66.2	321,300	1,277	93.3	55,313	13.7	4.7
3350260	Nashua city, New Hampshire........	90,266	84.8	9.6	36,986	54.6	65.3	355,000	1,555	94.1	40,218	12.7	5.9
34000	**NEW JERSEY**	9,174,117	89.4	5.7	3,497,945	64.4	64.3	389,800	1,457	92.0	3,437,038	10.6	11.2
3403580	Bayonne city, New Jersey	NA	NA	NA	28,375	34.6	NA	404,100	1,389	88.3	25,457	10.8	13.6
3410000	Camden city, New Jersey..............	70,877	86.5	5.8	24,276	35.2	58.7	106,000	1,060	83.2	22,573	11.7	5.0

STATE and place code	STATE Place	Total population 1 year and over	Lived in the same house 1 year ago (percent)	Did not live in the same city 1 year ago (percent)	Total occupied housing units	Owner-occupied units (percent)	Percent with a mortgage, contract to purchase, or similar debt	Median value of owner-occupied units (dollars; owner estimated)	Median gross rent of renter-occupied units paying cash rent	Households with Internet access (percent)	Number of workers who commuted to work	Commute of less than 10 minutes (percent)	Commute of 60 minutes or more (percent)
ACS table number:		C07204	C07204	C07204	B25003	B25003	B25081	B25097	B25064	S2801	B08012	B08012	B08012
FIPS	column number:	1	2	3	4	5	6	7	8	9	10	11	12
	NEW JERSEY—Cont.												
3413690	Clifton city, New Jersey	88,854	90.8	7.8	32,408	59.9	NA	427,100	1,553	85.2	38,174	6.0	7.8
3419390	East Orange city, New Jersey	67,494	86.6	7.2	28,318	32.5	NA	283,800	1,286	87.6	25,847	6.8	10.7
3421000	Elizabeth city, New Jersey	133,012	92.0	3.2	46,107	24.5	63.2	405,800	1,253	90.0	56,266	7.8	8.1
3436000	Jersey City city, New Jersey	280,504	85.3	8.9	119,158	28.8	58.1	487,400	1,739	91.6	92,325	4.2	15.7
3438580	Lakewood CDP, New Jersey	NA	NA	NA	13,701	41.1	69.2	481,300	1,739	52.3	NA	NA	NA
3451000	Newark city, New Jersey	304,271	88.8	6.4	115,145	20.8	NA	323,200	1,215	83.2	108,139	4.7	14.4
3456550	Passaic city, New Jersey	68,254	94.6	2.8	20,446	22.7	NA	350,800	1,256	91.5	24,761	9.2	6.6
3457000	Paterson city, New Jersey	156,276	92.9	2.9	51,612	24.7	73.1	311,700	1,302	83.9	59,145	4.9	1.9
3473110	Toms River CDP, New Jersey	92,687	90.0	7.2	35,128	79.6	NA	378,300	1,405	92.8	37,596	15.1	11.7
3474000	Trenton city, New Jersey	90,194	89.2	4.9	34,116	40.5	NA	95,400	964	82.2	29,760	6.1	7.6
3474630	Union City city, New Jersey	65,117	94.5	2.9	24,041	20.4	66.1	400,700	1,410	89.4	26,300	5.8	13.8
35000	**NEW MEXICO**	2,092,251	87.4	6.0	834,007	69.5	52.6	214,000	906	84.6	743,745	18.0	6.4
3502000	Albuquerque city, New Mexico	558,997	85.2	5.8	243,582	60.7	60.0	251,500	946	91.9	223,626	11.9	3.7
3539380	Las Cruces city, New Mexico	110,720	84.6	7.3	45,991	54.1	71.2	182,000	787	87.7	43,374	19.9	7.0
3563460	Rio Rancho city, New Mexico	104,170	84.7	9.2	40,013	81.0	57.5	247,200	1,223	95.0	36,681	14.4	12.6
3570500	Santa Fe city, New Mexico	87,752	85.9	9.3	40,641	68.6	58.9	349,900	1,245	92.1	30,539	21.2	5.2
36000	**NEW YORK**	19,626,300	89.6	4.1	7,652,666	55.4	58.2	368,800	1,409	90.6	7,246,571	10.8	15.5
3601000	Albany city, New York	97,816	80.3	12.7	44,279	39.1	49.8	206,800	1,086	86.4	37,590	14.0	2.6
3611000	Buffalo city, New York	273,904	85.9	6.5	122,569	44.1	63.0	155,200	877	88.3	101,006	13.2	4.6
3615000	Cheektowaga CDP, New York	75,714	92.3	7.0	33,247	71.6	61.2	162,500	863	87.3	32,905	13.9	1.8
3649121	Mount Vernon city, New York	72,107	93.3	3.7	26,465	49.0	NA	439,100	1,534	87.3	25,901	7.7	16.1
3650617	New Rochelle city, New York	81,299	92.0	6.6	32,877	53.5	55.4	615,300	1,811	89.6	30,342	11.9	16.2
3651000	New York city, New York	8,372,539	89.5	2.9	3,263,895	33.3	63.9	685,700	1,602	90.1	2,803,661	4.9	24.9
3663000	Rochester city, New York	207,927	85.3	8.5	93,263	40.9	NA	109,700	910	85.6	78,314	15.1	4.5
3665508	Schenectady city, New York	66,546	84.9	10.3	28,965	46.9	58.9	156,800	944	85.9	24,727	11.6	2.8
3673000	Syracuse city, New York	144,429	76.8	13.9	62,663	43.1	54.4	123,000	874	87.6	49,845	17.2	3.3
3684000	Yonkers city, New York	206,056	89.3	6.8	81,397	49.6	56.2	424,100	1,511	89.9	78,568	8.1	17.4
37000	**NORTH CAROLINA**	10,446,881	86.5	7.4	4,179,632	66.9	62.0	236,900	1,026	89.0	3,970,072	13.0	6.0
3702140	Asheville city, North Carolina	93,697	83.5	11.0	38,131	54.8	73.7	363,800	1,150	85.0	35,190	14.0	2.3
3710740	Cary town, North Carolina	177,130	83.9	12.5	65,254	68.6	73.7	463,200	1,426	97.2	51,037	10.7	2.9
3712000	Charlotte city, North Carolina	869,445	82.2	8.5	365,269	53.1	70.7	321,400	1,301	93.1	307,243	11.0	4.8
3714100	Concord city, North Carolina	106,628	88.6	9.6	33,859	72.7	76.0	298,600	1,152	92.6	41,870	8.2	5.0
3719000	Durham city, North Carolina	282,903	81.6	11.5	122,412	51.1	66.4	325,000	1,182	93.6	100,275	10.6	4.0
3722920	Fayetteville city, North Carolina	206,082	81.6	11.8	83,147	45.8	71.8	150,200	1,065	92.0	93,259	22.9	3.9
3725580	Gastonia city, North Carolina	80,965	91.2	6.0	33,292	53.6	64.3	231,300	1,027	85.4	32,145	9.7	5.2
3728000	Greensboro city, North Carolina	296,294	81.1	10.4	123,955	56.3	66.4	186,200	1,003	91.3	121,758	15.0	3.4
3728080	Greenville city, North Carolina	87,891	74.7	18.8	41,575	30.1	65.7	198,800	844	85.0	35,697	19.8	3.8
3731400	High Point city, North Carolina	113,193	85.9	9.0	42,738	57.0	64.4	180,300	939	91.6	42,103	15.4	5.6
3734200	Jacksonville city, North Carolina	71,754	69.4	23.8	22,024	35.0	76.4	175,800	1,064	95.1	39,517	40.7	2.4
3755000	Raleigh city, North Carolina	465,968	79.4	11.2	194,917	53.0	62.9	340,200	1,256	94.0	164,210	12.6	2.5
3774440	Wilmington city, North Carolina	117,118	77.7	14.9	59,341	46.3	63.5	334,900	1,142	90.7	49,283	19.0	3.6
3775000	Winston-Salem city, North Carolina	248,033	83.2	10.2	101,551	56.0	53.8	197,300	877	89.6	95,302	9.9	4.8
38000	**NORTH DAKOTA**	764,638	83.8	8.5	322,511	63.1	52.7	224,400	839	88.2	362,392	28.4	4.2
3807200	Bismarck city, North Dakota	73,319	85.4	8.2	31,426	64.9	61.3	254,800	834	88.5	35,427	25.9	0.9
3825700	Fargo city, North Dakota	123,151	72.9	15.1	58,269	43.8	60.1	238,600	784	90.3	60,821	19.8	3.4
39000	**OHIO**	11,660,200	87.6	5.1	4,832,922	67.2	61.4	180,200	870	89.1	4,677,145	15.2	4.8
3901000	Akron city, Ohio	187,720	87.8	5.0	84,914	50.3	59.5	106,300	791	88.0	72,843	13.4	4.1
3912000	Canton city, Ohio	70,065	84.2	8.1	31,168	54.3	66.3	88,300	759	77.0	24,865	21.2	2.9
3915000	Cincinnati city, Ohio	306,069	79.8	11.5	144,929	38.2	51.3	190,300	841	89.6	115,616	14.2	3.5
3916000	Cleveland city, Ohio	364,392	82.0	9.1	171,321	39.1	71.5	83,400	799	83.3	132,845	9.5	3.6
3918000	Columbus city, Ohio	895,229	79.0	9.2	390,605	44.9	58.1	219,200	1,098	92.8	357,884	11.1	3.1
3921000	Dayton city, Ohio	135,949	78.0	13.7	55,114	49.5	58.6	85,000	792	86.2	45,820	14.1	5.5
3944856	Lorain city, Ohio	64,574	91.9	4.5	27,852	56.5	62.7	113,700	783	76.9	24,495	12.1	4.1
3961000	Parma city, Ohio	79,401	87.8	8.1	33,401	74.7	55.5	148,000	891	90.4	33,393	10.6	2.8
3977000	Toledo city, Ohio	264,474	87.0	5.8	120,895	56.1	64.9	100,100	769	86.3	109,353	14.1	3.1

Table C-4. Cities — Where: Migration, Housing, and Transportation, 2021—*Continued*

STATE and place code	STATE Place	Total population 1 year and over	Lived in the same house 1 year ago (percent)	Did not live in the same city 1 year ago (percent)	Total occupied housing units	Owner-occupied units (percent)	Percent with a mortgage, contract to purchase, or similar debt	Median value of owner-occupied units (dollars; owner estimated)	Median gross rent of renter-occupied units paying cash rent	Households with Internet access (percent)	Number of workers who commuted to work	Commute of less than 10 minutes (percent)	Commute of 60 minutes or more (percent)
	ACS table number:	C07204	C07204	C07204	B25003	B25003	B25081	B25097	B25064	S2801	B08012	B08012	B08012
FIPS	column number:	1	2	3	4	5	6	7	8	9	10	11	12
40000	**OKLAHOMA**	3,943,443	84.9	6.8	1,547,967	65.5	53.7	168,500	855	88.0	1,589,401	17.9	4.8
4009050	Broken Arrow city, Oklahoma	116,061	84.8	10.1	45,138	72.8	65.3	211,600	1,100	93.5	49,510	11.4	4.2
4023200	Edmond city, Oklahoma	93,928	82.8	11.8	36,530	72.0	NA	283,800	1,233	94.3	38,100	12.7	5.1
4041850	Lawton city, Oklahoma	89,752	76.1	12.1	33,921	41.9	61.0	129,400	791	90.6	33,842	26.1	2.2
4052500	Norman city, Oklahoma	126,865	73.4	16.5	53,446	50.9	61.3	228,600	893	91.8	56,412	17.8	5.0
4055000	Oklahoma City city, Oklahoma	680,814	82.0	8.7	275,285	59.7	56.5	190,900	936	91.8	287,792	10.6	2.7
4075000	Tulsa city, Oklahoma	406,721	82.3	7.2	173,943	51.3	71.7	172,000	881	89.6	161,317	14.4	2.6
41000	**OREGON**	4,207,387	85.6	7.1	1,702,599	63.8	65.0	422,700	1,282	91.8	1,523,768	17.0	5.6
4105350	Beaverton city, Oregon	97,537	83.5	12.5	42,858	45.9	70.2	490,600	1,541	95.7	35,831	12.7	3.8
4105800	Bend city, Oregon	101,495	81.4	11.5	44,620	68.2	62.4	569,200	1,690	93.8	39,822	33.8	1.6
4123850	Eugene city, Oregon	173,771	77.4	13.7	74,740	51.1	73.1	394,800	1,182	93.4	68,588	16.4	4.5
4131250	Gresham city, Oregon	111,945	88.3	7.1	43,487	58.7	72.6	411,100	1,300	88.0	42,313	10.7	8.5
4134100	Hillsboro city, Oregon	105,340	86.0	10.9	40,891	50.0	66.9	432,600	1,661	94.2	39,840	15.3	3.8
4147000	Medford city, Oregon	85,402	84.0	10.6	36,525	60.8	71.1	363,800	1,139	85.8	34,448	15.3	3.7
4159000	Portland city, Oregon	637,452	81.3	8.9	286,734	53.4	70.1	520,200	1,394	94.0	229,478	9.7	4.5
4164900	Salem city, Oregon	176,466	81.5	9.4	64,959	55.7	59.4	351,300	1,179	93.6	62,101	13.7	7.2
42000	**PENNSYLVANIA**	12,842,522	89.2	5.1	5,228,956	69.9	58.6	222,300	1,036	89.1	4,938,027	13.8	7.5
4202000	Allentown city, Pennsylvania	124,482	85.1	6.7	47,204	41.7	53.0	173,400	1,131	79.5	43,864	10.1	5.7
4206088	Bethlehem city, Pennsylvania	75,031	88.1	9.3	30,099	52.7	54.7	214,800	1,063	86.1	28,509	10.4	6.0
4224000	Erie city, Pennsylvania	92,681	84.8	8.7	38,636	54.5	58.1	95,900	732	83.8	33,502	21.1	3.7
4260000	Philadelphia city, Pennsylvania	1,558,765	87.0	5.4	660,921	52.8	56.6	220,700	1,181	86.9	531,131	6.3	11.2
4261000	Pittsburgh city, Pennsylvania	298,278	79.8	12.7	136,747	48.8	54.2	181,100	1,074	89.7	103,298	10.5	3.3
4263624	Reading city, Pennsylvania	92,219	82.8	10.1	32,504	39.5	57.3	92,500	893	85.2	31,381	9.3	8.2
4269000	Scranton city, Pennsylvania	75,410	82.9	12.8	30,096	53.7	71.9	130,600	837	86.0	29,128	18.2	4.8
44000	**RHODE ISLAND**	1,085,539	88.4	6.2	440,170	63.3	67.9	348,100	1,142	90.9	439,664	11.7	6.3
4419180	Cranston city, Rhode Island	82,447	89.6	8.4	33,049	69.8	68.5	353,200	1,261	92.9	33,466	8.2	5.2
4454640	Pawtucket city, Rhode Island	74,801	90.8	7.3	29,735	49.8	73.6	275,200	996	89.7	33,479	10.9	6.5
4459000	Providence city, Rhode Island	187,243	86.0	9.5	68,179	40.6	69.3	291,200	1,218	89.1	71,101	8.5	4.1
4474300	Warwick city, Rhode Island	82,434	90.1	8.1	36,595	73.7	65.8	293,500	1,212	90.5	34,013	10.9	5.2
45000	**SOUTH CAROLINA**	5,142,137	86.4	7.4	2,049,972	71.8	57.2	213,500	976	87.9	2,049,352	11.7	6.5
4513330	Charleston city, South Carolina	150,153	84.3	10.5	63,391	58.1	65.6	420,800	1,395	94.9	63,512	10.9	4.9
4516000	Columbia city, South Carolina	136,703	67.9	25.8	51,455	45.8	69.6	218,500	1,049	89.6	58,451	29.7	2.3
4530850	Greenville city, South Carolina	71,548	71.7	21.1	34,154	39.6	72.5	389,700	1,073	88.8	31,974	13.4	3.9
4548535	Mount Pleasant town, South Carolina	91,687	84.1	8.3	37,983	74.1	62.2	591,900	1,866	87.9	34,082	7.2	2.2
4550875	North Charleston city, South Carolina	115,789	84.1	12.2	47,324	54.1	76.8	229,800	1,215	92.5	53,120	8.5	3.0
4561405	Rock Hill city, South Carolina	73,318	83.4	11.1	29,268	55.1	60.3	245,000	1,101	89.3	31,652	14.5	7.8
46000	**SOUTH DAKOTA**	884,616	85.9	7.0	356,887	69.4	54.7	219,900	830	88.3	396,212	29.0	3.3
4652980	Rapid City city, South Dakota	75,168	83.7	11.9	32,471	65.4	68.3	247,700	950	89.4	33,984	23.1	2.1
4659020	Sioux Falls city, South Dakota	194,078	81.9	7.2	83,498	61.1	59.3	249,600	893	93.1	94,023	18.3	2.6
47000	**TENNESSEE**	6,899,165	86.3	7.0	2,770,395	67.5	58.7	235,200	981	88.1	2,748,147	12.0	6.7
4714000	Chattanooga city, Tennessee	179,196	78.2	10.2	77,299	53.6	68.5	235,900	1,035	89.8	71,223	15.8	3.5
4715160	Clarksville city, Tennessee	168,533	73.9	15.4	63,787	54.2	75.0	211,100	1,099	92.0	71,317	10.2	10.5
4727740	Franklin city, Tennessee	84,495	81.3	12.8	33,275	66.4	58.3	592,200	1,625	96.1	31,628	14.1	0.5
4737640	Jackson city, Tennessee	67,736	84.6	5.9	26,505	52.4	56.7	170,400	947	87.0	25,874	16.3	6.1
4738320	Johnson City city, Tennessee	70,115	73.2	17.0	30,806	48.8	62.6	216,000	860	90.9	28,338	14.1	2.6
4740000	Knoxville city, Tennessee	190,825	82.3	10.5	85,151	47.6	59.7	193,600	967	85.2	84,345	11.2	2.2
4748000	Memphis city, Tennessee	620,039	87.7	4.5	256,968	46.6	69.0	142,800	989	87.3	244,301	9.3	2.1
4751560	Murfreesboro city, Tennessee	156,199	82.1	11.4	58,371	60.6	68.2	323,600	1,209	94.1	72,463	12.5	5.1
4752006	Nashville-Davidson metropolitan government (balance), Tennessee	668,586	79.1	10.5	305,247	53.2	57.5	346,700	1,316	92.9	281,929	11.7	4.3
48000	**TEXAS**	29,170,380	86.0	6.4	10,796,247	62.6	56.6	237,400	1,167	90.2	11,417,050	12.0	7.3
4801000	Abilene city, Texas	128,279	81.8	10.7	48,398	56.1	65.6	157,900	985	89.2	53,800	24.8	2.3
4801924	Allen city, Texas	105,758	87.8	9.8	37,461	70.1	57.1	392,000	1,674	97.3	33,676	13.0	4.6
4803000	Amarillo city, Texas	196,178	87.3	5.6	82,129	59.5	58.9	163,400	959	88.5	87,127	12.7	4.2
4804000	Arlington city, Texas	388,556	89.5	6.0	146,888	53.7	NA	254,700	1,211	89.8	169,699	7.7	5.4

STATE and place code	STATE Place	Total population 1 year and over	Lived in the same house 1 year ago (percent)	Did not live in the same city 1 year ago (percent)	Total occupied housing units	Owner-occupied units (percent)	Percent with a mortgage, contract to purchase, or similar debt	Median value of owner-occupied units (dollars; owner estimated)	Median gross rent of renter-occupied units paying cash rent	Households with Internet access (percent)	Number of workers who commuted to work	Commute of less than 10 minutes (percent)	Commute of 60 minutes or more (percent)
ACS table number:		C07204	C07204	C07204	B25003	B25003	B25081	B25097	B25064	S2801	B08012	B08012	B08012
FIPS	column number:	1	2	3	4	5	6	7	8	9	10	11	12
	TEXAS—Cont.												
4804462	Atascocita CDP, Texas....................	85,000	82.2	13.8	29,579	83.8	67.5	263,000	1,307	NA	39,203	4.4	14.4
4805000	Austin city, Texas........................	953,064	77.5	12.3	449,399	43.7	NA	482,900	1,426	93.6	346,080	10.3	4.7
4806128	Baytown city, Texas......................	78,493	80.0	10.2	28,264	50.8	48.6	173,200	1,153	88.5	28,408	7.0	10.7
4807000	Beaumont city, Texas....................	110,964	90.3	4.1	46,375	53.2	NA	150,100	939	91.6	50,580	14.0	5.7
4810768	Brownsville city, Texas..................	186,265	93.0	2.6	56,522	60.9	NA	104,100	801	84.2	67,801	8.4	2.7
4810912	Bryan city, Texas.........................	85,589	79.3	13.6	32,910	43.2	65.5	167,500	1,070	81.3	34,626	14.5	2.5
4813024	Carrollton city, Texas	131,199	90.3	8.0	50,308	56.4	73.3	302,800	1,399	96.6	55,743	8.5	3.4
4813552	Cedar Park city, Texas..................	78,067	87.6	9.5	30,407	65.6	62.4	448,600	1,463	94.5	23,858	16.8	3.9
4815976	College Station city, Texas	118,739	69.7	19.5	41,586	40.6	NA	291,300	1,033	83.9	51,429	18.3	1.8
4816432	Conroe city, Texas.......................	93,790	88.7	8.6	37,297	58.2	55.8	267,100	1,180	95.1	37,044	7.6	10.0
4817000	Corpus Christi city, Texas.............	313,987	85.2	4.8	117,366	57.8	54.4	171,500	1,111	88.7	135,167	8.6	2.5
4819000	Dallas city, Texas........................	1,270,447	83.9	8.1	536,008	42.8	NA	267,600	1,213	89.4	519,980	9.2	6.5
4819972	Denton city, Texas.......................	146,975	75.0	17.6	57,963	47.1	46.6	288,300	1,112	90.0	66,848	10.4	4.8
4822660	Edinburg city, Texas.....................	101,071	86.8	10.6	37,541	49.1	57.5	153,500	831	87.9	37,205	24.3	0.7
4824000	El Paso city, Texas.......................	669,399	86.6	5.1	242,529	60.9	69.1	152,800	904	89.1	264,694	10.6	4.2
4826232	Flower Mound town, Texas...........	77,619	90.1	6.7	27,696	82.5	65.4	475,300	1,854	97.9	26,885	9.6	1.4
4827000	Fort Worth city, Texas..................	927,955	87.2	7.1	334,286	55.4	76.3	249,000	1,240	92.8	379,700	8.2	6.3
4827684	Frisco city, Texas........................	209,438	83.6	10.4	72,282	64.9	60.1	520,200	1,696	98.7	63,873	10.7	4.2
4829000	Garland city, Texas......................	240,350	92.3	6.0	77,777	60.4	58.6	232,300	1,334	95.6	95,404	4.9	9.1
4829336	Georgetown city, Texas	74,190	78.7	14.7	30,207	70.1	61.2	351,600	1,582	95.2	23,123	15.1	6.1
4830464	Grand Prairie city, Texas...............	195,086	87.9	6.6	64,208	57.2	NA	242,200	1,309	93.4	80,230	5.1	4.9
4832372	Harlingen city, Texas....................	71,028	93.1	4.1	27,051	59.3	53.3	106,600	819	74.2	26,755	23.0	3.6
4835000	Houston city, Texas.....................	2,257,448	82.7	7.4	924,981	42.2	61.1	236,700	1,120	87.3	918,585	8.0	5.8
4837000	Irving city, Texas........................	249,332	84.8	7.8	95,309	36.2	NA	274,100	1,291	90.4	95,927	7.9	5.5
4839148	Killeen city, Texas.......................	153,475	79.9	11.5	57,875	47.3	NA	179,900	958	90.0	59,975	13.0	11.4
4841464	Laredo city, Texas.......................	253,900	89.0	1.5	76,095	63.3	66.2	157,400	866	83.8	97,320	14.8	3.1
4841980	League City city, Texas.................	113,446	83.9	10.5	44,419	74.7	NA	300,000	1,423	96.1	47,913	3.0	11.5
4842016	Leander city, Texas	68,152	82.8	15.4	24,031	76.1	NA	437,600	1,694	93.9	23,836	11.0	7.5
4842508	Lewisville city, Texas....................	111,883	85.8	11.4	46,897	45.0	NA	308,800	1,377	95.5	50,772	10.8	7.1
4843888	Longview city, Texas....................	80,770	86.5	6.8	31,072	52.6	55.3	164,200	893	90.2	35,393	20.1	6.2
4845000	Lubbock city, Texas.....................	258,361	77.5	10.4	104,426	51.4	49.0	171,400	969	87.7	120,426	22.9	3.4
4845384	McAllen city, Texas......................	142,055	89.4	5.4	48,438	59.1	77.3	164,300	906	90.7	54,117	16.6	4.9
4845744	McKinney city, Texas....................	199,634	85.0	10.9	73,357	64.2	NA	391,200	1,530	94.0	74,064	8.8	6.3
4846452	Mansfield city, Texas....................	73,760	85.9	8.3	25,327	70.3	61.2	345,700	1,502	94.4	32,669	15.5	4.6
4847892	Mesquite city, Texas....................	146,589	88.4	10.0	52,023	64.7	NA	208,900	1,216	93.3	62,528	5.8	12.5
4848072	Midland city, Texas......................	128,963	83.2	7.8	52,898	66.6	NA	276,100	978	93.1	62,477	14.4	4.2
4848768	Mission city, Texas.......................	84,953	88.9	7.2	28,128	65.6	NA	135,000	818	92.8	29,561	14.1	2.2
4848804	Missouri City city, Texas..............	NA	NA	NA	29,801	76.4	71.1	273,300	1,705	94.4	33,783	4.3	9.2
4850820	New Braunfels city, Texas	95,433	86.2	7.8	37,815	61.3	NA	285,600	1,369	96.2	42,092	9.0	9.1
4852356	North Richland Hills city, Texas.......	69,532	90.0	6.5	26,937	61.2	NA	314,000	1,332	93.2	29,607	8.7	10.8
4853388	Odessa city, Texas.......................	114,959	83.4	7.6	48,530	60.5	45.5	196,500	1,106	87.7	53,249	12.5	4.7
4856000	Pasadena city, Texas....................	147,016	82.4	9.7	50,598	57.2	72.2	192,300	1,100	90.0	53,351	11.8	5.9
4856348	Pearland city, Texas.....................	119,369	91.1	6.4	43,012	74.0	NA	307,800	1,450	97.4	49,957	7.1	6.7
4857176	Pflugerville city, Texas..................	65,630	88.5	6.0	23,875	72.9	NA	341,600	1,578	NA	25,348	6.9	1.7
4857200	Pharr city, Texas..........................	NA	NA	NA	24,797	58.1	60.9	91,200	916	82.4	25,227	17.6	5.0
4858016	Plano city, Texas.........................	284,192	84.6	11.6	108,472	56.1	59.2	387,200	1,592	96.7	99,424	9.9	5.7
4861796	Richardson city, Texas..................	114,496	84.4	10.9	45,148	56.4	70.3	358,000	1,523	94.7	43,112	6.8	4.1
4863500	Round Rock city, Texas.................	124,349	80.4	14.0	49,740	53.5	NA	355,600	1,512	95.9	46,928	8.7	2.3
4864472	San Angelo city, Texas.................	99,553	84.0	9.5	39,065	64.2	55.4	158,800	892	86.3	42,876	23.6	2.9
4865000	San Antonio city, Texas...............	1,433,641	83.5	6.6	549,245	52.8	NA	197,600	1,123	91.0	575,258	11.8	4.3
4865600	San Marcos city, Texas.................	67,873	66.5	20.7	27,015	25.9	NA	285,300	1,311	90.9	29,564	10.7	7.0
4869596	Spring CDP, Texas........................	70,668	86.4	10.6	23,096	75.2	54.7	188,500	1,680	95.1	28,678	3.8	7.1
4870808	Sugar Land city, Texas.................	108,615	89.2	5.8	37,008	81.5	NA	369,300	1,566	98.1	37,587	4.9	3.3
4872176	Temple city, Texas.......................	83,929	76.9	14.3	34,371	52.4	54.1	202,700	1,002	87.8	35,488	21.5	5.0
4872656	The Woodlands CDP, Texas	115,880	86.1	11.5	43,992	75.5	NA	429,500	1,494	96.8	36,329	13.5	12.2
4874144	Tyler city, Texas..........................	105,439	84.8	9.0	36,169	55.1	NA	195,900	969	90.9	45,288	14.2	3.6
4875428	Victoria city, Texas......................	64,411	82.6	4.8	25,410	55.1	NA	179,400	1,000	78.5	27,475	15.3	1.3
4876000	Waco city, Texas.........................	137,522	77.9	11.5	53,286	48.9	NA	177,300	1,014	89.4	55,017	18.0	3.9
4879000	Wichita Falls city, Texas	102,117	77.5	10.9	38,051	57.7	68.5	118,900	885	87.3	44,904	30.5	2.9

Table C-4. Cities — Where: Migration, Housing, and Transportation, 2021—*Continued*

STATE and place code	STATE Place	Total population 1 year and over	Lived in the same house 1 year ago (percent)	Did not live in the same city 1 year ago (percent)	Total occupied housing units	Owner-occupied units (percent)	Percent with a mortgage, contract to purchase, or similar debt	Median value of owner-occupied units (dollars; owner estimated)	Median gross rent of renter-occupied units paying cash rent	Households with Internet access (percent)	Number of workers who commuted to work	Commute of less than 10 minutes (percent)	Commute of 60 minutes or more (percent)
ACS table number:		C07204	C07204	C07204	B25003	B25003	B25081	B25097	B25064	S2801	B08012	B08012	B08012
FIPS	column number:	1	2	3	4	5	6	7	8	9	10	11	12
49000	**UTAH**..................	3,295,561	85.5	6.3	1,101,499	69.7	69.6	421,700	1,208	93.6	1,306,378	17.2	4.6
4943660	Layton city, Utah..................	82,824	90.1	8.3	27,176	69.9	83.3	409,200	1,308	91.8	35,968	12.6	5.1
4944320	Lehi city, Utah..................	78,725	88.8	9.9	22,067	77.3	70.3	536,600	1,657	NA	26,002	10.1	2.7
4955980	Ogden city, Utah..................	85,036	84.4	10.6	32,631	61.3	60.0	296,500	929	93.9	37,280	14.8	7.9
4957300	Orem city, Utah..................	96,277	76.9	18.4	32,398	61.1	72.1	404,200	1,148	93.6	42,810	17.1	4.1
4962470	Provo city, Utah..................	112,685	62.4	24.7	32,518	37.5	60.7	418,800	1,020	85.5	51,594	22.9	4.1
4965330	St. George city, Utah..................	99,333	87.7	7.1	35,656	63.3	65.6	447,900	1,167	90.2	35,905	19.5	2.7
4967000	Salt Lake City city, Utah..................	198,609	79.1	12.1	89,839	47.5	68.0	459,800	1,192	93.2	89,310	18.9	3.4
4967440	Sandy city, Utah..................	93,792	89.0	8.6	33,587	77.4	71.6	516,400	1,489	94.2	36,048	12.8	5.1
4970850	South Jordan city, Utah..................	79,119	84.4	13.1	25,502	82.0	78.9	603,500	1,584	95.0	28,203	14.5	3.8
4982950	West Jordan city, Utah..................	115,193	91.7	6.8	36,309	75.7	70.5	410,600	1,507	97.2	45,558	6.8	1.9
4983470	West Valley City city, Utah..................	137,071	82.4	10.2	42,003	70.5	77.8	343,300	1,289	94.6	60,267	7.9	4.2
50000	**VERMONT**..................	641,007	88.1	7.1	270,163	72.7	60.5	271,500	1,115	89.7	263,683	19.3	5.7
51000	**VIRGINIA**..................	8,557,020	86.3	8.8	3,331,461	67.6	68.0	330,600	1,331	90.8	3,312,668	11.2	7.9
5101000	Alexandria city, Virginia..................	153,119	82.2	13.2	72,024	43.2	75.0	630,500	1,823	93.9	57,037	6.3	4.7
5103000	Arlington CDP, Virginia..................	230,062	75.8	14.8	108,396	43.9	79.0	779,400	1,975	96.7	73,060	12.7	2.4
5114440	Centreville CDP, Virginia..................	74,476	86.7	11.3	24,957	74.2	75.6	526,800	1,921	98.4	28,551	5.6	3.2
5116000	Chesapeake city, Virginia..................	249,243	84.3	12.1	93,849	73.7	76.8	320,600	1,294	93.8	107,685	8.6	3.9
5121088	Dale City CDP, Virginia..................	78,618	93.2	5.9	22,465	82.2	69.4	371,800	1,526	96.8	32,820	1.9	14.4
5135000	Hampton city, Virginia..................	136,419	83.6	10.3	58,181	54.4	59.5	211,900	1,182	91.2	62,369	10.9	3.3
5147672	Lynchburg city, Virginia..................	78,144	79.4	14.5	28,346	52.1	72.4	175,600	946	93.8	31,631	23.5	2.2
5156000	Newport News city, Virginia..................	182,175	86.3	8.4	77,489	47.1	74.6	227,200	1,125	91.6	80,310	15.3	3.3
5157000	Norfolk city, Virginia..................	232,197	78.8	12.9	97,596	46.0	71.0	250,300	1,108	89.7	112,597	11.5	4.4
5164000	Portsmouth city, Virginia..................	96,664	87.7	9.5	40,827	56.1	70.4	221,500	1,111	87.1	39,852	11.4	3.0
5167000	Richmond city, Virginia..................	224,801	81.1	12.1	99,929	45.0	60.2	311,700	1,144	85.1	86,807	10.7	5.0
5168000	Roanoke city, Virginia..................	98,043	83.4	5.7	42,455	51.8	77.5	160,000	848	85.7	40,413	15.5	3.0
5176432	Suffolk city, Virginia..................	95,138	89.3	7.5	37,383	71.3	74.5	302,200	1,231	91.6	40,938	8.0	9.7
5182000	Virginia Beach city, Virginia..................	452,133	84.9	8.2	182,775	65.2	69.9	328,500	1,431	95.1	203,785	10.9	3.2
53000	**WASHINGTON**..................	7,657,350	84.6	6.7	3,022,255	64.0	66.7	485,700	1,484	93.6	2,780,613	13.1	8.1
5303180	Auburn city, Washington..................	85,858	89.9	7.8	31,836	59.0	58.9	474,600	1,437	94.5	35,648	8.0	11.1
5305210	Bellevue city, Washington..................	147,899	82.9	12.2	61,440	52.6	58.1	1,107,200	2,220	96.6	38,441	11.2	4.6
5305280	Bellingham city, Washington..................	91,971	76.1	14.5	40,653	40.8	72.3	586,700	1,324	95.3	40,379	21.8	1.9
5322640	Everett city, Washington..................	109,936	82.8	12.8	45,029	47.3	72.3	496,900	1,471	92.9	47,035	11.1	6.8
5323515	Federal Way city, Washington..................	97,740	88.7	6.9	35,047	56.1	64.2	461,000	1,600	94.4	35,855	6.7	11.4
5335275	Kennewick city, Washington..................	83,706	86.6	8.2	30,679	56.1	71.5	330,200	1,072	87.7	31,663	16.6	6.3
5335415	Kent city, Washington..................	133,928	81.6	12.9	46,036	56.8	66.8	523,000	1,628	95.7	53,115	8.1	11.2
5335940	Kirkland city, Washington..................	91,024	85.7	11.7	37,746	60.5	75.3	939,900	2,082	95.9	25,539	12.8	2.6
5343955	Marysville city, Washington..................	69,846	85.3	12.2	25,906	72.8	73.3	461,100	1,667	94.3	30,244	7.9	8.9
5353545	Pasco city, Washington..................	82,432	85.2	8.3	25,084	74.3	77.2	322,200	1,071	94.8	35,769	7.3	4.4
5357535	Redmond city, Washington..................	75,541	80.5	14.5	31,181	41.4	68.7	1,120,300	2,061	96.3	17,805	12.8	4.3
5357745	Renton city, Washington..................	103,937	80.4	14.5	41,997	51.3	77.6	587,300	1,753	95.0	39,733	5.7	8.4
5361115	Sammamish city, Washington..................	65,908	90.7	7.8	22,090	83.3	71.5	1,158,000	2,542	NA	17,180	12.2	4.4
5363000	Seattle city, Washington..................	727,859	75.3	11.0	351,650	46.0	80.8	848,100	1,787	95.1	233,291	8.7	7.1
5365922	South Hill CDP, Washington..................	66,270	83.5	14.7	22,379	79.3	67.1	462,200	1,807	96.7	27,275	8.4	12.8
5367000	Spokane city, Washington..................	226,745	80.0	9.3	94,748	57.5	67.6	318,200	986	92.9	86,330	12.9	4.6
5367167	Spokane Valley city, Washington...	104,647	85.3	11.5	44,047	57.8	75.4	323,800	1,142	88.1	44,993	10.7	5.6
5370000	Tacoma city, Washington..................	216,616	82.8	9.9	88,819	57.6	63.4	435,700	1,429	93.6	86,608	10.5	10.4
5374060	Vancouver city, Washington..................	190,718	84.2	9.6	81,814	50.7	61.1	399,100	1,431	94.2	73,046	11.1	4.1
5380010	Yakima city, Washington..................	95,433	90.7	5.5	37,282	55.2	60.5	260,500	850	81.4	33,277	25.4	4.6
54000	**WEST VIRGINIA**..................	1,767,792	89.6	5.5	722,201	75.2	46.2	143,200	767	85.2	635,030	15.3	9.1
55000	**WISCONSIN**..................	5,838,954	87.7	5.7	2,449,970	68.1	61.6	230,700	921	89.9	2,508,056	18.6	4.6
5502375	Appleton city, Wisconsin..................	71,678	85.9	11.2	29,204	66.7	58.3	193,800	781	94.1	29,026	22.7	6.3
5522300	Eau Claire city, Wisconsin..................	68,379	77.3	13.5	28,218	56.6	59.4	220,300	858	95.3	32,836	25.8	2.0
5531000	Green Bay city, Wisconsin..................	106,353	86.4	7.4	46,857	58.0	62.9	174,400	756	91.6	47,471	16.4	2.3
5537825	Janesville city, Wisconsin..................	65,404	87.2	5.6	28,236	67.0	67.5	183,600	858	92.9	31,995	21.2	2.9
5539225	Kenosha city, Wisconsin..................	97,872	84.6	9.1	38,438	58.9	69.1	206,700	1,045	92.4	42,756	19.0	5.5
5548000	Madison city, Wisconsin..................	266,909	74.1	14.0	123,938	48.6	64.1	321,800	1,227	92.9	111,619	15.7	1.5

Table C-4. Cities — Where: Migration, Housing, and Transportation, 2021—*Continued*

STATE and place code	STATE Place	Total population 1 year and over	Lived in the same house 1 year ago (percent)	Did not live in the same city 1 year ago (percent)	Total occupied housing units	Owner-occupied units (percent)	Percent with a mortgage, contract to purchase, or similar debt	Median value of owner-occupied units (dollars; owner estimated)	Median gross rent of renter-occupied units paying cash rent	Households with Internet access (percent)	Number of workers who commuted to work	Commute of less than 10 minutes (percent)	Commute of 60 minutes or more (percent)
	ACS table number:	C07204	C07204	C07204	B25003	B25003	B25081	B25097	B25064	S2801	B08012	B08012	B08012
FIPS	column number:	1	2	3	4	5	6	7	8	9	10	11	12
	WISCONSIN—Cont.												
5553000	Milwaukee city, Wisconsin	562,597	85.9	5.3	232,362	41.3	61.7	160,100	935	86.1	214,462	11.8	3.4
5560500	Oshkosh city, Wisconsin	66,024	81.8	12.7	28,532	53.1	61.8	152,100	755	90.7	29,482	21.8	5.2
5566000	Racine city, Wisconsin	76,163	84.5	6.5	30,885	52.8	70.7	144,100	862	88.6	31,639	16.8	4.0
5584250	Waukesha city, Wisconsin	70,810	84.8	9.7	31,139	59.4	72.9	252,500	1,032	93.4	32,990	18.1	3.4
56000	**WYOMING**...............................	573,476	83.9	7.5	242,763	71.4	58.2	266,400	889	90.4	258,246	33.3	5.7
5613900	Cheyenne city, Wyoming	64,589	84.7	8.4	28,727	62.3	47.0	276,100	918	88.3	30,224	20.9	5.8
72000	**PUERTO RICO**.............................	NA	NA	NA	1,165,982	68.7	36.9	114,100	504	77.6	977,274	9.5	9.9
7206593	Bayamón zona urbana, Puerto Rico...	NA	NA	NA	61,688	69.1	NA	123,600	630	77.1	52,582	7.6	6.5
7210334	Caguas zona urbana, Puerto Rico .	NA	NA	NA	29,970	59.9	54.3	118,200	608	83.5	24,116	10.8	13.7
7214290	Carolina zona urbana, Puerto Rico	NA	NA	NA	54,012	65.5	NA	138,400	645	90.8	47,059	6.6	7.6
7232522	Guaynabo zona urbana, Puerto Rico...	NA	NA	NA	26,979	75.2	NA	213,900	997	84.7	24,121	2.9	4.4
7263820	Ponce zona urbana, Puerto Rico....	NA	NA	NA	42,404	68.7	46.4	102,500	535	81.6	30,089	8.3	7.2
7276770	San Juan zona urbana, Puerto Rico...	NA	NA	NA	129,554	51.3	NA	149,100	530	74.1	106,404	7.7	4.1

NA = Not available.

Appendixes

A: Geographic Concepts and Codes

B: Source Notes and Explanations

C: Metropolitan Statistical Areas, Metropolitan Divisions, and Components

APPENDIX A:
GEOGRAPHIC CONCEPTS AND CODES

GEOGRAPHIC AREAS COVERED

The Who, What, and Where of America presents American Community Survey (ACS) data for the United States, all states, all metropolitan areas, and all counties and cities with populations of 65,000 or more. ACS population sizes are based on the most recent population estimates from the Census Bureau's Population Estimates Program. A few counties and cities may show populations below the 65,000 threshold. If a geographic area met the threshold for a previous period but dropped below the threshold for the current period, it will continue to be published as long as the population does not drop more than five percent below the threshold. Additionally, the Census Bureau uses housing unit estimates to distribute the county population among subcounty areas within the county (cities.) Housing unit estimates use building permits, mobile home shipments, and estimates of housing unit loss to update housing unit change since the last census. The Census Bureau does use vital statistics data in producing the initial county estimates, but not for the town and city numbers, so the estimates do not always seem consistent. All estimates are based on the geographic boundaries as they existed on January 1 of the sample year.

STATES AND COUNTIES

Data are presented for each of the 50 states, the District of Columbia, and the United States as a whole. The states are arranged alphabetically and counties are arranged alphabetically within each state. Data are presented for 841 counties and county equivalents with populations of 65,000 or more.

County Equivalents

In Louisiana, the primary divisions of the state are known as parishes rather than counties. In Alaska, the county equivalents are the organized boroughs, together with the census areas that were developed for general statistical purposes by the state of Alaska and the U.S. Census Bureau. Four states—Maryland, Missouri, Nevada, and Virginia—have one or more incorporated places that are legally independent of any county and thus constitute primary divisions of their states. Within each state, independent cities are listed alphabetically following the list of counties. The District of Columbia is not divided into counties or county equivalents—data for the entire district are presented as a county equivalent. New York City contains five counties: Bronx, Kings, New York, Queens, and Richmond.

METROPOLITAN AREAS

Data are included for 392 metropolitan statistical areas and 31 metropolitan divisions, which are located within 11 of the largest metropolitan statistical areas. The metropolitan statistical areas are listed alphabetically, and the metropolitan divisions are listed alphabetically under the metropolitan statistical area of which they are components.

Appendix C is an alphabetical listing of the metropolitan areas, together with their metropolitan divisions and component counties and their 2010 census populations. (2020 totals were not available at the time of publication.)

The U.S. Office of Management and Budget (OMB) defines metropolitan and micropolitan statistical areas according to published standards. The major purpose of defining these areas is to enable all U.S. government agencies to use the same geographic definitions in tabulating and publishing data. The general concept of a metropolitan or micropolitan statistical area is that of a core area containing a substantial population nucleus, together with adjacent communities that have a high degree of economic and social integration with the core.

New delineations of these Core Based Statistical Areas (CBSAs) based on the 2010 census were first released in February 2013. Standard definitions of metropolitan areas were first issued in 1949 by the Bureau of the Budget (the predecessor of OMB), under the designation "standard metropolitan area" (SMA). The term was changed to "standard metropolitan statistical area" (SMSA) in 1959, and to "metropolitan statistical area" (MSA) in 1983. The term "metropolitan area" (MA) was adopted in 1990 and referred collectively to metropolitan statistical areas (MSAs), consolidated metropolitan statistical areas (CMSAs), and primary metropolitan statistical areas (PMSAs). The term "core based statistical area" (CBSA) became effective in 2000 and refers collectively to metropolitan and micropolitan statistical areas.

The 2010 standards provide that each CBSA must contain at least one urban area of 10,000 or more population. Each metropolitan statistical area must have at least one urbanized area of 50,000 or more inhabitants. Each micropolitan statistical area must have at least one urban cluster of at least 10,000 but less than 50,000 people.

Under the standards, A metro area contains a core urban area of 50,000 or more population, and a micro area contains an urban core of at least 10,000 (but less than 50,000) population. Each metro or micro area consists of one or more counties and includes the counties containing the core urban area, as well as any adjacent counties that have a high degree of social and economic integration (as measured by commuting to work) with the urban core.

If specified criteria are met, a metropolitan statistical area containing a single core with a population of 2.5 million or more may be subdivided to form smaller groupings of counties referred to as "metropolitan divisions."

The largest city in each metropolitan or micropolitan statistical area is designated a "principal city." Additional cities qualify if specified requirements are met concerning population size and employment. The title of each metropolitan statistical area consists of the names of up to three of its principal cities and the name of each state into which the metropolitan or micropolitan statistical area extends. Titles of metropolitan divisions also typically are based on principal city names, but in certain cases consist of county names. The principal city need not be an incorporated place if it meets the requirements of population size and employment. Usually such a principal city is a census designated place (CDP.)

In view of the importance of cities and towns in New England, the 2010 standards also provide for a set of geographic areas that are defined using cities and towns in the six New England states. These New England city and town areas (NECTAs) are not included in this volume.

CITIES

This book presents data for 634 cities (called "places") with estimated populations of 65,000 or more in 2021. Corresponding data for states are also provided. The states are arranged alphabetically and the cities are ordered alphabetically within each state.

As used in this volume, the term *city* refers to *places* as defined by the Census Bureau. These include places that have been incorporated as cities, boroughs, towns, or villages under the laws of their respective states, as well as census designated places (CDPs). CDPs are delineated by the Census Bureau, in cooperation with states and localities,

as statistical counterparts of incorporated places for purposes of the decennial census and the ACS. CDPs comprise densely settled concentrations of population that are identifiable by name but are not legally incorporated places.

Included with the incorporated cities are the principal portions of seven consolidated cities. A consolidated city is an incorporated place that has combined its government functions with a county or subcounty entity but contains one or more other semi-independent incorporated places that continue to function as local governments within the consolidated government. Consolidated cities are not included in this book, but the "consolidated city (balance)" portions are treated as incorporated places in the ACS data. Consolidated city (balance) portions included in this volume are Milford, Connecticut; Athens-Clarke County, Georgia Augusta-Richmond County, Georgia; Indianapolis, Indiana; Louisville-Jefferson County, Kentucky; Butte-Silver Bow, Montana; and Nashville-Davidson, Tennessee.

Towns in the New England states and New York are treated as minor civil divisions (MCDs) and are not included in this book.

GEOGRAPHIC CODES

The tables in this book provide a geographic code or codes for each area.

For counties, a five-digit state and county code is given for each state and county. The first two digits indicate the state; the remaining three represent the county. Within each state, the counties are listed in order, beginning with 001, with even numbers usually omitted. Independent cities follow the counties and begin with the number 510. In the state-level tables, a two-digit state code is provided. The state code is a sequential numbering, with some gaps, of the states and the District of Columbia in alphabetical order from Alabama (01) to Wyoming (56).

These codes have been established by the U.S. government as Federal Information Processing Standards and are often referred to as *FIPS codes*. They are used by U.S. government agencies and many other organizations for data presentation. The codes are provided in this volume for use in matching the data given here with other data sources in which counties are identified by FIPS code.

The metropolitan area tables provide metro area codes for each metropolitan area, as well as metropolitan division codes where appropriate.

For cities, a seven-digit state and place code is included. The first two digits identify the state and are the same as the FIPS codes described above. The remaining five digits are the place FIPS codes established by the U.S. government.

INDEPENDENT CITIES

The following independent cities are not included in any county; their data are presented separately in this volume.

MARYLAND
Baltimore (separate from Baltimore County)

MISSOURI
St. Louis (separate from St. Louis County)

VIRGINIA
Alexandria
Chesapeake
Hampton
Lynchburg
Newport News
Norfolk
Portsmouth
Richmond
Roanoke
Suffolk
Virginia Beach

APPENDIX B:
SOURCE NOTES AND EXPLANATIONS

With one exception, all data in this book are from the American Community Survey (ACS). The sole exception is the population change between 2010 and 2019, which comes from the Census Bureau's Population Estimates Program, the official source for population totals.

Annual ACS data are released for all geographic entities with populations of 65,000 or more. Until 2014, 3-year estimates were released for counties and cities with populations between 20,000 and 65,000, while only 5-year estimates were available for smaller areas. In the first four editions of this book, the county and city tables included the 3-year data. Beginning with the 2014 data, the 3-year releases were discontinued and replaced by 1-year Supplemental Estimates which were used for the county and city tables in this book. These 1-year Supplemental Estimates have less precise categories but are more timely than the 5-year estimates also available for these areas. This is the third edition of this book to use the 1-year Supplemental Estimates.

This section of source notes is generally excerpted from https://www2.census.gov/programs-surveys/acs/tech_docs/ subject_definitions/2021_ACSSubjectDefinitions.pdf.

The data were assembled from the ACS detailed tables and the following notes reference the numbers of those detailed tables. Also included with each table number and title is the table's universe, which is the total number of units (e.g., individuals, households, businesses, in the population of interest). Many of the data items can also be found in ACS profiles, subject tables, geographic comparison tables, and other formats available on the ACS website.

Symbols

A "-" in a cell indicates that either there were no sample cases or the number of sample cases was too small.

Part A: WHO

Table A-1. Who — Age, Race/Ethnicity, and Household Structure

Table A-1 presents 61 items for the United States as a whole and for each individual state and the District of Columbia

POPULATION AND POPULATION CHANGE, Items 1 and 2

Source: Table B01003. Total Population
Universe: Total Population

In the 2021 1-year ACS, the total population for states is the official estimate from the Population Estimates Program. The 2010 1-year ACS used the total population from the 2010 census.

RACE, Items 3–8, 10–11

Sources: Table B02001. Race; Table B02008. White Alone or in Combination with One or More Other Races; Table B02009. Black or African American Alone or in Combination with One or More Other Races; Table B02010. American Indian and Alaska Native alone or in Combination with One or More Other Races; Table B02011. Asian Alone or in Combination with One or More Other Races; Table B02012. Native Hawaiian and Other Pacific Islander Alone or in Combination with One or More Other Races; Table B02013. Some Other Race Alone or in Combination with One or More Other Races; and Table B01001H. Sex by Age (White Alone, not Hispanic or Latino)
Universe: Total Population

The concept of race, as used by the Census Bureau, reflects self-identification by people according to the race or races with which they most closely identify. These categories are socio-political constructs and should not be interpreted as being scientific or anthropological in nature. Furthermore, the race categories include both racial and national-origin groups. The racial classifications used by the Census Bureau adhere to the October 30, 1997, *Federal Register Notice* entitled, "Revisions to the Standards for the Classification of Federal Data on Race and Ethnicity," issued by the Office of Management and Budget (OMB). These standards govern the categories used to collect and present federal data on race and ethnicity. The OMB requires five minimum categories (White, Black or African American, American Indian or Alaska Native, Asian, and Native Hawaiian or Other Pacific Islander) for race. The race categories are described below with a sixth category, "Some other race," added with OMB approval. In addition to the five race groups, the OMB also states that respondents should be offered the option of selecting one or more races.

The concept "race alone or in combination" includes people who reported a single race alone (e.g., Asian) and people who reported that race in combination with one or more of the other major race groups (e.g., White, Black or African American, American Indian and Alaska Native, Native Hawaiian and Other Pacific Islander, and Some Other Race). The "race alone or in combination" concept, therefore, represents the maximum number of people who reported as that race group, either alone, or in combination with another race(s). The sum of the six individual race "alone or in combination" categories may add to more than the total population because people who reported more than one race were tallied in each race category.

The **White** population includes persons having origins in any of the original peoples of Europe, the Middle East, or North Africa. It includes people who indicate their race as "White" or report entries such as Irish, German, Italian, Lebanese, Near Easterner, Arab, or Polish.

The **Black or African American** population includes persons having origins in any of the Black racial groups of Africa. It includes people who indicate their race as "Black, African American, or Negro," or provide written entries such as African American, Afro-American, Kenyan, Nigerian, or Haitian.

The **American Indian or Alaska Native** population includes persons having origins in any of the original peoples of North and South America (including Central America) and who maintain tribal affiliation or community attachment. It includes people who classified themselves as Canadian Indian, French-American Indian, Spanish-American Indian, Eskimo, Aleut, Alaska Indian, or any of the American Indian or Alaska Native tribes.

The **Asian** population includes persons having origins in any of the original peoples of the Far East, Southeast Asia, or the Indian subcontinent including, for example, Cambodia, China, India, Japan, Korea, Malaysia, Pakistan, the Philippine Islands, Thailand, and Vietnam. It includes Asian Indian, Chinese, Filipino, Korean, Japanese, Vietnamese, and Other Asian.

The **Native Hawaiian or Other Pacific Islander** population includes persons having origins in any of the original peoples of Hawaii, Guam, Samoa, or other Pacific Islands. It includes people who indicate their race as Native Hawaiian, Guamanian or Chamorro, Samoan, and Other Pacific Islander.

Some Other Race includes all other responses not included in the "White," "Black or African American," "American Indian or Alaska Native," "Asian," and "Native Hawaiian or Other Pacific Islander" race categories described above. Respondents providing write-in entries such as multiracial, mixed, interracial, or a Hispanic/Latino group (for example, Mexican, Puerto Rican, or Cuban) in the "Some other race" write-in space are included in this category.

Two or More Races. People may have chosen to provide two or more races either by checking two or more race response check boxes, by providing multiple write-in responses, or by some combination of check boxes and write-in responses. These people are included in each of the "race alone or in combination" categories that they selected.

HISPANIC ORIGIN, Item 9
Source: Table B03003. Hispanic or Latino Origin
Universe: Total Population

The data on the **Hispanic or Latino** population was asked of all people. The terms "Spanish," "Hispanic," and "Latino" are used interchangeably. Some respondents identify with all three terms, while others may identify with only one of these three specific terms. Hispanics or Latinos who identify with the terms "Spanish," "Hispanic," or "Latino" are those who classify themselves in one of the specific Hispanic or Latino categories listed on the questionnaire—"Mexican," "Puerto Rican," or "Cuban"—as well as those who indicate that they are "other Spanish/Hispanic/Latino." People who do not identify with one of the specific origins listed on the questionnaire but indicate that they are "other Spanish/Hispanic/Latino" are those whose origins are from Spain, the Spanish-speaking countries of Central or South America, the Dominican Republic, or people identifying themselves generally as Spanish, Spanish-American, Hispanic, Hispano, Latino, and so on.

AGE, Items 12–21, 23–31
Sources: Table B01001. Sex by Age; Table B01002. Median Age by Sex; Table B01002H. Median Age by Sex (White Alone, not Hispanic or Latino); Table B01002B. Median Age by Sex (Black or African American Alone); Table B01002C. Median Age by Sex (American Indian and Alaska Native); Table B01002D. Median Age by Sex (Asian Alone); Table B01002E. Median Age by Sex (Native Hawaiian and Other Pacific Islander Alone); Table B01002F. Median Age by Sex (Some Other Race Alone); Table B01002G. Median Age by Sex (Two or More Races); and Table B01002I. Median Age by Sex (Hispanic or Latino)
Universe: Total Population

The age classification is based on the age of the person in complete years at the time of interview. Both age and date of birth are used in combination to calculate the most accurate age at the time of the interview. Inconsistently reported and missing values are assigned or imputed based on the values of other variables for that person, from other people in the household, or from people in other households ("hot deck" imputation). Data on age are used to determine the applicability of other questions for a particular individual and to classify other characteristics in tabulations. Age data are needed to interpret most social and economic characteristics used to plan and analyze programs and policies. Therefore, age data are tabulated by many different age groupings, such as 5-year age groups.

The median age is the age that divides the population into two equal-size groups. Half of the population is older than the median age and half is younger. Median age is based on a standard distribution of the population by single years of age and is shown to the nearest tenth of a year.

PERCENT FEMALE, Item 22
Source: Table B01001. Sex by Age
Universe: Total Population

The female population is shown as a percentage of the total population.

MARITAL STATUS, Items 32–36
Source: Table B12001. Sex by Marital Status for the Population 15 Years and Over
Universe: Population 15 Years and Over

The **marital status** classification refers to the status at the time of interview. Data on marital status are tabulated only for people 15 years old and over. All people were asked whether they were "now married," "widowed," "divorced," "separated," or "never married." Couples who live together (unmarried people, people in common-law marriages) were allowed to report the marital status they considered the most appropriate. When marital status was not reported, it was imputed according to the relationship to the householder and sex and age of the person. Differences in the number of currently married males and females occur because there is no step in the weighting process to equalize the weighted estimates of husbands and wives.

Never married includes all people who have never been married, including people whose only marriage(s) was annulled.

Now married includes all people whose current marriage has not ended by widowhood or divorce. This category includes people defined as "separated" and "spouse absent." The category may also include couples who live together or people in common-law marriages if they consider this category the most appropriate. Beginning in 2013, same-sex married couples are included in the married spouse present category.

Widowed includes widows and widowers who have not remarried.

Divorced includes people who are legally divorced and who have not remarried.

Differences between the number of currently married males and the number of currently married females occur because of reporting differences, because some husbands and wives have their usual residence in different areas, and because husbands and wives do not have the same weights.

FOREIGN BORN, Item 37
Source: Table C05002. Place of Birth by Citizenship Status
Universe: Total Population

The **foreign-born** population includes anyone who was not a U.S. citizen or a U.S. national at birth. This includes respondents who indicated they were a U.S. citizen by naturalization or not a U.S. citizen.

LANGUAGES SPOKEN, Items 38–41
Source: Table C16002. Household Language by Household Limited English Speaking Status
Universe: Households

Language Spoken at Home. Questions on language spoken at home were asked only of persons 5 years of age and older. Instructions mailed with the American Community Survey questionnaire instructed respondents to mark "Yes" if they sometimes or always spoke a language other than English at home, and "No" if a language was spoken only at school—or if speaking was limited to a few expressions or slang. Respondents printed the name of the non-English language they spoke at home. If the person spoke more than one non-English language, they reported the language spoken most often. If the language spoken most frequently could not be determined, the respondent reported the language learned first.

The questions referred to languages spoken at home in an effort to measure the current use of languages other than English. This category excluded respondents who spoke a language other than English exclusively outside of the home.

Most respondents who reported speaking a language other than English also spoke English. The questions did not permit a determination of the primary language of persons who spoke both English and another language.

Household Language. In households where one or more people spoke a language other than English, the household language assigned to all household members was the non-English language spoken by the first person with a non-English language. This assignment scheme ranked household members in the following order: householder, spouse, parent, sibling, child, grandchild, other relative, stepchild, unmarried partner, housemate or roommate, and other nonrelatives. Therefore, a person who spoke only English may have had a non-English household language assigned during tabulations by household language.

Ability to Speak English. Respondents who reported speaking a language other than English were asked to indicate their English ability based on one of the following categories: "Very well," "Well," "Not well," or "Not at all." Ideally, the data on ability to speak English represented a person's perception of their own ability. However, because one household member usually completes American Community Survey questionnaires, the responses may have represented the perception of another household member.

Limited English Speaking Household. A "limited English speaking household" is one in which no member 14 years old and over (1) speaks only English or (2) speaks a non-English language and speaks English "very well." In other words, all members 14 years old and over have at least some difficulty with English. By definition, English-only households cannot belong to this group. Previous Census Bureau data products referred to these households as "linguistically isolated" and "Household where no one age 14 and over speaks English only or speaks English 'very well.'"

HOUSEHOLDS AND HOUSEHOLD TYPE, Item 42–61
Sources: Table B11001. Household Type (Including Living Alone); Table B11006. Households by Presence of People 60 Years and Over by Household Type; Table B11009. Unmarried-Partner Households by Sex of Partner; B11010. Nonfamily Households by Sex of Householder by Living Alone by Age of Householder; Table C11005. Households by Presence of People Under 18 Years by Household Type; and Table B25010. Average Household Size of Occupied-Housing Units by Tenure
Universe: Households

A **household** includes all the people who occupy a housing unit. (People not living in households are classified as living in group quarters.) A housing unit is a house, an apartment, a mobile home, a group of rooms, or a single room that is occupied (or if vacant, is intended for occupancy) as separate living quarters. Separate living quarters are those in which the occupants live separately from any other people in the building and which have direct access from the outside of the building or through a common hall. The occupants may be a single family, one person

living alone, two or more families living together, or any other group of related or unrelated people who share living arrangements.

A **family household** consists of a householder and one or more other people living in the same household who are related to the householder by birth, marriage, or adoption. All people in a household who are related to the householder are regarded as members of his or her family. A family household may contain people not related to the householder, but those people are not included as part of the householder's family in tabulations. Thus, the number of family households is equal to the number of families, but family households may include more members than do families. A household can contain only one family for purposes of tabulations.

A **married-couple family** is one in which the householder and his or her spouse are listed as members of the same household.

The category **male family households** includes only male-headed family households with no spouse present. Similarly, the category **female family households** includes only female-headed family households with no spouse present.

A **nonfamily household** consists of a group of unrelated people or of one person living alone.

An unmarried-partner household is a household other than a "married-couple household" that includes a householder and an "unmarried partner." An "unmarried partner" can be of the same sex or of the opposite sex as the householder. An "unmarried partner" in an "unmarried-partner household" is an adult who is unrelated to the householder, but shares living quarters and has a close personal relationship with the householder. An unmarried-partner household also may be a family household or a nonfamily household, depending on the presence or absence of another person in the household who is related to the householder. There may be only one unmarried partner per household, and an unmarried partner may not be included in a married-couple household, as the householder cannot have both a spouse and an unmarried partner.

Tables A-2, A-3, and A-4. Who—Age, Race/Ethnicity, and Household Structure

Table A-2 presents 24 items for the United States as a whole, each individual state and the District of Columbia, and 841 counties, county equivalents, and independent cities with a 2021 estimated population of 65,000 or more. This table is from the 2021 1-year file, from ACS tables beginning with "B" and "C," as the supplemental estimates were not available.

Table A-3 presents 24 items for 392 Metropolitan Statistical Areas and 31 Metropolitan Divisions within the 12 largest Metropolitan Statistical Areas. This table is from the 2021 1-year file, from ACS tables beginning with "B" and "C."

Table A-4 presents 24 items for 634 cities, Census Designated Places, and the principal portions of consolidated cities with a 2021 estimated population of 65,000 or more. This table is from the 2021 1-year file, from ACS tables beginning with "B" and "C," as the supplemental estimates were not available.

POPULATION, Item 1
Source: Table B01003. Total Population; Table K200104. Population by Age.
Universe: Total Population

In the 2021 ACS, the total population is based on the official estimate from the Population Estimates Program.

POPULATION CHANGE, Item 2
Source: U.S. Census Bureau—Population Estimates Program

The population change data for 2010 through 2019 are from the official estimates of the Population Estimates Program which estimates the population as of July 1 each year.

AGE, Items 3–8
Sources: Table B01001. Sex by Age; Table B01002. Median Age by Sex; Table K200104. Population by Age; Table K200103. Median Age by Sex.
Universe: Total Population

The age classification is based on the age of the person in complete years at the time of interview. Both age and date of birth are used in combination to calculate the most accurate age at the time of the interview. Inconsistently reported and missing values are assigned or imputed based on the values of other variables for that person, from other people in the household, or from people in other households ("hot deck" imputation). Data on age are used to determine the applicability of other questions for a particular individual and to classify other characteristics in tabulations. Age data are needed to interpret most social and economic characteristics used to plan and analyze programs and policies. Therefore, age data are tabulated by many different age groupings, such as 5-year age groups.

The median age is the age that divides the population into two equal-size groups. Half of the population is older than the median age and half is younger. Median age is based on a standard distribution of the population by single years of age and is shown to the nearest tenth of a year.

RACE, Items 9–12
Sources: Table B02008. White Alone or in Combination with One or More Other Races; Table B02009. Black or African American Alone or in Combination with One or More Other Races; Table B02010. American Indian and Alaska Native alone or in Combination with One or More Other Races; Table B02011. Asian Alone or in Combination with One or More Other Races; Table B02012. Native Hawaiian and Other Pacific Islander Alone or in Combination with One or More Other Races; and Table B02013. Some Other Race Alone or in Combination with One or More Other Races; Table K200201. Race.
Universe: Total Population

The concept of race, as used by the Census Bureau, reflects self-identification by people according to the race or races with which they most closely identify. These categories are socio-political constructs and should not be interpreted as being scientific or anthropological in nature. Furthermore, the race categories include both racial and national-origin groups. The racial classifications used by the Census Bureau adhere to the October 30, 1997, *Federal Register Notice* entitled, "Revisions to the Standards for the Classification of Federal Data on Race and Ethnicity," issued by the Office of Management and Budget (OMB). These standards govern the categories used to collect and present federal data on race and ethnicity. The OMB requires five minimum categories (White, Black or African American, American Indian or Alaska Native, Asian, and Native Hawaiian or Other Pacific Islander) for race. The race categories are described below with a sixth category, "Some other race," added with OMB approval. In addition to the five race groups, the OMB also states that respondents should be offered the option of selecting one or more races.

There are several concepts used to display and tabulate race information for the six major race categories (White; Black or African American; American Indian or Alaska Native; Asian; Native Hawaiian or Other Pacific Islander; and Some Other Race) and the various details within these groups.

The concept "race alone" includes people who reported a single entry (e.g., Korean) and no other race, as well as people who reported two or more entries within the same major race group (e.g., Asian). For example, respondents who reported Korean and Vietnamese are part of the larger "Asian alone" race group. Items 9 through 12 in

Tables A-2 and A-4 use the concept of "race alone."

The concept "race alone or in combination" includes people who reported a single race alone (e.g., Asian) and people who reported that race in combination with one or more of the other major race groups (e.g., White, Black or African American, American Indian and Alaska Native, Native Hawaiian and Other Pacific Islander, and Some Other Race). The "race alone or in combination" concept, therefore, represents the maximum number of people who reported as that race group, either alone, or in combination with another race(s). The sum of the six individual race "alone or in combination" categories may add to more than the total population because people who reported more than one race were tallied in each race category. Items 9 through 12 in Table A-3 use the concept of "race alone or in combination."

The **White** population includes persons having origins in any of the original peoples of Europe, the Middle East, or North Africa. It includes people who indicate their race as "White" or report entries such as Irish, German, Italian, Lebanese, Near Easterner, Arab, or Polish.

The **Black or African American** population includes persons having origins in any of the Black racial groups of Africa. It includes people who indicate their race as "Black, African American, or Negro," or provide written entries such as African American, Afro-American, Kenyan, Nigerian, or Haitian.

The **American Indian or Alaska Native** population includes persons having origins in any of the original peoples of North and South America (including Central America) and who maintain tribal affiliation or community attachment. It includes people who classified themselves as Canadian Indian, French-American Indian, Spanish-American Indian, Eskimo, Aleut, Alaska Indian, or any of the American Indian or Alaska Native tribes.

The **Asian and Pacific Islander** population combines two census groupings: Asian and Native Hawaiian or Other Pacific Islander. The **Asian** population includes persons having origins in any of the original peoples of the Far East, Southeast Asia, or the Indian subcontinent including, for example, Cambodia, China, India, Japan, Korea, Malaysia, Pakistan, the Philippine Islands, Thailand, and Vietnam. It includes Asian Indian, Chinese, Filipino, Korean, Japanese, Vietnamese, and Other Asian. The **Native Hawaiian or Other Pacific Islander** population includes persons having origins in any of the original peoples of Hawaii, Guam, Samoa, or other Pacific Islands. It includes people who indicate their race as Native Hawaiian, Guamanian or Chamorro, Samoan, and Other Pacific Islander. Because Table A-3 uses the "race alone or in combination" concept, this combination results in double-counting of individuals who combine these two racial groups. While the groups are combined in Tables A-2, A-3, and A-4, the separate populations are shown in Table A-1, States.

Some Other Race. Includes all other responses not included in the "White," "Black or African American," "American Indian or Alaska Native," "Asian," and "Native Hawaiian or Other Pacific Islander" race categories described above. Respondents reporting entries such as multiracial, mixed, interracial, or a Hispanic, Latino, or Spanish group (for example, Mexican, Puerto Rican, Cuban, or Spanish) in response to the race question are included in this category. In Tables A-2 through A-4, this group is combined with the **American Indian or Alaska Native** group. The **Some Other Race** alone or in combination is shown separately in Table A-1, States.

HISPANIC ORIGIN, Item 13
Source: Table B03003. Hispanic or Latino Origin; Table K200301. Hispanic or Latino Origin.
Universe: Total Population

The data on the **Hispanic or Latino** population was asked of all people. The terms "Spanish," "Hispanic," and "Latino" are used interchangeably. Some respondents identify with all three terms, while others may identify with only one of these three specific terms. Hispanics or Latinos who identify with the terms "Spanish," "Hispanic," or "Latino" are those who classify themselves in one of the specific Hispanic or Latino categories listed on the questionnaire—"Mexican," "Puerto Rican," or "Cuban"—as well as those who indicate that they are "other Spanish/Hispanic/Latino." People who do not identify with one of the specific origins listed on the questionnaire but indicate that they are "other Spanish/Hispanic/Latino" are those whose origins are from Spain, the Spanish-speaking countries of Central or South America, the Dominican Republic, or people identifying themselves generally as Spanish, Spanish-American, Hispanic, Hispano, Latino, and so on.

BORN IN STATE OF RESIDENCE, Item 14.
Source: Table B05002. Place of Birth by Nativity and Citizenship Status; Table K200503. Place of Birth in the United States.
Universe: Total Population

Respondents were asked to select one of two categories: (1) in the United States, or (2) outside the United States. In the ACS, respondents selecting category (1) were then asked to report the name of the state while respondents selecting category (2) were then asked to report the name of the foreign country, or Puerto Rico, Guam, etc. People not reporting a place of birth were assigned the state or country of birth of another family member, or were allocated the response of another individual with similar characteristics. People born outside the United States were asked to report their place of birth according to current international boundaries.

FOREIGN-BORN, Item 15
Source: Table B05002. Place of Birth by Nativity and Citizenship Status; Table K200503. Place of Birth in the United States.
Universe: Total Population

The **foreign-born** population includes anyone who was not a U.S. citizen or a U.S. national at birth. This includes respondents who indicated they were a U.S. citizen by naturalization or not a U.S. citizen.

NON-CITIZENS, Item 16
Source: Table B05002. Place of Birth by Nativity and Citizenship; Table K200501. Citizenship Status in the United States.
Universe: Total Population

Respondents who indicated that they were born in the United States, Puerto Rico, a U.S. Island Area (such as Guam), or abroad of American (U.S. citizen) parent or parents are considered U.S. citizens at birth. Foreign-born people who indicated that they were U.S. citizens through naturalization also are considered U.S. citizens. Respondents who indicated that they were not U.S. citizens at the time of the survey were considered **non-citizens**.

HOUSEHOLDS AND HOUSEHOLD TYPE, Items 17–24
Sources: Table B11001. Household Type (Including Living Alone); Table B11006. Households by Presence of People 60 Years and Over by Household Type; Table K200901. Household Type; Table K201102. Households by Presence of People 60 Years and Over by Household Type
Universe: Households

A **household** includes all the people who occupy a housing unit. (People not living in households are classified as living in group quarters.) A housing unit is a house, an apartment, a mobile home, a group of rooms, or a single room that is occupied (or if vacant, is intended for occupancy) as separate living quarters. Separate living quarters are those in which the occupants live separately from any other people in the building and which have direct access from the outside of the building or through a common hall. The occupants may be a single family, one person

living alone, two or more families living together, or any other group of related or unrelated people who share living arrangements.

A **family household** consists of a householder and one or more other people living in the same household who are related to the householder by birth, marriage, or adoption. All people in a household who are related to the householder are regarded as members of his or her family. A family household may contain people not related to the householder, but those people are not included as part of the householder's family in tabulations. Thus, the number of family households is equal to the number of families, but family households may include more members than do families. A household can contain only one family for purposes of tabulations.

A **married-couple family** is one in which the householder and his or her spouse are listed as members of the same household.

The category **male family households** includes only male-headed family households with no spouse present. Similarly, the category **female family households** includes only female-headed family households with no spouse present.

A **nonfamily household** consists of a group of unrelated people or of one person living alone.

Part B — WHAT

Table B-1. What — Education, Employment, and Income

Table B-1 presents 158 items for the United States as a whole and for each individual state and the District of Columbia.

EDUCATIONAL ATTAINMENT, Items 1–6
Source: Table C15003. Educational Attainment for the Population 25 Years and Over
Universe: Population 25 Years and Over

Data on **educational attainment** were derived from a question that asked respondents for the highest level of school completed or the highest degree received. Persons currently enrolled in school are instructed to report the level of the previous grade attended or the highest degree received. Persons who had passed a high school equivalency examination were considered high school graduates. Schooling received in foreign schools was to be reported as the equivalent grade or years in the regular American school system.

Specifically excluded are vocational and technical training, such as barber school training; business, trade, technical, and vocational schools; or other training for a specific trade.

No high school diploma includes all persons who have not received a high school diploma.

High school graduate includes persons whose highest degree was a high school diploma or its equivalent, including those who passed a high school equivalency examination.

Some college or associate degree includes people who attended college but did not receive a degree or received an associate degree.

Bachelor's degree includes persons who have received bachelor's degrees.

Graduate or professional degree includes persons who have received master's degrees, professional school degrees (such as law school or medical school degrees), or doctoral degrees.

SCHOOL ENROLLMENT, Items 7–17
Source: Table C14002. School Enrollment by Level of School by Type of School by for the Population 3 Years and Over
Universe: Population 3 Years and Over

People were classified as **enrolled in school** if they were attending a "regular" public or private school or college at any time during the 3 months prior to the time of interview. The question included instructions to "include only nursery or preschool, kindergarten, elementary school, and schooling that leads to a high school diploma, or a college degree" as regular school or college. Respondents who did not answer the enrollment question were assigned the enrollment status and type of school of a person with the same age, sex, race, and Hispanic or Latino origin whose residence was in the same or nearby area.

A regular school advances a person toward an elementary school certificate, a high school diploma, or a college, university, or professional school (such as law or medicine) degree. Tutoring or correspondence schools are included if credit can be obtained in a "regular school." People enrolled in "vocational, technical, or business school" were not reported as enrolled in regular school. Field interviewers were instructed to classify individuals who were home schooled as enrolled in private school. The guide sent out with the mail questionnaire does not include explicit instructions for how to classify home schoolers.

Enrolled in public and private school includes people who attended school in the reference period and indicated they were enrolled by marking one of the questionnaire categories for "public school, public college," or "private school, private college." The instruction guide defines a public school as "any school or college controlled and supported primarily by a local, county, state, or federal government." Private schools are defined as schools supported and controlled primarily by religious organizations or other private groups. Respondents who marked both the "public" and "private" boxes are edited to the first entry, "public."

Grade in which enrolled. Since 1999, in the American Community Survey, people reported to be enrolled in "public school, public college" or "private school, private college" were classified by grade or level according to responses to the question "What grade or level was this person attending?" Seven levels were identified: **nursery school, preschool**; **kindergarten**; **elementary grade 1 to grade 4** or **grade 5 to grade 8**; **high school grade 9 to grade 12**; **college undergraduate** years (freshman to senior); and **graduate or professional school** (*for example: medical, dental, or law school*).

EMPLOYMENT STATUS, Items 18–40
Sources: Table C23001. Sex by Age by Employment status for the Population 16 Years and Over
Universe: Population 16 Years and Over

Table B23006. Educational Attainment by Employment Status for the Population 25 to 64 Years
Universe: Population 25 to 64 Years;

Table C14005. Sex by School Enrollment by Educational Attainment by Employment Status for the Population 16 to 19 Years
Universe: Population 16 to 19 Years

Table C23022. Sex by Full-Time Work Status in the Past 12 Months for the Population 16 To 64 Years
Universe: Population 16 to 64 Years

Table B08202. Household Size by Number of Workers in Household
Universe: Households

Total employment includes all civilians 16 years old and over who were either (1) "at work"—those who did any work at all during the reference week as paid employees, worked in either their own business or profession, worked on their own farm, or worked 15 hours or more as unpaid workers in a family farm or business; or were (2) "with a job, but not at work"—those who had a job but were not at work that week due to illness, weather, industrial dispute, vacation, or other personal reasons.

The **labor force** consists of all persons 16 years old and over who are either employed or unemployed, including those in the armed forces.

The **unemployment rate** represents the number of unemployed people as a percentage of the labor force.

Unemployment includes all persons who did not work during the survey week, made specific efforts to find a job during the previous four weeks, and were available for work during the survey week (except for temporary illness). Persons waiting to be called back to a job from which they had been laid off and those waiting to report to a new job within the next 30 days are included in unemployment figures.

Full-time, year-round includes all persons 16 years old and over who usually worked 35 hours or more per week for 50 to 52 weeks in the past 12 months.

Households with no worker. The term "worker" as used here refers to work status in the past 12 months.

Not enrolled, not high school graduate. This category includes people of compulsory school attendance age or slightly above (ages 16 to 19) who were not enrolled in school and were not high school graduates. These people may be referred to as "high school dropouts." There is no restriction on when they "dropped out" of school; therefore, they may have dropped out before high school and never attended high school.

CHILDREN IN FAMILIES BY LIVING ARRANGEMENTS AND EMPLOYMENT STATUS OF PARENTS, Items 41–60
Sources: Table C23008. Age of Own Children Under 18 Years in Families and Subfamilies by Living Arrangements by Employment Status of Parents
Universe: Own Children Under 18 Years in Families and Subfamilies

Table C23007. Presence of Own Children Under 18 Years by Family Type by Employment Status
Universe: Families

Table B23003. Presence of Own Children Under 18 Years by Age of Own children Under 18 Years by Employment Status for Females 20 to 64 Years
Universe: Females 20 to 64 Years in Households

An own child is a never-married child under 18 years who is a son or daughter by birth, a stepchild, or an adopted child of the householder. Own children are further classified as living with two parents or with one parent only. Own children of the householder living with two parents are by definition found only in married-couple families. In the employment status tabulations in this book, own child refers to a never married child under the age of 18 in a family or a subfamily who is a son or daughter, by birth, marriage, or adoption, of a member of the householder's family, but not necessarily of the householder.

CLASS OF WORKER, Items 61–64
Source: Table C24080. Sex by Class of Worker for the Civilian Employed Population 16 Years and Over
Universe: Civilian Employed Population 16 Years and Over

For employed people, the data on **class of worker** refer to the person's job during the previous week. For those who worked two or more jobs, the data refer to the job where the person worked the greatest number of hours. The information on **class of worker** refers to the same job as a respondent's industry and occupation and categorizes people according to the type of ownership of the employing organization. The class of worker categories are defined as follows:

Private wage and salary workers includes people who worked for wages, salary, commission, tips, pay-in-kind, or piece rates for a private for-profit employer or a private not-for-profit, tax-exempt or charitable organization. Self-employed people whose business was incorporated are included with private wage and salary workers because they are paid employees of their own companies.

Government workers includes people who were employees of any local, state, or federal governmental unit, regardless of the activity of the particular agency. Employees of foreign governments, the United Nations, or other formal international organizations controlled by governments were classified as "federal government workers." The class of worker government categories includes all government workers, though government workers may work in different industries. For example, people who work in a public elementary or secondary school are coded as local government class of workers.

Self-employed includes people who worked for profit or fees in their own unincorporated business, profession, or trade, or who operated a farm.

Unpaid family workers includes people who worked 15 hours or more a week without pay in a business or on a farm operated by a relative.

OCCUPATION, Items 65–70
Source: Table C24060. Occupation by Class of Worker for the Civilian Employed Population 16 Years and Over
Universe: Civilian Employed Population 16 Years and Over

For employed people, the data on **occupation** refer to the person's job during the previous week. For those who worked two or more jobs, the data refer to the job where the person worked the greatest number of hours.

Written responses to the occupation questions are coded using the occupational classification system developed for the 2000 census and modified in 2010. This system consists of 539 specific occupational categories, including military, for employed people, arranged into 23 major occupational groups. This classification was developed based on the *Standard Occupational Classification (SOC) Manual: 2010*, published by the Executive Office of the President, Office of Management and Budget.

This table uses the standard ACS groupings of occupations.

INDUSTRY, Items 71–83
Source: Table C24070. Industry by Class of Worker for Civilian Employed Population 16 Years and Over
Universe: Civilian Employed Population 16 Years and Over

For employed people, the data on **industry** refer to the person's job during the previous week. For those who worked two or more jobs, the data refer to the job where the person worked the greatest number of hours.

Written responses to the industry questions are coded using the industry classification system developed for Census 2000. This system consists of 269 categories for employed people, including military, classified into 20 sectors. The NAICS was developed to increase comparability in industry definitions between the United States, Mexico, and Canada. It provides industry classifications that group establishments into industries based on the activities in which they are primarily engaged. The NAICS was created for establishment designations and provides detail about the smallest operating establishment, while the American Community Survey data are collected from households and differ in detail and nature from those obtained from establishment surveys. Because of disclosure issues, ACS data cannot be released in great detail, and the industry classification system, while defined in NAICS terms, cannot reflect the full detail for all categories.

The industry category, "Public administration," is limited to regular government functions such as legislative, judicial, administrative, and regulatory activities. Other government organizations such as public schools, public hospitals, liquor stores, and bus lines are classified by industry according to the activity in which they are engaged.

This table uses the standard ACS groupings of industries. The detailed NAICS industry code list, together with

the corresponding NAICS codes, can be found at https://www2.census.gov/programs-surveys/acs/tech_docs/code_lists/2021_ACS_Code_Lists.pdf?#

VETERAN STATUS, Item 84
Source: Table B21001. Sex by Age by Veteran Status for the Civilian Population 18 Years and Over
Universe: Civilian Population 18 Years and Over

A "civilian veteran" is a person 18 years old or over who has served (even for a short time), but is not now serving, on active duty in the U.S. Army, Navy, Air Force, Marine Corps, or the Coast Guard, or who served in the U.S. Merchant Marines during World War II. People who served in the National Guard or military Reserves are classified as veterans only if they were ever called or ordered to active duty, not counting the 4–6 months for initial training or yearly summer camps. All other civilians 18 years old and over are classified as nonveterans.

HOUSEHOLD INCOME, Items 85–98, 112–137
Sources: Table B19049. Median Household Income in the Past 12 Months (in 2021 Inflation-Adjusted Dollars) By Age of Householder; Table B19013A through B19013I Median Household Income in the Past 12 Months (in 2021 Inflation-Adjusted Dollars) for 9 Race and Hispanic Origin Groups; Table B19052. Wage or Salary Income in the Past 12 Months for Households; Table B19053. Self-Employment Income in the Past 12 Months for Households; Table B19054. Interest, Dividends, or Net Rental Income in the Past 12 Months for Households; Table B19055. Social Security Income in the Past 12 Months for Households; Table B19056. Supplemental Security Income (SSI) in the Past 12 Months for Households; Table B19057. Public Assistance Income in the Past 12 Months for Households; Table B19058. Public Assistance Income or Food Stamps in the Past 12 Months for Households; Table B19059. Retirement Income in the Past 12 Months for Households; Table B19060. Other Types of Income in the Past 12 Months for Households; Table B19001. Household Income in the Past 12 Months (in 2021 Inflation-Adjusted Dollars); and Table C19037. Age of Householder by Household Income in the Past 12 Months (in 2021 Inflation-Adjusted Dollars)
Universe: Households

Income of households includes the income of the householder and all other individuals 15 years old and over in the household, whether they are related to the householder or not. Because many households consist of only one person, average household income is usually less than average family income. Although the household income statistics cover the past 12 months, the characteristics of individuals and the composition of households refer to the time of interview. Thus, the income of the household does not include amounts received by individuals who were members of the household during all or part of the past 12 months if these individuals no longer resided in the household at the time of interview. Similarly, income amounts reported by individuals who did not reside in the household during the past 12 months but who were members of the household at the time of interview are included. However, the composition of most households was the same during the past 12 months as at the time of interview.

Income components were reported for the 12 months preceding the interview month. Monthly Consumer Price Indices (CPI) factors were used to inflation-adjust these components to a reference calendar year (January through December). For example, a household interviewed in March 2021 reports their income for March 2020 through February 2021. Their income is adjusted to the 2021 reference calendar year by multiplying their reported income by 2021 average annual CPI (January–December 2021) and then dividing by the average CPI for March 2020–February 2021.

In order to inflate income amounts from previous years, the dollar values on individual records are inflated to the latest year's dollar values by multiplying by a factor equal to the average annual CPI-U-RS factor for the current year, divided by the average annual CPI-U-RS factor for the earlier/earliest year.

Median income divides the income distribution into two equal parts, with half of all cases below the median income level and half of all cases above the median income level. For households and families, the median income is based on the distribution of the total number of households and families, including those with no income. Median income for households is computed on the basis of a standard distribution with a minimum value of less than $2,500 and a maximum value of $250,000 or more and is rounded to the nearest whole dollar.

The eight types of income reported in the American Community Survey are defined as follows:

1. **Wage or salary income:** Wage or salary income includes total money earnings received for work performed as an employee during the past 12 months. It includes wages, salary, armed forces pay, commissions, tips, piece-rate payments, and cash bonuses earned before deductions were made for taxes, bonds, pensions, union dues, etc.

2. **Self-employment income:** Self-employment income includes both farm and non-farm self-employment income.

Farm self-employment income includes net money income (gross receipts minus operating expenses) from the operation of a farm by a person on his or her own account, as an owner, renter, or sharecropper. Gross receipts include the value of all products sold, government farm programs, money received from the rental of farm equipment to others, and incidental receipts from the sale of wood, sand, gravel, etc. Operating expenses include cost of feed, fertilizer, seed, and other farming supplies, cash wages paid to farmhands, depreciation charges, cash rent, interest on farm mortgages, farm building repairs, farm taxes (not state and federal personal income taxes), etc. The value of fuel, food, or other farm products used for family living is not included as part of net income.

Non-farm self-employment income includes net money income (gross receipts minus expenses) from one's own business, professional enterprise, or partnership. Gross receipts include the value of all goods sold and services rendered. Expenses include costs of goods purchased, rent, heat, light, power, depreciation charges, wages and salaries paid, business taxes (not personal income taxes), etc.

3. **Interest, dividends, or net rental income:** Interest, dividends, or net rental income includes interest on savings or bonds, dividends from stockholdings or membership in associations, net income from rental of property to others and receipts from boarders or lodgers, net royalties, and periodic payments from an estate or trust fund.

4. **Social Security income:** Social Security income includes Social Security pensions and survivor benefits, permanent disability insurance payments made by the Social Security Administration prior to deductions for medical insurance, and railroad retirement insurance checks from the U.S. government. Medicare reimbursements are not included.

5. **Supplemental Security Income (SSI):** Supplemental Security Income (SSI) is a nationwide U.S. assistance program administered by the Social Security Administration that guarantees a minimum level of income for needy aged, blind, or disabled individuals.

6. **Public assistance income:** Public assistance income includes general assistance and Temporary Assistance to Needy Families (TANF). Separate payments received for hospital or other medical care, (vendor payments) are excluded. This does not include Supplemental Security Income (SSI) or noncash benefits such as Food Stamps. The terms "public assistance income" and "cash public assistance" are used interchangeably in the 2021 ACS data products.

7. **Retirement, survivor, or disability income:** Retirement income includes: (1) retirement pensions and survivor benefits from a former employer; labor union; or federal, state, or local government; and the U.S. military; (2)

disability income from companies or unions; federal, state, or local government; and the U.S. military; (3) periodic receipts from annuities and insurance; and (4) regular income from IRA and Keogh plans. This does not include Social Security income.

8. **All other income:** All other income includes unemployment compensation, Veterans' Administration (VA) payments, alimony and child support, contributions received periodically from people not living in the household, military family allotments, and other kinds of periodic income other than earnings.

Receipts from the following sources are not included as income: capital gains, money received from the sale of property (unless the recipient was engaged in the business of selling such property); the value of income "in kind" from food stamps, public housing subsidies, medical care, employer contributions for individuals, etc.; withdrawal of bank deposits; money borrowed; tax refunds; exchange of money between relatives living in the same household; gifts and lump-sum inheritances, insurance payments, and other types of lump-sum receipts.

Although receipt of **food stamps** is included in an income table, the data on Food Stamp benefits were obtained from a Housing Question in the 2021 American Community Survey. The Food Stamp Act of 1977 defines this federally-funded program as one intended to "permit low-income households to obtain a more nutritious diet" (from Title XIII of Public Law 95-113, The Food Stamp Act of 1977, declaration of policy). Food purchasing power is increased by providing eligible households with coupons or cards that can be used to purchase food. The Food and Nutrition Service (FNS) of the U.S. Department of Agriculture (USDA) administers the Food Stamp Program through state and local welfare offices. The Food Stamp Program is the major national income support program to which all low-income and low-resource households, regardless of household characteristics, are eligible. In 2008, the Federal Food Stamp program was renamed SNAP (Supplemental Nutrition Assistance Program). Respondents were asked if one or more of the current members received food stamps or a food stamp benefit card during the past 12 months. Respondents were also asked to include benefits from the Supplemental Nutrition Assistance Program (SNAP) in order to incorporate the program name change.

The questions on participation in the Food Stamp Program were designed to identify households in which one or more of the current members received food stamps during the past 12 months. Once a food stamp household was identified, a question was asked about the total value of all food stamps received for the household during that 12-month period.

FAMILY INCOME, Items 99–105
Source: Table B19126. Median Family Income in the Past 12 Months (in 2021 Inflation-Adjusted Dollars) by Family Type by Presence of Own Children Under 18 Years
Universe: Families

In compiling statistics on **family income**, the incomes of all members 15 years old and over related to the householder are summed and treated as a single amount. Although the family income statistics cover the past 12 months, the characteristics of individuals and the composition of families refer to the time of interview. Thus, the income of the family does not include amounts received by individuals who were members of the family during all or part of the past 12 months if these individuals no longer resided with the family at the time of interview. Similarly, income amounts reported by individuals who did not reside with the family during the past 12 months but who were members of the family at the time of interview are included. However, the composition of most families was the same during the past 12 months as at the time of interview.

NONFAMILY HOUSEHOLD INCOME, Items 106–108
Source: Table B19215. Median Nonfamily Household Income in the Past 12 Months (in 2021 Inflation-Adjusted Dollars) by Sex of Householder by Living Alone by Age of Householder Universe: Nonfamily Households

Nonfamily household income includes the income of the householder and all other individuals 15 years old and over in the nonfamily household. Although the household income statistics cover the past 12 months, the characteristics of individuals and the composition of households refer to the time of interview. Thus, the income of the household does not include amounts received by individuals who were members of the household during all or part of the past 12 months if these individuals no longer resided in the household at the time of interview. Similarly, income amounts reported by individuals who did not reside in the household during the past 12 months but who were members of the household at the time of interview are included. However, the composition of most households was the same during the past 12 months as at the time of interview.

INCOME OF INDIVIDUALS, Items 109–110
Source: Table B19326. Median Income in the Past 12 Months (in 2021 Inflation-Adjusted Dollars) by Sex by Work Experience in the Past 12 Months for the Population 15 Years and Over with Income
Universe: Population 15 Years and Over with Income in the Past 12 Months

Income of individuals. Income for individuals is obtained by summing the eight types of income for each person 15 years old and over. The characteristics of individuals are based on the time of interview even though the amounts are for the past 12 months.

PER CAPITA INCOME, Item 111
Source: Table B19301. Per Capita Income in the Past 12 Months (in 2021 Inflation-Adjusted Dollars)
Universe: Total Population

Per capita income is the mean income computed for every man, woman, and child in a particular group including those living in group quarters. It is derived by dividing the aggregate income of a particular group by the total population in that group. Per capita income is rounded to the nearest whole dollar.

POVERTY STATUS, Items 138–153
Sources: Table C17017. Poverty Status in the Past 12 Months by Household Type
Universe: Households

Table C17001. Poverty Status in the Past 12 Months by Sex by Age: Table C17001H, C17001B, C17001D, and C17001I. Poverty Status in the Past 12 Months by Sex by Age for specific race/Hispanic origin groups.
Universe: Population for Whom Poverty Status is Determined

The **poverty status** data were derived from data collected on the number of persons in the household, from questionnaire item 3, which provides data on each person's relationship to the householder, and items 47 and 48, the same questions used to derive the income data. The Social Security Administration (SSA) developed the original poverty definition in 1964, which federal interagency committees subsequently revised in 1969 and 1980. The Office of Management and Budget's (OMB) *Directive 14* prescribes the SSA's definition as the official poverty measure for federal agencies to use in their statistical work. Poverty statistics presented in American Community Survey products adhere to the standards defined by OMB in *Directive 14*.

The poverty thresholds vary depending on three criteria: size of family, number of children, and, for one- and two-person families, age of householder. In determining the poverty status of families and unrelated individuals, the Census Bureau uses thresholds (income cutoffs) arranged in a two-dimensional matrix. The matrix consists of family size (from one person to nine or more persons), cross-classified by presence and number of family members under 18 years old (from no children present to eight or more

children present). Unrelated individuals and two-person families are further differentiated by age of reference person (under 65 years old and 65 years old and over). To determine a person's poverty status, the person's total family income in the last 12 months is compared to the poverty threshold appropriate for that person's family size and composition. If the total income of that person's family is less than the threshold appropriate for that family, then the person is considered poor or "below the poverty level," together with every member of his or her family. If a person is not living with anyone related by birth, marriage, or adoption, then the person's own income is compared with his or her poverty threshold. The average poverty threshold for a four-person family was $26,500 in 2021.

Since ACS is a continuous survey, people respond throughout the year. Because the income questions specify a period covering the last 12 months, the appropriate poverty thresholds are determined by multiplying the base-year poverty thresholds (1982) by the average of the monthly inflation factors for the 12 months preceding the data collection.

HEALTH INSURANCE, Items 154–158
Source: Table C27010. Types of Health Insurance Coverage by Age
Universe: Civilian Non-institutionalized Population

In 2021, respondents were instructed to report their current health insurance coverage and to mark "yes" or "no" for each of the eight types listed:

a. Insurance through a current or former employer or union (of this person or another family member)
b. Insurance purchased directly from an insurance company (by this person or another family member)
c. Medicare, for people 65 and older, or people with certain disabilities
d. Medicaid, Medical Assistance, or any kind of government-assistance plan for those with low incomes or a disability
e. TRICARE or other military health care
f. VA (including those who have ever used or enrolled for VA health care)
g. Indian Health Service
h. Any other type of health insurance or health coverage plan (Respondents who answered "yes" were asked to provide their other type of coverage type in a write-in field.)

Health insurance coverage in the ACS and other Census Bureau surveys define coverage to include plans and programs that provide comprehensive health coverage. Plans that provide insurance for specific conditions or situations such as cancer and long-term care policies are not considered coverage. Likewise, other types of insurance like dental, vision, life, and disability insurance are not considered health insurance coverage.

In defining types of coverage, write-in responses were reclassified into one of the first seven types of coverage or determined not to be a coverage type. Write-in responses that referenced the coverage of a family member were edited to assign coverage based on responses from other family members. As a result, only the first seven types of health coverage are included in the four categories in this table.

An eligibility edit was applied to give Medicaid, Medicare, and TRICARE coverage to individuals based on program eligibility rules. TRICARE or other military health care was given to active-duty military personnel and their spouses and children. Medicaid or other means-tested public coverage was given to foster children, certain individuals receiving Supplementary Security Income or Public Assistance, and the spouses and children of certain Medicaid beneficiaries. Medicare coverage was given to people 65 and older who received Social Security or Medicaid benefits.

People were considered insured if they reported at least one "yes". People who had no reported health coverage, or those whose only health coverage was Indian Health Service, were considered uninsured. For reporting purposes, the Census Bureau broadly classifies health insurance coverage as private health insurance or public coverage. Private health insurance is a plan provided through an employer or union, a plan purchased by an individual from a private company, or TRICARE or other military health care. Respondents reporting a "yes" to the types listed in parts a, b, or e were considered to have private health insurance. Public health coverage includes the federal programs Medicare, Medicaid, and VA Health Care (provided through the Department of Veterans Affairs); the Children's Health Insurance Program (CHIP); and individual state health plans. Respondents reporting a "yes" to the types listed in c, d, or f were considered to have public coverage. The types of health insurance are not mutually exclusive; people may be covered by more than one at the same time.

Tables B-2, B-3, and B-4. What — Education, Employment, and Income

Table B-2 presents 12 items for the United States as a whole, each individual state and the District of Columbia, and 841 counties, county equivalents, and independent cities with a 2021 population of 65,000 or more. This table is from the 2021 1-year file, from ACS tables beginning with "B" and "C," as the supplemental estimates were not available.

Table B-3 presents 12 items for 392 Metropolitan Statistical Areas and 31 Metropolitan Divisions within the 12 largest Metropolitan Statistical Areas. This table is from the 2021 1-year file, from ACS tables beginning with "B."

Table B-4 presents 12 items for 634 cities, Census Designated Places, and the principal portions of consolidated cities with a 2021 population of 65,000 or more. This table is from the 2021 1-year file, from ACS tables beginning with "B" and "C," as the supplemental estimates were not available.

EDUCATIONAL ATTAINMENT, Items 1–3
Source: Table C15002. Sex by Educational Attainment for the Population 25 Years and Over; Table K201501. Educational Attainment for the Population 25 Years and Over.
Universe: Population 25 Years and Over

Data on **educational attainment** were derived from a question that asked respondents for the highest level of school completed or the highest degree received. Persons currently enrolled in school are instructed to report the level of the previous grade attended or the highest degree received. Persons who had passed a high school equivalency examination were considered high school graduates. Schooling received in foreign schools was to be reported as the equivalent grade or years in the regular American school system.

Specifically excluded are vocational and technical training, such as barber school training; business, trade, technical, and vocational schools; or other training for a specific trade.

High school diploma or less. This category includes persons whose highest degree was a high school diploma or its equivalent, and those who reported any level lower than a high school diploma.

Bachelor's degree or more. This category includes persons who have received bachelor's degrees, master's degrees, professional school degrees (such as law school or medical school degrees), or doctoral degrees.

EMPLOYMENT STATUS, Items 4–8
Sources: Table B23025. Employment Status for the Population 16 Years and Over;

Table K202301. Employment Status for the Population 16 Years and Over
Universe: Population 16 Years and Over

Table B23022. Sex By Work Status In The Past 12 Months By Usual Hours Worked Per Week In The Past 12 Months By Weeks Worked In The Past 12 Months For The Population 16 To 64 Years

Table K202302. Sex By Full-Time Work Status In The Past 12 Months For The Population 16 To 64 Years
Universe: Population 16 to 64 Years

Total employment includes all persons 16 years old and over who were either (1) "at work"—those who did any work at all during the reference week as paid employees, worked in either their own business or profession, worked on their own farm, or worked 15 hours or more as unpaid workers in a family farm or business; or were (2) "with a job, but not at work"—those who had a job but were not at work that week due to illness, weather, industrial dispute, vacation, or other personal reasons.

The **labor force** consists of all persons 16 years old and over who are either employed or unemployed, including those in the armed forces.

The **unemployment rate** represents the number of unemployed people as a percentage of the labor force.

Unemployment includes all persons who did not work during the survey week, made specific efforts to find a job during the previous four weeks, and were available for work during the survey week (except for temporary illness). Persons waiting to be called back to a job from which they had been laid off and those waiting to report to a new job within the next 30 days are included in unemployment figures.

Full-time, year-round includes all persons 16 to 64 years old who usually worked 35 hours or more per week for 50 to 52 weeks in the past 12 months.

INCOME AND BENEFITS, Items 9–12
Sources: Table B19013. Median Household Income in the Past 12 Months (in 2021 Inflation-Adjusted Dollars); Table K201902. Median Household Income in the Past 12 Months (in 2021 Inflation-Adjusted Dollars); B19001. Household Income in the Past 12 Months (in 2021 Inflation-Adjusted Dollars); Table K201901. Household Income in the Past 12 Months (in 2021 Inflation-Adjusted Dollars); Table C22001. Receipt Of Food Stamps/Snap In The Past 12 Months For Households; Table K202201. Receipt Of Food Stamps/Snap In The Past 12 Months By Presence Of Children Under 18 Years For Households
Universe: Households

Household income includes the income of the householder and all other individuals 15 years old and over in the household, whether or not they are related to the householder. Since many households consist of only one person, average household income is usually less than average family income. Although the household income statistics cover the past 12 months, the characteristics of individuals and the composition of households refer to the time of enumeration. Thus, the income of the household does not include amounts received by individuals who were members of the household during all or part of the past 12 months if these individuals no longer resided in the household at the time of enumeration. Similarly, income amounts reported by individuals who did not reside in the household during the past 12 months but who were members of the household at the time of enumeration are included. However, the composition of most households was the same during the past 12 months as at the time of enumeration.

Median income divides the income distribution into two equal parts, with half of all cases below the median income level and half of all cases above the median income level. For households and families, the median income is based on the distribution of the total number of households and families, including those with no income. Median income for households is computed on the basis of a standard distribution with a minimum value of less than $2,500 and a maximum value of $250,000 or more and is rounded to the nearest whole dollar.

Income in the American Community Survey is for the past 12 months as opposed to a single reference year.

Part C — WHERE

Table C-1. Where — Migration, Housing, and Transportation

Table C-1 presents 87 items for the United States as a whole and for each individual state and the District of Columbia.

PLACE OF RESIDENCE, Items 1–7
Source: Table C07204. Geographical Mobility in the Past Year for Current Residence—State, County, and Place Level in the United States
Universe: Population 1 Year and Over in the United States

Residence one year ago is used in conjunction with location of current residence to determine the extent of residential mobility of the population and the resulting redistribution of the population across the various states, metropolitan areas, and regions of the country.

Same house includes all people 1 year and over who did not move during the 1 year as well as those who had moved and returned to their residence 1 year ago.

Different house in the United States includes people who lived in the United States 1 year ago but in a different house or apartment from the one they occupied at the time of interview. These movers are then further subdivided according to the type of move. Movers within the U.S. are divided into groups according to their previous residence: **Different house, same city or town; Different house, different city, same county; Different house, different county, same state; and Different state.**

Abroad includes those whose previous residence was in a foreign country, Puerto Rico, American Samoa, Guam, the Northern Marianas, or the U.S. Virgin Islands, including members of the armed forces and their dependents.

HOME-OWNERSHIP BY RACE, HISPANIC ORIGIN, AGE OF HOUSEHOLDER, AND HOUSEHOLD TYPE, Items 8–35

Sources: Table B25003. Tenure; Table B25003H. Tenure (White alone, Not Hispanic or Latino Householder); Table B25003B. Tenure (Black or African American Alone Householder); Table B25003C. Tenure (American Indian and Alaska Native Alone Householder); Table B25003D. Tenure (Asian Alone Householder); Table B25003E. Tenure (Native Hawaiian and Other Pacific Islander Alone Householder); Table B25003I. Tenure (Hispanic or Latino Householder); Table B25007. Tenure by Age of Householder; and Table B25115. Tenure by Household Type And Presence And Age Of Own Children
Universe: Occupied Housing Units

A **housing unit** is a house, apartment, mobile home or trailer, group of rooms, or single room occupied or, if vacant, intended for occupancy as separate living quarters. Separate living quarters are those in which the occupants do not live and eat with any other person in the structure and which have direct access from the outside of the building or through a common hall. For vacant units, the criteria of separateness and direct access are applied to the intended occupants whenever possible. If that information cannot be obtained, the criteria are applied to the previous occupants.

The occupants of a housing unit may be a single family, one person living alone, two or more families living together, or any other group of related or unrelated persons who share living arrangements. Both occupied and vacant housing units are included in the housing inventory, although recreational vehicles, tents, caves, boats, railroad cars, and the like are included only if they are occupied as a person's usual place of residence.

Occupied housing units are classified as either owner occupied or renter occupied. A housing unit is classified as occupied if it is the usual place of residence of the person or group of persons living in it at the time of enumeration, or if the occupants are only temporarily absent from the residence for two months or less, that is, away on vacation or a business trip. If all the people staying in the unit at the time of the interview are staying there for two months or less, the unit is considered to be temporarily occupied and classified as "vacant."

A housing unit is **owner occupied** if the owner or co-owner lives in the unit even if it is mortgaged or not fully paid for. The owner or co-owner must live in the unit and usually is Person 1 on the questionnaire. The unit is "Owned by you or someone in this household with a mortgage or loan" if it is being purchased with a mortgage or some other debt arrangement such as a deed of trust, trust deed, contract to purchase, land contract, or purchase agreement. The unit also is considered owned with a mortgage if it is built on leased land and there is a mortgage on the unit. Mobile homes occupied by owners with installment loan balances also are included in this category.

All occupied housing units which are not owner occupied, whether they are rented for cash rent or occupied without payment of cash rent, are classified as **renter occupied.** "No cash rent" units are separately identified in the rent tabulations. Such units are generally provided free by friends or relatives or in exchange for services such as resident manager, caretaker, minister, or tenant farmer. Housing units on military bases also are classified in the "No cash rent" category. "Rented for cash rent" includes units in continuing care, sometimes called life care arrangements. These arrangements usually involve a contract between one or more individuals and a health services provider guaranteeing the individual shelter, usually a house or apartment, and services, such as meals or transportation to shopping or recreation.

HOUSEHOLD SIZE, Items 36–38
Source: Table B25010. Average Household Size of Occupied Housing Units by Tenure
Universe: Occupied Housing Units

Household size is based on the count of people in occupied housing units. All people occupying the housing unit are counted, including the householder, occupants related to the householder, and lodgers, roomers, boarders, and so forth.

Average household size of occupied units is obtained by dividing the number of people living in occupied housing units by the total number of occupied housing units. This measure is rounded to the nearest hundredth.

Average household size of owner-occupied units is obtained by dividing the number of people living in owner-occupied housing units by the total number of owner-occupied housing units. This measure is rounded to the nearest hundredth.

Average household size of renter-occupied units is obtained by dividing the number of people living in renter-occupied housing units by the total number of renter-occupied housing units. This measure is rounded to the nearest hundredth.

UNITS THAT ARE CROWDED OR LACKING COMPLETE PLUMBING, Item 39
Source: Table C25016. Tenure by Plumbing Facilities by Occupants per Room
Universe: Occupied Housing Units

Item 39 shows the percentage of housing units in the state that are **crowded** or **lacking complete plumbing facilities.**

Occupants per room is obtained by dividing the number of people in each occupied housing unit by the number of rooms in the unit. Although the Census Bureau has no official definition of **crowded** units, many users consider units with more than one occupant per room to be crowded, the measure used in this item.

The question on plumbing facilities was asked at both occupied and vacant housing units. Complete plumbing facilities include: (1) hot and cold piped water, (2) a flush toilet, and (3) a bathtub or shower. All three facilities must be located inside the house, apartment, or mobile home, but not necessarily in the same room. Housing units are classified as **lacking complete plumbing facilities** when any of the three facilities is not present.

MEDIAN HOUSEHOLD INCOME IN THE PAST 12 MONTHS, Items 40–44
Sources: Table B25119. Median Household Income the Past 12 Months (in 2021 Inflation-Adjusted Dollars) by Tenure
Universe: Occupied Housing Units

Table B25099. Mortgage Status by Median Household Income in the Past 12 Months (in 2021 Inflation-Adjusted Dollars)
Universe: Owner-Occupied Housing Units

The data on **mortgage status** were obtained from questions that were asked at owner-occupied units. The category **with a mortgage** refers to all forms of debt where the property is pledged as security for repayment of the debt, including deeds of trust; trust deeds; contracts to purchase; land contracts; junior mortgages; and home equity loans.

The category **without a mortgage** comprises housing units owned free and clear of debt.

A detailed definition of income and types of income is included above under Table B-1.

HOUSING VALUES AND COSTS, Items 45–51, 54–64
Sources: Table B25097. Mortgage Status by Median Value (Dollars); Table B25081. Mortgage Status; Table B25092. Median Selected Monthly Owner Costs as a Percentage of Household Income in the Past 12 Months; Table B25088. Median Selected Monthly Owner Costs (Dollars) by Mortgage Status; Table B25103. Mortgage Status by Median Real Estate Taxes Paid (Dollars); and Table C25093. Age of Householder by Selected Monthly Owner costs as a Percentage of Household Income in the Past 12 Months
Universe: Owner-Occupied Housing Units

Table B25105. Median Monthly Housing Costs (Dollars)
Universe: Occupied Housing Units with Monthly Housing Cost

Median value is the dollar amount that divides the distribution of specified owner-occupied housing units into two equal parts, with half of all units below the median value and half above the median value. Value is defined as the respondent's estimate of what the house would sell for if it were for sale. If the house or mobile home was owned or being bought, but the land on which it sits was not, the respondent was asked to estimate the combined value of the house or mobile home and the land. For vacant units, value was the price asked for the property. Value was tabulated separately for all owner-occupied and vacant-for-sale housing units, as well as owner-occupied and vacant-for-sale mobile homes.

Housing cost, as a percentage of income, is shown separately for owners with mortgages, owners without mortgages, and renters. Selected owner costs include utilities and fuels, mortgage payments, insurance, taxes, etc. In each case, the ratio of housing cost to income is computed separately for each housing unit. The housing cost ratios for half of all units are above the median shown in this book, and half are below the median shown in the book.

The data for monthly housing costs in item 51 are developed from a distribution of **selected monthly owner costs** for owner-occupied units and **gross rent** for renter-occupied units.

Selected monthly owner costs are the sum of payments for mortgages, deeds of trust, contracts to purchase, or similar debts on the property (including payments for the first mortgage, second mortgages, home equity loans, and other junior mortgages); real estate taxes; fire, hazard, and flood insurance on the property; utilities (electricity, gas, and water and sewer); and fuels (oil, coal, kerosene, wood, etc.). It also includes, where appropriate, the monthly condominium fee for condominiums and mobile home costs (installment loan payments, personal property taxes, site rent, registration fees, and license fees). Selected monthly owner costs were tabulated for all owner-occupied units, and usually are shown separately for units "with a mortgage" and for units "not mortgaged."

Real estate taxes include state, local, and all other real estate taxes even if delinquent, unpaid, or paid by someone who is not a member of the household. However, taxes due from prior years are not included. If taxes are paid on other than a yearly basis, the payments are converted to a yearly basis.

RENT, Items 52–53, 65–68
Sources: Table B25064. Median Gross Rent (Dollars); and Table B25071. Median Gross Rent as a Percentage of Household Income in the Past 12 Months (Dollars)
Universe: Renter-Occupied Housing Units Paying Cash Rent

Table B25072. Age of Householder by Gross Rent as a Percentage of Household Income in the Past 12 Months
Universe: Renter-Occupied Housing Units

Median gross rent divides the distribution of renter-occupied housing units into two equal parts: one-half of the cases falling below the median gross rent and one-half above the median.

Gross rent is the **contract rent** plus the estimated average monthly cost of **utilities** (electricity, gas, and water and sewer) and fuels (oil, coal, kerosene, wood, etc.) if these are paid by the renter (or paid for the renter by someone else). Gross rent is intended to eliminate differentials that result from varying practices with respect to the inclusion of utilities and fuels as part of the rental payment. The estimated costs of water and sewer, and fuels are reported on a 12-month basis but are converted to monthly figures for the tabulations. Renter units occupied without payment of cash rent are not included in the tabulations.

Gross rent as a percentage of household income is a computed ratio of monthly gross rent to monthly household income (total household income divided by 12). Median gross rent divides the gross rent as a percentage of household income distribution into two equal parts: one-half of the cases falling below the median gross rent as a percentage of household income and one-half above the median.

MEANS OF TRANSPORTATION TO WORK, ITEMS 69–76
Source: Table B08301. Means of Transportation to Work
Universe: Workers 16 Years and Over

Means of transportation to work refers to the principal mode of travel or type of conveyance that the worker usually used to get from home to work during the reference week. People who used different means of transportation on different days of the week were asked to specify the one they used most often, that is, the greatest number of days. People who used more than one means of transportation to get to work each day were asked to report the one used for the longest distance during the work trip.

The category, **car, truck, or van**, includes workers using a car (including company cars but excluding taxicabs), a truck of one-ton capacity or less, or a van. A question on vehicle occupancy was asked of people who indicated that they worked at some time during the reference week and who reported that their means of transportation to work was **car, truck, or van**. The category, **drove alone**, includes people who usually drove alone to work as well as people who were driven to work by someone who then drove back home or to a nonwork destination. The category, **carpooled**, includes workers who reported that two or more people usually rode to work in the vehicle during the reference week.

The category, **public transportation**, includes workers who used a bus or trolley bus, streetcar or trolley car, subway or elevated, railroad, or ferryboat, even if each mode is not shown separately in the tabulation. The category, "Other means," includes workers who used a mode of travel that is not identified separately within the data distribution.

MEAN TRAVEL TIME TO WORK, Items 77–81
Sources: Table C08301. Means of Transportation to Work
Universe: Workers 16 Years and Over

Table C08136. Aggregate Travel Time to Work (in Minutes) of Workers by Means of Transportation to Work
Universe: Workers 16 Years and Over Whom Did Not Work at Home

Travel time to work refers to the total number of minutes that it usually took the worker to get from home to work during the reference week. The elapsed time includes time spent waiting for public transportation, picking up passengers in carpools, and time spent in other activities related to getting to work.

Mean travel time to work (in minutes) is the average travel time that workers usually took to get from home to work (one way) during the reference week. This measure is obtained by dividing the total number of minutes taken to get from home to work (the aggregate travel time) by the number of workers 16 years old and over who did not work at home.

VEHICLES AVAILABLE, Items 83–87
Sources: Table B08201. Household Size by Vehicles Available; and Table B25046. Aggregate Number of Vehicles Available by Tenure
Universe: Occupied Housing Units

The data on vehicles available show the number of passenger cars, vans, and pickup or panel trucks of one-ton capacity or less kept at home and available for the use of household members. Vehicles rented or leased for one month or more, company vehicles, and police and government vehicles are included if kept at home and used for non-business purposes. Dismantled or immobile vehicles are excluded. Vehicles kept at home but used only for business purposes also are excluded.

Tables C-2, C-3, and C-4. Where — Migration, Housing, and Transportation

Table C-2 presents 12 items for the United States as a whole, each individual state and the District of Columbia, and 841 counties, county equivalents, and independent cities with a 2021 population of 65,000 or more. This table is from the 2021 1-year file, from ACS tables beginning with "B" and "C."

Table C-3 presents 12 items for 392 Metropolitan Statistical Areas and 31 Metropolitan Divisions within the 12 largest Metropolitan Statistical Areas. This table includes data from the 2021 1-year file, from ACS tables beginning with "B" and "C."

Table C-4 presents 12 items for 634 cities, Census Designated Places, and the principal portions of consolidated cities with a 2021 population of 65,000 or more. This table is from the 2021 1-year file, from ACS tables beginning with "B" and "C," as the supplemental estimates were not available.

PLACE OF RESIDENCE, Items 1-3
Sources: Table B07201. Geographical Mobility in the Past Year for Current Residence—Metropolitan Statistical Area Level in the United States
Universe: Population 1 year and over living in a Metropolitan Statistical Area in the United States

Table K200701. Geographical Mobility in the Past Year in the United States
Universe: Population 1 Year and Over in the United States

Residence one year ago is used in conjunction with location of current residence to determine the extent of residential mobility of the population and the resulting redistribution of the population across the various states, metropolitan areas, and regions of the country. **Same house** includes all people 1 year old and over who, a year earlier, lived in the same house or apartment that they occupied at the time of interview.

Did not live in same county one year ago includes all persons who did not live in the same county 1 year ago, whether their previous residence was in the same

metropolitan area, the same state, a different state, Puerto Rico, or abroad. Persons who moved within the county but to a new city cannot be identified as movers in Table C-4.

Did not live in same metropolitan area one year ago includes all persons who did not live in the same metropolitan area 1 year ago, whether their previous residence was in the same state, a different state, Puerto Rico, or abroad.

OCCUPIED HOUSING UNITS, Items 4-5
Source: Table B25003. Housing Tenure; Table K202502. Housing Tenure
Universe: Occupied Housing Units

A **housing unit** is a house, apartment, mobile home or trailer, group of rooms, or single room occupied or, if vacant, intended for occupancy as separate living quarters. Separate living quarters are those in which the occupants do not live and eat with any other person in the structure and which have direct access from the outside of the building or through a common hall. For vacant units, the criteria of separateness and direct access are applied to the intended occupants whenever possible. If that information cannot be obtained, the criteria are applied to the previous occupants.

The occupants of a housing unit may be a single family, one person living alone, two or more families living together, or any other group of related or unrelated persons who share living arrangements. Both occupied and vacant housing units are included in the housing inventory, although recreational vehicles, tents, caves, boats, railroad cars, and the like are included only if they are occupied as a person's usual place of residence.

Occupied housing units are classified as either owner occupied or renter occupied. A housing unit is classified as occupied if it is the usual place of residence of the person or group of persons living in it at the time of enumeration, or if the occupants are only temporarily absent from the residence for two months or less, that is, away on vacation or a business trip. If all the people staying in the unit at the time of the interview are staying there for two months or less, the unit is considered to be temporarily occupied and classified as "vacant."

A housing unit is **owner occupied** if the owner or co-owner lives in the unit even if it is mortgaged or not fully paid for. The owner or co-owner must live in the unit and usually is Person 1 on the questionnaire. The unit is "Owned by you or someone in this household with a mortgage or loan" if it is being purchased with a mortgage or some other debt arrangement such as a deed of trust, trust deed, contract to purchase, land contract, or purchase agreement. The unit also is considered owned with a mortgage if it is built on leased land and there is a mortgage on the unit. Mobile homes occupied by owners with installment loan balances also are included in this category.

All occupied housing units that are not owner occupied, whether they are rented for cash rent or occupied without payment of cash rent, are classified as **renter occupied**. "No cash rent" units are separately identified in the rent tabulations. Such units are generally provided free by friends or relatives or in exchange for services such as resident manager, caretaker, minister, or tenant farmer. Housing units on military bases also are classified in the "No cash rent" category. "Rented for cash rent" includes units in continuing care, sometimes called life care arrangements. These arrangements usually involve a contract between one or more individuals and a health services provider guaranteeing the individual shelter, usually a house or apartment, and services, such as meals or transportation to shopping or recreation.

HOUSING VALUES AND COSTS, Items 6-7
Sources: Table B25081. Mortgage Status; Table B25077. Median Value (dollars); Table K202508. Mortgage Status; Table K202510. Median Value (dollars).
Universe: Owner-Occupied Housing Units

The data on **mortgage status** were obtained from questions that were asked at owner-occupied units. The category **with a mortgage** refers to all forms of debt where the property is pledged as security for repayment of the debt, including deeds of trust; trust deeds; contracts to purchase; land contracts; junior mortgages; and home equity loans.

Housing value is defined as the respondent's estimate of what the house would sell for if it were for sale. If the house or mobile home was owned or being bought, but the land on which it sits was not, the respondent was asked to estimate the combined value of the house or mobile home and the land. For vacant units, value was the price asked for the property. Value was tabulated separately for all owner-occupied and vacant-for-sale housing units, as well as owner-occupied and vacant-for-sale mobile homes.

Median value is the dollar amount that divides the distribution of specified owner-occupied housing units into two equal parts, with half of all units below the median value and half above the median value. Value is defined as the respondent's estimate of what the house would sell for if it were for sale. If the house or mobile home was owned or being bought, but the land on which it sits was not, the respondent was asked to estimate the combined value of

the house or mobile home and the land. For vacant units, value was the price asked for the property. Value was tabulated separately for all owner-occupied and vacant-for-sale housing units, as well as owner-occupied and vacant-for-sale mobile homes.

RENT, Item 8

Table K202511. Median Gross Rent (dollars). Table B25064. Median Gross Rent (dollars)
Universe: Renter-Occupied Housing Units

Gross rent is the contract rent plus the estimated average monthly cost of utilities (electricity, gas, and water and sewer) and fuels (oil, coal, kerosene, wood, etc.) if these are paid by the renter (or paid for the renter by someone else). Gross rent is intended to eliminate differentials that result from varying practices with respect to the inclusion of utilities and fuels as part of the rental payment. The estimated costs of water and sewer, and fuels are reported on a 12-month basis but are converted to monthly figures for the tabulations. Renter units occupied without payment of cash rent are not included in the tabulations.

Median gross rent divides the distribution of renter-occupied housing units into two equal parts: one-half of the cases falling below the median gross rent and one-half above the median.

Gross rent is the **contract rent** plus the estimated average monthly cost of **utilities** (electricity, gas, and water and sewer) and fuels (oil, coal, kerosene, wood, etc.) if these are paid by the renter (or paid for the renter by someone else). Gross rent is intended to eliminate differentials that result from varying practices with respect to the inclusion of utilities and fuels as part of the rental payment. The estimated costs of water and sewer, and fuels are reported on a 12-month basis but are converted to monthly figures for the tabulations. Renter units occupied without payment of cash rent are not included in the tabulations.

INTERNET ACCESS, Item 9
Source: Table K202801. Presence Of A Computer And Type Of internet Subscription In Household; B28003. Presence Of A Computer And Type Of internet Subscription In Household.
Universe: Households

The computer use question asked if anyone in the household owned or used a computer and included three response categories for a desktop/laptop, a handheld computer, or some other type of computer. The Category

Households with Internet Access includes housing units where someone pays to access the internet through a service such as a data plan for a mobile phone, a cable modem, DSL or other type of service. This will normally refer to a service that someone is billed for directly for internet alone or sometimes as part of a bundle. Not included in this category are those respondents who may live in a city or town that provides free internet services for their residents, or attend a university that provides internet services. These persons may be able to access the internet without a subscription, but are not included in the total in Item 9.

TRAVEL TIME TO WORK, Items 10-12
Sources: Table K200802. Travel Time to Work; B08303. Travel Time to Work.
Universe: Workers 16 Years and Over Who Did Not Work at Home

Travel time to work refers to the total number of minutes that it usually took the worker to get from home to work during the reference week. The elapsed time includes time spent waiting for public transportation, picking up passengers in carpools, and time spent in other activities related to getting to work.

Core based statistical area	State/ County FIPS code	Title and Geographic Components	2010 Census Population
CBSA	FIPS	AREANAME	C0021
10180		Abilene, TX	165252
10180	48059	Callahan County	13544
10180	48253	Jones County	20202
10180	48441	Taylor County	131506
10420		Akron, OH	703200
10420	39133	Portage County	161419
10420	39153	Summit County	541781
10500		Albany, GA	157308
10500	13007	Baker County	3451
10500	13095	Dougherty County	94565
10500	13177	Lee County	28298
10500	13273	Terrell County	9315
10500	13321	Worth County	21679
10540		Albany, OR	116672
10540	41043	Linn County	116672
10580		Albany-Schenectady-Troy, NY	870716
10580	36001	Albany County	304204
10580	36083	Rensselaer County	159429
10580	36091	Saratoga County	219607
10580	36093	Schenectady County	154727
10580	36095	Schoharie County	32749
10740		Albuquerque, NM	887077
10740	35001	Bernalillo County	662564
10740	35043	Sandoval County	131561
10740	35057	Torrance County	16383
10740	35061	Valencia County	76569
10780		Alexandria, LA	153922
10780	22043	Grant Parish	22309
10780	22079	Rapides Parish	131613
10900		Allentown-Bethlehem-Easton, PA-NJ	821173
10900	34041	Warren County	108692
10900	42025	Carbon County	65249
10900	42077	Lehigh County	349497
10900	42095	Northampton County	297735
11020		Altoona, PA	127089
11020	42013	Blair County	127089
11100		Amarillo, TX	251933
11100	48011	Armstrong County	1901
11100	48065	Carson County	6182
11100	48359	Oldham County	2052
11100	48375	Potter County	121073
11100	48381	Randall County	120725
11180		Ames, IA	89542
11180	19169	Story County	89542
11260		Anchorage, AK	380821
11260	02020	Anchorage Municipality	291826
11260	02170	Matanuska-Susitna Borough	88995
11460		Ann Arbor, MI	344791
11460	26161	Washtenaw County	344791
11500		Anniston-Oxford-Jacksonville, AL	118572
11500	01015	Calhoun County	118572
11540		Appleton, WI	225666
11540	55015	Calumet County	48971
11540	55087	Outagamie County	176695
11700		Asheville, NC	424858
11700	37021	Buncombe County	238318
11700	37087	Haywood County	59036
11700	37089	Henderson County	106740
11700	37115	Madison County	20764
12020		Athens-Clarke County, GA	192541
12020	13059	Clarke County	116714
12020	13195	Madison County	28120
12020	13219	Oconee County	32808
12020	13221	Oglethorpe County	14899
12060		Atlanta-Sandy Springs-Roswell, GA	5286728
12060	13013	Barrow County	69367
12060	13015	Bartow County	100157
12060	13035	Butts County	23655
12060	13045	Carroll County	110527
12060	13057	Cherokee County	214346
12060	13063	Clayton County	259424
12060	13067	Cobb County	688078
12060	13077	Coweta County	127317
12060	13085	Dawson County	22330
12060	13089	DeKalb County	691893
12060	13097	Douglas County	132403
12060	13113	Fayette County	106567
12060	13117	Forsyth County	175511
12060	13121	Fulton County	920581
12060	13135	Gwinnett County	805321
12060	13143	Haralson County	28780
12060	13149	Heard County	11834
12060	13151	Henry County	203922
12060	13159	Jasper County	13900
12060	13171	Lamar County	18317
12060	13199	Meriwether County	21992
12060	13211	Morgan County	17868
12060	13217	Newton County	99958
12060	13223	Paulding County	142324
12060	13227	Pickens County	29431
12060	13231	Pike County	17869
12060	13247	Rockdale County	85215
12060	13255	Spalding County	64073
12060	13297	Walton County	83768
12100		Atlantic City-Hammonton, NJ	274549
12100	34001	Atlantic County	274549
12220		Auburn-Opelika, AL	140247
12220	01081	Lee County	140247
12260		Augusta-Richmond County, GA-SC	564873
12260	13033	Burke County	23316
12260	13073	Columbia County	124053
12260	13181	Lincoln County	7996
12260	13189	McDuffie County	21875
12260	13245	Richmond County	200549
12260	45003	Aiken County	160099
12260	45037	Edgefield County	26985
12420		Austin-Round Rock, TX	1716289
12420	48021	Bastrop County	74171
12420	48055	Caldwell County	38066
12420	48209	Hays County	157107
12420	48453	Travis County	1024266
12420	48491	Williamson County	422679
12540		Bakersfield, CA	839631
12540	06029	Kern County	839631
12580		Baltimore-Columbia-Towson, MD	2710489
12580	24003	Anne Arundel County	537656
12580	24005	Baltimore County	805029
12580	24013	Carroll County	167134
12580	24025	Harford County	244826
12580	24027	Howard County	287085

Core based statistical area	State/County FIPS code	Title and Geographic Components	2010 Census Population	Core based statistical area	State/County FIPS code	Title and Geographic Components	2010 Census Population
12580	24035	Queen Anne's County	47798	14260	16073	Owyhee County	11526
12580	24510	Baltimore city	620961	14460		Boston-Cambridge-Newton, MA-NH	4552402
12620		Bangor, ME	153923	14460		Boston, MA Div 14454	1887792
12620	23019	Penobscot County	153923	14460	25021	Norfolk County	670850
12700		Barnstable Town, MA	215888	14460	25023	Plymouth County	494919
12700	25001	Barnstable County	215888	14460	25025	Suffolk County	722023
12940		Baton Rouge, LA	802484	14460		Cambridge-Newton-Framingham, MA Div 15764	2246244
12940	22005	Ascension Parish	107215				
12940	22033	East Baton Rouge Parish	440171	14460	25009	Essex County	743159
12940	22037	East Feliciana Parish	20267	14460	25017	Middlesex County	1503085
12940	22047	Iberville Parish	33387	14460		Rockingham County-Strafford County, NH Div 40484	418366
12940	22063	Livingston Parish	128026				
12940	22077	Pointe Coupee Parish	22802	14460	33015	Rockingham County	295223
12940	22091	St. Helena Parish	11203	14460	33017	Strafford County	123143
12940	22121	West Baton Rouge Parish	23788	14500		Boulder, CO	294567
12940	22125	West Feliciana Parish	15625	14500	08013	Boulder County	294567
12980		Battle Creek, MI	136146	14540		Bowling Green, KY	158599
12980	26025	Calhoun County	136146	14540	21003	Allen County	19956
13020		Bay City, MI	107771	14540	21031	Butler County	12690
13020	26017	Bay County	107771	14540	21061	Edmonson County	12161
13140		Beaumont-Port Arthur, TX	403190	14540	21227	Warren County	113792
13140	48199	Hardin County	54635	14740		Bremerton-Silverdale, WA	251133
13140	48245	Jefferson County	252273	14740	53035	Kitsap County	251133
13140	48351	Newton County	14445	14860		Bridgeport-Stamford-Norwalk, CT	916829
13140	48361	Orange County	81837	14860	09001	Fairfield County	916829
13220		Beckley, WV	124898	15180		Brownsville-Harlingen, TX	406220
13220	54019	Fayette County	46039	15180	48061	Cameron County	406220
13220	54081	Raleigh County	78859	15260		Brunswick, GA	112370
13380		Bellingham, WA	201140	15260	13025	Brantley County	18411
13380	53073	Whatcom County	201140	15260	13127	Glynn County	79626
13460		Bend-Redmond, OR	157733	15260	13191	McIntosh County	14333
13460	41017	Deschutes County	157733	15380		Buffalo-Cheektowaga-Niagara Falls, NY	1135509
13740		Billings, MT	158934	15380	36029	Erie County	919040
13740	30009	Carbon County	10078	15380	36063	Niagara County	216469
13740	30037	Golden Valley County	884	15500		Burlington, NC	151131
13740	30111	Yellowstone County	147972	15500	37001	Alamance County	151131
13780		Binghamton, NY	251725	15540		Burlington-South Burlington, VT	211261
13780	36007	Broome County	200600	15540	50007	Chittenden County	156545
13780	36107	Tioga County	51125	15540	50011	Franklin County	47746
13820		Birmingham-Hoover, AL	1128047	15540	50013	Grand Isle County	6970
13820	01007	Bibb County	22915	15680		California-Lexington Park, MD	105151
13820	01009	Blount County	57322	15680	24037	St. Mary's County	105151
13820	01021	Chilton County	43643	15940		Canton-Massillon, OH	404422
13820	01073	Jefferson County	658466	15940	39019	Carroll County	28836
13820	01115	St. Clair County	83593	15940	39151	Stark County	375586
13820	01117	Shelby County	195085	15980		Cape Coral-Fort Myers, FL	618754
13820	01127	Walker County	67023	15980	12071	Lee County	618754
13900		Bismarck, ND	114778	16020		Cape Girardeau, MO-IL	96275
13900	38015	Burleigh County	81308	16020	17003	Alexander County	8238
13900	38059	Morton County	27471	16020	29017	Bollinger County	12363
13900	38065	Oliver County	1846	16020	29031	Cape Girardeau County	75674
13900	38085	Sioux County	4153	16060		Carbondale-Marion, IL	126575
13980		Blacksburg-Christiansburg-Radford, VA	178237	16060	17077	Jackson County	60218
13980	51063	Floyd County	15279	16060	17199	Williamson County	66357
13980	51071	Giles County	17286	16180		Carson City, NV	55274
13980	51121	Montgomery County	94392	16180	32510	Carson City	55274
13980	51155	Pulaski County	34872	16220		Casper, WY	75450
13980	51750	Radford city	16408	16220	56025	Natrona County	75450
14010		Bloomington, IL	186133	16300		Cedar Rapids, IA	257940
14010	17039	De Witt County	16561	16300	19011	Benton County	26076
14010	17113	McLean County	169572	16300	19105	Jones County	20638
14020		Bloomington, IN	159549	16300	19113	Linn County	211226
14020	18105	Monroe County	137974	16540		Chambersburg-Waynesboro, PA	149618
14020	18119	Owen County	21575	16540	42055	Franklin County	149618
14100		Bloomsburg-Berwick, PA	85562	16580		Champaign-Urbana, IL	231891
14100	42037	Columbia County	67295	16580	17019	Champaign County	201081
14100	42093	Montour County	18267	16580	17053	Ford County	14081
14260		Boise City, ID	616561	16580	17147	Piatt County	16729
14260	16001	Ada County	392365	16620		Charleston, WV	227078
14260	16015	Boise County	7028	16620	54005	Boone County	24629
14260	16027	Canyon County	188923	16620	54015	Clay County	9386
14260	16045	Gem County	16719	16620	54039	Kanawha County	193063

Core based statistical area	State/ County FIPS code	Title and Geographic Components	2010 Census Population
16700		Charleston-North Charleston, SC	664607
16700	45015	Berkeley County	177843
16700	45019	Charleston County	350209
16700	45035	Dorchester County	136555
16740		Charlotte-Concord-Gastonia, NC-SC	2217012
16740	37025	Cabarrus County	178011
16740	37071	Gaston County	206086
16740	37097	Iredell County	159437
16740	37109	Lincoln County	78265
16740	37119	Mecklenburg County	919628
16740	37159	Rowan County	138428
16740	37179	Union County	201292
16740	45023	Chester County	33140
16740	45057	Lancaster County	76652
16740	45091	York County	226073
16820		Charlottesville, VA	218705
16820	51003	Albemarle County	98970
16820	51029	Buckingham County	17146
16820	51065	Fluvanna County	25691
16820	51079	Greene County	18403
16820	51125	Nelson County	15020
16820	51540	Charlottesville city	43475
16860		Chattanooga, TN-GA	528143
16860	13047	Catoosa County	63942
16860	13083	Dade County	16633
16860	13295	Walker County	68756
16860	47065	Hamilton County	336463
16860	47115	Marion County	28237
16860	47153	Sequatchie County	14112
16940		Cheyenne, WY	91738
16940	56021	Laramie County	91738
16980		Chicago-Naperville-Elgin, IL-IN-WI	9461105
16980		Chicago-Naperville-Arlington Heights, IL Div 16974	7262718
16980	17031	Cook County	5194675
16980	17043	DuPage County	916924
16980	17063	Grundy County	50063
16980	17093	Kendall County	114736
16980	17111	McHenry County	308760
16980	17197	Will County	677560
16980		Elgin, IL Div 20994	620429
16980	17037	DeKalb County	105160
16980	17089	Kane County	515269
16980		Gary, IN Div 23844	708070
16980	18073	Jasper County	33478
16980	18089	Lake County	496005
16980	18111	Newton County	14244
16980	18127	Porter County	164343
16980		Lake County-Kenosha County, IL-WI Div 29404	869888
16980	17097	Lake County	703462
16980	55059	Kenosha County	166426
17020		Chico, CA	220000
17020	06007	Butte County	220000
17140		Cincinnati, OH-KY-IN	2114580
17140	18029	Dearborn County	50047
17140	18115	Ohio County	6128
17140	18161	Union County	7516
17140	21015	Boone County	118811
17140	21023	Bracken County	8488
17140	21037	Campbell County	90336
17140	21077	Gallatin County	8589
17140	21081	Grant County	24662
17140	21117	Kenton County	159720
17140	21191	Pendleton County	14877
17140	39015	Brown County	44846
17140	39017	Butler County	368130
17140	39025	Clermont County	197363
17140	39061	Hamilton County	802374
17140	39165	Warren County	212693
17300		Clarksville, TN-KY	260625
17300	21047	Christian County	73955
17300	21221	Trigg County	14339
17300	47125	Montgomery County	172331
17420		Cleveland, TN	115788
17420	47011	Bradley County	98963
17420	47139	Polk County	16825
17460		Cleveland-Elyria, OH	2077240
17460	39035	Cuyahoga County	1280122
17460	39055	Geauga County	93389
17460	39085	Lake County	230041
17460	39093	Lorain County	301356
17460	39103	Medina County	172332
17660		Coeur d'Alene, ID	138494
17660	16055	Kootenai County	138494
17780		College Station-Bryan, TX	228660
17780	48041	Brazos County	194851
17780	48051	Burleson County	17187
17780	48395	Robertson County	16622
17820		Colorado Springs, CO	645613
17820	08041	El Paso County	622263
17820	08119	Teller County	23350
17860		Columbia, MO	162642
17860	29019	Boone County	162642
17900		Columbia, SC	767598
17900	45017	Calhoun County	15175
17900	45039	Fairfield County	23956
17900	45055	Kershaw County	61697
17900	45063	Lexington County	262391
17900	45079	Richland County	384504
17900	45081	Saluda County	19875
17980		Columbus, GA-AL	294865
17980	01113	Russell County	52947
17980	13053	Chattahoochee County	11267
17980	13145	Harris County	32024
17980	13197	Marion County	8742
17980	13215	Muscogee County	189885
18020		Columbus, IN	76794
18020	18005	Bartholomew County	76794
18140		Columbus, OH	1901974
18140	39041	Delaware County	174214
18140	39045	Fairfield County	146156
18140	39049	Franklin County	1163414
18140	39073	Hocking County	29380
18140	39089	Licking County	166492
18140	39097	Madison County	43435
18140	39117	Morrow County	34827
18140	39127	Perry County	36058
18140	39129	Pickaway County	55698
18140	39159	Union County	52300
18580		Corpus Christi, TX	428185
18580	48007	Aransas County	23158
18580	48355	Nueces County	340223
18580	48409	San Patricio County	64804
18700		Corvallis, OR	85579
18700	41003	Benton County	85579
18880		Crestview-Fort Walton Beach-Destin, FL	235865
18880	12091	Okaloosa County	180822
18880	12131	Walton County	55043
19060		Cumberland, MD-WV	103299
19060	24001	Allegany County	75087
19060	54057	Mineral County	28212
19100		Dallas-Fort Worth-Arlington, TX	6426214
19100		Dallas-Plano-Irving, TX Div 19124	4230520
19100	48085	Collin County	782341
19100	48113	Dallas County	2368139
19100	48121	Denton County	662614
19100	48139	Ellis County	149610
19100	48231	Hunt County	86129
19100	48257	Kaufman County	103350
19100	48397	Rockwall County	78337
19100		Fort Worth-Arlington, TX Div 23104	2195694
19100	48221	Hood County	51182
19100	48251	Johnson County	150934

Core based statistical area	State/ County FIPS code	Title and Geographic Components	2010 Census Population	Core based statistical area	State/ County FIPS code	Title and Geographic Components	2010 Census Population
19100	48367	Parker County	116927	20700	42089	Monroe County	169842
19100	48425	Somervell County	8490	20740		Eau Claire, WI	161151
19100	48439	Tarrant County	1809034	20740	55017	Chippewa County	62415
19100	48497	Wise County	59127	20740	55035	Eau Claire County	98736
19140		Dalton, GA	142227	20940		El Centro, CA	174528
19140	13213	Murray County	39628	20940	06025	Imperial County	174528
19140	13313	Whitfield County	102599	21060		Elizabethtown-Fort Knox, KY	148338
19180		Danville, IL	81625	21060	21093	Hardin County	105543
19180	17183	Vermilion County	81625	21060	21123	Larue County	14193
19300		Daphne-Fairhope-Foley, AL	182265	21060	21163	Meade County	28602
19300	01003	Baldwin County	182265	21140		Elkhart-Goshen, IN	197559
19340		Davenport-Moline-Rock Island, IA-IL	379690	21140	18039	Elkhart County	197559
19340	17073	Henry County	50486	21300		Elmira, NY	88830
19340	17131	Mercer County	16434	21300	36015	Chemung County	88830
19340	17161	Rock Island County	147546	21340		El Paso, TX	804123
19340	19163	Scott County	165224	21340	48141	El Paso County	800647
19380		Dayton, OH	799232	21340	48229	Hudspeth County	3476
19380	39057	Greene County	161573	21420		Enid, OK	60580
19380	39109	Miami County	102506	21420	40047	Garfield County	60580
19380	39113	Montgomery County	535153	21500		Erie, PA	280566
19460		Decatur, AL	153829	21500	42049	Erie County	280566
19460	01079	Lawrence County	34339	21660		Eugene, OR	351715
19460	01103	Morgan County	119490	21660	41039	Lane County	351715
19500		Decatur, IL	110768	21780		Evansville, IN-KY	311552
19500	17115	Macon County	110768	21780	18129	Posey County	25910
19660		Deltona-Daytona Beach-Ormond Beach, FL	590289	21780	18163	Vanderburgh County	179703
19660	12035	Flagler County	95696	21780	18173	Warrick County	59689
19660	12127	Volusia County	494593	21780	21101	Henderson County	46250
19740		Denver-Aurora-Lakewood, CO	2543482	21820		Fairbanks, AK	97581
19740	08001	Adams County	441603	21820	02090	Fairbanks North Star Borough	97581
19740	08005	Arapahoe County	572003	22020		Fargo, ND-MN	208777
19740	08014	Broomfield County	55889	22020	27027	Clay County	58999
19740	08019	Clear Creek County	9088	22020	38017	Cass County	149778
19740	08031	Denver County	600158	22140		Farmington, NM	130044
19740	08035	Douglas County	285465	22140	35045	San Juan County	130044
19740	08039	Elbert County	23086	22180		Fayetteville, NC	366383
19740	08047	Gilpin County	5441	22180	37051	Cumberland County	319431
19740	08059	Jefferson County	534543	22180	37093	Hoke County	46952
19740	08093	Park County	16206	22220		Fayetteville-Springdale-Rogers, AR-MO	463204
19780		Des Moines-West Des Moines, IA	569633	22220	05007	Benton County	221339
19780	19049	Dallas County	66135	22220	05087	Madison County	15717
19780	19077	Guthrie County	10954	22220	05143	Washington County	203065
19780	19121	Madison County	15679	22220	29119	McDonald County	23083
19780	19153	Polk County	430640	22380		Flagstaff, AZ	134421
19780	19181	Warren County	46225	22380	04005	Coconino County	134421
19820		Detroit-Warren-Dearborn, MI	4296250	22420		Flint, MI	425790
19820		Detroit-Dearborn-Livonia, MI Div 19804	1820584	22420	26049	Genesee County	425790
19820	26163	Wayne County	1820584	22500		Florence, SC	205566
19820		Warren-Troy-Farmington Hills, MI 47664	2475666	22500	45031	Darlington County	68681
19820	26087	Lapeer County	88319	22500	45041	Florence County	136885
19820	26093	Livingston County	180967	22520		Florence-Muscle Shoals, AL	147137
19820	26099	Macomb County	840978	22520	01033	Colbert County	54428
19820	26125	Oakland County	1202362	22520	01077	Lauderdale County	92709
19820	26147	St. Clair County	163040	22540		Fond du Lac, WI	101633
20020		Dothan, AL	145639	22540	55039	Fond du Lac County	101633
20020	01061	Geneva County	26790	22660		Fort Collins, CO	299630
20020	01067	Henry County	17302	22660	08069	Larimer County	299630
20020	01069	Houston County	101547	22900		Fort Smith, AR-OK	280467
20100		Dover, DE	162310	22900	05033	Crawford County	61948
20100	10001	Kent County	162310	22900	05131	Sebastian County	125744
20220		Dubuque, IA	93653	22900	40079	Le Flore County	50384
20220	19061	Dubuque County	93653	22900	40135	Sequoyah County	42391
20260		Duluth, MN-WI	279771	23060		Fort Wayne, IN	416257
20260	27017	Carlton County	35386	23060	18003	Allen County	355329
20260	27137	St. Louis County	200226	23060	18179	Wells County	27636
20260	55031	Douglas County	44159	23060	18183	Whitley County	33292
20500		Durham-Chapel Hill, NC	504357	23420		Fresno, CA	930450
20500	37037	Chatham County	63505	23420	06019	Fresno County	930450
20500	37063	Durham County	267587	23460		Gadsden, AL	104430
20500	37135	Orange County	133801	23460	01055	Etowah County	104430
20500	37145	Person County	39464	23540		Gainesville, FL	264275
20700		East Stroudsburg, PA	169842	23540	12001	Alachua County	247336

Core based statistical area	State/County FIPS code	Title and Geographic Components	2010 Census Population
23540	12041	Gilchrist County	16939
23580		Gainesville, GA	179684
23580	13139	Hall County	179684
23900		Gettysburg, PA	101407
23900	42001	Adams County	101407
24020		Glens Falls, NY	128923
24020	36113	Warren County	65707
24020	36115	Washington County	63216
24140		Goldsboro, NC	122623
24140	37191	Wayne County	122623
24220		Grand Forks, ND-MN	98461
24220	27119	Polk County	31600
24220	38035	Grand Forks County	66861
24260		Grand Island, NE	81850
24260	31079	Hall County	58607
24260	31081	Hamilton County	9124
24260	31093	Howard County	6274
24260	31121	Merrick County	7845
24300		Grand Junction, CO	146723
24300	08077	Mesa County	146723
24340		Grand Rapids-Wyoming, MI	988938
24340	26015	Barry County	59173
24340	26081	Kent County	602622
24340	26117	Montcalm County	63342
24340	26139	Ottawa County	263801
24420		Grants Pass, OR	82713
24420	41033	Josephine County	82713
24500		Great Falls, MT	81327
24500	30013	Cascade County	81327
24540		Greeley, CO	252825
24540	08123	Weld County	252825
24580		Green Bay, WI	306241
24580	55009	Brown County	248007
24580	55061	Kewaunee County	20574
24580	55083	Oconto County	37660
24660		Greensboro-High Point, NC	723801
24660	37081	Guilford County	488406
24660	37151	Randolph County	141752
24660	37157	Rockingham County	93643
24780		Greenville, NC	168148
24780	37147	Pitt County	168148
24860		Greenville-Anderson-Mauldin, SC	824112
24860	45007	Anderson County	187126
24860	45045	Greenville County	451225
24860	45059	Laurens County	66537
24860	45077	Pickens County	119224
25060		Gulfport-Biloxi-Pascagoula, MS	370702
25060	28045	Hancock County	43929
25060	28047	Harrison County	187105
25060	28059	Jackson County	139668
25180		Hagerstown-Martinsburg, MD-WV	251599
25180	24043	Washington County	147430
25180	54003	Berkeley County	104169
25220		Hammond, LA	121097
25220	22105	Tangipahoa Parish	121097
25260		Hanford-Corcoran, CA	152982
25260	06031	Kings County	152982
25420		Harrisburg-Carlisle, PA	549475
25420	42041	Cumberland County	235406
25420	42043	Dauphin County	268100
25420	42099	Perry County	45969
25500		Harrisonburg, VA	125228
25500	51165	Rockingham County	76314
25500	51660	Harrisonburg city	48914
25540		Hartford-West Hartford-East Hartford, CT	1212381
25540	09003	Hartford County	894014
25540	09007	Middlesex County	165676
25540	09013	Tolland County	152691
25620		Hattiesburg, MS	142842
25620	28035	Forrest County	74934
25620	28073	Lamar County	55658
25620	28111	Perry County	12250
25860		Hickory-Lenoir-Morganton, NC	365497
25860	37003	Alexander County	37198
25860	37023	Burke County	90912
25860	37027	Caldwell County	83029
25860	37035	Catawba County	154358
25940		Hilton Head Island-Bluffton-Beaufort, NC	187010
25940	45013	Beaufort County	162233
25940	45053	Jasper County	24777
25980		Hinesville, GA	77917
25980	13179	Liberty County	63453
25980	13183	Long County	14464
26140		Homosassa Springs, FL	141236
26140	12017	Citrus County	141236
26300		Hot Springs, AR	96024
26300	05051	Garland County	96024
26380		Houma-Thibodaux, LA	208178
26380	22057	Lafourche Parish	96318
26380	22109	Terrebonne Parish	111860
26420		Houston-The Woodlands-Sugar Land, TX	5920416
26420	48015	Austin County	28417
26420	48039	Brazoria County	313166
26420	48071	Chambers County	35096
26420	48157	Fort Bend County	585375
26420	48167	Galveston County	291309
26420	48201	Harris County	4092459
26420	48291	Liberty County	75643
26420	48339	Montgomery County	455746
26420	48473	Waller County	43205
26580		Huntington-Ashland, WV-KY-OH	364908
26580	21019	Boyd County	49542
26580	21089	Greenup County	36910
26580	39087	Lawrence County	62450
26580	54011	Cabell County	96319
26580	54043	Lincoln County	21720
26580	54079	Putnam County	55486
26580	54099	Wayne County	42481
26620		Huntsville, AL	417593
26620	01083	Limestone County	82782
26620	01089	Madison County	334811
26820		Idaho Falls, ID	133265
26820	16019	Bonneville County	104234
26820	16023	Butte County	2891
26820	16051	Jefferson County	26140
26900		Indianapolis-Carmel-Anderson, IN	1887877
26900	18011	Boone County	56640
26900	18013	Brown County	15242
26900	18057	Hamilton County	274569
26900	18059	Hancock County	70002
26900	18063	Hendricks County	145448
26900	18081	Johnson County	139654
26900	18095	Madison County	131636
26900	18097	Marion County	903393
26900	18109	Morgan County	68894
26900	18133	Putnam County	37963
26900	18145	Shelby County	44436
26980		Iowa City, IA	152586
26980	19103	Johnson County	130882
26980	19183	Washington County	21704
27060		Ithaca, NY	101564
27060	36109	Tompkins County	101564
27100		Jackson, MI	160248
27100	26075	Jackson County	160248
27140		Jackson, MS	567122
27140	28029	Copiah County	29449
27140	28049	Hinds County	245285
27140	28089	Madison County	95203
27140	28121	Rankin County	141617
27140	28127	Simpson County	27503
27140	28163	Yazoo County	28065
27180		Jackson, TN	130011
27180	47023	Chester County	17131
27180	47033	Crockett County	14586

Core based statistical area	State/County FIPS code	Title and Geographic Components	2010 Census Population	Core based statistical area	State/County FIPS code	Title and Geographic Components	2010 Census Population
27180	47113	Madison County	98294	28940	47105	Loudon County	48556
27260		Jacksonville, FL	1345596	28940	47129	Morgan County	21987
27260	12003	Baker County	27115	28940	47145	Roane County	54181
27260	12019	Clay County	190865	28940	47173	Union County	19109
27260	12031	Duval County	864263	29020		Kokomo, IN	82752
27260	12089	Nassau County	73314	29020	18067	Howard County	82752
27260	12109	St. Johns County	190039	29100		La Crosse-Onalaska, WI-MN	133665
27340		Jacksonville, NC	177772	29100	27055	Houston County	19027
27340	37133	Onslow County	177772	29100	55063	La Crosse County	114638
27500		Janesville-Beloit, WI	160331	29180		Lafayette, LA	466750
27500	55105	Rock County	160331	29180	22001	Acadia Parish	61773
27620		Jefferson City, MO	149807	29180	22045	Iberia Parish	73240
27620	29027	Callaway County	44332	29180	22055	Lafayette Parish	221578
27620	29051	Cole County	75990	29180	22099	St. Martin Parish	52160
27620	29135	Moniteau County	15607	29180	22113	Vermilion Parish	57999
27620	29151	Osage County	13878	29200		Lafayette-West Lafayette, IN	201789
27740		Johnson City, TN	198716	29200	18007	Benton County	8854
27740	47019	Carter County	57424	29200	18015	Carroll County	20155
27740	47171	Unicoi County	18313	29200	18157	Tippecanoe County	172780
27740	47179	Washington County	122979	29340		Lake Charles, LA	199607
27780		Johnstown, PA	143679	29340	22019	Calcasieu Parish	192768
27780	42021	Cambria County	143679	29340	22023	Cameron Parish	6839
27860		Jonesboro, AR	121026	29420		Lake Havasu City-Kingman, AZ	200186
27860	05031	Craighead County	96443	29420	04015	Mohave County	200186
27860	05111	Poinsett County	24583	29460		Lakeland-Winter Haven, FL	602095
27900		Joplin, MO	175518	29460	12105	Polk County	602095
27900	29097	Jasper County	117404	29540		Lancaster, PA	519445
27900	29145	Newton County	58114	29540	42071	Lancaster County	519445
27980		Kahului-Wailuku-Lahaina, HI	154924	29620		Lansing-East Lansing, MI	464036
27980	15005	Kalawao County	90	29620	26037	Clinton County	75382
27980	15009	Maui County	154834	29620	26045	Eaton County	107759
28020		Kalamazoo-Portage, MI	326589	29620	26065	Ingham County	280895
28020	26077	Kalamazoo County	250331	29700		Laredo, TX	250304
28020	26159	Van Buren County	76258	29700	48479	Webb County	250304
28100		Kankakee, IL	113449	29740		Las Cruces, NM	209233
28100	17091	Kankakee County	113449	29740	35013	Dona Ana County	209233
28140		Kansas City, MO-KS	2009342	29820		Las Vegas-Henderson-Paradise, NV	1951269
28140	20091	Johnson County	544179	29820	32003	Clark County	1951269
28140	20103	Leavenworth County	76227	29940		Lawrence, KS	110826
28140	20107	Linn County	9656	29940	20045	Douglas County	110826
28140	20121	Miami County	32787	30020		Lawton, OK	130291
28140	20209	Wyandotte County	157505	30020	40031	Comanche County	124098
28140	29013	Bates County	17049	30020	40033	Cotton County	6193
28140	29025	Caldwell County	9424	30140		Lebanon, PA	133568
28140	29037	Cass County	99478	30140	42075	Lebanon County	133568
28140	29047	Clay County	221939	30300		Lewiston, ID-WA	60888
28140	29049	Clinton County	20743	30300	16069	Nez Perce County	39265
28140	29095	Jackson County	674158	30300	53003	Asotin County	21623
28140	29107	Lafayette County	33381	30340		Lewiston-Auburn, ME	107702
28140	29165	Platte County	89322	30340	23001	Androscoggin County	107702
28140	29177	Ray County	23494	30460		Lexington-Fayette, KY	472099
28420		Kennewick-Richland, WA	253340	30460	21017	Bourbon County	19985
28420	53005	Benton County	175177	30460	21049	Clark County	35613
28420	53021	Franklin County	78163	30460	21067	Fayette County	295803
28660		Killeen-Temple, TX	405300	30460	21113	Jessamine County	48586
28660	48027	Bell County	310235	30460	21209	Scott County	47173
28660	48099	Coryell County	75388	30460	21239	Woodford County	24939
28660	48281	Lampasas County	19677	30620		Lima, OH	106331
28700		Kingsport-Bristol-Bristol, TN-VA	309544	30620	39003	Allen County	106331
28700	47073	Hawkins County	56833	30700		Lincoln, NE	302157
28700	47163	Sullivan County	156823	30700	31109	Lancaster County	285407
28700	51169	Scott County	23177	30700	31159	Seward County	16750
28700	51191	Washington County	54876	30780		Little Rock-North Little Rock-Conway, AR	699757
28700	51520	Bristol city	17835	30780	05045	Faulkner County	113237
28740		Kingston, NY	182493	30780	05053	Grant County	17853
28740	36111	Ulster County	182493	30780	05085	Lonoke County	68356
28940		Knoxville, TN	837571	30780	05105	Perry County	10445
28940	47001	Anderson County	75129	30780	05119	Pulaski County	382748
28940	47009	Blount County	123010	30780	05125	Saline County	107118
28940	47013	Campbell County	40716	30860		Logan, UT-ID	125442
28940	47057	Grainger County	22657	30860	16041	Franklin County	12786
28940	47093	Knox County	432226	30860	49005	Cache County	112656

Appendix C: Metropolitan Statistical Areas, Metropolitan Divisions, and Components (as defined July 2015)—*Continued*

Core based statistical area	State/County FIPS code	Title and Geographic Components	2010 Census Population
30980		Longview, TX	214369
30980	48183	Gregg County	121730
30980	48401	Rusk County	53330
30980	48459	Upshur County	39309
31020		Longview, WA	102410
31020	53015	Cowlitz County	102410
31080		Los Angeles-Long Beach-Anaheim, CA	12828837
31080		Anaheim-Santa Ana-Irvine, CA Div 11244	3010232
31080	06059	Orange County	3010232
31080		Los Angeles-Long Beach-Glendale, CA Div 31084	9818605
31080	06037	Los Angeles County	9818605
31140		Louisville/Jefferson County, KY-IN	1235708
31140	18019	Clark County	110232
31140	18043	Floyd County	74578
31140	18061	Harrison County	39364
31140	18143	Scott County	24181
31140	18175	Washington County	28262
31140	21029	Bullitt County	74319
31140	21103	Henry County	15416
31140	21111	Jefferson County	741096
31140	21185	Oldham County	60316
31140	21211	Shelby County	42074
31140	21215	Spencer County	17061
31140	21223	Trimble County	8809
31180		Lubbock, TX	290805
31180	48107	Crosby County	6059
31180	48303	Lubbock County	278831
31180	48305	Lynn County	5915
31340		Lynchburg, VA	252634
31340	51009	Amherst County	32353
31340	51011	Appomattox County	14973
31340	51019	Bedford County	68676
31340	51031	Campbell County	54842
31340	51515	Bedford city	6222
31340	51680	Lynchburg city	75568
31420		Macon, GA	232293
31420	13021	Bibb County	155547
31420	13079	Crawford County	12630
31420	13169	Jones County	28669
31420	13207	Monroe County	26424
31420	13289	Twiggs County	9023
31460		Madera, CA	150865
31460	06039	Madera County	150865
31540		Madison, WI	605435
31540	55021	Columbia County	56833
31540	55025	Dane County	488073
31540	55045	Green County	36842
31540	55049	Iowa County	23687
31700		Manchester-Nashua, NH	400721
31700	33011	Hillsborough County	400721
31740		Manhattan, KS	92719
31740	20149	Pottawatomie County	21604
31740	20161	Riley County	71115
31860		Mankato-North Mankato, MN	96740
31860	27013	Blue Earth County	64013
31860	27103	Nicollet County	32727
31900		Mansfield, OH	124475
31900	39139	Richland County	124475
32580		McAllen-Edinburg-Mission, TX	774769
32580	48215	Hidalgo County	774769
32780		Medford, OR	203206
32780	41029	Jackson County	203206
32820		Memphis, TN-MS-AR	1324829
32820	05035	Crittenden County	50902
32820	28009	Benton County	8729
32820	28033	DeSoto County	161252
32820	28093	Marshall County	37144
32820	28137	Tate County	28886
32820	28143	Tunica County	10778
32820	47047	Fayette County	38413
32820	47157	Shelby County	927644
32820	47167	Tipton County	61081
32900		Merced, CA	255793
32900	06047	Merced County	255793
33100		Miami-Fort Lauderdale-West Palm Beach, FL	5564635
33100		Fort Lauderdale-Pompano Beach-Deerfield Beach, FL Div 22744	1748066
33100	12011	Broward County	1748066
33100		Miami-Miami Beach-Kendall, FL Div 33124	2496435
33100	12086	Miami-Dade County	2496435
33100		West Palm Beach-Boca Raton-Delray Beach, FL Div 48424	1320134
33100	12099	Palm Beach County	1320134
33140		Michigan City-La Porte, IN	111467
33140	18091	LaPorte County	111467
33220		Midland, MI	83629
33220	26111	Midland County	83629
33260		Midland, TX	141671
33260	48317	Martin County	4799
33260	48329	Midland County	136872
33340		Milwaukee-Waukesha-West Allis, WI	1555908
33340	55079	Milwaukee County	947735
33340	55089	Ozaukee County	86395
33340	55131	Washington County	131887
33340	55133	Waukesha County	389891
33460		Minneapolis-St. Paul-Bloomington, MN	3348859
33460	27003	Anoka County	330844
33460	27019	Carver County	91042
33460	27025	Chisago County	53887
33460	27037	Dakota County	398552
33460	27053	Hennepin County	1152425
33460	27059	Isanti County	37816
33460	27079	Le Sueur County	27703
33460	27095	Mille Lacs County	26097
33460	27123	Ramsey County	508640
33460	27139	Scott County	129928
33460	27141	Sherburne County	88499
33460	27143	Sibley County	15226
33460	27163	Washington County	238136
33460	27171	Wright County	124700
33460	55093	Pierce County	41019
33460	55109	St. Croix County	84345
33540		Missoula, MT	109299
33540	30063	Missoula County	109299
33660		Mobile, AL	412992
33660	01097	Mobile County	412992
33700		Modesto, CA	514453
33700	06099	Stanislaus County	514453
33740		Monroe, LA	176441
33740	22073	Ouachita Parish	153720
33740	22111	Union Parish	22721
33780		Monroe, MI	152021
33780	26115	Monroe County	152021
33860		Montgomery, AL	374536
33860	01001	Autauga County	54571
33860	01051	Elmore County	79303
33860	01085	Lowndes County	11299
33860	01101	Montgomery County	229363
34060		Morgantown, WV	129709
34060	54061	Monongalia County	96189
34060	54077	Preston County	33520
34100		Morristown, TN	113951
34100	47063	Hamblen County	62544
34100	47089	Jefferson County	51407
34580		Mount Vernon-Anacortes, WA	116901
34580	53057	Skagit County	116901
34620		Muncie, IN	117671
34620	18035	Delaware County	117671
34740		Muskegon, MI	172188
34740	26121	Muskegon County	172188
34820		Myrtle Beach-Conway-North Myrtle Beach, NC-SC	376722
34820	37019	Brunswick County	107431

Core based statistical area	State/ County FIPS code	Title and Geographic Components	2010 Census Population
34820	45051	Horry County	269291
34900		Napa, CA	136484
34900	06055	Napa County	136484
34940		Naples-Immokalee-Marco Island, FL	321520
34940	12021	Collier County	321520
34980		Nashville-Davidson--Murfreesboro--Franklin, TN	1670890
34980	47015	Cannon County	13801
34980	47021	Cheatham County	39105
34980	47037	Davidson County	626681
34980	47043	Dickson County	49666
34980	47081	Hickman County	24690
34980	47111	Macon County	22248
34980	47119	Maury County	80956
34980	47147	Robertson County	66283
34980	47149	Rutherford County	262604
34980	47159	Smith County	19166
34980	47165	Sumner County	160645
34980	47169	Trousdale County	7870
34980	47187	Williamson County	183182
34980	47189	Wilson County	113993
35100		New Bern, NC	126802
35100	37049	Craven County	103505
35100	37103	Jones County	10153
35100	37137	Pamlico County	13144
35300		New Haven-Milford, CT	862477
35300	09009	New Haven County	862477
35380		New Orleans-Metairie, LA	1189866
35380	22051	Jefferson Parish	432552
35380	22071	Orleans Parish	343829
35380	22075	Plaquemines Parish	23042
35380	22087	St. Bernard Parish	35897
35380	22089	St. Charles Parish	52780
35380	22093	St. James Parish	22102
35380	22095	St. John the Baptist Parish	45924
35380	22103	St. Tammany Parish	233740
35620		New York-Newark-Jersey City, NY-NJ-PA	19567410
35620		Dutchess County-Putnam County, NY Div 20524	397198
35620	36027	Dutchess County	297488
35620	36079	Putnam County	99710
35620		Nassau County-Suffolk County, NY Div 35004	2832882
35620	36059	Nassau County	1339532
35620	36103	Suffolk County	1493350
35620		Newark, NJ-PA Div 35084	2471171
35620	34013	Essex County	783969
35620	34019	Hunterdon County	128349
35620	34027	Morris County	492276
35620	34035	Somerset County	323444
35620	34037	Sussex County	149265
35620	34039	Union County	536499
35620	42103	Pike County	57369
35620		New York-Jersey City-White Plains, NY-NJ Div 35614	13866159
35620	34003	Bergen County	905116
35620	34017	Hudson County	634266
35620	34023	Middlesex County	809858
35620	34025	Monmouth County	630380
35620	34029	Ocean County	576567
35620	34031	Passaic County	501226
35620	36005	Bronx County	1385108
35620	36047	Kings County	2504700
35620	36061	New York County	1585873
35620	36071	Orange County	372813
35620	36081	Queens County	2230722
35620	36085	Richmond County	468730
35620	36087	Rockland County	311687
35620	36119	Westchester County	949113
35660		Niles-Benton Harbor, MI	156813
35660	26021	Berrien County	156813
35840		North Port-Sarasota-Bradenton, FL	702281

Core based statistical area	State/ County FIPS code	Title and Geographic Components	2010 Census Population
35840	12081	Manatee County	322833
35840	12115	Sarasota County	379448
35980		Norwich-New London, CT	274055
35980	09011	New London County	274055
36100		Ocala, FL	331298
36100	12083	Marion County	331298
36140		Ocean City, NJ	97265
36140	34009	Cape May County	97265
36220		Odessa, TX	137130
36220	48135	Ector County	137130
36260		Ogden-Clearfield, UT	597159
36260	49003	Box Elder County	49975
36260	49011	Davis County	306479
36260	49029	Morgan County	9469
36260	49057	Weber County	231236
36420		Oklahoma City, OK	1252987
36420	40017	Canadian County	115541
36420	40027	Cleveland County	255755
36420	40051	Grady County	52431
36420	40081	Lincoln County	34273
36420	40083	Logan County	41848
36420	40087	McClain County	34506
36420	40109	Oklahoma County	718633
36500		Olympia-Tumwater, WA	252264
36500	53067	Thurston County	252264
36540		Omaha-Council Bluffs, NE-IA	865350
36540	19085	Harrison County	14928
36540	19129	Mills County	15059
36540	19155	Pottawattamie County	93158
36540	31025	Cass County	25241
36540	31055	Douglas County	517110
36540	31153	Sarpy County	158840
36540	31155	Saunders County	20780
36540	31177	Washington County	20234
36740		Orlando-Kissimmee-Sanford, FL	2134411
36740	12069	Lake County	297052
36740	12095	Orange County	1145956
36740	12097	Osceola County	268685
36740	12117	Seminole County	422718
36780		Oshkosh-Neenah, WI	166994
36780	55139	Winnebago County	166994
36980		Owensboro, KY	114752
36980	21059	Daviess County	96656
36980	21091	Hancock County	8565
36980	21149	McLean County	9531
37100		Oxnard-Thousand Oaks-Ventura, CA	823318
37100	06111	Ventura County	823318
37340		Palm Bay-Melbourne-Titusville, FL	543376
37340	12009	Brevard County	543376
37460		Panama City, FL	184715
37460	12005	Bay County	168852
37460	12045	Gulf County	15863
37620		Parkersburg-Vienna, WV	92673
37620	54105	Wirt County	5717
37620	54107	Wood County	86956
37860		Pensacola-Ferry Pass-Brent, FL	448991
37860	12033	Escambia County	297619
37860	12113	Santa Rosa County	151372
37900		Peoria, IL	379186
37900	17123	Marshall County	12640
37900	17143	Peoria County	186494
37900	17175	Stark County	5994
37900	17179	Tazewell County	135394
37900	17203	Woodford County	38664
37980		Philadelphia-Camden-Wilmington, PA-NJ-DE-MD	5965343
37980		Camden, NJ Div 15804	1250679
37980	34005	Burlington County	448734
37980	34007	Camden County	513657
37980	34015	Gloucester County	288288
37980		Montgomery County-Bucks County-Chester County, PA Div 33874	1924009

Appendix C: Metropolitan Statistical Areas, Metropolitan Divisions, and Components (as defined July 2015)—Continued

Core based statistical area	State/County FIPS code	Title and Geographic Components	2010 Census Population
37980	42017	Bucks County	625249
37980	42029	Chester County	498886
37980	42091	Montgomery County	799874
37980		Philadelphia, PA Div 37964	2084985
37980	42045	Delaware County	558979
37980	42101	Philadelphia County	1526006
37980		Wilmington, DE-MD-NJ Div 48864	705670
37980	10003	New Castle County	538479
37980	24015	Cecil County	101108
37980	34033	Salem County	66083
38060		Phoenix-Mesa-Scottsdale, AZ	4192887
38060	04013	Maricopa County	3817117
38060	04021	Pinal County	375770
38220		Pine Bluff, AR	100258
38220	05025	Cleveland County	8689
38220	05069	Jefferson County	77435
38220	05079	Lincoln County	14134
38300		Pittsburgh, PA	2356285
38300	42003	Allegheny County	1223348
38300	42005	Armstrong County	68941
38300	42007	Beaver County	170539
38300	42019	Butler County	183862
38300	42051	Fayette County	136606
38300	42125	Washington County	207820
38300	42129	Westmoreland County	365169
38340		Pittsfield, MA	131219
38340	25003	Berkshire County	131219
38540		Pocatello, ID	82839
38540	16005	Bannock County	82839
38860		Portland-South Portland, ME	514098
38860	23005	Cumberland County	281674
38860	23023	Sagadahoc County	35293
38860	23031	York County	197131
38900		Portland-Vancouver-Hillsboro, OR-WA	2226009
38900	41005	Clackamas County	375992
38900	41009	Columbia County	49351
38900	41051	Multnomah County	735334
38900	41067	Washington County	529710
38900	41071	Yamhill County	99193
38900	53011	Clark County	425363
38900	53059	Skamania County	11066
38940		Port St. Lucie, FL	424107
38940	12085	Martin County	146318
38940	12111	St. Lucie County	277789
39140		Prescott, AZ	211033
39140	04025	Yavapai County	211033
39300		Providence-Warwick, RI-MA	1600852
39300	25005	Bristol County	548285
39300	44001	Bristol County	49875
39300	44003	Kent County	166158
39300	44005	Newport County	82888
39300	44007	Providence County	626667
39300	44009	Washington County	126979
39340		Provo-Orem, UT	526810
39340	49023	Juab County	10246
39340	49049	Utah County	516564
39380		Pueblo, CO	159063
39380	08101	Pueblo County	159063
39460		Punta Gorda, FL	159978
39460	12015	Charlotte County	159978
39540		Racine, WI	195408
39540	55101	Racine County	195408
39580		Raleigh, NC	1130490
39580	37069	Franklin County	60619
39580	37101	Johnston County	168878
39580	37183	Wake County	900993
39660		Rapid City, SD	134598
39660	46033	Custer County	8216
39660	46093	Meade County	25434
39660	46103	Pennington County	100948
39740		Reading, PA	411442
39740	42011	Berks County	411442
39820		Redding, CA	177223
39820	06089	Shasta County	177223
39900		Reno, NV	425417
39900	32029	Storey County	4010
39900	32031	Washoe County	421407
40060		Richmond, VA	1208101
40060	51007	Amelia County	12690
40060	51033	Caroline County	28545
40060	51036	Charles City County	7256
40060	51041	Chesterfield County	316236
40060	51053	Dinwiddie County	28001
40060	51075	Goochland County	21717
40060	51085	Hanover County	99863
40060	51087	Henrico County	306935
40060	51101	King William County	15935
40060	51127	New Kent County	18429
40060	51145	Powhatan County	28046
40060	51149	Prince George County	35725
40060	51183	Sussex County	12087
40060	51570	Colonial Heights city	17411
40060	51670	Hopewell city	22591
40060	51730	Petersburg city	32420
40060	51760	Richmond city	204214
40140		Riverside-San Bernardino-Ontario, CA	4224851
40140	06065	Riverside County	2189641
40140	06071	San Bernardino County	2035210
40220		Roanoke, VA	308707
40220	51023	Botetourt County	33148
40220	51045	Craig County	5190
40220	51067	Franklin County	56159
40220	51161	Roanoke County	92376
40220	51770	Roanoke city	97032
40220	51775	Salem city	24802
40340		Rochester, MN	206877
40340	27039	Dodge County	20087
40340	27045	Fillmore County	20866
40340	27109	Olmsted County	144248
40340	27157	Wabasha County	21676
40380		Rochester, NY	1079671
40380	36051	Livingston County	65393
40380	36055	Monroe County	744344
40380	36069	Ontario County	107931
40380	36073	Orleans County	42883
40380	36117	Wayne County	93772
40380	36123	Yates County	25348
40420		Rockford, IL	349431
40420	17007	Boone County	54165
40420	17201	Winnebago County	295266
40580		Rocky Mount, NC	152392
40580	37065	Edgecombe County	56552
40580	37127	Nash County	95840
40660		Rome, GA	96317
40660	13115	Floyd County	96317
40900		Sacramento--Roseville--Arden-Arcade, CA	2149127
40900	06017	El Dorado County	181058
40900	06061	Placer County	348432
40900	06067	Sacramento County	1418788
40900	06113	Yolo County	200849
40980		Saginaw, MI	200169
40980	26145	Saginaw County	200169
41060		St. Cloud, MN	189093
41060	27009	Benton County	38451
41060	27145	Stearns County	150642
41100		St. George, UT	138115
41100	49053	Washington County	138115
41140		St. Joseph, MO-KS	127329
41140	20043	Doniphan County	7945
41140	29003	Andrew County	17291
41140	29021	Buchanan County	89201
41140	29063	DeKalb County	12892
41180		St. Louis, MO-IL	2787701
41180	17005	Bond County	17768

Core based statistical area	State/ County FIPS code	Title and Geographic Components	2010 Census Population	Core based statistical area	State/ County FIPS code	Title and Geographic Components	2010 Census Population
41180	17013	Calhoun County	5089	42540	42131	Wyoming County	28276
41180	17027	Clinton County	37762	42660		Seattle-Tacoma-Bellevue, WA	3439809
41180	17083	Jersey County	22985	42660		Seattle-Bellevue-Everett, WA Div 42644	2644584
41180	17117	Macoupin County	47765	42660	53033	King County	1931249
41180	17119	Madison County	269282	42660	53061	Snohomish County	713335
41180	17133	Monroe County	32957	42660		Tacoma-Lakewood, WA Div 45104	795225
41180	17163	St. Clair County	270056	42660	53053	Pierce County	795225
41180	29071	Franklin County	101492	42680		Sebastian-Vero Beach, FL	138028
41180	29099	Jefferson County	218733	42680	12061	Indian River County	138028
41180	29113	Lincoln County	52566	42700		Sebring, FL	98786
41180	29183	St. Charles County	360485	42700	12055	Highlands County	98786
41180	29189	St. Louis County	998954	43100		Sheboygan, WI	115507
41180	29219	Warren County	32513	43100	55117	Sheboygan County	115507
41180	29510	St. Louis city	319294	43300		Sherman-Denison, TX	120877
41420		Salem, OR	390738	43300	48181	Grayson County	120877
41420	41047	Marion County	315335	43340		Shreveport-Bossier City, LA	439811
41420	41053	Polk County	75403	43340	22015	Bossier Parish	116979
41500		Salinas, CA	415057	43340	22017	Caddo Parish	254969
41500	06053	Monterey County	415057	43340	22031	De Soto Parish	26656
41540		Salisbury, MD-DE	373802	43340	22119	Webster Parish	41207
41540	10005	Sussex County	197145	43420		Sierra Vista-Douglas, AZ	131346
41540	24039	Somerset County	26470	43420	04003	Cochise County	131346
41540	24045	Wicomico County	98733	43580		Sioux City, IA-NE-SD	168563
41540	24047	Worcester County	51454	43580	19149	Plymouth County	24986
41620		Salt Lake City, UT	1087873	43580	19193	Woodbury County	102172
41620	49035	Salt Lake County	1029655	43580	31043	Dakota County	21006
41620	49045	Tooele County	58218	43580	31051	Dixon County	6000
41660		San Angelo, TX	111823	43580	46127	Union County	14399
41660	48235	Irion County	1599	43620		Sioux Falls, SD	228261
41660	48451	Tom Green County	110224	43620	46083	Lincoln County	44828
41700		San Antonio-New Braunfels, TX	2142508	43620	46087	McCook County	5618
41700	48013	Atascosa County	44911	43620	46099	Minnehaha County	169468
41700	48019	Bandera County	20485	43620	46125	Turner County	8347
41700	48029	Bexar County	1714773	43780		South Bend-Mishawaka, IN-MI	319224
41700	48091	Comal County	108472	43780	18141	St. Joseph County	266931
41700	48187	Guadalupe County	131533	43780	26027	Cass County	52293
41700	48259	Kendall County	33410	43900		Spartanburg, SC	313268
41700	48325	Medina County	46006	43900	45083	Spartanburg County	284307
41700	48493	Wilson County	42918	43900	45087	Union County	28961
41740		San Diego-Carlsbad, CA	3095313	44060		Spokane-Spokane Valley, WA	527753
41740	06073	San Diego County	3095313	44060	53051	Pend Oreille County	13001
41860		San Francisco-Oakland-Hayward, CA	4335391	44060	53063	Spokane County	471221
41860		Oakland-Hayward-Berkeley, CA Div 36084	2559296	44060	53065	Stevens County	43531
41860	06001	Alameda County	1510271	44100		Springfield, IL	210170
41860	06013	Contra Costa County	1049025	44100	17129	Menard County	12705
41860		San Francisco-Redwood City-South San Francisco, CA Div 41884	1523686	44100	17167	Sangamon County	197465
41860	06075	San Francisco County	805235	44140		Springfield, MA	621570
41860	06081	San Mateo County	718451	44140	25013	Hampden County	463490
41860		San Rafael, CA Div 42034	252409	44140	25015	Hampshire County	158080
41860	06041	Marin County	252409	44180		Springfield, MO	436712
41940		San Jose-Sunnyvale-Santa Clara, CA	1836911	44180	29043	Christian County	77422
41940	06069	San Benito County	55269	44180	29059	Dallas County	16777
41940	06085	Santa Clara County	1781642	44180	29077	Greene County	275174
42020		San Luis Obispo-Paso Robles-Arroyo Grande, CA	269637	44180	29167	Polk County	31137
				44180	29225	Webster County	36202
42020	06079	San Luis Obispo County	269637	44220		Springfield, OH	138333
42100		Santa Cruz-Watsonville, CA	262382	44220	39023	Clark County	138333
42100	06087	Santa Cruz County	262382	44300		State College, PA	153990
42140		Santa Fe, NM	144170	44300	42027	Centre County	153990
42140	35049	Santa Fe County	144170	44420		Staunton-Waynesboro, VA	118502
42200		Santa Maria-Santa Barbara, CA	423895	44420	51015	Augusta County	73750
42200	06083	Santa Barbara County	423895	44420	51790	Staunton city	23746
42220		Santa Rosa, CA	483878	44420	51820	Waynesboro city	21006
42220	06097	Sonoma County	483878	44700		Stockton-Lodi, CA	685306
42340		Savannah, GA	347611	44700	06077	San Joaquin County	685306
42340	13029	Bryan County	30233	44940		Sumter, SC	107456
42340	13051	Chatham County	265128	44940	45085	Sumter County	107456
42340	13103	Effingham County	52250	45060		Syracuse, NY	662577
42540		Scranton--Wilkes-Barre--Hazleton, PA	563631	45060	36053	Madison County	73442
42540	42069	Lackawanna County	214437	45060	36067	Onondaga County	467026
42540	42079	Luzerne County	320918	45060	36075	Oswego County	122109
				45220		Tallahassee, FL	367413

Core based statistical area	State/ County FIPS code	Title and Geographic Components	2010 Census Population
45220	12039	Gadsden County	46389
45220	12065	Jefferson County	14761
45220	12073	Leon County	275487
45220	12129	Wakulla County	30776
45300		Tampa-St. Petersburg-Clearwater, FL	2783243
45300	12053	Hernando County	172778
45300	12057	Hillsborough County	1229226
45300	12101	Pasco County	464697
45300	12103	Pinellas County	916542
45460		Terre Haute, IN	172425
45460	18021	Clay County	26890
45460	18153	Sullivan County	21475
45460	18165	Vermillion County	16212
45460	18167	Vigo County	107848
45500		Texarkana, TX-AR	149198
45500	05081	Little River County	13171
45500	05091	Miller County	43462
45500	48037	Bowie County	92565
45540		The Villages, FL	93420
45540	12119	Sumter County	93420
45780		Toledo, OH	610001
45780	39051	Fulton County	42698
45780	39095	Lucas County	441815
45780	39173	Wood County	125488
45820		Topeka, KS	233870
45820	20085	Jackson County	13462
45820	20087	Jefferson County	19126
45820	20139	Osage County	16295
45820	20177	Shawnee County	177934
45820	20197	Wabaunsee County	7053
45940		Trenton, NJ	366513
45940	34021	Mercer County	366513
46060		Tucson, AZ	980263
46060	04019	Pima County	980263
46140		Tulsa, OK	937478
46140	40037	Creek County	69967
46140	40111	Okmulgee County	40069
46140	40113	Osage County	47472
46140	40117	Pawnee County	16577
46140	40131	Rogers County	86905
46140	40143	Tulsa County	603403
46140	40145	Wagoner County	73085
46220		Tuscaloosa, AL	230162
46220	01065	Hale County	15760
46220	01107	Pickens County	19746
46220	01125	Tuscaloosa County	194656
46340		Tyler, TX	209714
46340	48423	Smith County	209714
46520		Urban Honolulu, HI	953207
46520	15003	Honolulu County	953207
46540		Utica-Rome, NY	299397
46540	36043	Herkimer County	64519
46540	36065	Oneida County	234878
46660		Valdosta, GA	139588
46660	13027	Brooks County	16243
46660	13101	Echols County	4034
46660	13173	Lanier County	10078
46660	13185	Lowndes County	109233
46700		Vallejo-Fairfield, CA	413344
46700	06095	Solano County	413344
47020		Victoria, TX	94003
47020	48175	Goliad County	7210
47020	48469	Victoria County	86793
47220		Vineland-Bridgeton, NJ	156898
47220	34011	Cumberland County	156898
47260		Virginia Beach-Norfolk-Newport News, VA-NC	1676822
47260	37053	Currituck County	23547
47260	37073	Gates County	12197
47260	51073	Gloucester County	36858
47260	51093	Isle of Wight County	35270
47260	51095	James City County	67009
47260	51115	Mathews County	8978
47260	51199	York County	65464
47260	51550	Chesapeake city	222209
47260	51650	Hampton city	137436
47260	51700	Newport News city	180719
47260	51710	Norfolk city	242803
47260	51735	Poquoson city	12150
47260	51740	Portsmouth city	95535
47260	51800	Suffolk city	84585
47260	51810	Virginia Beach city	437994
47260	51830	Williamsburg city	14068
47300		Visalia-Porterville, CA	442179
47300	06107	Tulare County	442179
47380		Waco, TX	252772
47380	48145	Falls County	17866
47380	48309	McLennan County	234906
47460		Walla Walla, WA	62859
47460	53013	Columbia County	4078
47460	53071	Walla Walla County	58781
47580		Warner Robins, GA	179605
47580	13153	Houston County	139900
47580	13225	Peach County	27695
47580	13235	Pulaski County	12010
47900		Washington-Arlington-Alexandria, DC-VA-MD-WV	5636232
47900		Silver Spring-Frederick-Rockville, MD Div 43524	1205162
47900	24021	Frederick County	233385
47900	24031	Montgomery County	971777
47900		Washington-Arlington-Alexandria, DC-VA-MD-WV Div 47894	4431070
47900	11001	District of Columbia	601723
47900	24009	Calvert County	88737
47900	24017	Charles County	146551
47900	24033	Prince George's County	863420
47900	51013	Arlington County	207627
47900	51043	Clarke County	14034
47900	51047	Culpeper County	46689
47900	51059	Fairfax County	1081726
47900	51061	Fauquier County	65203
47900	51107	Loudoun County	312311
47900	51153	Prince William County	402002
47900	51157	Rappahannock County	7373
47900	51177	Spotsylvania County	122397
47900	51179	Stafford County	128961
47900	51187	Warren County	37575
47900	51510	Alexandria city	139966
47900	51600	Fairfax city	22565
47900	51610	Falls Church city	12332
47900	51630	Fredericksburg city	24286
47900	51683	Manassas city	37821
47900	51685	Manassas Park city	14273
47900	54037	Jefferson County	53498
47940		Waterloo-Cedar Falls, IA	167819
47940	19013	Black Hawk County	131090
47940	19017	Bremer County	24276
47940	19075	Grundy County	12453
48060		Watertown-Fort Drum, NY	116229
48060	36045	Jefferson County	116229
48140		Wausau, WI	134063
48140	55073	Marathon County	134063
48260		Weirton-Steubenville, WV-OH	124454
48260	39081	Jefferson County	69709
48260	54009	Brooke County	24069
48260	54029	Hancock County	30676
48300		Wenatchee, WA	110884
48300	53007	Chelan County	72453
48300	53017	Douglas County	38431
48540		Wheeling, WV-OH	147950
48540	39013	Belmont County	70400
48540	54051	Marshall County	33107
48540	54069	Ohio County	44443

Core based statistical area	State/ County FIPS code	Title and Geographic Components	2010 Census Population
48620		Wichita, KS..	630919
48620	20015	Butler County...................................	65880
48620	20079	Harvey County..................................	34684
48620	20095	Kingman County................................	7858
48620	20173	Sedgwick County...............................	498365
48620	20191	Sumner County..................................	24132
48660		Wichita Falls, TX.................................	151306
48660	48009	Archer County...................................	9054
48660	48077	Clay County......................................	10752
48660	48485	Wichita County..................................	131500
48700		Williamsport, PA.................................	116111
48700	42081	Lycoming County...............................	116111
48900		Wilmington, NC..................................	254884
48900	37129	New Hanover County..........................	202667
48900	37141	Pender County...................................	52217
49020		Winchester, VA-WV.............................	128472
49020	51069	Frederick County................................	78305
49020	51840	Winchester city..................................	26203
49020	54027	Hampshire County..............................	23964
49180		Winston-Salem, NC.............................	640595
49180	37057	Davidson County................................	162878

Core based statistical area	State/ County FIPS code	Title and Geographic Components	2010 Census Population
49180	37059	Davie County.....................................	41240
49180	37067	Forsyth County..................................	350670
49180	37169	Stokes County...................................	47401
49180	37197	Yadkin County...................................	38406
49340		Worcester, MA-CT...............................	916980
49340	09015	Windham County...............................	118428
49340	25027	Worcester County..............................	798552
49420		Yakima, WA.......................................	243231
49420	53077	Yakima County..................................	243231
49620		York-Hanover, PA...............................	434972
49620	42133	York County......................................	434972
49660		Youngstown-Warren-Boardman, OH-PA........	565773
49660	39099	Mahoning County..............................	238823
49660	39155	Trumbull County...............................	210312
49660	42085	Mercer County..................................	116638
49700		Yuba City, CA....................................	166892
49700	06101	Sutter County...................................	94737
49700	06115	Yuba County.....................................	72155
49740		Yuma, AZ..	195751
49740	04027	Yuma County....................................	195751

CPSIA information can be obtained
at www.ICGtesting.com
Printed in the USA
BVHW061609010223
657177BV00002B/7

9 781636 710785